PHILIP'S

STREET ATLAS
North
Yorkshire

First published in 2002 by

Philip's, a division of
Octopus Publishing Group Ltd
2–4 Heron Quays, London E14 4JP

First edition 2002
Third impression 2002

ISBN 0-540-08143-4 (spiral)

© Philip's 2002

Ordnance Survey®

This product includes mapping data licensed
from Ordnance Survey® with the permission of
the Controller of Her Majesty's Stationery Office.
© Crown copyright 2002. All rights reserved.
Licence number 100011710

Printed and bound in Spain
by Cayfosa-Quebecor

Contents

III	**Key to map symbols**
IV	**Key to map pages**
VI	**Route planning**
X	**Administrative and Postcode boundaries**
1	**Street maps** at 1¾ inches to 1 mile
208	**Street maps** at 3½ inches to 1 mile
233	**Street map of York city centre** at 7 inches to 1 mile
234	**Index** of towns and villages
238	**Index** of streets, hospitals, industrial estates, railway stations, schools, shopping centres, universities and places of interest

Digital Data

The exceptionally high-quality mapping found in this atlas is available as digital data in TIFF format, which is easily convertible to other bit mapped (raster) image formats.

The index is also available in digital form as a standard database table. It contains all the details found in the printed index together with the National Grid reference for the map square in which each entry is named.

For further information and to discuss your requirements, please contact Philip's on 020 7531 8439 or ruth.king@philips-maps.co.uk

Motorway with junction number	**Railway station** Walsall
Primary route – dual/single carriageway	**Private railway station**
A road – dual/single carriageway	**Bus, coach station**
B road – dual/single carriageway	**Ambulance station**
Minor road – dual/single carriageway	**Coastguard station**
Other minor road – dual/single carriageway	**Fire station**
Road under construction	**Police station**
Pedestrianised area	**Accident and Emergency entrance to hospital**
DY7 **Postcode boundaries**	**Hospital**
County and unitary authority boundaries	**Place of worship**
Railway	**Information Centre** (open all year)
Railway under construction	**Parking**
Tramway, miniature railway	**Park and Ride**
Rural track, private road or narrow road in urban area	**Post Office**
Gate or obstruction to traffic (restrictions may not apply at all times or to all vehicles)	**Camping site**
Path, bridleway, byway open to all traffic, road used as a public path	**Caravan site**
The representation in this atlas of a road, track or path is no evidence of the existence of a right of way	**Golf course**
177	**Picnic site**
32	
229 **Adjoining page indicators** (The colour of the arrow indicates the scale of the adjoining page - see scales below)	**Important buildings, schools, colleges, universities and hospitals** Prim Sch
233	River Medway **Water name**
213 **The map areas within the pink and blue bands are shown at a larger scale on the page, indicated by the red and blue blocks and arrows**	**River, stream**
	Lock, weir
	Water
	Tidal water
	Woods
	Houses
	Church **Non-Roman antiquity**
	ROMAN FORT **Roman antiquity**

Acad	**Academy**	Mkt	**Market**
Allot Gdns	**Allotments**	Meml	**Memorial**
Cemy	**Cemetery**	Mon	**Monument**
C Ctr	**Civic Centre**	Mus	**Museum**
CH	**Club House**	Obsy	**Observatory**
Coll	**College**	Pal	**Royal Palace**
Crem	**Crematorium**	PH	**Public House**
Ent	**Enterprise**	Recn Gd	**Recreation Ground**
Ex H	**Exhibition Hall**	Resr	**Reservoir**
Ind Est	**Industrial Estate**	Ret Pk	**Retail Park**
IRB Sta	**Inshore Rescue Boat Station**	Sch	**School**
		Sh Ctr	**Shopping Centre**
Inst	**Institute**	TH	**Town Hall/House**
Ct	**Law Court**	Trad Est	**Trading Estate**
L Ctr	**Leisure Centre**	Univ	**University**
LC	**Level Crossing**	Wks	**Works**
Liby	**Library**	YH	**Youth Hostel**

■ The small numbers around the edges of the maps identify the 1 kilometre National Grid lines ■ The dark grey border on the inside edge of some pages indicates that the mapping does not continue onto the adjacent page

The scale of the maps on the pages numbered in blue is 5.52 cm to 1 km • 3½ inches to 1 mile • 1: 18103

0	¼	½	¾	1 mile
0	250 m	500 m	750 m	1 kilometre

The scale of the maps on pages numbered in green is 2.76 cm to 1 km • 1¾ inches to 1 mile • 1: 36206

0	¼	½	¾	1 mile
0	250m 500m 750m	1kilometre		

The scale of the maps on pages numbered in red is 11.04 cm to 1 km • 7 inches to 1 mile • 1: 9051.4

0	220 yards	440 yards	660 yards	½ mile
0	125 m	250 m	375 m	½ kilometre

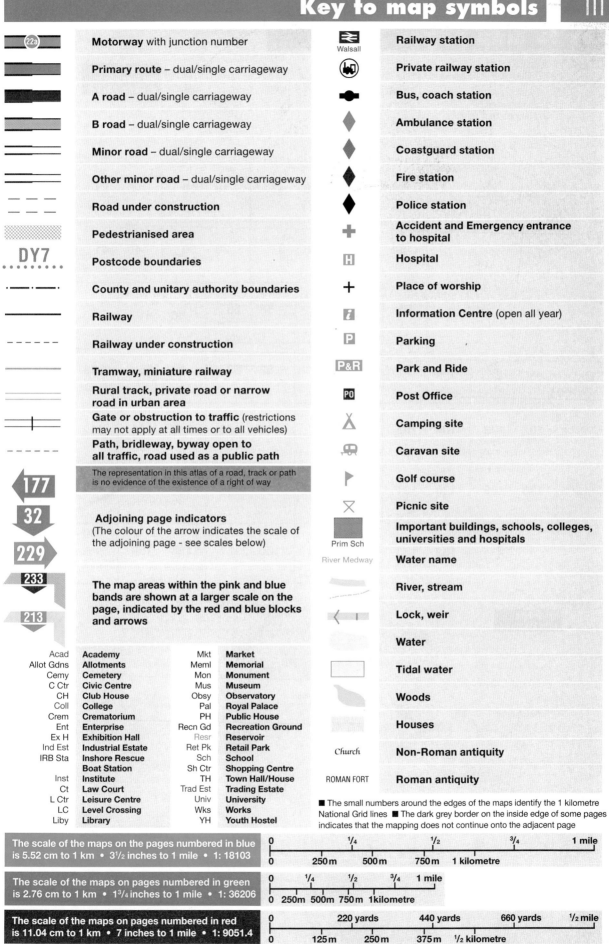

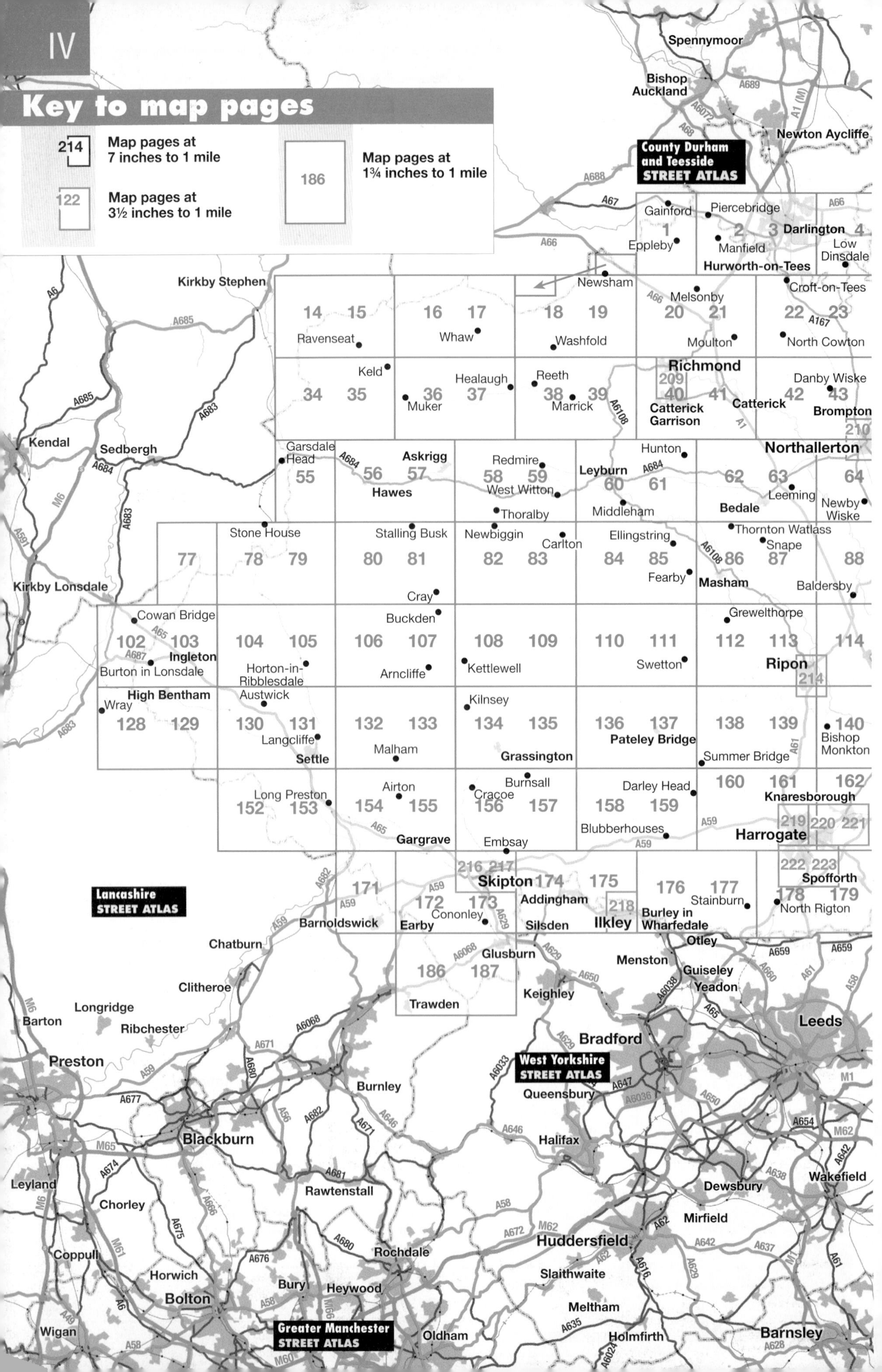

Key to map pages

IV

214	Map pages at 7 inches to 1 mile
122	Map pages at 3½ inches to 1 mile
186	Map pages at 1¾ inches to 1 mile

County Durham and Teesside STREET ATLAS

Spennymoor
Bishop Auckland
Newton Aycliffe
Gainford Piercebridge
Eppleby Manfield Darlington Low Dinsdale
Hurworth-on-Tees
Newsham Melsonby Croft-on-Tees

Kirkby Stephen

| 14 | 15 | 16 | 17 | 18 | 19 | 20 | 21 | 22 | 23 |
Ravenseat Whaw Washfold Moulton North Cowton

Keld Healaugh Reeth Richmond Danby Wiske
| 34 | 35 | 36 | 37 | 38 | 39 | 209 40 | 41 | 42 | 43 |
Muker Marrick Catterick Garrison Catterick Brompton

A6 Kendal Sedbergh
Garsdale Head Askrigg Redmire Hunton Northallerton
| 55 | 56 | 57 | 58 | 59 | Leyburn 60 | 61 | 62 | 63 | 64 |
Hawes West Witton Middleham Bedale Leeming Newby Wiske
Thoralby

Stone House Stalling Busk Newbiggin Ellingstring Thornton Watlass
Kirkby Lonsdale
| 77 | 78 | 79 | 80 | 81 | 82 | 83 | 84 | 85 | 86 | 87 | 88 |
Carlton Fearby Snape Baldersby
Masham

Cowan Bridge Buckden Grewelthorpe
| 102 | 103 | 104 | 105 | 106 | 107 | 108 | 109 | 110 | 111 | 112 | 113 | 114 |
Ingleton Horton-in-Ribblesdale Arncliffe Kettlewell Swetton Ripon
Burton in Lonsdale 214

High Bentham Austwick Kilnsey Bishop Monkton
Wray
| 128 | 129 | 130 | 131 | 132 | 133 | 134 | 135 | 136 | 137 | 138 | 139 | 140 |
Langcliffe Malham Grassington Pateley Bridge Summer Bridge
Settle

Burnsall Darley Head Knaresborough
| 152 | 153 | 154 | 155 | 156 | 157 | 158 | 159 | 160 | 161 | 162 |
Long Preston Airton Cracoe Blubberhouses 219 220 221
Gargrave Embsay Harrogate 222 223

Lancashire STREET ATLAS

| 171 | 172 | 173 | 174 | 175 | 176 | 177 | 178 | 179 |
Skipton Addingham Stainburn Spofforth
Barnoldswick Cononley Silsden Ilkley North Rigton
Chatburn Earby Burley in Wharfedale 218
Clitheroe Glusburn Otley
| 186 | 187 | Menston Guiseley
Barton Ribchester Trawden Keighley Yeadon
Longridge Bradford
Preston **West Yorkshire STREET ATLAS** Leeds
Queensbury
Burnley

Blackburn Halifax Dewsbury Wakefield
Leyland Mirfield
Chorley Rawtenstall
Coppull Rochdale Huddersfield
Horwich Bury Heywood Slaithwaite
Wigan Bolton Meltham Barnsley
Greater Manchester STREET ATLAS Oldham Holmfirth

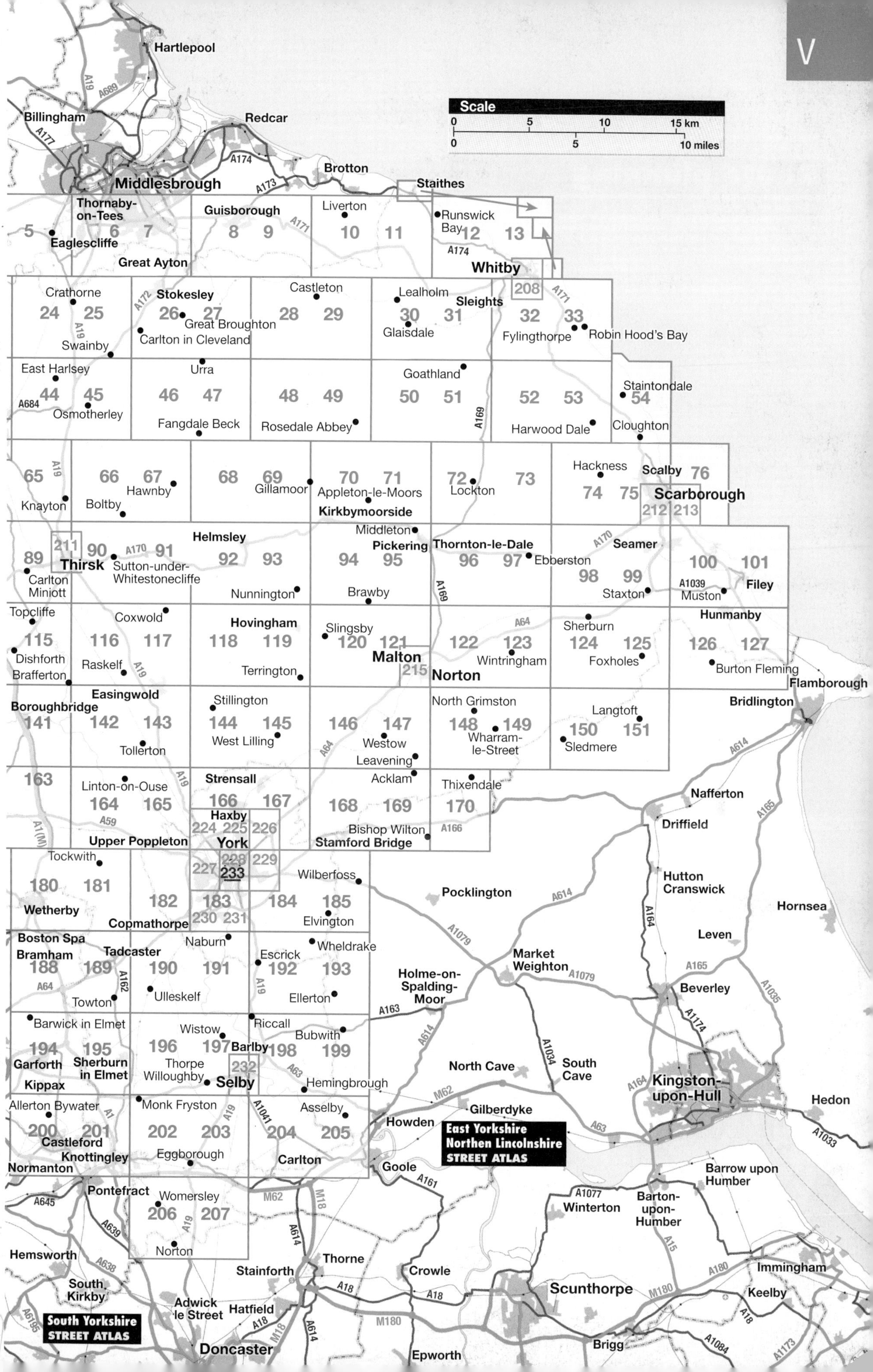

Scale

0 ... 5 ... 10 ... 15 km
0 ... 5 ... 10 miles

Hartlepool

Billingham

Redcar

Middlesbrough

Thornaby-on-Tees

5 Eaglescliffe **6** **7**

Guisborough **8** **9**

Liverton **10** **11**

Brotton

Staithes

Runswick Bay **12** **13**

Whitby

Great Ayton

Crathorne **24** **25**

Stokesley **26** **27** Great Broughton **28** Castleton **29**

Lealholm **30** **31** Sleights **32** **33**

Swainby

Carlton in Cleveland

Glaisdale

Fylingthorpe

Robin Hood's Bay

208

East Harsley **44** **45**

Urra **46** **47**

48 **49**

Goathland **50** **51**

52 **53** Staintondale **54**

Osmotherley

Fangdale Beck

Rosedale Abbey

Harwood Dale

Cloughton

65 **66** **67** Hawnby **68** **69** Gillamoor **70** **71**

72 Lockton **73**

Hackness **74** **75** Scalby **76**

Knayton

Boltby

Appleton-le-Moors

Kirkbymoorside

Scarborough

212 213

89 211 **90** Helmsley **91** **92** **93**

Middleton

Pickering **94** **95**

Thornton-le-Dale **96** **97** Ebberston

Seamer **98** **99**

100 **101** Filey

Thirsk

Sutton-under-Whitestonecliffe

Nunnington

Brawby

Staxton

Muston

Topcliffe

Coxwold

Hovingham **118** **119**

Slingsby **120** **121**

Sherburn **122** **123** **124** **125**

Hunmanby **126** **127**

Carlton Miniott **115** **116** **117**

Dishforth

Brafferton

Raskelf

Terrington

Malton

Norton

Wintringham

Foxholes

Burton Fleming

Flamborough

Boroughbridge **141** Easingwold **142** **143**

Stillington **144** **145**

146 **147**

North Grimston **148** **149**

Langtoft **150** **151**

Bridlington

Tollerton

West Lilling

Westow

Leavening

Wharram-le-Street

Sledmere

163

Linton-on-Ouse **164** **165**

Strensall **166** **167**

Acklam

Thixendale **170**

168 **169**

Nafferton

Driffield

Haxby

224 225 226

York

Upper Poppleton

227 228 229

233

Wilberfoss

Hutton Cranswick

Tockwith **180** **181**

182 **183** **184** **185**

230 231

Pocklington

A614

Hornsea

Wetherby

Copmathorpe

Elvington

Market Weighton

Leven

Beverley

Boston Spa **188** **189** Tadcaster **190** **191**

Naburn

Escrick **192** **193** Wheldrake

Holme-on-Spalding-Moor

Bramham

Towton

Ulleskelf

Ellerton

South Cave

Kingston-upon-Hull

Barwick in Elmet **194** **195**

Wistow **196** **197** Barlby **198** **199**

Riccall

Bubwith

North Cave

Hedon

Garforth

Sherburn in Elmet

Thorpe Willoughby

Selby

Hemingbrough

232

Kippax

Allerton Bywater

Monk Fryston **202** **203**

Asselby **204** **205**

Howden

Gilberdyke

Barrow upon Humber

200 **201** Castleford

Knottingley

Eggborough

Carlton

Goole

Barton-upon-Humber

Normanton

Pontefract

Womersley **206** **207**

Winterton

Hemsworth

South Kirkby

Norton

Thorne

Crowle

Scunthorpe

Keelby

Adwick le Street

Stainforth

Hatfield

Immingham

Doncaster

Epworth

Brigg

East Yorkshire Northen Lincolnshire STREET ATLAS

South Yorkshire STREET ATLAS

Route planning

Scale
0 5 10 15 20 km
0 5 10 miles

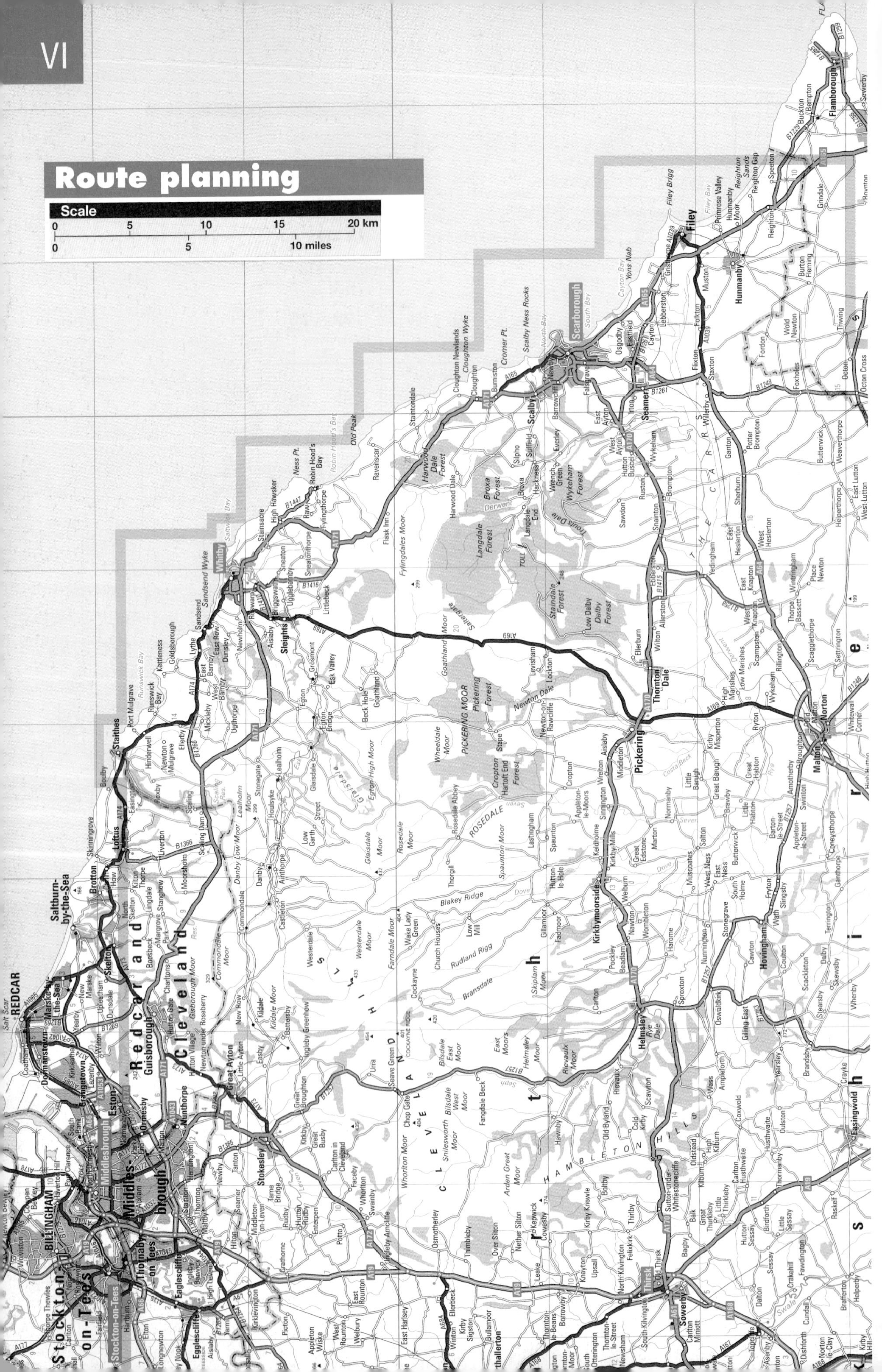
REDCAR
Saltburn-by-the-Sea
Middlesbrough
Stockton-on-Tees
Billingham
Guisborough
Redcar and Cleveland
Great Ayton
Stokesley
Thornaby-on-Tees
Yarm
Eaglescliffe
Loftus
Staithes
Whitby
Sleights
Robin Hood's Bay
Scarborough
Scalby
Seamer
Filey
Filey Brigg
Hunmanby
Flamborough
Pickering
Thornton Dale
Kirkbymoorside
Helmsley
Thirsk
Sowerby
Malton
Norton
Hovingham
Easingwold
Northallerton
North York Moors
Cleveland Hills
Hambleton Hills
Rosedale
Pickering Moor
Fylingdales Moor
Goathland Moor
Glaisdale Moor
Farndale Moor
Bilsdale
Dalby Forest
Langdale Forest
Broxa Forest
Wykeham Forest
Cropton Forest
A19
A169
A170
A171
A172
A173
A174
A64
A165

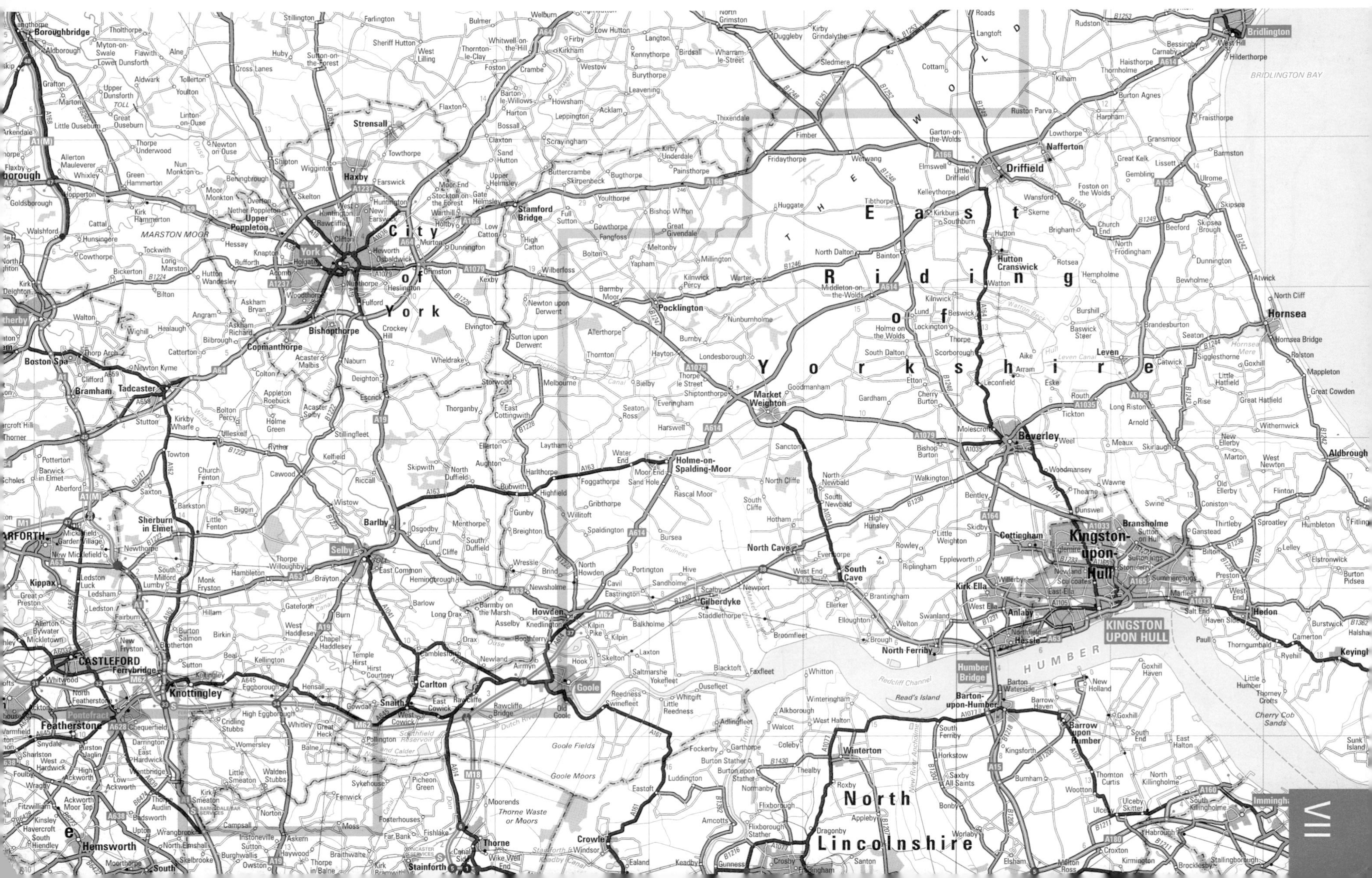
East Riding of Yorkshire
City of York
North Lincolnshire
THE WOLDS
Bridlington
BRIDLINGTON BAY
Driffield
Nafferton
Hornsea
Aldbrough
Beverley
Cottingham
Kingston-upon-Hull
KINGSTON UPON HULL
HUMBER
Humber Bridge
Hessle
Anlaby
Hedon
Keyingham
Barton-upon-Humber
Barrow upon Humber
Winterton
North Ferriby
South Cave
North Cave
Market Weighton
Pocklington
Holme-on-Spalding-Moor
Gilberdyke
Howden
Goole
Selby
Barlby
Snaith
Carlton
Thorne
Crowle
Stainforth
Hemsworth
Featherstone
Pontefract
CASTLEFORD
Ferrybridge
Knottingley
Sherburn in Elmet
Tadcaster
Bramham
Boston Spa
Wetherby
Boroughbridge
Upper Poppleton
York
Haxby
Strensall
Stamford Bridge
Bishopthorpe
Copmanthorpe
MARSTON MOOR
Leven
Hutton Cranswick
Goole Fields
Goole Moors
Thorne Waste or Moors
Read's Island
Redcliff Channel
Cherry Cob Sands
Immingham

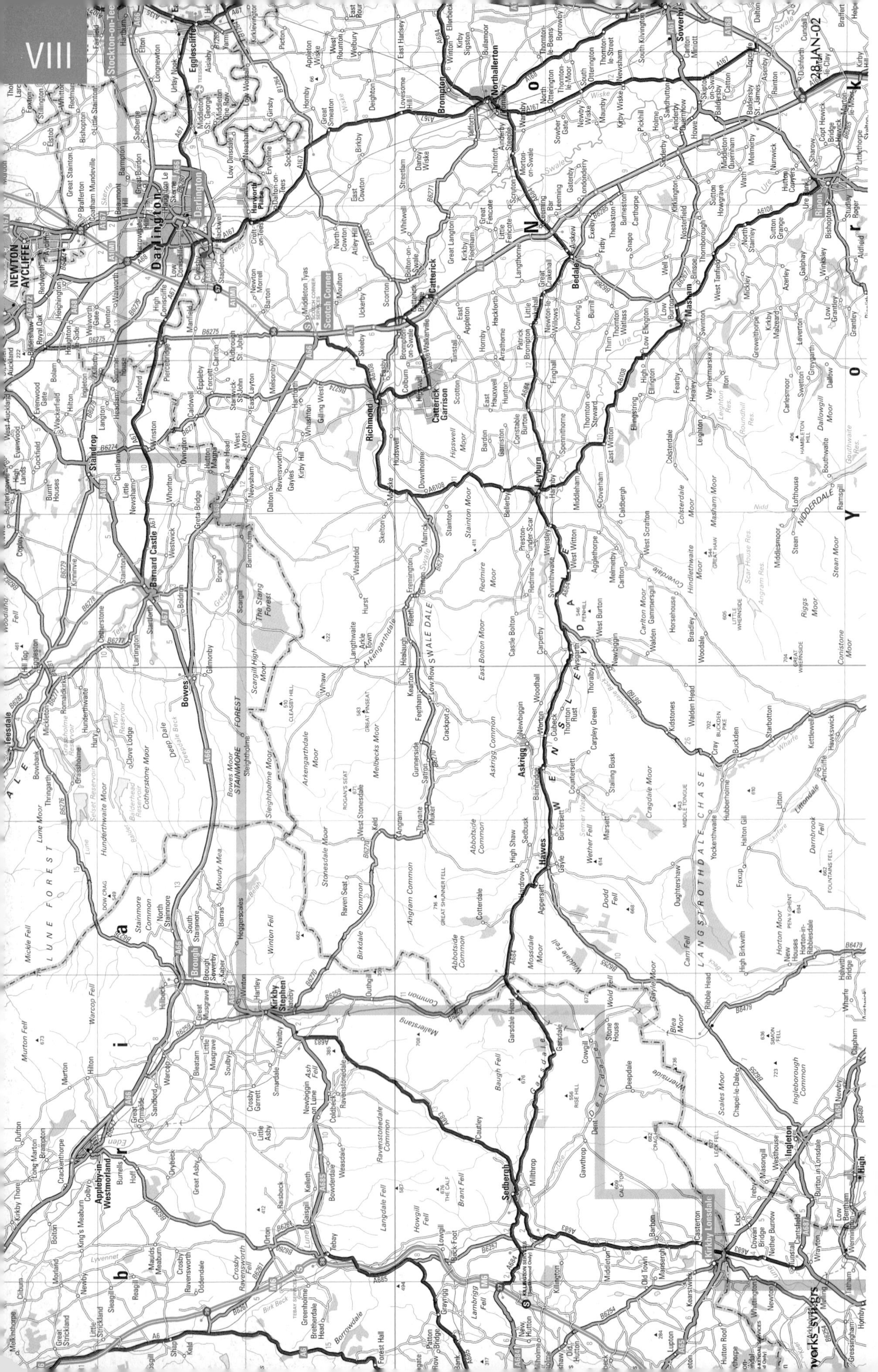
28-JAN-02
Darlington
Northallerton
Stockton-on-Tees
Newton Aycliffe
Richmond
Catterick
Catterick Garrison
Bedale
Masham
Ripon
Leyburn
Barnard Castle
Bowes
Staindrop
Hawes
Askrigg
Sedbergh
Kirkby Stephen
Brough
Appleby-in-Westmorland
Kirkby Lonsdale
Ingleton
Tebay
Thirsk
Scotch Corner
Eaglescliffe
Hurworth Place
Middleton Tyas
Sowerby
WENSLEYDALE
SWALE DALE
LANGSTROTHDALE CHASE
NIDDERDALE
LUNE FOREST
STAINMORE FOREST
The Stang Forest
Mallerstang
Dentdale
Garsdale
Howgill Fell
Baugh Fell
Great Shunner Fell
Whernside
Ingleborough Common
Kilnsey
Kettlewell
Buckden
Middleham
West Witton
Aysgarth
West Burton
Reeth
Muker
Keld
Gunnerside
Dent
Garsdale Head
Killington Services
Tebay Services
Scotch Corner Services

Knaresborough
Harrogate
Wetherby
Boston Spa
Collingham
GARFORTH
LEEDS
Kippax
Rothwell
Normanton
Wakefield
Featherstone
Otley
Ilkley
Burley in Wharfedale
Menston
Guiseley
Yeadon
Horsforth
Bramhope
Pudsey
Morley
Batley
Dewsbury
Ossett
Horbury
Crigglestone
Middleton
Shipley
Baildon
Bingley
Bradford
Keighley
Silsden
Skipton
Addingham
Cleckheaton
Heckmondwike
Liversedge
Mirfield
Brighouse
Elland
Halifax
Huddersfield
Queensbury
Illingworth
Sowerby Bridge
Hebden Bridge
Mytholmroyd
Todmorden
Littleborough
Milnrow
Rochdale
Heywood
Wardle
Whitworth
Bacup
Rawtenstall
Haslingden
Ramsbottom
Tottington
Edgworth
Horwich
Chorley
Adlington
Coppull
Darwen
Blackburn
Accrington
Oswaldtwistle
Church
Clayton-le-Moors
Great Harwood
Rishton
Whalley
Clitheroe
Chatburn
Padiham
Burnley
Brierfield
Nelson
Colne
Barrowford
Trawden
Foulridge
Earby
Barnoldswick
Gisburn
Settle
Giggleswick
Bentham
Grassington
Pateley Bridge
Gargrave
Ribchester
Longridge
Ribbleton
Pendle Hill
Forest of Bowland
Gisburn Forest
Ilkley Moor
Forest of Rossendale
The Forest of Trawden
Keighley Moor
Haworth
Wadsworth Moor
Barden Fell
Ribblesdale
West Yorkshire
Lancashire

Administrative and Postcode boundaries

County and unitary authority boundaries
Postcode boundaries
Area covered by this atlas

Scale
0 5 10 15 20 25 30 35 40 km
0 5 10 15 20 25 miles

NY
SD
NZ OV
OV
TA
SD SE

County Durham
Darlington
Redcar and Cleveland
Scarborough
Cumbria
Richmondshire
Hambleton
Ryedale
North Yorkshire
Harrogate
Craven
Lancashire
Bradford
Leeds
Selby
Wakefield
East Riding of Yorkshire
Kingston-upon-Hull
York

DL12 CA17 DL11 DL10 DL9 DL8 DL7 DL6 DL2 DL1 DL3
TS21 TS18 TS5 TS4 TS3 TS6 TS16 TS17 TS7 TS8 TS14 TS12 TS13 TS15 TS9
YO21 YO22 YO13 YO18 YO62 YO11 YO12 YO14 YO16 YO17 YO25 YO61 YO60 YO7 YO51 YO30 YO32 YO26 YO41 YO42 YO31 YO1 YO24 YO10 YO19 YO23 YO8
LA10 LA6 LA2 BD24 BD23 BB7 BB18 BB8 BD20 BB22 LS29 LS21 LS17 LS22 LS23 LS14 LS15 LS24 LS25 LS26
HG4 HG3 HG5 HG1 HG2
WF6 WF10 WF11 WF8 WF7 DN14 DN6

Staithes, Runswick Bay, Whitby, Sleights, Robin Hood's Bay, Fylingthorpe, Goathland, Lealholm, Castleton, Liverton, Guisborough, Great Ayton, Stokesley, Carlton in Cleveland, Urra, Swainby, East Harlsey, Crathorne, Longnewton, Darlington, Low Dinsdale, Croft-on-Tees, Hurworth-on-Tees, Manfield, Gainford, Eppleby, Melsonby, Moulton, Richmond, North Cowton, Newsham, Whaw, Washfold, Ravenseat, Keld, Muker, Reeth, Marrick, Catterick Garrison, Catterick, Danby Wiske, Brompton, Osmotherley, Northallerton, Fangdale Beck, Rosedale Abbey, Staintondale, Harwood Dale, Cloughton, Scalby, Scarborough, Hackness, Lockton, Gillamoor, Kirkbymoorside, Pickering, Seamer, Eastfield, Filey, Staxton, Hunmanby, Sherburn, Ebberston, Thornton-le-Dale, Brawby, Helmsley, Hawnby, Boltby, Knayton, Leeming, Bedale, Snape, Thirsk, Sutton-under-Whitestonecliffe, Coxwold, Nunnington, Slingsby, Hovingham, Malton, Norton, Wintringham, Foxholes, Burton Fleming, Langtoft, North Grimston, Wharram-le-Street, Sledmere, Westow, Terrington, Raskelf, Easingwold, Stillington, Tollerton, West Lilling, Strensall, Acklam, Thixendale, Stamford Bridge, Bishop Wilton, Haxby, Linton-on-Ouse, Upper Poppleton, Tockwith, York, Copmanthorpe, Elvington, Wheldrake, Naburn, Escrick, Ellerton, Bubwith, Riccall, Barlby, Hemingbrough, Selby, Asselby, Goole, Carlton, Wistow, Ulleskelf, Tadcaster, Towton, Sherburn in Elmet, Barwick in Elmet, Garforth, Kippax, Allerton Bywater, Castleford, Normanton, Pontefract, Knottingley, Womersley, Norton, Bramham, Boston Spa, Wetherby, Spofforth, North Rigton, Knaresborough, Harrogate, Hampsthwaite, Summer Bridge, Pateley Bridge, Darley Head, Blubberhouses, Stainburn, Burley in Wharfedale, Addingham, Ilkley, Silsden, Glusburn, Earby, Barnoldswick, Skipton, Embsay, Gargrave, Airton, Cracoe, Burnsall, Grassington, Malham, Settle, Langcliffe, Long Preston, Austwick, Horton-in-Ribblesdale, Kilnsey, Arncliffe, Kettlewell, Buckden, Cray, Stalling Busk, Hawes, Bainbridge, Askrigg, Garsdale Head, Stone House, Redmire, West Witton, Leyburn, Hunton, Middleham, Carlton, Ellingstring, Fearby, Masham, Swetton, Ripon, Dishforth, Brafferton, Boroughbridge, Ingleton, High Bentham, Wray, Cowan Bridge

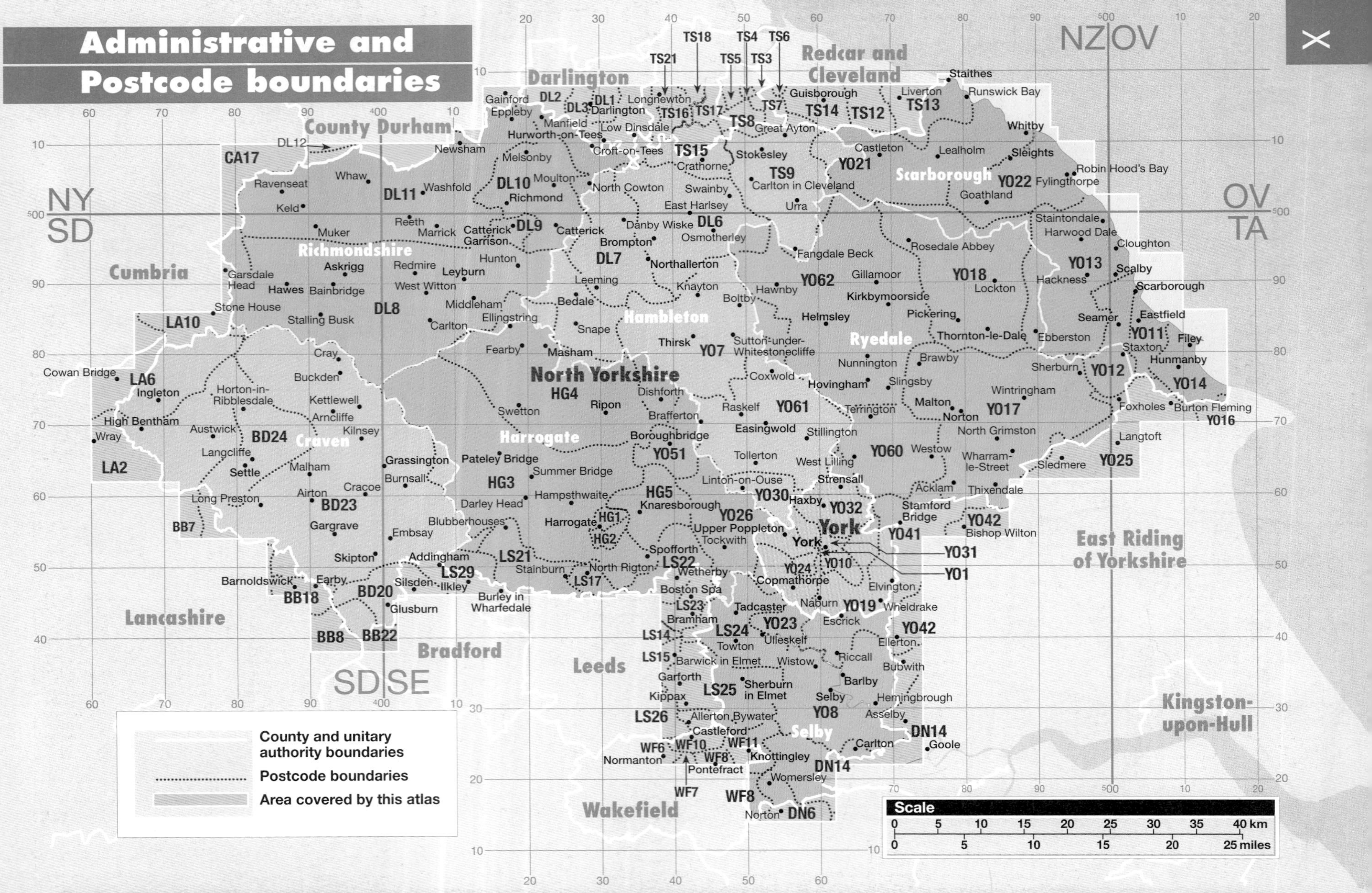

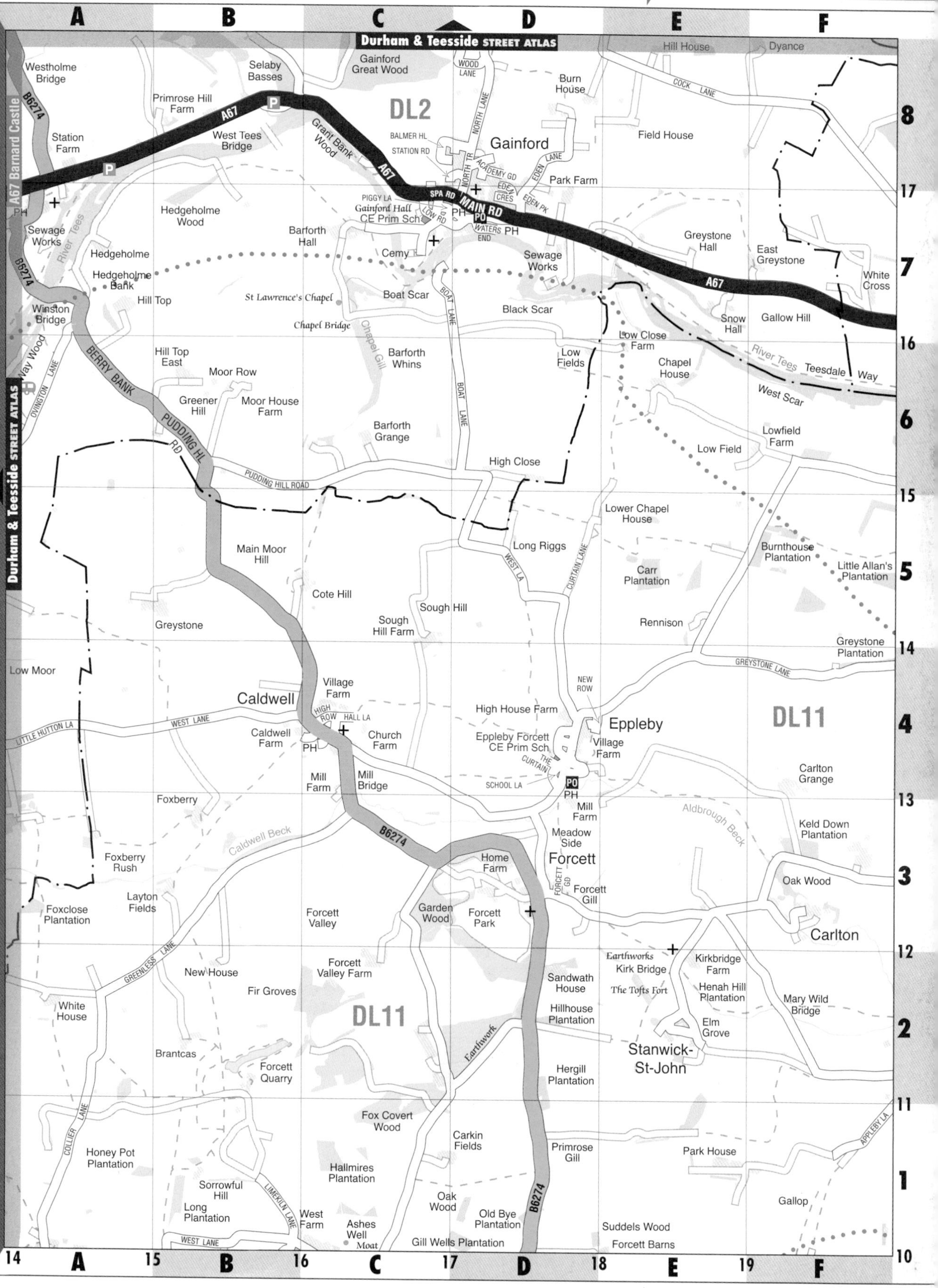

Scale: 1¾ inches to 1 mile

0 ¼ ½ mile
0 250m 500m 750m 1 km

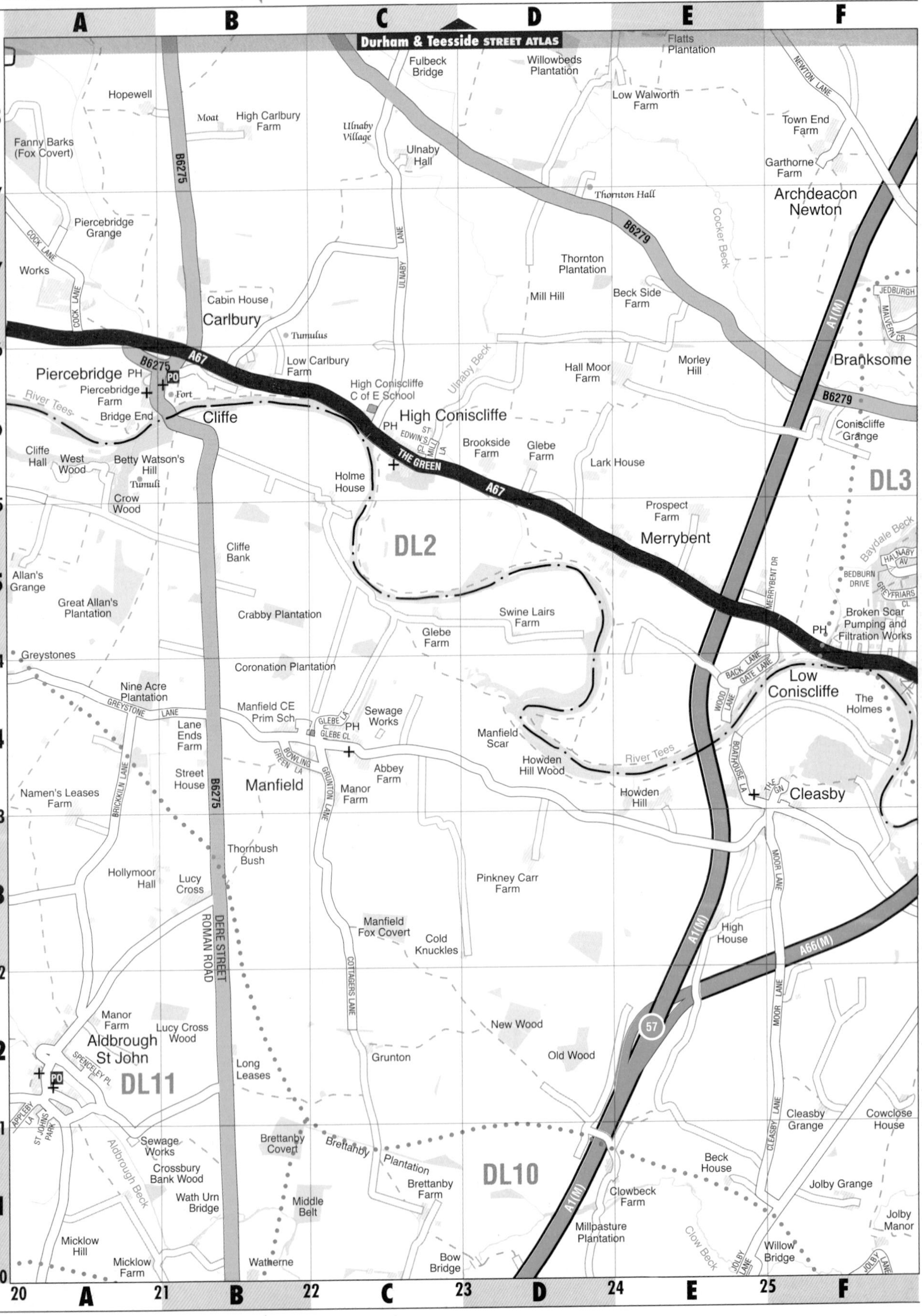

A B C D E F

Durham & Teesside STREET ATLAS

Flatts Plantation

Hopewell

Fulbeck Bridge

Willowbeds Plantation

Low Walworth Farm

Town End Farm

8

Fanny Barks (Fox Covert)

Moat

High Carlbury Farm

Ulnaby Village

Ulnaby Hall

Garthorne Farm

B6275

17

Thornton Hall

B6279

Archdeacon Newton

Piercebridge Grange

Cocker Beck

COCK LANE

ULNABY LANE

Thornton Plantation

JEDBURGH MALVERN CR

7

Works

Cabin House

Carlbury

Mill Hill

Beck Side Farm

A1(M)

Branksome

A67

Piercebridge PH

B6275

PO

Low Carlbury Farm

Tumulus

Hall Moor Farm

Morley Hill

B6279

Conscliffe Grange

16

Piercebridge Farm

Fort

High Coniscliffe C of E School

Ulnaby Beck

Bridge End

Cliffe

PH

ST EDWIN'S MILL CL

High Coniscliffe

DL3

6

River Tees

Cliffe Hall

West Wood

Betty Watson's Hill

Tumuli

Holme House

THE GREEN

Brookside Farm

Glebe Farm

Lark House

A67

15

Crow Wood

Cliffe Bank

DL2

Prospect Farm

Baydale Beck

HALNABY AV GREYFRIARS CL

5

Allan's Grange

Great Allan's Plantation

Crabby Plantation

Glebe Farm

Swine Lairs Farm

Merrybent

MERRYBENT DR

BEDBURN DRIVE

14

Greystones

Coronation Plantation

Broken Scar Pumping and Filtration Works

PH

Low Coniscliffe

4

Nine Acre Plantation

GREYSTONE LANE

Manfield CE Prim Sch

GLEBE CL

PH

Sewage Works

Manfield Scar

River Tees

Howden Hill Wood

WOOD LANE

BACK LANE

GATE LANE

The Holmes

BROCKLIN LANE

Lane Ends Farm

Street House

B6275

BOWLING GREEN LA

GRUNTON LANE

Abbey Farm

Manor Farm

Manfield

Howden Hill

BOATHOUSE LA

Cleasby

13

Namen's Leases Farm

Thornbush Bush

3

Hollymoor Hall

Lucy Cross

Manfield Fox Covert

Cold Knuckles

Pinkney Carr Farm

High House

A66(M)

DERE STREET ROMAN ROAD

COTTAGERS LANE

A1(M)

MOOR LANE

12

Cleasby Grange

Cowclose House

2

Manor Farm

Aldbrough St John

SPENCELEY PL

Lucy Cross Wood

DL11

Long Leases

Grunton

New Wood

Old Wood

57

CLEASBY LANE

11

PO

APPLEBY LANE

ST JOHNS PARK

Aldbrough Beck

Sewage Works

Crossbury Bank Wood

Brettanby Covert

Brettanby

Plantation

Beck House

Jolby Grange

1

Micklow Hill

Wath Urn Bridge

Middle Belt

Brettanby Farm

DL10

Clowbeck Farm

Millpasture Plantation

Clow Beck

JOLBY LANE

Willow Bridge

Jolby Manor

JOLBY LANE

10

Micklow Farm

Watherne

Bow Bridge

20 A 21 B 22 C 23 D 24 E 25 F

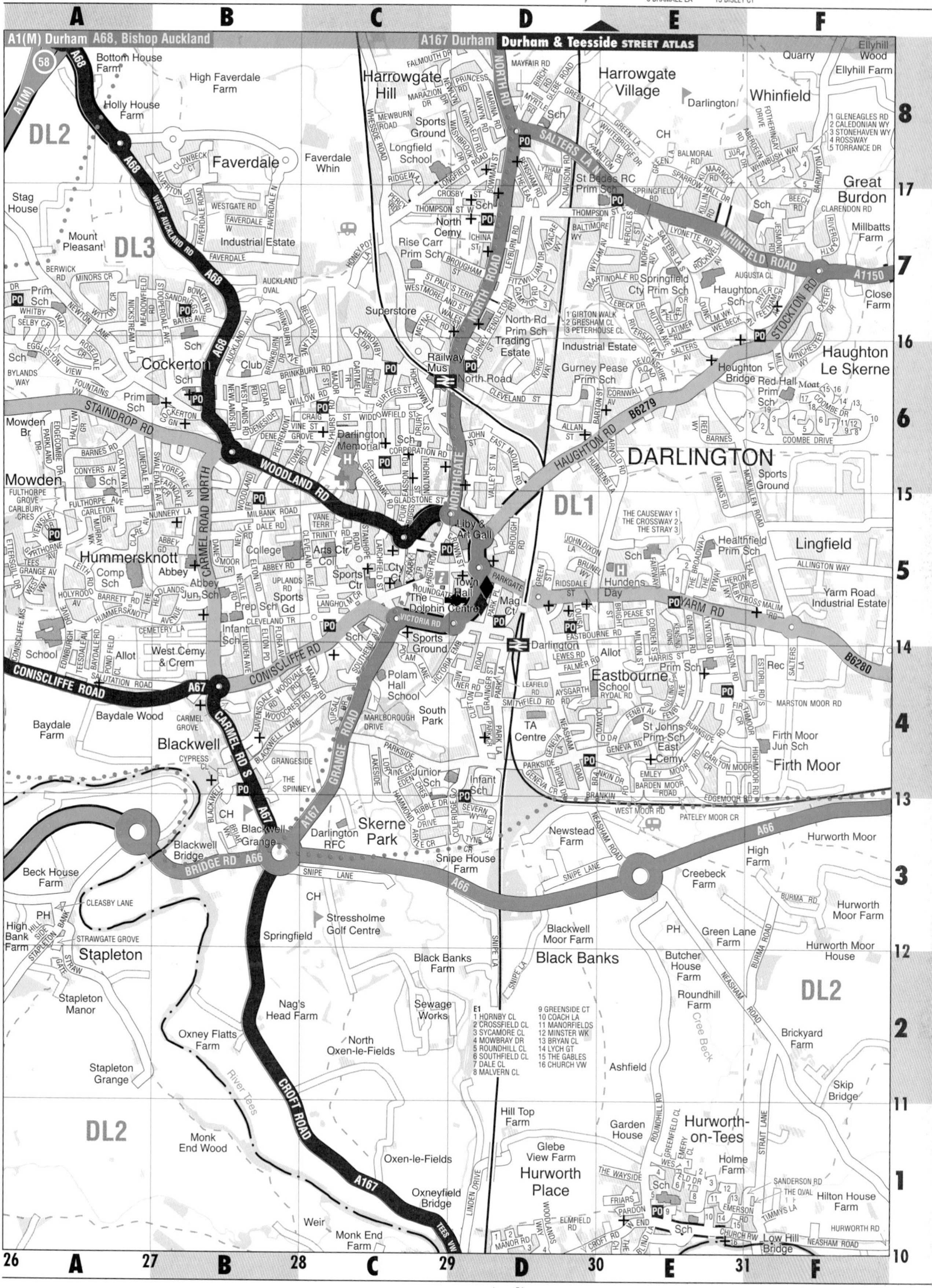

F6
1 AYRESOME WY
2 WIMBLEDON CL
3 HEADINGLEY CR
4 WHITE HART CR
5 MURRAYFIELD WY
6 BRAMALL LA
7 DEEPDALE WY
8 ANFIELD CT
9 AINTREE CT
10 AVIEMORE T
11 EPSOM CT
12 ELLAND CT
13 BISLEY CT
14 CHEPSTOW CT
15 KEMPTON CT
16 HICKSTEAD CT
17 MALLORY CT
18 BADMINTON CT
19 TRAFFORD CT

A1(M) Durham A68, Bishop Auckland   A167 Durham   **Durham & Teesside** STREET ATLAS

DL2

DL3

Bottom House Farm
High Faverdale Farm
Holly House Farm
Faverdale
Faverdale Whin
Faverdale N
Faverdale Industrial Estate
Westgate Rd

Stag House
Mount Pleasant
Cockerton

Staindrop Rd

Mowden

Hummersknott
Comp Sch

Mowden Br

Harrowgate Hill
Harrowgate Village
Whinfield

Darlington

Great Burdon
Millbatts Farm

1 GLENEAGLES RD
2 CALEDONIAN WY
3 STONEHAVEN WY
4 ROSSWAY
5 TORRANCE DR

Salters La
St Bedes RC Prim Sch
Springfield Cty Prim Sch
Haughton Sch
Whinfield Road
A1150
Close Farm

North Cemy
Rise Carr Prim Sch
Superstore
Railway Mus
North Road
North-Rd Prim Sch Trading Estate
Industrial Estate
Gurney Pease Prim Sch
Haughton Le Skerne
Houghton Bridge
Red Hall Prim Sch

1 GIRTON WALK
2 GRESHAM CL
3 PETERHOUSE CT

B6279
Coombe Drive

Woodland Rd
Darlington Memorial
College
Abbey Jun Sch
Cemetery La

DARLINGTON

DL1

Lingfield

Healthfield Prim Sch
Allington Way
Yarm Road Industrial Estate

THE CAUSEWAY 1
THE CROSSWAY 2
THE STRAY 3

Hundens Day

Conscliffe Rd
West Cemy & Crem
Infant Sch

Yarm Rd
Eastbourne
School
St Johns Prim Sch East Cemy
Firth Moor Jun Sch
Firth Moor

Coniscliffe Road
A67
Baydale Wood
Baydale Farm
Blackwell
Carmel Grove
Cypress Cl
The Spinney

Grange Road
Marlborough Drive
South Park
Polam Hall School
Junior Sch
Infant Sch
TA Centre

B6280

WEST MOOR RD
PATELEY MOOR CR
Newstead Farm
A66

Hurworth Moor
High Farm
Creebeck Farm
Hurworth Moor Farm
Hurworth Moor House

Beck House Farm
High Bank Farm
Stapleton
Stapleton Manor
Stapleton Grange

DL2

Bridge Rd A66
Blackwell Grange
Blackwell Bridge
Darlington RFC
Skerne Park
Snipe House Farm

Cleasby Lane
Strawgate Grove

Springfield
Nag's Head Farm
Oxney Flatts Farm
Stressholme Golf Centre
North Oxen-le-Fields

Black Banks Farm
Sewage Works

Black Banks
Blackwell Moor Farm

Green Lane Farm
Butcher House Farm
Roundhill Farm
Ashfield
Cree Beck

DL2
Brickyard Farm
Skip Bridge

E1
1 HORNBY CL
2 CROSSFIELD CL
3 SYCAMORE CL
4 MOWBRAY DR
5 ROUNDHILL CL
6 SOUTHFIELD CL
7 DALE CL
8 MALVERN CL
9 GREENSIDE CT
10 COACH LA
11 MANORFIELDS
12 MINSTER WK
13 BRYAN CL
14 LYCH GT
15 THE GABLES
16 CHURCH VW

Monk End Wood

Croft Road
A167

Oxen-le-Fields
Oxneyfield Bridge
Weir
Monk End Farm

Hill Top Farm
Glebe View Farm
Hurworth Place

Garden House
Hurworth-on-Tees
Holme Farm
The Wayside
Friars Pardon
Hilton House Farm
Hurworth Rd
Low Hill Bridge
Neasham Road

D1
1 HAWKSWOOD
2 EDEN CL
3 GRANGE AVE
4 HUNTERS CL

For full street detail of Darlington see Philip's **STREET ATLAS of Co. Durham and Teesside**

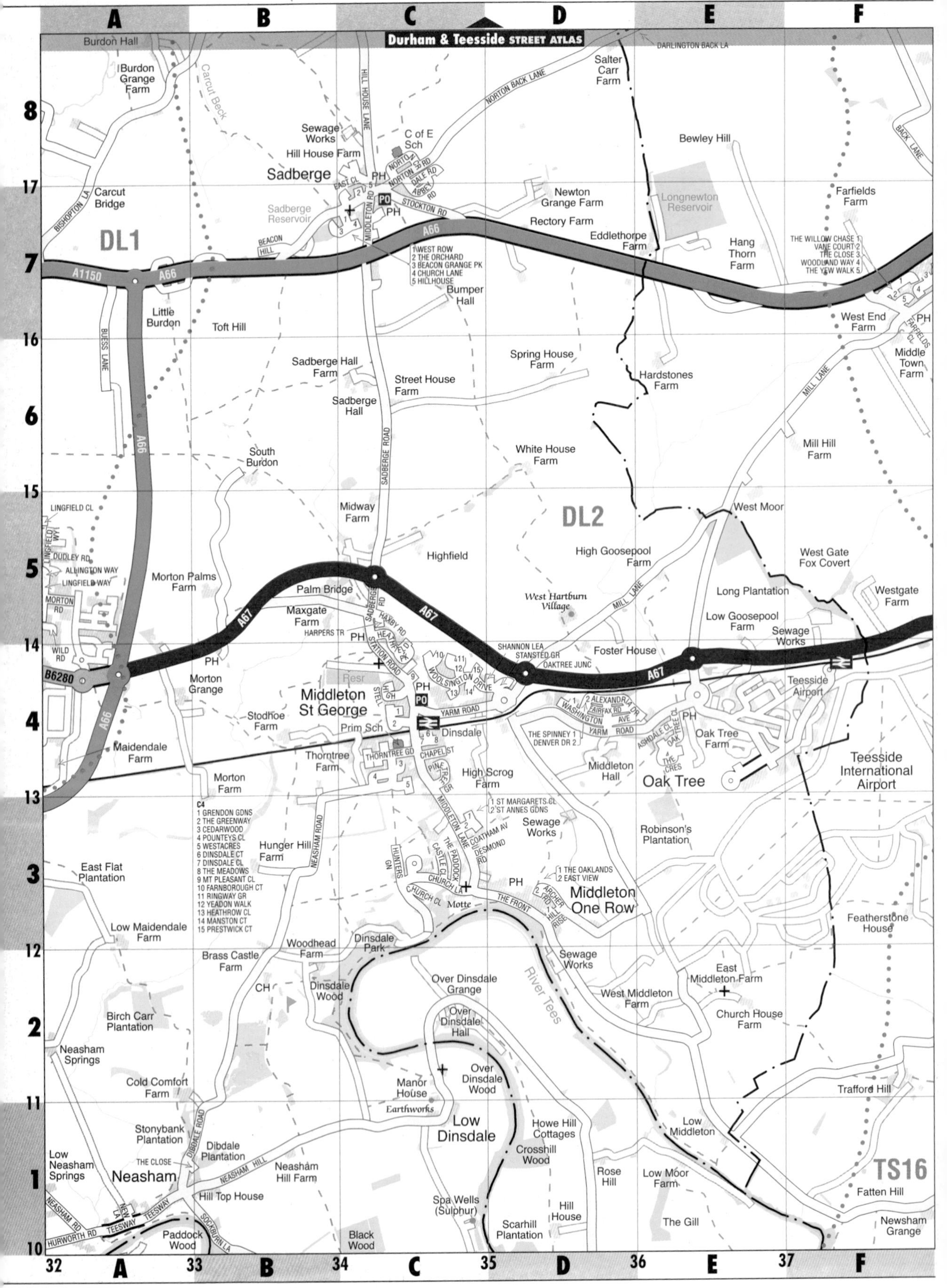

3

Scale: 1¾ inches to 1 mile

| 0 | ¼ | ½ | mile |

| 0 | 250m | 500m | 750m | 1 km |

Durham & Teesside STREET ATLAS

A B C D E F

Burdon Hall

Burdon Grange Farm

Carcut Back

Sewage Works

Hill House Farm

Sadberge

C of E Sch

PH

Salter Carr Farm

DARLINGTON BACK LA

Bewley Hill

Farfields Farm

8

BISHOPTON LA

Carcut Bridge

HILL HOUSE LANE

NORTON BACK LANE

NORTON S RD

DALE RD

ABBEY RD

STOCKTON RD

Newton Grange Farm

Rectory Farm

Longnewton Reservoir

Hang Thorn Farm

BACK LANE

THE WILLOW CHASE 1
VANE COURT 2
THE CLOSE 3
WOODLAND WAY 4
THE YEW WALK 5

17

DL1

Sadberge Reservoir

PO
PH

EAST CL

MIDDLETON RD

A66

Eddlethorpe Farm

West End Farm

FARFIELDS CL

PH

7

A1150

A66

BLUESS LANE

Little Burdon

Toft Hill

BEACON HILL

1 WEST ROW
2 THE ORCHARD
3 BEACON GRANGE PK
4 CHURCH LANE
5 HILLHOUSE

Bumper Hall

Spring House Farm

Hardstones Farm

MILL LANE

Middle Town Farm

16

A66

Sadberge Hall Farm

Street House Farm

Sadberge Hall

SADBERGE ROAD

White House Farm

DL2

West Moor

West Gate Fox Covert

Westgate Farm

6

South Burdon

Midway Farm

Highfield

High Goosepool Farm

MILL LANE

Long Plantation

Low Goosepool Farm

Sewage Works

15

LINGFIELD CL

LINGFIELD WY

DUDLEY RD

ALLINGTON WAY

LINGFIELD WAY

Morton Palms Farm

Palm Bridge

A67

Maxgate Farm

HARPERS TR

PH

SADBERGE RD

HANBY AV

A67

West Hartburn Village

Westgate Farm

5

MORTON RD

WILD RD

PH

Morton Grange

STATION ROAD

Resr

WOOLSINGTON DRIVE

SHANNON LEA
STANSTED GR
OAKTREE JUNC

Foster House

A67

Teesside Airport

14

B6280

A66

Maidendale Farm

Stodhoe Farm

Morton Farm

Middleton St George

Prim Sch

STEEL

PH
PO

YARM ROAD

Dinsdale

WASHINGTON

2 ALEXANDRA
FAIRFAX RD
AVE

YARM ROAD

THE SPINNEY 1
DENVER DR 2

Middleton Hall

ASHDALE CL

OAK

THE CRES

PH

Oak Tree Farm

Oak Tree

Teesside International Airport

4

Thorntree Farm

THORNTREE GD

CHAPEL ST

PINE TREE GR

High Scrog Farm

13

C4
1 GRENDON GDNS
2 THE GREENWAY
3 CEDARWOOD
4 POUNTEYS CL
5 WESTACRES
6 DINSDALE CT
7 DINSDALE CL
8 THE MEADOWS
9 MT PLEASANT CL
10 FARNBOROUGH CT
11 RINGWAY GR
12 YEADON WALK
13 HEATHROW CL
14 MANSTON CT
15 PRESTWICK CT

East Flat Plantation

Hunger Hill Farm

NEASHAM ROAD

HUNTERS GN

CASTLE CL

THE PADDOCK

CHURCH CL

COATHAM AV

DESMOND RD

1 ST MARGARETS CL
2 ST ANNES GDNS

Sewage Works

Robinson's Plantation

Featherstone House

3

Low Maidendale Farm

Brass Castle Farm

Woodhead Farm

CH

Dinsdale Park

Dinsdale Wood

CHURCH CL

MIDDLETON ROAD

Motte

THE FRONT

ARCHER RD

HILL RISE

1 THE OAKLANDS
2 EAST VIEW

Middleton One Row

12

Birch Carr Plantation

DIBDALE ROAD

Over Dinsdale Grange

River Tees

Sewage Works

West Middleton Farm

East Middleton Farm

Church House Farm

2

Neasham Springs

Cold Comfort Farm

Stonybank Plantation

Dibdale Plantation

Neasham Hill Farm

THE CLOSE

Dinsdale Wood

Over Dinsdale Hall

Manor House

Earthworks

Over Dinsdale Wood

Low Dinsdale

Howe Hill Cottages

Crosshill Wood

Low Middleton

Trafford Hill

11

Low Neasham Springs

Neasham

NEASHAM RD

HURWORTH RD

VIEW

TEESWAY
TEESWAY

SOCKBURN LA

NEASHAM HILL

Paddock Wood

Hill Top House

Black Wood

Spa Wells (Sulphur)

Scarhill Plantation

Hill House

Rose Hill

Low Moor Farm

The Gill

Fatten Hill

TS16

Newsham Grange

10

A B C D E F

3 23

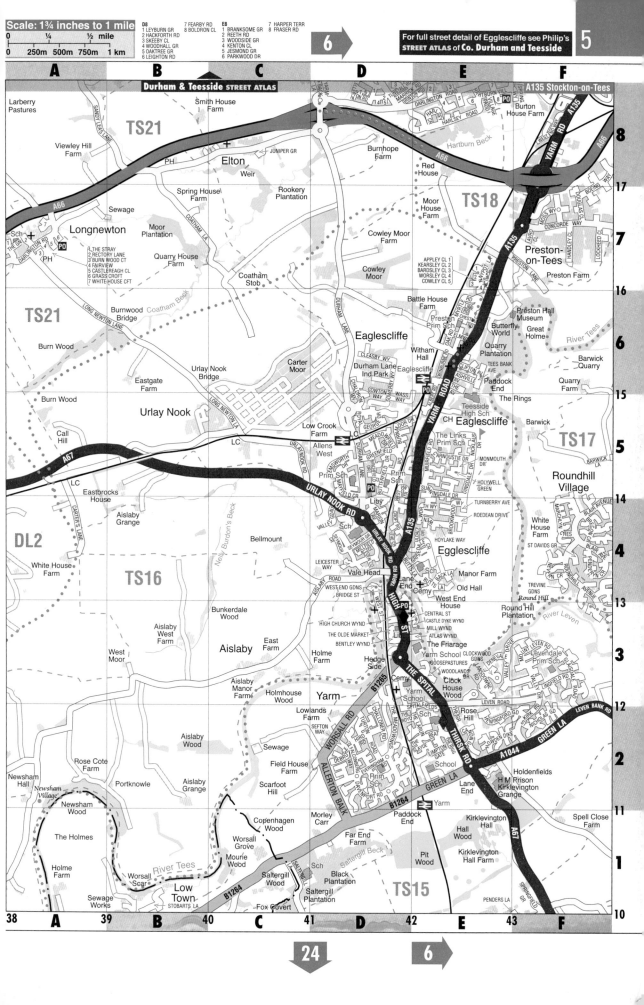

D8
1 LEYBURN GR
2 HACKFORTH RD
3 SKEEBY CL
4 WOODHALL GR
5 OAKTREE GR
6 LEIGHTON RD
7 FEARBY RD
8 BOLDRON CL

E8
1 BRANSOME GR
2 REETH RD
3 WOODSIDE GR
4 KENTON CL
5 JESMOND GR
6 PARKWOOD DR
7 HARPER TERR
8 FRASER RD

6 →

For full street detail of Egglescliffe see Philip's
STREET ATLAS of Co. Durham and Teesside

5

Durham & Teesside STREET ATLAS

A   B   C   D   E   F

A135 Stockton-on-Tees

Larberry Pastures

Smith House Farm

TS21

Viewley Hill Farm

Elton
Weir

Juniper Gr

Burnhope Farm

Red House

TS18

8

17

Hartburn Beck

Spring House Farm

Rookery Plantation

Moor House Farm

Burton House Farm

A66 Longnewton

Moor Plantation

1 THE STRAY
2 RECTORY LANE
3 BURN WOOD CT
4 FAIRVIEW
5 CASTLEREAGH CL
6 GRASS CROFT
7 WHITE HOUSE CFT

Cowley Moor Farm

Preston-on-Tees

Preston Farm

7

Quarry House Farm

Coatham Stob

Cowley Moor

APPLEY CL 1
KEARSLEY CL 2
BARDSLEY CL 3
WORSLEY CL 4
COWLEY CL 5

16

TS21

Long Newton Lane

Burnwood Bridge

Coatham Beck

Carter Moor

Battle House Farm

Preston Prim Sch

Preston Hall Museum

Great Holme

River Tees

6

Burn Wood

Eastgate Farm

Eaglescliffe

Witham Hall

Butterfly World

Quarry Plantation

Barwick Quarry

Urlay Nook Bridge

Durham Lane Ind Park

Eaglescliffe

Paddock End

The Rings

Quarry Farm

15

Call Hill

Burn Wood

Urlay Nook

Low Crook Farm

Allens West

Teesside High Sch

Eaglescliffe

Barwick

TS17

A67

The Links Prim Sch

Roundhill Village

5

LC

Eastbrocks House

Prim Sch

Greenfield

MONMOUTH DR

HOLYWELL GREEN

White House Farm

14

DL2

Aislaby Grange

Bellmount

PO

Liby

TURNBERRY AVE

ROEDEAN DRIVE

Round Hill

TS16

Egglescliffe

13

Bunkerdale Wood

LEICESTER WAY

Vale Head

Manor Farm

Old Hall

West End House

Round Hill Plantation

River Leven

West End Gdns

Bridge St

West Moor

Aislaby West Farm

East Moor

Aislaby

Holme Farm

Hedge Side

HIGH CHURCH WYND
THE OLDE MARKET
BENTLEY WYND

CENTRAL ST
CASTLE DYKE WYND
MILL WYND
ATLAS WYND

The Friarage

Yarm School

Clock House Wood

3

West Moor

Holmhouse Wood

Yarm

THE SPITAL

Yarm School

Cemy

2

Aislaby Manor Farm

Lowlands Farm

SEFTON WAY

B1265

Cemy

Rose Hill

12

Rose Cote Farm

Field House Farm

Sewage

School

H M Prison Kirklevington Grange

Holdenfields

GREEN LA

A1044

Newsham Hall

Newsham Village

Portknowle

Aislaby Wood

Scarfoot Hill

B1264

Yarm

Paddock End

Far End Farm

Kirklevington Hall

Hall Wood

Spell Close Farm

11

Newsham Wood

Aislaby Grange

Copenhagen Wood

Morley Carr

Kirklevington Hall Farm

A67

The Holmes

Worsall Grove

Mourie Wood

Pit Wood

1

Holme Farm

River Tees

Low Town

Saltergill Wood

Black Plantation

TS15

PENDERS LA

Sewage Works

STOBARTS LA

B1264

Fox Covert

Saltergill Plantation

SPRINGFIELD

10

38   A   39   B   40   C   41   D   42   E   43   F   10

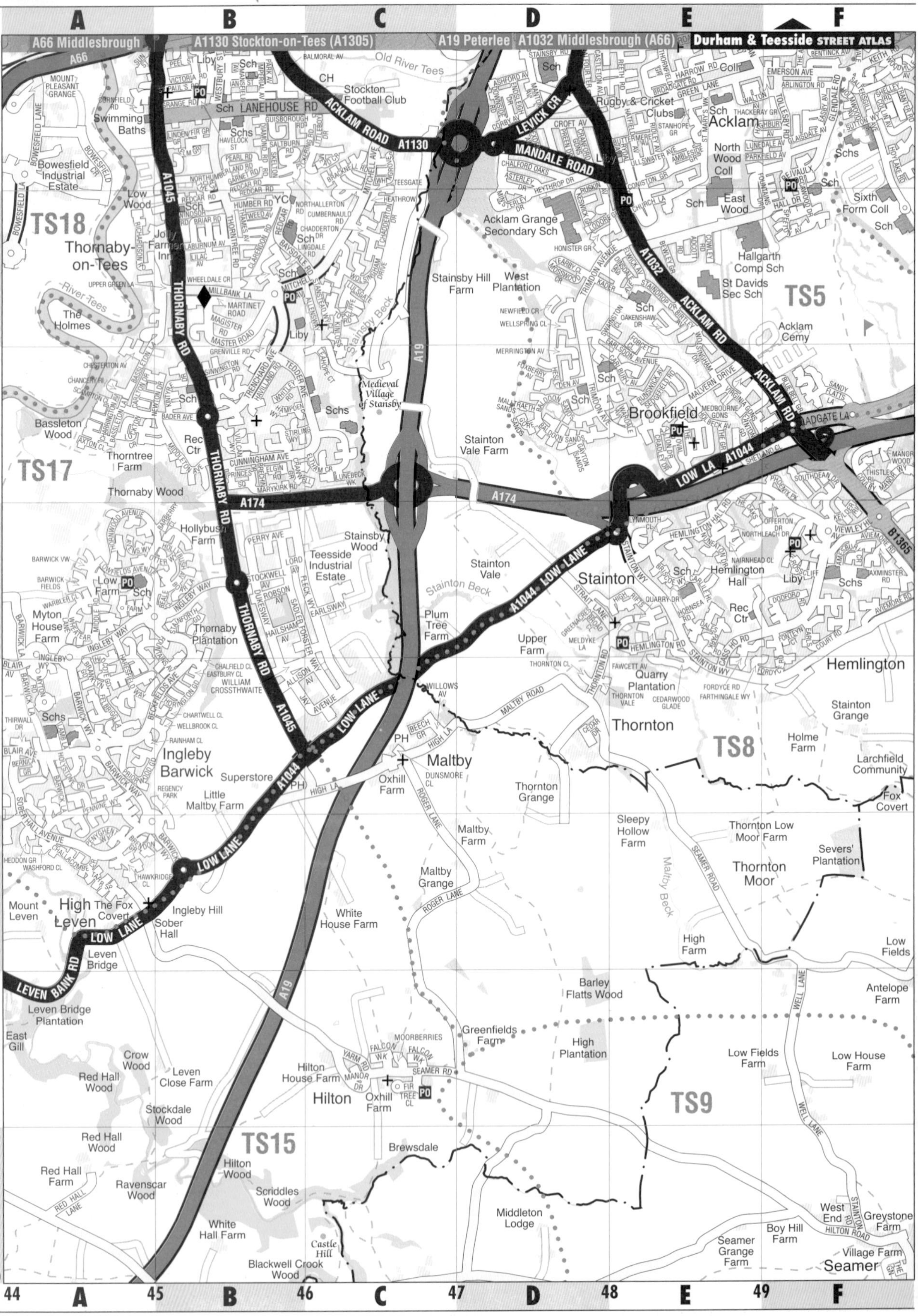

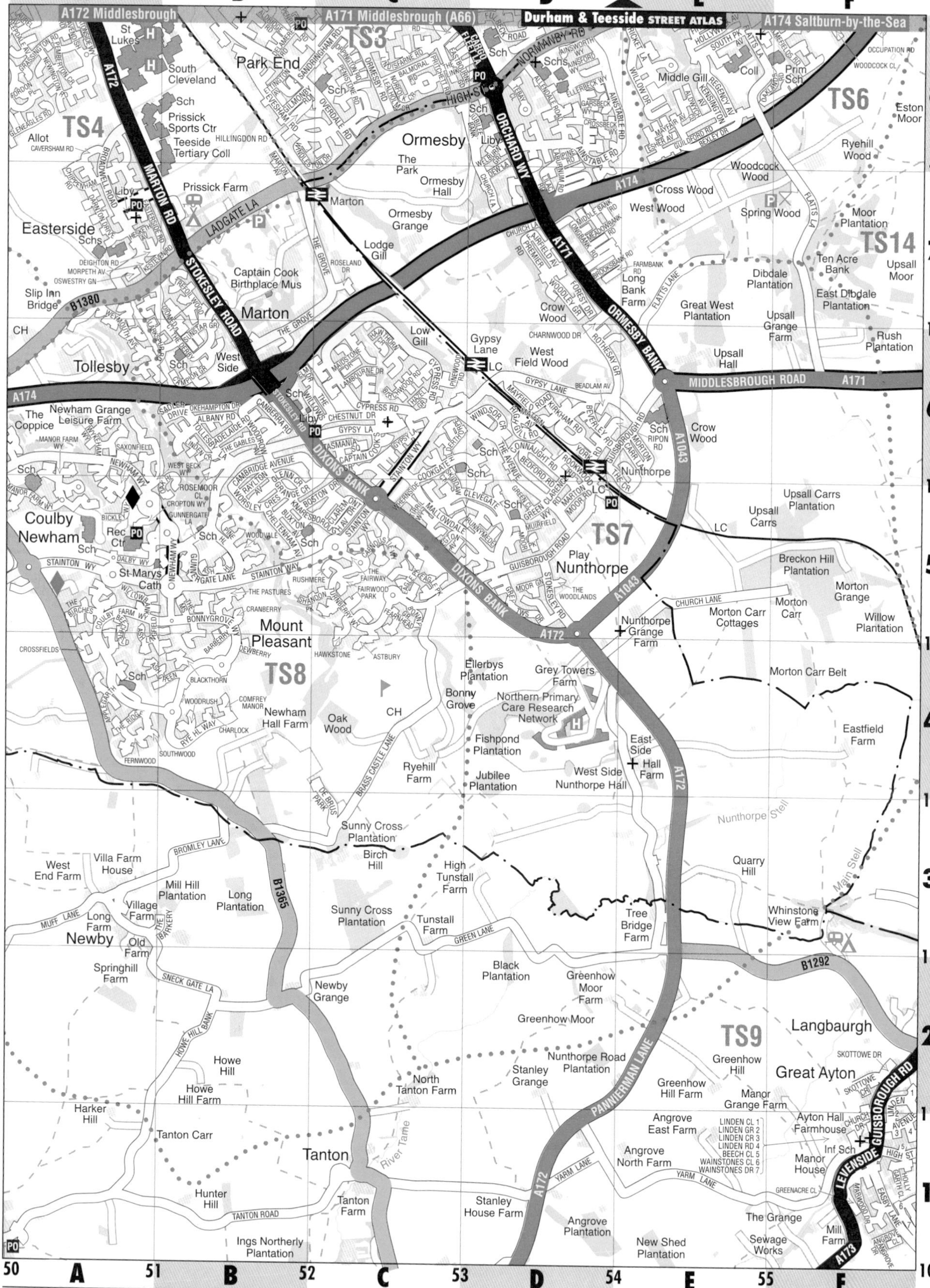

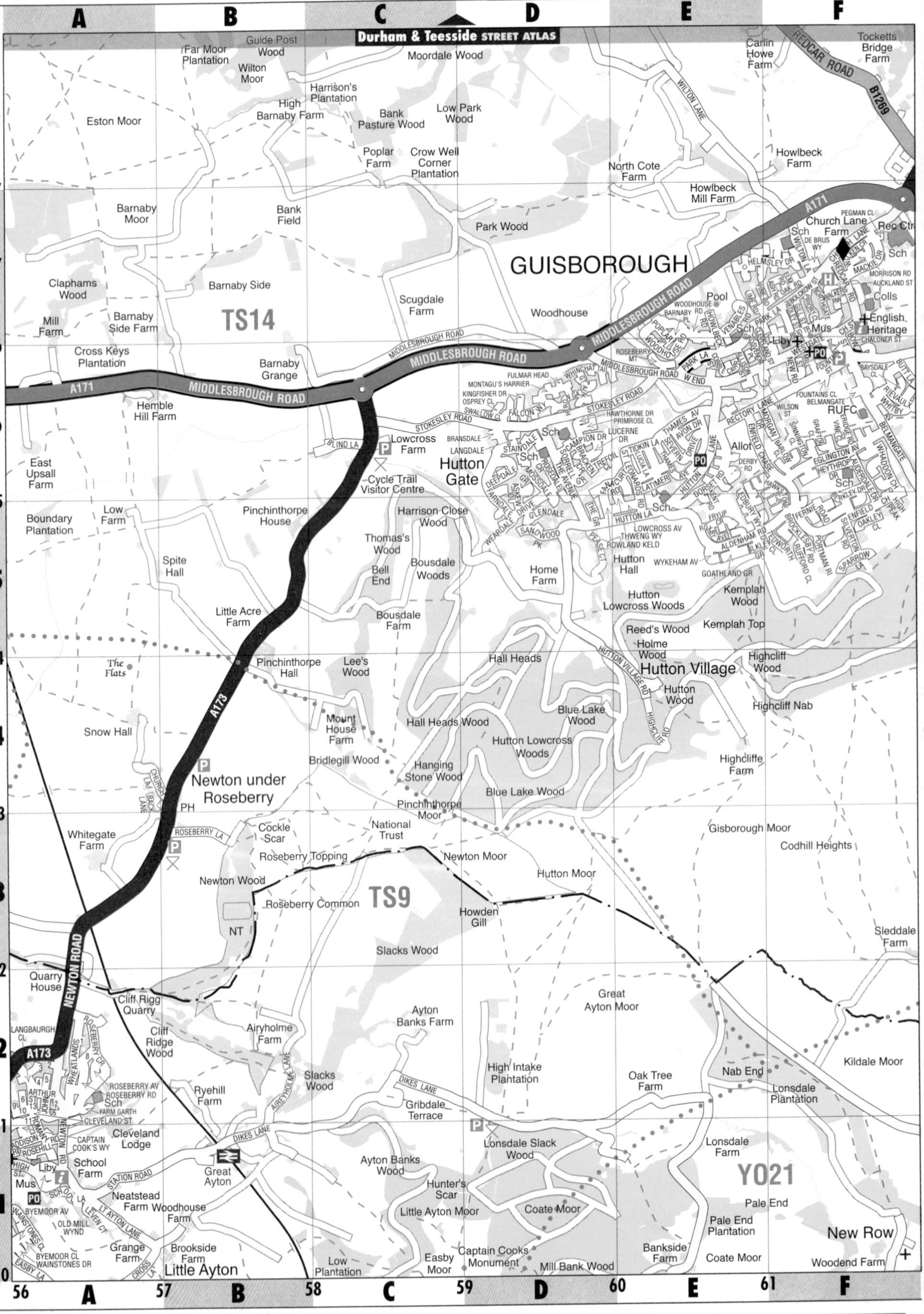

Scale: 1¾ inches to 1 mile

0 ¼ ½ mile
0 250m 500m 750m 1 km

Durham & Teesside STREET ATLAS

A B C D E F

Far Moor Plantation
Guide Post Wood
Moordale Wood
Wilton Moor
Harrison's Plantation
High Barnaby Farm
Bank Pasture Wood
Low Park Wood
Carlin Howe Farm
Tocketts Bridge Farm
REDCAR ROAD
B1269

Eston Moor
Poplar Farm
Crow Well Corner Plantation
North Cote Farm
Howlbeck Farm

WILTON LANE

8

17

Barnaby Moor
Bank Field
Park Wood
Howlbeck Mill Farm
A171
Church Lane Farm
Sch
Mus
PEGMAN CL
Rec Ctr
Sch

7

Claphams Wood
Barnaby Side
Scugdale Farm
GUISBOROUGH
Woodhouse
Pool
English Heritage
Colls

Mill Farm
Barnaby Side Farm
TS14
MIDDLESBROUGH ROAD
MIDDLESBROUGH ROAD
Liby
PO

16

Cross Keys Plantation
Barnaby Grange
Barnaby Grange
MIDDLESBROUGH ROAD
RUFC

A171 MIDDLESBROUGH ROAD

6

Hemble Hill Farm
BLIND LA
Lowcross Farm
Fulmar Head
Montagu's Harrier
Kingfisher Dr
Osprey Cl
Swallow Cl
Falcon Cl
Hawthorne Dr
Primrose Cl
Thames Av
PO

East Upsall Farm
Lowcross
Cycle Trail Visitor Centre
Hutton Gate
Stokesley Road
Stokesley Road
Sch
Sch

15

Boundary Plantation
Low Farm
Pinchinthorpe House
Harrison Close Wood
Home Farm
Hutton Lowcross Woods
Kemplah Wood

Spite Hall
Thomas's Wood
Bell End
Bousdale Woods
Hutton Hall
Wykeham Av
Kemplah Top

5

Little Acre Farm
Bousdale Farm
Reed's Wood
Holme Wood
Highcliff Wood

The Flats
Pinchinthorpe Hall
Lee's Wood
Hall Heads
Hutton Wood
Hutton Village
Highcliff Nab

14

Snow Hall
Mount House Farm
Hall Heads Wood
Blue Lake Wood
Highcliffe Farm

A173
Bridlegill Wood
Hanging Stone Wood
Hutton Lowcross Woods
Highcliffe

4

Newton under Roseberry
Pinchinthorpe Moor
Blue Lake Wood
Gisborough Moor
Codhill Heights

13

Whitegate Farm
Cockle Scar
National Trust
Newton Moor
Hutton Moor

ROSEBERRY LA
Roseberry Topping
Sleddale Farm

3

Newton Wood
Roseberry Common
NT
TS9
Howden Gill

Quarry House
NEWTON ROAD
Slacks Wood

12

Cliff Rigg Quarry
Ayton Banks Farm
Great Ayton Moor

LANGBAURGH CL
Cliff Ridge Wood
Airyholme Farm
High Intake Plantation
Nab End
Lonsdale Plantation
Kildale Moor

A173
Ryehill Farm
Slacks Wood
Oak Tree Farm

2

ROSEBERRY AV
ROSEBERRY RD
FARM GARTH
CLEVELAND ST
DIKES LANE
Gribdale Terrace
Lonsdale Farm

CAPTAIN COOK'S WY
Cleveland Lodge
Lonsdale Slack Wood
YO21

11

School Farm
Great Ayton
Ayton Banks Wood
Pale End

Neatstead Farm
Woodhouse Farm
Hunter's Scar
Pale End Plantation
New Row

BYEMOOR AV
OLD MILL WYND
Grange Farm
Brookside Farm
Little Ayton
Little Ayton Moor
Captain Cooks Monument
Low Plantation
Easby Moor
Coate Moor
Mill Bank Wood
Bankside Farm
Coate Moor
Woodend Farm

1

10

56 57 58 59 60 61
A B C D E F

A2
1 ORCHARD CL
2 BRADLEYS TR
3 CHURCHILL CL
4 SPENCE CT
5 ROWAN DR
6 CENTRAL WY
7 CALIFORNIA GR
8 ROSEBERRY DR
9 OAKLANDS
10 THE HAWTHORNS
11 ROMANY RD
12 WOODBINE CL
13 WHINSTONE VW

For full street detail of Guisborough see Philip's
STREET ATLAS of Co. Durham and Teesside

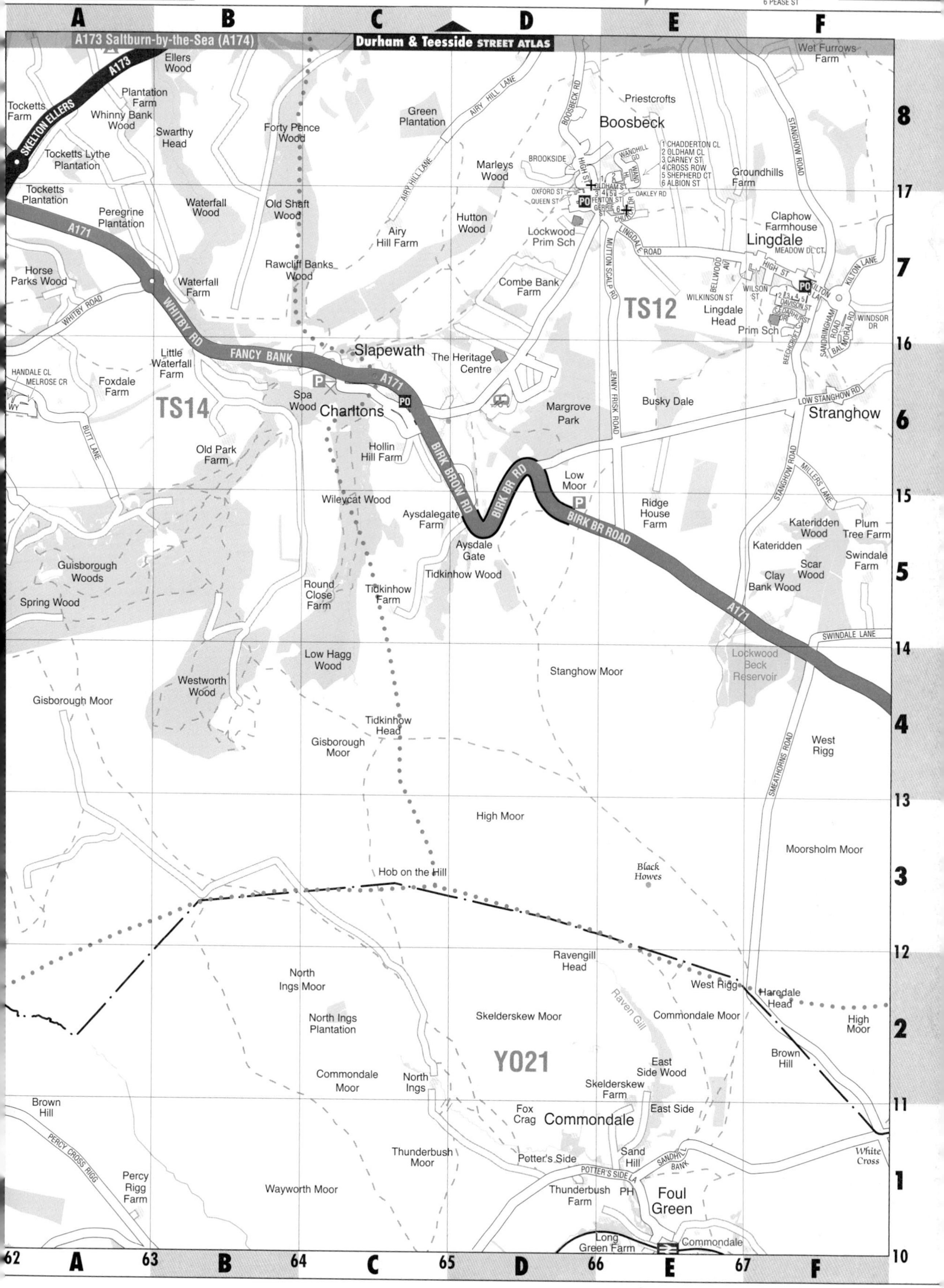

Scale: 1¾ inches to 1 mile

0   ¼   ½   mile
0   250m 500m 750m 1 km

10 →

9

F7
1 PROSPECT TR
2 CATHERINE ST
3 SCARTH CL
4 PEASE CT
5 COCKBURN ST
6 PEASE ST

A173 Saltburn-by-the-Sea (A174)

Durham & Teesside STREET ATLAS

A173

Tocketts Farm

SKELTON ELLERS

Ellers Wood

Plantation Farm

Whinny Bank Wood

Swarthy Head

Forty Pence Wood

Tocketts Lythe Plantation

Green Plantation

Boosbeck

Priestcrofts

1 CHADDERTON CL
2 OLDHAM CL
3 CARNEY ST
4 CROSS ROW
5 SHEPHERD CT
6 ALBION ST

BOOSBECK RD

STANGHOW ROAD

Groundhills Farm

Tocketts Plantation

A171

Peregrine Plantation

Waterfall Wood

Old Shaft Wood

Marleys Wood

BROOKSIDE

HIGH ST

WANDHILL GD

OLDHAM ST

Claphow Farmhouse

Lingdale

Horse Parks Wood

WHITBY ROAD

Waterfall Farm

Airy Hill Farm

AIRY HILL LANE

Hutton Wood

OXFORD ST
Queen St

FENTON ST

GERRIE

OAKLEY RD

Oakley Rd

TS12

MEADOW DR CT.

WILKINSON ST

WILSON ST

HIGH ST

Lingdale Head

Prim Sch

BELLWOOD

SANDRINGHAM ROAD

KILTON LANE

WINDSOR DR

HANDALE CL
MELROSE CR

WY

Foxdale Farm

Little Waterfall Farm

FANCY BANK

Slapewath

A171

The Heritage Centre

Lockwood Prim Sch

MUTTON SCALP RD

LINGDALE ROAD

CHURCH

BEECHWOOD

BAL MORAL

Stranghow

TS14

Spa Wood

Charltons

P

PO

Combe Bank Farm

JENNY FRISK ROAD

Margrove Park

Busky Dale

LOW STANGHOW RD

Old Park Farm

Hollin Hill Farm

BIRK BROW RD

BIRK BR RD

Low Moor

Ridge House Farm

MILLERS LANE

Kateridden Wood

Plum Tree Farm

Wileycat Wood

Aysdalegate Farm

Aysdale Gate

Tidkinhow Wood

BIRK BR ROAD

P

SMEATHORNS ROAD

STANGHOW ROAD

Kateridden

Scar Wood

Clay Bank Wood

Swindale Farm

Guisborough Woods

Round Close Farm

Tidkinhow Farm

A171

SWINDALE LANE

Spring Wood

Low Hagg Wood

Westworth Wood

Lockwood Beck Reservoir

Gisborough Moor

Tidkinhow Head

Gisborough Moor

Stanghow Moor

West Rigg

High Moor

Moorsholm Moor

Hob on the Hill

Black Howes

North Ings Moor

Ravengill Head

West Rigg

Haredale Head

High Moor

North Ings Plantation

Skelderskew Moor

Raven Gill

Commondale Moor

Brown Hill

Commondale Moor

North Ings

YO21

East Side Wood

Skelderskew Farm

East Side

Brown Hill

Fox Crag

Commondale

PERCY CROSS RIGG

Percy Rigg Farm

Thunderbush Moor

Potter's Side

POTTER'S SIDE LA

Sand Hill

SANDHILL BANK

White Cross

Wayworth Moor

Thunderbush Farm

Thunderbush PH

Foul Green

Long Green Farm

Commondale

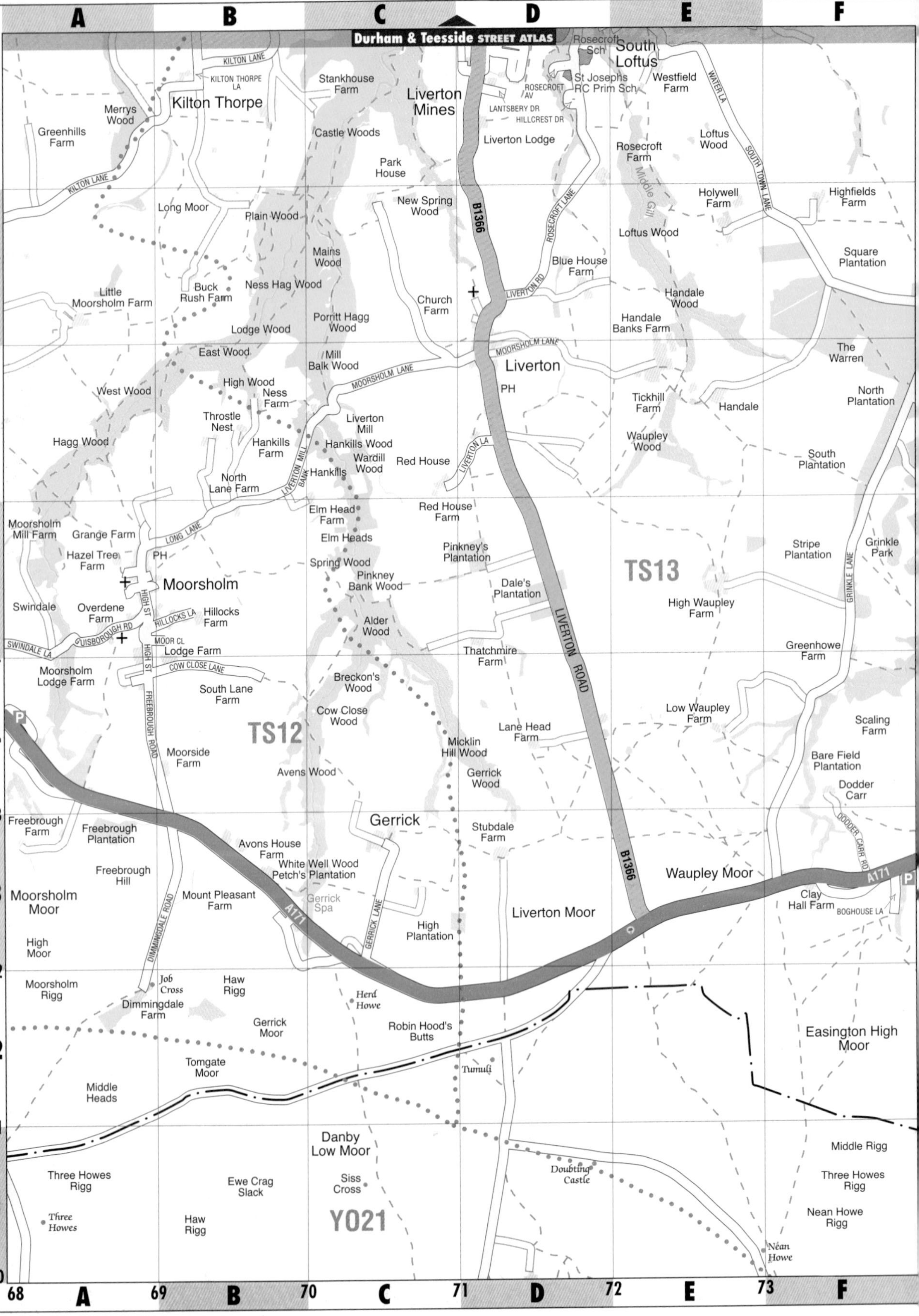

Scale: 1¾ inches to 1 mile

0 ¼ ½ mile
0 250m 500m 750m 1 km

Durham & Teesside STREET ATLAS

A **B** **C** **D** **E** **F**

KILTON LANE
KILTON THORPE LA

Stankhouse Farm

Rosecroft Sch

South Loftus

Liverton Mines

St Josephs RC Prim Sch

Westfield Farm

WATER LA

8

Greenhills Farm

Merrys Wood

Kilton Thorpe

Castle Woods

ROSECROFT AV
LANTSBERY DR
HILLCREST DR

Rosecroft Farm

Loftus Wood

Liverton Lodge

Middle Gill

SOUTH TOWN LANE

17

KILTON LANE

Long Moor

Plain Wood

Park House

New Spring Wood

B1366

Loftus Wood

Holywell Farm

Highfields Farm

7

Little Moorsholm Farm

Buck Rush Farm

Mains Wood

Ness Hag Wood

Church Farm

Blue House Farm

LIVERTON RD

Handale Wood

Square Plantation

16

Lodge Wood

East Wood

Porritt Hagg Wood

Mill Balk Wood

Moorsholm Lane

MOORSHOLM LANE

Liverton

PH

Handale Banks Farm

The Warren

North Plantation

6

Hagg Wood

West Wood

High Wood
Ness Farm

Throstle Nest

Liverton Mill

Hankills Wood
Wardill Wood

Red House

LIVERTON LA

Tickhill Farm

Waupley Wood

Handale

South Plantation

15

Moorsholm Mill Farm

Grange Farm

Hazel Tree Farm

PH

Hankills Farm

North Lane Farm

BANK MILL

Hankills

Elm Head Farm

Elm Heads

Red House Farm

Pinkney's Plantation

Stripe Plantation

Grinkle Park

5

Swindale

Overdene Farm

HILLOCKS LA

MOOR CL

LONG LANE

HIGH ST

Moorsholm

Hillocks Farm

Spring Wood

Pinkney Bank Wood

Dale's Plantation

TS13

GRINKLE LANE

High Waupley Farm

Greenhowe Farm

14

SWINDALE LA

GUISBOROUGH RD

Moorsholm Lodge Farm

HIGH ST

COW CLOSE LANE

Lodge Farm

South Lane Farm

Alder Wood

Thatchmire Farm

Lane Head Farm

Low Waupley Farm

Scaling Farm

Bare Field Plantation

Dodder Carr

4

P

FREEBROUGH ROAD

Moorside Farm

TS12

Breckon's Wood

Cow Close Wood

Avens Wood

Micklin Hill Wood

Gerrick Wood

LIVERTON ROAD

DODDER CARR RD

13

Freebrough Farm

Freebrough Plantation

DIMMINGDALE ROAD

Avons House Farm
White Well Wood
Petch's Plantation

Gerrick

Stubdale Farm

B1366

Waupley Moor

A171

Clay Hall Farm

P

BOGHOUSE LA

3

Moorsholm Moor

Freebrough Hill

Mount Pleasant Farm

A171

GERRICK LANE

Gerrick Spa

High Plantation

Liverton Moor

High Moor

Job Cross

Haw Rigg

Herd Howe

2

Moorsholm Rigg

Dimmingdale Farm

Gerrick Moor

Robin Hood's Butts

Easington High Moor

Tomgate Moor

Tumuli

Middle Heads

Danby Low Moor

Middle Rigg

11

Three Howes Rigg

Ewe Crag Slack

Siss Cross

Doubting Castle

Three Howes Rigg

1

Three Howes

Haw Rigg

YO21

Nean Howe Rigg

Nean Howe

10

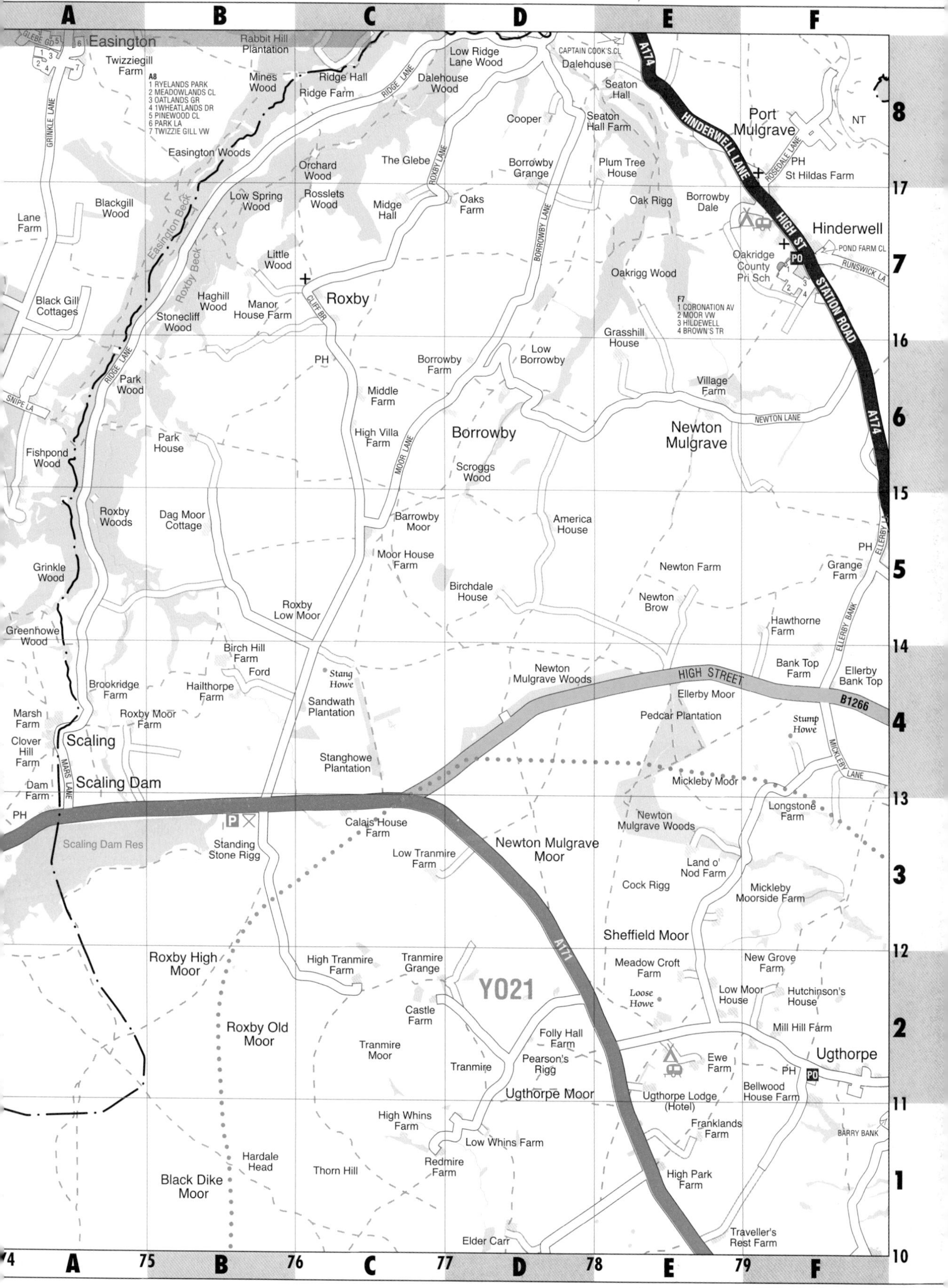

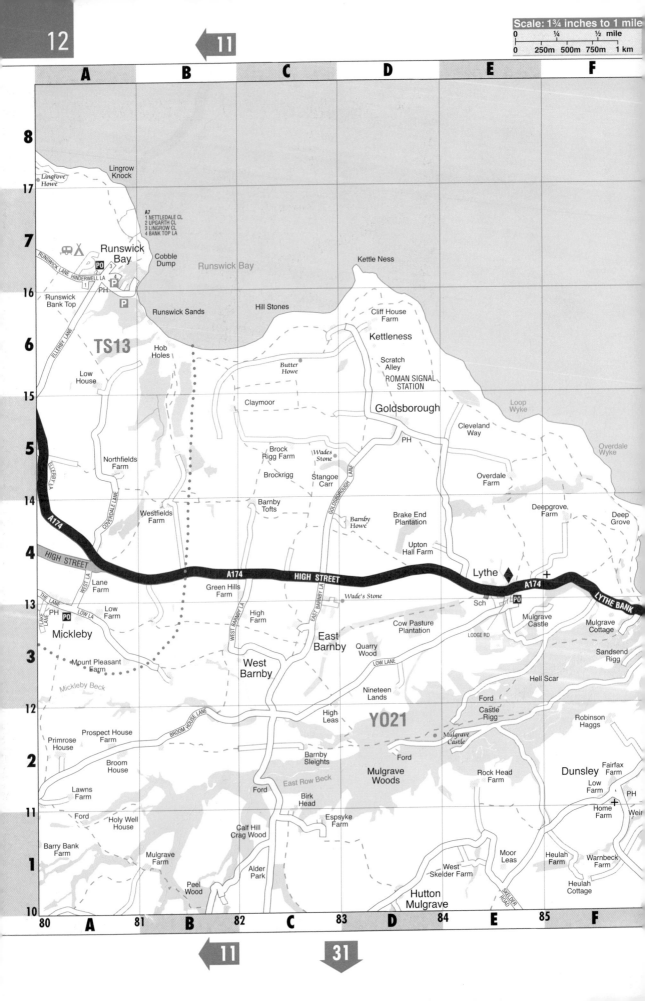

Scale: 1¾ inches to 1 mile
0   ¼   ½   mile
0   250m 500m 750m   1 km

A   B   C   D   E   F

8

Lingrove Howe

Lingrow Knock

17

A7
1 NETTLEDALE CL
2 UPGARTH CL
3 LINGROW CL
4 BANK TOP LA

7

Runswick Bay

Cobble Dump

Kettle Ness

Runswick Bay

16

Runswick Bank Top

PH

Runswick Sands

Hill Stones

Cliff House Farm

6

TS13

Hob Holes

Butter Howe

Kettleness

Scratch Alley

ROMAN SIGNAL STATION

Low House

Claymoor

15

Goldsborough

Loop Wyke

ELLERBY LANE

5

Northfields Farm

Brock Rigg Farm

Wades Stone

PH

Cleveland Way

Overdale Wyke

Brockrigg

Stangoe Carr

Overdale Farm

14

ELLERBY LA

Westfields Farm

Barnby Tofts

GOLDSBOROUGH LANE

Barnby Howe

Brake End Plantation

Deepgrove Farm

Deep Grove

A174

4

HIGH STREET

A174   HIGH STREET

Upton Hall Farm

Lythe

A174

LYTHE BANK

WEST LA

Lane Farm

Green Hills Farm

EAST BARNBY LA

Wade's Stone

Sch

PO

Mulgrave Castle

Mulgrave Cottage

THE LANE

13

PH   PO

Low LA

Low Farm

High Farm

Cow Pasture Plantation

LODGE RD

Sandsend Rigg

FLAKE LANE

Mickleby

WEST BARNBY LA

East Barnby

Quarry Wood

LOW LANE

Hell Scar

3

Mount Pleasant Farm

West Barnby

Nineteen Lands

Ford

Castle Rigg

Robinson Haggs

Mickleby Beck

BROOM HOUSE LANE

High Leas

YO21

Mulgrave Castle

12

Primrose House

Prospect House Farm

Barnby Sleights

Ford

Dunsley

Fairfax Farm

2

Broom House

East Row Beck

Mulgrave Woods

Rock Head Farm

Low Farm

PH

Lawns Farm

Ford

Birk Head

Home Farm

Weir

11

Ford

Holy Well House

Calf Hill Crag Wood

Espsyke Farm

Moor Leas

Heulah Farm

Warnbeck Farm

Barry Bank Farm

Mulgrave Farm

Alder Park

West Skelder Farm

SKELDER ROAD

Heulah Cottage

1

Peel Wood

Hutton Mulgrave

10

80   A   81   B   82   C   83   D   84   E   85   F

Scale: 1¾ inches to 1 mile

¼   ½ mile
250m 500m 750m 1 km

A   B   C   D   E   F

H   J   K   L

Durham & Teesside STREET ATLAS

A174 Saltburn-by-the-Sea

COWBAR BANK 1
WESLEY SQ 2
HIGH ST 3
BECKSIDE 4
CHURCH ST 5
THE OLD STUBBLE 6
WHITEGATE CL 7

Saltburn-by-the-Sea

Red House Farm
COWBAR LANE
Cowbar
Staithes
Harbour
PO
SEATON GARTH
Old Nab
TS13
Captain Cook & Staithes Her Ctr
Thorndale Shaft
A174
Cliff Farm
Brackenberry Wyke
FAIRFIELD RD
Athletic Club
CLIFF RD
SEATON CR
Limekiln Gill
PH
WHITBY RD
Seaton CP Sch
Ford
RIDGE LANE
OAKHOUSE BANK
Roxby Woods
ROXBY LANE
BORROWBY LANE
Captain Cooks Cl
Seaton Hall
HINDERWELL LA
NT
ROSEDALE LA

Red House Farm

H 77   J 78   K 79   L 80

92

Saltwick Nab

NT
Saltwick Bay
The Headlands
Black Nab
Knowles Farm
Brook House Farm
Y022
HAWSKER LANE
Highgate Howe

92

Sandsend Ness

Sandsend Wyke

A174
Sandsend
PO
East Row
MEADOWFIELD
SANDSEND RD
SANDSEND ROAD
Raven Hill Farm
DUNSLEY LANE
Home Farm
Moss Brow Farm
A174
CH
Upgang Beach
Whitby Sands
West Pier
208
East Pier
Sandfield House
PO
NORTH PR
Raithwaite
High Straggleton Farm
NORTH TERRACE
P
Lifeboat
Mus
Remains of Benedictine Abbey
NT
Saltwick Nab
CLIFF LANE
LOVE LA
WHITE BR RD
UPGANG LA
ARGYLE
GREEN AV
West Cliff
PO
Abbey House
Heritage Centre
The Headlands
Saltwick Bay
Y021
208
Ewe Cote
STAKESBY ROAD
ST HILDA'S TR
Whitby
CHURCH STREET
Knowles Farm
Watt's Wood
CASTLE RD
BYLAND RD
Sch
KIRKHAM RD
Mus
ABBEY LANE
GREEN LANE
208
Brook House Farm
Greystone Farm
BACK LA
B1460
RUNSWICK AV
Coll
H
Whitby
Business Centre
Highgate Howe
Newholm
PH
BENNISON LA
HOWLGATE LA
Stakesby Vale Farm
B1416
High Stakesby
PO
WATERSTEAD LA
A174
PO
EAST PIER
FLOWERGATE
WHITBY
Y022
Crow Gill
DUNSLEY LA
Bannial Flat Farm
BARKER'S LANE
GUISBOROUGH RD
B1460
A171
MAYFIELD RD A171
Caedmon Sch
A171
HAWSKER LANE

86 A 87 B 88 C 89 D 90 E 91 F

For full street detail of the highlighted area see page 208.

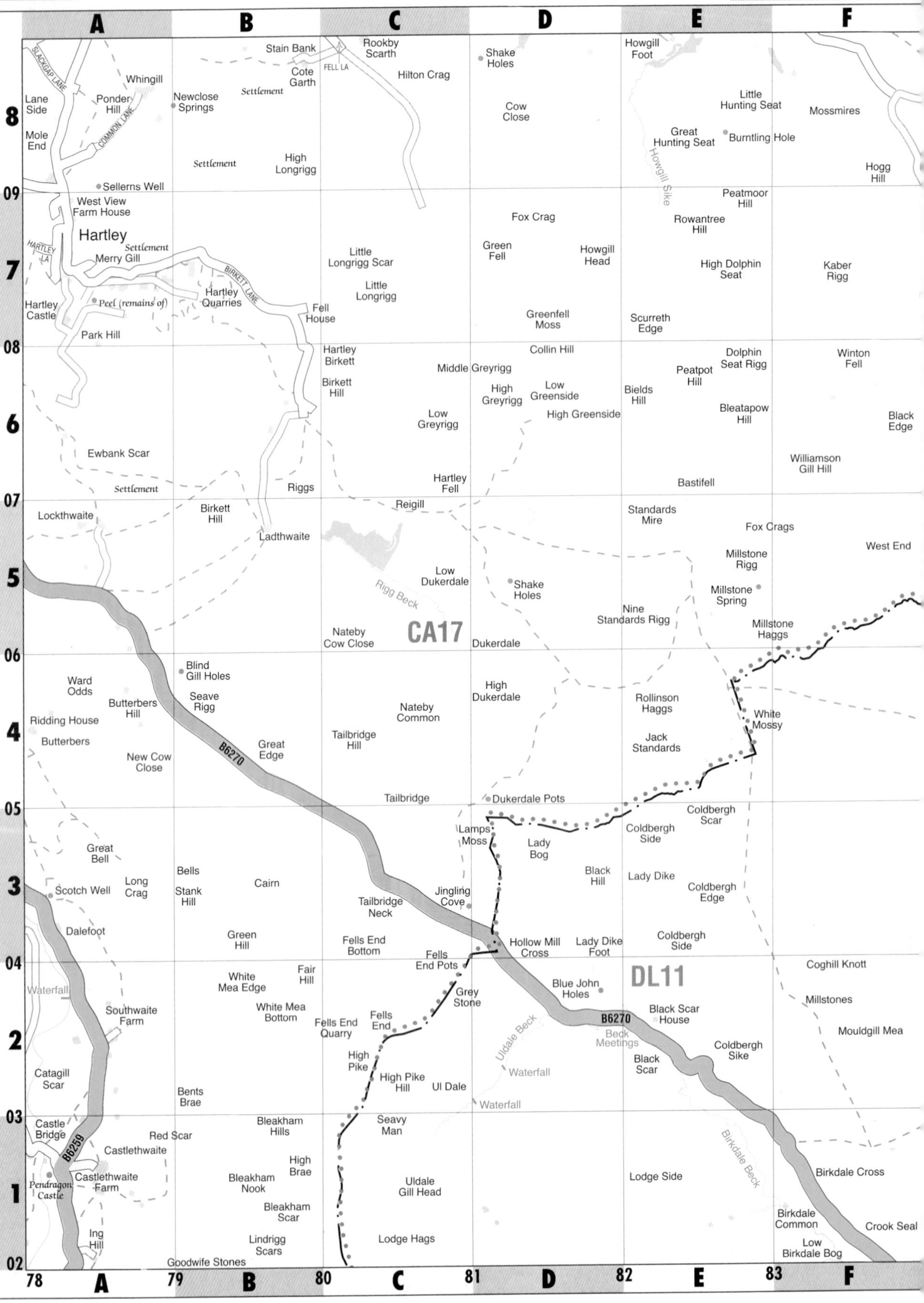

A

Slackgate Lane

Lane Side

Mole End

Whingill

Ponder Hill

Common Lane

Sellerns Well

West View Farm House

Hartley

Hartley La

Merry Gill

Settlement

Hartley Castle

Peel (remains of)

Hartley Quarries

Park Hill

Ewbank Scar

Settlement

Lockthwaite

Ward Odds

Ridding House

Butterbers

Butterbers Hill

New Cow Close

B6270

Great Bell

Scotch Well

Long Crag

Dalefoot

Waterfall

Southwaite Farm

Catagill Scar

Castle Bridge

B6259

Castlethwaite

Pendragon Castle

Castlethwaite Farm

Ing Hill

B

Stain Bank

Cote Garth

Fell La

Newclose Springs

Settlement

High Longrigg

Settlement

Birkett Lane

Fell House

Hartley Birkett

Birkett Hill

Riggs

Birkett Hill

Ladthwaite

Blind Gill Holes

Seave Rigg

Great Edge

Bells Stank Hill

Cairn

Green Hill

White Mea Edge

Fair Hill

White Mea Bottom

Bleakham Hills

Bents Brae

Bleakham Nook

High Brae

Bleakham Scar

Lindrigg Scars

Goodwife Stones

C

Rookby Scarth

Hilton Crag

Little Longrigg Scar

Little Longrigg

Hartley Fell

Reigill

Rigg Beck

Low Dukerdale

Nateby Cow Close

CA17

Nateby Common

Tailbridge Hill

Tailbridge

Tailbridge Neck

Fells End Bottom

Fells End Pots

Fells End Quarry

Fells End

High Pike

High Pike Hill

Seavy Man

Uldale Gill Head

Lodge Hags

D

Shake Holes

Cow Close

Fox Crag

Green Fell

Greenfell Moss

Collin Hill

Middle Greyrigg

High Greyrigg

Low Greyrigg

Low Greenside

High Greenside

Shake Holes

Dukerdale

High Dukerdale

Dukerdale Pots

Lamps Moss

Lady Bog

Jingling Cove

Hollow Mill Cross

Grey Stone

Blue John Holes

Uldale Beck

Waterfall

Beck Meetings

Waterfall

Ul Dale

E

Howgill Foot

Howgill Sike

Great Hunting Seat

Little Hunting Seat

Burntling Hole

Peatmoor Hill

Rowantree Hill

Howgill Head

High Dolphin Seat

Scurreth Edge

Peatpot Hill

Dolphin Seat Rigg

Bields Hill

Bleatapow Hill

Bastifell

Standards Mire

Fox Crags

Millstone Rigg

Millstone Spring

Nine Standards Rigg

Rollinson Haggs

Jack Standards

Coldbergh Scar

Coldbergh Side

Black Hill

Lady Dike

Coldbergh Edge

Lady Dike Foot

Coldbergh Side

DL11

B6270

Black Scar House

Black Scar

Coldbergh Sike

Lodge Side

Birkdale Beck

F

Mossmires

Hogg Hill

Kaber Rigg

Winton Fell

Black Edge

Williamson Gill Hill

West End

Millstone Haggs

White Mossy

Coghill Knott

Millstones

Mouldgill Mea

Birkdale Cross

Birkdale Common

Crook Seal

Low Birkdale Bog

Grid numbers: 8, 09, 7, 08, 6, 07, 5, 06, 4, 05, 3, 04, 2, 03, 1, 02

Bottom scale: 78 A 79 B 80 C 81 D 82 E 83 F

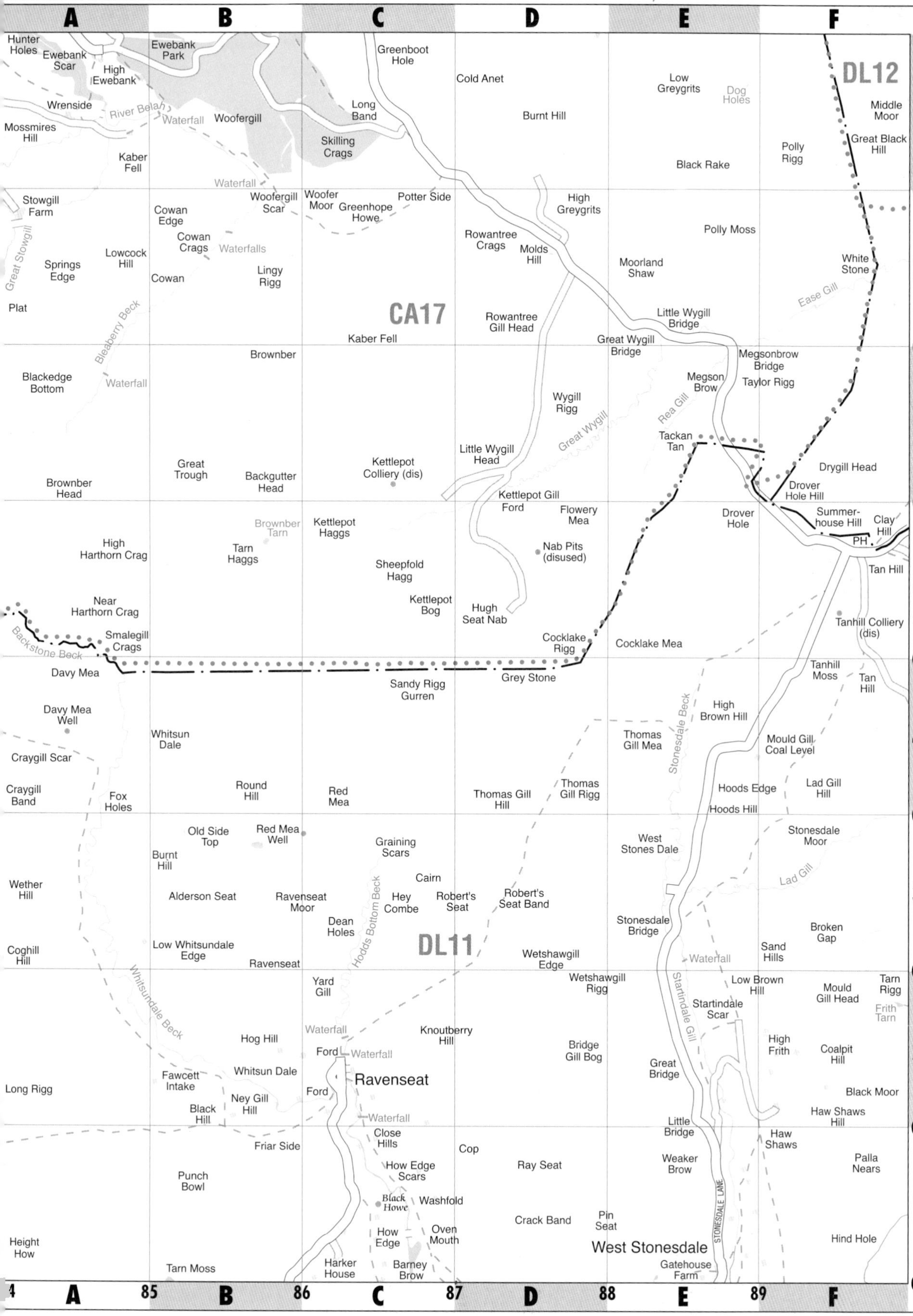

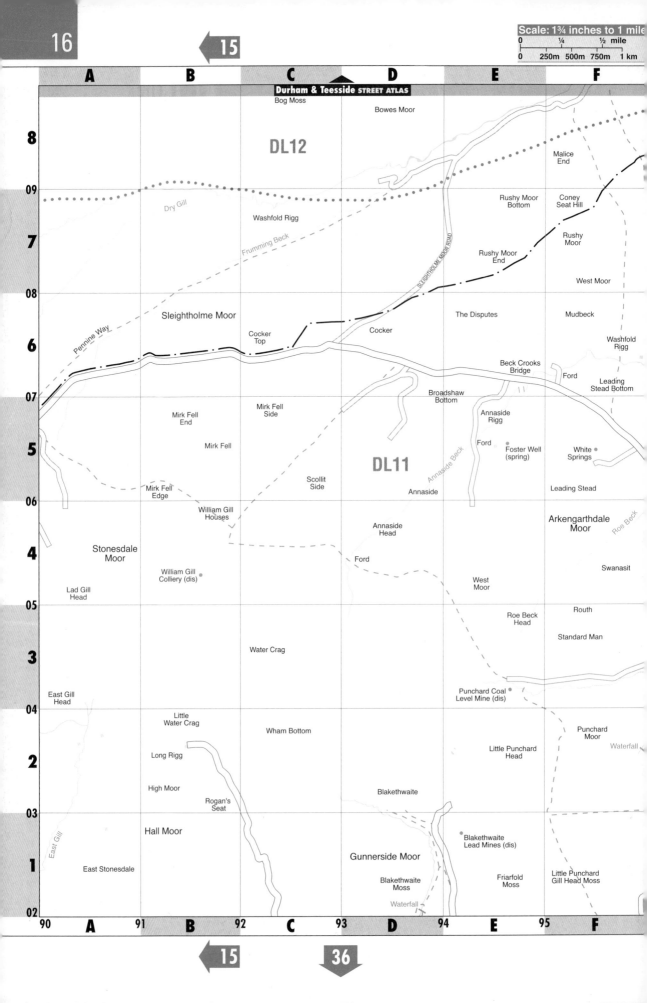

Durham & Teesside STREET ATLAS

Bog Moss

Bowes Moor

DL12

Malice End

Dry Gill

Rushy Moor Bottom

Coney Seat Hill

Washfold Rigg

Frumming Beck

Rushy Moor

Rushy Moor End

West Moor

Sleightholme Moor

The Disputes

Mudbeck

Pennine Way

Cocker Top

Cocker

Washfold Rigg

Beck Crooks Bridge

Ford

Leading Stead Bottom

Broadshaw Bottom

Mirk Fell Side

Annaside Rigg

Mirk Fell End

Annaside Beck

Ford

Foster Well (spring)

White Springs

Mirk Fell

DL11

Scollit Side

Leading Stead

Mirk Fell Edge

Annaside

William Gill Houses

Arkengarthdale Moor

Roe Beck

Annaside Head

Stonesdale Moor

Ford

West Moor

Swanasit

William Gill Colliery (dis)

Lad Gill Head

Roe Beck Head

Routh

East Gill Head

Standard Man

Water Crag

Punchard Coal Level Mine (dis)

Little Water Crag

Punchard Moor

Wham Bottom

Waterfall

Long Rigg

Little Punchard Head

High Moor

Blakethwaite

Rogan's Seat

East Gill

Hall Moor

Blakethwaite Lead Mines (dis)

Gunnerside Moor

Friarfold Moss

Little Punchard Gill Head Moss

East Stonesdale

Blakethwaite Moss

Waterfall

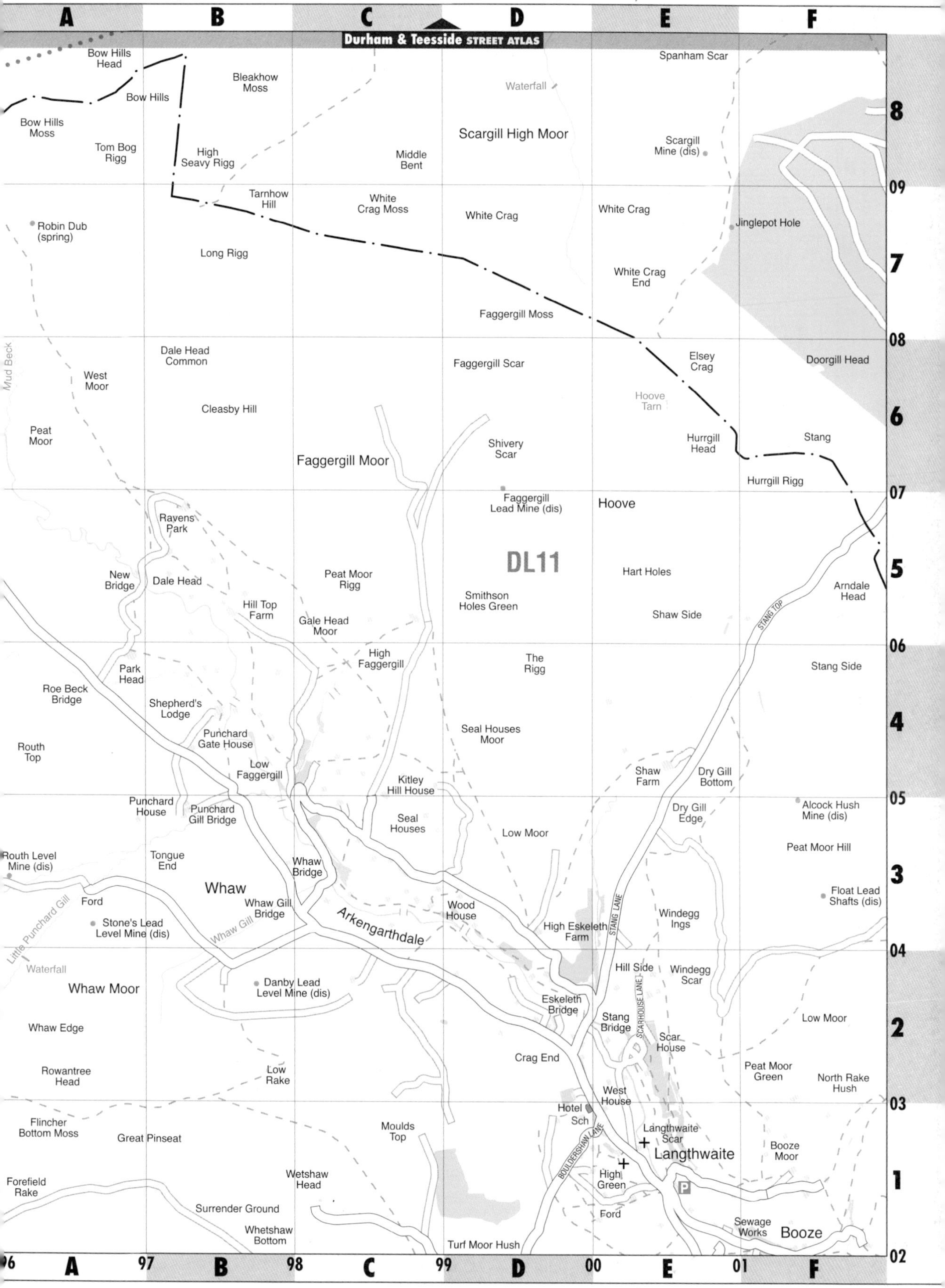

A B C D E F

Bow Hills Head

Bow Hills Moss

Bow Hills

Tom Bog Rigg

High Seavy Rigg

Bleakhow Moss

Spanham Scar

Waterfall

Scargill High Moor

Scargill Mine (dis)

8

Robin Dub (spring)

Tarnhow Hill

Long Rigg

Middle Bent

White Crag Moss

White Crag

White Crag

White Crag

Jinglepot Hole

09

7

Mud Beck

West Moor

Dale Head Common

Cleasby Hill

Faggergill Moss

Faggergill Scar

White Crag End

Elsey Crag

Doorgill Head

08

6

Peat Moor

Faggergill Moor

Shivery Scar

Hoove Tarn

Hurrgill Head

Stang

Hurrgill Rigg

Ravens Park

Faggergill Lead Mine (dis)

Hoove

5

New Bridge

Dale Head

Hill Top Farm

Peat Moor Rigg

Gale Head Moor

DL11

Smithson Holes Green

Hart Holes

Shaw Side

Arndale Head

07

Park Head

High Faggergill

The Rigg

Stang Side

06

4

Roe Beck Bridge

Shepherd's Lodge

Punchard Gate House

Low Faggergill

Seal Houses Moor

Shaw Farm

Dry Gill Bottom

STANG TOP

Route Top

Kitley Hill House

Dry Gill Edge

Alcock Hush Mine (dis)

05

Punchard House

Punchard Gill Bridge

Seal Houses

Low Moor

Peat Moor Hill

Route Level Mine (dis)

Tongue End

Whaw Bridge

Float Lead Shafts (dis)

3

Ford

Whaw

Whaw Gill Bridge

Arkengarthdale

Wood House

High Eskeleth Farm

STANG LANE

Windegg Ings

04

Stone's Lead Level Mine (dis)

Little Punchard Gill

Whaw Gill

Hill Side

Windegg Scar

Waterfall

Whaw Moor

Danby Lead Level Mine (dis)

Eskeleth Bridge

Stang Bridge

SCARHOUSE LANE

Scar House

Low Moor

2

Whaw Edge

Crag End

West House

Peat Moor Green

North Rake Hush

Rowantree Head

Low Rake

Hotel Sch

Langthwaite Scar

Booze Moor

03

Flincher Bottom Moss

Great Pinseat

Moulds Top

BOULDERSHAW LANE

High Green

Langthwaite

1

Forefield Rake

Wetshaw Head

Surrender Ground

Whetshaw Bottom

Turf Moor Hush

Ford

P

Sewage Works

Booze

02

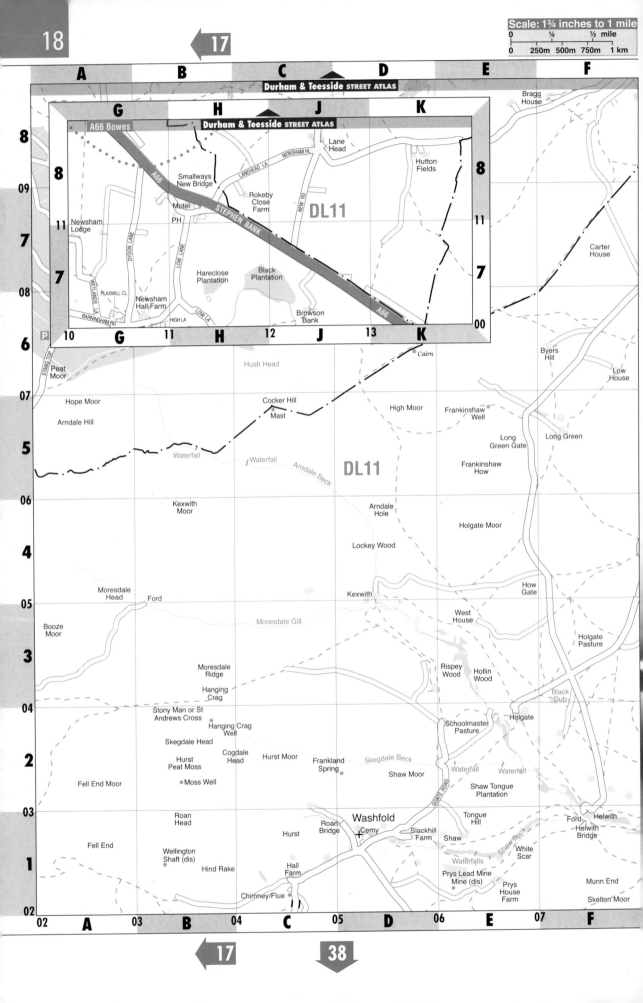

Scale: 1¾ inches to 1 mile

0   ¼   ½ mile

0   250m 500m 750m 1 km

A   B   C   D   E   F

Bragg
House

G   H   J   K

A66 Bowes

Durham & Teesside STREET ATLAS

8

8

NEWSHAM HL

Lane
Head

Hutton
Fields

8

Smallways
New Bridge

LANEHEAD LA

Rokeby
Close
Farm

NEW RD

DL11

Motel

PH

STEPHEN BANK

Newsham
Lodge

DYSON LANE

Carter
House

11

11

11

7

7

LOW LANE

Hareclose
Plantation

Black
Plantation

7

WETLANDS LA

PLAXMILL CL

Newsham
Hall Farm

LOW LA

Browson
Bank

A66

BARNINGHAM RD

HIGH LA

00

08

10   G   11   H   12   J   13   K

P

6

STANG TOP

Peat
Moor

Hush Head

Cairn

Byers
Hill

Low
House

07

Hope Moor

Cocker Hill

High Moor

Frankinshaw
Well

Arndale Hill

Mast

Long
Green Gate

Long Green

5

Waterfall

Waterfall

Arndale Beck

DL11

Frankinshaw
How

06

Kexwith
Moor

Arndale
Hole

Holgate Moor

Lockey Wood

4

How
Gate

05

Moresdale
Head

Ford

Kexwith

West
House

Holgate
Pasture

Moresdale Gill

Booze
Moor

3

Moresdale
Ridge

Rispey
Wood

Hollin
Wood

Black
Dub

Hanging
Crag

04

Stony Man or St
Andrews Cross

Schoolmaster
Pasture

Holgate

Hanging Crag
Well

2

Skegdale Head

Cogdale
Head

Hurst Moor

Frankland
Spring

Skegdale Beck

Waterfall

Waterfall

Hurst
Peat Moss

Shaw Moor

Shaw Tongue
Plantation

Fell End Moor

Moss Well

GOATS ROAD

03

Roan
Head

Washfold

Tongue
Hill

Ford   Helwith

Cemy

Slackhill
Farm

Shaw

Helwith
Bridge

Fell End

Hurst

Roan
Bridge

Shaw Beck

White
Scar

1

Wellington
Shaft (dis)

Hind Rake

Hall
Farm

Waterfalls

Prys Lead Mine
Mine (dis)

Munn End

Prys
House
Farm

Skelton Moor

02

Chimney/Flue

02   A   03   B   04   C   05   D   06   E   07   F

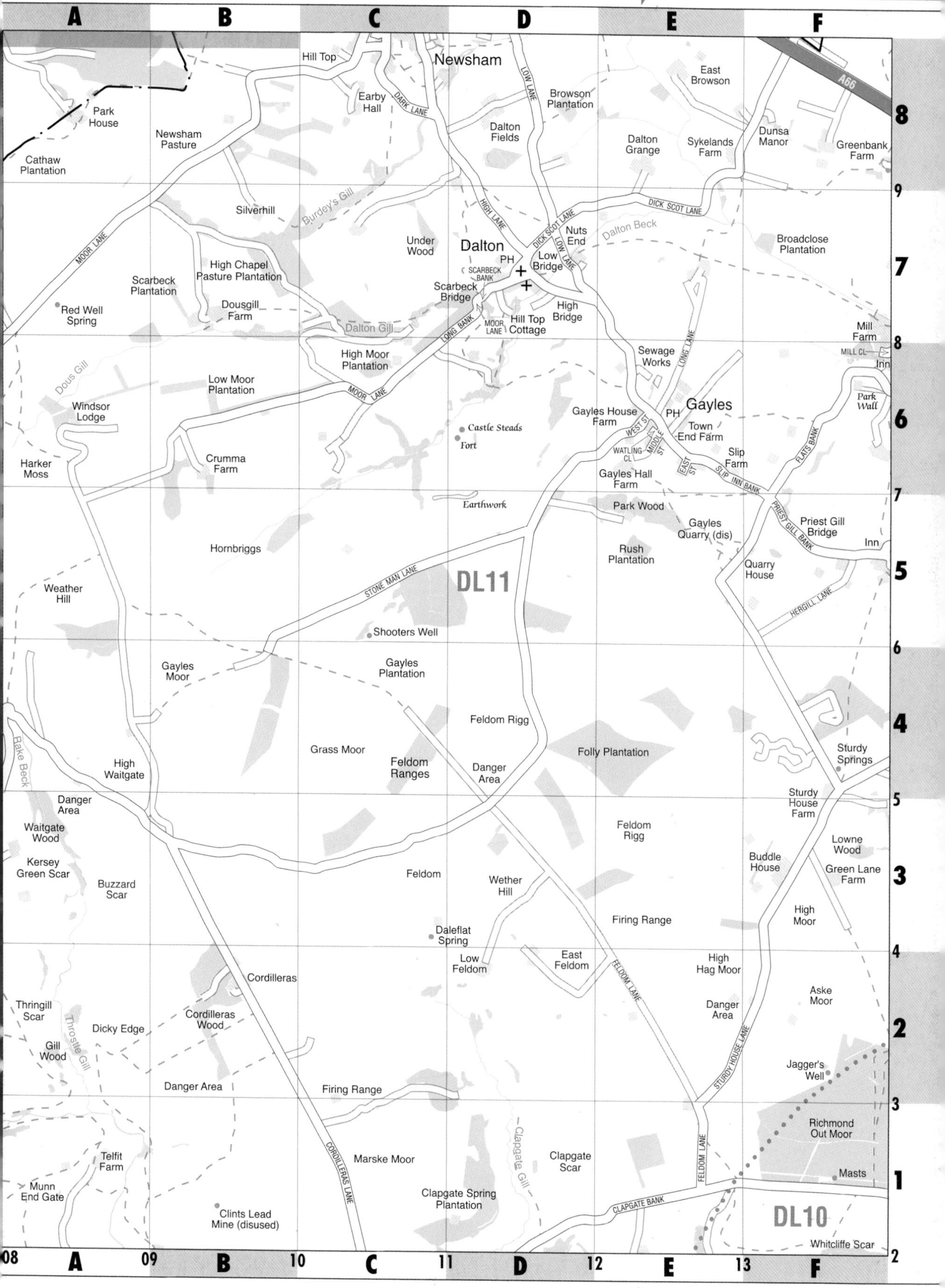

19
1

Scale: 1¾ inches to 1 mile

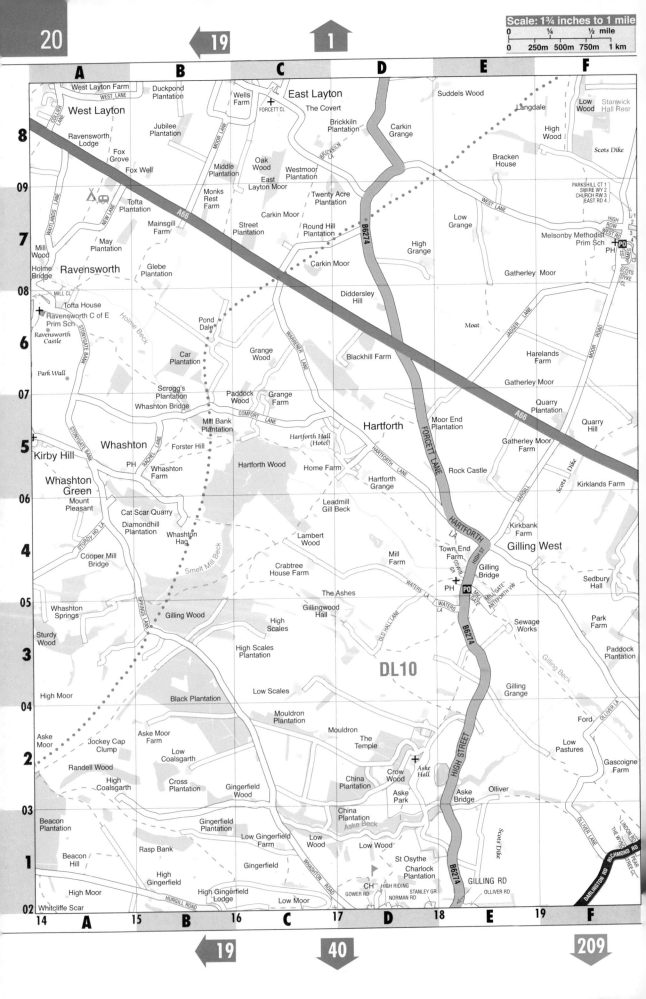
West Layton Farm
West Layton
Duckpond Plantation
Wells Farm
East Layton
The Covert
Suddels Wood
Langdale
Low Wood
Stanwick Hall Resr
Jubilee Plantation
Brickkiln Plantation
Carkin Grange
High Wood
Scots Dike
Ravensworth Lodge
Fox Grove
Fox Well
Middle Plantation
Oak Wood
Westmoor Plantation
Bracken House
East Layton Moor
Monks Rest Farm
Twenty Acre Plantation
Tofta Plantation
Carkin Moor
Low Grange
Mainsgill Farm
Street Plantation
Round Hill Plantation
Melsonby Methodist Prim Sch
May Plantation
High Grange
Mill Wood
Holme Bridge
Ravensworth
Glebe Plantation
Carkin Moor
Gatherley Moor
Diddersley Hill
Tofta House
Ravensworth C of E Prim Sch
Pond Dale
Moat
Ravensworth Castle
Holme Beck
Car Plantation
Grange Wood
Blackhill Farm
Harelands Farm
Park Wall
Scrogg's Plantation
Paddock Wood
Grange Farm
Gatherley Moor
Whashton Bridge
Quarry Plantation
Mill Bank Plantation
Moor End Plantation
Quarry Hill
Hartforth
Hartforth Hall (Hotel)
Whashton
Forster Hill
Kirby Hill
Gatherley Moor Farm
Hartforth Wood
Home Farm
Rock Castle
Whashton Farm
Whashton Green
Hartforth Grange
Kirklands Farm
Mount Pleasant
Leadmill Gill Beck
Cat Scar Quarry
Diamondhill Plantation
Kirkbank Farm
Whashton Hag
Lambert Wood
Gilling West
Town End Farm
Cooper Mill Bridge
Mill Farm
Smelt Mill Beck
Crabtree House Farm
Gilling Bridge
Sedbury Hall
The Ashes
Whashton Springs
Gillingwood Hall
Gilling Wood
High Scales
Sewage Works
Park Farm
Sturdy Wood
High Scales Plantation
Paddock Plantation
DL10
Gilling Beck
Low Scales
Gilling Grange
High Moor
Black Plantation
Mouldron Plantation
Ford
Aske Moor
Aske Moor Farm
Mouldron
Jockey Cap Clump
The Temple
Low Pastures
Low Coalsgarth
Randell Wood
Gascoigne Farm
Crow Wood
Aske Hall
High Coalsgarth
Cross Plantation
Gingerfield Wood
China Plantation
Aske Park
Aske Bridge
Olliver
Beacon Plantation
Gingerfield Plantation
China Plantation
Aske Beck
Low Gingerfield Farm
Low Wood
Scots Dike
Rasp Bank
Low Wood
Beacon Hill
St Osythe
Gingerfield
Charlock Plantation
High Gingerfield
High Moor
High Gingerfield Lodge
Low Moor
Whitcliffe Scar
A66
B6274
FORCETT LANE
HIGH STREET
HARTFORTH LA
GILLING RD
WASHTON ROAD
SPRINGS LANE
COMFORT LANE
WARRENER LANE
MOOR LANE
MOOR ROAD
JAGGER LANE
WEST LANE
HARBILL
OLLIVER LANE
RICHMOND RD
DARLINGTON RD
HURGILL ROAD
WAITLANDS LANE
NEW LANE
STONYGATE BANK
RACHEL LANE
STURDY HO LA
WATERS LA
OLD HALL LANE
PH
PO
CH
FORCETT CL
PARKSHILL CT 1
SWIRE WY 2
CHURCH RW 3
EAST RD 4
HIGH ROW
WEST RD
SCOTS DYKE CL
HIGH ST
OSWIN GR
MILL GATE
ANTEFORTH VW
HIGH RIDING
STANLEY GR
GOWER RD
NORMAN RD
OLLIVER RD
LINDON RD
THE WYND
PEAR TREE CL
OLLIVER LA

19
40
209

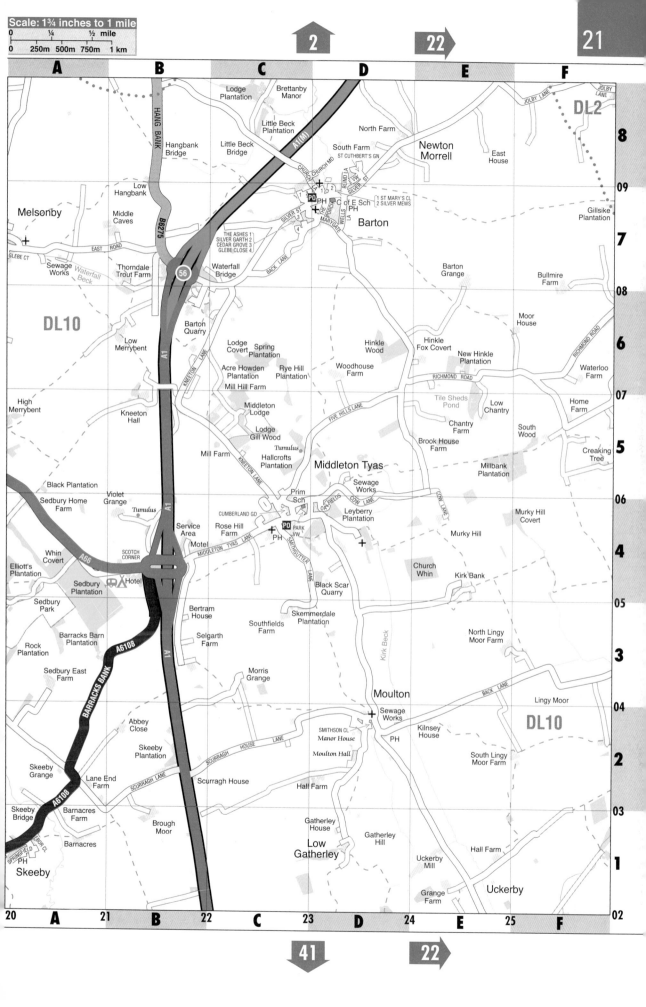

22

21

3

C8
1 LEWIS CL
2 CARROLL PL
3 RECTORY LA
4 THE MILL RACE

D8
1 LINDEN DRIVE
2 BAXBY TERRACE
3 BELGRAVE TERR
4 CEDAR MEWS
5 GRANGE AVE
6 FOX CL

7 WOODLANDS WAY
8 AVON ROAD
9 ASHVILLE DRIVE

Scale: 1¾ inches to 1 mile
0   ¼   ½ mile
0   250m 500m 750m 1 km

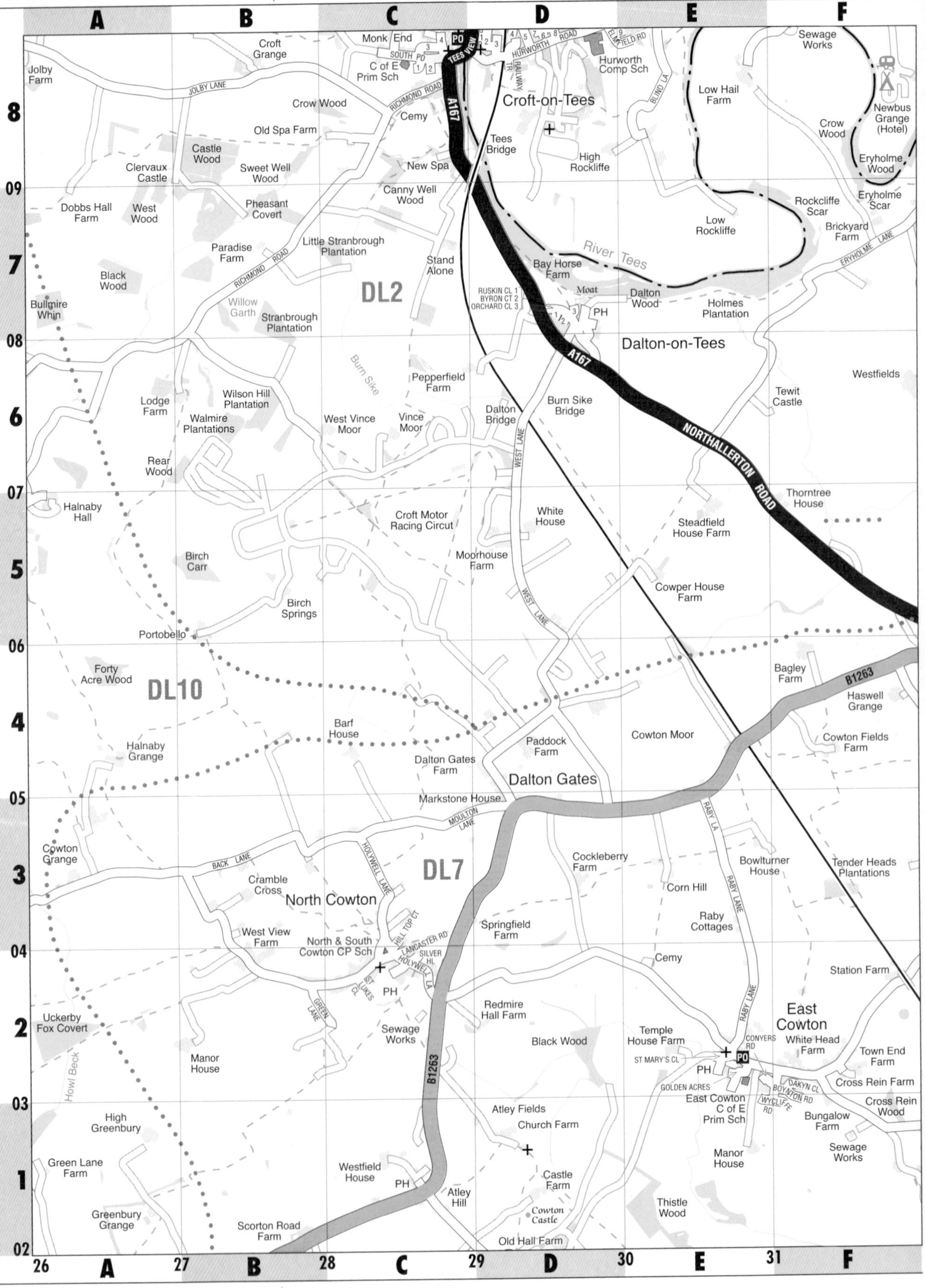

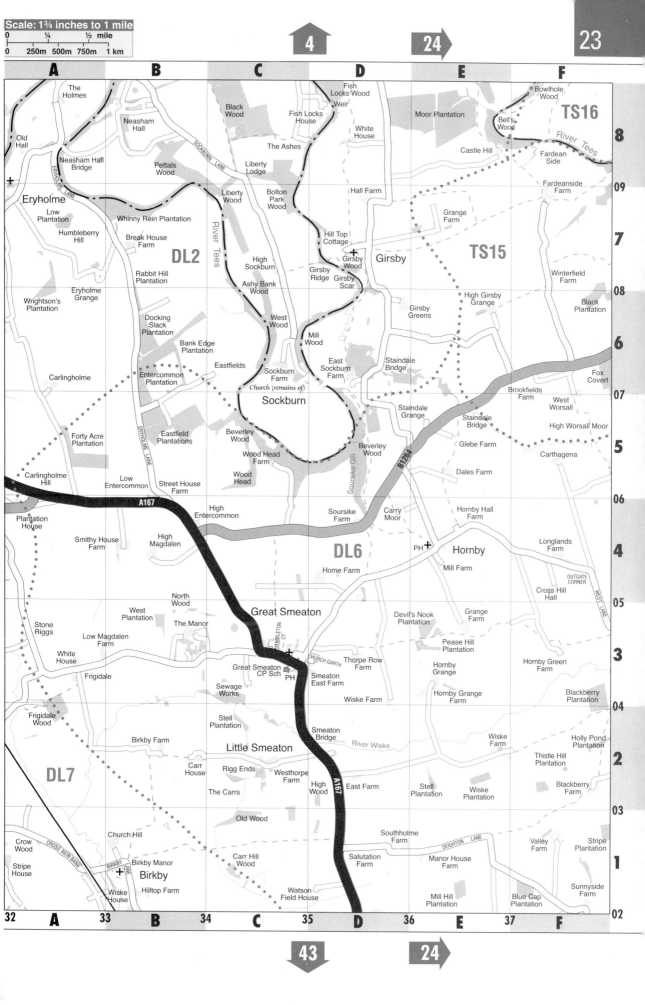

	A	B	C	D	E	F

8 — The Holmes, Old Hall, Neasham Hall, Black Wood, Fish Locks Wood, Weir, Fish Locks House, White House, Moor Plantation, Bowlhole Wood, Bell's Wood, Castle Hill, Fardean Side, TS16, River Tees

09 — Eryholme, Neasham Hall Bridge, The Ashes, Liberty Lodge, Hall Farm, Grange Farm, Fardeanside Farm

7 — Low Plantation, Humbleberry Hill, Whinny Rein Plantation, Break House Farm, DL2, Liberty Wood, Bolton Park Wood, Hill Top Cottage, Girsby Wood, Girsby, TS15, Winterfield Farm

08 — Wrightson's Plantation, Eryholme Grange, Rabbit Hill Plantation, High Sockburn, Ashy Bank Wood, Girsby Ridge, Girsby Scar, Girsby Greens, High Girsby Grange, Black Plantation

6 — Carlingholme, Docking Slack Plantation, Bank Edge Plantation, West Wood, Mill Wood, East Sockburn Farm, Staindale Bridge, Fox Covert

07 — Entercommon Plantation, Eastfields, Sockburn Farm, Church (remains of), Sockburn, Staindale Grange, Staindale Bridge, Brookfields Farm, West Worsall

5 — Forty Acre Plantation, Eastfield Plantations, Beverley Wood, Wood Head Farm, Beverley Wood, Soursike Gill, B1264, Glebe Farm, Dales Farm, High Worsall Moor, Carthagena

06 — Carlingholme Hill, Low Entercommon, Street House Farm, Wood Head, Soursike Farm, Carry Moor, Hornby Hall Farm, A167

4 — Plantation House, Smithy House Farm, High Magdalen, High Entercommon, DL6, PH, Hornby, Mill Farm, Longlands Farm, Outgate Corner, West Lane

05 — North Wood, Home Farm, Cross Hill Hall

3 — Stone Riggs, White House, Low Magdalen Farm, West Plantation, The Manor, North Wood, Great Smeaton, HAMBLETON CT, Church Garth, PH, Thorpe Row Farm, Smeaton East Farm, Devil's Nook Plantation, Grange Farm, Pease Hill Plantation, Hornby Grange, Hornby Green Farm, Hornby Grange Farm, Blackberry Plantation

04 — Frigidale, Great Smeaton CP Sch, Sewage Works, Wiske Farm, Wiske Farm

2 — Frigidale Wood, Birkby Farm, Little Smeaton, Carr House, Rigg Ends, Westhorpe Farm, Stell Plantation, Smeaton Bridge, River Wiske, East Farm, Stell Plantation, Wiske Plantation, Wiske Farm, Holly Pond Plantation, Thistle Hill Plantation, Blackberry Farm

03 — DL7, The Carrs, Old Wood, High Wood, Southholme Farm, DEIGHTON LANE, Manor House Farm, Valley Farm, Stripe Plantation

1 — Crow Wood, Stripe House, Church Hill, CROSS REIN BANK, BIRKBY LANE, Birkby Manor, Birkby, Hilltop Farm, Carr Hill Wood, Salutation Farm, Mill Hill Plantation, Blue Cap Plantation, Sunnyside Farm, Wiske House, Watson Field House

02

E8
1 ASH GR
2 BIRCH CL
3 BRAESIDE
4 GR BANK
5 KNOWLES CL
6 WESTLANDS
7 HALL MOOR CL
8 THE GN
9 STRATHMORE DR
10 MOOR CL
11 ST MARTINS WY
12 MANOR GARTH

Scale: 1¾ inches to 1 mile
0   ¼   ½ mile
0   250m   500m   750m   1 km

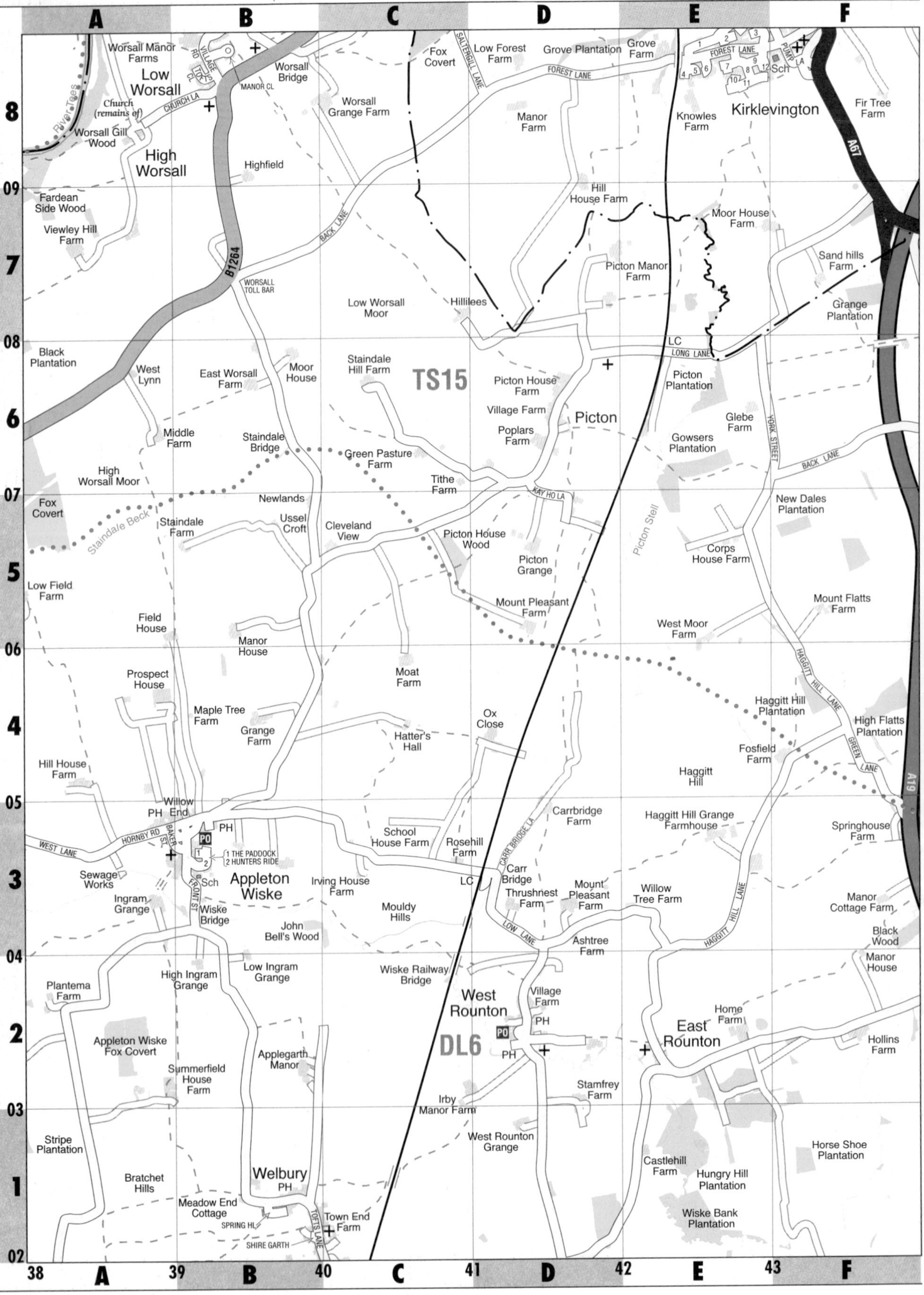

A B C D E F

Worsall Manor Farms
Low Worsall
Worsall Bridge
MANOR CL
Church (remains of)
CHURCH LA
Worsall Grange Farm
Fox Covert
Low Forest Farm
Grove Plantation
Grove Farm
FOREST LANE
FOREST LANE
Sch
Kirklevington
Fir Tree Farm
PUMP LA
A67

8

Worsall Gill Wood
High Worsall
Highfield
Manor Farm
Knowles Farm

09

Fardean Side Wood
Viewley Hill Farm
Hill House Farm
Moor House Farm
Sand hills Farm

River Tees
B1264
BACK LANE
WORSALL TOLL BAR
Low Worsall Moor
Hillilees
Picton Manor Farm
Grange Plantation

08

7

Black Plantation
West Lynn
East Worsall Farm
Moor House
Staindale Hill Farm
TS15
Picton House Farm
LC
LONG LANE
Picton Plantation

6

Middle Farm
Staindale Bridge
Village Farm
Picton
Glebe Plantation
YORK STREET
BACK LANE

High Worsall Moor
Green Pasture Farm
Poplars Farm
Gowsers Plantation
New Dales Plantation

07

Fox Covert
Staindale Farm
Newlands
Tithe Farm
KAY HO LA
Picton Stell
Corps House Farm

Staindale Beck
Ussel Croft
Cleveland View
Picton House Wood
Picton Grange

5

Low Field Farm
Field House
Mount Pleasant Farm
West Moor Farm
Mount Flatts Farm

06

Prospect House
Manor House
Moat Farm
HAGGITT HILL LANE

4

Hill House Farm
Maple Tree Farm
Grange Farm
Hatter's Hall
Ox Close
Haggitt Hill
Fosfield Farm
Haggitt Hill Plantation
High Flatts Plantation

GREEN LANE
A19

05

Willow End
PH
PH
PO
Carrbridge Farm
Haggitt Hill Grange Farmhouse
Springhouse Farm

WEST LANE
HORNBY RD
BAKER ISL
FRONT ST
1 THE PADDOCK
2 HUNTERS RIDE
School House Farm
Rosehill Farm
CARR BRIDGE LA

3

Sewage Works
Sch
Appleton Wiske
Irving House Farm
LC
Carr Bridge
Thrushnest Farm
Mount Pleasant Farm
Willow Tree Farm
HAGGITT HILL LANE
Manor Cottage Farm

Ingram Grange
Wiske Bridge
John Bell's Wood
Mouldy Hills
LOW LANE
Ashtree Farm
Black Wood

04

Manor House

2

Plantema Farm
High Ingram Grange
Low Ingram Grange
Wiske Railway Bridge
West Rounton
DL6
Village Farm
PH
PO
PH
East Rounton
Home Farm
Hollins Farm

03

Appleton Wiske Fox Covert
Summerfield House Farm
Applegarth Manor
Irby Manor Farm
Stamfrey Farm

1

Stripe Plantation
Bratchet Hills
Welbury
PH
West Rounton Grange
Castlehill Farm
Hungry Hill Plantation
Horse Shoe Plantation

Meadow End Cottage
SPRING HL
Town End Farm
TOFTS LANE
SHIRE GARTH
Wiske Bank Plantation

02

38 A 39 B 40 C 41 D 42 E 43 F

Scale: 1¾ inches to 1 mile
0 ¼ ½ mile
0 250m 500m 750m 1 km

C5
1 CODLIN RD
2 N END
3 NORTHCLIFFE CR
4 NORTHFIELDS
5 HUNDALE RD
6 LEVENDALE
7 DEEPDALE
8 THE WICKETS
9 GLENDALE
10 WESTHOLME
11 COLDIE HL
12 WYND CL
13 WILLINS CL

6

D5
1 THE GR
2 S VW
3 HUTTON BANK
4 LEVENSIDE
5 E SIDE
6 POPLAR AV

26

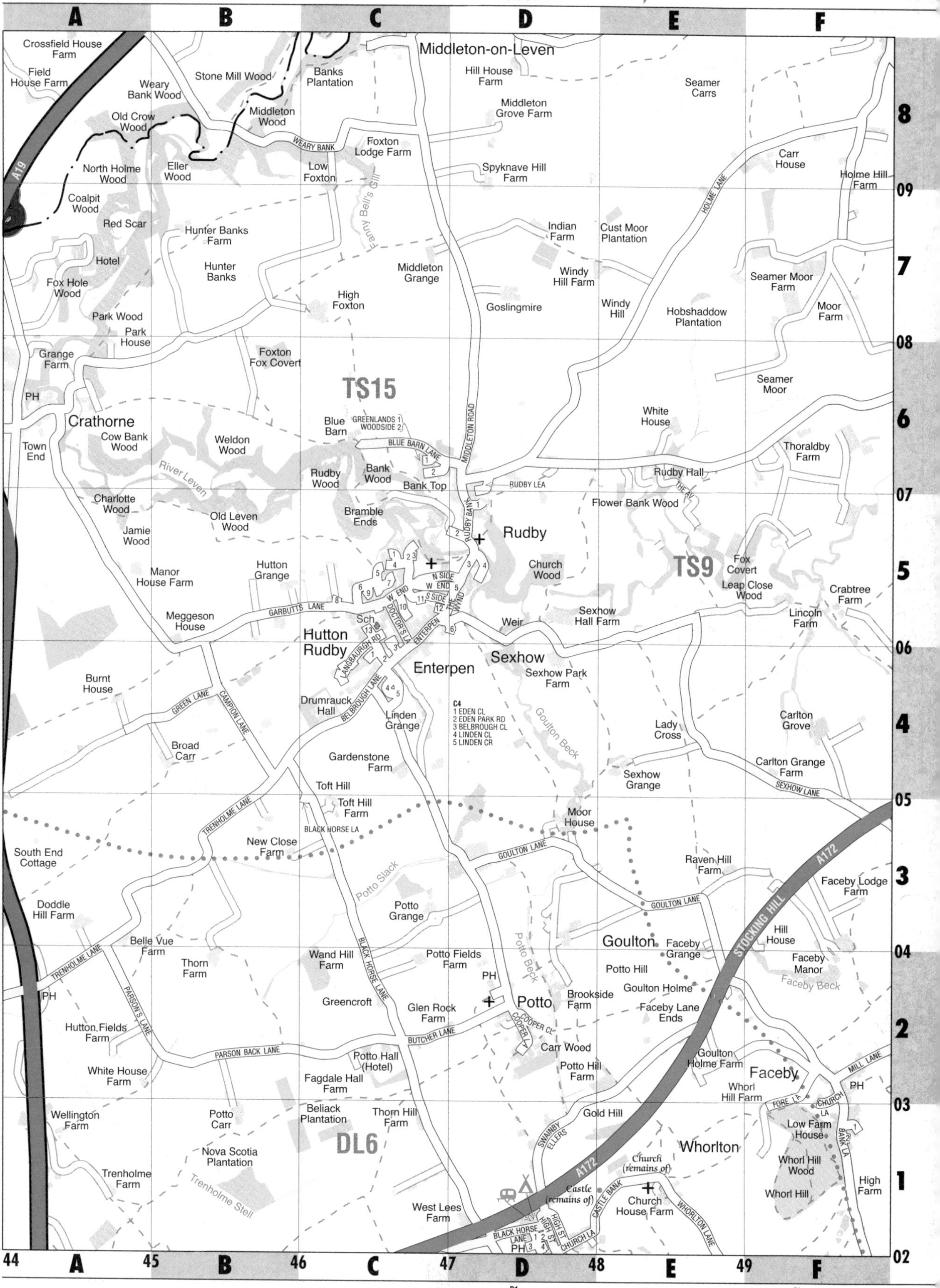

D1
1 GARBUTT LA
2 EMERSON CL
3 HEATHER CL
4 GARBUTT LA

F1
1 CLEVELAND VW
2 BIRCH DR

45

26

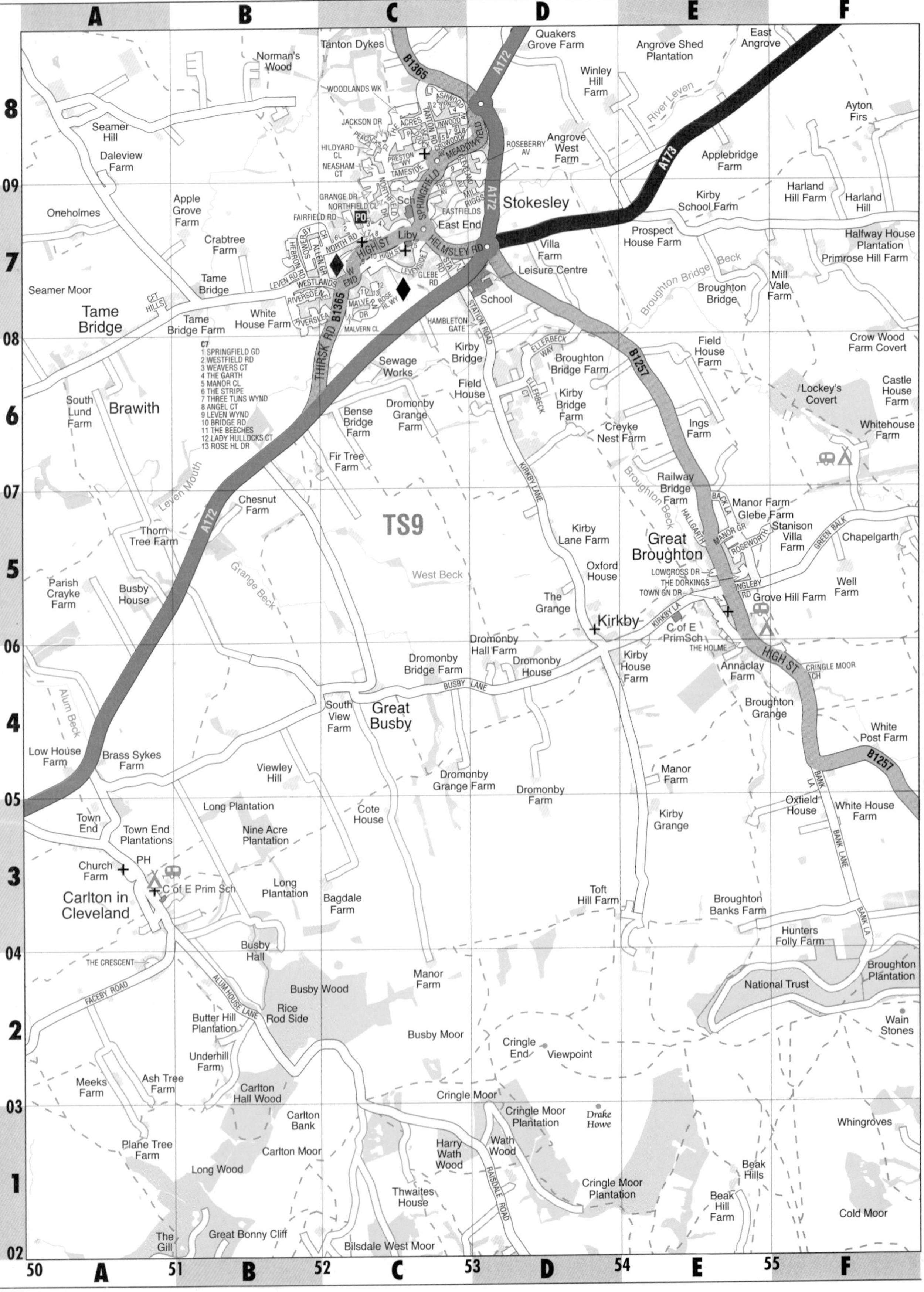

C8
1 CEDARWOOD AV
2 BEECHWOOD AV
3 DALEWOOD WK
4 CHERRYWOOD AV
5 COPSEWOOD WK
6 ELMWOOD CL
7 PINEWOOD WK
8 MEADOWFIELD
9 QUEENS DR

Scale: 1¾ inches to 1 mile

0   ¼   ½   mile
0 250m 500m 750m 1 km

Map labels

Tanton Dykes
Quakers Grove Farm
Angrove Shed Plantation
East Angrove
Norman's Wood
Winley Hill Farm
WOODLANDS WK
River Leven
Ayton Firs
JACKSON DR
Roseberry AV
Angrove West Farm
Applebridge Farm
Harland Hill Farm
Harland Hill
Oneholmes
Apple Grove Farm
Sch
Stokesley
Kirby School Farm
Halfway House Plantation
Primrose Hill Farm
Crabtree Farm
PO
East End
Prospect House Farm
Seamer Moor
Tame Bridge
Villa Farm
Broughton Bridge
Mill Vale Farm
Tame Bridge
White House Farm
Leisure Centre
Broughton Bridge
Crow Wood Farm Covert
Tame Bridge Farm
School
Field House Farm
Castle House Farm
Sewage Works
Kirby Bridge
Broughton Bridge Farm
Lockey's Covert
Whitehouse Farm
Bense Bridge Farm
Dromonby Grange Farm
Field House
Kirby Bridge Farm
Ings Farm
Fir Tree Farm
Creyke Nest Farm
Chesnut Farm
TS9
Railway Bridge Farm
Manor Farm
Glebe Farm
Stanison Villa Farm
Chapelgarth
Thorn Tree Farm
West Beck
Kirby Lane Farm
Great Broughton
Well Farm
Parish Crayke Farm
Busby House
Oxford House
Grove Hill Farm
The Grange
Kirby
C of E PrimSch
THE HOLME
Annaclay Farm
Dromonby Hall Farm
Kirby House Farm
Broughton Grange
Low House Farm
Brass Sykes Farm
Viewley Hill
Dromonby Bridge Farm
Dromonby House
BUSBY LANE
White Post Farm
Town End
Town End Plantations
South View Farm
Great Busby
Manor Farm
Kirby Grange
Oxfield House
White House Farm
Church Farm
PH
Long Plantation
Cote House
Dromonby Grange Farm
Dromonby Farm
C of E Prim Sch
Nine Acre Plantation
Carlton in Cleveland
Long Plantation
Bagdale Farm
Toft Hill Farm
Broughton Banks Farm
Hunters Folly Farm
THE CRESCENT
Busby Hall
Busby Wood
Manor Farm
Broughton Plantation
FACEBY ROAD
National Trust
Butter Hill Plantation
Rice Rod Side
Busby Moor
Wain Stones
Underhill Farm
Cringle End
Viewpoint
Whingroves
Meeks Farm
Ash Tree Farm
Carlton Hall Wood
Cringle Moor
Beak Hills
Plane Tree Farm
Carlton Bank
Carlton Moor
Long Wood
Harry Wath Wood
Wath Wood
Drake Howe
Cringle Moor Plantation
Beak Hill Farm
Cold Moor
Thwaites House
Cringle Moor Plantation
The Gill
Great Bonny Cliff
Bilsdale West Moor

C7
1 SPRINGFIELD GD
2 WESTFIELD RD
3 WEAVERS CT
4 THE GARTH
5 THE STRIPE
6 MANOR CL
7 THREE TUNS WYND
8 ANGEL CT
9 LEVEN WYND
10 BRIDGE RD
11 THE BEECHES
12 LADY HULLOCKS CT
13 ROSE HL DR

Scale: 1¾ inches to 1 mile

0   ¼   ½   mile
0   250m 500m 750m 1 km

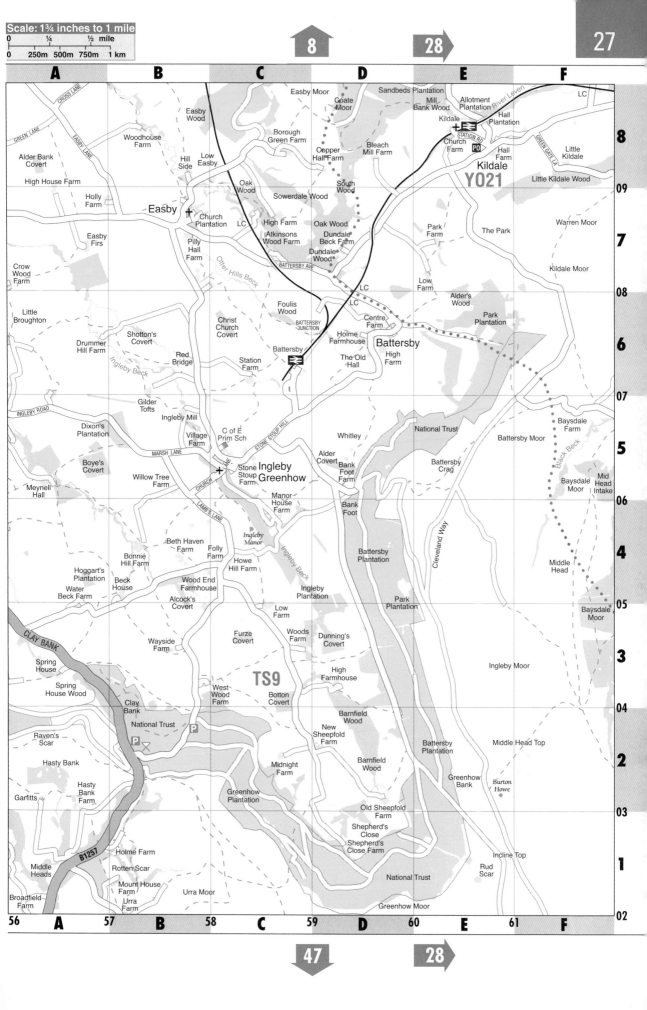

A   B   C   D   E   F

8
09
7
08
6
07
5
4
06
05
3
04
2
03
1
02

CROSS LANE
GREEN LANE
EASBY LANE
Alder Bank Covert
Woodhouse Farm
High House Farm
Holly Farm
Easby Firs
Easby
Hill Side
Low Easby
Easby Wood
Oak Wood
Church Plantation
LC
High Farm
Atkinsons Wood Farm
Sowerdale Wood
Borough Green Farm
Easby Moor
Goate Moor
Copper Hall Farm
South Wood
Oak Wood
Dundale Beck Farm
Dundale Wood
Sandbeds Plantation
Bleach Mill Farm
Mill Bank Wood
Allotment Plantation
River Leven
LC
Hall Plantation
Kildale
Church Farm
STATION RD
PO
Kildale
YO21
Hall Farm
Little Kildale
Little Kildale Wood
GREEN GATE LA
Warren Moor
Park Farm
The Park
Kildale Moor
BATTERSBY AVE
Foulis Wood
BATTERSBY JUNCTION
LC
LC
Centre Farm
Holme Farmhouse
Battersby
Low Farm
Alder's Wood
Park Plantation
Crow Wood Farm
Little Broughton
Shotton's Covert
Drummer Hill Farm
Ingleby Beck
Otter Hills Beck
Pilly Hall Farm
Christ Church Covert
Station Farm
Battersby
Red Bridge
The Old Hall
High Farm
National Trust
Baysdale Farm
Black Beck
Battersby Moor
INGLEBY ROAD
Dixon's Plantation
Gilder Tofts
Ingleby Mill
Village Farm
C of E Prim Sch
STONE STOUP HILL
MARSH LANE
Whitley
Alder Covert
Bank Foot Farm
Battersby Crag
Baysdale Moor
Mid Head Intake
Boye's Covert
Willow Tree Farm
Ingleby Greenhow
Stone Stoup Farm
CHURCH LANE
Manor House Farm
Bank Foot
Cleveland Way
Middle Head
Meynell Hall
LAMB'S LANE
Beth Haven Farm
Folly Farm
Ingleby Manor
Howe Hill Farm
Ingleby Beck
Ingleby Plantation
Battersby Plantation
Hoggart's Plantation
Water Beck Farm
Bonnie Hill Farm
Beck House
Wood End Farmhouse
Alcock's Covert
Low Farm
Park Plantation
Baysdale Moor
CLAY BANK
Spring House
Spring House Wood
Wayside Farm
Furze Covert
Woods Farm
Dunning's Covert
Ingleby Moor
Middle Head
Raven's Scar
Hasty Bank
TS9
West Wood Farm
Botton Covert
High Farmhouse
Barnfield Wood
Battersby Plantation
Middle Head Top
Clay Bank
National Trust
P
P
Midnight Farm
New Sheepfold Farm
Barnfield Wood
Greenhow Bank
Burton Howe
Garfitts
Hasty Bank Farm
Greenhow Plantation
Old Sheepfold Farm
Incline Top
Rud Scar
B1257
Holme Farm
Rotten Scar
Mount House Farm
Urra Farm
Urra Moor
Shepherd's Close
Shepherd's Close Farm
National Trust
Greenhow Moor
Middle Heads
Broadfield Farm

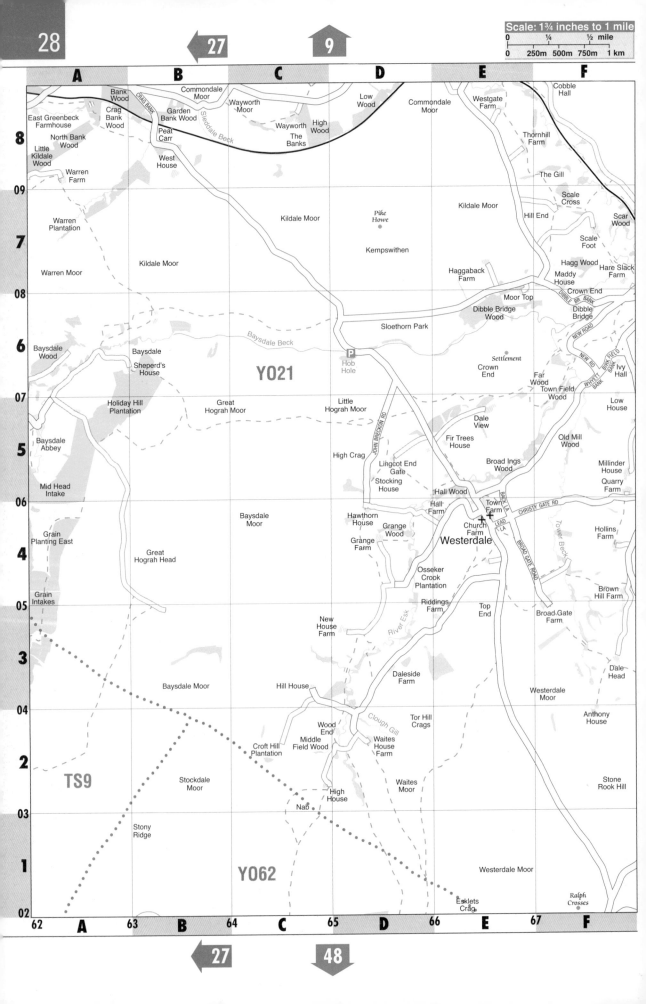

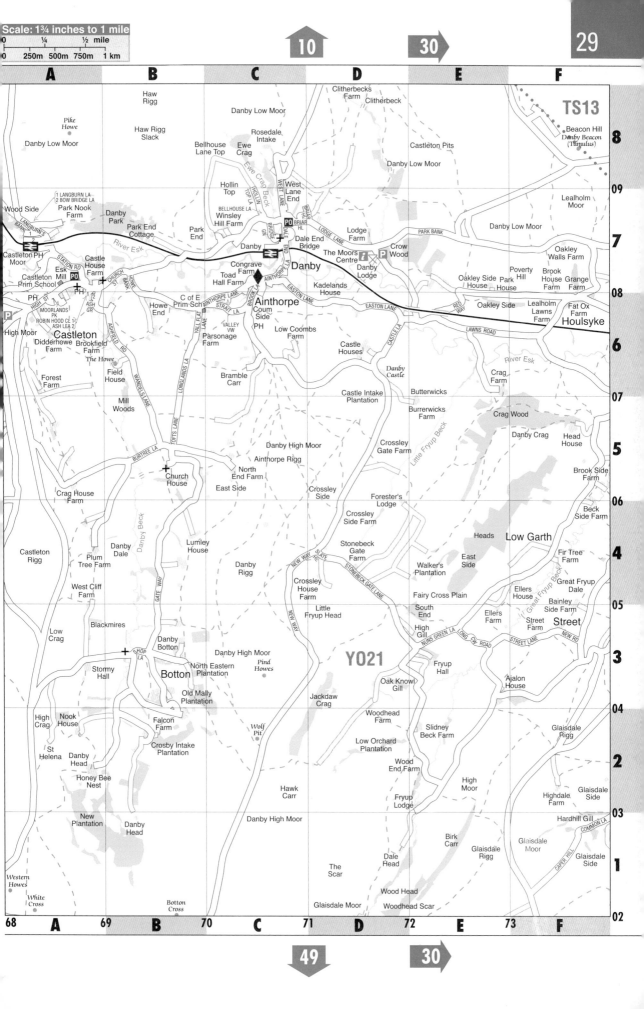

A   B   C   D   E   F

Haw Rigg
Danby Low Moor
TS13

Pike Howe
Haw Rigg Slack
Rosedale Intake
Clitherbecks Farm   Clitherbeck
Beacon Hill
Danby Beacon (Tumulus)

Danby Low Moor
Bellhouse Lane Top
Ewe Crag
Castleton Pits

Danby Low Moor   **8**

Hollin Top
West Lane End
Danby Low Moor
Lealholm Moor   **09**

1 LANGBURN LA
2 BOW BRIDGE LA
Wood Side
Park Nook Farm
Danby Park
Winsley Hill Farm
BELLHOUSE LA
PO
BRIAR HL
Lodge Farm
Danby Low Moor
PARK BANK
Oakley Walls Farm   **7**

Castleton PH Moor
Park End Cottage
Park End
Danby
Dale End Bridge
Crow Wood
STATION RD
Esk Mill
PO
Castle House Farm
CHURCH BANK
Congrave Farm
Toad Hall Farm
The Moors Centre
P
Danby Lodge
Poverty Hill
Brook House Farm
Grange Farm   **08**

Castleton Prim School
PH
River Esk
C of E Prim Sch
Kadelands House
Oakley Side House
Park House
Lealholm Lawns Farm
Fat Ox Farm   **7**

High Moor
P
PH
HIGH ST
MOORLANDS PK
ROBIN HOOD CL 1
ASH LEA 2
ASH GR
Howe End
Ainthorpe
Coum Side
PH
EASTON LANE
RED WAY
Oakley Side
Houlsyke

Castleton
Didderhowe Farm
Brookfield Farm
The Howe
Field House
Parsonage Farm
VALL FLAT LANE
STRAIT LA
VALLEY VW
Low Coombs Farm
CASTLE LA
LAWNS ROAD   **6**

Forest Farm
Mill Woods
Bramble Carr
Castle Houses
Danby Castle
Crag Farm
River Esk   **07**

LONGLANDS LA
WANDER LANE
ASHFIELD RD
Castle Intake Plantation
Burrerwicks Farm
Butterwicks
Crag Wood   **5**

BURTREE LA
TOFTS LANE
Church House
Danby High Moor
Ainthorpe Rigg
North End Farm
East Side
Crossley Side
Crossley Gate Farm
Little Fryup Beck
Danby Crag
Head House   **5**

Crag House Farm
Danby Beck
Lumley House
Danby Rigg
Crossley Side Farm
Forester's Lodge
Heads
Low Garth
Brook Side Farm   **06**

Castleton Rigg
Plum Tree Farm
Danby Dale
GATE WAY
NEW WAY
SLITE HL
Stonebeck Gate Farm
STONEBECK GATE LANE
Walker's Plantation
East Side
Ellers House
Fir Tree Farm
Great Fryup Dale   **4**

West Cliff Farm
Blackmires
Danby Botton
Crossley House Farm
Little Fryup Head
Fairy Cross Plain
South End
High Gill
Ellers Farm
Street Farm
GREAT FRYUP BECK
Bainley Side Farm
Street   **05**

Low Crag
CHOP LA
Botton
North Eastern Plantation
Danby High Moor
Pind Howes
Y021
NUNS GREEN LA
LONG LW ROAD
STREET LANE
NEW RD   Fryup Hall
Ajalon House   **04**

Stormy Hall
Old Mally Plantation
Jackdaw Crag
Oak Knowl Gill
Slidney Beck Farm
Glaisdale Rigg   **04**

High Crag
Nook House
Falcon Farm
Wolf Pit
Woodhead Farm
Low Orchard Plantation
High Moor   **2**

St Helena
Danby Head
Crosby Intake Plantation
Wood End Farm
Highdale Farm
Glaisdale Side   **2**

Honey Bee Nest
Hawk Carr
Fryup Lodge
Hardhill Gill
COMMON LA   **03**

New Plantation
Danby Head
Danby High Moor
Birk Carr
Glaisdale Rigg
Glaisdale Moor
CAPER HILL
Glaisdale Side   **1**

Western Howes
White Cross
Botton Cross
The Scar
Dale Head
Wood Head
Woodhead Scar
Glaisdale Moor   **02**

Scale: 1¾ inches to 1 mile

0 ¼ ½ mile
0 250m 500m 750m 1 km

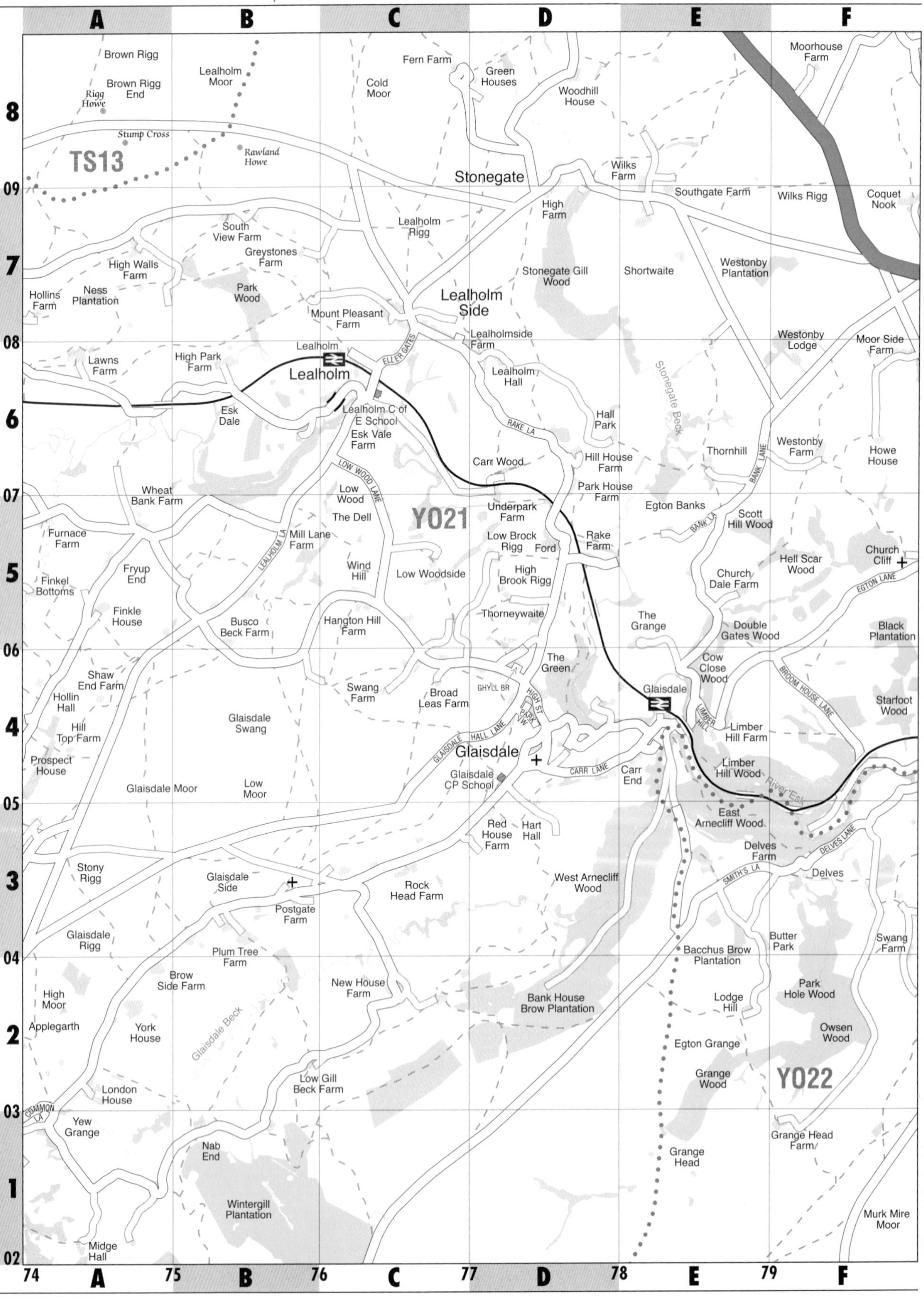

A B C D E F

8
Brown Rigg
Brown Rigg End
Lealholm Moor
Rigg Howe
Fern Farm
Green Houses
Cold Moor
Woodhill House
Moorhouse Farm

Stump Cross
Rawland Howe
TS13

09
Stonegate
High Farm
Wilks Farm
Southgate Farm
Wilks Rigg
Coquet Nook

7
South View Farm
Greystones Farm
Lealholm Rigg
Stonegate Gill Wood
Shortwaite
Westonby Plantation
High Walls Farm
Ness Plantation
Park Wood
Hollins Farm

Lealholm Side

Mount Pleasant Farm
Lealholmside Farm
Westonby Lodge
Moor Side Farm

08
Lawns Farm
High Park Farm
High Walls
Lealholm
Lealholm Hall
Thornhill
Westonby Farm
Howe House

6
Esk Dale
Lealholm C of E School
Esk Vale Farm
Hall Park
Rake La
Hill House Farm
Stonegate Beck
Bank La

07
Wheat Bank Farm
Low Wood Lane
Low Wood
The Dell
YO21
Carr Wood
Underpark Farm
Park House Farm
Egton Banks
Scott Hill Wood

Furnace Farm
Mill Lane Farm
Low Brock Rigg
Ford
Rake Farm
Church Dale Farm
Hell Scar Wood
Church Cliff

5
Finkel Bottoms
Fryup End
Wind Hill
Low Woodside
High Brook Rigg
Double Gates Wood
Black Plantation
Finkle House

Shaw End Farm
Busco Beck Farm
Hangton Hill Farm
Thorneywaite
The Grange

06
Hollin Hall
The Green
Cow Close Wood
Broom House Lane
Starfoot Wood

4
Hill Top Farm
Glaisdale Swang
Swang Farm
Broad Leas Farm
Ghyll Br
High St
Glaisdale
Limber Hill Farm
Prospect House
Glaisdale
Carr Lane
Carr End
Limber Hill Wood
River Esk
Delves Lane

Glaisdale Hall Lane
Glaisdale CP School
Delves Farm
Delves

05
Glaisdale Moor
Low Moor
Red House Farm
Hart Hall
East Arncliff Wood
Smith's La

3
Stony Rigg
Glaisdale Side
Postgate Farm
Rock Head Farm
West Arncliff Wood
Butter Park
Swang Farm

Glaisdale Rigg
Plum Tree Farm
New House Farm
Bacchus Brow Plantation
Lodge Hill
Park Hole Wood

04
High Moor
Brow Side Farm
Bank House Brow Plantation
Egton Grange
Owsen Wood
YO22

2
Applegarth
York House
Glaisdale Beck
Low Gill Beck Farm
Grange Wood
Grange Head Farm

03
Common La
Yew Grange
London House
Nab End
Grange Head
Murk Mire Moor

1
Midge Hall
Wintergill Plantation

02
74 A 75 B 76 C 77 D 78 E 79 F

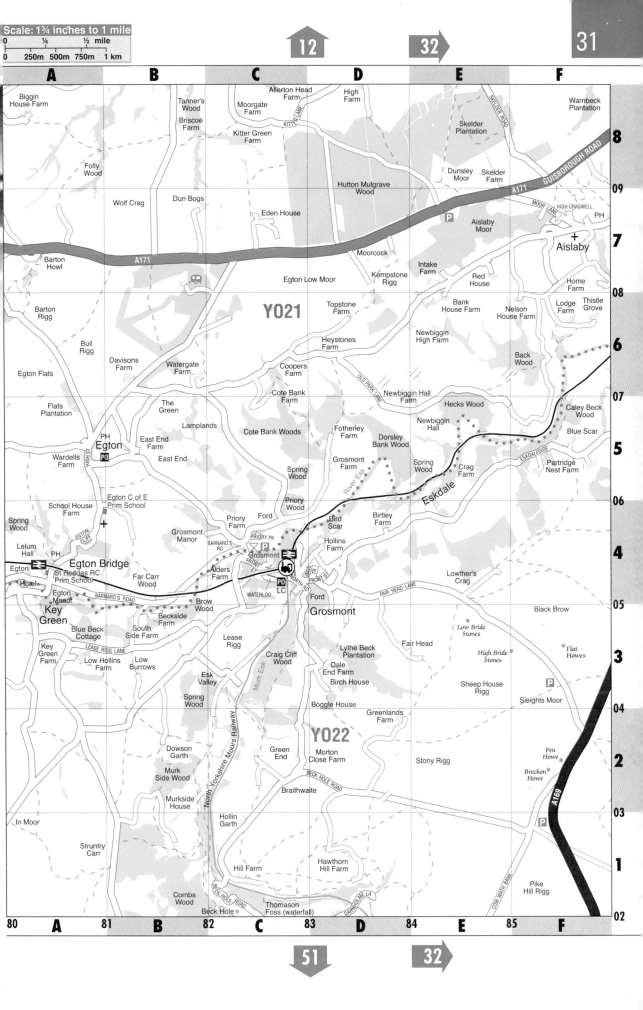

A6
1 THE AV
2 BANK CL
3 ORCHARD RD
4 LOWDALE CT
5 SMIDDYFIELDS
6 NETHERBY CL
7 SELSTONE CR
8 NARROWFIELD
9 HALL PASTURE
10 BIRCH CR
11 FOURACRE DR
12 SPRING CL
13 YEWTREE CL

31

13

E8
1 LARPOOL CR
2 HELREDALE GD
3 ST PETER'S RD
4 ST PETER'S CT
5 FAIRMEAD WY
6 ELLERBECK WY
7 QUEENS DR
8 BRACKEN CL
9 STAINSACRE LA
10 PLEASANT MOUNT
11 KINGFISHER DR
12 HEATHER DR
13 CHOLMLEY WY

Scale: 1¾ inches to 1 mile
0 ¼ ½ mile
0 250m 500m 750m 1 km

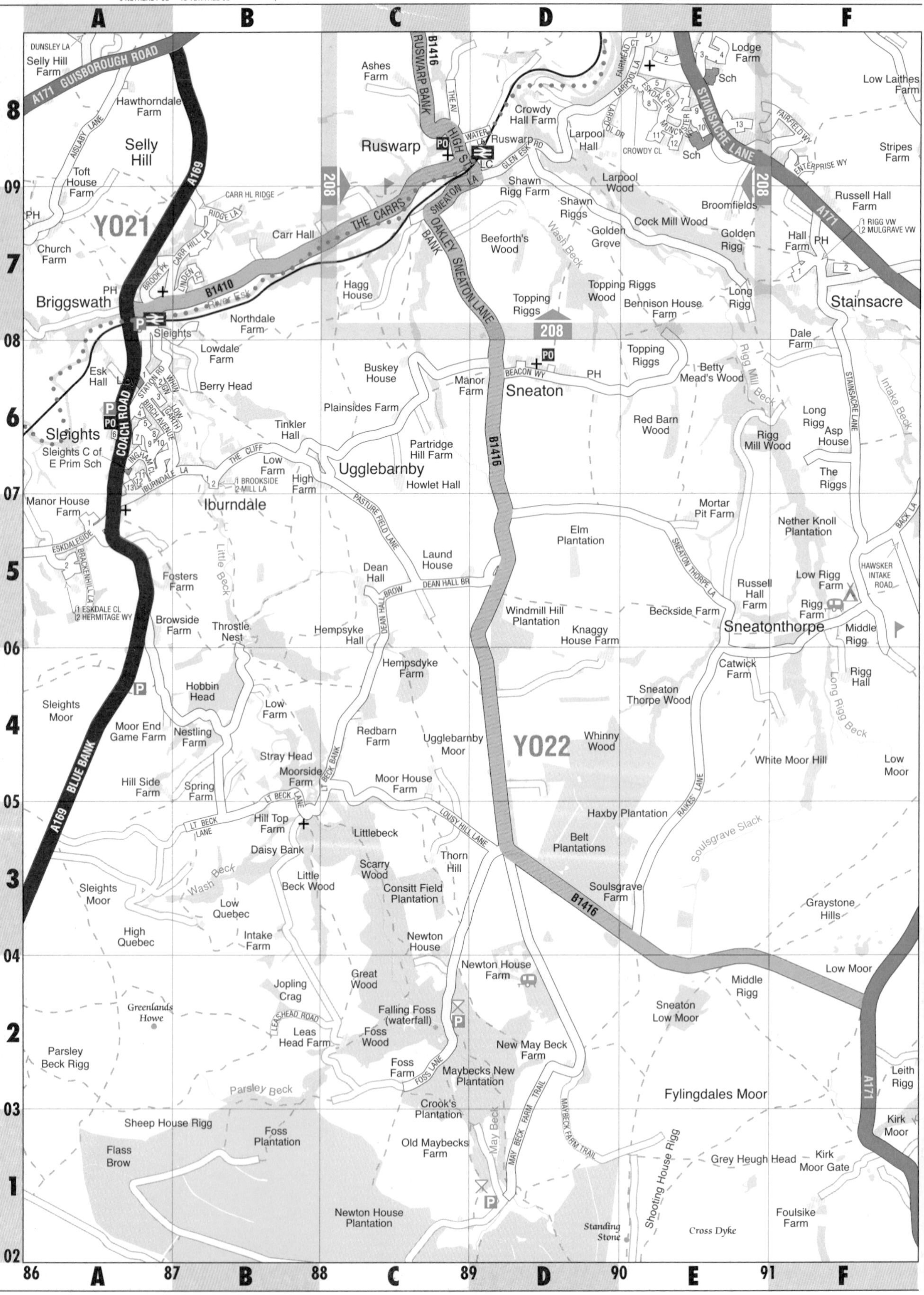

31

52

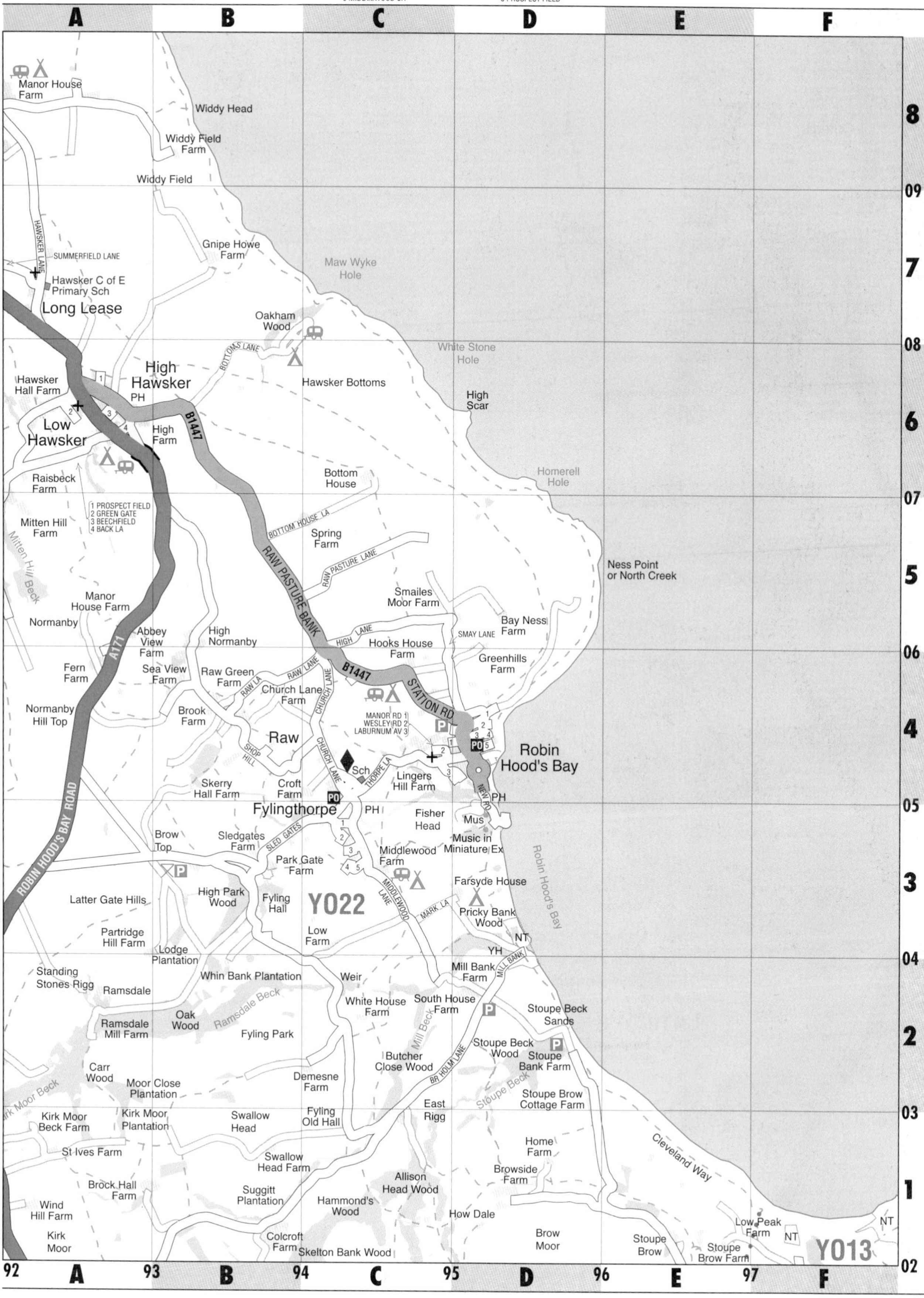

Scale: 1¼ inches to 1 mile

0   ¼   ½   mile
0   250m 500m 750m 1 km

C3
1 THORPE GN BANK
2 KINGSTON GARTH
3 MIDDLEWOOD CL
4 MIDDLEWOOD GARTH
5 MIDDLEWOOD CR

D4
1 MOUNT PLEASANT N
2 MOUNT PLEASANT E
3 MOUNT PLEASANT S
4 THE CL
5 PROSPECT FIELD

Manor House Farm
Widdy Head
Widdy Field Farm
Widdy Field
Summerfield Lane
Gnipe Howe Farm
Maw Wyke Hole
HAWSKER LANE
Hawsker C of E Primary Sch
Long Lease
Oakham Wood
White Stone Hole
Hawsker Hall Farm
High Hawsker PH
High Scar
BOTTOMS LANE
Hawsker Bottoms
Low Hawsker
High Farm
B1447
Bottom House
Homerell Hole
Raisbeck Farm
1 PROSPECT FIELD
2 GREEN GATE
3 BEECHFIELD
4 BACK LA
Mitten Hill Farm
BOTTOM HOUSE LA
Spring Farm
Mitten Hill Beck
RAW PASTURE LANE
Ness Point or North Creek
Manor House Farm
Normanby
Smailes Moor Farm
Bay Ness Farm
A171
Abbey View Farm
High Normanby
SMAY LANE
Fern Farm
Sea View Farm
RAW LA
HIGH LANE
Hooks House Farm
Greenhills Farm
Raw Green Farm
B1447
Normanby Hill Top
Brook Farm
CHURCH LANE
Church Lane Farm
STATION RD.
MANOR RD 1
WESLEY RD 2
LABURNUM AV 3
P
Robin Hood's Bay
Raw
Sch
ROBIN HOOD'S BAY ROAD
SHOP HILL
Croft Farm
THORPE LA
Lingers Hill Farm
PO
PH
NEW RD
PH
Skerry Hall Farm
Fylingthorpe
PO
PH
Fisher Head
Mus
Music in Miniature Ex
Brow Top
Sledgates Farm
SLED GATES
Middlewood Farm
Farsyde House
Latter Gate Hills
High Park Wood
Park Gate Farm
MARK LA
Pricky Bank Wood
NT
YO22
Fyling Hall
MIDDLEWOOD LANE
Low Farm
Robin Hood's Bay
Partridge Hill Farm
Lodge Plantation
YH
Standing Stones Rigg
Ramsdale
Whin Bank Plantation
Weir
Mill Bank Farm
MILL BANK
Ramsdale Beck
White House Farm
South House Farm
P
Stoupe Beck Sands
Ramsdale Mill Farm
Oak Wood
Fyling Park
Mill Beck
Butcher Close Wood
Stoupe Beck Wood
Stoupe Bank Farm
P
Carr Wood
Moor Close Plantation
Demesne Farm
BR HOLM LANE
East Rigg
Stoupe Beck
Stoupe Brow Cottage Farm
Kirk Moor Beck
Swallow Head
Fyling Old Hall
Kirk Moor Beck Farm
Kirk Moor Plantation
Home Farm
Browside Farm
Cleveland Way
St Ives Farm
Swallow Head Farm
Allison Head Wood
How Dale
Wind Hill Farm
Suggitt Plantation
Hammond's Wood
Brow Moor
Low Peak Farm
NT
NT
Kirk Moor
Colcroft Farm
Skelton Bank Wood
Stoupe Brow
Stoupe Brow Farm
YO13

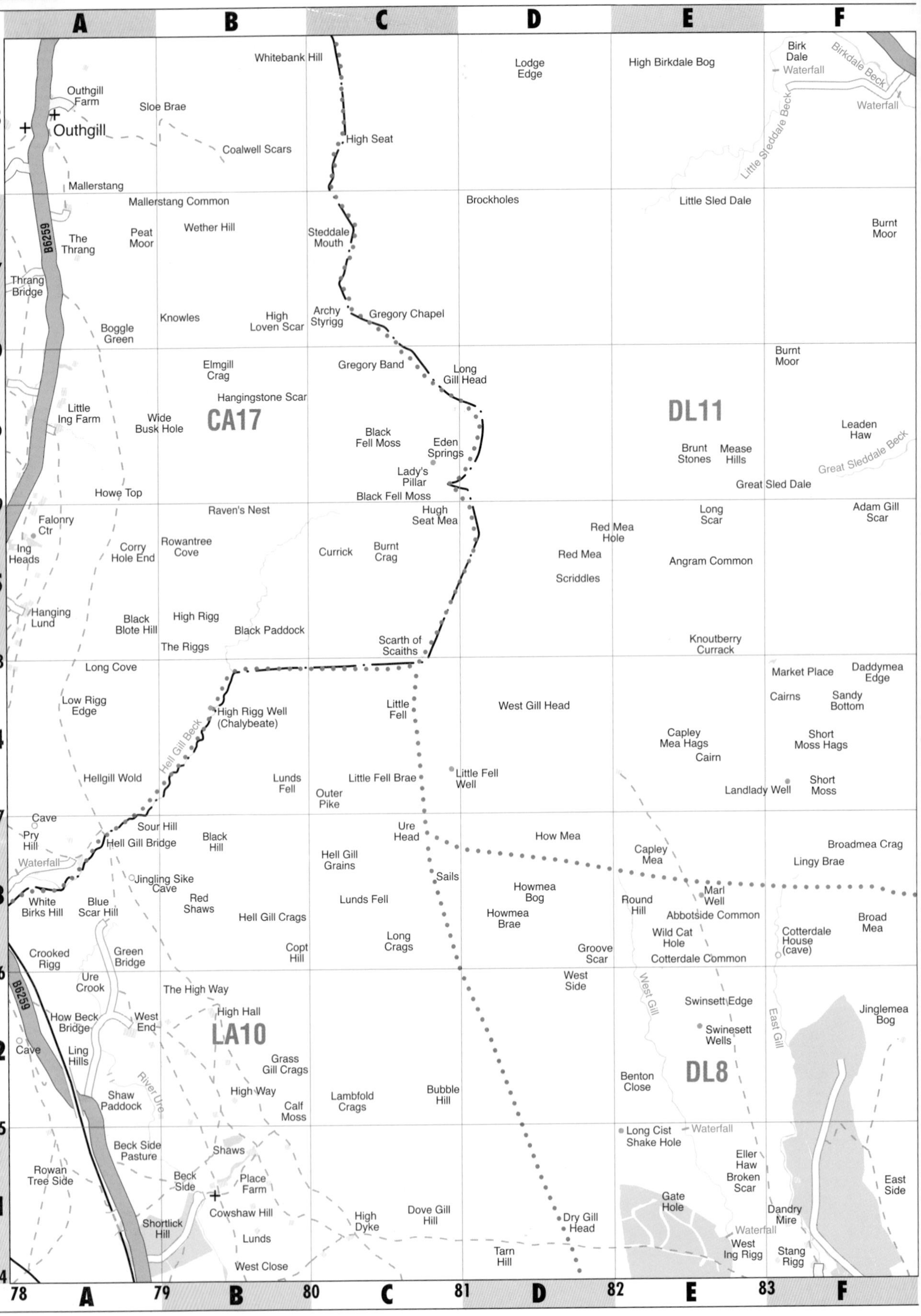

Scale: 1¾ inches to 1 mile

0 ¼ ½ mile
0 250m 500m 750m 1 km

A **B** **C** **D** **E** **F**

8
Whitebank Hill
Lodge Edge
High Birkdale Bog
Birk Dale
Birkdale Beck
Waterfall
Waterfall

Outhgill Farm
Sloe Brae
Outhgill
Coalwell Scars
High Seat
Little Steddale Beck

01
Mallerstang
Mallerstang Common
Brockholes
Little Sled Dale
Burnt Moor

7
The Thrang
Peat Moor
Wether Hill
Steddale Mouth

Thrang Bridge
Knowles
High Loven Scar
Archy Styrigg
Gregory Chapel

00
Boggle Green
Elmgill Crag
Gregory Band
Long Gill Head
Burnt Moor

Hangingstone Scar
CA17
DL11

6
Little Ing Farm
Wide Busk Hole
Black Fell Moss
Eden Springs
Leaden Haw

Howe Top
Lady's Pillar
Brunt Stones
Mease Hills
Great Sleddale Beck

99
Falonry Ctr
Raven's Nest
Black Fell Moss
Hugh Seat Mea
Great Sled Dale

Ing Heads
Corry Hole End
Rowantree Cove
Currick
Burnt Crag
Red Mea Hole
Long Scar
Adam Gill Scar

5
Red Mea
Angram Common

Hanging Lund
Black Blote Hill
High Rigg
Scriddles

98
The Riggs
Black Paddock
Scarth of Scaiths
Knoutberry Currack

Long Cove
High Rigg Well (Chalybeate)
Little Fell
West Gill Head
Market Place
Daddymea Edge

4
Low Rigg Edge
Cairns
Sandy Bottom

Hellgill Wold
Lunds Fell
Little Fell Brae
Little Fell Well
Capley Mea Hags Cairn
Short Moss Hags

Outer Pike
Landlady Well
Short Moss

97
Cave
Pry Hill
Sour Hill
Hell Gill Bridge
Black Hill
Ure Head
How Mea
Capley Mea
Broadmea Crag

Waterfall
Hell Gill Grains
Sails
Lingy Brae

3
White Birks Hill
Blue Scar Hill
Jingling Sike Cave
Red Shaws
Lunds Fell
Howmea Bog
Round Hill
Marl Well
Abbotside Common
Broad Mea

Hell Gill Crags
Howmea Brae
Wild Cat Hole
Cotterdale House (cave)

Crooked Rigg
Green Bridge
Copt Hill
Long Crags
Groove Scar
Cotterdale Common

96
Ure Crook
The High Way
West Side
Swinsett Edge
Jinglemea Bog

How Beck Bridge
West End
High Hall
LA10
DL8
Swinesett Wells

2
Cave
Ling Hills
Grass Gill Crags
Benton Close

Shaw Paddock
High Way
Calf Moss
Lambfold Crags
Bubble Hill

95
Beck Side Pasture
Long Cist Shake Hole
Waterfall

Rowan Tree Side
Shaws
Beck Side
Place Farm
Eller Haw Broken Scar

1
Shortlick Hill
Cowshaw Hill
High Dyke
Dove Gill Hill
Dry Gill Head
Gate Hole
Dandry Mire
East Side

Lunds
West Ing Rigg
Waterfall
Stang Rigg

94
West Close
Tarn Hill

78 **A** **79** **B** **80** **C** **81** **D** **82** **E** **83** **F**

Scale: 1¾ inches to 1 mile

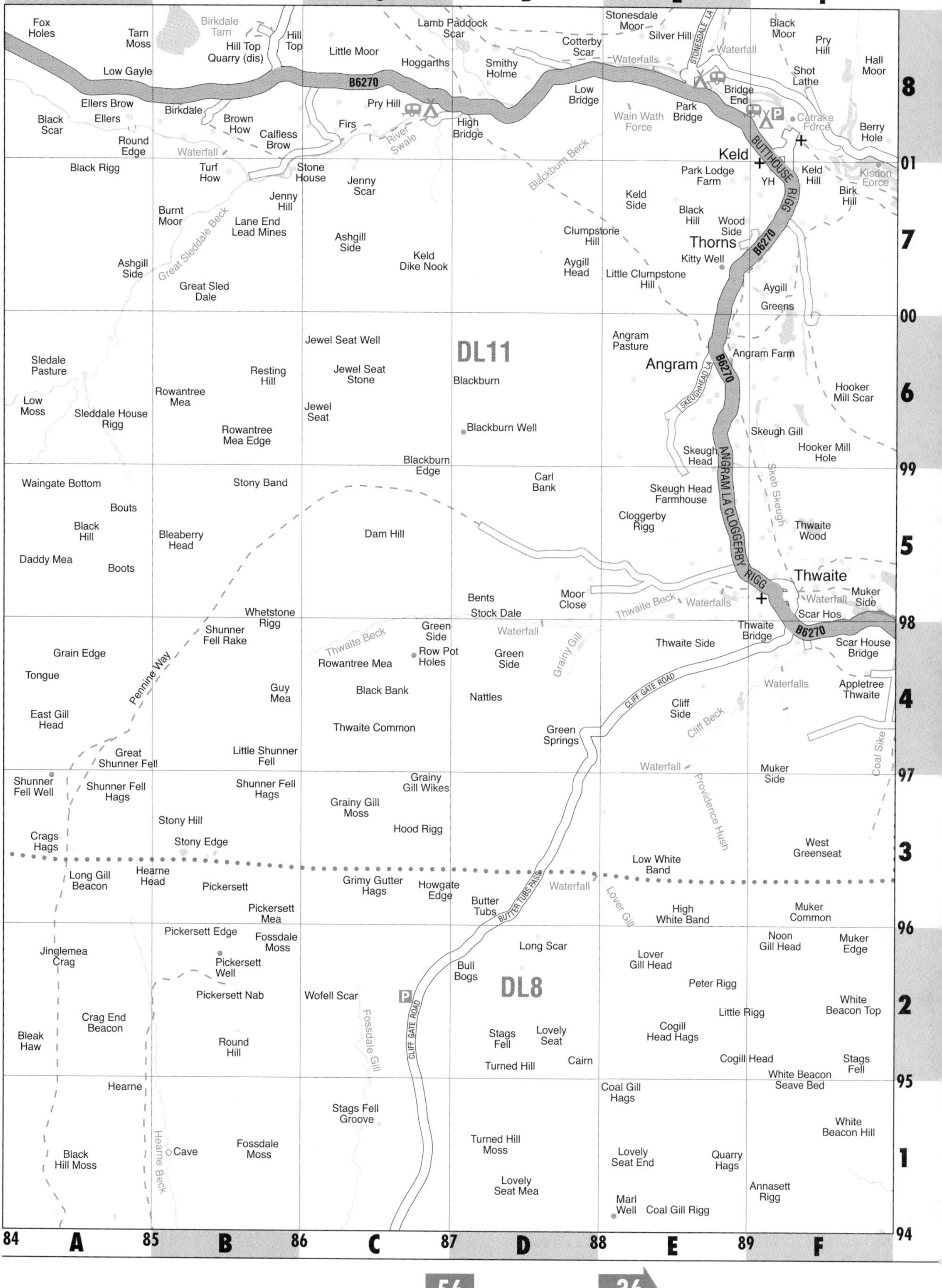
15
36
A B C D E F
8 01 7 00 6 99 5 98 4 97 3 96 2 95 1 94
84 85 86 87 88 89
Fox Holes
Tarn Moss
Birkdale Tarn
Hill Top Quarry (dis)
Hill Top
Little Moor
Lamb Paddock Scar
Hoggarths
Smithy Holme
Cotterby Scar
Stonesdale Moor
Silver Hill
Stonesdale La
Waterfall
Waterfalls
Black Moor
Pry Hill
Hall Moor
Shot Lathe
Low Gayle
B6270
Ellers Brow
Ellers
Black Scar
Birkdale
Brown How
Calfless Brow
Pry Hill
Firs
River Swale
High Bridge
Low Bridge
Wain Wath Force
Park Bridge
Bridge End
Catrake Force
Berry Hole
Round Edge
Waterfall
Black Rigg
Turf How
Stone House
Jenny Scar
Blackburn Beck
Keld
Park Lodge Farm
YH
Butthouse Rigg
Keld Hill
Kisdon Force
Birk Hill
Jenny Hill
Burnt Moor
Lane End Lead Mines
Great Sleddale Beck
Keld Side
Black Hill
Wood Side
Clumpstone Hill
Thorns
Kitty Well
Ashgill Side
Ashgill Side
Keld Dike Nook
Aygill Head
Little Clumpstone Hill
Aygill
Greens
Great Sled Dale
Jewel Seat Well
DL11
Angram Pasture
Angram
Angram Farm
Sledale Pasture
Resting Hill
Jewel Seat Stone
Blackburn
Skeughead La
Hooker Mill Scar
Rowantree Mea
Low Moss
Sleddale House Rigg
Jewel Seat
Rowantree Mea Edge
Blackburn Well
Skeugh Gill
Skeugh Head
Angram La Cloggerby Rigg
Hooker Mill Hole
Blackburn Edge
Waingate Bottom
Stony Band
Carl Bank
Skeugh Head Farmhouse
Skeb Skeugh
Bouts
Cloggerby Rigg
Black Hill
Bleaberry Head
Dam Hill
Thwaite Wood
Daddy Mea
Boots
Thwaite
Muker Side
Moor Close
Bents
Thwaite Beck
Waterfalls
Waterfall
Whetstone Rigg
Stock Dale
Scar Hos
Shunner Fell Rake
Green Side
Waterfall
Thwaite Bridge
Scar House Bridge
Grain Edge
Thwaite Beck
Row Pot Holes
Green Side
Thwaite Side
Rowantree Mea
Grainy Gill
Cliff Gate Road
Tongue
Pennine Way
Guy Mea
Black Bank
Cliff Side
Waterfalls
Appletree Thwaite
Nattles
Cliff Beck
East Gill Head
Thwaite Common
Green Springs
Great Shunner Fell
Little Shunner Fell
Waterfall
Muker Side
Coal Sike
Shunner Fell Well
Shunner Fell Hags
Shunner Fell Hags
Grainy Gill Wikes
Grainy Gill Moss
Providence Hush
Stony Hill
Hood Rigg
Crags Hags
Stony Edge
West Greenseat
Low White Band
Long Gill Beacon
Hearne Head
Pickersett
Grimy Gutter Hags
Howgate Edge
Butter Tubs
Butter Tubs Pass
Waterfall
Lover Gill
Pickersett Mea
High White Band
Muker Common
Pickersett Edge
Fossdale Moss
Long Scar
Noon Gill Head
Muker Edge
Jinglemea Crag
Pickersett Well
Bull Bogs
Lover Gill Head
Peter Rigg
Pickersett Nab
Wofell Scar
DL8
Fossdale Gill
White Beacon Top
Crag End Beacon
Little Rigg
Cliff Gate Road
Stags Fell
Lovely Seat
Cogill Head Hags
Bleak Haw
Round Hill
Cairn
Turned Hill
Cogill Head
Stags Fell
White Beacon Seave Bed
Coal Gill Hags
Hearne
Stags Fell Groove
White Beacon Hill
Turned Hill Moss
Black Hill Moss
Cave
Fossdale Moss
Hearne Beck
Lovely Seat End
Quarry Hags
Lovely Seat Mea
Annasett Rigg
Marl Well
Coal Gill Rigg
56
36

35
16

Scale: 1¾ inches to 1 mile

0 ¼ ½ mile
0 250m 500m 750m 1 km

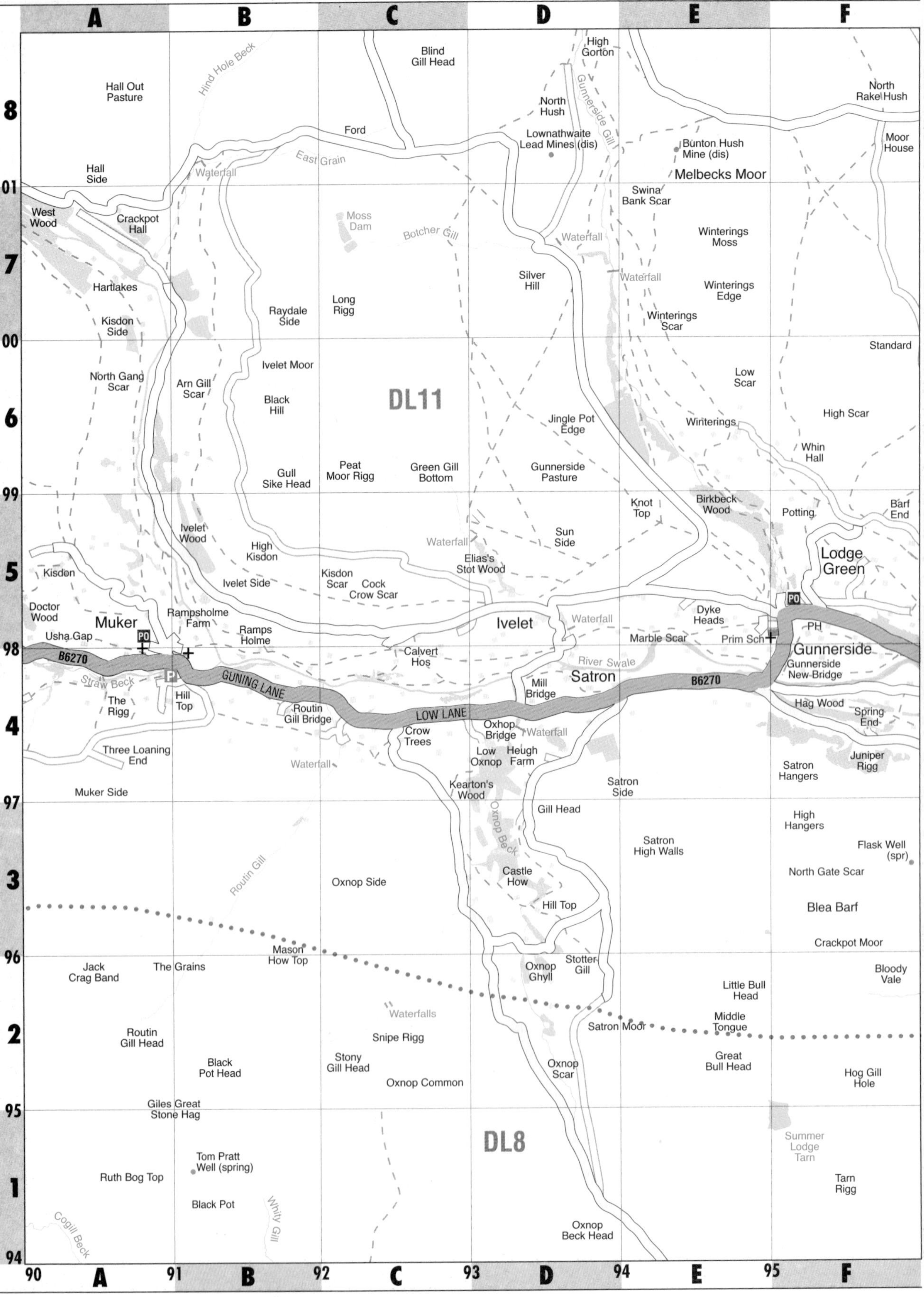

A B C D E F

8

Hall Out
Pasture

Blind
Gill Head

High
Gorton

North
Rakel Hush

Hind Hole Beck

Gunnerside Gill

North
Hush

Moor
House

Hall
Side

Ford

Lownathwaite
Lead Mines (dis)

Bunton Hush
Mine (dis)

01

East Grain

Waterfall

Melbecks Moor

West
Wood

Crackpot
Hall

Swina
Bank Scar

7

Moss
Dam

Winterings
Moss

Hartlakes

Botcher Gill

Silver
Hill

Winterings
Edge

Kisdon
Side

Raydale
Side

Long
Rigg

Waterfall

Winterings
Scar

Waterfall

00

North Gang
Scar

Standard

Arn Gill
Scar

Ivelet Moor

DL11

Low
Scar

High Scar

6

Black
Hill

Jingle Pot
Edge

Winterings

Whin
Hall

Gull
Sike Head

Peat
Moor Rigg

Green Gill
Bottom

Gunnerside
Pasture

Birkbeck
Wood

Barf
End

99

Sun
Side

Knot
Top

Potting

Ivelet
Wood

Waterfall

Elias's
Stot Wood

Lodge
Green

5

Kisdon

High
Kisdon

Kisdon
Scar

Cock
Crow Scar

Dyke
Heads

PO

PH

Doctor
Wood

Ivelet Side

Rampsholme
Farm

Ramps
Holme

Ivelet

Waterfall

Marble Scar

Prim Sch

Gunnerside

98

Muker
PO

Calvert Hos

River Swale

Satron

Gunnerside
New-Bridge

B6270

GUNING LANE

Mill
Bridge

B6270

Usha Gap

Straw Beck

Hill
Top

P

LOW LANE

Hag Wood

Spring
End

4

The
Rigg

Routin
Gill Bridge

Crow
Trees

Oxhop
Bridge

Waterfall

Satron
Hangers

Juniper
Rigg

Three Loaning
End

Low
Oxnop

Heugh
Farm

Satron
Side

Waterfall

Kearton's
Wood

Gill Head

High
Hangers

Muker Side

Satron
High Walls

Flask Well
(spr)

3

Routin Gill

Oxnop Side

Castle
How

North Gate Scar

Blea Barf

Oxnop Beck

Hill Top

Crackpot Moor

96

Mason
How Top

Stotter
Gill

Bloody
Vale

Jack
Crag Band

The Grains

Oxnop
Ghyll

Little Bull
Head

2

Waterfalls

Snipe Rigg

Satron Moor

Middle
Tongue

Routin
Gill Head

Stony
Gill Head

Great
Bull Head

Hog Gill
Hole

Black
Pot Head

Oxnop
Scar

Oxnop Common

95

Giles Great
Stone Hag

Summer
Lodge
Tarn

DL8

1

Tom Pratt
Well (spring)

Ruth Bog Top

Tarn
Rigg

Black Pot

Whity Gill

Oxnop
Beck Head

Cogill Beck

94

90 A 91 B 92 C 93 D 94 E 95 F

35
57

Scale: 1¾ inches to 1 mile
¼ ½ mile
250m 500m 750m 1 km

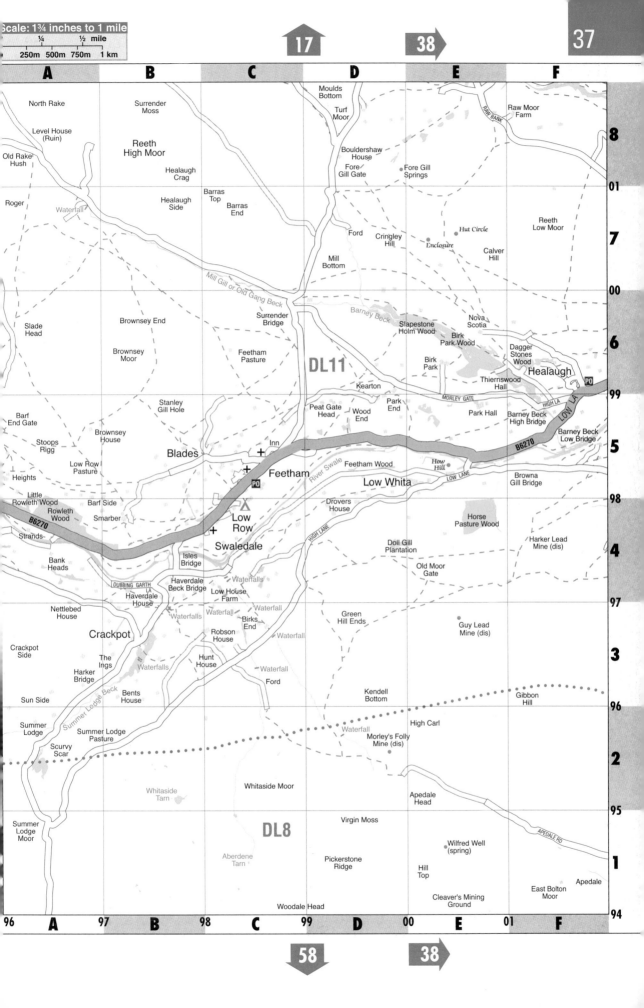

A **B** **C** **D** **E** **F**

North Rake

Surrender Moss

Level House (Ruin)

Reeth High Moor

Old Rake Hush

Healaugh Crag

Roger

Healaugh Side

Barras Top

Barras End

Moulds Bottom

Turf Moor

Bouldershaw House

Fore Gill Gate

Fore Gill Springs

Raw Moor Farm

RAW BANK

8

01

Ford

Cringley Hill

Enclosure

Hut Circle

Calver Hill

Reeth Low Moor

7

Waterfall

Mill Bottom

00

Slade Head

Brownsey End

Mill Gill or Old Gang Beck

Surrender Bridge

Feetham Pasture

DL11

Barney Beck

Slapestone Holm Wood

Birk Park Wood

Nova Scotia

Dagger Stones Wood

6

Brownsey Moor

Birk Park

Healaugh

PO

Barf End Gate

Stanley Gill Hole

Kearton

Peat Gate Head

Wood End

Park End

MORLEY GATE

Park Hall

Thiernswood Hall

HIGH LA

Barney Beck High Bridge

LOW LA

99

Stoops Rigg

Brownsey House

Blades

Inn

Feetham

River Swale

Feetham Wood

How Hill

LOW LANE

Barney Beck Low Bridge

B6270

Browna Gill Bridge

5

Barf End Gate

Low Row Pasture

PO

Low Whita

98

Heights

Little Rowleth Wood

Rowleth Wood

Barf Side

Smarber

Low Row

Swaledale

Drovers House

HIGH LANE

Horse Pasture Wood

Harker Lead Mine (dis)

4

B6270

Strands

Bank Heads

Isles Bridge

Haverdale Beck Bridge

Low House Farm

Waterfalls

Doll Gill Plantation

Old Moor Gate

97

DUBBING GARTH LA

Haverdale House

Waterfalls

Waterfall

Birks End

Waterfall

Green Hill Ends

Guy Lead Mine (dis)

Nettlebed House

Robson House

Gibbon Hill

3

Crackpot

The Ings

Hunt House

Waterfall

Kendell Bottom

96

Crackpot Side

Waterfalls

Ford

Harker Bridge

Bents House

Summer Lodge Beck

Waterfall

Morley's Folly Mine (dis)

High Carl

2

Sun Side

Summer Lodge

Scurvy Scar

Summer Lodge Pasture

Apedale Head

APEDALE RD

95

Whitaside Tarn

Whitaside Moor

Virgin Moss

Wilfred Well (spring)

Summer Lodge Moor

DL8

Hill Top

Aberdene Tarn

Pickerstone Ridge

Cleaver's Mining Ground

East Bolton Moor

Apedale

1

Woodale Head

94

96 **A** **97** **B** **98** **C** **99** **D** **00** **E** **01** **F**

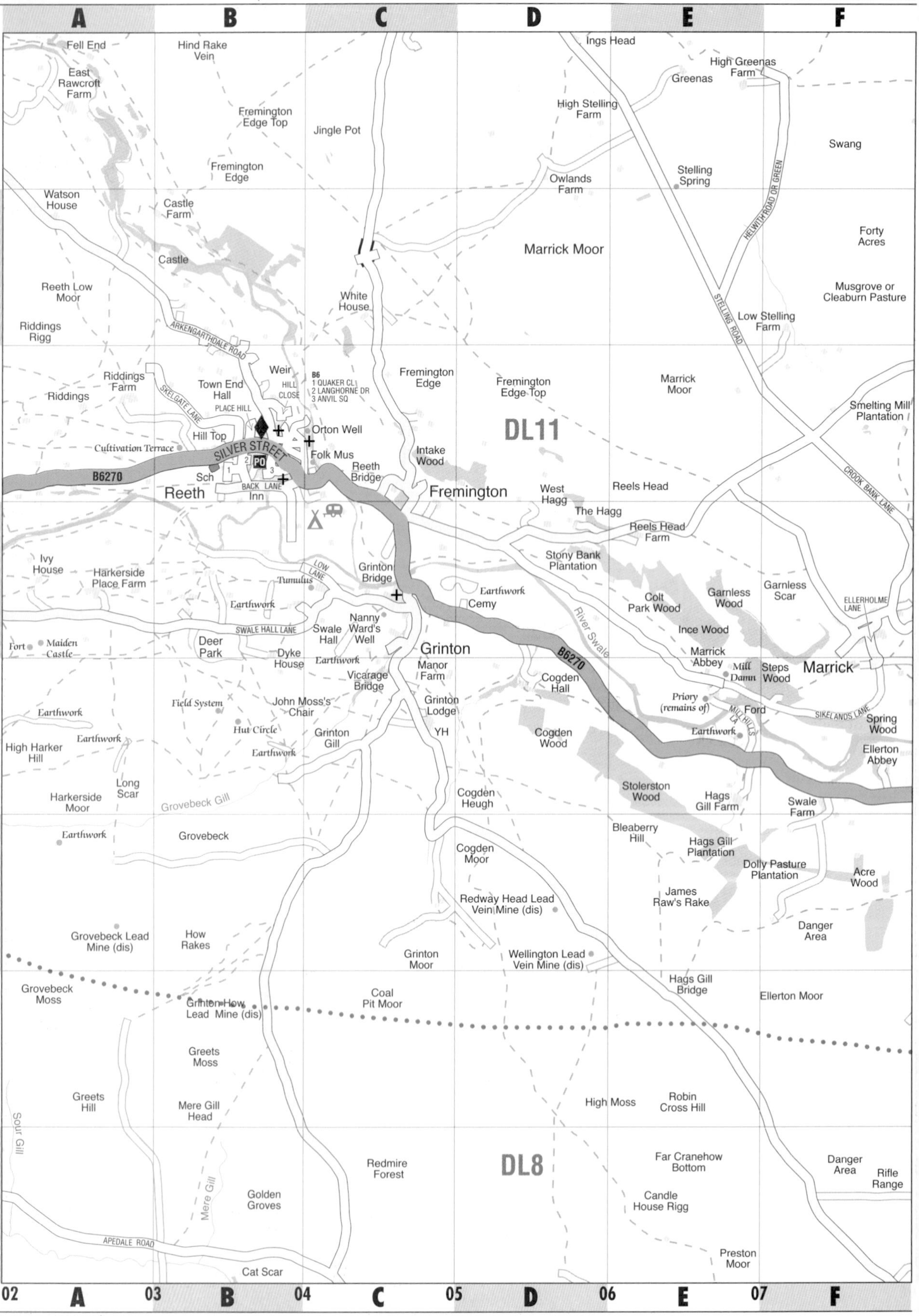

A   B   C   D   E   F

8

01

7

00

6

99

5

98

4

97

3

96

2

95

1

94

Fell End
East Rawcroft Farm
Hind Rake Vein
Ings Head
High Greenas Farm
Greenas
Swang

Fremington Edge Top
Jingle Pot
High Stelling Farm
Stelling Spring
Forty Acres

Watson House
Castle Farm
Fremington Edge
Owlands Farm
Marrick Moor
Low Stelling Farm
Musgrove or Cleaburn Pasture

Castle
White House
Smelting Mill Plantation

Reeth Low Moor
ARKENGARTHDALE ROAD
Weir
Fremington Edge
Fremington Edge Top
Marrick Moor
DL11

Riddings Rigg
Riddings Farm
Town End Hall
HILL CLOSE
B6
1 QUAKER CL
2 LANGHORNE DR
3 ANVIL SQ

Riddings
SKELGATE LANE
PLACE HILL
Orton Well
Fremington
Reels Head

Hill Top
SILVER STREET
Folk Mus
Intake Wood
West Hagg
The Hagg
Reels Head Farm

Cultivation Terrace
B6270
Sch
PO
BACK LANE
Reeth Bridge

Reeth
Inn

Ivy House
LOW LANE
Grinton Bridge
Stony Bank Plantation
River Swale
Colt Park Wood
Garnless Wood
Garnless Scar
ELLERHOLME LANE

Harkerside Place Farm
Tumulus
Earthwork
Cemy
Ince Wood

Earthwork
SWALE HALL LANE
Swale Hall
Nanny Ward's Well
Grinton
B6270
Marrick Abbey
Mill Dam
Steps Wood
Marrick

Fort
Maiden Castle
Deer Park
Dyke House
Vicarage Bridge
Manor Farm
Cogden Hall
Priory (remains of)
Ford
MILL HILLS
SIKELANDS LANE
Spring Wood

Earthwork
Field System
John Moss's Chair
Earthwork
Grinton Lodge
Cogden Wood
Earthwork
Ellerton Abbey

High Harker Hill
Earthwork
Hut Circle
Grinton Gill
Earthwork
YH
Stolerston Wood
Hags Gill Farm
Swale Farm

Harkerside Moor
Long Scar
Grovebeck Gill
Cogden Heugh
Bleaberry Hill
Hags Gill Plantation
Dolly Pasture Plantation
Acre Wood

Earthwork
Grovebeck
Cogden Moor
James Raw's Rake
Danger Area

Grovebeck Lead Mine (dis)
How Rakes
Redway Head Lead Vein Mine (dis)
Wellington Lead Vein Mine (dis)
Hags Gill Bridge

Grovebeck Moss
Grinton How Lead Mine (dis)
Coal Pit Moor
Grinton Moor
Ellerton Moor

Greets Moss

Greets Hill
Mere Gill Head
High Moss
Robin Cross Hill

Sour Gill
Mere Gill
Golden Groves
Redmire Forest
DL8
Far Cranehow Bottom
Candle House Rigg
Danger Area
Rifle Range

APEDALE ROAD
Cat Scar
Preston Moor

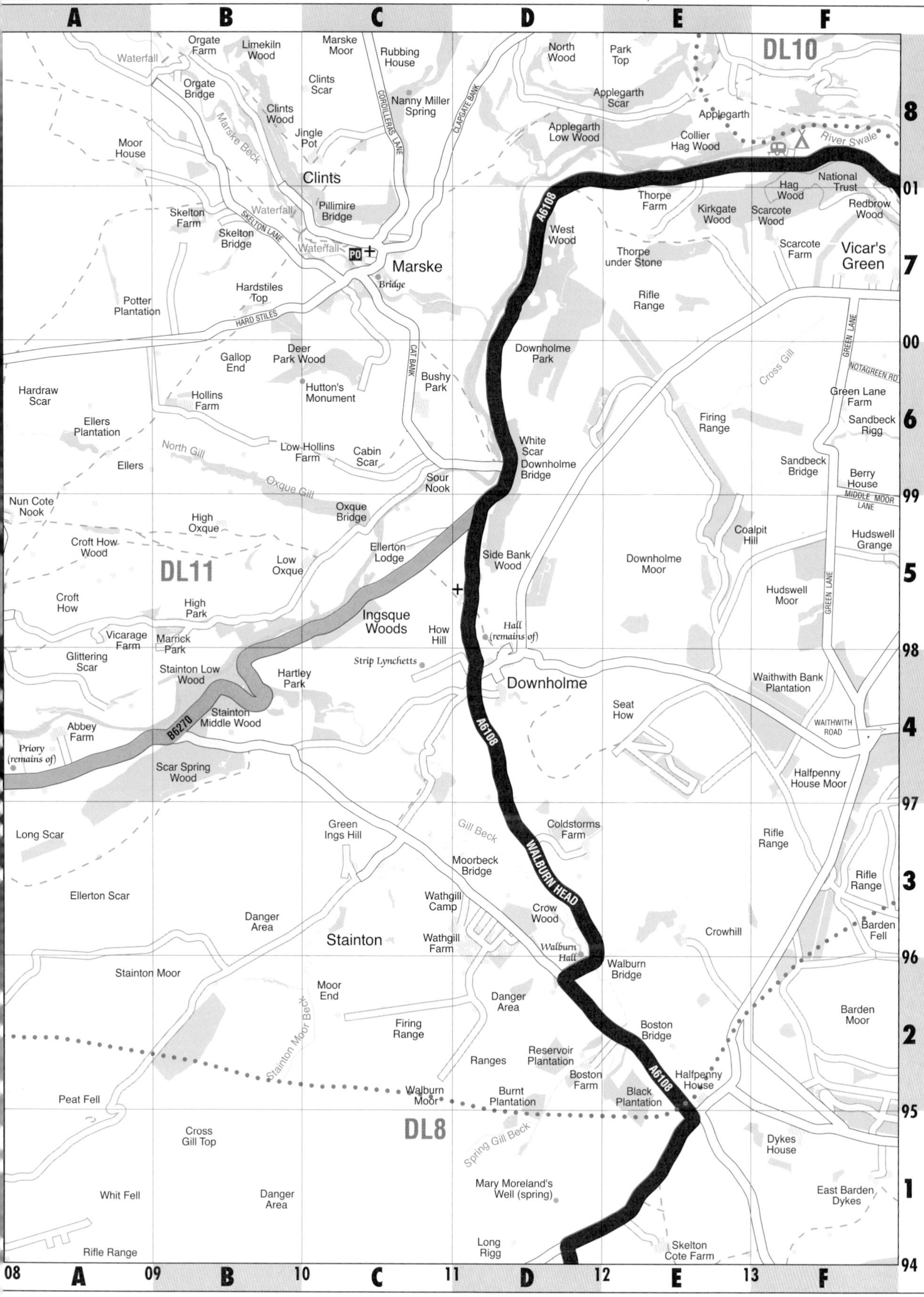
A
B
C
D
E
F
DL10
DL11
DL8
Waterfall
Orgate Farm
Limekiln Wood
Marske Moor
Rubbing House
North Wood
Park Top
Orgate Bridge
Clints Scar
Nanny Miller Spring
Applegarth Scar
Applegarth
CORDILLERAS LANE
CLAPGATE BANK
Marske Beck
Clints Wood
Jingle Pot
Applegarth Low Wood
Collier Hag Wood
River Swale
Moor House
Clints
National Trust
Hag Wood
Redbrow Wood
A6108
Thorpe Farm
Kirkgate Wood
Scarcote Wood
Skelton Farm
Waterfall
Pillimire Bridge
West Wood
SKELTON LANE
Skelton Bridge
Waterfall
PO
Marske
Bridge
Thorpe under Stone
Scarcote Farm
Vicar's Green
Hardstiles Top
Rifle Range
Potter Plantation
HARD STILES
GREEN LANE
Gallop End
Deer Park Wood
Downholme Park
Cross Gill
NOTAGREEN RD
Hardraw Scar
Hutton's Monument
CAT BANK
Bushy Park
Green Lane Farm
Hollins Farm
Firing Range
Ellers Plantation
Sandbeck Rigg
North Gill
White Scar
Low Hollins Farm
Cabin Scar
Downholme Bridge
Ellers
Sandbeck Bridge
Berry House
Oxque Gill
Sour Nook
MIDDLE MOOR LANE
Nun Cote Nook
Oxque Bridge
High Oxque
Coalpit Hill
Hudswell Grange
Croft How Wood
Ellerton Lodge
Side Bank Wood
Downholme Moor
Low Oxque
Hudswell Moor
Croft How
High Park
Ingsque Woods
How Hill
Hall (remains of)
GREEN LANE
Vicarage Farm
Marrick Park
Glittering Scar
Strip Lynchetts
Stainton Low Wood
Hartley Park
Downholme
Waithwith Bank Plantation
Seat How
Abbey Farm
Stainton Middle Wood
B6270
WAITHWITH ROAD
Priory (remains of)
Scar Spring Wood
Halfpenny House Moor
Long Scar
Green Ings Hill
Gill Beck
Coldstorms Farm
Rifle Range
Moorbeck Bridge
WALBURN HEAD
Rifle Range
Ellerton Scar
Wathgill Camp
Crow Wood
Barden Fell
Danger Area
Stainton
Wathgill Farm
Walburn Hall
Crowhill
Walburn Bridge
Stainton Moor
Moor End
Stainton Moor Beck
Danger Area
Barden Moor
Firing Range
Boston Bridge
Ranges
Reservoir Plantation
Boston Farm
Halfpenny House
Peat Fell
Walburn Moor
Burnt Plantation
Black Plantation
Cross Gill Top
Spring Gill Beck
Dykes House
Mary Moreland's Well (spring)
Whit Fell
Danger Area
East Barden Dykes
Long Rigg
Skelton Cote Farm
Rifle Range
8
01
7
00
6
99
5
98
4
97
3
96
2
95
1
94
08
09
10
11
12
13

39
20
For full street detail of the highlighted area see page 209.

F5
1 WESTRIDGE CR
2 FALKLAND RD
3 ALBERMARLE DR
4 CRAVENDALE RD
5 MAPLE CL
6 CHESTNUT CL
7 GRANGE RD
8 MANOR GR

Scale: 1¾ inches to 1 mile
0 ¼ ½ mile
0 250m 500m 750m 1 km

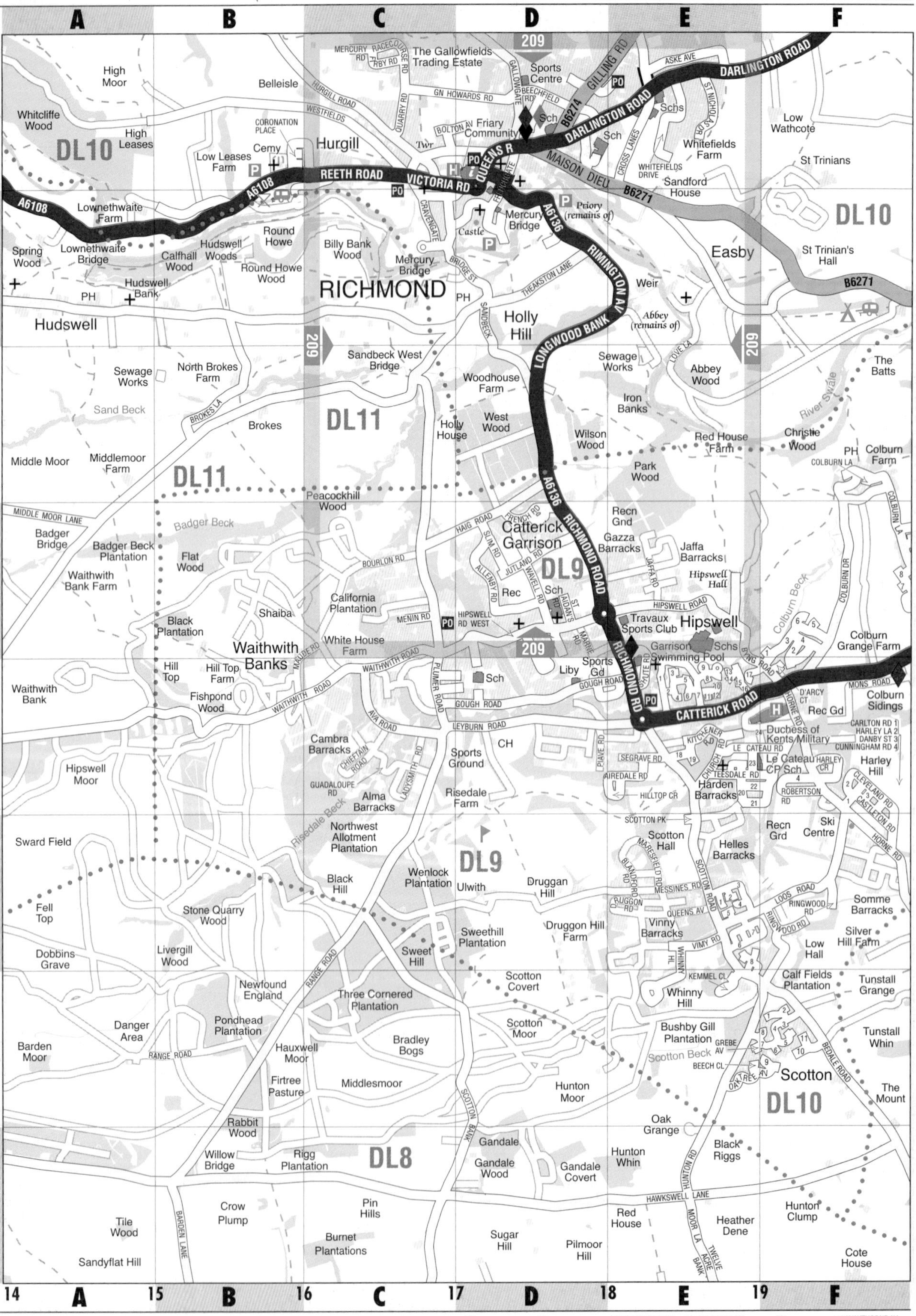

39
61

E3
1 SAN CARLOS CL
2 GOOSE GN CL
3 GOODWOOD RD
4 STANLEY CL
5 TUMBLEDOWN CL
6 HAMBLETON RD
7 FIELD GR
8 SCOTTON GD

E4
1 HEATHERDENE RD
2 VICKERS RD
3 BROWNING CL
4 ENFIELD CL
5 MAXIM CL
6 WESSON CL
7 BELTON PK DR
8 DUMFRIES SQ
9 SIDMOUTH SQ
10 FELIXSTOWE DR
11 WATCHET RD
12 FILEY CL
13 ST OSWALDS RD
14 ST OSWALDS CL
15 ST MARTINS CL
16 VICARAGE RD
17 LINTON RI
18 BERWICK RD
19 QUENTIN RD
20 WEARDALE RD
21 WENSLEYDALE ROAD
22 SWALEDALE RD
23 BROUGHRD
24 WINDSOR RD

F2
1 FALCON CL
2 CURLEW CR
3 KINGFISHER CT
4 MALLARD RD
5 OSPREY CL
6 HERON CT
7 KESTREL DR
8 WOODCOCK DR
9 BIRCH CL
10 HAWTHORNE AV
11 MEANEERD

Scale: 1¾ inches to 1 mile
0 ¼ ½ mile
0 250m 500m 750m 1 km

A5
1 ST GILES' CLOSE
2 ST PETER'S CL
3 BRIDGE CL
4 ST CUTHBERT'S AV
5 BROUGH AV
6 CORONATION AV
7 SUTTON AV
8 COLVILLE CR
9 MEADOWFIELD RD
10 CONSTANTINE AV
11 CONSTANTINE GR
12 COLVILLE RD
13 DAISY CL
14 CHERRY TREE WY
15 PEPPERMINT DR
16 POPPY CT
17 ORCHID CT
18 PRIMROSE CT
19 FOXGLOVE CT
20 CROCUS CT
21 LAVENDER CT
22 WALKERVILLE AV
23 FIRSTAV
24 FIFTH AV
25 BLUENILEWY
26 FOURTHAV

21

C7
1 CAXTON CL
2 STEPHENSON RD
3 SHAKESPEARE CL
4 WELLINGTON WY
5 CITADILLA CL

D5
1 WILLOW VW
2 SYCAMORE CT
3 CHESTNUT CL
4 BROUGH MS
5 MOWBRAY RD
6 ELM WK
7 ASH CFT
8 ROWAN CT
9 KING'S CL
10 PALLET HL
11 GARTH CL
12 ARENA VW
13 GARTH MS

42

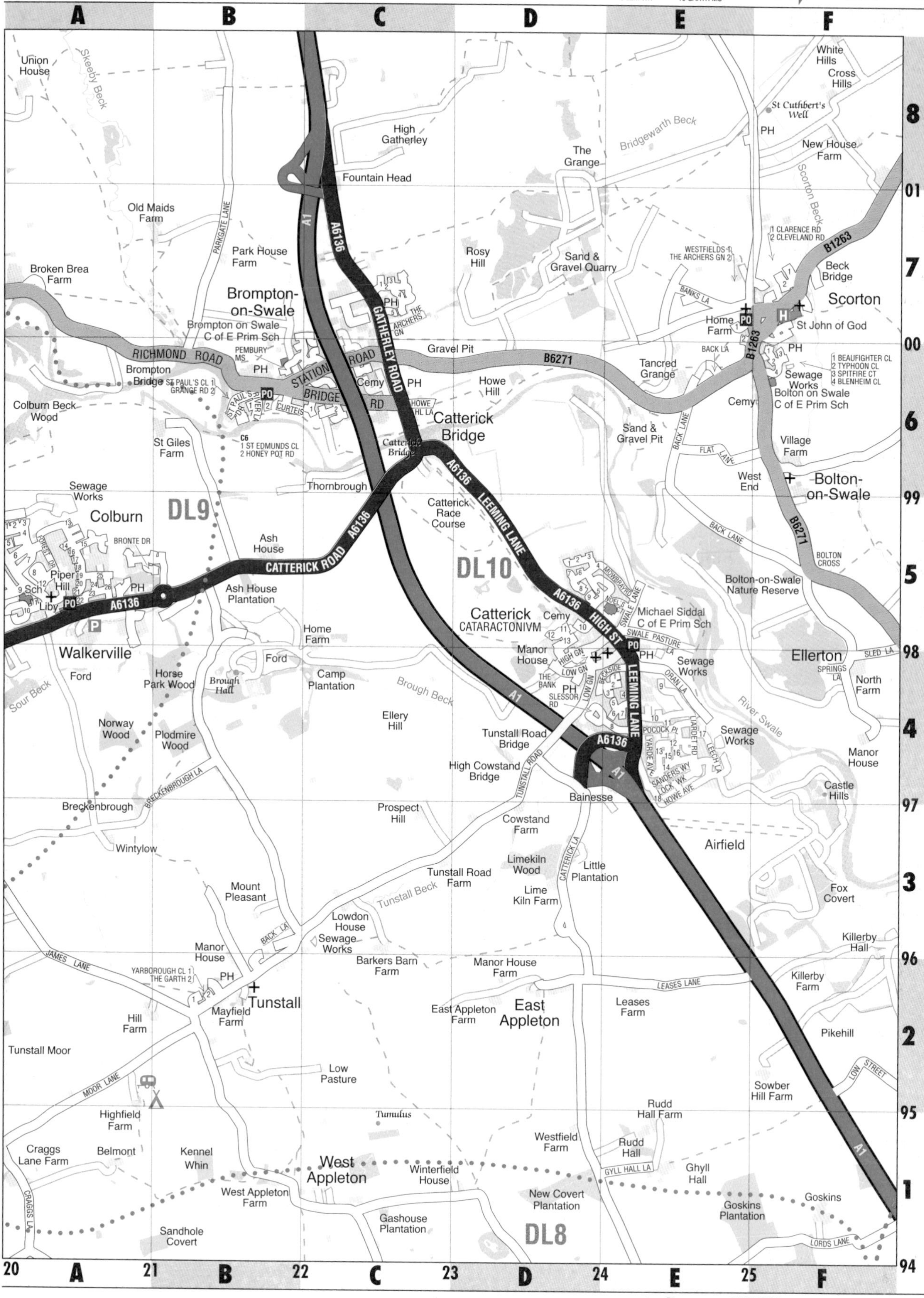

62

42

E4
1 SYDALL'S WY
2 KILLERBY DR
3 ST ANNE'S CR
4 CHAPEL RIGGS
5 BENNIONS WY
6 PER ARDUA WY
7 CENTURIAN CL
8 SLESSOR RD
9 HARRIS DR
10 YOUNGS WY
11 GRUNDY WY
12 GODFREY RD
13 ROBINSON RD
14 FULLER-GOOD RD
15 STRAFFORD RD
16 MELLERSH RD
17 CHACKSFIELD RD
18 LYDFORD RD

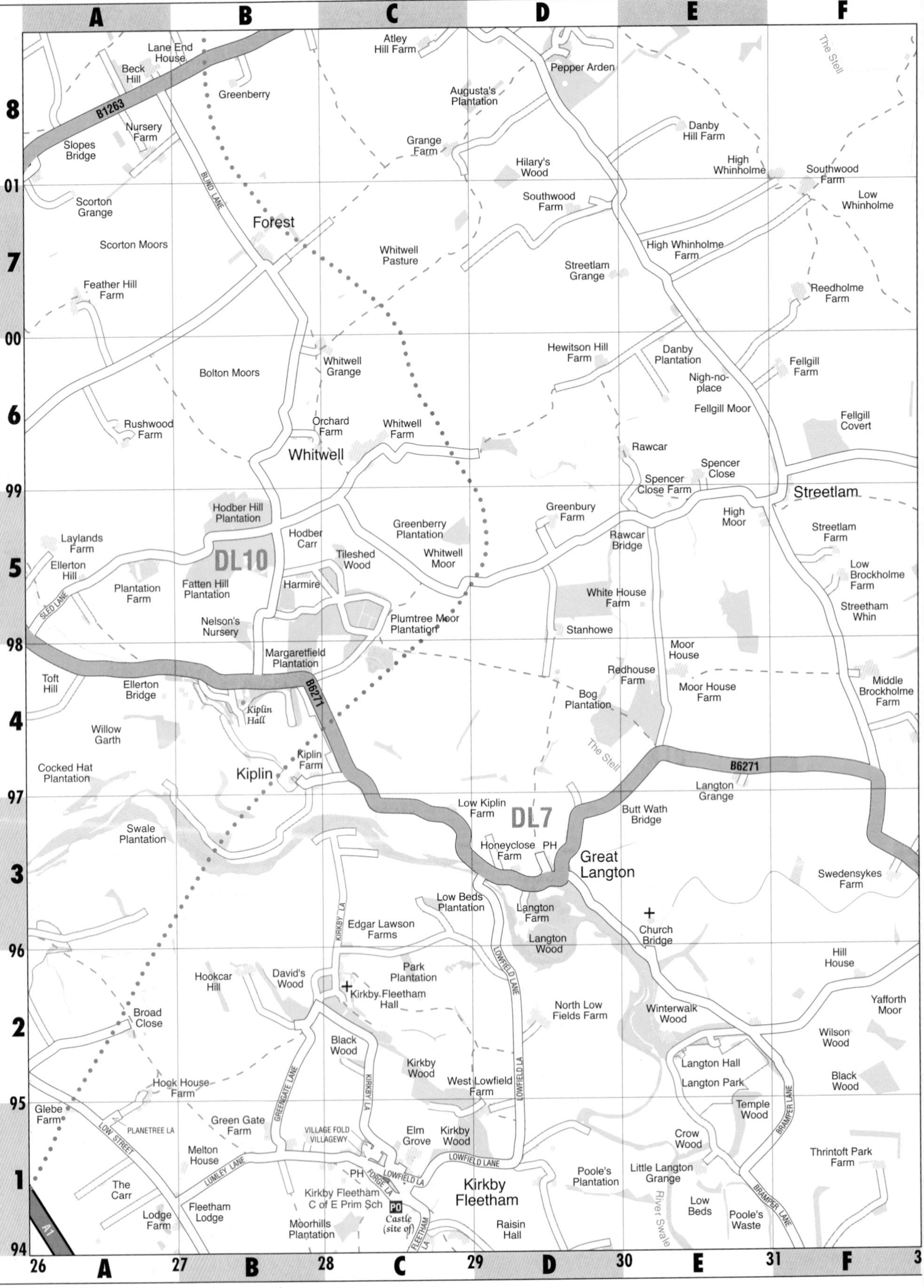

Scale: 1¾ inches to 1 mile
¼ ½ mile
250m 500m 750m 1 km

23
44

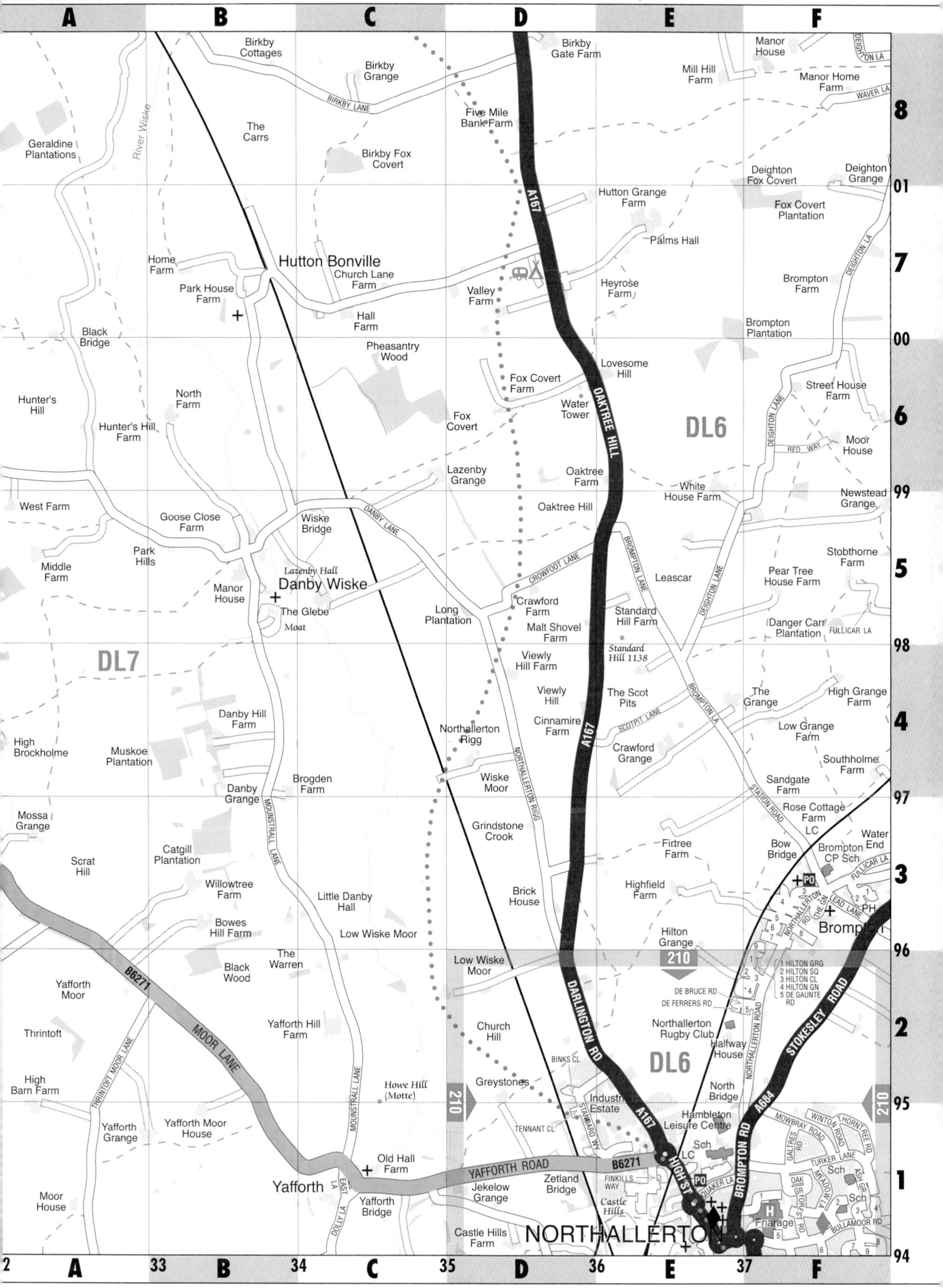

64
44

F1
1 BYLAND AV
2 MOORVIEW RD
3 SCHOLLA VW
4 LEWIS RD
5 DENE RD
6 ELM AV
7 ASHLANDS RD
8 HAILSTONE DV
9 BANKHEAD RD

F3
1 DANELAW FIELDS
2 DANELAW
3 CHURCH VW
4 ORCHARD GR
5 LODGE LA
6 VIKINGS CT
7 CORBER HL
8 MILL HL CL
9 FERNWOOD CL

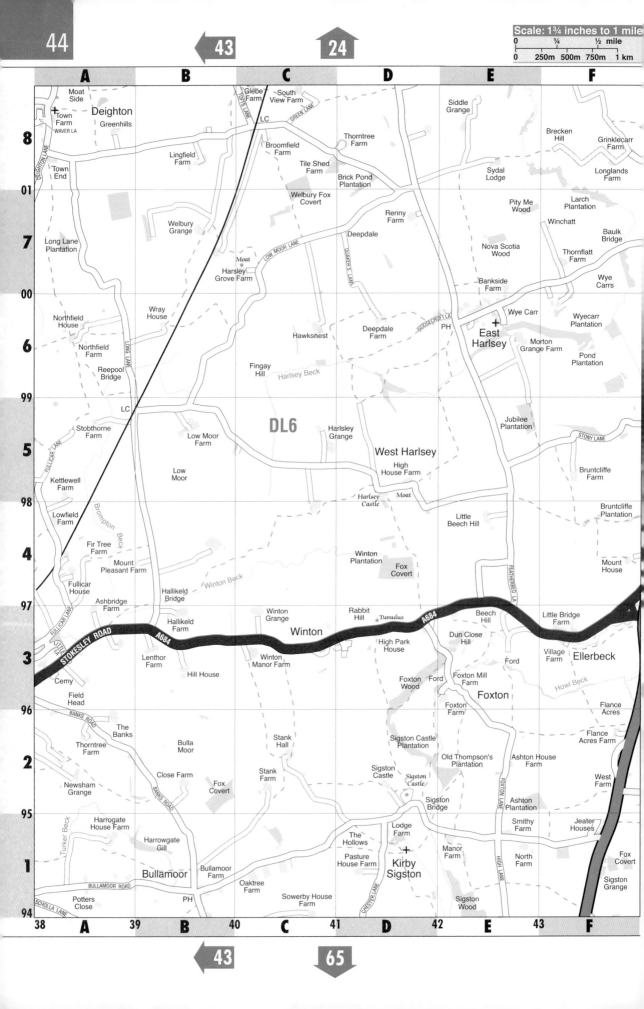

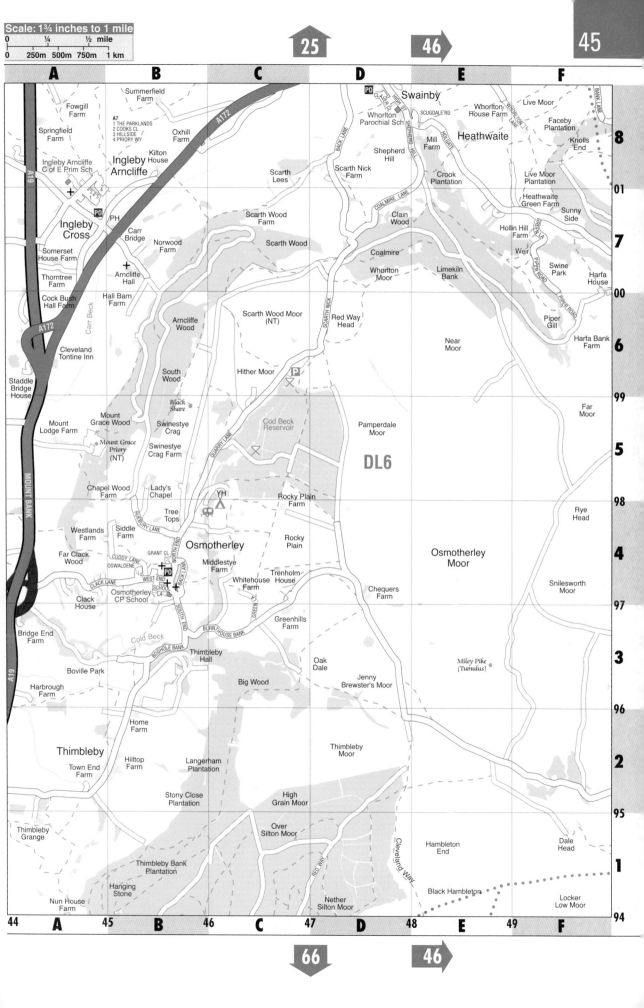

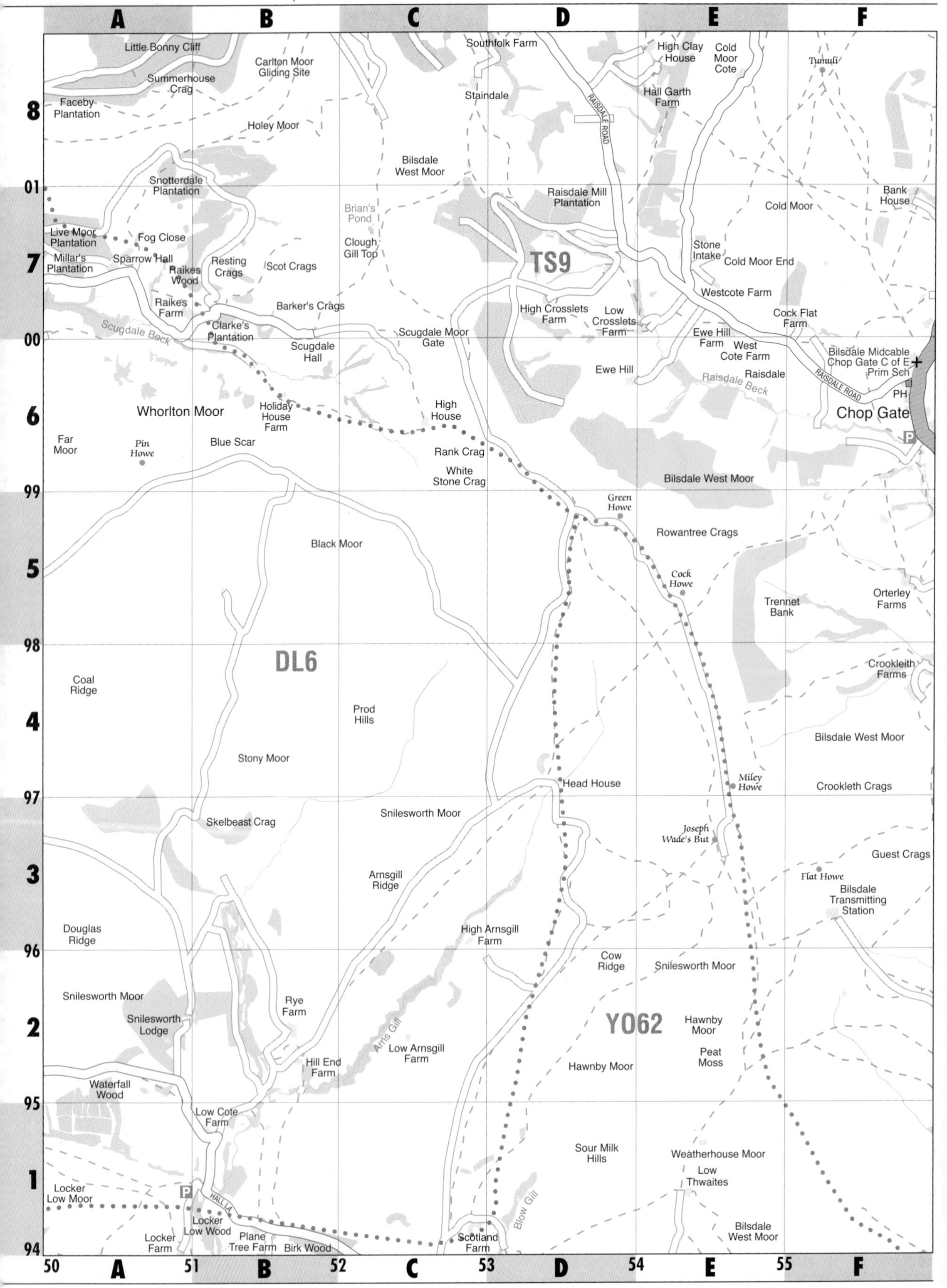

A **B** **C** **D** **E** **F**

8
01
7
00
6
99
5
98
4
97
3
96
2
95
1
94

Little Bonny Cliff
Summerhouse Crag
Carlton Moor Gliding Site
Southfolk Farm
High Clay House
Cold Moor Cote
Tumuli
Faceby Plantation
Holey Moor
Staindale
Hall Garth Farm
Bank House
Snotterdale Plantation
Bilsdale West Moor
Raisdale Mill Plantation
Cold Moor
Live Moor Plantation
Fog Close
Clough Gill Top
TS9
Stone Intake
Cold Moor End
Millar's Plantation
Sparrow Hall
Raikes Wood
Resting Crags
Scot Crags
Westcote Farm
Scugdale Beck
Raikes Farm
Clarke's Plantation
Barker's Crags
High Crosslets Farm
Low Crosslets Farm
Cock Flat Farm
Scugdale Hall
Scugdale Moor Gate
Ewe Hill Farm
West Cote Farm
Bilsdale Midcable Chop Gate C of E Prim Sch
Whorlton Moor
Holiday House Farm
High House
Ewe Hill
Raisdale
RAISDALE ROAD
PH
Chop Gate
Far Moor
Pin Howe
Blue Scar
Rank Crag
Raisdale Beck
P
White Stone Crag
Bilsdale West Moor
Green Howe
Black Moor
Rowantree Crags
Cock Howe
Orterley Farms
Trennet Bank
Coal Ridge
DL6
Crookleith Farms
Prod Hills
Bilsdale West Moor
Stony Moor
Head House
Miley Howe
Crookleith Crags
Skelbeast Crag
Snilesworth Moor
Joseph Wade's But
Guest Crags
Arnsgill Ridge
Flat Howe
Bilsdale Transmitting Station
Douglas Ridge
High Arnsgill Farm
Cow Ridge
Snilesworth Moor
Snilesworth Moor
Rye Farm
YO62
Hawnby Moor
Snilesworth Lodge
Arns Gill
Low Arnsgill Farm
Peat Moss
Hill End Farm
Hawnby Moor
Waterfall Wood
Low Cote Farm
Sour Milk Hills
Weatherhouse Moor
Low Thwaites
Locker Low Moor
HALL LA
Blow Gill
Bilsdale West Moor
P
Locker Low Wood
Locker Farm
Plane Tree Farm
Birk Wood
Scotland Farm

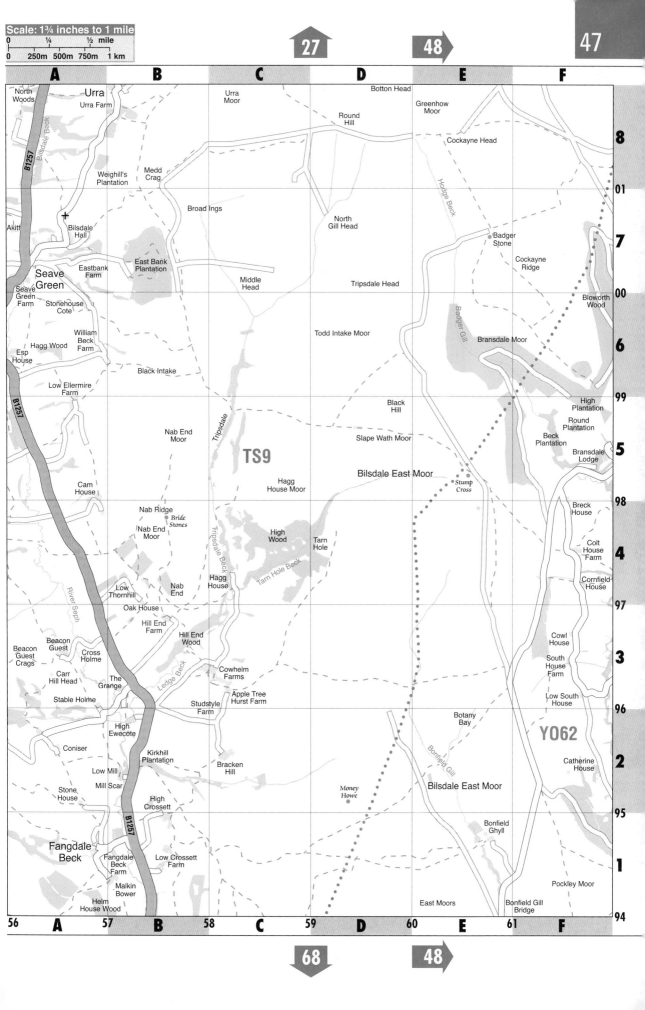

A   B   C   D   E   F

North Woods
Urra
Urra Farm
Urra Moor
Botton Head
Greenhow Moor
8

Weighill's Plantation
Medd Crag
Round Hill
Cockayne Head
01

Broad Ings
North Gill Head
Badger Stone
Cockayne Ridge
7

Akitt
Bilsdale Hall
East Bank Plantation
Middle Head
Tripsdale Head
Bloworth Wood
00

Seave Green
Eastbank Farm
Badger Gill
Bransdale Moor
High Plantation
99

Seave Green Farm
Stonehouse Cote
William Beck Farm
Todd Intake Moor
Black Hill
Round Plantation
6

Esp House
Hagg Wood
Black Intake
Slape Wath Moor
Beck Plantation
Bransdale Lodge
5

Low Ellermire Farm
Nab End Moor
Tripsdale
Bilsdale East Moor
Stump Cross
Breck House
98

Cam House
TS9
Hagg House Moor
Colt House Farm
4

Nab Ridge
Bride Stones
Tripsdale Beck
High Wood
Tarn Hole
Cornfield House
97

Nab End Moor
Tarn Hole Beck
Hagg House
Cowl House
3

Low Thornhill
Nab End
South House Farm
96

Oak House
Hill End Farm
Hill End Wood
Cowhelm Farms
Botany Bay
Bonfield Gill
YO62

Beacon Guest Crags
Beacon Guest
Cross Holme
Apple Tree Hurst Farm
Catherine House
2

Carr Hill Head
The Grange
Ledge Beck
Studstyle Farm
Low South House

Stable Holme
High Ewecote
Bilsdale East Moor
95

Coniser
Kirkhill Plantation
Bracken Hill
Money Howe
Bonfield Ghyll
1

Low Mill
Mill Scar
High Crossett

Stone House
River Seph
B1257

Fangdale Beck
Fangdale Beck Farm
Low Crossett Farm
East Moors
Bonfield Gill Bridge
Pockley Moor

Malkin Bower
Helm House Wood

56   57   58   59   60   61   94

A   B   C   D   E   F

B1257

Scale: 1¾ inches to 1 mile

0   ¼   ½ mile

0   250m 500m 750m 1 km

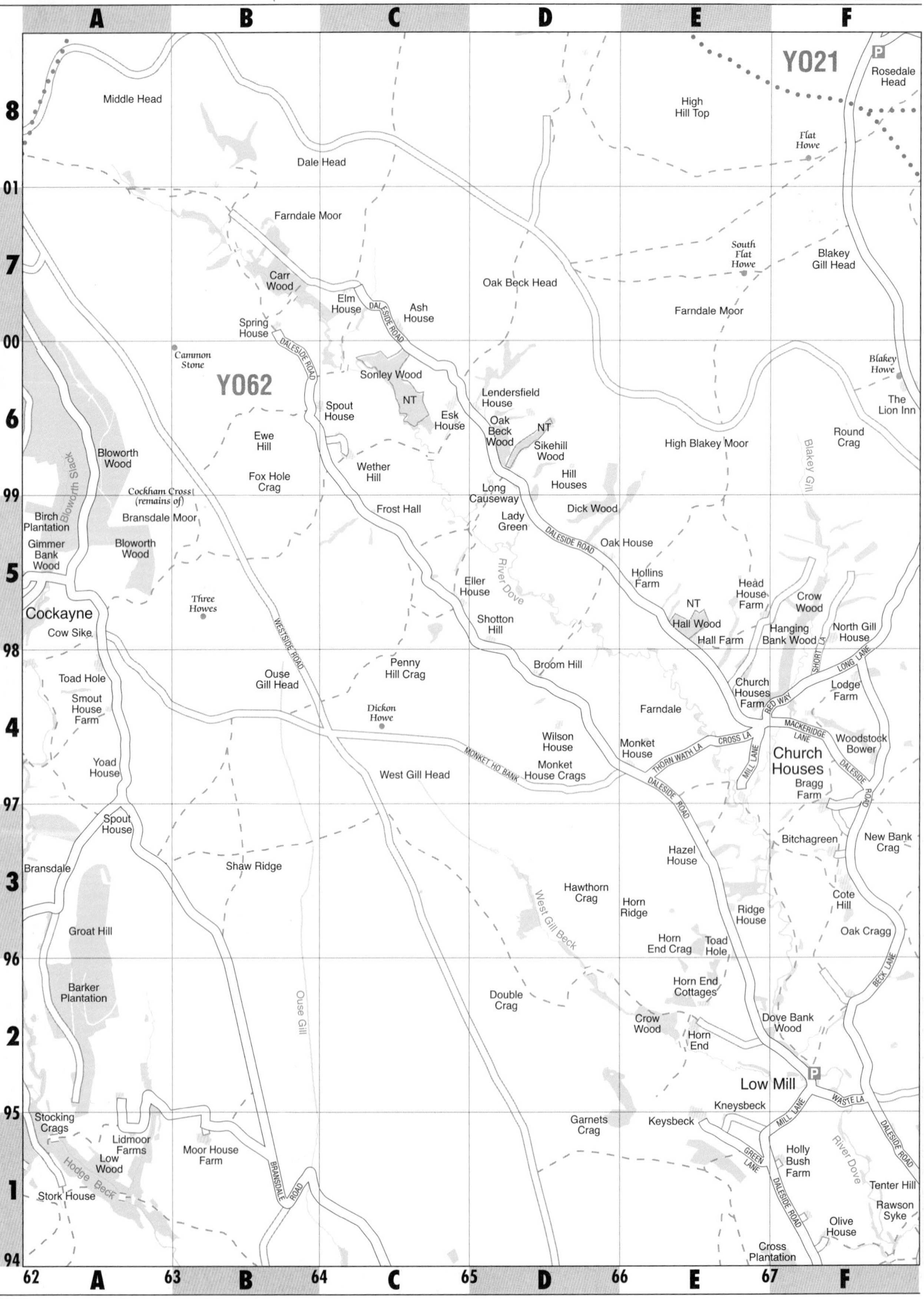

A   B   C   D   E   F

YO21

P
Rosedale Head

8   Middle Head   High Hill Top   Flat Howe

Dale Head

01   Farndale Moor   South Flat Howe   Blakey Gill Head

7   Carr Wood   Oak Beck Head   Farndale Moor

Elm House   Ash House

Spring House   DALESIDE ROAD

00   Cammon Stone   Blakey Howe

YO62   Sonley Wood   Lendersfield House   The Lion Inn

6   Spout House   NT   Esk House   Oak Beck Wood   NT Sikehill Wood   High Blakey Moor   Round Crag

Ewe Hill   Wether Hill   Hill Houses   Blakey Gill

Fox Hole Crag

99   Cockham Cross (remains of)   Frost Hall   Long Causeway   Dick Wood   Oak House

Bransdale Moor   Lady Green   DALESIDE ROAD

Birch Plantation

Bloworth Wood   Eller House   Hollins Farm   Head House Farm   Crow Wood

Gimmer Bank Wood   Bloworth Wood

5   Cockayne   Three Howes   Shotton Hill   NT Hall Wood   Hall Farm   Hanging Bank Wood   North Gill House

Cow Sike   WESTSIDE ROAD   Penny Hill Crag   Broom Hill   Church Houses Farm   Lodge Farm

98   Toad Hole   Ouse Gill Head   Farndale   RED WAY   MACKERIDGE LANE   Woodstock Bower

Smout House Farm   Dickon Howe   Wilson House   Monket House   THORN WATH LA   CROSS LA   Church Houses   Bragg Farm

4   Yoad House   MONKET HO BANK   Monket House Crags   DALESIDE ROAD   MILL LANE   DALESIDE ROAD   Bitchagreen   New Bank Crag

West Gill Head   Hazel House

97   Spout House   Shaw Ridge   Horn Ridge   Ridge House   Cote Hill   Oak Cragg

3   Bransdale   Hawthorn Crag   WEST GILL BECK   Horn End Crag   Toad Hole   BECK LANE

Groat Hill   Ouse Gill   Horn End Cottages

96   Barker Plantation   Double Crag   Crow Wood   Dove Bank Wood

2   Horn End   P Low Mill

Stocking Crags   BRANSDALE ROAD   Kneysbeck   WASTE LA

95   Lidmoor Farms   Garnets Crag   Keysbeck   GREEN LANE   MILL LANE   River Dove   DALESIDE ROAD

Low Wood   Moor House Farm   Holly Bush Farm   Tenter Hill

1   Hodge Beck   Stork House   Olive House   Rawson Syke

Cross Plantation

94   62   A   63   B   64   C   65   D   66   E   67   F

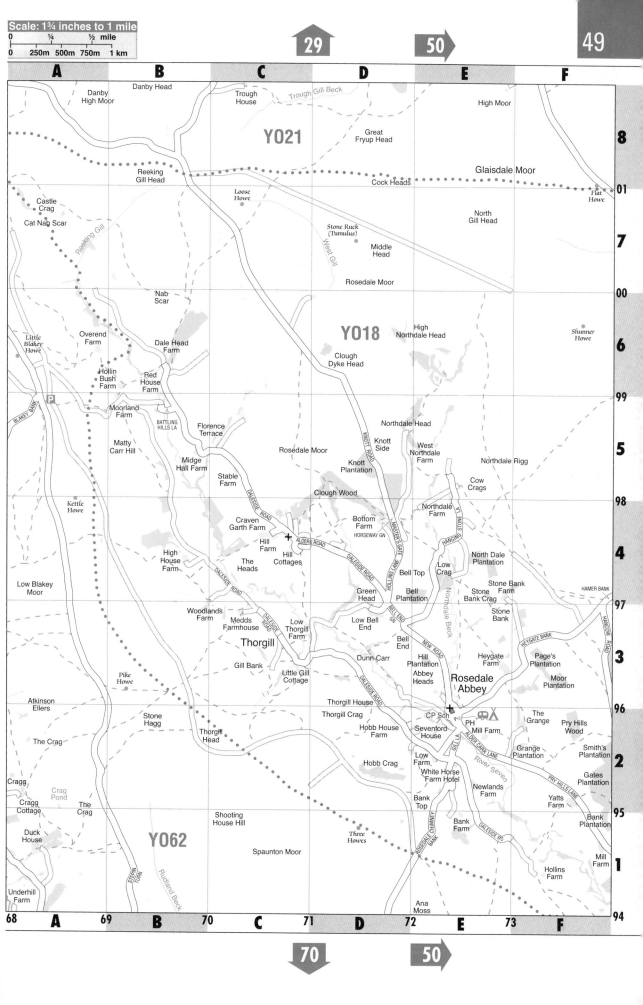

49 30

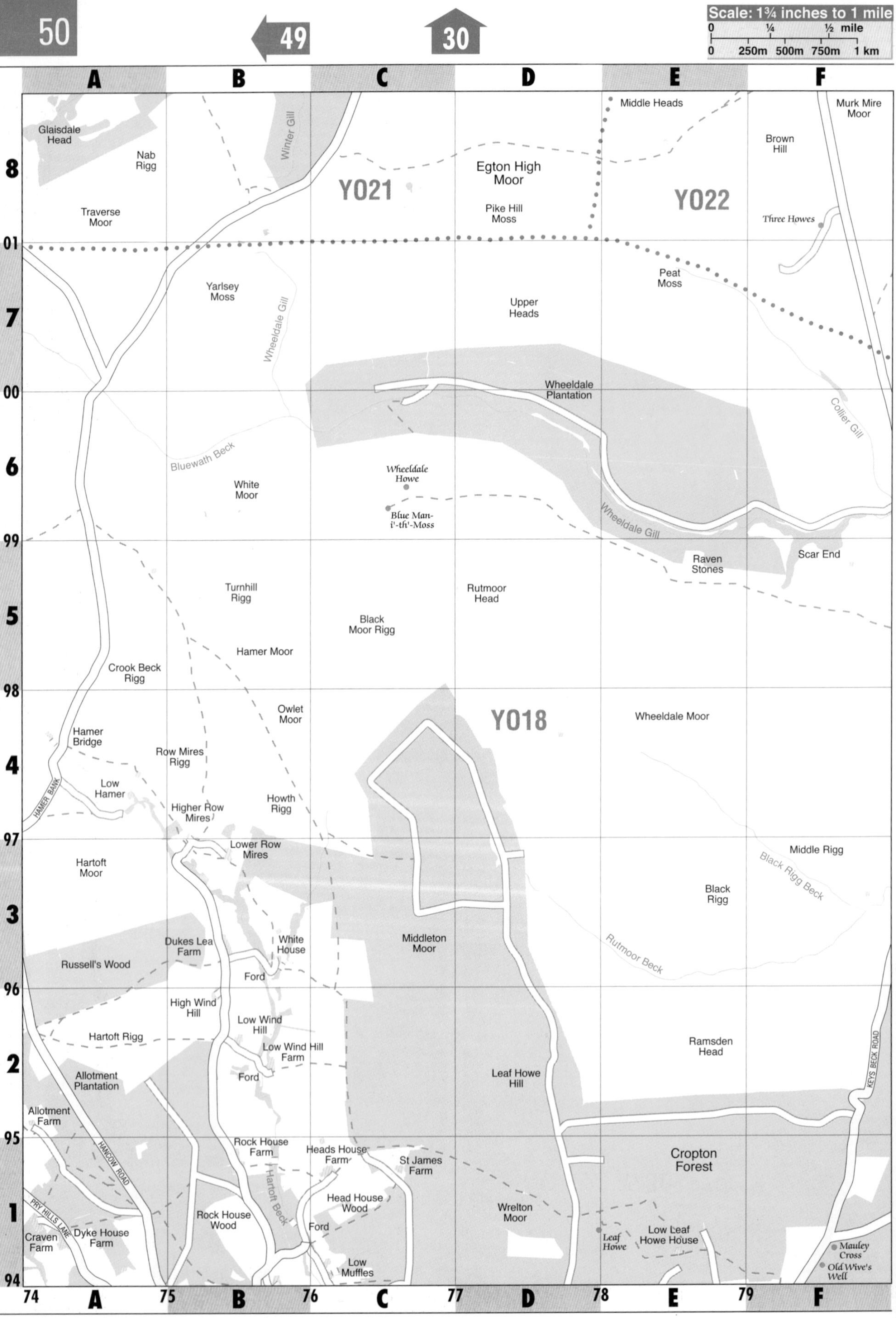
Scale: 1¾ inches to 1 mile
0 ¼ ½ mile
0 250m 500m 750m 1 km
A B C D E F
8 01 7 00 6 99 5 98 4 97 3 96 2 95 1 94
74 75 76 77 78 79
Glaisdale Head
Nab Rigg
Winter Gill
YO21
Egton High Moor
Middle Heads
Murk Mire Moor
Brown Hill
YO22
Three Howes
Pike Hill Moss
Traverse Moor
Yarlsey Moss
Wheeldale Gill
Upper Heads
Peat Moss
Wheeldale Plantation
Collier Gill
Bluewath Beck
White Moor
Wheeldale Howe
Blue Man-i'-th'-Moss
Wheeldale Gill
Raven Stones
Scar End
Turnhill Rigg
Rutmoor Head
Black Moor Rigg
Hamer Moor
Crook Beck Rigg
Owlet Moor
YO18
Wheeldale Moor
Hamer Bridge
Row Mires Rigg
Low Hamer
HAMER BANK
Higher Row Mires
Howth Rigg
Lower Row Mires
Hartoft Moor
Middle Rigg
Black Rigg Beck
Black Rigg
Dukes Lea Farm
White House
Middleton Moor
Russell's Wood
Rutmoor Beck
Ford
High Wind Hill
Low Wind Hill
Hartoft Rigg
Low Wind Hill Farm
Ramsden Head
Allotment Plantation
Ford
Leaf Howe Hill
KEYS BECK ROAD
Allotment Farm
HANCOW ROAD
Rock House Farm
Heads House Farm
St James Farm
Cropton Forest
Hartoft Beck
Head House Wood
PRY HILLS LANE
Rock House Wood
Wrelton Moor
Ford
Craven Farm
Dyke House Farm
Leaf Howe
Low Leaf Howe House
Mauley Cross
Old Wive's Well
Low Muffles

49 71

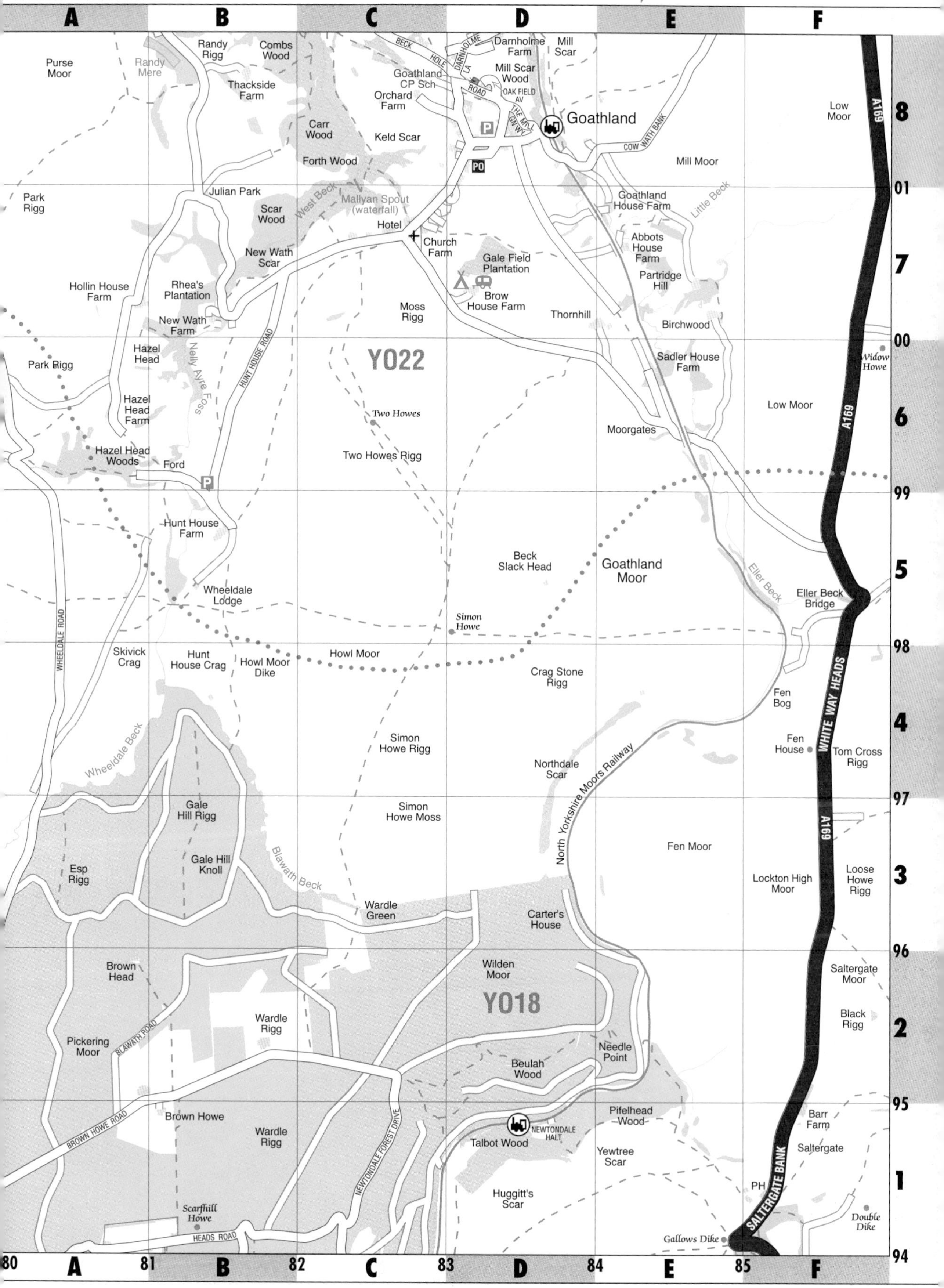

Scale: 1¾ inches to 1 mile

¼ ½ mile
250m 500m 750m 1 km

A **B** **C** **D** **E** **F**

Purse Moor

Randy Mere

Randy Rigg

Combs Wood

Thackside Farm

Carr Wood

Keld Scar

Forth Wood

DARNHOLME LA

BECK HOLE ROAD

Darnholme Farm

Mill Scar

Goathland CP Sch

Orchard Farm

Mill Scar Wood

OAK FIELD AV

THE INTAK

Goathland

Low Moor

Park Rigg

Julian Park

Scar Wood

New Wath Scar

Mallyan Spout (waterfall)

Hotel

Church Farm

Gale Field Plantation

Brow House Farm

Thornhill

Mill Moor

Goathland House Farm

Abbots House Farm

Partridge Hill

Birchwood

COW WATH BANK

Little Beck

Hollin House Farm

Rhea's Plantation

New Wath Farm

Hazel Head

Hazel Head Farm

Moss Rigg

YO22

Sadler House Farm

Low Moor

Widow Howe

Park Rigg

Nelly Ayre Foss

West Beck

HUNT HOUSE ROAD

Two Howes

Two Howes Rigg

Moorgates

A169

Hazel Head Woods

Ford

Hunt House Farm

P

Beck Slack Head

Goathland Moor

Eller Beck

Eller Beck Bridge

Wheeldale Lodge

WHEELDALE ROAD

Skivick Crag

Hunt House Crag

Howl Moor Dike

Howl Moor

Simon Howe

Crag Stone Rigg

Fen Bog

WHITE WAY HEADS

Fen House

Tom Cross Rigg

Wheeldale Beck

Simon Howe Rigg

Northdale Scar

North Yorkshire Moors Railway

Gale Hill Rigg

Gale Hill Knoll

Blawath Beck

Simon Howe Moss

Fen Moor

Lockton High Moor

Loose Howe Rigg

A169

Esp Rigg

Wardle Green

Brown Head

Pickering Moor

BLAWATH ROAD

Wardle Rigg

YO18

Wilden Moor

Carter's House

Needle Point

Saltergate Moor

Black Rigg

Brown Howe

BROWN HOWE ROAD

Wardle Rigg

NEWTONDALE FOREST DRIVE

Beulah Wood

Talbot Wood

NEWTONDALE HALT

Pifelhead Wood

Yewtree Scar

Barr Farm

Saltergate

SALTERGATE BANK

PH

Scarfhill Howe

HEADS ROAD

Huggitt's Scar

Gallows Dike

Double Dike

A **B** **C** **D** **E** **F**

80 81 82 83 84 85

8
01
7
00
6
5
98
4
97
3
96
2
95
1
94

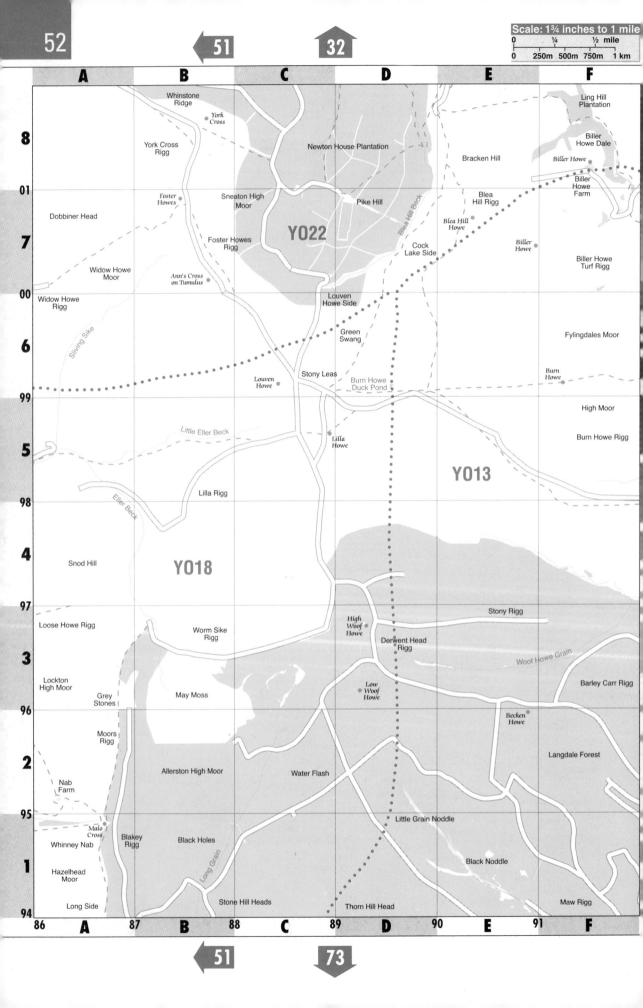

Scale: 1¾ inches to 1 mile

0   ¼   ½   mile
0 250m 500m 750m 1 km

A   B   C   D   E   F

8

Whinstone Ridge
York Cross
York Cross Rigg
Newton House Plantation
Ling Hill Plantation
Bracken Hill
Biller Howe Dale
Biller Howe

01

Foster Howes
Sneaton High Moor
Pike Hill
YO22
Blea Hill Beck
Blea Hill Rigg
Biller Howe Farm

7

Dobbiner Head
Foster Howes Rigg
Blea Hill Howe
Biller Howe
Biller Howe Turf Rigg
Cock Lake Side

Widow Howe Moor
Ann's Cross on Tumulus

00

Widow Howe Rigg
Louven Howe Side

Sliving Sike
Green Swang
Fylingdales Moor

6

Stony Leas
Burn Howe
Louven Howe
Burn Howe Duck Pond
High Moor

99

Little Eller Beck
Lilla Howe
Burn Howe Rigg

5

Eller Beck
Lilla Rigg
YO13

98

YO18

4

Snod Hill

97

Loose Howe Rigg
Stony Rigg
Worm Sike Rigg
High Woof Howe

3

Derwent Head Rigg
Woof Howe Grain
Barley Carr Rigg

Lockton High Moor
Grey Stones
May Moss
Low Woof Howe
Becken Howe

96

Moors Rigg
Langdale Forest

2

Nab Farm
Allerston High Moor
Water Flash

95

Malo Cross
Little Grain Noddle
Blakey Rigg
Black Holes
Black Noddle

Whinney Nab

1

Hazelhead Moor
Long Grain
Stone Hill Heads
Thorn Hill Head
Maw Rigg

94

Long Side

86   A   87   B   88   C   89   D   90   E   91   F

Scale: 1¾ inches to 1 mile

33
54

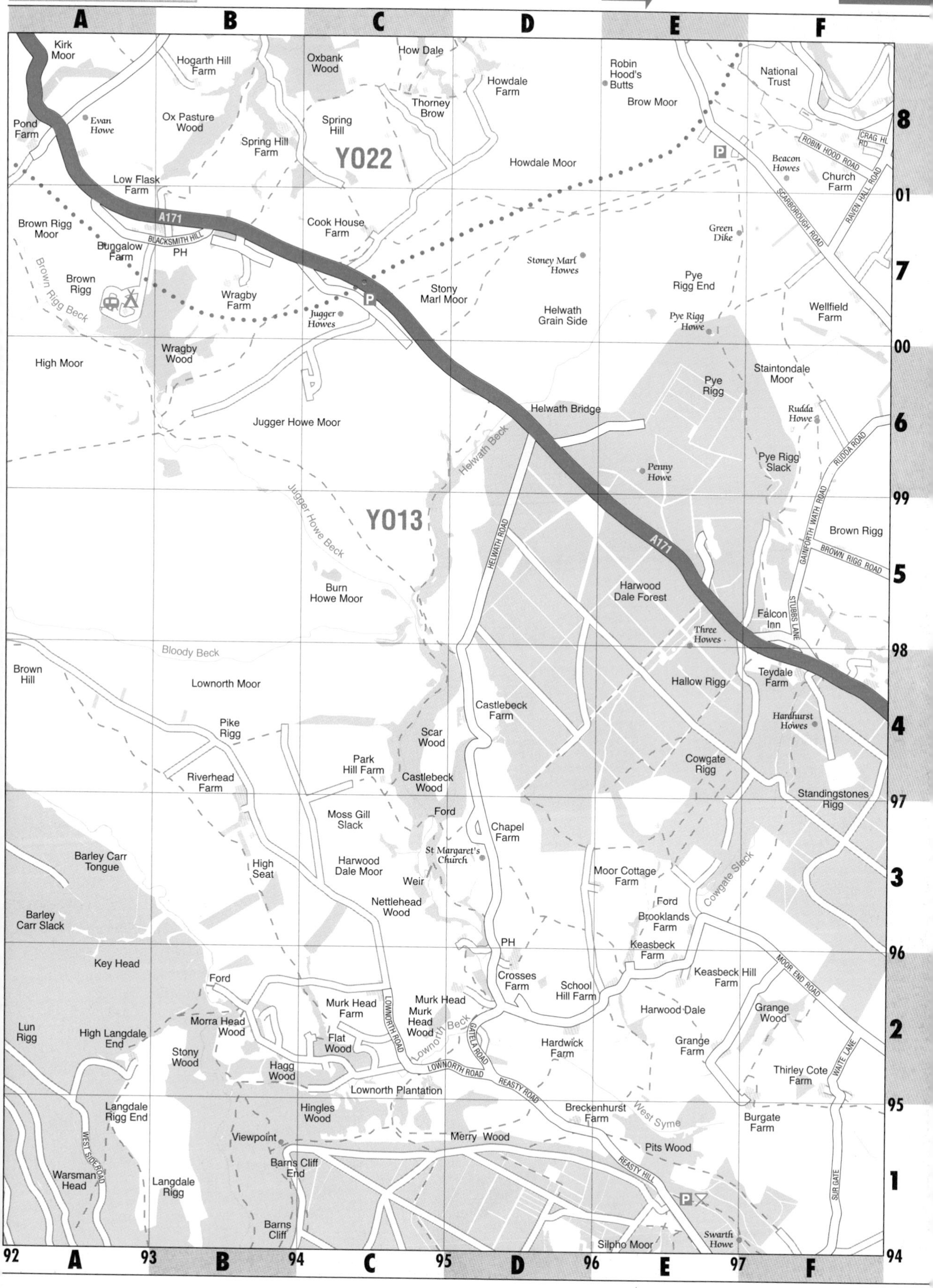
Kirk Moor
Hogarth Hill Farm
Oxbank Wood
How Dale
Robin Hood's Butts
National Trust
Howdale Farm
Thorney Brow
Brow Moor
Pond Farm
Evan Howe
Ox Pasture Wood
Spring Hill
Spring Hill Farm
YO22
Howdale Moor
Beacon Howes
Church Farm
CRAG HL RD
ROBIN HOOD ROAD
RAVEN HALL ROAD
SCARBOROUGH ROAD
Low Flask Farm
A171
Brown Rigg Moor
BLACKSMITH HILL
Cook House Farm
Green Dike
Bungalow Farm
PH
Stoney Marl Howes
Brown Rigg
Brown Rigg Beck
Wragby Farm
Jugger Howes
Stony Marl Moor
Helwath Grain Side
Pye Rigg End
Pye Rigg Howe
Wellfield Farm
High Moor
Wragby Wood
Staintondale Moor
Pye Rigg
Helwath Bridge
Rudda Howe
Jugger Howe Moor
Helwath Beck
Penny Howe
Pye Rigg Slack
RUDDA ROAD
Jugger Howe Beck
YO13
HELWATH ROAD
GAINFORTH WATH ROAD
Brown Rigg
BROWN RIGG ROAD
Burn Howe Moor
Harwood Dale Forest
Falcon Inn
STUBBS LANE
Three Howes
Bloody Beck
Brown Hill
Lownorth Moor
Hallow Rigg
Teydale Farm
Castlebeck Farm
Hardhurst Howes
Pike Rigg
Scar Wood
Cowgate Rigg
Park Hill Farm
Riverhead Farm
Castlebeck Wood
Standingstones Rigg
Moss Gill Slack
Ford
Chapel Farm
Barley Carr Tongue
High Seat
St Margaret's Church
Harwood Dale Moor
Weir
Moor Cottage Farm
Cowgate Slack
Nettlehead Wood
Ford
Barley Carr Slack
Brooklands Farm
PH
Keasbeck Farm
Key Head
MOOR END ROAD
Ford
Keasbeck Hill Farm
Murk Head Farm
Murk Head
Crosses Farm
School Hill Farm
Morra Head Wood
Murk Head Wood
Harwood Dale
Grange Wood
Lun Rigg
High Langdale End
LOWNORTH ROAD
Lownorth Beck
GATELA ROAD
Flat Wood
Hardwick Farm
Grange Farm
Stony Wood
WAITE LANE
Hagg Wood
LOWNORTH ROAD
REASTY ROAD
Thirley Cote Farm
Lownorth Plantation
Langdale Rigg End
Hingles Wood
Breckenhurst Farm
West Syme
Burgate Farm
Viewpoint
Merry Wood
WEST SIDE ROAD
Barns Cliff End
Pits Wood
Warsman Head
Langdale Rigg
REASTY HILL
SUR GATE
Barns Cliff
Silpho Moor
Swarth Howe
A B C D E F
8 01 7 00 6 99 5 98 4 97 3 96 2 95 1 94
92 93 94 95 96 97 94

74
54

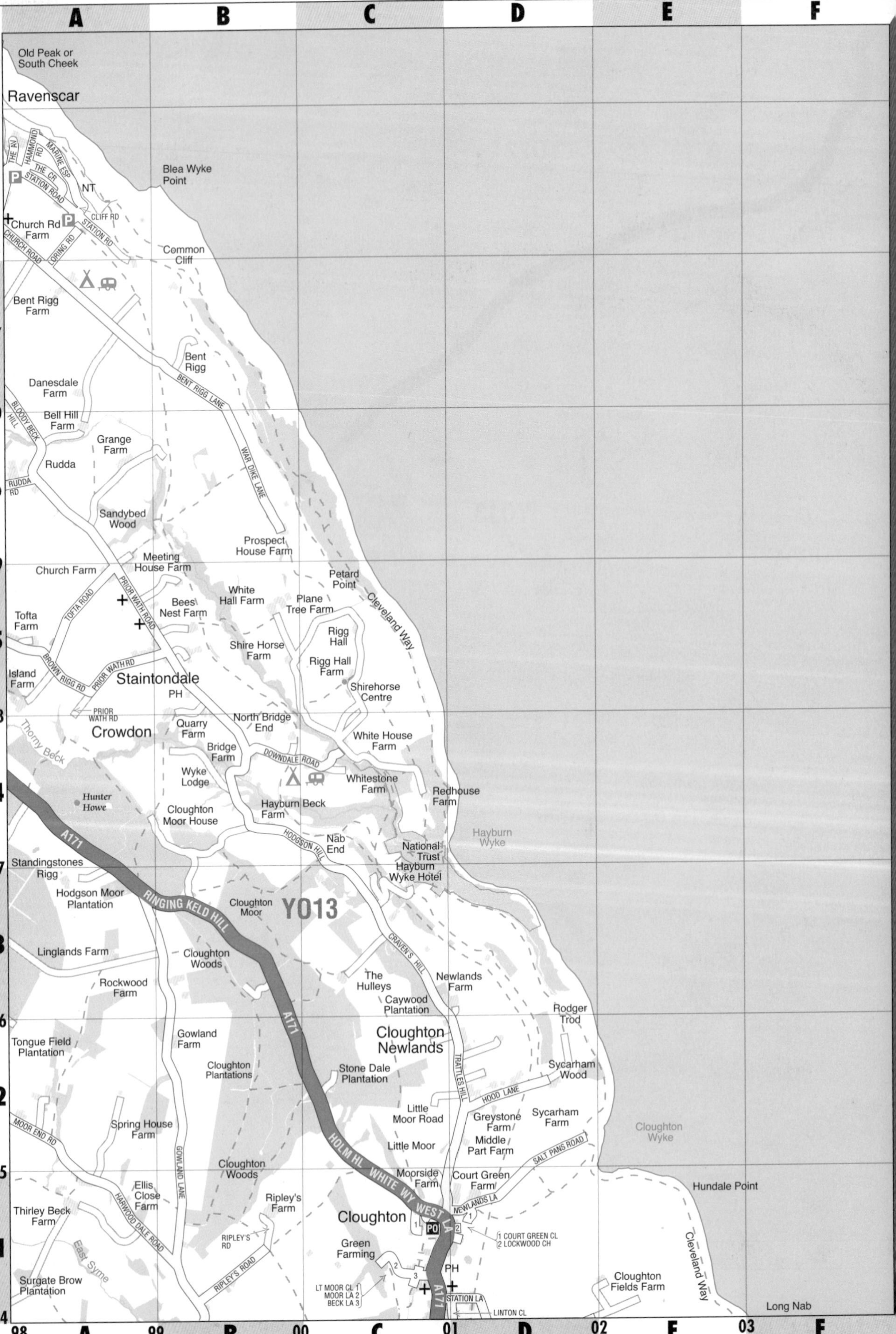

A   B   C   D   E   F

Old Peak or
South Cheek

Ravenscar

02

THE AV
HAMMOND RD
MARINE ESP
THE CR
STATION ROAD

Blea Wyke
Point

8

NT

P
Church Rd
Farm
P
SPRING RD
CLIFF RD
STATION RD

Common
Cliff

01

CHURCH ROAD

Bent Rigg
Farm

7

Bent
Rigg

BENT RIGG LANE

Danesdale
Farm

00

BLOODY BECK HILL

Bell Hill
Farm

Grange
Farm

WAR DIKE LANE

Rudda

6

RUDDA RD

Sandybed
Wood

Prospect
House Farm

Meeting
House Farm

99

Church Farm

TOFTA ROAD

Bees
Nest Farm

White
Hall Farm

Plane
Tree Farm

Petard
Point

Cleveland Way

Tofta
Farm

PRIOR WATH ROAD

Shire Horse
Farm

Rigg
Hall

Rigg Hall
Farm

5

Island
Farm

BROWN RIGG RD

PRIOR WATH RD

Staintondale

PH

Shirehorse
Centre

PRIOR WATH RD

98

Crowdon

Quarry
Farm

North Bridge
End

White House
Farm

Bridge
Farm

DOWNDALE ROAD

Hunter
Howe

Wyke
Lodge

Whitestone
Farm

Redhouse
Farm

4

Cloughton
Moor House

Hayburn Beck
Farm

HODGSON HILL

Nab
End

Hayburn
Wyke

Standingstones
Rigg

National
Trust
Hayburn
Wyke Hotel

97

A171

Hodgson Moor
Plantation

RINGING KELD HILL

Cloughton
Moor

YO13

CRAVEN'S HILL

3

Linglands Farm

Cloughton
Woods

Rockwood
Farm

The
Hulleys

Newlands
Farm

Caywood
Plantation

Rodger
Trod

96

Tongue Field
Plantation

A171

Gowland
Farm

Cloughton
Newlands

TRATLES HILL

Sycarham
Wood

Cloughton
Plantations

Stone Dale
Plantation

HOOD LANE

2

GOWLAND LANE

Spring House
Farm

MOOR END RD

Little
Moor Road

Greystone
Farm /
Middle
Part Farm

Sycarham
Farm

Cloughton
Wyke

Cloughton
Woods

Little Moor

SALT PANS ROAD

95

HOLM HL WHITE WY WEST

Ellis
Close
Farm

Ripley's
Farm

Moorside
Farm

Court Green
Farm

Hundale Point

Thirley Beck
Farm

HARWOOD DALE ROAD

RIPLEY'S RD

Cloughton

PO

NEWLANDS LA

1 COURT GREEN CL
2 LOCKWOOD CH

1

EAST SYME

Green
Farming

Cleveland Way

RIPLEY'S ROAD

PH

A171

Cloughton
Fields Farm

Surgate Brow
Plantation

LT MOOR CL 1
MOOR LA 2
BECK LA 3

STATION LA

LINTON CL

Long Nab

94

98   A   99   B   00   C   01   D   02   E   03   F

Scale: 1¾ inches to 1 mile

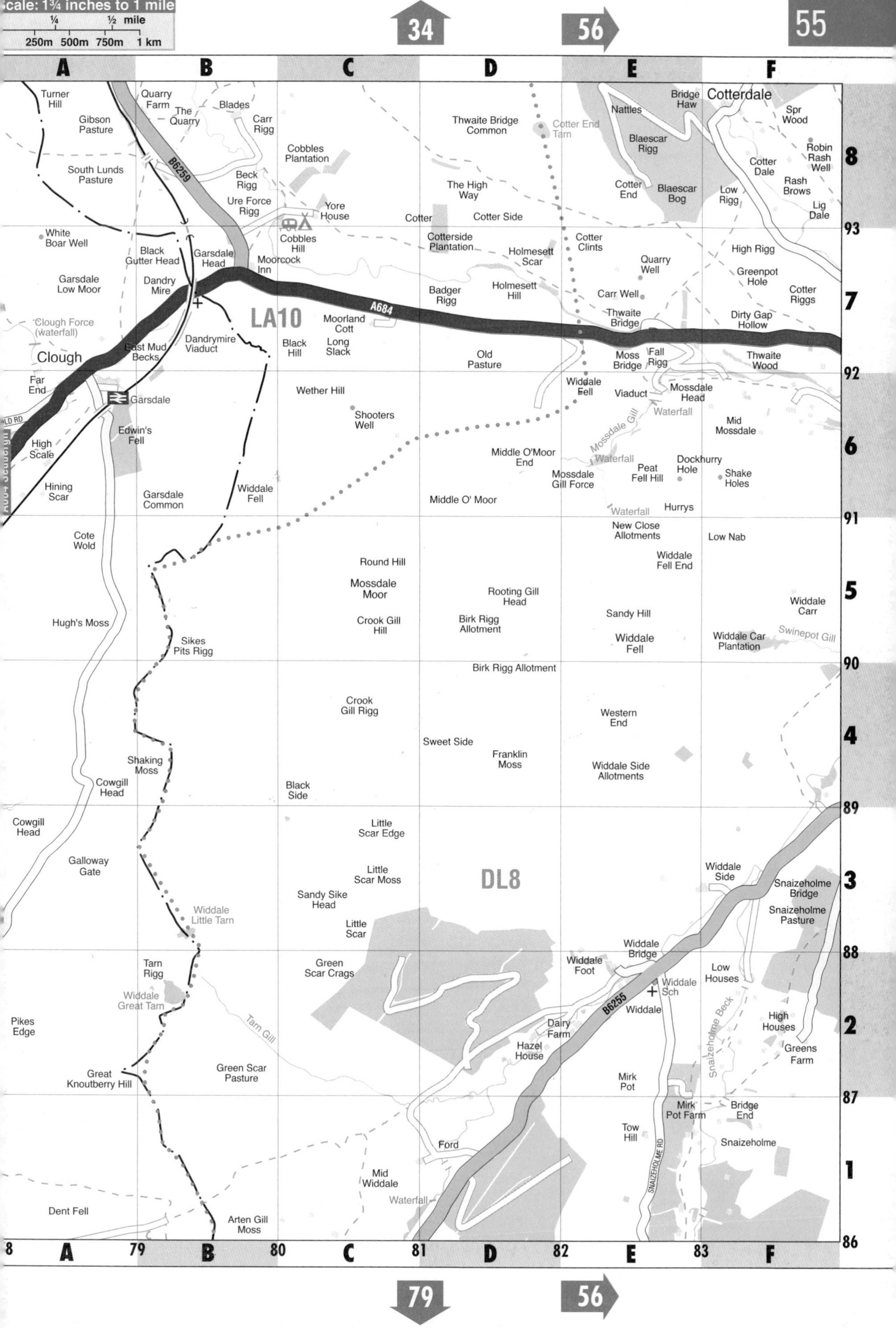
34
56
A B C D E F
Turner Hill
Quarry Farm
The Quarry
Blades
Carr Rigg
Gibson Pasture
Cobbles Plantation
Thwaite Bridge Common
Cotter End Tarn
Nattles
Bridge Haw
Cotterdale
Spr Wood
Robin Rash Well
Blaescar Rigg
Cotter Dale
South Lunds Pasture
B6259
Beck Rigg
Ure Force Rigg
Yore House
The High Way
Cotter End
Blaescar Bog
Low Rigg
Rash Brows
Lig Dale
Cotter
Cotter Side
White Boar Well
Black Gutter Head
Garsdale Head
Cobbles Hill
Moorcock Inn
Cotterside Plantation
Holmesett Scar
Cotter Clints
Quarry Well
High Rigg
Greenpot Hole
Garsdale Low Moor
Dandry Mire
LA10
Moorland Cott
A684
Badger Rigg
Holmesett Hill
Carr Well
Cotter Riggs
Clough Force (waterfall)
Thwaite Bridge
Dirty Gap Hollow
Clough
East Mud Becks
Dandrymire Viaduct
Black Hill
Long Slack
Old Pasture
Moss Bridge
Fall Rigg
Thwaite Wood
Far End
Garsdale
Wether Hill
Widdale Fell
Viaduct
Mossdale Head
Waterfall
Shooters Well
Mid Mossdale
Edwin's Fell
Mossdale Gill
High Scale
Middle O'Moor End
Waterfall
Dockhurry Hole
Peat Fell Hill
Shake Holes
Mossdale Gill Force
Hining Scar
Garsdale Common
Widdale Fell
Middle O' Moor
Hurrys
Waterfall
New Close Allotments
Low Nab
Cote Wold
Widdale Fell End
Round Hill
Mossdale Moor
Rooting Gill Head
Widdale Carr
Sandy Hill
Crook Gill Hill
Birk Rigg Allotment
Hugh's Moss
Widdale Fell
Widdale Car Plantation
Swinepot Gill
Sikes Pits Rigg
Birk Rigg Allotment
Crook Gill Rigg
Western End
Sweet Side
Franklin Moss
Shaking Moss
Widdale Side Allotments
Cowgill Head
Black Side
Cowgill Head
Little Scar Edge
Galloway Gate
Little Scar Moss
DL8
Widdale Side
Snaizeholme Bridge
Sandy Sike Head
Snaizeholme Pasture
Widdale Little Tarn
Little Scar
Widdale Bridge
Tarn Rigg
Green Scar Crags
Widdale Foot
Low Houses
Widdale Sch
Widdale Great Tarn
B6255
Widdale
Snaizeholme Beck
Pikes Edge
Tarn Gill
Dairy Farm
High Houses
Hazel House
Greens Farm
Great Knoutberry Hill
Green Scar Pasture
Mirk Pot
Mirk Pot Farm
Bridge End
Tow Hill
Snaizeholme
Ford
SNAIZEHOLME RD
Mid Widdale
Waterfall
Dent Fell
Arten Gill Moss
8 93 7 92 6 91 5 90 4 89 3 88 2 87 1 86
78 79 80 81 82 83
79
56

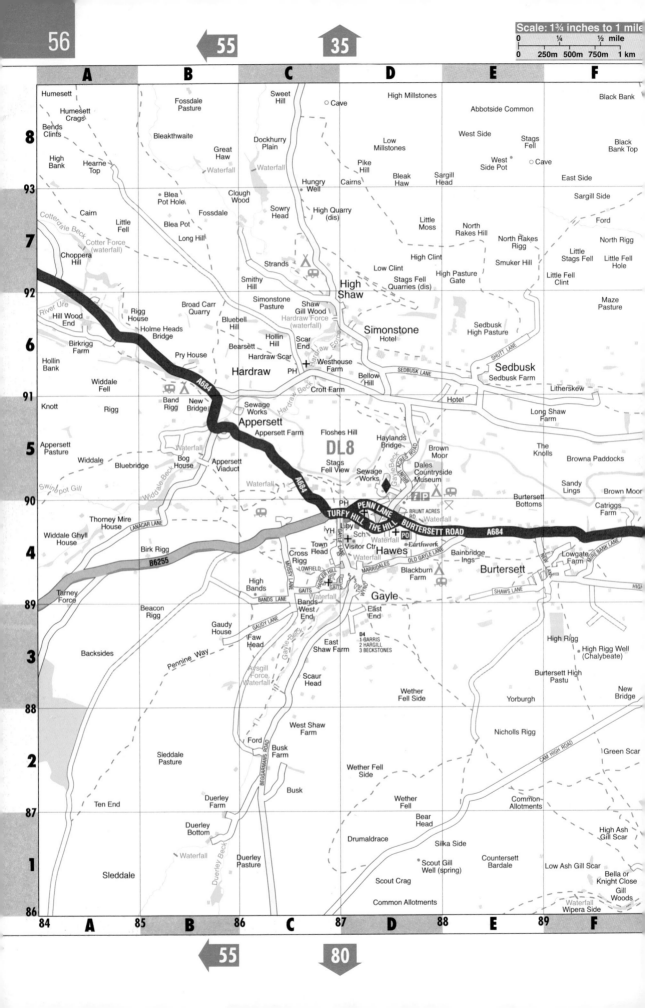

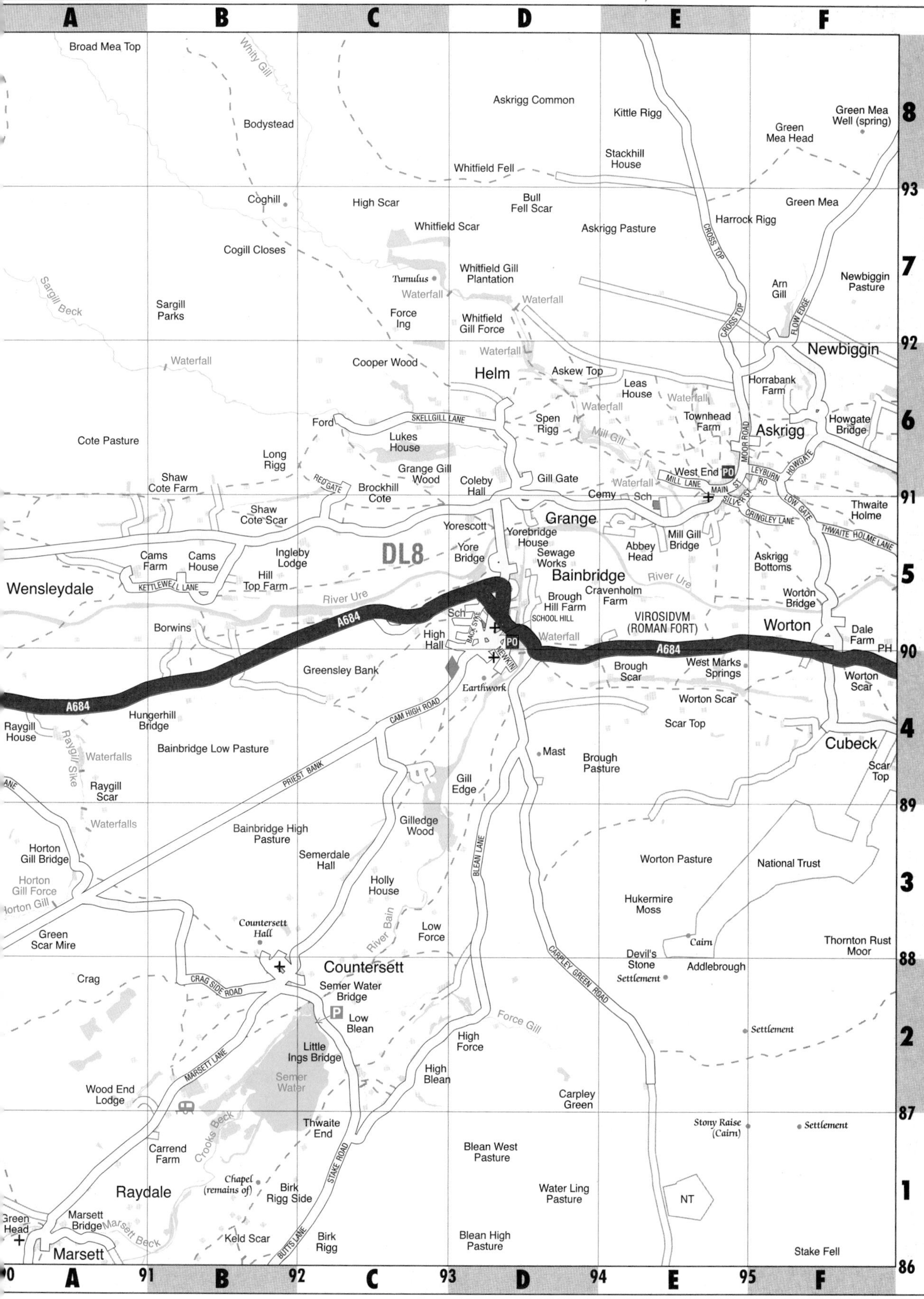
A B C D E F
8 93 7 92 6 91 5 90 4 89 3 88 2 87 1 86
90 91 92 93 94 95
Broad Mea Top
Whity Gill
Bodystead
Askrigg Common
Kittle Rigg
Stackhill House
Green Mea Head
Green Mea Well (spring)
Whitfield Fell
Coghill
High Scar
Bull Fell Scar
Whitfield Scar
Askrigg Pasture
Green Mea
Harrock Rigg
CROSS TOP
Cogill Closes
Tumulus
Whitfield Gill Plantation
Waterfall
Arn Gill
Newbiggin Pasture
Sargill Beck
Sargill Parks
Force Ing
Whitfield Gill Force
FLOW EDGE
Newbiggin
Cooper Wood
Helm
Askew Top
Leas House
Horrabank Farm
Spen Rigg
Mill Gill
Townhead Farm
Askrigg
Howgate Bridge
Ford
SKELLGILL LANE
Lukes House
MOOR ROAD
Cote Pasture
Long Rigg
Grange Gill Wood
Coleby Hall
Gill Gate
West End
PO
LEYBURN RD
HOWGATE
MILL LANE
MAIN ST
Shaw Cote Farm
RED GATE
Brockhill Cote
Cemy
Sch
SILVER ST
LOW GATE
Thwaite Holme
Shaw Cote Scar
Grange
ORINGLEY LANE
Yorescott
Yorebridge House
Mill Gill Bridge
THWAITE HOLME LANE
DL8
Yore Bridge
Sewage Works
Abbey Head
Askrigg Bottoms
Cams Farm
Cams House
Ingleby Lodge
Bainbridge
River Ure
Wensleydale
KETTLEWELL LANE
Hill Top Farm
Brough Hill Farm
Cravenholm Farm
Worton Bridge
A684
Sch
BACK SYKE
SCHOOL HILL
VIROSIDVM (ROMAN FORT)
Worton
Borwins
High Hall
NEWKIN
Dale Farm
PH
Greensley Bank
Brough Scar
West Marks Springs
Worton Scar
Earthwork
Raygill House
Hungerhill Bridge
CAM HIGH ROAD
Scar Top
Cubeck
Raygill Sike
Waterfalls
Bainbridge Low Pasture
Mast
Brough Pasture
Scar Top
PRIEST BANK
Raygill Scar
Gill Edge
Gilledge Wood
Bainbridge High Pasture
Horton Gill Bridge
Semerdale Hall
BLEAN LANE
Worton Pasture
National Trust
Horton Gill Force
Horton Gill
Holly House
Hukermire Moss
Countersett Hall
River Bain
Low Force
Green Scar Mire
Cairn
Thornton Rust Moor
Devil's Stone
CARPLEY GREEN ROAD
Countersett
Addlebrough
Settlement
Crag
CRAG SIDE ROAD
Semer Water Bridge
Low Blean
Force Gill
Settlement
High Force
Little Ings Bridge
MARSETT LANE
High Blean
Semer Water
Wood End Lodge
Carpley Green
Thwaite End
Stony Raise (Cairn)
Settlement
Carrend Farm
Crooks Beck
STAKE ROAD
Blean West Pasture
Chapel (remains of)
Raydale
Birk Rigg Side
Water Ling Pasture
NT
Green Head
Marsett Bridge
Marsett Beck
Keld Scar
BUTTS LANE
Birk Rigg
Blean High Pasture
Stake Fell
Marsett

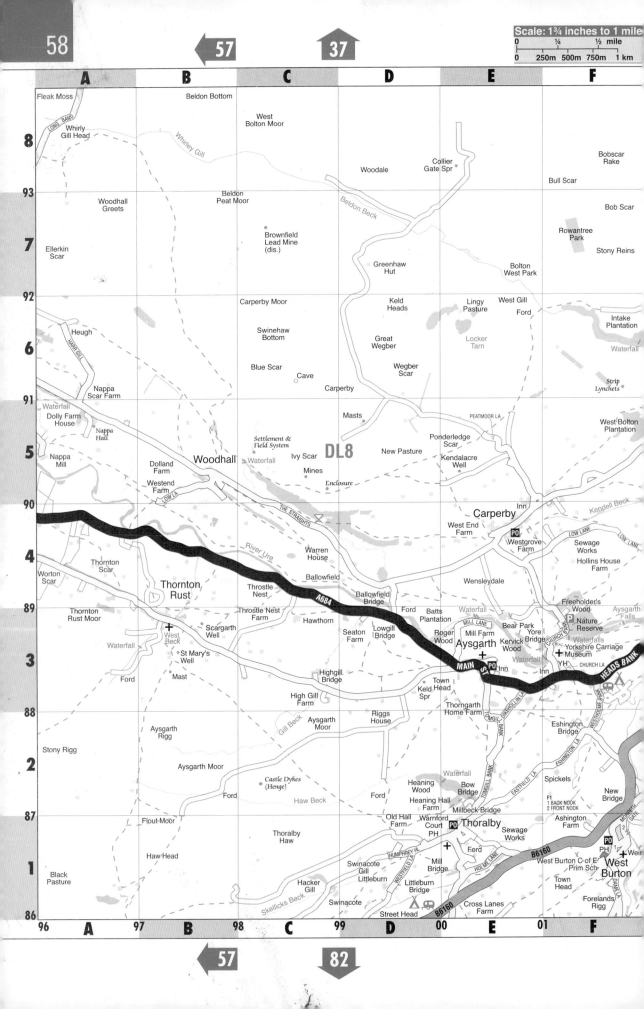

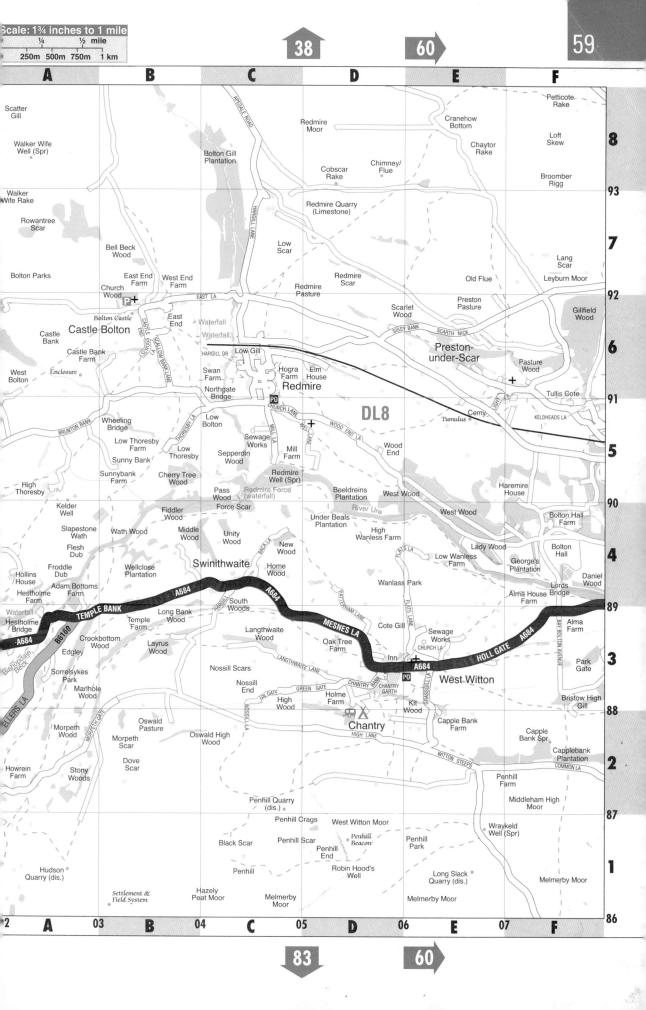

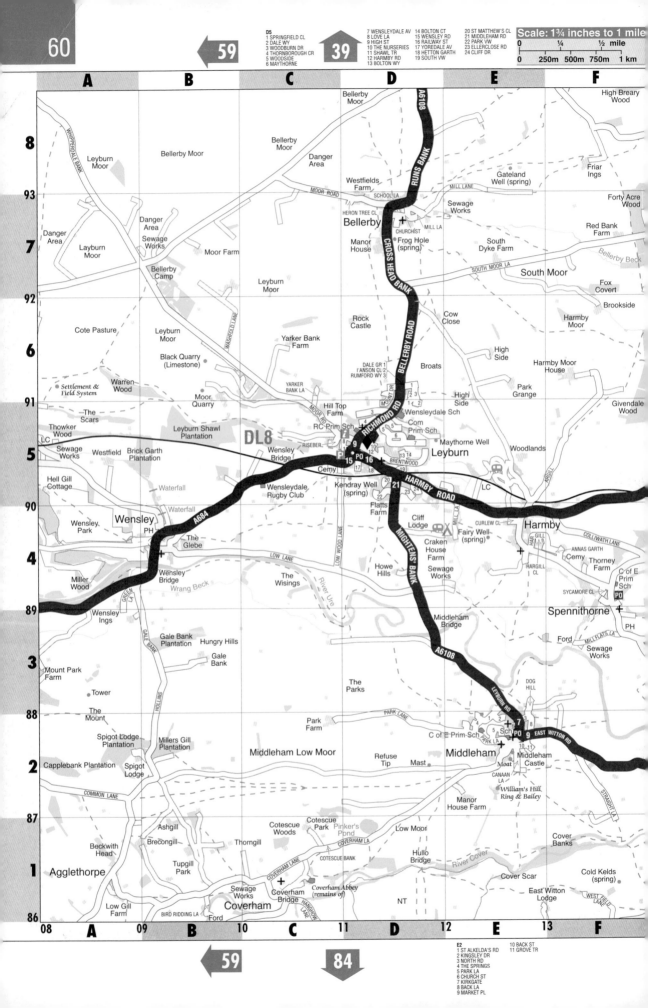

59   39

Scale: 1¾ inches to 1 mile

0   ¼   ½   mile

0   250m   500m   750m   1 km

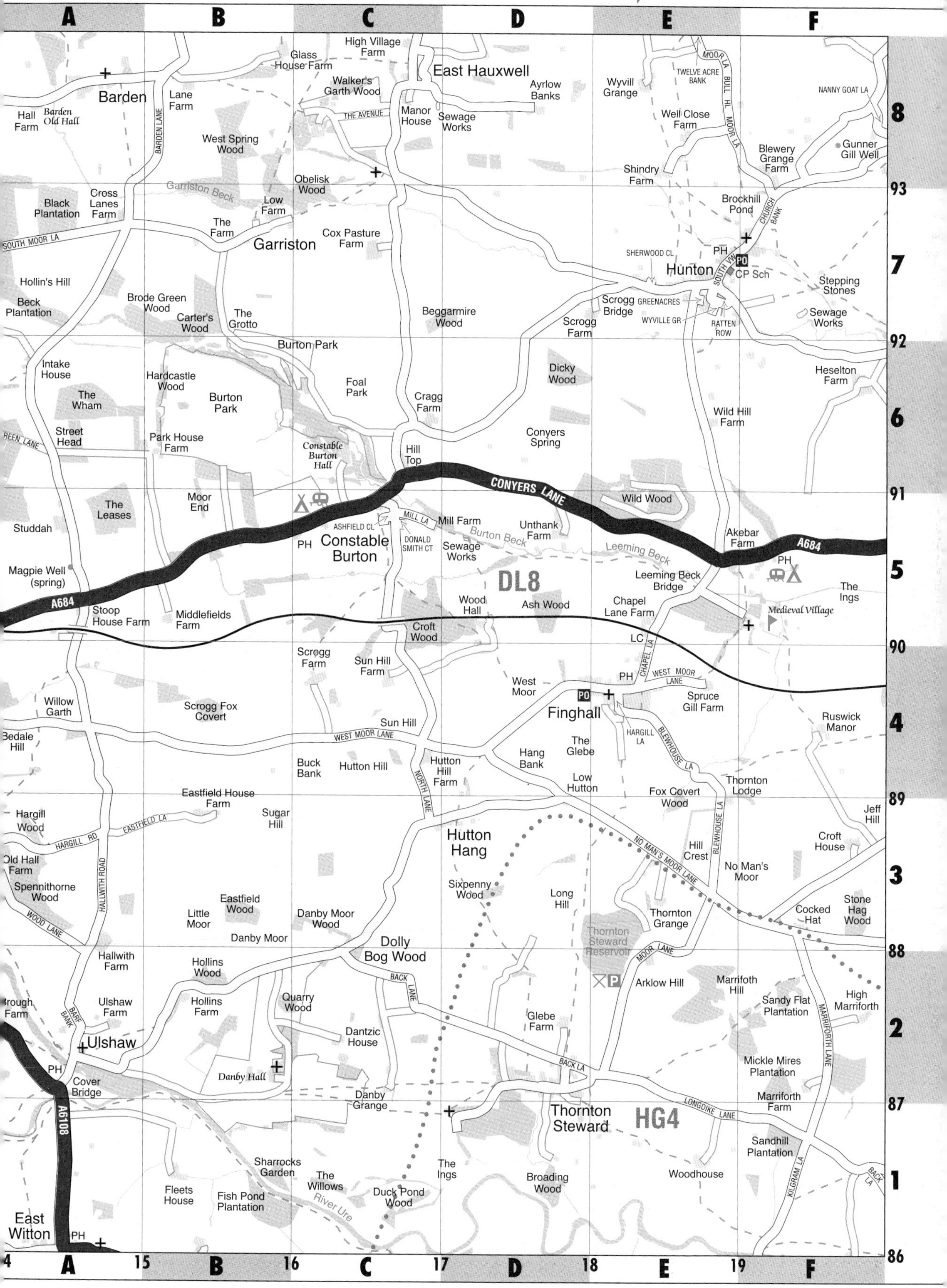
A
B
C
D
E
F
Barden
Barden Old Hall
Hall Farm
Lane Farm
BARDEN LANE
Glass House Farm
High Village Farm
Walker's Garth Wood
East Hauxwell
Ayrlow Banks
Manor House
Sewage Works
THE AVENUE
West Spring Wood
Wyvill Grange
TWELVE ACRE BANK
MOOR LA
BULL HL
MOOR LA
Well Close Farm
NANNY GOAT LA
Blewery Grange Farm
Gunner Gill Well
Shindry Farm
Brockhill Pond
CHURCH BANK
Obelisk Wood
Garriston Beck
Black Plantation
Cross Lanes Farm
Low Farm
The Farm
Garriston
Cox Pasture Farm
SOUTH MOOR LA
SHERWOOD CL
PH
PO
Hunton
SOUTH VW
CP Sch
Hollin's Hill
Beck Plantation
Brode Green Wood
Carter's Wood
The Grotto
Beggarmire Wood
Scrogg Bridge
GREENACRES
WYVILLE GR
Scrogg Farm
RATTEN ROW
Stepping Stones
Sewage Works
Burton Park
Intake House
Hardcastle Wood
Dicky Wood
Heselton Farm
The Wham
Burton Park
Foal Park
Cragg Farm
Wild Hill Farm
Street Head
GREEN LANE
Park House Farm
Constable Burton Hall
Hill Top
Conyers Spring
CONYERS LANE
The Leases
Moor End
Wild Wood
Studdah
ASHFIELD CL
MILL LA
Mill Farm
Unthank Farm
Burton Beck
PH
Constable Burton
DONALD SMITH CT
Sewage Works
Leeming Beck
Akebar Farm
A684
Magpie Well (spring)
DL8
Leeming Beck Bridge
The Ings
A684
Stoop House Farm
Middlefields Farm
Wood Hall
Ash Wood
Chapel Lane Farm
Medieval Village
Croft Wood
LC
Scrogg Farm
Sun Hill Farm
CHAPEL LA
West Moor
PH
WEST MOOR LANE
Spruce Gill Farm
Willow Garth
Scrogg Fox Covert
Sun Hill
Finghall
Ruswick Manor
Bedale Hill
WEST MOOR LANE
HARGILL LA
The Glebe
BLEWHOUSE LA
Buck Bank
Hutton Hill
Hutton Hill Farm
NORTH LANE
Hang Bank
Low Hutton
Thornton Lodge
Eastfield House Farm
Fox Covert Wood
Hargill Wood
EASTFIELD LA
Sugar Hill
Jeff Hill
HARGILL RD
Hutton Hang
NO MAN'S MOOR LANE
Hill Crest
BLEWHOUSE LA
Croft House
Old Hall Farm
HALLWITH ROAD
No Man's Moor
Spennithorne Wood
Sixpenny Wood
Long Hill
Eastfield Wood
Stone Hag Wood
WOOD LANE
Little Moor
Danby Moor Wood
Thornton Grange
Cocked Hat
Danby Moor
Dolly Bog Wood
Thornton Steward Reservoir
MOOR LANE
Hallwith Farm
Hollins Wood
BACK LANE
Arklow Hill
Marrifoth Hill
High Marriforth
Brough Farm
BARE BANK
Ulshaw Farm
Hollins Farm
Quarry Wood
Sandy Flat Plantation
MARRIFORTH LANE
Glebe Farm
Ulshaw
Dantzic House
PH
Danby Hall
BACK LA
Mickle Mires Plantation
Cover Bridge
Danby Grange
LONGDIKE LANE
Marrifoth Farm
A6108
Thornton Steward
HG4
Sharrocks Garden
Sandhill Plantation
The Willows
The Ings
Broading Wood
Woodhouse
KILGRAM LA
BACK LA
Fleets House
Fish Pond Plantation
Duck Pond Wood
River Ure
East Witton
PH
8
93
7
92
6
91
5
90
4
89
3
88
2
87
1
86
14
15
16
17
18
19

61 41

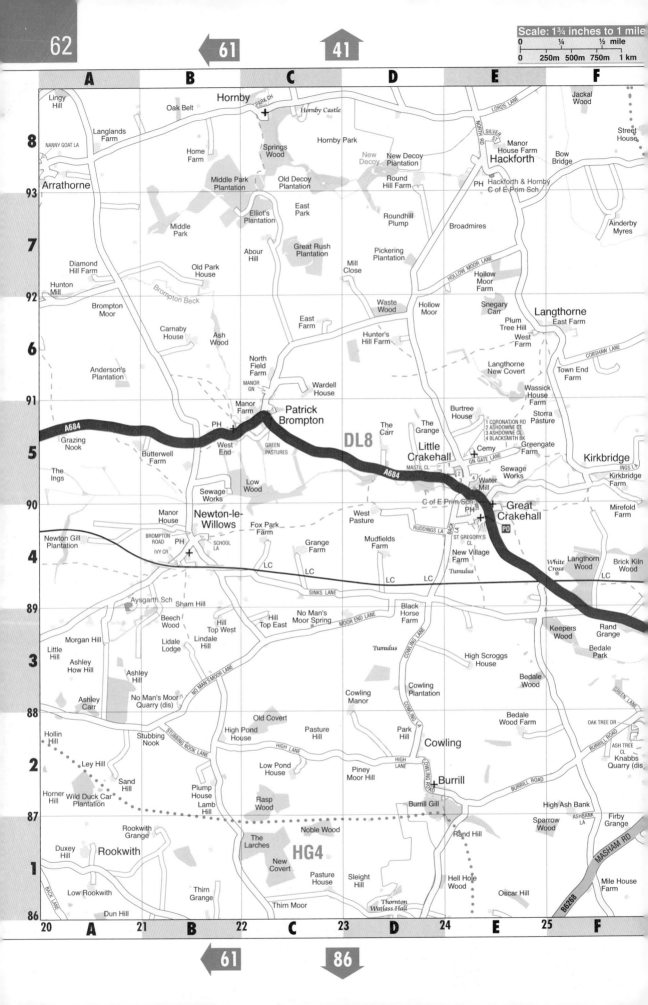
Scale: 1¾ inches to 1 mile
Hornby
Hornby Castle
Oak Belt
Lingy Hill
Langlands Farm
Home Farm
Springs Wood
Hornby Park
New Decoy
New Decoy Plantation
Manor House Farm
Hackforth
Bow Bridge
Jackal Wood
Street House
Arrathorne
Middle Park Plantation
Old Decoy Plantation
Round Hill Farm
Hackforth & Hornby C of E Prim Sch
Elliot's Plantation
East Park
Roundhill Plump
Broadmires
Ainderby Myres
Middle Park
Great Rush Plantation
Abour Hill
Pickering Plantation
Mill Close
Diamond Hill Farm
Old Park House
Hunton Mill
Brompton Beck
Hollow Moor Farm
Brompton Moor
Waste Wood
Hollow Moor
Snegary Carr
Langthorne
East Farm
Plum Tree Hill
West Farm
Carnaby House
Ash Wood
Hunter's Hill Farm
Anderson's Plantation
North Field Farm
Wardell House
Langthorne New Covert
Town End Farm
Wassick House Farm
Manor Farm
Patrick Brompton
Burtree House
Storra Pasture
A684
Grazing Nook
West End
The Carr
The Grange
DL8
Little Crakehall
Cemy
Greengate Farm
Kirkbridge
Butterwell Farm
Green Pastures
Sewage Works
Kirkbridge Farm
The Ings
Low Wood
Water Mill
Manor House
Newton-le-Willows
Fox Park Farm
West Pasture
C of E Prim Sch
Great Crakehall
Mirefold Farm
Newton Gill Plantation
Brompton Road
Ivy Cr
School La
Grange Farm
Mudfields Farm
St Gregory's Cl
New Village Farm
Tumulus
White Cross
Langthorn Wood
Brick Kiln Wood
Sinks Lane
Aysgarth Sch
Sham Hill
Black Horse Farm
Beech Wood
Hill Top West
Hill Top East
No Man's Moor Spring
Moor End Lane
Keepers Wood
Rand Grange
Morgan Hill
Lidale Lodge
Lindale Hill
Cowling Lane
High Scroggs House
Bedale Park
Little Hill
Ashley How Hill
Ashley Hill
No Man's Moor Lane
Bedale Wood
Ashley Carr
No Man's Moor Quarry (dis)
Cowling Manor
Cowling Plantation
Green Lane
Old Covert
Bedale Wood Farm
Oak Tree Dr
Hollin Hill
Stubbing Nook
Stubbing Nook Lane
High Pond House
Pasture Hill
Park Hill
Cowling
Ash Tree Cl
Burrill Road
Knabbs Quarry (dis)
High Lane
Ley Hill
Low Pond House
Piney Moor Hill
Burrill
Sand Hill
Horner Hill
Wild Duck Car Plantation
Plump House
Lamb Hill
Rasp Wood
Burrill Gill
High Ash Bank
Sparrow Wood
Ashbank La
Firby Grange
Rookwith Grange
Noble Wood
Rand Hill
Duxey Hill
Rookwith
The Larches
HG4
Masham Rd
New Covert
Pasture House
Sleight Hill
Hell Hole Wood
Mile House Farm
Back Lane
Low Rookwith
Thirn Grange
Thirn Moor
Thornton Watlass Hall
Oscar Hill
B6268
Dun Hill
1 Coronation Rd
2 Ashdowne Ct
3 Ashdowne Cl
4 Blacksmith Bk
Mastil Cl
Gn Gate Lane
Ruddings La
Back La
Lords Lane
North Rd
Silver St
Park Ch
Nanny Goat La
Hollow Moor Lane
Cobshaw Lane
Ings La
Manor Gn
Cowling Rd

61 86

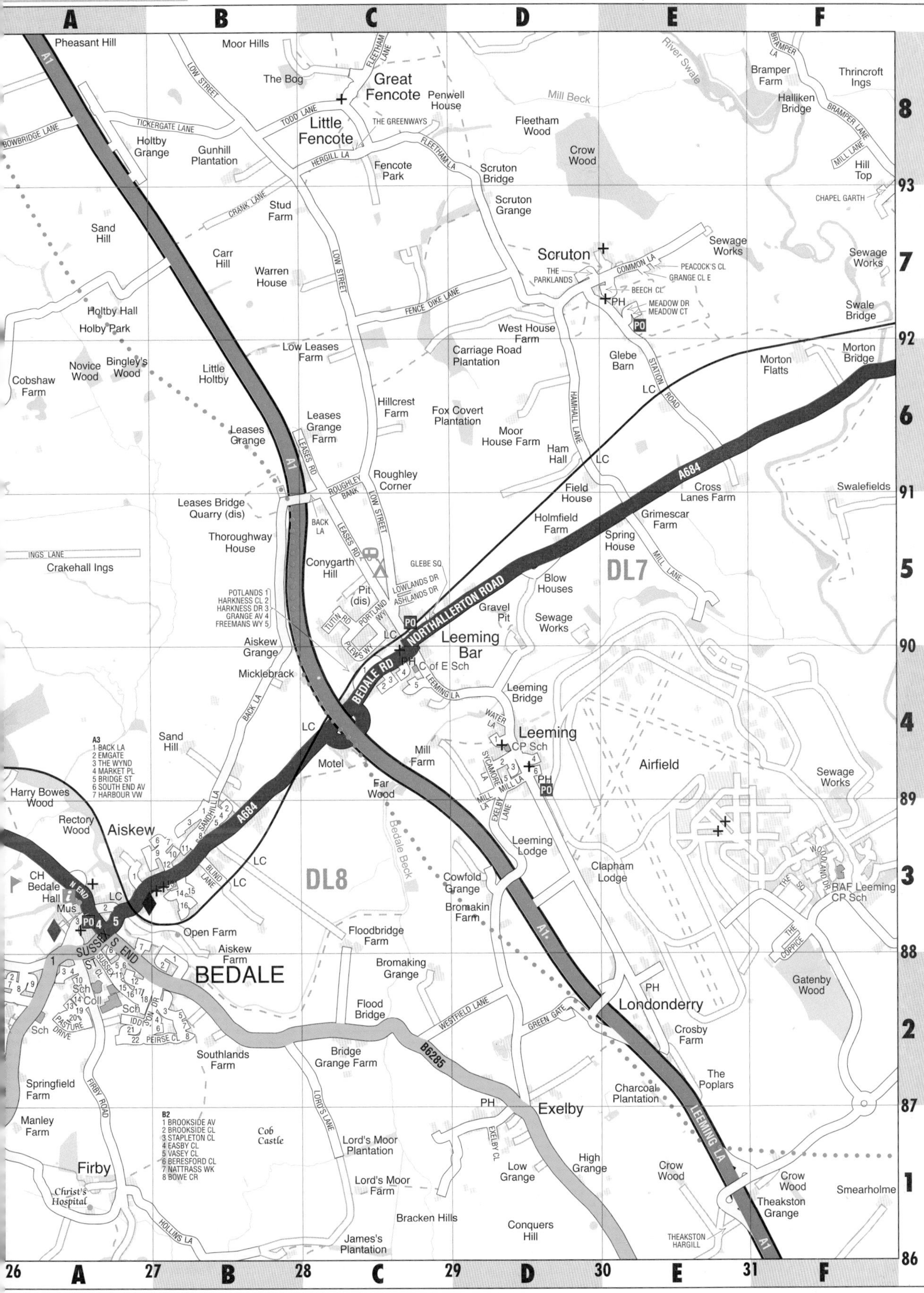

A2
1 WYCAR
2 OAK TREE CL
3 QUEEN ANNE'S CT
4 QUEEN ANNE'S DR
5 HARBOUR RI
6 THE COURT
7 OAK TREE RD
8 ASH TREE RD
9 SYCAMORE DR
10 GRANGE CL
11 KENDREW C
12 TOM HALL CTL
13 PINEWOOD GR
14 BEECHWOOD CL
15 GLEBE CL
16 BENKHILL DR
17 MOWBRAY CR
18 FITZALAN RD
19 GRANGE RD
20 MEADOW GR
21 PARKER DR
22 HIRD AV

B3
1 HERON CL
2 INGS VW
3 KINGFISHER DR
4 SPRUCE GILL AV
5 SPRUCE GILL DR
6 WILLOW DR
7 CHERRY GR
8 BIELBY CL
9 MEADOWFIELD
10 HOLLY RD
11 HAXEL CT
12 NEWSTEADS
13 THE CRESCENT
14 BADGER HILL DR
15 FOX COVERT CL
16 OTTERBECK WY

D4
1 MILLFIELD CL
2 ST JOHN'S RD
3 ST JOHN'S CR
4 NEWTON CR
5 PROSPECT WY
6 HARGILL LA

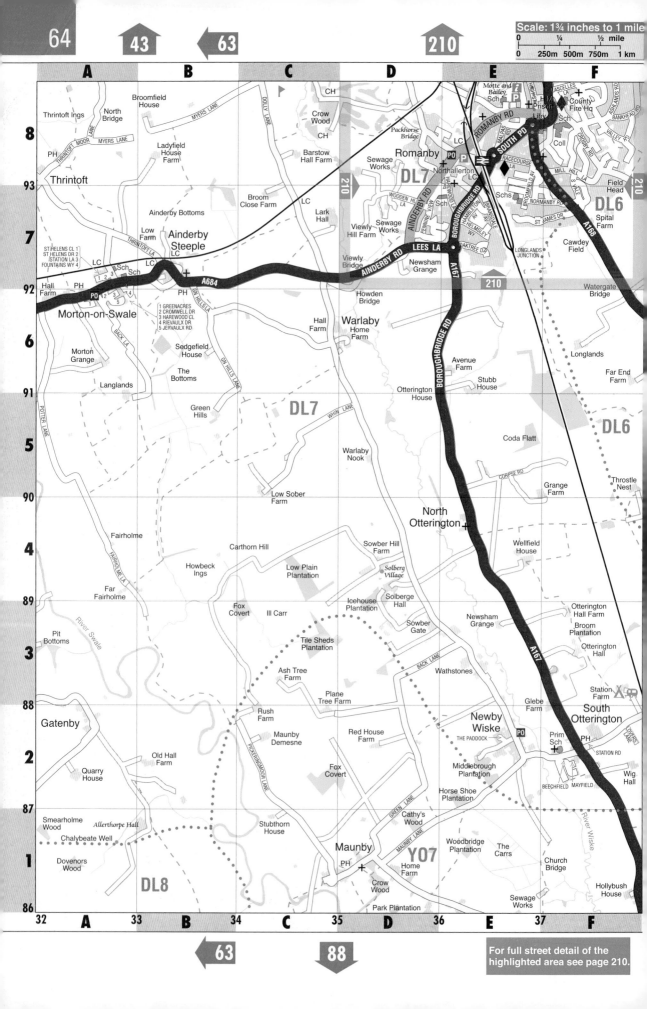

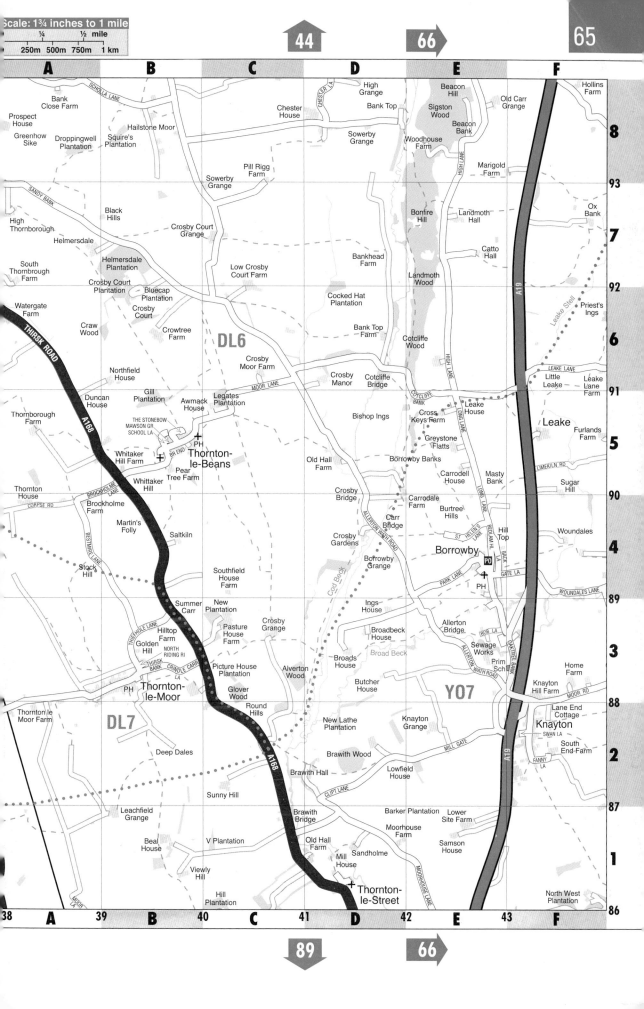

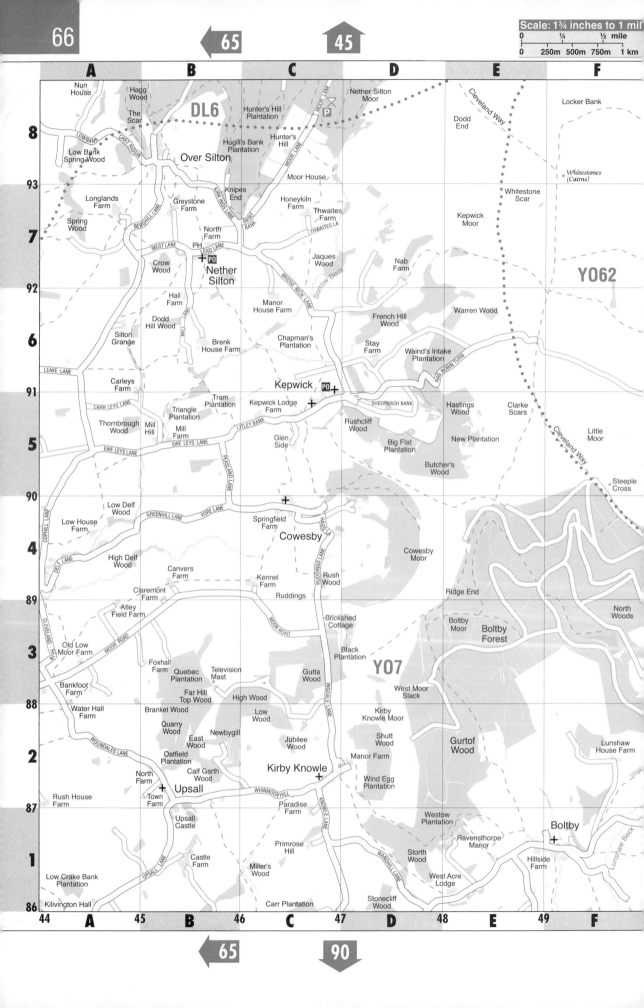

A   B   C   D   E   F

Nun House
Hagg Wood
The Scar
DL6
Hunter's Hill Plantation
Nether Silton Moor
Cleveland Way
Dodd End
Locker Bank

Low Bank Spring Wood
LOWBANK
CART RIGGIN
Over Silton
Hugill's Bank Plantation
Hunter's Hill
MOOR LANE
P
Whitestones (Cairns)

8

93
Longlands Farm
Greystone Farm
Knipes End
Moor House
Honeykiln Farm
Thwaites Farm
Whitestone Scar

Spring Wood
BERGHILL LANE
KIRK INGS LANE
SKYRT BANK
THWAITES LA
Kepwick Moor
YO62

7
North Farm
WEST LANE
PH
LEAD LANE
Crow Wood
PO
Nether Silton
BRIDGE BECK LANE
Sorrow Beck
Jaques Wood
Nab Farm

92
Hall Farm
Manor House Farm
French Hill Wood
Warren Wood

6
Dodd Hill Wood
MILL LANE
Brenk House Farm
Chapman's Plantation
Stay Farm
Waind's Intake Plantation
RAG ROBIN TURN

Silton Grange
Carleys Farm
LEAKE LANE
CARR LEYS LANE
Triangle Plantation
Tram Plantation
Kepwick
PO
SHEEPWASH BANK
Hastings Wood
Clarke Scars
Little Moor

91
Thornbrough Wood
Mill Hill
Mill Farm
Kepwick Lodge Farm
LITLEY BANK
Rushcliff Wood
New Plantation
Cleveland Way

5
EWE LEYS LANE
EWE LEYS LANE
Glen Side
Big Flat Plantation
Butcher's Wood
Steeple Cross

COPHILL LANE
PEASLAND LANE
Low Delf Wood
GREENHILL LANE
FORE LANE
Springfield Farm
HAGG LA
Cowesby Moor

90
Low House Farm
Cowesby
Ridge End

4
DELF LANE
High Delf Wood
Canvers Farm
Kennel Farm
RUDDINGS LANE
Rush Wood
Boltby Moor
Boltby Forest
North Woods

Claremont Farm
Ruddings

89
Atley Field Farm
MOOR ROAD
Brickshed Cottage

CLEVELAND RIGG
Old Low Moor Farm
MOOR ROAD
Foxhall Farm
Black Plantation
YO7
West Moor Slack

3
Bankfoot Farm
Quebec Plantation
Television Mast
Gutta Wood
INGDALE LANE

Far Hill Top Wood
High Wood
Kirby Knowle Moor

88
Water Hall Farm
Branket Wood
Low Wood
Shutt Wood
Gurtof Wood
Lunshaw House Farm

2
WOUNDALES LANE
Quarry Wood
Newbygill
Jubilee Wood
Manor Farm

East Wood
Kirby Knowle
Wind Egg Plantation

Oatfield Plantation
Calf Garth Wood
North Farm
Upsall
WHINMOOR HILL
Westow Plantation
Boltby

87
Rush House Farm
Town Farm
Paradise Farm
KNOWLE LANE
Ravensthorpe Manor
Hillside Farm

Upsall Castle
Primrose Hill
Storth Wood
LUNSHAW BECK

1
UPSALL LANE
Castle Farm
Miller's Wood
WARDHILL LANE
West Acre Lodge

Low Crake Bank Plantation
Carr Plantation
Stonecliff Wood

86
Kilivington Hall

44   A   45   B   46   C   47   D   48   E   49   F

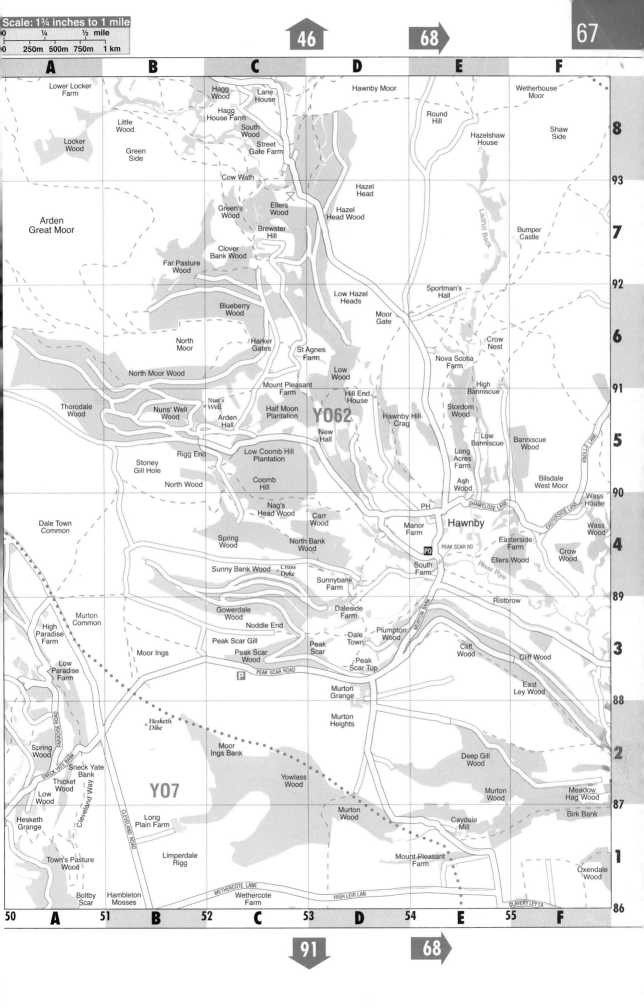

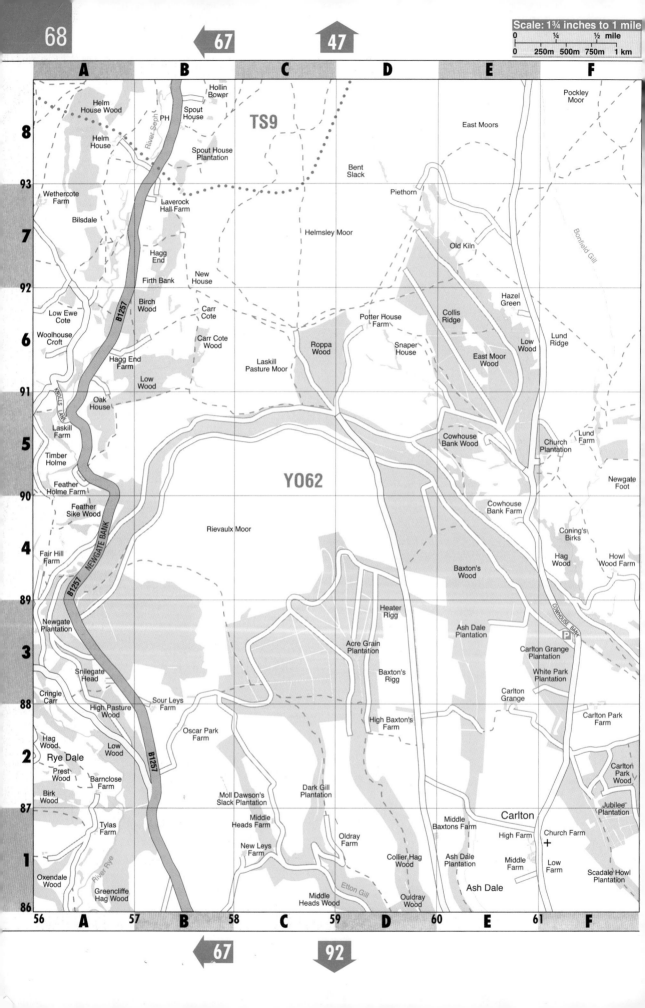

Scale: 1¾ inches to 1 mile

0   ¼   ½   mile
0   250m 500m 750m   1 km

A   B   C   D   E   F

Pockley Moor

Helm House Wood
Hollin Bower
PH
Spout House
TS9

8

East Moors

Bonfield Gill

Helm House
River Seph
Spout House Plantation

93

Wethercote Farm
Laverock Hall Farm
Bent Slack
Piethorn

Bilsdale
Helmsley Moor

7

Hagg End
Old Kiln

92

Firth Bank
New House
Hazel Green

Low Ewe Cote
Birch Wood
Carr Cote
Potter House Farm
Collis Ridge
Low Wood
Lund Ridge

6

Woolhouse Croft
Carr Cote Wood
Roppa Wood
Snaper House
East Moor Wood

B1257
Hagg End Farm
Laskill Pasture Moor

91

Low Wood

Oak House
Cowhouse Bank Wood
Church Plantation
Lund Farm

5

Laskill Farm
KNOLLS LANE
Newgate Foot

Timber Holme

YO62

90

Feather Holme Farm
Cowhouse Bank Farm

Feather Sike Wood
Coning's Birks

4

Fair Hill Farm
NEWGATE BANK
Rievaulx Moor
Baxton's Wood
Hag Wood
Howl Wood Farm

B1257

89

Heater Rigg
Ash Dale Plantation
COWHOUSE BANK
P

Newgate Plantation

3

Acre Grain Plantation
Carlton Grange Plantation

Snilegate Head
Baxton's Rigg
White Park Plantation

Cringle Carr
Sour Leys Farm
High Baxton's Farm
Carlton Grange
Carlton Park Farm

88

High Pasture Wood
Oscar Park Farm

Hag Wood
Rye Dale
Low Wood
B1257

2

Prest Wood
Barnclose Farm
Carlton Park Wood

Birk Wood
Moll Dawson's Slack Plantation
Dark Gill Plantation
Middle Baxtons Farm
Carlton
Church Farm
Jubilee Plantation

87

Tylas Farm
Middle Heads Farm
Oldray Farm
Middle Baxtons Farm
High Farm
+

New Leys Farm
Collier Hag Wood
Ash Dale Plantation
Middle Farm
Low Farm
Scadale Howl Plantation

1

River Rye
Oxendale Wood
Ash Dale

Greencliffe Hag Wood
Middle Heads Wood
Etton Gill
Ouldray Wood

86

56   57   58   59   60   61
A   B   C   D   E   F

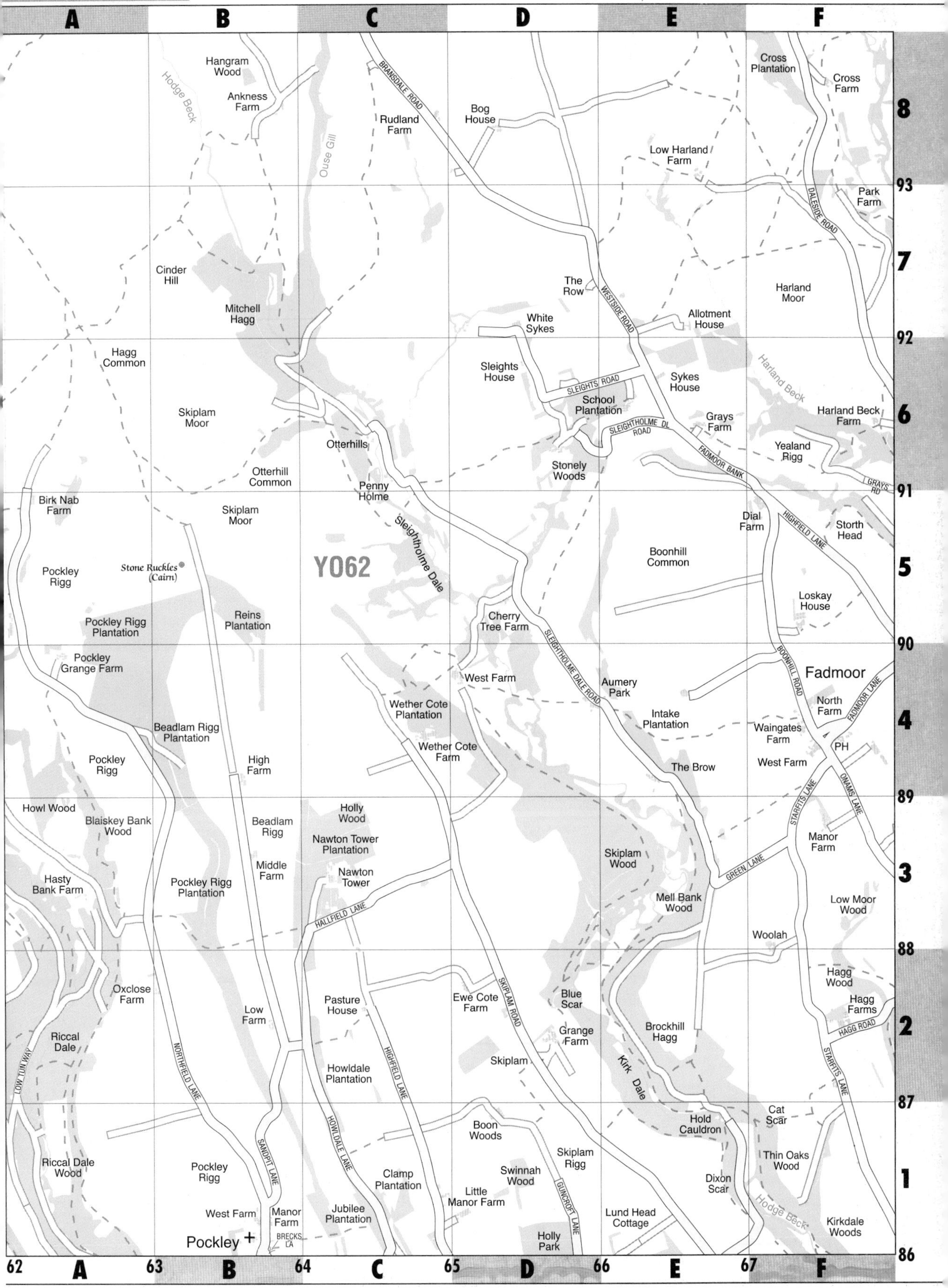
A
B
C
D
E
F
Hangram Wood
Ankness Farm
Hodge Beck
Ouse Gill
Rudland Farm
BRANSDALE ROAD
Bog House
Cross Plantation
Cross Farm
Low Harland Farm
Park Farm
DALESIDE ROAD
Cinder Hill
Mitchell Hagg
The Row
WESTSIDE ROAD
White Sykes
Allotment House
Harland Moor
Hagg Common
Sleights House
SLEIGHTS ROAD
Sykes House
Harland Beck
Skiplam Moor
School Plantation
SLEIGHTHOLME DL ROAD
Grays Farm
Harland Beck Farm
Otterhills
Yealand Rigg
FADMOOR BANK
Stonely Woods
Otterhill Common
GRAYS RD
Penny Holme
Birk Nab Farm
Skiplam Moor
Dial Farm
HIGHFIELD LANE
Storth Head
Sleightholme Dale
Boonhill Common
Pockley Rigg
Stone Ruckles (Cairn)
YO62
Loskay House
Reins Plantation
Cherry Tree Farm
Pockley Rigg Plantation
SLEIGHTHOLME DALE ROAD
BOONHILL ROAD
Fadmoor
Pockley Grange Farm
West Farm
Aumery Park
North Farm
FADMOOR LANE
Wether Cote Plantation
Intake Plantation
Waingates Farm
Beadlam Rigg Plantation
PH
Pockley Rigg
Wether Cote Farm
West Farm
High Farm
The Brow
STARFITS LANE
OMANS LANE
Howl Wood
Holly Wood
Blaiskey Bank Wood
Beadlam Rigg
Nawton Tower Plantation
Manor Farm
Skiplam Wood
Middle Farm
Nawton Tower
GREEN LANE
Hasty Bank Farm
Pockley Rigg Plantation
Low Moor Wood
Mell Bank Wood
HALLFIELD LANE
Woolah
Hagg Wood
Oxclose Farm
Pasture House
Ewe Cote Farm
SKIPLAM ROAD
Blue Scar
Hagg Farms
Low Farm
Brockhill Hagg
HAGG ROAD
Riccal Dale
Grange Farm
LOW TUN WAY
NORTHFIELD LANE
HIGHFIELD LANE
Skiplam
Kirk Dale
Howdale Plantation
STARFITS LANE
HOWDALE LANE
Cat Scar
Hold Cauldron
Boon Woods
Thin Oaks Wood
Riccal Dale Wood
Skiplam Rigg
Pockley Rigg
SANDPIT LANE
Clamp Plantation
Swinnah Wood
Dixon Scar
GUINCROFT LANE
Little Manor Farm
Hodge Beck
West Farm
Manor Farm
Jubilee Plantation
Lund Head Cottage
Kirkdale Woods
Pockley
BRECKS LA
Holly Park
8
93
7
92
6
91
5
90
4
89
3
88
2
87
1
86
62
63
64
65
66
67

69
49

Scale: 1¾ inches to 1 mile
0 ¼ ½ mile
0 250m 500m 750m 1 km

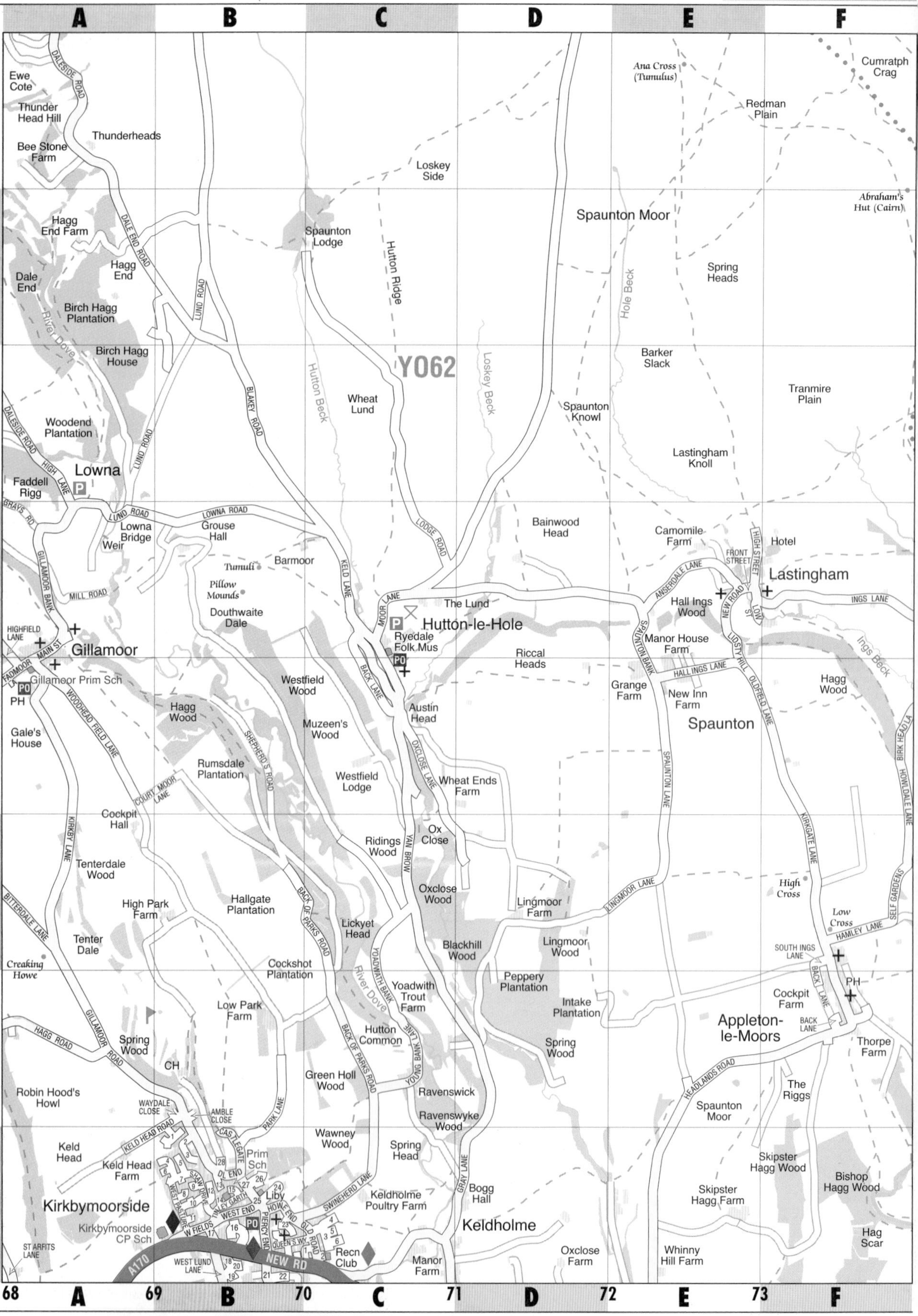

B1
1 KELD HEAD OR
2 RYEDALE VW
3 RYEDALE CR
4 POPLAR AV
5 WILLOW RI
6 BEECH DR
7 ASH GR
8 CEDAR VALE
9 OAK CL
10 LIME CH
11 RIPLEY CL
12 BROOKE CL
13 MANOR CL
14 TINLEY GD
15 TOWN FARM CL
16 FEVERSHAM DR
17 W LUND
18 SHERBROOKE CL
19 SLINGSBY GARTH
20 PARKERS MT
21 INGS LA
22 CARTER LA
23 OXCROFT
24 CHURCH ST
25 MARKET PL
26 CROWN SQ
27 HIGH MKT PL
28 MANOR VALE LA

C1
1 VIVERS PL
2 EASTWAY CL
3 SPRINGFIELD LA
4 STUTEVILLE CL
5 KILDARE GARTH
6 DUNA WY

69
94

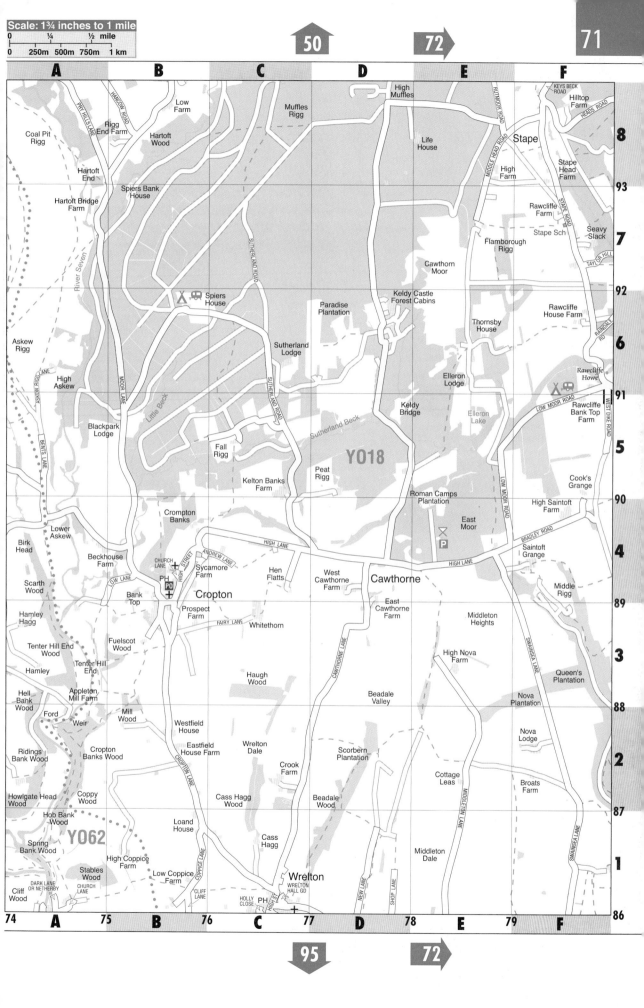

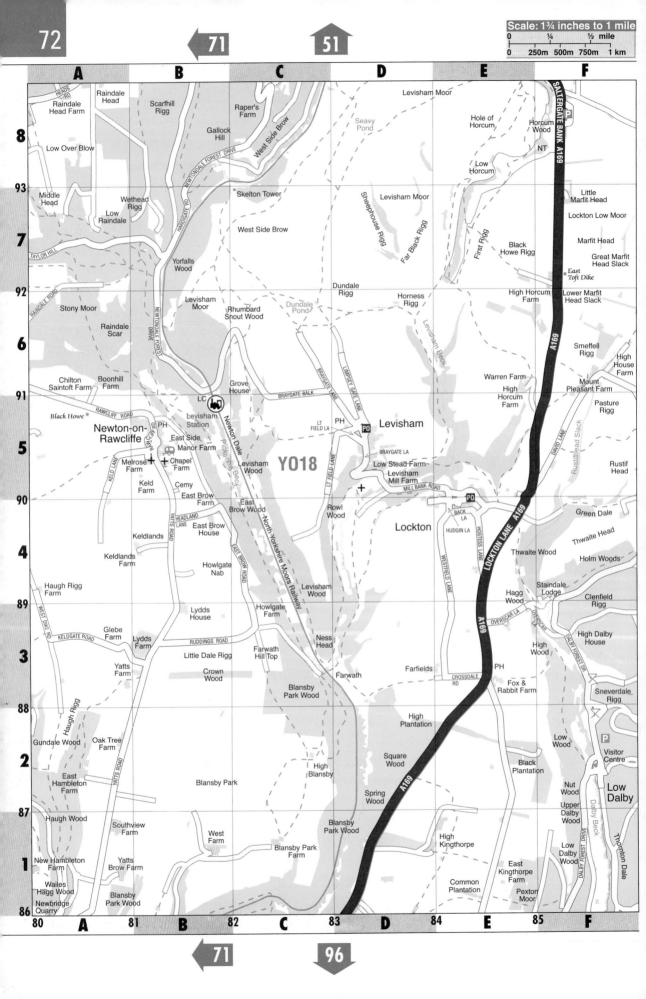

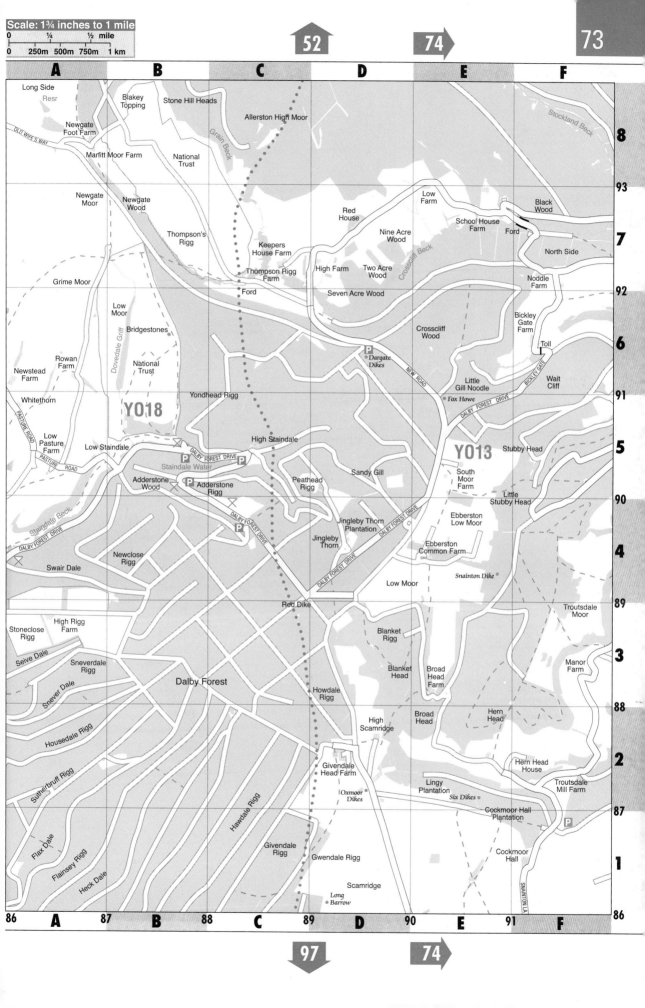

A   B   C   D   E   F

Long Side Resr
Newgate Foot Farm
Blakey Topping
Stone Hill Heads
Allerston High Moor
Stockland Beck

8

Marfitt Moor Farm
National Trust
Grain Beck

Newgate Moor
Newgate Wood
Thompson's Rigg
Red House
Low Farm
Black Wood
School House Farm
Ford
North Side

93

7

Grime Moor
Keepers House Farm
Thompson Rigg Farm
High Farm
Nine Acre Wood
Two Acre Wood
Crossliff Beck
Noddle Farm

Ford
Seven Acre Wood
Bickley Gate Farm
Toll

92

6

Low Moor
Bridgestones
Dovedale Griff
Crosscliff Wood
Dargate Dikes
NEW ROAD
Little Gill Noodle
Wait Cliff
BICKLEY GATE

Newstead Farm
Rowan Farm
National Trust
Yondhead Rigg
Fox Howe
DALBY FOREST DRIVE

91

Whitethorn
YO18
High Staindale
Stubby Head

5

Low Pasture Farm
PASTURE ROAD
Low Staindale
Staindale Water
P   P
Adderstone Rigg
Sandy Gill
YO13
South Moor Farm
Little Stubby Head

Adderstone Wood
P
Peathead Rigg
Ebberston Low Moor

90

Staindale Beck
DALBY FOREST DRIVE
P
Jingleby Thorn Plantation
Jingleby Thorn
DALBY FOREST DRIVE
Ebberston Common Farm

4

DALBY FOREST DRIVE
Swair Dale
Newclose Rigg
Low Moor
Snainton Dike

Red Dike
Troutsdale Moor

89

Stoneclose Rigg
High Rigg Farm
Blanket Rigg

3

Seive Dale
Sneverdale Rigg
Blanket Head
Broad Head Farm
Manor Farm

Sneaver Dale
Dalby Forest
Howdale Rigg
Broad Head
Hern Head

88

Housedale Rigg
High Scamridge
Hern Head House

2

Sutherbruff Rigg
Givendale Head Farm
Lingy Plantation
Troutsdale Mill Farm

Oxmoor Dikes
Six Dikes
Cockmoor Hall Plantation

87

Hawdale Rigg
Gwendale Rigg
Cockmoor Hall
P

Flax Dale
Givendale Rigg
SNAINTON LA

1

Flainsey Rigg
Heck Dale
Scamridge
Long Barrow

86   A   87   B   88   C   89   D   90   E   91   F   86

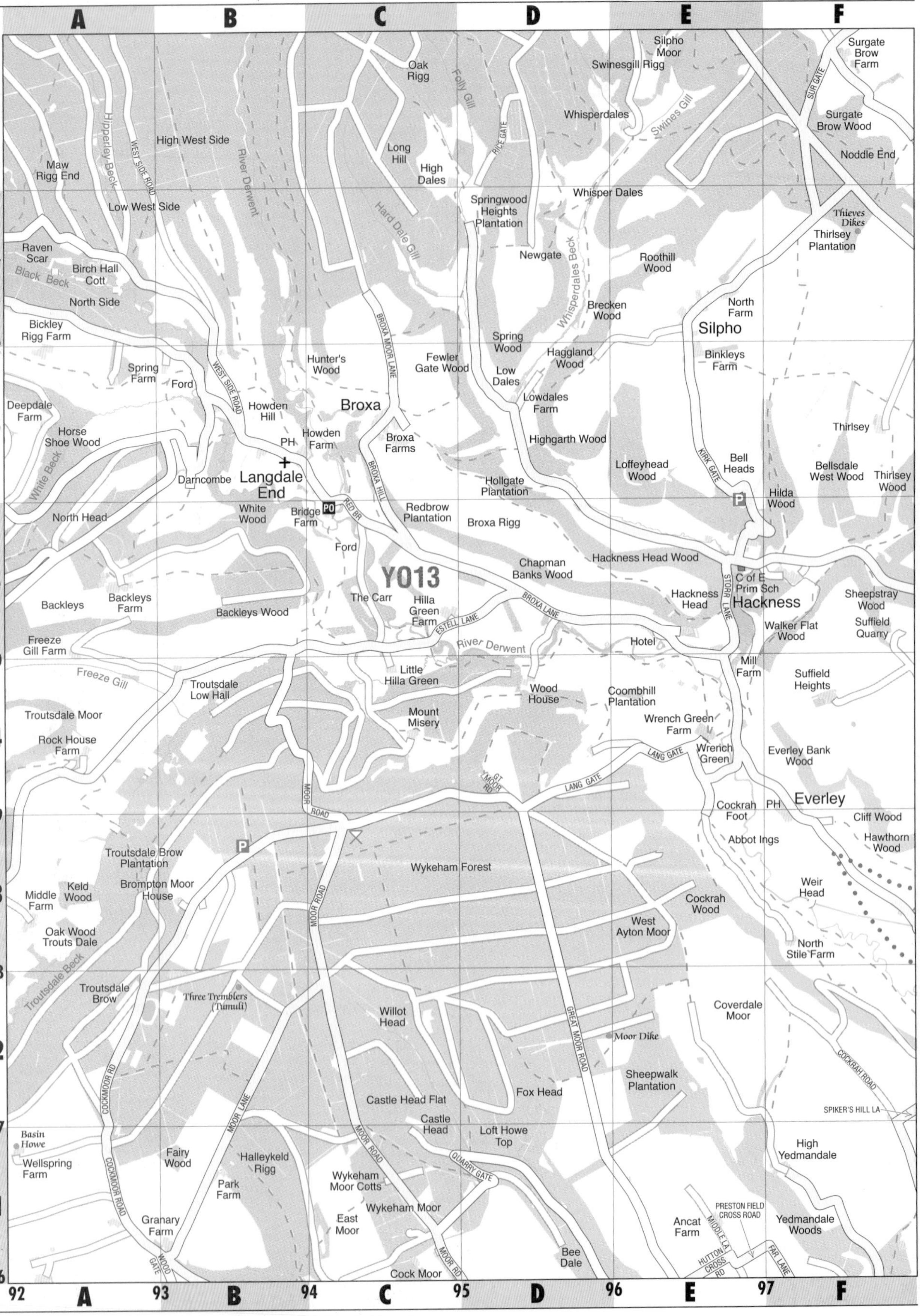

Scale: 1¾ inches to 1 mile

0   ¼   ½ mile
0   250m 500m 750m 1 km

8

93

7

92

6

91

5

90

4

89

3

88

2

87

1

86

A   B   C   D   E   F

Maw Rigg End

High West Side

Oak Rigg

Silpho Moor

Swinesgill Rigg

Surgate Brow Farm

Low West Side

Long Hill

High Dales

Whisperdales

Surgate Brow Wood

Noddle End

Hippeley Beck

WEST SIDE ROAD

River Derwent

Hard Dale Gill

Folly Gill

RICE GATE

Whisper Dales

Swines Gill

Whisperdales Beck

SUR GATE

Raven Scar

Birch Hall Cott.

Springwood Heights Plantation

Newgate

Roothill Wood

Thieves Dikes

Thirlsey Plantation

Black Beck

North Side

Bickley Rigg Farm

Spring Farm

Ford

Howden Hill

Broxa

Fewler Gate Wood

Spring Wood

Haggland Wood

Brecken Wood

Silpho

North Farm

Thirlsey

Deepdale Farm

Horse Shoe Wood

Howden Farm

Low Dales

Lowdales Farm

Binkleys Farm

WHITE BECK

WEST SIDE ROAD

Darncombe

PH

Howden Farm

Broxa Farms

Highgarth Wood

Loffeyhead Wood

Bell Heads

Bellsdale West Wood

Thirlsey Wood

BROXA MOOR LANE

BROXA HILL

Langdale End

White Wood

Bridge Farm

PO

RED BR

Redbrow Plantation

Hollgate Plantation

KIRK GATE

Hilda Wood

North Head

Ford

Broxa Rigg

Hackness Head Wood

Hackness Head

Hilda Wood

YO13

Chapman Banks Wood

STORR LANE

C of E Prim Sch

Hackness

Sheepstray Wood

Backleys

Backleys Farm

The Carr

Hilla Green Farm

Hotel

Walker Flat Wood

Suffield Quarry

Backleys Wood

BROXA LANE

ESTELL LANE

River Derwent

Mill Farm

Suffield Heights

Freeze Gill Farm

Freeze Gill

Troutsdale Low Hall

Little Hilla Green

Wood House

Coombhill Plantation

Wrench Green Farm

Everley Bank Wood

Troutsdale Moor

Mount Misery

Wrench Green

Rock House Farm

MOOR ROAD

Lang Gate

Cockrah Foot

PH

Everley

LANG GATE

Abbot Ings

Cliff Wood

Hawthorn Wood

Troutsdale Brow Plantation

P

Brompton Moor House

GT TMOOR RD

Wykeham Forest

Cockrah Wood

Weir Head

Middle Farm

Keld Wood

West Ayton Moor

North Stile Farm

Oak Wood Trouts Dale

Troutsdale Brow

Three Tremblers (Tumuli)

Willot Head

Coverdale Moor

COCKRAH ROAD

Troutsdale Beck

COCKMOOR RD

MOOR LANE

Castle Head Flat

Fox Head

Moor Dike

GREAT MOOR ROAD

Sheepwalk Plantation

SPIKER'S HILL LA

Basin Howe

Fairy Wood

Castle Head

Loft Howe Top

High Yedmandale

Wellspring Farm

Halleykeld Rigg

Park Farm

Wykeham Moor Cotts

QUARRY GATE

PRESTON FIELD CROSS ROAD

Granary Farm

WOOD GATE

East Moor

Wykeham Moor

MOOR RD

Bee Dale

Ancat Farm

MIDDLE LA CROSS RD

HUTTON LA CROSS RD

FAR LANE

Yedmandale Woods

Cock Moor

Scale: 1¾ inches to 1 mile

0 ¼ ½ mile

0 250m 500m 750m 1 km

D5
1 ANNADALE GR
2 WREA HEAD CL
3 COOKS GD
4 IVY BANK CT
5 STONY CT
6 ELLIS GD
7 CASTLE VW
8 STONY LA
9 LANCASTER CL
10 QUEEN ELIZABETH DR
11 DUCHY AV
12 BEECH DR
13 WEST PARK RD
14 THE PARK
15 EAST PARK RD
16 FIELD CL RD
17 LANCASTER WY
18 CHICHESTER CL
19 WEST AV
20 SOUTH AV
21 EAST AV
22 LOW ST
23 HALL PK CL
24 FLOCK LEYS
25 HALL PK GR
26 TIBBY BUTTS
27 SCALBY BECK RD
28 RIVERSIDE
39 THOMPSON CL
30 COW WATH CL
31 HAGUE AV
32 ELLISON AV
33 BIELBY CL
34 DANES DYKE
35 NEWBY FARM CL
36 NEWBY FARM CR

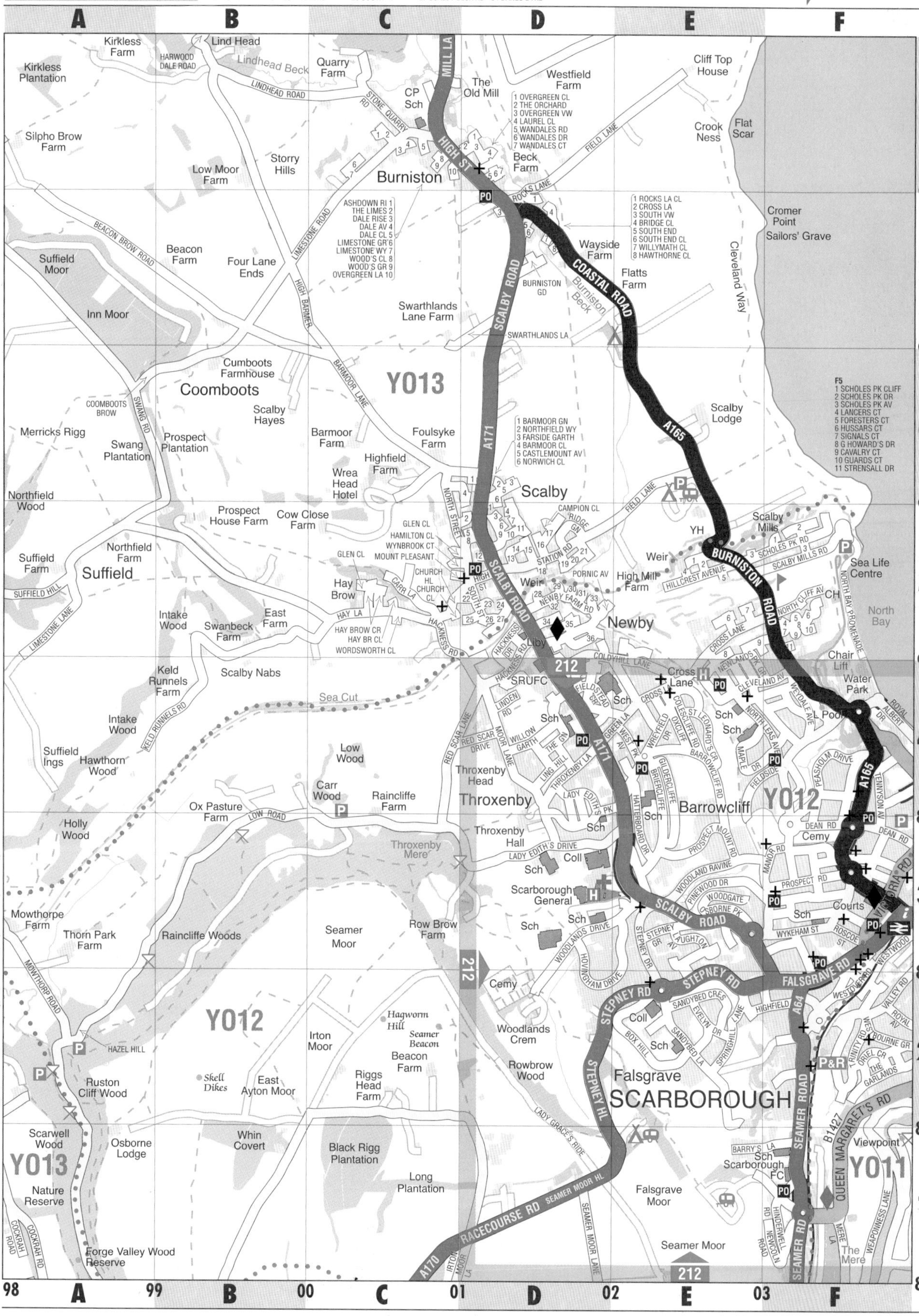

F5
1 SCHOLES PK CLIFF
2 SCHOLES PK DR
3 SCHOLES PK AV
4 LANCERS CT
5 FORESTERS CT
6 HUSSARS CT
7 SIGNALS CT
8 G HOWARD'S DR
9 CAVALRY CT
10 GUARDS CT
11 STRENSALL DR

E5
1 HIGH MILL DR
2 HILLCREST GR
3 RYCROFT RD
4 FAIRWAY
5 SEAVIEW AV
6 WESTFIELD AV
7 MAYFIELD AV
8 HAREWOOD AV
9 BRIARDENE AV

For full street detail of the highlighted area see page 212.

A   B   C   D   E   F

8

93

7

92

6

91

5

90

213

North
Bay

4

Y012

Castle Cliff

Castle

ROYAL ALBERT DRIVE

MARINE DRIVE

P

Chapel Of
Our Lady

Hall

P

89

PO

CASTLE RD

Y011

LONGWESTGATE
Sch

PO

QUEEN ST

ST THOMAS ST

SANDSIDE

FORESHORE RD

Old & East
Harbours

PO

3

Sh Ctr

SCARBOROUGH

Mus

VERNON RD

Art Gall

South
Sands

88

The Spa Complex

ALBION RD

RAMSHILL RD

WEST ST

The Spa

South Bay

213

FILEY RD

2

PO

AV VICTORIA

ESPLANADE

Sch

HOLBECK RD

87

Coll

Black
Rocks

P

A165

WEAPONNESS PK

Sports
Ctr

BESDALE AVE

Coll

HOLBECK HILL

Schs

FILEY RD

Y011

White Nab

Raven Scar

1

COLLEGE LA

CH

KNOX LA

Univ
of Hull

PO

Cornelian Bay

86

04   A   05   B   06   C   07   D   08   E   09   F

213

For full street detail of the highlighted area see page 213.

← 212   ↓ 100

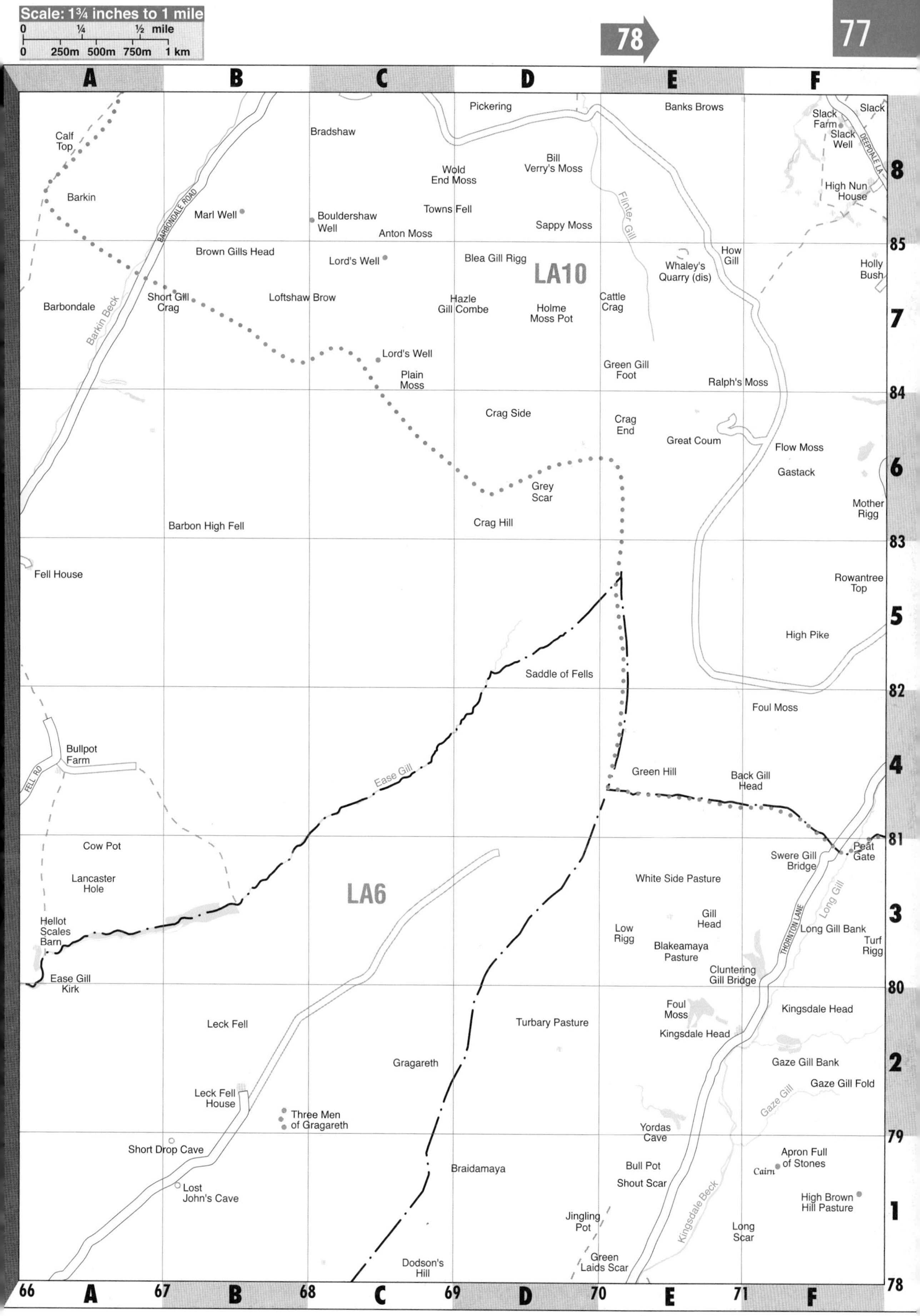

A   B   C   D   E   F

Calf Top

Barkin

Marl Well

Bradshaw

Pickering

Banks Brows

Slack Farm
Slack Well

DEEPDALE LA.

8

Wold End Moss

Bill Verry's Moss

High Nun House

Barbondale

Brown Gills Head

Bouldershaw Well

Towns Fell

Sappy Moss

85

Anton Moss

Short Gill Crag

Lord's Well

Blea Gill Rigg

LA10

Whaley's Quarry (dis)

How Gill

Holly Bush

7

Loftshaw Brow

Hazle Gill Combe

Holme Moss Pot

Cattle Crag

Green Gill Foot

Ralph's Moss

84

Lord's Well

Plain Moss

Crag Side

Crag End

Great Coum

Flow Moss

Gastack

6

Barbon High Fell

Crag Hill

Grey Scar

Mother Rigg

83

Fell House

Rowantree Top

5

High Pike

Saddle of Fells

82

Foul Moss

Bullpot Farm

FELL RD

Green Hill

Back Gill Head

4

Ease Gill

81

Cow Pot

Lancaster Hole

LA6

White Side Pasture

Swere Gill Bridge

Peat Gate

THORNTON LANE

Long Gill

Long Gill Bank

3

Hellot Scales Barn

Low Rigg

Gill Head

Blakeamaya Pasture

Cluntering Gill Bridge

Turf Rigg

Ease Gill Kirk

80

Leck Fell

Turbary Pasture

Foul Moss

Kingsdale Head

Kingsdale Head

Gragareth

Gaze Gill Bank

Gaze Gill Fold

2

Leck Fell House

Three Men of Gragareth

Yordas Cave

Gaze Gill

79

Short Drop Cave

Bull Pot

Shout Scar

Apron Full of Stones

Cairn

Braidamaya

Lost John's Cave

Kingsdale Beck

High Brown Hill Pasture

1

Jingling Pot

Long Scar

Dodson's Hill

Green Laids Scar

78

66   A   67   B   68   C   69   D   70   E   71   F   78

77

Scale: 1¾ inches to 1 mile

0   ¼   ½   mile
0 250m 500m 750m 1 km

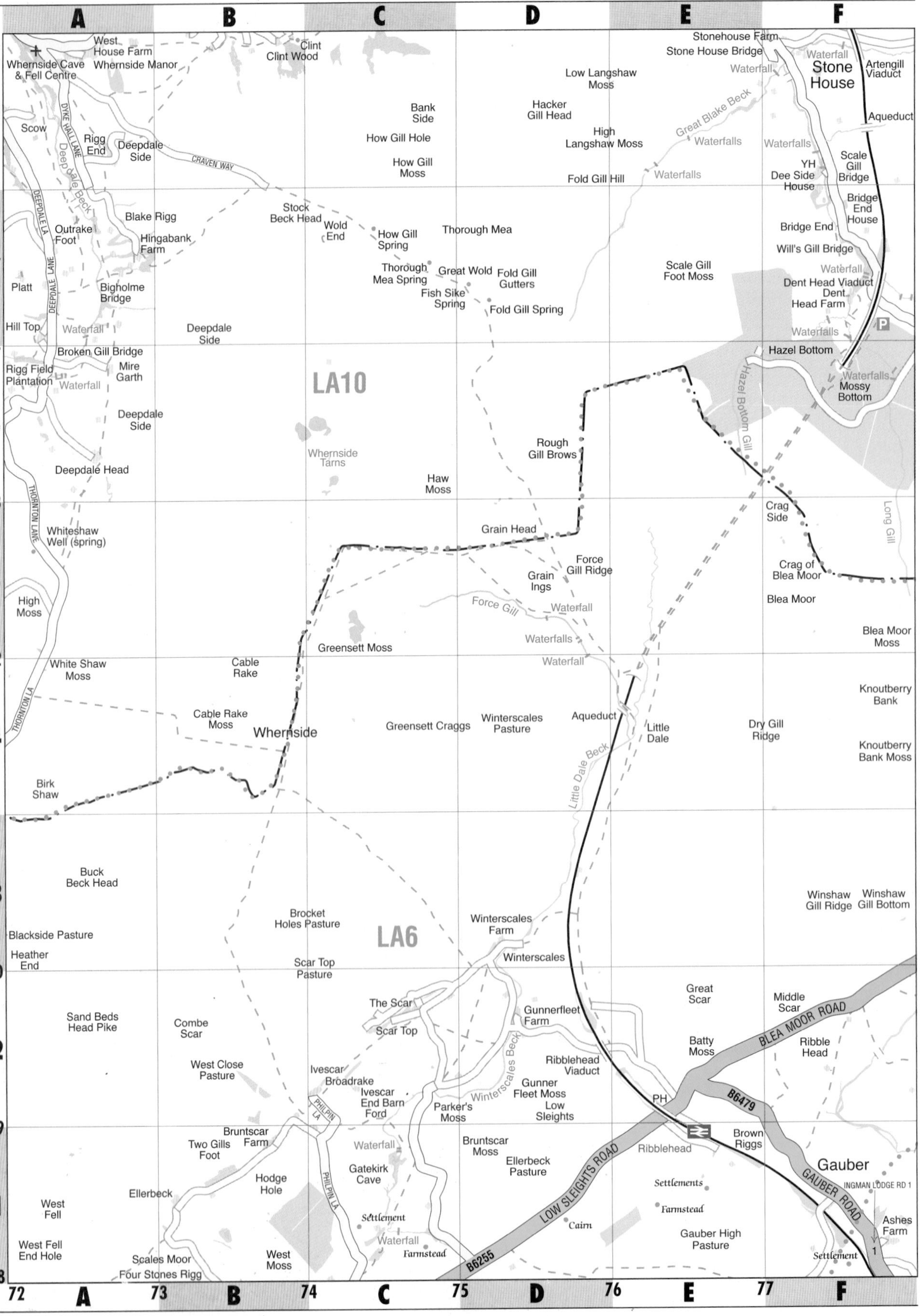

A **B** **C** **D** **E** **F**

Whernside Cave & Fell Centre
West House Farm
Whernside Manor
Clint
Clint Wood

Stonehouse Farm
Stone House Bridge
Waterfall
Waterfall
Stone House
Artengill Viaduct

8

Scow
Rigg End
Deepdale Side
Bank Side
How Gill Hole
Low Langshaw Moss
Hacker Gill Head
Aqueduct

CRAVEN WAY
How Gill Moss
High Langshaw Moss
Waterfalls
Waterfalls
Scale Gill Bridge
YH Dee Side House

85

Outrake Foot
Blake Rigg
Hingabank Farm
Stock Beck Head
Wold End
How Gill Spring
Fold Gill Hill
Waterfalls
Bridge End House
Bridge End
Will's Gill Bridge

7

Platt
Bigholme Bridge
Thorough Mea Spring
Great Wold
Fold Gill Gutters
Thorough Mea
Scale Gill Foot Moss
Waterfall
Dent Head Viaduct
Dent Head Farm

Hill Top
Fish Sike Spring
Fold Gill Spring
Waterfalls

84

Rigg Field Plantation
Broken Gill Bridge
Mire Garth
Deepdale Side
Hazel Bottom
Mossy Bottom

Waterfall
Waterfall

6

Deepdale Side
Rough Gill Brows
Waterfalls

Deepdale Head
Whernside Tarns
Haw Moss
Crag Side

83

Whiteshaw Well (spring)
Grain Head
Crag of Blea Moor

5

High Moss
Force Gill Ridge
Blea Moor
Blea Moor Moss

White Shaw Moss
Cable Rake
Greensett Moss
Grain Ings
Force Gill
Waterfall
Waterfalls

82

Cable Rake Moss
Whernside
Greensett Craggs
Winterscales Pasture
Aqueduct
Little Dale
Dry Gill Ridge
Knoutberry Bank

4

Birk Shaw
Little Dale Beck
Knoutberry Bank Moss

81

Buck Beck Head
Winshaw Gill Ridge
Winshaw Gill Bottom

3

Blackside Pasture
Brocket Holes Pasture
Winterscales Farm

Heather End
Scar Top Pasture
LA6

80

The Scar
Gunnerfleet Farm
Great Scar
Middle Scar

2

Sand Beds Head Pike
Combe Scar
Scar Top
Ribblehead Viaduct
Batty Moss
Ribble Head
BLEA MOOR ROAD

West Close Pasture
Ivescar Broadrake
Ivescar End Barn Ford
Parker's Moss
Gunner Fleet Moss
Low Sleights
PH
B6479
Brown Riggs

79

Two Gills Foot
Bruntscar Farm
Waterfall
Bruntscar Moss
Ribblehead
Gauber
INGMAN LODGE RD 1

Ellerbeck
Hodge Hole
Gatekirk Cave
Ellerbeck Pasture
Settlements
Farmstead
GAUBER ROAD
Ashes Farm

1

West Fell
Settlement
Cairn
Gauber High Pasture
Settlement

West Fell End Hole
Scales Moor
Four Stones Rigg
West Moss
Waterfall
Farmstead
B6255

78

72 **A** **73** **B** **74** **C** **75** **D** **76** **E** **77** **F**

LA10

LA6

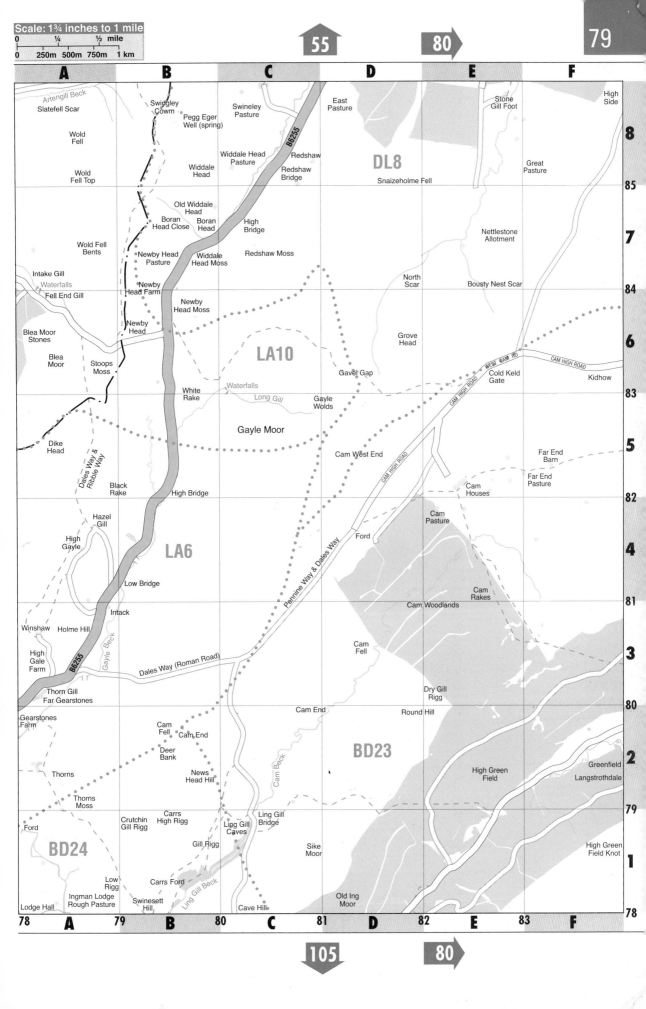

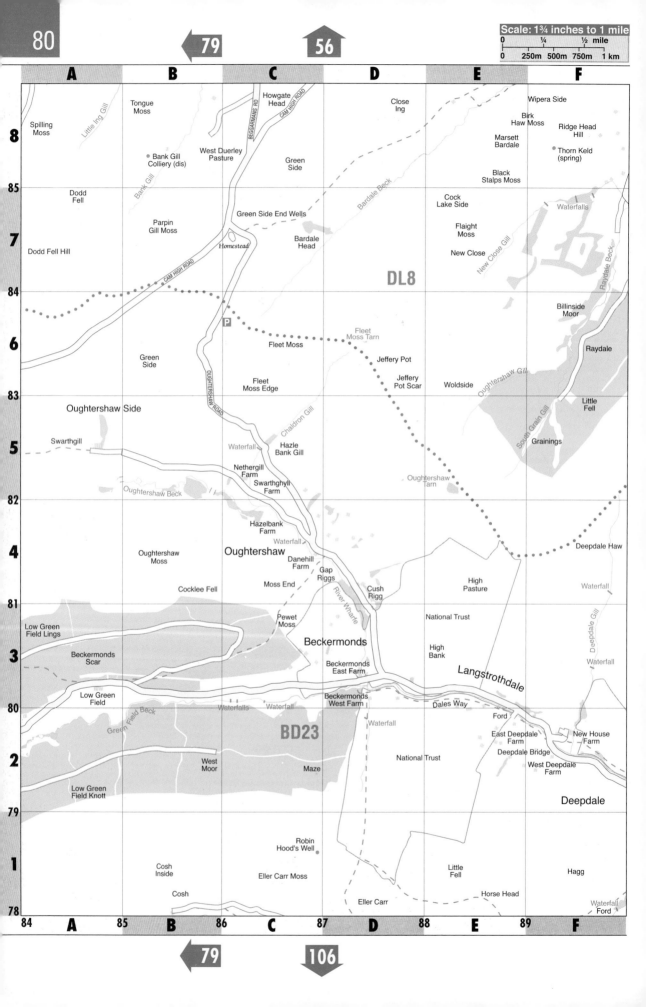

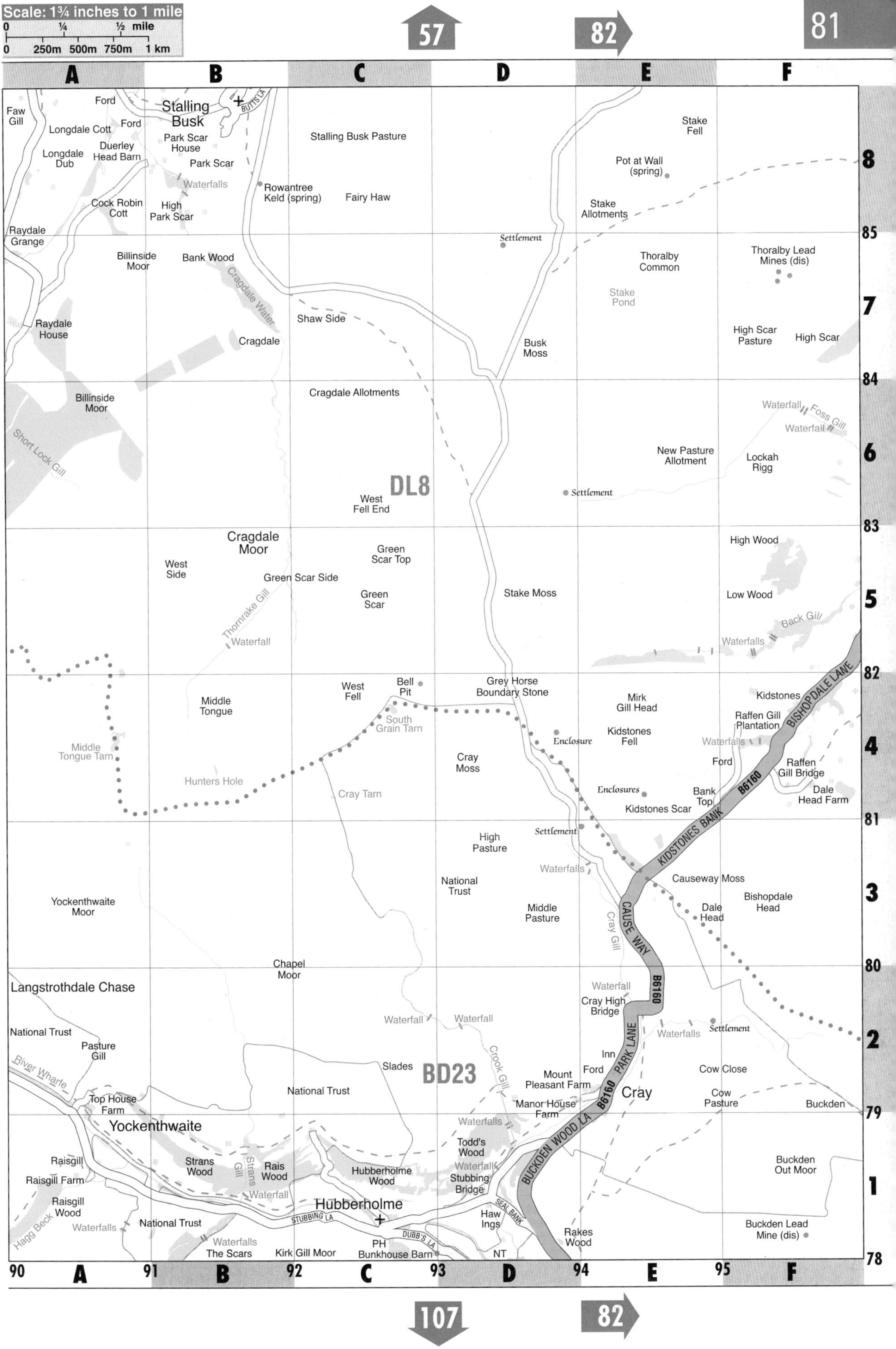

Scale: 1¾ inches to 1 mile
0 ¼ ½ mile
0 250m 500m 750m 1 km
57
82
A B C D E F
Faw Gill
Ford
Stalling Busk
BUTTS LA
Longdale Cott
Ford
Park Scar House
Stalling Busk Pasture
Stake Fell
Longdale Dub
Duerley Head Barn
Park Scar
Pot at Wall (spring)
Waterfalls
Rowantree Keld (spring)
Fairy Haw
Cock Robin Cott
High Park Scar
Stake Allotments
Raydale Grange
Settlement
Billinside Moor
Bank Wood
Thoralby Common
Thoralby Lead Mines (dis)
Cragdale Water
Stake Pond
Raydale House
Shaw Side
Cragdale
Busk Moss
High Scar Pasture
High Scar
Billinside Moor
Cragdale Allotments
Waterfall
Foss Gill
Waterfall
Short Lock Gill
New Pasture Allotment
Lockah Rigg
DL8
West Fell End
Settlement
Cragdale Moor
Green Scar Top
High Wood
West Side
Green Scar Side
Green Scar
Stake Moss
Low Wood
Thornrake Gill
Back Gill
Waterfall
Waterfalls
West Fell
Bell Pit
Grey Horse Boundary Stone
Mirk Gill Head
Kidstones
Middle Tongue
BISHOPDALE LANE
South Grain Tarn
Raffen Gill Plantation
Enclosure
Kidstones Fell
Middle Tongue Tarn
Waterfalls
Cray Moss
Ford
Raffen Gill Bridge
Hunters Hole
Cray Tarn
Enclosures
B6160
Bank Top
Dale Head Farm
Kidstones Scar
KIDSTONES BANK
High Pasture
Settlement
Waterfalls
National Trust
Causeway Moss
Bishopdale Head
Yockenthwaite Moor
Middle Pasture
Cray Gill
CAUSE WAY
Dale Head
Chapel Moor
B6160
Langstrothdale Chase
Waterfall
Cray High Bridge
National Trust
Waterfall
Waterfall
PARK LANE
Waterfalls
Settlement
Pasture Gill
Crook Gill
Inn
River Wharfe
Slades
BD23
Ford
Cow Close
Mount Pleasant Farm
National Trust
Cray
Cow Pasture
Buckden
Top House Farm
B6160
Manor House Farm
Yockenthwaite
Waterfalls
Todd's Wood
Raisgill
Strans Wood
Strans Gill
Rais Wood
Hubberholme Wood
Waterfall
BUCKDEN WOOD LA
Buckden Out Moor
Raisgill Farm
Stubbing Bridge
Waterfall
Raisgill Wood
Hubberholme
SEAL BANK
Hagg Beck
Waterfalls
National Trust
STUBBING LA
Haw Ings
Rakes Wood
Buckden Lead Mine (dis)
Waterfalls
DUBB'S LA
The Scars
Kirk Gill Moor
PH
Bunkhouse Barn
NT
8
85
7
84
6
83
5
82
4
81
3
80
2
79
1
78
90 91 92 93 94 95

A   B   C   D   E   F

Side Well

Lopsey Keld
(spr)

East
Farm

B6160

Newbiggin

Forelands

Cote
Bridge
Cote

8

Heck
Brow

Cote
Bottom

Hargarth
Farm

Forelands
Rigg

Barker

Bishopdale

B6160

Millbeck
Springs

85

Odlin Holes
Wood

Howsyke

East Lane
House

Newbiggin
Pasture

7

Faw
Wood

West Lane
House

Burton
Pasture

Dale
Foot

Dalefoot
Plantation

Wasset Fell
End

84

Scar
Top

Waterfall

Floutgate
Scar

The
Rookery

BISHOPDALE LANE

Wasset Fell
Edge

White
Scar

Whiterow
Farm

6

New
House

New
Bridge

Wasset
Fell

Cross
Farm

Cowstone
Gill House

Low Pur
Plantation

Ribba
Hall

Newhouse
Gill Pasture

Lady Wasset
Well

Whiterow
Plantation

Langrigg

Myers
Garth

Haw
Farm

Hargill
Farm

83

Skell Gill
Plantation

Smelter

Mile
Stone Hill

Cowstone
Gill Bottom

Walden Beck

Walden

Dove
Scar

5

B6160

DL8

Dewersit
Well

Wildgath
End

Bridge
End Farm

Low
Dovescar

Dovescar
Moss

Smelter
Plantation

Bishopdale
Edge

Bunkhouse
Barn

Hill Top
Farm

Ashes

82

Naughtberry
Hill

Petticoat
Rake

4

Waterfall

Routengil

Waterfall

Little
Fell Pot

Tomlin Haw
Tip (dis)

81

Fairy Scar

Waterfall

Waterfall
Walden
Head

TEMPLE LANE

Great
Fell Pot

Braidley
Moor

3

West Pasture
Scar

Waterfall

Kentucky
House

Grange
Farm

Precious Hull
Tip (dis)

Cranshaw
Ridge

Crag
Brea

80

White Moor

Greens
End

Waterfall

Brown
Haw

Woodale
Moor

Waterfall

Fall Gill

Fow Mere
Hill

Deepdale
Scar

Deepdale Gill

Green Haw
Well (spr)

Waterfall

2

Deepdale
Head

Walden Moor

West Gill

Waterfall

Fell
Bottom Rigg

Waterfall

Waterfall

79

Fosse
Gill Pike

Waterfall

Grove
End

Flat
Moss

Cover
Bridge

River Cover

Buckden
Pike

Raven
Scar

Cover Head
Bents

Coverhead
Farm

1

North
Moor

78

96   A   97   B   98   C   99   D   00   E   01   F

Throsly Gill

WHITEROW ROAD

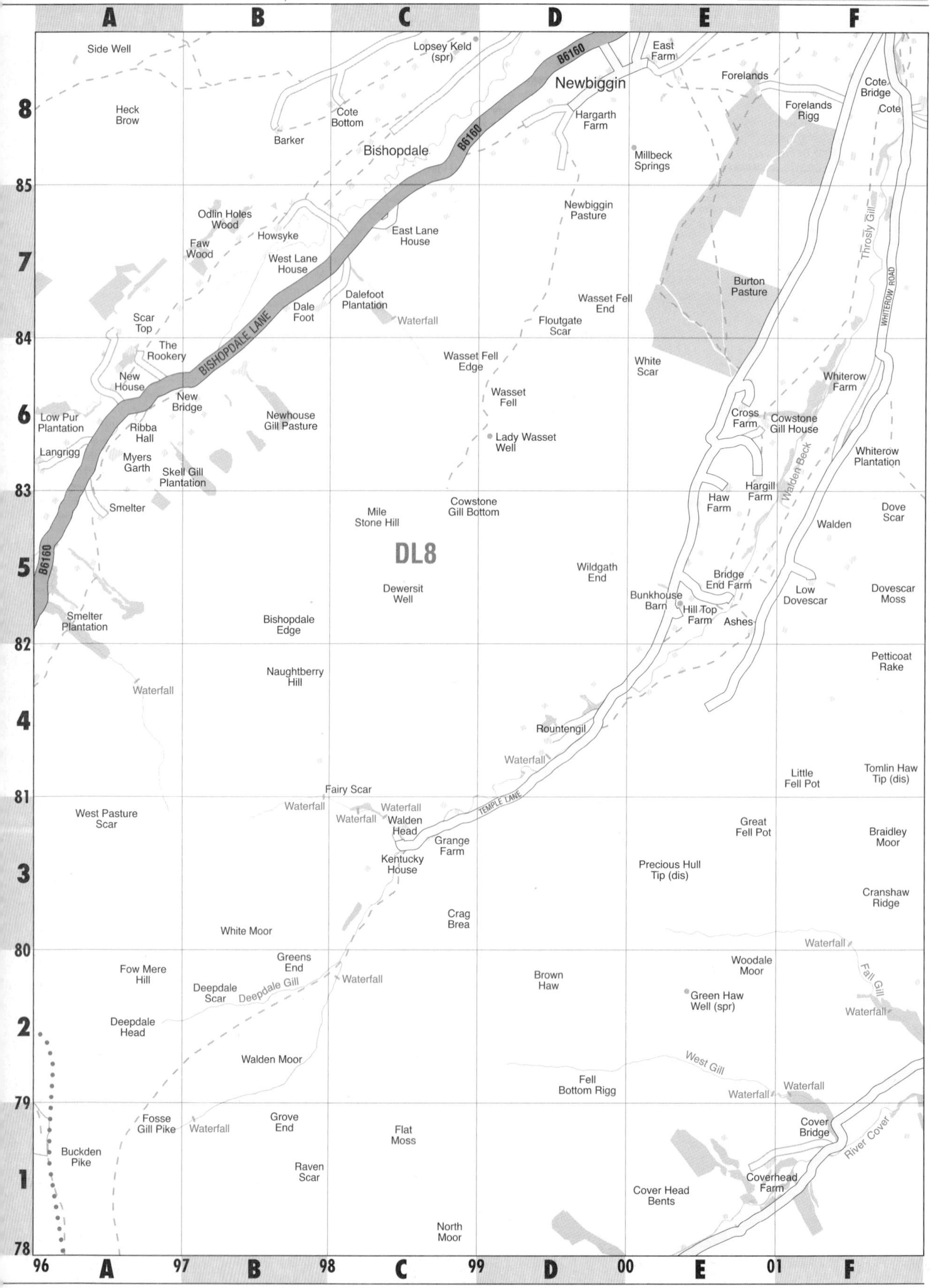

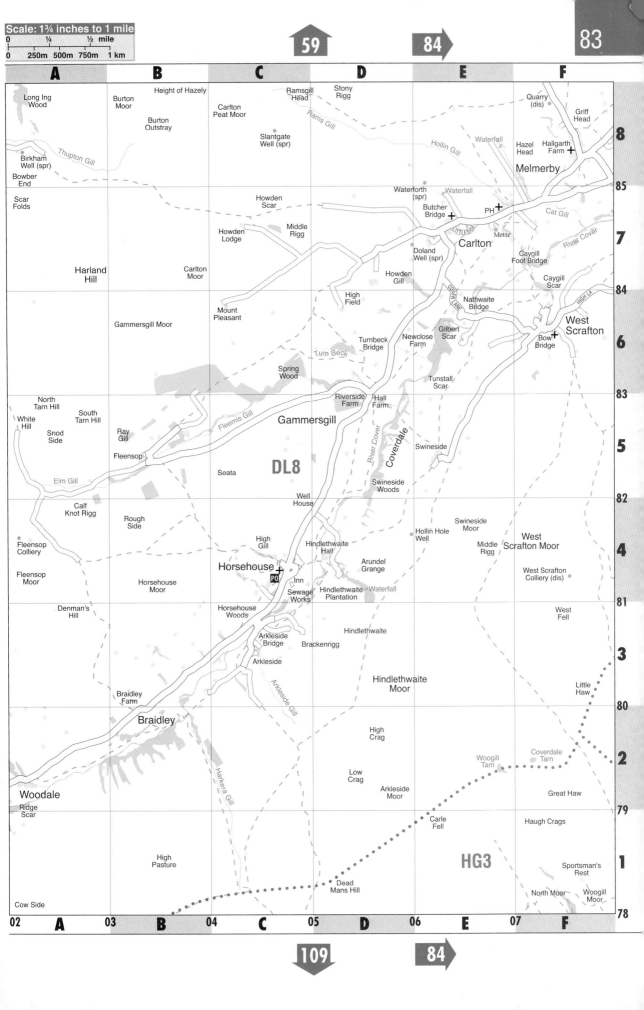

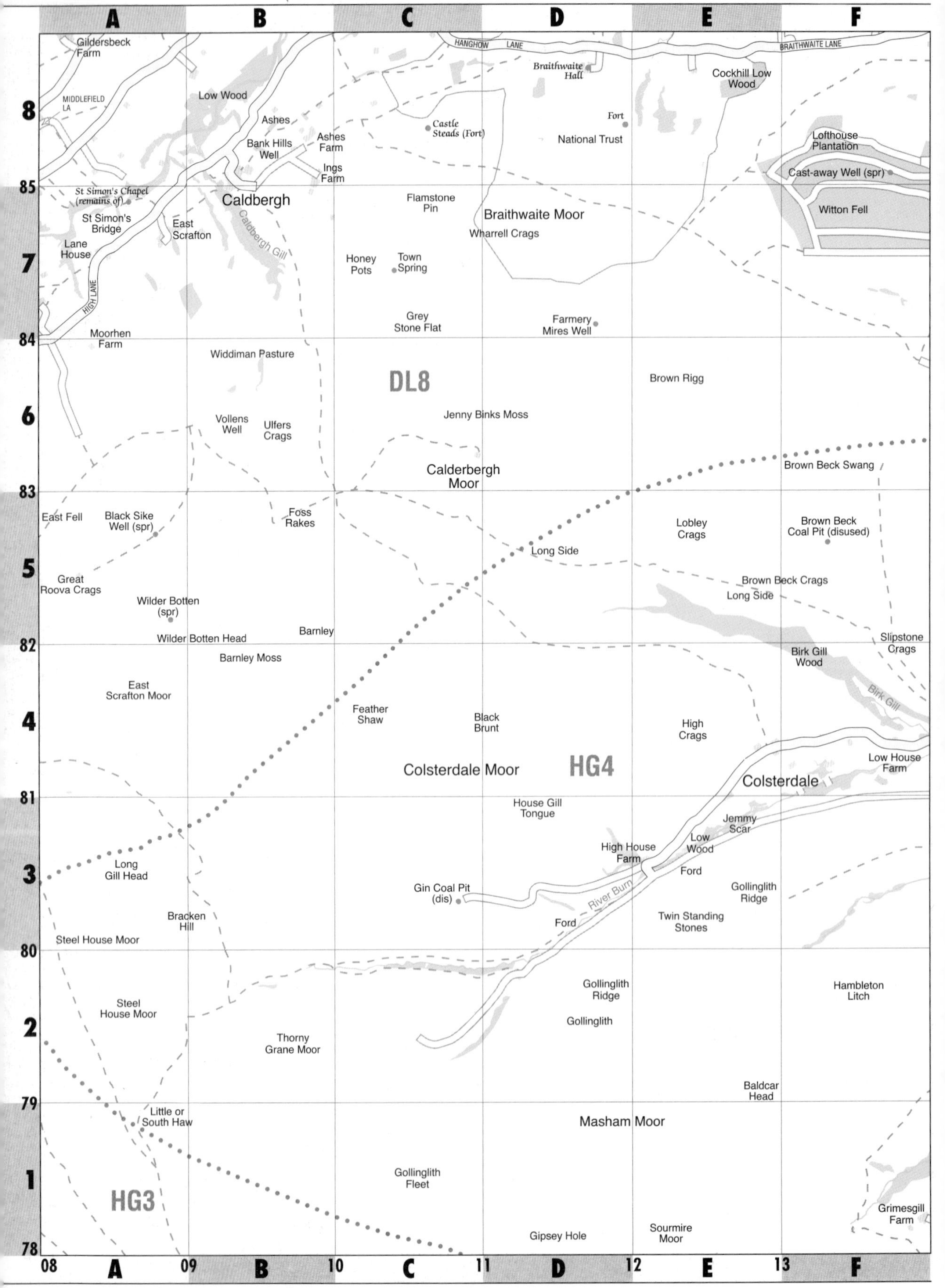

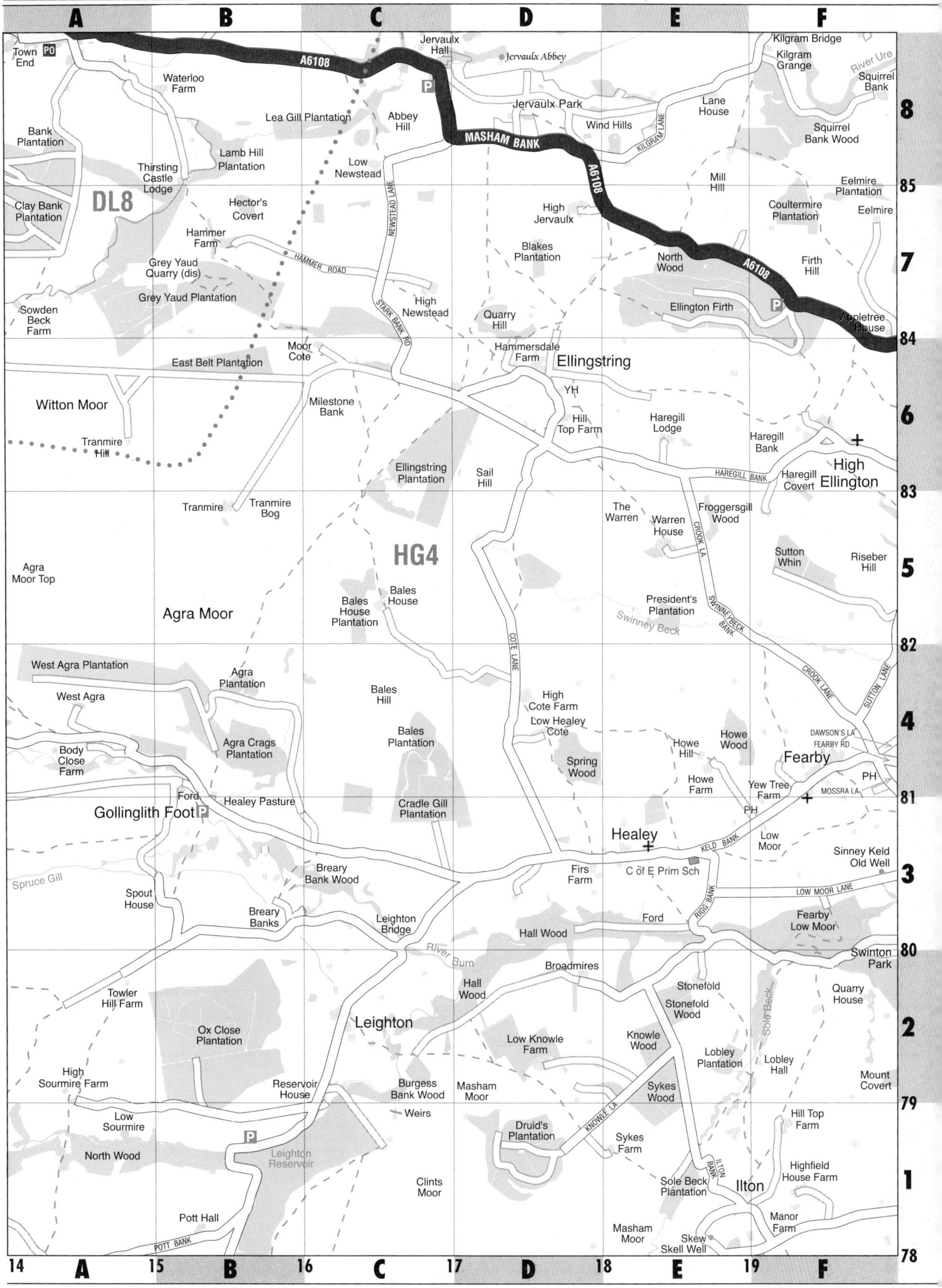

Scale: 1¾ inches to 1 mile

0   ¼   ½   mile
0   250m 500m 750m 1 km

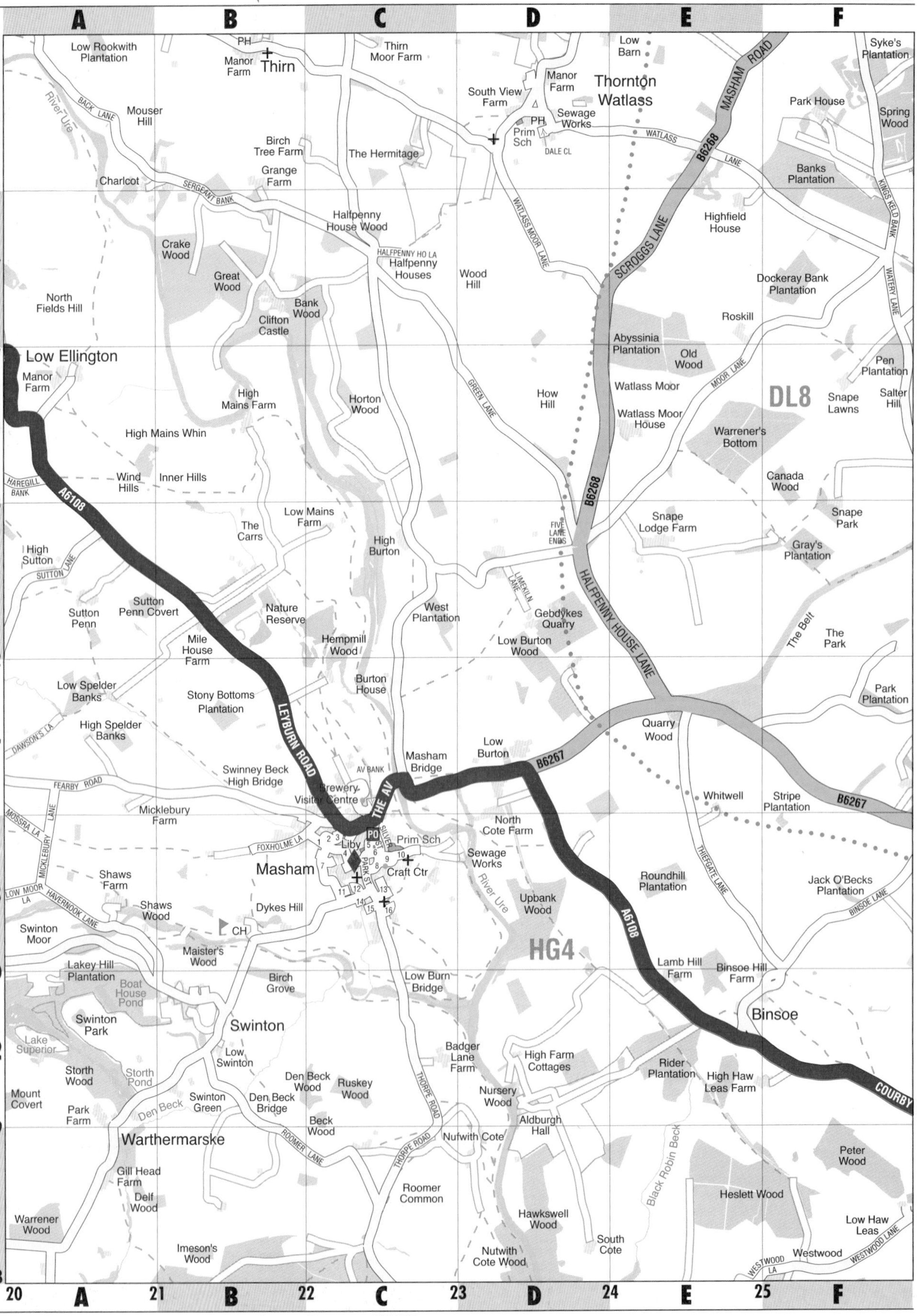

Grid columns: A B C D E F
Grid rows: 8 85 7 84 6 83 5 82 4 81 3 80 2 1 78
Bottom scale: 20 A 21 B 22 C 23 D 24 E 25 F

Low Rookwith Plantation
Manor Farm
PH
Thirn
Thirn Moor Farm
Low Barn
Thornton Watlass
Manor Farm
South View Farm
PH
Prim Sch
DALE CL.
Sewage Works
MASHAM ROAD
Syke's Plantation
Park House
Spring Wood
Mouser Hill
BACK LANE
River Ure
Charlcot
Birch Tree Farm
Grange Farm
The Hermitage
SERGEANT BANK
WATLASS LANE
B6268
Banks Plantation
Highfield House
KINGS KELD BANK
Crake Wood
Great Wood
Halfpenny House Wood
HALFPENNY HO LA
Halfpenny Houses
Wood Hill
WATLASS MOOR LANE
SCROGGS LANE
Dockeray Bank Plantation
Roskill
WATERY LANE
North Fields Hill
Clifton Castle
Bank Wood
Abyssinia Plantation
Old Wood
Watlass Moor
MOOR LANE
DL8
Snape Lawns
Pen Plantation
Salter Hill
Low Ellington
Manor Farm
High Mains Farm
Horton Wood
GREEN LANE
How Hill
Watlass Moor House
Warrener's Bottom
Canada Wood
HAREGILL BANK
A6108
High Mains Whin
Wind Hills
Inner Hills
The Carrs
Low Mains Farm
High Burton
FIVE LANE ENDS
B6268
Snape Lodge Farm
Snape Park
The Belt
Gray's Plantation
The Park
High Sutton
SUTTON LANE
Sutton Penn
Sutton Penn Covert
Nature Reserve
Hempmill Wood
West Plantation
LIME KILN LANE
Gebdykes Quarry
Low Burton Wood
HALFPENNY HOUSE LANE
DAWSON'S LA
Low Spelder Banks
High Spelder Banks
Mile House Farm
Stony Bottoms Plantation
Burton House
Quarry Wood
Park Plantation
FEARBY ROAD
MOSSRA LA
Swinney Beck High Bridge
LEYBURN ROAD
AV BANK
Masham Bridge
Low Burton
B6267
Whitwell
Stripe Plantation
B6267
Micklebury Farm
THE AV
Brewery Visitor Centre
North Cote Farm
THEEGATE LANE
MICKLEBURY LA
FOXHOLME LA
PO
Prim Sch
Sewage Works
LOW MOOR LA
HAVERNOOK LANE
Shaws Farm
Masham
Craft Ctr
River Ure
Roundhill Plantation
BINSOE LANE
Jack O'Becks Plantation
Shaws Wood
Dykes Hill
CH
Upbank Wood
A6108
Swinton Moor
Maister's Wood
Birch Grove
Low Burn Bridge
HG4
Lamb Hill Farm
Binsoe Hill Farm
Lakey Hill Plantation
Boat House Pond
Swinton Park
Lake Superior
Storth Wood
Storth Pond
Low Swinton
Swinton
Den Beck Wood
Ruskey Wood
THORPE ROAD
Badger Lane Farm
High Farm Cottages
Rider Plantation
Binsoe
High Haw Leas Farm
COURBY
Mount Covert
Park Farm
Swinton Green
Den Beck Bridge
DEN Beck
ROOMER LANE
Beck Wood
Nutwith Cote
Aldburgh Hall
Nursery Wood
Warthermarske
Gill Head Farm
Delf Wood
Imeson's Wood
Roomer Common
Nutwith Cote Wood
Hawkswell Wood
South Cote
Black Robin Beck
Heslett Wood
Peter Wood
Warrener Wood
WESTWOOD LA
Low Haw Leas
Westwood
WESTWOOD LANE

C3
1 WESTHOLME RD
2 WESTHOLME CR
3 WESTHOLME CT
4 RED LA
5 COLLEGE LA
6 CHURCH ST
7 THE OAKS
8 CHAPMAN LA
9 MARKET PL
10 MILLGATE
11 SWINBURN RD
12 SWINBURN CT
13 PARK DR
14 FISHER ROW
15 RODNEY TR
16 IBBETSON CL

Scale: 1¾ inches to 1 mile

63
88

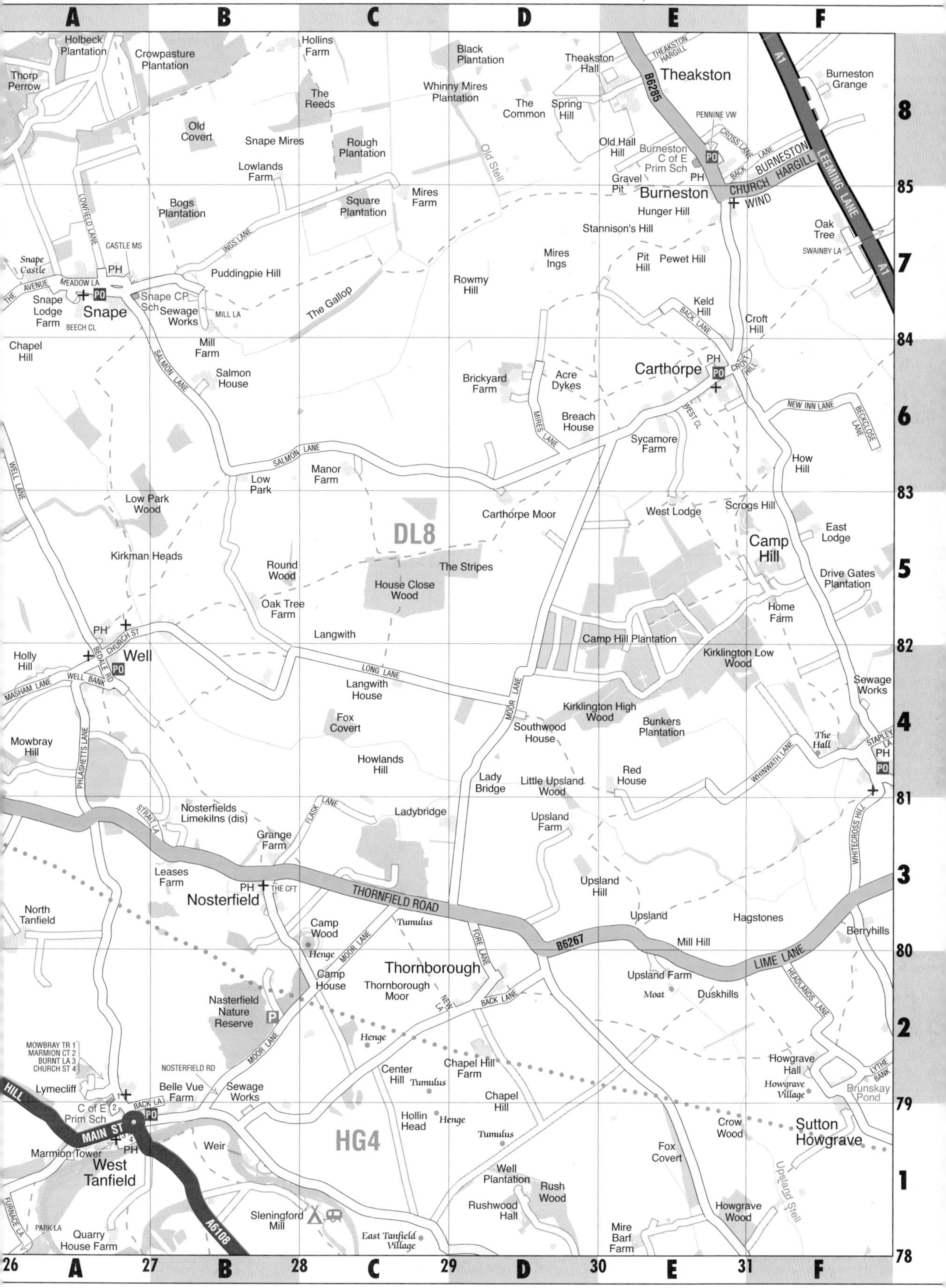
Holbeck Plantation
Thorp Perrow
Crowpasture Plantation
Hollins Farm
Black Plantation
Whinny Mires Plantation
Theakston Hall
Theakston
Burneston Grange
The Reeds
The Common
Spring Hill
Old Covert
Snape Mires
Rough Plantation
Old Hall Hill
Burneston C of E Prim Sch
Lowlands Farm
Gravel Pit
Burneston
Bogs Plantation
Square Plantation
Mires Farm
Hunger Hill
Stannison's Hill
Oak Tree
Snape Castle
Puddingpie Hill
Mires Ings
Pit Hill
Pewet Hill
Snape Lodge Farm
Snape
Snape CP Sch
Sewage Works
The Gallop
Rowmy Hill
Keld Hill
Croft Hill
Chapel Hill
Mill Farm
Salmon House
Brickyard Farm
Acre Dykes
Carthorpe
Breach House
Sycamore Farm
How Hill
Low Park
Manor Farm
Low Park Wood
Carthorpe Moor
West Lodge
Scrogs Hill
East Lodge
DL8
Camp Hill
Kirkman Heads
Round Wood
The Stripes
House Close Wood
Drive Gates Plantation
Oak Tree Farm
Home Farm
Langwith
Camp Hill Plantation
Holly Hill
Well
Kirklington Low Wood
Langwith House
Sewage Works
Fox Covert
Kirklington High Wood
Southwood House
Bunkers Plantation
Mowbray Hill
The Hall
Howlands Hill
Lady Bridge
Little Upsland Wood
Red House
Nosterfields Limekilns (dis)
Ladybridge
Upsland Farm
Grange Farm
Leases Farm
Nosterfield
Upsland Hill
North Tanfield
Camp Wood
Tumulus
Upsland
Hagstones
Berryhills
Mill Hill
Henge
Thornborough
Camp House
Upsland Farm
Thornborough Moor
Moat
Duskhills
Nasterfield Nature Reserve
Henge
Howgrave Hall
Center Hill
Chapel Hill Farm
Howgrave Village
Lymecliff
Belle Vue Farm
Sewage Works
Tumulus
Brunskay Pond
C of E Prim Sch
Chapel Hill
Hollin Head
Henge
Crow Wood
Sutton Howgrave
Marmion Tower
Weir
HG4
Tumulus
West Tanfield
Fox Covert
Upsland Stell
Well Plantation
Rush Wood
Rushwood Hall
Howgrave Wood
Sleningford Mill
Quarry House Farm
East Tanfield Village
Mire Barf Farm
Old Stell
THEAKSTON HARGILL
B6285
PENNINE VW
CROSS LANE
BACK LANE
BURNESTON
CHURCH HARGILL
WIND
A1
LEEMING LANE
SWAINBY LA
LOWFIELD LANE
CASTLE MS
INGS LANE
THE AVENUE
MEADOW LA
BEECH CL
MILL LA
BACK LANE
CROFT HILL
SALMON LANE
WEST CL
NEW INN LANE
BECKCLOSE LANE
MIRES LANE
WELL LANE
CHURCH ST
BEDALE RD
WELL BANK
MASHAM LANE
LONG LANE
MOOR LANE
PHLASHETTS LANE
STAPLEY LA
WHINWATH LANE
STRAIT LA
FLASK LANE
WHITECROSS HILL
THE CFT
THORNFIELD ROAD
B6267
LIME LANE
FORE LANE
MOOR LANE
HEADLANDS LANE
NEW LA
BACK LANE
MOOR LANE
MOWBRAY TR
MARMION CT
BURNT LA
CHURCH ST
NOSTERFIELD RD
LYTHE BANK
HILL
BACK LA
MAIN ST
A6108
FURNACE LA
PARK LA
A
B
C
D
E
F
8
85
7
84
6
83
5
82
4
81
3
80
2
79
1
78
26
27
28
29
30
31

113
88

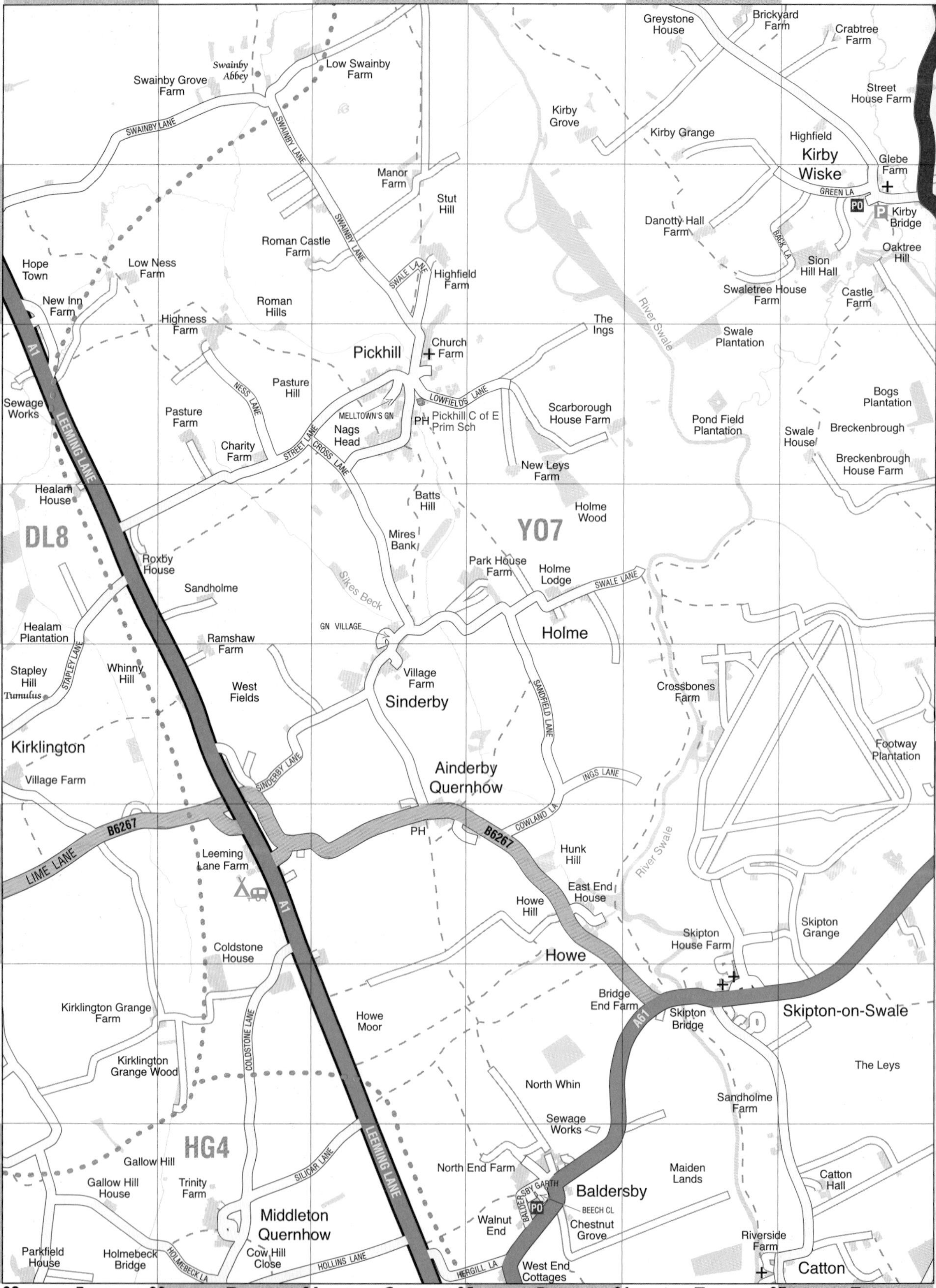

Scale: 1¾ inches to 1 mile

0   ¼   ½ mile
0   250m 500m 750m 1 km

A   B   C   D   E   F

8

Greystone House
Brickyard Farm
Crabtree Farm

Swainby Abbey
Low Swainby Farm
Kirby Grove
Street House Farm

85

Swainby Grove Farm
Swainby Lane
Kirby Grange
Highfield
Kirby Wiske
Glebe Farm
Green La
PO
P
Kirby Bridge

Manor Farm
Stut Hill

7

Hope Town
Low Ness Farm
Roman Castle Farm
Swainby Lane
Danotty Hall Farm
Sion Hill Hall
Oaktree Hill

New Inn Farm
Roman Hills
Swale La
Highfield Farm
Swaletree House Farm
Castle Farm

84

Highness Farm
A1
Leeming Lane
Pasture Hill
Ness Lane
Pickhill
Church Farm
The Ings
River Swale
Swale Plantation
Bogs Plantation

6

Sewage Works
Pasture Farm
Charity Farm
Street Lane
Cross Lane
Nags Head
Melltown's Gn
PH
Pickhill C of E Prim Sch
Lowfields Lane
Scarborough House Farm
Pond Field Plantation
Breckenbrough
Swale House
Breckenbrough House Farm

83

Healam House
DL8
Roxby House
Sandholme
Batts Hill
YO7
Holme Wood

5

Healam Plantation
Ramshaw Farm
Mires Bank
Sikes Beck
Park House Farm
Holme Lodge
Swale Lane
Holme

82

Stapley Hill
Tumulus
Whinny Hill
GN VILLAGE
Crossbones Farm

4

Kirklington
Stapley Lane
West Fields
Village Farm
Sinderby
Ainderby Quernhow
Sandfield Lane
Ings Lane
Footway Plantation

Village Farm
Sinderby Lane
A1

81

B6267
Lime Lane
Leeming Lane Farm
PH
B6267
Cowland La
River Swale

3

Coldstone House
Hunk Hill
East End House
Skipton Grange

80

Howe Hill
Howe
Bridge End Farm
Skipton House Farm
A61
Skipton Bridge
Skipton-on-Swale

2

Kirklington Grange Farm
Coldstone Lane
Howe Moor
North Whin
The Leys

Kirklington Grange Wood
Sandholme Farm

79

HG4
Gallow Hill
Silican Lane
Sewage Works
Maiden Lands
Catton Hall

1

Gallow Hill House
Trinity Farm
Leeming Lane
North End Farm
Baldersby Garth
PO
Baldersby
Chestnut Grove
Beech Cl
Maiden Lands
Riverside Farm

Parkfield House
Holmebeck Bridge
Holmebeck La
Middleton Quernhow
Cow Hill Close
Hollins Lane
Hergill La
Walnut End
West End Cottages
Catton

78

32   A   33   B   34   C   35   D   36   E   37   F

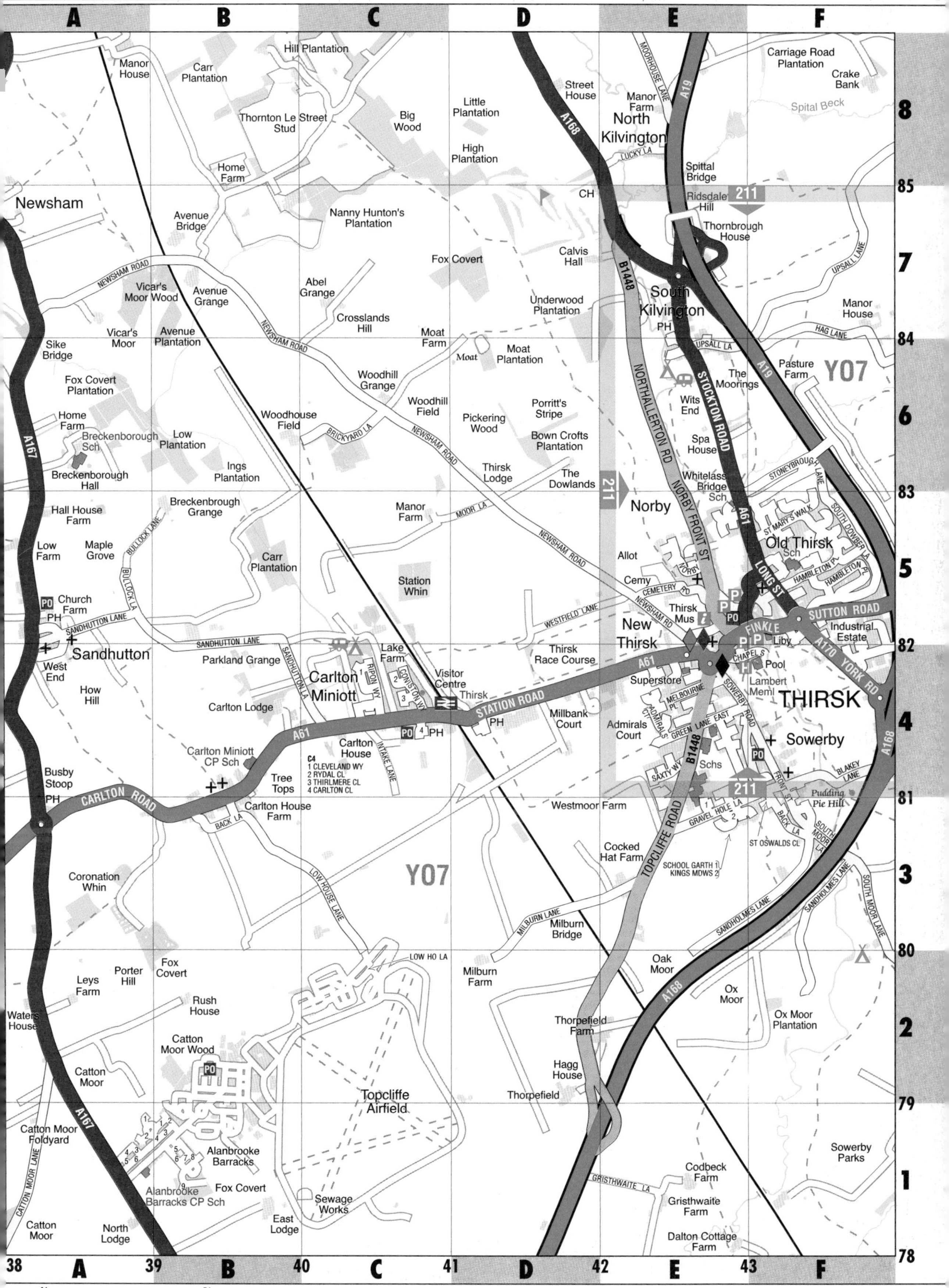
A B C D E F
8 85 7 84 6 83 5 82 4 81 3 80 2 79 1 78
38 39 40 41 42 43
Manor House
Carr Plantation
Hill Plantation
Thornton Le Street Stud
Big Wood
Little Plantation
High Plantation
Street House
Manor Farm
North Kilvington
MOORHOUSE LANE
LUCKY LA
A19
A168
Carriage Road Plantation
Crake Bank
Spital Beck
Spittal Bridge
Ridsdale Hill
211
Thornbrough House
Home Farm
Newsham
Avenue Bridge
Nanny Hunton's Plantation
CH
Calvis Hall
Fox Covert
NEWSHAM ROAD
Vicar's Moor Wood
Avenue Grange
Abel Grange
Crosslands Hill
Underwood Plantation
B1448
South Kilvington
PH
UPSALL LANE
Manor House
HAG LANE
Sike Bridge
Vicar's Moor
Avenue Plantation
Moat Farm
Moat
Moat Plantation
UPSALL LA
STOCKTON ROAD
The Moorings
Pasture Farm
YO7
Fox Covert Plantation
Woodhill Grange
Woodhill Field
Wits End
NORTHALLERTON RD
Home Farm
Breckenborough Sch
Low Plantation
Woodhouse Field
BRICKYARD LA
Pickering Wood
Porritt's Stripe
Bown Crofts Plantation
Spa House
A167
Breckenborough Hall
Ings Plantation
Thirsk Lodge
The Dowlands
Whitelass Bridge
Sch
STONEYBROUGH LANE
NORBY FRONT ST
A61
Hall House Farm
Breckenbrough Grange
Manor Farm
MOOR LA
Norby
ST MARY'S WALK
SOUTH DOWBER LA
Old Thirsk
Sch
Low Farm
Maple Grove
BULLOCK LANE
Carr Plantation
Station Whin
Allot
NORBY
LONG ST
HAMBLETON PL
Cemy
CEMETERY RD
Church Farm
PO
PH
SANDHUTTON LANE
Sandhutton
WESTFIELD LANE
Thirsk Mus
New Thirsk
SUTTON ROAD
Industrial Estate
FINKLE
Liby
A170 YORK RD
West End
Parkland Grange
SANDHUTTON LA
Lake Farm
RIPON WY
CONISTON WY
Carlton Miniott
Visitor Centre
Thirsk
STATION ROAD
Thirsk Race Course
CHAPEL S
Pool
Superstore
Lambert Meml
THIRSK
How Hill
Carlton Lodge
MELBOURNE PL
Millbank Court
Admirals Court
ADMIRALS CT
GREEN LANE EAST
SOWERBY ROAD
Sowerby
Carlton Miniott CP Sch
Carlton House
INTAKE LANE
C4
1 CLEVELAND WY
2 RYDAL CL
3 THIRLMERE CL
4 CARLTON CL
Schs
SAXTY WY
Busby Stoop
CARLTON ROAD
Tree Tops
Carlton House Farm
BACK LA
Westmoor Farm
GRAVEL HOLE LA
FRONT ST
BLAKEY LANE
Pudding Pie Hill
BACK LA
SOUTH MOOR LA
ST OSWALDS CL
Cocked Hat Farm
TOPCLIFFE ROAD
SCHOOL GARTH 1
KINGS MDWS 2
Coronation Whin
YO7
LOW HOUSE LANE
MILBURN LANE
Milburn Bridge
SANDHOLMES LANE
SOUTH MOOR LANE
LOW HO LA
Oak Moor
Fox Covert
Porter Hill
Leys Farm
Milburn Farm
Ox Moor
Ox Moor Plantation
Waters House
Rush House
Thorpefield Farm
Catton Moor Wood
Catton Moor
Hagg House
Thorpefield
Topcliffe Airfield
Catton Moor Foldyard
Alanbrooke Barracks
Sowerby Parks
Codbeck Farm
CATTON MOOR LANE
GRISTHWAITE LA
Alanbrooke Barracks CP Sch
Fox Covert
Sewage Works
Gristhwaite Farm
Catton Moor
North Lodge
East Lodge
Dalton Cottage Farm

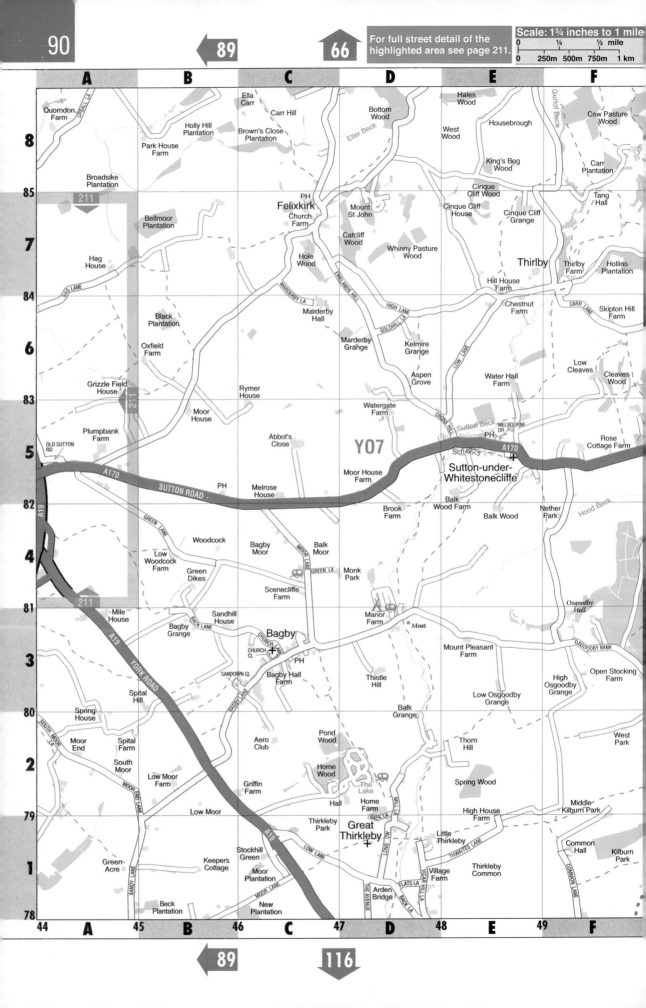

90

89

66

For full street detail of the highlighted area see page 211.

Scale: 1¾ inches to 1 mile
0   ¼   ½   mile
0 250m 500m 750m 1 km

A **B** **C** **D** **E** **F**

8

Quorndon Farm

Ella Carr

Carr Hill

Bottom Wood

Hales Wood

West Wood

Housebrough

Cow Pasture Wood

Holly Hill Plantation

Brown's Close Plantation

Eller Beck

King's Bog Wood

Carr Plantation

Park House Farm

Broadsike Plantation

85

Bellmoor Plantation

Felixkirk

Church Farm

Mount St John

Catcliff Wood

Cinque Cliff Wood

Cinque Cliff House

Cinque Cliff Grange

Tang Hall

7

Hag House

PH

Hole Wood

Whinny Pasture Wood

Thirlby

Thirlby Farm

Hollins Plantation

84

Black Plantation

MARDERBY LA

Marderby Hall

ENGLANDS HILL

HIGH LANE

Hill House Farm

Chestnut Farm

CARR LANE

Skipton Hill Farm

6

Oxfield Farm

Marderby Grange

GOLDHILL LA

Kelmire Grange

LOW LANE

Water Hall Farm

Low Cleaves

Cleaves Wood

Grizzle Field House

Rymer House

Aspen Grove

83

Plumpbank Farm

Moor House

Watergate Farm

CROSS HILL

Sutton Beck

Melbourne DR

PH

Rose Cottage Farm

5

OLD SUTTON RD

A170

Abbot's Close

Y07

Moor House Farm

Sch

Sutton-under-Whitestonecliffe

A170

82

A19

SUTTON ROAD

PH

Melrose House

Brook Farm

Balk Wood Farm

Balk Wood

Nether Park

Hood Beck

GREEN LANE

Woodcock

Bagby Moor

Balk Moor

4

Low Woodcock Farm

Green Dikes

Scenecliffe Farm

GREEN LA

Monk Park

Osgoodby Hall

81

Mile House

Sandhill House

Manor Farm

Moat

OSGOODBY BANK

Bagby Grange

BACK LANE

Bagby

CHURCH LA

CL

PH

Mount Pleasant Farm

High Osgoodby Grange

Open Stocking Farm

3

SANDOWN CL

Bagby Hall Farm

Thistle Hill

Low Osgoodby Grange

Spital Hill

BAGBY LANE

Balk Grange

80

Spring House

SOUTH MOOR LA

Moor End

Spital Farm

Aero Club

Pond Wood

Thorn Hill

West Park

2

YORK ROAD

MOOR END LANE

South Moor

Low Moor Farm

Griffin Farm

Home Wood

The Lake

Spring Wood

Middle Kilburn Park

Low Moor

Hall

Home Farm

MILL LA

High House Farm

79

A19

Thirkleby Park

Great Thirkleby

Little Thirkleby

THWAITES LANE

Common Hall

1

SANDY LANE

Green Acre

Keepers Cottage

Stockhill Green

Moor Plantation

LOW LANE

A19

B1378

Village Farm

VICAR HILL LA

Thirkleby Farm

Thirkleby Common

COMMON LANE

Kilburn Park

Beck Plantation

MOOR LANE

New Plantation

THE AVENUE

Arden Bridge

FLATS LA

BACK LA

78

44 **A** **45** **B** **46** **C** **47** **D** **48** **E** **49** **F**

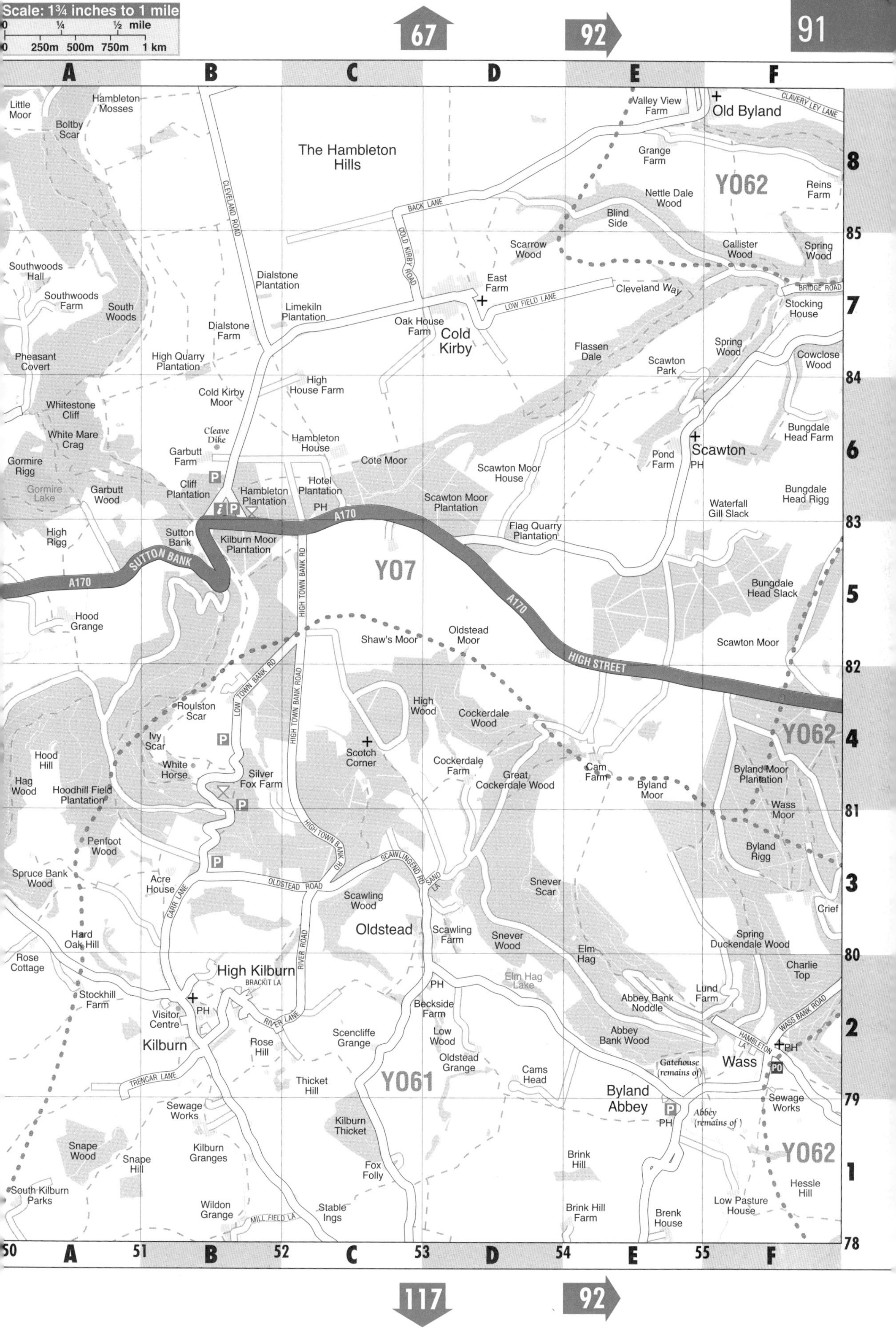
Scale: 1¾ inches to 1 mile
0 ¼ ½ mile
0 250m 500m 750m 1 km
67
92
A B C D E F
Little Moor
Hambleton Mosses
Boltby Scar
The Hambleton Hills
Valley View Farm
Old Byland
CLAVERY LEY LANE
Grange Farm
Y062
Reins Farm
Nettle Dale Wood
BACK LANE
CLEVELAND ROAD
Blind Side
OLD KIRBY ROAD
Scarrow Wood
Callister Wood
Spring Wood
Southwoods Hall
Dialstone Plantation
East Farm
Cleveland Way
BRIDGE ROAD
Southwoods Farm
South Woods
LOW FIELD LANE
Stocking House
Limekiln Plantation
Dialstone Farm
Oak House Farm
Cold Kirby
Flassen Dale
Spring Wood
Cowclose Wood
Pheasant Covert
High Quarry Plantation
Scawton Park
High House Farm
Cold Kirby Moor
Whitestone Cliff
Bungdale Head Farm
Cleave Dike
White Mare Crag
Hambleton House
Garbutt Farm
Pond Farm
Scawton
PH
Gormire Rigg
Cote Moor
Scawton Moor House
Gormire Lake
Garbutt Wood
Cliff Plantation
Hambleton Plantation
Hotel Plantation
Scawton Moor Plantation
Waterfall Gill Slack
Bungdale Head Rigg
PH
A170
High Rigg
Sutton Bank
Kilburn Moor Plantation
Flag Quarry Plantation
SUTTON BANK
Y07
HIGH TOWN BANK RD
Bungdale Head Slack
A170
A170
Hood Grange
Oldstead Moor
Shaw's Moor
Scawton Moor
HIGH STREET
LOW TOWN BANK RD
HIGH TOWN BANK ROAD
Roulston Scar
High Wood
Cockerdale Wood
Ivy Scar
Scotch Corner
Y062
Hood Hill
White Horse
Cockerdale Farm
Cam Farm
Byland Moor Plantation
Hag Wood
Hoodhill Field Plantation
Silver Fox Farm
Great Cockerdale Wood
Byland Moor
Wass Moor
HIGH TOWN BANK RD
Penfoot Wood
Byland Rigg
SCAWLINGEND RD
SAND LA
Spruce Bank Wood
Acre House
OLDSTEAD ROAD
Snever Scar
CARR LANE
Scawling Wood
Crief
Hard Oak Hill
Oldstead
Scawling Farm
Snever Wood
Elm Hag
Spring Duckendale Wood
Rose Cottage
RIVER ROAD
Charlie Top
High Kilburn
Elm Hag Lake
BRACKIT LA
PH
Stockhill Farm
PH
Beckside Farm
Abbey Bank Noddle
Lund Farm
WASS BANK ROAD
Visitor Centre
RIVER LANE
Low Wood
Abbey Bank Wood
HAMBLETON LA
PH
Kilburn
Rose Hill
Scencliffe Grange
Oldstead Grange
Gatehouse (remains of)
Wass
PO
TRENCAR LANE
Thicket Hill
Y061
Cams Head
Byland Abbey
Sewage Works
Sewage Works
PH
Abbey (remains of)
Kilburn Thicket
Snape Wood
Snape Hill
Kilburn Granges
Brink Hill
Y062
Fox Folly
South Kilburn Parks
Hessle Hill
Wildon Grange
Stable Ings
Brink Hill Farm
Low Pasture House
Brenk House
MILL FIELD LA
8
85
7
84
6
83
5
82
4
81
3
80
2
79
1
78
50 A 51 B 52 C 53 D 54 E 55 F
117
92

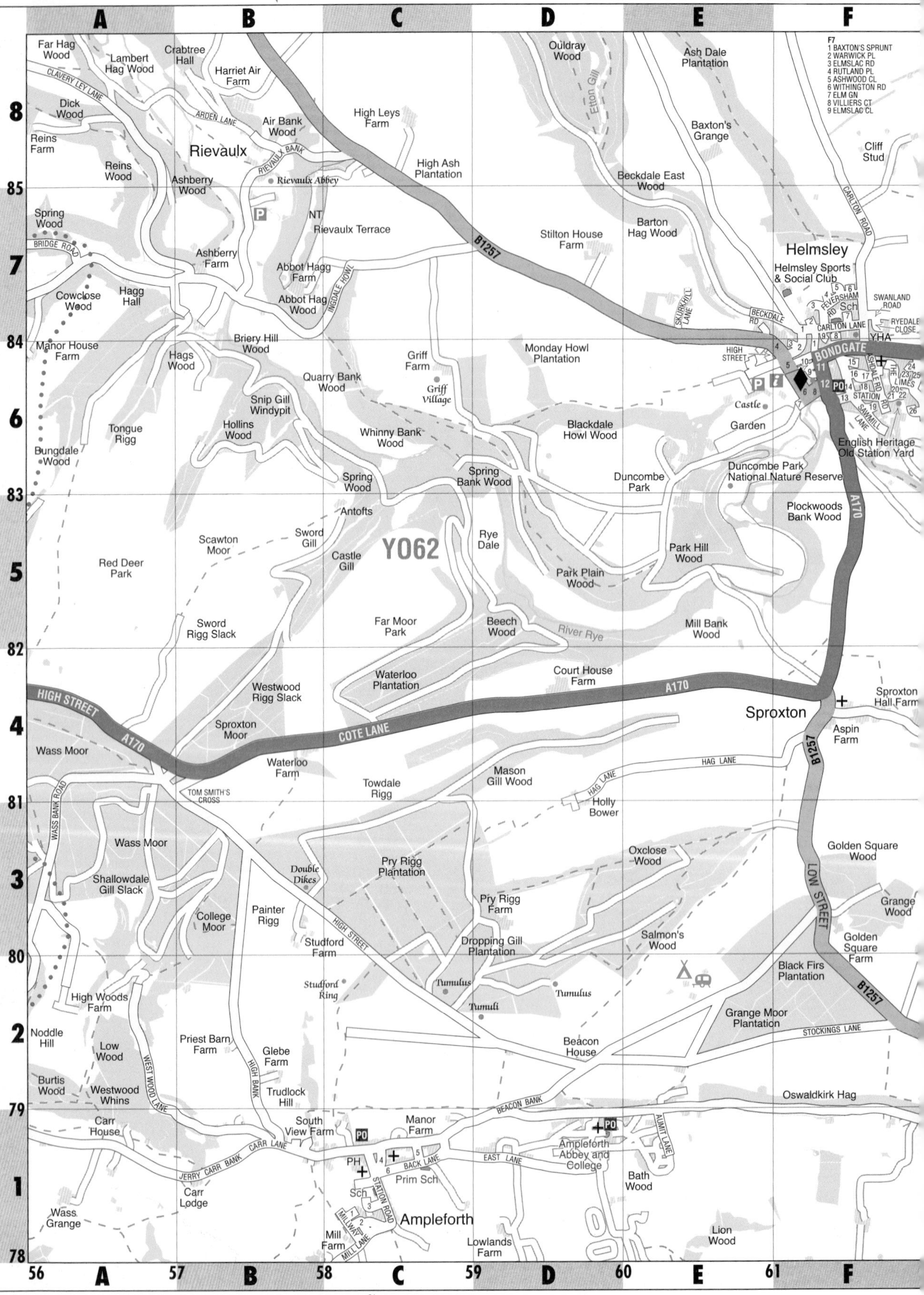

F6
1 ELMSLAC CL
2 CANONS GARTH LA
3 STONE GARTH
4 HIGH ST
5 CHURCH ST
6 CASTLEGATE

7 BUCKINGHAM SQ
8 BUCKINGHAM SQ
9 BOROGATE
10 MARKET PL
11 MARKET PL
12 BRIDGE ST
13 RYEGATE

14 POTTERGATE
15 BELL'S CT
16 EASTGATE
17 THE CR
18 SOUTH GATE
19 SOUTHLANDS
20 ALLENBY RD

21 CHAPEL CL
22 CROSLAND CL
23 CONOWL CL
24 ACRES CL
25 RICCAL DR
26 STOREY CL

Scale: 1¾ inches to 1 mile

0   ¼   ½   mile
0   250m 500m 750m 1 km

F7
1 BAXTON'S SPRUNT
2 WARWICK PL
3 ELMSLAC RD
4 RUTLAND PL
5 ASHWOOD CL
6 WITHINGTON RD
7 ELM GN
8 VILLIERS CT
9 ELMSLAC CL

Far Hag Wood
Lambert Hag Wood
Crabtree Hall
Harriet Air Farm
CLAVERY LEY LANE
ARDEN LANE
Dick Wood
Air Bank Wood
Rievaulx
High Leys Farm
Ouldray Wood
Ash Dale Plantation
Reins Farm
Reins Wood
Ashberry Wood
RIEVAULX BANK
Rievaulx Abbey
High Ash Plantation
Baxton's Grange
Beckdale East Wood
Cliff Stud
Helmsley
Spring Wood
BRIDGE ROAD
Ashberry Farm
P NT
Rievaulx Terrace
B1257
Stilton House Farm
Barton Hag Wood
Helmsley Sports & Social Club
CARLTON ROAD
Cowclose Wood
Hagg Hall
Abbot Hagg Farm
Abbot Hagg Wood
Monday Howl Plantation
SKURIGHILL LANE
BECKDALE RD
FEVERSHAM
SWANLAND ROAD
RYEDALE CLOSE
Manor House Farm
Briery Hill Wood
Hags Wood
INGDALE HOWL
Griff Farm
CARLTON LANE
HIGH STREET
BONDGATE
Snip Gill Windypit
Quarry Bank Wood
Griff Village
Blackdale Howl Wood
Castle Garden
English Heritage Old Station Yard
A170
Tongue Rigg
Hollins Wood
Whinny Bank Wood
Spring Bank Wood
Duncombe Park
Duncombe Park National Nature Reserve
Plockwoods Bank Wood
Bungdale Wood
Spring Wood
Antofts
YO62
Rye Dale
Park Plain Wood
Park Hill Wood
Red Deer Park
Scawton Moor
Sword Gill
Castle Gill
Beech Wood
River Rye
Mill Bank Wood
Sword Rigg Slack
Far Moor Park
Court House Farm
A170
Sproxton Hall Farm
HIGH STREET
A170
Westwood Rigg Slack
Waterloo Plantation
Sproxton
Aspin Farm
Wass Moor
Sproxton Moor
COTE LANE
Waterloo Farm
Mason Gill Wood
HAG LANE
HAG LANE
B1257
WASS BANK ROAD
TOM SMITH'S CROSS
Towdale Rigg
Holly Bower
Golden Square Wood
Wass Moor
Double Dikes
Pry Rigg Plantation
Oxclose Wood
LOW STREET
Grange Wood
Shallowdale Gill Slack
College Moor
Painter Rigg
HIGH STREET
Pry Rigg Farm
Salmon's Wood
Golden Square Wood
High Woods Farm
Studford Farm
Dropping Gill Plantation
Black Firs Plantation
B1257
Noddle Hill
Low Wood
Studford Ring
Tumulus
Tumulus
Tumulus
Grange Moor Plantation
STOCKINGS LANE
Burtis Wood
Priest Barn Farm
Glebe Farm
Tumuli
Beacon House
WEST WOOD LANE
HIGH BANK
Trudlock Hill
BEACON BANK
Oswaldkirk Hag
Westwood Whins
Carr House
South View Farm
PO
Manor Farm
PO
Ampleforth Abbey and College
AUMIT LANE
Carr Lodge
JERRY CARR BANK
CARR LANE
BACK LANE
PH
Sch
Prim Sch
EAST LANE
Bath Wood
Wass Grange
STATION ROAD
Ampleforth
Mill Farm
MILL LANE
Lowlands Farm
Lion Wood

C1
1 BIRDFORTH WY
2 FAIRFAX CL
3 VALLEY VW
4 OLD STATION RD
5 THE ORCHARD
6 ST HILDA'S WK

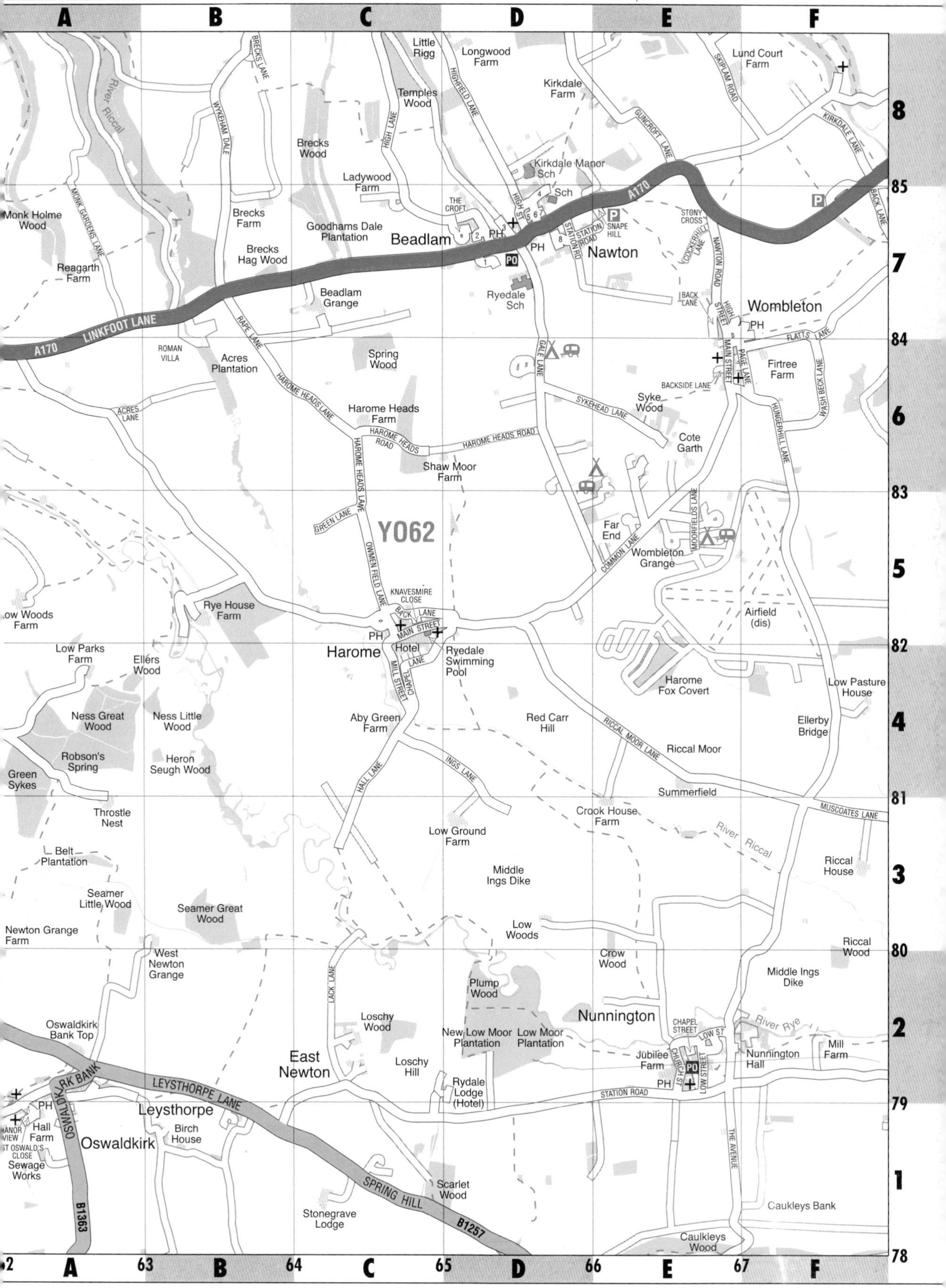

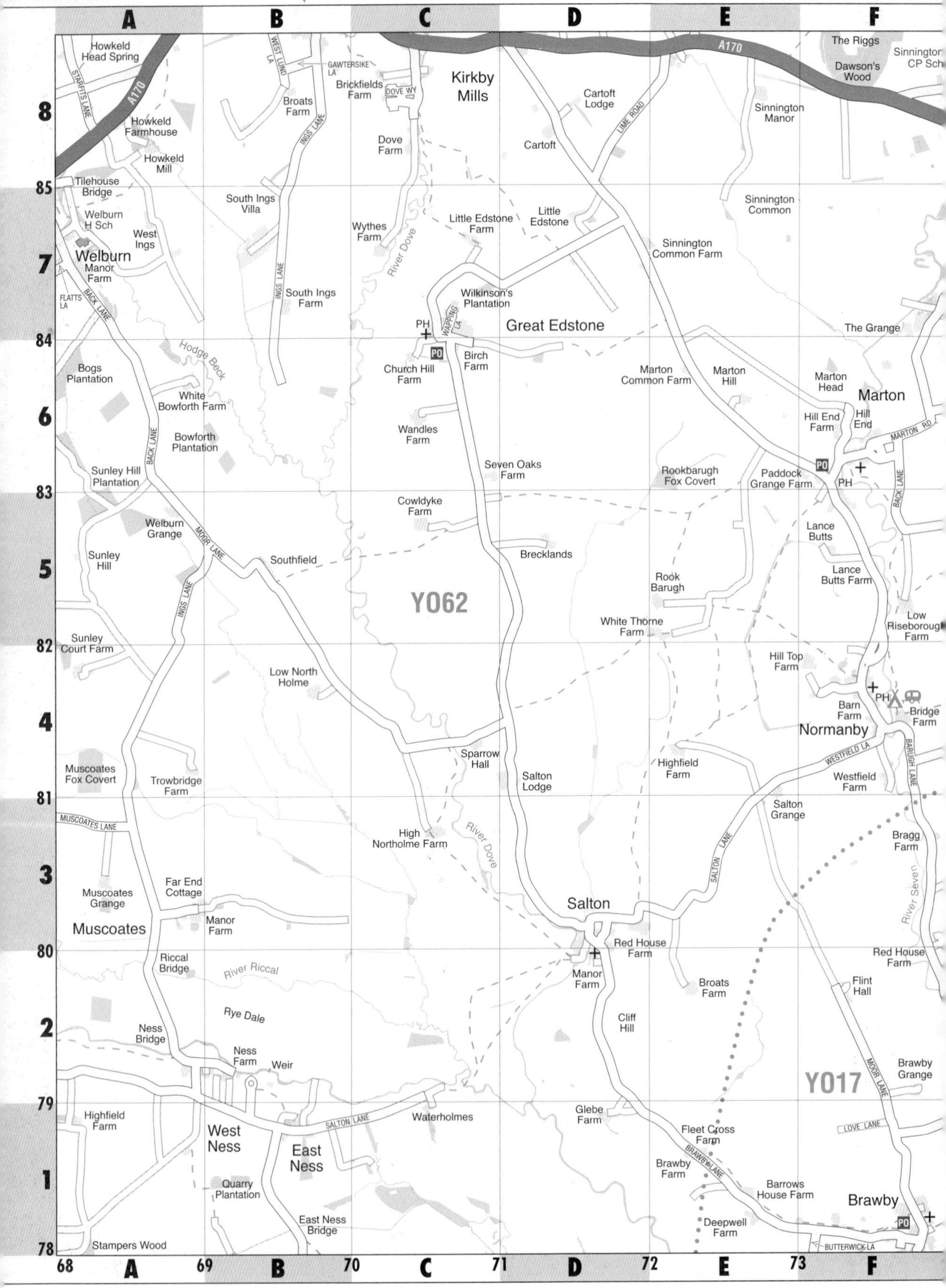

Scale: 1¾ inches to 1 mile

0   ¼   ½   mile
0   250m 500m 750m 1 km

A   B   C   D   E   F

The Riggs
Sinnington
CP Sch
Dawson's
Wood

Howkeld
Head Spring
A170

8

Broats
Farm
Gawtersike La
Brickfields
Farm
Dove Wy
Kirkby
Mills
Cartoft
Lodge
Sinnington
Manor

Howkeld
Farmhouse
Dove
Farm
Cartoft

Howkeld
Mill

Tilehouse
Bridge
South Ings
Villa
Wythes
Farm
River Dove
Little Edstone
Farm
Little
Edstone
Sinnington
Common

85

Welburn
H Sch
West
Ings
Sinnington
Common Farm

7

Welburn
Manor
Farm
South Ings
Farm
Wilkinson's
Plantation
Great Edstone
The Grange

Flatts
La
Back Lane
Hodge Beck
PH
Wapping La
Marton
Head
Marton

84

PO
Birch
Farm
Church Hill
Farm
Marton
Common Farm
Marton
Hill
Hill End
Farm
Hill
End

Bogs
Plantation
White
Bowforth Farm
Wandles
Farm
PO
PH

6

Bowforth
Plantation
Seven Oaks
Farm
Rookbarugh
Fox Covert
Paddock
Grange Farm
Back Lane
Marton Rd

Sunley Hill
Plantation
Cowldyke
Farm
Lance
Butts

83

Moor Lane
Southfield
Breaklands
Rook
Barugh
Lance
Butts Farm

Welburn
Grange
YO62

5

Sunley
Hill
White Thorne
Farm
Low
Riseborough
Farm

Ings Lane
Sunley
Court Farm
Low North
Holme
Hill Top
Farm

82

PH
Barn
Farm
Bridge
Farm

4

Muscoates
Fox Covert
Trowbridge
Farm
Sparrow
Hall
Highfield
Farm
Normanby
Westfield La
Westfield
Farm
Barugh Lane

Muscoates Lane
Salton
Lodge
Salton
Grange

81

High
Northolme Farm
River Dove
Bragg
Farm

3

Muscoates
Grange
Far End
Cottage
River Seven
Salton Lane

Muscoates
Manor
Farm
Salton
Red House
Farm
Red House
Farm

80

Riccal
Bridge
River Riccal
Manor
Farm
Flint
Hall
Moor Lane

Rye Dale
Broats
Farm
YO17

2

Ness
Bridge
Ness
Farm
Weir
Cliff
Hill
Brawby
Grange
Love Lane

Highfield
Farm
Salton Lane
Waterholmes
Glebe
Farm
Fleet Cross
Farm

79

West
Ness
East
Ness
Brawby
Lane
Brawby
Farm
Barrows
House Farm
Brawby

1

Quarry
Plantation
East Ness
Bridge
Deepwell
Farm
PO

Stampers Wood
Butterwick-La

78

68   A   69   B   70   C   71   D   72   E   73   F

F6
1 FIELD DR
2 PADDOCK CL
3 GARDEN WY
4 WESTERDALE
5 BRUCE WY
6 INGS CL
7 W PASTURE
8 PIKE RD
9 GOSLIPGATE
10 FISHERS GARTH
11 TROUTBECK CL
12 MALLARD CL
13 OTTER DR
14 KINGFISHER DR
15 MOLE END
16 WILLOW CT
17 RECREATION RD
18 KEEPERS GATE
19 SMIDDY HL
20 POOL CT
21 OUTGANG RD
22 CROSSGATE LA

71 96

F7
1 WESTERN WY
2 MEADOW RD
3 SWAINSEA DR
4 PIPERS ACRE
5 OLD FARM CL
6 TEAL LA
7 ANCHORITE LA
8 WESTBOURNE GR
9 SECOND AV
10 FIRST AV
11 POTTER HL
12 LAMBS LA
13 WELLS WK
14 TRAIN LA
15 THE ROPERY
16 BRIDGE ST
17 UNDER CLIFFE
18 CASTLE RD
19 CASTLEGATE
20 HERISSON CL
21 ROSAMUND AV
22 NORMAN CL
23 HATCASE LA
24 WILLOWGATE
25 HALL GARTH

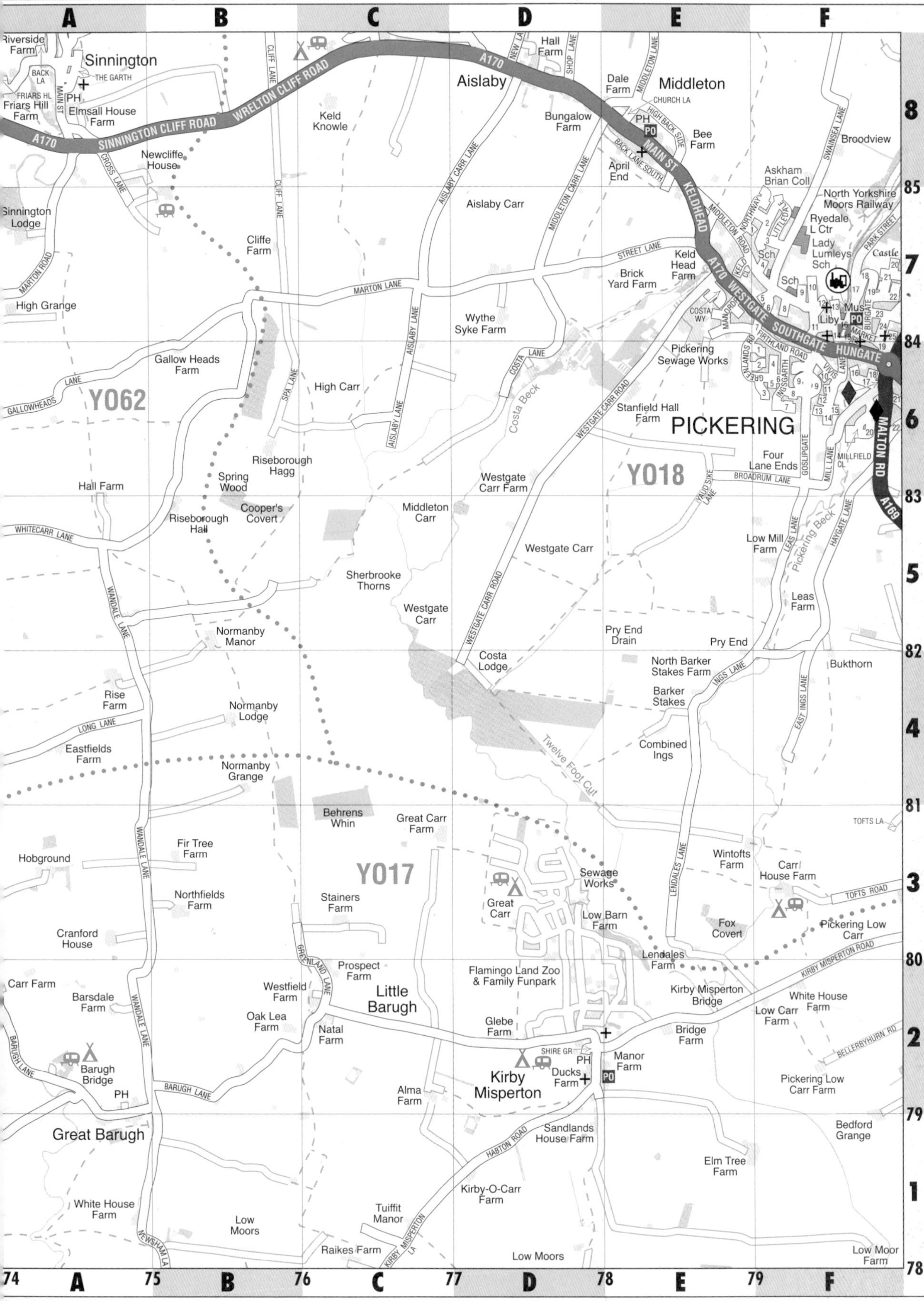

121 96

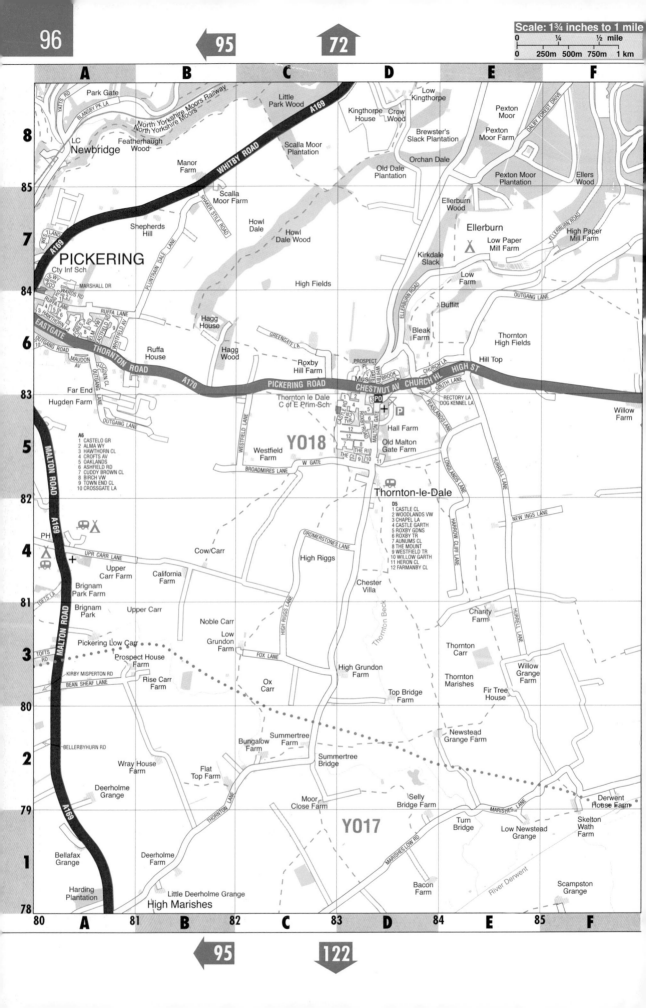

A   B   C   D   E   F

8

YATTS RD
Park Gate
BLANSBY PK. LA
North Yorkshire Moors Railway
North Yorkshire Moors
Little Park Wood
A169
WHITBY ROAD
Scalla Moor Plantation
Low Kingthorpe
Kingthorpe House
Crow Wood
Pexton Moor
LC
Newbridge
Featherhaugh Wood
Manor Farm
Brewster's Slack Plantation
Orchan Dale
Pexton Moor Farm
DALBY FOREST DRIVE

85

SHAKER STILE ROAD
Scalla Moor Farm
Old Dale Plantation
Ellerburn Wood
Pexton Moor Plantation
Ellers Wood

7

WESTLAND LA
A169
Shepherds Hill
PLUNTINGTON DALE LANE
Howl Dale
Howl Dale Wood
Ellerburn
Low Paper Mill Farm
Kirkdale Slack
High Paper Mill Farm
ELLERBURN ROAD

PICKERING
Cty Inf Sch

84

PK WY
WARDS RD
MARSHALL DR
High Fields
Low Farm

ELLERBURN ROAD
RUFFA LANE
HAWTHORN CL
RUFFA LANE
WHITFIELD AV
Hagg House
Buffitt
Thornton High Fields

6

EASTGATE
OUTGANG ROAD
MAUDON AV
Ruffa House
THORNTON ROAD
A170
Hagg Wood
GREENGATE LA
Roxby Hill Farm
PROSPECT PL
Bleak Farm
Hill Top

OUTGANG LANE
Far End
Hugden Farm
OUTGANG LANE
PICKERING ROAD
CHESTNUT AV
CHURCH HL
HIGH ST
Mus
Willow Farm

83

MALTON ROAD
A169
A6
1 CASTELO GR
2 ALMA WY
3 HAWTHORN CL
4 CROFTS AV
5 OAKLANDS
6 ASHFIELD RD
7 CUDDY BROWN CL
8 BIRCH VW
9 TOWN END CL
10 CROSSGATE LA
Thornton le Dale
C of E Prim Sch
WESTFIELD LANE
Hall Farm
RECTORY LA
DOG KENNEL LA

5

Westfield Farm
YO18
Old Malton Gate Farm
HURRELL LANE

BROADMIRES LANE
W GATE
THE RI
THE CL
Thornton-le-Dale

82

D5
1 CASTLE CL
2 WOODLANDS VW
3 CHAPEL LA
4 CASTLE GARTH
5 ROXBY GDNS
6 ROXBY TR
7 AUNUMS CL
8 THE MOUNT
9 WESTFIELD TR
10 WILLOW GARTH
11 HERON CL
12 FARMANBY CL
NEW INGS LANE

4

PH
UPR CARR LANE
Cow Carr
ORDMERSTONES LANE
High Riggs
HARROW CLIFF LANE

TOFTS LA
Upper Carr Farm
California Farm
HIGH RIGGS LANE
Charity Farm
HURRELL LANE

81

Brignam Park Farm
Brignam Park
Upper Carr
Noble Carr
Chester Villa
Thornton Carr

3

TOFTS RD
Pickering Low Carr
Low Grundon Farm
FOX LANE
High Grundon Farm
Thornton Marishes
Willow Grange Farm

KIRBY MISPERTON RD
BEAN SHEAF LANE
Prospect House Farm
Rise Carr Farm
Ox Carr
Thornton Beck
Top Bridge Farm
Fir Tree House

80

Summertree Farm
Newstead Grange Farm

2

BELLERBYHURN RD
Wray House Farm
Flat Top Farm
Bungalow Farm
Summertree Bridge
MARISHES LANE
Derwent House Farm

79

Deerholme Grange
Moor Close Farm
YO17
Selly Bridge Farm
Turn Bridge
Low Newstead Grange
Skelton Wath Farm

1

Bellafax Grange
Deerholme Farm
THORNTON LANE
MARISHES LOW RD
Bacon Farm
River Derwent
Scampston Grange

78

Harding Plantation
Little Deerholme Grange
High Marishes

80   A   81   B   82   C   83   D   84   E   85   F

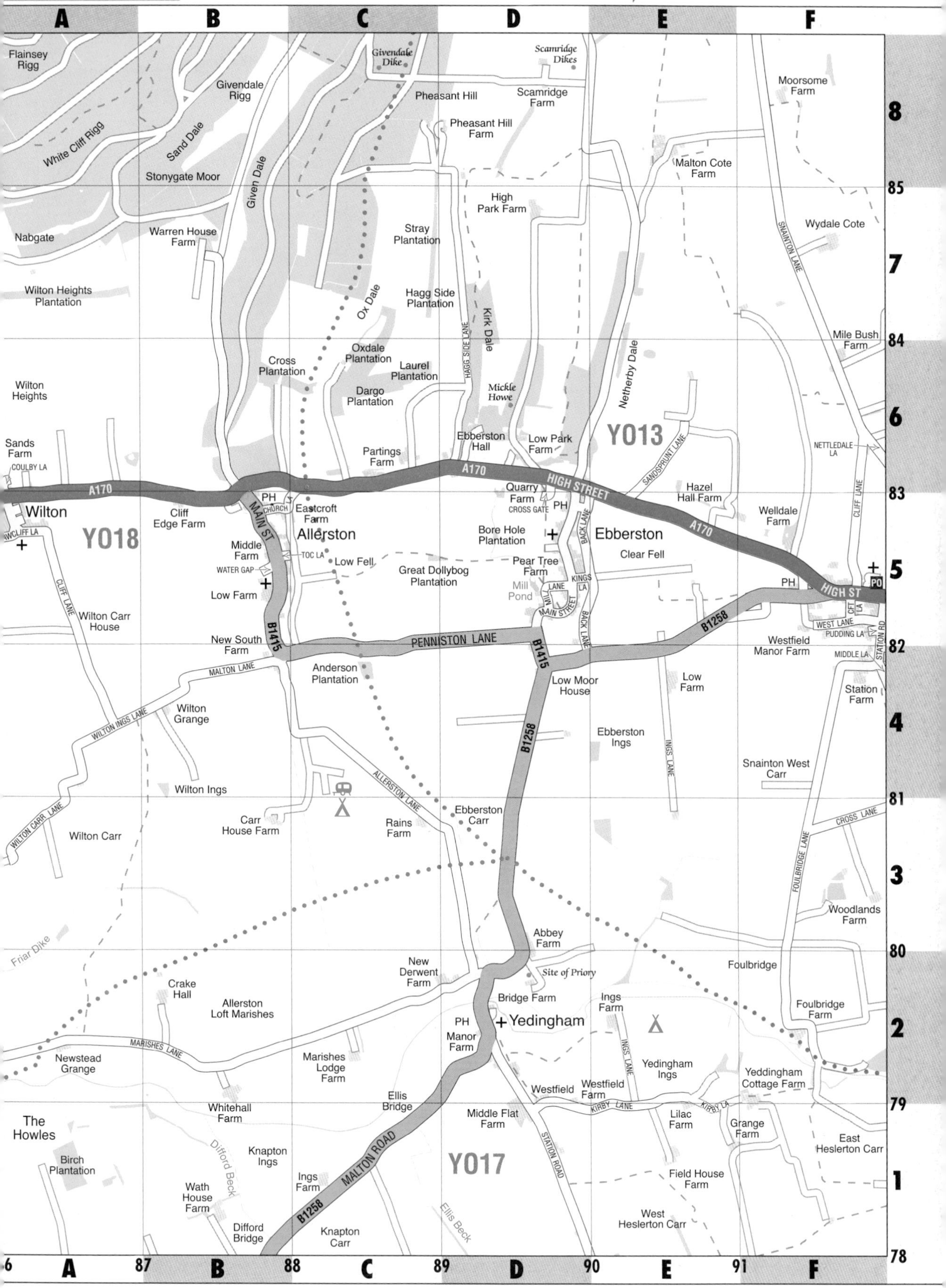
A
B
C
D
E
F
Flainsey Rigg
Givendale Dike
Scamridge Dikes
Givendale Rigg
Pheasant Hill
Scamridge Farm
Moorsome Farm
White Cliff Rigg
Sand Dale
Pheasant Hill Farm
Stonygate Moor
Given Dale
Malton Cote Farm
High Park Farm
Wydale Cote
SNAINTON LANE
Nabgate
Warren House Farm
Stray Plantation
Wilton Heights Plantation
Hagg Side Plantation
Ox Dale
Kirk Dale
HAGG SIDE LANE
Mile Bush Farm
Cross Plantation
Oxdale Plantation
Laurel Plantation
Netherby Dale
Wilton Heights
Dargo Plantation
Mickle Howe
YO13
Sands Farm
COULBY LA
Partings Farm
Ebberston Hall
Low Park Farm
SANDSPRUNT LANE
NETTLEDALE LA
A170
A170
HIGH STREET
Quarry Farm
CROSS GATE
PH
Hazel Hall Farm
Welldale Farm
CLIFF LANE
PH
CHURCH
Eastcroft Farm
Wilton
Cliff Edge Farm
MAIN ST
Allerston
Bore Hole Plantation
BACK LANE
Ebberston
A170
YO18
CLIFF LA
Middle Farm
TOC LA
Low Fell
Clear Fell
WATER GAP
Great Dollybog Plantation
Pear Tree Farm
Mill Pond
LANE
KINGS LA
MILL
MAIN STREET
PH
HIGH ST
PO
CFT LA
CLIFF LANE
Low Farm
Wilton Carr House
BACK LANE
B1258
WEST LANE
PUDDING LA
New South Farm
B1415
PENNISTON LANE
B1415
Westfield Manor Farm
MIDDLE LA
STATION RD
MALTON LANE
Anderson Plantation
Low Moor House
Low Farm
Station Farm
WILTON INGS LANE
Wilton Grange
Ebberston Ings
B1258
INGS LANE
Snainton West Carr
Wilton Ings
ALLERSTON LANE
WILTON CARR LANE
Carr House Farm
Ebberston Carr
Rains Farm
CROSS LANE
Wilton Carr
FOULBRIDGE LANE
Woodlands Farm
Abbey Farm
Friar Dike
New Derwent Farm
Site of Priory
Foulbridge
Crake Hall
Allerston Loft Marishes
Bridge Farm
Ings Farm
Foulbridge Farm
PH
Yedingham
MARISHES LANE
Manor Farm
INGS LANE
Newstead Grange
Marishes Lodge Farm
Yedingham Ings
Yeddingham Cottage Farm
Westfield
Westfield Farm
The Howles
Whitehall Farm
Ellis Bridge
Middle Flat Farm
KIRBY LANE
KIRBY LA
Lilac Farm
Grange Farm
East Heslerton Carr
Birch Plantation
Difford Beck
Knapton Ings
MALTON ROAD
YO17
STATION ROAD
Field House Farm
Wath House Farm
Ings Farm
B1258
Ellis Beck
West Heslerton Carr
Difford Bridge
Knapton Carr
8
85
7
84
6
83
5
82
4
81
3
80
2
79
1
78
86
87
88
89
90
91

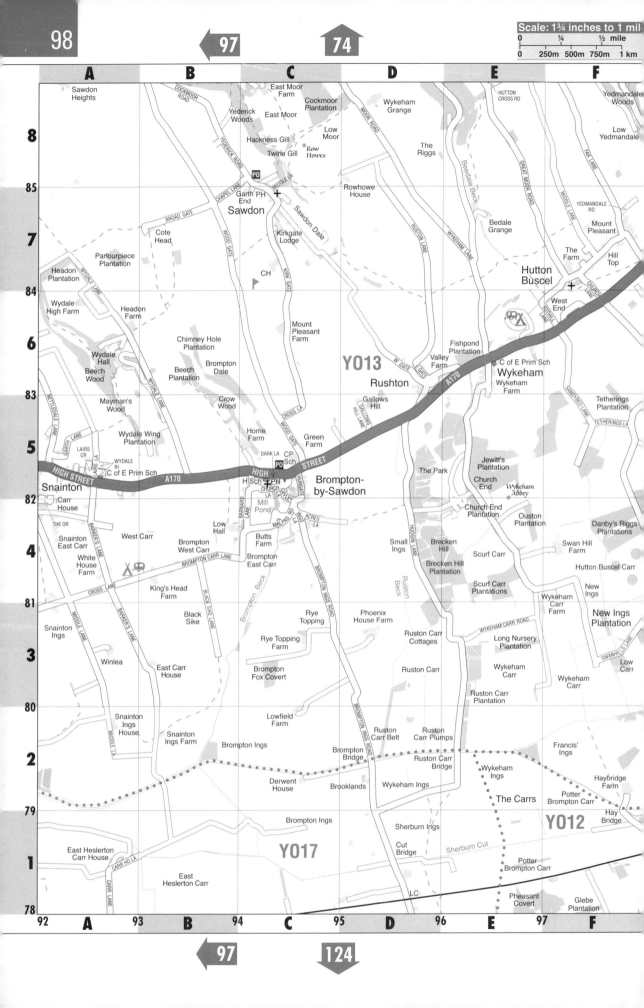

Scale: 1¾ inches to 1 mile
¼ ½ mile
250m 500m 750m 1 km

A7 1 CASTLE RI 2 YEDMANDALE RD 3 MILL LA 4 DREAKEN FOLD 5 WILSON'S LA 6 STATION CL 7 WEST ACRES CL 8 BEECH LA 9 HEWLEY DR 10 MORLEY DR 11 BROUGHTON RD 12 CANDLER AV

D6 1 THE GROVE 2 PASTURE LA 3 EASTGATE 4 MAYFIELD DR 5 BELL CL 6 THE GREEN 7 RAINFORD CL 8 DENISON AV 9 WHITE HORSE LA 10 LONDESBOROUGH PK 11 STAPLETON CL 12 WELBOURN DR

F7 1 BURTONDALE RD 2 DUNCOMBE CL 3 CONISTON WY 4 ROXBY GD 5 DAWNAY CL 6 CONISTON GD 7 RYDALE CR 8 THE LEAS 9 LINGHOLM CR 10 RIDGEWAY 11 DALE EDGE 12 RYEFIELD CL

75 212 100

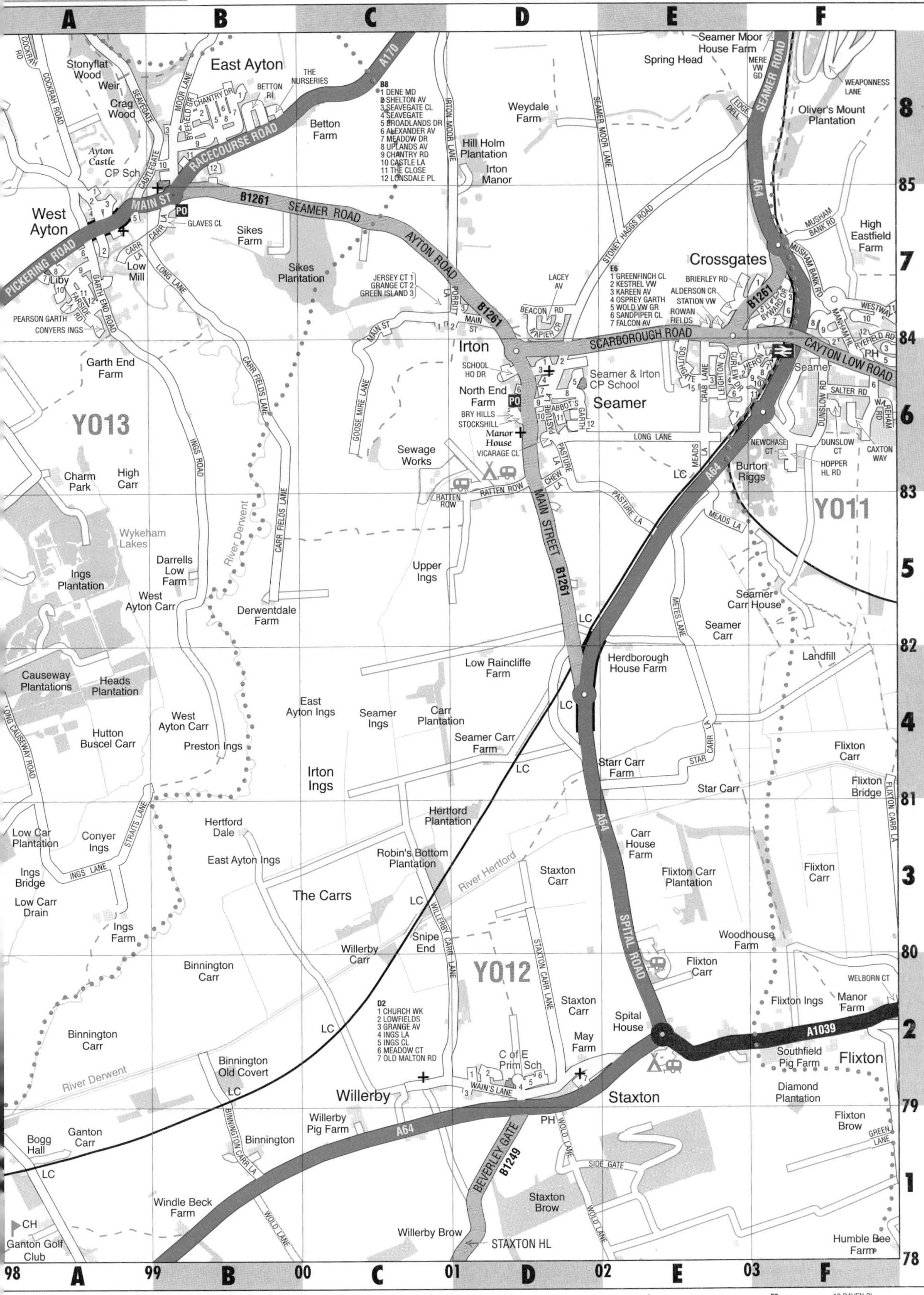

125 100

F6 1 PLOVER GD 2 CARRSIDE 2 THE MEADS 4 MALLARD WY 5 LODERS GREEN 6 THORNBURH RD 7 KINGFISHER CL 8 BLACKBIRD WY 9 NIGHTINGALE LA 10 RAVEN CL 11 AVOCET CR

B6
1 FENWICK CL
2 ESTILL CL
3 MOUNT VW RD
4 WEST END VW
5 WEST END CT
6 IVY HOUSE CL
7 LODGE CL
8 LIMEKILN LA
9 BECK HOLE
10 SPRING GD
11 BEVERLEY RD
12 BEVERLEY CL
13 CHAPEL LA
14 GREEN PARK RD
15 GREEN PARK AV
16 THE PASTURES
17 NESFIELD CL
18 EAST CARR
19 FLOWER CT
20 PENTON RD
21 EAST LEA VW
22 STANLEY CL
23 WEST GARTH GD
24 GREEN CROFT GD

99

213

B7
1 SEAVIEW AV
2 BRADWORTH DR
3 BRADWORTH CL
4 STUART CL
5 SOUTHWOLD CL
6 SOUTHWOLD RI
7 SOUTHWOLD
8 SOUTHWOLD CR
9 HAWSON CL
10 FENTON CL
11 KNOLLS CL
12 REDCLIFF CL
13 SHEPHERDS DR
14 PLOUGHMANS CT
15 WAIN CL
16 THE FURROWS
17 SHIRE CFT
18 SHIRE CL

Scale: 1¾ inches to 1 mile
0 ¼ ½ mile
0 250m 500m 750m 1 km

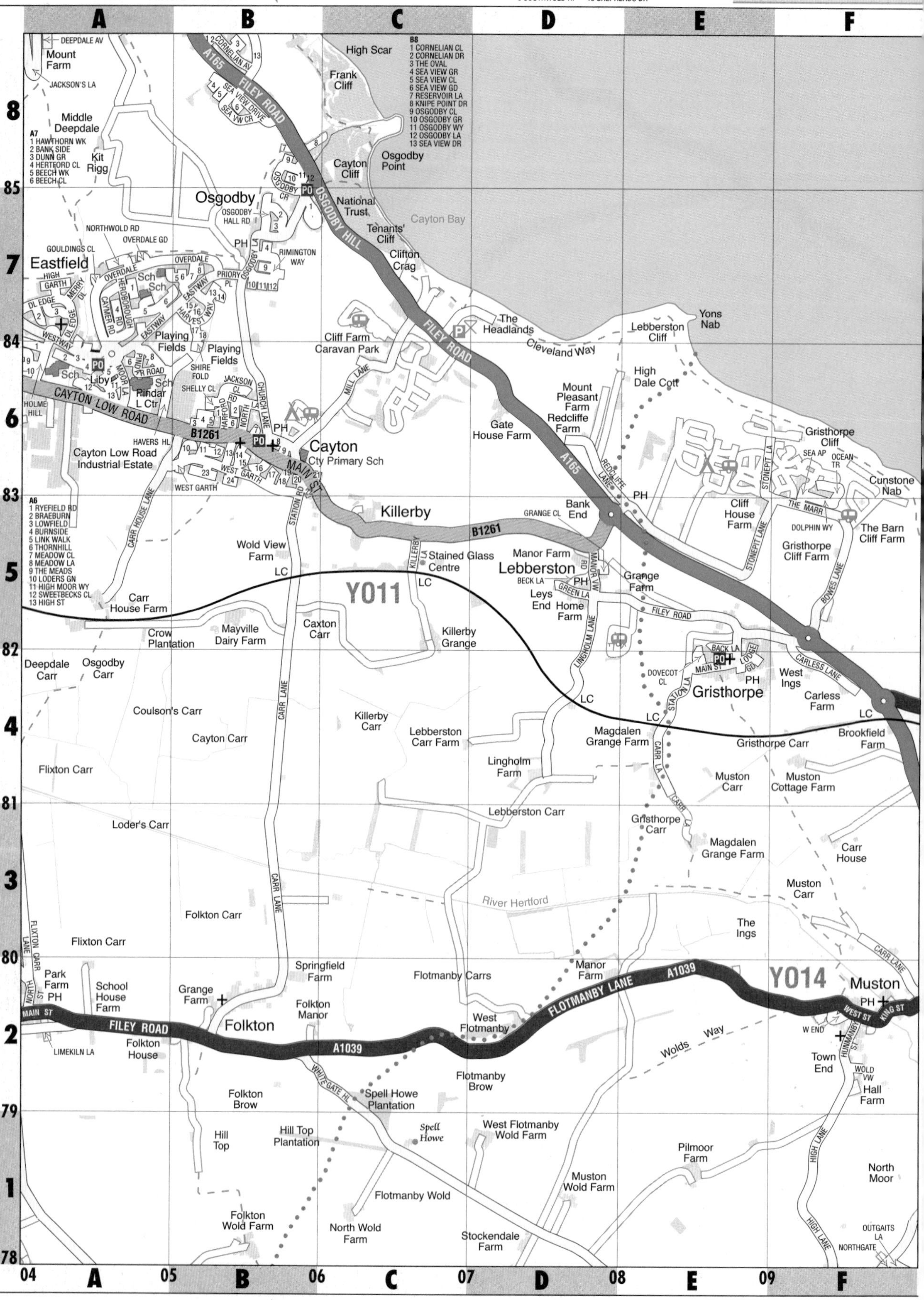

Scale: 1¾ inches to 1 mile

¼ ½ mile
250m 500m 750m 1 km

The Wyke

Cloakhouse End

Newbiggin

A4
1 COPSE HL
2 HAZEL RD
3 ROWAN AV
4 WIDGEON CL
5 SNIPE CL
6 HERON CT
7 CYGNET CL
8 MALLARD CL
9 SHELDRAKE CL

Club Point

North Cliff

Cleveland Way

Filey Field

Newbiggin Farm West

Moat

CHERRY TREE DR

PINEWOOD AV

Filey Spa

North Cliff Ctry Park

Filey Brigg Nature Reserve

SCARBOROUGH ROAD

PLANE TREE WY

WOOLDALE DR

FIR TRE

Crayke House Farm

WEST RD

OAK CL

Filey Sands

Wolds Way

Y014

Nature Reserve

Filey

P

Lifeboat Station

B3
1 THE CROFT
2 ASHLEY CT
3 QUEEN'S TR
4 LAUNDRY RD
5 CHURCH ST
6 ST OSWALDS CT
7 RAVINE TOP
8 BIRCH CL
9 CARLTON RD
10 VICTORIA AV
11 NORMAN CR
12 WEST RD
13 PROVIDENCE PL
14 QUEEN ST
15 REYNOLDS ST
16 MARINER'S TR
17 WHITKIRK PL
18 WHISTON DR

19 LINTON CL
20 STATION AV
21 GRANVILLE RD
22 CROMWELLAV
22 CLAREMONT
24 MITFORD ST
25 CLIFFORD'S TR
26 THE AVENUE
27 CHAPEL ST
28 UNION ST
29 RAINCLIFFE AV
30 HOPE ST
31 MURRAY ST
32 CARGATE HL
33 BELLE VUE CR
34 BELLE VUE ST
35 JOHN ST
36 WELFORD RD

37 WEST VALE
38 RUTLAND ST
39 HINDLE DR
40 FLOWER GARTH
41 HALLAM CL
42 ST JOHN'S AV
43 BROOKLANDS
44 BROOKLANDS CL
45 DORAN CL
46 PADBURY CL
46 CLARENCE AV
47 SOUTHDENE
48 COOPER RD
50 PADBURY AV
51 SOUTH CR CL
52 MELVILLE TR
53 CRESCENT HL
54 SOUTH CR AV

FILEY

Sun Lounge Theatre

Beacon Hill

Swimming Pool

A165

MUSTON ROAD

GRANGE AV

Cemy

Inf Sch

LC

Filey School

Allison Field Farm

KING HILL

MOUNT VW

MOOR RD

MILL LA

Mill Farm

P

CH

Filey Bay

Muston Grange

Muston Sands

North Moor

Centenary Way

MOOR ROAD

A165

Lowfield Farm

Filey Golf Club

North Moor Farm

The Dams

LC

PH

SOUTH CLIFF DR

VALLEY ROAD

PRIMROSE AVENUE

SEA VW

FLAT CLIFFS

1 BACK SEA VW
2 THE CLOSE
3 HAWTHORN WY

Hunmanby Sands

Primrose Valley

HIGHLANDS CL

PRIMROSE DR

PRIMROSE VALLEY RD

PRIMROS

LAKESIDE

PH

A3
1 SANDPIPER CL
2 TEAL CL
3 CURLEW DR
4 HAREWOOD DR
5 SILVERWOOD AV
6 BURNSALL CL
7 LANGSETT AV
8 LEYBURN PL
9 BARDEN PL

10 RIVELIN WY
11 FEWSTON CL
12 COLLINGHAM WY
13 WASHBURN CL
14 WHARNCLIFFE PL
15 MIDHOPE WY
16 EWDEN CL

B4
1 LARCH GR
2 WILLOW CL
3 CEDAR GR
4 GROVE HILL RD
5 HORNDALE RD
6 THORN TREE AV
7 ALMOND CL
8 ARNDALE WY
9 CHURCH CLIFF DR

10 ELM CL
11 ALMOND GR
12 ASH GR
13 ASH RD
14 GROVE RD
15 THE GARDENS
16 THE CROFT
17 RAVINE HL
18 CHURCH CL

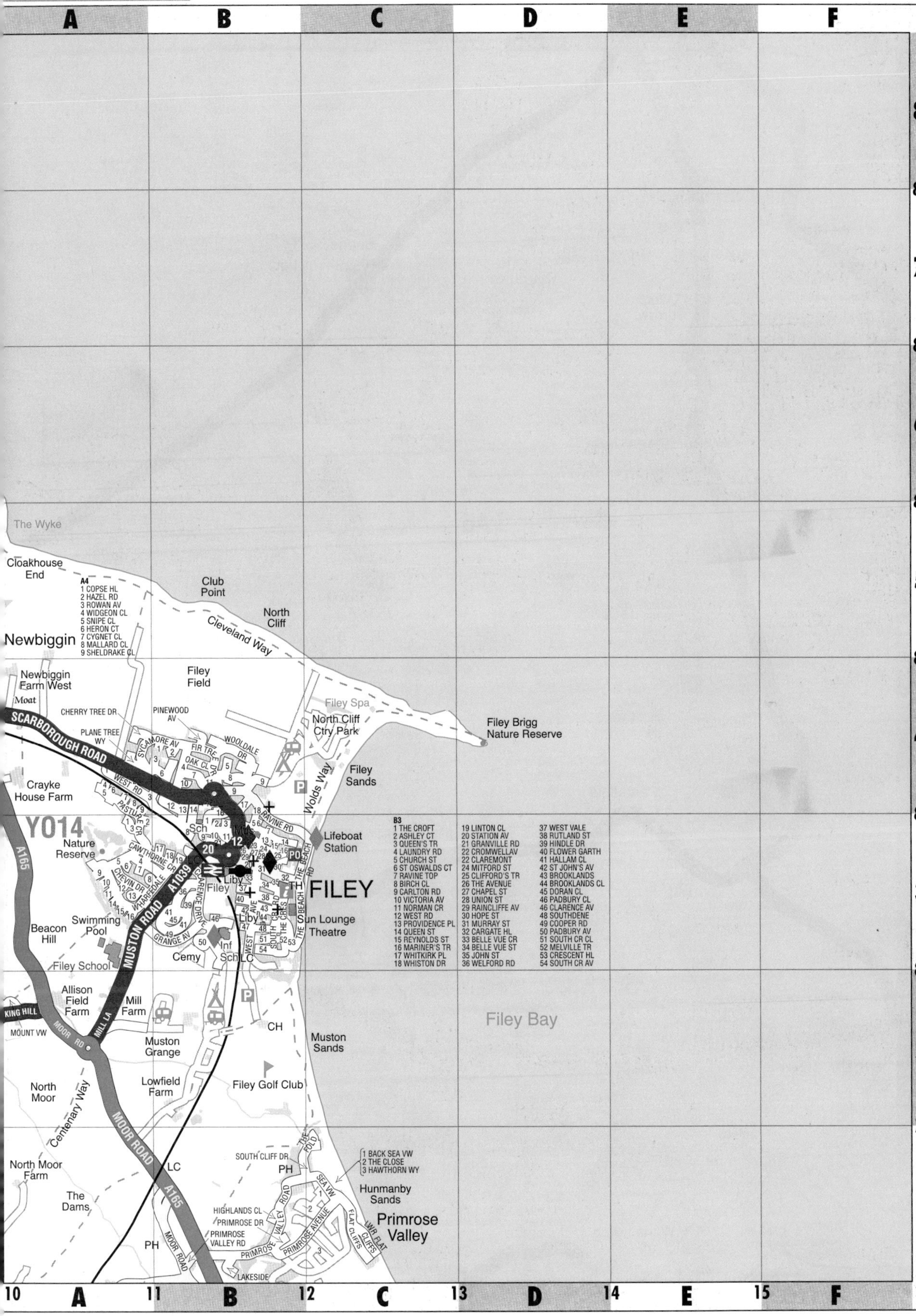

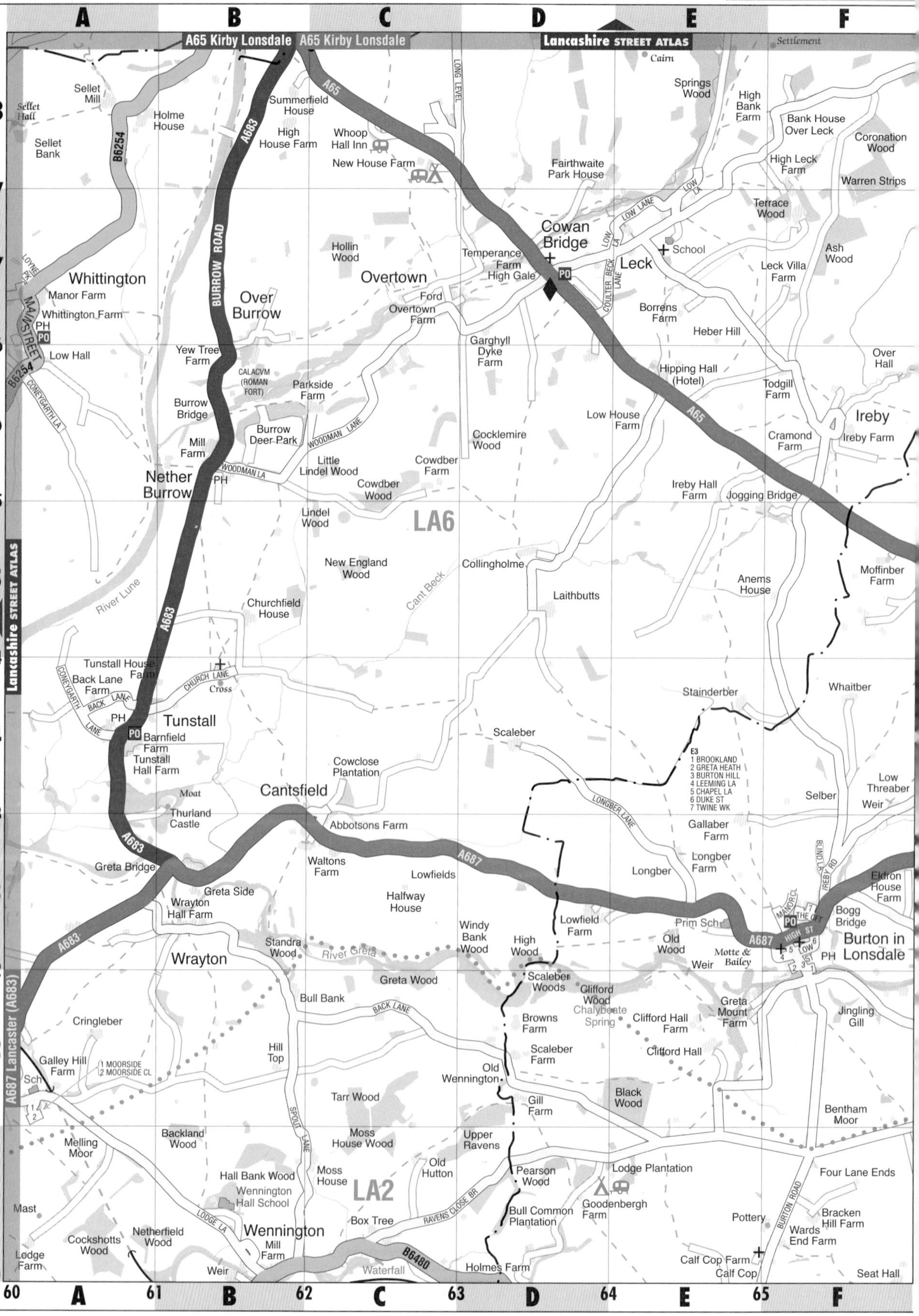

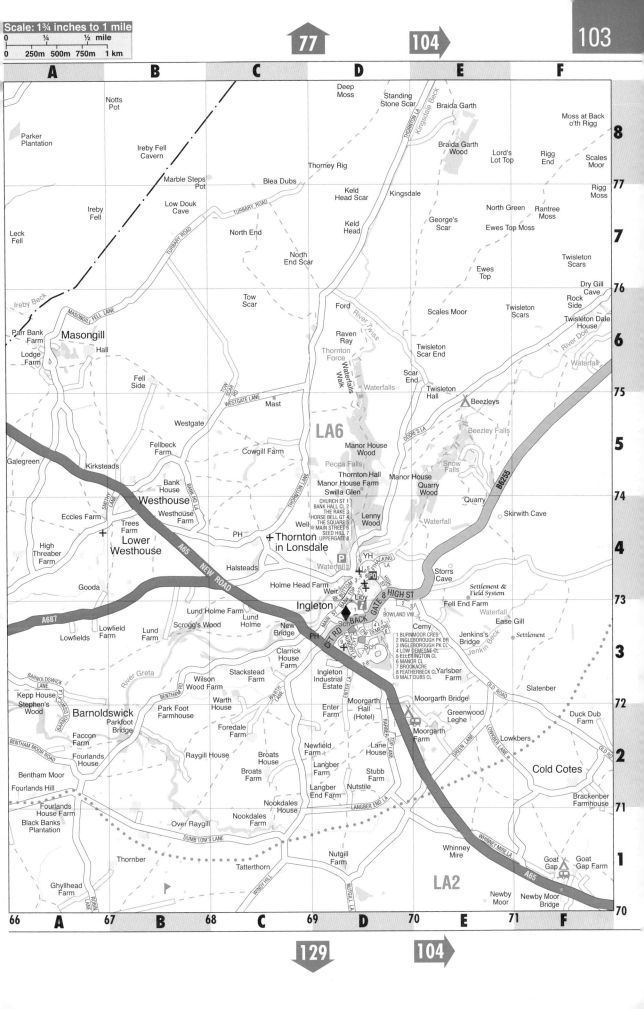

A   B   C   D   E   F

8

Blake Bank Moss

Four Stones Rigg   West Moss

Philpin   B6255

Scar Close

Colt Park   New Bridge
Colt Park Farm

Hard Rigg

Scales Moor

Weathercote

PH

Settlement

Fell Close

Colt Park Wood

Settlement

Twisleton Scars   Hurtle Pot

Low Hill Farm

Chapel-le-Dale

Nature Reserve

Stone House

77

Great Hard Rigg Moss
Scales Moor

Settlement

Settlement

Southerscales Scars

Park Fell

Park Fell Rocks

7

Springcote
Spring Cote Farm

Ullet Gill Cave

Settlement

God's Bridge

Highwood Pasture

Souther Scales Fell

South House Moor

Washfold Pot

BD24

Raven Scar

Great Douk Cave

76

Dale House

Raven Scar Cave

Harry Hallam's Moss   Meregill Hole

South House Moor

Settlement

Borrins Moor Rocks

6

B6255

High Howeth

LA6

Black Shiver Moss

Top Cow Pasture

75

Raven Scar

Tatham Wife Moss

Ingleborough

Simon Fell

Borrins Moor

Fell Close

5

Fort

Simon Fell Breast

Lead Mine Moss

Fell Beck Head

74

Quaking Pot

White Scars   Gait Head

Clapham Bents
Sware Gill Head
Sware Gill

Brunt Riggs

Nick Pot   Sulber Pot

Settlement & Field System

4

Ingleborough Common

Little Ingleborough

Fell Beck

Juniper Gulf
The Allotment

Thieves Moss

Dowlass Moss

Bottoms Rigg

73

Boggarts Roaring Hole

Grange Rigg

3

Long Kin West Pot

Hurnel Moss

Clapham Bottoms

Settlement   Moughton Scars

72

Grey Scars

Newby Moss

Long Scar

Crummack Dale

Gill Head

Austwick Beck Head

2

Bleak Bank

LA2

Clapdale Scars

Rayside Plantation

Ingleborough Cave

Crummack Farm

71

Crooklands Spring

Newby Cote

Hagg

Clapdale

Thwaite Scars

Ford

Scale Mire

Newby Cote Farm

CLAPDALE RD

Clapdale

1

Newby Moor   Town Head

Newby

Ryecroft Farm

LAITHBUTTS LA

Flatts Farm

Clapdale Wood

Clapham Beck

Thwaite

Enclosures

Waterfall

70

A65

72   A   73   B   74   C   75   D   76   E   77   F

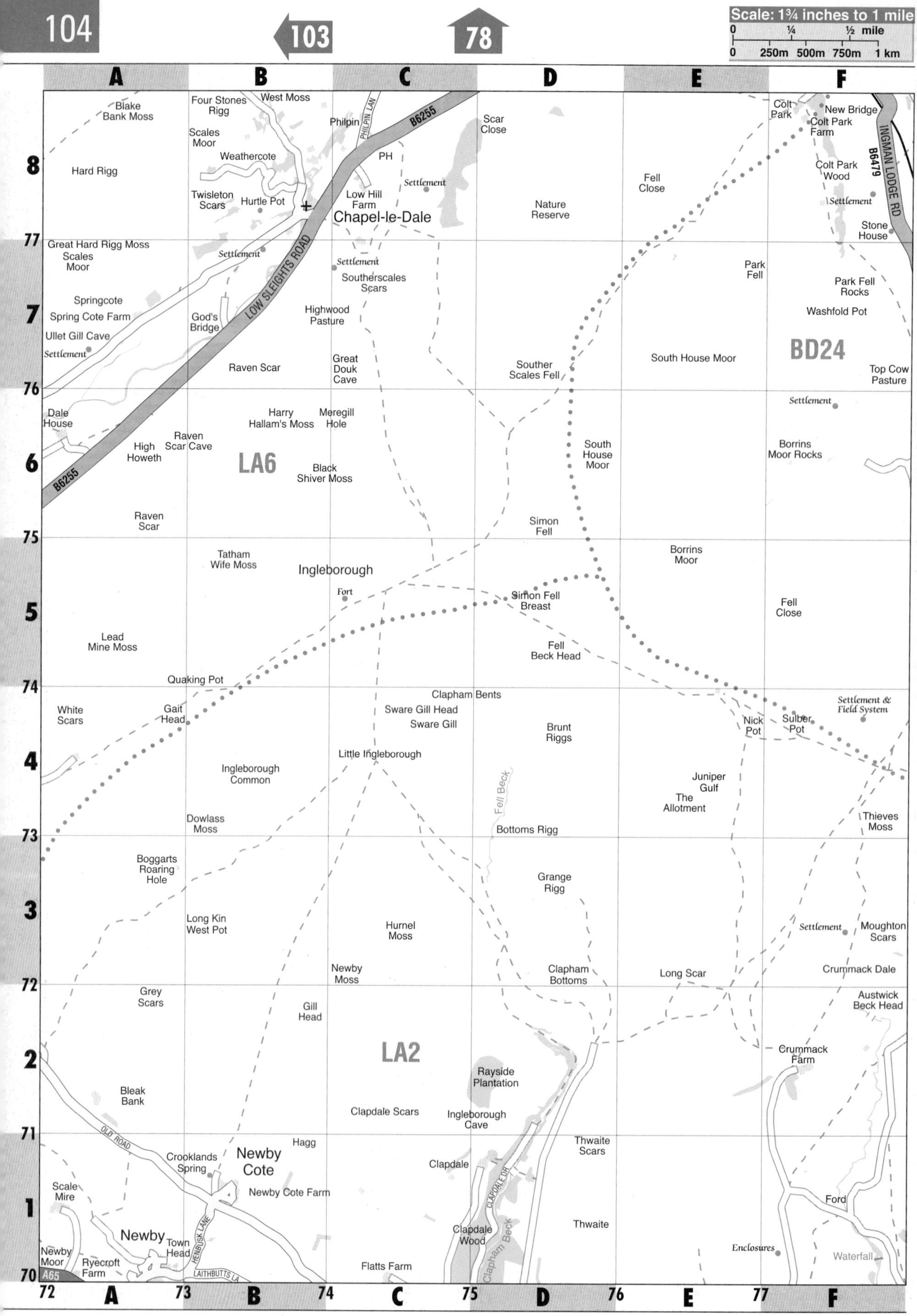

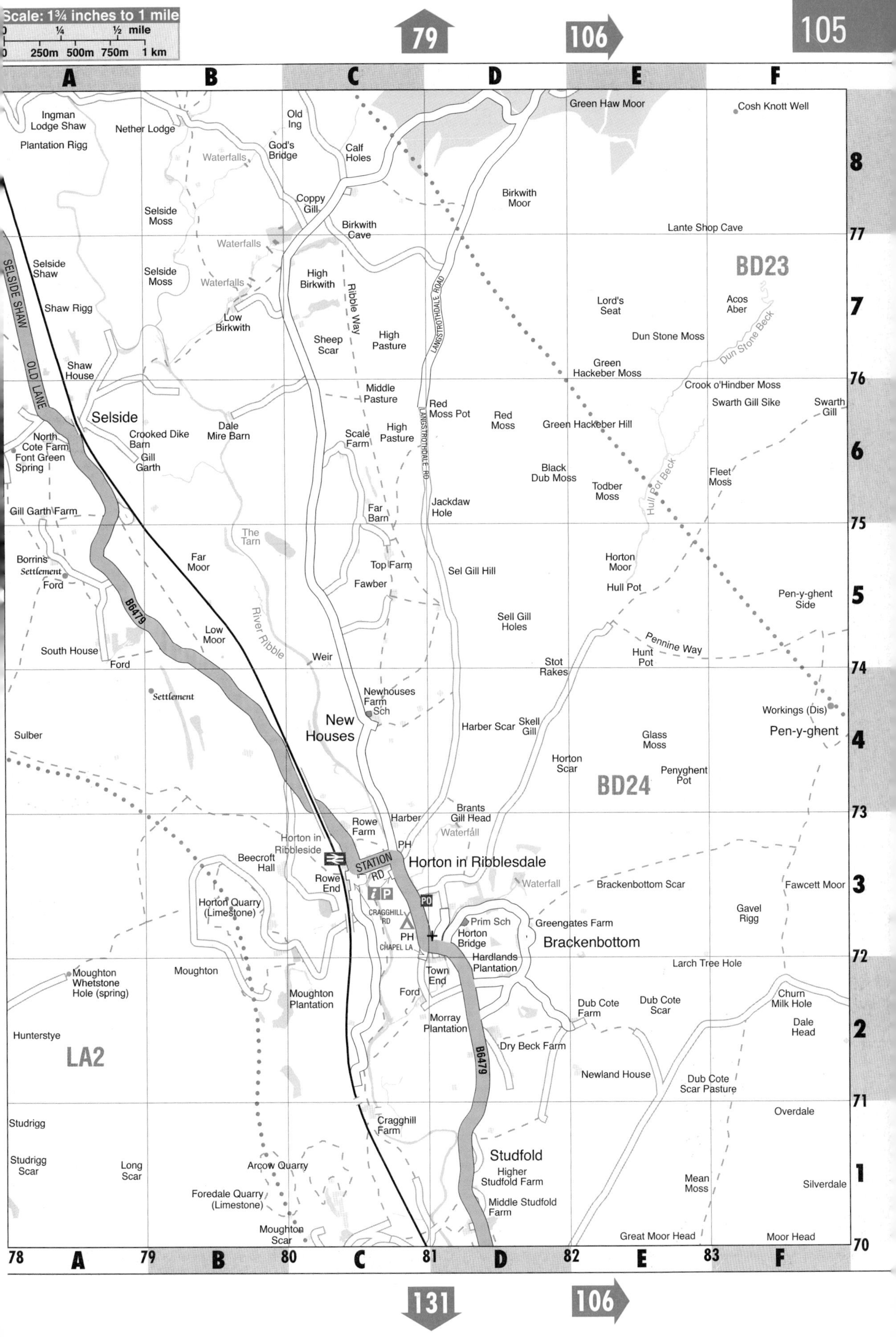

Scale: 1¾ inches to 1 mile
79
106
A B C D E F
Ingman Lodge Shaw
Plantation Rigg
Nether Lodge
Waterfalls
Old Ing
God's Bridge
Calf Holes
Green Haw Moor
Cosh Knott Well
Coppy Gill
Selside Moss
Birkwith Cave
Birkwith Moor
Lante Shop Cave
BD23
Selside Shaw
Selside Moss
High Birkwith
Ribble Way
LANGSTROTHDALE ROAD
Lord's Seat
Acos Aber
Shaw Rigg
Low Birkwith
Sheep Scar
High Pasture
Dun Stone Moss
Dun Stone Beck
SELSIDE SHAW
OLD LANE
Shaw House
Green Hackeber Moss
Crook o'Hindber Moss
Middle Pasture
Swarth Gill Sike
Swarth Gill
Selside
Red Moss Pot
Red Moss
Green Hackeber Hill
North Cote Farm
Crooked Dike Barn
Dale Mire Barn
Scale Farm
High Pasture
LANGSTROTHDALE RD
Font Green Spring
Gill Garth
Black Dub Moss
Hull Pot Beck
Fleet Moss
Todber Moss
Jackdaw Hole
Gill Garth Farm
Far Barn
The Tarn
Borrins Settlement
Far Moor
Top Farm
Sel Gill Hill
Horton Moor
Ford
Fawber
Hull Pot
Pen-y-ghent Side
B6479
River Ribble
Sell Gill Holes
Low Moor
Pennine Way
South House
Hunt Pot
Ford
Weir
Stot Rakes
Settlement
Newhouses Farm
Sch
Workings (Dis)
Sulber
New Houses
Harber Scar
Skell Gill
Glass Moss
Pen-y-ghent
Horton Scar
Penyghent Pot
BD24
Brants Gill Head
Rowe Farm
Harber
Waterfall
Horton in Ribbleside
PH
Beecroft Hall
Horton in Ribblesdale
STATION RD
Rowe End
Waterfall
Brackenbottom Scar
Fawcett Moor
Horton Quarry (Limestone)
PO
CRAGGHILL RD
Prim Sch
Gavel Rigg
Greengates Farm
PH
Horton Bridge
CHAPEL LA
Brackenbottom
Hardlands Plantation
Moughton Whetstone Hole (spring)
Moughton
Town End
Larch Tree Hole
Moughton Plantation
Ford
Dub Cote Farm
Dub Cote Scar
Churn Milk Hole
Morray Plantation
Dale Head
Hunterstye
LA2
B6479
Dry Beck Farm
Newland House
Dub Cote Scar Pasture
Studrigg
Cragghill Farm
Overdale
Studrigg Scar
Long Scar
Arcow Quarry
Studfold
Higher Studfold Farm
Mean Moss
Silverdale
Foredale Quarry (Limestone)
Middle Studfold Farm
Moughton Scar
Great Moor Head
Moor Head
8 77 7 76 6 75 5 74 4 73 3 72 2 71 1 70
78 79 80 81 82 83
131
106

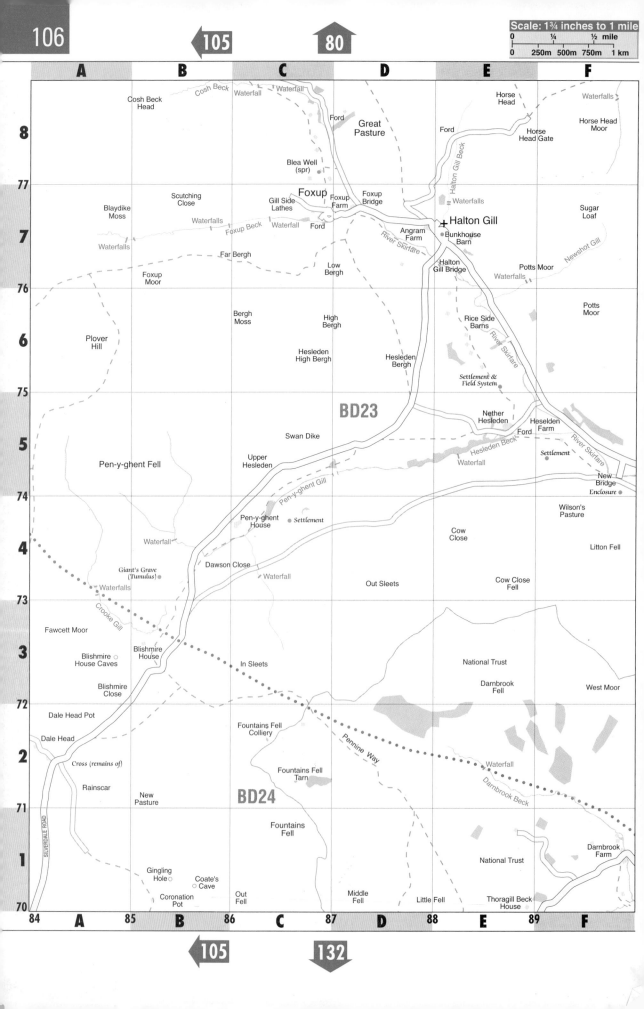

105

80

Scale: 1¾ inches to 1 mile

0 ¼ ½ mile
0 250m 500m 750m 1 km

A   **B**   **C**   **D**   **E**   **F**

Cosh Beck Head

Cosh Beck

Waterfall

Waterfall

Ford

Great Pasture

Horse Head

Ford

Horse Head Gate

Waterfalls

Horse Head Moor

8

Blea Well (spr)

Scutching Close

77

Gill Side Lathes

Foxup

Foxup Farm

Foxup Bridge

Halton Gill Beck

Waterfalls

Sugar Loaf

Blaydike Moss

Waterfalls

Foxup Beck

Waterfall

Ford

✝ **Halton Gill**

7

Waterfalls

Far Bergh

Angram Farm

Bunkhouse Barn

River Skirfare

Newshot Gill

Foxup Moor

Low Bergh

Halton Gill Bridge

Potts Moor

Waterfalls

76

Bergh Moss

High Bergh

Rice Side Barns

River Skirfare

Potts Moor

6

Plover Hill

Hesleden High Bergh

Hesleden Bergh

Settlement & Field System

75

BD23

Nether Hesleden

Heselden Farm

Swan Dike

Ford

5

Upper Hesleden

Waterfall

Settlement

River Skirfare

Pen-y-ghent Fell

Pen-y-ghent Gill

New Bridge

Enclosure

74

Pen-y-ghent House

Settlement

Waterfall

Wilson's Pasture

Waterfall

Dawson Close

Waterfall

Cow Close

Litton Fell

4

Giant's Grave (Tumulus)

Out Sleets

Cow Close Fell

Waterfalls

Crooke Gill

73

Fawcett Moor

Blishmire House

National Trust

Darnbrook Fell

West Moor

3

Blishmire House Caves

In Sleets

Blishmire Close

72

Dale Head Pot

Fountains Fell Colliery

Dale Head

Pennine Way

Waterfall

Darnbrook Beck

2

Cross (remains of)

Fountains Fell Tarn

Rainscar

BD24

New Pasture

71

SILVERDALE ROAD

Fountains Fell

Darnbrook Farm

1

Gingling Hole

Coate's Cave

National Trust

Coronation Pot

Out Fell

Middle Fell

Little Fell

Thoragill Beck House

70

84   **A**   85   **B**   86   **C**   87   **D**   88   **E**   89   **F**

105

132

A   B   C   D   E   F

8

Mooring
Head
Waterfalls
Blue
Haw
Kirk
Gill Moor
Rakes
Wood
Cairn   Settlement
Buckden Beck
Waterfall
Waterfalls
Kirk
Gill Moor
East Side
River Wharfe
DUBB'S LA
Dale
Head
Nab
End
Ford
Waterfall
P
East Side
77
Waterfall
Kirk
Gill Moor
Birks
Fell
Redmire
B6160
Inn
Buckden

7
High Combe
Stoop
Water Gill
Sewage
Works
Eastside
Wood
East
Side
East
Side
Waterfalls
Moss
Top
Birks
Fell
Water Gill
Wood
Waterfalls
Wharfdale
Knuckle Bone
Pasture
76
National Trust
Birks Wood
Eshber
Wood
Cross (remains of)
Out Moor
Birks Tarn
Step Gill
Waterfall
Cave
Step Gill Pot
Firth
Wood
Eshber
Wood
Waterfalls
River Wharfe
Cam Gill Beck
6
Waterfall

75
Capple
Stones
Firth
Fell
Lord's
Wood
B6160
Hill Top
High
Side
Hill Side
COATES LA
Starbotton
Potts Beck
Middle
Moor
Crystal Beck
Haw
Fell
National Trust
Fosse
Wood
Inn
Low
Side
5
Waterfalls
Litton
Waterfall
Ford
Calfhalls
Wood
Springs
Wood
Armistead
Farm
West
Farm
Inn
Sawyers
Garth Farm
Ackerley
Moor
Old Cote
Moor Top
Foss Gill Pot
Slater Barn
Hall
Ings
74
Spittle
Croft
Ford
PO
Ford
Smearbeck
Wood
Moor
End Fell
East
Garth
Roselber
Wood
Brearland Farm
House
Old Cote High Moor
Moor End
Fell
Wibbertons
Fields
4
Stonelands
White Sike
Wood
Cave
Wood
Moor
End
Springs
Wood
73
Great Scoska Moor
Flat Wood
Littondale
Ackerley
Moor
Old Cote
Moor
National Trust
Scoska
Moor
Scoska Wood
3
Little
Scoska Moor
Settlement &
Field System
Bown
Scar Wood
Bown Scar
Old Cote
Low Moor
Brayshaw
Scar
Park
Scar
Old Cote Little Moor
Bown Scar Cave
Waterfalls
Old Cote
Farm
Blea Head
Byre
Bank Wood
Hawkswick
Moor
72
Littondale
Sch
Arncliffe
West
Moor
Field
System
Brootes
Barn
BROOTES LA
1 MONK'S RD
2 GOOSELANDS HL
Arnberg
Scar
Field Ho
Barn
River Skirfare
Hawkswick
Wood
2
Field
House Wood
Garth
End
71
Nab End
Yew Cogar
Scar
Settlement
Blue
Scar
Cairns
Hazelhead
Farm
Field
System
OUT GANG LANE
Hawkswick
Hawkswick
Bridge
1
Cowside Beck
Blue
Scar
Arncliffe
Cote
Hawkswick
Cote
70
Clowder

90   A   91   B   92   C   93   D   94   E   95   F

BD23

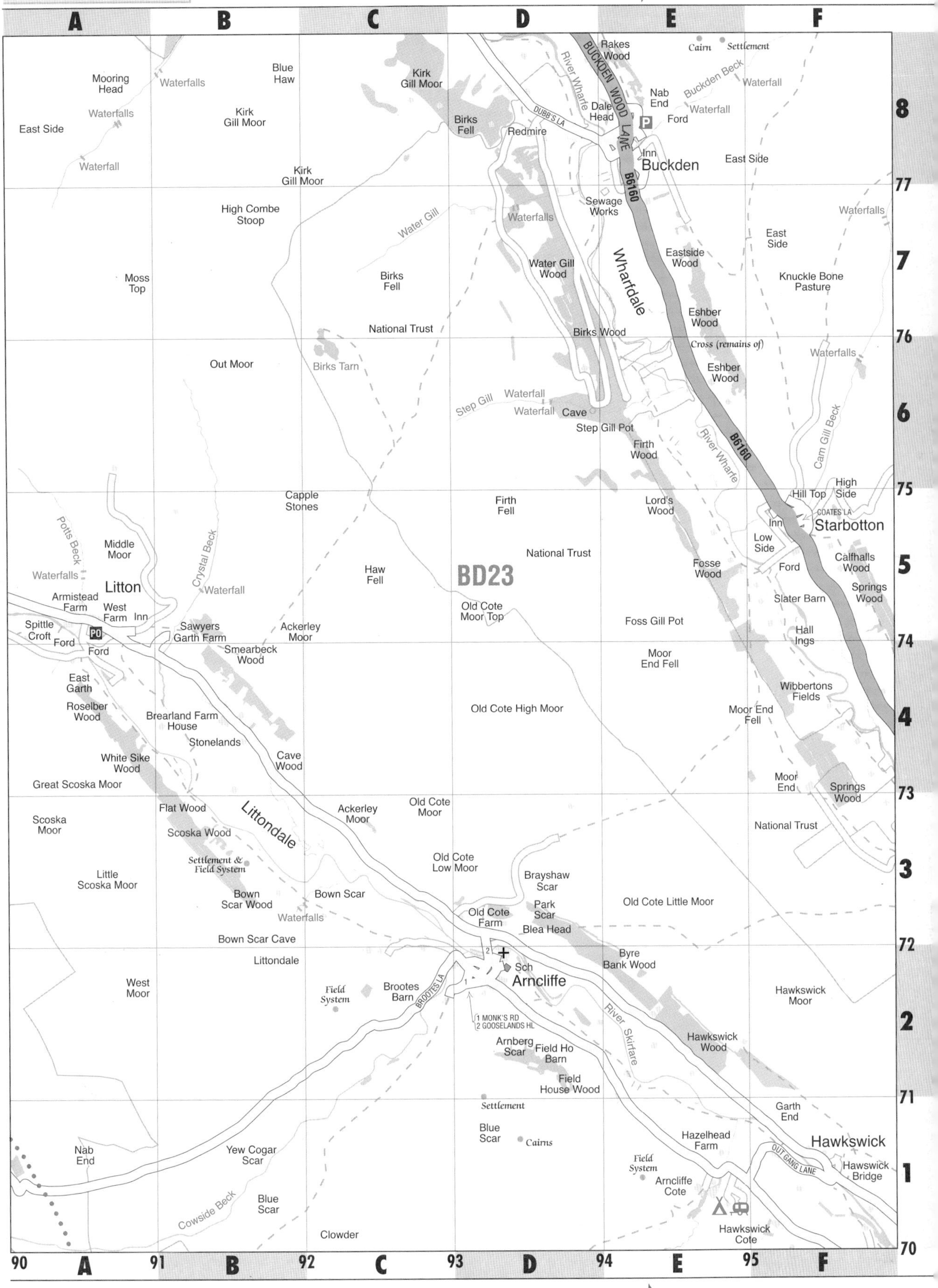

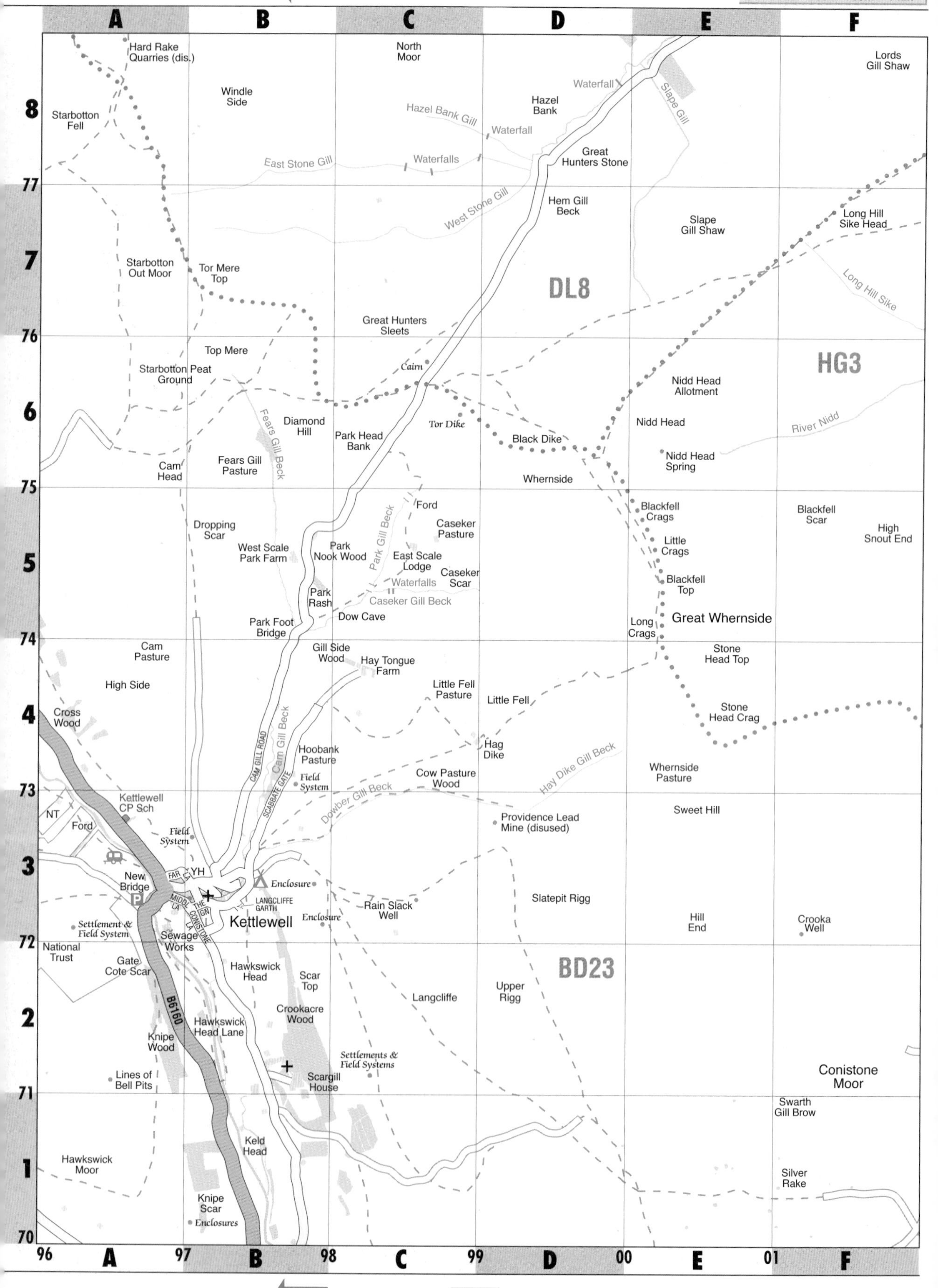

Scale: 1¾ inches to 1 mile

0   ¼   ½ mile

0   250m 500m 750m 1 km

A · **B** · **C** · **D** · **E** · **F**

8

Hard Rake
Quarries (dis.)

North
Moor

Waterfall

Lords
Gill Shaw

Windle
Side

Hazel
Bank

Starbotton
Fell

Hazel Bank Gill

Waterfall

Great
Hunters Stone

Slape Gill

77

East Stone Gill

Waterfalls

Hem Gill
Beck

Slape
Gill Shaw

Long Hill
Sike Head

West Stone Gill

7

Starbotton
Out Moor

Tor Mere
Top

DL8

Long Hill Sike

76

Great Hunters
Sleets

Nidd Head
Allotment

HG3

Top Mere

Starbotton Peat
Ground

Cairn

Nidd Head

River Nidd

6

Diamond
Hill

Park Head
Bank

Tor Dike

Black Dike

Nidd Head
Spring

Fears Gill Beck

Cam
Head

Fears Gill
Pasture

Whernside

75

Dropping
Scar

Ford

Caseker
Pasture

Blackfell
Crags

Blackfell
Scar

High
Snout End

West Scale
Park Farm

Park
Nook Wood

Park Gill Beck

East Scale
Lodge

Caseker
Scar

Little
Crags

5

Park
Rash

Waterfalls

Caseker Gill Beck

Blackfell
Top

Park Foot
Bridge

Dow Cave

Long
Crags

Great Whernside

74

Cam
Pasture

Gill Side
Wood

Hay Tongue
Farm

Stone
Head Top

High Side

Little Fell
Pasture

Little Fell

Cam Gill Beck

Stone
Head Crag

4

Cross
Wood

Hoobank
Pasture

Hag
Dike

Whernside
Pasture

CAM GILL ROAD

Field
System

Hay Dike Gill Beck

73

Kettlewell
CP Sch

Cow Pasture
Wood

Sweet Hill

NT

Ford

Field
System

SCARBATE GATE

Dowber Gill Beck

Providence Lead
Mine (disused)

3

New
Bridge

YH

Enclosure

LANGCLIFFE
GARTH

Slatepit Rigg

Hill
End

Crooka
Well

FAR

MIDDLE

THE

GN

Kettlewell

Enclosure

Rain Slack
Well

Settlement &
Field System

Sewage
Works

72

National
Trust

Gate
Cote Scar

Hawkswick
Head

BD23

Hawkswick
Head Lane

Scar
Top

Langcliffe

Upper
Rigg

Conistone
Moor

2

Knipe
Wood

Crookacre
Wood

B6160

Lines of
Bell Pits

Scargill
House

Settlements &
Field Systems

Swarth
Gill Brow

71

Hawkswick
Moor

Keld
Head

Silver
Rake

1

Knipe
Scar

Enclosures

70

96 · **A** · 97 · **B** · 98 · **C** · 99 · **D** · 00 · **E** · 01 · **F**

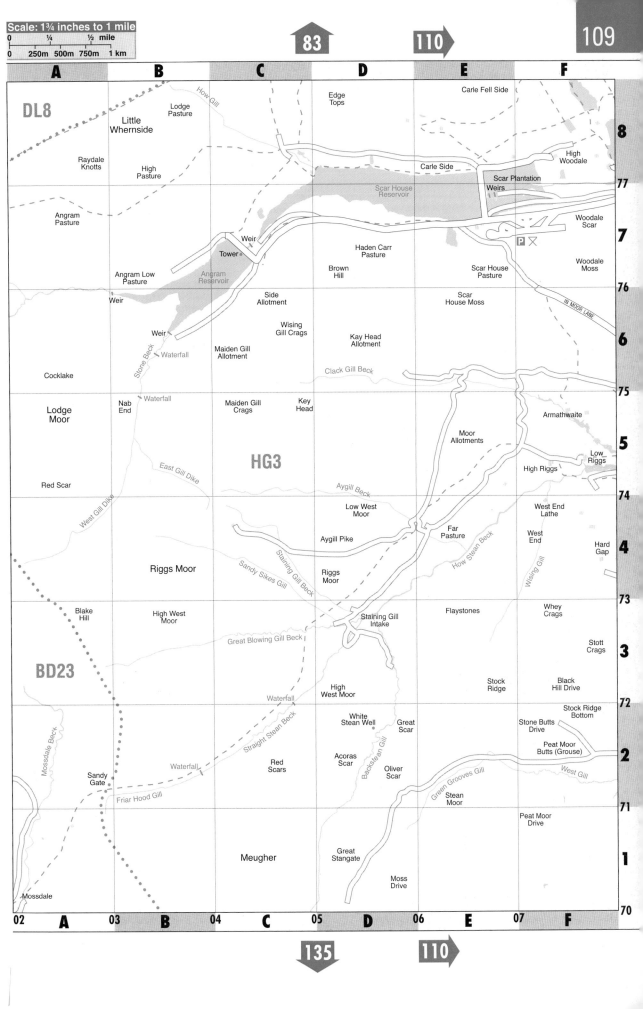

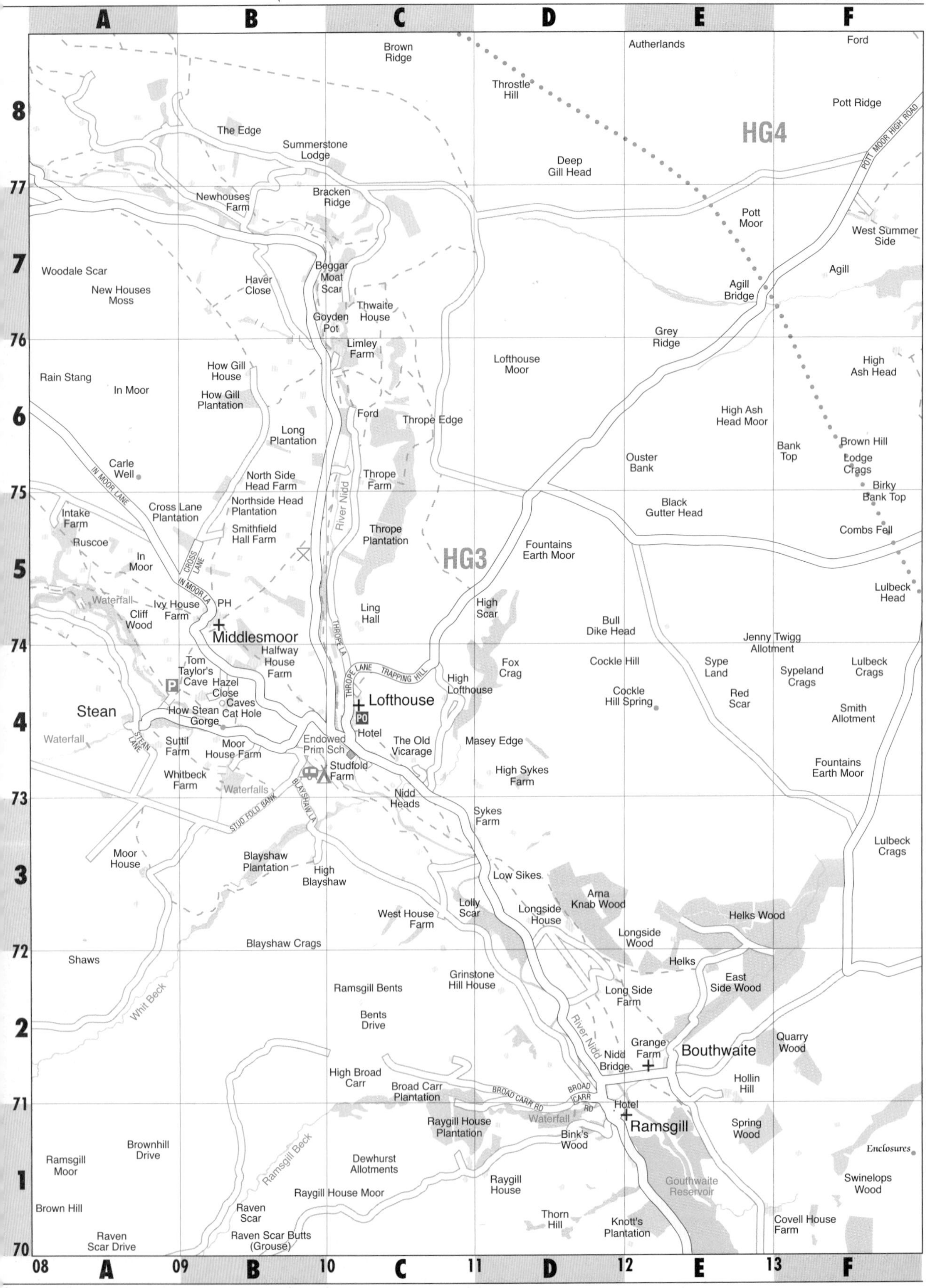

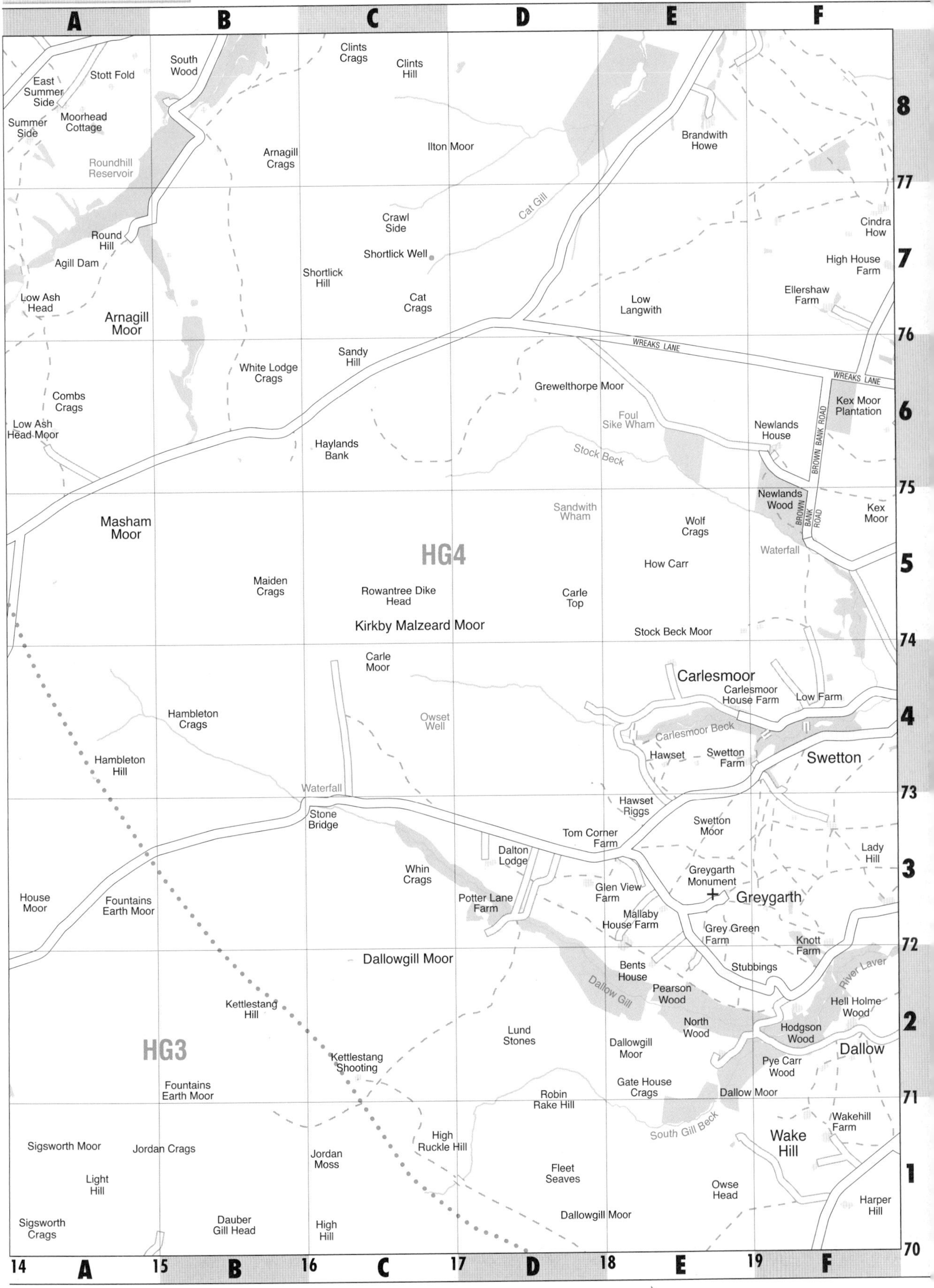
A
B
C
D
E
F
Clints Crags
Clints Hill
South Wood
Stott Fold
East Summer Side
Summer Side
Moorhead Cottage
Roundhill Reservoir
Arnagill Crags
Ilton Moor
Brandwith Howe
8
77
Cat Gill
Crawl Side
Round Hill
Agill Dam
Shortlick Well
Shortlick Hill
Cindra How
High House Farm
7
Ellershaw Farm
Low Ash Head
Arnagill Moor
Cat Crags
Low Langwith
76
WREAKS LANE
Sandy Hill
White Lodge Crags
Grewelthorpe Moor
Kex Moor Plantation
Combs Crags
Foul Sike Wham
Newlands House
BROWN BANK ROAD
6
Low Ash Head Moor
Haylands Bank
Stock Beck
75
Newlands Wood
Kex Moor
Sandwith Wham
Wolf Crags
Masham Moor
HG4
Waterfall
5
How Carr
Maiden Crags
Rowantree Dike Head
Carle Top
Kirkby Malzeard Moor
Stock Beck Moor
74
Carle Moor
Carlesmoor
Carlesmoor House Farm
Low Farm
Hambleton Crags
Owset Well
Carlesmoor Beck
4
Hambleton Hill
Hawset
Swetton Farm
Swetton
Waterfall
73
Hawset Riggs
Stone Bridge
Swetton Moor
Tom Corner Farm
Lady Hill
Dalton Lodge
Whin Crags
Greygarth Monument
3
Glen View Farm
House Moor
Fountains Earth Moor
Potter Lane Farm
Greygarth
Mallaby House Farm
Grey Green Farm
Knott Farm
72
Dallowgill Moor
Stubbings
River Laver
Bents House
Dallow Gill
Pearson Wood
Hell Holme Wood
Kettlestang Hill
North Wood
Hodgson Wood
2
Lund Stones
HG3
Dallowgill Moor
Dallow
Kettlestang Shooting
Pye Carr Wood
Gate House Crags
Fountains Earth Moor
Robin Rake Hill
Dallow Moor
71
Wakehill Farm
South Gill Beck
Wake Hill
High Ruckle Hill
Sigsworth Moor
Jordan Crags
Jordan Moss
1
Light Hill
Fleet Seaves
Owse Head
Harper Hill
Sigsworth Crags
Dauber Gill Head
High Hill
Dallowgill Moor
70
14
15
16
17
18
19

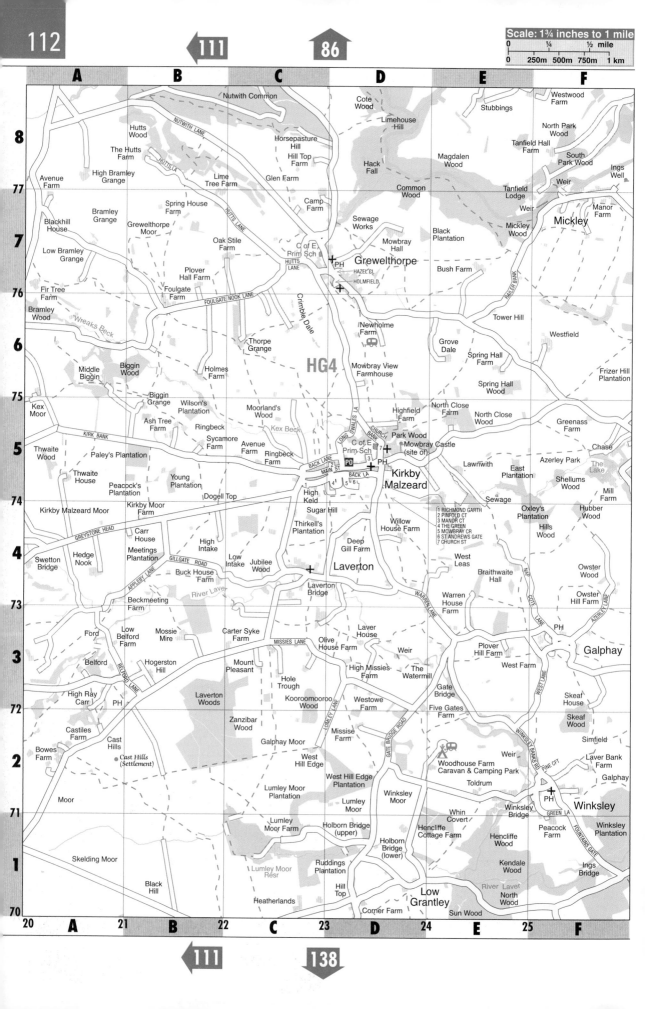

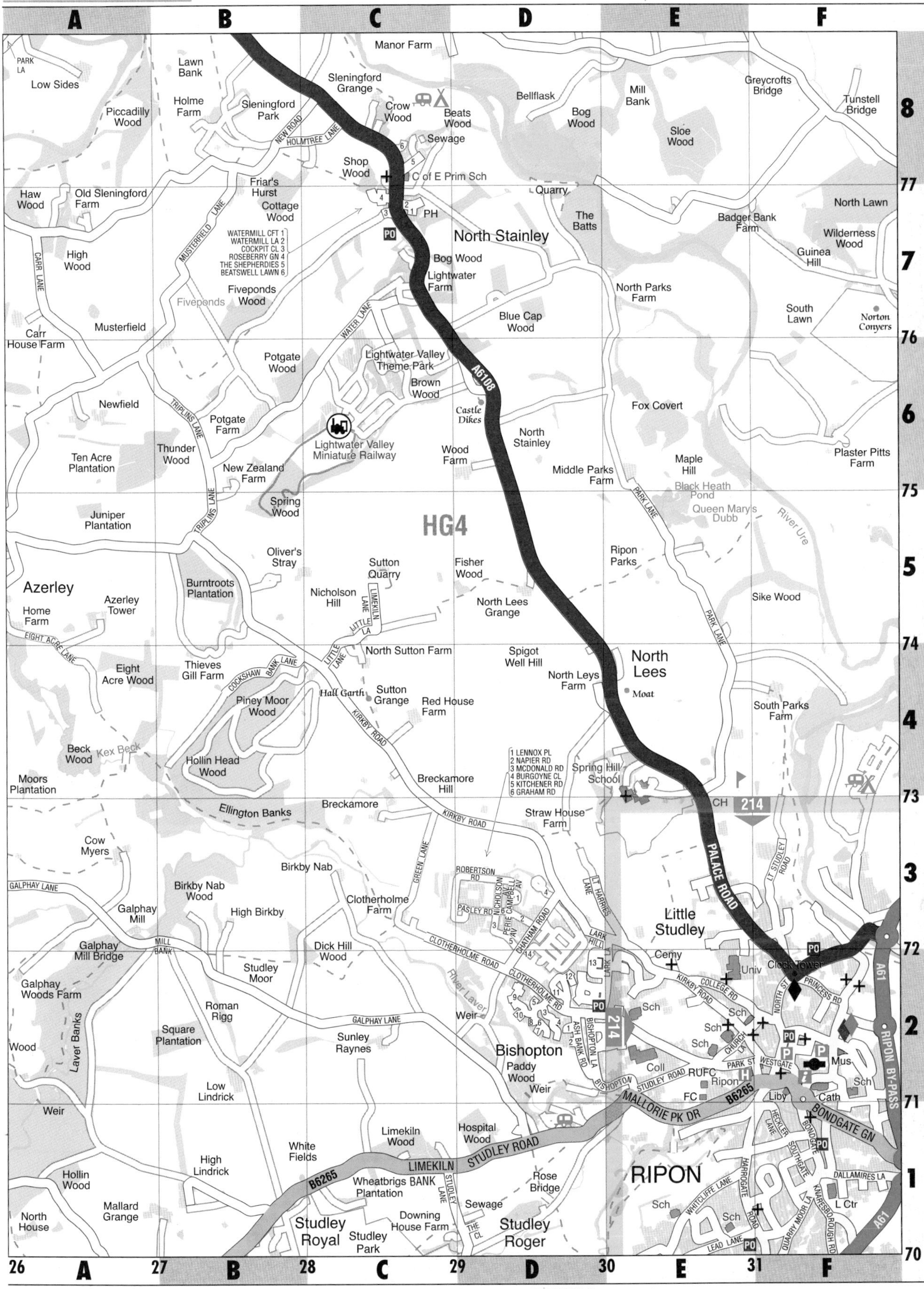

114

◄ 113

▲ 88

Scale: 1¾ inches to 1 mile

0 ¼ ½ mile
0 250m 500m 750m 1 km

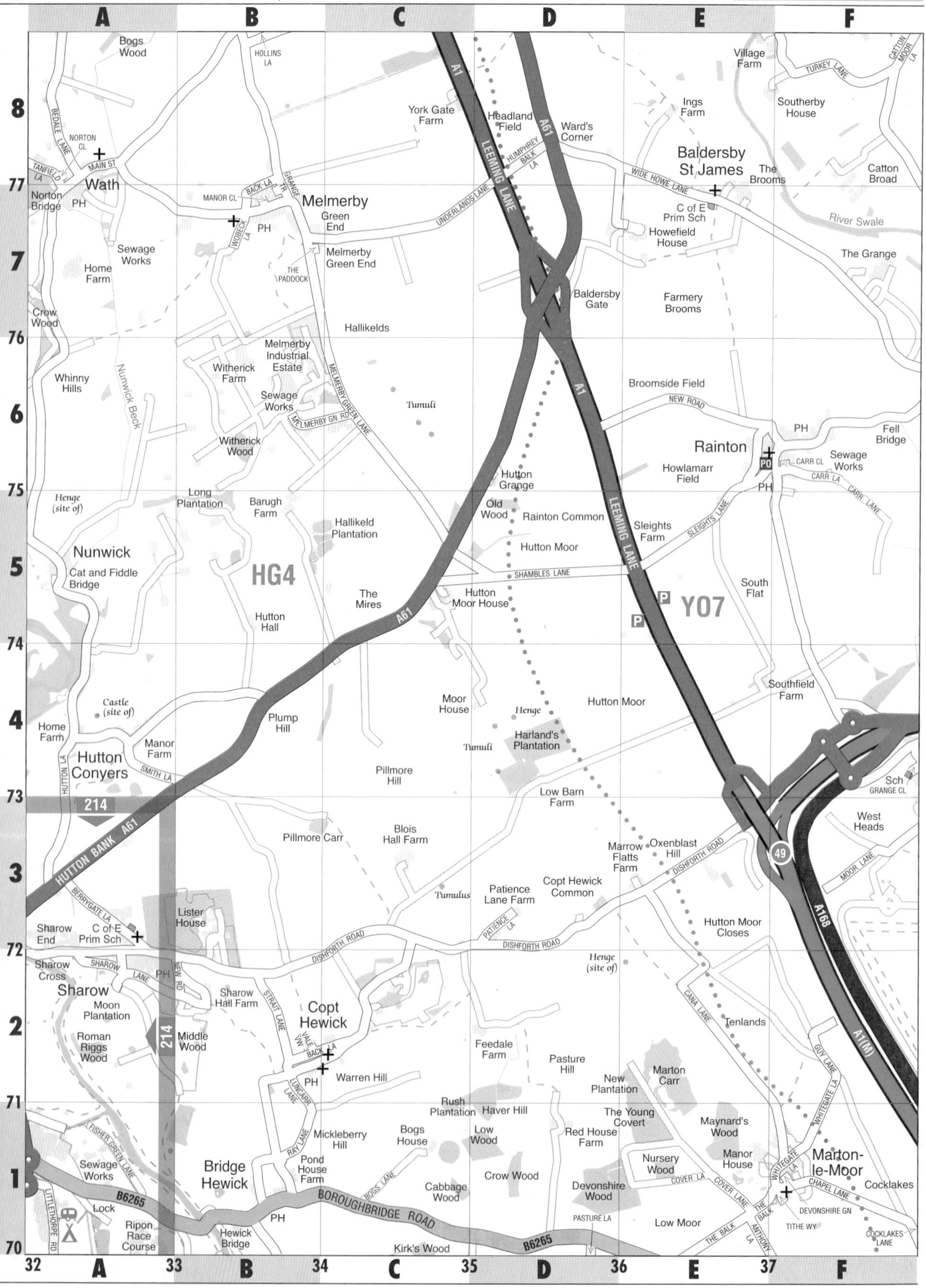

8

Bogs Wood

HOLLINS LA

Village Farm

TURKEY LANE

CATTON MOOR LA

York Gate Farm

Headland Field

Ward's Corner

Ings Farm

Southerby House

Catton Broad

BEDALE LANE

NORTON CL

MAIN ST

77

Wath

PH

MANOR CL

BACK LA

BRAMGE

Melmerby

Green End

HUMPREY BALK LA

WIDE HOWE LANE

Baldersby St James

The Brooms

TANFIELD LA

Norton Bridge

PH

IVYBECK LA

PH

THE PADDOCK

Melmerby Green End

C of E Prim Sch

Howefield House

River Swale

7

Home Farm

Sewage Works

LEEMING LANE

UNDERLANDS LANE

Baldersby Gate

Farmery Brooms

The Grange

Crow Wood

Hallikelds

76

Whinny Hills

Nunwick Back

Witherick Farm

Melmerby Industrial Estate

Tumuli

A1

Broomside Field

NEW ROAD

PH

Fell Bridge

Sewage Works

Witherick Wood

MELMERBY GN LANE

MELMERBY GREEN LANE

Rainton

CARR CL

PO

PH

CARR LA

CARR LANE

6

Nunwick

Long Plantation

Barugh Farm

Hutton Grange

Howlamarr Field

SLEIGHTS LANE

Sleights Farm

75

Henge (site of)

Hallikeld Plantation

Old Wood

Rainton Common

A1

South Flat

Cat and Fiddle Bridge

HG4

The Mires

Hutton Moor

SHAMBLES LANE

LEEMING LANE

5

Hutton Hall

Hutton Moor House

Hutton Moor

P

P

YO7

Southfield Farm

74

Home Farm

Castle (site of)

Manor Farm

Plump Hill

Moor House

Henge

Hutton Moor

Sch

GRANGE CL

4

Hutton Conyers

SMITH LA

Tumuli

Harland's Plantation

West Heads

HUTTON LA

214

Pillmore Hill

Low Barn Farm

A168

73

HUTTON BANK A61

Pillmore Carr

Blois Hall Farm

Marrow Flatts Farm

Oxenblast Hill

DISHFORTH ROAD

MOOR LANE

49

3

BERRYGATE LA

Tumulus

Patience Lane Farm

Copt Hewick Common

PATIENCE LA

Hutton Moor Closes

Sharow End

C of E Prim Sch

Lister House

DISHFORTH ROAD

Henge (site of)

CANA LANE

72

Sharow Cross

SHAROW LANE

PH

Sharow Hall Farm

DISHFORTH ROAD

Tenlands

A1(M)

GUY LANE

Sharow

Moon Plantation

NEW RD

Sharow Hall Farm

STRAIT LANE

Feedale Farm

Pasture Hill

New Plantation

Marton Carr

WHITEGATE LANE

2

Roman Riggs Wood

214

Middle Wood

VALE VW

BACK LA

PH

Maynard's Wood

Marton-le-Moor

WHITEGATE

CHAPEL LANE

Cocklakes

71

LONGGATE

PH

Warren Hill

Rush Plantation

Haver Hill

The Young Covert

Red House Farm

Nursery Wood

Manor House

COVER LA

COVER LANE

THE BALK

DEVONSHIRE GN

COCKLAKES LANE

RAY LANE

Mickleberry Hill

Bogs House

Low Wood

Devonshire Wood

Low Moor

ANTHONY LA

TITHE WY

1

LITTLETHORPE RD

Sewage Works

Bridge Hewick

Pond House Farm

BOGS LANE

Cabbage Wood

Crow Wood

PASTURE LA

THE BALK

Lock

B6265

PH

BOROUGHBRIDGE ROAD

70

Ripon Race Course

Hewick Bridge

Kirk's Wood

B6265

32 **A** 33 **B** 34 **C** 35 **D** 36 **E** 37 **F**

For full street detail of the highlighted area see page 214.

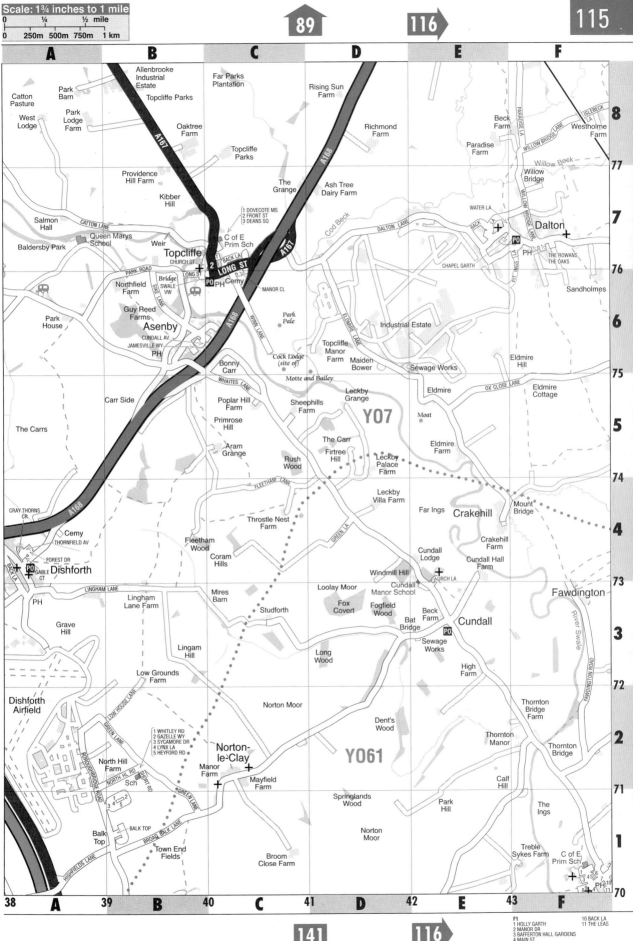

Scale: 1¾ inches to 1 mile

89 116 115

A B C D E F

8
77
7
76
6
75
5
74
4
73
3
72
2
71
1
70

Catton Pasture
Park Barn
Allenbrooke Industrial Estate
Topcliffe Parks
Far Parks Plantation
Rising Sun Farm
Beck Farm
Paradise Farm
Westholme Farm

West Lodge
Park Lodge Farm
Oaktree Farm
Richmond Farm
Paradise Farm
Willow Bridge
Willow Beck

A167
Providence Hill Farm
Topcliffe Parks
Kibber Hill
The Grange
Ash Tree Dairy Farm
A168
Water La
Willow Bridge
Dalton

Salmon Hall
CATTON LANE
Queen Marys School
Weir
1 DOVECOTE MS
2 FRONT ST
3 DEANS SQ
C of E Prim Sch
Cod Beck
DALTON LANE
Chapel Garth
PO
PH
THE ROWANS
THE OAKS

Baldersby Park
Northfield Farm
Topcliffe
CHURCH ST
LONG ST
Cemy
A167
MANOR CL
Sandholmes

Park House
Guy Reed Farms
Asenby
PARK ROAD
SIKE LANE
Bridge SWALE VW
PO
PH
WINN LANE
Eldmire Lane
Industrial Estate
Eldmire Hill

CUNDALL AV
JAMESVILLE WY
PH
A168
Bonny Carr
Park Pale
Cock Lodge (site of)
Topcliffe Manor Farm
Maiden Bower
Sewage Works
Eldmire
OX CLOSE LANE
Eldmire Cottage

Carr Side
WHAITES LANE
Poplar Hill Farm
Motte and Bailey
Sheephills Farm
Leckby Grange
YO7
Eldmire
Eldmire Farm

The Carrs
Primrose Hill
Aram Grange
Rush Wood
The Carr
Firtree Hill
Moat
Leckby Palace Farm
Eldmire Farm
Mount Bridge

Carr Side
FLEETHAM LANE
Leckby Villa Farm
Far Ings
Crakehill

CRAY THORNS CR.
A168
Cemy
THORNFIELD AV
Throstle Nest Farm
Fleetham Wood
GREEN LA
Cundall Lodge
Crakehill Farm
Cundall Hall Farm

FOREST DR
GABLE CT
Dishforth
LINGHAM LANE
Mires Barn
Coram Hills
Windmill Hill
CHURCH LA
Fawdington

PH
Grave Hill
Lingham Lane Farm
Studforth
Loolay Moor
Fox Covert
Fogfield Wood
Cundall Manor School
Beck Farm
Cundall
River Swale

Lingam Hill
Long Wood
Bat Bridge
PO
Sewage Works
Thornton Bridge Farm

Low Grounds Farm
LOW HOUSE LANE
Norton Moor
Dent's Wood
High Farm
Thornton Manor
Thornton Bridge

Dishforth Airfield
GREEN LANE
North Hill Farm
NORTH HL RD
Sch
SHORT RD
1 WHITLEY RD
2 GAZELLE WY
3 SYCAMORE DR
4 LYNX LA
5 HEYFORD RD
Norton-le-Clay
Manor Farm
Mayfield Farm
YO61
Calf Hill

BOROUGHBRIDGE ROAD
GREEN LANE
Balk Top
BALK TOP
BROAD BALK LANE
Town End Fields
Broom Close Farm
Springlands Wood
Park Hill
The Ings

HIGHFIELDS LANE
Norton Moor
Treble Sykes Farm
C of E Prim Sch
PH

F1
1 HOLLY GARTH
2 MANOR DR
3 BAFFERTON HALL GARDENS
4 MAIN ST
5 FOX GARTH
6 THE ORCHARDS
7 RASKELF RD
8 THE MALTINGS
9 BRIDGE ST
10 BACK LA
11 THE LEAS

38 39 40 41 42 43
A B C D E F

A   B   C   D   E   F

8

77

7

76

6

75

5

74

4

73

3

72

2

71

1

70

Sowerby Parks Farm
SANDY LA
MOOR LANE
ISLEBECK LANE
Islebeck Grange
New Plantation
Islebeck Farm
Isle Beck
Bruce House
Bridge Farm
Thirkleby Bridge
THE AVE
BACK LA
VICAR HL LA
Sewage Works
Little Bridge
Sandhill Farm
LOW ROAD
COMMON LANE
MILL DIKE LA
Islebeck Bridge
Rush Wood
Crowtree House
Plane Tree House
Thirkleby Barugh
Burtree House
Quarry Wood
SPRING LANE
CROFT LANE
CROFT CL
BUTT LA
PH
Dalton Moor
SCAIFE SHAY LANE
Scaife Shay Bridge
Hutton Moor
LOW LANE
HUTTON RAE LANE
Windmere Hill
A19
QUARRY BANKS
Cross Lanes
PO
BACK LA
The Barugh
Carlton Husthwaite
PH
Moor Share Plantation
Low Lane
LOW LANE
Hutton Sessay
Hall Farm
Birdforth House Farm
Little Hutton
PO
YO7
Highfield Farm
PH
Birdforth
Birdforth Bridge
Cold Harbour Farm
Sessay
CHURCH LANE
Birdforth Beck
1 BACK LA
2 WENTWORTH AV
3 BACK RD
4 CHURCH LA
OX CLOSE LANE
Broughton Farm
Cop Hall
Fullans
Sycamore Grange Farm
PH
Thormanby
Eldmire Moor
C of E Prim Sch
Little Sessay
MILL LA
MOOR LANE
Clarkwood Farm
Clark Wood
Dimple Wells
The Heights
Sessay Park
Watson Hill
BLIND PIECE LANE
Clark Wood
RACE LANE
Thormanby Hill Farm
New Mills
Enterprise Farm
High Wood
Wood End
Briar Hill Farm
White Carrs
Thormanby Carr
CARR LANE
West Moor
Ox Close Farm
Sessay Wood
Owlet Nest Farm
Throstle Nest
Cold Harbour Farm
A19
Tibet Plantation
Pilmoor Hall
East Moor
Jobbing Cross Bridge
Low Wood
NEW ROAD
Fawdington House
JOBBING CROSS
Pilmoor Cottages
Oak Tree Farm
Moor Plantation
Rush Plantation
Spring House Farm
Buskey Closes
Pilmoor
Pilmoor Grange
Raskelf Moor
YO61
Brafferton Spring Wood
Ellekers Wood
Sun Beck
Raskelf Bridge
West Moor
WEST MOOR ROAD
West Moor
HOWKER LA
West Moor
PH
SOMMERSET PASTURES
Bishop House
WEST MOOR ROAD
Moor House Farm
MOORFIELDS
BACK LA
West Moor
Parks Plantation
Park House
Old Burrow Hill
Raskelf
Little Meerut Plantation
Moorhouse Farm
MOOR HO LANE
Helperby Moor
The Parks
Fish Pond
Glebe Farm
FLAG LANE
The Green
Sewage Works
Brafferton
Sewage Works
RAGHILL LANE
Meerut Plantation
Leys Bridge
Leys Barn
Mill Farm

44 45 46 47 48 49

A   B   C   D   E   F

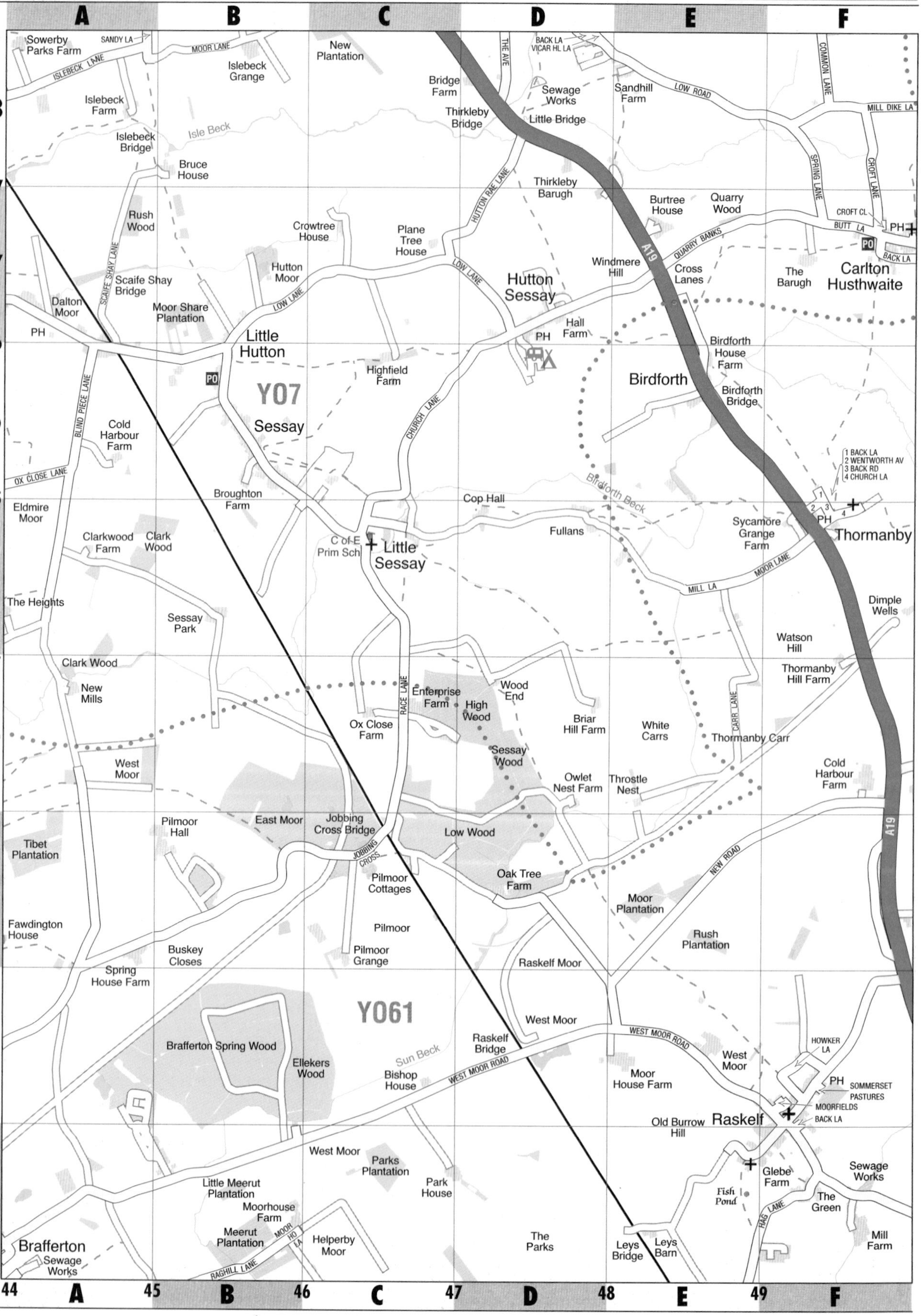

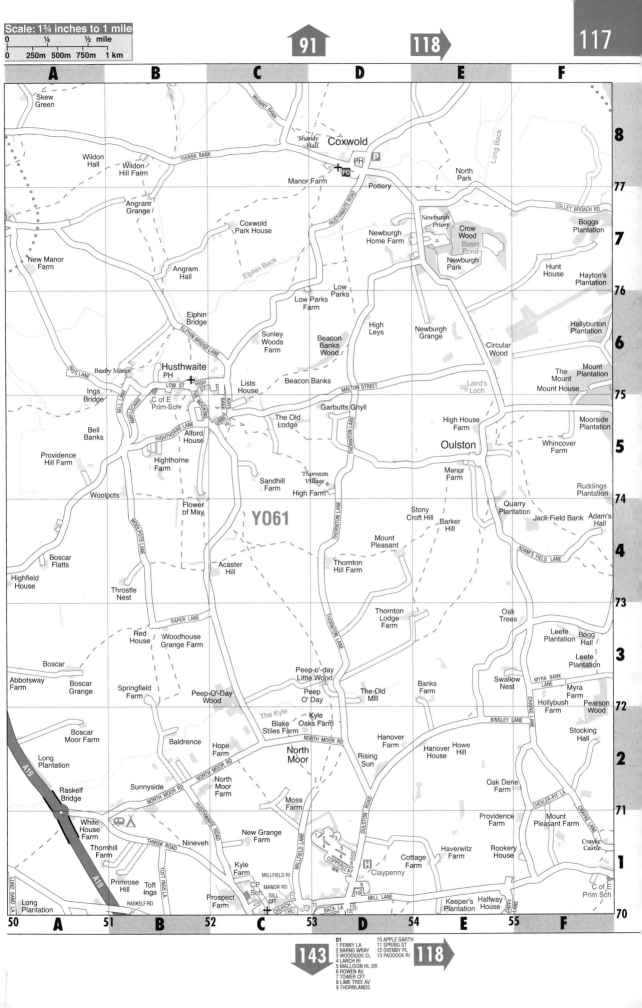

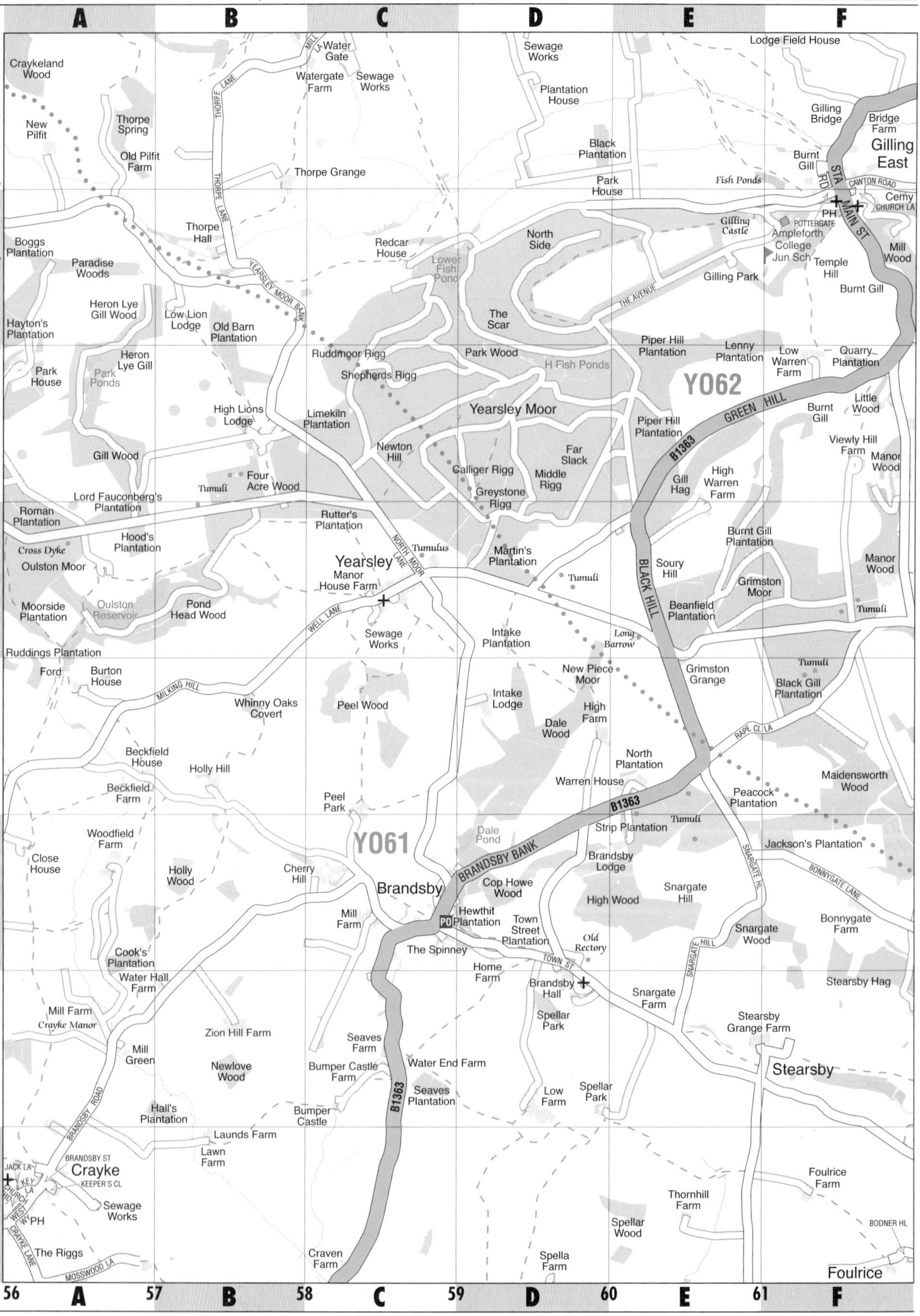

A B C D E F

8

Craykeland Wood

New Pilfit

Thorpe Spring

Old Pilfit Farm

Mill Lane

Water Gate

Watergate Farm

Sewage Works

Sewage Works

Lodge Field House

Gilling Bridge

Bridge Farm

Gilling East

Burnt Gill

77

Thorpe Grange

Thorpe Lane

Thorpe Hall

Plantation House

Black Plantation

Park House

Fish Ponds

Gilling Castle

AMPLEFORTH COLLEGE JUN SCH

POTTERGATE

Ampleforth College Jun Sch

STA RD

MAIN ST

CAWTON ROAD

PH

Cemy CHURCH LA

Mill Wood

Boggs Plantation

Paradise Woods

Redcar House

North Side

Piper Hill Plantation

Lenny Plantation

Low Warren Farm

Quarry Plantation

Temple Hill

Burnt Gill

7

Hayton's Plantation

Heron Lye Gill Wood

Low Lion Lodge

Old Barn Plantation

Yearsley Moor Bank

Lower Fish Pond

The Scar

THE AVENUE

Gilling Park

YO62

76

Park House

Heron Lye Gill

Park Ponds

Ruddmoor Rigg

Shepherds Rigg

Park Wood

H Fish Ponds

Piper Hill Plantation

GREEN HILL

B1363

Burnt Gill

Little Wood

Viewly Hill Farm

Manor Wood

6

Gill Wood

High Lions Lodge

Limekiln Plantation

Newton Hill

Yearsley Moor

Calliger Rigg

Far Slack

Piper Hill Plantation

Gill Hag

High Warren Farm

75

Lord Fauconberg's Plantation

Tumuli

Four Acre Wood

Rutter's Plantation

Greystone Rigg

Middle Rigg

BLACK HILL

Burnt Gill Plantation

Manor Wood

Roman Plantation

Hood's Plantation

North Moor Lane

Tumulus

Martin's Plantation

Tumuli

Soury Hill

Grimston Moor

Tumuli

5

Cross Dyke

Oulston Moor

Yearsley

Manor House Farm

Beanfield Plantation

Moorside Plantation

Oulston Reservoir

Pond Head Wood

WELL LANE

Sewage Works

Intake Plantation

Long Barrow

Grimston Grange

Tumuli

Black Gill Plantation

74

Ruddings Plantation

New Piece Moor

RAPE CL LA

Ford

Burton House

MILKING HILL

Whinny Oaks Covert

Peel Wood

Intake Lodge

Dale Wood

High Farm

North Plantation

Maidensworth Wood

4

Beckfield House

Holly Hill

Warren House

Peacock Plantation

Beckfield Farm

Peel Park

B1363

Strip Plantation

Tumuli

Jackson's Plantation

73

Woodfield Farm

YO61

Dale Pond

BRANDSBY BANK

Brandsby Lodge

SNARGATE HL

BONNYGATE LANE

Close House

Holly Wood

Cherry Hill

Brandsby

Cop Howe Wood

High Wood

Snargate Hill

Bonnygate Farm

3

Mill Farm

PO Hewthit Plantation

Town Street Plantation

Snargate Wood

Cook's Plantation

The Spinney

Home Farm

Old Rectory

Snargate Hill

Stearsby Hag

72

Water Hall Farm

Brandsby Hall

Snargate Farm

Stearsby Grange Farm

Mill Farm

Crayke Manor

Zion Hill Farm

Spellar Park

Stearsby

2

Mill Green

Newlove Wood

Bumper Castle Farm

Seaves Farm

Water End Farm

Low Farm

Spellar Park

Hall's Plantation

B1363

Seaves Plantation

71

BRANDSBY ROAD

Launds Farm

Lawn Farm

Bumper Castle

Foulrice Farm

JACK LA KEY

Crayke

KEEPER'S CL

BRANDSBY ST

Thornhill Farm

BODNER HL

1

CHURCH

PH

Sewage Works

Spellar Wood

CRAYKE LANE

The Riggs

MOSSWOOD LA

Craven Farm

Spella Farm

Foulrice

70

56 A 57 B 58 C 59 D 60 E 61 F

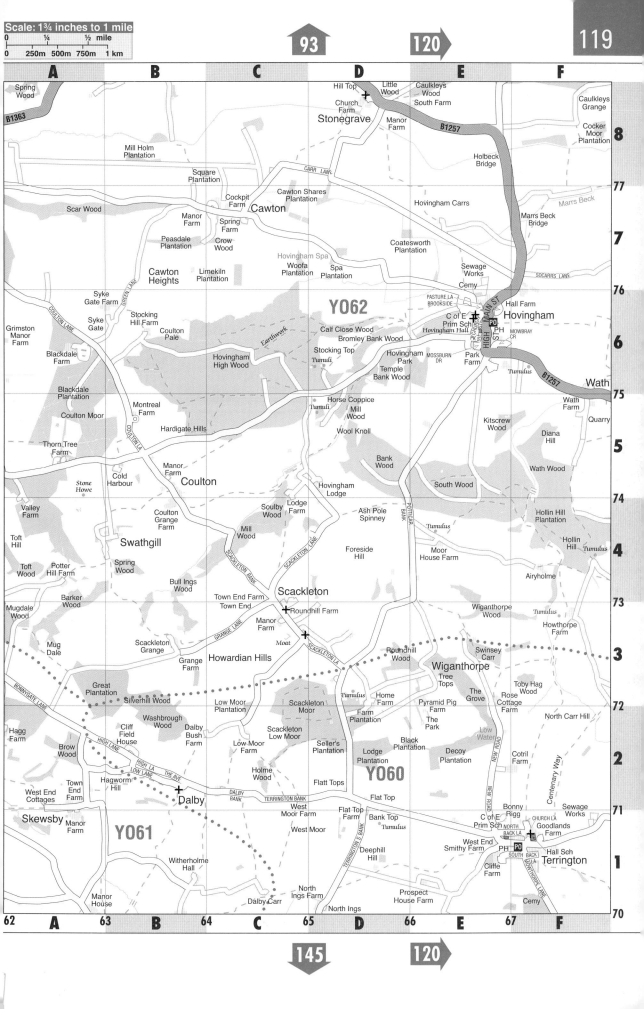

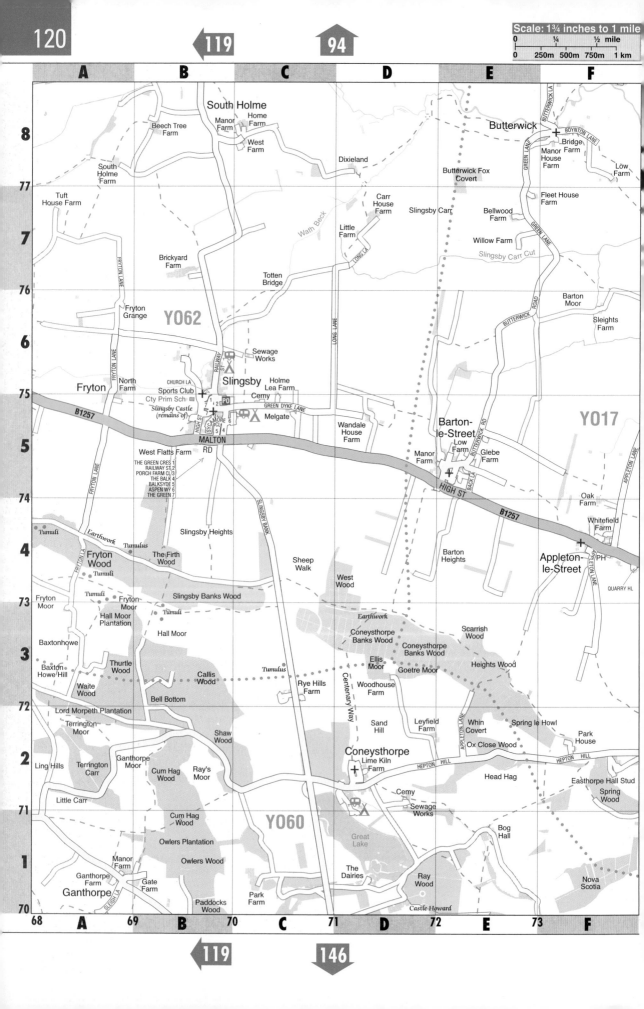

119
94

Scale: 1¾ inches to 1 mile

0   ¼   ½   mile
0   250m   500m   750m   1 km

A   B   C   D   E   F

8

South Holme

Butterwick

Home
Farm

Manor
Farm

West
Farm

Beech Tree
Farm

BUTTERWICK LA

BOYNTON LANE

Bridge
Farm

Manor
House
Farm

Low
Farm

77

South
Holme
Farm

Dixieland

Butterwick Fox
Covert

GREEN LANE

Tuft
House Farm

Carr
House
Farm

Slingsby Carr

Fleet House
Farm

Bellwood
Farm

7

Brickyard
Farm

Little
Farm

LONG LA

Slingsby Carr Cut

Willow Farm

76

Totten
Bridge

Wath Beck

Barton
Moor

Fryton
Grange

BUTTERWICK ROAD

Sleights
Farm

YO62

6

FRYTON LANE

LONG LANE

Sewage
Works

75

RAILWAY ST

Fryton

North
Farm

CHURCH LA
Sports Club
Cty Prim Sch

Slingsby

Holme
Lea Farm

Cemy

Barton-
le-Street

YO17

B1257

Slingsby Castle
(remains of)

HIGH ST
SYC
MORE
2 1
CL
5 4
6

PO

Melgate

GREEN DYKE LANE

BUTTERWICK RD

Manor
Farm

Low
Farm

BACK LA

Glebe
Farm

5

MALTON
RD

West Flatts Farm

Wandale
House
Farm

HIGH ST

74

THE GREEN CRES 1
RAILWAY ST 2
PORCH FARM CL 3
THE BALK 4
BALKSYDE 5
ASPEN WY 6
THE GREEN 7

B1257

Oak
Farm

Whitefield
Farm

Tumuli

Earthwork

Slingsby Heights

SLINGSBY BANK

Appleton-
le-Street

APPLETON LANE

PH

4

Fryton
Wood

Tumulus

The Firth
Wood

Sheep
Walk

West
Wood

Barton
Heights

QUARRY HL

FRYTON LA

Tumulus

73

Fryton
Moor

Tumuli

Fryton
Moor

Slingsby Banks Wood

Earthwork

Coneysthorpe
Banks Wood

Scarrish
Wood

Hall Moor
Plantation

Tumuli

Hall Moor

Coneysthorpe
Banks Wood

Heights Wood

3

Baxtonhowe

Ellis
Moor

Goetre Moor

Baxton
Howe Hill

Thurtle
Wood

Callis
Wood

Rye Hills
Farm

Woodhouse
Farm

Waite
Wood

Tumulus

Bell Bottom

72

Lord Morpeth Plantation

Centenary Way

Sand
Hill

Leyfield
Farm

APPLETON LANE

Whin
Covert

Spring le Howl

Park
House

Terrington
Moor

Shaw
Wood

Ox Close Wood

2

Ling Hills

Terrington
Carr

Ganthorpe
Moor

Cum Hag
Wood

Ray's
Moor

Coneysthorpe

Lime Kiln
Farm

HEPTON HILL

Head Hag

HEPTON HILL

Eastthorpe Hall Stud

Little Carr

Cemy

Spring
Wood

71

Cum Hag
Wood

YO60

Sewage
Works

Bog
Hall

Owlers Plantation

Great
Lake

Manor
Farm

Owlers Wood

The
Dairies

Ray
Wood

Nova
Scotia

1

Ganthorpe
Farm

Gate
Farm

SLEIGH LA

Park
Farm

Paddocks
Wood

Castle Howard

70

68   A   69   B   70   C   71   D   72   E   73   F

119
146

121
96

Scale: 1¾ inches to 1 mile

0	¼		½	mile
0	250m	500m 750m		1 km

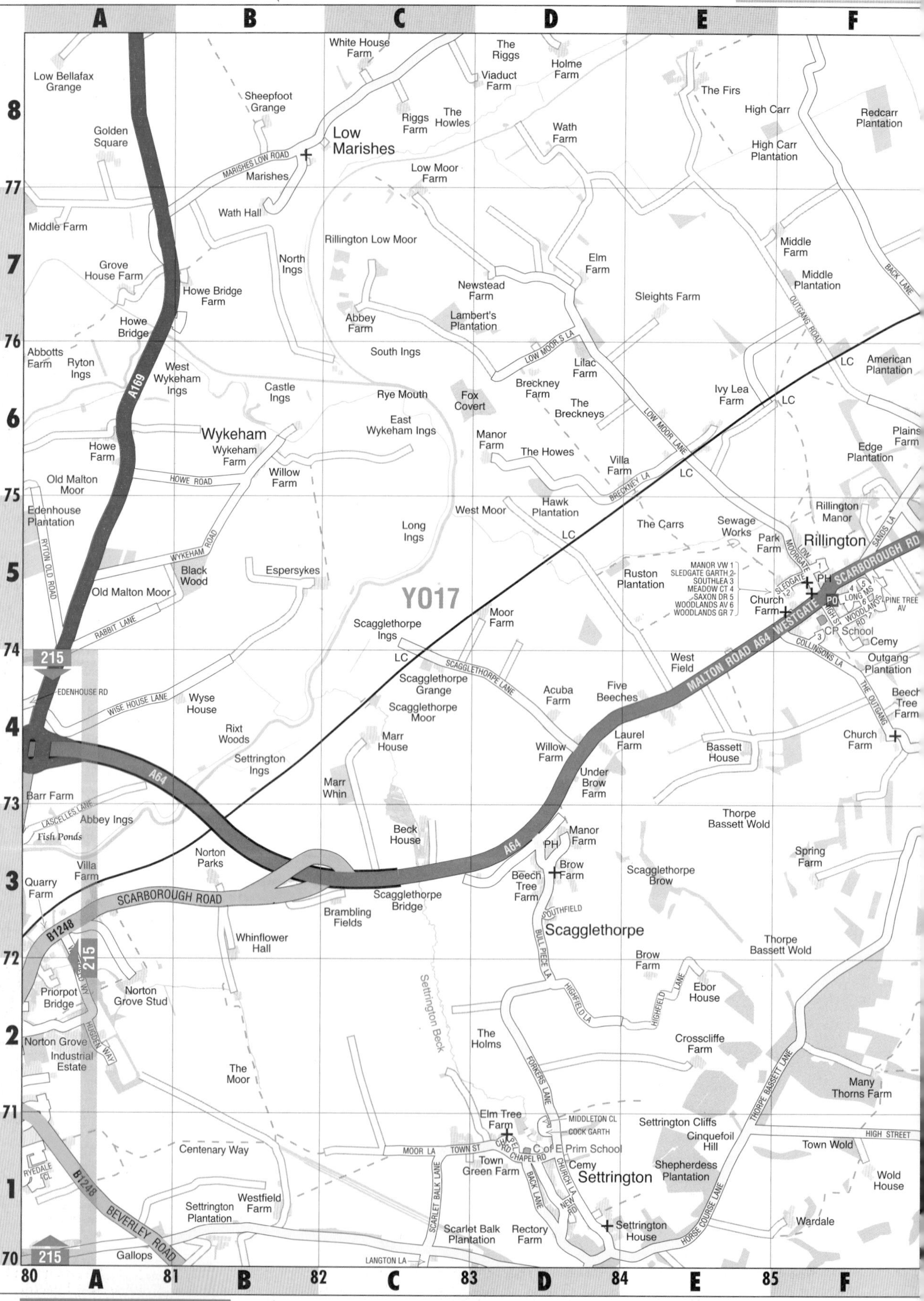

8

Low Bellafax Grange

Golden Square

White House Farm

Sheepfoot Grange

Riggs Farm

The Howes

The Riggs

Viaduct Farm

Holme Farm

The Firs

High Carr

Redcarr Plantation

Low Marishes

MARISHES LOW ROAD

Marishes

Wath Farm

High Carr Plantation

77

Middle Farm

Wath Hall

Low Moor Farm

Middle Farm

7

Grove House Farm

Howe Bridge Farm

North Ings

Rillington Low Moor

Elm Farm

Sleights Farm

Middle Plantation

BACK LANE

Howe Bridge

Abbey Farm

Lambert's Plantation

Newstead Farm

OUTGANG ROAD

76

Abbotts Farm

Ryton Ings

West Wykeham Ings

Castle Ings

South Ings

Breckney Farm

Lilac Farm

LC

American Plantation

A169

The Breckneys

Ivy Lea Farm

LOW MOOR S LA

LC

6

Howe Farm

Wykeham

Wykeham Farm

Rye Mouth

Fox Covert

East Wykeham Ings

Manor Farm

The Howes

Villa Farm

LOW MOOR LANE

LC

Plains Farm

Edge Plantation

75

Old Malton Moor

Edenhouse Plantation

HOWE ROAD

Willow Farm

WYKEHAM ROAD

Long Ings

West Moor

Hawk Plantation

BRECKNEY LA

LC

Rillington Manor

Rillington

SANDS LA

5

RYTON OLD ROAD

Black Wood

Espersykes

YO17

Moor Farm

The Carrs

Ruston Plantation

Sewage Works

Park Farm

SLEDGATE

MANOR VW 1
SLEDGATE GARTH 2
SOUTHLEA 3
MEADOW CT 4
SAXON DR 5
WOODLANDS AV 6
WOODLANDS GR 7

MOORGATE

SCARBOROUGH RD

PH

Old Malton Moor

RABBIT LANE

LC

SCAGGLETHORPE LANE

Scagglethorpe Ings

West Field

Church Farm

PO

LONG MS

PINE TREE AV

74

215

EDENHOUSE RD

WISE HOUSE LANE

Wyse House

Scagglethorpe Grange

Scagglethorpe Moor

Acuba Farm

Five Beeches

MALTON ROAD A64 WESTGATE

CP School

COLLINSONS LA

Cemy

Outgang Plantation

THE OUTGANG

4

A64

Rixt Woods

Settrington Ings

Marr House

Willow Farm

Laurel Farm

Bassett House

Church Farm

Beech Tree Farm

Barr Farm

Marr Whin

Under Brow Farm

Thorpe Bassett Wold

73

LASCELLES LANE

Abbey Ings

Fish Ponds

Beck House

A64

Manor Farm

Spring Farm

3

Quarry Farm

Villa Farm

Norton Parks

SCARBOROUGH ROAD

Brambling Fields

Scagglethorpe Bridge

PH

Beech Tree Farm

Brow Farm

Scagglethorpe Brow

Scagglethorpe

SOUTHFIELD

BULL PIECE LA

Thorpe Bassett Wold

72

B1248

215

Whinflower Hall

Settrington Beck

Brow Farm

HIGHFIELD LA

HIGHFIELD LANE

Ebor House

THORPE BASSETT LANE

2

Norton Grove Industrial Estate

HUDSON WAY

Priorpot Bridge

Norton Grove Stud

The Moor

The Holms

FORGERS LANE

Crosscliffe Farm

Many Thorns Farm

71

RYEDALE CL

B1248

Centenary Way

Elm Tree Farm

MOOR LA

TOWN ST

MIDDLETON CL

COOK GARTH

C of E Prim School

Settrington Cliffs

Cinquefoil Hill

HIGH STREET

Town Wold

1

BEVERLEY ROAD

Settrington Plantation

Westfield Farm

SCARLET BALK LANE

CHAPEL RD

Town Green Farm

BACK LANE

CHURCH LANE

Cemy

Settrington

Shepherdess Plantation

HORSE COURSE LANE

Wold House

Wardale

70

215

Gallops

LANGTON LA

Scarlet Balk Plantation

Rectory Farm

NEW RD

Settrington House

215
148

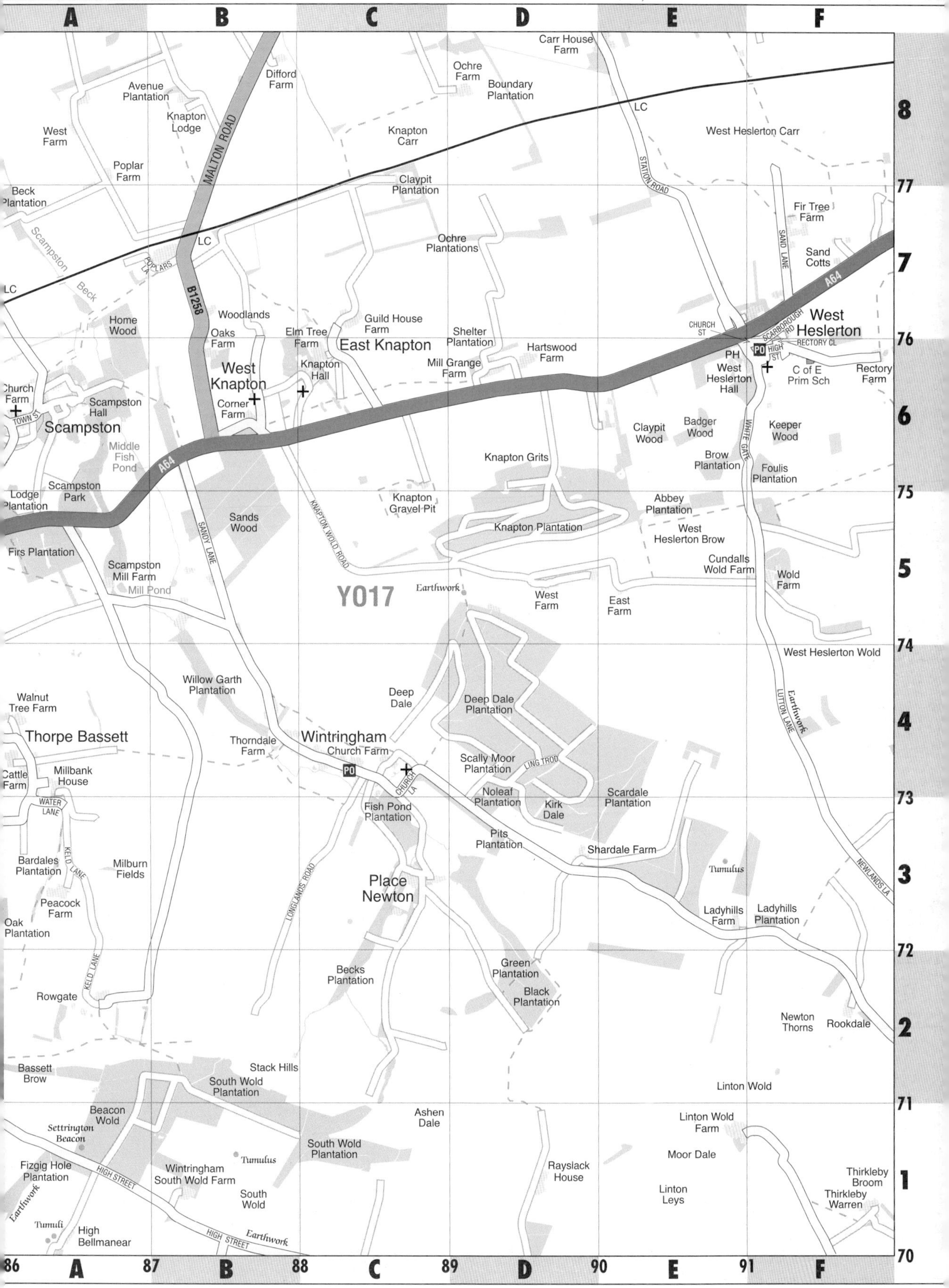
Scale: 1¾ inches to 1 mile
¼
½ mile
250m 500m 750m 1 km
97
124
A
B
C
D
E
F
Carr House Farm
Ochre Farm
Boundary Plantation
Difford Farm
Avenue Plantation
Knapton Lodge
MALTON ROAD
West Farm
Poplar Farm
Knapton Carr
LC
West Heslerton Carr
STATION ROAD
Beck Plantation
Claypit Plantation
Scampston Beck
LC
Ochre Plantations
Fir Tree Farm
SAND LANE
Sand Cotts
POPLARS LA
LC
B1258
A64
Home Wood
Woodlands
Oaks Farm
Elm Tree Farm
Guild House Farm
East Knapton
Shelter Plantation
Hartswood Farm
CHURCH ST
SCARBOROUGH RD
West Heslerton
HIGH ST
RECTORY CL
PH
West Heslerton Hall
C of E Prim Sch
Rectory Farm
West Knapton
Knapton Hall
Mill Grange Farm
Church Farm
Scampston Hall
Corner Farm
TOWN ST
Scampston
Middle Fish Pond
Claypit Wood
Badger Wood
WHITE GATE
Keeper Wood
A64
Knapton Grits
Brow Plantation
Foulis Plantation
Lodge Plantation
Scampston Park
Knapton Gravel Pit
Abbey Plantation
Sands Wood
Knapton Plantation
West Heslerton Brow
SANDY LANE
KNAPTON WOLD ROAD
Firs Plantation
Scampston Mill Farm
Mill Pond
Cundalls Wold Farm
Wold Farm
YO17
Earthwork
West Farm
East Farm
West Heslerton Wold
Willow Garth Plantation
Walnut Tree Farm
Deep Dale
Deep Dale Plantation
LUTTON LANE
Earthwork
Thorpe Bassett
Thorndale Farm
Wintringham
Church Farm
Scally Moor Plantation
LING TROD
Cattle Farm
Millbank House
CHURCH LA
WATER LANE
Noleaf Plantation
Kirk Dale
Scardale Plantation
Fish Pond Plantation
Pits Plantation
Shardale Farm
Tumulus
Bardales Plantation
KELD LANE
Milburn Fields
NEWLANDS LA
Place Newton
LONGLANDS ROAD
Peacock Farm
Ladyhills Farm
Ladyhills Plantation
Oak Plantation
Green Plantation
Becks Plantation
KELD LANE
Rowgate
Black Plantation
Newton Thorns
Rookdale
Bassett Brow
Stack Hills
South Wold Plantation
Linton Wold
Beacon Wold
Settrington Beacon
Ashen Dale
Linton Wold Farm
South Wold Plantation
Tumulus
Moor Dale
Fizgig Hole Plantation
HIGH STREET
Wintringham South Wold Farm
Rayslack House
Thirkleby Broom
Earthwork
South Wold
Linton Leys
Thirkleby Warren
Tumuli
High Bellmanear
HIGH STREET
Earthwork
8
77
7
76
6
75
5
74
4
73
3
72
2
71
1
70
86
87
88
89
90
91
149
124

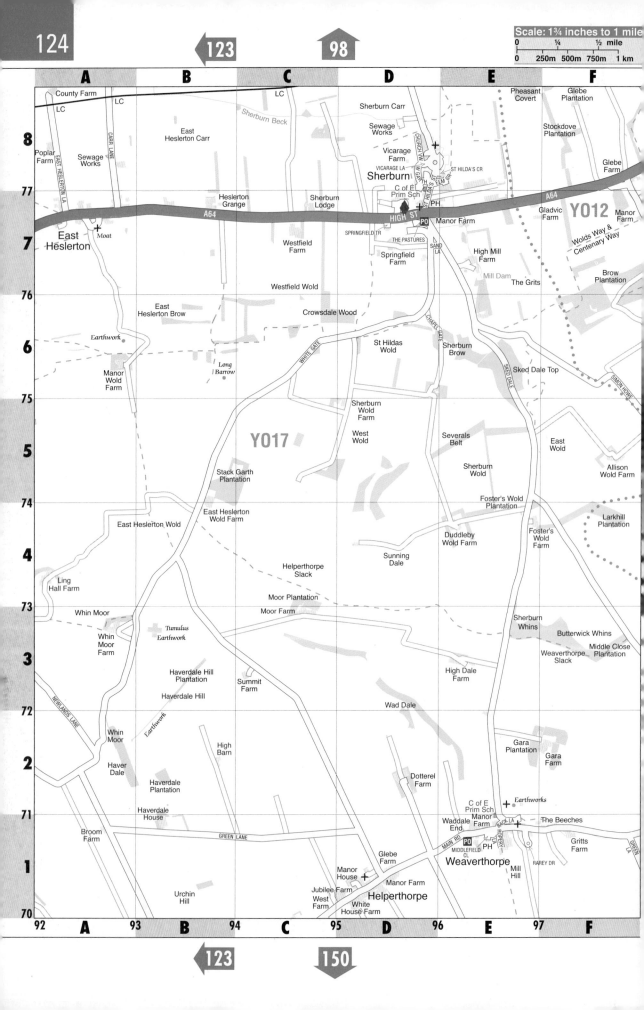

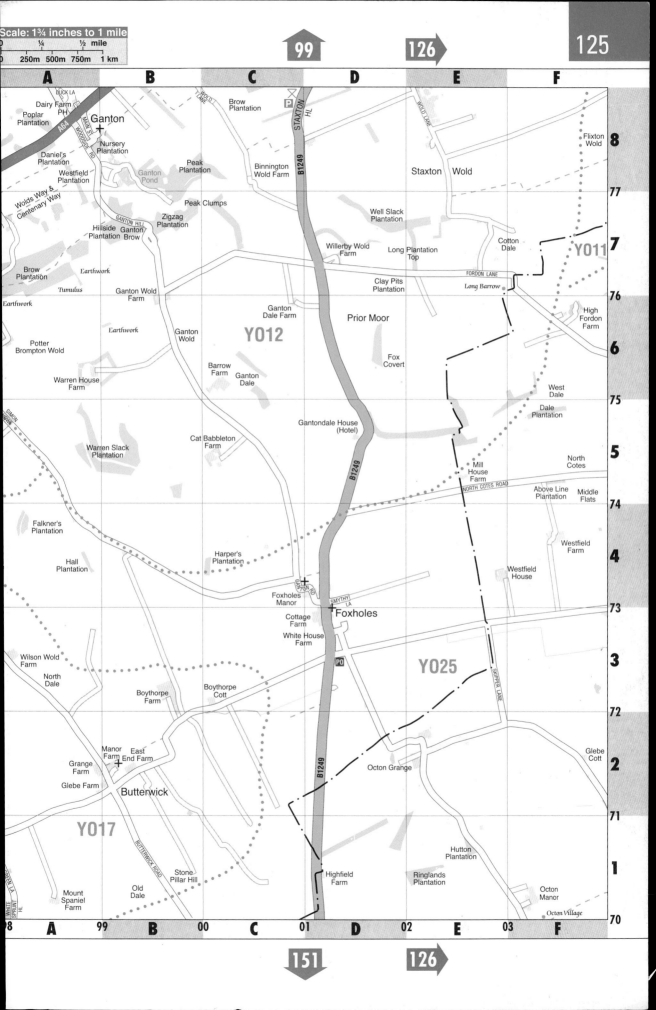

F8
1 OWSTON RD
2 MITFORD RD
3 MITFORD CL
4 OUTGAITS CL
5 WENTWORTH WY
6 SIMPSON AV

7 HIGH CFT
8 CASTLE HL
9 BOWLING GN LA
10 CHURCH HL
11 HUNGATE CT
12 VICARAGE CL
13 FONTAYNE RD

14 BARDNEY RD
15 ROWEDALE CL
16 AMBREY CL
17 PARK RISE
18 OLIVER'S CL
19 ROSEMOOR CL
20 HARBOROUGH CL

Scale: 1¾ inches to 1 mile

0   ¼   ½   mile

0   250m   500m   750m   1 km

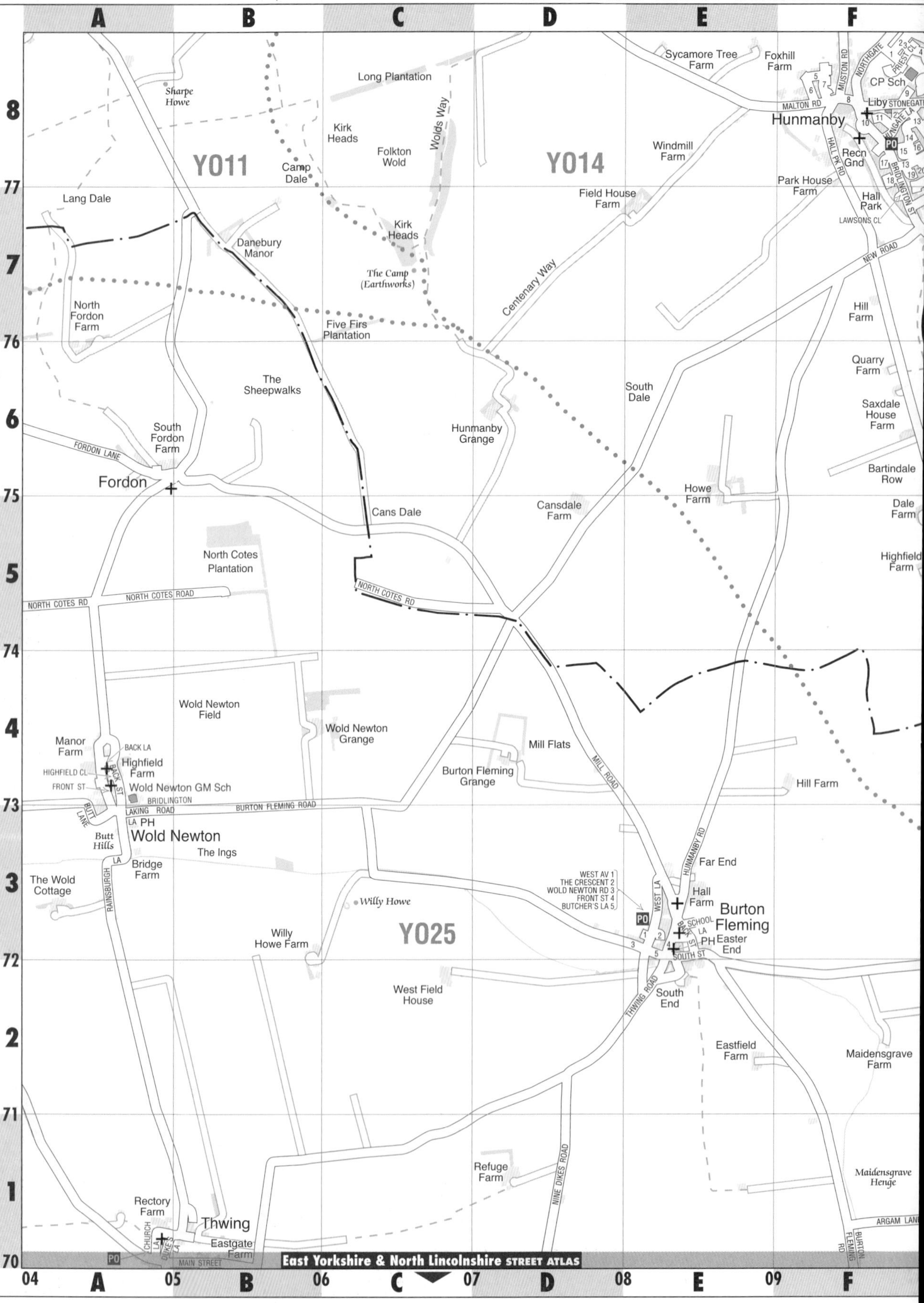

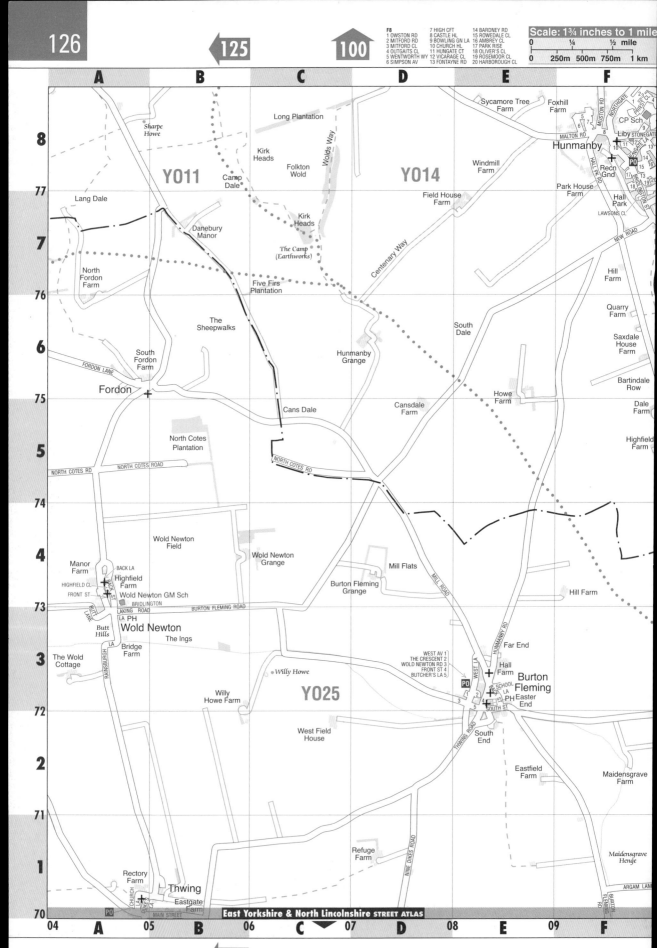

YO11

YO14

Sharpe Howe

Lang Dale

Long Plantation

Kirk Heads

Folkton Wold

Camp Dale

Danebury Manor

North Fordon Farm

The Camp (Earthworks)

Kirk Heads

Wolds Way

Five Firs Plantation

The Sheepwalks

Sycamore Tree Farm

Foxhill Farm

CP Sch

Hunmanby

Windmill Farm

Park House Farm

Hall Park

Field House Farm

Centenary Way

South Dale

Hill Farm

Quarry Farm

Saxdale House Farm

Bartindale Row

Dale Farm

South Fordon Farm

Fordon

Fordon Lane

Hunmanby Grange

Cans Dale

Cansdale Farm

Howe Farm

Highfield Farm

North Cotes Plantation

North Cotes Rd

North Cotes Road

North Cotes Road

Wold Newton Field

Wold Newton Grange

Mill Flats

Burton Fleming Grange

Mill Road

Hill Farm

Manor Farm

BACK LA

Highfield Farm

HIGHFIELD CL

FRONT ST

Wold Newton GM Sch

BRIDLINGTON

LAKING ROAD

BURTON FLEMING ROAD

Butt Hills

LA PH

Wold Newton

The Ings

RAINSBURGH LA

BUTT LANE

The Wold Cottage

Bridge Farm

Willy Howe

Willy Howe Farm

YO25

West Field House

WEST AV 1
THE CRESCENT 2
WOLD NEWTON RD 3
FRONT ST 4
BUTCHER'S LA 5

PO

WEST LA

SCHOOL LA

Far End

Hall Farm

HUNMANBY RD

Burton Fleming

PH Easter End

SOUTH ST

South End

THWING ROAD

Eastfield Farm

Maidensgrave Farm

Refuge Farm

NINE DIKES ROAD

Maidensgrave Henge

ARGAM LANE

BURTON FLEMING RD

Rectory Farm

Thwing

CHURCH LA

NINE DIKES LA

Eastgate Farm

PO

MAIN STREET

cale: 1¾ inches to 1 mile

| | ¼ | ½ mile |
| | 250m 500m 750m | 1 km |

A8
1 WRANGHAM DR
2 LENNOX CL
3 BURLYN RD
4 CHERRY RD
5 HAWKE GARTH
6 MANOR GD
7 CECIL RD
8 HOWES RD
9 WATSON CL
10 HAMERTON RD
11 HAMERTON CL
12 GRIMSTON RD
13 STRICKLAND RD
14 PERCY RD
15 HAVERCROFT RD
16 COWLINGS CL

101

127

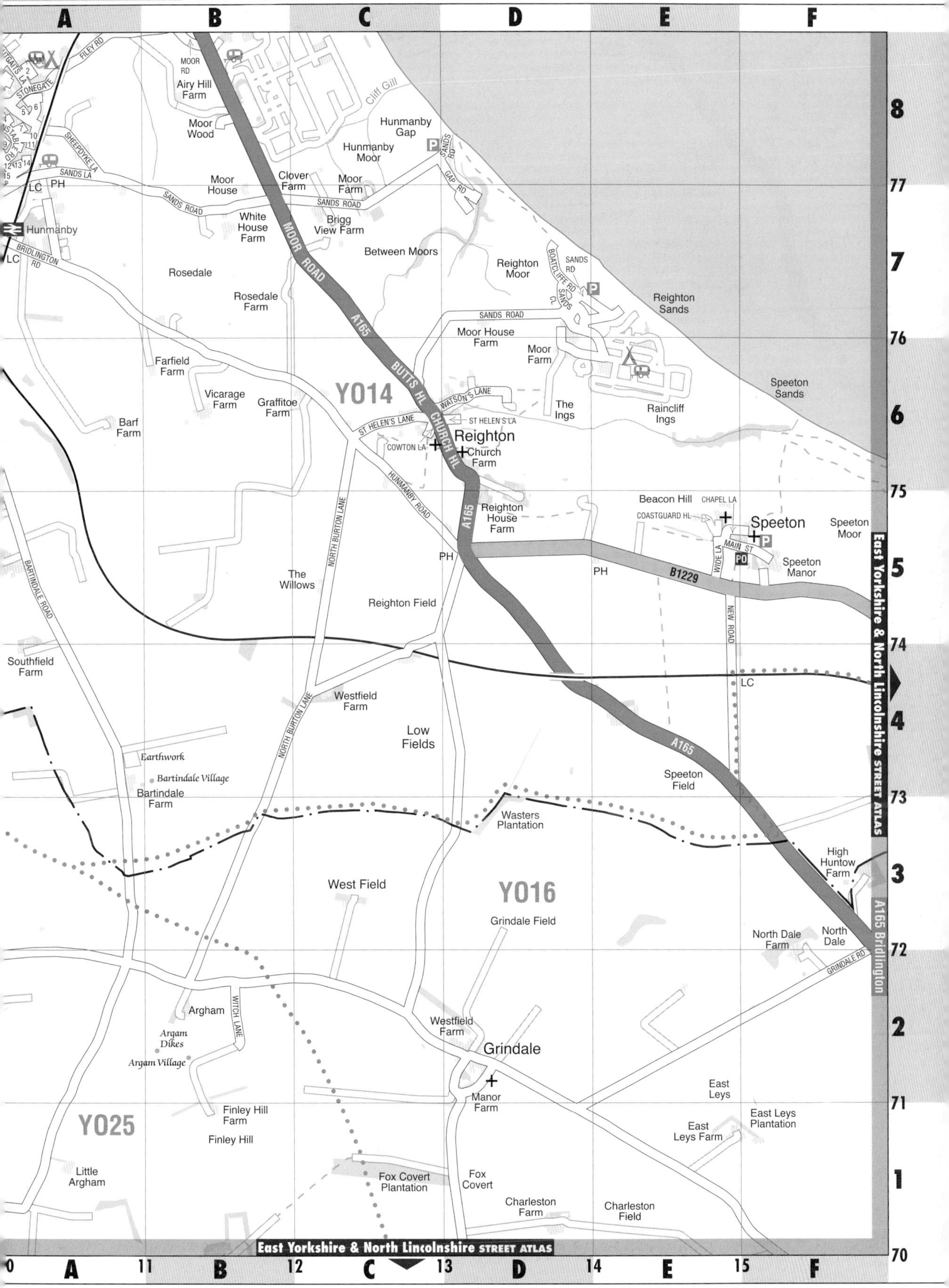

E8
1 CROWTREES
2 DOCTOR'S HL

F8
1 YEWTREE DR
2 HILLSIDE RD
3 HARLEY CL

Scale: 1¾ inches to 1 mile

0   ¼   ½   mile
0   250m 500m 750m 1 km

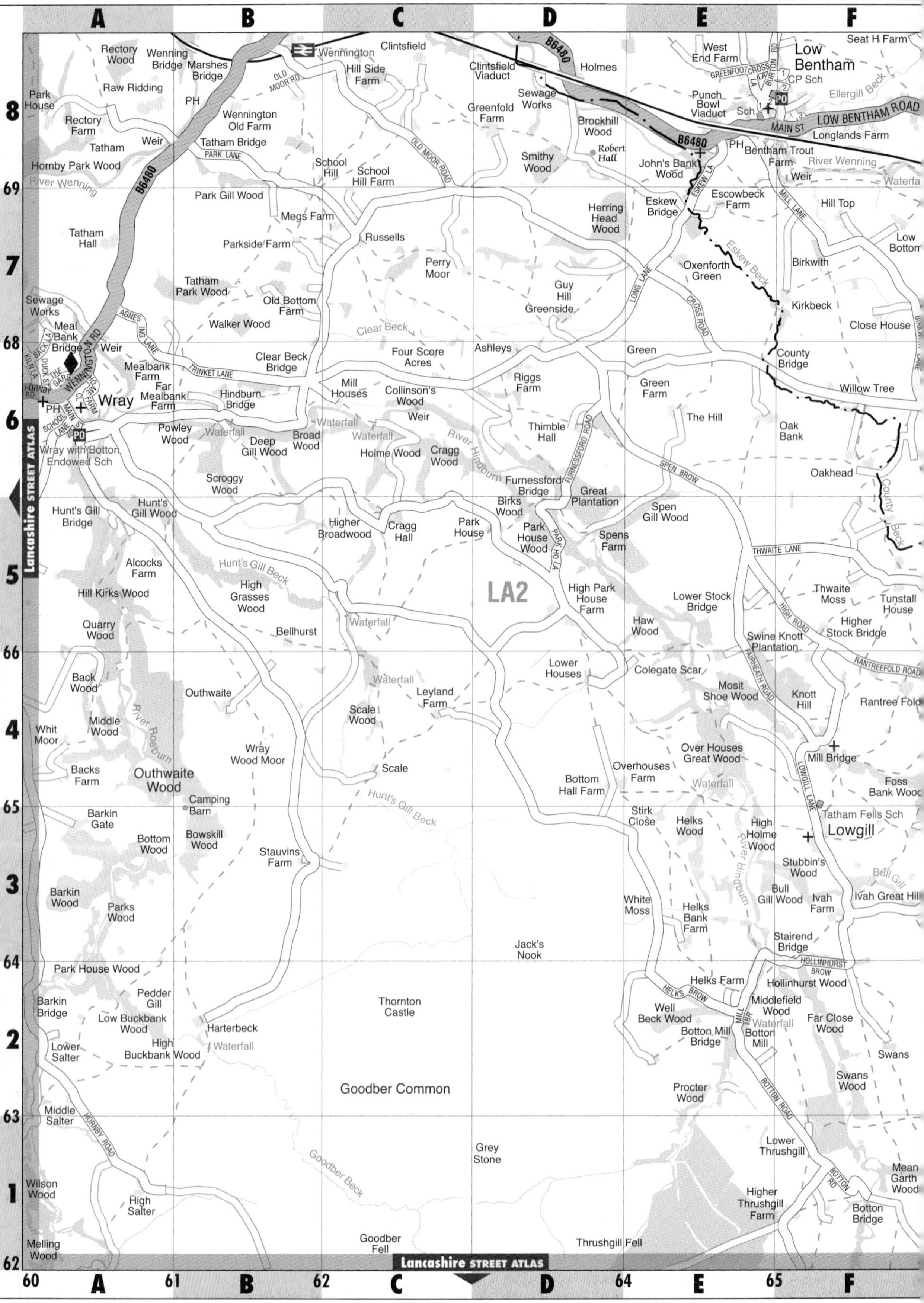

scale: 1¾ inches to 1 mile

¼   ½ mile
250m 500m 750m 1 km

A7
1 MAYFIELD RD
2 MILLHOLME DR
3 HOLME PK
4 HILLCROFT

A8
1 WESLEY CL
2 GOODENBER CR
3 BANKS HEAD RD
4 BANKS WY
5 BANKS RI
6 TWEED ST

7 GRASMERE DR
8 KING ST
9 LAKEBER CL

103

130

129

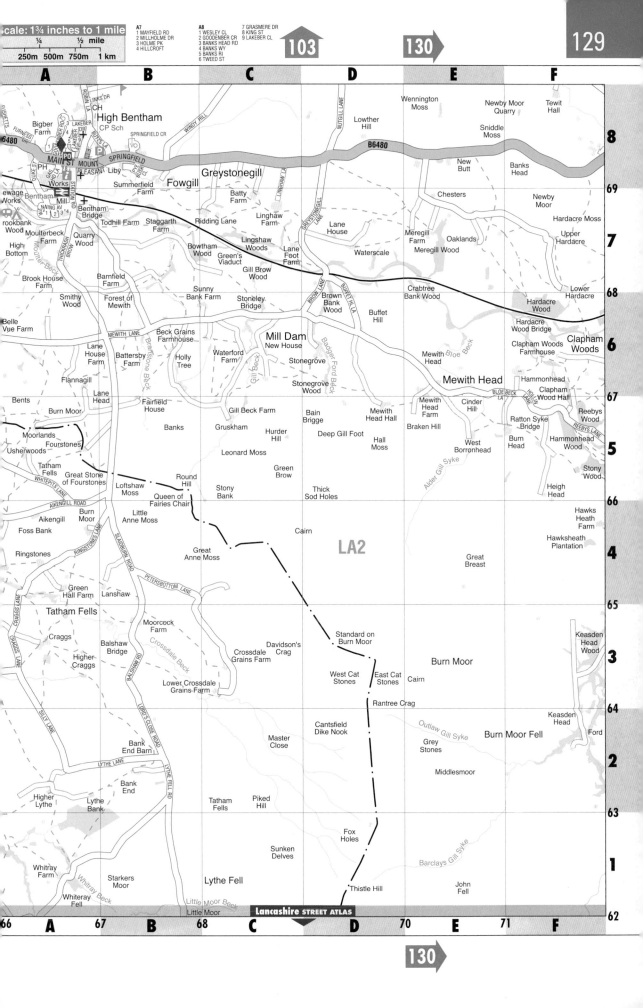

High Bentham
CP Sch

Bigber
Farm
Furness
6480
PH
Works
Main St
PO
Springfield
Mount
Pleasant
Liby
Bentham
Mill
Bentham
Bridge

Wennington
Moss
Newby Moor
Quarry
Tewit
Hall

Lowther
Hill
Sniddle
Moss

B6480

New
Butt
Banks
Head

Greystonegill
Fowgill
Summerfield
Farm
Batty
Farm
Lingham
Farm
Linghaw
Woods
Lane
House

Chesters

Newby
Moor

Todhill Farm
Staggarth
Farm
Ridding Lane
Lingshaw
Woods
Lane
Foot
Farm

Meregill
Farm
Oaklands
Meregill Wood

Waterscale

Hardacre Moss

Upper
Hardacre

Bowtham
Wood
Green's Viaduct
Gill Brow
Wood

Brook House
Farm
Barnfield
Farm
Sunny
Bank Farm
Stoneley
Bridge
Brown
Bank
Wood
Buffet Hill

Crabtree
Bank Wood

Lower
Hardacre

Hardacre
Wood

Smithy
Wood
Forest of
Mewith
Belle
Vue Farm
Moulterbeck
Farm
High
Bottom

Mewith Lane

Beck Grains
Farmhouse

Mill Dam
New House

Mewith
Head

Hardacre
Wood Bridge

Clapham
Woods

Lane
House
Farm
Battersby
Farm
Holly
Tree
Waterford
Farm
Stonegrove
Clapham Woods
Farmhouse

Clapham
Wood Hall

Flannagill
Lane
Head
Fairfield
House
Stonegrove
Wood
Mewith
Head Hall
Mewith Head

Hammonhead

Bents
Burn Moor
Banks
Gill Beck Farm
Bain
Brigge
Deep Gill Foot
Mewith
Head
Farm
Cinder
Hill
Ratton Syke
Bridge
Reebys
Wood

Moorlands
Fourstones
Usherwoods
Gruskham
Hurder
Hill
Hall
Moss
Braken Hill
Burn
Head
Hammonhead
Wood

Tatham
Fells
Great Stone
of Fourstones
Leonard Moss
Green
Brow
West
Borronhead
Stony
Wood

Loftshaw
Moss
Round
Hill
Stony
Bank
Thick
Sod Holes
Heigh
Head

Aikengill
Burn
Moor
Queen of
Fairies Chair
Cairn
Hawks
Heath
Farm

Foss Bank
Little
Anne Moss
Great
Anne Moss
LA2
Hawksheath
Plantation

Ringstones
Petersbottom Lane
Great
Breast

Green
Hall Farm
Lanshaw

Tatham Fells
Moorcock
Farm
Standard on
Burn Moor
Keasden
Head
Wood

Craggs
Balshaw
Bridge
Crossdale
Grains Farm
Davidson's
Crag
Burn Moor

Higher
Craggs
Lower Crossdale
Grains Farm
West Cat
Stones
East Cat
Stones
Cairn

Rantree Crag

Bank
End Barn
Master
Close
Cantsfield
Dike Nook
Grey
Stones
Burn Moor Fell
Keasden
Head
Ford

Lythe Lane
Middlesmoor

Bank
End

Higher
Lythe
Lythe
Bank
Tatham
Fells
Piked
Hill

Fox
Holes

Whitray
Farm
Starkers
Moor
Lythe Fell
Sunken
Delves
John
Fell

Whiteray
Fell
Little Moor Beck
Little Moor
Thistle Hill

130

129

104

C8
1 THE GN
2 CLAPDALE WY
3 CROSS HAW LA

Scale: 1¾ inches to 1 mile

0   ¼   ½   mile
0   250m 500m 750m 1 km

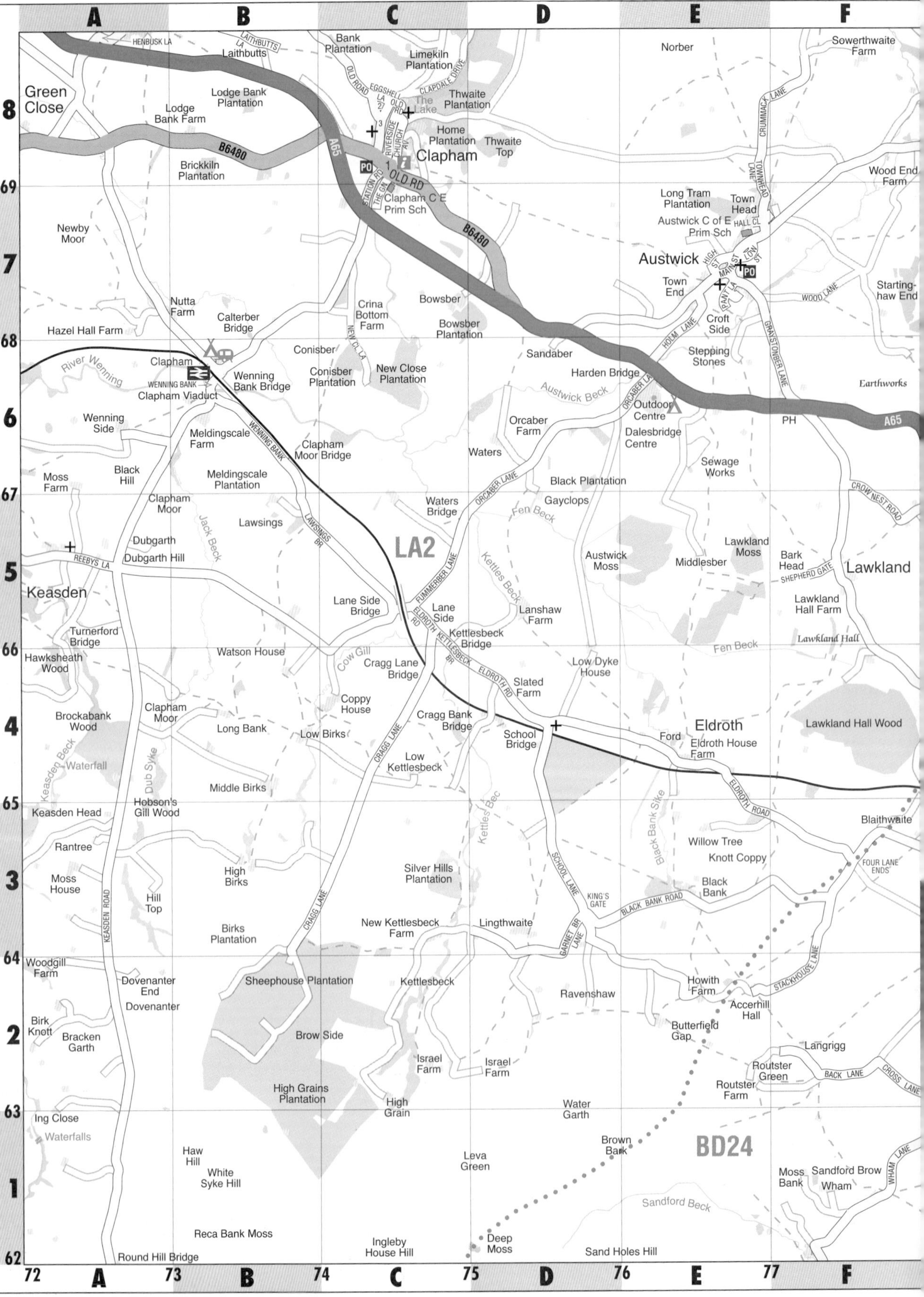

A B C D E F

8

Green
Close

Henbusk La
Laithbutts La
Laithbutts

Bank
Plantation

Limekiln
Plantation

Norber

Sowerthwaite
Farm

Lodge Bank
Plantation

Lodge
Bank Farm

Eggshell La
Old Rd

Thwaite
Plantation

Crummack Lane

B6480

Brickkiln
Plantation

A65

The Lake

Home
Plantation

Clapham

Thwaite
Top

Downhead Lane

Wood End
Farm

69

PO

Old Rd

Station Rd

The Gn

Riverside Church

Clapham C E
Prim Sch

Long Tram
Plantation

Austwick C of E
Prim Sch

Town
Head

Hall Cl

B6480

High St

Pant La

PO

7

Newby
Moor

Austwick

Town
End

Wood Lane

Starting-
haw End

Nutta
Farm

Calterber
Bridge

Crina
Bottom
Farm

Bowsber

New Cl La

Bowsber
Plantation

Hollin Lane

Town
End

Croft
Side

Graystonber Lane

68

Hazel Hall Farm

Clapham

Conisber

Sandaber

Harden Bridge

Stepping
Stones

Earthworks

River Wenning

Wenning
Bank Bridge

Conisber
Plantation

New Close
Plantation

Austwick Beck

Outdoor
Centre

PH

A65

Wenning Bank

Clapham Viaduct

6

Wenning
Side

Meldingscale
Farm

Wenning Bank

Clapham
Moor Bridge

Waters

Orcaber
Farm

Dalesbridge
Centre

Sewage
Works

Moss
Farm

Black
Hill

Meldingscale
Plantation

Jack Beck

Clapham
Moor

Lawsings

Lawsings Br

Waters
Bridge

Orcaber Lane

Black Plantation

Gayclops

Crow Nest Road

67

Fen Beck

Lawkland
Moss

Bark
Head

Lawkland

Dubgarth

Dubgarth Hill

LA2

Austwick
Moss

Middlesber

Shepherd Gate

Lawkland
Hall Farm

5

Reebys La

Keasden

Lane Side
Bridge

Lane
Side

Lanshaw
Farm

Fen Beck

Lawkland Hall

Kettlesbeck
Bridge

Kummerber Lane

Kettles Beck

Low Dyke
House

66

Hawksheath
Wood

Turnerford
Bridge

Watson House

Cow Gill

Cragg Lane
Bridge

Eldroth Rd

Kettlesbeck Br

Eldroth Rd

Slated
Farm

Brockabank
Wood

Clapham
Moor

Long Bank

Low Birks

Coppy
House

Cragg Bank
Bridge

School
Bridge

Ford

Eldroth

Eldroth House
Farm

Lawkland Hall Wood

4

Keasden Beck

Dub Syke

Cragg Lane

Low
Kettlesbeck

Middle Birks

Eldroth Road

65

Waterfall

Keasden Head

Hobson's
Gill Wood

Kettles Beck

Black Bank Sike

Blaithwaite

Rantree

High
Birks

Willow Tree
Knott Coppy

Four Lane
Ends

3

Moss
House

Hill
Top

School Lane

King's
Gate

Black Bank Road

Black
Bank

Keasden Road

Birks
Plantation

Cragg Lane

New Kettlesbeck
Farm

Silver Hills
Plantation

Lingthwaite

Garnet Br Lane

64

Woodgill
Farm

Dovenanter
End

Dovenanter

Sheephouse Plantation

Kettlesbeck

Ravenshaw

Howith
Farm

Accerhill
Hall

Stackhouse Lane

2

Birk
Knott

Bracken
Garth

Brow Side

Israel
Farm

Israel
Farm

Butterfield
Gap

Langrigg

Routster
Green

Back Lane

Cross Lane

High Grains
Plantation

High
Grain

Water
Garth

Routster
Farm

63

Ing Close

Waterfalls

Haw
Hill

White
Syke Hill

Leva
Green

Brown
Bank

BD24

Moss
Bank

Sandford Brow

Wham

Wham Lane

1

Reca Bank Moss

Sandford Beck

Sand Holes Hill

62

Round Hill Bridge

Ingleby
House Hill

Deep
Moss

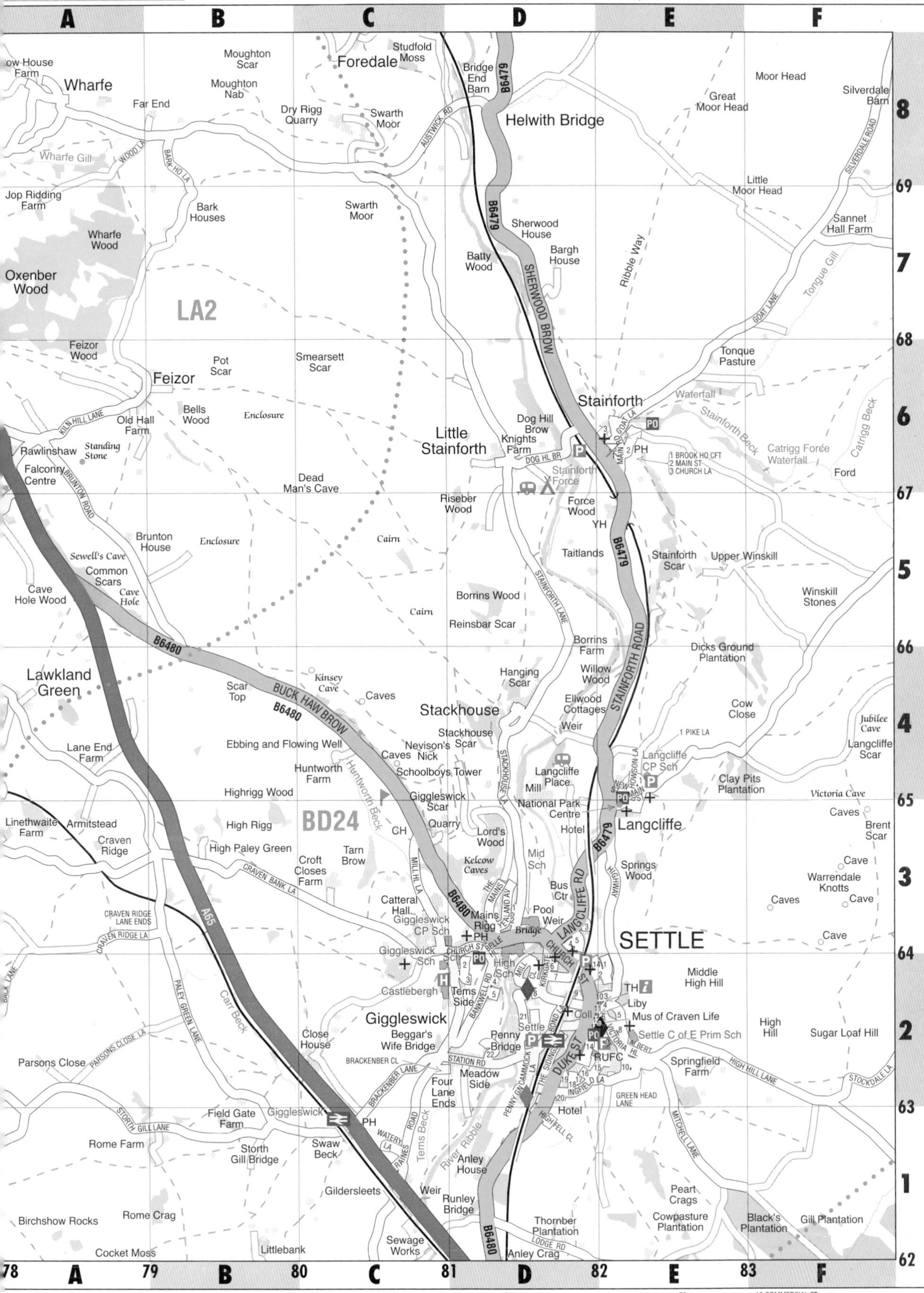

D2
1 BUCKS LA
2 TEMS ST
3 TEMS SIDE
4 KENDALMANS
5 RIVERSDALE
6 TILLMAN CL
7 MARSHFIELD RD
8 KINGS MILL LA
9 WHITEFRIARS CT
10 MARKET PL
11 CHEAPSIDE
12 CHAPEL ST
13 CRAGDALE
14 HIGH HL GR ST
15 LWR GREENFOOT
16 BIRCHWOOD CL
17 FALCON CL
18 LONGDALE AV
19 DELANEY CL
20 FALCON GD
21 SOWARTH FIELD
22 SANDHOLME CL

D3
1 MAINSFIELD CL
2 MAINSFIELD RI
3 SYKES BARREL
4 NORTHFIELDS AV
5 NORTHFIELDS CR

E2
1 TOWN HEAD AV
2 TOWNHEAD
3 CONSTITUTION HL
4 CASTLE HI
5 CASTLEBERGH LA
6 HIGH ST
7 CHAPEL SQ
8 SCHOOL HL
9 G HEAD LA
10 COMMERCIAL ST

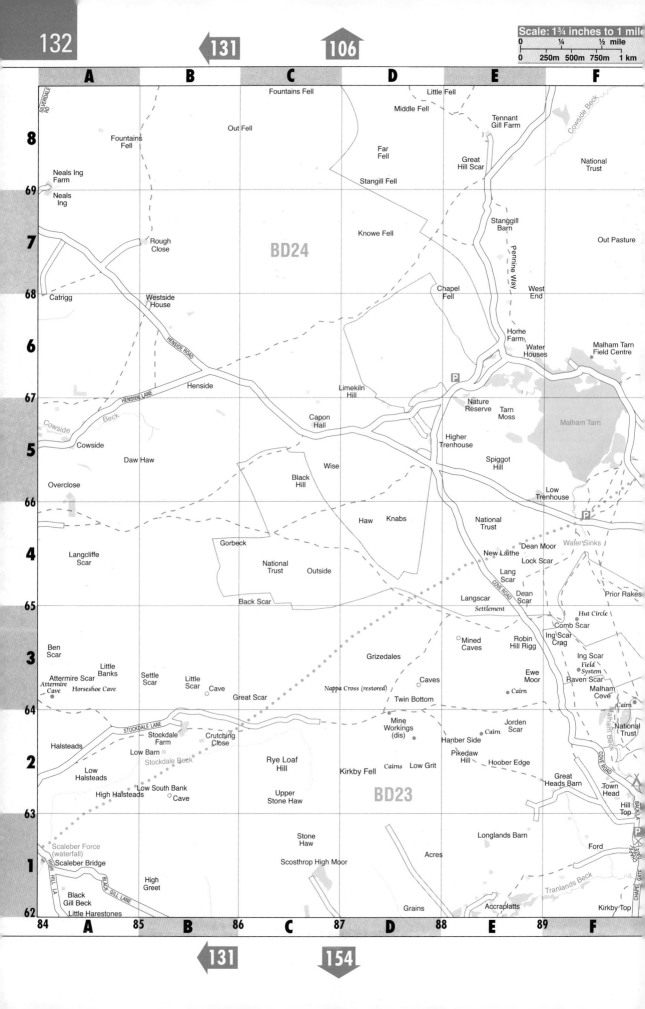

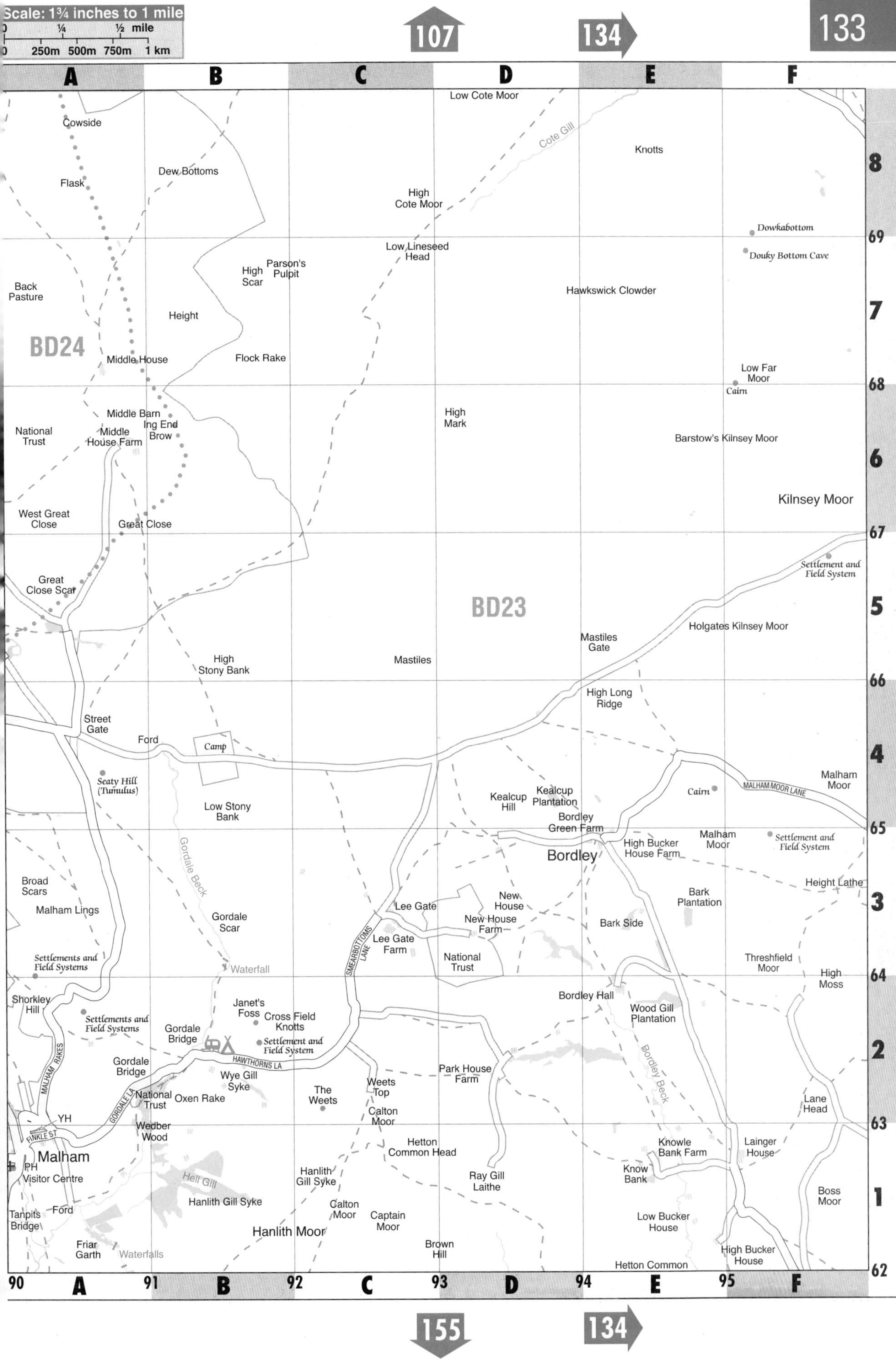

Scale: 1¾ inches to 1 mile

0   ¼   ½ mile
0 250m 500m 750m 1 km

A **B** **C** **D** **E** **F**

Low Cote Moor

Cowside

Cote Gill

Knotts

8

Dew Bottoms

Flask

Dowkabottom

69

High
Cote Moor

Douky Bottom Cave

Low Lineseed
Head

Back
Pasture

High
Scar

Parson's
Pulpit

Hawkswick Clowder

7

BD24

Height

Middle House

Flock Rake

Low Far
Moor

68

Cairn

Middle Barn
Ing End
Brow

High
Mark

Barstow's Kilnsey Moor

6

National
Trust

Middle
House Farm

West Great
Close

Great Close

Kilnsey Moor

Great
Close Scar

67

Settlement and
Field System

BD23

5

High
Stony Bank

Mastiles

Mastiles
Gate

Holgates Kilnsey Moor

High Long
Ridge

66

Street
Gate

Ford

Camp

Malham
Moor

MALHAM MOOR LANE

4

Seaty Hill
(Tumulus)

Low Stony
Bank

Kealcup
Hill

Kealcup
Plantation

Cairn

Malham
Moor

Bordley
Green Farm

Settlement and
Field System

65

Gordale Beck

High Bucker
House Farm

Broad
Scars

Gordale
Scar

Bordley

Height Lathe

Malham Lings

New
House

Bark
Plantation

3

Settlements and
Field Systems

Lee Gate

New House
Farm

Bark Side

Threshfield
Moor

High
Moss

Waterfall

SMEARBOTTOMS LANE

Lee Gate
Farm

National
Trust

64

Shorkley
Hill

Settlements and
Field Systems

Janet's
Foss

Cross Field
Knotts

Bordley Hall

Wood Gill
Plantation

MALHAM RAKES

Gordale
Bridge

Settlement and
Field System

Bordley Beck

Lane
Head

2

Gordale
Bridge

HAWTHORNS LA

Park House
Farm

GORDALE LN

Wye Gill
Syke

Weets
Top

National
Trust

Oxen Rake

The
Weets

Calton
Moor

Knowle
Bank Farm

Lainger
House

63

YH

Wedber
Wood

Boss
Moor

FINKLE ST

Malham

Hetton
Common Head

Know
Bank

PH
Visitor Centre

Hell Gill

Hanlith
Gill Syke

Ray Gill
Laithe

Low Bucker
House

1

Tanpits
Bridge

Ford

Hanlith Gill Syke

Calton
Moor

Captain
Moor

High Bucker
House

Friar
Garth

Waterfalls

Hanlith Moor

Brown
Hill

Hetton Common

62

A **B** **C** **D** **E** **F**

90   91   92   93   94   95

Scale: 1¾ inches to 1 mile

0   ¼   ½   mile

0 250m 500m 750m 1 km

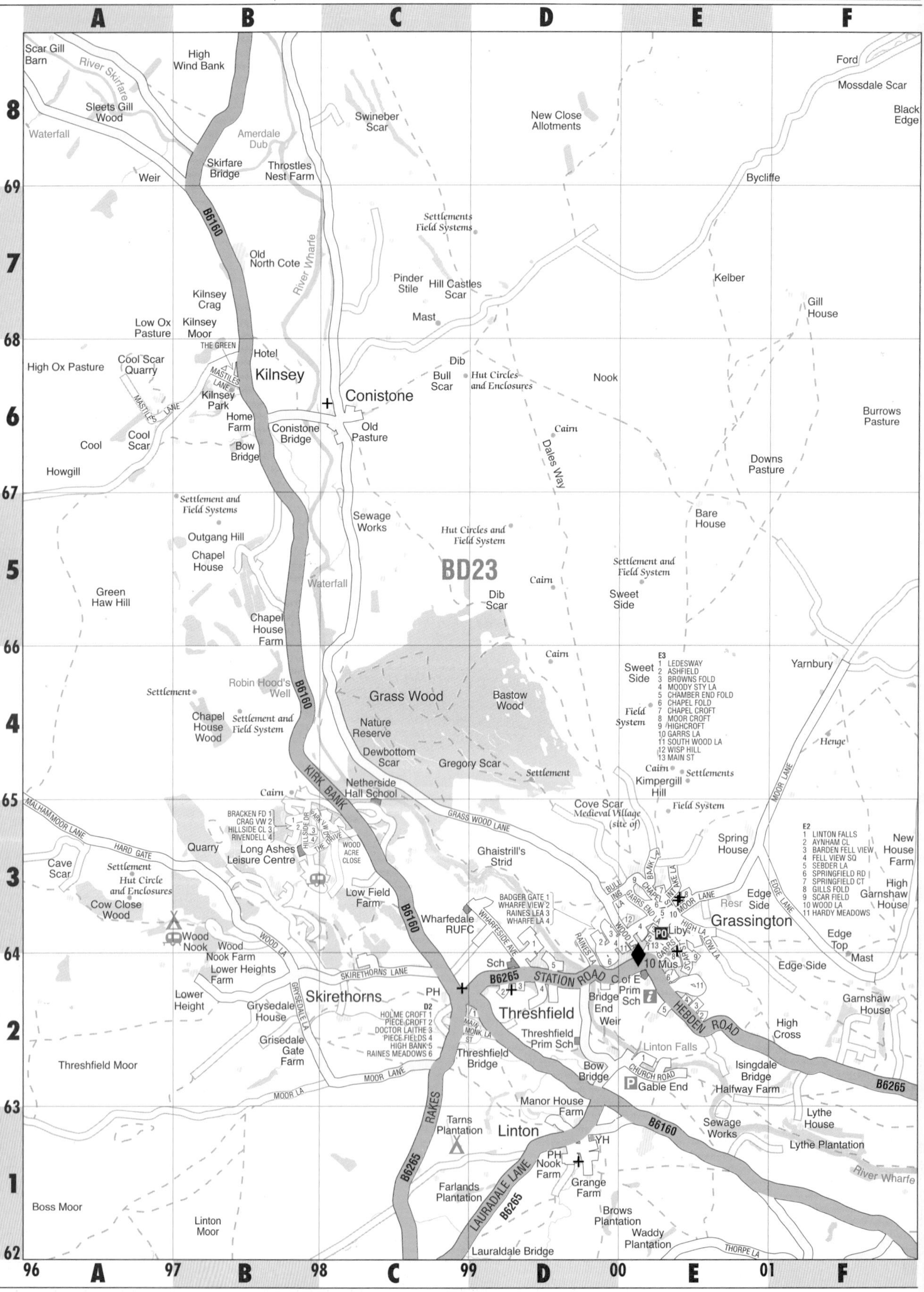

A · B · C · D · E · F (top)

8
Scar Gill Barn
River Skirfare
High Wind Bank
Ford
Mossdale Scar
Black Edge
Sleets Gill Wood
Waterfall
Amerdale Dub
Swineber Scar
New Close Allotments
Bycliffe

69
Weir
Skirfare Bridge
Throstles Nest Farm
Settlements Field Systems
Kelber
Gill House

7
Old North Cote
River Wharfe
Pinder Stile
Hill Castles Scar
Mast

68
Kilnsey Crag
Kilnsey Moor
THE GREEN
Hotel
Kilnsey
Conistone
Dib
Bull Scar
Hut Circles and Enclosures
Nook
Burrows Pasture

6
High Ox Pasture
Low Ox Pasture
Cool Scar Quarry
MASTILES LANE
Kilnsey Park
Home Farm
Conistone Bridge
Old Pasture
Cairn
Downs Pasture

67
Cool
Cool Scar
MASTILES LANE
Bow Bridge
Howgill
Dales Way
Bare House

5
Green Haw Hill
Settlement and Field Systems
Outgang Hill
Chapel House
Sewage Works
Hut Circles and Field System
Settlement and Field System
Sweet Side

BD23

66
Waterfall
Chapel House Farm
Dib Scar
Cairn
Sweet Side
Yarnbury

E3
1 LEDESWAY
2 ASHFIELD
3 BROWNS FOLD
4 MOODY STY LA
5 CHAMBER END FOLD
6 CHAPEL FOLD
7 CHAPEL CROFT
8 MOOR CROFT
9 HIGHCROFT
10 GARRS LA
11 SOUTH WOOD LA
12 WISP HILL
13 MAIN ST

4
Chapel House Wood
Robin Hood's Well
Settlement
Settlement and Field System
Grass Wood
Nature Reserve
Bastow Wood
Cairn
Field System
Henge

65
MALHAM MOOR LANE
Cairn
KIRK BANK
Dewbottom Scar
Gregory Scar
Settlement
Netherside Hall School
GRASS WOOD LANE
Cove Scar Medieval Village (site of)
Field System
Kimpergill Hill
Settlements

3
Cave Scar
HARD GATE
Quarry
BRACKEN FD 1
CRAG VW 2
HILLSIDE CL 3
RIVENDELL 4
Long Ashes Leisure Centre
WOOD ACRE CLOSE
Ghaistrill's Strid
Spring House
E2
1 LINTON FALLS
2 AYNHAM CL
3 BARDEN FELL VIEW
4 FELL VIEW SQ
5 SEBDER LA
6 SPRINGFIELD RD
7 SPRINGFIELD CT
8 GILLS FOLD
9 SCAR FIELD
10 WOOD LA
11 HARDY MEADOWS
New House Farm
High Garnshaw House

Settlement Hut Circle and Enclosures
Cow Close Wood
Wood Nook
Wood Nook Farm
Lower Heights Farm
Low Field Farm
Wharfedale RUFC
BADGER GATE 1
WHARFE VIEW 2
RAINES LEA 3
WHARFE LA 4
Grassington
Edge Side
Edge Top
Mast

64
SKIRETHORNS LANE
BRIGSDALE LA
WOOD LA
Skirethorns
PH
Sch
B6265
STATION ROAD
C of E Prim Sch
10 Mus.
Edge Side
Garnshaw House

Lower Height
Grysedale House
D2
HOLME CROFT 1
PIECE CROFT 2
DOCTOR LAITHE 3
PIECE FIELDS 4
HIGH BANK 5
RAINES MEADOWS 6
Threshfield
Threshfield Prim Sch
Bridge End Weir
Linton Falls
High Cross

2
Threshfield Moor
Grisedale Gate Farm
MOOR LANE
Threshfield Bridge
MAIN ST
MONK LA
Bow Bridge
CHURCH ROAD
Gable End
Isingdale Bridge
Halfway Farm
B6265

63
MOOR LA
RAKES
Tarns Plantation
Manor House Farm
Gable End
P
Sewage Works
Lythe House
Lythe Plantation

1
Boss Moor
Linton Moor
B6265
Farlands Plantation
LAURALDALE LANE
Linton
PH Nook Farm
YH
Grange Farm
Brows Plantation
River Wharfe

62
Lauraldale Bridge
B6265
Waddy Plantation
THORPE LA

A · B · C · D · E · F (bottom)
96 · 97 · 98 · 99 · 00 · 01

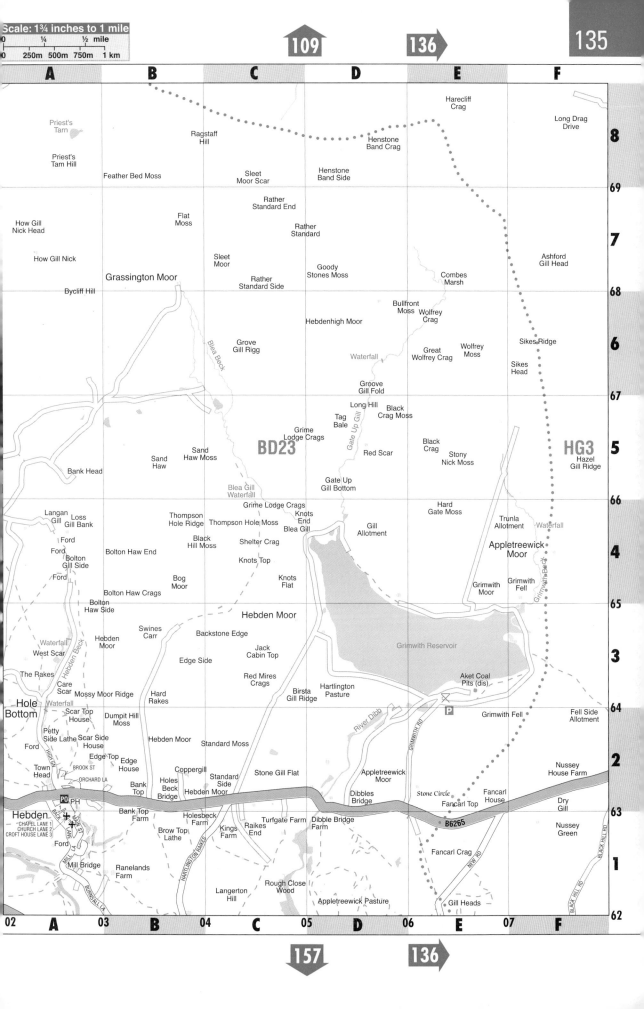
Scale: 1¾ inches to 1 mile
0 ¼ ½ mile
0 250m 500m 750m 1 km
109
136
A B C D E F
Priest's Tarn
Priest's Tarn Hill
Ragstaff Hill
Feather Bed Moss
Sleet Moor Scar
Henstone Band Side
Henstone Band Crag
Harecliff Crag
Long Drag Drive
Rather Standard End
How Gill Nick Head
Flat Moss
Rather Standard
How Gill Nick
Sleet Moor
Goody Stones Moss
Ashford Gill Head
Grassington Moor
Rather Standard Side
Combes Marsh
Bycliff Hill
Bullfront Moss
Wolfrey Crag
Hebdenhigh Moor
Blea Beck
Grove Gill Rigg
Waterfall
Great Wolfrey Crag
Wolfrey Moss
Sikes Ridge
Sikes Head
Groove Gill Fold
Long Hill
Black Crag Moss
Tag Bale
Gate Up Gill
Grime Lodge Crags
BD23
HG3
Sand Haw Moss
Sand Haw
Red Scar
Black Crag
Stony Nick Moss
Hazel Gill Ridge
Bank Head
Gate Up Gill Bottom
Blea Gill Waterfall
Grime Lodge Crags
Hard Gate Moss
Langan Gill
Loss Gill Bank
Thompson Hole Ridge
Thompson Hole Moss
Knots End
Blea Gill
Gill Allotment
Trunla Allotment
Waterfall
Ford
Black Hill Moss
Shelter Crag
Appletreewick Moor
Ford
Bolton Haw End
Bolton Gill Side
Knots Top
Ford
Bog Moor
Knots Flat
Grimwith Moor
Grimwith Fell
Grimwith Beck
Bolton Haw Crags
Bolton Haw Side
Hebden Moor
Swines Carr
Backstone Edge
Waterfall
Hebden Moor
Hebden Beck
Grimwith Reservoir
West Scar
Jack Cabin Top
Edge Side
The Rakes
Red Mires Crags
Aket Coal Pits (dis)
Care Scar
Mossy Moor Ridge
Hard Rakes
Birsta Gill Ridge
Hartlington Pasture
Hole Bottom
Waterfall
Scar Top House
Dumpit Hill Moss
River Dibb
P
Grimwith Fell
Fell Side Allotment
Petty Side Lathe
Scar Side House
GRIMWITH RD
Ford
Hebden Moor
Standard Moss
HIGH GN
Edge Top
Edge House
Town Head
BROOK ST
Coppergill
Standard Side
Stone Gill Flat
Appletreewick Moor
Nussey House Farm
ORCHARD LA
Bank Top
Holes Beck Bridge
Hebden Moor
Dibbles Bridge
Stone Circle
Fancarl House
Fancarl Top
PO
PH
Dry Gill
Hebden
Bank Top Farm
Holesbeck Farm
Turfgate Farm
Dibble Bridge Farm
B6265
BACK LANE
MAIN ST
CHAPEL LANE 1
CHURCH LANE 2
CROFT HOUSE LANE 3
Brow Top Lathe
Kings Farm
Raikes End
Nussey Green
Ford
Fancarl Crag
NEW RD
BLACK HILL RD
MILL LA
Mill Bridge
HARTLINGTON RAIKES
Ranelands Farm
Rough Close Wood
Langerton Hill
BURNSALL LA
Appletreewick Pasture
Gill Heads
BLACK HILL RD
8 69 7 68 6 67 5 66 4 65 3 64 2 63 1 62
02 A 03 B 04 C 05 D 06 E 07 F
157
136

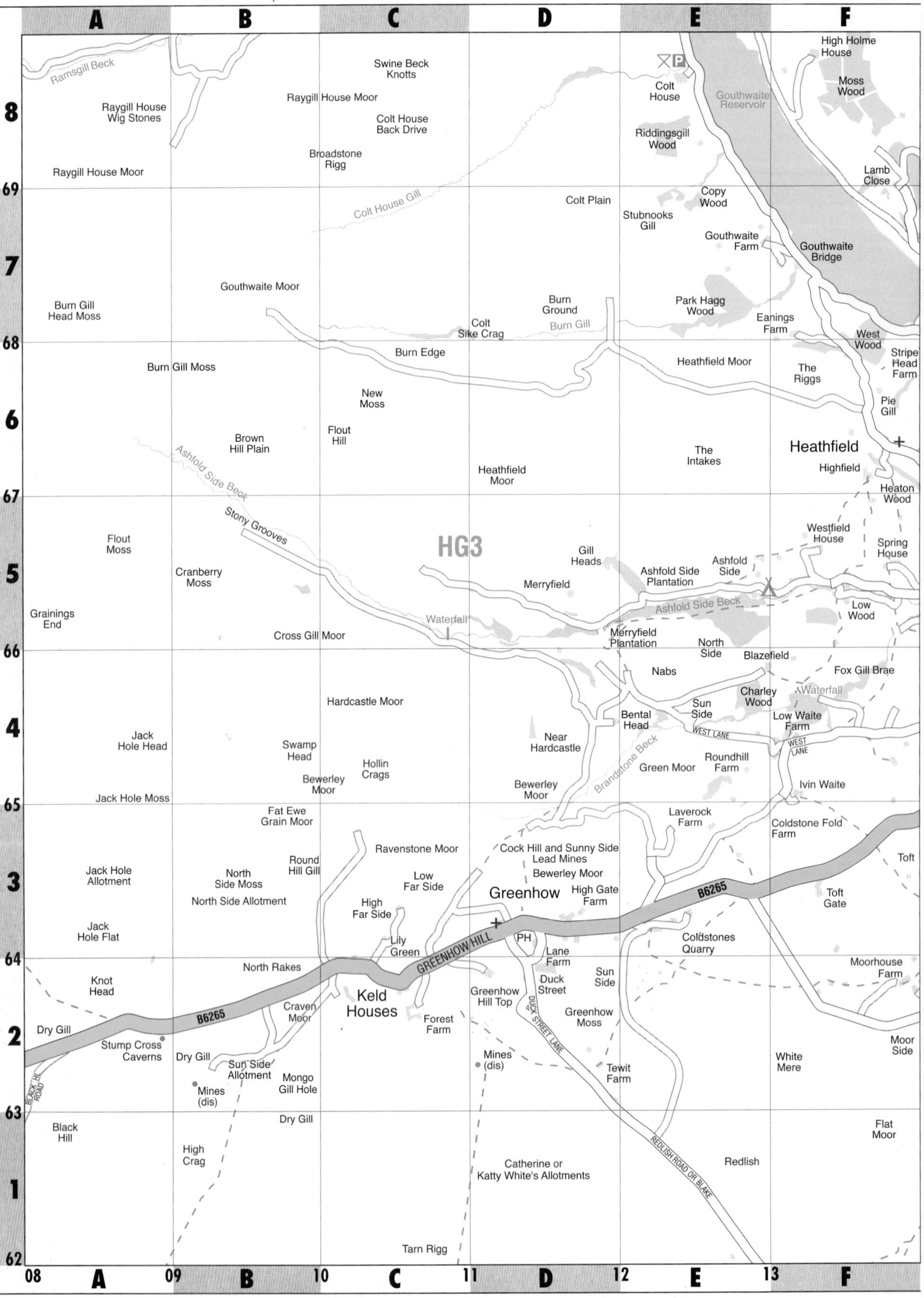

Scale: 1¾ inches to 1 mile
0   ¼   ½   mile
0   250m 500m 750m 1 km

8

Ramsgill Beck

Raygill House
Wig Stones

Raygill House Moor

Swine Beck
Knotts

Raygill House Moor

Colt House
Back Drive

Broadstone
Rigg

Colt
House

High Holme
House

Moss
Wood

Goulthwaite
Reservoir

Riddingsgill
Wood

Lamb
Close

69

Colt House Gill

Colt Plain

Stubnooks
Gill

Copy
Wood

Goulthwaite
Bridge

Goulthwaite
Farm

7

Gouthwaite Moor

Burn Gill
Head Moss

Burn
Ground

Colt
Sike Crag

Burn Gill

Park Hagg
Wood

Eanings
Farm

West
Wood

Stripe
Head
Farm

68

Burn Gill Moss

Burn Edge

Heathfield Moor

The
Riggs

Pie
Gill

6

New
Moss

Brown
Hill Plain

Flout
Hill

Heathfield
Moor

The
Intakes

Heathfield

Highfield

Heaton
Wood

67

Ashfold Side Beck

Stony Grooves

HG3

Gill
Heads

Ashfold Side
Plantation

Ashfold
Side

Westfield
House

Spring
House

5

Flout
Moss

Cranberry
Moss

Merryfield

Ashfold Side Beck

Low
Wood

Grainings
End

Cross Gill Moor

Waterfall

Merryfield
Plantation

North
Side

Blazefield

Fox Gill Brae

66

Hardcastle Moor

Nabs

Charley
Wood

Waterfall

4

Jack
Hole Head

Swamp
Head

Hollin
Crags

Near
Hardcastle

Bental
Head

Sun
Side

Low Waite
Farm

WEST LANE

WEST
LANE

Bewerley
Moor

Green Moor

Roundhill
Farm

Ivin Waite

Jack Hole Moss

Bewerley
Moor

Brandstone Beck

Laverock
Farm

Coldstone Fold
Farm

65

Fat Ewe
Grain Moor

Round
Hill Gill

Ravenstone Moor

Cock Hill and Sunny Side
Lead Mines

Toft

3

Jack Hole
Allotment

North
Side Moss

Low
Far Side

Bewerley Moor

High Gate
Farm

B6265

Toft
Gate

North Side Allotment

High
Far Side

Greenhow

Coldstones
Quarry

Moorhouse
Farm

Jack
Hole Flat

Lily
Green

GREENHOW HILL

Lane
Farm

PH

Sun
Side

64

North Rakes

Knot
Head

Craven
Moor

Keld
Houses

Forest
Farm

Greenhow
Hill Top

Duck
Street

Greenhow
Moss

DUCK STREET LANE

2

Dry Gill

B6265

Stump Cross
Caverns

Dry Gill

Sun Side
Allotment

Mongo
Gill Hole

Mines
(dis)

Tewit
Farm

White
Mere

Moor
Side

BACK LA. ROAD

Mines
(dis)

63

Black
Hill

Dry Gill

Flat
Moor

High
Crag

Catherine or
Katty White's Allotments

Redlish

REDLISH ROAD OR BLAZE

1

Tarn Rigg

62

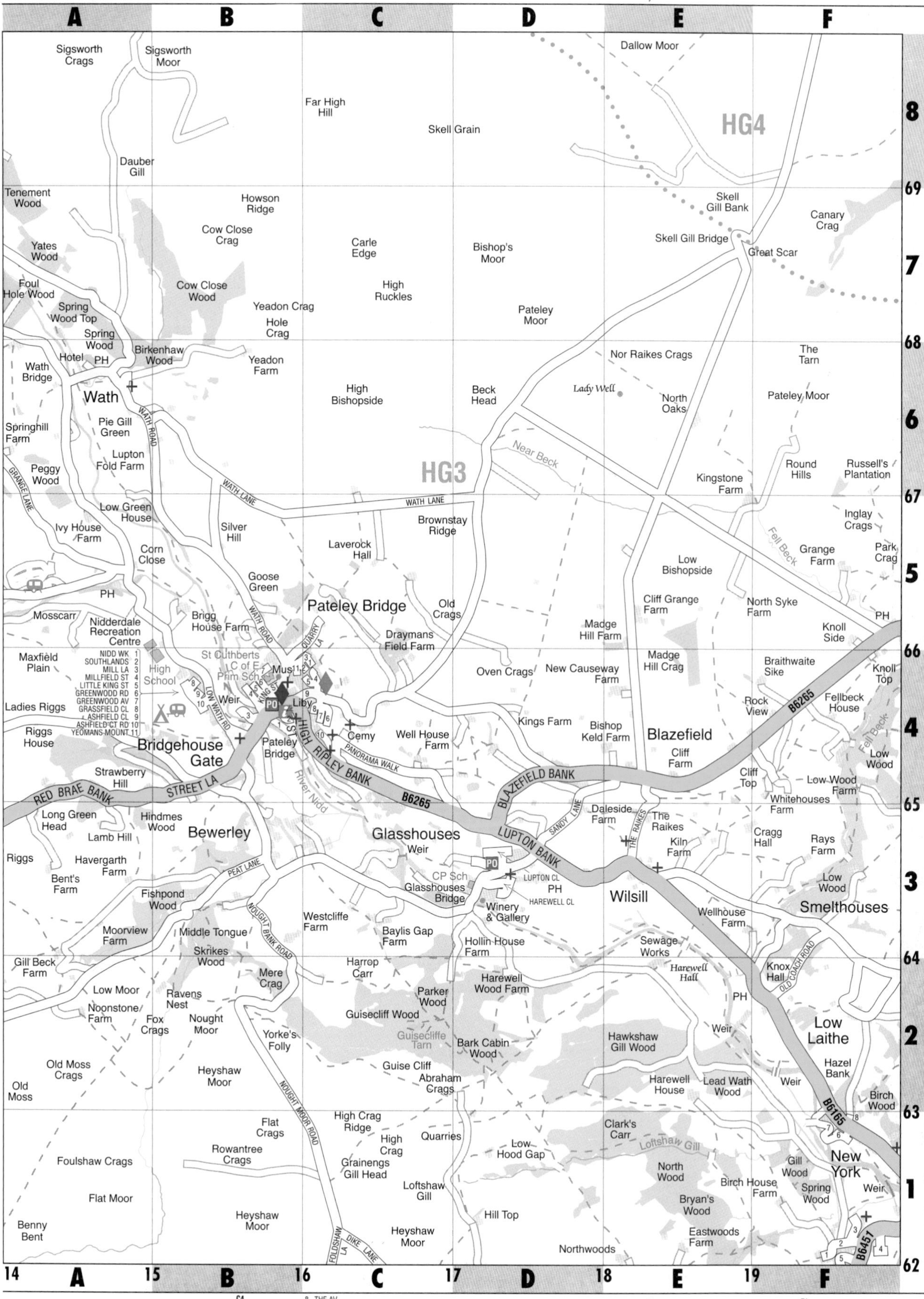

C4
1 BISHOP CL
2 BISHOP GARTH
3 BISHOP WY
4 SPRINGFIELD WY
5 SPRINGFIELD CL
6 HIGH CREST
7 THE DR
8 THE AV
9 OLD CHURCH LA
10 PANORAMA CL

F1
1 GRANGE LA
2 CABIN LA
3 HAREWELL LA
4 CHURCH AV
5 GRANGE RD
6 ORCHARD CL
7 THOMAS GILL RD
8 RIGGS SPRING

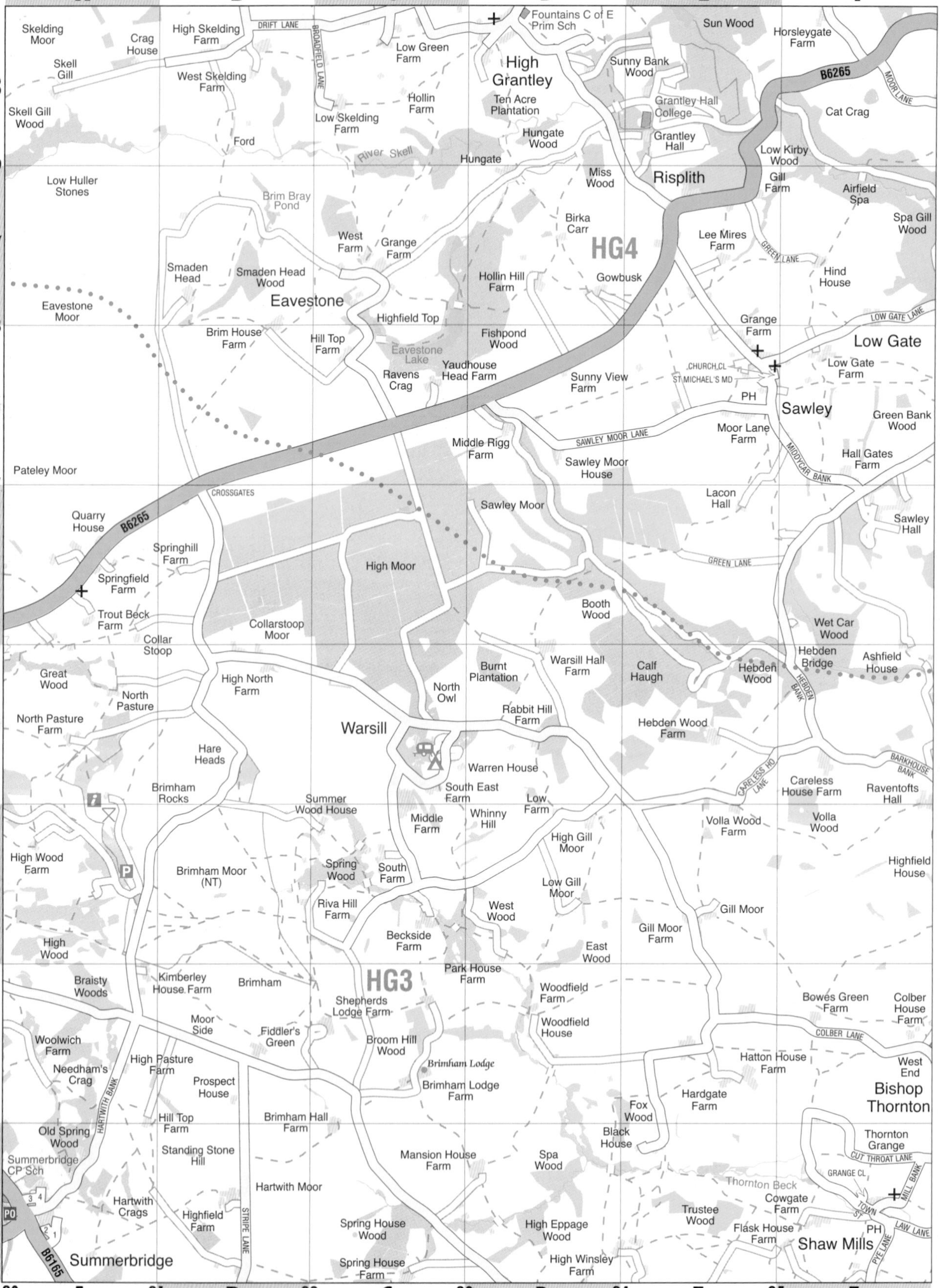

Scale: 1¾ inches to 1 mile

0   ¼   ½   mile
0 250m 500m 750m 1 km

A   B   C   D   E   F

8
Skelding Moor
Skell Gill
Skell Gill Wood
Crag House
High Skelding Farm
West Skelding Farm
Ford
Low Skelding Farm
DRIFT LANE
BROADFIELD LANE
Low Green Farm
Hollin Farm
Fountains C of E Prim Sch
High Grantley
Ten Acre Plantation
Hungate Wood
Sun Wood
Sunny Bank Wood
Grantley Hall College
Grantley Hall
Horsleygate Farm
B6265
Cat Crag
MOOR LANE

69
Low Huller Stones
River Skell
Hungate
Miss Wood
Risplith
Low Kirby Wood
Gill Farm
Airfield Spa
Spa Gill Wood

7
Brim Bray Pond
West Farm
Grange Farm
Birka Carr
HG4
Gowbusk
Lee Mires Farm
GREEN LANE
Hind House
Eavestone Moor
Smaden Head
Smaden Head Wood
Eavestone
Hollin Hill Farm

68
Brim House Farm
Hill Top Farm
Highfield Top
Eavestone Lake
Ravens Crag
Fishpond Wood
Yaudhouse Head Farm
Sunny View Farm
Grange Farm
CHURCH CL
ST MICHAEL'S MD
PH
Sawley
Low Gate Farm
LOW GATE LANE
Low Gate
Green Bank Wood

6
Pateley Moor
SAWLEY MOOR LANE
Middle Rigg Farm
Sawley Moor House
Moor Lane Farm
Lacon Hall
Hall Gates Farm
MIDDYCAR BANK

67
CROSSGATES
Sawley Moor
GREEN LANE
Sawley Hall

5
Quarry House
B6265
Springhill Farm
Springfield Farm
Trout Beck Farm
Collar Stoop
Collarstoop Moor
High Moor
High North Farm
Booth Wood
Wet Car Wood
Hebden Bridge
Hebden Wood
Ashfield House
HEBDEN BANK

66
Great Wood
North Pasture
North Pasture Farm
Burnt Plantation
North Owl
Warsill Hall Farm
Calf Haugh
Hebden Wood Farm
CARELESS HO LANE
BARKHOUSE BANK

4
Warsill
Hare Heads
Brimham Rocks
North Owl
Rabbit Hill Farm
Warren House
South East Farm
Low Farm
Careless House Farm
Raventofts Hall

65
Summer Wood House
Middle Farm
Whinny Hill
High Gill Moor
Volla Wood Farm
Volla Wood
Highfield House

3
High Wood Farm
Brimham Moor (NT)
Spring Wood
South Farm
Low Gill Moor
Gill Moor
Gill Moor Farm
P
Riva Hill Farm
West Wood
East Wood

64
High Wood
Beckside Farm
Park House Farm
Woodfield Farm
Bowes Green Farm
Colber House Farm

2
Braisty Woods
Kimberley House Farm
Brimham
HG3
Shepherds Lodge Farm
Woodfield House
COLBER LANE
West End
Bishop Thornton
Woolwich Farm
Needham's Crag
Moor Side
Fiddler's Green
Broom Hill Wood
Brimham Lodge
Hatton House Farm
HARTWITH BANK

63
Old Spring Wood
High Pasture Farm
Prospect House
Hill Top Farm
Brimham Hall Farm
Brimham Lodge Farm
Fox Wood
Black House
Hardgate Farm
Thornton Grange
CUT THROAT LANE
GRANGE CL

1
Summerbridge CP Sch
PO
3 4
2 1
B6165
Hartwith Crags
Highfield Farm
Standing Stone Hill
Hartwith Moor
STRIPE LANE
Mansion House Farm
Spa Wood
Thornton Beck
Trustee Wood
Cowgate Farm
Flask House Farm
PH
Shaw Mills
TOWN ST
MILL BANK
LAW LANE

62
Summerbridge
Spring House Wood
Spring House Farm
High Eppage Wood
High Winsley Farm
PYE LANE

20   A   21   B   22   C   23   D   24   E   25   F

A1
1 THE WHINFIELDS
2 THE CR
3 HARTWITH AV
4 HARTWITH GN

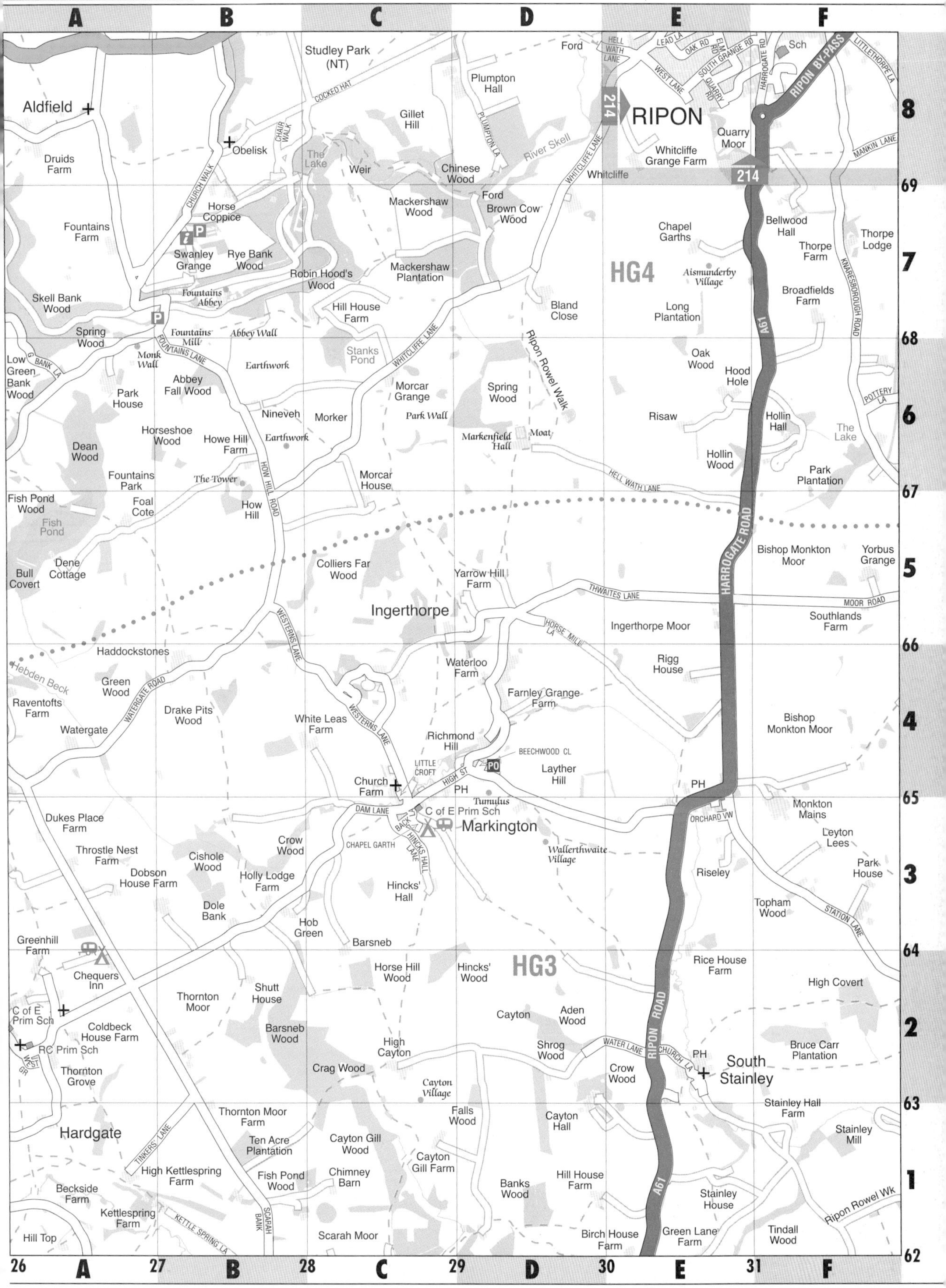

Scale: 1¾ inches to 1 mile

0   ¼   ½   mile

0   250m   500m   750m   1 km

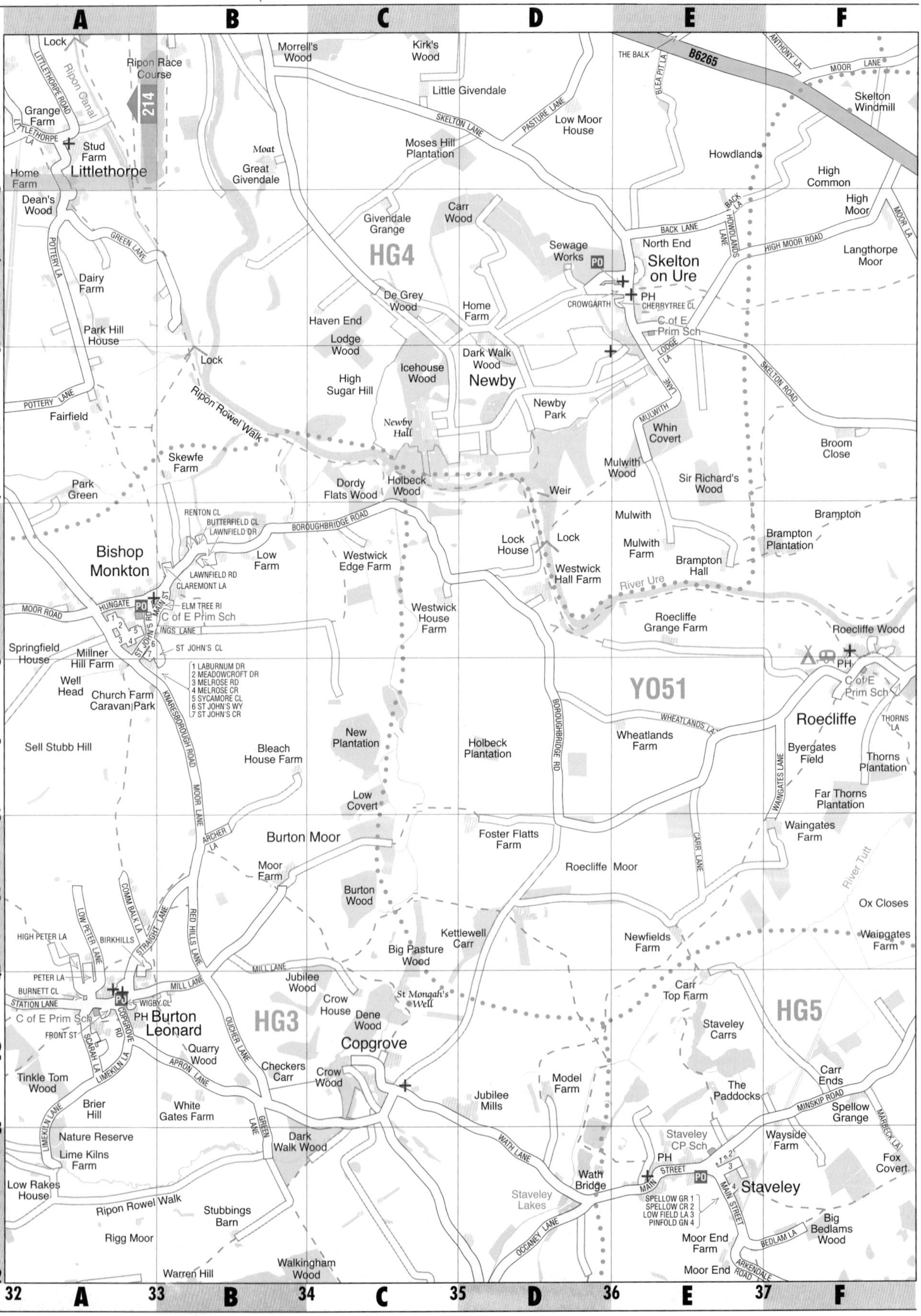

Grid columns: A B C D E F
Grid rows: 8 69 7 68 6 67 5 66 4 65 3 64 2 63 1 62

Lock

Ripon Canal

LITTLETHORPE ROAD

Ripon Race Course

214

Morrell's Wood

Kirk's Wood

Little Givendale

THE BALK

BLEA PIT LA

B6265

ANTHONY LA

MOOR LANE

Skelton Windmill

Grange Farm

LITTLETHORPE LA

Home Farm

Stud Farm

Littlethorpe

Moat

Great Givendale

SKELTON LANE

PASTURE LANE

Moses Hill Plantation

Low Moor House

Howdlands

High Common

Dean's Wood

Givendale Grange

Carr Wood

HG4

BACK LANE

HOWDLANDS LANE

High Moor

High Moor Road

MOOR LA

High Moor

Langthorpe Moor

POTTERY LA

GREEN LANE

Dairy Farm

Sewage Works

PO

North End

Skelton on Ure

Park Hill House

De Grey Wood

Home Farm

CROWGARTH

PH

C. of E Prim Sch

LODGE LA

SKELTON ROAD

Lock

Ripon Rowel Walk

Haven End

Lodge Wood

Icehouse Wood

Dark Walk Wood

Newby

Newby Park

MULWITH LANE

Whin Covert

Broom Close

POTTERY LANE

Fairfield

High Sugar Hill

Newby Hall

Mulwith Wood

Sir Richard's Wood

Skewfe Farm

Dordy Flats Wood

Holbeck Wood

Weir

Mulwith

Brampton

Park Green

BOROUGHBRIDGE ROAD

Lock House

Lock

Mulwith Farm

Brampton Plantation

RENTON CL
BUTTERFIELD CL
LAWNFIELD DR

Low Farm

Westwick Edge Farm

Westwick Hall Farm

Westwick House Farm

River Ure

Brampton Hall

Bishop Monkton

LAWNFIELD RD
CLAREMONT LA

ELM TREE RI
C of E Prim Sch

PO

Roecliffe Grange Farm

Roecliffe Wood

MOOR ROAD

HUNGATE

KINGS LANE

ST JOHN'S CL

Y051

Roecliffe

THORNS LA

Springfield House

Millner Hill Farm

1 LABURNUM DR
2 MEADOWCROFT DR
3 MELROSE RD
4 MELROSE CR
5 SYCAMORE CL
6 ST JOHN'S WY
7 ST JOHN'S CR

WHEATLANDS LA

Wheatlands Farm

PH
C of E Prim Sch

Well Head

Church Farm Caravan Park

New Plantation

Holbeck Plantation

BOROUGHBRIDGE RD

Byergates Field

Thorns Plantation

Sell Stubb Hill

Bleach House Farm

Low Covert

Far Thorns Plantation

KNARESBOROUGH ROAD

ARCHER LA

Burton Moor

MOOR LANE

Moor Farm

Foster Flatts Farm

Roecliffe Moor

CARR LANE

WAINGATES LA

Waingates Farm

River Tutt

Ox Closes

COMM BALK LA

STRAIGHT LANE

RED HILLS LANE

Burton Wood

Newfields Farm

Waingates Farm

High Peter La

LOW PETER LANE

BIRKHILLS

MILL LANE

Big Pasture Wood

Kettlewell Carr

St Mongah's Well

Carr Top Farm

Staveley Carrs

HG5

Peter La
BURNETT CL
STATION LANE

Jubilee Wood

Crow House

Dene Wood

Model Farm

The Paddocks

Carr Ends

MINSKIP ROAD

MARBECK LA

C of E Prim Sch

PH Burton Leonard

HG3

Checkers Carr

Crow Wood

Copgrove

Jubilee Mills

Spellow Grange

FRONT ST

LIMEKILN LA

SCRAFLN LA

Quarry Wood

APRON LANE

OUCHER LANE

GREEN LANE

White Gates Farm

Dark Walk Wood

WATH LANE

Staveley CP Sch

Wayside Farm

Fox Covert

Tinkle Tom Wood

Brier Hill

Nature Reserve

Lime Kilns Farm

Wath Bridge

PH

MAIN ST

PO

Staveley

LIMEKILN LANE

Stubbings Barn

Ripon Rowel Walk

Staveley Lakes

SPELLOW GR 1
SPELLOW CR 2
LOW FIELD LA 3
PINFOLD GN 4

MAIN STREET

Big Bedlams Wood

Low Rakes House

Rigg Moor

OCCANEY LANE

Moor End Farm

Moor End

BEDLAM LA

ARKENDALE ROAD

Warren Hill

Walkingham Wood

32 A 33 B 34 C 35 D 36 E 37 F

For full street detail of the highlighted area see page 214.

◄ 139   162

Scale: 1¾ inches to 1 mile

0 ¼ ½ mile

0 250m 500m 750m 1 km

B5
1 VALUATION LA
2 HORSEFAIR
3 FISHERGATE
4 CHATSWORTH GR
5 HALL SQ
6 HIGH ST
7 BACK LA
8 DRUIDS MEADOW
9 ARROWS TR
10 ARROWS CR
11 ST HELENA
12 FLORENCE CT
13 CHURCH MS
14 MALLARD WK
15 NEW ROW
16 ST JAMES' MD
17 KINGFISHER REACH
18 SPRINGFIELD RD
19 SPRINGFIELD DR
20 SPRINGFIELD CL
21 SPRINGFIELD GR
22 SOUTHOLME CL
23 SOUTHOLME WK

115
142

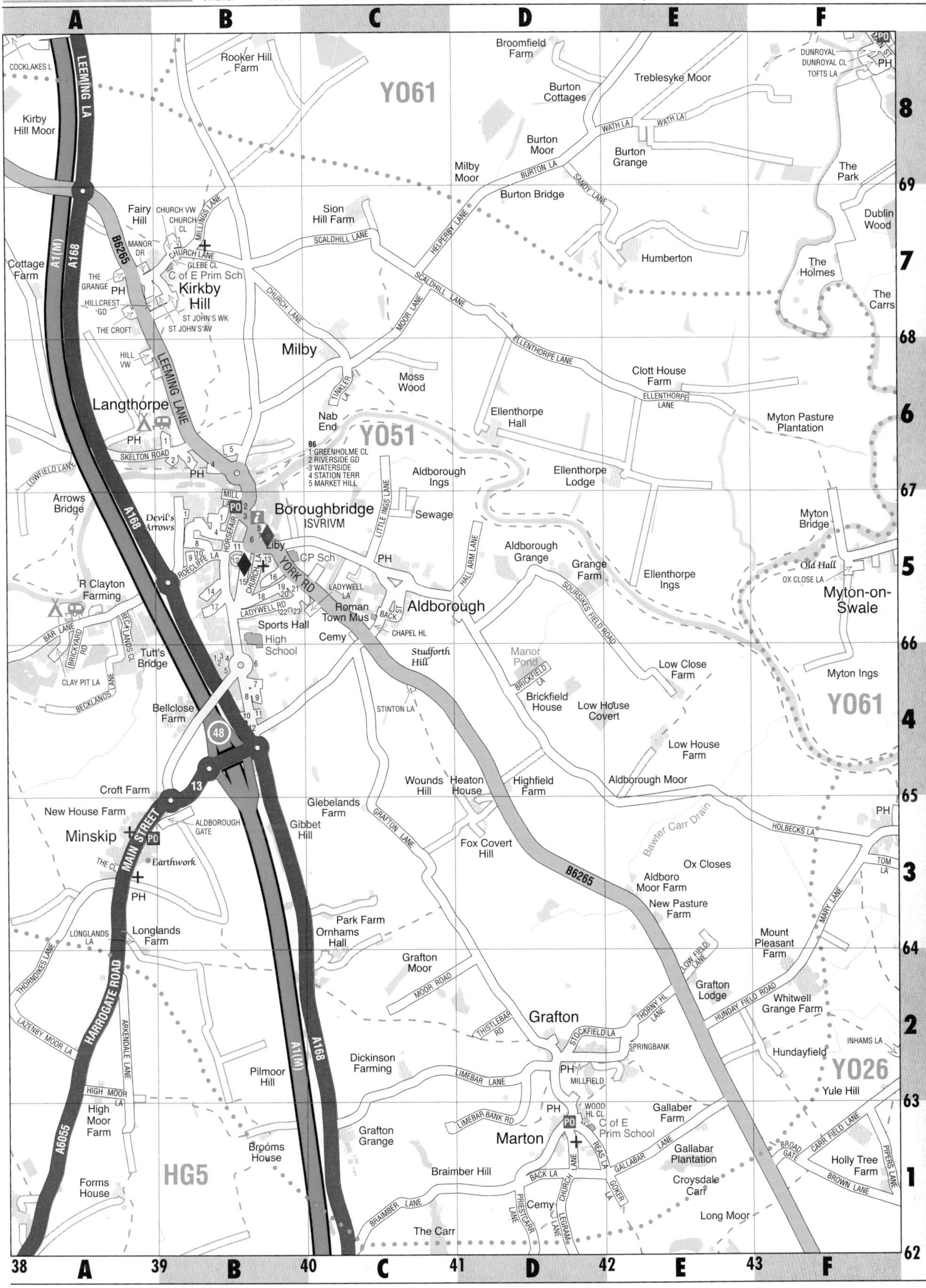

B4
1 LAWSON AV
2 HAZEL RD
3 FOTHERGILL WY
4 SMITHSON GR
5 CRAVEN WY
6 HUNTERS ROW
7 THE RIDINGS
8 WETHERBY RD
9 HARNESS LA
10 ASHBOURNE RD
11 THE CHASE
12 ASHBOURNE CL
13 ALDBOROUGH GATE

163
142

141
116

Scale: 1¾ inches to 1 mile

0   ¼   ½   mile
0   250m   500m   750m   1 km

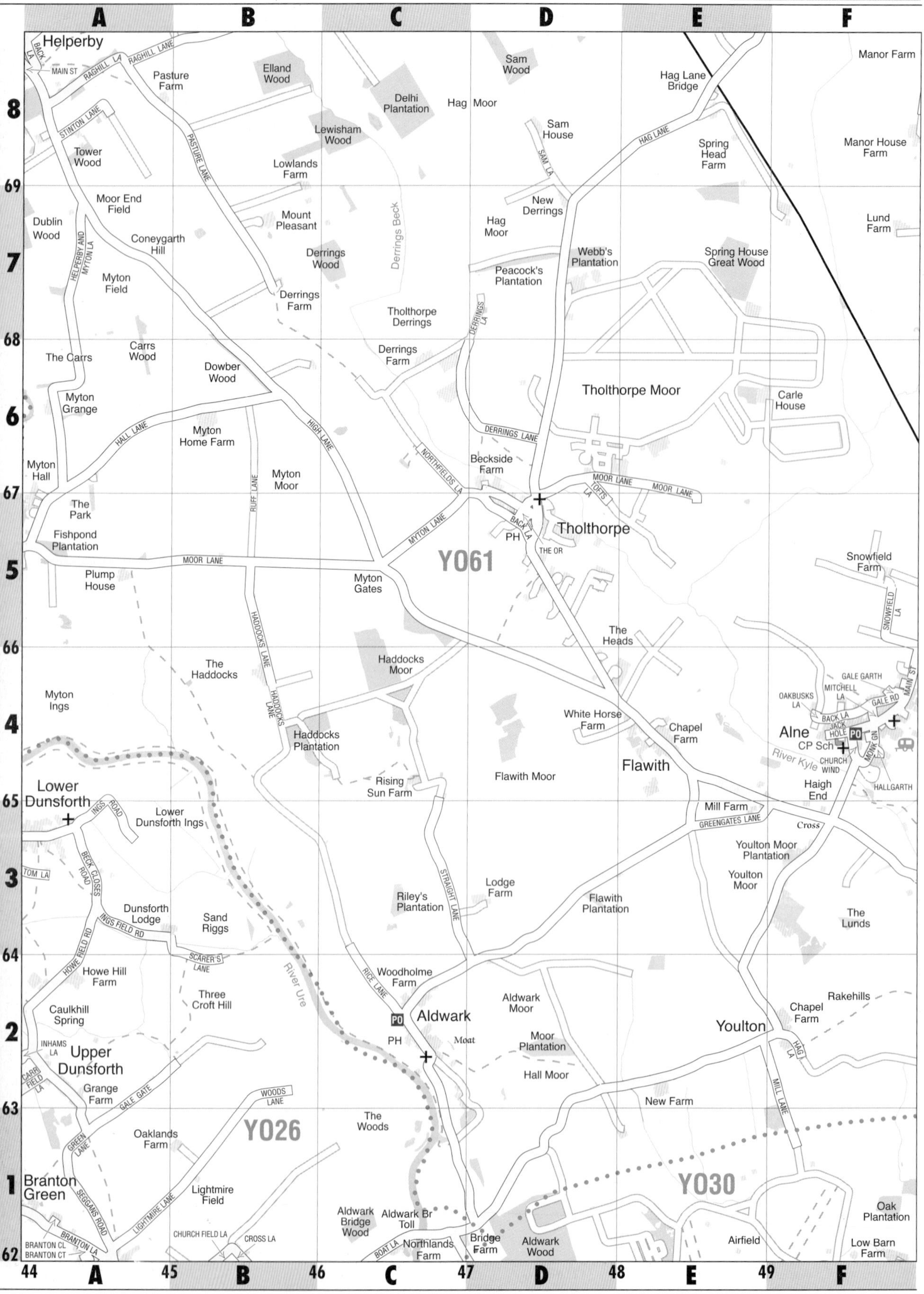

A **B** **C** **D** **E** **F**

Helperby
MAIN ST
BACK LA
RAGHILL LANE
RAGHILL LA
STINTON LANE
Pasture Farm
Elland Wood
Delhi Plantation
Sam Wood
Hag Lane Bridge
Manor Farm

8

Tower Wood
Lewisham Wood
Lowlands Farm
Hag Moor
Sam House
Sam La
Spring Head Farm
Manor House Farm

69

Moor End Field
PASTURE LANE
HELPERBY AND MYTON LA
Mount Pleasant
New Derrings
Dublin Wood
Coneygarth Hill
Derrings Wood
Hag Moor
Webb's Plantation
Spring House Great Wood
Lund Farm

7

Myton Field
Derrings Farm
DERRINGS BECK
Peacock's Plantation

The Carrs
Carrs Wood
Dowber Wood
Tholthorpe Derrings
Derrings Farm
Tholthorpe Moor
Carle House

68

HIGH LANE
HALL LANE
RUFF LANE
DERRINGS LA
Myton Grange
Myton Home Farm
Derrings Farm
DERRINGS LANE

6

Myton Hall
The Park
Myton Moor
NORTHFIELDS LA
Beckside Farm
MOOR LANE
MOOR LANE
Snowfield Farm

Fishpond Plantation
MOOR LANE
Myton Gates
MYTON LANE
BACK LA
TOFTS LA
Tholthorpe
PH
THE OR

67

Plump House
YO61
The Heads
SNOWFIELD LA

5

HADDOCKS LANE
The Haddocks
Haddocks Moor
Gale Garth
OAKBUSKS LA
MITCHELL LA
BACK LA
MAIN ST
GALE RD

66

Myton Ings
Haddocks Plantation
White Horse Farm
Chapel Farm
Alne
CP Sch
JACK HOLE
MONK GR
PO
HALLGARTH

4

Lower Dunsforth
Lower Dunsforth Ings
Rising Sun Farm
Flawith Moor
Flawith
River Kyle
CHURCH WIND
Haigh End

TOM LA
BECK CLOSES ROAD
INGS ROAD
Mill Farm
GREENGATES LANE
Cross

65

Dunsforth Lodge
Sand Riggs
Riley's Plantation
STRAIGHT LANE
Lodge Farm
Flawith Plantation
Youlton Moor Plantation
Youlton Moor
The Lunds

3

HOWE FIELD RD
INGS FIELD RD
SCARER'S LANE
Howe Hill Farm
Woodholme Farm
RICE LANE
Aldwark Moor

64

Caulkhill Spring
Three Croft Hill
River Ure
PO
Aldwark
PH
Moat
Moor Plantation
Youlton
Chapel Farm
Rakehills
MILL LA

2

Upper Dunsforth
INHAMS LA
CARBI FIELD LA
Grange Farm
GALE GATE
WOODS LANE
Hall Moor
New Farm

63

GREEN LANE
SEGRAMS ROAD
Oaklands Farm
YO26
The Woods
YO30

1

Branton Green
LIGHTMIRE LANE
Lightmire Field
Aldwark Bridge Wood
Aldwark Br Toll
Bridge Farm
Aldwark Wood
Airfield
Oak Plantation
Low Barn Farm

BRANTON CL
BRANTON CT
BRANTON LA
CHURCH FIELD LA
CROSS LA
BOAT LA
Northlands Farm

62

44 **A** 45 **B** 46 **C** 47 **D** 48 **E** 49 **F**

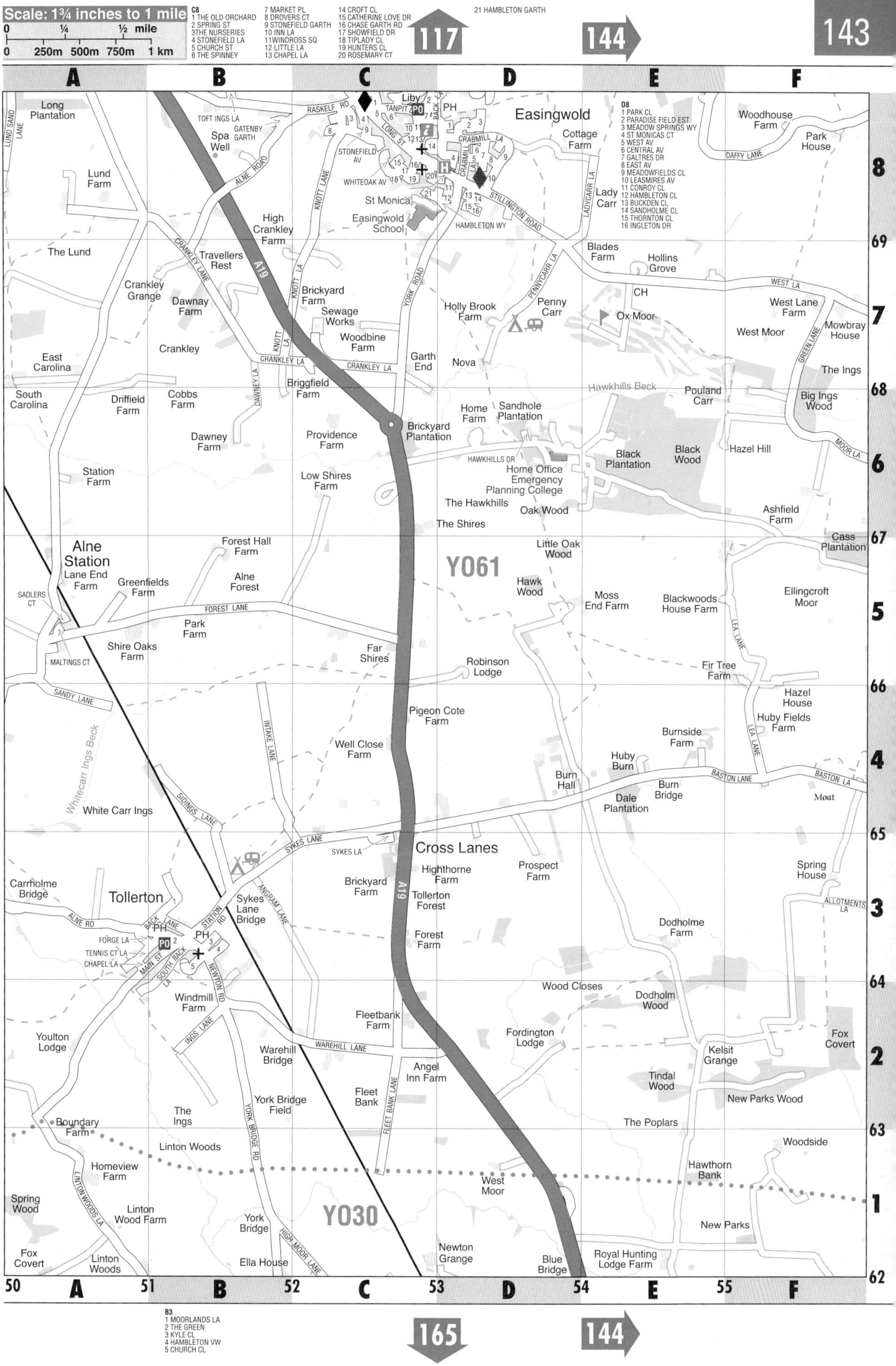

Scale: 1¾ inches to 1 mile

0   ¼   ½   mile
0   250m 500m 750m 1 km

117
144

C8
1 THE OLD ORCHARD
2 SPRING ST
3 THE NURSERIES
4 STONEFIELD LA
5 CHURCH ST
6 THE SPINNEY
7 MARKET PL
8 DROVERS CT
9 STONEFIELD GARTH
10 INN LA
11 WINDROSS SQ
12 LITTLE LA
13 CHAPEL LA
14 CROFT CL
15 CATHERINE LOVE DR
16 CHASE GARTH RD
17 SHOWFIELD DR
18 TIPLADY CL
19 HUNTERS CL
20 ROSEMARY CT
21 HAMBLETON GARTH

D8
1 PARK CL
2 PARADISE FIELD EST
3 MEADOW SPRINGS WY
4 ST MONICAS CT
5 WEST AV
6 CENTRAL AV
7 GALTRES DR
8 EAST AV
9 MEADOWFIELDS CL
10 LEASMIRES AV
11 CONROY CL
12 HAMBLETON CL
13 BUCKDEN CL
14 SANDHOLME CL
15 THORNTON CL
16 INGLETON DR

B3
1 MOORLANDS LA
2 THE GREEN
3 KYLE CL
4 HAMBLETON VW
5 CHURCH CL

165
144

143
118

Scale: 1¾ inches to 1 mile

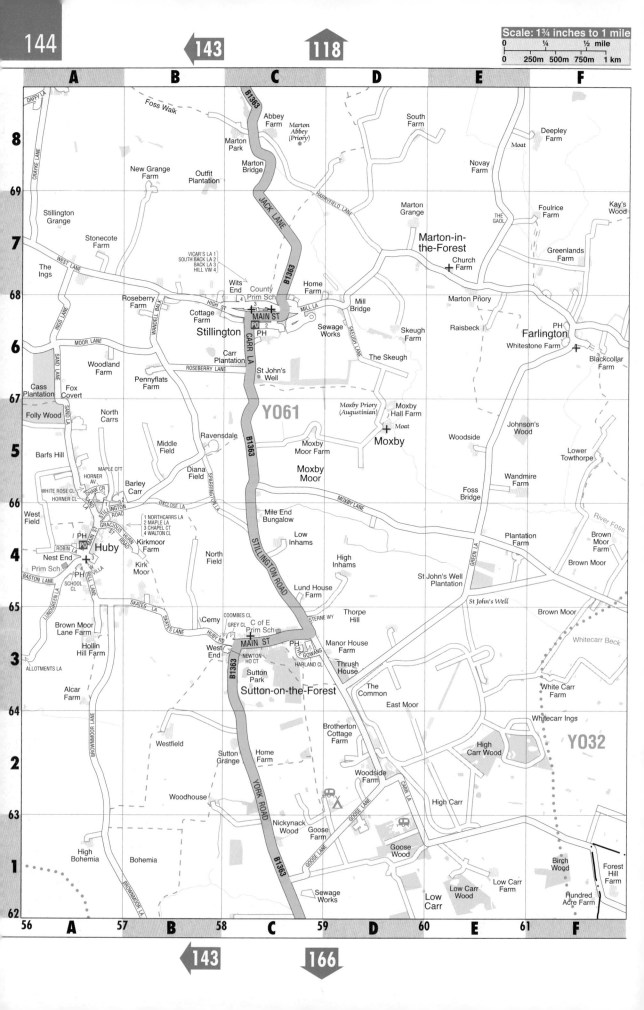
Foss Walk
Abbey Farm
Marton Abbey (Priory)
Marton Park
Marton Bridge
New Grange Farm
Outfit Plantation
South Farm
Deepley Farm
Moat
Novay Farm
JACK LANE
HARRYFIELD LANE
Marton Grange
Foulrice Farm
Kay's Wood
THE GAOL
Stillington Grange
Stonecote Farm
Marton-in-the-Forest
Church Farm
Greenlands Farm
The Ings
WEST LANE
VICAR'S LA 1
SOUTH BACK LA 2
BACK LA 3
HILL VW 4
Wits End
County Prim Sch
Home Farm
B1363
Roseberry Farm
HIGH ST
MAIN ST
MILL LA
Mill Bridge
Marton Priory
Cottage Farm
WANDELL BALK
Sewage Works
Skeugh Farm
Raisbeck
PH
Farlington
Stillington
PO
CARR LA
Whitestone Farm
Blackcollar Farm
MOOR LANE
Carr Plantation
SKEUGH LANE
The Skeugh
Woodland Farm
ROSEBERRY LANE
St John's Well
Pennyflats Farm
Cass Plantation
Fox Covert
SAND LANE
YO61
Moxby Priory (Augustinian)
Moxby Hall Farm
North Carrs
Folly Wood
SAND LA
Johnson's Wood
Moat
Ravensdale
Moxby
Woodside
Middle Field
Moxby Moor Farm
Barfs Hill
Lower Towthorpe
MAPLE CFT
HORNER AV
Diana Field
Moxby Moor
Wandmire Farm
WHITE ROSE CL
SHAW CR
Barley Carr
HORNER CL
Foss Bridge
OXCLOSE LA
SPARRINGTON LA
MOXBY LANE
STILLINGTON ROAD
Mile End Bungalow
River Foss
West Field
GRACIOUS ST
1 NORTHCARRS LA
2 MAPLE LA
3 CHAPEL CT
4 WALTON CL
HURN ROAD
Low Inhams
Plantation Farm
Brown Moor Farm
ROBIN LA
Kirkmoor Farm
Huby
North Field
GREEN LA
Nest End
STILLINGTON ROAD
High Inhams
Brown Moor
Prim Sch
Kirk Moor
St John's Well Plantation
BASTON LANE
SCHOOL CL
W VILLA
BELL LANE
Lund House Farm
LUNDGREEN LA
SKATES LA
St John's Well
Brown Moor
Cemy
COOMBES CL
Thorpe Hill
GREY CL
C of E Prim Sch
STERNE WY
Brown Moor Lane Farm
SKATES LANE
HUBY RD
Whitecarr Beck
Hollin Hill Farm
West End
Manor House Farm
THE GOWANS
NEWTON HO CT
HARLAND CL
Thrush House
ALLOTMENTS LA
Sutton Park
White Carr Farm
Alcar Farm
Sutton-on-the-Forest
The Common
East Moor
BROWNMOOR LANE
Whitecarr Ings
Brotherton Cottage Farm
Westfield
Sutton Grange
Home Farm
High Carr Wood
YO32
YORK ROAD
Woodside Farm
CARR LA
Woodhouse
GOOSE LANE
High Carr
Nickynack Wood
Goose Farm
High Bohemia
Goose Wood
Bohemia
Birch Wood
Forest Hill Farm
GOOSE LANE
BROWNMOOR LA
Sewage Works
Low Carr Wood
Low Carr Farm
Hundred Acre Farm
Low Carr

143
166

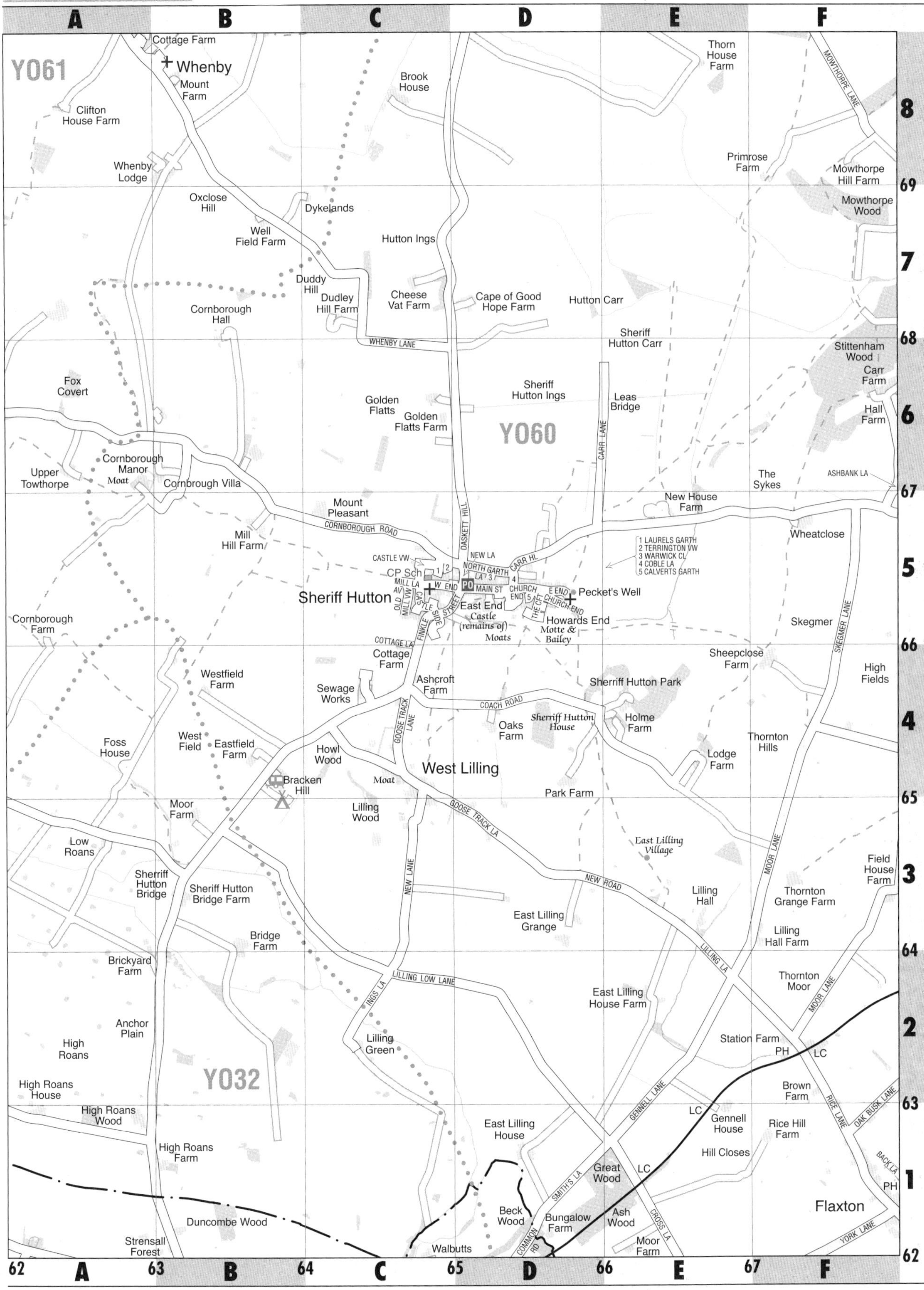

145
120

Scale: 1¾ inches to 1 mile

| 0 | ¼ | ½ mile |
| 0 | 250m | 500m | 750m | 1 km |

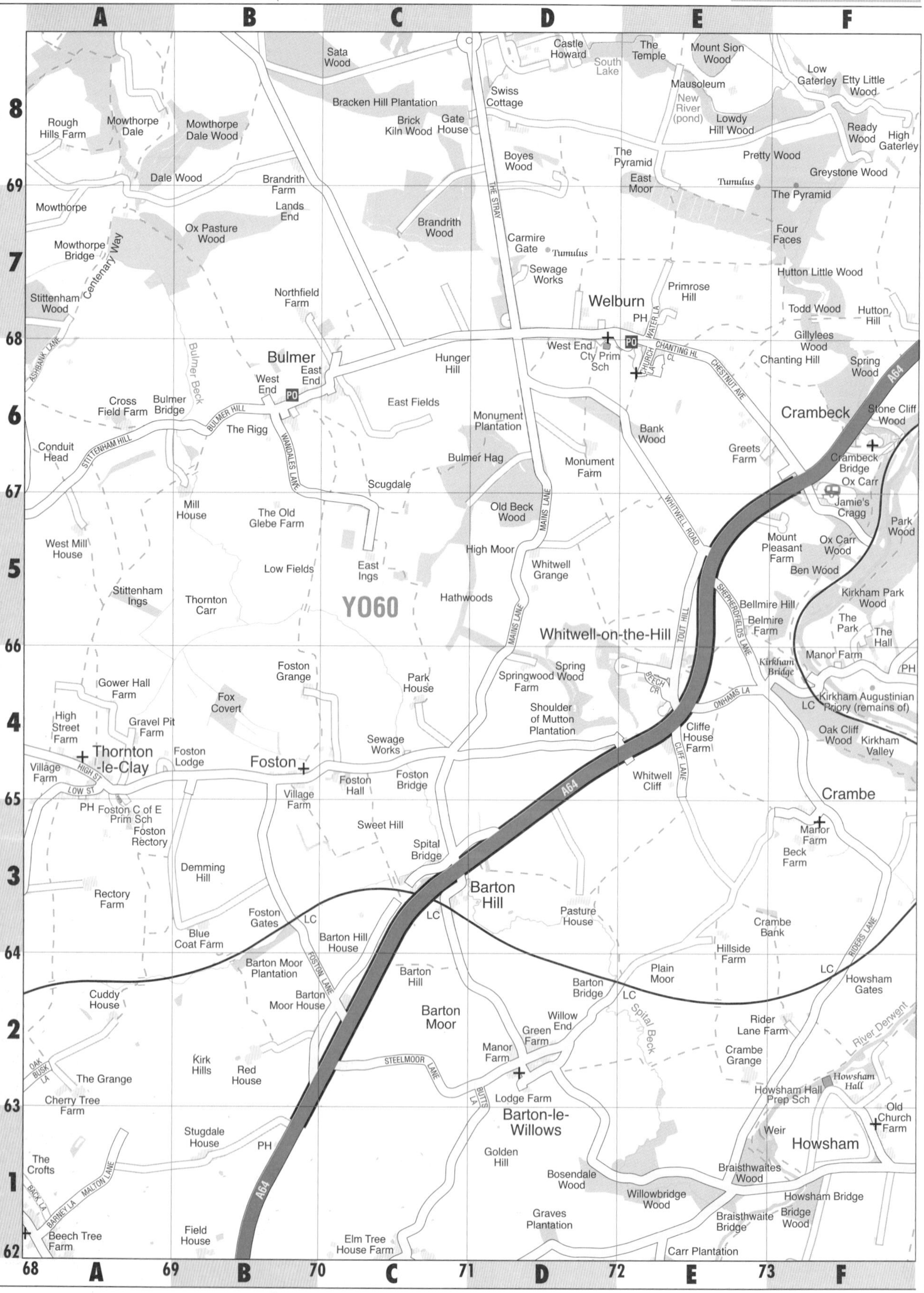

A B C D E F

8
Rough Hills Farm
Mowthorpe Dale
Mowthorpe Dale Wood
Sata Wood
Bracken Hill Plantation
Brick Kiln Wood
Gate House
Swiss Cottage
Castle Howard
South Lake
The Temple
Mount Sion Wood
Mausoleum
New River (pond)
Lowdy Hill Wood
Low Gaterley
Etty Little Wood
Ready Wood
High Gaterley

69
Dale Wood
Brandrith Farm
Lands End
Boyes Wood
The Pyramid
East Moor
Pretty Wood
Tumulus
The Pyramid
Greystone Wood
Four Faces

7
Mowthorpe
Mowthorpe Bridge
Stittenham Wood
Centenary Way
Ox Pasture Wood
Northfield Farm
Brandrith Wood
Carmire Gate
Tumulus
Sewage Works
Welburn
PH
Primrose Hill
Hutton Little Wood
Todd Wood
Hutton Hill

68
ASHBANK LANE
Bulmer Beck
Bulmer
West End
East End
PO
Hunger Hill
West End
Cty Prim Sch
PO
CHURCH
WATER LA
CHANTING HL
CL
CHESTNUT AVE
Gillylees Wood
Chanting Hill
Spring Wood
Crambeck
A64

6
Cross Field Farm
Bulmer Bridge
The Rigg
Bulmer Hill
West End
East Fields
WANDALES LANE
STITTENHAM HILL
Conduit Head
Monument Plantation
Bulmer Hag
Monument Farm
Bank Wood
Greets Farm
Stone Cliff Wood
Crambeck Bridge
Ox Carr

67
Mill House
The Old Glebe Farm
Scugdale
Old Beck Wood
MAINS LANE
Jamie's Cragg
Mount Pleasant Farm
Ox Carr Wood
Ben Wood
Park Wood

5
West Mill House
Stittenham Ings
Thornton Carr
Low Fields
East Ings
High Moor
Hathwoods
Whitwell Grange
WHITWELL ROAD
Bellmire Hill
Belmire Farm
Kirkham Park Wood
The Park
The Hall

YO60

66
Gower Hall Farm
Fox Covert
Foston Grange
Park House
Whitwell-on-the-Hill
THE TOLL
SHEPHERDSFIELDS LANE
Kirkham Bridge
Manor Farm
PH

4
High Street Farm
Gravel Pit Farm
Foston Lodge
Sewage Works
Springwood Farm
Spring
Shoulder of Mutton Plantation
BEECH CR
ONHAMS LA
Cliffe House Farm
CLIFF LANE
LC
Kirkham Augustinian Priory (remains of)
Oak Cliff Wood
Kirkham Valley

65
Village Farm
Thornton-le-Clay
HIGH ST
LOW ST
Foston
Village Farm
Foston Hall
Foston Bridge
Whitwell Cliff
A64
Crambe
Manor Farm
Beck Farm

3
PH
Foston C of E Prim Sch
Foston Rectory
Demming Hill
Sweet Hill
Spital Bridge
Barton Hill
Pasture House
Crambe Bank
Hillside Farm
RIDERS LANE

64
Rectory Farm
Foston Gates
LC
Blue Coat Farm
Barton Hill House
Barton Hill
FOSTON LANE
LC
Barton Bridge
LC
Plain Moor
Howsham Gates
Howsham

2
OAK BUSK LA
Cuddy House
Kirk Hills
Red House
Barton Moor Plantation
Barton Moor House
Barton Moor
STEELMOOR LANE
Willow End Green Farm
Manor Farm
BUTTS LA
Spital Beck
Rider Lane Farm
Crambe Grange
River Derwent
Howsham Hall

63
The Grange
Cherry Tree Farm
Stugdale House
Lodge Farm
Barton-le-Willows
Howsham Hall Prep Sch
Weir
Old Church Farm
Howsham

1
BACK LA
BARNEY LA
MALTON LANE
The Crofts
PH
A64
Golden Hill
Bosendale Wood
Willowbridge Wood
Braithwaites Wood
Braithwaite Bridge
Howsham Bridge
Bridge Wood

62
Beech Tree Farm
Field House
Elm Tree House Farm
Graves Plantation
Carr Plantation

68 A 69 B 70 C 71 D 72 E 73 F

145
168

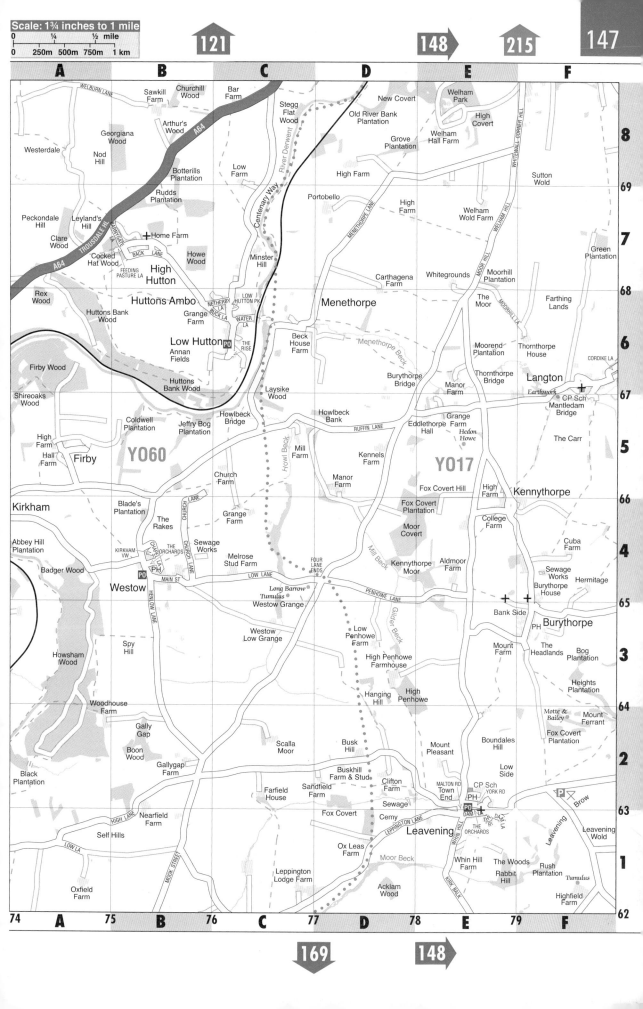

Scale: 1¾ inches to 1 mile

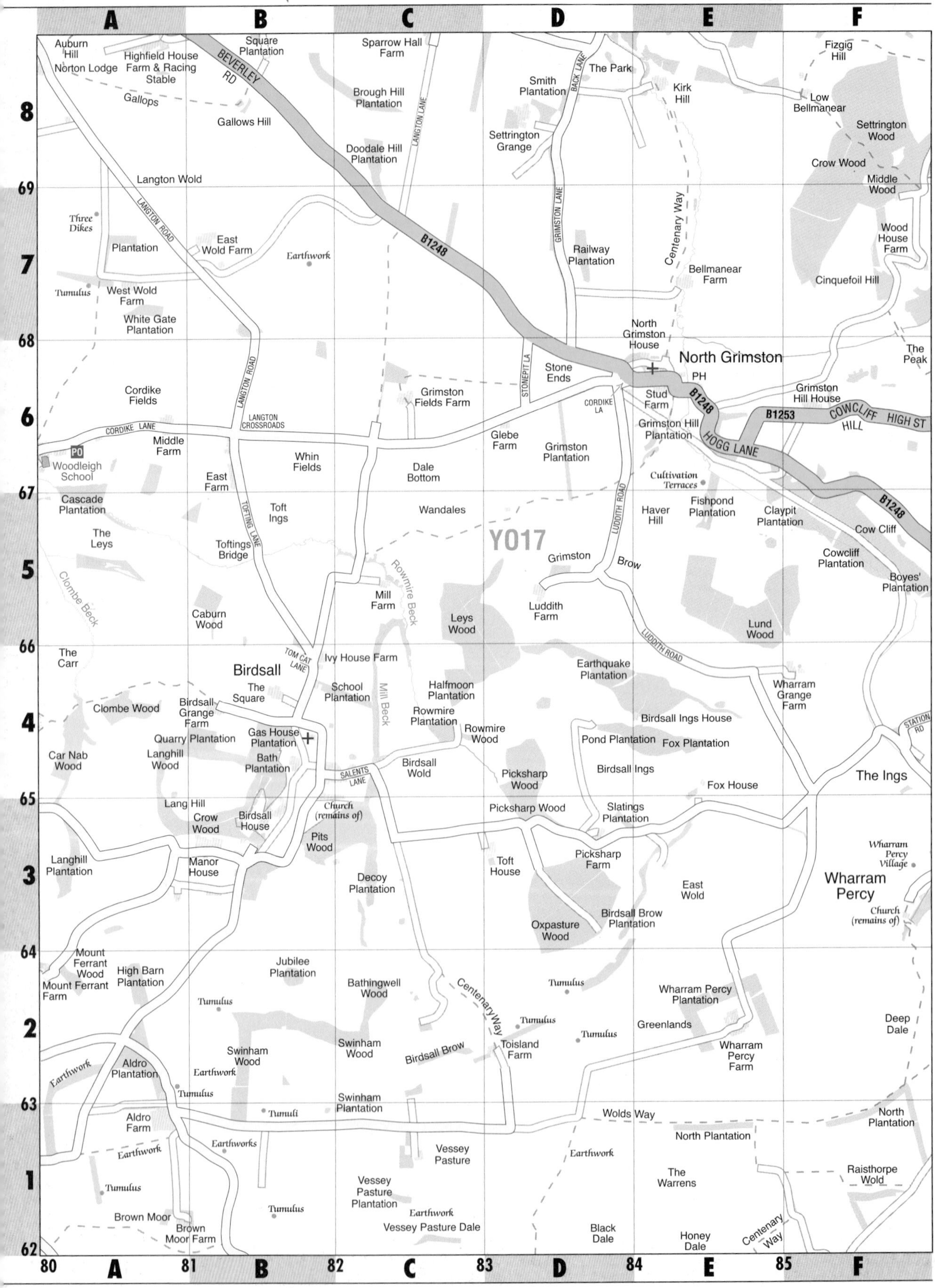

A **B** **C** **D** **E** **F**

Auburn Hill
Norton Lodge
Highfield House Farm & Racing Stable
Square Plantation
Sparrow Hall Farm
Smith Plantation
The Park
Kirk Hill
Fizgig Hill
Low Bellmanear

Gallops
Gallows Hill
Brough Hill Plantation
Settrington Wood

8

Doodale Hill Plantation
Settrington Grange
Crow Wood
Middle Wood

69
Langton Wold
Three Dikes
Wood House Farm

7
Plantation
East Wold Farm
Earthwork
Railway Plantation
Bellmanear Farm
Cinquefoil Hill

Tumulus
West Wold Farm
White Gate Plantation
North Grimston House
The Peak

68
Cordike Fields
Stone Ends
Grimston Fields Farm
North Grimston
PH
Grimston Hill House
B1253
Cowcliff High St

6
Cordike Lane
Langton Crossroads
Middle Farm
Whin Fields
Dale Bottom
Glebe Farm
Grimston Plantation
Stud Farm
Grimston Hill Plantation
Hogg Lane
B1248

Woodleigh School
PO
East Farm
Toft Ings
Cultivation Terraces
Haver Hill
Fishpond Plantation
Claypit Plantation
Cow Cliff

67
Cascade Plantation
Toftings Bridge
Wandales
Grimston
Brow
Cowcliff Plantation
Boyes' Plantation

The Leys

5
Clombe Beck
Caburn Wood
Mill Farm
Leys Wood
Luddith Farm
Luddith Road
Lund Wood

66
The Carr
Tom Cat Lane
Ivy House Farm
Earthquake Plantation
Wharram Grange Farm

Clombe Wood
Birdsall Grange Farm
Birdsall
The Square
School Plantation
Halfmoon Plantation
Birdsall Ings House
Pond Plantation
Fox Plantation
Station Rd

4
Quarry Plantation
Gas House Plantation
Rowmire Plantation
Rowmire Wood
Birdsall Ings
Fox House
The Ings

Car Nab Wood
Langhill Wood
Bath Plantation
Birdsall Wold
Picksharp Wood
Slatings Plantation

65
Lang Hill
Crow Wood
Birdsall House
Church (remains of)
Pits Wood
Picksharp Wood
Picksharp Farm
Wharram Percy Village

Langhill Plantation
Manor House
Decoy Plantation
Toft House
East Wold
Wharram Percy
Church (remains of)

3

64
Mount Ferrant Wood
High Barn Plantation
Jubilee Plantation
Bathingwell Wood
Oxpasture Wood
Birdsall Brow Plantation
Wharram Percy Plantation

Mount Ferrant Farm
Tumulus
Centenary Way
Tumulus
Greenlands
Deep Dale

2
Earthwork
Aldro Plantation
Swinham Wood
Swinham Wood
Birdsall Brow
Toisland Farm
Tumulus
Wharram Percy Farm

Tumulus
Earthwork
Swinham Plantation

63
Aldro Farm
Tumuli
Wolds Way
North Plantation

Earthwork
Earthworks
Vessey Pasture
Earthwork
North Plantation

1
Tumulus
Vessey Pasture Plantation
The Warrens
Raisthorpe Wold

Brown Moor
Brown Moor Farm
Tumulus
Earthwork
Vessey Pasture Dale
Black Dale
Honey Dale
Centenary Way

62

80 **A** **81** **B** **82** **C** **83** **D** **84** **E** **85** **F**

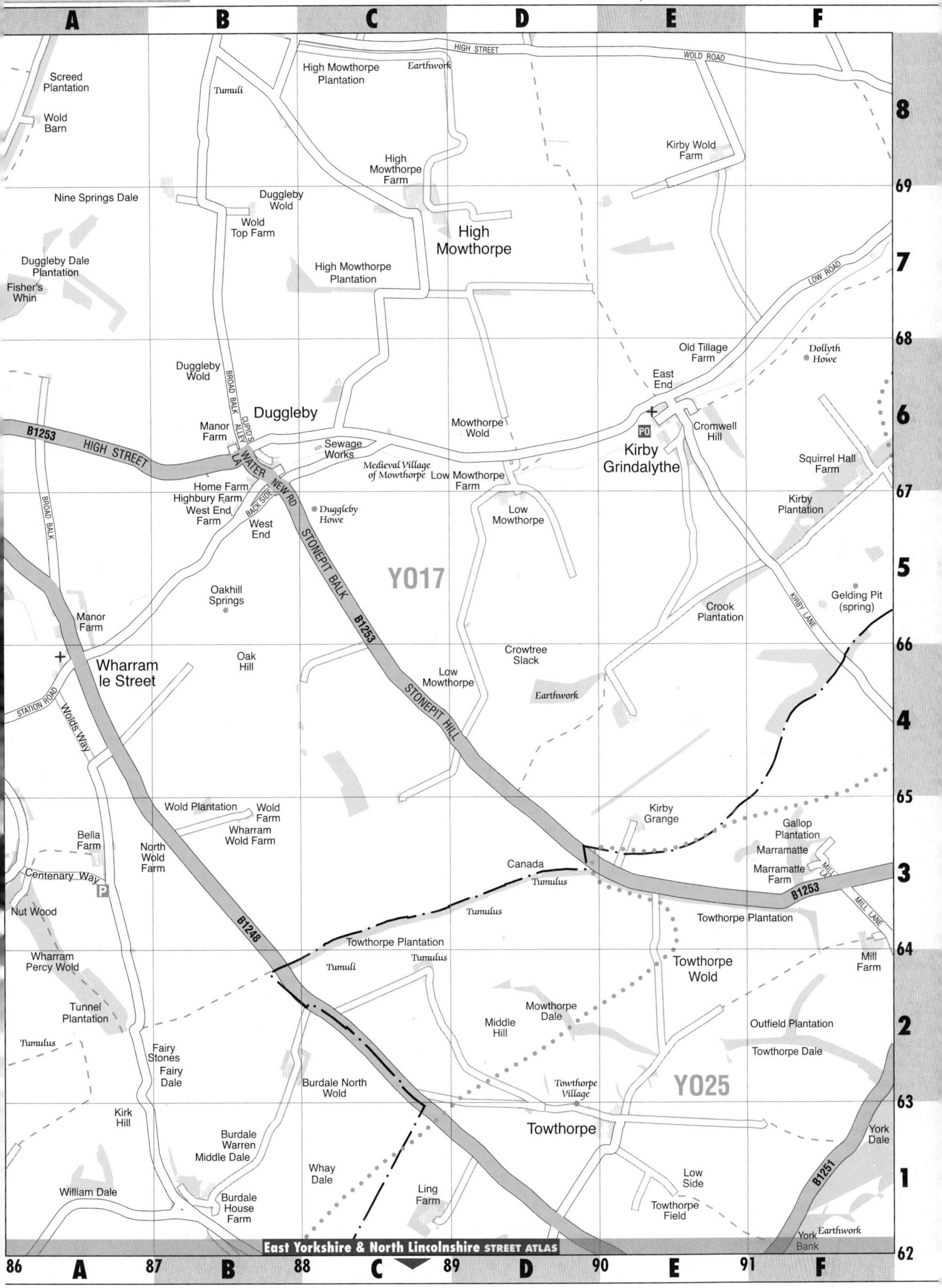
A
B
C
D
E
F
8
69
7
68
6
67
5
66
4
65
3
64
2
63
1
62
86
87
88
89
90
91
HIGH STREET
WOLD ROAD
Screed Plantation
Wold Barn
Tumuli
High Mowthorpe Plantation
Earthwork
High Mowthorpe Farm
Kirby Wold Farm
Nine Springs Dale
Duggleby Wold
Wold Top Farm
High Mowthorpe
Duggleby Dale Plantation
Fisher's Whin
High Mowthorpe Plantation
LOW ROAD
Old Tillage Farm
Dollyth Howe
East End
Duggleby Wold
BROAD BALK
Duggleby
CUPIDS ALLEY
Manor Farm
B1253
HIGH STREET
WATER LA
Sewage Works
Mowthorpe Wold
PO
Kirby Grindalythe
Cromwell Hill
Squirrel Hall Farm
Medieval Village of Mowthorpe
Low Mowthorpe Farm
Home Farm
Highbury Farm
West End Farm
BACK SIDE
NEW RD
Duggleby Howe
West End
Low Mowthorpe
Kirby Plantation
BROAD BALK
STONEPIT BALK
YO17
Oakhill Springs
Manor Farm
Crook Plantation
KIRBY LANE
Gelding Pit (spring)
B1253
Wharram le Street
Oak Hill
Crowtree Slack
Low Mowthorpe
STATION ROAD
Wolds Way
Earthwork
STONEPIT HILL
Wold Plantation
Wold Farm
Wharram Wold Farm
Kirby Grange
Gallop Plantation
Bella Farm
North Wold Farm
Marramatte
Canada
Marramatte Farm
Centenary Way
P
Tumulus
MILL LA
B1253
Nut Wood
Tumulus
Towthorpe Plantation
MILL LANE
B1248
Towthorpe Plantation
Wharram Percy Wold
Tumuli
Tumulus
Towthorpe Wold
Mill Farm
Tunnel Plantation
Mowthorpe Dale
Middle Hill
Outfield Plantation
Tumulus
Towthorpe Dale
Fairy Stones
Fairy Dale
Burdale North Wold
Towthorpe Village
YO25
Kirk Hill
Towthorpe
York Dale
Burdale Warren
Middle Dale
Whay Dale
Low Side
B1251
William Dale
Burdale House Farm
Ling Farm
Towthorpe Field
York Bank
Earthwork

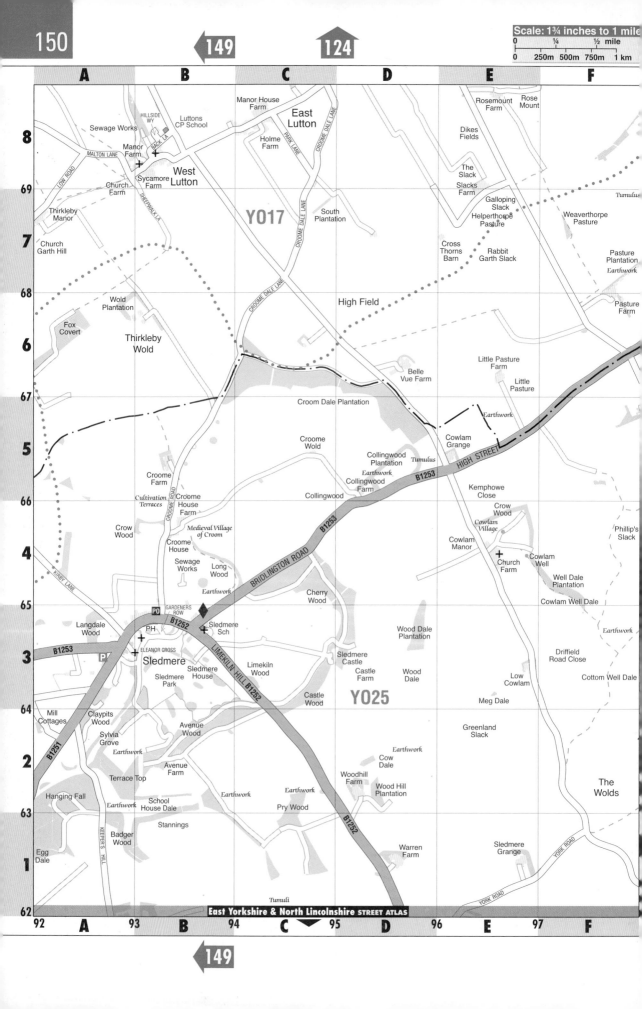

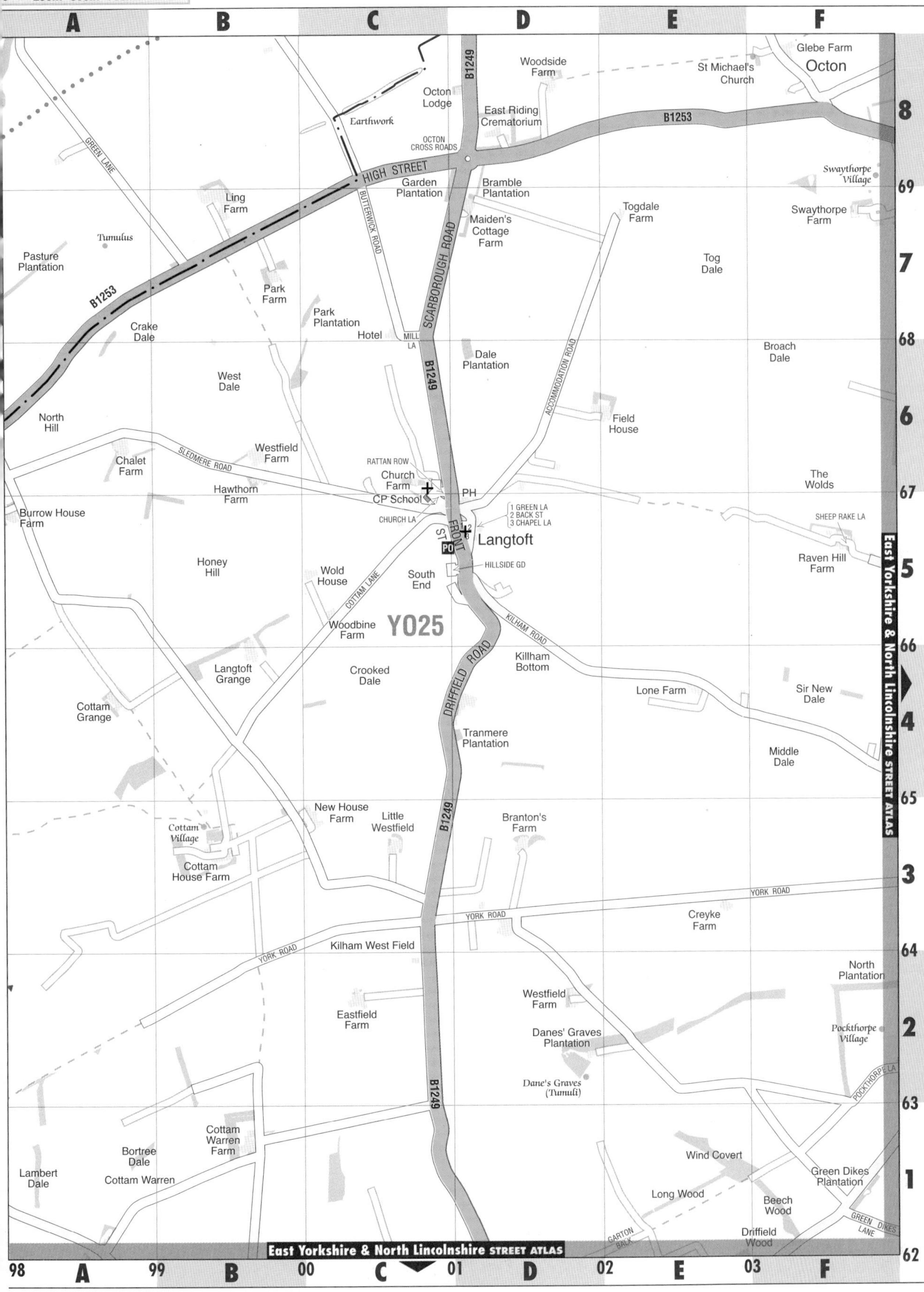

A B C D E F

8

Woodside Farm

Octon Lodge

Earthwork

St Michael's Church

Glebe Farm

Octon

East Riding Crematorium

B1253

OCTON CROSS ROADS

69

Swaythorpe Village

HIGH STREET

Garden Plantation

Bramble Plantation

Togdale Farm

Swaythorpe Farm

Ling Farm

Tumulus

Maiden's Cottage Farm

7

Tog Dale

Pasture Plantation

B1253

Park Farm

Park Plantation

Hotel

Dale Plantation

68

Broach Dale

West Dale

Crake Dale

MILL LA

North Hill

6

Field House

Westfield Farm

SLEDMERE ROAD

Chalet Farm

Hawthorn Farm

RATTAN ROW
Church Farm
CP School

PH

67

The Wolds

SHEEP RAKE LA

Burrow House Farm

CHURCH LA

FRONT ST

1 GREEN LA
2 BACK ST
3 CHAPEL LA

Honey Hill

Wold House

Langtoft

PO

Langtoft

HILLSIDE GD

Raven Hill Farm

5

South End

COTTAM LANE

Woodbine Farm

KILHAM ROAD

YO25

Killham Bottom

66

Lone Farm

Sir New Dale

Langtoft Grange

Crooked Dale

Cottam Grange

DRIFFIELD ROAD

Tranmere Plantation

Middle Dale

4

65

New House Farm

Little Westfield

Branton's Farm

Cottam Village

B1249

3

Cottam House Farm

YORK ROAD

YORK ROAD

Creyke Farm

York Road

York Road

Kilham West Field

64

North Plantation

Eastfield Farm

Westfield Farm

Danes' Graves Plantation

Pockthorpe Village

2

POCKTHORPE LA

B1249

Dane's Graves (Tumuli)

63

Cottam Warren Farm

Wind Covert

Green Dikes Plantation

Bortree Dale

Lambert Dale

Cottam Warren

Long Wood

Beech Wood

1

GREEN DIKES LANE

GARTON BECK

Driffield Wood

62

98 A 99 B 00 C 01 D 02 E 03 F

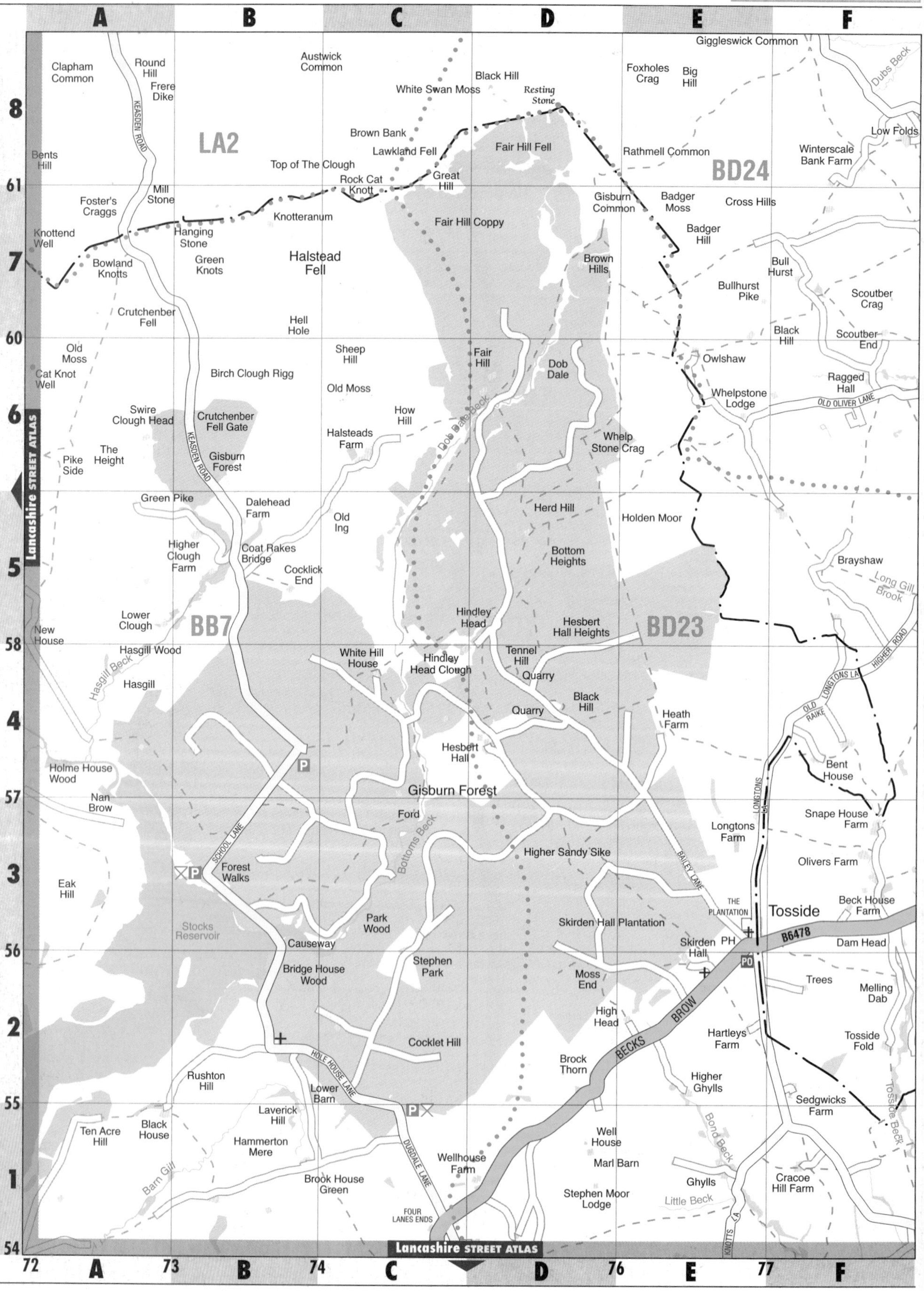

Scale: 1¾ inches to 1 mile

0 ¼ ½ mile
0 250m 500m 750m 1 km

Lancashire STREET ATLAS

Clapham Common
Round Hill
Frere Dike
KEASDEN ROAD
Bents Hill
LA2
Austwick Common
White Swan Moss
Brown Bank
Lawkland Fell
Top of The Clough
Rock Cat Knott
Great Hill
Black Hill
Resting Stone
Fair Hill Fell
Foxholes Crag
Big Hill
Giggleswick Common
Low Folds
Winterscale Bank Farm
BD24
Foster's Craggs
Mill Stone
Knotteranum
Fair Hill Coppy
Gisburn Common
Rathmell Common
Badger Moss
Cross Hills
Knottend Well
Hanging Stone
Green Knots
Halstead Fell
Brown Hills
Badger Hill
Bullhurst Pike
Bull Hurst
Scoutber Crag
Bowland Knotts
Black Hill
Scoutber End
Crutchenber Fell
Hell Hole
Fair Hill
Dob Dale
Owlshaw
Whelpstone Lodge
OLD OLIVER LANE
Ragged Hall
Old Moss
Cat Knot Well
Birch Clough Rigg
Sheep Hill
Old Moss
How Hill
Whelp Stone Crag
Swire Clough Head
Crutchenber Fell Gate
Halsteads Farm
Herd Hill
Holden Moor
Brayshaw
Long Gill Brook
Pike Side
The Height
Green Pike
Gisburn Forest
Dalehead Farm
Old Ing
Bottom Heights
Higher Clough Farm
Coat Rakes Bridge
Cocklick End
Hindley Head
Hesbert Hall Heights
BD23
Lower Clough
BB7
White Hill House
Hindley Head Clough
Tennel Hill
Quarry
New House
Hasgill Wood
Hasgill Beck
Hasgill
Quarry
Black Hill
Heath Farm
Higher Road
Longtons La
Old Raike
Bent House
Holme House Wood
Hesbert Hall
Snape House Farm
Nan Brow
Gisburn Forest
Ford
Higher Sandy Sike
Longtons Farm
Olivers Farm
Eak Hill
Forest Walks
SCHOOL LANE
Bottoms Beck
THE PLANTATION
Tosside
Beck House Farm
Stocks Reservoir
Park Wood
Skirden Hall Plantation
Skirden Hall
PH
B6478
Dam Head
Causeway
Bridge House Wood
Stephen Park
Moss End
Trees
Melling Dab
Rushton Hill
HOLE HOUSE LANE
Cocklet Hill
High Head
Hartleys Farm
Tosside Fold
Laverick Hill
Lower Barn
Brock Thorn
BECKS BROW
BAILEY LANE
Higher Ghylls
Sedgwicks Farm
Ten Acre Hill
Black House
Hammerton Mere
Wellhouse Farm
Well House
Marl Barn
Bond Beck
Ghylls
Cracoe Hill Farm
Barn Gill
Brook House Green
DUGDALE LANE
FOUR LANES ENDS
Stephen Moor Lodge
Little Beck
Tosside Beck
KNOTTS LA

Lancashire STREET ATLAS

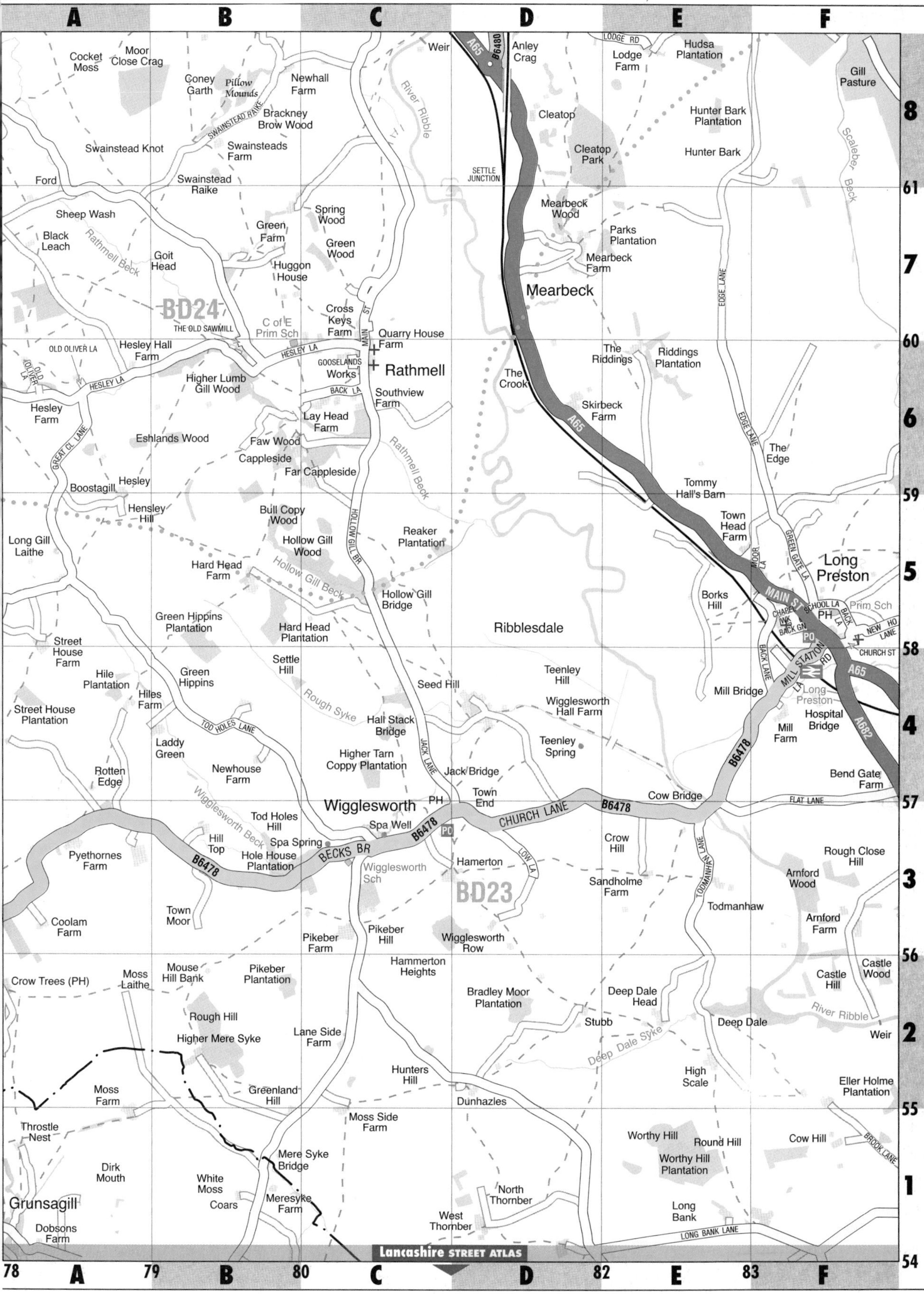

Scale: 1¾ inches to 1 mile

0   ¼   ½   mile

0   250m 500m 750m 1 km

A   B   C   D   E   F

Cocket Moss

Moor Close Crag

Coney Garth

Pillow Mounds

Newhall Farm

Weir

A65

B6480

Anley Crag

LODGE RD

Lodge Farm

Hudsa Plantation

Gill Pasture

8

Brackney Brow Wood

Cleatop

Hunter Bark Plantation

SWAINSTEAD RAIKE

Swainstead Knot

Swainsteads Farm

Cleatop Park

Hunter Bark

Scaleber Beck

61

Ford

Swainstead Raike

SETTLE JUNCTION

7

Sheep Wash

Spring Wood

Mearbeck Wood

Black Leach

Goit Head

Green Farm

Green Wood

Parks Plantation

EDGE LANE

BD24

THE OLD SAWMILL

Huggon House

Mearbeck Farm

60

OLD OLIVER LA

Hesley Hall Farm

C of E Prim Sch

HESLEY LA

Cross Keys Farm

Quarry House Farm

Mearbeck

The Riddings

Riddings Plantation

Higher Lumb Gill Wood

MAIN ST

Rathmell

7

Hesley Farm

HESLEY LA

Gooselands Works

BACK LA

Southview Farm

The Crook

Skirbeck Farm

The Edge

6

Boostagill

Hesley

Eshlands Wood

Lay Head Farm

A65

EDGE LANE

Hensley Hill

Faw Wood

Cappleside

Far Cappleside

Rathmell Beck

59

Long Gill Laithe

Bull Copy Wood

Reaker Plantation

Tommy Hall's Barn

Town Head Farm

GREEN GATE LA

Long Preston

5

Hollow Gill Wood

HOLLOW GILL BR

Hard Head Farm

Hollow Gill Beck

Hollow Gill Bridge

Borks Hill

MOOR LA

MAIN ST

Prim Sch

Green Hippins Plantation

Hard Head Plantation

Ribblesdale

CHAPEL LA

SCHOOL LA

PH

NEW HO LANE

58

Street House Farm

Settle Hill

Seed Hill

Teenley Hill

BACK GRN

PO

CHURCH ST

Hile Plantation

Rough Syke

Wigglesworth Hall Farm

Mill Bridge

MILL STATION LA

Long Preston

A65

Street House Plantation

Green Hippins

Hiles Farm

Hall Stack Bridge

JACK LANE

Teenley Spring

Mill Farm

Hospital Bridge

A682

4

Laddy Green

Higher Tarn Coppy Plantation

Jack Bridge

Town End

B6478

Cow Bridge

FLAT LANE

Bend Gate Farm

57

Rotten Edge

TOD HOLES LANE

Newhouse Farm

Wigglesworth

PH

CHURCH LANE

B6478

Pyethornes Farm

Tod Holes Hill

Spa Well

Spa Spring

BECKS BR

B6478

LOW LA

Hamerton

Crow Hill

TODMANHAW LANE

Rough Close Hill

3

B6478

Hole House Plantation

Wigglesworth Sch

BD23

Sandholme Farm

Todmanhaw

Arnford Wood

Wigglesworth Beck

Town Moor

Wigglesworth Row

Arnford Farm

Coolam Farm

Pikeber Farm

Pikeber Hill

Castle Hill

Castle Wood

56

Crow Trees (PH)

Moss Laithe

Mouse Hill Bank

Pikeber Plantation

Hammerton Heights

Bradley Moor Plantation

Deep Dale Head

River Ribble

2

Rough Hill

Lane Side Farm

Stubb

Deep Dale

Higher Mere Syke

Deep Dale Syke

Weir

Moss Farm

Greenland Hill

Hunters Hill

High Scale

Eller Holme Plantation

55

Throstle Nest

Dunhazles

Worthy Hill

Round Hill

Cow Hill

BROOK LANE

Dirk Mouth

Mere Syke Bridge

Moss Side Farm

Worthy Hill Plantation

White Moss Coars

Meresyke Farm

North Thornber

Long Bank

1

Grunsagill

West Thornber

LONG BANK LANE

Dobsons Farm

78   A   79   B   80   C   D   82   E   83   F   54

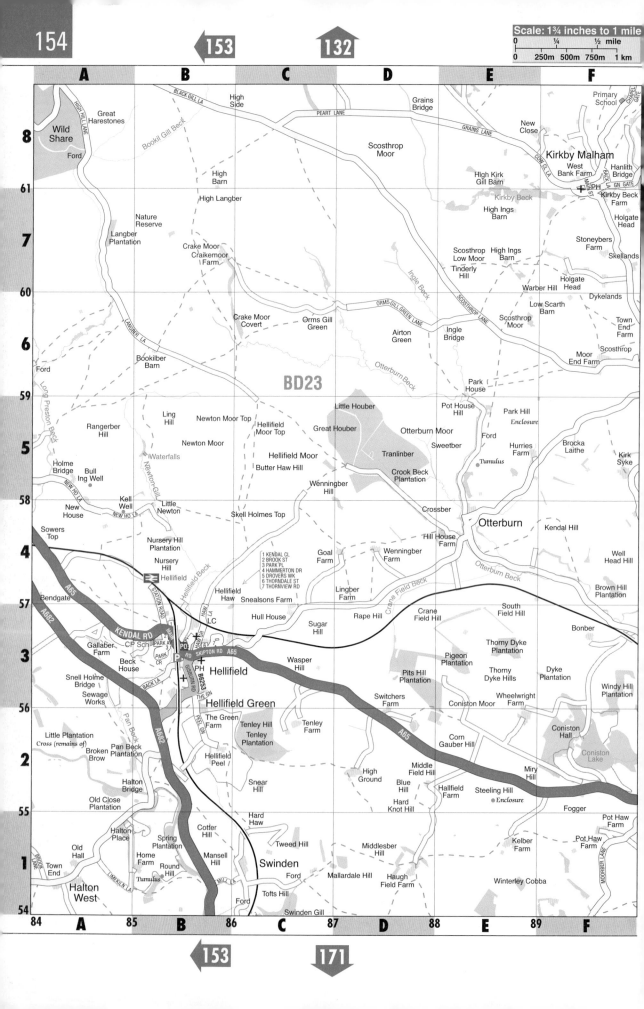

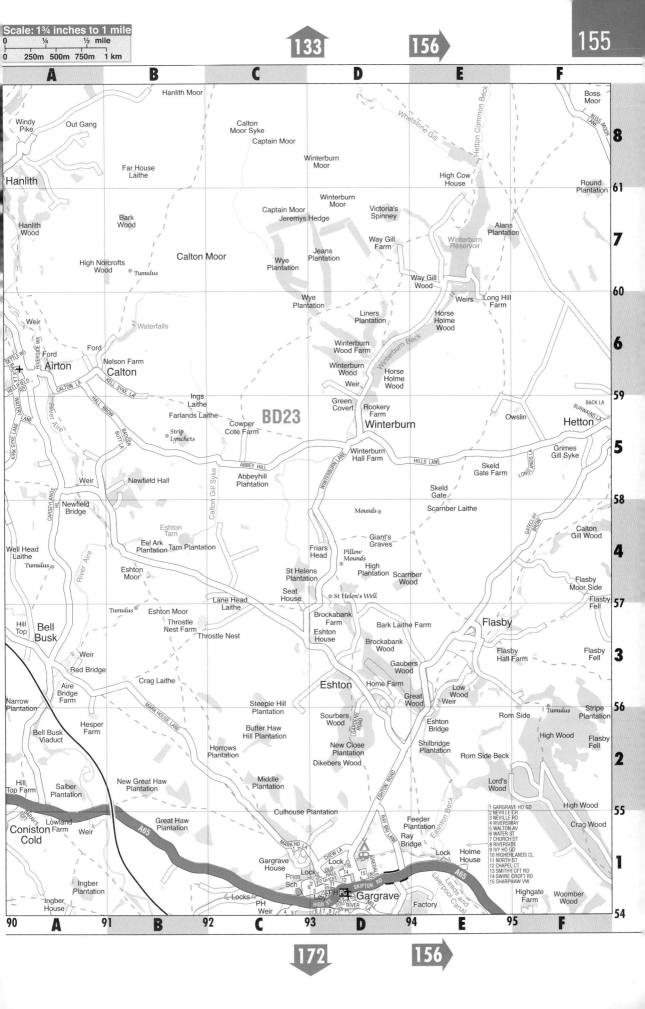

Scale: 1¾ inches to 1 mile

| 0 | ¼ | ½ mile |
| 0 | 250m | 500m | 750m | 1 km |

A   **B**   **C**   **D**   **E**   **F**

Boss Moor

Catchall Farm

B6265

Ings House

Cockerham

Elbolton

Holly Tree Farm

Thorpe
Kale Farm

Skulberts Wood

8

Ford

Swinden Quarry (Limestone)

Escoe House

Elbolton Cave

Kail Hill

61

Cowpasture Plantation

BOSS MOOR LA

Eller Beck

Threaplands House Farm

Langerton Farm

Far Langerton

THORPE LANE

Stebden Hill

Raven Nest Crags

Shafts (dis)

7

Sun Hill Farm
Gill Plantation

Gill Wood

Fleets

New Laithe

Threapland

THORPE LANE

Garden Lead Mines (dis)

Rolling Gate Crags

Threapland Fell

60

Black Hill Plantation

Green End PH

Town End

Cracoe

BACK LANE

FELL LANE

Fell Side

Ford

Hill Top Laithe

Skelterton Hill

Threapland Gill

Bartle Crag

Burnsall & Thorpe Fell

Cracoe Prim-Sch

B6265

6

FLEETS LANE

Skirse Gill Beck

LC

Skirse Gill Bridge

RAIKES LANE

Fell Side Laithe

Three Thorn Well

In Fell

Cracoe Fell

The Crags

Peter's Crag

Threapland Peat Pits (dis)

Thorpe Fell Top

Gill Beck Head

Burnsall Peat Pits (dis)

59

PH

Burton House Farm

BACK LA

Willowlands Laithe

Fish Ponds

Watt Crag

5

Manor House

Rylstone

BACK LA

Green Farm

Crutching Close

Hall Dentesne

Hall Fell

Water Crag

Rylstone Fell

Gutter Stones

The Whams

Weir

BD23

58

Calton Gill Wood

Out Fell

Weir

Upper Barden Reservoir

Weir

4

Tumulus

Flasby Fell

Rylstone Fell

Yethersgill Head or Padmire

Brown Bank Brow

Brown Bank Brow

Cross Gill Head

Lumb Gill Wham

Brown Bank

Peggy Wests Well

57

Far Fell Plantation

Scale Hill Farm

Tumulus

Norton Twr

Pillow Mounds

Sun Moor

Norton Tower Wood

Gill Head

Bilton Ings

Lumb Gill Head

3

Ten Acre Plantation

Flasby Fell

B6265

Scale House

Sun Moor Wood

Hellifield Crag

Sun Moor Plantation

Stone Ridge Plain

Stoneridge Quarries (dis)

Embsay Moor

Hut Crag

Brayshaw Top

Embsay Moor

Rotten Park

56

Rough Haw

Bents Wood

Sandy Beck

Nettlehole Wood

Crookrise

Crag Top

Crookrise Wood

Deer Gallows Plain

Wayshaw Bogs

Rams Gill Head

Tewit Bogs

2

Hollin Wood

LC

Crookrise Crag

White Stones

Heugh Ground Head

55

Owlet House

Eller Beck

LC

Crag Nook

Embsay Crag

Crow Crag

Waterfall

Heugh Farm

Bondcroft Farm

Eastby

1

Enclosure

Skyrakes Farm

Crag Nook Farm

Hill Top

Embsay Moor Resr

Good Intent

Chimney

Monk's Well

MOOR LANE

HUNTERS CFT PH

None-Go-Bye Farm

B6265

Bog Wood

B6265

Hagg Farm

Intake Farm

PASTURE

ROAD

Crown Cottage Farm

Embsay Kirk

KIRK LANE

54

96   **A**   **97**   **B**   **98**   **C**   **99**   **D**   **00**   **E**   **01**   **F**   **0**

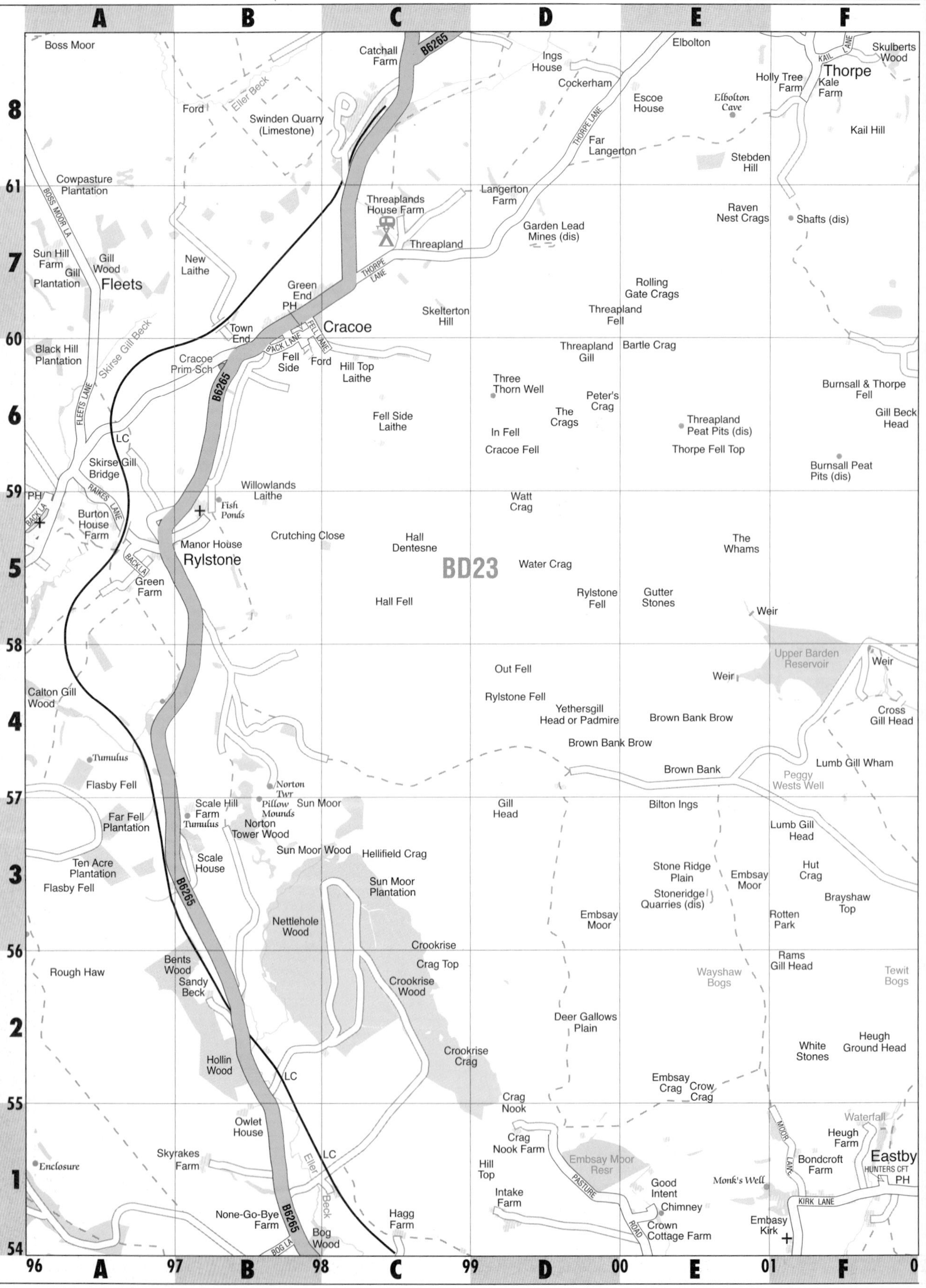

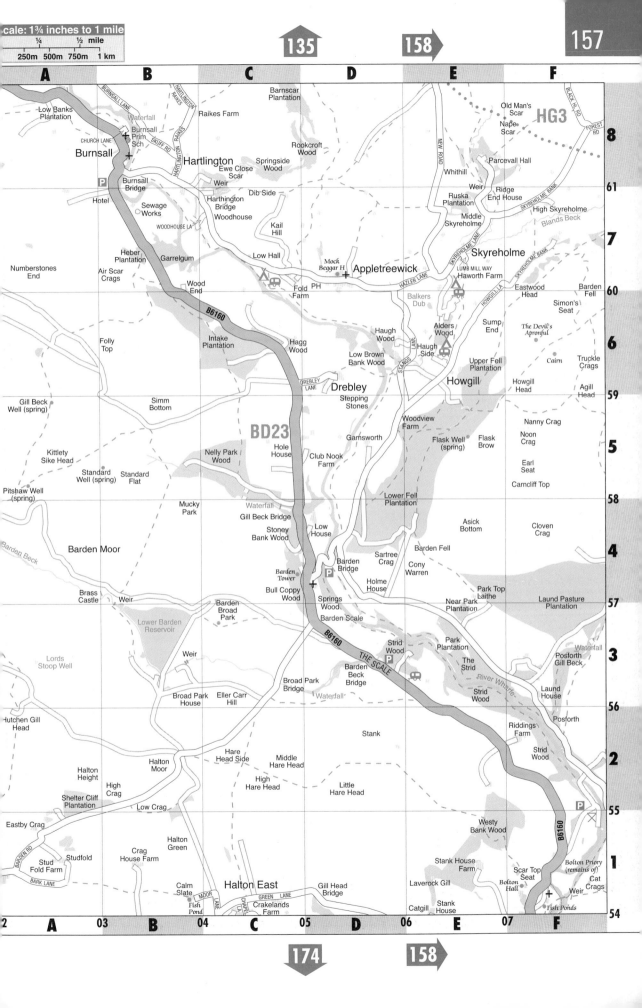

Scale: 1¾ inches to 1 mile

¼   ½ mile

250m 500m 750m 1 km

135

158

157

8
61
7
60
6
59
5
58
4
57
3
56
2
55
1
54

A   B   C   D   E   F

Low Banks
Plantation

BURNSALL LANE

Waterfall

HARTLINGTON RAKES

Raikes Farm

Barnscar
Plantation

Old Man's
Scar

Nape
Scar

HG3

BLACK HILL RD

FOREST RD

Burnsall
Prim
Sch

CHURCH LANE

Burnsall

SKUFF RD

HARTLINGTON LANE

Hartlington

Rookcroft
Wood

Springside
Wood

Ewe Close
Scar

Whithill

Parcevall Hall

NEW ROAD

Burnsall
Bridge

Hotel

P

Weir

Dib Side

Weir

Ridge
End House

Ruska
Plantation

High Skyreholme

SKYREHOLME BANK

Blands Beck

Sewage
Works

WOODHOUSE LA

Hartlington
Bridge
Woodhouse

Kail
Hill

Middle
Skyreholme

Heber
Plantation

Garrelgum

Low Hall

Mock
Beggar H

Appletreewick

HAZLER LANE

SKYREHOLME LANE

Skyreholme

Air Scar
Crags

Numberstones
End

Wood
End

PH

Fold
Farm

Haworth Farm

HOWGILL LA

SKYREHOLME BANK

Eastwood
Head

Barden
Fell

B6160

Balkers
Dub

Alders
Wood

Simon's
Seat

The Devil's
Apronful

Intake
Plantation

Hagg
Wood

Haugh
Wood

STANGS LANE

Haugh
Side

Sump
End

Cairn

Truckle
Crags

Folly
Top

Low Brown
Bank Wood

Upper Fell
Plantation

Howgill
Head

Agill
Head

DREBLEY
LANE

Drebley

Howgill

Gill Beck
Well (spring)

Simm
Bottom

Stepping
Stones

Woodview
Farm

Nanny Crag

Noon
Crag

BD23

Gamsworth

Flask Well
(spring)

Flask
Brow

Kittlety
Sike Head

Hole
House

Nelly Park
Wood

Club Nook
Farm

Earl
Seat

Standard
Well (spring)

Standard
Flat

Carncliff Top

Pitshaw Well
(spring)

Waterfall

Lower Fell
Plantation

Asick
Bottom

Cloven
Crag

Barden Beck

Mucky
Park

Gill Beck Bridge

Low
House

Stoney
Bank Wood

Barden Fell

Barden Moor

Barden
Tower

Barden
Bridge

Sartree
Crag

Cony
Warren

Park Top
Laithe

Laund Pasture
Plantation

Brass
Castle

Weir

Bull Coppy
Wood

P

Springs
Wood

Holme
House

Near Park
Plantation

Lower Barden
Reservoir

Barden
Broad
Park

Barden Scale

Park
Plantation

Laund
Pasture

Lords
Stoop Well

Weir

B6160

THE SCALE

Strid
Wood

P

Posforth
Gill Beck

Waterfall

Broad Park
Bridge

Barden
Beck
Bridge

Waterfall

River Wharfe

The
Strid

Strid
Wood

Laund
House

Hutchen Gill
Head

Broad Park
House

Eller Carr
Hill

Stank

Riddings
Farm

Strid
Wood

Posforth

Halton
Height

Hare
Head Side

Middle
Hare Head

High
Crag

Halton
Moor

High
Hare Head

Little
Hare Head

P

Shelter Cliff
Plantation

Low Crag

Eastby Crag

Westy
Bank Wood

B6160

Stud
Fold Farm

BARDEN RD

Studfold

Halton
Green

Crag
House Farm

Calm
Slate

MOOR LANE

Halton East

Crakelands
Farm

Gill Head
Bridge

Stank House
Farm

Laverock Gill

Catgill

Stank
House

Scar Top
Seat

Bolton
Hall

Bolton Priory
(remains of)

Cat
Crags

Weir

BARK LANE

Fish
Pond

CHAPEL LANE

GREEN LANE

Fish Ponds

2   A   03   B   04   C   05   D   06   E   07   F

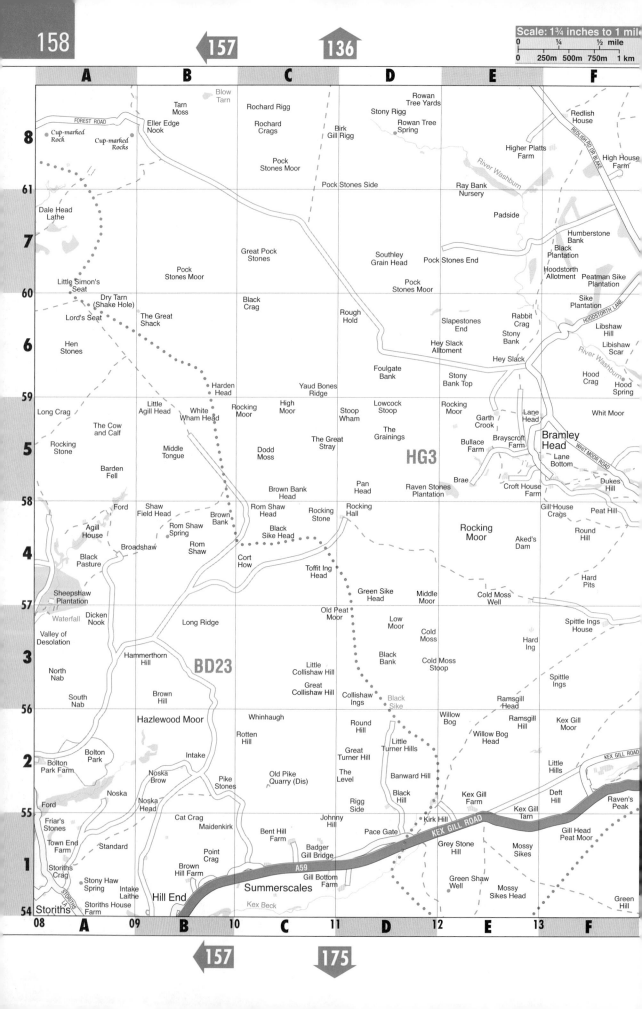

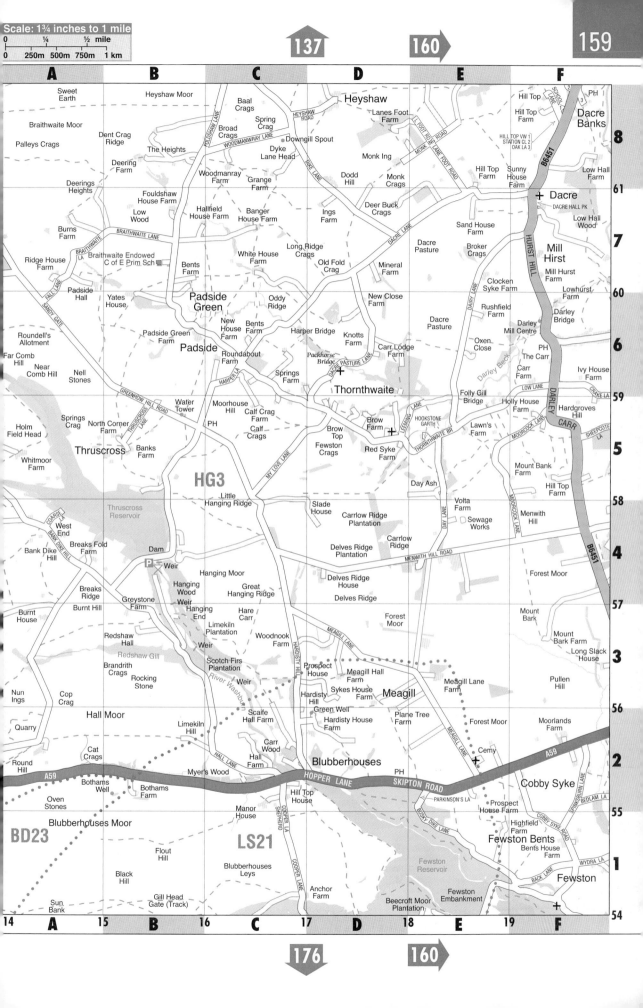

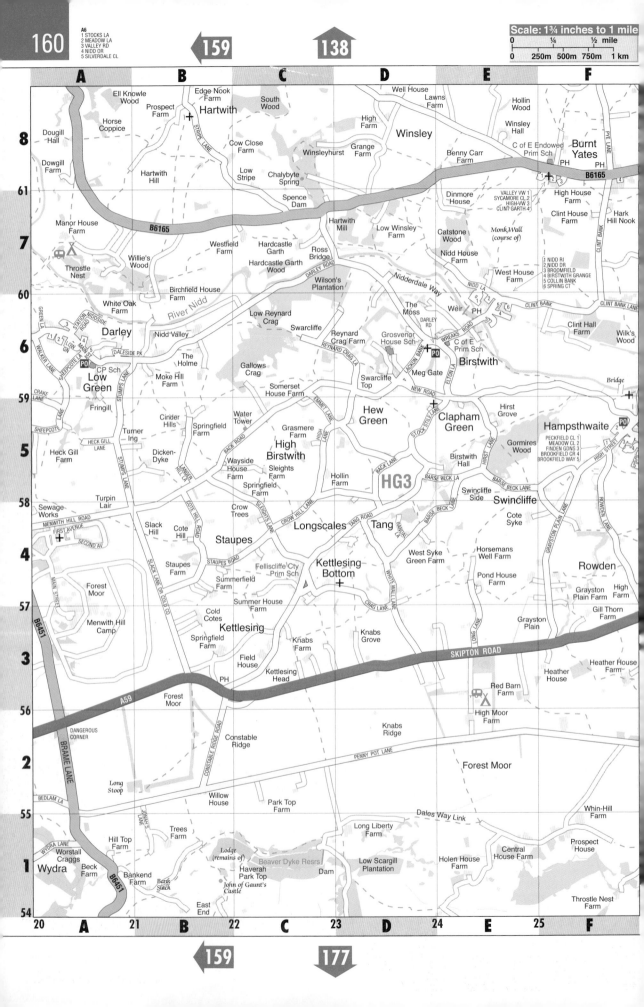

Scale: 1¾ inches to 1 mile

0   ¼   ½ mile
0 250m 500m 750m 1 km

Map labels

Dougill Hall
Ell Knowle Wood
Horse Coppice
Prospect Farm
Edge Nook Farm
Hartwith
South Wood
Well House
Lawns Farm
Hollin Wood
Winsley Hall
C of E Endowed Prim Sch
Burnt Yates
PH
PH
Pye Lane

Dowgill Farm
Hartwith Hill
Cow Close Farm
Low Stripe
Winsleyhurst
Grange Farm
Chalybyte Spring
Winsley
Benny Carr Farm
B6165
VALLEY VW 1
SYCAMORE CL 2
HIGH VW 3
CLINT GARTH 4
High House Farm

Manor House Farm
B6165
Spence Dam
Hartwith Mill
Low Winsley Farm
Dinmore House
Catstone Wood
Nidd House Farm
Monk Wall (course of)
Clint House Farm
Hark Hill Nook
Clint Bank

Throstle Nest
Willie's Wood
Westfield Farm
Hardcastle Garth
Hardcastle Garth Wood
Ross Bridge
DARLEY ROAD
Wilson's Plantation
Nidderdale Way
NIDD LA
West House Farm
Weir
PH
1 NIDD RI
2 NIDD DR
3 BROOMFIELD
4 BIRSTWITH GRANGE
5 COLLIN BANK
6 SPRING CT
Clint Bank
Clint Hall Farm
Wilk's Wood
Clint Bank

Birchfield House Farm
River Nidd
Low Reynard Crag
Swarcliffe
Reynard Crag Farm
The Moss
Grosvenor House Sch
DARLEY RD
WREAKS ROAD
C of E Prim Sch
Birstwith
Bridge

White Oak Farm
Darley
Nidd Valley
The Holme
Reynard Crag La
Gallows Crag
Swarcliffe Top
JACKSON BANK
Meg Gate
New Road
ELTON LA
Hirst Grove
Hampsthwaite
PO

GREEN LA
STATION
NIDDSIDE
LOW MAIN ROAD
LOW GN
PO
CP Sch
Low Green
DALESIDE PK
Moke Hill Farm
Somerset House Farm
FAWNET LANE
HIGH LANE
Hew Green
STOCK STILE LANE
Clapham Green
Birstwith Hall
Gormires Wood
PECKFIELD CL 1
MEADOW CL 2
FINDEN GDNS 3
BROOKFIELD CR 4
BROOKFIELD WAY 5
HIGH STREET

WALKER LANE
SHEEPCOTE LA
Fringill
Cinder Hills
Springfield Farm
Water Tower
Grasmere Farm
High Birstwith
Hollin Farm
HG3
HIRST LANE
Swincliffe Side
Swincliffe
Cote Syke
ROWDEN LANE

CRAKE LANE
SHEEPCOTE LANE
STUMPS LANE
HECK GILL LANE
Heck Gill Farm
Turner Ing
Dicken-Dyke
LANGER HILL LA
Wayside House Farm
Sleights Farm
Springfield Farm
BACK ROAD
CROW HILL LANE
SLEIGHTS LANE
Crow Trees
Longscales
Tang
TANG ROAD
RANDAL LANE
BARSE BECK LA
BARSE BECK LANE
West Syke Green Farm
Horsemans Well Farm
Grayston Plain Farm
High Farm
Rowden
GRAYSTON PLAIN LANE

Sewage Works
Turpin Lair
MENWITH HILL ROAD
FIRST AVENUE
SECOND AV
Slack Hill
COTE HILL ROAD
Cote Hill
Staupes
Felliscliffe Cty Prim Sch
Kettlesing Bottom
Pond House Farm
Gill Thorn Farm

Forest Moor
SLACK LANE OR COLD CO
Staupes Farm
STAUPES ROAD
Summerfield Farm
Summer House Farm
WHITE WALL LANE
Grayston Plain
Grayston Plain Farm

MAIN STREET
B6451
Menwith Hill Camp
Cold Cotes
Kettlesing
Springfield Farm
Field House
Knabs Farm
Knabs Grove
CRAG LANE
LONG LANE
Heather House Farm
Heather House

Forest Moor
Kettlesing Head
PH
SKIPTON ROAD
Red Barn Farm
High Moor Farm

BRAME LANE
A59
DANGEROUS CORNER
Constable Ridge
CONSTABLE RIDGE ROAD
Knabs Ridge
PENNY POT LANE
Forest Moor

BEDLAM LA
Long Stoop
Willow House
Park Top Farm
Dales Way Link
Whin-Hill Farm

WYDRA LANE
Worstall Craggs
JONAH'S LANE
Trees Farm
Hill Top Farm
Lodge (remains of)
Beaver Dyke Resrs
Long Liberty Farm
Holen House Farm
Central House Farm
Prospect House

Wydra
Beck Farm
Bankend Farm
Bank Slack
B6451
Haverah Park Top
John of Gaunt's Castle
Dam
Low Scargill Plantation
Throstle Nest Farm
East End

Scale: 1¾ inches to 1 mile

0 ¼ ½ mile

0 250m 500m 750m 1 km

139

162

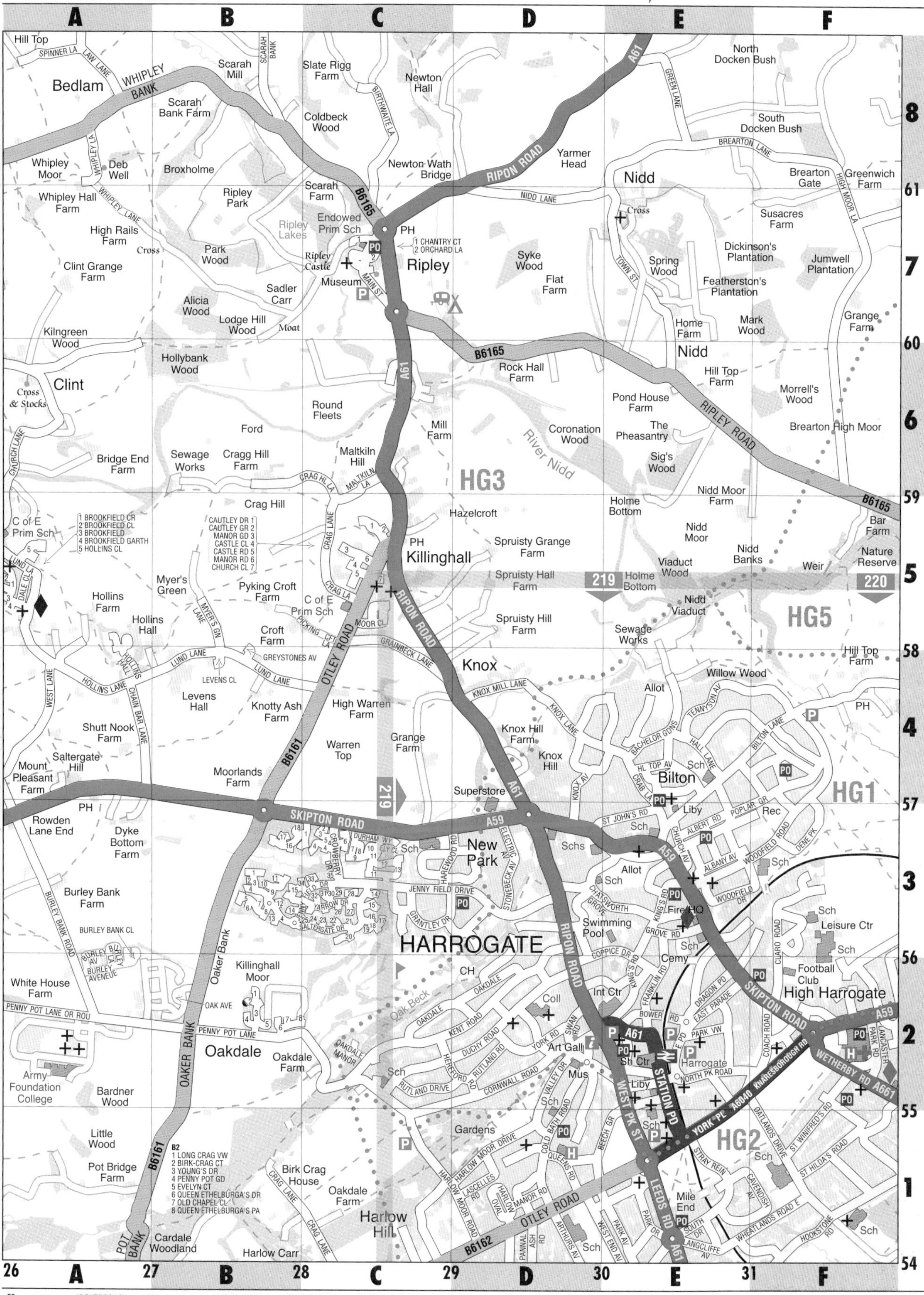

B3
1 CORNFLOWER WY
2 FOXGLOVE CL
3 OAKRIDGE VW
4 TREFOIL DR
5 STONECROP AV
6 BUTTERCUP CL
7 PENNY ROYAL CL
8 ORCHID WY
9 CLOVER WY
10 BURDOCK CL
11 BRAMBLE CL
12 ANGELICA CL
13 PRIMROSE CL
14 LARKSPUR GR
15 PENNYWORT GR
16 HEATHER WY
17 HAREBELL CL
18 BLUEBELL WK

C3
1 STONECROP DR
2 TANSY CL
3 TANSY RD
4 BRYONY RD
5 BRYONY WY
6 CAMPION GR
7 TRURO RD
8 TRURO CR
9 SALISBURY DR
10 EXETER CR
11 NORWICH DR
12 LINCOLN GR
13 LICHFIELD GR
14 SPEEDWELL GLADE
15 BLUEBELL MDW
16 SALLOW HEATH
17 GENTIAN GLADE
18 SWEET BRIAR
19 SAFFRON MDW
20 BARBERRY CL
21 WINTER GN
22 STONE BRAMBLE
23 CARLINE MEAD
24 SUNDEW HEATH
25 PETTY WHIN CL
26 CORNEL RI
27 WOODRUFF CL
28 JUNIPER WY
29 SORREL GR
30 BORAGE RD
31 TEASEL GR
32 COMFREY CL
33 COLUMBINE GR
34 BUTTERBUR WY
35 WOOD AVEN CL

178

220

For full street detail of the highlighted area see pages 219, 220, 222 and 223.

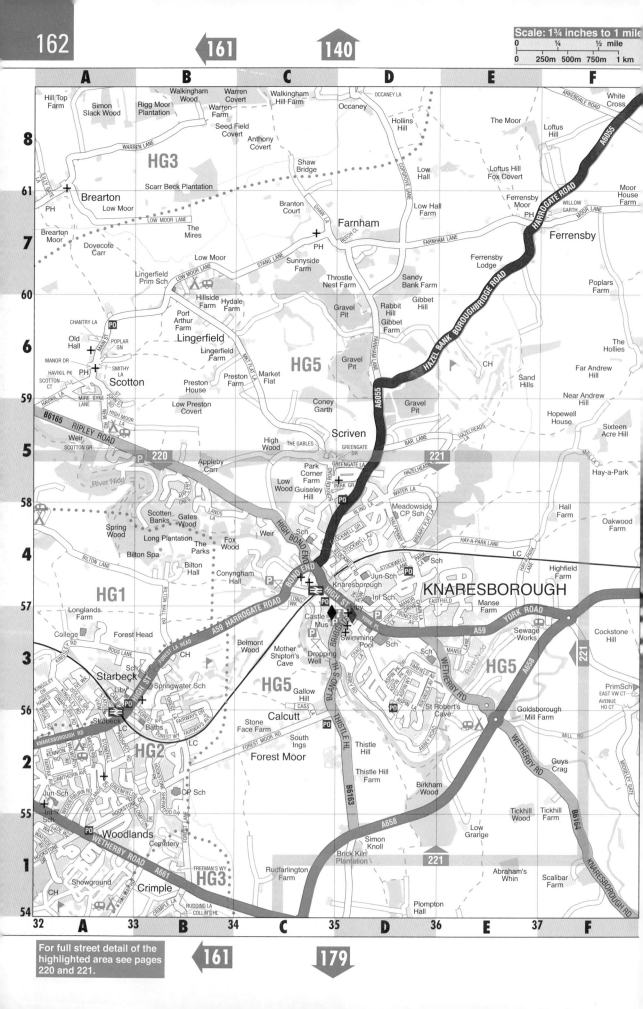

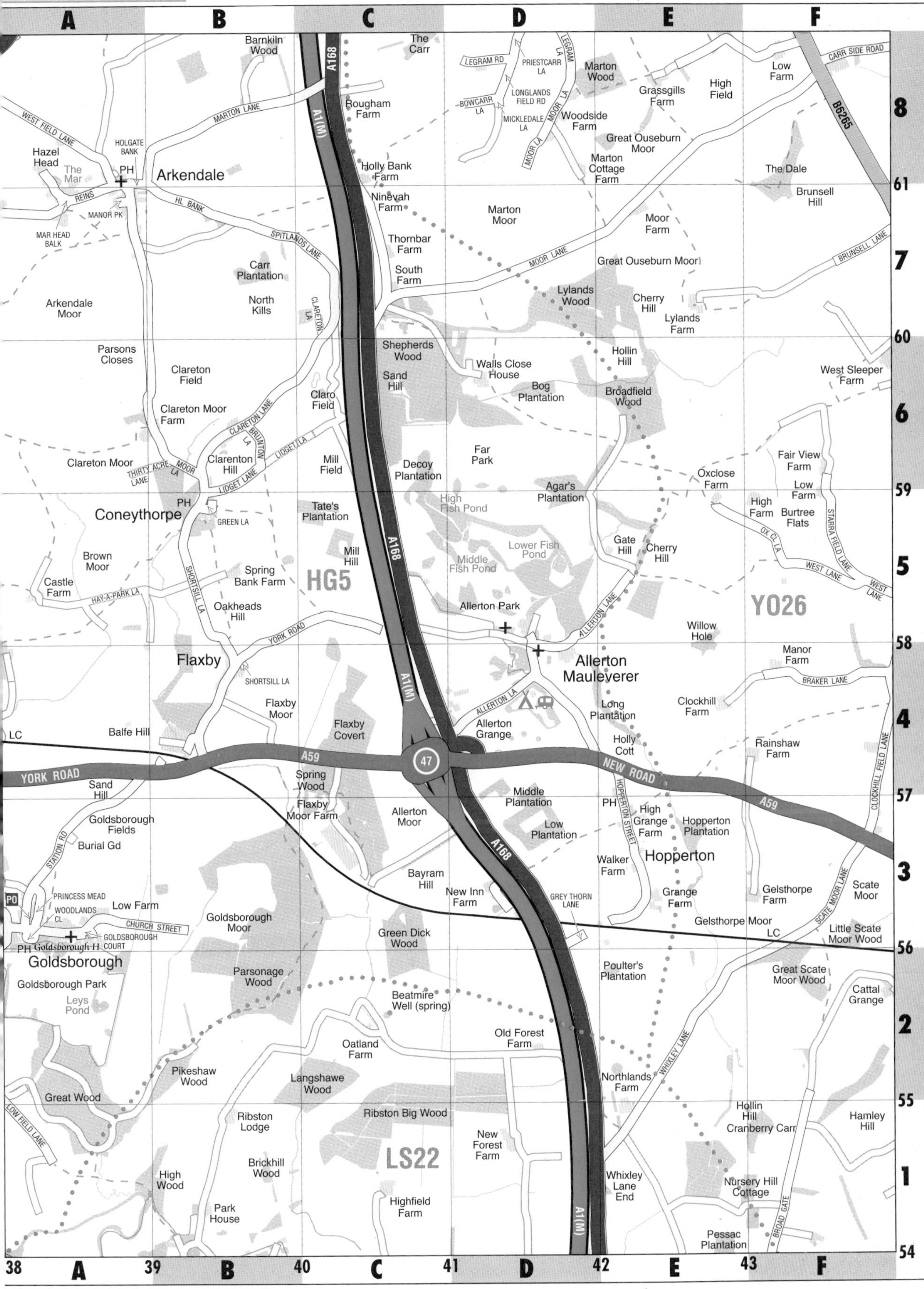
A
B
C
D
E
F
Barnkiln Wood
The Carr
A168
LEGRAM RD
PRIESTCARR LA
LEGRAM LA
Marton Wood
Low Farm
CARR SIDE ROAD
High Field
Grassgills Farm
B6265
8
WEST FIELD LANE
MARTON LANE
Rougham Farm
BOWCARR LA
LONGLANDS FIELD RD
MICKLEDALE LA
MOOR LA
Woodside Farm
A1(M)
Great Ouseburn Moor
HOLGATE BANK
Hazel Head
The Mar
PH
Arkendale
Holly Bank Farm
MOOR LA
Marton Cottage Farm
The Dale
Brunsell Hill
61
REINS
MANOR PK
HL BANK
Ninevah Farm
Marton Moor
MAR HEAD BALK
Moor Farm
SPITLANDS LANE
Thornbar Farm
BRUNSELL LANE
South Farm
MOOR LANE
Great Ouseburn Moor
7
Carr Plantation
Lylands Wood
Cherry Hill
Arkendale Moor
North Kills
CLARETON LA
Lylands Farm
60
Parsons Closes
Shepherds Wood
Hollin Hill
Clareton Field
Walls Close House
West Sleeper Farm
Sand Hill
Bog Plantation
Broadfield Wood
Claro Field
Clareton Moor Farm
6
CLARETON LANE
BRUNTON LA
Far Park
Fair View Farm
LIDGET LA
Clareton Moor
MOOR LA
Clarenton Hill
Mill Field
Decoy Plantation
Oxclose Farm
THIRTY ACRE LANE
LIDGET LANE
Low Farm
Agar's Plantation
59
PH
High Fish Pond
High Farm
Burtree Flats
Coneythorpe
Tate's Plantation
STARRA FIELD LANE
GREEN LA
OX CL LA
Lower Fish Pond
Gate Hill
Cherry Hill
Brown Moor
Mill Hill
Middle Fish Pond
WEST LANE
5
Spring Bank Farm
HG5
SHORTSILL LA
WEST LANE
Castle Farm
HAY-A-PARK LA
Y026
Oakheads Hill
Allerton Park
ALLERTON LANE
Willow Hole
YORK ROAD
58
Flaxby
Allerton Mauleverer
Manor Farm
SHORTSILL LA
BRAKER LANE
Flaxby Moor
ALLERTON LA
Long Plantation
Clockhill Farm
4
Flaxby Covert
Allerton Grange
LC
Balfe Hill
Holly Cott
Rainshaw Farm
CLOCKHILL FIELD LANE
A59
47
YORK ROAD
NEW ROAD
Sand Hill
Spring Wood
57
Flaxby Moor Farm
Middle Plantation
PH
High Grange Farm
HOPPERTON STREET
Hopperton Plantation
Goldsborough Fields
Allerton Moor
A59
Low Plantation
Burial Gd
STATION RD
A168
Hopperton
Walker Farm
3
Bayram Hill
SCATE MOOR LANE
Scate Moor
PO
PRINCESS MEAD
New Inn Farm
GREY THORN LANE
Grange Farm
Gelsthorpe Farm
WOODLANDS CL
Low Farm
Goldsborough Moor
Gelsthorpe Moor
CHURCH STREET
Little Scate Moor Wood
GOLDSBOROUGH COURT
Green Dick Wood
LC
PH
Goldsborough H
56
Goldsborough
Poulter's Plantation
Great Scate Moor Wood
Parsonage Wood
Goldsborough Park
Cattal Grange
Leys Pond
Beatmire Well (spring)
2
Old Forest Farm
Oatland Farm
WHIXLEY LANE
Pikeshaw Wood
Northlands Farm
Langshawe Wood
Great Wood
Hollin Hill
55
Ribston Lodge
Ribston Big Wood
Hamley Hill
LOW FIELD LANE
Cranberry Carr
New Forest Farm
LS22
Brickhill Wood
1
High Wood
Whixley Lane End
Nursery Hill Cottage
Highfield Farm
Park House
A1(M)
BROAD GATE
Pessac Plantation
54
38
39
40
41
42
43

A8
1 SPRINGFIELD RI
2 CHURCH FIELD LA
3 TOWNEND CT

163

142

F7
1 HALF MOON ST
2 BEECH TREE CT
3 GARTH GRANGE
4 LINTON PL
5 LINTON MDW
6 MILL LA
7 MAPLE GR
8 WHITE ROSE CL

F8
1 THE PADDOCK
2 GREEN CL
3 GROSVENOR SQ

Scale: 1¾ inches to 1 mile
0 ¼ ½ mile
0 250m 500m 750m 1 km

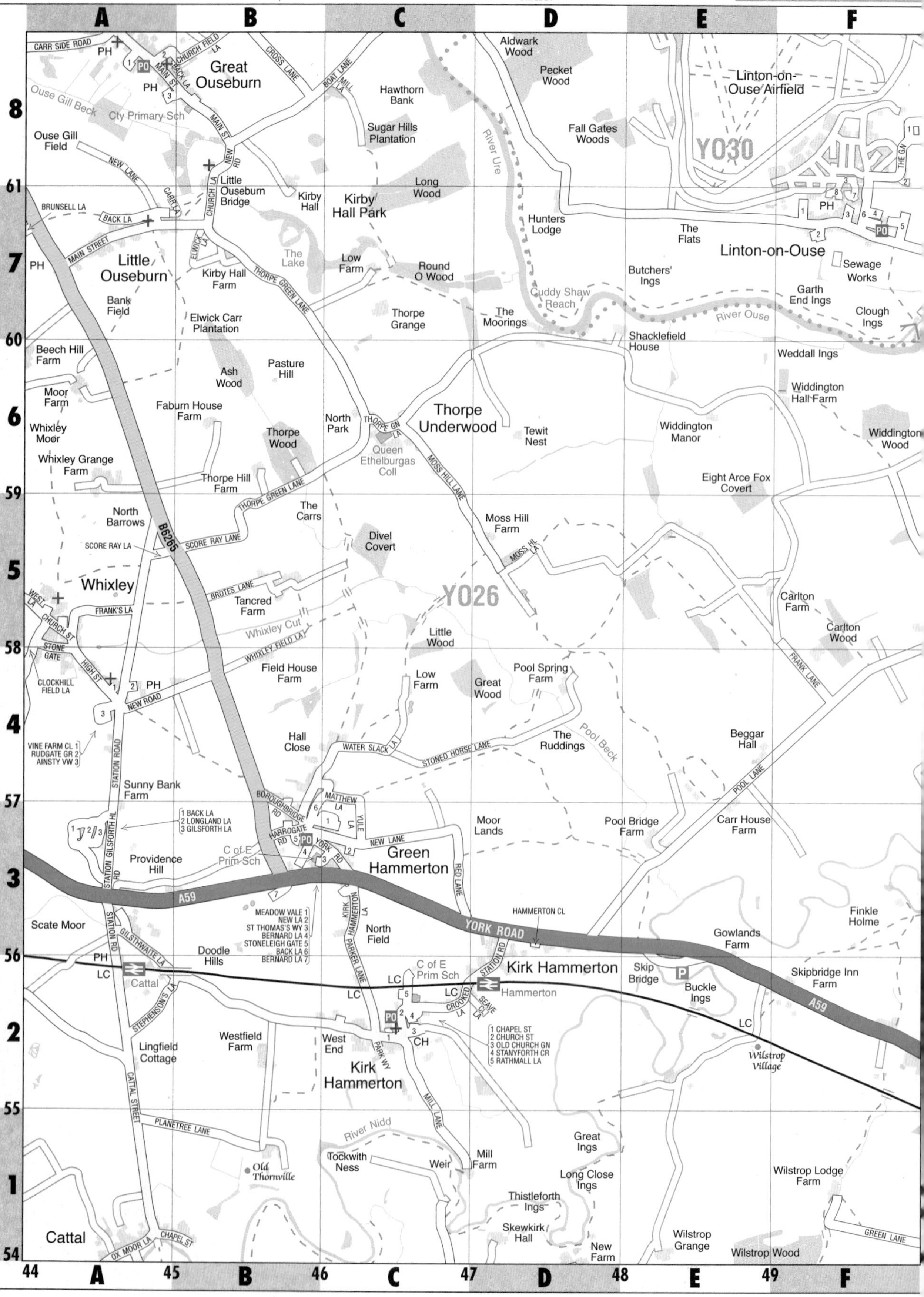

163

181

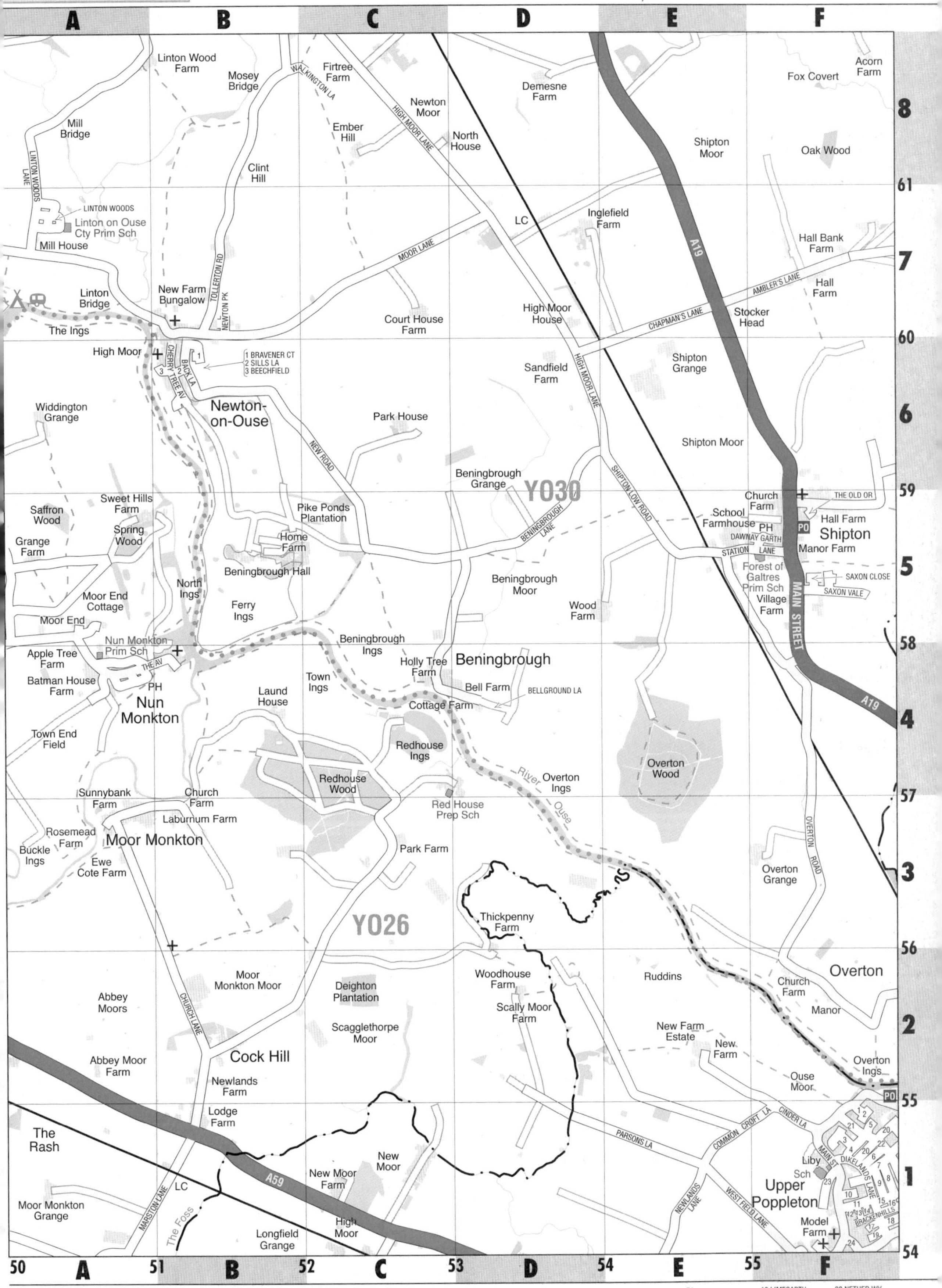

F1
1 RIVERSIDE WALK
2 RIVERSIDE GD
3 BANKSIDE CL
4 SPRINGFIELD RD
5 LITTLEFIELD CL
6 MONTAGUE WALK
7 EBOR WAY
8 PEAR TREE AV
9 ELM TREE AV
10 LIMEGARTH
11 CHANTRY GAP
12 GROVE GD
13 CHANTRY GR
14 CHANTRY AV
15 APPLE GARTH
16 CHERRY GROVE
17 SYCAMORE VIEW
18 FAIRWAY DR
19 DIKELANDS CL
20 NETHER WY
21 RIVERSVALE DR
22 ALLERTON DR
23 SCHOOL LA
24 STATION RD

Scale: 1¾ inches to 1 mile

0   ¼   ½   mile
0   250m   500m   750m   1 km

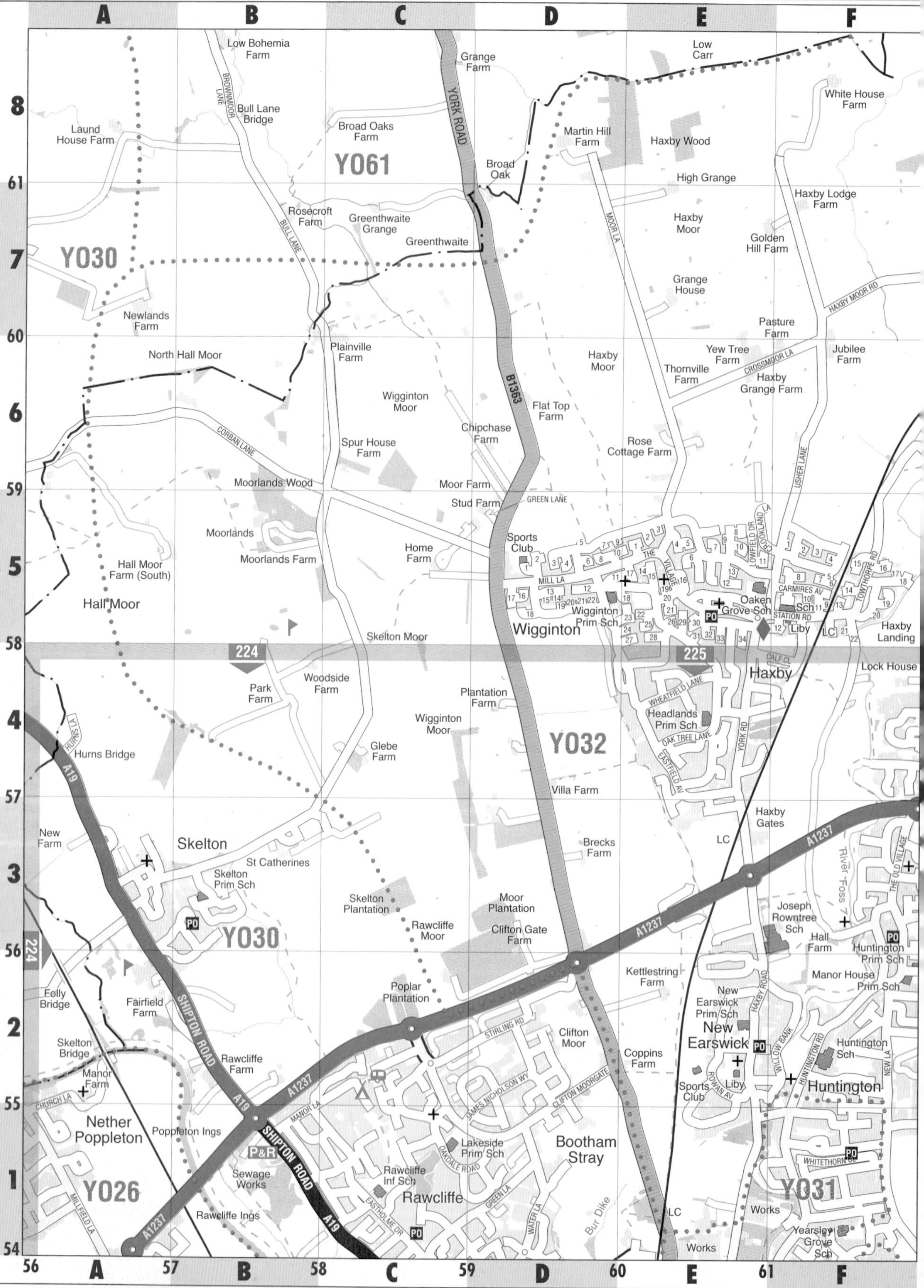

Grid references (left margin): 8, 61, 7, 60, 6, 59, 5, 58, 4, 57, 3, 56, 2, 55, 1, 54

Column letters: A B C D E F

Row numbers (bottom): 56 57 58 59 60 61

YO61, YO30, YO32, YO30, YO26, YO31

Low Bohemia Farm, Brownmoor Lane, Bull Lane Bridge, Broad Oaks Farm, York Road, Grange Farm, Low Carr, White House Farm, Laund House Farm, Martin Hill Farm, Haxby Wood, High Grange, Haxby Lodge Farm, Broad Oak, Rosecroft Farm, Greenthwaite Grange, Greenthwaite, Haxby Moor, Golden Hill Farm, Newlands Farm, North Hall Moor, Plainville Farm, B1363, Grange House, Moor La, Pasture Farm, Usher Lane, Jubilee Farm, Wigginton Moor, Haxby Moor, Yew Tree Farm, Thornton Farm, Haxby Grange Farm, Crossmoor La, Spur House Farm, Chipchase Farm, Flat Top Farm, Moorlands Wood, Moor Farm Cl, Green Lane, Rose Cottage Farm, Moorlands, Stud Farm, Sports Club, Moorlands Farm, Home Farm, Mill La, The Village, Carmires Av, Tonthorpe Rd, Haxby Landing, Hall Moor Farm (South), Wigginton Prim Sch, Oaken Grove Sch, Liby, Hall Moor, Skelton Moor, Wigginton, Haxby, Lock House, Woodside Farm, Plantation Farm, 224, Headlands Prim Sch, 225, Park Farm, Wigginton Moor, Oak Tree Lane, Wheatfield Lane, York Rd, Eastfield La, Glebe Farm, Villa Farm, Brecks Farm, Haxby Gates, New Farm, Skelton, St Catherines, Skelton Prim Sch, Skelton Plantation, Moor Plantation, A1237, River Foss, The Old Village, Joseph Rowntree Sch, Hall Farm, Huntington Prim Sch, YO30, Rawcliffe Moor, Clifton Gate Farm, Kettlestring Farm, Manor House Prim Sch, Folly Bridge, Fairfield Farm, Poplar Plantation, New Earswick Prim Sch, Huntington Sch, Skelton Bridge, Manor Farm, Rawcliffe Farm, Shipton Road, A19, Manor La, James Nicholson Wy, Stirling Rd, Clifton Moor, Coppins Farm, New Earswick, Sports Club, Liby, Huntington, Church La, Nether Poppleton, Poppleton Ings, A1237, Lakeside Prim Sch, Bootham Stray, P&R, Sewage Works, Rawcliffe Inf Sch, Rawcliffe, Water La, Green La, Bur Dike, Works, YO31, Whitethorn, Yearsley Grove Sch, Millfield La, Rawcliffe Ings, Eastholme Dr, Oakdale Road, Works

For full street detail of the highlighted area see pages 224 and 225.

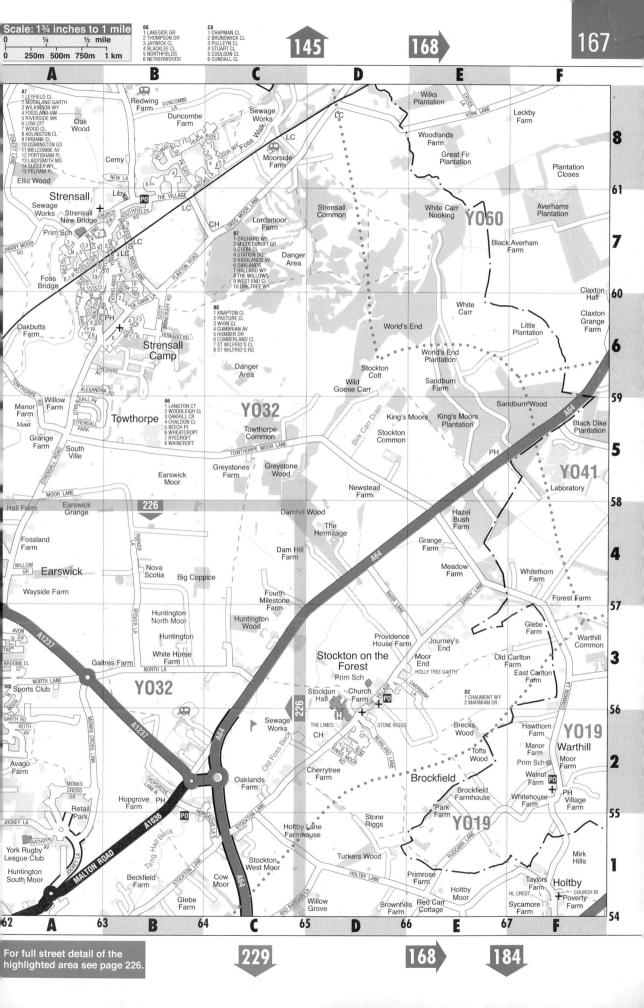

Scale: 1¾ inches to 1 mile

0 ¼ ½ mile
0 250m 500m 750m 1 km

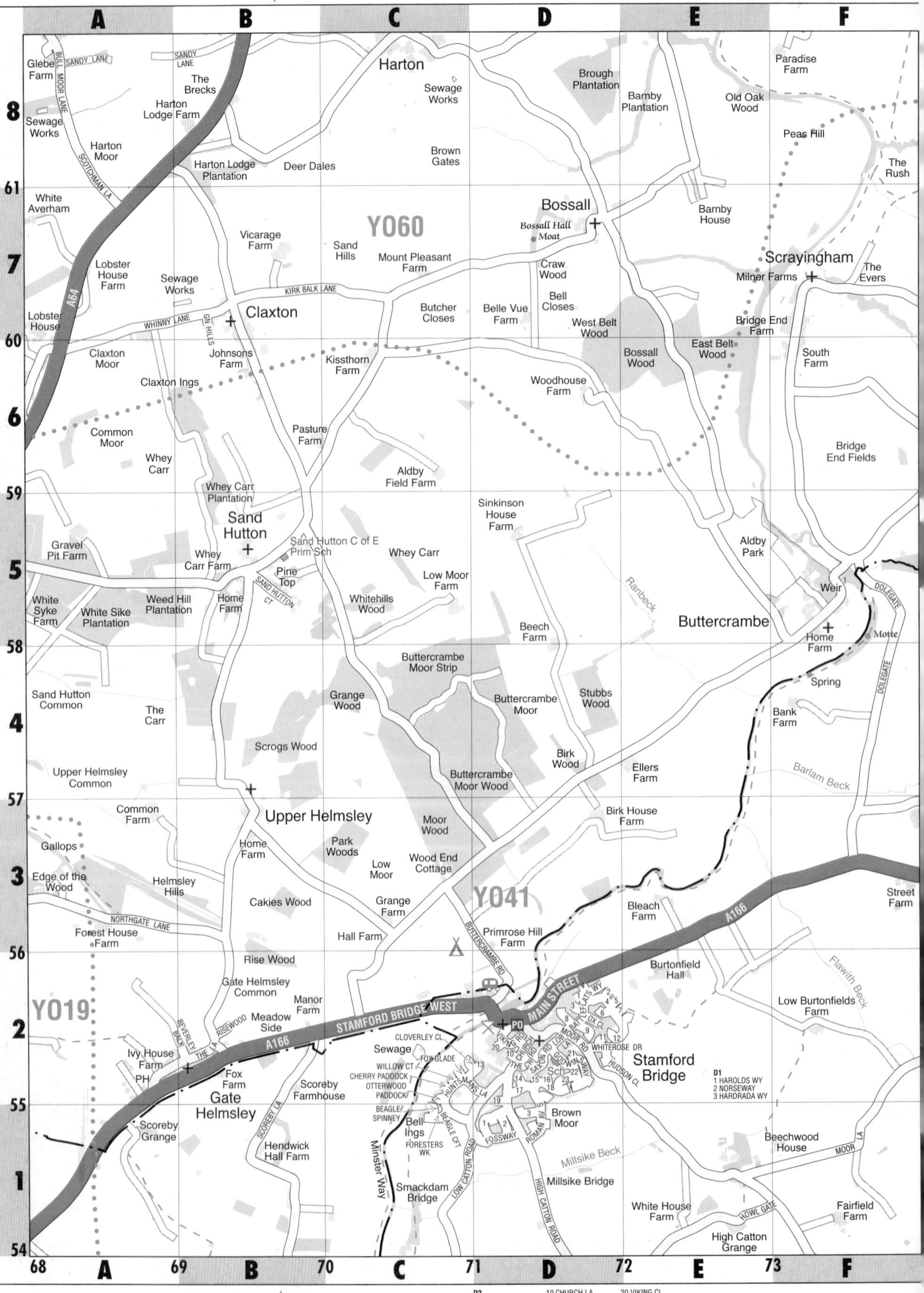

A B C D E F

8

61

7

60

6

59

5

58

4

57

56

3

2

Y019

1

54

Glebe Farm
SANDY LANE
Sewage Works
Harton Moor
BULL MOOR LANE
SCOTCHMAN LA
White Averham
Lobster House Farm
Lobster House
A64
Claxton Moor
Common Moor
Whey Carr
WHINNY LANE
GH HILLS
Gravel Pit Farm
White Syke Farm
White Sike Plantation
Weed Hill Plantation
Sand Hutton Common
The Carr
Upper Helmsley Common
Common Farm
Gallops
Edge of the Wood
Helmsley Hills
NORTHGATE LANE
Forest House Farm
THE LA
BEVERLEY BALK
RISEWOOD
Ivy House Farm
PH
Fox Farm
Gate Helmsley
Scoreby Grange
SCOREBY LA

SANDY LANE
The Brecks
Harton Lodge Farm
Harton Lodge Plantation
Deer Dales
Vicarage Farm
Claxton
Johnsons Farm
Claxton Ings
KIRK BALK LANE
Sewage Works
Pasture Farm
Whey Carr Plantation
Sand Hutton
Sand Hutton C of E Prim Sch
Whey Carr Farm
Pine Top
Home Farm
SAND HUTTON CT
Scrogs Wood
Upper Helmsley
Home Farm
Cakies Wood
Rise Wood
Gate Helmsley Common
Meadow Side
Manor Farm
Scoreby Farmhouse
Hendwick Hall Farm

Harton
Sewage Works
Brown Gates
YO60
Sand Hills
Mount Pleasant Farm
Butcher Closes
Kissthorn Farm
Aldby Field Farm
Whey Carr
Whitehills Wood
Buttercrambe Moor Strip
Grange Wood
Buttercrambe Moor Wood
Moor Wood
Park Woods
Low Moor
Grange Farm
Hall Farm
Manor Farm
Sewage
WILLOW CT
CLOVERLEY CL.
CHERRY PADDOCK
OTTERWOOD PADDOCK
FOX GLADE
BEAGLE SPINNEY
Bell Ings
FORESTERS WK
Smackdam Bridge
Minster Way
STAMFORD BRIDGE WEST
A166

Brough Plantation
Barnby Plantation
Bossall
Bossall Hall Moat
Craw Wood
Belle Vue Farm
Bell Closes
West Belt Wood
Bossall Wood
Woodhouse Farm
Sinkinson House Farm
Ranbeck
Beech Farm
Buttercrambe Moor
Stubbs Wood
Birk Wood
Ellers Farm
Birk House Farm
Wood End Cottage
YO41
BUTTERCRAMBE RD
Primrose Hill Farm
Bleach Farm
MAIN STREET
LOW CATTON ROAD
HUNTSMANS LA
ROMAN AV
FOSSWAY
BEAGLE CT
Brown Moor
Millsike Beck
Millsike Bridge
HUDSON CL
PO
Stamford Bridge
WHITEROSE DR
Burtonfield Hall
Low Burtonfields Farm
HOWL GATE
White House Farm
High Catton Grange

Old Oak Wood
Paradise Farm
Peas Hill
The Rush
Scrayingham
Milner Farms
The Evers
Bridge End Farm
South Farm
Bridge End Fields
Aldby Park
Weir
DOLEGATE
Buttercrambe
Home Farm
Motte
Spring
Bank Farm
Barlam Beck
A166
Street Farm
Flawith Beck
Beechwood House
MOOR LA
Fairfield Farm

D1
1 HAROLDS WY
2 NORSEWAY
3 HARDRADA WY

YO19

68 A 69 B 70 C 71 D 72 E 73 F

D2
1 BRIDLINGTON RD
2 DERWENT CL
3 DANESWELL CL
4 BURTON FIELDS RD
5 GARROWBY VW
6 KINGSWAY
7 DARLEY CL
8 WHARTON RD
9 ST JOHN'S RD
10 CHURCH LA
11 EGREMONT CL
12 BURTON FIELDS CL
13 HEATHER BANK
14 TOSTIG CL
15 FAIRFAX
16 SCHOOL CL
17 ROMAN AV N
18 GODWINSWAY
19 BUTTS CL
20 VIKING CL
21 MIDGLEY CL
22 BROWN MOOR
23 FURLONG RD

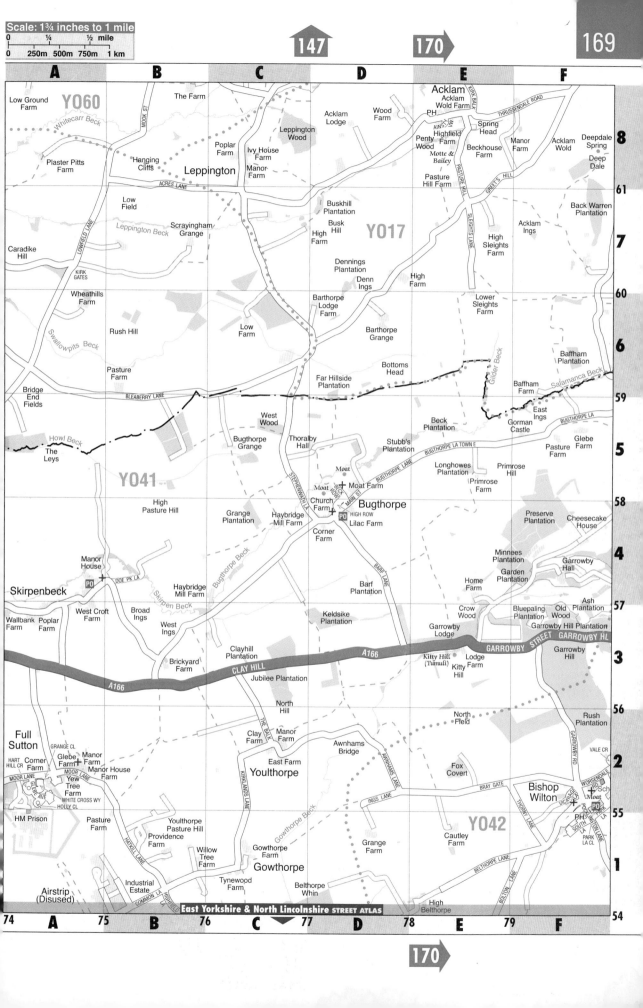

170

169

148

Scale: 1¾ inches to 1 mile

0   ¼   ½   mile
0   250m 500m 750m 1 km

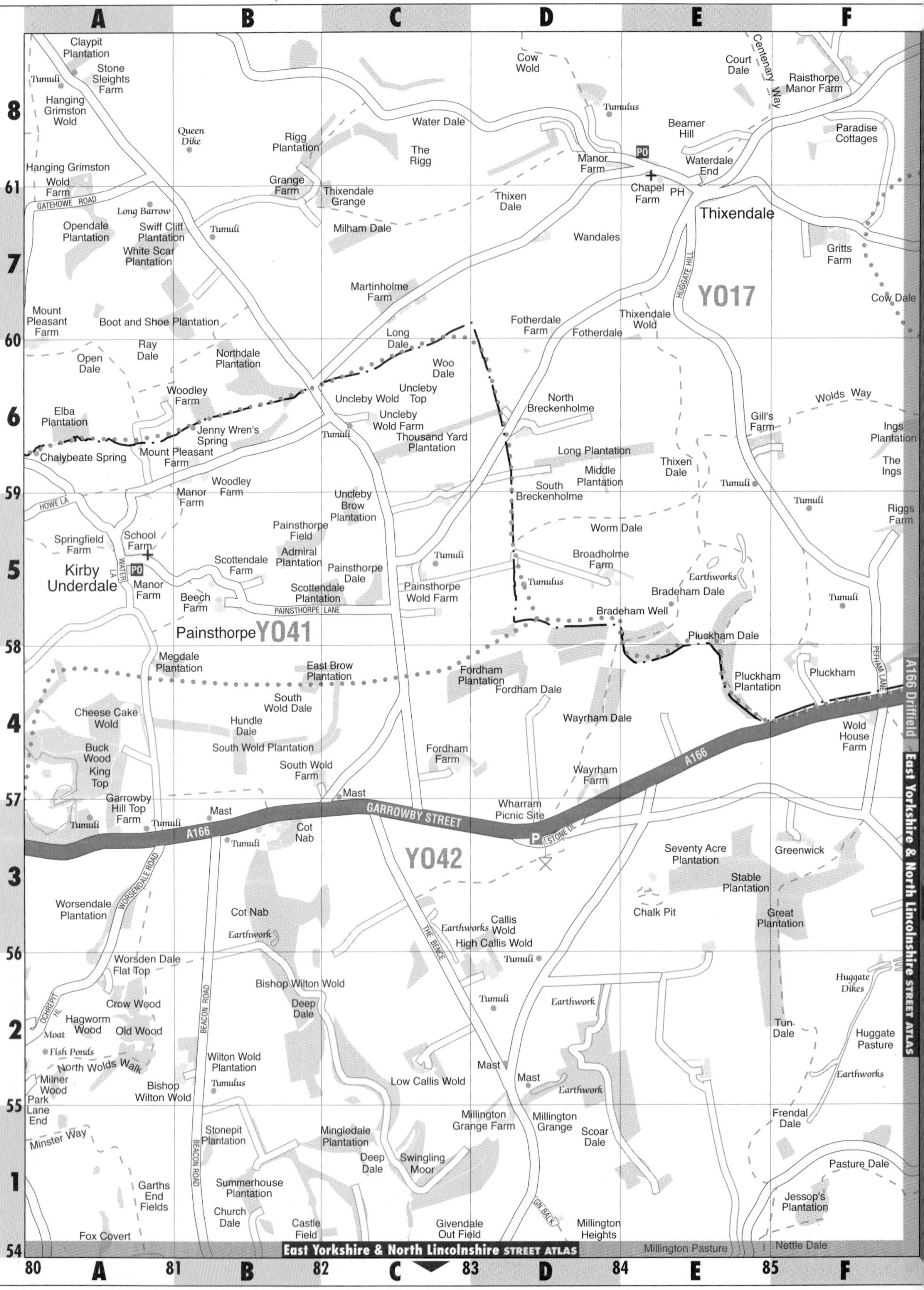

A   B   C   D   E   F

8

Claypit Plantation

Tumuli

Stone Sleights Farm

Hanging Grimston Wold

Queen Dike

Rigg Plantation

Cow Wold

Water Dale

The Rigg

Court Dale

Cenetary Way

Raisthorpe Manor Farm

Tumulus

Beamer Hill

Paradise Cottages

61

Hanging Grimston Wold Farm

GATEHOWE ROAD

Long Barrow

Grange Farm

Thixendale Grange

Milham Dale

Manor Farm

Thixen Dale

Chapel Farm

PH

Waterdale End

PO

Thixendale

7

Opendale Plantation

Swiff Cliff Plantation

White Scar Plantation

Tumuli

Martinholme Farm

Wandales

Gritts Farm

Boot and Shoe Plantation

Long Dale

Woo Dale

Fotherdale Farm

Fotherdale

Thixendale Wold

Y017

Wolds Way

Cow Dale

Mount Pleasant Farm

Open Dale

Ray Dale

Northdale Plantation

Uncleby Top

Gill's Farm

Ings Plantation

60

Elba Plantation

Woodley Farm

Jenny Wren's Spring

Uncleby Wold

Uncleby Wold Farm

Thousand Yard Plantation

North Breckenholme

Long Plantation

Thixen Dale

Tumuli

The Ings

6

Chalybeate Spring

Mount Pleasant Farm

Tumuli

Middle Plantation

Tumuli

HOWE LA

Woodley Farm

South Breckenholme

Riggs Farm

59

Manor Farm

Springfield Farm

School Farm

Uncleby Brow Plantation

Worm Dale

PO

WATER LA

Painsthorpe Field

Tumuli

Broadholme Farm

Earthworks

Tumuli

5

Kirby Underdale

Manor Farm

Scottendale Farm

Admiral Plantation

Painsthorpe Dale

Painsthorpe Wold Farm

Tumulus

Bradeham Dale

Beech Farm

Scottendale Plantation

Bradeham Well

Pluckham Dale

Painsthorpe **Y041**

PAINSTHORPE LANE

Pluckham Plantation

Pluckham

58

Megdale Plantation

East Brow Plantation

Fordham Plantation

Fordham Dale

Wayrham Dale

PERFAM LANE

A166 Driffield

Cheese Cake Wold

South Wold Dale

Hundle Dale

Fordham Farm

Wayrham Farm

A166

Wold House Farm

4

Buck Wood King Top

South Wold Plantation

South Wold Farm

Mast

Wharram Picnic Site

Garrowby Hill Top Farm

Tumuli

Mast

GARROWBY STREET

STONE DL

Seventy Acre Plantation

Greenwick

57

Tumuli

A166

Cot Nab

P

Y042

Stable Plantation

Great Plantation

3

Worsendale Plantation

Cot Nab

Earthwork

THE BECK

Earthworks

Callis Wold

High Callis Wold

Chalk Pit

Huggate Dikes

56

Worsden Dale Flat Top

Crow Wood

Bishop Wilton Wold

Deep Dale

Tumuli

Earthwork

Tun Dale

Huggate Pasture

2

Hagworm Wood

Old Wood

OCHREPIT HL

Moat

Fish Ponds

North Wolds Walk

Wilton Wold Plantation

Tumulus

Low Callis Wold

Mast

Mast

Earthwork

Earthworks

Milner Wood

BEACON ROAD

Bishop Wilton Wold

Frendal Dale

55

Park Lane End

Stonepit Plantation

Mingledale Plantation

Millington Grange Farm

Millington Grange

Scoar Dale

Pasture Dale

Minster Way

Deep Dale

Swingling Moor

Jessop's Plantation

1

Garths End Fields

Summerhouse Plantation

Church Dale

Castle Field

Givendale Out Field

GN BECK

Millington Heights

Fox Covert

54

East Yorkshire & North Lincolnshire STREET ATLAS

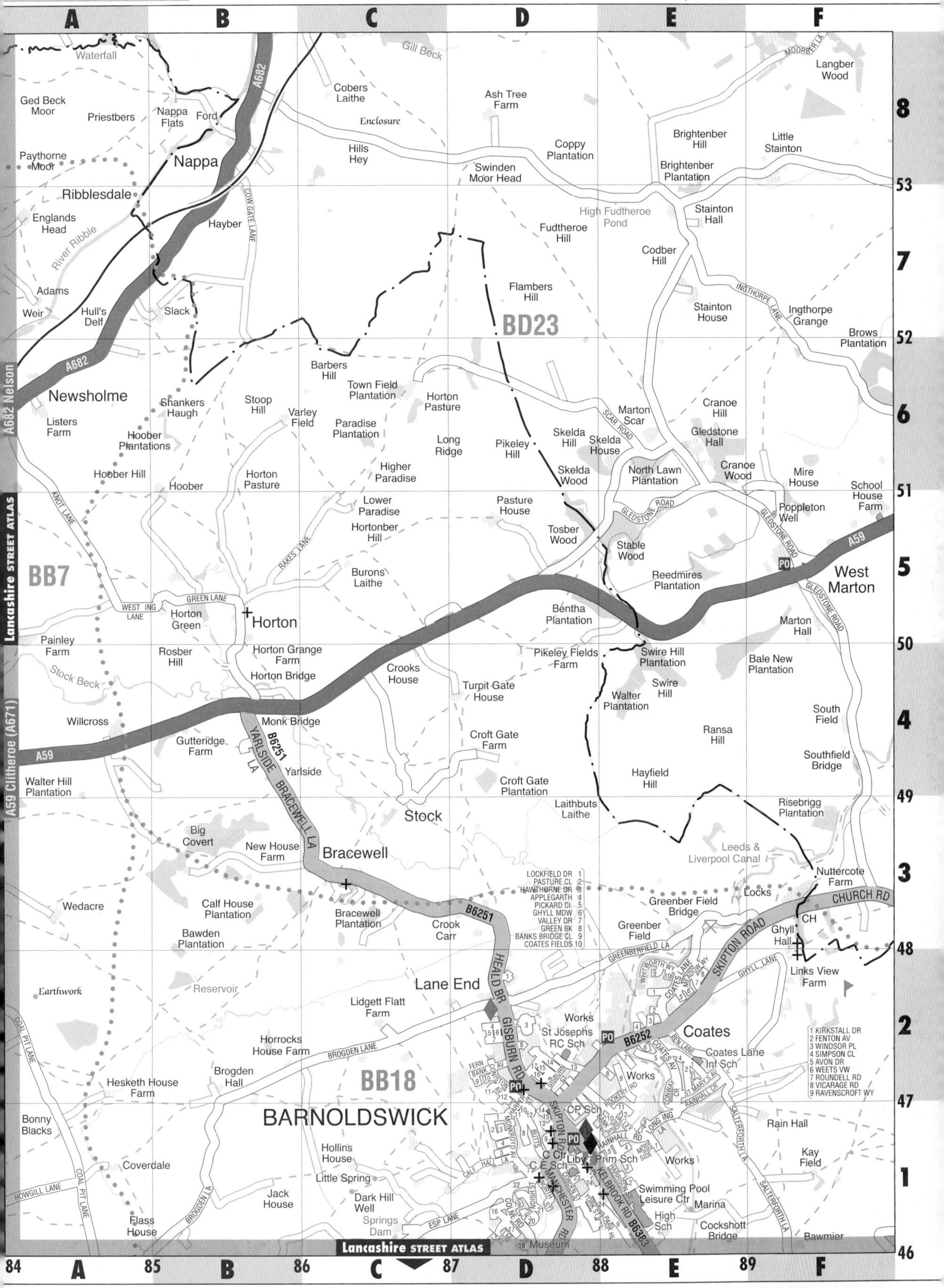

D1
1 RYLSTONE DR
2 GARNBROOK RD
3 GORDALE CL
4 INGLEBOROUGH DR
5 PEN-Y-GHENT WY
6 MILL ST
7 PARROCK ST
8 TAYLOR ST
9 COMMERCIAL ST
10 HOLLINS RD
11 PENNINE WY
12 FEDERATION ST
13 ASH GR
14 DAM HEAD RD
15 LEONARD ST
16 SYCAMORE WY
17 CHESTNUT DR
18 BANCROFT FOLD
19 SMITH ST
20 SACKVILLE ST
21 LONGFIELD CT
22 WESTGATE
23 BEECH ST
24 FRANK ST
25 ROOK ST

D2
1 BANKS HL
2 WEST FIELD RD
3 BLAKELEY CR
4 FOSTER RD
5 LEONARD ST
6 ARTHUR ST
7 CARR RD
8 GLEDSTONE VW
9 GREAT CROFT CL
10 AMBLESIDE AV
11 MILTON GROVE
12 RICHMOND RD
13 WEST CLO RD
14 COLIN ST
15 BRACEWELL ST
16 BOLLAND ST
17 EDMONDSON ST

E1
1 VICTORIA RD
2 CLARENCE ST
3 CLIFFORD ST
4 RIDING CL
5 WELLHOUSE ST
6 HILL ST
7 CLAYTON ST
8 CORONATION ST
9 FRANK ST
10 STUART ST
11 HAVRE PK
12 ETHEL ST

172

For full street detail of Barnoldswick see Philip's STREET ATLAS of Lancashire

Scale: 1¾ inches to 1 mile
0 ¼ ½ mile
0 250m 500m 750m 1 km

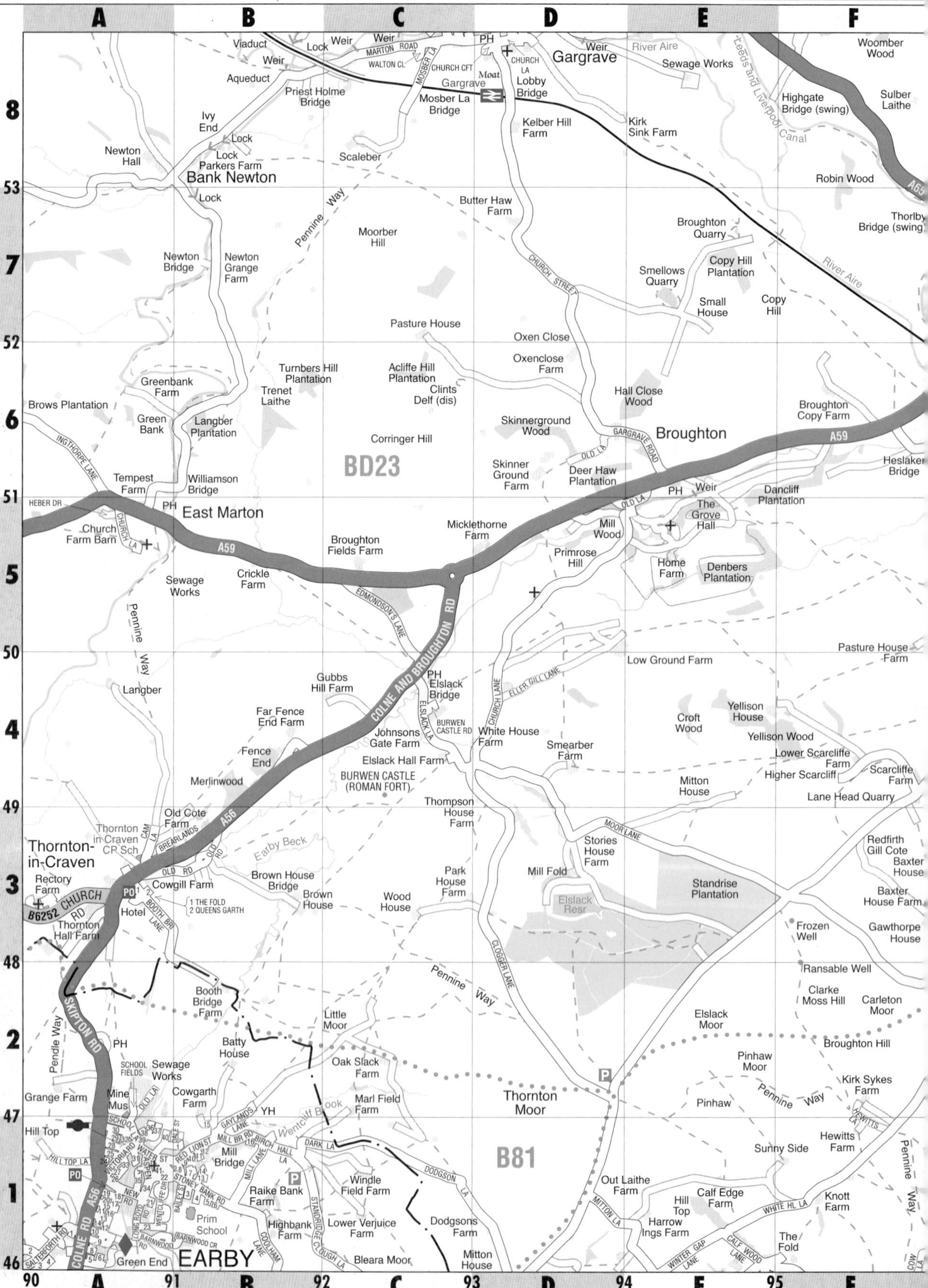

A B C D E F

8
53
7
52
6
51
5
50
4
49
3
48
2
47
1
46

90 A 91 B 92 C 93 D 94 E 95 F

Woomber Wood
Viaduct Lock Weir Weir PH Weir Gargrave
MARTON ROAD WALTON CL CHURCH CFT CHURCH LA Sewage Works
Aqueduct MOSBER LA Gargrave Moat Lobby Highgate Sulber Laithe
Priest Holme Bridge Mosber La Bridge Bridge Bridge (swing)
Ivy End Lock Kelber Hill Farm Kirk Sink Farm Thorlby Bridge (swing)
Newton Hall Lock Parkers Farm Scaleber Robin Wood
Bank Newton Lock
Butter Haw Farm
Pennine Way Moorber Hill Broughton Quarry Copy Hill Plantation
Newton Bridge Newton Grange Farm Smellows Quarry Small House Copy Hill
Pasture House Church Street Oxen Close Hall Close Wood Broughton Copy Farm
Greenbank Farm Turnbers Hill Plantation Acliffe Hill Plantation Oxenclose Farm
Brows Plantation Trenet Laithe Clints Delf (dis) Skinnerground Wood Broughton Heslaker Bridge
Green Bank Langber Plantation Corringer Hill Skinner Ground Farm Deer Haw Plantation Old La Gargrave Road A59
BD23 Williamson Bridge Micklethorne Farm Danclif Plantation The Grove Hall Denbers Plantation
Tempest Farm PH East Marton Weir
HEBER DR CHURCH LA A59 Broughton Fields Farm Mill Wood PH Home Farm
Church Farm Barn Crickle Farm Primrose Hill
Sewage Works EDMONDSON'S LANE COLNE AND BROUGHTON RD Low Ground Farm Pasture House Farm
Pennine Way Gubbs Hill Farm PH Elslack Bridge Church Lane Eller Gill Lane
Langber Far Fence End Farm BURWEN CASTLE RD White House Farm Croft Wood Yellison House
Fence End Johnsons Gate Farm Smearber Farm Yellison Wood Lower Scarcliffe Farm
Merlinwood Elslack Hall Farm BURWEN CASTLE (ROMAN FORT) Mitton House Higher Scarcliff Scarcliffe Farm
Thompson House Farm MOOR LANE Lane Head Quarry
Thornton in Craven CR Sch Old Cote Farm A56 CLOGGER LANE Stories House Farm Redfirth Gill Cote Baxter House
Thornton-in-Craven CAM LA BREARLANDS OLD RD Earby Beck Mill Fold Standrise Plantation Baxter House Farm
Rectory Farm PO Cowgill Farm Brown House Bridge Park House Farm Elslack Resr Gawthorpe House
B6252 CHURCH RD Hotel 1 THE FOLD Brown House Wood House Frozen Well
Thornton Hall Farm BOOTH BR LANE 2 QUEENS GARTH Ransable Well
Clarke Moss Hill Carleton Moor
Booth Bridge Farm Pennine Way Elslack Moor Broughton Hill
SKIPTON RD Little Moor Pinhaw Moor
Pendle Way PH Batty House Oak Slack Farm P Kirk Sykes Farm
SCHOOL FIELDS Sewage Works Marl Field Farm Thornton Moor Pinhaw Pennine Way
Grange Farm Mine Mus Cowgarth Farm YH Sunny Side Hewitts Farm
Hill Top SCHOOL GAYLANDS LANE Wentclif Brook DARK LA B81 Calf Edge Farm Knott Farm
PO Mill Bridge Windle Field Farm DODGSON LA Out Laithe Farm Hill Top The Fold
HILL TOP LA Raike Bank Farm STANDRIDGE CLOUGH LA Dodgsons Farm Harrow Ings Farm
COLNE RD A56 Prim School Highbank Farm Lower Verjuice Farm MITTON LA WINTER GAP LANE CALF WOOD LA WHITE HL LA Pennine Way
EARBY Green End Bleara Moor Mitton House

A1
1 BEECH AVE
2 WARWICK DR
3 KENILWORTH DR
4 TYSELEY GR
5 GREEN WLK
6 DALE VW
7 BROOKFIELD WY
8 JAGOE RD
9 LINDEN RD
10 ROSTLE TOP RD
11 JOHN ST
12 HARTLEY ST
13 BARRET ST
14 CROSS ST
15 APPLEGARTH ST
16 WILLIAM ST
17 COWGILL ST
18 BROOK ST
19 GEORGE ST
20 JAMES ST
21 RUSHTON AVE
22 CHAPEL ST
23 BAWHEAD RD
24 VICTORIA ST
25 ALBION RD
26 BOOT ST
27 EDWARD ST
28 ALBION ST
29 HIGHFIELD RD
30 LINCOLN RD
31 GOODALL CL
32 VALLEY RD
33 ALBERT ST
34 GREEN END RD
35 GREEN END AVE
36 SHUTTLEWORTH ST
37 WADDINGTON ST
38 GROVE ST
39 LOWER CROFT ST
40 CEMETERY RD
41 RILEY ST

B1
1 ALDER HILL ST
2 WELBURY CL
3 SPRINGMOUNT
4 SPRINGFIELD AVE
5 PLEASANT VW
6 MOORLAND AVE
7 LONG GREEN
8 STOOPES HL
9 SELBOURNE
10 EARLHAM ST
11 DUXBURY ST
12 CROFT ST
13 REEVAL CL
14 BROWNROYD
15 COWGARTH ST
16 HEATHER BROW

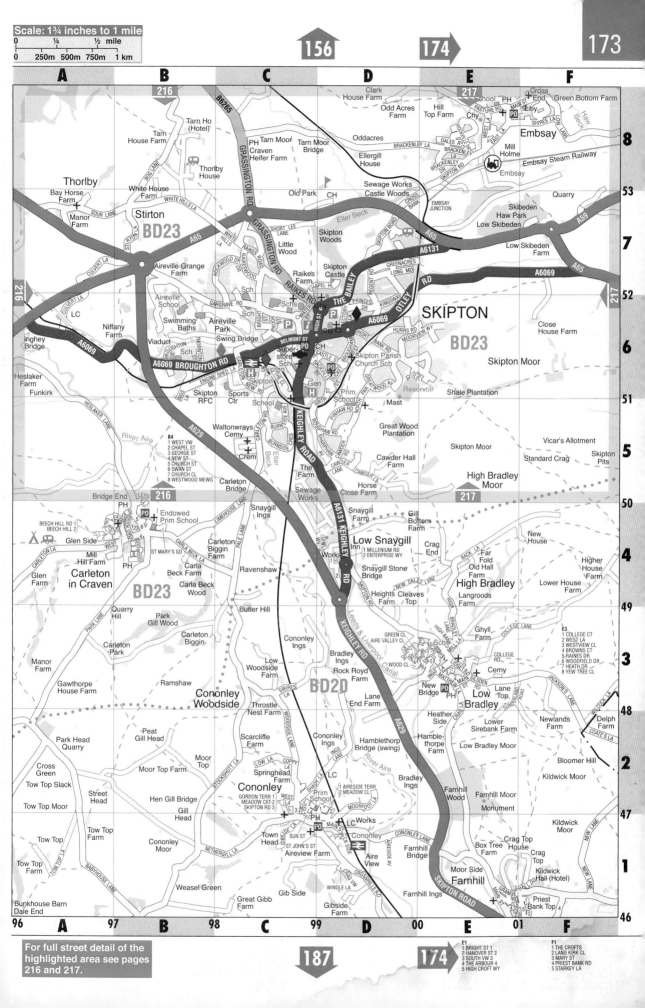

Scale: 1¾ inches to 1 mile
0   ¼   ½   mile
0   250m   500m   750m   1 km

For full street detail of the
highlighted area see pages
216 and 217.

Clark House Farm
Odd Acres Farm
Hill Top Farm
Oddacres
Ellergill House
Tarn Moor
Tarn Moor Bridge
Craven Heifer Farm
Tarn Ho (Hotel)
Tarn House Farm
White House Farm
Thorlby House
Thorlby
Bay Horse Farm
Manor Farm
Stirton
BD23
Sour Lane
White Hills La
Aireville Grange Farm
Aireville School
Niffany Farm
Heslaker Farm
Funkirk
Inghey Bridge
Swimming Baths
Aireville Park
Viaduct
Skipton RFC
Sports Ctr
Waltonwrays Cemy
Crem
Carleton Bridge
River Aire

Cross End
Green Bottom Farm
Liby
Embsay
Mill Holme
Embsay Steam Railway
Quarry
Skibeden Haw Park
Low Skibeden
Low Skibeden Farm
Castle Woods
Sewage Works
Embsay Junction
Skipton Woods
Skipton Castle
Little Wood
Raikes Road

SKIPTON
BD23
Close House Farm
Skipton Moor
Shale Plantation
Great Wood Plantation
Skipton Moor
Vicar's Allotment
Standard Crag
Skipton Pits
Reservoir
Mast
Cawder Hall Farm
High Bradley Moor
Prim School
Skipton Parish Church Sch

B4
1 WEST VW
2 CHAPEL ST
3 GEORGE ST
4 NEW ST
5 CHURCH ST
6 SWAN ST
7 CHURCH CL
8 WESTWOOD MEWS

Bridge End
BEECH HILL RD 1
BEECH HILL 2
Glen Side
Glen Farm
Mill Hill Farm
Endowed Prim School
Carleton in Craven
BD23
Manor Farm
Gawthorpe House Farm
Park Head Quarry
Carleton Park
Carleton Biggin
Park Gill Wood
Quarry Hill
Ramshaw
Cononley Woodside
Peat Gill Head
Carla Beck Farm
Carleton Biggin Farm
Ravenshaw
Butler Hill
Carla Beck Wood
Low Woodside Farm
Snaygill Ings
Snaygill Ings
Gill Bottom Farm
Low Snaygill
1 MILLENIUM RD
2 ENTERPRISE WY
Snaygill Stone Bridge
Crag End
New House
Far Fold Old Hall Farm
Back La
Higher House Farm
Lower House Farm
High Bradley
Langroods Farm
Ghyll Farm
College Lane

E3
1 COLLEGE CT
2 WEST LA
3 WESTVIEW CL
4 BROWNS CT
5 RAINES DR
6 WOODFIELD DR
7 HEATH DR
8 YEW TREE CL

Heights Cleaves Farm Top
New Dales Lane
Green Cl
Aire Valley Cl
Wood Cl
Bradley Ings
Rock Royd Farm
Cononley Ings
Lane End Farm
Cononley Woodside
Throstle Nest Farm
Cemy
New Bridge
Low Bradley
College Rd
Jackson's La
Heather Side
Lower Sirebank Farm
Low Bradley Moor
Newlands Farm
Delph Farm
Scarcliffe Farm
Moor Top Farm
Moor Top
Springhead Farm
Cononley Ings
Hamblethorpe Bridge (swing)
Hamble-thorpe Farm
Bloomer Hill
Kildwick Moor
Cononley Moor
Hen Gill Bridge
Gill Head
Cross Green
Tow Top Slack
Tow Top Moor
Street Head
Tow Top Farm
Tow Top
Tow Top Farm
Bunkhouse Barn
Dale End
Weasel Green
Great Gibb Farm
Gib Side
Gibside Farm
Windle La
Cononley
GORDON TERR 1
MEADOW CFT 2
SKIPTON RD 3
Prim School
Town Head
St John's St
Aireview Farm
Aire View
1 AIRESIDE TERR
2 MEADOW CL
Bradley Ings
Farnhill Wood
Farnhill
Moor Side
Farnhill Moor Monument
Farnhill Bridge
Farnhill Ings
Box Tree Farm
Crag Top House
Crag Top
Kildwick Moor
Kildwick Hall (Hotel)
Priest Bank Top
SKIPTON ROAD

E1
1 BRIGHT ST 1
2 HANOVER ST 2
3 SOUTH VW 3
4 THE ARBOUR 4
5 HIGH CROFT WY

F1
1 THE CROFTS
2 LANG KIRK CL
3 MARY ST
4 PRIEST BANK RD
5 STARKEY LA

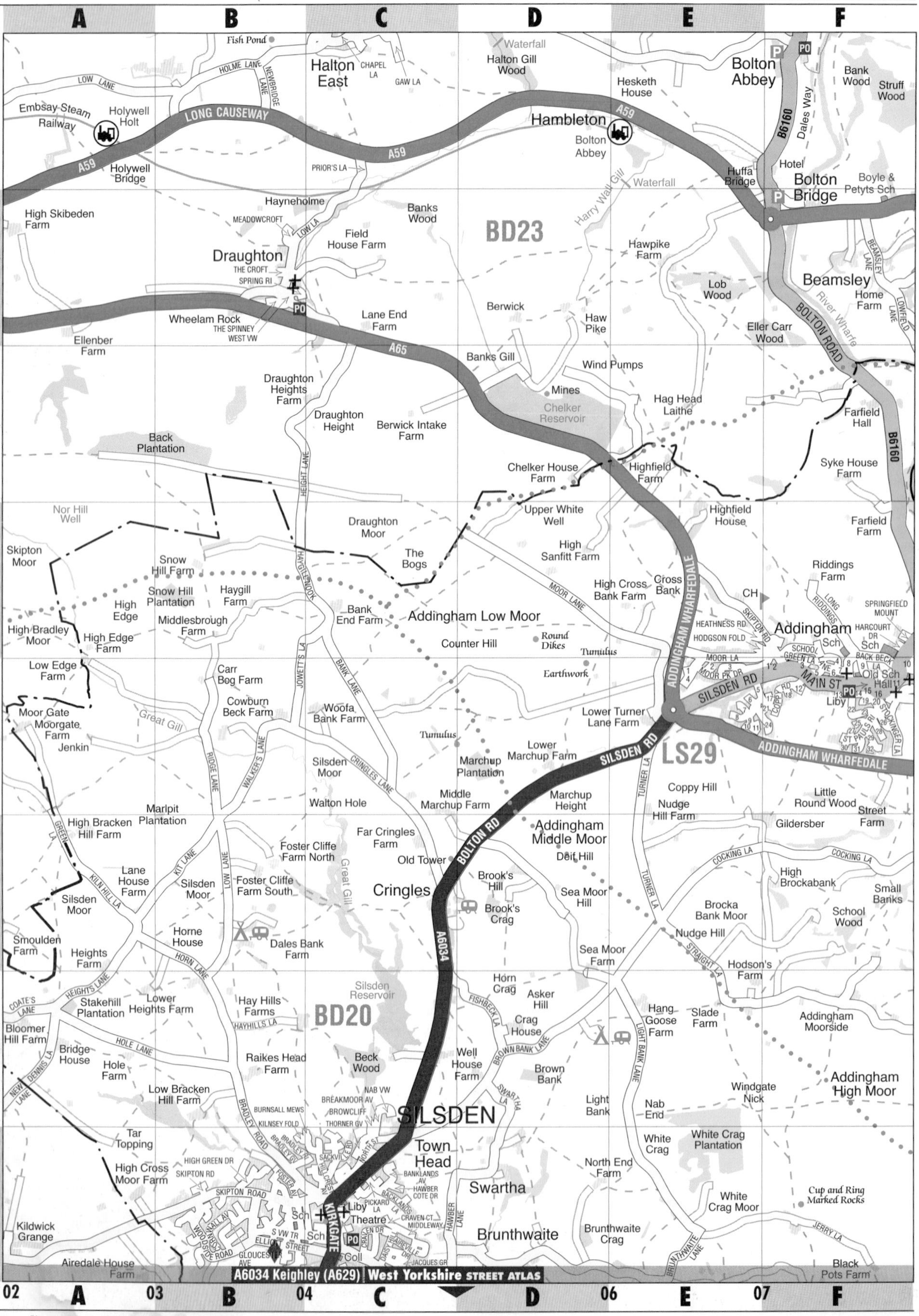

173
157

E4
1 PARSON'S LA
2 MOOR PK CL
3 MOOR PK CR
4 TURNER LA
5 BIG MD DR
6 GILL CL
7 STAMP HL CL
8 THE STREET
9 BROADFIELD WY
10 LIME CL
11 HAWTHORN CL

Scale: 1¾ inches to 1 mile
0   ¼   ½   mile
0   250m   500m   750m   1 km

For full street detail of Silsden see
Philip's STREET ATLAS of West Yorkshire

Scale: 1¾ inches to 1 mile
0 ¼ ½ mile
0 250m 500m 750m 1 km

158
176

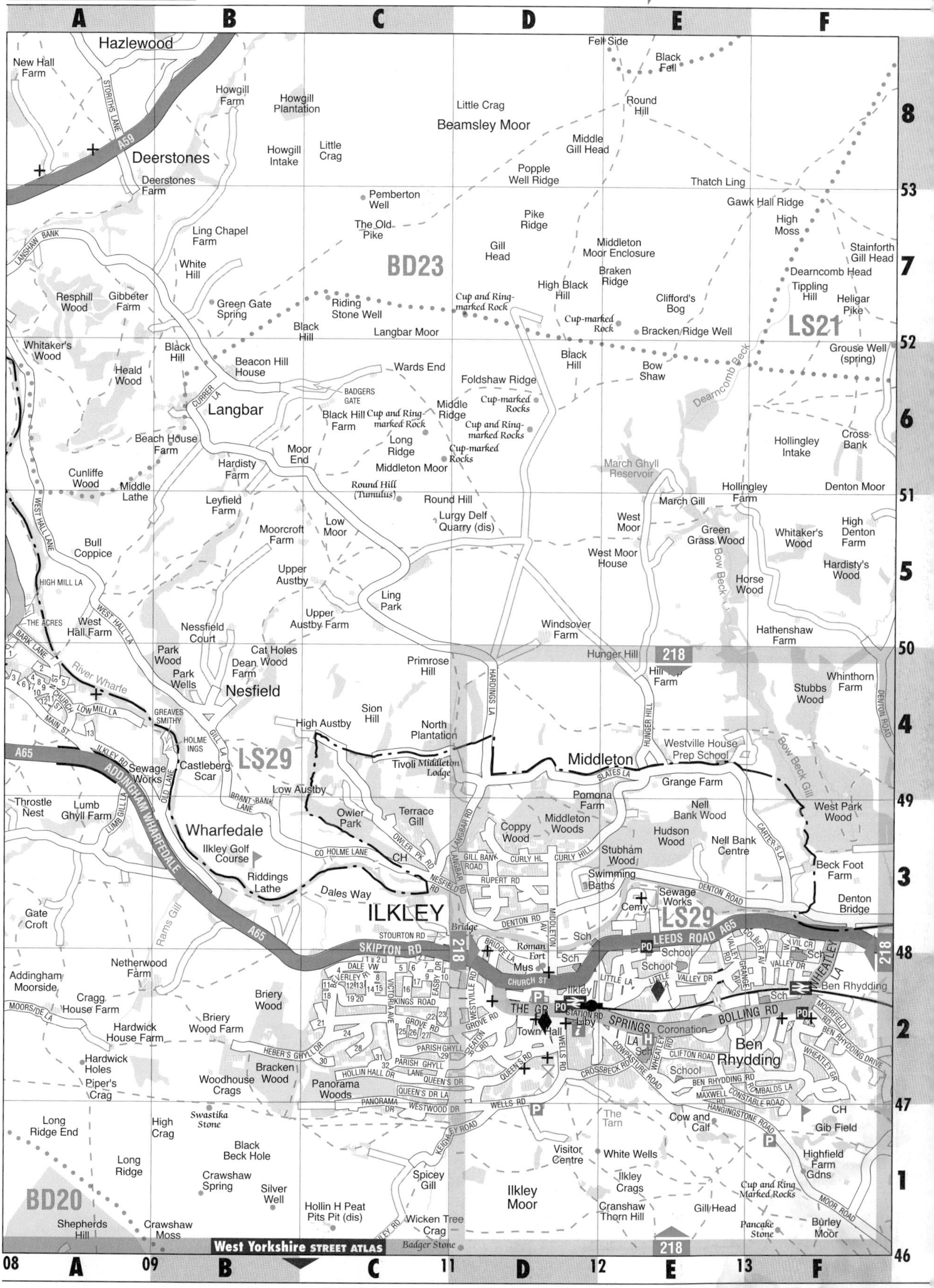

For full street detail of the highlighted area see page 218.

A4
1 AYNHOLME DR
2 WHARFE PK
3 CROSS END FOLD
4 NURSERY LA
5 BEACON ST
6 CROSS CR
7 LILAC CL
8 ORCHARD LA
9 SAWYERS GARTH
10 CROFT HO FOLD
11 SYCAMORE DR
12 ABBEY CL
13 HALLCROFT DR

C2
1 ASH CL
2 CHERRY GR
3 APPLE TREE GD
4 BEACON RI
5 VICTORIA GR
6 THE BRAMBLES
7 EASBY CL
8 WOODLANDS GR
9 VICTORIA DR
10 VICTORIA RD
11 CURLEW CL
12 NESFIELD VW
13 BEAMSLEY VW
14 WOODLANDS RI
15 WOODLANDS CL
16 BEECHWOOD GR
17 VICTORIA GD
18 BRIERY CL
19 KINGS CL
20 DALE CFT
21 HEBER'S GR
22 THE LUTYENS
23 WARLBECK
24 HEBER'S GHYLL DR
25 GROVE AV
26 SHANNON CL
27 HEATH PK
28 GHYLL WOOD
29 PINES GD
30 PREMIERE PK
31 HOLLINGWOOD GATE
32 HOLLINGWOOD RI

176

175
159

Scale: 1¾ inches to 1 mile
0 ¼ ½ mile
0 250m 500m 750m 1 km

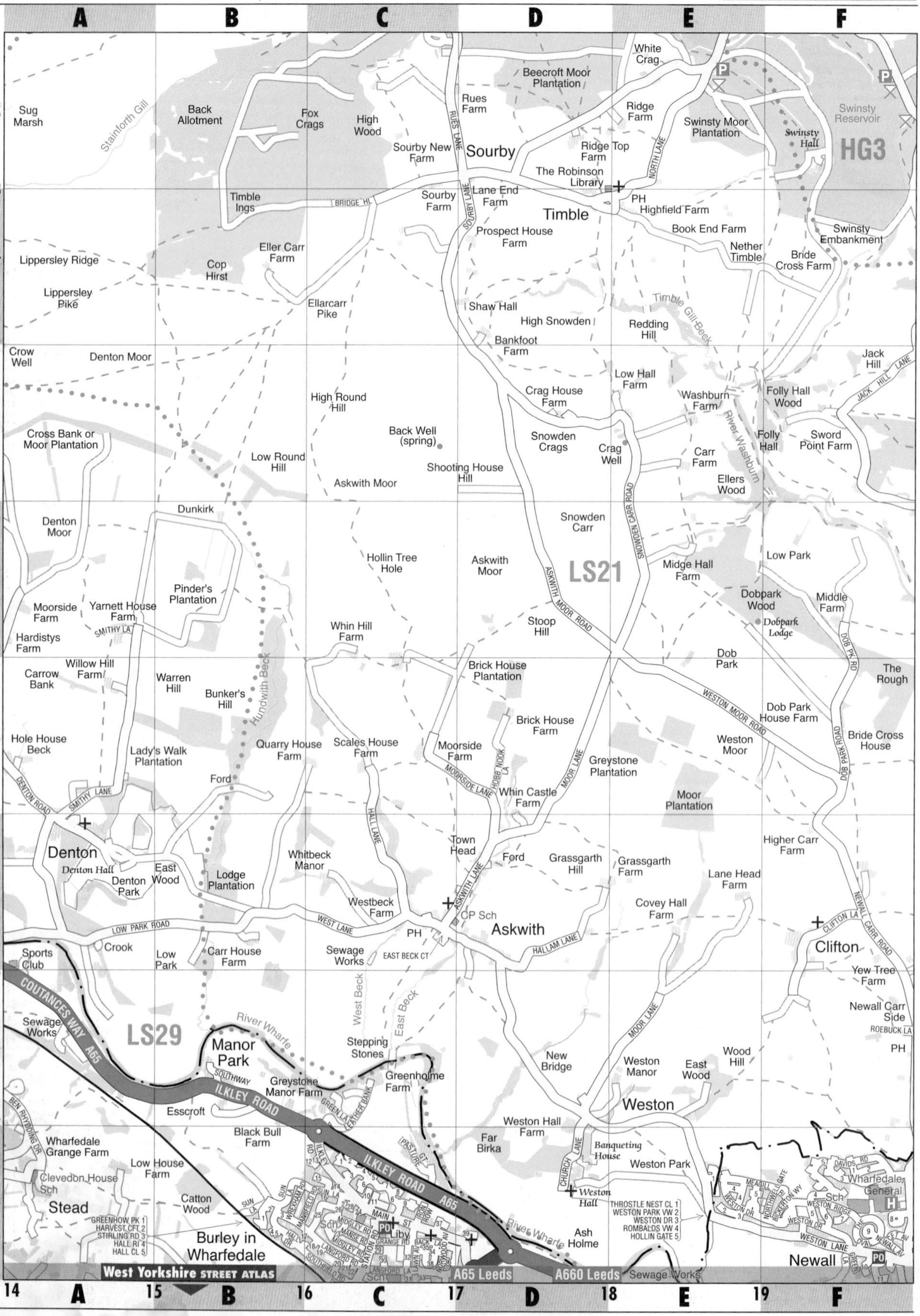

West Yorkshire STREET ATLAS
218

C1
1 TANFIELD DR
2 GREYSTONE CL
3 FAR MEAD CRF
4 PASTURE FOLD
5 MILL VW
6 LONG MDWS
7 GREENHOLME CL
8 OLD MILL CL
9 WILLOW TREE GD
10 NORTH PAR
11 PEEL PL
12 WOODPECKER RD
13 WELLFIELD LA
14 THORNTON ST
15 MARIA ST
16 MELROSE DR
17 LANGFORD CT
18 MIDGE HALL CL
19 LANGFORD MS
20 WILLOW CL
21 LANGFORD CL
22 ASH TREE WK
23 MANSE CR
24 HILL TOP
25 WEST VIEW AV
26 WEST VIEW RD
27 BOOTH ST
28 VICTORIA RD
29 BECKSIDE CL
30 LANGFORD RIDE
31 FOSTER CL
32 GRANGEFIELD AV
33 ST PHILIP'S WY
34 CROWN ST
35 LAWN RD
36 NORWOOD CL
37 YORK RD
38 FENTON ST
39 CORN MILL LA

F1
1 KELL BECK
2 ST MARTINS AV
3 ST RICHARDS RD
4 RUMPLE CFT
5 RIDDING GATE
6 WILKINSON WY
7 WESTON CR
8 CROFT HOUSE DR
9 THE GREEN
10 BELMONT AV
11 GRANGE VW

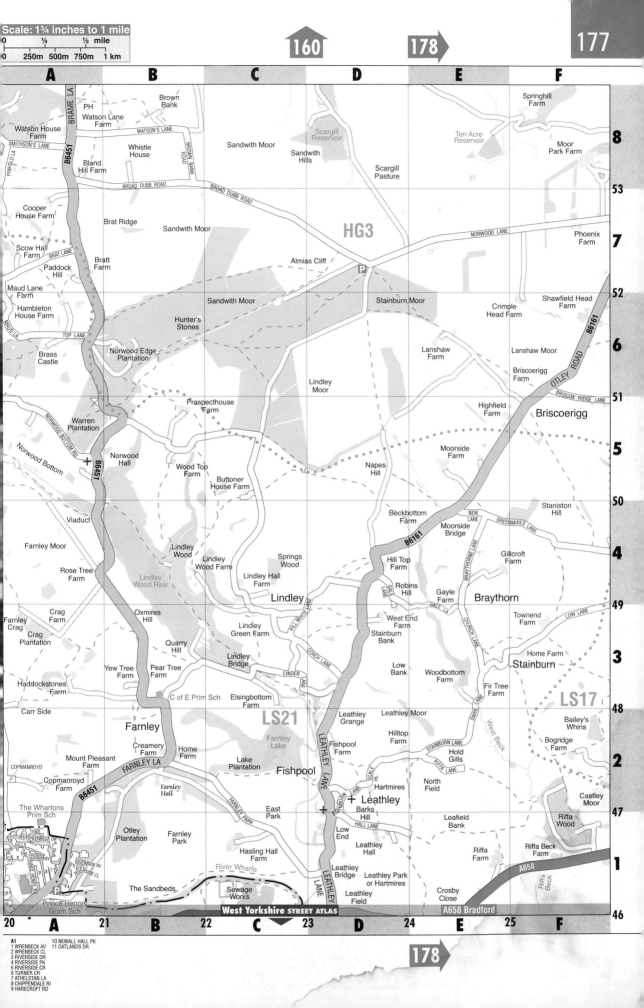

177
161

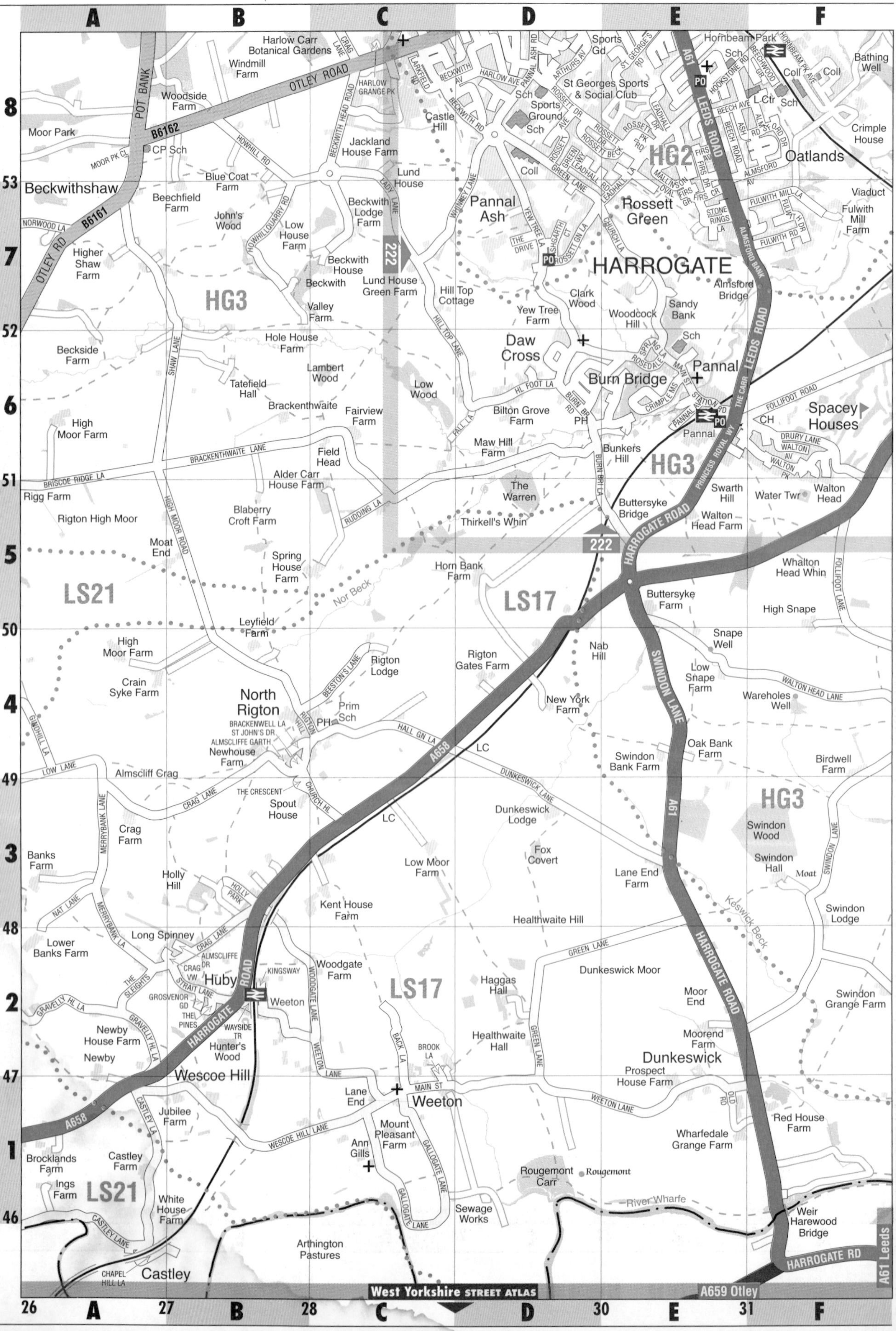
A
B
C
D
E
F
8
53
7
52
6
51
5
50
4
49
3
48
2
47
1
46
26
27
28
30
31
Harlow Carr Botanical Gardens
Windmill Farm
CRAG LANE
OTLEY ROAD
POT BANK
Woodside Farm
HARLOW GRANGE PK
LARKFIELD RD
BECKWITH HEAD ROAD
BECKWITH AV
HARLOW AVE
PANNAL ASH RD
ARTHURS AV
Sports Gd
ST GEORGE'S RD
Hornbeam Park
HORNBEAM PK AVE
Bathing Well
Sch
Coll
A61
PO
LEEDS ROAD
HOOKSTONE RD
BEECHWOOD GR
St Georges Sports & Social Club
Sports Ground
Castle Hill
ROSSETT DR
ROSSETT PK RD
BEECH AVE
L Ctr
Crimple House
Moor Park
B6162
MOOR PK CL
CP Sch
HOWHILL RD
Jackland House Farm
Lund House
LADY LANE
Coll
ROSSETT GREEN LANE
LEADHALL RD
MALLINSON OVAL
FIRS AV
FIRS DR
FIRS CR
BEECH ROAD
ASH RD
ALMSFORD DR
ALMSFORD AV
HG2
Oatlands
Viaduct
Beckwithshaw
Blue Coat Farm
Beechfield Farm
B6161
NORWOOD LA
OTLEY RD
John's Wood
HOWHILLQUARRY RD
Low House Farm
Beckwith Lodge Farm
222
WHINNEY LANE
Pannal Ash
YEW TREE LA
THE DRIVE
ROSSETT CT
HIGHGARTH
CHURCH LA
Rossett Green
STONE RINGS LA
FULWITH MILL LA
FULWITH DR
FULWITH RD
Fulwith Mill Farm
ALMSFORD BANK
Higher Shaw Farm
Beckwith House
Beckwith
Lund House Green Farm
Hill Top Cottage
HARROGATE
Clark Wood
Almsford Bridge
HG3
Valley Farm
Yew Tree Farm
Woodcock Hill
Sandy Bank
Beckside Farm
Hole House Farm
SHAW LANE
HILL TOP LANE
Daw Cross
SPRING LA
ROSEDALE
MAIN ST
Pannal
Lambert Wood
Tatefield Hall
Low Wood
HL FOOT LA
Burn Bridge
CRIMPLE MS
THE CARR
FOLLIFOOT ROAD
Spacey Houses
Brackenthwaite
Fairview Farm
Bilton Grove Farm
BURN BR RD
PH
PANNAL STATION RD
High Moor Farm
FALL LA
Maw Hill Farm
Bunkers Hill
CH
DRURY LANE
WALTON AV
WALTON PK
BRACKENTHWAITE LANE
Field Head
BURN BRI LA
PRINCESS ROYAL WY
BRISCOE RIDGE LA
Alder Carr House Farm
The Warren
Swarth Hill
Water Twr
Walton Head
Rigg Farm
HIGH MOOR ROAD
Blaberry Croft Farm
RUDDING LA
Buttersyke Bridge
HARROGATE ROAD
Walton Head Farm
Rigton High Moor
Thirkell's Whin
Moat End
Spring House Farm
Horn Bank Farm
Whalton Head Whin
FOLLIFOOT LANE
LS21
Nor Beck
LS17
Buttersyke Farm
High Snape
Leyfield Farm
High Moor Farm
Nab Hill
Snape Well
Rigton Lodge
BEESTON'S LANE
Rigton Gates Farm
SWINDON LANE
Crain Syke Farm
Low Snape Farm
WALTON HEAD LANE
North Rigton
Prim Sch
New York Farm
Wareholes Well
GINDHILL LA
BRACKENWELL LA
ST JOHN'S DR
ALMSCLIFFE GARTH
RIGTON HILL
HALL GN LA
A658
LC
Oak Bank Farm
Newhouse Farm
Swindon Bank Farm
Birdwell Farm
LOW LANE
Almscliff Crag
DUNKESWICK LANE
CRAG LANE
THE CRESCENT
CHURCH HL
MERRYBANK LANE
Spout House
Dunkeswick Lodge
HG3
Swindon Wood
Crag Farm
Banks Farm
LC
Low Moor Farm
Fox Covert
Lane End Farm
Swindon Hall
Moat
SWINDON LANE
Holly Hill
HOLLY PARK
NAT LANE
Kent House Farm
Keswick Beck
Swindon Lodge
MERRYBANK LA
Long Spinney
Healthwaite Hill
Lower Banks Farm
ALMSCLIFFE DR
CRAG VW
GREEN LANE
Dunkeswick Moor
THE SLEIGHTS
Huby
KINGSWAY
Woodgate Farm
LS17
Haggas Hall
Moor End
Swindon Grange Farm
GRAVELLY HL LA
STRAIT LANE
GROSVENOR GD
THE PINES
Weeton
WOODGATE LANE
WAYSIDE TR
Hunter's Wood
Newby House Farm
Newby
BACK LA
BROOK LA
Healthwaite Hall
GREEN LANE
Moorend Farm
Dunkeswick
Prospect House Farm
Wescoe Hill
WEETON LANE
MAIN ST
Lane End
Weeton
OLD RD
Jubilee Farm
CASTLEY LA
WESCOE HILL LANE
Mount Pleasant Farm
Red House Farm
Ann Gills
GALLOGATE LANE
Wharfedale Grange Farm
Brocklands Farm
Castley Farm
Rougemont Carr
Rougemont
Ings Farm
White House Farm
Sewage Works
River Wharfe
Weir
Harewood Bridge
CASTLEY LANE
GALLOGATE LANE
Arthington Pastures
HARROGATE RD
A61 Leeds
CHAPEL HILL LA
Castley
A659 Otley

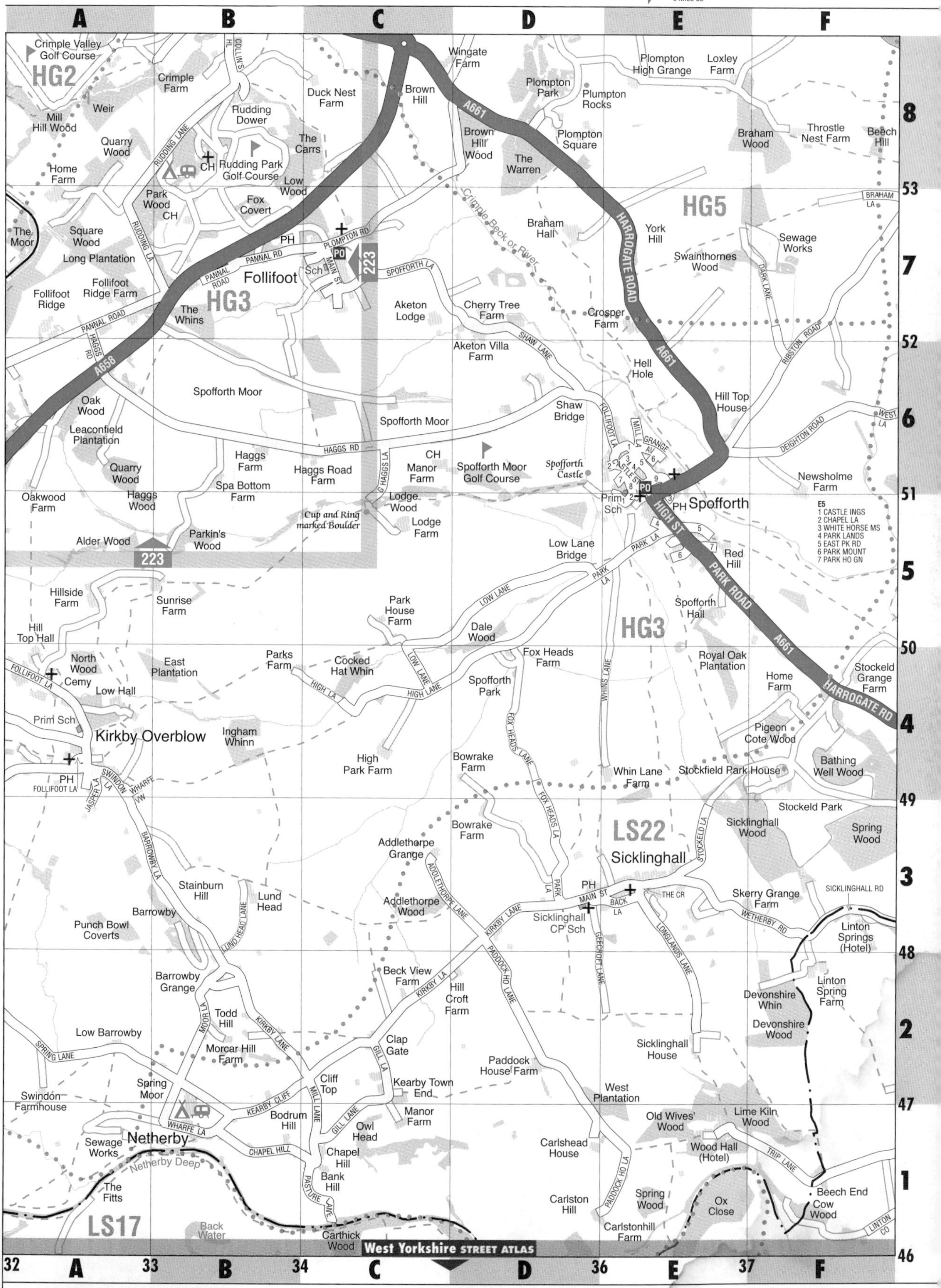

162

180

179

E6
1 CLIVE RD
2 CASTLE CL
3 BEECH CL
4 CANBY LA
5 CHURCH HL
6 MILL CL

7 MANOR GARTH
8 SCHOOL LA
9 CHURCH LA

A   B   C   D   E   F

HG2

Crimple Valley
Golf Course

Crimple
Farm

Duck Nest
Farm

Brown
Hill

Wingate
Farm

Plompton
High Grange

Loxley
Farm

8

Mill
Hill Wood

Weir

Rudding
Dower

The
Carrs

Brown
Hill Wood

Plompton
Park

Plumpton
Rocks

Braham
Wood

Throstle
Nest Farm

Beech
Hill

Quarry
Wood

Rudding Park
Golf Course

Plumpton
Square

A661

53

Home
Farm

Park
Wood CH

Low
Wood

The
Warren

Braham
Hall

York
Hill

HG5

BRAHAM LA

The
Moor

Square
Wood

Fox
Covert

Crosper
Farm

Swainthornes
Wood

Sewage
Works

DARK LANE

7

Long Plantation

PH

Cherry Tree
Farm

RIBSTON ROAD

52

Follifoot
Ridge

Follifoot
Ridge Farm

PO
Sch

Follifoot

Aketon
Lodge

Hell
Hole

Hill Top
House

DEIGHTON ROAD

WEST LA

6

HG3

The
Whins

Aketon Villa
Farm

Shaw
Bridge

Newsholme
Farm

Oak
Wood

HAGGS RD

Spofforth
Moor

Spofforth
Castle

51

Leaconfield
Plantation

Haggs
Farm

CH

Manor
Farm

Spofforth Moor
Golf Course

Prim
Sch

PO

PH Spofforth

E5
1 CASTLE INGS
2 CHAPEL LA
3 WHITE HORSE MS
4 PARK LANDS
5 EAST PK RD
6 PARK MOUNT
7 PARK HO GN

Quarry
Wood

Haggs Road
Farm

Lodge
Wood

Spa Bottom
Farm

HIGH ST

Oakwood
Farm

Haggs
Wood

Lodge
Farm

Low Lane
Bridge

Red
Hill

5

Alder Wood

Parkin's
Wood

Cup and Ring
marked Boulder

Low Lane
Bridge

PARK LA

Hill

PARK ROAD

A661

223

Hillside
Farm

Sunrise
Farm

Park
House
Farm

Dale
Wood

Fox Heads
Farm

Spofforth
Hall

50

Hill
Top Hall

Parks
Farm

Cocked
Hat Whin

LOW LANE

HG3

Royal Oak
Plantation

Home
Farm

Stockeld
Grange
Farm

North
Wood

East
Plantation

Ingham
Whinn

Spofforth
Park

Whin Lane
Farm

Stockfield Park House

Pigeon
Cote Wood

Bathing
Well Wood

4

Cemy

Low Hall

HIGH LA

High
Park Farm

Bowrake
Farm

Prim Sch

Kirkby Overblow

Bowrake
Farm

LS22

Stockeld Park

49

PH
Follifoot La

Stainburn
Hill

Lund
Head

Addlethorpe
Grange

Sicklinghall

Sicklinghall
Wood

Spring
Wood

SICKLINGHALL RD

3

Barrowby

Addlethorpe
Wood

Sicklinghall
CP Sch

THE CR

Skerry Grange
Farm

Linton
Springs
(Hotel)

Punch Bowl
Coverts

Beck View
Farm

Hill
Croft
Farm

WETHERBY RD

48

Barrowby
Grange

Todd
Hill

Kirkby Town
End

Paddock
House Farm

West
Plantation

Devonshire
Whin

Linton
Spring
Farm

2

Low Barrowby

Morcar Hill
Farm

Clap
Gate

Sicklinghall
House

Devonshire
Wood

Spring Lane

Spring
Moor

Cliff
Top

Kearby Town
End

Manor
Farm

Old Wives'
Wood

Lime Kiln
Wood

47

Swindon
Farmhouse

Netherby

Bodrum
Hill

Owl
Head

Carlshead
House

Wood Hall
(Hotel)

TRIP LANE

Beech End
Cow Wood

1

Sewage
Works

Chapel
Hill

Bank
Hill

Spring
Wood

Ox
Close

LS17

The
Fitts

Back
Water

Carthick
Wood

Carlston
Hill

Carlstonhill
Farm

46

32   A   33   B   34   C   D   36   E   37   F

For full street detail of the
highlighted area see pages
222 and 223.

Scale: 1¾ inches to 1 mile

0   ¼   ½   mile
0   250m   500m   750m   1 km

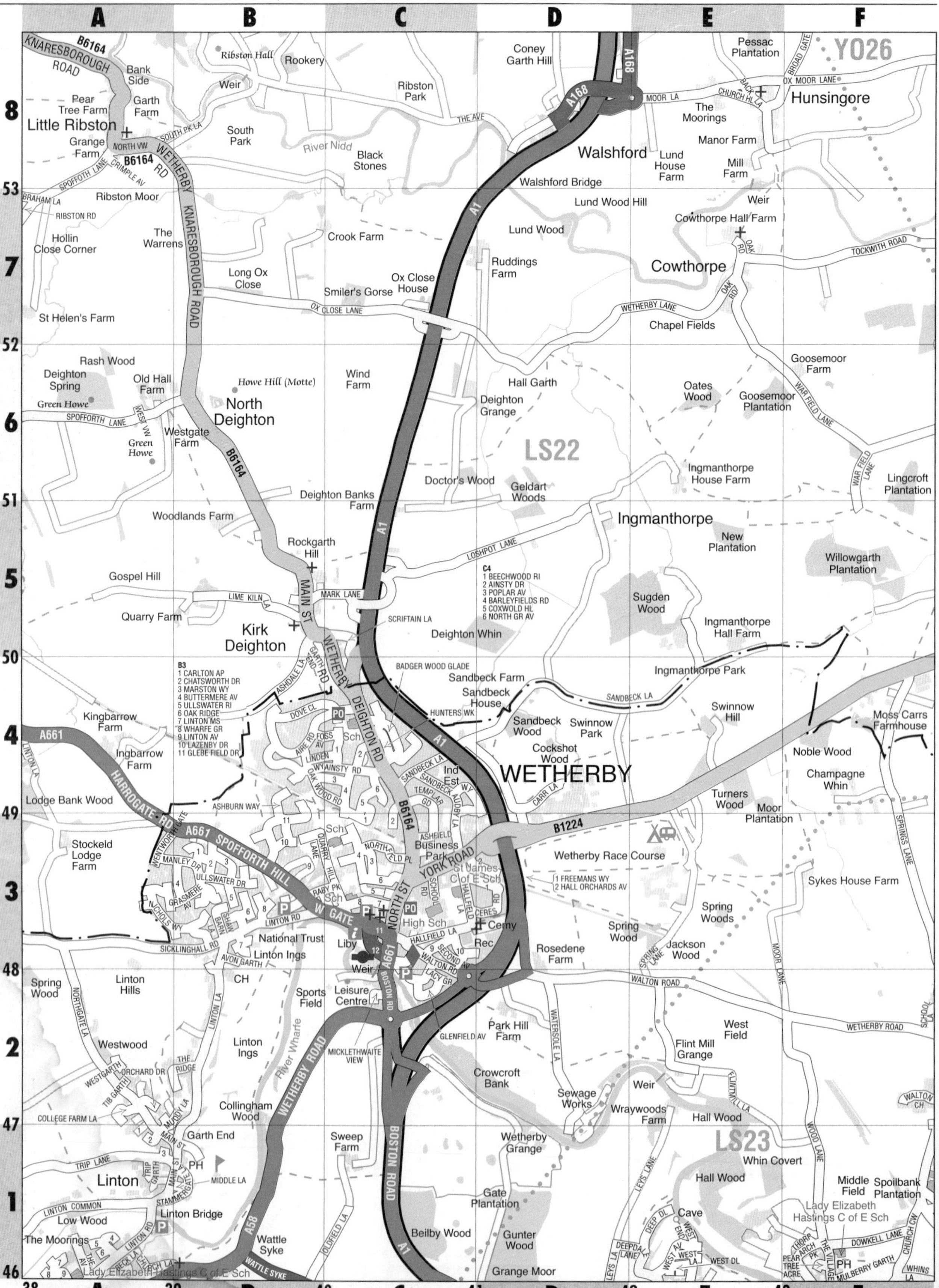

KNARESBOROUGH ROAD
B6164
Bank Side
Garth Farm
Pear Tree Farm
Garth Farm
Little Ribston
Grange Farm
SOUTH PK LA
SPOFFORTH LANE
CRIMPLE LA
NORTH VW
WETHERBY RD
Ribston Hall
Rookery
Weir
South Park
Ribston Park
Coney Garth Hill
A168
A168
MOOR LA
BROAD GATE
OX MOOR LANE
Y026
Pessac Plantation
CHURCH HI LA
BACK LA
Hunsingore
River Nidd
Black Stones
The Moorings
Walshford
Manor Farm
Mill Farm
Lund House Farm
BRAHAM LA
RIBSTON RD
Ribston Moor
The Warrens
Walshford Bridge
Lund Wood Hill
Weir
Cowthorpe Hall Farm
TOCKWITH ROAD
Hollin Close Corner
Long Ox Close
Crook Farm
Lund Wood
Cowthorpe
OAK RD
OAK RD
St Helen's Farm
Smiler's Gorse
Ox Close House
OX CLOSE LANE
WETHERBY LANE
Chapel Fields
Rash Wood
Deighton Spring
Green Howe
SPOFFORTH LANE
WEST VW
Old Hall Farm
Howe Hill (Motte)
Wind Farm
Hall Garth
Deighton Grange
Oates Wood
Goosemoor Plantation
Goosemoor Farm
WAR FIELD LANE
North Deighton
B6164
Westgate Farm
Green Howe
LS22
Ingmanthorpe House Farm
Lingcroft Plantation
Woodlands Farm
Deighton Banks Farm
Doctor's Wood
Geldart Woods
Ingmanthorpe
Willowgarth Plantation
WAR FIELD LANE
Gospel Hill
Rockgarth Hill
MAIN ST
LIME KILN
MARK LANE
LOSHPOT LANE
New Plantation
Sugden Wood
Quarry Farm
SCRIFTAIN LA
Deighton Whin
Ingmanthorpe Hall Farm
Kirk Deighton
WETHERBY RD
GARTH RD
C4
1 BEECHWOOD RI
2 AINSTY DR
3 POPLAR AV
4 BARLEYFIELDS RD
5 COXWOLD HL
6 NORTH GR AV
Ingmanthorpe Park
ASHDALE RD
DOVE CL
BADGER WOOD GLADE
HUNTERS WK
Sandbeck Farm
Sandbeck House
SANDBECK LA
Swinnow Hill
Moss Carrs Farmhouse
B3
1 CARLTON AP
2 CHATSWORTH DR
3 MARSTON WY
4 BUTTERMERE AV
5 ULLSWATER RI
6 OAK RIDGE
7 LINTON MS
8 WHARFE GR
9 LINTON AV
10 LAZENBY DR
11 GLEBE FIELD DR
Sandbeck Wood
Swinnow Park
Cockshot Wood
Noble Wood
Champagne Whin
Kingbarrow Farm
AIRE RD
FOSS
LINDEN AV
WAINSTY RD
Sch
Ind Est
SANDBECK LA
SANDBECK AUDBY LA
CARR LA
WETHERBY
Turners Wood
Moor Plantation
A661
Ingbarrow Farm
WOOD RD
ASHBURN WAY
DEIGHTON RD
A1
B6164
Business Park
B1224
Wetherby Race Course
LINTON CL
Lodge Bank Wood
HARROGATE RD
A667
SPOFFORTH HILL
MANLEY DR
ULLSWATER DR
GRASMERE AV
NICHOLS WY
QUARRY LANE
RABY PK
ASHFIELD
St James C of E Sch
NORTH ST
SCHOOL
HALLFIELD LA
1 FREEMANS WY
2 HALL ORCHARDS AV
Spring Woods
Sykes House Farm
Stockeld Lodge Farm
SICKLINGHALL RD
W GATE
LINTON RD
P0
High Sch
CERES
Spring Wood
Jackson Wood
National Trust
Linton Ings
AVON GARTH
CH
WALTON RD
LADY GR
Cmty
Rec
Rosedene Farm
SPRING LANE
WETHERBY ROAD
Spring Wood
Linton Hills
Weir
Liby
Sports Field
Leisure Centre
BOSTON RD
GLENFIELD AV
WATERSOLE LA
WALTON ROAD
West Field
Westwood
Linton Ings
THE RIDGE
WETHERBY ROAD
River Wharfe
MICKLETHWAITE VIEW
Park Hill Farm
Flint Mill Grange
ORCHARD DR
TIB GARTH
Collingham Wood
Crowcroft Bank
Sewage Works
Weir
Wraywoods Farm
Hall Wood
COLLEGE FARM LA
Garth End
Sweep Farm
Wetherby Grange
LS23
NORTHGATE LA
WESTGARTH
MUDDY LA
TRIP LANE
MAIN ST
PH
MIDDLE LA
BOSTON ROAD
Gate Plantation
Hall Wood
Whin Covert
Middle Field
Spoilbank Plantation
Linton
LINTON COMMON
Low Wood
Linton Bridge
A58
Wattle Syke
COLDFIELD LA
Beilby Wood
Gunter Wood
Grange Moor
WATTLE SYKE
Lady Elizabeth Hastings C of E Sch
Cave
Lady Elizabeth Hastings C of E Sch
LEYS LANE
DEEP DL
DEEPDALE LANE
WEST EN
WEST LA
WEST DL
DOWKELL LANE
MULBERRY GARTH
WHINS GR

179 | 188
For full street detail of Wetherby see
Philip's STREET ATLAS of West Yorkshire

A1
1 NORTHGATE LA
2 NORTHGATE RI
3 NORTHCOTE FOLD
4 OSPREY CL
5 KINGFISHER REACH
6 TERN PK
7 BISHOPDALE DR
8 GARSDALE FOLD
9 COTTERDALE HOLT

C3
1 COXWOLD VW
2 NORTH GR
3 WOODHILL VW
4 BARLEYFIELDS RD
5 BARLEYFIELDS LA
6 SANDRINGHAM RD
7 ST JAMES'S ST
8 CROSSLEY ST
9 FIRST AV
10 THIRD AV
11 BANK ST
12 MARKET PL

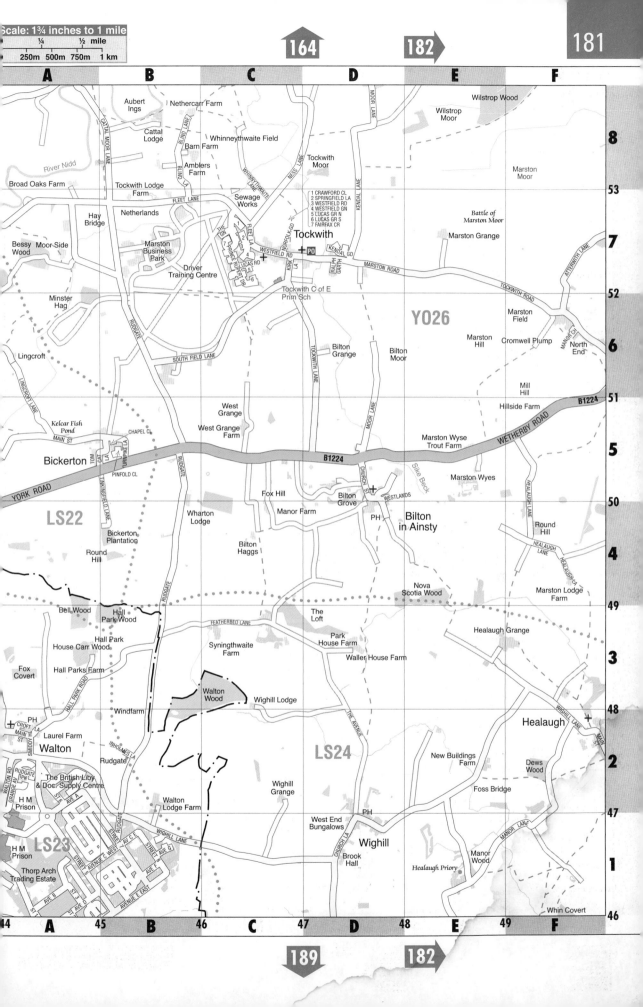

181
165

Scale: 1¾ inches to 1 mile

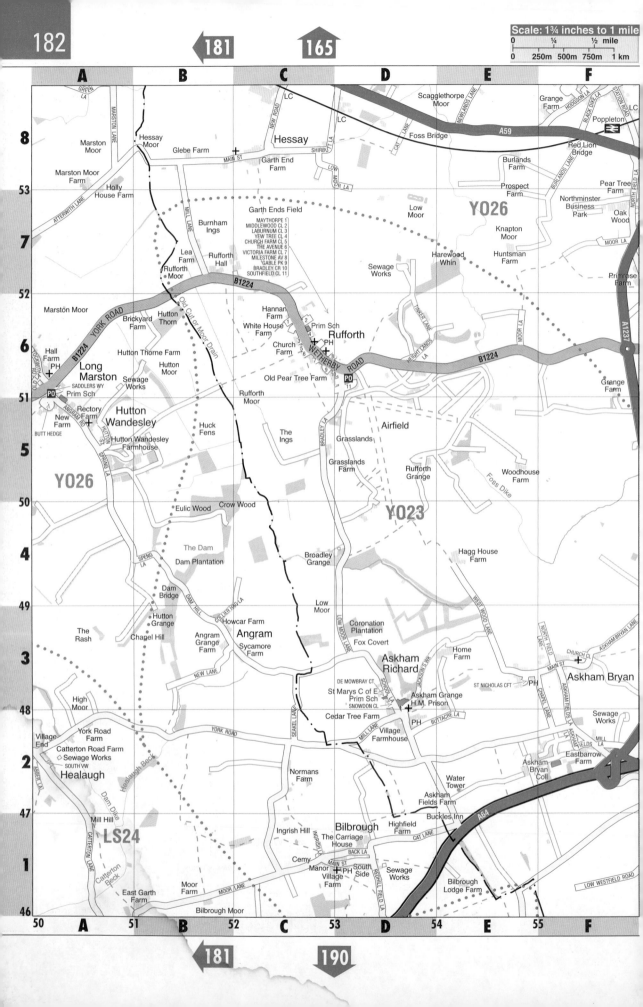
A B C D E F
8 7 6 5 4 3 2 1
53 52 51 50 49 48 47 46
50 51 52 53 54 55
Hessay
Hessay Moor
Glebe Farm
Garth End Farm
Marston Moor
Marston Moor Farm
Holly House Farm
Scagglethorpe Moor
Foss Bridge
A59
Poppleton
Red Lion Bridge
Grange Farm
Burlands Farm
Prospect Farm
Pear Tree Farm
Northminster Business Park
Oak Wood
YO26
Low Moor
Knapton Moor
Huntsman Farm
Harewood Whin
Garth Ends Field
Burnham Ings
Lea Farm
Rufforth Hall
Rufforth Moor
MAYTHORPE 1
MIDDLEWOOD CL 2
LABURNUM CL 3
YEW TREE CL 4
CHURCH FARM CL 5
THE AVENUE 6
VICTORIA FARM CL 7
MILESTONE AV 8
GABLE PK 9
BRADLEY CR 10
SOUTHFIELD CL 11
Sewage Works
Primrose Farm
B1224
Hannah Farm
White House Farm
Church Farm
Prim Sch
Rufforth
Old Pear Tree Farm
Brickyard Farm
Hutton Thorn
Hutton Thorne Farm
Hutton Moor
Long Marston
Hall Farm
Sewage Works
Prim Sch
Rectory Farm
New Farm
Hutton Wandesley
Hutton Wandesley Farmhouse
Huck Fens
Rufforth Moor
The Ings
Grasslands
Airfield
Grasslands Farm
Rufforth Grange
Woodhouse Farm
Foss Dike
Grange Farm
A1237
YO26
YO23
Eulic Wood
Crow Wood
The Dam
Dam Plantation
Broadley Grange
Hagg House Farm
Dam Bridge
Hutton Grange
Chapel Hill
The Rash
Low Moor
Howcar Farm
Angram
Angram Grange Farm
Sycamore Farm
Coronation Plantation
Fox Covert
Askham Richard
Home Farm
Askham Bryan
St Marys C of E Prim Sch
Askham Grange H.M. Prison
Cedar Tree Farm
Village Farmhouse
Sewage Works
High Moor
York Road Farm
Village End
Catterton Road Farm
Sewage Works
Healaugh
Healaugh Beck
Dam Dike
Mill Hill
LS24
Normans Farm
Water Tower
Askham Bryan Coll
Eastbarrow Farm
Askham Fields Farm
Buckles Inn
A64
Ingrish Hill
Bilbrough
The Carriage House
Highfield Farm
Cemy
Manor
Village Farm
South Side
Sewage Works
Bilbrough Lodge Farm
Catterton Beck
East Garth Farm
Moor Farm
Bilbrough Moor
Old Cut or Moor Drain
YORK ROAD
WETHERBY ROAD
LOW WESTFIELD ROAD

181
190

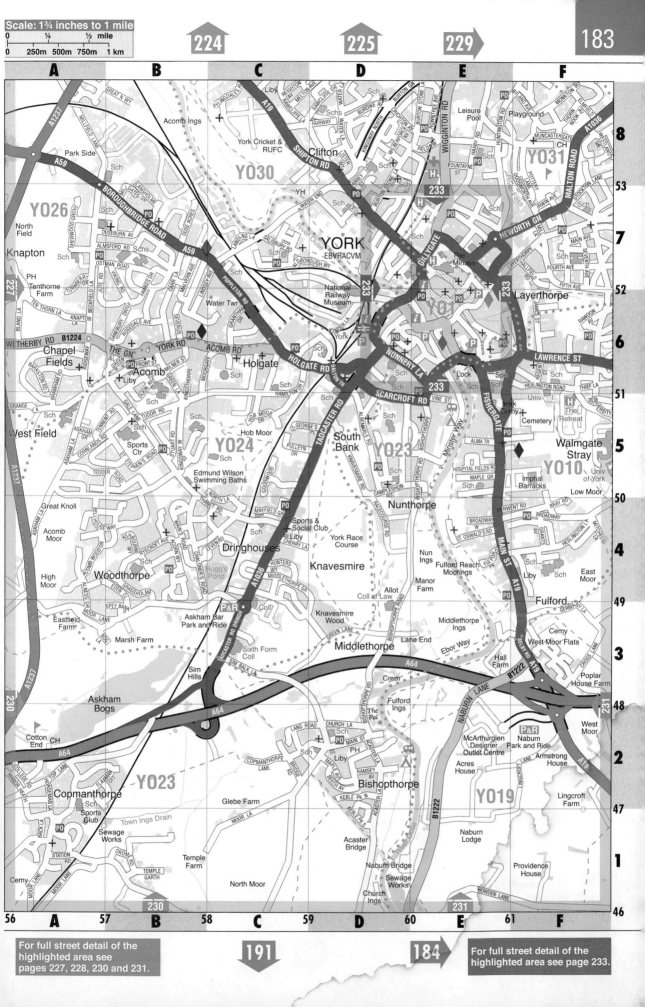

F7
1 GORSE HL
2 HOLLY TREE CFT
3 ASPEN CL
4 ORCHARD CTS
5 PETERCROFT CL
6 KENDAL CL
7 UNDERCROFT
8 THORNCROFT
9 SAWYERS WK
10 CONEYCROFT
11 KEEPERS WY
12 WESTWOOD MS
13 SCAUDERCROFT
14 GREENCROFT CT
15 LIME TREE MS
16 OX CALDER CL
17 GREENCROFT LA
18 GREENSIDE
19 ASHDALE RD
20 THE GREEN
21 HUNTERS WOOD WY
22 DEERSTONE WY
23 GREENSIDE WLK
24 GREENSIDE CL

Scale: 1¾ inches to 1 mile
0 ¼ ½ mile
0 250m 500m 750m 1 km

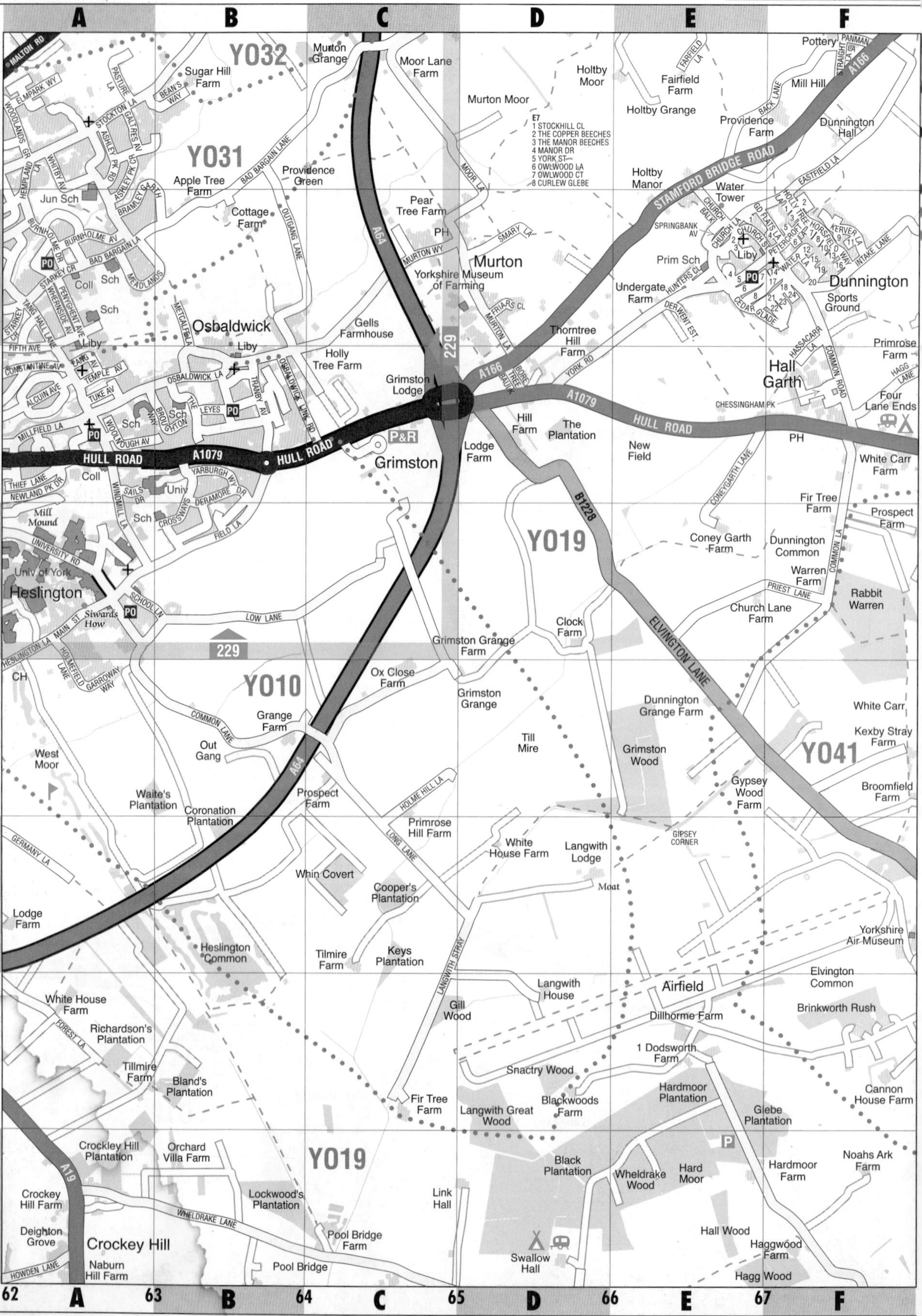

For full street detail of the highlighted area see page 229.

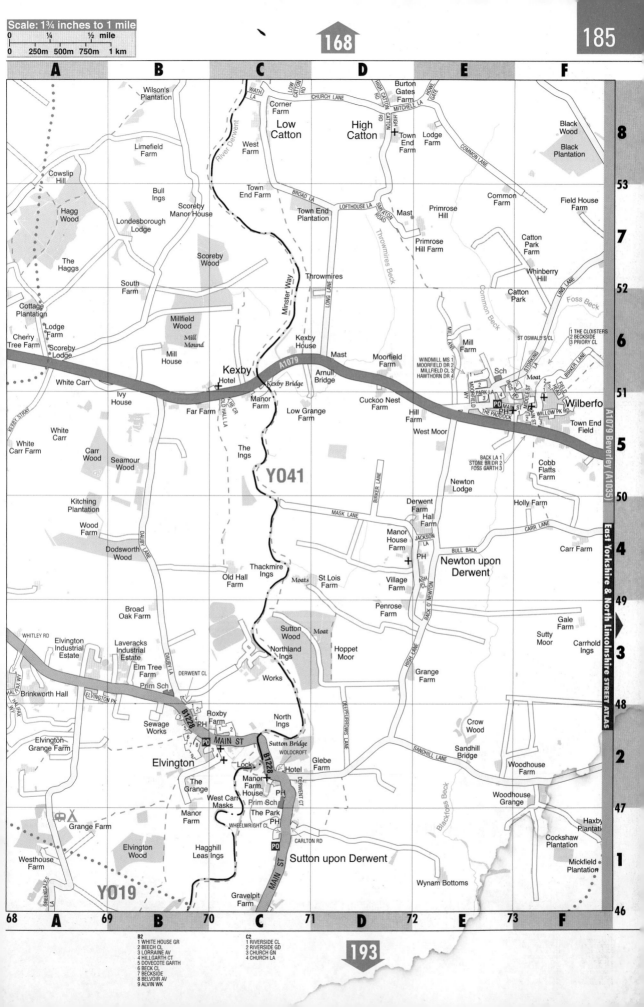

A **B** **C** **D** **E** **F**

8

Wilson's Plantation

Burton Gates Farm

Corner Farm

Low Catton

High Catton

Black Wood

Black Plantation

West Farm

Limefield Farm

Town End Farm

Lodge Farm

CHURCH LANE

WATH LA

LOW CATTON RD

HIGH CATTON RD

MITCHELL LA

HOWE GATE

Cowslip Hill

53

Bull Ings

Scoreby Manor House

Town End Farm

Town End Plantation

LOFTHOUSE LA

SMEATON ROAD

Mast

Primrose Hill

Common Farm

Field House Farm

Hagg Wood

Londesborough Lodge

BROAD LA

7

Scoreby Wood

Primrose Hill Farm

Catton Park Farm

The Haggs

South Farm

Throwmires

Minster Way

Long Lane

Whinberry Hill

Catton Park

LONG LANE

FOSS Beck

52

Cottage Plantation

Millfield Wood

Common Beck

Throwmires Beck

MILL LANE

Common Beck

St OSWALD'S/CL

1 THE CLOISTERS
2 BECKSIDE
3 PRIORY CL

6

Lodge Farm

Mill Mound

Kexby House

Mast

Moorfield Farm

Mill Farm

WINDMILL MS 1
MOORFIELD DR 2
MILLFIELD CL 3
HAWTHORN DR 4

Sch

Moat

Cherry Tree Farm

Scoreby Lodge

Mill House

Kexby

Hotel

A1079

Arnull Bridge

MOORFIELD

PARK LA

INGS LA

STORKING LA

BIRKER LANE

Wilberfo

White Carr

Ivy House

Kexby Bridge

OLD HALL LA

Manor Farm

Low Grange Farm

Cuckoo Nest Farm

Hill Farm

PO

MAIN ST

WILLOW PK RD

THE PADDOCK

Town End Field

A1079 Beverley (A1035)

51

Far Farm

West Moor

KCKBY STRAY

White Carr

The Ings

BACK LA 1
STONE BR DR 2
FOSS GARTH 3

Cobb Flatts Farm

5

White Carr Farm

Carr Wood

Seamour Wood

YO41

Newton Lodge

Holly Farm

50

Kitching Plantation

MASK LANE

BIRKER LANE

Derwent Farm

Hall Farm

CARR LANE

Wood Farm

DALBY LANE

Manor House Farm

JACKSON LA

BULL BALK

PH

Carr Farm

Dodsworth Wood

Thackmire Ings

Old Hall Farm

Moats

St Lois Farm

Village Farm

Newton upon Derwent

ASH CL

BACK O' NEWTON

4

Broad Oak Farm

Penrose Farm

Gale Farm

49

Sutton Wood

Moat

Hoppet Moor

Sutty Moor

Carrhold Ings

WHITLEY RD

Elvington Industrial Estate

Laveracks Industrial Estate

Northland Ings

HIGH LANE

East Yorkshire & North Lincolnshire STREET ATLAS

3

Elm Tree Farm

Prim Sch

DALBY LA

DERWENT CL

Works

Grange Farm

Brinkworth Hall

ELVINGTON PK

B1228

PH

Roxby Farm

North Ings

DEEPFURROWS LANE

48

Sewage Works

PO

MAIN ST

Sutton Bridge

Woldcroft

Crow Wood

Sandhill Bridge

SANDHILL LANE

Woodhouse Farm

2

Elvington Grange Farm

Elvington

Lock

Manor Farm House

Glebe Farm

Blackfoss Beck

Woodhouse Grange

HALIFAX WAY

The Grange

B1228

Hotel

DERWENT CT

47

West Carr Masks

Prim Sch

PH

Haxby Plantati

Grange Farm

Manor Farm

The Park

WHEELWRIGHT CL

PH

PO

CARLTON RD

Cockshaw Plantation

1

Westhouse Farm

Elvington Wood

Hagghill Leas Ings

MAIN ST

Sutton upon Derwent

Wynam Bottoms

Mickfield Plantation

GREENGALES LA

YO19

Gravelpit Farm

46

B2
1 WHITE HOUSE GR
2 BEECH CL
3 LORRAINE AV
4 HILLGARTH CT
5 DOVECOTE GARTH
6 BECK CL
7 BECKSIDE
8 BELVOIR AV
9 ALVIN WK

C2
1 RIVERSIDE CL
2 RIVERSIDE GD
3 CHURCH GN
4 CHURCH LA

A7
1 UNITY ST
2 SCHOOL ST
3 VICARAGE RD

172

Scale: 1¾ inches to 1 mile
0 ¼ ½ mile
0 250m 500m 750m 1 km

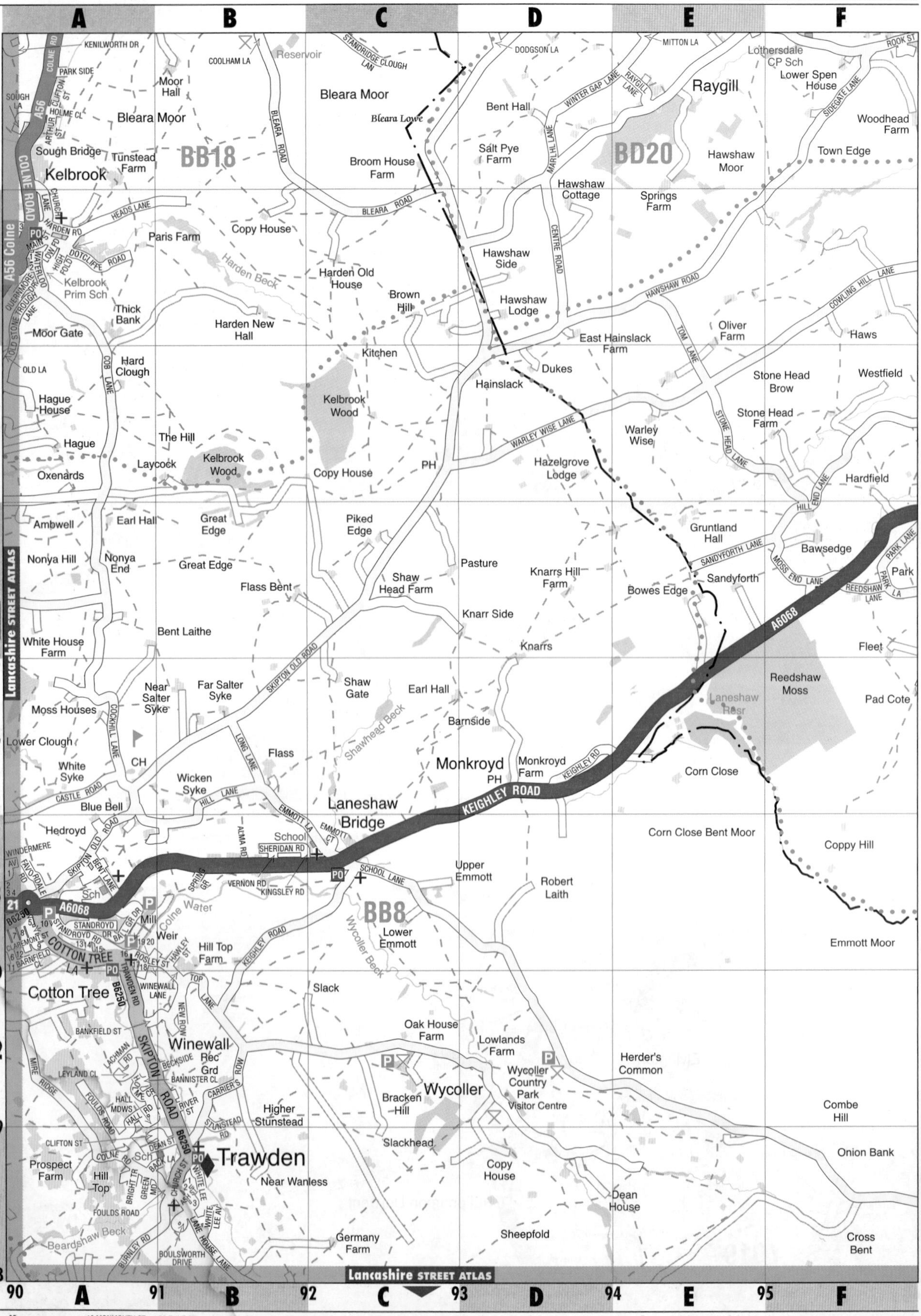

A3
1 CONISTON GR
2 DERWENT CL
3 RYDAL PLACE
4 GRASMERE CL
5 KEIGHLEY RD
6 CLARENCE ST
7 AVONDALE ST
8 CRAVEN ST
9 BOULSWORTH GR
10 MONMOUTH ST
11 ACRESFIELD
12 LONG MEADOW
13 LAMBETH ST
14 HOLLINGTON ST
15 CLARENDON ST
16 WINEWALL RD
17 HOLME ST
18 BRIGHT ST
19 HARTINGTON ST
20 DUKE ST
21 BYRON RD

B1
1 CLARENCE ST
2 LAMBERT ST
3 EAST VIEW

Scale: 1¾ inches to 1 mile
0 ¼ ½ mile
0 250m 500m 750m 1 km

B6
1 ACRE MEADOW
2 ACRE RD
3 WOODLAND ST
4 SUN ST
5 WALTON ST
6 CROSS ST
7 GREEN ST
8 SPRINGWELL CL
9 COLLINGE RD
10 QUEEN ST

173

E8
1 BLACK ABBEY LA
2 RYECROFT WY
3 VALLEY VW
4 WASHBURN DR
5 BEANLANDS PL
6 HOPP'S RD
7 WHEATLANDS LA
8 WHEATLANDS AVE
9 RYELAND RD
10 JAMES ST
11 CAMPBELL ST
12 YORK ST
13 CHURCH ST
14 NORTH ST
15 PARKER S
16 PARK S
17 BACK STATION RD
18 ANDERTON ST

F8
1 AIREDALE VW
2 NEWLANDS DR
3 ELMFIELD RD
4 CHURCHILL WY
5 SPENCER CL
6 LYNNDALE AV

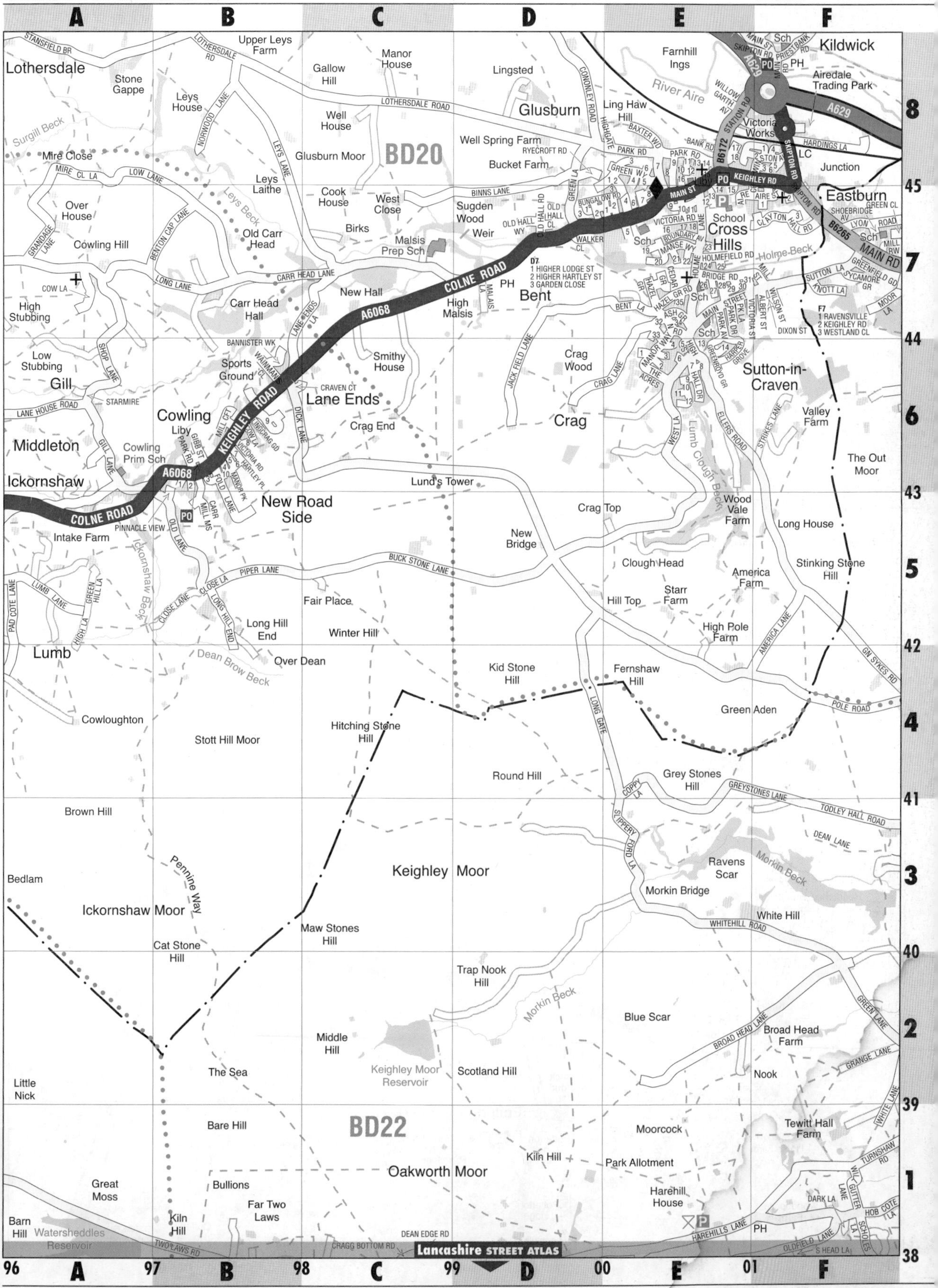

E6
1 THE CROFTS
2 THE POPLARS
3 EARLS VW
4 WILLOW WY
5 LISTER HILL
6 WEST CROFT
7 HARPERS SQ
8 OVERBURN RD
9 HALL WAY
10 HALL AVE
11 HALL CL
12 NORTH AVE
13 GREENROYD DR
14 DOVELANDS

E7
1 CROFT ST
2 CROFT HEAD TERR
3 MAYFIELD CL
4 INSTITUTE ST
5 TOWNEND PL
6 SUNNY BANK RD
7 BEANLANDS DR
8 BEANLANDS PL
9 BACK COLNE RD
10 BEECH ST
11 ASH ST
12 ALBERT RD
13 EAST AVE
14 PROSPECT ST
15 FIELDHEAD DR
16 TOWN END CL
17 BURNROYD AV
18 ROYD CL
19 THE COPPICE
20 THE HAWTHORNS
21 MEADOW LEA
22 ROWAN GARTH
23 HOLME CL
24 JACKSON ST
25 WIGHILL ST
26 CHURCH RD
27 KING EDWARD ST
28 GORDON ST
29 SPENCER ST
30 WRIGHT ST
31 NORTH ST
32 CROFT HILL
33 CRAG CL
34 ELM RD
35 SCOTT CL

A8
1 BISHOPDALE DR
2 COVERDALE GARTH
3 LANGWITH AV
4 GREEN LA
5 THE CROFT
6 THE CLOSE
7 MILLGARTH CT
8 THE GARTH
9 LOWCROFT
10 THE VALE

180

E7
1 MOOR AV
2 BRIDGE GARTH
3 WILLOW GR
4 ASHMEAD
5 WILLOW GLADE
6 ST LUKE'S CL
7 CHURCH VW MS
8 NURSERY WY
9 ALBION TR

Scale: 1¾ inches to 1 mile
0 ¼ ½ mile
0 250m 500m 750m 1 km

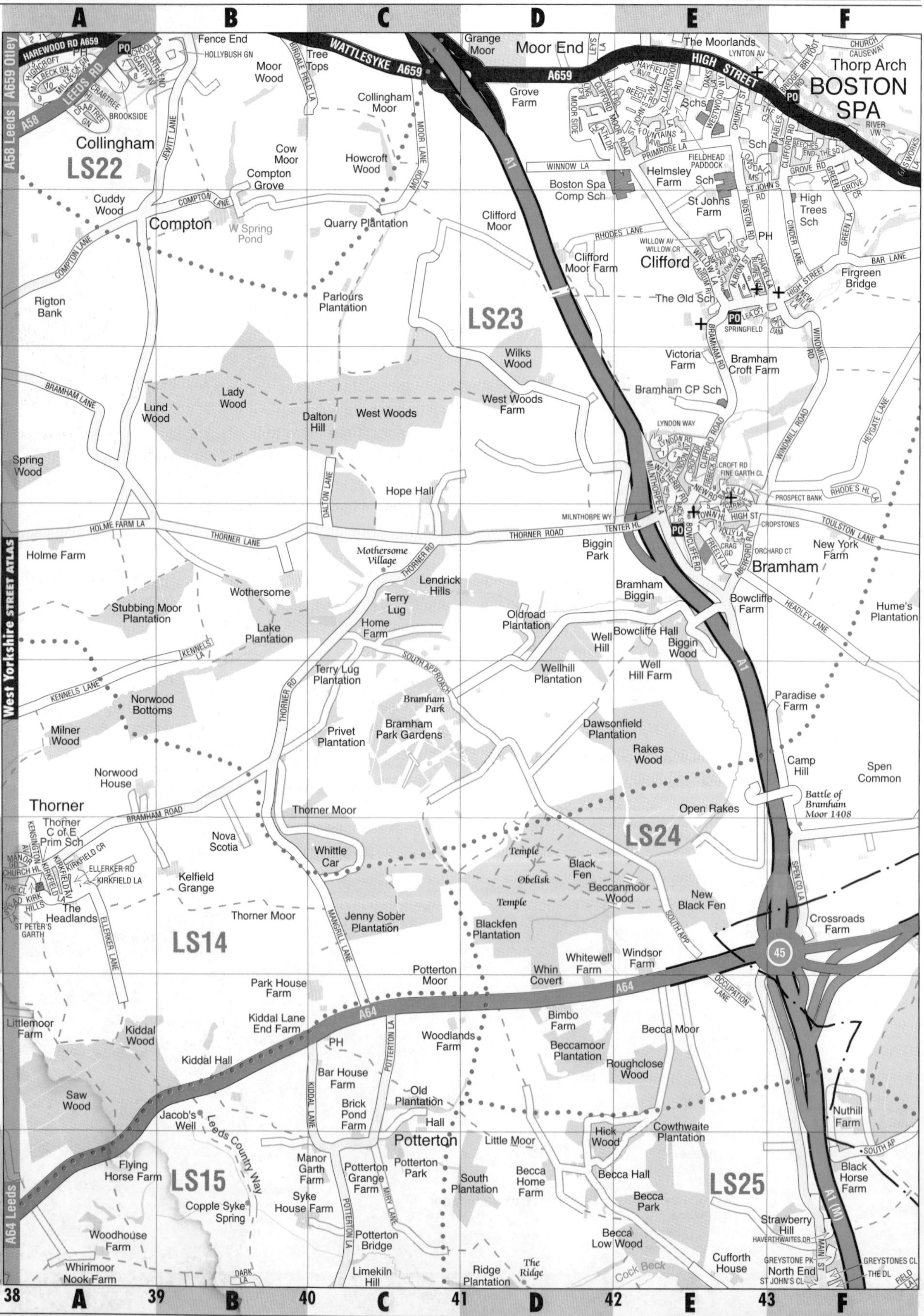

194

E5
1 ALMSHOUSE HL
2 FOLLY VW
3 THE CRAG
4 CHURCH HL
5 LOW WY
6 FRONT ST

E6
1 LYNDON CL
2 LYNDON SQ
3 THE KNOLL
4 LYNDON CR
5 MILNTHORPE GD
6 MILNTHORPE CL
7 MILNTHORPE GARTH
8 BRADFORDS CL
9 CHURCH MS

For full street detail of Boston Spa see Philip's STREET ATLAS of West Yorkshire

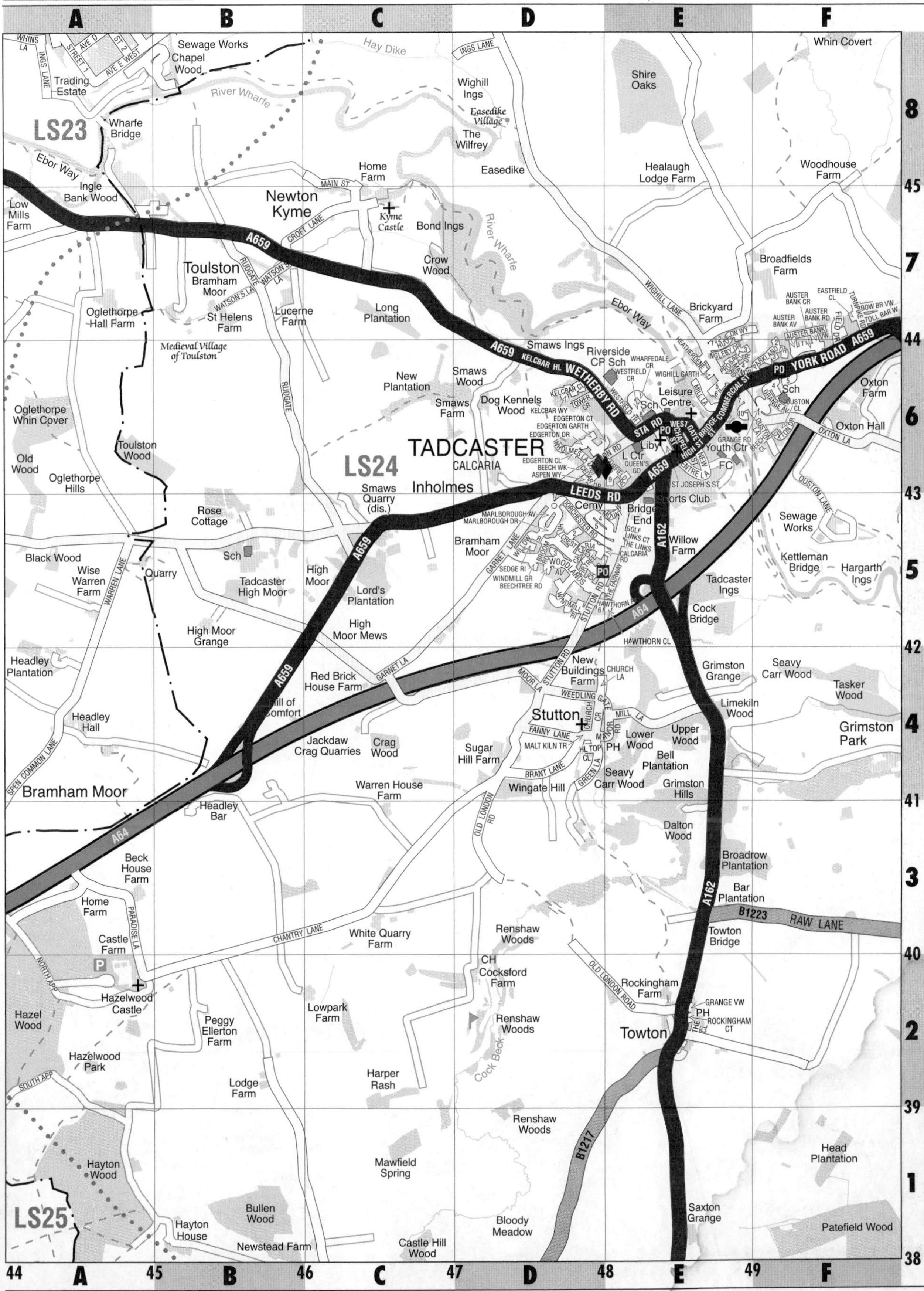
A
B
C
D
E
F
8
45
7
44
6
43
5
42
4
41
3
40
2
39
1
38
44
45
46
47
48
49
Sewage Works
Chapel Wood
Trading Estate
INGS LANE
River Wharfe
Hay Dike
LS23
Wharfe Bridge
Ebor Way
Ingle Bank Wood
Low Mills Farm
Wighill Ings
Easedike Village
The Wilfrey
Easedike
Shire Oaks
Whin Covert
Healaugh Lodge Farm
Woodhouse Farm
Home Farm
MAIN ST
Newton Kyme
Kyme Castle
Bond Ings
CROFT LANE
A659
Toulston
Bramham Moor
Crow Wood
Broadfields Farm
WIGHILL LANE
Brickyard Farm
Oglethorpe Hall Farm
St Helens Farm
WATSON'S LA
RUDGATE
Lucerne Farm
Long Plantation
Medieval Village of Toulston
Smaws Ings
Riverside CP Sch
KELCBAR HL
WETHERBY RD
YORK ROAD
PO
New Plantation
Smaws Wood
Smaws Farm
Dog Kennels Wood
Leisure Centre
Sch
Oxton Farm
Oxton Hall
OXTON LA
Oglethorpe Whin Cover
Old Wood
Toulston Wood
Oglethorpe Hills
TADCASTER
CALCARIA
LS24
Inholmes
Smaws Quarry (dis.)
LEEDS RD
Liby
L Ctr
Youth Ctr
FC
Sports Club
Cemy
Bridge End
Rose Cottage
A162
Willow Farm
Sewage Works
OUSTON LANE
Black Wood
Sch
Wise Warren Farm
WARREN LANE
Quarry
Tadcaster High Moor
High Moor
Lord's Plantation
Bramham Moor
GARNET LANE
Kettleman Bridge
Hargarth Ings
Tadcaster Ings
Cock Bridge
High Moor Grange
High Moor Mews
A64
HAWTHORN CL
Headley Plantation
Red Brick House Farm
GARNET LA
New Buildings Farm
Grimston Grange
Seavy Carr Wood
Tasker Wood
Hill of Comfort
Headley Hall
Stutton
Limekiln Wood
Grimston Park
Jackdaw Crag Quarries
Crag Wood
Sugar Hill Farm
Lower Wood
Upper Wood
Bell Plantation
SPEN COMMON LANE
Bramham Moor
Warren House Farm
Wingate Hill
Seavy Carr Wood
Grimston Hills
Headley Bar
OLD LONDON RD
Dalton Wood
Beck House Farm
Broadrow Plantation
Home Farm
Bar Plantation
B1223
RAW LANE
Castle Farm
PARADISE LA
CHANTRY LANE
White Quarry Farm
Renshaw Woods
Towton Bridge
NORTH APP
CH
Cocksford Farm
OLD LONDON ROAD
Rockingham Farm
Hazelwood Castle
Hazel Wood
Peggy Ellerton Farm
Lowpark Farm
Renshaw Woods
GRANGE VW
PH
ROCKINGHAM CT
Towton
Hazelwood Park
SOUTH APP
Lodge Farm
Cock Beck
Harper Rash
B1217
Renshaw Woods
Hayton Wood
Mawfield Spring
Head Plantation
LS25
Bullen Wood
Hayton House
Newstead Farm
Castle Hill Wood
Bloody Meadow
Saxton Grange
Patefield Wood

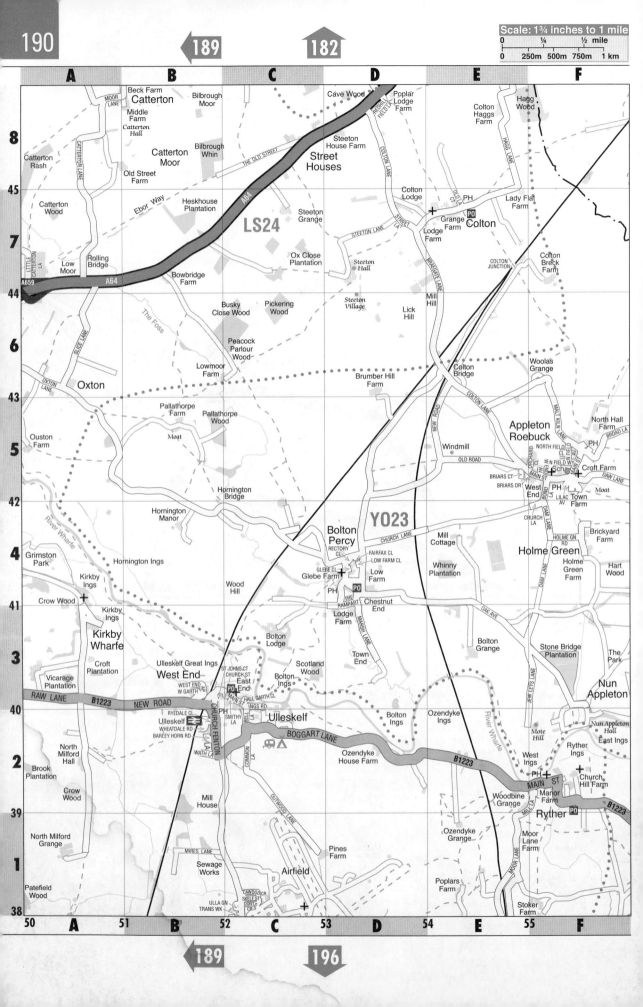

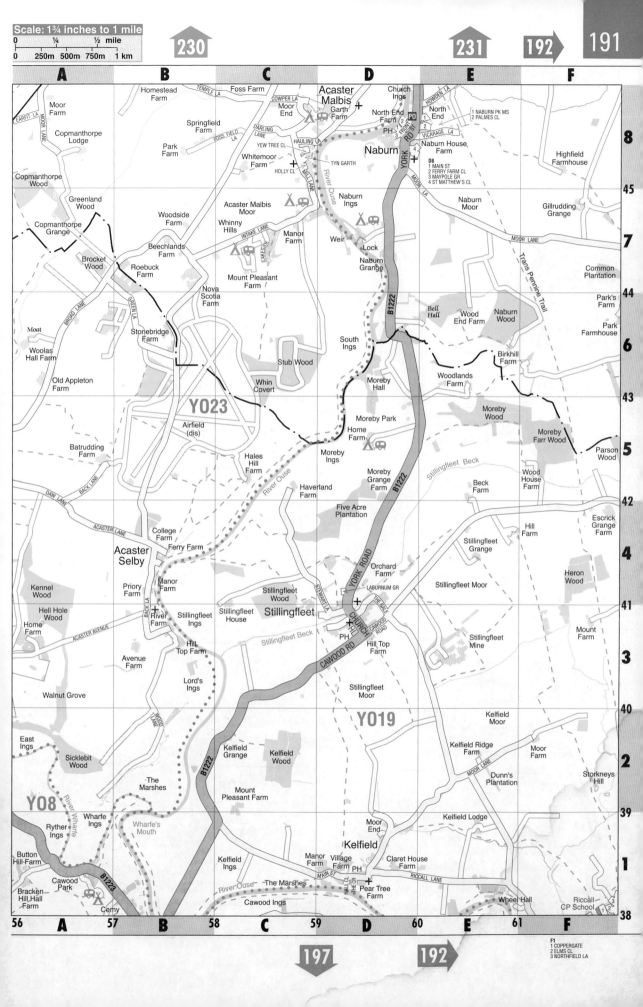

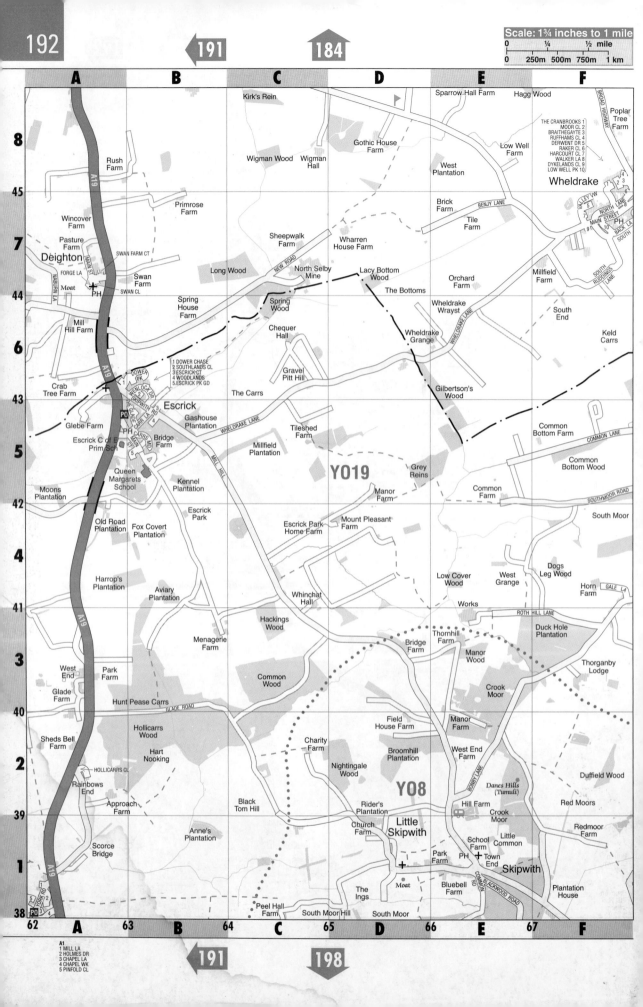

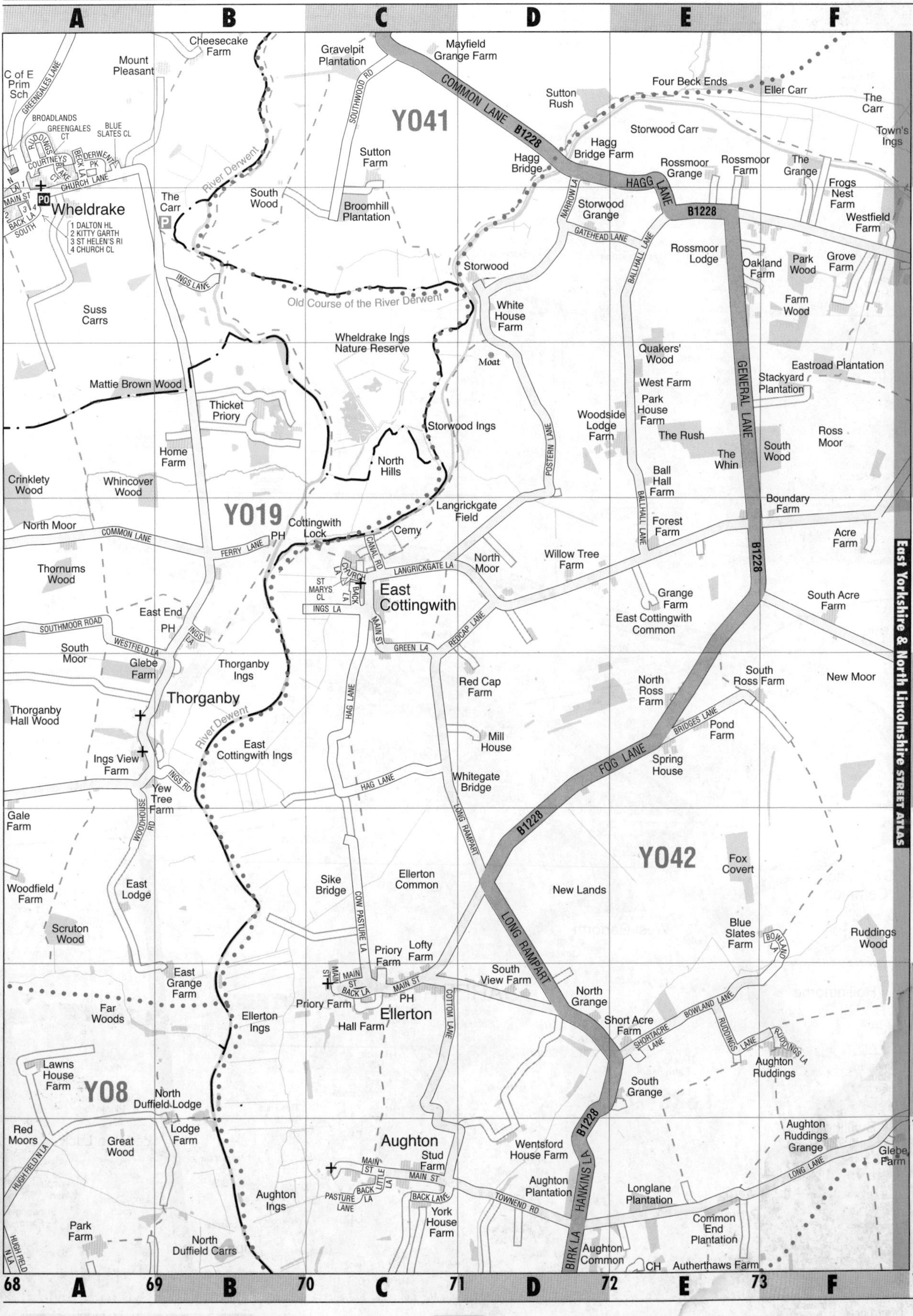

A   B   C   D   E   F

Mount Pleasant
Cheesecake Farm
Gravelpit Plantation
Mayfield Grange Farm
Four Beck Ends
Eller Carr
The Carr
C of E Prim Sch
GREENGALES LANE
SOUTHWOOD RD
COMMON LANE B1228
Sutton Rush
Storwood Carr
Town's Ings
YO41
8
Broadlands
GREENGALES CT
BLUE SLATES CL
BIRCHWENT CL
COURTNEYS
PK
CHURCH LANE
Sutton Farm
South Wood
Broomhill Plantation
Hagg Bridge
Hagg Bridge Farm
Rossmoor Grange
Rossmoor Farm
The Grange
Frogs Nest Farm
45
MAIN ST
BACK LA SOUTH
PO
Wheldrake
The Carr
River Derwent
P
NARROW LA
Storwood Grange
HAGG LANE
B1228
Westfield Farm
1 DALTON HL
2 KITTY GARTH
3 ST HELEN'S RI
4 CHURCH CL
INGS LANE
GATEHEAD LANE
Rossmoor Lodge
Oakland Farm
Park Wood
Grove Farm
7
Suss Carrs
Storwood
White House Farm
BALLHALL LANE
Farm Wood
44
Mattie Brown Wood
Wheldrake Ings Nature Reserve
Moat
Quakers' Wood
Eastroad Plantation
Stackyard Plantation
Thicket Priory
West Farm
GENERAL LANE
6
Crinklety Wood
Whincover Wood
Home Farm
Storwood Ings
North Hills
Woodside Lodge Farm
Park House Farm
The Rush
South Wood
Ross Moor
The Whin
43
North Moor
COMMON LANE
YO19
FERRY LANE
PH
Cottingwith Lock
Langrickgate Field
POSTERN LANE
Ball Hall Farm
Forest Farm
Boundary Farm
Acre Farm
5
Thornums Wood
Cemy
North Moor
Willow Tree Farm
B1228
South Acre Farm
East End PH
ST MARYS CL
CHURCH BACK
East Cottingwith
LANGRICKGATE LA
Grange Farm
42
SOUTHMOOR ROAD
WESTFIELD LA
INGS LA
INGS LA
East Cottingwith Common
South Moor
Glebe Farm
Thorganby Ings
GREEN LA
Red Cap Farm
REDCAP LANE
MAIN ST
North Ross Farm
South Ross Farm
New Moor
Thorganby
HAG LANE
BRIDGES LANE
Pond Farm
4
Thorganby Hall Wood
East Cottingwith Ings
Mill House
FOG LANE
Spring House
Ings View Farm
River Derwent
WOODHOUSE RD
Yew Tree Farm
Whitegate Bridge
HAG LANE
41
Gale Farm
LONG RAMPART
YO42
Fox Covert
Woodfield Farm
East Lodge
Sike Bridge
Ellerton Common
New Lands
Blue Slates Farm
BOWLAND
Ruddings Wood
3
Scruton Wood
COW PASTURE LA
Priory Farm
Lofty Farm
B1228
South View Farm
North Grange
Short Acre Farm
BOWLAND LANE
RUDDINGS LANE
RUDDINGS LA
40
East Grange Farm
Ellerton Ings
MAIN ST
BACK LA
Priory Farm
Ellerton PH
COTTAM LANE
SHORTACRE LANE
Aughton Ruddings
Far Woods
Hall Farm
South Grange
2
Lawns House Farm
YO8
North Duffield Lodge
Wentsford House Farm
B1228
South Grange
Aughton Ruddings Grange
Glebe Farm
39
Red Moors
HUGHFIELD LA
Great Wood
Lodge Farm
Aughton Ings
BACK LA
Aughton
Stud Farm
MAIN ST
LITTLE LA
MAIN ST
Aughton Plantation
HANKINS LA
Longlane Plantation
LONG LANE
1
Park Farm
HUGHFIELD LA
North Duffield Carrs
PASTURE LANE
BACK LA
York House Farm
TOWNEND RD
BIRK LA
Aughton Common
CH
Common End Plantation
Autherhaws Farm
38

68   A   69   B   70   C   71   D   72   E   73   F

East Yorkshire & North Lincolnshire STREET ATLAS

188

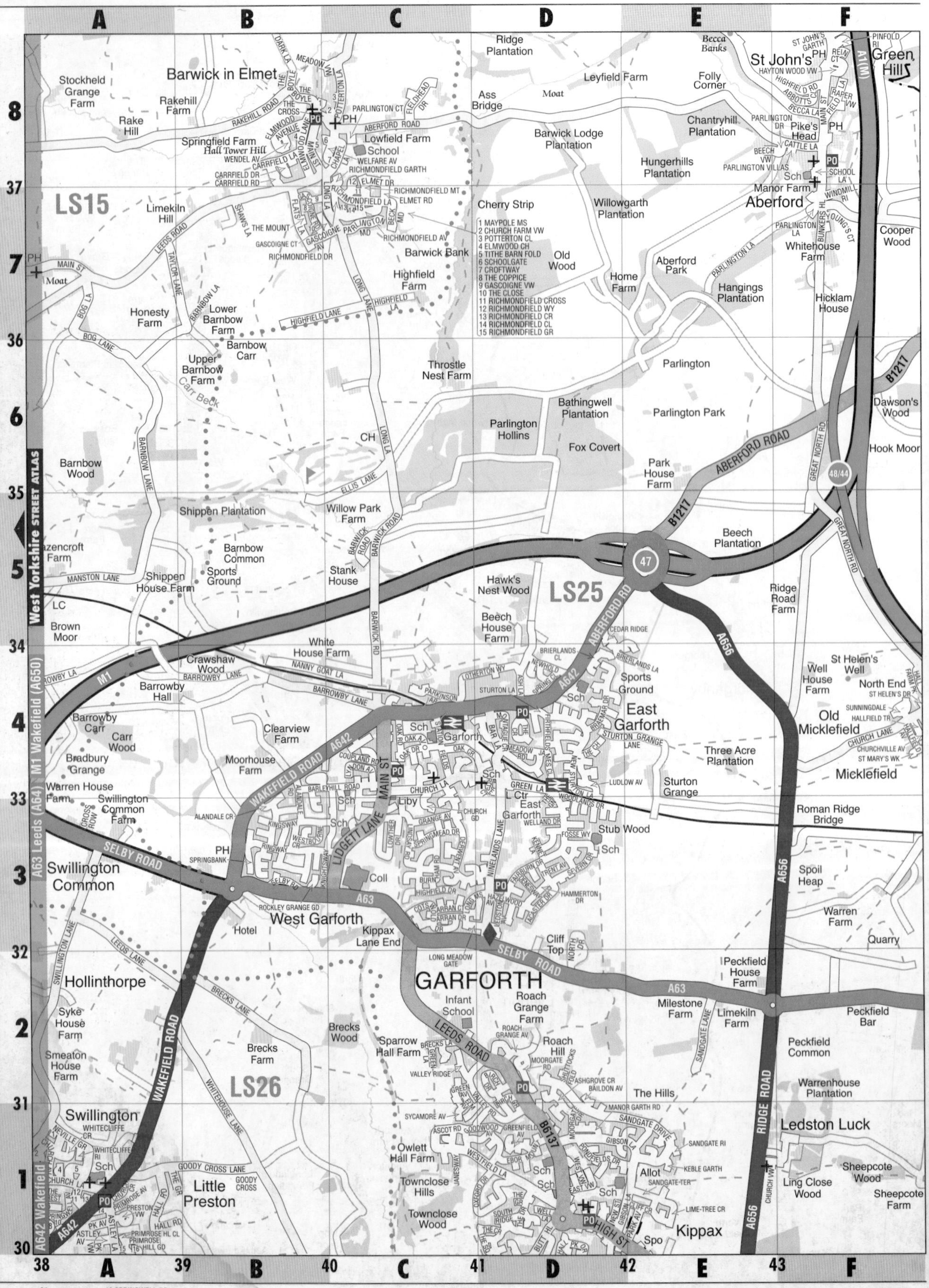

A **B** **C** **D** **E** **F**

St John's
Green Hills

Ridge Plantation
Leyfield Farm
Becca Banks
St John's Garth
HAYTON WOOD VW
Folly Corner
A1(M)

Barwick in Elmet
Ass Bridge
Moat
Barwick Lodge Plantation
Chantryhill Plantation
Pike's Head
PINFOLD RI

Stockheld Grange Farm
Rakehill Farm
Rake Hill
Springfield Farm
Hall Tower Hill
Lowfield Farm
School
Hungerhills Plantation
PH
Manor Farm
Aberford
School LA

LS15
Limekiln Hill
Richmondfield Garth
ELMET RD
Cherry Strip
Willowgarth Plantation
Whitehouse Farm
Cooper Wood

THE MOUNT
Barwick Bank
Highfield Farm
1 MAYPOLE MS
2 CHURCH FARM VW
3 POTTERTON CL
4 ELMWOOD GR
5 TITHE BARN FOLD
6 SCHOOLGATE
7 CROFTWAY
8 THE COPPICE
9 GASCOIGNE VW
10 THE CLOSE
11 RICHMONDFIELD CROSS
12 RICHMONDFIELD WY
13 RICHMONDFIELD CR
14 RICHMONDFIELD CL
15 RICHMONDFIELD GR

Old Wood
Home Farm
Aberford Park
Hangings Plantation
Hicklam House

PH
Moat
Honesty Farm
Lower Barnbow Farm
HIGHFIELD LANE
Throstle Nest Farm
Parlington
Parlington LA
Dawson's Wood

Upper Barnbow Farm
Barnbow Carr
Bathingwell Plantation
Parlington Park
Hook Moor

Barnbow Wood
Parlington Hollins
Fox Covert
Park House Farm
ABERFORD ROAD
48/44

Shippen Plantation
Willow Park Farm
Beech Plantation

Brown Moor
Barnbow Common Sports Ground
Stank House
Hawk's Nest Wood
LS25
47
Ridge Road Farm

LC
White House Farm
Beech House Farm
Brierlands LA
Sports Ground
Well House Farm
St Helen's Well
North End

M1
Crawshaw Wood
Barrowby Lane
NANNY GOAT LA
Lotherton Wy
East Garforth
Three Acre Plantation
Old Micklefield

Barrowby Hall
BARROWBY LANE
Sturton LA
Sturton Grange
Micklefield

Barrowby Carr
Carr Wood
Clearview Farm
A642
Garforth
OAK LA
Ludlow AV
Churchville AV
St Mary's WK

Bradbury Grange
Moorhouse Farm
PO
East Garforth
Roman Ridge Bridge

Warren House Farm
Swillington Common Farm
BARLEYHILL ROAD
CHURCH LA
GREEN LA
Stub Wood
A656

Swillington Common
PH
SPRINGBANK
ALANDALE CR
Coll
A63
Spoil Heap

SELBY ROAD
West Garforth
Kippax Lane End
Hammerton DR
Warren Farm

Hollinthorpe
BRECKS LANE
Long Meadow Gate
Cliff Top
SELBY ROAD
A63
Peckfield House Farm
Quarry

Syke House Farm
Brecks Wood
GARFORTH
Roach Grange Farm
Milestone Farm
Limekiln Farm
Peckfield Bar

Smeaton House Farm
LS26
Brecks Farm
Sparrow Hall Farm
Valley Ridge
Roach Hill
Roach Grange AV
The Hills
Peckfield Common

Swillington
WAKEFIELD ROAD
WHITEHOUSE LANE
Townclose Hills
LEEDS ROAD
B6137
Manor Garth RD
SANDGATE LANE
RIDGE ROAD
Warrenhouse Plantation

WHITECLIFFE CR
GOODY CROSS LANE
Owlett Hall Farm
Townclose Wood
Ling Close Wood
Ledston Luck

A642 Wakefield
PO
Little Preston
Goody Cross
SYCAMORE AV
Allot
Keble Garth
LIME-TREE CR
A656
Sheepcote Wood
Sheepcote Farm

GARFORTH
HIGH ST
Kippax
Spo

A 38 **B** 39 **C** 40 **D** 41 **E** 42 **F** 43

200

A1
1 WHITECLIFFE DR
2 LOWTHER DR
3 LOWTHER CR
4 CHURCH CL
5 SMEATON GR
6 THE PLEASANCE
7 WOODLAND GR
8 WOODLAND CR
9 WOODLAND AV
10 SPRINGWELL RD
11 SPRINGWELL AV
12 THE DR
13 SCOTT CL
14 ST MARY'S AV
15 PRIMROSE HL DR
16 PRIMROSE HL GR

For full street detail of Garforth see
Philip's **STREET ATLAS** of **West Yorkshire**

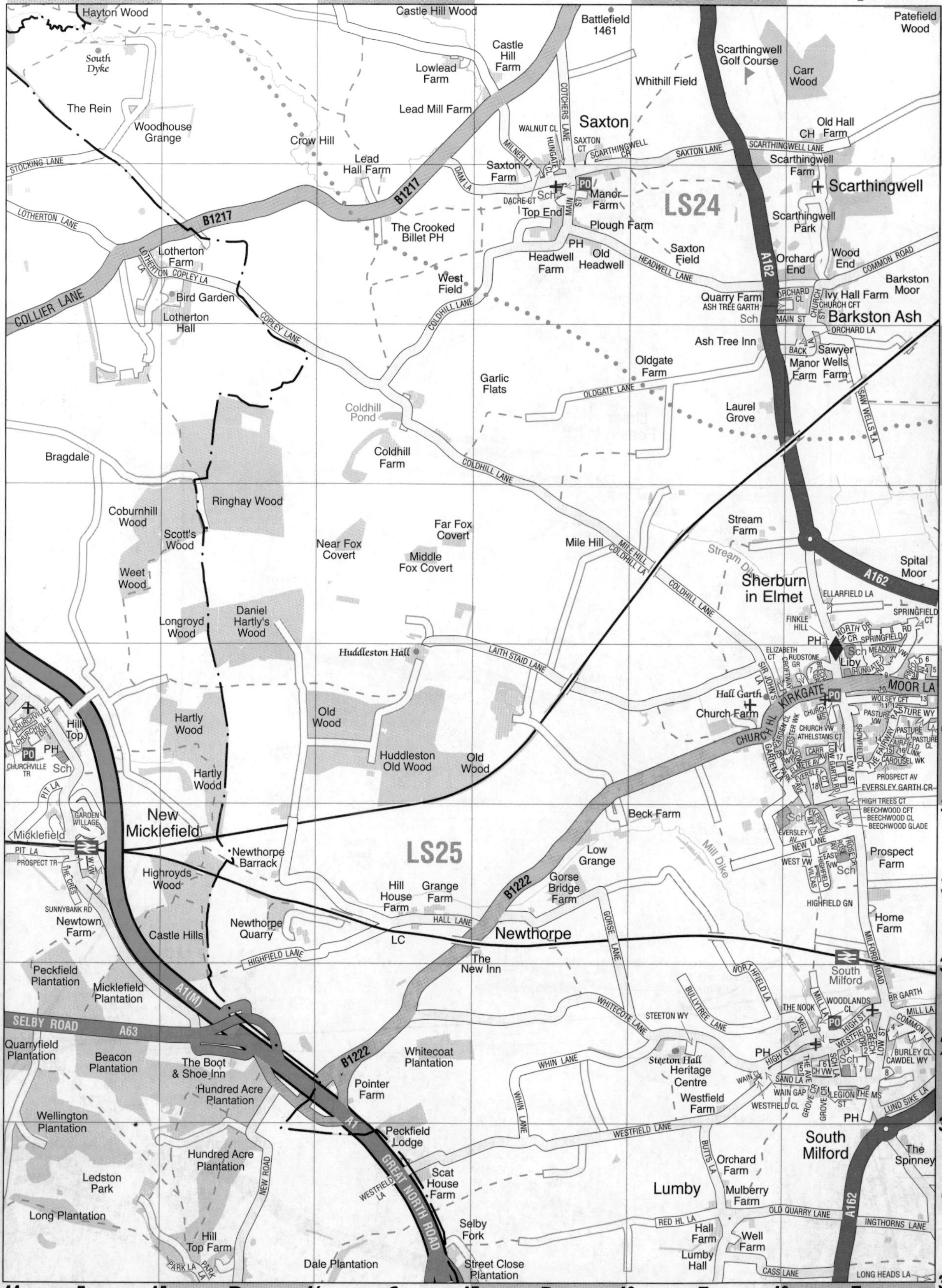

F2
1 WESTFIELD CT
2 MAPLE CL
3 BEECH CL
4 CAWDEL CL
5 THE HAVEN
6 ORCHARD CL
7 STEINCROFT RD
8 SOUTHLANDS CL

F4
1 DUFFIELD CR
2 E BANK
3 PINFOLD CL
4 PINFOLD CT
5 PINFOLD WY
6 PINFOLD GARTH
7 BEECH CL
8 CRICKETERS WY
9 MOOR RD
10 APPLETREE WY
11 WOLSEY CL
12 WOLSEY GD
13 CARDINAL CL
14 THE COPPICE
15 FAIRWAY CL
16 FAIRFIELD CL
17 LOW GARTH LINK
18 DEIGHTON AV

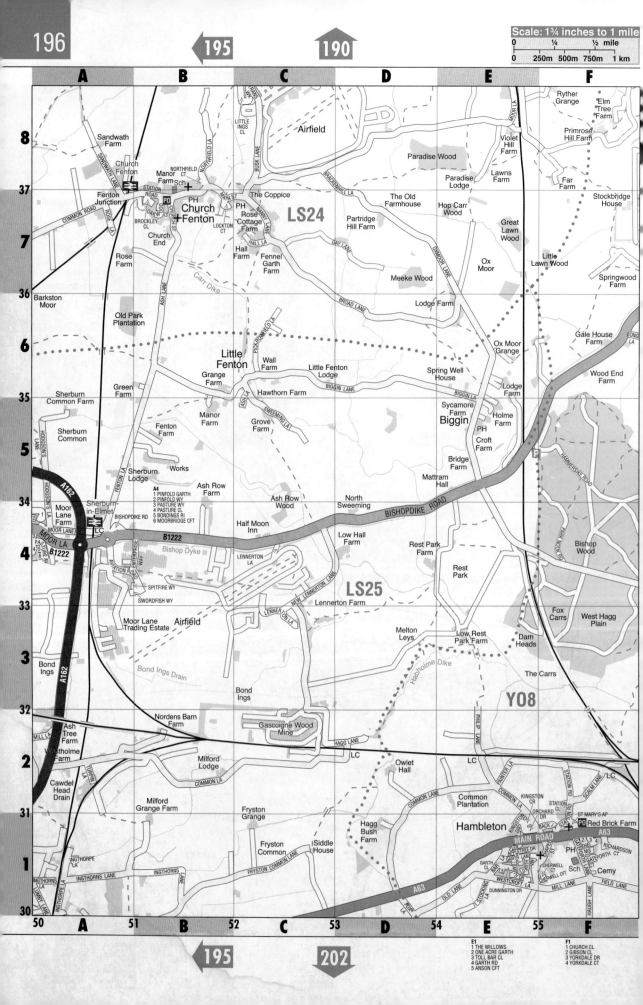

Scale: 1¾ inches to 1 mile

0   ¼   ½   mile
0   250m 500m 750m 1 km

Map labels:

Ryther Grange
Elm Tree Farm
Primrose Hill Farm
Sandwath Farm
Violet Hill Farm
Far Farm
Stockbridge House
Church Fenton
Manor Farm
Sch
NORTHFIELD CT
Paradise Wood
Paradise Lodge
Lawns Farm
Airfield
LITTLE INGS CL
NORTHFIELD LA
BUSK LANE
BRACKENHILL LA
MOOR LA
Fenton Junction
Station Road
PO
PH
The Coppice
MANN ST
The Old Farmhouse
Hop Carr Wood
Great Lawn Wood
LS24
Little Lawn Wood
Springwood Farm
Brockley Cl
Church End
Rose Cottage Farm
PH
Lockton Ct
Partridge Hill Farm
Ox Moor
Church Fenton
Hall Farm
Fennel Garth Farm
GAY LANE
Meeke Wood
COMMOOR LANE
Rose Farm
ROSE LA
HALL LA
Carr Dike
ASH LANE
Lodge Farm
Gale House Farm
LONG LA
Barkston Moor
BROAD LANE
Ox Moor Grange
Wood End Farm
Old Park Plantation
Little Fenton
Wall Farm
Little Fenton Lodge
Spring Well House
Ox Moor Grange
Lodge Farm
PICK ROWFIELD LA
Grange Farm
Little Fenton Lodge
BIGGIN LANE
BIGGIN LA
Sherburn Common Farm
Green Farm
Hawthorn Farm
Sycamore Farm
Holme Farm
HODGSON'S LANE
FENTON LA
ASH LA
SWEEMING LA
Biggin
PH
Sherburn Common
Fenton Farm
Manor Farm
Grove Farm
Croft Farm
Sherburn Lodge
Works
Ash Row Farm
Bridge Farm
Mattram Hall
A162
A4
1 PINFOLD GARTH
2 PINFOLD WY
3 PASTURE WY
4 PASTURE CL
5 BONDINGS RI
6 MOORBRIDGE CFT
Ash Row Wood
North Sweeming
P
HAMMERSIKE ROAD
Moor Lane Farm
Sherburn-in-Elmet
BISHOPDIKE RD
Half Moon Inn
BISHOPDIKE ROAD
Bishop Wood
HODGSON'S LA
LC
Low Hall Farm
Rest Park Farm
PARK NOOK LANE
PASTURE AV
B1222
Bishop Dyke
B1222
LENNERTON LA
Rest Park
Fox Carrs
West Hagg Plain
MOOR LA
ENTERPRISE WAY
LS25
AVIATION ROAD
SPITFIRE WY
Lennerton Farm
Melton Leys
Low Rest Park Farm
Dam Heads
SWORDFISH WY
NEW LENNERTON LA
LENNERTON LA
Habholme Dike
The Carrs
Moor Lane Trading Estate
Airfield
YO8
Bond Ings
Bond Ings Drain
Bond Ings
Nordens Barn Farm
Gascoigne Wood Mine
HAGG LANE
LC
PHILIP LANE
Ash Tree Farm
MILL LANE
Milford Lodge
Wastholme Farm
COMMON LA
Owlet Hall
Common Plantation
LC
PRINTER LA
STATION RD
SCALM LANE
LC
Cawdel Head Drain
TUPPIN LA
Milford Grange Farm
Fryston Grange
COMMON LANE
KINGSTON CR
STATION CL
Hambleton
ORCHARD DR
ST MARY'S AP
PO
Red Brick Farm
A63
A162
Fryston Common
Siddle House
Hagg Bush Farm
MAIN ROAD
PH
Sch
Cemy
RICHARDSON CL
Ingthorpe La
INGTHORPE LA
INGTHORNS LANE
FRYSTON COMMON LA
CHERWELL CR
CHERWELL CFT
WESTCROFT LA
GATEFORTH LANE
FIELD LANE
LIMBY LANE
A63
OLD LANE
MILL LANE
DUNNINGTON DR
HAUGH LANE

E1
1 THE WILLOWS
2 ONE ACRE GARTH
3 TOLL BAR CL
4 GARTH RD
5 ANSON CFT

F1
1 CHURCH CL
2 GIBSON CL
3 YORKDALE DR
4 YORKDALE CT

Scale: 1¾ inches to 1 mile
0 ¼ ½ mile
0 250m 500m 750m 1 km

B8
1 SHERBURN ST
2 MARKET PL
3 CARDINALS CL
4 OLD BOYS SCHOOL LA
5 GOLD THREAD LA
6 KING ST

D6
1 GREENWAYS DR
2 GREEN WAYS
3 MOORFIELDS
4 HILL TOP RD
5 CHURCH WK
6 GARTH CL
7 GEORGE ST
8 CHURCH HL
9 WOODALL CT

191

198

F8
1 ASH GR
2 HAWTHORNS
3 CHURCH ST
4 HALL FARM CL
5 VIKING DR
6 THE CRESCENT
7 NORSEMAN CL
8 WEST CT
9 KELFIELD RD

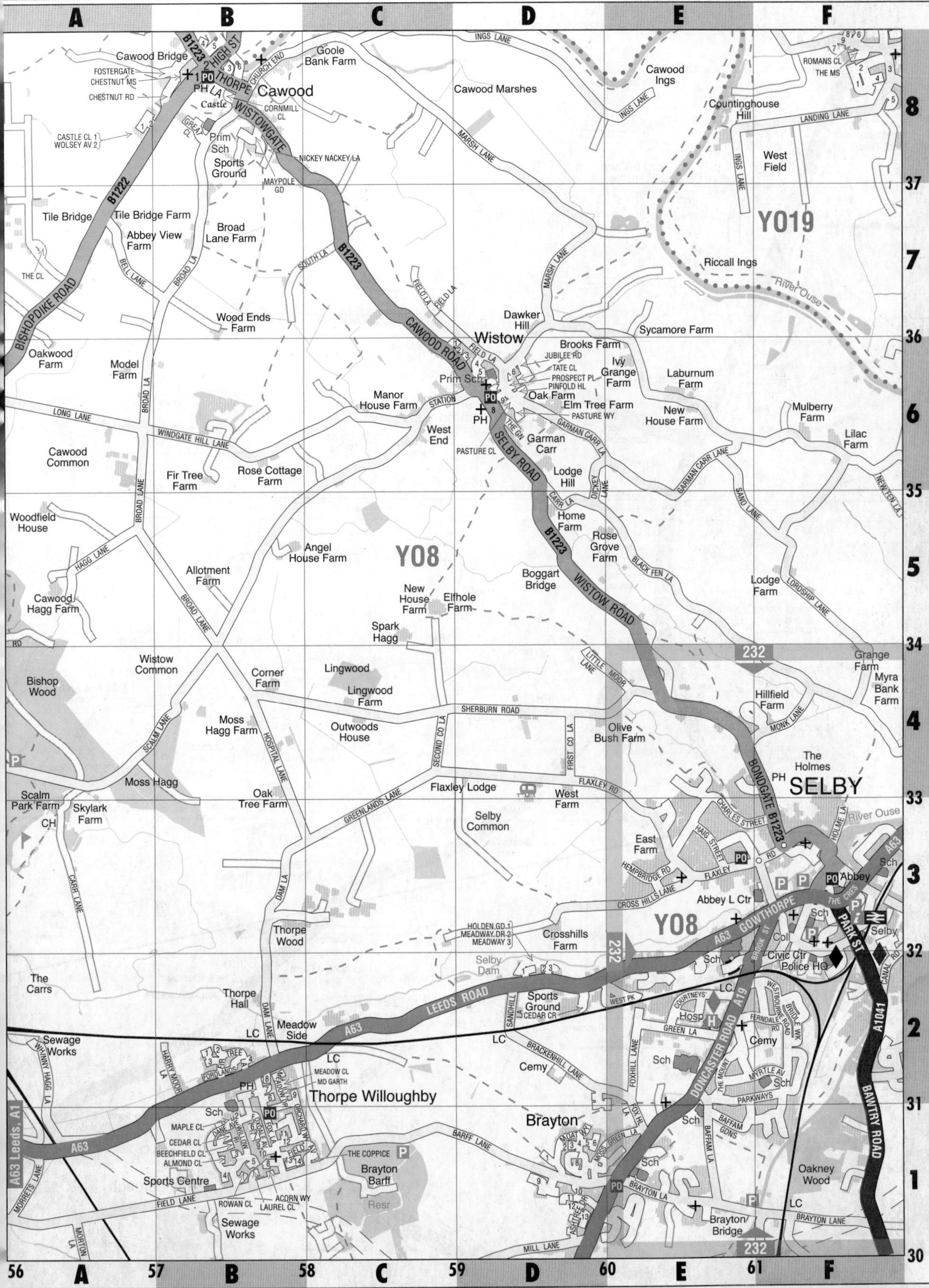

B1
1 SANDWAY DR
2 LIMETREE CL
3 LABURNUM CL
4 BIRCH CL
5 OAK DR
6 SAXON CL
7 NORMAN CL
8 BRAMBLES
9 STUART GR
10 TUDOR CL
11 SANDWAY CL
12 SANDWAY AV
13 WOOD LA
14 WOOD CL

B2
1 FIR TREE WY
2 PINE TREE CL
3 THE FIR TREES
4 FIR TREE CL
5 LONDESBOROUGH GR
6 BARFF GR
7 FRANCIS CT
8 HOLLY GR
9 LINDEN WY

203

D1
1 EVERGREEN WY
2 CONIFERS CL
3 GREENACRES GR
4 GREENACRES DR
5 SANDIACRES
6 GREENFIELD DR
7 GREENACRES CR
8 GREENACRES CL
9 ST WILFRID'S CR
10 BARFF CL
11 THE POPLARS
12 MAPLE GR
13 CHERRY TREE CL

232

For full street detail of the highlighted area see page 232.

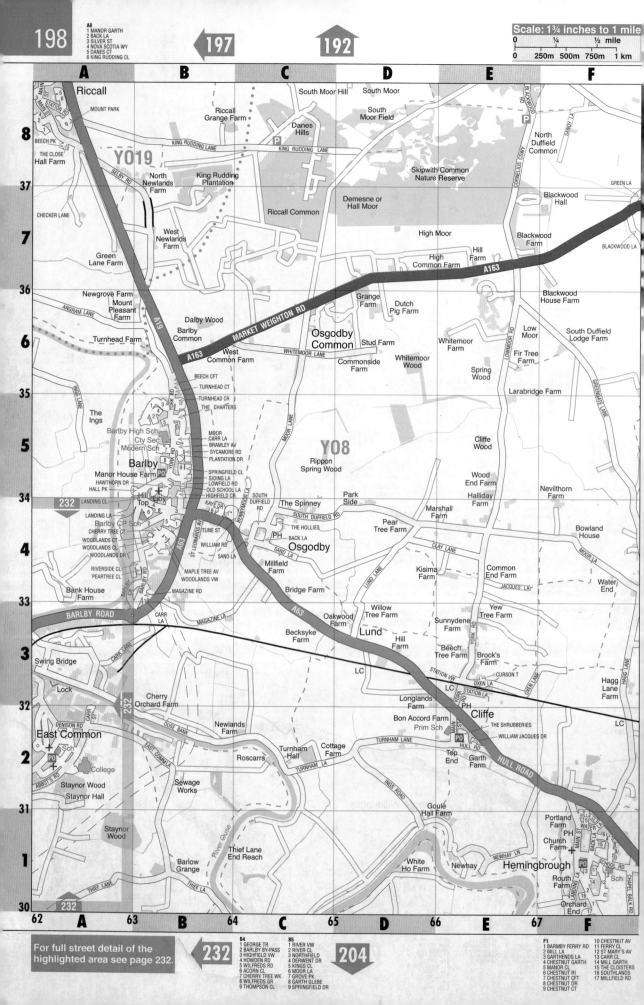

198

A8
1 MANOR GARTH
2 BACK LA
3 SILVER ST
4 NOVA SCOTIA WY
5 DANES CT
6 KING RUDDING CL

197   192

Scale: 1¾ inches to 1 mile

0   ¼   ½   mile
0   250m   500m   750m   1 km

Riccall

MOUNT PARK

YO19

BEECH PK

THE CLOSE
Hall Farm

CHECKER LANE

North Newlands
Farm

Riccall
Grange Farm

Danes
Hills

South Moor Hill   South Moor

South
Moor Field

King Rudding Lane

King Rudding
Plantation

Skipwith Common
Nature Reserve

North
Duffield
Common

Blackwood
Hall

West
Newlands
Farm

Riccall Common

Demesne or
Hall Moor

High Moor

Blackwood
Farm

GREEN LA

BLACKWOOD LA

Green
Lane Farm

Newgrove Farm
Mount
Pleasant
Farm

ANGRAM LANE

Turnhead Farm

Dalby Wood

Barlby
Common

West
Common Farm

WHITEMOOR LANE

High
Common Farm

Hill
Farm

A163

Blackwood
House Farm

Osgodby
Common

Grange
Farm

Dutch
Pig Farm

Low
Moor

Fir Tree
Farm

South Duffield
Lodge Farm

MARKET WEIGHTON RD

A163

BEECH CFT
Turnhead CT
Turnhead CR
THE CHARTERS

The
Ings

Barlby High Sch
Cty Sec
Modern Sch

Barlby

Manor House Farm
HAWTHORN DR
HALL PK

Hill
Top   Lby

Commonside
Farm

Whitemoor
Wood

Whitemoor
Farm

Spring
Wood

Larabridge Farm

YO8

Rippon
Spring Wood

Cliffe
Wood

Wood
End Farm

Nevilthorn
Farm

232   LANDING CL

LANDING LA
Barlby CP Sch
CHERRY TREE CT
WOODLANDS CT
WOODLANDS CL
WOODLANDS DR

MOOR
CARR LA
BRAMLEY AV
SYCAMORE RD
PLANTATION DR

SPRINGFIELD CL
SIDING LA
LOWFIELD RD
OLD SCHOOL LA
HIGHFIELD CR

SOUTH
DUFFIELD
RD

KAYE DR

BENTLEY LA

TUNE ST

WILLIAM RD

SAND LA

The Spinney

SOUTH DUFFIELD RD

THE HOLLIES

PH   BACK LA

Osgodby

Millfield
Farm

Park
Side

Marshall
Farm

Halliday
Farm

Pear
Tree Farm

CLAY LANE

Common
End Farm

Bowland
House

JACQUES' LA

Water
End

RIVERSIDE CL
PEARTREE CL

Bank House
Farm

ST LEONARDS AV

A63

BARLBY CR

BARLBY RD

MAPLE TREE AV
WOODLANDS VW

MAGAZINE RD

Bridge Farm

Kisima
Farm

LUND LANE

Willow
Tree Farm

Oakwood
Farm

Lund

Becksyke
Farm

Hill
Farm

Sunnydene
Farm

Beech
Tree Farm

YORK RD

Brock's
Farm

Yew
Tree Farm

MOOR LA

BARLBY ROAD

CARR
LA

MAGAZINE LA

A63

STATION VW

LC

OXEN LA

OXEN LANE

CURSON T

LC

STATION LA

Hagg
Lane
Farm

HAGG LANE

Swing Bridge

CARR LANE

LC

Longlands
Farm

STATION VW

YORK RD

LC

Lock

232

Cherry
Orchard Farm

OUSE BANK

Newlands
Farm

Bon Accord Farm
Prim Sch

PH

Cliffe

THE SHRUBBERIES

WILLIAM JACQUES DR

LC

DENISON RD

CARR ST

East Common

PO   Sch

College

ABBOT'S RD

EAST COMM LA

Roscarrs

Turnham
Hall

TURNHAM LA

Cottage
Farm

TURNHAM LANE

PO   HULL RD

Top
End

Garth
Farm

HULL ROAD

Staynor Wood

Staynor Hall

Sewage
Works

River Ouse

INGS ROAD

Goulé
Hall Farm

Portland
Farm

VILLA

WATER

PH
Church
Farm

BACK LA

Staynor
Wood

Barlow
Grange

THIEF LANE

Thief Lane
End Reach

THIEF LA

White
Ho Farm

NEWHAY LN

Newhay

Hemingbrough

LANDING RD

PO

Routh
Farm

Orchard
End

SCHOOL RD

Sch

CHAPEL BALK RD

232

62   A   63   B   64   C   65   D   66   E   67   F

For full street detail of the
highlighted area see page 232.

232   204

B4
1 GEORGE TR
2 BARLBY BY-PASS
3 HIGHFIELD VW
4 HOWDEN RD
5 WILFREDS RD
6 ACORN CL
7 CHERRY TREE WK
8 WILFREDS GR
9 THOMPSON CL

B5
1 RIVER VW
2 RIVER CL
3 NORTHFIELD
4 DERWENT DR
5 KINGS CL
6 MOOR LA
7 GROVE PK
8 GARTH GLEBE
9 SPRINGFIELD DR

F1
1 BARMBY FERRY RD
2 MILL LA
3 GARTHENDS LA
4 CHESTNUT GARTH
5 MANOR CL
6 CHESTNUT RI
7 CHESTNUT CFT
8 CHESTNUT DR
9 CHESTNUT CT
10 CHESTNUT AV
11 FERRY CL
12 ST MARY'S AV
13 CARR CL
14 MILL GARTH
15 THE CLOISTERS
16 SOUTHLANDS
17 MILLFIELD RD

193

Scale: 1¾ inches to 1 mile

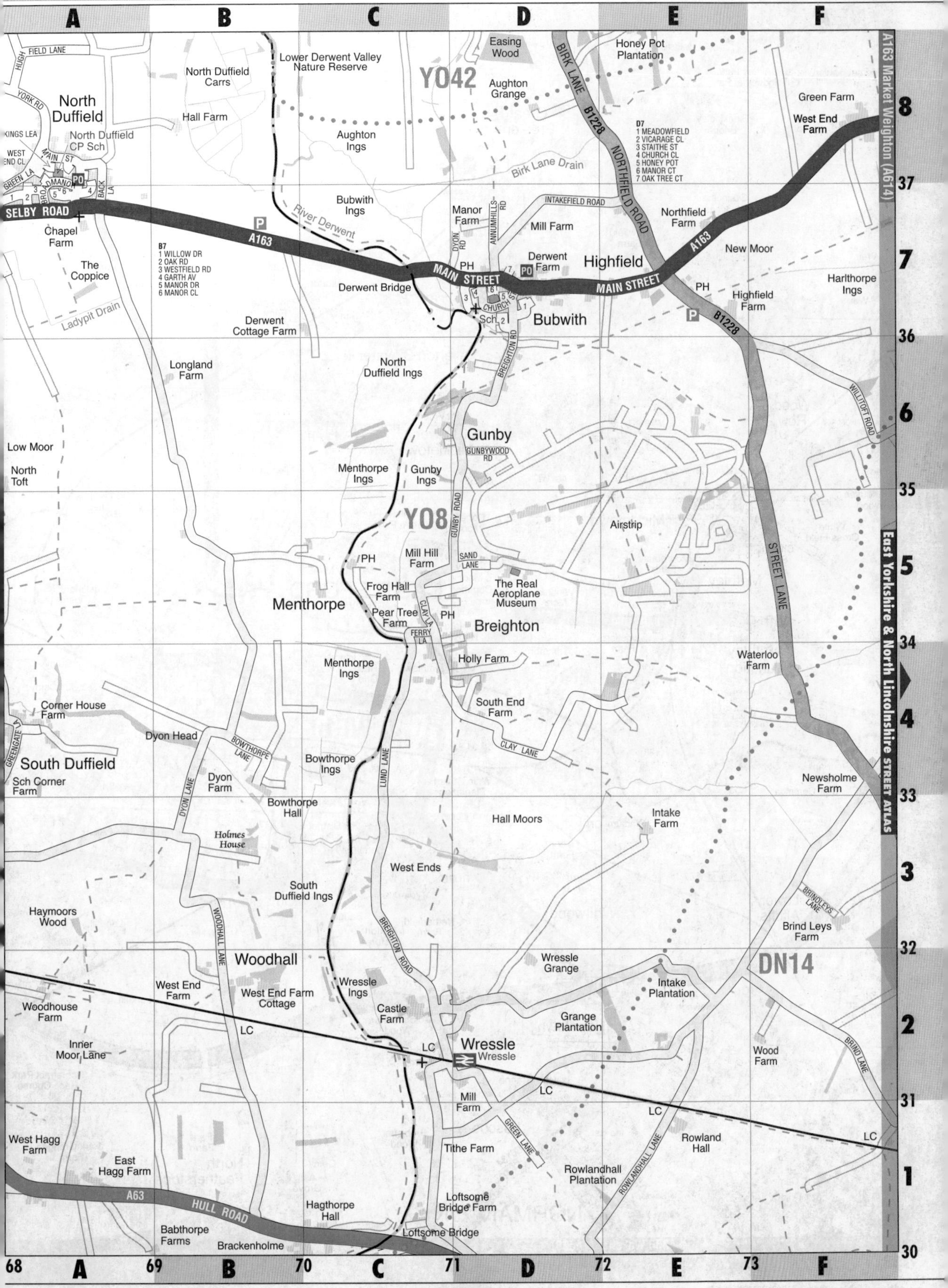
A
B
C
D
E
F
North Duffield
North Duffield Carrs
Lower Derwent Valley Nature Reserve
Easing Wood
Honey Pot Plantation
YO42
Aughton Grange
Green Farm
West End Farm
Hall Farm
North Duffield CP Sch
Aughton Ings
D7
1 MEADOWFIELD
2 VICARAGE CL
3 STAITHE ST
4 CHURCH CL
5 HONEY POT
6 MANOR CT
7 OAK TREE CT
Birk Lane Drain
SELBY ROAD
Chapel Farm
Bubwith Ings
River Derwent
Manor Farm
Mill Farm
INTAKEFIELD ROAD
Northfield Farm
B7
1 WILLOW DR
2 OAK RD
3 WESTFIELD RD
4 GARTH AV
5 MANOR DR
6 MANOR CL
A163
The Coppice
Derwent Farm
Highfield
New Moor
MAIN STREET
Derwent Bridge
Harlthorpe Ings
Highfield Farm
Ladypit Drain
Bubwith
B1228
Derwent Cottage Farm
North Duffield Ings
Longland Farm
BIRK LANE
NORTHFIELD ROAD
Low Moor
North Toft
Gunby
GUNBYWOOD RD
Menthorpe Ings
Gunby Ings
YO8
GUNBY ROAD
Airstrip
STREET LANE
Mill Hill Farm
SAND LANE
The Real Aeroplane Museum
Frog Hall Farm
Menthorpe
Pear Tree Farm
Breighton
CLAY LA
FERRY LA
Holly Farm
Menthorpe Ings
Waterloo Farm
Corner House Farm
South End Farm
Dyon Head
BOWTHORPE LANE
CLAY LANE
South Duffield
Bowthorpe Ings
Sch Corner Farm
Dyon Farm
Newsholme Farm
Bowthorpe Hall
LUND LANE
DYON LANE
Hall Moors
Intake Farm
Holmes House
West Ends
South Duffield Ings
BRINDLEYS LANE
Haymoors Wood
Brind Leys Farm
Woodhall
WOODHALL LANE
Wressle Grange
DN14
BREIGHTON ROAD
West End Farm
West End Farm Cottage
Wressle Ings
Intake Plantation
Castle Farm
Woodhouse Farm
Grange Plantation
LC
Wressle
Inner Moor Lane
Wood Farm
BRIND LANE
Mill Farm
West Hagg Farm
GREEN LANE
Tithe Farm
Rowland Hall
ROWLANDHALL LANE
East Hagg Farm
Rowlandhall Plantation
A63
HULL ROAD
Loftsome Bridge Farm
Hagthorpe Hall
Babthorpe Farms
Loftsome Bridge
Brackenholme
A163 Market Weighton (A614)
East Yorkshire & North Lincolnshire STREET ATLAS
68
69
70
71
72
73
30
31
32
33
34
35
36
37
1
2
3
4
5
6
7
8

205

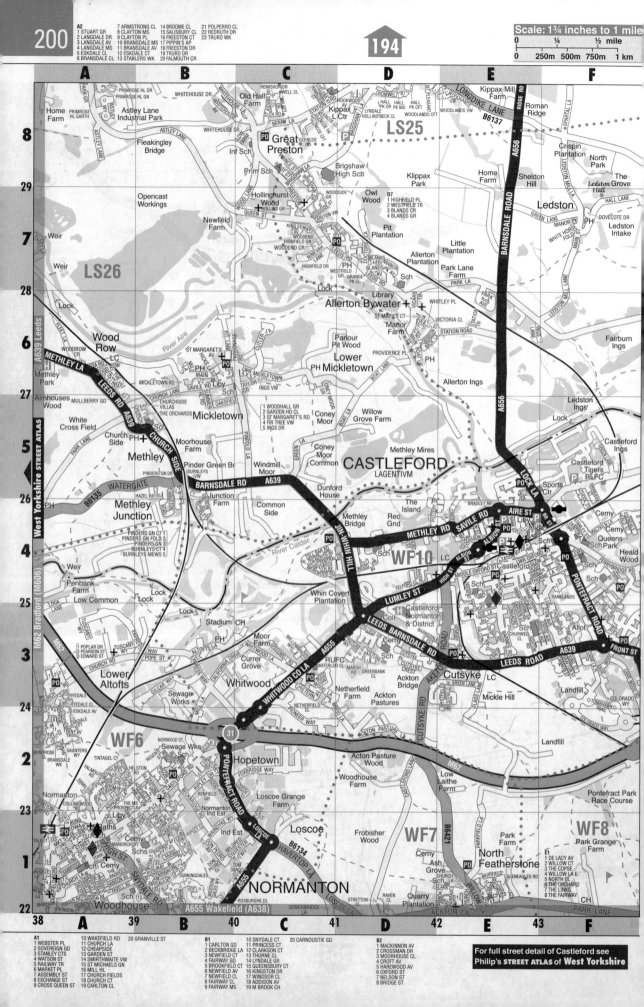

A2
1 STUART GR
2 LANGDALE DR
3 LANGDALE AV
4 LANGDALE MS
5 ESKDALE CL
6 BRANSDALE CL
7 ARMSTRONG CL
8 CLAYTON MS
9 CLAYTON PL
10 BRANSDALE AV
11 BRANSDALE MS
12 ESKDALE CT
13 STABLERS WK
14 BROOME CL
15 SALISBURY CL
16 FREESTON CT
17 PIPPIN'S AP
18 FREESTON DR
19 TRURO DR
20 FALMOUTH CR
21 POLPERRO CL
22 REDRUTH CT
23 TRURO WK

Scale: 1¾ inches to 1 mile

A1
1 WEBSTER PL
2 SOVEREIGN GD
3 STANLEY CTS
4 WATSON ST
5 RAILWAY TR
6 MARKET PL
7 ASSEMBLY ST
8 EXCHANGE ST
9 CROSS QUEEN ST
10 WAKEFIELD RD
11 CHURCH LA
12 CHEAPSIDE
13 GARDEN ST
14 SMITHWAITE VW
15 ST MICHAELS GN
16 MILL HL
17 CHURCH FIELDS
18 CHURCH CT
19 CARLTON CL
20 GRANVILLE ST

B1
1 CARLTON GD
2 BECKBRIDGE LA
3 NEWFIELD CT
4 FAIRWAY WY
5 BROOKFIELD CT
6 NEWFIELD AV
7 NEWFIELD CL
8 FAIRWAY CL
9 FAIRWAY MS
10 SNYDALE CT
11 PRINCESS CT
12 CLARKSON CT
13 THORNE CL
14 LYNDALE CL
15 QUEENSBURY CT
16 KINGSTON DR
17 WINDSOR CL
18 ADDISON AV
19 M BROOK CH
20 CARNOUSTIE GD

B2
1 MACKINNON AV
2 CROSSMAN DR
3 MOORHOUSE CL
4 CROFT AV
5 HAREWOOD AV
6 OXFORD ST
7 NELSON ST
8 BRIDGE ST

E1
1 DE LACY AV
2 WILLOW CT
3 THE COPSE
4 WILLOW LA E
5 NORTH CL
6 THE ORCHARD
7 THE LINKS
8 THE FAIRWAY

D7
1 HIGHFIELD PL
2 WESTFIELD TR
3 BLANDS GR
4 BLANDS GR

1 WOODHALL GR
2 GARDEN HO CL
3 ST MARGARET'S RD
4 FIR TREE VW
5 INGS DR

For full street detail of Castleford see Philip's STREET ATLAS of West Yorkshire

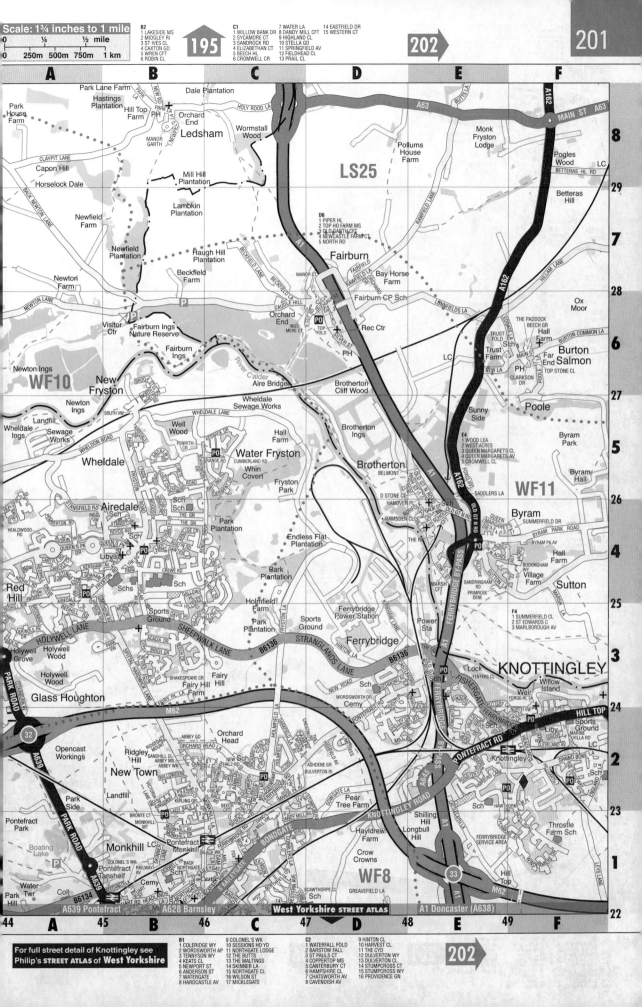

Scale: 1¾ inches to 1 mile

0 ¼ ½ mile
0 250m 500m 750m 1 km

195
202
202

B2
1 LAKESIDE MS
2 MIDGLEY RI
3 ST IVES CL
4 CAXTON GD
5 WREN CFT
6 ROBIN CL

C1
1 WILLOW BANK DR
2 SYCAMORE CT
3 SANDROCK RD
4 ELIZABETHAN CT
5 BEECH HL
6 CROMWELL CR

7 WATER LA
8 DANDY MILL CFT
9 HIGHLAND CL
10 STELLA GD
11 SPRINGFIELD AV
12 FIELDHEAD CL
13 PRAIL CL

14 EASTFIELD DR
15 WESTERN CT

D6
1 PIPER HL
2 TOP HO FARM MS
3 OLD GARTH CFT
4 NEWCASTLE FARM CT
5 NORTH RD

E4
1 WOOD LEA
2 WEST ACRES
3 QUEEN MARGARETS CL
4 QUEEN MARGARETS AV
5 CROMWELL CL

F4
1 SUMMERFIELD CL
2 ST EDWARDS C
3 MARLBOROUGH AV

LS25

WF10

WF11

Byram

Sutton

Ferrybridge

KNOTTINGLEY

Knottingley

WF8

For full street detail of Knottingley see
Philip's STREET ATLAS of West Yorkshire

West Yorkshire STREET ATLAS

B1
1 COLERIDGE WY
2 WORDSWORTH AP
3 TENNYSON WY
4 KEATS CL
5 NEWPORT ST
6 ANDERSON ST
7 WATERGATE
8 HARDCASTLE AV

9 COLONEL'S WK
10 SESSIONS HO YD
11 NORTHGATE LODGE
12 THE BUTTS
13 THE MALTINGS
14 SKINNER LA
15 NORTHGATE CL
16 WILSON ST
17 MICKLEGATE

C2
1 WATERFALL FOLD
2 BARSTOW FALL
3 ST PAULS CT
4 COPPERTOP MS
5 CANTERBURY CT
6 HAMPSHIRE CL
7 CHATSWORTH AV
8 CAVENDISH AV

9 HINTON CL
10 HARVEST CL
11 THE CYD
12 DULVERTON WY
13 DULVERTON CL
14 STUMPCROSS CT
15 STUMPCROSS GN
16 PROVIDENCE WY

A8
1 DEER PK CT
2 PRIORY PARK GR
3 PRIORY PARK CL
4 CHURCH LA
5 OLD VICARAGE LA
6 ORCHARD CL
7 THE MEADOWS
8 HILLCREST
9 HILLSIDE CL

201

A7
1 PINE TREE LA
2 ROSE LEA CL
3 HILLAM HALL VW
4 HILLAM HALL LA
5 HILLIAM HALL CL
6 BEDFORDS FOLD

196

Scale: 1¾ inches to 1 mile
0 ¼ ½ mile
0 250m 500m 750m 1 km

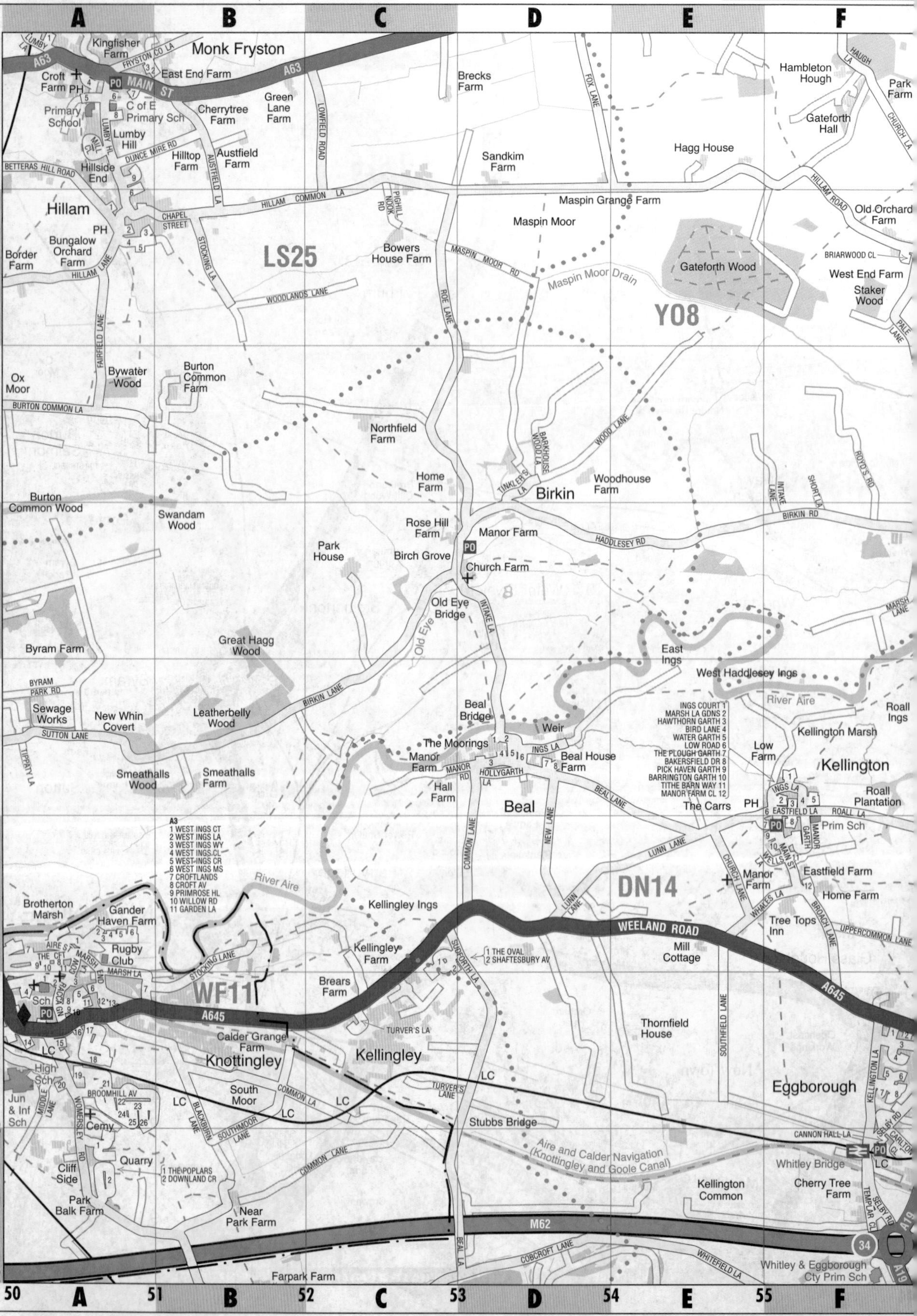

A3
1 WEST INGS CT
2 WEST INGS LA
3 WEST INGS WY
4 WEST INGS CL
5 WEST INGS CR
6 WEST INGS MS
7 CROFTLANDS
8 CROFT AV
9 PRIMROSE HL
10 WILLOW RD
11 GARDEN LA

E4
INGS COURT 1
MARSH LA GDNS 2
HAWTHORN GARTH 3
BIRD LANE 4
WATER GARTH 5
LOW ROAD 6
THE PLOUGH GARTH 7
BAKERSFIELD DR 8
PICK HAVEN GARTH 9
BARRINGTON GARTH 10
TITHE BARN WAY 11
MANOR FARM CL 12

A2
1 PRIMROSE VALE
2 TITHE BARN RD
3 SUNNY BANK
4 ST BOLTOPHS CL
5 FOUNDRY LA
6 FERNLEY GREEN CL
7 TRUNDLES LA
8 GRENLEY ST
9 LAMB INN RD
10 EAST VW
11 RACCA AV
12 HARKER ST
13 LOW GN
14 MIDDLE LA
15 GILLANN ST
16 WEELAND CT
17 SPRINGFIELDS AV
18 SPRINGFIELDS
19 BROOMHILL GR
20 QUARRY AV
21 BROOMHILL WK
22 BROOMHILL PL
23 BROOMHILL CL
24 BROOMHILL SQ
25 BROOMHILL CR
26 BROOMHILL DR

201

206

D4
1 GARTH MILL
2 MARSH LA
3 MAIN ST
4 RIVERDALE
5 CRAVEN GARTH
6 BROAD LA
7 VILLAGE FARM CT
8 GABLES CL

F2
1 WESTFIELD RD
2 WESTFIELD CL
3 WESTFIELD AV
4 WESTFIELD GR
5 TABARD HAMLET
6 TABARD RD
7 THE TABARDS
8 THE HAMLET

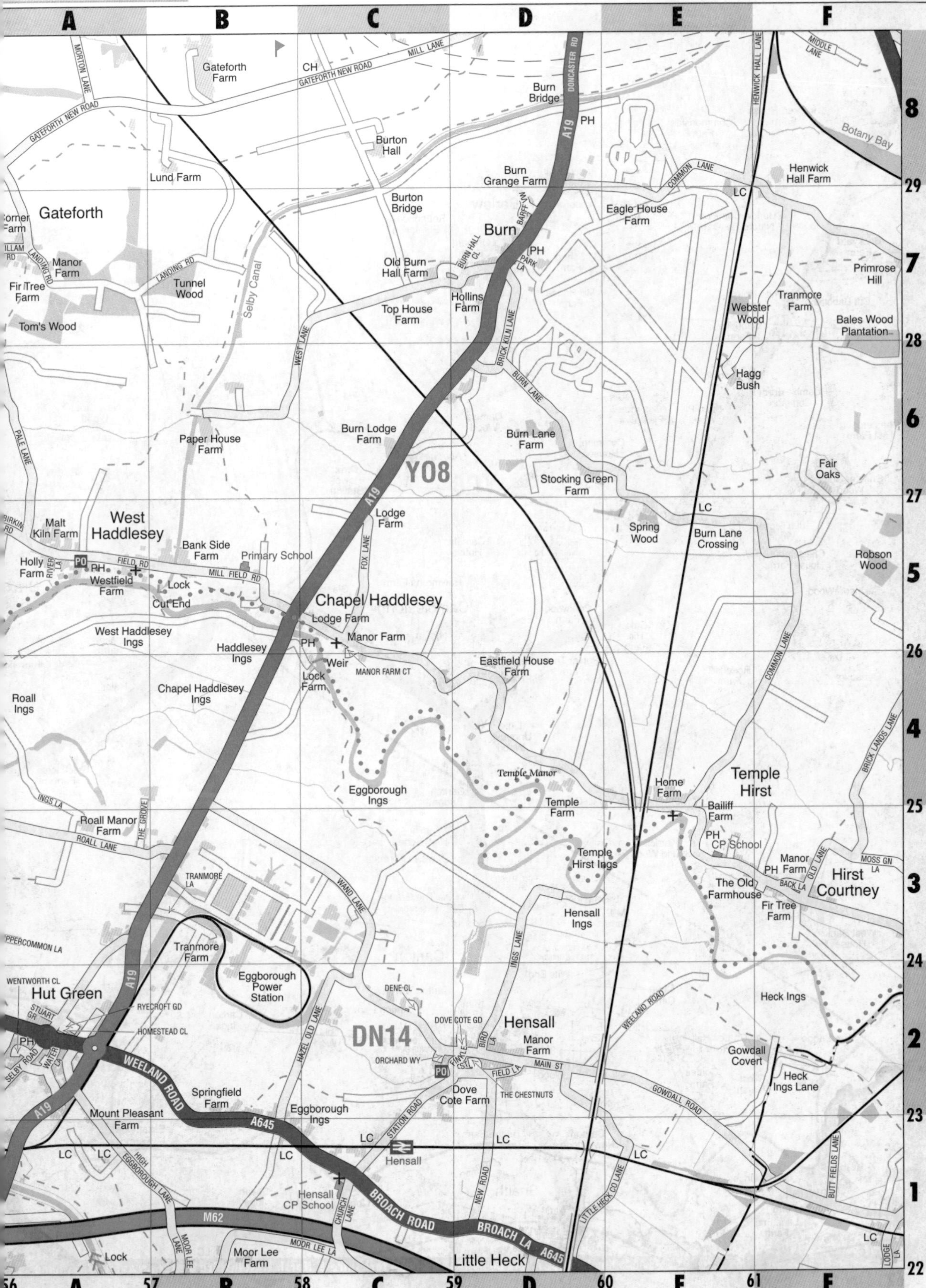
A
B
C
D
E
F
Gateforth Farm
CH
Gateforth New Road
Mill Lane
Morton Lane
Gateforth New Road
Burn Bridge
Doncaster Rd
A19
PH
Burton Hall
Lund Farm
Burn Grange Farm
Common Lane
Henwick Hall Farm
Henwick Hall Lane
Middle Lane
Botany Bay
LC
Gateforth
Corner Farm
Burton Bridge
Eagle House Farm
Burn
Manor Farm
Landing Rd
Old Burn Hall Farm
PH
Primrose Hill
Fir Tree Farm
Tunnel Wood
Selby Canal
Hollins Farm
Tranmore Farm
Top House Farm
Webster Wood
Bales Wood Plantation
Tom's Wood
West Lane
Brick Kiln Lane
Burn Lane
Hagg Bush
Pale Lane
Paper House Farm
Burn Lodge Farm
Burn Lane Farm
YO8
Fair Oaks
Stocking Green Farm
Malt Kiln Farm
West Haddlesey
Lodge Farm
LC
Spring Wood
Burn Lane Crossing
Bank Side Farm
Primary School
Fox Lane
Robson Wood
Holly Farm
PO
PH
Field Rd
Westfield Farm
Mill Field Rd
Lock
Chapel Haddlesey
Cut End
Lodge Farm
West Haddlesey Ings
Manor Farm
PH
Haddlesey Ings
Weir
Manor Farm Ct
Eastfield House Farm
Lock Farm
Common Lane
Chapel Haddlesey Ings
Roall Ings
Brick Lands Lane
Temple Manor
Eggborough Ings
Temple Hirst
Home Farm
Temple Farm
Bailiff Farm
Ings La
Roall Manor Farm
The Grove
Roall Lane
PH
CP School
Temple Hirst Ings
Manor Farm
PH
Old Lane
Moss Gn La
Tranmore La
Wand Lane
Back La
Hirst Courtney
The Old Farmhouse
Fir Tree Farm
Hensall Ings
Ings Lane
Tranmore Farm
Eggborough Power Station
Heck Ings
Wentworth Cl
Hut Green
Ryecroft Gd
Dene Cl
Weeland Road
Stuart Gr
Homestead Cl
Hazel Old Lane
Dove Cote Gd
Hensall
PH
Manor Farm
DN14
Gowdall Covert
Selby Road
Water La
Orchard Wy
PO
Main St
Field La
Heck Ings Lane
Weeland Road
Springfield Farm
Dove Cote Farm
The Chestnuts
Gowdall Road
A19
Mount Pleasant Farm
A645
Eggborough Ings
Station Road
LC
LC
LC
LC
LC
Hensall
LC
High Eggborough Lane
Butt Fields Lane
Hensall CP School
New Road
Little Heck Co Lane
M62
Church Lane
Broach Road
Broach La
LC
Moor Lee Lane
Lock
Moor Lee Farm
Moor Lee La
Little Heck
A645
Lodge La
8
29
7
28
6
27
5
26
4
25
3
24
2
23
1
22
56
57
58
59
60
61

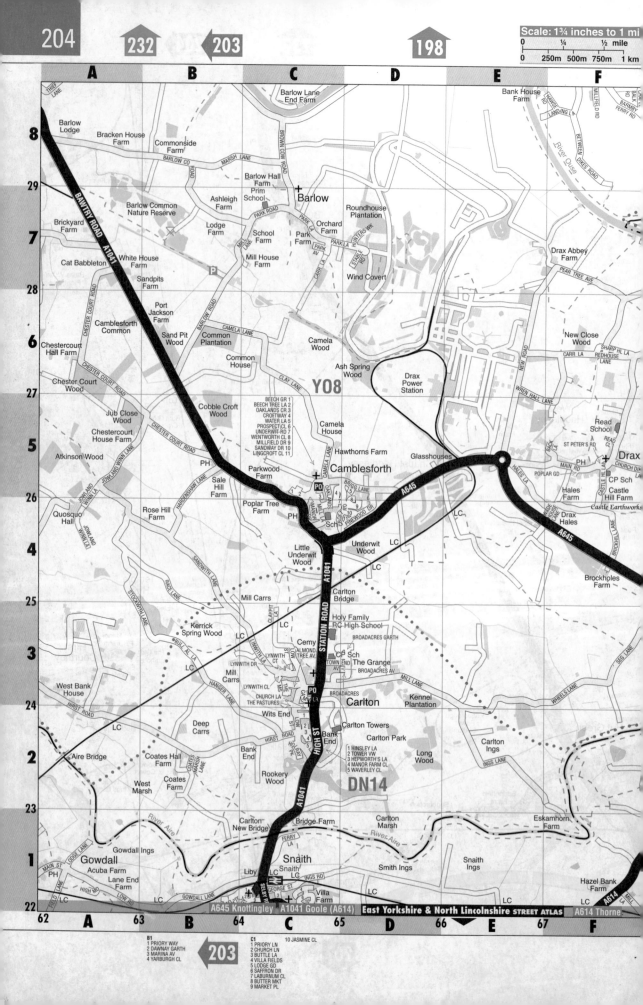

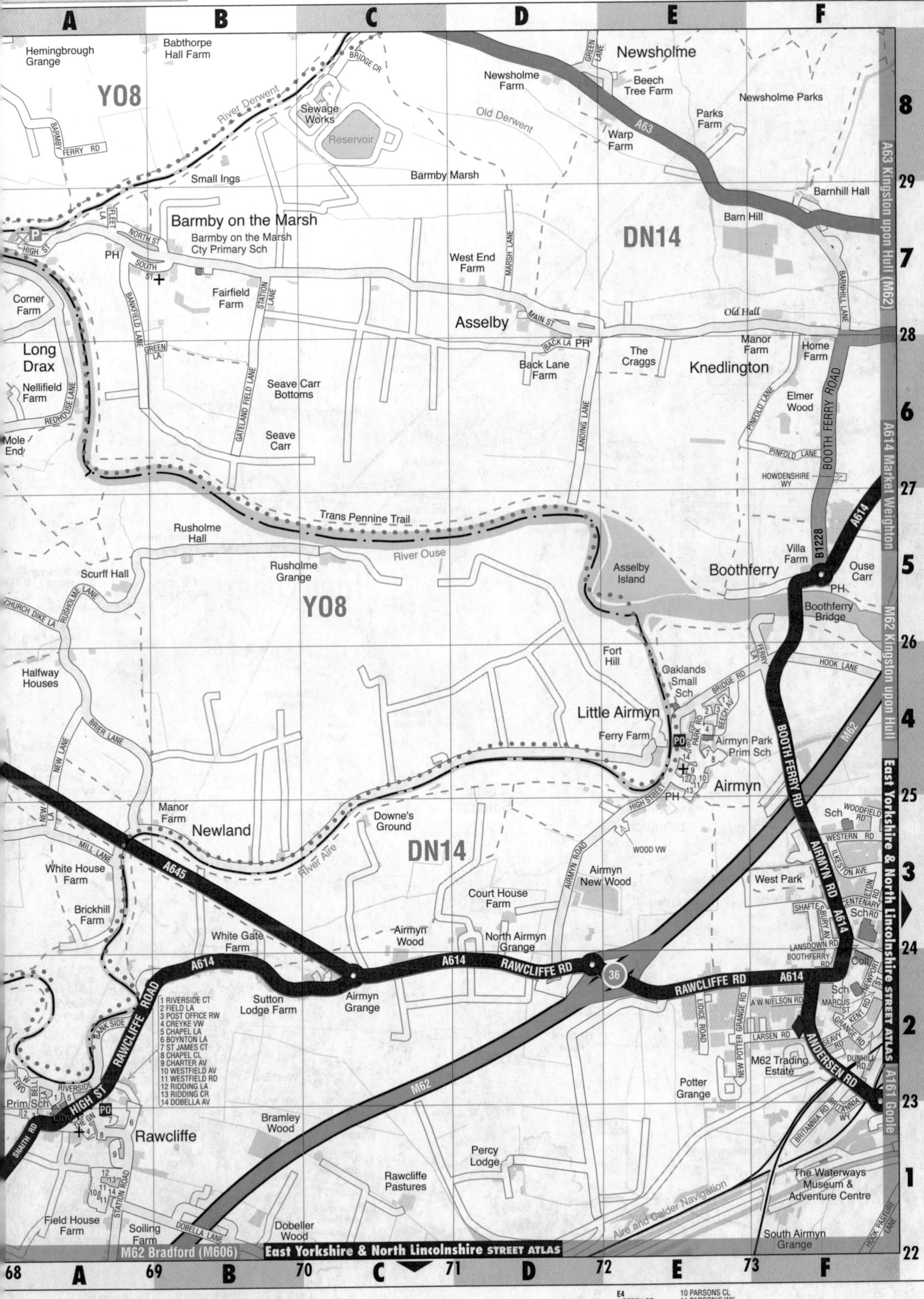

Hemingbrough Grange

Babthorpe Hall Farm

YO8

Newsholme

Newsholme Farm

Beech Tree Farm

Newsholme Parks

Parks Farm

BRIDGE CR

Sewage Works

Reservoir

Old Derwent

Warp Farm

A63

Small Ings

Barmby Marsh

Barnhill Hall

DN14

Barn Hill

Barmby on the Marsh

Barmby on the Marsh Cty Primary Sch

Fairfield Farm

West End Farm

MARSH LANE

Asselby

Old Hall

Manor Farm

Home Farm

Corner Farm

Back La PH

The Craggs

Knedlington

Elmer Wood

Long Drax

Back Lane Farm

Nellifield Farm

Seave Carr Bottoms

Landing Lane

Pinfold Lane

Mole End

Seave Carr

Pinfold Lane

Howdenshire Wy

Trans Pennine Trail

Rusholme Hall

River Ouse

Asselby Island

Villa Farm

Boothferry

Ouse Carr

Scurff Hall

Rusholme Grange

YO8

Boothferry Bridge

Fort Hill

Oaklands Small Sch

Hook Lane

Halfway Houses

Little Airmyn

Ferry Farm

Airmyn Park Prim Sch

Airmyn

Manor Farm

Newland

Downe's Ground

DN14

Airmyn New Wood

West Park

White House Farm

Court House Farm

Airmyn Road

Wood Vw

Brickhill Farm

Airmyn Wood

North Airmyn Grange

White Gate Farm

A614

A614 RAWCLIFFE RD

36

RAWCLIFFE RD A614

Sutton Lodge Farm

Airmyn Grange

M62

Bramley Wood

Rawcliffe

Rawcliffe Pastures

Percy Lodge

Potter Grange

M62 Trading Estate

The Waterways Museum & Adventure Centre

Field House Farm

Soiling Farm

Dobella Lane

Dobeller Wood

Aire and Calder Navigation

South Airmyn Grange

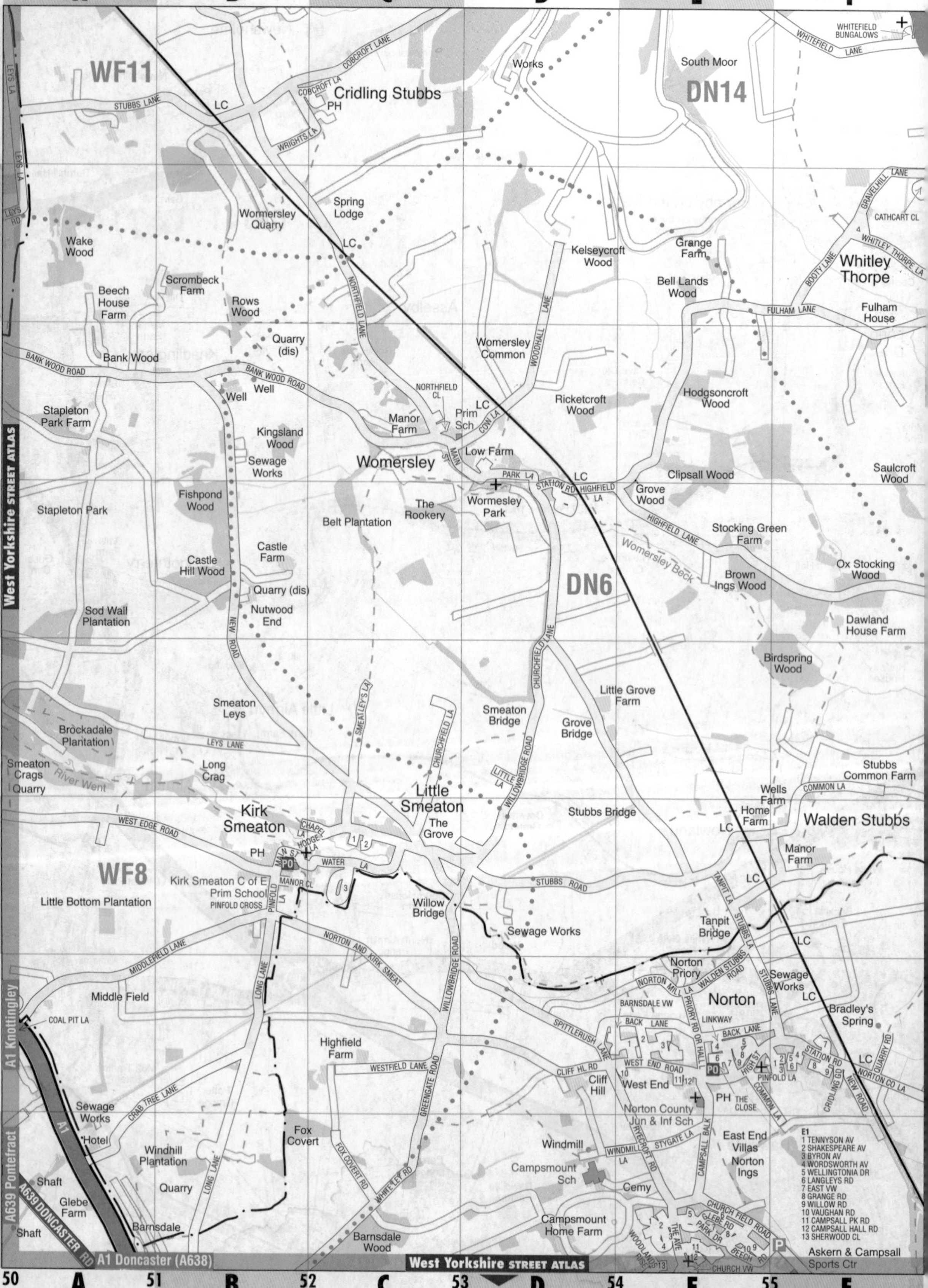

Scale: 1¾ inches to 1 mile

| 0 | ¼ | ½ | mile |
| 0 | 250m | 500m | 750m | 1 km |

WF11

DN14

Cridling Stubbs

WHITEFIELD BUNGALOWS

South Moor

Whitley Thorpe

Womersley Quarry

Spring Lodge

Wake Wood

Kelseycroft Wood

Grange Farm

Bell Lands Wood

Fulham House

Beech House Farm

Scrombeck Farm

Rows Wood

Womersley Common

Bank Wood

Quarry (dis)

Northfield CL

Ricketcroft Wood

Hodgsoncroft Wood

Stapleton Park Farm

Well

Well

Manor Farm

Prim Sch

Low Farm

Clipsall Wood

Saulcroft Wood

Kingsland Wood

Sewage Works

Womersley

Park La

Grove Wood

Stocking Green Farm

Ox Stocking Wood

Stapleton Park

Fishpond Wood

The Rookery

Wormesley Park

Highfield La

Womersley Beck

Brown Ings Wood

Belt Plantation

Castle Hill Wood

Castle Farm

Highfield Lane

Dawland House Farm

Sod Wall Plantation

Quarry (dis)

Nutwood End

Birdspring Wood

Smeaton Leys

Smeaton Bridge

Grove Bridge

Little Grove Farm

Stubbs Common Farm

Brockadale Plantation

Leys Lane

Long Crag

Churchfield La

Little La

Wells Home Farm

Common La

Smeaton Crags Quarry

River Went

Kirk Smeaton

Little Smeaton

The Grove

Stubbs Bridge

Walden Stubbs

West Edge Road

PH

Manor Farm

WF8

Kirk Smeaton C of E Prim School

Pinfold Cross

Willow Bridge

Stubbs Road

Norton Priory

Tanpit Bridge

Sewage Works

Little Bottom Plantation

Sewage Works

Norton

Bradley's Spring

Middle Field

Coal Pit La

Barnsdale Vw

Linkway

Highfield Farm

Westfield Lane

Cliff Hl Rd

West End Road

Cliff Hill

West End

PH The Close

East End Villas Norton Ings

Sewage Works

Hotel

Windhill Plantation

Fox Covert

Norton County Jun & Inf Sch

Shaft

Glebe Farm

Quarry

Windmill

Campsmount Sch

Cemy

Campsmount Home Farm

Barnsdale Wood

Askern & Campsall Sports Ctr

Shaft

Barnsdale

A1 Doncaster (A638)

West Yorkshire STREET ATLAS

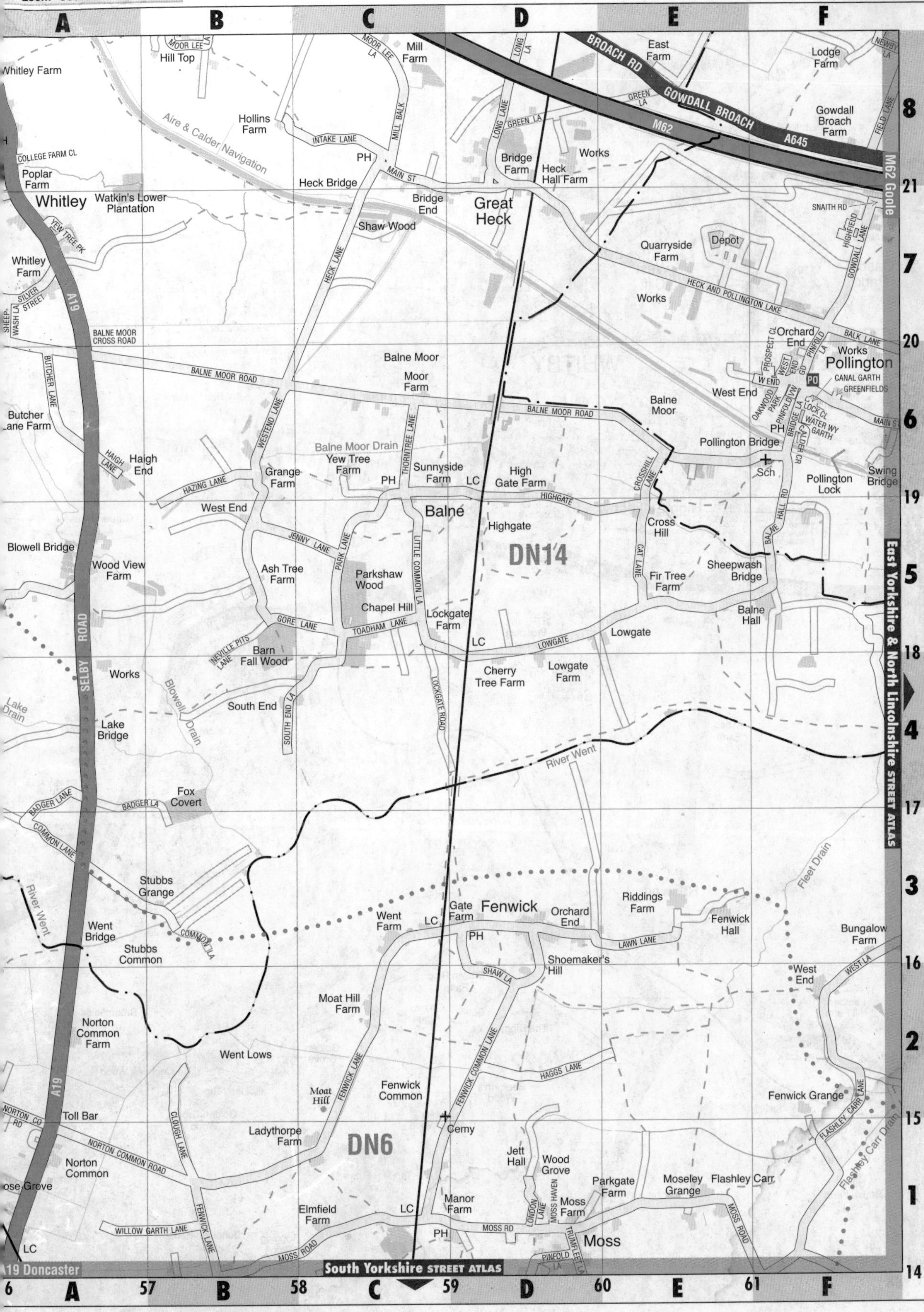

Scale: 1¾ inches to 1 mile

¼   ½   mile

250m 500m 750m   1 km

A   B   C   D   E   F

8

MOOR LEE LA

Whitley Farm

Hill Top

MOOR LEE LA

Mill Farm

BROACH RD

East Farm

Lodge Farm

NEWBY LA

Hollins Farm

Aire & Calder Navigation

INTAKE LANE

GREEN LA

GOWDALL BROACH

M62

A645

Gowdall Broach Farm

FIELD LANE

M62 Goole

21

College Farm Cl

PH

Heck Bridge

MILL BALK

MAIN ST

Long Green La

LONG LA

Bridge Farm

Works

SNAITH RD

Poplar Farm

Whitley

Watkin's Lower Plantation

Bridge End

Shaw Wood

Great Heck

Heck Hall Farm

7

Whitley Farm

YEW TREE PK

A19

HECK LANE

Quarryside Farm

Depot

HIGHFIELD

GOWDALL LANE

SILVER STREET

SHEEP WASH LA

Works

HECK AND POLLINGTON LAKE

BALK LANE

20

BALNE MOOR CROSS ROAD

BALNE MOOR ROAD

Balne Moor

Orchard End

Works

W END

PROSPECT CL

DAKWOOD

WEST

Pollington

PO

Canal Garth

Greenfields

Butcher Lane Farm

BUTCHER LANE

Moor Farm

BALNE MOOR ROAD

Balne Moor

West End

PINFOLD

BRIDGE

LOCK CL

WATER GARTH

MAIN S

6

HAIGH LANE

Haigh End

WESTEND LANE

YEW TREE FARM

THORNTREE LANE

Grange Farm

PH

Sunnyside Farm

LC

High Gate Farm

HIGHGATE

CROSSHILL

LANE

Pollington Bridge

Sch

PH

BRIDGE CR

BUTCHER CR

Pollington Lock

Swing Bridge

19

HAZING LANE

West End

JENNY LANE

PARK LANE

Balné

Highgate

HIGHGATE

CAT LANE

Cross Hill

Fir Tree Farm

Sheepwash Bridge

BALNE HALL RD

5

Blowell Bridge

Wood View Farm

Ash Tree Farm

LITTLE COMMON LA

Parkshaw Wood

Chapel Hill

GORE LANE

TOADHAM LANE

Lockgate Farm

LC

DN14

Lowgate

Balne Hall

Lake Drain

NEVILLE PITS LANE

Barn Fall Wood

Cherry Tree Farm

LOWGATE

Lowgate Farm

18

Works

BLOWELL DRAIN

SOUTH END LA

South End

LOCKGATE ROAD

River Went

4

Lake Bridge

BADGER LANE

COMMON LANE

BADGER LA

Fox Covert

East Yorkshire & North Lincolnshire STREET ATLAS

17

River Went

Stubbs Grange

COMMON LA

Went Farm

LC

Gate Farm

Fenwick

Orchard End

Riddings Farm

Fenwick Hall

Fleet Drain

Bungalow Farm

3

Went Bridge

Stubbs Common

PH

LAWN LANE

WEST LA

16

SHAW LA

Shoemaker's Hill

West End

A19

Norton Common Farm

Moat Hill Farm

FENWICK LANE

HAGGS LANE

2

Went Lows

FENWICK COMMON LANE

Fenwick Grange

FLASHLEY CARR LANE

A19

Moat Hill

Fenwick Common

Cemy

Moseley Grange

Flashley Carr

FLASHLEY CARR DRAIN

15

Toll Bar

NORTON COMMON ROAD

CLOUGH LANE

Ladythorpe Farm

DN6

Cemy

Jett Hall

Wood Grove

Parkgate Farm

1

Norton Common

ose Grove

FENWICK LANE

Elmfield Farm

LC

Manor Farm

CONDON LANE

MOSS HAVEN

Moss Farm

TRUMBLETT LA

MOSS RD

Moss

LC

WILLOW GARTH LANE

MOSS ROAD

PH

PINFOLD LA

14

B6
1 ABBEVILLE AV
2 HOLLY TREE CT
3 THE NURSERIES
4 ELM GR
5 BYLAND CT
6 SUTCLIFFE CT

13

C6
1 FOUNTAINS CL
2 HARROWING DR
3 ROSEDALE CL
4 LIME GR
5 PINEWOOD CL
6 KIRKHAM CL
7 AUCKLAND WY
8 SOUTHEND GD
9 ARUNDEL PL

13

D5
1 WATERSTEAD CR
2 SCORESBY TR
3 RAGLAN TR
4 FISHBURN RD
5 OSWY ST

D6
1 ANGEL YD
2 WELINGTON RD
3 VICTORIA PL
4 STATION SQ
5 PRINCESS PL
6 ENDEAVOUR WHARF
7 WINDSOR CR
8 PANNETT WY
9 LYNDHURST CL
10 SPRING HL TR
11 FALCON TR
12 GEORGE ST
13 GRAY ST
14 ALBION PL
15 GROVE ST
16 ELGIN ST
17 MEADOWFIELDS CT

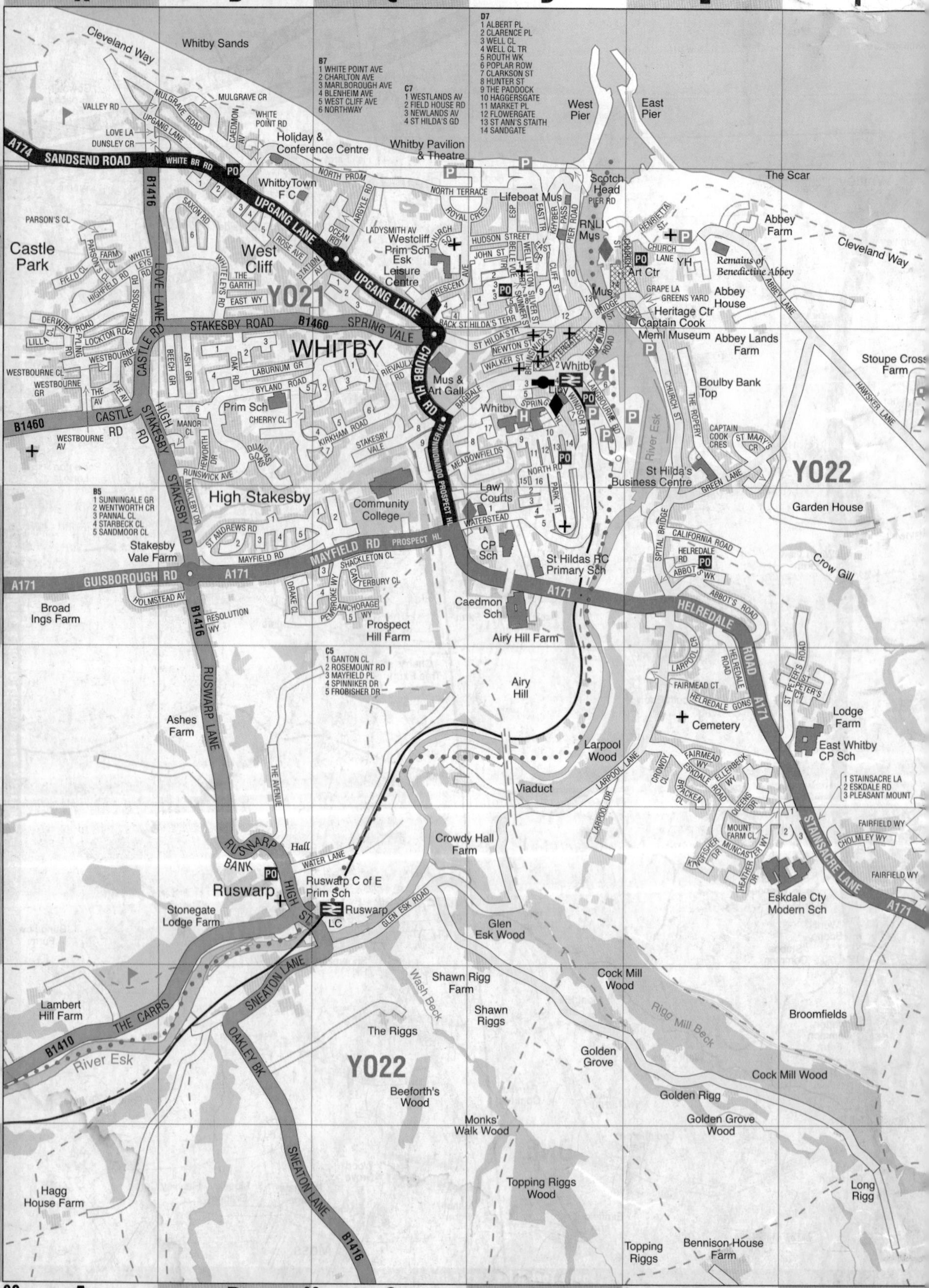

32
32
32

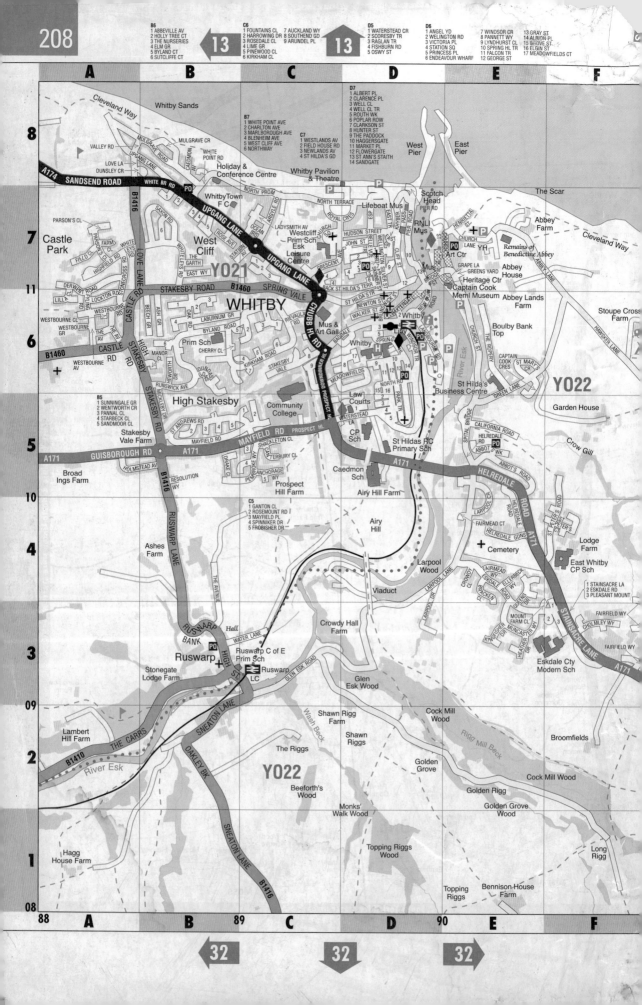

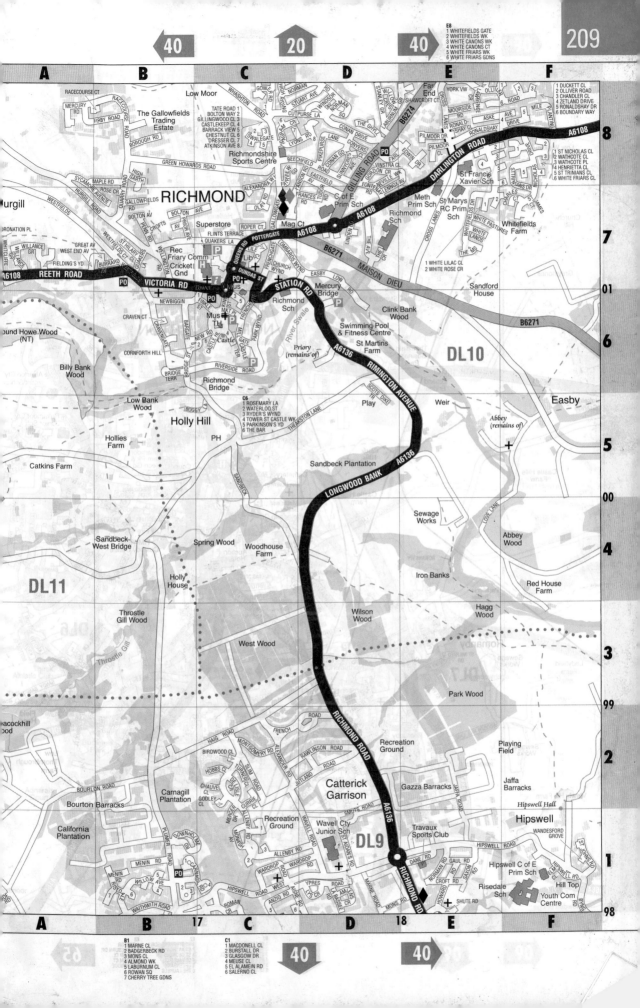

209

E8
1 WHITEFIELDS GATE
2 WHITEFIELDS WK
3 WHITE CANONS WK
4 WHITE CANONS CT
5 WHITE FRIARS WK
6 WHITE FRIARS GDNS

40   20   40

A   B   C   D   E   F

8

7

01

6

5

00

4

3

99

2

1

98

RICHMOND

RACECOURSE CT

MERCURY RD

FIRBY ROAD

BOROUGH RD

The Gallowfields Trading Estate

Low Moor

TATE ROAD 1
BOLTON WAY 2
GILLINGWOOD CL 3
CASTLEKEEP CL 4
BARRACK VIEW 5
CHESTNUT CL 6
DRESSER CL 7
ATKINSON AVE 8

WHASTHON ROAD

GREEN HOWARDS ROAD

Richmondshire Sports Centre

Farm End

B6274

York VW

A6108

DARLINGTON ROAD

1 DUCKETT CL
2 OLLIVER ROAD
3 CHANDLER CL
4 ZETLAND DRIVE
5 RONALDSHAY DR
6 BOUNDARY WAY

St Francis Xavier Sch

St Marys RC Prim Sch

Meth Prim Sch

1 ST NICHOLAS CL
2 WATHCOTE CL
3 WATHCOTE PL
4 HENRIETTA CL
5 ST TRINIANS CL
6 WHITE FRIARS CL

Richmond Sch

Whitefields Farm

urgill

WESTFIELDS

A6108 REETH ROAD

Superstore

FLINTS TERRACE

Rec Friary Comm Cricket Gnd

VICTORIA RD

Power

Mag Ct

A6108 POTTERGATE

Lib

DUNDAS ST

STATION RD

B6271

Richmond Sch

MAISON DIEU

1 WHITE LILAC CL
2 WHITE ROSE CR

Sandford House

B6271

DL10

Mus TH

Castle

Richmond Bridge

RIVERSIDE ROAD

River Swale

Priory (remains of)

A6136 RIMINGTON AVENUE

Mercury Bridge

Swimming Pool & Fitness Centre

St Martins Farm

Clink Bank Wood

Weir

Abbey (remains of)

Easby

Billy Bank Wood

ound Howe Wood (NT)

Low Bank Wood

Holly Hill

C6
1 ROSEMARY LA
2 WATERLOO ST
3 RYDER'S WYND
4 TOWER ST CASTLE WK
5 PARKINSON'S YD
6 THE BAR

Play

Hollies Farm

Catkins Farm

Sandbeck Plantation

A6136 LONGWOOD BANK

Sewage Works

Abbey Wood

DL11

Sandbeck West Bridge

Spring Wood

Woodhouse Farm

Iron Banks

Red House Farm

Holly House

Throstle Gill Wood

West Wood

Wilson Wood

Hagg Wood

Park Wood

acockhill ood

French ROAD

Catterick Garrison

Recreation Ground

Playing Field

Bourlon Road

Bourton Barracks

Carnagill Plantation

HAIG ROAD

BIRDWOOD CL

HOBBS CL

RAWLINSON ROAD

RICHMOND ROAD

Gazza Barracks

Jaffa Barracks

Hipswell Hall

California Plantation

Recreation Ground

Wavell Cty Junior Sch

DL9

A6136

Travaux Sports Club

Hipswell

Hipswell C of E Prim Sch

Youth Com Centre

Risedale Sch

A   B   17   C   D   18   E   F

B1
1 MARNE CL
2 BADGERBECK RD
3 MONS CL
4 ALMOND WK
5 LABURNUM CL
6 ROWAN SQ
7 CHERRY TREE GDNS

C1
1 MACDONELL CL
2 BURSTALL DR
3 GLASGOW DR
4 MEUSE CL
5 EL ALAMEIN RD
6 SALERNO CL

40   40

90 75 75

C8
1 ST MARK'S CL
2 ST JOSEPHS CL
3 GREYLANDS PK GR
4 GREYLANDS PK RD
5 HEATHCLIFF GD

D8
1 HAREWOOD AV
2 NEWLANDS PK GR
3 WOODVILLE AV
4 VERNON GR
5 HIGHDALE AV

E5
1 FAIRFAX ST
2 BRITANNIA ST
3 IRETON ST
4 BRINKBURN RD
5 HARLEY ST
6 FALSGRAVE MS

F6
1 WREA LA
2 LWR CLARK ST
3 LWR WILLIAM ST
4 MELROSE ST
5 CLIFTON ST
6 VINE ST
7 FRANKLIN ST
8 MURCHISON PL
9 PROSPECT RD
10 ALBEMARLE BK RD
11 NORTHWAY
12 BROOK ST

F7
1 VICTORIA PARK
2 VICTORIA PARK AV
3 LANGDALE RD
4 SANDRINGHAM ST
5 SYDNEY ST
6 DURHAM ST

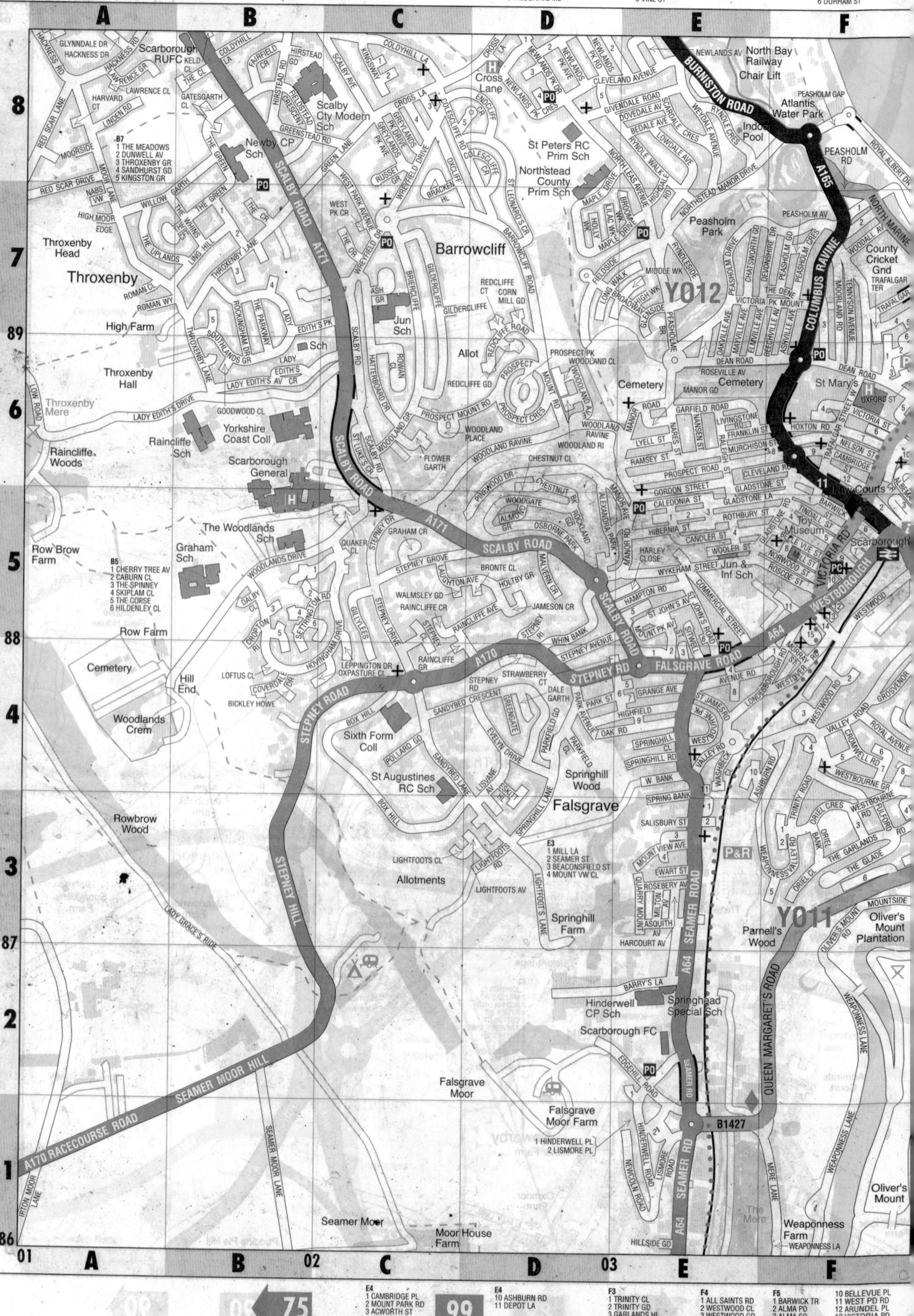

E4
1 CAMBRIDGE PL
2 MOUNT PARK RD
3 ACWORTH ST
4 NEW PK RD
5 DERWENT AV
6 PARK RD
7 DERWENT ST
8 NEW PARKS CR
9 ELM RD

E4
10 ASHBURN RD
11 DEPOT LA

F3
1 TRINITY CL
2 TRINITY GD
3 GARLANDS HL
4 PRINCESS ROYAL LA
5 WEAPONNESS VALLEY CL
6 QUEEN MARGARET'S RD

F4
1 ALL SAINTS RD
2 WESTWOOD CL
3 WESTWOOD GD
4 COLLEGE CT
5 CROMWELL PD
6 CROMWELL GD
7 CROMWELL TR
8 ROYAL CRES LA

F5
1 BARWICK TR
2 ALMA PD
3 ALMA SQ
4 MORGAN ST
5 SHERWOOD ST
6 HANNOVER RD
7 WEST SQ
8 NORWOOD PL
9 BELLEVUE PD
10 BELLEVUE PL
11 WEST PD RD
12 ARUNDEL PL
13 VICTORIA PD
14 BELGRAVE TR
15 BELGRAVE CR

90 90 75 99

A6
1 REGENT ST
2 JAMES PL
3 GEORGE ST
4 NORTH TR
5 AUBOROUGH ST
6 LANCASTER ST
7 CLARENCE PL
8 SILVER ST
9 MARIAS CT
10 FRIAR'S GD
11 FRIARS WY
12 UNION ST
13 BEDFORD ST
14 SUSSEX ST
15 PROVIDENCE PL
16 ABERDEEN WK
17 ABERDEEN ST
18 ALBERMARLE CR
19 ABERDEEN LA
20 ABERDEEN PL
21 ABERDEEN TR
22 NORTH ST LA
23 CHAPEL RD
24 MARKET ST
25 MARKET WY
26 ST HELEN'S SQ
27 BLAND'S CLIFF
28 PROSPECT PL
29 WATERHOUSE LA

76 76

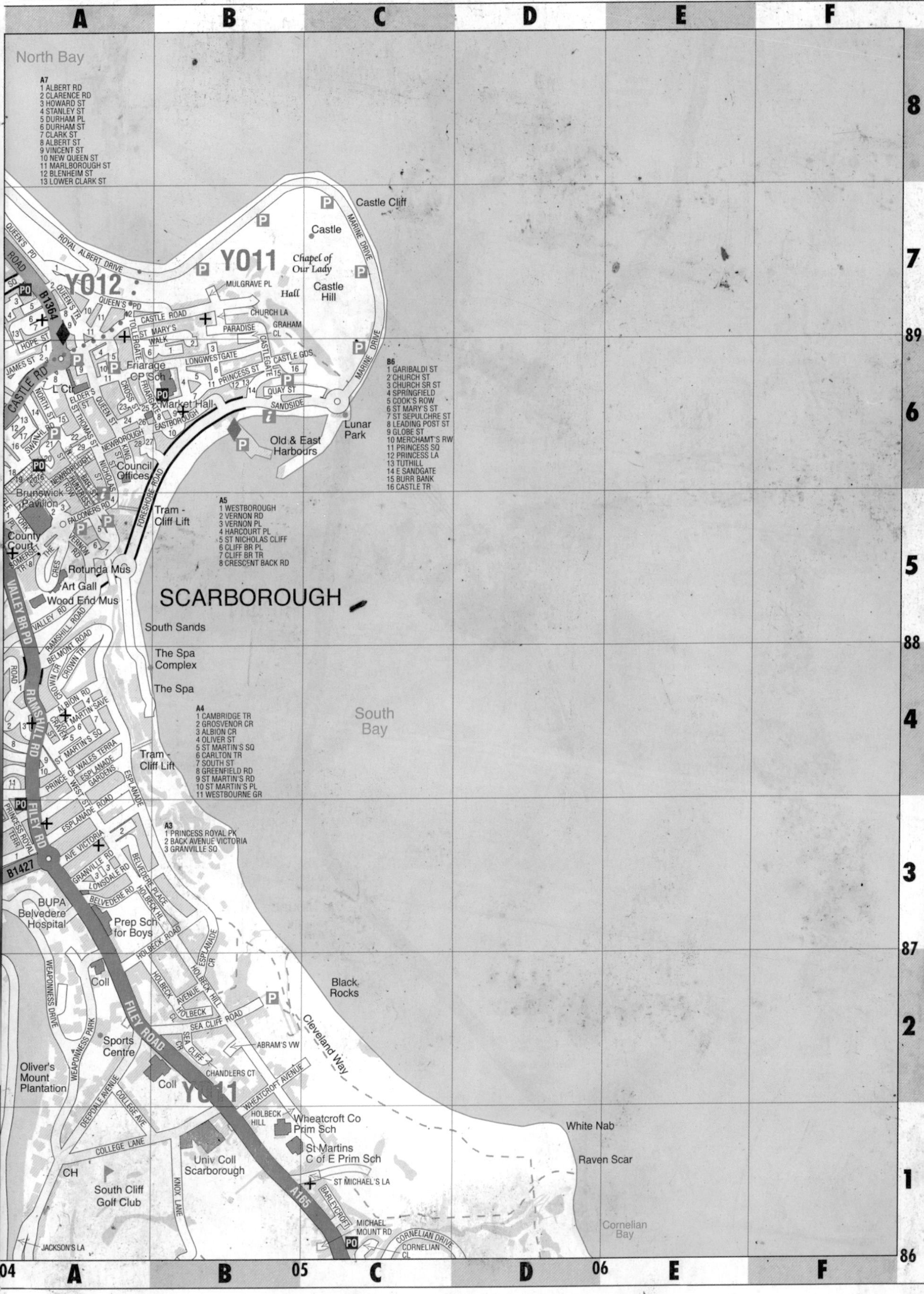

100 76

113 113 114

C5
1 ST WILFRID'S RD
2 ST WILFRID'S PL
3 WESTBOURNE GR
4 FINKLE CL
5 FINKLE ST
6 OLD MARKET PL

7 HIGH SKELLGATE
8 WILLIAMSON DR
9 WELLINGTON MS
10 WELLINGTON ST
11 KIRKGATE
12 BEDERN BANK
13 MINSTER CL

14 WILLIAMSON CL
15 LOWSKELLGATE
16 BEDERN CT
17 FISHERGATE
18 QUEEN ST
19 MARKET PLACE NORTH
20 MARKET PLACE EAST

21 MARKET PLACE SOUTH
22 MARKET PLACE WEST
23 MINSTER CLOSE

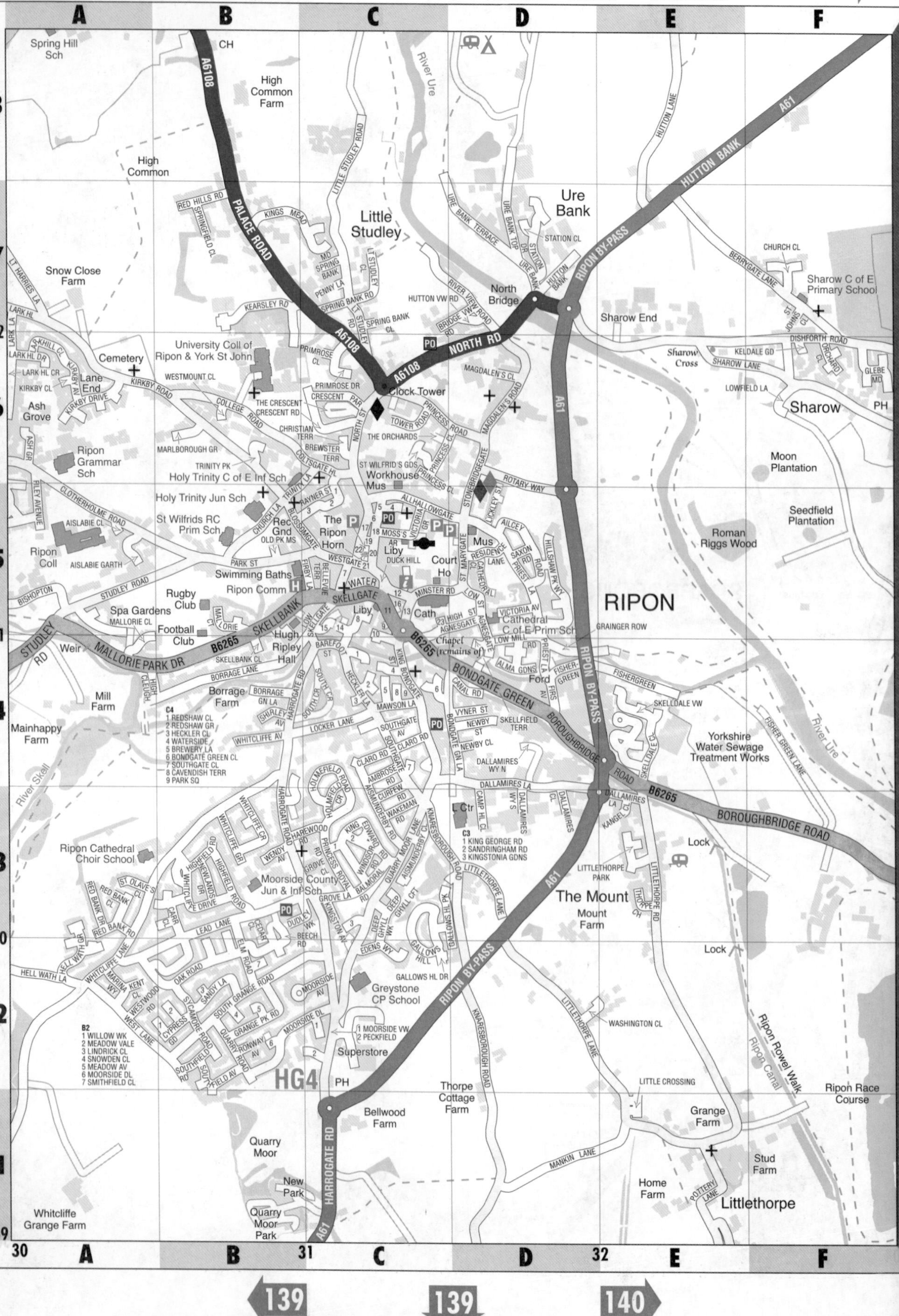

Spring Hill Sch

High Common Farm

High Common

Little Studley

Ure Bank

River Ure

Snow Close Farm

Cemetery

Lane End

Ash Grove

Ripon Grammar Sch

University Coll of Ripon & York St John

Westmount Cl

The Crescent

Clock Tower

North Bridge

Sharow End

Sharow Cross

Sharow C of E Primary School

Sharow

Moon Plantation

Seedfield Plantation

Roman Riggs Wood

RIPON

Holy Trinity C of E Inf Sch

Holy Trinity Jun Sch

St Wilfrids RC Prim Sch

Workhouse Mus

The Ripon Horn

Ripon Coll

Swimming Baths

Ripon Comm

Rugby Club

Spa Gardens

Football Club

Mill Farm

Mainhappy Farm

Ripon Cathedral Choir School

Moorside County Jun & Inf Sch

Greystone CP School

Superstore

C4
1 REDSHAW CL
2 REDSHAW GR
3 HECKLER CL
4 WATERSIDE
5 BREWERY LA
6 BONDGATE GREEN CL
7 SOUTHGATE CL
8 CAVENDISH TERR
9 PARK SQ

C3
1 KING GEORGE RD
2 SANDRINGHAM RD
3 KINGSTONIA GDNS

B2
1 WILLOW WK
2 MEADOW VALE
3 LINDRICK CL
4 SNOWDEN CL
5 MEADOW AV
6 MOORSIDE DL
7 SMITHFIELD CL

1 MOORSIDE VW
2 PECKFIELD

HG4

Cathedral C of E Prim Sch

Court Ho

Bondgate Green

Boroughbridge Road

Yorkshire Water Sewage Treatment Works

The Mount

Mount Farm

Lock

Littlethorpe Park

Ripon Rowel Walk

Ripon Canal

Ripon Race Course

Stud Farm

Littlethorpe

Home Farm

Grange Farm

Little Crossing

Thorpe Cottage Farm

Bellwood Farm

Quarry Moor

New Park

Quarry Moor Park

Whitcliffe Grange Farm

Borrage Farm

Hugh Ripley Hall

Chapel (remains of)

Ford

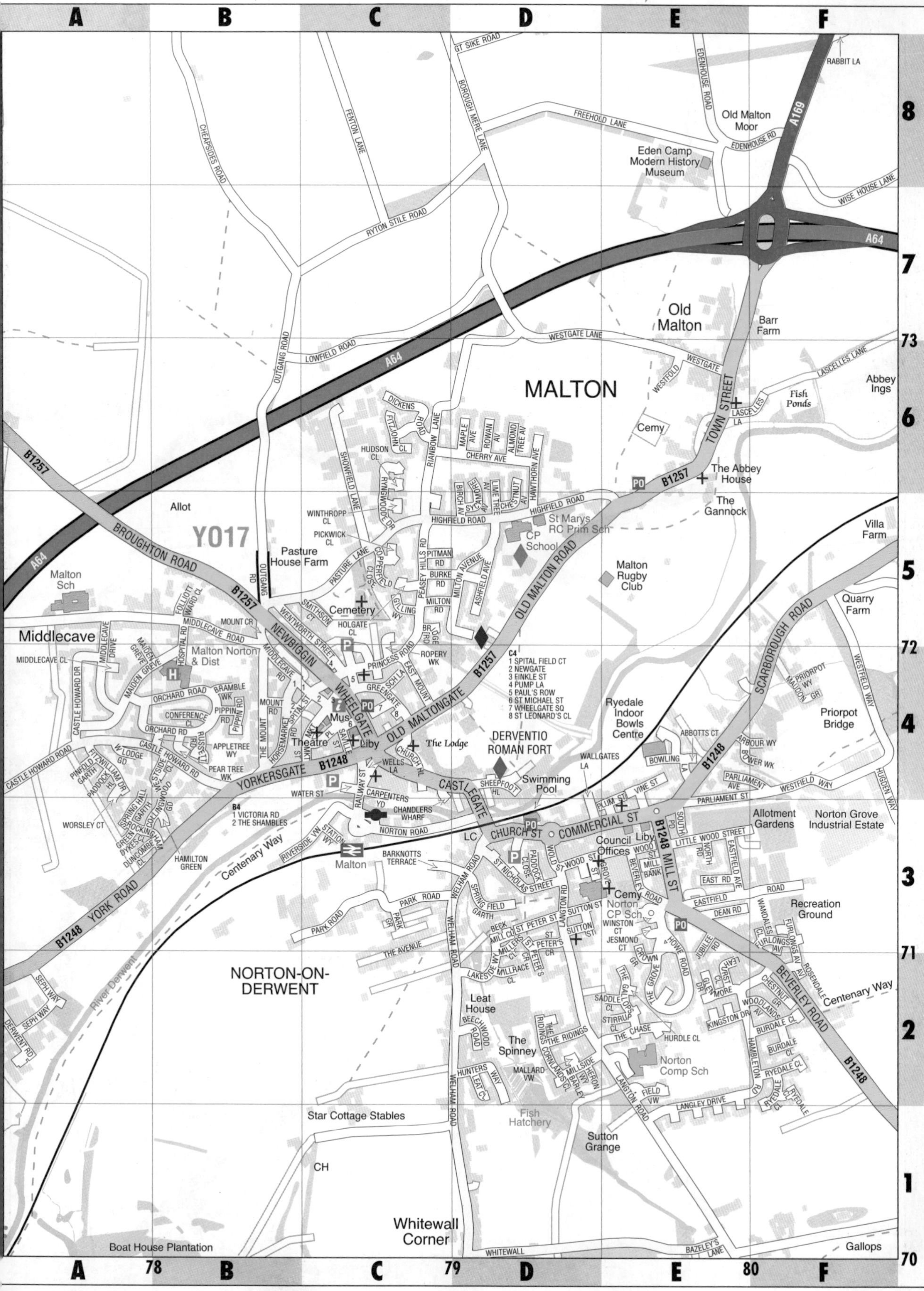
A
B
C
D
E
F
8
7
73
6
5
72
4
3
71
2
1
70
78
79
80
MALTON
Old Malton
Old Malton Moor
Eden Camp Modern History Museum
NORTON-ON-DERWENT
Y017
Middlecave
Malton Sch
Allot
Pasture House Farm
Cemetery
Malton Norton & Dist
Mus
Theatre
Liby
The Lodge
DERVENTIO ROMAN FORT
Swimming Pool
St Marys RC Prim Sch
CP School
Malton Rugby Club
Ryedale Indoor Bowls Centre
Council Offices
Cemy
Norton CP Sch
Norton Comp Sch
Allotment Gardens
Norton Grove Industrial Estate
Recreation Ground
Priorpot Bridge
Quarry Farm
Villa Farm
Abbey Ings
Fish Ponds
The Abbey House
The Gannock
Barr Farm
Leat House
The Spinney
Fish Hatchery
Sutton Grange
Star Cottage Stables
CH
Whitewall Corner
Boat House Plantation
Gallops
Malton
Centenary Way
River Derwent
A64
A169
B1257
B1248
BROUGHTON ROAD
YORK ROAD
YORKERSGATE
OLD MALTONGATE
OLD MALTON ROAD
SCARBOROUGH ROAD
BEVERLEY ROAD
TOWN STREET
COMMERCIAL ST
CHURCH ST
CASTLEGATE
WHEELGATE
NEWBIGGIN
MILL ST
WELHAM ROAD
LANGTON ROAD
OUTGANG ROAD
CHEAPSIDES ROAD
FENTON LANE
BOROUGH MERE LANE
FREEHOLD LANE
RYTON STILE ROAD
LOWFIELD ROAD
WESTGATE LANE
WESTGATE
EDENHOUSE ROAD
WISE HOUSE LANE
RABBIT LA
LASCELLES LANE
GT SIKE ROAD
HIGHFIELD ROAD
CHERRY AVE
PEASEY HILLS RD
SHOWFIELD LANE
MIDDLECAVE ROAD
CASTLE HOWARD RD
CASTLE HOWARD DR
ORCHARD ROAD
PARK ROAD
THE AVENUE
NORTON ROAD
WESTFIELD WAY
PARLIAMENT ST
LITTLE WOOD STREET
EASTFIELD ROAD
LANGLEY DRIVE
WHITEWALL
BAZELEY'S LANE
HUGDEN WAY
C4
1 SPITAL FIELD CT
2 NEWGATE
3 FINKLE ST
4 PUMP LA
5 PAUL'S ROW
6 ST MICHAEL ST
7 WHEELGATE SQ
8 ST LEONARD'S CL
B4
1 VICTORIA RD
2 THE SHAMBLES

172
156

F4
1 PARK ST
2 PRIMROSE HL
3 VICTORIA TR
4 HALLAM'S YD
5 THE PINFOLD
6 BACK O THE BECK
7 WATSON'S HO
8 CANAL YD
9 BAY HORSE YD
10 VICTORIA ST
11 SHEEP ST
12 DEVONSHIRE PL
13 COACH ST YD
14 GLADSTONE ST

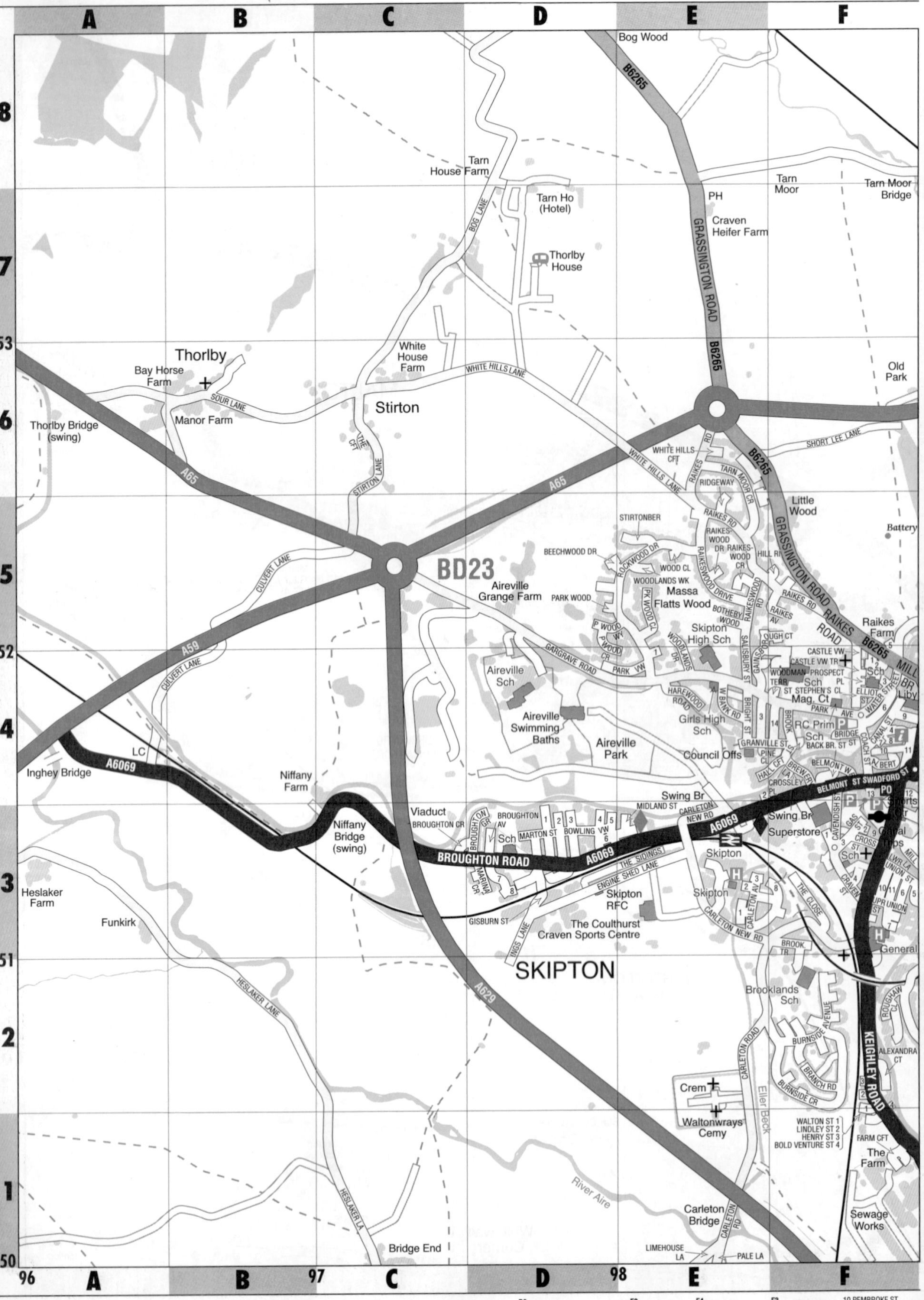

D3
1 SAWLEY ST
2 CLITHEROE ST
3 THORNTON ST
4 PENDLE ST
5 GREENFIELD ST
6 RUSKIN AVE
7 NIFFANY GDNS
8 STATION VW

E3
1 AIREDALE MS
2 GLYNWED CT
3 ELLER MS

E4
1 ROCKWOOD CL
2 BELLEVUE TERR
3 BELGRA. ST

F3
1 CLIFFORD ST
2 HIRDS YD
3 CARLETON ST
4 CHURCH ST
5 UNION TR
6 CUMBERLAND ST
7 SOUTHFIELD TR
8 LINTON CT
9 THANET'S CT
10 PEMBROKE ST
11 BENNETT ST

172
173

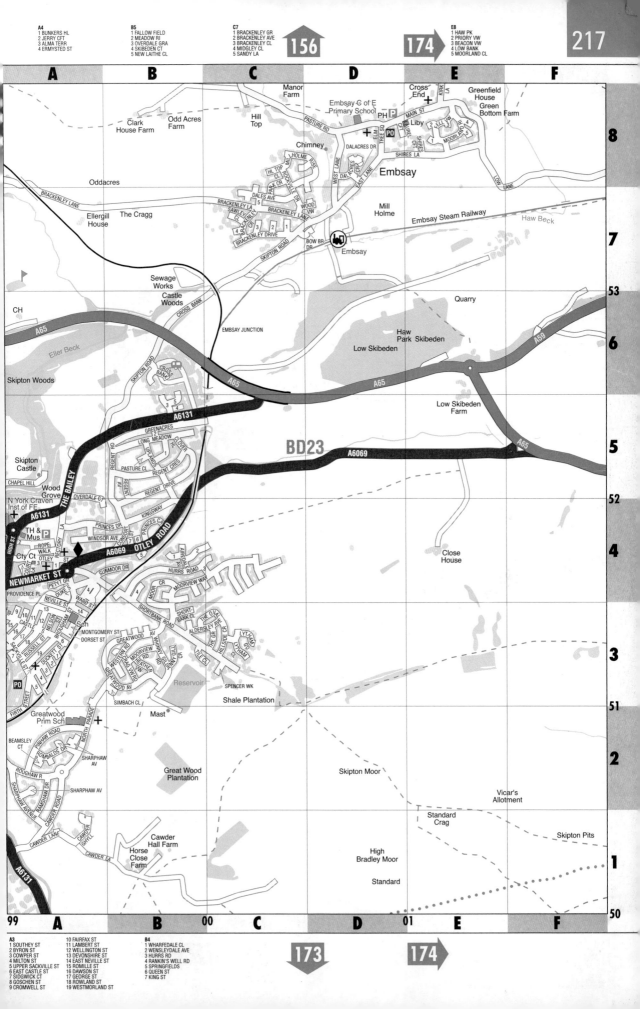

156
174

A4
1 BUNKERS HL
2 JERRY CFT
3 ALMA TERR
4 ERMYSTED ST

B5
1 FALLOW FIELD
2 MEADOW RI
3 OVERDALE GRA
4 SKIBEDEN CT
5 NEW LAITHE CL

C7
1 BRACKENLEY GR
2 BRACKENLEY AVE
3 BRACKENLEY CL
4 MIDGLEY CL
5 SANDY LA

E8
1 HAW PK
2 PRIORY VW
3 BEACON VW
4 LOW BANK
5 MOORLAND CL

A3
1 SOUTHEY ST
2 BYRON ST
3 COWPER ST
4 MILTON ST
5 UPPER SACKVILLE ST
6 EAST CASTLE ST
7 SIDGWICK CT
8 GOSCHEN ST
9 CROMWELL ST
10 FAIRFAX ST
11 LAMBERT ST
12 WELLINGTON ST
13 DEVONSHIRE ST
14 EAST NEVILLE ST
15 ROMILLE ST
16 DAWSON ST
17 GEORGE ST
18 ROWLAND ST
19 WESTMORLAND ST

B4
1 WHARFEDALE CL
2 WENSLEYDALE AVE
3 HURRS RD
4 RANKIN'S WELL RD
5 SPRINGFIELDS
6 QUEEN ST
7 KING ST

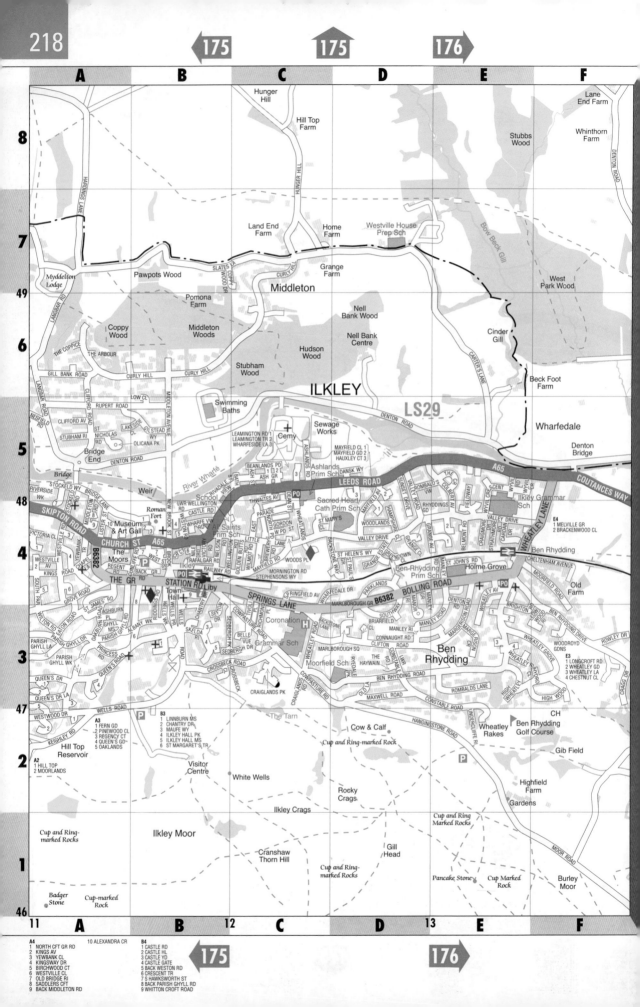

175 175 176

A B C D E F

8
7
49
6
5
48
4
3
47
2
1
46

Hunger Hill
Hill Top Farm
Land End Farm
Home Farm
Westville House Prep Sch
Lane End Farm
Whinthorn Farm
Stubbs Wood

Myddelton Lodge
Pawpots Wood
Grange Farm
Middleton
West Park Wood
Bow Beck Gill
DENTON ROAD

Pomona Farm
Coppy Wood
Middleton Woods
Nell Bank Wood
Cinder Gill
CARTER'S LANE

THE COPPICE
THE ARBOUR
Stubham Wood
Hudson Wood
Nell Bank Centre
Beck Foot Farm

GILL BANK ROAD
CURLY HILL
CURLY HILL
ILKLEY
LS29
Wharfedale
LANGBAR RD
LANGBAR ROAD
NESFIELD RD
CLIFFORD ROAD
LOW CL
MIDDLETON AVENUE
DENTON ROAD
A65

Swimming Baths
Sewage Works
Denton Bridge

Bridge End
DENTON ROAD
ST NICHOLAS RD
OLICANA PK
LAKESIDE
GYLSTEAD WY
Cemy
Leamington Rd 1
Leamington Tr 2
Wharfeside La 3
Mayfield Cl 1
Mayfield Gd 2
Hauxley Ct 3

Bridge
Weir
River Wharfe
LEEDS ROAD
Ilkley Grammar Sch

SKIPTON ROAD
48
Roman Fort
SCHWDALE VIEW
BATH
THWAITES AV
PO
Sacred Heart Cath Prim Sch
St Mary's
RHYDDINGS GD
VALLEY DRIVE
E4
1 MELVILLE GR
2 BRACKENWOOD CL

Museum & Art Gall
CASTLE RD
LWR WELLINGTON
Ashlands Prim Sch
DANSK WY
WOODLANDS
Ben Rhydding

CHURCH ST
A65
B6382
All Saints Prim Sch
WHARFE VW
GORDON
St Helen's Wy
VALLEY DRIVE
St John's Rd
Holme Grove
CHELTENHAM AVENUE

The Moors
WEST ST
BROOK
RAILWAY RD
MAYFIELD RD
Ben-Rhydding Prim Sch
Old Farm

THE GR
STATION RD
Liby
PO
Ringfield Av
Wharfedale Dr
B6382
BOLLING ROAD
MOORFIELD ROAD

SPRINGS LANE
Town Hall
SKELDA RI
Coronation
Marlborough Gr
DENTON RD
E3
1 LONGCROFT RD
2 WHEATLEY GD
3 WHEATLEY LA
4 CHESTNUT CL

Grammar Sch
BELLE VUE
SEDBERGH DR
Marlborough Sq
Ben Rhydding

Moorfield Sch
THE HAYWAIN
Ben Rhydding Road
ROMBALDS LANE

PARISH GHYLL LA
PARISH GHYLL WK
CROSSBECK ROAD
CRAIGLANDS PK
Maxwell Road
CONSTABLE ROAD
CH

QUEEN'S DR
QUEEN'S DR LA
WELLS ROAD
The Tarn
HANGINGSTONE ROAD
Ben Rhydding Golf Course

WESTWOOD DR
B3
1 LINNBURN MS
2 CHANTRY DR
3 MAUFE WY
4 ILKLEY HALL PK
5 ILKLEY HALL MS
6 ST MARGARET'S TR
Cow & Calf
Cup and Ring-marked Rock
Wheatley Rakes
Gib Field

Hill Top Reservoir
A3
1 FERN GD
2 PINEWOOD CL
3 REGENCY CT
4 QUEEN'S GD
5 OAKLANDS
Highfield Farm

A2
1 HILL TOP
2 MOORLANDS
Visitor Centre
White Wells
Rocky Crags
Gardens

Ilkley Crags
Cup and Ring Marked Rocks

Cup and Ring-marked Rocks
Ilkley Moor
Cranshaw Thorn Hill
Gill Head
Pancake Stone
Cup Marked Rock
Burley Moor
MOOR ROAD

Badger Stone
Cup-marked Rock
Cup and Ring-marked Rocks

175 176

A4
1 NORTH CFT GR RD
2 KINGS AV
3 YEWBANK CL
4 KINGSWAY DR
5 BIRCHWOOD CT
6 WESTVILLE CL
7 OLD BRIDGE RI
8 SADDLERS CFT
9 BACK MIDDLETON RD

10 ALEXANDRA CR

B4
1 CASTLE RD
2 CASTLE HL
3 CASTLE YD
4 CASTLE GATE
5 BACK WESTON RD
6 CRESCENT TR
7 S HAWKSWORTH ST
8 BACK PARISH GHYLL RD
9 WHITTON CROFT ROAD

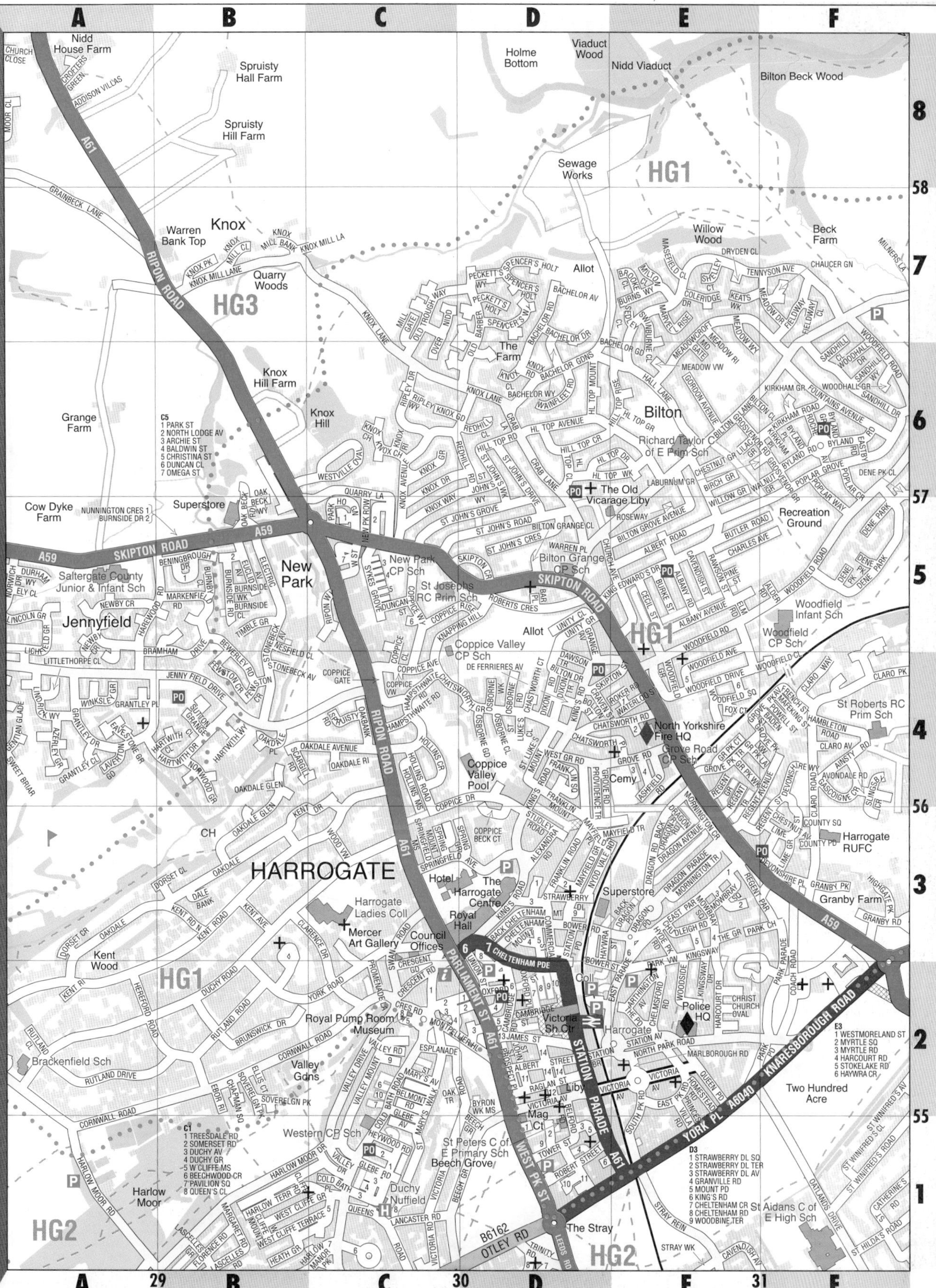

C2
1 MONTPELLIER RD
2 MONTPELLIER GDNS
3 MONTPELLIER MS
4 MONTPELLIER ST
5 BACK ROYAL PD
6 WELLINGTON SQ
7 ST PETER'S SQ
8 ROYAL PAR
9 WELLINGTON CT
10 KENSINGTON SQ

D1
1 BRUNSWICK PL
2 OXFORD TR
3 BELFORD PL
4 ST ROBERTS MS
5 ALBERT TR
6 BACK YORK PL
7 PARK DR
8 PARK RD
9 BELFORD SQ
10 TRAFALGAR CT
11 TRAFALGAR RD

D2
1 THE GINNEL
2 PARLIAMENT TR
3 MONTPELLIER SQ
4 CAMBRIDGE TR
5 CAMBRIDGE CR
6 CHELTENHAM CR
7 CAMBRIDGE PL
8 NORTHUMBERLAND CT
9 EBENEZER TR
10 BEULAH ST
11 JOHN ST
12 PRINCES SQ
13 PROSPECT CR
14 ST PRINCES SQ

E4
1 WEYMOUTH RD
2 CHATSWORTH TR
3 BACK ELMWOOD ST
4 ELMWOOD ST
5 WOODFIELD GD
6 WOODFIELD PL

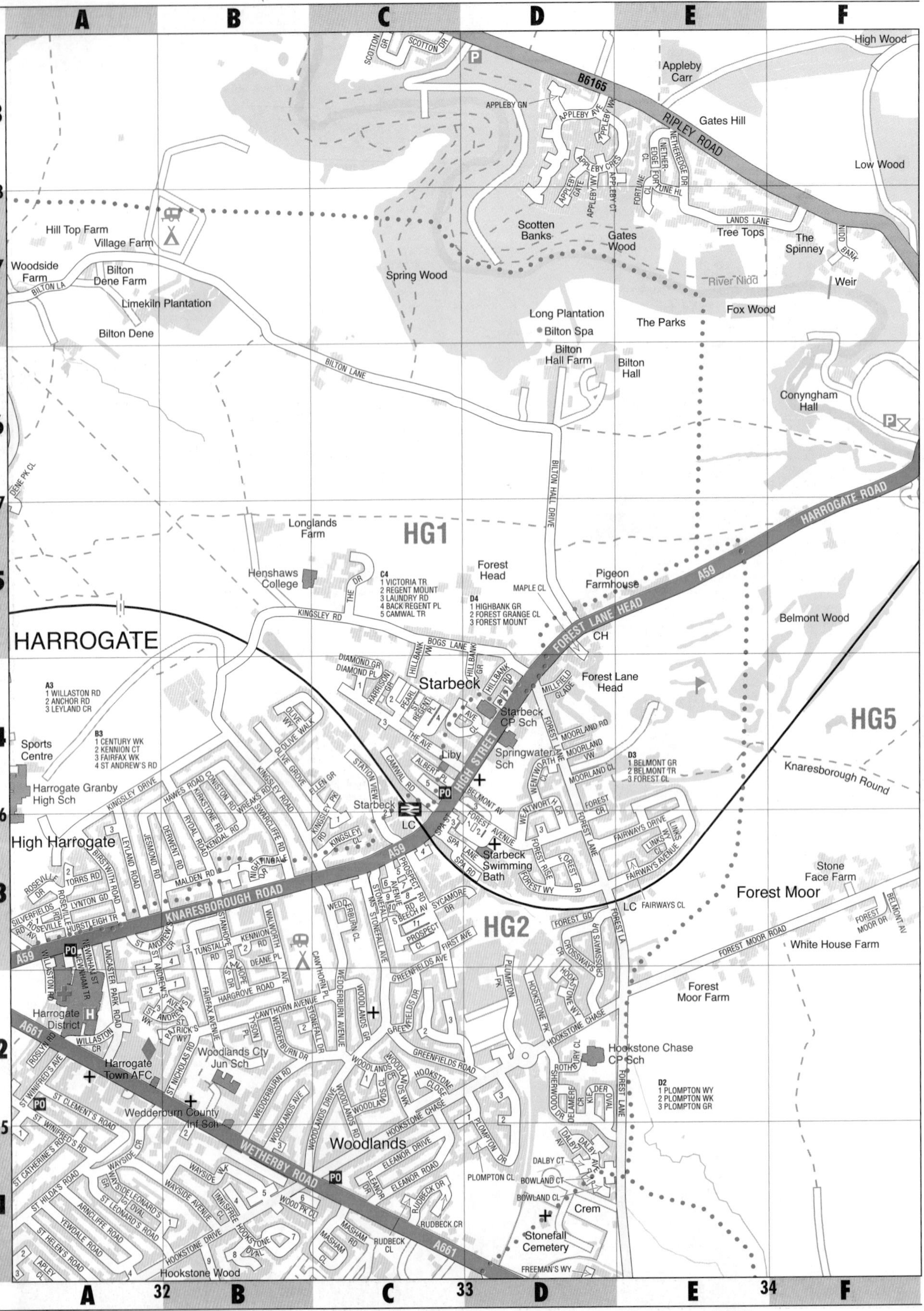

A   B   C   D   E   F

8
58
7
6
57
5
4
56
3
2
55
1

HARROGATE

HG1

HG2

HG5

High Harrogate

Forest Moor

Starbeck

Woodlands

High Wood
Low Wood
Appleby Carr
Gates Hill
Scotten Banks
Gates Wood
Tree Tops
The Spinney
Weir
Spring Wood
River Nidd
Long Plantation
Bilton Spa
The Parks
Fox Wood
Bilton Hall Farm
Bilton Hall
Conyngham Hall
Belmont Wood
Knaresborough Round
Stone Face Farm
White House Farm
Forest Moor Farm
Forest Moor Road
Hill Top Farm
Village Farm
Woodside Farm
Bilton Dene Farm
Limekiln Plantation
Bilton Dene
Bilton Lane
Longlands Farm
Henshaws College
Forest Head
Pigeon Farmhouse
Forest Lane Head
Sports Centre
Harrogate Granby High Sch
Starbeck CP Sch
Springwater Sch
Starbeck Swimming Bath
Hookstone Chase CP Sch
Harrogate District
Harrogate Town AFC
Woodlands Cty Jun Sch
Wedderburn County Inf Sch
Hookstone Wood
Stonefall Cemetery
Crem

B6165
RIPLEY ROAD
HARROGATE ROAD
A59
KNARESBOROUGH ROAD
WETHERBY ROAD
A661

A   32   B   33   C   D   34   E   F

← **219**   **223**

A6
1 ST MARGARET'S GD
2 ST MARGARET'S GARTH
3 ST MARGARET'S CL
4 PUMP HL
5 JOCKEY LA
6 BEECH HL
8 WATER BAG BANK
9 STATION RD
10 VICARAGE LA
11 THE PARSONAGE
12 FINKLE ST

B5
1 WELLINGTON ST
2 CHEAPSIDE
3 CASTLEGATE
4 SILVER ST
5 HIGH ST
6 FISHER ST
7 GRACIOUS ST
8 ORCHARD CT
9 STOCKDALE CL
10 TANNERY CT
11 ROSEHILL SQ

162

B6
1 COMMERCIAL YD
2 PARK SQ
3 MARKET PL
4 PARK PL
5 BERRY'S AV
6 WHINCUP CL
7 WHINCUP GR
8 PARK CL
9 STOCKWELL CT
10 CHARLTON CT
11 HOLLY CT
12 CHARLTON GR
13 CHARLTON MANOR DR

163

B7
1 NORWOOD CT
2 HAWTHORN AV
3 PASTURE CR
4 FROGMIRE CL
5 STOCKWELL CR

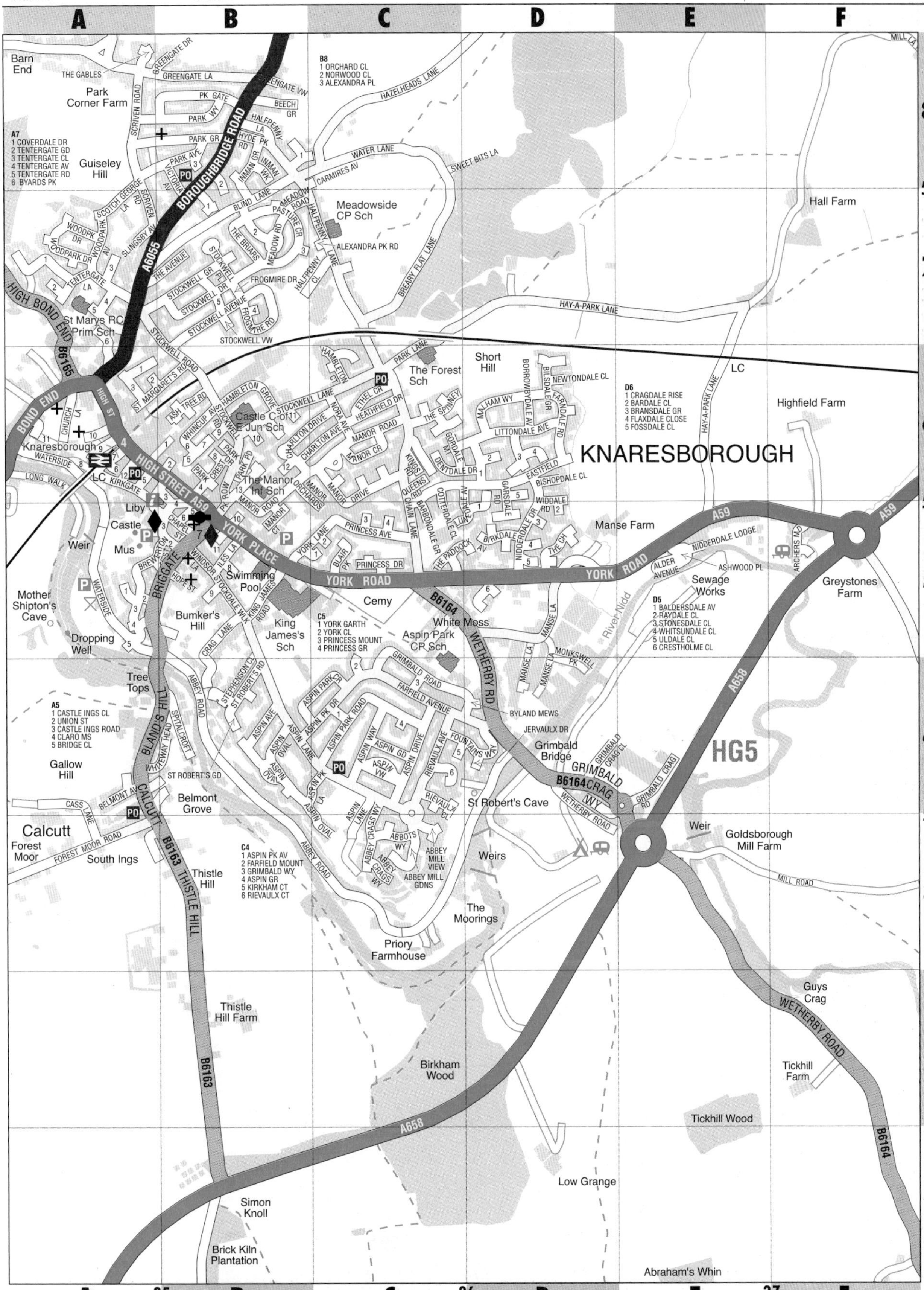

179
163

178 219

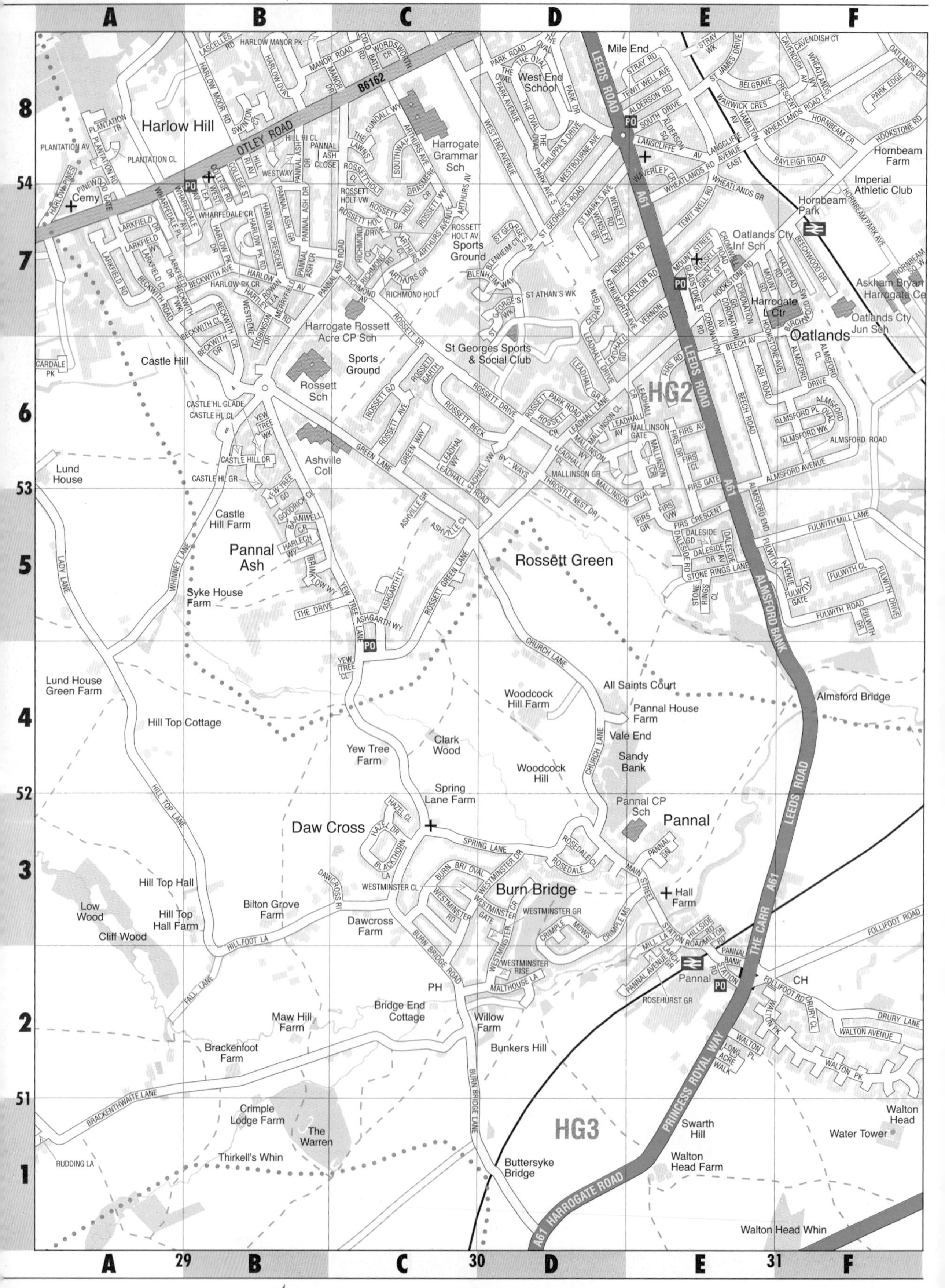
Harlow Hill
Otley Road
B6162
Harrogate Grammar Sch
West End School
Mile End
Leeds Road
A61
Hornbeam Farm
Imperial Athletic Club
Hornbeam Park
Oatlands Cty Inf Sch
Sports Ground
Harrogate L Ctr
Oatlands
Oatlands Cty Jun Sch
Askham Bryan Harrogate Ce
Cemy
Harrogate Rosset Acre CP Sch
Castle Hill
Rossett Sch
St Georges Sports & Social Club
HG2
Lund House
Ashville Coll
Castle Hill Farm
Pannal Ash
Rossett Green
Syke House Farm
Almsford Bank
Lund House Green Farm
All Saints Court
Woodcock Hill Farm
Pannal House Farm
Almsford Bridge
Hill Top Cottage
Vale End
Yew Tree Farm
Clark Wood
Sandy Bank
Woodcock Hill
Spring Lane Farm
Pannal CP Sch
Daw Cross
Pannal
Burn Bridge
Hill Top Hall
Hall Farm
Low Wood
Bilton Grove Farm
Hill Top Hall Farm
Dawcross Farm
Cliff Wood
The Carr
PH
CH
Maw Hill Farm
Bridge End Cottage
Willow Farm
Brackenfoot Farm
Bunkers Hill
Princess Royal Way
Crimple Lodge Farm
The Warren
HG3
Swarth Hill
Walton Head
Water Tower
Thirkell's Whin
Buttersyke Bridge
Walton Head Farm
Harrogate Road
Walton Head Whin
Brackenthwaite Lane
Rudding La
Burn Bridge Lane
Lady Lane
Whinney Lane
Hill Top Lane
Church Lane
Spring Lane
Follifoot Road
Drury Lane
Walton Avenue
Fulwith Mill Lane
Almsford Avenue
Almsford Road
A B C D E F
8 7 6 5 4 3 2 1
54 53 52 51
29 30 31

178 178

220
179

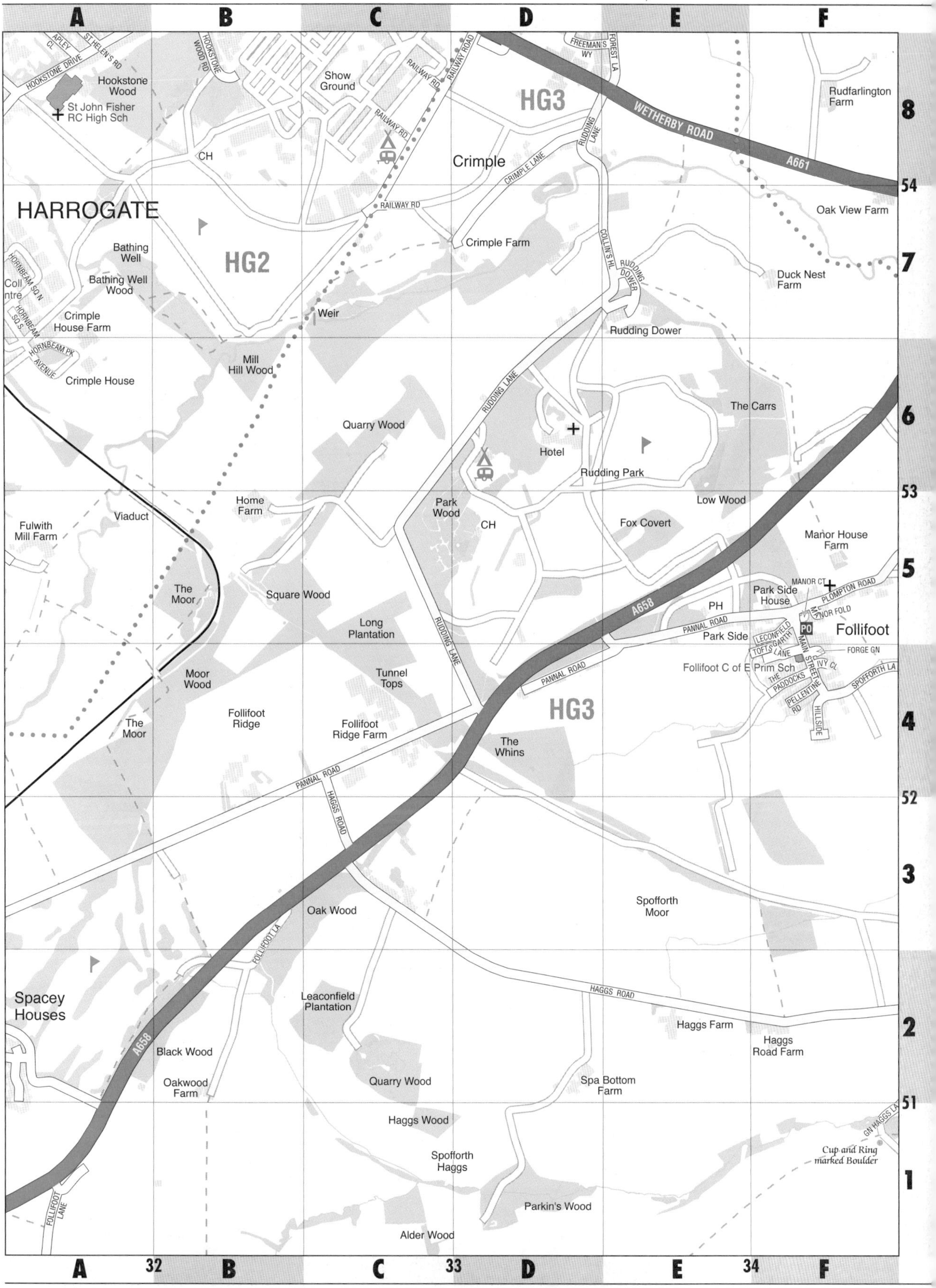
A
B
C
D
E
F
HARROGATE
HG2
HG3
HG3
Hookstone Wood
St John Fisher RC High Sch
HOOKSTONE DRIVE
APLEY CL
ST HELEN'S RD
HOOKSTONE WOOD RD
Show Ground
RAILWAY RD
RAILWAY ROAD
FREEMAN'S WY
FOREST LA
WETHERBY ROAD
A661
Rudfarlington Farm
CH
Crimple
CRIMPLE LANE
RUDDING LANE
Oak View Farm
Bathing Well
Bathing Well Wood
Crimple Farm
COLLIN'S HL
RUDDING DOWER
Duck Nest Farm
HORNBEAM SQ N
HORNBEAM SQ S
HORNBEAM PK
AVENUE
Crimple House Farm
Crimple House
Weir
Mill Hill Wood
Rudding Dower
Quarry Wood
The Carrs
Hotel
Rudding Park
Home Farm
Park Wood
Viaduct
Fulwith Mill Farm
Low Wood
Fox Covert
Manor House Farm
The Moor
Square Wood
Long Plantation
A658
PH
PANNAL ROAD
Park Side House
MANOR CT
PLOMPTON ROAD
MANOR FOLD
PO
Follifoot
Park Side
LECONFIELD GARTH
TOFTS LANE
MAIN STREET
FORGE GN
Follifoot C of E Prim Sch
IVY CL
THE PADDOCKS
PELLENTINE RD
HILLSIDE
SPOFFORTH LA
Moor Wood
Tunnel Tops
Follifoot Ridge
Follifoot Ridge Farm
The Whins
HAGGS ROAD
Spofforth Moor
Oak Wood
FOLLIFOOT LA
Spacey Houses
Leaconfield Plantation
Haggs Farm
Haggs Road Farm
Black Wood
Oakwood Farm
Quarry Wood
Spa Bottom Farm
Haggs Wood
GN HAGGS LA
Spofforth Haggs
Cup and Ring marked Boulder
Parkin's Wood
Alder Wood
FOLLIFOOT LANE
8
7
6
5
4
3
2
1
54
53
52
51
32
33
34

179
179

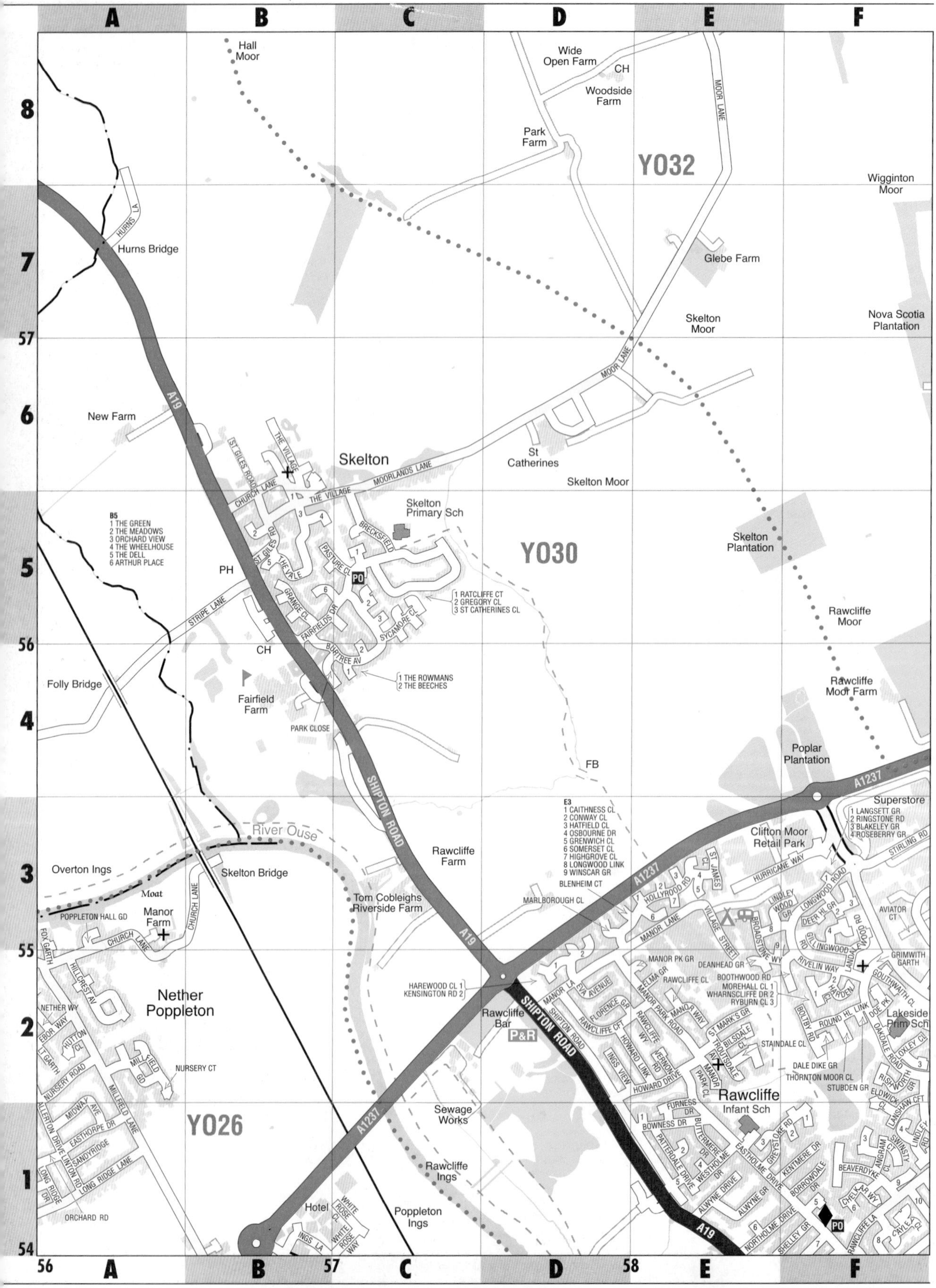

B5
1 THE GREEN
2 THE MEADOWS
3 ORCHARD VIEW
4 THE WHEELHOUSE
5 THE DELL
6 ARTHUR PLACE

1 RATCLIFFE CT
2 GREGORY CL
3 ST CATHERINES CL

1 THE ROWMANS
2 THE BEECHES

E3
1 CAITHNESS CL
2 CONWAY CL
3 HATFIELD CL
4 OSBOURNE DR
5 GRENWICH CL
6 SOMERSET CL
7 HIGHGROVE CL
8 LONGWOOD LINK
9 WINSCAR GR
BLENHEIM CT

MARLBOROUGH CL

HAREWOOD CL 1
KENSINGTON RD 2

E1
1 CONISTON CL
2 WASDALE CL
3 GARBURN GR
4 SCAFELL CL
5 LOWESWATER RD
6 FYLINGDALES AV

F1
1 EMBLETON DR
2 COLEDALE CL
3 LEIGHTON CFT
4 BARMBY CL
5 GRASMERE GR
6 BARDEN CT
7 SOUTHOLME DR
8 MILTON CARR
9 FEWSTON DR

10 REIGHTON DR

Hall Moor

Wide Open Farm

CH

Woodside Farm

Park Farm

YO32

Wigginton Moor

Hurns Bridge

Glebe Farm

Nova Scotia Plantation

New Farm

Skelton Moor

THE VILLAGE

Skelton

St Catherines

Skelton Moor

Skelton Plantation

MOORLANDS LANE

Skelton Primary Sch

YO30

PH

Rawcliffe Moor

STRIPE LANE

CH

Rawcliffe Moor Farm

Folly Bridge

Fairfield Farm

PARK CLOSE

FB

Poplar Plantation

SHIPTON ROAD

Rawcliffe Farm

A1237

Superstore

Clifton Moor Retail Park

River Ouse

Overton Ings

Skelton Bridge

Tom Cobleighs Riverside Farm

A19

Hurricane Way

Moat

POPPLETON HALL GD

Manor Farm

CHURCH LANE

Rawcliffe Bar
P&R

SHIPTON ROAD

Nether Poppleton

NURSERY CT

Rawcliffe Infant Sch

Lakeside Prim Sch

YO26

Sewage Works

Rawcliffe Ings

Hotel

Poppleton Ings

A1237

A19

PO

ORCHARD RD

166 226

C7
1 PLOUGHLANDS
2 THE GREENWAY
3 FOXCROFT

C8
1 DEALTRY AVE
2 ARENHALL CL
3 MINSTER CL
4 UPPERCROFT
5 BECKS CL
6 THE CHESTNUTS

7 COPWOOD GR
8 HESLIN CL
9 RUDDINGS CL
10 HUNTERS CL
11 CORNWOOD WY

D8
1 MEADOW LN
2 CHERRY OR
3 ORCHARD PADDOCK
4 CHERRY PADDOCK

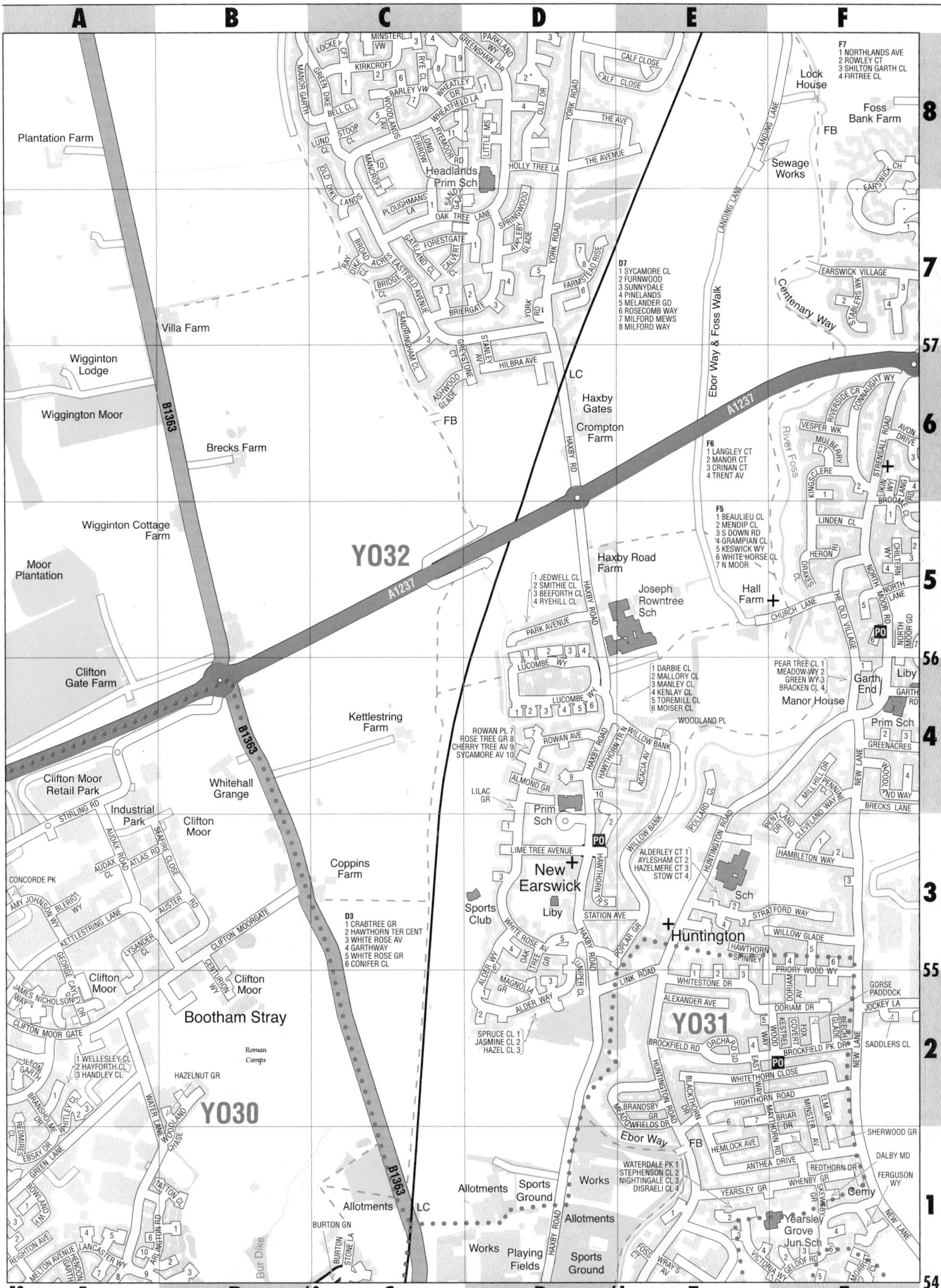

A1
1 CALDBECK CL
2 STONELANDS CT
3 BELMONT CL
4 HASTINGS CL
5 HARROW GLADE
6 WIMPOLE CL
7 HALIFAX CT
8 WATER LA
9 TAMWORTH RD
10 LUNDY CL

B1
1 HERDWICK CL
2 HEADLEY CL
3 MINCHIN CL

E2
1 SCAWTON AV
2 GORMIRE AV
3 ROLSTON AV
4 HEATHER CFT
5 BADGER PADDOCK
6 PINEWOOD GR
7 THORNFIELD DR

F1
1 DICKENS CL
2 HOMESTEAD CL
3 CARRNOCK CT
4 ANDREW DR
5 MONKTON RD
6 THERESA AV

F3
1 CHEVIOT CL
2 CAMBRIAN CL
3 KENDREW CL
4 MERLIN COVERT
5 FIRWOOD WHIN
6 OAK GLADE

228 226

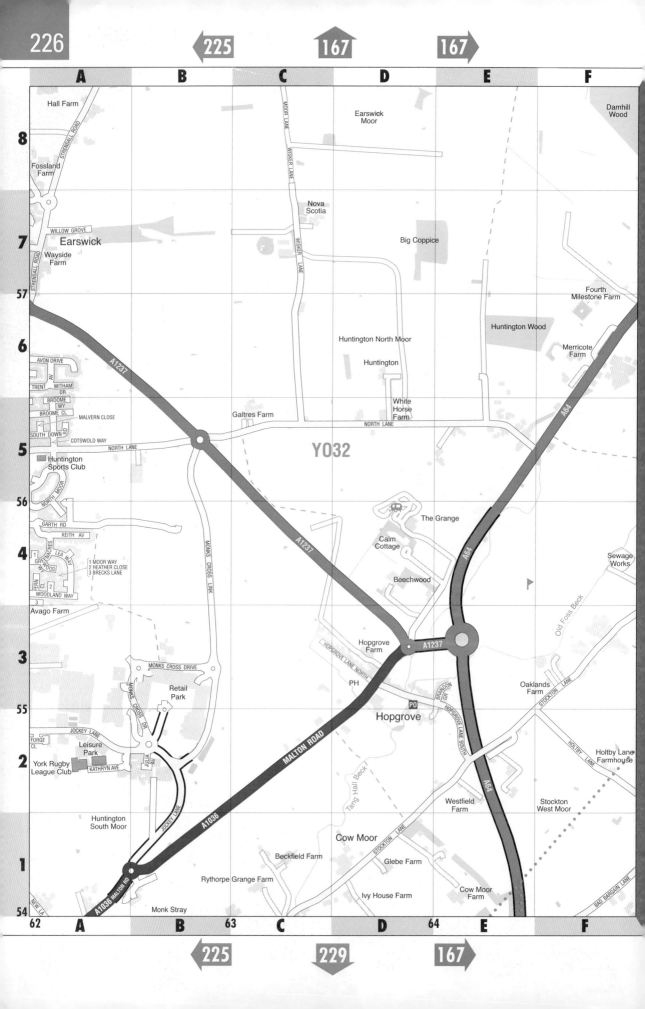

225
167
167

A   B   C   D   E   F

8

Hall Farm

Damhill
Wood

Earswick
Moor

Fossland
Farm

Nova
Scotia

7

Willow Grove

Earswick

Big Coppice

Wayside
Farm

Fourth
Milestone Farm

57

6

A1237

Huntington North Moor

Huntington Wood

Merricote
Farm

Huntington

AVON DRIVE

TRENT AV   WITHAM DR

BROOME WY

BROOME CL   MALVERN CLOSE

White
Horse
Farm

Galtres Farm

North Lane

SOUTH DOWN RD   COTSWOLD WAY

A64

5

NORTH LANE

YO32

Huntington
Sports Club

NORTH MOOR

56

GARTH RD

The Grange

KEITH AV

Calm
Cottage

4

GREENACRES   LEA WAY

1 MOOR WAY
2 HEATHER CLOSE
3 BRECKS LANE

A64

Sewage
Works

FERN WOOD

FERN CL   2

Beechwood

WOODLAND WAY   3

MONKS CROSS LINK

Avago Farm

Old Foss Beck

3

HOPGROVE LANE NORTH

Hopgrove
Farm

A1237

MONKS CROSS DRIVE

Oaklands
Farm

STOCKTON LANE

Retail
Park

MONKS CROSS DR

PH

BRANDON GR

HOPGROVE LANE SOUTH

55

JOCKEY LANE

PO

FORGE CL

Leisure
Park

JULIA AV

Hopgrove

HOLTBY LANE

Holtby Lane
Farmhouse

2

York Rugby
League Club

KATHRYN AVE

MALTON ROAD

A64

Westfield
Farm

Stockton
West Moor

JOCKEY LANE

Huntington
South Moor

A1036

Cow Moor

STOCKTON LANE

1

Beckfield Farm

Glebe Farm

A1036 MALTON RD

Rythorpe Grange Farm

Ivy House Farm

Cow Moor
Farm

BAD BARGAIN LANE

54

NEW LA

Monk Stray

62   A   B   63   C   D   64   E   F

225
229
167

F5
1 CHUDLEIGH RD
2 BROMLEY ST
3 ALBANY ST
4 WALWORTH ST N
5 HANOVER ST E
6 UPR HANOVER ST
7 HANOVER ST W
8 STAMFORD ST W
9 WALWORTH ST S
10 STAMFORD ST E
11 KINGSLAND TR
12 BRUNNEL CT
13 ST BARNABAS CT
14 REGENTS CT
15 VICTORIA CT
16 CARLISLE ST
17 CARLETON ST

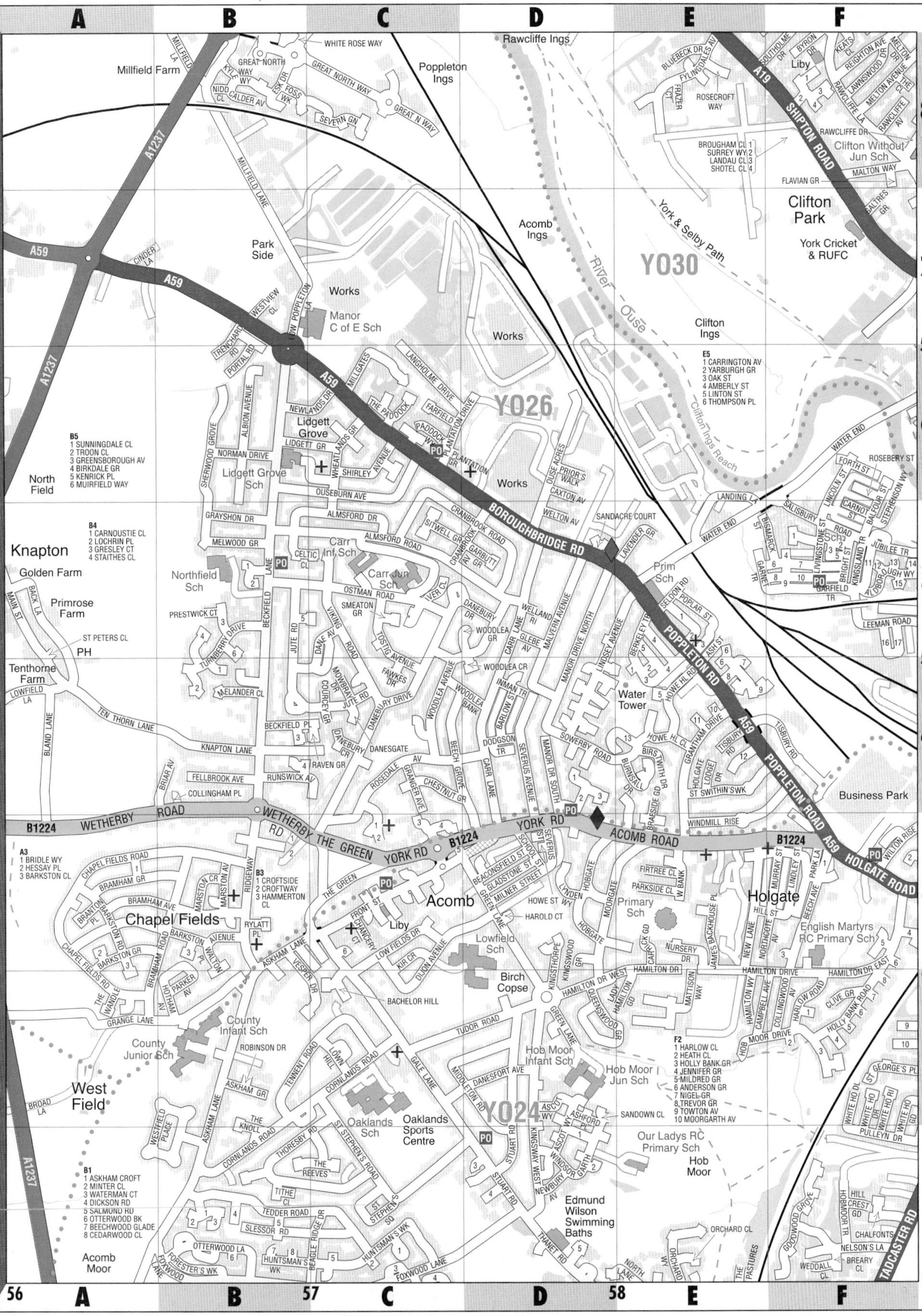

C1
1 THORNWOOD COVERT
2 MAPLEWOOD PADDOCK
3 FOXWOOD LANE
4 HERMAN WALK
5 FIR HEATH CL

C3
1 KIRK VIEW
2 CHURCH MEWS
3 ELMTREE GDNS
4 OAK RISE
5 CROSS ST
6 GALE FARM CT

D1
1 WOODFORD PL
2 KEMPTON C
3 CLAY PL
4 CHESNEY FIELDS
5 ST JAMES PLACE

D4
1 PATELY PL
2 HEBDON RISE
3 BAILDON CL

E4
1 WINCHESTER GR
2 GARLAND ST
3 WINCHESTER AV
4 CHATSWORTH TR
5 DILYS GR
6 PEPPERCORN CL
7 BONINGTON CT
8 RENSHAW GDNS
9 HILLARY GARTH
10 SEGRAVE WALK
11 MANTHORPE WK
12 CHELWOOD WK
13 BOUTHWAITE DR

F3
1 FALCONER ST
2 ENFIELD CR
3 BARRETT AVE
4 BARBARA GR
5 CAROLINE CL
6 ROBIN GR

A8
1 LINDEN GROVE
2 MARTEN CLOSE
3 RAINSBOROUGH WAY

A7
1 BELCOMBE WAY
2 HUDSON CRESCENT
3 CLIFTON PLACE
4 PINFOLD COURT

227

C7
1 UPR NEWBOROUGH ST
2 ALLAN ST
3 MURROUGH WILSON PL
4 FEVERSHAM CR
5 HILLSBOROUGH TR
6 HUDSON ST

225

E8
1 KIRKHAM AV
2 THE CROSSWAY
3 LILLING AV

E5
1 HAWTHORN ST
2 EMMERSON ST
3 FLEMING AV
4 SCROPE AV

F8
1 ALBERT CL
2 VICTORIA WY
3 MORRITT CL
4 FOSTON GR
5 THORNFIELD AV
6 LABURNUM GARTH

For full street detail of the highlighted area see page 233.

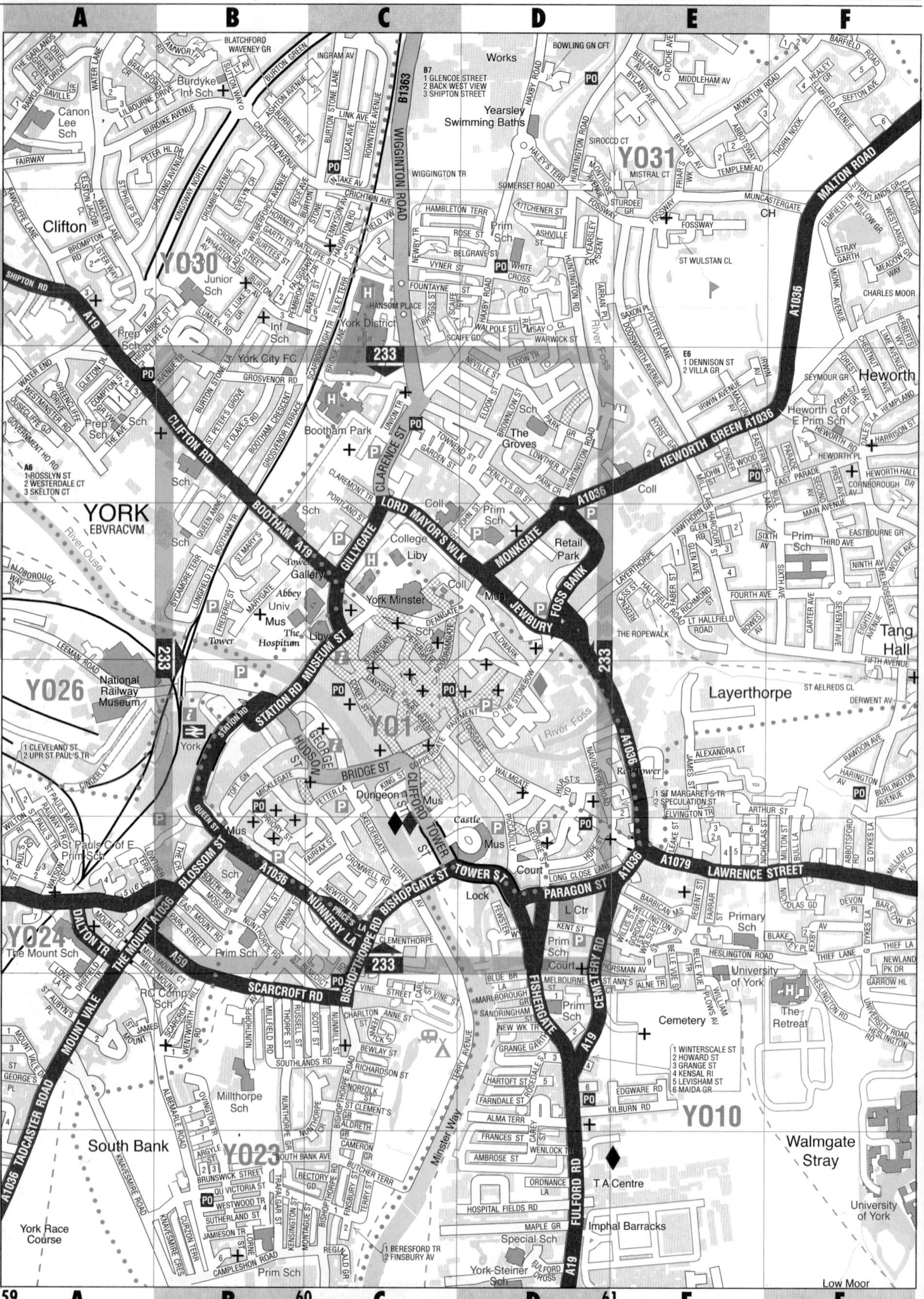

A2
1 TOWTON AV
2 TRENTHOLME DR
3 MOORGARTH AV
4 WHITE HO GD

A3
1 ENFIELD CR
2 WATSON TR
3 CECILIA PL
4 CAMBRIDGE ST
5 OXFORD ST
6 MOUNT EPHRAIM
7 HOLGATE BR GD

227

B1
1 WINDSOR ST
2 HUBERT ST
3 RUBY ST
4 COUNT DE BURGH TR
5 BALMORAL TR
6 LICHFIELD CT

231

B2
1 TELFORD TR
2 PHILADELPHIA TR
3 ADELAIDE ST

E3
1 BRINKWORTH TR
2 THOMAS ST
3 HILDA ST
4 GRANVILLE TR
5 LANSDOWNE TR
6 HERBERT ST
7 CHAUCER ST
8 DAYSFOOT CT
9 APOLLO ST

F3
1 ST NICHOLAS PL
2 ARNSIDE PL

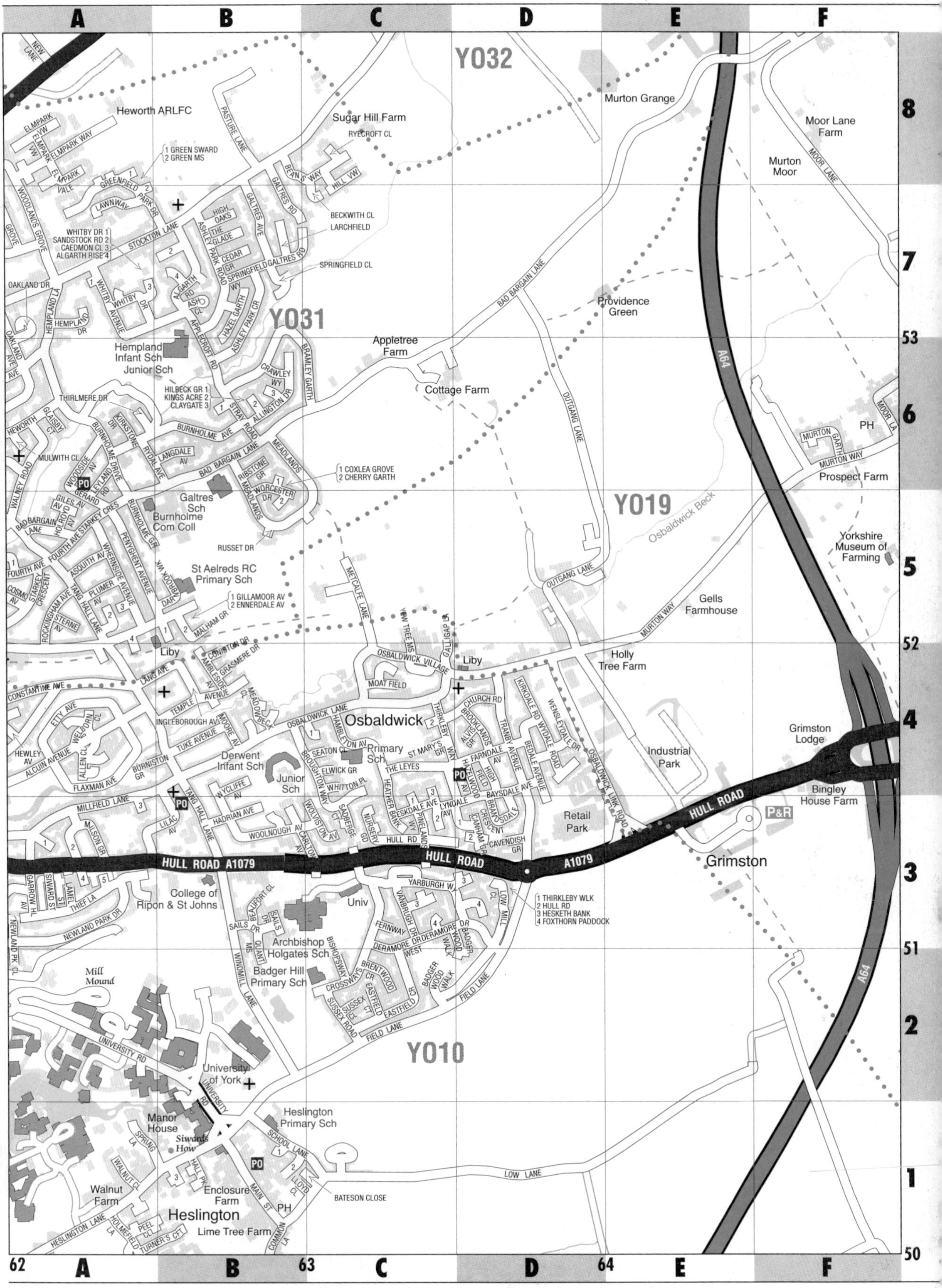

A5
1 MELROSE CL
2 APPLEBY PL
3 INGLETON WK
4 WOODHOUSE GR

A   B   C   D   E   F

YO32

Murton Grange

Moor Lane Farm

Heworth ARLFC

8

Sugar Hill Farm
RYECROFT CL

Murton Moor

1 GREEN SWARD
2 GREEN MS

ELMPARK
VW
ELMPARK WAY
BEAN'S WAY
HILL VW

MOOR LANE

PASTURE LANE

GALTRES RD

7

GREENFIELD PARK DR
LAWNWAY
STOCKTON LANE
HIGH OAKS
THE GLADE
CEDAR
GALTRES AVE
BECKWITH CL
LARCHFIELD

WHITBY DR 1
SANDSTOCK RD 2
CAEDMON CL 3
ALGARTH RISE 4

SPRINGFIELD CL

Bad Bargain Lane

Providence Green

53

OAKLAND DR

WHITBY AVENUE
WHITBY DR
HEMPLAND DR
HEMPLAND LA

ALGARTH RD

ASHLEY PARK RD

SPRINGFIELD WY

A64

YO31

Appletree Farm

6

OAKLAND RD
HEMPLAND AVE

HAZEL GARTH
CRAWLEY WY
BRAMLEY GARTH
ALLINGTON DR

Cottage Farm

MURTON
MURTON WAY
MURTON GARTH RD

PH

Hempland Infant Sch
Junior Sch

Prospect Farm

HILBECK GR 1
KINGS ACRE 2
CLAYGATE 3

STRAY RD
MEADLANDS

YO19

Osbaldwick Beck

THIRLMERE DR
HEWORTH
GLASBY
KIRKSTONE DR
BURNHOLME DR
RYDAL AV
LANGDALE AV
BURNHOLME AVE

RIBSTONE GR
WORCESTER DR

1 COXLEA GROVE
2 CHERRY GARTH

Yorkshire Museum of Farming

5

MULWITH CL
PO
WALNEY ROAD
CLELAND ST

Galtres Sch
Burnholme Corn Coll

OUTGANG LANE

OUTGANG RD

Gells Farmhouse

BAD BARGAIN LANE

RUSSET DR

MURTON WAY

GILES AV
BOROUGHBRIDGE
FOURTH AVE STARKEY CRES

St Aelreds RC Primary Sch

METCALFE LANE

52

FOURTH AVE
COSMO AV
ASQUITH AVENUE
WENLOCK AVE
PLUMER AVENUE
STEANE

1 GILLAMOOR AV
2 ENNERDALE AV

MALHAM GR

YEW TREE MS
GILL GAP YD

Holly Tree Farm

Grimston Lodge

4

ROCKINGHAM AV
FIFTH AVE
HALL LANE

Liby
CONISTON DR
GRASMERE DR

OSBALDWICK VILLAGE

Liby

MOAT FIELD

CHURCH RD

Bingley House Farm

CONSTANTINE AVE

LANG AVE

OSBALDWICK LANE

CHURCH RD
KIRKDALE DR
THRIANBY
WOLDALE RD
WENSLEYDALE DR
BEDALE AVENUE

Industrial Park

HULL ROAD

P&R

ETTY AVE
HEWLEY AV
ALCUIN AVENUE
ALLEN CL

Osbaldwick

3

TEMPLE AVENUE
INGLEBOROUGH AV
TUKE AVENUE
MEADOW DR

Derwent Infant Sch

HAMBLETON AV
BOGTON AV

Primary Sch
ST MARY'S
THE LEYES

FARNDALE AVENUE

Retail Park

Grimston

A64

BURNSTON GR
FLAXMAN AVE

Junior Sch
WYCLIFFE AVE

SEATON CL
ELWICK GR
WHITTON PL

HEATHER BANK
BESKDALE AVE

BAYSDALE AVE
BRANDSDALE
CRESCENT
CANHAM GR
CAVENDISH GR

MILLFIELD LANE
HADRIAN AVE
PO
LILAC AV

WOOLNOUGH AVE
WOOLNOUGH AV

NURSERY
SADBERGE
HULL RD
LYNDALE AV

1 THIRKLEBY WLK
2 HULL RD
3 HESKETH BANK
4 FOXTHORN PADDOCK

HULL ROAD A1079

HULL ROAD

HULL ROAD

A1079

3

NELSON GR
SIWARD ST
GARROW HL
JAMES ST
THIEF LA

College of Ripon & St Johns

AIRPORT CL
SAILS DR

Univ

YARBURGH WY

LOW MILL

51

NEWLAND PK DR

SAILS DR
WINDMILL LANE
BISHOPSWAY

Archbishop Holgates Sch

FERNWAY
DERAMORE DR

DERAMORE DR WEST

BADGER WOOD WALK
FIELD LANE

Mill Mound

NEWLAND PK CL

Badger Hill Primary Sch

CROSSWAYS
SUSSEX CL
SUSSEX ROAD
EASTFIELD

BRENTWOOD
FASTFIELD CR
EASTFIELD AVE
BADGER WOOD WALK

2

YO10

UNIVERSITY RD

University of York

FIELD LANE

Heslington Primary Sch

MAIN ST

1

Manor House
Siwards How

UNIVERSITY RD

SCHOOL LANE

Walnut Farm

SPRUCE LA
WALNUT CL
HALL LANE
PO
LIME TREE AVE

Enclosure Farm

PH

LOW LANE

50

HESLINGTON LANE
HOLMES CL
PEEL CL
TURNER'S CFT

Heslington

Lime Tree Farm

62   A   B   63   C   D   64   E   F

A3
1 HEATHFIELD RD
2 OWSTON AV
3 WAYNEFLEET GR
4 CYCLE ST
5 NORMAN ST

B1
1 ENCLOSURE GD
2 HESLINGTON CT
3 HOLBURNS CFT

C3
1 SHALLOWDALE GR
2 BRACKEN HILL
3 KIMBERLOWS WOOD HILL
4 PINEWOOD HILL

C4
1 VICARAGE GD
2 ST THOMAS'S CL
3 GIVENDALE GR

182

227

C8
1 HINTON AV
2 LYDHAM CT
3 MARTIN CHEESEMAN CT
4 CRANFIELD PL

D8
1 FARMLANDS RD
2 DRINGFIELD CL
3 HERDSMAN RD
4 SANDCROFT CL
5 DEEPDALE

E8
1 TURNMIRE RD
2 SOUTHFIELD CR
3 MEADOW CT
4 THE PASTURES
5 ST HELEN'S RD

F8
1 KENSINGTON CT
2 REGENCY MS

A B C D E F

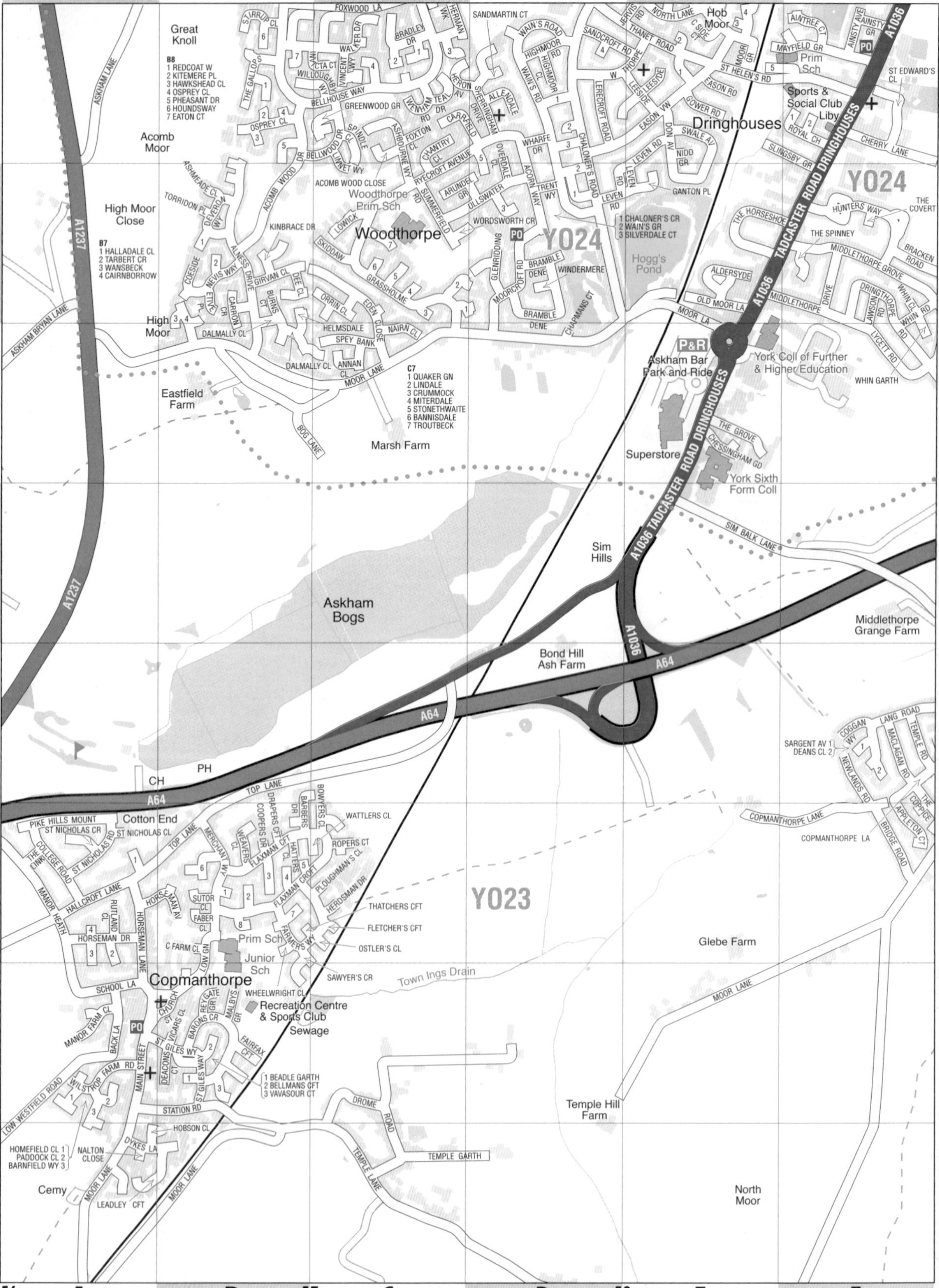

A B C D E F

A3
1 LARKFIELD CL
2 HORSEMAN CL
3 LYNWOOD AV
4 LYNWOOD VW

B3
1 SADDLERS CL
2 FARRIERS CFT
3 WAGGONERS DR
4 POTTERS DR
5 WAINERS CL
6 MILLERS CFT
7 LORINERS DR
8 GARDENERS CL

182

191

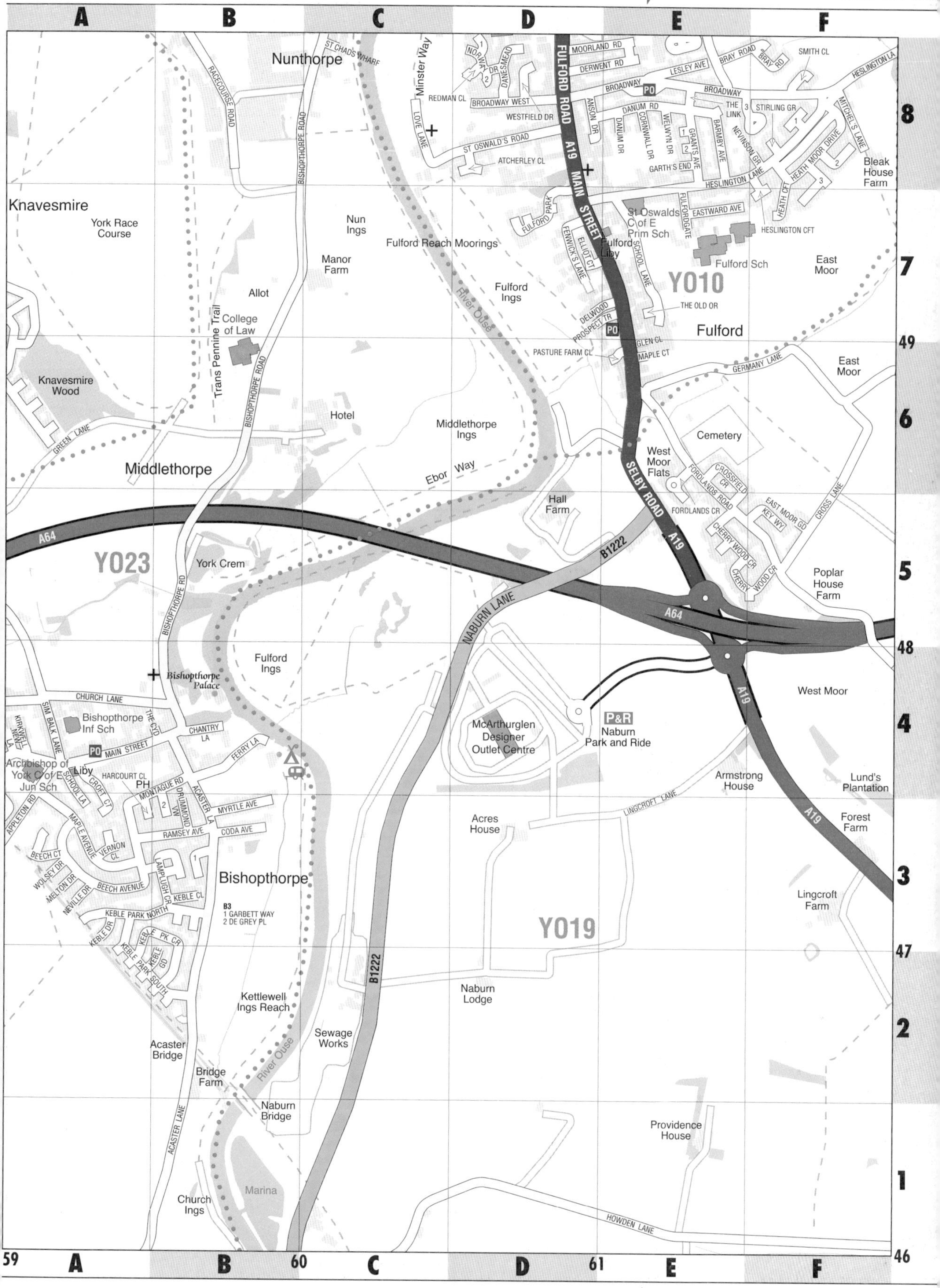

C5
1 YORK ST
2 HARPER ST
3 DOUGLAS ST
4 RAINCLIFFE ST
5 LONDESBOROUGH ST
6 HILDA ST
7 PORTHOLME CR
8 SOUTH PAR
9 TURNERS SQ
10 AUDUS ST
11 MARKET PL

D5
1 MICKLEGATE
2 WREN LA
3 CHURCH HL
4 CHURCH LA

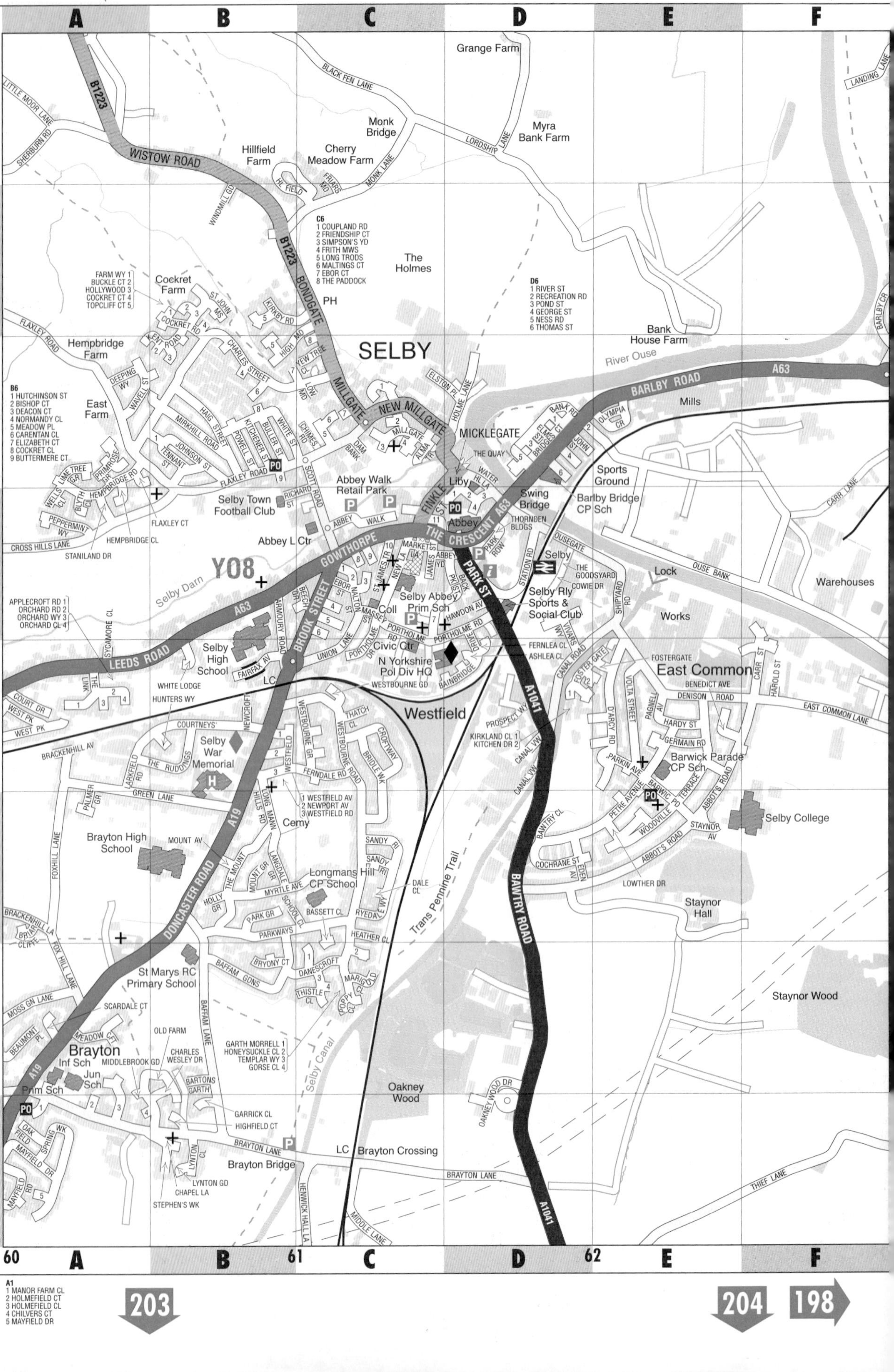

A1
1 MANOR FARM CL
2 HOLMEFIELD CT
3 HOLMEFIELD CL
4 CHILVERS CT
5 MAYFIELD DR

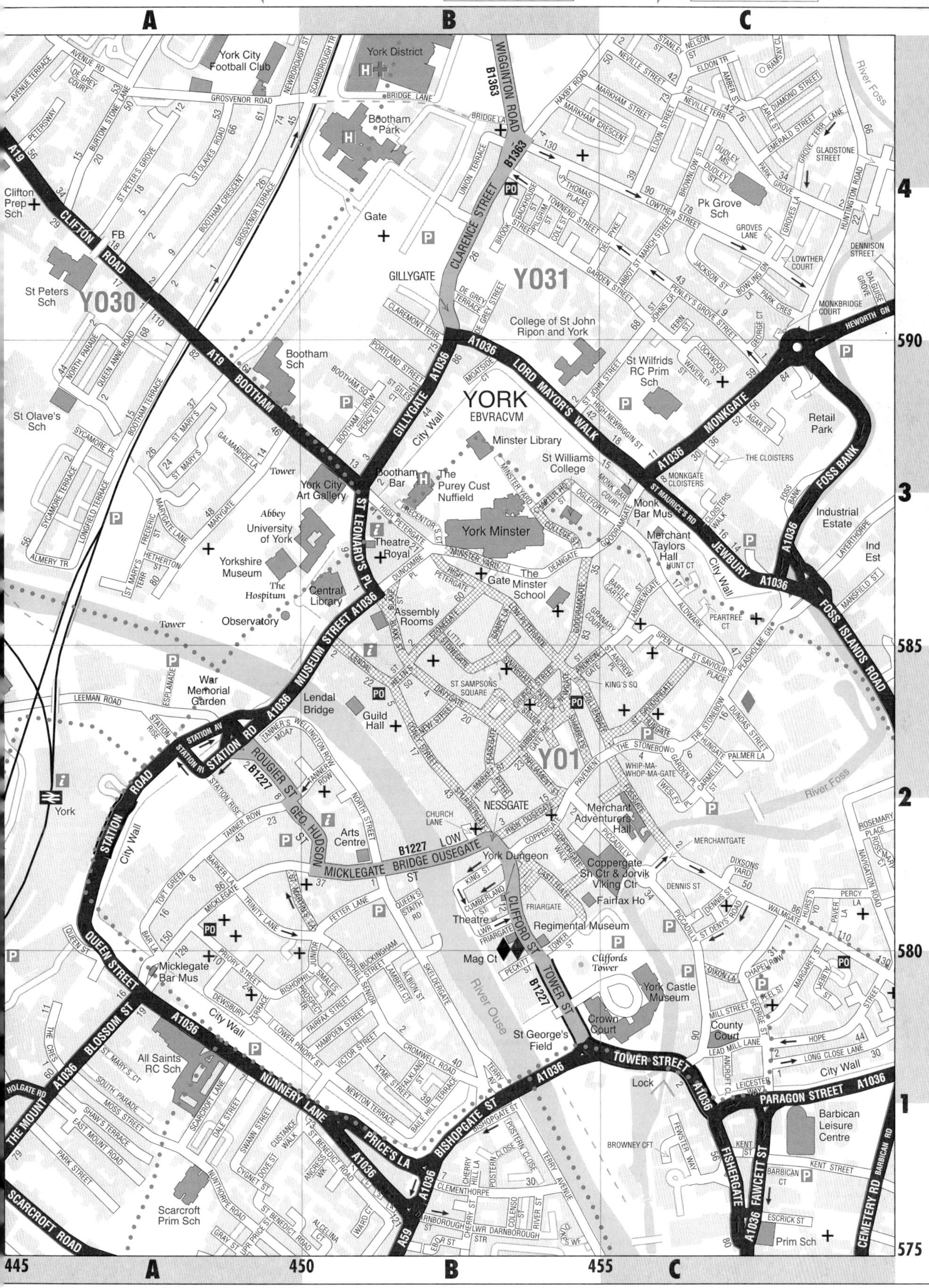

Index

Church Rd **6** Beckenham BR2..........**53** C6

Place name	Location number	Locality, town or village	Postcode district	Page and grid square
May be abbreviated on the map	Present when a number indicates the place's position in a crowded area of mapping	Shown when more than one place has the same name	District for the indexed place	Page number and grid reference for the standard mapping

Public and commercial buildings are highlighted in magenta   **Places of interest** are highlighted in blue with a star★

Abbreviations used in the index

Acad	Academy	Comm	Common	Gd	Ground	L	Leisure
App	Approach	Cott	Cottage	Gdn	Garden	La	Lane
Arc	Arcade	Cres	Crescent	Gn	Green	Liby	Library
Ave	Avenue	Cswy	Causeway	Gr	Grove	Mdw	Meadow
Bglw	Bungalow	Ct	Court	H	Hall	Meml	Memorial
Bldg	Building	Ctr	Centre	Ho	House	Mkt	Market
Bsns, Bus	Business	Ctry	Country	Hospl	Hospital	Mus	Museum
Bvd	Boulevard	Cty	County	HQ	Headquarters	Orch	Orchard
Cath	Cathedral	Dr	Drive	Hts	Heights	Pal	Palace
Cir	Circus	Dro	Drove	Ind	Industrial	Par	Parade
Cl	Close	Ed	Education	Inst	Institute	Pas	Passage
Cnr	Corner	Emb	Embankment	Int	International	Pk	Park
Coll	College	Est	Estate	Intc	Interchange	Pl	Place
Com	Community	Ex	Exhibition	Junc	Junction	Prec	Precinct

Prom	Prom
Rd	Road
Recn	Recreation
Ret	Retail
Sh	Shopping
Sq	Square
St	Street
Sta	Station
Terr	Terrace
TH	Town Hall
Univ	University
Wk, Wlk	Walk
Wr	Water
Yd	Yard

Index of localities, towns and villages

A

Aberford	194	F7
Acaster Malbis	191	D8
Acaster Selby	191	B4
Acklam	169	E8
Acklam	6	E8
Acomb	227	C3
Addingham	174	F5
Agglethorpe	60	A1
Ainderby Quernhow	88	C4
Ainderby Steeple	64	B7
Ainthorpe	29	C6
Aire View	173	D1
Airedale	201	B4
Airmyn	205	E4
Airton	155	A6
Airy Hill	208	D4
Aiskew	63	A3
Aislaby	5	C3
Aislaby	31	F7
Aislaby	95	D8
Aldborough	141	C5
Aldbrough St John	2	A2
Aldfield	139	A8
Aldwark	142	C2
Allerston	97	C5
Allerton Bywater	200	D6
Allerton Mauleverer	163	E4
Alne	142	F4
Alne Station	143	A5
Amotherby	121	B4
Ampleforth	92	C1
Angram	182	C3
Angram	35	E6
Appersett	56	C5

Appleton Roebuck	190	F5
Appleton Wiske	24	B3
Appleton-le-Moors	70	F2
Appleton-le-Street	120	F4
Appletreewick	157	D7
Archdeacon Newton	2	F7
Arkendale	163	B8
Arncliffe	107	D2
Arrathorne	62	A8
Asenby	115	B6
Askham Bryan	182	F3
Askham Richard	182	D3
Askrigg	57	F6
Askwith	176	D3
Asselby	205	D7
Aughton	193	C1
Austwick	130	E7
Aysgarth	58	E3
Azerley	113	A5

B

Bagby	90	C3
Bainbridge	57	D5
Baldersby	88	D1
Baldersby St James	114	E8
Balne	207	C5
Bank Newton	172	B8
Barden	61	A8
Barkston Ash	195	F7
Barlby	198	B5
Barlow	204	C7
Barmby on the Marsh	205	B7
Barnoldswick	171	D1
Barnoldswick	103	A2

Barrowcliff	212	D7
Barton	21	D7
Barton Hill	146	D3
Barton-le-Street	120	E5
Barton-le-Willows	146	D1
Barwick in Elmet	194	B8
Battersby	27	D6
Beadlam	93	C7
Beal	202	D4
Beamsley	174	F7
Beckermonds	80	D3
Beckwithshaw	178	A7
Bedale	63	B2
Bedlam	161	A8
Bell Busk	155	A3
Bellerby	60	D7
Ben Rhydding	218	E3
Beningbrough	165	D4
Bent	187	D7
Bewerley	137	B3
Bickerton	181	A5
Biggin	196	F5
Bilbrough	182	D1
Bilton	219	E6
Bilton in Ainsty	181	E4
Binsoe	86	F2
Birdforth	116	E6
Birdsall	148	B4
Birkby	23	B1
Birkin	202	D6
Birstwith	160	E6
Bishop Monkton	140	A5
Bishop Thornton	138	F2
Bishop Wilton	169	F2
Bishopthorpe	231	B3
Bishopton	113	D2
Black Banks	3	D2

Blackwell	3	B4
Blades	37	B5
Blazefield	137	E4
Blubberhouses	159	D2
Boltby	66	F1
Bolton Abbey	174	E8
Bolton Bridge	174	F8
Bolton Percy	190	D4
Bolton-on-Swale	41	F6
Boosbeck	9	E8
Bootham Stray	225	B2
Boothferry	205	F5
Booze	17	F1
Bordley	133	D3
Boroughbridge	141	C5
Borrowby	11	D6
Borrowby	65	E4
Bossall	168	D7
Boston Spa	188	F8
Botton	29	B3
Bouthwaite	110	E2
Bracewell	171	C3
Brackenbottom	105	E3
Brafferton	116	A1
Braidley	83	B2
Bramham	188	F5
Brandsby	118	C3
Branksome	2	F6
Branton Green	142	A1
Brawby	94	F1
Brawith	26	A6
Braythorn	177	E4
Brayton	232	A2
Brearton	162	A7
Breighton	199	D5
Bridge Hewick	114	B1
Bridgehouse Gate	137	B4

Briggswath	32	B7
Briscoerigg	177	F5
Brockfield	167	E2
Brompton	43	F3
Brompton-by-Sawdon	98	C5
Brompton-on-Swale	41	B7
Brookfield	6	E5
Brotherton	201	D5
Broughton	121	D4
Broughton	172	E6
Broxa	74	C6
Brunthwaite	174	D1
Bubwith	199	D7
Buckden	107	E8
Bugthorpe	169	D4
Bullamoor	44	B1
Bulmer	146	B6
Burley in Wharfedale	176	B1
Burn	203	D7
Burn Bridge	222	D3
Burneston	87	C7
Burniston	75	C8
Burnsall	157	B8
Burnt Yates	160	F8
Burrill	62	E2
Burtersett	56	E4
Burton Fleming	126	E3
Burton in Lonsdale	102	F3
Burton Leonard	140	B2
Burton Salmon	201	F6
Burythorpe	147	F3
Buttercrambe	168	F5
Butterwick	120	E8
Butterwick	125	B2
Byland Abbey	91	E1
Byram	201	F4

C

Calcutt ...221 A3
Caldbergh ...84 B7
Caldwell ...1 B4
Calton ...155 B6
Camblesforth ...204 D5
Camp Hill ...87 F5
Cantsfield ...102 B4
Carlbury ...2 E7
Carlesmoor ...111 E4
Carleton in Craven ...173 A4
Carlton ...1 F3
Carlton ...204 D3
Carlton ...83 E7
Carlton ...68 E1
Carlton Husthwaite ...116 F7
Carlton in Cleveland ...26 A3
Carlton Miniott ...89 C4
Carperby ...58 E4
Carthorpe ...87 E6
Castle Bolton ...59 A6
Castleford ...200 E4
Castleton ...29 A6
Castley ...178 A1
Cattal ...164 A1
Catterick ...41 D5
Catterick Bridge ...41 D6
Catterick Garrison ...209 D2
Catterton ...190 B8
Catton ...88 F1
Cawood ...197 B8
Cawthorne ...71 D4
Cawton ...119 C7
Cayton ...100 C6
Chantry ...59 D2
Chapel Fields ...227 B3
Chapel Haddlesey ...203 C5
Chapel-le-Dale ...104 C4
Charltons ...9 C6
Chop Gate ...46 F6
Church Fenton ...196 B7
Church Houses ...48 F4
Clapham ...130 C8
Clapham Green ...160 E5
Claxton ...168 B7
Cleasby ...2 F4
Cliffe ...198 E2
Cliffe ...2 B6
Clifford ...188 E2
Clifton ...176 F3
Clifton ...228 A2
Clifton Park ...227 F7
Clint ...161 A6
Clints ...39 C8
Clough ...55 A7
Cloughton ...54 C1
Cloughton Newlands ...54 C2
Coates ...171 E2
Cobby Syke ...159 F2
Cock Hill ...165 B2
Cockayne ...48 A5
Cockerton ...3 B6
Colburn ...41 A5
Cold Cotes ...103 F2
Cold Kirby ...91 D7
Collingham ...188 A8
Colsterdale ...84 E4
Colton ...190 E7
Commondale ...9 D1
Coneysthorpe ...120 D2
Coneythorpe ...163 A5
Coniston Cold ...155 A1
Conistone ...134 C6
Cononley ...173 C2
Cononley Woodside ...173 C3
Constable Burton ...61 C5
Coomboots ...75 B6
Copgrove ...140 C2
Copmanthorpe ...230 B2
Copt Hewick ...114 C2
Cotterdale ...55 F8
Cotton Tree ...186 A2
Coulby Newham ...7 A5
Coulton ...119 B5
Countersett ...57 C2
Coverham ...60 C1
Cowan Bridge ...102 D7
Cowesby ...66 C4
Cowling ...62 D2
Cowling ...187 B6
Cowthorpe ...180 E7
Coxwold ...117 D8
Crackpot ...37 B3
Cracoe ...156 C7
Crag ...187 D6
Crakehill ...115 E4
Crambe ...146 F3
Crambeck ...146 F6
Crathorne ...25 A6
Cray ...81 E2
Crayke ...118 A1
Cridling Stubbs ...206 C8
Crimple ...223 D8
Cringles ...174 C3
Crockey Hill ...184 A1

Croft-on-Tees ...22 D8
Cropton ...71 B4
Crosby Court ...65 B6
Cross Hills ...187 E7
Cross Lanes ...143 D3
Crossgates ...99 E7
Crowdon ...54 A4
Cubeck ...57 F7
Cundall ...115 E3
Cutsyke ...200 E3

D

Dacre ...159 F7
Dacre Banks ...159 F8
Dalby ...119 B2
Dalesbridge Centre ...130 E6
Dallow ...111 F2
Dalton ...19 D7
Dalton ...115 F7
Dalton Gates ...22 D4
Dalton-on-Tees ...22 E6
Danby ...29 C7
Danby Wiske ...43 C5
Darley ...160 A6
Darlington ...3 E6
Daw Cross ...222 B3
Deepdale ...80 F2
Deerstones ...175 B8
Deighton ...44 A8
Deighton ...192 A7
Denton ...176 A3
Dishforth ...115 A4
Downholme ...39 D4
Draughton ...174 B7
Drax ...204 F5
Drebley ...157 D6
Dringhouses ...230 E8
Duggleby ...149 B6
Dunkeswick ...178 E2
Dunnington ...184 F7
Dunsley ...12 F2

E

Eaglescliffe ...5 E5
Earby ...172 B1
Earswick ...226 A7
Easby ...27 B7
Easby ...209 F5
Easington ...11 A8
Easingwold ...143 D8
East Appleton ...41 D2
East Ayton ...99 B8
East Barnby ...12 C3
East Common ...232 E4
East Cottingwith ...193 C5
East Cowton ...22 F2
East Garforth ...194 E4
East Harlsey ...44 E6
East Hauxwell ...61 D8
East Heslerton ...124 A7
East Knapton ...123 C6
East Layton ...20 C8
East Lutton ...150 C8
East Marton ...172 B6
East Ness ...94 B1
East Newton ...93 C2
East Rounton ...24 E2
East Row ...13 A3
East Witton ...61 A1
Eastbourne ...3 E4
Eastburn ...187 F7
Eastby ...156 F1
Easterside ...7 A7
Eastfield ...100 A7
Eavestone ...138 B7
Ebberston ...97 E5
Eggborough ...202 F2
Egglescliffe ...5 E4
Egton ...31 B5
Egton Bridge ...31 A4
Eldroth ...130 E4
Ellerbeck ...44 F3
Ellerburn ...96 E7
Ellerton ...193 C2
Ellerton ...41 E4
Ellingstring ...85 D6
Elton ...5 C8
Elvington ...185 B2
Embsay ...217 D8
Enterpen ...25 C4
Eppleby ...1 E4
Eryholme ...23 A7
Escrick ...192 B5
Eshton ...155 D3
Everley ...74 F4
Exelby ...63 D1

F

Faceby ...25 F2
Fadmoor ...69 F4
Fairburn ...201 D7
Falsgrave ...212 D3
Fangdale Beck ...47 A1
Farlington ...144 F6
Farnham ...162 D7
Farnhill ...173 E1
Farnley ...177 B2
Faverdale ...3 B8
Fawdington ...115 F3
Fearby ...85 F4
Feetham ...37 C5
Feizor ...131 B6
Felixkirk ...90 C7
Fenwick ...207 B3
Ferrensby ...162 F7
Ferrybridge ...201 D3
Fewston ...159 F1
Fewston Bents ...159 F1
Filey ...101 C3
Finghall ...61 D4
Firby ...63 A1
Firby ...147 A5
Firth Moor ...3 F4
Fishpool ...177 C2
Flasby ...155 E3
Flawith ...142 E4
Flaxby ...163 B4
Flaxton ...145 E4
Fleets ...156 A7
Flixton ...99 F2
Folkton ...100 B2
Follifoot ...223 F5
Forcett ...1 D3
Fordon ...126 A6
Foredale ...131 C8
Forest ...42 B7
Forest Moor ...220 F1
Foston ...146 B4
Foul Green ...9 D1
Foulrice ...118 F1
Fowgill ...129 B8
Foxholes ...125 D3
Foxton ...44 E3
Foxup ...106 C7
Fremington ...38 D6
Fryton ...120 A6
Fulford ...231 E7
Full Sutton ...169 A2
Fylingthorpe ...33 B3

G

Gainford ...1 F3
Galphay ...112 F3
Gammersgill ...83 C5
Ganthorpe ...120 A1
Ganton ...125 A8
Garforth ...194 C4
Gargrave ...155 D1
Garriston ...61 B7
Gate Helmsley ...168 B2
Gateforth ...203 A7
Gatenby ...64 A2
Gauber ...78 F1
Gayle ...56 D4
Gayles ...19 E6
Gerrick ...10 C3
Giggleswick ...131 C2
Gill ...187 A6
Gillamoor ...70 A6
Gilling East ...118 F8
Gilling West ...20 E4
Girsby ...23 D7
Glaisdale ...30 D4
Glass Houghton ...201 D4
Glasshouses ...137 C3
Glusburn ...187 D8
Goathland ...51 E8
Goldsborough ...163 A2
Goldsborough ...12 D5
Gollinglith Foot ...85 B3
Goulton ...25 E3
Gowdall ...204 A1
Gowthorpe ...169 C1
Grafton ...141 D2
Grange ...57 D5
Grassington ...134 E3
Great Ayton ...7 F2
Great Barugh ...95 A1
Great Broughton ...26 E5
Great Burdon ...3 D7
Great Busby ...26 C4
Great Crakehall ...62 E4
Great Edstone ...94 C7
Great Fencote ...63 C8
Great Habton ...121 B7
Great Heck ...207 D2
Great Langton ...42 D3
Great Ouseburn ...164 B8
Great Preston ...200 C8

Great Smeaton ...23 C3
Great Thirkleby ...90 D1
Green Close ...130 A8
Green Hammerton ...164 C3
Green Hill ...194 F8
Greenhow ...136 D3
Grewelthorpe ...112 D7
Greygarth ...111 F3
Greystonegill ...129 C8
Grimston ...229 E3
Grindale ...127 D2
Grinton ...38 C5
Gristhorpe ...100 E4
Grosmont ...31 D3
Grunsagill ...153 A1
Guisborough ...8 D7
Gunby ...199 D6
Gunnerside ...36 F4

H

Hackforth ...62 E8
Hackness ...74 F5
Hall Garth ...184 F6
Halton East ...174 C8
Halton Gill ...106 E7
Halton West ...154 A1
Hambleton ...174 D8
Hambleton ...196 F1
Hampsthwaite ...160 F5
Hanlith ...155 A8
Hardgate ...139 A1
Hardraw ...56 C6
Harlow Hill ...222 A3
Harmby ...60 E4
Harome ...93 C4
Harrogate ...219 D1
Harrogate Hill ...3 C8
Harrowgate Village ...3 E8
Hartforth ...20 D5
Hartlington ...157 C8
Harton ...168 C3
Hartwith ...160 B8
Haughton Le Skerne ...3 F6
Hawes ...56 D4
Hawkswick ...107 F1
Hawnby ...67 E4
Hazlewood ...175 A8
Healaugh ...182 A2
Healaugh ...37 F6
Healey ...85 E3
Heathfield ...136 F6
Heathwaite ...45 E8
Hebden ...135 A1
Hellifield ...154 B3
Hellifield Green ...154 B3
Helm ...57 D6
Helmsley ...92 F7
Helperby ...142 A8
Helperthorpe ...124 D1
Helwith Bridge ...131 D8
Hemingbrough ...198 F1
Hemlington ...6 F4
Hensall ...203 D2
Heslington ...229 B1
Hessay ...182 C8
Hetton ...155 F5
Hew Green ...160 D5
Heworth ...228 F6
Heyshaw ...159 D8
High Bentham ...129 B8
High Birstwith ...160 E5
High Bradley ...173 E4
High Catton ...185 D8
High Coniscliffe ...2 C6
High Ellington ...85 F6
High Grantley ...138 D8
High Harrogate ...220 A3
High Hawsker ...33 B6
High Hutton ...147 B7
High Kilburn ...91 B2
High Leven ...6 A3
High Marishes ...96 B1
High Mowthorpe ...149 D7
High Shaw ...56 D7
High Stakesby ...208 B5
High Worsall ...24 A8
Highfield ...199 E7
Hillam ...202 A7
Hilton ...6 C2
Hinderwell ...11 F7
Hipswell ...209 F1
Hirst Courtney ...203 F3
Hole Bottom ...135 A3
Holgate ...227 F3
Hollinthorpe ...194 A2
Holly Hill ...209 B5
Holme ...88 D5
Holme Green ...190 F4
Holtby ...167 F1
Hopetown ...200 C2
Hopgrove ...226 D2
Hopperton ...163 E3
Hornby ...23 E4

Hornby ...62 B8
Horsehouse ...83 C4
Horton ...171 B5
Horton in Ribblesdale ...105 C3
Houlsyke ...29 F6
Hovingham ...119 F6
Howe ...88 E3
Howgill ...157 E6
Howsham ...146 F1
Hubberholme ...81 C1
Huby ...144 A4
Huby ...178 B2
Hudswell ...40 A7
Hummersknott ...3 A5
Hunmanby ...126 F8
Hunsingore ...180 F8
Huntington ...225 E3
Hunton ...61 E7
Hurgill ...209 A7
Hurworth Place ...3 D1
Hurworth-on-Tees ...3 E1
Hut Green ...203 A2
Hutton Bonville ...43 C7
Hutton Buscel ...98 E7
Hutton Conyers ...114 A4
Hutton Gate ...8 D6
Hutton Hang ...61 D3
Hutton Mulgrave ...12 D1
Hutton Rudby ...25 C5
Hutton Sessay ...116 D7
Hutton Village ...8 E4
Hutton Wandesley ...182 A5
Hutton-le-Hole ...70 C5
Huttons Ambo ...147 B6

I

Ickornshaw ...187 A6
Ilkley ...218 B4
Ilton ...85 E1
Ingerthorpe ...139 C5
Ingleby Arncliffe ...45 B8
Ingleby Barwick ...6 B4
Ingleby Cross ...45 A7
Ingleby Greenhow ...27 C5
Ingleton ...103 D3
Ingmanthorpe ...180 E5
Inholmes ...189 C6
Ireby ...102 F6
Irton ...99 D6
Ivelet ...36 D5

J

Jennyfield ...219 A5
Junction ...187 F8

K

Keasden ...130 A5
Kelbrook ...186 A8
Keld ...35 E8
Keld Houses ...136 C2
Keldholme ...70 D1
Kelfield ...191 D1
Kellingley ...202 C2
Kellington ...202 F4
Kennythorpe ...147 F5
Kepwick ...66 C6
Kettleness ...12 D6
Kettlesing ...160 C3
Kettlesing Bottom ...160 D4
Kettlewell ...108 B3
Kexby ...185 C6
Key Green ...31 A3
Kilburn ...91 B2
Kildale ...27 E8
Kildwick ...187 F8
Killerby ...100 C5
Killinghall ...161 C5
Kilnsey ...134 B6
Kilton Thorpe ...10 B8
Kiplin ...42 B4
Kippax ...194 E1
Kirby Grindalythe ...149 E6
Kirby Hill ...20 A5
Kirby Knowle ...66 C2
Kirby Misperton ...95 D2
Kirby Sigston ...44 D1
Kirby Underdale ...170 A5
Kirby Wiske ...88 F8
Kirk Deighton ...180 B5
Kirk Hammerton ...164 C2
Kirk Smeaton ...206 B3
Kirkbridge ...62 F5
Kirkby ...26 D5
Kirkby Fleetham ...42 D1
Kirkby Hill ...141 B7
Kirkby Malham ...154 F8
Kirkby Malzeard ...112 D5
Kirkby Mills ...94 C8

L

Kirkby Overblow 179 A4
Kirkby Wharfe 190 A3
Kirkbymoorside 70 B1
Kirkham 147 A4
Kirklevington 24 F8
Kirklington 88 A4
Knapton 227 A5
Knaresborough 221 A6
Knavesmire 230 F7
Knayton 65 F2
Knedlington 205 F6
Knottingley 201 F3
Knottingley 202 B2
Knox 219 B7

L

Lane End 171 C2
Lane Ends 187 C6
Laneshaw Bridge 186 C4
Langbar 175 B6
Langbaurgh 7 F2
Langcliffe 131 E3
Langthorne 62 F6
Langthorpe 141 A6
Langthwaite 17 E1
Langtoft 151 D5
Langton 147 F6
Lastingham 70 F5
Laverton 112 D4
Lawkland 130 F5
Lawkland Green 131 A4
Layerthorpe 228 E4
Leake 65 F5
Lealholm 30 B6
Lealholm Side 30 C4
Leathley 177 D2
Leavening 147 E1
Lebberston 100 D5
Leck 102 E7
Ledsham 201 B8
Ledston 200 F7
Ledston Luck 194 E1
Leeming 63 D4
Leeming Bar 63 C5
Leighton 85 C2
Leppington 169 C8
Levisham 72 D5
Leyburn 60 D5
Leysthorpe 93 B1
Lindley 177 C4
Lingdale 9 F7
Lingerfield 162 B6
Lingfield 3 F5
Linton 180 A1
Linton 134 D1
Linton-on-Ouse 164 E7
Little Airmyn 205 E4
Little Ayton 8 B1
Little Barugh 95 C2
Little Crakehall 62 D5
Little Fencote 63 C8
Little Fenton 196 B6
Little Habton 121 A8
Little Heck 203 D1
Little Hutton 116 B7
Little Ouseburn 164 A7
Little Preston 194 B1
Little Ribston 180 A8
Little Sessay 116 C5
Little Skipwith 192 E1
Little Smeaton 23 C2
Little Smeaton 206 C3
Little Stainforth 131 D6
Little Studley 214 C7
Littlethorpe 214 F1
Litton 107 A5
Liverton 10 D6
Liverton Mines 10 C8
Lockton 72 D4
Lodge Green 36 F5
Lofthouse 110 C4
Londonderry 63 E2
Long Drax 205 A6
Long Lease 33 A7
Long Marston 182 A6
Long Preston 153 F5
Longnewton 5 A7
Longscales 160 C4
Loscoe 200 C1
Lothersdale 187 A8
Low Bentham 128 F8
Low Bradley 173 E3
Low Coniscliffe 2 F4
Low Dalby 72 F2
Low Dinsdale 4 C1
Low Ellington 86 A6
Low Garth 29 F4
Low Gate 138 F6
Low Gatherley 21 D1
Low Green 160 A6
Low Grantley 112 E1
Low Hawsker 33 A6
Low Hutton 147 C6

M

Low Laithe 137 F2
Low Marishes 122 C8
Low Mill 48 E2
Low Row 37 C4
Low Snaygill 173 D4
Low Town 5 B1
Low Whita 37 D5
Low Worsall 24 A8
Lower Altofts 200 A3
Lower Dunsforth 142 A4
Lower Mickletown 200 D6
Lower Westhouse 103 B4
Lowgill 128 F3
Lowna 70 A6
Lumb 187 A4
Lumby 195 E1
Lund 198 D3
Lythe 12 E4

M

Malham 133 A1
Maltby 6 C4
Malton 215 C4
Manfield 2 B4
Manor Park 176 B2
Margrove Park 9 D6
Markington 139 D3
Marrick 38 F4
Marsett 57 A1
Marske 39 C7
Marton 94 F6
Marton 141 D1
Marton 7 B7
Marton-in-the-Forest 144 E2
Marton-le-Moor 114 F1
Masham 86 B3
Masongill 103 A6
Maunby 64 D1
Meagill 159 D3
Mearbeck 153 D7
Melmerby 83 F8
Melmerby 114 C7
Melsonby 21 A7
Menethorpe 147 D6
Menthorpe 199 C5
Merrybent 2 E5
Methley 200 B5
Methley Junction 200 A4
Mewith Head 129 E6
Mickleby 12 A4
Micklefield 194 F4
Mickletown 200 B5
Mickley 112 F7
Middlecave 215 A5
Middleham 60 E2
Middlesmoor 110 B5
Middlethorpe 231 B6
Middleton 187 A6
Middleton 218 C7
Middleton 95 E8
Middleton One Row 4 D3
Middleton Quernhow 88 B1
Middleton St George 4 B4
Middleton Tyas 21 D5
Middleton-on-Leven 25 D8
Milby 141 B6
Mill Dam 129 C6
Mill Hirst 159 F7
Minskip 141 A3
Monk Fryston 202 B8
Monkhill 201 B1
Monkroyd 186 D4
Moor End 188 D8
Moor Monkton 165 A3
Moorsholm 10 B5
Morton-on-Swale 64 A6
Moss 207 D1
Moulton 21 D3
The Mount 214 D3
Mount Pleasant 7 B5
Mowden 3 A6
Moxby 144 D5
Muker 36 A5
Murton 184 D7
Muscoates 94 A3
Muston 100 F2
Myton-on-Swale 141 F5

N

Naburn 191 D8
Nappa 171 B8
Nawton 93 E7
Neasham 4 A1
Nesfield 175 B4
Nether Burrow 102 B6
Nether Poppleton 224 A2
Nether Silton 66 B7
Netherby 179 B1
New Earswick 225 D3
New Fryston 201 B6
New Houses 105 C4

N

New Micklefield 195 A3
New Park 219 B5
New Road Side 187 B5
New Row 8 F1
New Thirsk 211 A3
New Town 201 B2
New York 137 F1
Newall 176 F1
Newbiggin 57 F6
Newbiggin 101 A5
Newbiggin 82 D8
Newbridge 96 A8
Newby 104 A1
Newby 7 A3
Newby 75 E5
Newby 140 D6
Newby Cote 104 B1
Newby Wiske 64 E2
Newholm 13 A1
Newland 205 B3
Newsham 19 D8
Newsham 89 A8
Newsholme 171 A6
Newsholme 205 E8
Newthorpe 195 D3
Newton Kyme 189 B7
Newton Morrell 21 E8
Newton Mulgrave 11 E6
Newton under Roseberry 8 B4
Newton upon Derwent 185 E4
Newton-le-Willows 62 B4
Newton-on-Ouse 165 B6
Newton-on-Rawcliffe 72 A5
Nidd 161 E6
Norby 211 A4
Normanby 94 F4
Normanton 200 C1
North Cowton 22 C3
North Deighton 180 B6
North Duffield 199 A4
North Featherstone 200 E1
North Grimston 148 E6
North Ings 119 D1
North Kilvington 89 E8
North Lees 113 D4
North Otterington 64 D4
North Rigton 178 B5
North Stainley 113 D7
Northallerton 210 D4
Norton 206 E2
Norton-le-Clay 115 C2
Norton-on-Derwent 215 D3
Nosterfield 87 B3
Nun Appleton 190 F3
Nun Monkton 165 A4
Nunnington 93 E2
Nunthorpe 7 D5
Nunthorpe 231 C8
Nunwick 114 A5

O

Oak Tree 4 E4
Oakdale 161 B2
Oatlands 222 F6
Octon 151 F8
Old Byland 91 F8
Old Malton 215 E7
Old Micklefield 194 F4
Old Thirsk 211 C4
Oldstead 91 C3
Ormesby 7 C8
Osbaldwick 229 C4
Osgodby 198 C4
Osgodby 100 B7
Osgodby Common 198 C6
Osmotherley 45 C4
Oswaldkirk 93 A1
Otterburn 154 E4
Oughtershaw 80 C4
Oulston 117 E5
Outhgill 34 A8
Over Burrow 102 B7
Over Silton 66 B8
Overton 165 F2
Overtown 102 C7
Oxton 190 A6

P

Padside 159 B6
Padside Green 159 C6
Painsthorpe 170 B5
Pannal 222 E3
Pannal Ash 222 B5
Park 186 F5
Park End 7 B8
Parlington 194 E6
Pateley Bridge 137 C5
Patrick Brompton 62 C5
Pickering 95 E6
Pickhill 88 C6
Picton 24 D6

R

Piercebridge 2 A6
Place Newton 123 C3
Pockley 69 B1
Pollington 207 F6
Poole 201 F5
Port Mulgrave 11 F8
Potterton 188 C1
Potto 25 D2
Preston-on-Tees 5 F7
Preston-under-Scar 59 E6
Primrose Valley 101 C1

R

Rainton 114 E6
Ramsgill 110 E1
Raskelf 116 E2
Rathmell 153 C6
Ravenseat 15 C2
Ravensworth 20 A7
Raw 33 B4
Rawcliffe 205 A1
Rawcliffe 224 E2
Raydale 57 A1
Raygill 186 E8
Red Hill 201 A4
Redmire 59 C6
Reeth 38 B6
Reighton 127 D6
Riccall 198 A8
Richmond 209 C7
Rievaulx 92 B8
Rillington 122 F5
Ripley 161 C7
Ripon 214 E5
Risplith 138 E7
Robin Hood's Bay 33 D4
Roecliffe 140 F4
Romanby 210 B3
Rookwith 62 A1
Rosedale Abbey 49 E3
Rossett Green 222 D5
Roundhill Village 5 F5
Rowden 160 F4
Roxby 11 C7
Rudby 25 D5
Rufforth 182 C6
Runswick Bay 12 A7
Rushton 98 D6
Ruswarp 208 B3
Rylstone 156 B5
Ryther 190 F1
Ryton 121 F6

S

Sadberge 4 B8
St John's 194 F8
Salton 94 D3
Sand Hutton 168 B5
Sandhutton 89 A4
Sandsend 13 A3
Satron 36 D4
Sawdon 98 C7
Sawley 138 F6
Saxton 195 D8
Scackleton 119 C4
Scagglethorpe 122 D3
Scalby 75 D6
Scaling 11 A4
Scaling Dam 11 A4
Scampston 123 A6
Scarborough 213 B5
Scarthingwell 195 F7
Scawton 91 E6
Scorton 41 F7
Scotton 40 F2
Scotton 162 A6
Scrayingham 168 F7
Scriven 162 D5
Scruton 63 D7
Seamer 6 F1
Seamer 99 E6
Seave Green 47 A7
Sedbusk 56 E6
Selby 232 C6
Selly Hill 32 A8
Selside 105 A6
Sessay 116 B6
Settle 131 E3
Settrington 122 D1
Sexhow 25 D4
Sharow 214 F6
Shaw Mills 138 F1
Sherburn 124 D8
Sherburn in Elmet 195 D5
Sheriff Hutton 145 C5
Shipton 165 F5
Sicklinghall 179 C3
Silpho 74 E7
Silsden 174 C5
Simonstone 56 D6
Sinderby 88 C4

T

Sinnington 95 A8
Skeeby 21 A1
Skelton 224 C6
Skelton on Ure 140 E7
Skerne Park 3 C3
Skewsby 119 A1
Skipton 216 F4
Skipton-on-Swale 88 C2
Skipwith 192 E1
Skirethorns 134 C2
Skirpenbeck 169 A4
Skyreholme 157 E7
Slapewath 9 C5
Sledmere 150 B3
Sleights 32 A4
Slingsby 120 C6
Small Banks 174 B7
Smelthouses 137 F3
Snainton 98 A5
Snaith 204 C1
Snape 87 A1
Sneaton 32 D6
Sneatonthorpe 32 F5
Sockburn 23 C5
Sourby 176 D8
South Bank 228 B5
South Duffield 199 A4
South Kilvington 211 B2
South Loftus 10 E4
South Milford 195 F1
South Otterington 64 E2
South Stainley 139 E2
Sowerby 211 C1
The Spa 213 B4
Spacey Houses 223 A2
Spaunton 70 E4
Speeton 127 F5
Spennithorne 60 E3
Spofforth 179 E5
Sproxton 92 F4
Stackhouse 131 D4
Stainburn 177 F3
Stainforth 131 E6
Stainsacre 32 F7
Stainton 39 C3
Stainton 6 D5
Staintondale 54 B5
Stalling Busk 81 B8
Stamford Bridge 168 D2
Stanwick-St-John 1 E7
Stape 71 F8
Stapleton 3 A2
Starbeck 220 C4
Starbotton 107 F5
Staupes 160 C4
Staveley 140 F7
Staxton 99 E2
Stead 176 A1
Stean 110 A4
Stearsby 118 F2
Stillingfleet 191 C3
Stillington 144 C6
Stirton 216 C6
Stock 171 C3
Stockton on the Forest 167 D2
Stokesley 26 C7
Stone House 78 F8
Stonegate 30 D8
Stonegrave 119 D8
Stranghow 9 F6
Street 29 F3
Street Houses 190 C8
Streetlam 42 F5
Strensall 167 A7
Strensall Camp 167 B6
Studfold 105 D1
Studley Roger 113 D1
Studley Royal 113 C5
Stutton 189 D4
Suffield 75 B4
Summerbridge 138 A1
Summerscales 158 C2
Sutton 201 F4
Sutton Howgrave 87 B2
Sutton upon Derwent 185 C1
Sutton-in-Craven 187 B4
Sutton-on-the-Forest 144 C4
Sutton-under-
  Whitestonecliffe 90 E5
Swainby 45 E8
Swaledale 37 C4
Swartha 174 C1
Swathgill 119 B4
Swetton 111 F1
Swillington 194 A1
Swillington Common 194 A3
Swincliffe 160 E4
Swinden 154 C1
Swinithwaite 59 C4
Swinton 121 C4
Swinton 86 C4

T

Tadcaster 189 D6

Tame Bridge 26 A7
Tang 160 D4
Tang Hall 228 F5
Tanton 7 C1
Temple Hirst 203 E4
Terrington 119 F1
Theakston 87 E8
Thimbleby 45 A2
Thirlby 90 E7
Thirn 86 B8
Thirsk 211 C2
Thixendale 170 E7
Tholthorpe 142 D5
Thoralby 58 E1
Thorganby 193 B4
Thorgill 49 C3
Thorlby 216 B6
Thormanby 116 F5
Thornaby-on-Tees 6 A7
Thornborough 87 C2
Thorns 35 E7
Thornthwaite 159 D6
Thornton 6 E4
Thornton in Lonsdale .103 C4
Thornton Rust 58 B4
Thornton Steward 61 D1
Thornton Watlass 86 D8
Thornton-in-Craven ..172 A3
Thornton-le-Beans ...65 B5
Thornton-le-Clay 146 A4
Thornton-le-Dale 96 D5
Thornton-le-Moor 65 B3
Thornton-le-Street ..65 D1
Thorp Arch 188 F8
Thorpe 156 F8
Thorpe Bassett 123 A4
Thorpe Underwood 164 C6
Thorpe Willoughby ...197 B2
Threshfield 134 D2
Thrintoft 64 A8
Throxenby 212 A7
Thruscross 159 A5

Thwaite 35 F5
Thwing 126 B1
Timble 176 D7
Tockwith 181 D7
Tollerton 143 A3
Tollesby 7 A6
Topcliffe 115 B7
Tosside 152 F3
Toulston 189 B7
Town Head 174 C1
Towthorpe 149 D1
Towthorpe 167 B5
Towton 189 E2
Trawden 186 B1
Tunstall 41 B2
Tunstall 102 B4

U

Uckerby 21 E1
Ugglebarnby 32 C6
Ugthorpe 11 F2
Ulleskelf 190 C2
Ulshaw 61 A2
Upper Dunsforth 142 A2
Upper Helmsley 168 B3
Upper Poppleton 165 F1
Upsall 66 B2
Ure Bank 214 D7
Urlay Nook 5 B5
Urra 47 A8

V

Vicar's Green 39 F7

W

Waithwith Banks 40 B5
Wake Hill 111 F1
Walden Stubbs 206 F3
Walkerville 41 A4
Walmgate Stray 228 F1
Walshford 180 D8
Walton 181 A2
Warlaby 64 D6
Warsill 138 C4
Warthermarske 86 A1
Warthill 167 F2
Washfold 18 D1
Wass 91 F2
Water Fryston 201 C5
Wath 137 A6
Wath 119 F6
Wath 114 A7
Weaverthorpe 124 E1
Weeton 178 C1
Welburn 94 A7
Welburn 146 D7
Welbury 24 B1
Well 87 A4
Wennington 102 B1
Wensley 60 A4
Wensleydale 57 A5
Wescoe Hill 178 B1
West Appleton 41 C1
West Ayton 99 A7
West Barnby 12 C3
West Burton 58 F1
West Cliff 208 B7
West Field 227 A2
West Garforth 194 B3
West Haddlesey 203 A5
West Harlsey 44 D5
West Heslerton 123 F7
West Knapton 123 B6
West Layton 20 A8

West Lilling 145 C4
West Lutton 150 B8
West Marton 171 F5
West Ness 94 B1
West Rounton 24 D2
West Scrafton 83 F6
West Stonesdale 15 E1
West Tanfield 87 A1
West Witton 59 E3
Westerdale 28 E4
Westfield 232 C4
Westhouse 103 C4
Weston 176 E2
Westow 147 B4
Wetherby 180 D4
Wharfe 131 A8
Wharram le Street ..149 A4
Whashton 20 A5
Whashton Green 20 A5
Whaw 17 B3
Wheldale 201 B5
Wheldrake 192 F8
Whenby 145 B8
Whinfield 3 F8
Whitby 208 C6
Whitewall Corner ...215 C1
Whitley 207 A7
Whitley Thorpe 206 F7
Whittington 102 A7
Whitwell 42 B6
Whitwell-on-the-Hill .146 E4
Whitwood 200 C3
Whixley 164 A5
Whorlton 25 E1
Wiganthorpe 119 E3
Wigginton 166 D5
Wigglesworth 153 C3
Wighill 181 D1
Wilberfoss 185 F5
Willerby 99 C2
Wilsill 137 E3
Wilton 97 A5

Winewall 186 B2
Winksley 112 F2
Winsley 160 D8
Winterburn 155 D5
Winton 44 C3
Wintringham 123 C4
Wistow 197 D6
Wold Newton 126 A3
Wombleton 93 F7
Womersley 206 C6
Wood Row 200 A6
Woodale 83 A2
Woodhall 58 B5
Woodhall 199 B2
Woodhouse 200 A1
Woodlands 220 C1
Woodthorpe 230 C7
Worton 57 F5
Wray 128 A6
Wrayton 102 B3
Wrelton 71 C1
Wressle 199 D2
Wycoller 186 C2
Wydra 160 A1
Wykeham 122 B6
Wykeham 98 E6

Y

Yafforth 43 C1
Yarm 5 D3
Yearsley 118 C5
Yedingham 97 D2
Yockenthwaite 81 A1
York 233 B3
Youlthorpe 169 C2
Youlton 142 E2

A

A W Nielson Rd DN14 ... 205 F2
Abber La LS24 ... 182 A2
Abbeville Ave 1 YO21 ... 208 B6
Abbey Cl 12 LS29 ... 175 A4
Abbey Crags Way
HG5 ... 221 C3
Abbey Cty Inf Sch DL3 ... 3 B5
Abbey Gdns
Darlington DL3 ... 3 B5
Pontefract WF8 ... 201 B2
Abbey Hill BD23 ... 155 C5
Abbey Jun Sch DL3 ... 3 B5
Abbey La YO22 ... 208 E7
Abbey Leisure Ctr
YO8 ... 232 C5
Abbey Mews WF8 ... 201 B2
Abbey Mill Gdns HG5 ... 221 C3
Abbey Mill View HG5 ... 221 C3
Abbey Rd Darlington DL3 ... 3 B5
Knaresborough HG5 ... 221 B3
Sadberge DL2 ... 4 C7
Abbey St YO30 ... 228 A7
Abbey Walk Ret Pk
YO8 ... 232 C6
Abbey Wlk
Pontefract WF8 ... 201 B2
Selby YO8 ... 232 C5
Abbey Yd YO8 ... 232 C5
Abbot St YO31 ... 233 C4
Abbot's Garth YO12 ... 99 D6
Abbot's Rd Selby YO8 ... 232 E3
Whitby YO22 ... 208 E5
Abbots Way HG5 ... 221 C3
Abbot's Wlk YO22 ... 208 E5
Abbotsford Rd YO10 ... 228 F3
Abbotsway YO31 ... 228 E8
Abbotts Cl LS25 ... 194 F8
Abbotts Ct YO17 ... 215 E4
Abelton Gr 33 YO32 ... 166 E5
Aberdeen La 19 YO11 ... 213 A6
Aberdeen Pl 20 YO11 ... 213 A6
Aberdeen Rd DL1 ... 3 E8
Aberdeen St 17 YO11 ... 213 A6
Aberdeen Terr 21 YO11 ... 213 A6
Aberdeen Wlk 16 YO11 ... 213 A6
Aberford C of E Prim Sch
LS25 ... 194 F8
Aberford Rd
Barwick in Elmet & Scholes
LS15 ... 194 C8
Bramham cum Oglethorpe
LS23 ... 188 E5
Garforth LS25 ... 194 D4
Abram's View YO11 ... 213 B2
Acacia Ave YO32 ... 225 E4
Acacia Dr WF10 ... 201 B3
Academy Gdns DL2 ... 1 D8
Acaster Ave YO23 ... 191 A3
Acaster Dr LS25 ... 194 D3
Acaster La
Acaster Malbis YO23 ... 231 B1
Acaster Selby YO23 ... 191 A4
Accommodation Rd
YO25 ... 151 D6
Acklam Grange Sec Sch
TS5 ... 6 D7
Acklam Rd TS17 ... 6 C8
Acklam Whin Prim Sch
TS5 ... 6 D6
Ackton La WF7 ... 200 D1
Ackton Pasture La
WF7 ... 200 D2
Ackton Pastures Jun & Inf
Sch WF10 ... 200 D3
Acomb Prim Sch
YO24 ... 227 E3
Acomb Rd YO24 ... 227 D3
Acomb Wood Cl YO24 ... 230 C7
Acomb Wood Dr YO24 ... 230 B7
Acorn Cl 6 YO8 ... 198 B4
Acorn Way
Gateforth YO8 ... 197 B1
York YO24 ... 230 D7
Acre Fold 21 LS29 ... 174 F4
Acre Mdw 1 BD22 ... 187 B6
Acre Rd 2 BD22 ... 187 B6
Acres Cl 24 YO62 ... 92 F6
Acres La Brompton YO13 ... 98 C4
Helmsley YO62 ... 93 A6
Scrayingham YO41 ... 169 B8
Acres The
Addingham LS29 ... 175 A5
Glusburn BD20 ... 187 E6
Stokesley TS9 ... 26 C8
Acresfield 11 BB8 ... 186 A3
Acworth St 3 YO12 ... 212 E4
Adam's Field La YO61 ... 117 F4
Adcott Rd TS5 ... 6 E7
Addingham Mid Sch
LS29 ... 174 F5
Addingham Prim Sch
LS29 ... 174 F5
Addingham Wharfedale
LS29 ... 174 E4
Addison Ave 18 WF6 ... 200 B1
Addison Rd TS9 ... 8 A1
Addison Villas HG3 ... 219 A8
Addlethorpe La LS22 ... 179 C3
Adelaide Rd
Middlesbrough TS7 ... 7 B6
6 Norton DN6 ... 206 E2
Adelaide St 3 YO23 ... 228 B2
Adlington Cl 8 YO32 ... 167 A7
Admirals Ct YO7 ... 211 A2
Admirals' Ct YO7 ... 211 A2
Agar St YO31 ... 233 C3
Agnes Ing La LA2 ... 128 A7
Agnesgate HG4 ... 214 D5
Aikengill Rd LA2 ... 129 A4
Ailcey Rd HG4 ... 214 D5
Ainderby Rd DL7 ... 210 B2
Ainsford Way TS7 ... 7 D8
Ainstable Rd TS7 ... 7 D8
Ainsty Ave YO24 ... 230 F8
Ainsty Dr 2 LS22 ... 180 C4
Ainsty Gr YO24 ... 230 F8
Ainsty Rd
Harrogate HG1 ... 219 F4
Wetherby LS22 ... 180 C4
Ainsty View
Acklam YO17 ... 169 E8
Whixley YO26 ... 164 A4
Ainsworth Way TS7 ... 7 D8
Ainthorpe La YO21 ... 29 C7
Aintree Ct
9 Darlington DL1 ... 3 F6
York YO24 ... 230 F8
Aire Cres BD20 ... 187 E7
Aire Rd LS22 ... 180 B4
Aire St Castleford WF10 ... 200 E4
Glusburn BD20 ... 187 F7
Knottingley WF11 ... 202 A3
Aire Valley Cl BD20 ... 173 D3
Aire Valley Dr BD20 ... 173 D3
Aire View Inf Sch
BD20 ... 174 C1
Airedale Ave
Gargrave BD23 ... 155 D1
Skipton BD23 ... 217 B4
Airedale Dr WF10 ... 201 B5
Airedale High Sch
WF10 ... 201 B4
Airedale Mews 1 BD23 ... 216 E3
Airedale Rd
Castleford WF10 ... 201 A4
Scotton DL9 ... 40 D4
Airedale Trading Pk
BD20 ... 187 F8
Airedale View 1 BD20 ... 187 F8
Aireside Ave BD20 ... 173 D1
Aireside Terr BD20 ... 173 D2
Aireville Dr BD20 ... 174 C1
Aireville Sch BD23 ... 216 D4
Aireville Swimming Baths
BD23 ... 216 D4
Aireyholme La TS9 ... 8 B2
Airmyn Park Prim Sch
DN14 ... 205 E4
Airmyn Rd DN14 ... 205 D3
Airy Hill CP Sch YO21 ... 208 D5
Airy Hill La TS12 ... 9 D8
Aiskew Leeming Bar C of E
Sch DL7 ... 63 C4
Aislabie Cl HG4 ... 214 A5
Aislabie Garth HG4 ... 214 A5
Aislaby Carr La YO18 ... 95 C7
Aislaby La Aislaby YO21 ... 32 A8
Aislaby YO18 ... 95 C6
Aislaby Rd TS16 ... 5 D4
Aismunderby Cl HG4 ... 214 C3
Aismunderby Rd HG4 ... 214 C4
Aisne Rd DL9 ... 209 C1
Aketon Rd WF10 ... 200 D3
Alanbrooke Barracks Cty
Prim Sch YO7 ... 89 A1
Alanbrooke Ind Est
YO7 ... 115 B8
Alandale Cres LS25 ... 194 B3
Alandale Rd LS25 ... 194 B4
Albany Ave HG1 ... 219 E5
Albany Rd
Harrogate HG1 ... 219 E5
Middlesbrough TS7 ... 7 B6
Albany St 3 YO26 ... 227 F5
Albany Wlk LS29 ... 218 A3
Albatross Way DL1 ... 3 E5
Albemarle Back Rd 10
YO11 ... 212 F6
Albemarle Cres 18
YO11 ... 213 A6
Albemarle Rd YO23 ... 228 B2
Albermarle Dr 3 DL9 ... 40 F5
Albert Cl 1 YO32 ... 228 F8
Albert Hill BD24 ... 131 E2
Albert Pl
Harrogate HG1 ... 220 C4
1 Whitby YO21 ... 208 D7
Albert Rd
Eaglescliffe TS16 ... 5 E5
12 Glusburn BD20 ... 187 E7
Harrogate HG1 ... 219 E5
1 Scarborough YO12 ... 213 A7
Albert St 33 Earby BB18 ... 172 A1
Glusburn BD20 ... 187 F7
Harrogate HG1 ... 219 D2
Normanton South WF6 ... 200 B2
8 Scarborough YO12 ... 213 A7
York YO10 ... 233 C1
Albert Terr
5 Harrogate HG1 ... 219 D1
Skipton BD23 ... 216 F4
Albion Ave YO26 ... 227 B6
Albion Cres 3 YO11 ... 213 A4
Albion Pl 14 YO21 ... 208 D6
Albion Rd 25 Earby BB18 ... 172 A1
Scarborough YO11 ... 213 A4
Albion St Boosbeck TS12 ... 9 E7
Boston Spa LS23 ... 188 E7
Castleford WF10 ... 200 E4
Albion St *continued*
28 Earby BB18 ... 172 A1
York YO1 ... 233 B1
Albion Terr 9 LS23 ... 188 E7
Alcelina Ct YO23 ... 233 B1
Alcuin Ave YO10 ... 229 A4
Aldborough Gate 13
YO51 ... 141 B4
Aldborough Way YO26 ... 227 F5
Aldbrough & Boroughbridge
CP Sch YO51 ... 141 C5
Aldenham Rd TS14 ... 8 E5
Alder Ave HG5 ... 221 E5
Alder Carr La YO18 ... 49 E2
Alder Hill St 1 BB18 ... 172 B1
Alder Rd HG1 ... 219 F5
Alder Way YO32 ... 225 D2
Alderley Ct YO32 ... 225 E3
Alderman Leach Inf Sch
DL3 ... 3 B6
Alders Rd YO18 ... 49 C4
Aldersley Ave BD23 ... 217 B3
Alderson Cres YO12 ... 99 E7
Alderson Rd HG2 ... 222 E8
Alderson Sq HG2 ... 222 E8
Aldersyde YO24 ... 230 E7
Aldreth Gr YO23 ... 228 C2
Aldridge Rd TS3 ... 7 B8
Aldwark YO1 ... 233 C3
Aldwych Cl TS6 ... 7 E8
Alexander Ave
6 East Ayton/West Ayton
YO13 ... 99 B8
York YO31 ... 225 E2
Alexander Cl YO7 ... 211 C4
Alexander Rd DL9 ... 209 C2
Alexandra Cres 10 LS29 ... 218 A4
Alexandra Ct
Skipton BD23 ... 216 F2
York YO10 ... 228 E4
Alexandra Park Rd
HG5 ... 221 C7
Alexandra Pk YO12 ... 212 D5
Alexandra Pl 3 HG5 ... 221 B8
Alexandra Rd
Harrogate HG1 ... 219 D3
Strensall YO32 ... 167 A6
Alexandra Way DL10 ... 209 C7
Alexandria Dr DL2 ... 4 D4
Algarth Rd YO31 ... 229 B7
Algarth Rise YO31 ... 229 B7
All Saints Jun & Inf Sch
WF7 ... 200 E1
All Saints Prim Sch
LS29 ... 218 B4
All Saints RC Comp Sch
YO24 ... 233 A1
All Saints RC Prim Sch
YO7 ... 211 B2
All Saints Rd 1 YO12 ... 212 F4
Allan St Darlington DL1 ... 3 D6
2 York YO30 ... 228 C7
Allen Cl YO10 ... 229 A4
Allen Gr TS9 ... 26 B7
Allenby Rd
20 Helmsley YO62 ... 92 F6
Hipswell DL9 ... 209 C1
Allendale YO24 ... 230 D8
Allendale Rd TS7 ... 7 D8
Allens West Sta TS16 ... 5 D5
Allensway TS17 ... 6 C7
Allerdale Cl YO7 ... 211 C4
Allerston La YO18 ... 97 C4
Allerton Balk TS15 ... 5 D2
Allerton Bywater Prim Sch
WF10 ... 200 D7
Allerton Dr
22 Poppleton YO26 ... 165 F1
Poppleton YO26 ... 224 A1
Allerton La HG5 ... 163 D4
Allerton Wath Rd DL6 ... 65 D4
Allertonshire Sch DL6 ... 210 D6
Allhallowgate HG4 ... 214 C5
Allington Dr YO31 ... 229 B6
Allington Way
Darlington DL1 ... 3 F5
Great Burdon DL1 ... 4 A5
Allison Ave TS17 ... 6 B4
Allison St TS14 ... 8 E6
Allotments La YO61 ... 143 F3
Alma Gdns HG4 ... 214 D4
Alma Par 2 YO11 ... 212 F5
Alma Rd BB8 ... 186 B3
Alma Sq 3 YO11 ... 212 F5
Alma Terr Selby YO8 ... 232 C6
3 Skipton BD23 ... 217 A4
York YO10 ... 228 D2
Alma Way 2 YO18 ... 96 A6
Almery Terr YO30 ... 233 A3
Almond Cl 7 Filey YO14 ... 101 B4
Hambleton YO8 ... 197 B1
Almond Gr 11 Filey YO14 ... 101 B4
Northallerton DL7 ... 210 D3
Scarborough YO12 ... 212 D5
York YO32 ... 225 D4
Almond Tree Ave
Carlton DN14 ... 204 C3
Malton YO17 ... 215 D6
Almond Wlk 4 DL9 ... 209 B1
Almscliffe Dr LS17 ... 178 B2
Almscliffe Garth LS17 ... 178 B4
Almsford Ave HG2 ... 222 E6
Almsford Bank HG2 ... 222 E5
Almsford Cl HG2 ... 222 F6
Almsford Dr
Harrogate HG2 ... 222 F6
York YO26 ... 227 C5
Almsford End HG2 ... 222 E6
Almsford Oval HG2 ... 222 F6
Almsford Pl HG2 ... 222 E6
Almsford Rd
Harrogate HG2 ... 222 F6
York YO26 ... 227 C5
Almsford Wlk HG2 ... 222 F6
Almshouse Hill 1 LS23 ... 188 E5
Alne CP Sch YO61 ... 142 F4
Alne Rd
Easingwold YO61 ... 143 B8
Tollerton YO61 ... 143 A3
Alne Terr YO10 ... 228 E2
Alness Dr YO24 ... 230 B7
Altofts La WF10 ... 200 B3
Altofts Rd WF6 ... 200 A1
Alum House La TS9 ... 26 B2
Alverton Cty Inf Sch
DL6 ... 210 F6
Alverton Dr DL3 ... 3 B8
Alverton La DL7 ... 210 D4
Alvin Wlk 9 YO41 ... 185 B2
Alvis Gr YO10 ... 229 D4
Alwyn Rd DL3 ... 3 D8
Alwyne Dr YO30 ... 224 E1
Alwyne Gr YO30 ... 224 E1
Amber St YO31 ... 233 C4
Amberly St 4 YO26 ... 227 E5
Amble Cl YO62 ... 70 B2
Ambler St WF10 ... 200 E4
Ambler's La YO30 ... 165 F7
Ambleside Ave
10 Barnoldswick BB18 ... 171 D2
York YO10 ... 229 B4
Ambleside Gr TS5 ... 6 E8
Ambrey Cl 16 YO14 ... 126 F8
Ambrose Rd HG4 ... 214 C4
Ambrose St YO10 ... 228 D1
America La BD20 ... 187 F4
Amesbury Cres TS8 ... 6 F5
Amiens Cres DL9 ... 209 D1
Amotherby CP Sch
YO17 ... 121 A4
Amotherby La YO17 ... 121 A6
Amplecarr YO61 ... 117 B5
Ampleforth Abbey & Coll
YO62 ... 92 D1
Ampleforth Coll Jun Sch
YO62 ... 118 F7
Ampleforth St Benedicts RC
Prim Sch YO62 ... 92 C1
Amy Johnson Way
YO30 ... 225 A3
Anchor Rd 2 HG1 ... 220 A3
Anchorage La DL7 ... 210 C5
Anchorage Way YO21 ... 208 C5
Anchorite La 7 YO18 ... 95 F7
Ancress Wlk YO23 ... 233 B1
Ancroft Cl YO1 ... 233 C1
Andersen Rd DN14 ... 205 F2
Anderson Gr 6 YO24 ... 227 F2
Anderson St 6 WF8 ... 201 B1
Anderton St 18 BD20 ... 187 E8
Andrew Dr 4 YO32 ... 225 F1
Andrew La YO18 ... 71 B4
Anfield Ct 8 DL1 ... 3 F6
Angel Ct 8 TS9 ... 26 C7
Angel Yd 1 YO21 ... 208 D6
Angelica Cl 12 HG3 ... 161 B3
Angram Cl YO30 ... 224 F1
Angram La
Barlby with Osgodby
YO19 ... 198 A6
Muker DL11 ... 35 E6
Tollerton YO61 ... 143 B3
Angram Rd YO26 ... 182 A5
Angrove Cl TS9 ... 7 F1
Angrove Dr TS9 ... 7 F1
Annan Cl YO24 ... 230 C6
Annandale Gr 1 YO13 ... 75 D5
Annas Garth DL8 ... 60 F4
Anne St YO23 ... 228 C2
Annumhills Rd YO8 ... 199 D7
Anserdale La YO62 ... 70 E5
Anson Croft 5 YO8 ... 196 E1
Anson Dr YO10 ... 231 D8
Anteforth View DL10 ... 20 E3
Anthea Dr YO31 ... 225 E1
Anthony La HG4 ... 114 E1
Anvil Sq 3 DL11 ... 38 B6
Anzio Rd DL9 ... 209 C1
Apedale Rd
Castle Bolton with East &
West Bolton DL8 ... 37 F1
Redmire DL8 ... 59 C8
Apley Cl HG2 ... 220 A1
Apollo St 9 YO10 ... 228 E3
Apple Garth
10 Easingwold YO61 ... 117 D1
15 Poppleton YO26 ... 165 F1
Apple Tree Gdns 2
LS29 ... 175 C2
Appleby Ave HG5 ... 220 D8
Appleby Cres HG5 ... 220 D8
Appleby Ct HG5 ... 220 D8
Appleby Gate HG5 ... 220 D7
Appleby Glade YO32 ... 225 D7
Appleby Gn HG5 ... 220 D8
Appleby La
Aldbrough DL11 ... 1 F1
Kirkby Malzeard HG4 ... 112 B4
Appleby Pl 2 YO31 ... 229 A5
Appleby Way HG5 ... 220 D7
Appleby Wlk HG5 ... 220 D8
Applecroft Rd
Selby YO8 ... 232 A4
York YO31 ... 229 B7
Applegarth
Barnoldswick BB18 ... 171 E2
Applegarth *continued*
Coulby Newham TS8 ... 7 A4
Applegarth Ct DL7 ... 210 D5
Applegarth St 15 BB18 ... 172 A1
Applegartn CP Prim Sch
DL7 ... 210 D4
Appleton Ct YO23 ... 230 F3
Appleton La
Appleton-le-Street with
Easthorpe YO17 ... 120 F4
Coneysthorpe YO60 ... 120 E2
Appleton Rd YO23 ... 231 A3
Appleton Roebuck CP Sch
YO23 ... 190 F5
Appleton Wiske CP Sch
DL6 ... 24 B3
Appletree Dr YO8 ... 196 E1
Appletree Way
Malton YO17 ... 215 B4
10 Sherburn in Elmet LS25 ... 195 F4
Appletreewick Stone Circle*
BD23 ... 135 E2
Appley Cl TS16 ... 5 E7
Apron La HG3 ... 140 B2
Arbour The
4 Glusburn BD20 ... 173 E1
Ilkley LS29 ... 218 A6
Arbour Way YO17 ... 215 E4
Archbishop Holgates Sch
YO10 ... 229 B3
Archbishop of York C of E
Jun Sch YO23 ... 231 A4
Archer La HG3 ... 140 B3
Archer Rd DL2 ... 4 D3
Archers Gn The DL10 ... 41 C7
Archers Mdw HG5 ... 221 F5
Archie St 3 HG1 ... 219 C5
Arden La YO62 ... 92 B8
Arena View 12 DL10 ... 41 D5
Arenhall Cl 2 YO32 ... 225 C8
Argam La YO25 ... 126 F1
Argill DL8 ... 60 F5
Argyle Rd YO21 ... 208 C7
Argyle St YO23 ... 228 B1
Arkendale La HG5 ... 141 A2
Arkendale Rd HG5 ... 162 F8
Arkengarthdale C of E Prim
Sch DL11 ... 17 D1
Arkengarthdale Rd
DL11 ... 38 B7
Arkle Cres DL1 ... 3 C3
Arlington Rd
Middlesbrough TS5 ... 6 F8
York YO30 ... 225 A1
Armoury Rd YO8 ... 232 B5
Armstrong Cl 7 WF6 ... 200 A2
Army Foundation Coll
HG3 ... 161 A2
Arncliffe C of E Prim Sch
BD23 ... 107 D2
Arncliffe Dr WF11 ... 201 D2
Arncliffe Rd HG2 ... 220 A1
Arndale Way 8 YO14 ... 101 B4
Arnold Rd DL1 ... 3 E6
Arnside Cres WF10 ... 201 B4
Arnside Pl 2 YO10 ... 228 F3
Arran Ct LS25 ... 194 C3
Arran Dr LS25 ... 194 C3
Arran Pl YO31 ... 228 D7
Arrows Cres 10 YO51 ... 141 B5
Arrows Terr 9 YO51 ... 141 B5
Arthington Ave HG1 ... 219 E2
Arthur Pl 6 YO30 ... 224 B5
Arthur St
6 Barnoldswick BB18 ... 171 D2
Earby BB18 ... 186 A8
Great Ayton TS9 ... 8 A2
York YO10 ... 228 E4
Arthurs Ave HG2 ... 222 C7
Arthurs Cl HG2 ... 222 C7
Arthurs Gr HG2 ... 222 C7
Arundel Gr YO24 ... 230 C7
Arundel Pl
12 Scarborough YO11 ... 212 F5
9 Whitby YO21 ... 208 C6
Arundel Rd 5 DN6 ... 206 E2
Ascot Rd LS25 ... 194 C1
Ascot Way YO24 ... 227 D1
Ash Bank Ave 2 HG4 ... 113 D2
Ash Bank Cl 1 HG4 ... 113 D2
Ash Bank Rd HG4 ... 113 D2
Ash Cl 1 Ilkley LS29 ... 175 C2
Newton on Derwent
YO41 ... 185 E4
York YO31 ... 229 B7
Ash Croft 7 DL10 ... 41 D5
Ash Gn TS8 ... 7 A4
Ash Gr
13 Barnoldswick BB18 ... 171 D1
Danby YO21 ... 29 A6
12 Filey YO14 ... 101 B4
Glusburn BD20 ... 187 E7
Ilkley LS29 ... 218 C5
7 Kirkbymoorside YO62 ... 70 B1
1 Kirklevington TS15 ... 24 E8
Northallerton DL6 ... 210 F5
1 Riccall YO19 ... 197 F8
Ripon HG4 ... 214 A6
Scarborough YO12 ... 212 C7
Whitby YO21 ... 208 B6
Ash Hill TS8 ... 7 B5
Ash La
Church Fenton LS24 ... 196 B6
Garforth LS25 ... 194 D4
8 Haxby YO32 ... 166 E5
Little Fenton LS25 ... 196 C5
Ash Lea YO21 ... 29 A6
Ash Rd 13 Filey YO14 ... 101 B4

Ash - Ban 239

Ash Rd *continued*
Guisborough TS14 8 F7
Harrogate HG2 222 E6
Ash Ridge 5 DL6 210 E3
Ash St 11 Glusburn BD20 187 E7
Ilkley LS29 218 C5
Trawden BB8 186 B1
York YO26 227 E4
Ash Tree Cl DL8 62 F2
Ash Tree Garth LS24 195 E7
Ash Tree Rd
8 Bedale DL8 63 A2
Knaresborough HG5 221 B6
Ash Tree Wlk 22 LS29 176 C1
Ashbank La Firby DL8 62 F1
Sheriff Hutton YO60 145 F6
Ashbourne Cl 12 YO51 141 B4
Ashbourne Rd 10 YO51 141 B4
Ashbourne Way YO24 230 C8
Ashburn Pl LS29 218 A3
Ashburn Rd YO11 212 E4
Ashburn Rise 10 YO11 212 E4
Ashburn Way LS22 180 B4
Ashburnham Cl 4 DN6 206 F2
Ashburnham Wlk 5
DN6 206 F2
Ashdale Cl DL2 4 E4
Ashdale La LS22 180 B4
Ashdale Rd
19 Dunnington YO19 184 F7
Helmsley YO62 92 F6
Ashdene Gr WF8 201 D2
Ashdown Rise YO13 75 C8
Ashdowne Cl DL8 62 E5
Ashdowne Ct DL8 62 E5
Ashes The DL10 21 C7
Ashfield
2 Grassington BD23 134 E3
Wetherby LS22 180 C3
Ashfield Ave YO17 215 D5
Ashfield Cl
Constable Burton DL8 61 C5
Pateley Bridge HG3 137 B4
Ashfield Court Rd
HG3 137 B4
Ashfield Rd Danby YO21 29 B6
Harrogate HG1 219 E4
6 Pickering YO18 96 A6
Ashfield St WF6 200 A2
Ashford Ave TS5 6 D8
Ashford Pl YO24 227 D2
Ashgap La WF6 200 A2
Ashgarth Ct HG2 222 C5
Ashgarth Way HG2 222 C5
Ashgrove Cres LS25 194 D2
Ashlands Cl DL6 210 F4
Ashlands Ct DL6 210 F4
Ashlands Dr DL7 63 C5
Ashlands Prim Sch
LS29 218 C5
Ashlands Rd
Ilkley LS29 218 C5
Northallerton DL6 210 F4
Ashlea Cl YO8 232 D4
Ashlea Rd DL7 210 D4
Ashley Ct 2 YO14 101 B3
Ashley Park Cres
YO31 229 B6
Ashley Park Rd YO31 229 B7
Ashmead 4 LS23 188 E7
Ashmeade Cl YO24 230 B8
Ashton Ave YO30 228 B8
Ashton Rd WF10 200 E3
Ashtree Dr YO8 197 D1
Ashville Ave
Eaglescliffe TS16 5 E6
Scarborough YO12 212 F6
Ashville Cl HG2 222 C5
Ashville Coll HG2 222 B6
Ashville Dr 9 DL2 22 E8
Ashville Gr HG2 222 C5
Ashville St YO31 228 D7
Ashwood Cl 5 YO62 92 F7
Ashwood Dr TS9 26 C8
Ashwood Glade YO32 225 C6
Ashwood Pl HG5 221 E5
Ashworth Rd WF8 201 C2
Askam Ave WF8 201 C2
Askam Bryan Coll TS14 8 F7
Aske Ave DL10 209 E8
Aske Hall* DL10 20 D2
Askern & Campsall Sports Ctr
DN6 206 F1
Askew Dale TS14 8 D6
Askew Rigg La YO18 71 A5
Askham Bryan Coll
Askham Bryan YO23 182 F2
Bedale DL8 63 A2
Pickering YO18 95 F8
Askham Bryan Coll Harrogate
Ctr HG2 223 A7
Askham Bryan La
YO23 230 A6
Askham Croft 1 YO24 227 B1
Askham Fields La
YO23 182 F2
Askham Gr YO24 227 B2
Askham La
Askham Bryan YO24 230 A8
York YO24 227 B1
Askrigg Prim Sch DL8 57 E5
Askwith CP Sch LS21 176 D3
Askwith La LS21 176 D3
Askwith Moor Rd
LS21 176 D5
Aspen Cl 3 YO19 184 F7
Aspen La BB18 172 A1
Aspen Way
Slingsby YO62 120 B5
Tadcaster LS24 189 D6
Aspin Ave HG5 221 B4
Aspin Dr HG5 221 C4
Aspin Gdns HG5 221 C4
Aspin Gr 4 HG5 221 C4
Aspin La HG5 221 C3
Aspin Oval HG5 221 B4
Aspin Park Ave 1 HG5 221 C4
Aspin Park CP Sch
HG5 221 C5
Aspin Park Cres HG5 221 B4
Aspin Park Dr HG5 221 B4
Aspin Park La HG5 221 C4
Aspin Park Rd HG5 221 C4
Aspin View HG5 221 C4
Aspin Way HG5 221 C4
Asquith Ave
Scarborough YO12 212 E3
York YO31 229 A5
Assembly St 7 WF6 200 A1
Astbury TS8 7 C4
Asterley Dr TS5 6 D8
Astley Ave LS26 194 A1
Astley La
Great & Little Preston
LS26 200 B8
Swillington LS26 194 A1
Astley Lane Ind Pk
LS26 200 B8
Astley Way LS26 200 A8
Atcherley Cl YO10 231 D8
Athelstan CP Sch
LS25 195 F3
Athelstan La 7 LS21 177 A1
Athelstans Ct LS25 195 F4
Atkinson Ave DL10 209 D8
Atkinson Ct WF6 200 A1
Atkinson La WF8 201 C1
Atlantis Water Pk*
YO12 212 F8
Atlas Rd YO30 225 A3
Atlas Wynd TS16 5 E3
Attermire Cave*
BD24 132 A3
Atterwith La YO26 182 A7
Auborough St 5 YO11 213 A6
Auckland Ave DL3 3 B6
Auckland Oval DL3 3 B7
Auckland St TS14 8 F7
Auckland Way 7 YO21 208 C6
Audax Cl YO30 225 A3
Audax Rd YO30 225 A3
Audby La LS22 180 C4
Audus St 10 YO8 232 C5
Augusta Cl DL1 3 F7
Aumit La YO62 92 E1
Aunums Cl 7 YO18 96 D5
Auster Bank Ave LS24 189 F7
Auster Bank Cres
LS24 189 F7
Auster Bank Rd LS24 189 F7
Auster Bank View
LS24 189 F7
Auster Rd YO30 225 B3
Austfield La LS25 202 B8
Austin Rd WF10 201 B4
Austwick C of E Prim Sch
LA2 130 E7
Austwick Rd BD24 131 C8
Ava Rd DL9 40 C4
Avens Way TS17 6 A5
Avenue A LS23 181 A2
Avenue B LS23 181 A1
Avenue Bank HG4 86 C4
Avenue C E LS23 181 B1
Avenue C W LS23 181 A1
Avenue Cl HG2 220 D4
Avenue D LS23 181 A1
Avenue E E LS23 181 B1
Avenue E W LS23 189 A8
Avenue F LS23 181 B1
Avenue G LS23 181 B1
Avenue Gr 11 HG2 220 C3
Avenue House Ct HG5 162 F3
Avenue Pl 7 HG2 220 C3
Avenue Prim Sch The
TS7 7 D6
Avenue Rd
Harrogate HG2 220 C3
Scarborough YO12 212 E4
York YO30 233 A4
Avenue St 8 HG2 220 C3
Avenue Terr
5 Harrogate HG2 220 C3
York YO30 233 A4
Avenue The
Campsall DN6 206 E1
Collingham LS22 180 A1
Dalby-cum-Skewsby
YO60 119 B2
Eaglescliffe TS16 5 E6
26 Filey YO14 101 B3
Gilling East YO62 118 E7
Great Ribston with Walshford
LS22 180 C8
Guisborough TS14 8 D6
Harrogate HG1 220 C4
5 Haxby YO32 166 E5
Haxby YO32 225 D8
Knaresborough HG5 221 A7
Masham HG4 86 C3
Middlesbrough TS5 6 F8
Middlesbrough TS7 7 D6
Norton YO17 215 C2
Nun Monkton YO26 165 A4
Nunnington YO62 93 E1
Avenue The *continued*
8 Pateley Bridge HG3 137 C4
Richmond DL10 209 D7
Rufforth YO23 182 C6
Skutterskelfe TS15 25 E6
1 Sleights YO22 32 A6
Snape with Thorp DL8 87 A7
South Milford LS25 195 F2
Stainton Dale YO13 54 A8
Stokesley TS9 26 C7
Thirkleby High & Low
with Osgodby YO7 116 D8
West Hauxwell DL8 61 C8
Whitby YO21 208 B4
Wighill LS24 181 D2
York YO30 228 A6
Avenue Victoria YO11 213 A3
Aviation Rd LS25 196 A4
Aviator Ct YO30 224 F3
Aviemore Ct 10 DL1 3 F6
Aviemore Rd TS8 6 F5
Avocet Cres 11 YO12 99 F6
Avon Dr
Barnoldswick BB18 171 E2
Guisborough TS14 8 E6
York YO32 225 F6
Avon Garth LS22 180 B3
Avon Rd 8 DL2 22 D8
Avondale Rd HG1 219 F4
Avondale St 7 BB8 186 A3
Avro Cl TS18 5 F7
Awnhams La YO42 169 D2
Axminster Rd TS8 6 F5
Axton Cl TS17 6 A6
Aylesham Ct YO32 225 E3
Aylton Dr TS5 6 E6
Aynham Cl 2 BD23 134 E2
Aynholme Cl 10 LS29 174 F4
Aynholme Dr 1 LS29 175 A4
Ayresome Way 1 DL1 3 F6
Aysgarth Gr DL7 210 B2
Aysgarth Rd DL1 3 D4
Aysgarth Sch DL8 62 A4
Ayton Castle* YO13 99 A8
Ayton Rd YO12 99 C7
Azerley Gr HG3 219 A4
Azerley La HG4 112 F3

B

Babyhouse La BD20 173 A1
Bachelor Ave HG1 219 D7
Bachelor Dr HG1 219 D7
Bachelor Gdns HG1 219 D6
Bachelor Hill YO24 227 C2
Bachelor Rd HG1 219 D6
Bachelor Way HG1 219 D6
Back Ave Victoria 2
YO11 213 A3
Back Beck La LS29 174 F4
Back Bridge St BD23 216 F4
Back Cheltenham Mount
HG1 219 D3
Back Colne Rd 9 BD20 187 E7
Back Dragon Par HG1 219 E3
Back Dragon Rd HG1 219 E3
Back Elmwood St 3
HG1 219 E4
Back Gate LA6 103 D3
Back Gn BD23 153 F5
Back Grove Rd LS29 218 B4
Back La
Acaster Selby YO23 191 B3
Airton BD23 155 A6
Aiskew DL7 63 C5
Alne YO61 142 F4
Ampleforth YO62 92 C1
Appleton Roebuck YO23 191 A5
Appleton-le-Moors YO62 70 F2
Asselby DN14 205 D6
Bagby YO7 90 B3
Barkston Ash LS24 195 F6
Barlby with Osgodby
YO8 198 C4
Barton DL10 21 C7
Barton-le-Street YO17 120 E5
1 Bedale DL8 63 A3
Bilbrough YO23 182 D1
Birstwith HG3 160 D5
Bolton-on-Swale DL10 41 E5
7 Boroughbridge YO51 141 B5
Borrowby YO7 65 E4
Bradleys Both BD20 173 E4
10 Brafferton YO61 115 F1
Bramham LS23 188 E6
Burley in Warfedale
LS29 176 C1
Carlton Miniott YO7 89 B3
Carthorpe DL8 87 E7
Cawood YO8 197 A8
Cold Kirby YO7 91 C8
Copmanthorpe YO23 230 A2
Copt Hewick HG4 114 B2
Cottingwith YO42 193 C5
Crakehall DL8 62 E4
Crathorne TS15 24 F6
Dalton YO7 115 E7
Dishforth YO7 115 A4
Drax YO8 204 F5
Eaglescliffe TS16 5 E4
Easingwold YO61 117 D1
East Tanfield DL8 87 D2
Ebberston & Yedingham
YO13 97 D5
Ellerton YO42 193 C1
Fewston HG3 159 F1
Flaxton YO60 145 F1
Back La *continued*
Giggleswick BD24 130 F2
Great & Little Broughton
TS9 26 E5
Great Ouseburn YO26 164 A8
Great Preston WF10 200 D6
Gristlthorp YO14 100 E5
Guisborough TS9 8 A4
Hambleton YO8 196 F1
Harome YO62 93 C5
Hawsker-cum-Stainsacre
YO22 32 F5
11 Haxby YO32 166 D5
Hebden BD23 135 A2
Hellifield BD23 154 B3
Hemingbrough YO8 198 F1
Hetton BD23 155 F5
Hirst Courtney YO8 203 F3
Holtby YO19 184 E8
Hunsingore LS22 180 E8
Hutton-le-Hole YO62 70 C4
Huttons Ambo YO60 147 B7
Kirby Wiske YO7 88 E7
Kirkby Malham BD23 154 F8
Kirkby Malzeard HG4 112 C5
Lockton YO18 72 E4
Long Preston BD23 153 F5
Longnewton TS21 4 F8
Low Coniscliffe & Merrybent
DL2 2 E4
Low Worsall TS15 24 C7
Luttons YO17 150 B8
Malham BD23 132 F2
Markington with Wallerthwaite
HG3 139 C3
Marton YO62 94 F5
Marton cum Grafton
YO51 141 D1
Melmerby HG4 114 B7
8 Middleham DL8 60 E2
Morton-on-Swale DL7 64 A6
Moulton DL10 21 E3
Newby Wiske DL7 64 D3
Newholm-cum-Dunsley
YO21 13 A1
Newton-on-Ouse YO30 165 B6
North Cowton DL7 22 B3
North Duffield YO8 199 A7
Norton DN6 206 E2
Osmotherley DL6 45 B4
Raskelf YO61 116 F2
Rathmell BD24 153 C6
Reeth, Fremington & Healaugh
DL11 38 B6
2 Riccall YO19 198 A8
Rookwith HG4 86 A8
Scorton DL10 41 E6
Settrington YO17 148 D8
Sicklinghall LS22 179 E3
Sinnington YO62 95 A8
Skelton HG4 140 E7
Stillington YO61 144 C6
Sutton-under-Whitestonecliffe
YO7 90 E5
Thirkleby High & Low
with Osgodby YO7 116 D8
Thirsk YO7 211 B1
Tholthorpe YO61 142 D5
Thormanby YO61 116 F6
Thornton Steward DL8 61 C2
Topcliffe YO7 115 C7
Trawden BB8 186 A1
Tunstall DL10 41 B3
Tunstall LA6 102 A4
Weaverthorpe YO17 124 E1
Weeton LS17 178 C2
Wennington LA2 102 C2
West Tanfield HG4 87 A1
West Witton DL8 59 C4
Westerdale YO21 28 E5
Whixley YO26 164 A3
Whorlton DL6 45 D8
Wilberfoss YO41 185 F5
Wold Newton YO25 126 A4
Wombleton YO62 93 E7
Wray-with-Botton LA2 128 A6
York YO26 227 A5
Back La S
Middleton YO18 95 E8
Wheldrake YO19 192 F7
Back Middleton Rd 9
LS29 218 A4
Back Newton La
WF10 201 A7
Back Nook 1 DL8 58 F1
Back Northgate WF8 201 B1
Back O' Newton YO41 185 A3
Back of Parks Rd YO62 70 C2
Back of the Beck 6
BD23 216 F4
Back Parish Ghyll Rd 8
LS29 218 B4
Back Park St YO8 232 D5
Back Rd Birstwith HG3 160 B5
Thormanby YO61 116 F5
Back Regent Pl 4 HG1 220 C4
Back Royal Par 5 HG1 219 C2
Back Sea View YO14 101 C1
Back Side YO17 149 B5
Back St
Boroughbridge YO51 141 C5
Bramham LS23 188 E6
Burton Fleming YO25 126 E3
Langtoft YO25 151 D5
10 Middleham DL8 60 E2
Wold Newton YO25 126 A4
Back St Hilda's Terr
YO21 208 D7
Back Station Rd 17
BD20 187 E8
Back Syke DL8 57 D5
Back West View 2
YO30 228 B7
Back Weston Rd 5
LS29 218 B4
Back York Pl 6 HG1 219 D1
Backhouse St YO31 233 B4
Backside La YO62 93 E6
Backstone La LS29 218 C3
Backstone Way LS29 218 C4
Bacon Ave WF6 200 B2
Bad Bargain La YO31 229 A5
Baden St HG1 219 F4
Bader Ave TS17 6 B6
Bader Prim Sch TS17 6 B6
Badger Butt La BD23 155 B5
Badger Gate BD23 134 D3
Badger Hill Dr 14 DL8 63 B3
Badger Hill Prim Sch
YO10 229 B2
Badger La DN6 207 A3
Badger Paddock 5
YO31 225 E2
Badger Wood Glade
LS22 180 C4
Badger Wood Wlk
YO10 229 D3
Badgerbeck Rd 2 DL9 209 B1
Badgers Gate LS29 175 C6
Badminton Ct 18 DL1 3 F6
Baffam Gdns YO8 232 B2
Baffam La YO8 232 B2
Bagby La YO7 90 B2
Bagdale YO21 208 C6
Baghill La WF8 201 C1
Baildon Ave LS25 194 D2
Baildon Cl 3 YO26 227 D4
Baile Hill Terr YO1 233 B1
Bailey Ct DL7 210 C4
Bailey La BD23 152 E3
Bailey St BB18 172 B1
Bailey The BD23 217 A4
Bainbridge C of E Prim Sch
DL8 57 D5
Bainbridge Dr YO8 232 C4
Bairnswood Sch YO12 212 B6
Baker St
Appleton Wiske DL6 24 A3
York YO30 228 C7
Bakersfield Dr DN14 202 F3
Baldersby Garth YO7 88 D1
Baldersby St James C of E
Prim Sch YO7 114 E7
Baldersdale Ave 1
HG5 221 D5
Baldoon Sands TS5 6 D6
Baldwin St 4 HG1 219 C5
Balfour St YO26 227 F5
Balfour Terr TS5 6 D8
Balfour Way YO32 167 A6
Balk La DN14 207 F7
Balk The
Bishop Wilton YO41 169 C2
Marton-le-Moor HG4 114 E1
Slingsby YO62 120 B5
Balk Top YO7 115 B1
Balksyde YO62 120 B5
Ball Grove Dr BB8 186 A3
Ballhall La YO42 193 E6
Balmer Hill DL2 1 C8
Balmoral Ave TS17 6 C8
Balmoral Rd
Barmpton DL1 3 E8
Lingdale TS12 9 F6
Middlesbrough TS3 7 C8
Ripon HG4 214 C3
Balmoral Terr 5 YO23 228 B1
Balne Hall Rd DN14 207 F5
Balne Moor Rd DN14 207 B6
Balshaw Rd LA2 129 B3
Baltimore Way DL1 3 D7
Banbury Rd WF8 201 C2
Bancroft Fold 18 BB18 171 D1
Bancroft Steam Mus*
BB18 171 D1
Bands La DL8 56 C4
Bank Bottom LA6 103 D3
Bank Cl 2 YO22 32 A6
Bank Dike Hill HG3 159 A4
Bank Hall Cl LA6 103 D4
Bank House La LA6 103 B5
Bank La Egton YO21 30 E5
Faceby TS9 25 F1
Grassington BD23 134 E3
Great & Little Broughton
TS9 26 F3
Silsden BD20 174 C4
Bank Rd Glusburn BD20 187 E8
Selby YO8 232 D6
Bank Side
2 Eastfield YO11 100 A7
Rawcliffe DN14 205 A2
Bank St
Barnoldswick BB18 171 D1
Castleford WF10 200 E4
11 Wetherby LS22 180 C3
Bank The DL10 41 D4
Bank Top LA6 103 D3
Bank Top La 4 TS13 12 A7
Bank Wood Rd WF8 206 A6
Bankfield La DN14 205 A7
Bankfield St BB8 186 A2
Bankhead Cl DL6 210 F4

Bankhead Rd DL6 .....210 F4
Banklands Ave BD20 ..174 C1
Banklands La BD20 ...174 C1
Banks Bridge Cl BB18 ..171 E2
Banks La DL10 ....41 E7
Banks Rd Brompton DL6 ..44 A2
  Darlington DL1 ....3 E6
Bankside Cl 3 YO26 ..165 F1
Bankwell Rd BD24 ...131 D2
Bannisdale 6 YO24 ...230 C7
Bannister Cl BB8 .....186 B2
Bannister Wlk BD22 ..187 B6
Banqueting House★
  LS21 ....176 D1
Bar La
  Bramham cum Oglethorpe
  LS23 ....188 F7
  Garforth LS25 ....194 D4
  Hambleton YO8 ......196 E1
  Knaresborough HG5 ..162 D5
  Roecliffe YO51 ......141 A5
  York YO1 ....233 A2
Bar Pl HG1 ....219 D5
Bar St YO11 ....213 A6
Bar The 6 DL10 ......209 C6
Barbara Gr 4 YO24 ...227 F3
Barbeck YO7 ....211 C3
Barbeck Cl YO7 ......211 D3
Barberry TS8 ....7 B4
Barberry Cl Ingleby TS17 ..6 B5
  20 Killinghall HG3 ...161 B3
Barbers Dr YO23 .....230 B4
Barbican Ctr YO10 ...233 C1
Barbican Leisure Ctr
  YO10 ....233 C1
Barbican Mews YO10 ..228 E3
Barbican Rd YO10 ....233 C1
Barbondale Gr HG5 ..221 C5
Barbondale Rd LA10 ..77 A7
Bardale Cl 2 HG5 ....221 D6
Barden Ct 6 YO30 ...224 F1
Barden Fell View 3
  BD23 ....134 E2
Barden La DL8 ....40 B1
Barden Moor Rd DL1 ..3 E4
Barden Pl 9 YO14 ....101 A3
Barden Rd BD23 .....157 A1
Barden Twr★ BD23 ...157 C4
Bardney Rd 14 YO14 ..126 F8
Bardsley Cl TS16 .....5 E7
Barefoot St HG4 .....214 C4
Barf Bank DL8 ....61 A2
Barf La YO41 ....169 D4
Barff Cl 10 YO8 ......197 D1
Barff Gr 8 YO8 ....197 B2
Barff La YO8 ....197 C1
Barff View YO8 ......203 D7
Barfield Rd YO31 ....228 F8
Bargate DL10 ....209 B6
Bark House La LA2 ...131 B8
Bark La
  Addingham LS29 .....175 A5
  Embsay with Eastby
  BD23 ....157 A1
Barker La YO1 ....233 A2
Barker's La
  Newholm-cum-Dunsley
  YO21 ....13 A1
  Snainton YO13 ....98 A4
Barkery The TS8 .....7 B3
Barkhouse Bank HG3 ..138 F4
Barkhouse Wood La
  WF11 ....202 D6
Barknotts Terr YO17 ..215 C3
Barkston Ash RC Prim Sch
  LS24 ....195 E7
Barkston Ave 4 YO26 ..227 B3
Barkston Cl 3 YO26 ..227 A3
Barkston Gr YO26 ....227 A3
Barkston Gr YO26 ....227 A3
Barlby Bridge CP Sch
  YO8 ....232 D5
Barlby By Pass 2 YO8 ..198 B4
Barlby CP Sch YO8 ...198 B4
Barlby Cres YO8 .....232 F7
Barlby High Sch YO8 ..198 B8
Barlby Rd YO8 ....232 E6
Barley Cl YO17 ......215 D2
Barley Horn Rd LS24 ..190 B2
Barley Rise YO32 ....167 A6
Barley View YO32 ....225 C8
Barleycroft YO11 ....213 C1
Barleyfields La 5 LS22 ..180 C3
Barleyfields Rd
  4 Wetherby LS22 ....180 C3
  4 Wetherby LS22 ....180 C3
Barleyhill Rd LS25 ...194 B4
Barley's Yd YO7 .....211 B3
Barlow C of E Prim Sch
  YO8 ....204 C7
Barlow Cl TS14 ......8 F6
Barlow Common Nature
  Reserve★ YO8 ......204 B7
Barlow Common Rd
  YO8 ....204 B8
Barlow Rd YO8 ......204 B6
Barlow St YO26 .....227 D4
Barmby Ave YO10 ...231 E8
Barmby Cl 13 YO30 ..224 F1
Barmby Ferry Rd 1
  YO8 ....198 F1
Barmby on the Marsh Cty
  Prim Sch DN14 .....205 B7
Barmoor Cl YO13 ....75 D6

Barmoor Gn YO13 ....75 D6
Barmoor La YO13 ....75 C6
Barmpton La DL1 ....3 F7
Barn Field Cl BB8 ....186 A3
Barnaby Pl TS14 .....8 E7
Barnard La YO13 .....98 C4
Barnard's La YO21 ...31 A4
Barnbow La LS15 ....194 A6
Barnes Rd
  Castleford WF10 .....200 E3
  Darlington DL3 ......3 A6
Barney La YO60 .....146 A1
Barnfield Way YO23 ..230 A2
Barnhill La DN14 ....205 F7
Barningham Rd DL11 ..18 G7
Barnoldswick CE Sch
  BB18 ....171 D1
Barnoldswick La 6 ...103 A2
Barns Wray 2 YO61 ..117 D1
Barnsdale Est WF10 ..200 D3
Barnsdale Rd
  Ledston WF10 ....200 E7
  Mickletown LS26 ....200 B5
Barnsdale View DN6 ..206 E4
Barnwell Cres HG4 ..222 B5
Barnwood Cres BB18 ..172 B1
Barnwood Rd BB18 ..172 A1
Barngate La YO60 ....147 A7
Barons Cres YO23 ...230 B2
Barr La YO32 ....167 D4
Barrack View DL10 ..209 C8
Barracks Bank DL10 ..21 A2
Barret St 15 BB18 ...172 A1
Barrett Ave 3 YO24 ..227 F3
Barrett Rd DL3 ......3 A5
Barrington Garth
  DN14 ....202 F3
Barrowby La
  Austhorpe LS15 .....194 A4
  Kirkby Overblow HG3 ..179 A3
Barrowcliff Cty Jun Sch
  YO12 ....212 C7
Barrowcliff Rd YO12 ..212 D7
Barry Bank YO21 ....11 F1
Barry's La YO12 .....212 E2
Barse Beck La HG3 ...160 D5
Barstow Ave YO30 ...228 F3
Barstow Fall 2 WF8 ..201 C2
Bartindale Rd YO14 ..127 A5
Bartle Garth YO1 ....233 C3
Barton C of E Sch DL10 ..21 D7
Barton St DL1 ......3 E6
Bartons Garth YO8 ..232 B2
Barugh La
  Barugh (Great & Little)
  YO17 ....95 B2
  Normanby YO62 .....94 F4
Barwic Par YO8 ......232 E5
Barwick Fields TS17 ..6 A5
Barwick Inf Sch LS15 ..194 C8
Barwick La Ingleby TS17 ..6 A4
  Ingleby Barwick TS17 ..5 F5
Barwick Parade CP Sch
  YO8 ....232 E4
Barwick Rd LS25 ....194 C5
Barwick St YO12 ....212 F5
Barwick Terr 1 YO12 ..212 F5
Barwick View TS17 ..6 A5
Barwick Way TS17 ...6 A4
Bassett Cl YO8 ......232 C3
Bassleton La TS17 ..6 A6
Baston La YO61 .....143 E4
Bates Ave DL3 ......3 B7
Bateson Cl YO10 ....229 C1
Bath St LS29 ....218 C5
Battersby Ave TS9 ...27 C7
Battersby Junc TS9 ..27 C6
Battersby Sta TS9 ...27 C6
Battle of Bramham Moor
  (site of)★ LS24 .....188 F4
Battle of Marston Moor (site
  of)★ YO26 ....181 B7
Battle of Standard Hill (site
  of)★ DL6 ....43 E4
Battle of Towton (site of)★
  LS24 ....195 D8
Battleflats Way YO41 ..168 D2
Battling Hills La YO18 ..49 B5
Bawhead Rd 28 BB18 ..172 A1
Bawtry Cl YO8 ......232 D3
Bawtry Rd YO8 .....232 D3
Baxby Manor★ YO61 ..117 B6
Baxby Terr 2 DL2 ...22 D8
Baxter Wood BD20 ..187 E8
Baxtergate YO21 ....208 D6
Baxton's Sprunt 1 YO62 ..92 F7
Bay Bolton Ave DL8 ..59 F3
Bay Horse Yd 9 BD23 ..216 F4
Baydale Rd DL3 .....3 A4
Baysdale Ave YO10 ..229 D3
Baysdale Cl TS14 ...8 F6
Baysdale Rd TS17 ...6 B7
Bazeley's La YO11 ...215 E1
Beach Rd The YO14 ..101 B3
Beach The YO14 ....101 B3
Beacon Bank YO62 ..92 D1
Beacon Brow Rd YO13 ..75 A7
Beacon Grange Pk DL2 ..4 C7
Beacon Hill DL2 ....4 B7
Beacon Rd
  Millington YO42 ....170 A1
  Seamer YO12 ....99 D7
Beacon Rise 4 LS25 ..175 C2
Beacon St 5 LS29 ...175 A4
Beacon View 3 BD23 ..217 C8
Beacon Way YO22 ...32 D6
Beaconsfield St
  Northallerton DL7 ...210 D4

Beaconsfield St continued
  3 Scarborough YO12 ..212 E3
  York YO10 ....227 B3
Beadlam Ave TS7 ....7 D6
Beadle Garth YO23 ..230 B2
Beagle Croft YO41 ..168 C1
Beagle Ridge Dr YO24 ..227 C1
Beagle Spinney YO41 ..168 C1
Beal La Beal DN14 ...202 D4
  Cridling Stubbs WF11 ..202 C1
Beale Cl TS17 ....5 B5
Beamsley Ct BD23 ..217 A2
Beamsley La BD23 ...174 F7
Beamsley View 13 LS29 ..175 C2
Bean Sheaf La YO17 ..96 A3
Beancroft Rd WF10 ..200 D3
Beancroft St WF10 ..200 D3
Beanland La YO32 ...167 D2
Beanlands Dr 7 BD20 ..187 E7
Beanlands Par LS29 ..218 C5
Beanlands Pl
  8 Glusburn BD20 ....187 E7
  5 Glusburn BD20 ....187 E8
Bean's Way YO31 ...229 B8
Beatswell Lawn HG4 ..113 C8
Beaufighter Cl DL10 ..41 F4
Beaufort Cl YO10 ...229 B3
Beaulieu Cl 1 YO32 ..225 F5
Beaumont Hill Sch DL1 ..3 D8
Beaumont Pl YO8 ...232 A2
Beaverdyke YO30 ...224 F1
Becca La LS25 ......194 F8
Beck Cl 6 YO41 .....185 B2
Beck Closes Rd YO26 ..142 A3
Beck Hole 5 YO11 ..100 B6
Beck Hole Rd YO22 ..31 C1
Beck Isle Mus of Rural Life★
  YO18 ....95 F7
Beck La Cloughton YO13 ..54 C1
  Collingham LS22 ....180 A1
  Farndale East YO62 ..48 D5
  Lebberston YO11 ....100 D5
  South Kilvington YO7 ..211 B6
  Wheldrake YO19 ....193 A8
Beck Mdw LS15 .....194 C2
Beck Mill Cl YO17 ...215 D3
Beck Row YO41 .....169 D5
Beck Side BD23 .....173 B4
Beck Side Cl BD20 ..173 D1
Beckbridge La 2 WF6 ..200 B1
Beckbridge Rd WF6 ..200 B1
Beckbridge Way WF6 ..200 B1
Beckclose La DL8 ...87 F6
Beckdale Rd YO62 ...92 E7
Beckett Cl 8 YO62 ..93 D7
Beckfield La
  Fairburn WF11 ......201 C7
  York YO26 ....227 B5
Beckfield Pl YO26 ...227 B4
Beckfields Ave TS17 ..6 A4
Becklands Cl YO51 ..141 A5
Becklands La YO51 ..141 A4
Becks Brow BD23 ...153 C3
Becks Cl 5 YO32 ....225 C8
Beckside Catterick DL10 ..41 E4
  7 Elvington YO41 ...185 B2
  Northallerton DL7 ...210 B4
  4 Staithes TS13 .....13 K2
  Trawden Forest BB8 ..186 B2
  Wilberfoss YO41 ....185 E6
Beckside Cl
  19 Addingham LS29 ..174 C1
  25 Burley in Warfedale
  LS29 ....176 C1
Beckwith Ave HG2 ..222 B7
Beckwith Cl
  Harrogate HG2 ......222 A6
  Heworth YO31 ......229 C7
Beckwith Cres HG2 ..222 B7
Beckwith Dr HG2 ...222 B6
Beckwith Head Rd
  HG3 ....178 C8
Beckwith Rd HG2 ...222 A7
Beckwith Wlk HG2 ..222 A7
Beckwithshaw CP Sch
  HG3 ....178 A8
Bedale Ave
  Scarborough YO12 ..212 E8
  York YO10 ....229 D4
Bedale C of E Prim Sch
  DL8 ....63 A2
Bedale High Sch DL8 ..63 A4
Bedale La HG4 ......114 A8
Bedale Mus★ DL8 ...63 A3
Bedale Rd Aiskew DL7 ..63 C4
  Scotton DL9 ....40 F2
  Well DL8 ....87 A4
Bedburn Dr DL3 ....2 B7
Bede Ave YO30 .....228 B7
Bedern Bank 13 HG4 ..214 C5
Bedern Ct 16 HG4 ...214 C5
Bedford Rd 17 ....7 D6
Bedford St 18 YO11 ..213 A6
Bedfords Fold 6 LS25 ..202 A7
Bedlam Hill YO7 ....65 E4
Bedlam La
  Fewston HG3 ....159 F2
  Staveley HG5 ....140 E1
Beech Ave
  3 Airmyn DN14 .....205 E4
  Bishopthorpe YO23 ..231 A3
  1 Earby BB18 ....172 A1
  Harrogate HG2 ......222 E6
  4 Topcliffe YO7 .....89 B1
  York YO24 ....227 B1
Beech Cl Baldersby YO7 ..88 D1
  3 Eastfield YO11 ....100 A7
  2 Elvington YO41 ...185 B2

Beech Cl continued
  Farnham HG5 ....162 D7
  Great Ayton TS9 ....7 F1
  Hunton DL9 ....40 E2
  Scruton DL7 ....63 E7
  7 Sherburn in Elmet LS25 ..195 F4
  Snape with Thorp DL8 ..87 A7
  3 South Milford LS25 ..195 F2
  Tadcaster LS24 .....189 F6
Beech Cres
  Castleford WF10 ....201 B3
  Whitwell-on-the-Hill
  YO60 ....146 E4
Beech Croft
  Barlby with Osgodby
  YO8 ....198 B6
  Pontefract WF8 .....201 C2
Beech Ct YO23 ......231 A3
Beech Dr
  6 Kirkbymoorside YO62 ..70 B1
  12 Scalby YO13 .....75 D5
  South Milford LS25 ..195 F2
Beech Glade YO31 ..225 F2
Beech Gr
  1 Airmyn DN14 .....205 E4
  Burton Salmon LS25 ..201 F6
  Camblesforth YO8 ..204 C5
  Harrogate HG2 ......219 C1
  Knaresborough HG5 ..221 B8
  Maltby TS8 ....6 C4
  Northallerton DL6 ...210 E5
  Selby YO8 ....232 C5
  Sherburn in Elmet LS25 ..195 F4
  Sowerby YO7 ....211 C1
  Whitby YO21 ....208 B6
  York YO26 ....227 C4
Beech Hill
  Carleton BD23 ......173 A4
  6 Knaresborough HG5 ..221 A6
  5 Pontefract WF8 ...201 C1
Beech Hill Rd BD23 ..173 A4
Beech La
  8 East Ayton/West Ayton
  YO13 ....99 A7
  3 Spofforth HG3 ....179 E6
Beech Pk 5 YO19 ...198 A8
Beech Pl 5 YO32 ...167 A6
Beech Rd
  Boston Spa LS23 ....188 E8
  Campsall DN6 ......206 E1
  Darlington DL1 .....3 F7
  Harrogate HG2 ......222 E6
  Ripon HG4 ....214 B3
Beech St
  23 Barnoldswick BB18 ..171 D1
  10 Glusburn BD20 ...187 E7
  6 Harrogate HG2 ....220 C3
Beech Tree Ct 2 YO30 ..164 F7
Beech Tree La YO8 ..204 C5
Beech View LS25 ....194 E8
Beech Wlk
  5 Eastfield YO11 ....100 A7
  Tadcaster LS24 .....189 D6
Beechcroft Cl TS12 ..9 F6
Beeches End LS23 ...188 F8
Beeches The
  Skelton YO30 ....224 C4
  11 Stokesley TS9 ...26 C7
Beechfield
  Coulby Newham TS8 ..7 A5
  Hawsker-cum-Stainsacre
  YO22 ....33 A6
  Newby Wiske DL7 ...64 F2
  Newton-on-Ouse YO30 ..165 B6
Beechfield Cl YO8 ...197 B1
Beechfield Rd DL10 ..209 C8
Beechnut La WF8 ...201 B1
Beechtree Rd LS24 ..189 D5
Beechville Ave YO12 ..212 F6
Beechwood Ave 2 TS9 ..26 C8
Beechwood Cl
  14 Bedale DL8 ......63 A2
  Markington with Wallerthwaite
  HG3 ....139 D4
  Sherburn in Elmet LS25 ..195 F3
Beechwood Cres 6
  HG2 ....219 C1
Beechwood Croft
  LS25 ....195 F3
Beechwood Dr BD23 ..216 D5
Beechwood Glade
  Sherburn in Elmet LS25 ..195 F3
  7 York YO24 ....227 B1
Beechwood Gr
  Harrogate HG2 ......222 F7
  16 Ilkley LS29 ......175 C2
Beechwood Rd YO17 ..215 D2
Beechwood Rise 1
  LS22 ....180 C4
Beeforth Cl YO32 ...225 D5
Beeston's La LS17 ..178 C4
Beggarmans Rd DL8 ..80 C8
Belbrough Cl 3 TS15 ..25 C4
Belbrough La TS15 ..25 C4
Belcombe Way 1 YO30 ..228 A7
Belford La HG4 .....112 A3
Belford Pl 3 HG1 ...219 D2
Belford Rd HG1 ....219 D2
Belford Sq 9 HG1 ...219 D1
Belgrave Cres
  Harrogate HG2 ......222 E8
  15 Scarborough YO12 ..212 F5
Belgrave St
  3 Skipton BD23 ....216 E4
  York YO24 ....228 C7
Belgrave Terr
  3 Hurworth-on-Tees DL2 ..22 D8
  14 Scarborough YO11 ..212 F5

Bell Cl Haxby YO32 ..225 C8
  5 Seamer YO12 .....99 D6
Bell End Gn YO18 ...49 G5
Bell La Cawood YO8 ..197 A7
  Huby YO61 ....144 A4
  Husthwaite YO61 ...117 B5
  Rawcliffe DN14 .....205 A4
  Ulleskelf LS24 ......190 C2
Bellaby Pk 7 YO62 ..93 D7
Bellburn La DL3 ....3 B7
Belle Hill BD24 .....131 D3
Belle Vue LS29 .....218 C3
Belle Vue Cres 33 YO14 ..101 B3
Belle Vue Par 9 YO11 ..212 F5
Belle Vue Pl 10 YO11 ..212 F5
Belle Vue St
  34 Filey YO14 ......101 B3
  Scarborough YO12 ..212 F5
  York YO10 ....228 E3
Belle Vue Terr
  Whitby YO21 ....208 D3
  York YO10 ....228 E3
Bellerby Camp DL8 ..60 B7
Bellerby Rd DL8 ....60 C6
Bellerbyhurn Rd YO17 ..95 F2
Bellevue Terr
  Ripon HG4 ....214 C5
  2 Skipton BD23 ....216 E4
Bellfarm Ave YO31 ..228 E8
Bellground La YO30 ..165 D4
Bellhouse La YO21 ..29 C7
Bellhouse Way YO24 ..230 B8
Bellingham Cl YO7 ..211 C3
Bellman Wlk 3 HG4 ..113 D2
Bellmans Croft YO23 ..230 B2
Bell's Ct 15 YO62 ...92 F5
Bellwood Ave
  Boston Spa LS23 ....188 E8
  Lockwood TS12 ....9 F7
Bellwood Dr YO24 ..230 B8
Belmangate TS14 ...8 F6
Belmont WF11 .....201 D5
Belmont Ave
  Harrogate HG2 ......220 D5
  10 Otley LS21 ......176 F1
Belmont Cl 3 YO30 ..225 A1
Belmont Gr 1 HG2 ..220 D3
Belmont Prim Sch TS14 ..8 F5
Belmont Rd
  Harrogate HG2 ......219 C2
  Ilkley LS29 ....218 E4
  Scarborough YO11 ..213 A4
Belmont St BD23 ...216 F4
Belmont Terr 2 HG2 ..220 D3
Belmont Wharf BD23 ..216 F4
Belthorpe La YO42 ..169 C4
Belton Park Dr 7 DL9 ..40 E4
Belvedere Pl YO11 ..213 A3
Belvedere Rd YO11 ..213 A3
Belvoir Ave 8 YO41 ..185 B2
Belvoir Dr WF11 ...201 F2
Ben La BB18 ....171 E2
Ben Rhydding Dr LS29 ..218 F3
Ben Rhydding Prim Sch
  LS29 ....218 E4
Ben Rhydding Rd
  LS29 ....218 E4
Ben Rhydding Sta
  LS29 ....218 F4
Bence The YO42 ....170 C3
Benedict Ave YO8 ..232 E4
Beningbrough Dr HG3 ..219 B5
Beningbrough La
  YO30 ....165 G5
Benjy La YO19 .....192 F2
Benkhill Dr 16 DL8 ..63 A2
Bennett St 11 BD23 ..216 F3
Bennions Way 5 DL10 ..41 E4
Bennison La YO21 ...13 L1
Bennymoor La YO8 ..198 C4
Bensham Rd DL1 ...3 D8
Benson La WF6 .....200 B2
Bent La Colne BB8 ..186 A3
  Sutton BD20 ....187 E2
Bent Rigg La YO13 ..54 B7
Bentham Moor Rd
  LA6 ....103 A2
Bentham St LA6 ....103 B3
Bentham Sta LA2 ..129 A7
Bentinck Ave TS5 ..6 F8
Bentley Wynd TS16 ..5 D3
Benton Cap La BD22 ..187 B7
Bents La YO18 .....71 A5
Beresford Cl 6 DL8 ..63 B2
Beresford Terr YO23 ..228 C1
Berghill La YO7 ....66 A4
Berkeley Terr YO26 ..227 E5
Berkley Dr TS14 ....8 F5
Bernard La YO60 ...164 B3
Bernica Gr TS17 ...6 A4
Berry Bank YO21 ...1 A6
Berry La LS26 ......200 C8
Berrygate La HG4 ..214 E2
Berry's Ave HG5 ...221 B6
Berwick Rd
  Archdeacon Newton DL3 ..3 A7
  18 Scotton DL9 .....40 E4
Bestmire La DL6 ...65 A4
Betteras Hill Rd LS25 ..202 A8
Betton Rise YO13 ..99 B8
Between Dikes Rd
  YO8 ....204 F8
Beulah St 10 HG1 ..219 D2
Beverley Balk YO41 ..168 B2
Beverley Cl 12 YO11 ..100 B6
Beverley Gate YO12 ..99 D1
Beverley Rd
  11 Eastfield YO11 ..100 A6

Beverley Rd *continued*
Middlesbrough TS7 7 D6
Norton YO17 215 E3
Beverley Rise LS29 175 C2
Beverley Sch TS4 6 F8
Bewerley Rd HG1 219 B5
Bewlay St YO23 228 C2
Bewley Gr TS5 6 E7
Bexhill Cl WF8 201 C1
Bexley Dr TS6 7 E8
Bickerton Way LS21 176 F1
Bickley Gate YO13 73 F6
Bickley Howe YO12 212 B4
Bickley Way TS8 7 A5
Bielby Cl 8 Bedale DL8 63 B3
33 Scalby YO12 75 D5
Big Meadow Dr 5 LS29 174 E4
Biggin La LS25 196 C6
Bilsdale Cl
Northallerton DL7 210 C2
York YO30 224 E2
Bilsdale Gr HG5 221 D6
Bilsdale Midcable Chop Gate C of E Prim Sch TS9 46 F6
Bilton Cl HG1 219 E6
Bilton Dr HG1 219 D4
Bilton Grange Cl HG1 219 D5
Bilton Grange CP Sch
HG1 219 D5
Bilton Grove Ave HG1 219 E5
Bilton Hall Dr HG1 220 D6
Bilton La HG1 219 E6
Binks Cl DL6 210 B7
Binnington Carr La
YO12 99 B1
Binns La BD20 187 D7
Binsley La YO61 117 E2
Binsoe La HG4 86 F3
Birch Ave Malton YO17 215 D6
Sleights YO22 32 A6
Birch Cl 8 Filey YO14 101 B3
9 Hunton DL9 40 F2
2 Kirklevington TS15 24 E8
4 Thorpe Willoughby YO8 197 B1
Birch Cres 10 YO22 32 A6
Birch Dr 2 Faceby TS9 25 F1
Kippax LS25 194 D2
Birch Gr
Castleford WF10 201 B3
Harrogate HG1 219 E6
Kippax LS25 194 D1
Birch Hall La BB18 172 B1
Birch La 13 YO32 166 E5
Birch Rd DL1 3 D8
Birch View 8 YO18 96 A6
Birches The TS8 7 A5
Birchfield Dr TS16 5 D5
Birchwood Cl 16 BD24 131 D2
Birchwood Ct 5 LS29 218 A4
Birchwood Mews HG2 222 F7
Birchwood Rd TS7 7 C6
Bird Gdn* LS25 195 B7
Bird La Hensall DN14 203 D2
Kellington DN14 202 F4
Bird Ridding La DL8 60 B1
Birdale Field La LS22 188 B8
Birdforth Way 1 YO62 92 C1
Birdwood Cl DL9 209 C2
Birk Brow Rd TS12 9 D5
Birk Field Bank YO21 28 F6
Birk Head La YO62 70 F4
Birk La YO42 199 D8
Birkby La DL7 23 B1
Birk-Crag Ct 2 HG3 161 B2
Birkdale Ave HG5 221 D5
Birkdale Gr 4 YO26 227 B5
Birker La
Newton on Derwent YO41 185 D4
Wilberfoss YO41 185 F6
Birkett La CA17 14 B7
Birkhills HG3 140 A3
Birkin La WF11 202 B4
Birkin Rd YO8 202 F5
Birklands 1 YO62 93 D7
Birkwith La LA2 128 F7
Birstwith C of E Prim Sch
HG3 160 E6
Birstwith Dr YO26 227 E4
Birstwith Grange HG3 160 E6
Birstwith Rd HG1 220 A3
Birthwaite La HG3 161 C8
Birtley Ave TS5 6 E7
Bishop Cl 1 HG3 137 C4
Bishop Ct 2 YO8 232 B6
Bishop Garth 2 HG3 137 C4
Bishop Monkton C of E Prim Sch HG3 140 B5
Bishop Thornton C of E Prim Sch HG3 139 A2
Bishop Thornton RC Prim Sch HG3 139 A2
Bishop Way 3 HG3 137 C4
Bishop Witton Sch
YO42 169 F2
Bishopdale Cl HG5 221 D6
Bishopdale Dr
7 Collingham LS22 180 A1
1 Collingham LS22 188 A8
Bishopdike Rd
Cawood YO8 197 A6
Sherburn in Elmet LS25 196 A4
Bishopgate St YO23 233 B1
Bishophill Jun YO1 233 A1
Bishophill Senior YO1 233 B1
Bishopsgarth DL7 210 C4
Bishopsway YO10 229 C3
Bishopthorpe Inf Sch
YO23 231 A4
Bishopthorpe Pal*
YO23 231 B4
Bishopthorpe Rd
YO23 231 B5
Bishopton HG4 214 A5
Bishopton La
Great Burdon DL1 4 A7
Ripon HG4 113 D2
Bisley Ct 13 DL1 3 F6
Bismarck St YO26 227 E5
Bitterdale La YO62 70 A3
Black Abbey La 1 BD20 187 E8
Black Bank Rd LA2 130 E3
Black Dike La YO26 182 F8
Black Fen La YO8 232 C8
Black Gill La
Airton BD23 154 B8
Settle BD23 132 A1
Black Hill YO62 118 E5
Black Hill Rd HG3 157 F8
Black Horse La TS15 25 C3
Black Sike La YO13 98 B4
Black Wlk WF8 201 B1
Blackbird Way 8 YO12 99 F6
Blackburn La WF11 202 B2
Blacklee Cl 4 YO32 167 B8
Blacksmith Bank DL8 62 E5
Blacksmith Hill YO22 53 A7
Blackthorn TS8 7 B4
Blackthorn Dr YO31 225 E2
Blackthorn La HG3 222 C3
Blackwell DL3 3 B3
Blackwell La DL3 3 B4
Blackwood La YO8 198 F7
Blackwood Rd YO8 198 E8
Blair Ave TS17 5 F4
Blair Pk HG5 221 C5
Blake Ct YO19 193 A8
Blake Gate HG3 136 E1
Blake St YO1 233 B3
Blakeley Cres 3 BB18 171 D2
Blakeley Gr YO30 224 F3
Blakeney Pl YO10 228 F3
Blakey Bank YO62 49 A5
Blakey Cl YO7 211 C1
Blakey La YO7 211 C1
Blakey Rd YO62 70 B6
Bland La YO26 227 A4
Blandford Rd DL9 40 E3
Blands Ave WF10 200 D7
Bland's Cliff 27 YO11 213 A6
Blands Cres 3 WF10 200 D7
Blands Gr 4 WF10 200 D7
Bland's Hill HG5 221 A4
Blands Terr WF10 200 D7
Blansby La YO17 121 C8
Blansby Park La YO18 96 A8
Blatchford YO30 228 B8
Blawath Rd YO18 51 A2
Blayshaw La HG3 110 B4
Blazefield Bank HG3 137 D3
Blea Moor Rd LA6 78 E2
Blea Pit La HG4 140 E8
Bleaberry La YO41 169 B5
Blean La DL8 57 D3
Bleara Rd BB18 186 B8
Blenheim Ave 4 YO21 208 B7
Blenheim Cl DL10 41 F6
Blenheim Ct
Harrogate HG2 222 D7
Rawcliffe YO30 224 D3
Blenheim St 12 YO12 213 A7
Blenheim Way HG2 222 C7
Bleriot Way YO30 225 A3
Blewhouse La DL8 61 E3
Blind La Aiskew DL8 63 B3
Barton DL10 21 D7
Burton in Lonsdale LA6 102 F3
Guisborough TS14 8 C6
Hurworth DL2 22 E8
Knaresborough HG5 221 B7
Scorton DL10 42 B8
Tockwith YO26 181 B8
Blind Piece La YO7 116 A6
Bloe Beck La LA2 129 E6
Bloody Beck Hill YO13 54 A7
Blossom St YO24 233 A1
Blossomgate HG4 214 B5
Blue Bank YO22 32 A4
Blue Barn La TS15 25 C6
Blue Bell Gr TS5 6 F6
Blue Bridge La YO10 228 D2
Blue Nile Way 25 DL9 41 A5
Blue Slates Cl YO19 193 A8
Bluebeck Dr YO30 227 E8
Bluebell Mdw 15 HG3 161 B3
Bluebell Wlk 18 HG3 161 B3
Blyth Cl YO8 232 A5
Boar La TS17 6 B5
Boat La Barforth DL11 1 C7
Great Ouseburn YO26 164 C8
Kirby Hall YO26 142 C1
Mickletown LS26 200 D5
Boatcliffe Rd YO14 127 D7
Boathouse La DL2 2 E4
Bob La YO7 65 E3
Bodmin Dr WF6 200 A2
Bodner Hill YO61 118 F1
Boeing Way TS18 5 F7
Bog La
Askham Bryan YO24 230 B6
Barwick in Elmet & Scholes LS15 194 A7
Stirton with Thorlby BD23 216 D7
Boggart La LS24 190 C2
Boggy La DL10 209 B5
Boghole Bank DL6 45 B3
Boghouse La TS13 10 F3
Bogs La
Bridge Hewick HG4 114 C1
Harrogate HG1 220 C5
Bolckow St TS14 8 F7
Bold Venture St BD23 216 F2
Boldron Cl 8 TS18 5 D8
Bolland St 16 BB18 171 D2
Bolling Rd LS29 218 D4
Boltby Rd YO30 224 F2
Bolton Abbey Sta
BD23 174 D8
Bolton Ave DL10 209 B7
Bolton Castle* DL8 59 B6
Bolton Cross DL10 41 F5
Bolton Ct 14 DL8 60 D5
Bolton Hall* BD23 157 F1
Bolton La YO42 169 E1
Bolton on Swale C of E Prim Sch DL10 41 F6
Bolton Priory (rems of)*
BD23 157 F1
Bolton Rd
Draughton BD23 174 F7
Silsden BD20 174 D3
Bolton St HG1 219 D4
Bolton Way
13 Leyburn DL8 60 D5
Richmond DL10 209 C8
Bolton-on-Swale Nature Reserve* DL10 41 F5
Bonby La YO8 192 E2
Bond End HG5 221 A6
Bond La
Appleton Roebuck YO23 190 F5
Settle BD24 131 D2
Bond St WF8 201 C1
Bondgate Helmsley YO62 92 F6
Pontefract WF8 201 C1
Ripon HG4 214 C4
Selby YO8 232 B7
Bondgate Gn HG4 214 D4
Bondgate Green Cl 6
HG4 214 C4
Bondgate Green La
HG4 214 C4
Bondings Rise 5 LS25 196 A4
Bonington Ct 7 YO26 227 E4
Bonny Gr TS8 7 C5
Bonnygate La YO61 118 F3
Bonnygrove Way TS8 7 B5
Boonhill Rd YO62 69 F4
Boosbeck Rd TS12 9 D8
Boot St 26 BB18 172 A1
Booth Bridge La BD23 172 A3
Booth Ferry Rd DN14 205 F4
Booth St 27 LS29 176 C1
Bootham YO30 233 A3
Bootham Bar* YO31 233 B3
Bootham Cres YO30 233 A4
Bootham Park Hospl
YO31 233 B4
Bootham Row YO31 233 B3
Bootham Sch YO31 233 A3
Bootham Sq YO31 233 B3
Bootham Terr YO30 233 A3
Boothferry Prim Sch
DN14 205 F2
Boothferry Rd DN14 205 F2
Boothwood Rd YO30 224 E2
Booty La DN14 206 F7
Borage Rd 30 HG3 161 B3
Bore Tree Baulk YO19 184 D6
Borogate 9 YO62 92 F6
Borough Mere La
YO17 215 D8
Borough Rd
Darlington DL1 3 D5
Richmond DL10 209 B8
Boroughbridge High Sch
YO51 141 B5
Boroughbridge Rd
Bishop Monkton HG3 140 B5
Bridge Hewick HG4 114 B1
Dishforth YO7 115 A2
Knaresborough HG5 221 B7
North Otterington DL7 64 E6
Northallerton DL7 210 C1
Ripon HG4 214 E3
Scriven HG5 162 E6
Westwick YO51 140 D4
Whixley YO26 164 B4
York YO26 227 D5
Borrage Green La
HG4 214 B4
Borrage La HG4 214 B4
Borrowby Ave DL6 210 F3
Borrowby La
Borrowby TS13 11 D7
Staithes TS13 13 J1
Borrowbydale Ave
HG5 221 D6
Borrowdale Dr
Castleford WF10 201 B5
York YO30 224 F1
Boss Moor La BD23 155 F8
Boston Dr TS7 7 B5
Boston Rd Clifford LS23 188 E7
Wetherby LS22 180 C2
Boston Spa C of E Sch
LS23 188 E8
Boston Spa Comp Sch
LS23 188 D8
Boston Spa Primrose Lane Jun & Infants Sch
LS23 188 E8
Botheby Wood BD23 216 E5
Bottom House La YO22 33 B5
Bottoms La YO22 33 B6
Botton Rd LA2 128 E2
Bouldershaw La DL11 17 D1
Boulsworth Dr BB8 186 B1
Boulsworth Gr 9 BB8 186 A3
Boundary Ave BD20 187 E7
Boundary Way DL10 209 F8
Bourlon Rd DL9 209 A2
Bournemouth Rd TS3 7 C8
Bouthwaite Dr 13 YO26 227 E4
Bow Bridge Dr BD23 217 D7
Bow Bridge La YO21 29 A7
Bow Bridge View
LS24 189 F7
Bow St TS14 8 F7
Bowbridge La DL7 63 A8
Bowcarr La YO26 163 D8
Bowcliffe Rd LS23 188 E5
Bowe Cres 8 DL8 63 B2
Bowen Rd DL3 3 B7
Bower Rd HG1 219 D3
Bower St HG1 219 D2
Bower Wlk YO17 215 E4
Bowes Ave YO31 228 E5
Bowes La YO14 100 F5
Bowesfield Cres TS18 6 A8
Bowesfield Ind Est TS18 6 A8
Bowesfield La TS18 6 A7
Bowland Cl HG2 220 D1
Bowland Ct HG2 220 D1
Bowland La YO42 193 E2
Bowland View LA6 103 E3
Bowland Way YO30 225 A1
Bowling Green Ct
YO31 228 D8
Bowling Green La
9 Hunmanby YO14 126 F8
Manfield DL2 2 B4
York YO31 233 C4
Bowling La YO17 215 E4
Bowling View BD23 216 D3
Bowman St DL3 3 D7
Bowness Dr YO30 224 E1
Bowthorpe La YO8 199 B4
Bowyers Cl YO23 230 C4
Box Hill YO12 212 C3
Box La WF8 201 C1
Boyle & Petyts Sch
BD23 174 F8
Boyle The LS15 194 B8
Boynton La
Barton-le-Street YO17 120 F8
Rawcliffe DN14 205 A1
Boynton Rd DL7 22 E2
Bracewell La BD23 171 B4
Bracewell St 15 BB18 171 D2
Bracken Cl
Whitby YO22 208 E4
York YO32 225 F4
Bracken Cres TS14 8 D6
Bracken Field BD23 134 B3
Bracken Hill
Scarborough YO12 212 C7
2 York YO10 229 C3
Bracken Rd YO24 230 F7
Brackenber Cl BD24 131 C2
Brackenber La BD24 131 C1
Brackenfield Sch HG1 219 A2
Brackenhill Ave YO8 232 A4
Brackenhill La
Brayton YO8 232 A3
Church Fenton LS24 196 C8
Sleights YO22 32 A5
Brackenhills YO26 165 F1
Brackenhoe Sec Sch
TS4 7 B8
Brackenley Ave 2
BD23 217 C7
Brackenley Cl 3 BD23 217 C7
Brackenley Cres BD23 217 C7
Brackenley Dr BD23 217 C7
Brackenley Gr 1 BD23 217 C7
Brackenley La BD23 217 A7
Brackenthwaite La
HG3 222 A1
Brackenwell La LS17 178 B4
Brackenwood Cl 2
LS29 218 E4
Brackit La YO61 91 B2
Bracknell Rd TS17 6 C8
Bradfords Cl 8 LS23 188 E6
Bradley Ave
Castleford WF10 200 E4
Northallerton DL6 210 F2
Bradley Cres YO23 182 D6
Bradley Dr YO24 230 C8
Bradley Gr BD20 174 B1
Bradley La YO23 182 C5
Bradley Rd
Pickering YO18 71 F4
Silsden BD20 174 B2
Bradley Rise BD20 174 B1
Bradleys Both CP Sch
BD20 173 E3
Bradleys Terr 2 TS9 8 A2
Bradworth Cl 3 YO11 100 B7
Bradworth Dr 2 YO11 100 B7
Braeburn Cty Jun Sch
YO11 100 A6
Braegate La LS24 190 E7
Braemar Dr LS25 194 D4
Braeside 3 TS15 24 E8
Braeside Gdns YO24 227 E3
Brafferton C of E Prim Sch
YO61 115 F1
Brafferton Hall Garde 3
YO61 115 F1
Braham La HG5 179 F7
Brailsford Cres YO30 228 A8
Braimber La YO51 141 C1
Braithegayte YO19 192 F8
Braithwaite Endowed C of E Prim Sch HG3 159 B7
Braithwaite Hall* DL8 84 D8
Braithwaite La
Dacre HG3 159 A7
East Witton Town DL8 84 E8
Braker La YO26 163 F4
Bramall La 6 DL1 3 F6
Bramble Cl 11 HG3 161 B3
Bramble Dene YO24 230 D7
Bramble Wlk YO17 215 B4
Brambles 8 YO8 197 B1
Brambles The 6 LS29 175 C2
Bramcote Prep Sch for Boys
YO11 213 A3
Brame La HG3 177 A8
Bramham Ave YO26 227 A3
Bramham CP Sch
LS23 188 E6
Bramham Dr HG3 219 A4
Bramham Gr YO26 227 A3
Bramham La LS23 188 A6
Bramham Park Gdns*
LS23 188 C4
Bramham Pk* LS23 188 C4
Bramham Rd
Boston Spa LS23 188 E7
Thorner LS14 188 A3
York YO26 227 A2
Bramley Ave YO8 198 B5
Bramley Garth YO31 229 B6
Bramper La DL7 42 E1
Branch Rd BD23 216 F2
Brandon Gr YO32 226 E3
Brandsby Bank YO61 118 D3
Brandsby Gr YO31 225 E2
Brandsby Rd YO61 118 A1
Brandsby St YO61 118 A1
Brandsdale Cres
YO10 229 D3
Brankin Dr DL1 3 E4
Brankin Rd DL1 3 D3
Branklyn Gdns TS17 6 A4
Branksome Comp Sch
DL3 3 A6
Branksome Gr 1 TS18 5 E8
Bransdale TS14 8 D6
Bransdale Ave
Northallerton DL7 210 C2
11 Pontefract WF6 200 A2
Bransdale Cl 6 WF6 200 A2
Bransdale Gr 3 HG5 221 D6
Bransdale Mews 10
WF6 200 A2
Bransdale Rd YO62 48 B1
Bransdale Wlk WF6 200 A2
Bransholme Dr YO30 225 A2
Brant Bank La LS29 175 B3
Brant La LS24 189 D4
Branton Cl YO26 142 A1
Branton Ct YO26 142 A1
Branton La YO26 142 A1
Branton Pl YO26 227 A3
Brass Castle La TS8 7 C3
Brat La LS21 177 A7
Bravener Ct YO30 165 B6
Brawby La YO62 94 E1
Bray Gate YO42 169 E2
Bray Rd YO10 231 F8
Braygate Balk YO18 72 C5
Braygate La YO18 72 D5
Braygate St YO17 121 A2
Braythorne La LS21 177 E4
Brayton C of E Prim Sch
YO8 232 A2
Brayton Cty Inf Sch
YO8 232 A2
Brayton Cty Jun Sch
YO8 232 A2
Brayton High Sch
YO8 232 A3
Brayton La YO8 232 B1
Breakmoor Ave BD20 174 C2
Brearlands BD23 172 A3
Brearton La HG3 161 E8
Breary Cl YO24 227 F1
Breary Flat La HG5 221 C7
Brechin Dr TS17 6 B6
Breckenbrough La
DL10 41 A3
Breckenbrough Sch
YO7 89 A6
Breckney La YO17 122 D5
Brecks La Kippax LS25 194 C2
Pockley YO62 93 B8
Strensall YO32 167 B7
Swillington LS26 194 B2
York YO32 225 F4
Brecksfield YO30 224 C5
Brecon Cres TS17 5 F4
Breedycroft La YO17 121 C4
Breighton Rd
Bubwith YO8 199 D6
Wressle YO8 199 C3
Brendon Gr TS17 6 A3
Brentwood DL8 60 D5
Brentwood Cres YO10 229 C2
Brewers Ct YO7 211 B3
Brewerton St HG5 221 A5

Brewery La
5 Ripon HG4 ....214 C4
Skipton BD23 ....216 F4
Brewery Rd LS29 ....218 C4
Brewster Terr HG4 ....214 C6
Briar Ave YO26 ....227 B4
Briar Cliffe YO8 ....232 A3
Briar Dr YO31 ....225 F2
Briar Pk 5 YO62 ....93 D7
Briar Rd TS17 ....6 B7
Briar Wlk DL3 ....3 B3
Briardene Ave 9 YO12 ....75 E5
Briarfield Cl LS29 ....218 D3
Briars Ct YO23 ....190 E5
Briars Dr YO23 ....190 E5
Briars The HG5 ....221 B7
Briarwood Cl YO8 ....202 F7
Brick Kiln La YO8 ....203 D6
Brick Lands La YO8 ....203 F4
Brickfield La YO51 ....141 D4
Brickhill La YO8 ....204 F4
Brickkiln La
Aldbrough DL11 ....2 A3
Forcett & Carkin DL11 ....20 C8
Brickyard La YO7 ....89 C6
Brickyard Rd YO51 ....141 A4
Bridge Beck La YO7 ....66 C7
Bridge Cl
Burniston YO13 ....75 D7
3 Colburn DL9 ....41 A5
Haxby YO32 ....225 C7
5 Knaresborough HG5 ....221 A5
Bridge Cres DN14 ....205 C8
Bridge End DL6 ....65 B5
Bridge Foot LS23 ....188 F8
Bridge Garth
2 Boston Spa LS23 ....188 E7
South Milford LS25 ....195 F2
Bridge Gn YO21 ....29 C7
Bridge Hill LS21 ....176 C7
Bridge Holm La YO22 ....33 C2
Bridge La Ilkley LS29 ....218 A5
Pollington DN14 ....207 F6
York YO30 ....233 B4
Bridge Rd Airmyn DN14 ....205 E4
Bishopthorpe YO23 ....230 F3
Boston Spa LS23 ....188 F8
Brompton-on-Swale DL10 ....41 B6
Glusburn BD20 ....187 E7
Hurworth DL2 ....3 B3
Malton YO17 ....215 C5
Old Byland & Scawton YO7 ....91 F7
10 Stokesley TS9 ....26 C7
Bridge St 5 Bedale DL8 ....63 A3
9 Brafferton YO61 ....115 F1
Castleford WF10 ....200 F4
Egglescliffe TS16 ....5 D4
12 Helmsley YO62 ....92 F6
8 Normanton South WF6 ....200 B2
16 Pickering YO18 ....95 F7
Richmond DL10 ....209 B6
Skipton BD23 ....216 F4
Tadcaster LS24 ....189 E6
Thirsk YO7 ....211 B3
Whitby YO22 ....208 D7
York YO1 ....233 B2
Bridge Terr DL10 ....209 B6
Bridge View Rd HG4 ....214 C7
Bridges Ct YO8 ....232 D6
Bridges La YO42 ....193 E4
Bridle Way 1 YO26 ....227 A3
Bridle Wlk YO8 ....232 C4
Bridlington Rd
Hunmanby YO14 ....127 A7
Sledmere YO25 ....150 C4
1 Stamford Bridge YO41 ....168 D2
Wold Newton YO25 ....126 A4
Bridlington St YO14 ....126 F8
Brier Hill YO21 ....29 C7
Brier La YO8 ....205 A4
Briercliffe YO12 ....212 C7
Briergate YO32 ....225 C7
Brierlands Cl LS25 ....194 D4
Brierlands La LS25 ....194 E4
Brierley Rd YO12 ....99 E7
Briery Cl 18 LS29 ....175 C2
Brigg La YO8 ....204 D5
Briggate HG5 ....221 B5
Brigg's Ave WF10 ....200 E3
Briggs St YO31 ....228 C7
Bright St 18 Colne BB8 ....186 A3
Darlington DL1 ....3 E5
1 Glusburn BD20 ....173 E1
Skipton BD23 ....216 E4
York YO26 ....227 F5
Bright Terr BB8 ....186 A1
Brighton Rd LS29 ....218 E3
Brigshaw Dr WF10 ....200 C8
Brigshaw High Sch WF10 ....200 C8
Brigshaw La WF10 ....200 C8
Brind La DN14 ....199 F2
Brindle Park Dr WF10 ....201 A3
Brindleys La DN14 ....199 F3
Brinkburn Ave DL3 ....3 B7
Brinkburn Dr DL3 ....3 B6
Brinkburn Rd
Darlington DL3 ....3 B6
4 Scarborough YO12 ....212 E5
Brinklow Way HG2 ....222 B5
Brinkworth Terr 1 YO10 ....228 E3
Briscoe Ridge La HG3 ....177 F6
Briscoe Way TS8 ....6 E5
Britannia Rd DN14 ....205 F1
Britannia St 2 YO12 ....212 E5
Britannia Way DN14 ....205 F2
Broach La Heck DN14 ....203 D1
Kellington DN14 ....202 F3
Broach Rd Heck DN14 ....207 D8
Hensall DN14 ....203 C1
Broad Acres YO32 ....225 C7
Broad Balk YO17 ....149 A5
Broad Balk La YO7 ....115 B1
Broad Carr Rd HG3 ....110 D2
Broad Cl TS8 ....6 D5
Broad Dubb Rd HG3 ....177 C8
Broad Gate
Brompton YO13 ....98 B7
Hunsingore LS22 ....180 F8
Marton cum Grafton YO26 ....141 F1
Broad Gate Rd YO21 ....28 E4
Broad Head La BD22 ....187 E2
Broad Highway YO19 ....192 F8
Broad La
Appleton Roebuck YO23 ....191 A6
6 Beal DN14 ....202 D4
Catton YO41 ....185 C7
Cawood YO8 ....197 A6
Church Fenton LS24 ....196 D6
Rufforth YO23 ....227 A2
Wistow YO8 ....197 A5
Broad Oak YO61 ....166 D8
Broad Oak La 18 YO32 ....166 E5
Broadacres DN14 ....204 D3
Broadacres Ave DN14 ....204 D3
Broadacres Garth DN14 ....204 D3
Broadfield La HG4 ....138 B8
Broadfield Way 9 LS29 ....174 E4
Broadgate Rd TS5 ....6 E8
Broadlands YO19 ....193 A8
Broadlands Dr 5 YO13 ....99 B8
Broadmanor YO8 ....199 A7
Broadmires La YO18 ....96 C5
Broadrum La YO18 ....95 E6
Broadstone Way YO30 ....224 E3
Broadway
Scarborough YO12 ....212 D7
York YO10 ....231 E8
Broadway Gr 3 YO10 ....231 E8
Broadway The DL1 ....3 E5
Broadway W YO10 ....231 D8
Broadwell Rd TS4 ....7 A8
Brockfield Pk Dr YO31 ....225 F2
Brockfield Rd YO31 ....225 E2
Brockholme La DL6 ....65 A4
Brocklesby Rd TS14 ....8 F5
Brockley Cl LS24 ....196 B7
Broc-o-Bank 1 DN6 ....206 E2
Brogden La BB18 ....171 B1
Brokes La DL11 ....40 B6
Bromley La TS8 ....7 B3
Bromley St 2 YO26 ....227 F5
Brompton Carr La YO13 ....98 B4
Brompton CP Sch DL6 ....43 F3
Brompton Hall Sch YO13 ....98 C5
Brompton Ings Rd YO13 ....98 D3
Brompton La DL6 ....43 E4
Brompton on Swale C of E Prim Sch DL10 ....41 B7
Brompton Rd
Newton-le-Willows DL8 ....62 B4
Northallerton DL6 ....210 D5
York YO30 ....228 A7
Brompton-by-Sawdon CP Sch YO13 ....98 C5
Bronte Cl YO12 ....212 D5
Bronte Ct WF8 ....201 B1
Bronte Dr DL9 ....41 A5
Brook House Croft BD24 ....131 E6
Brook La Danby YO21 ....29 C6
Halton West BD23 ....153 F1
Thornton Dale YO18 ....96 D6
Weeton LS17 ....178 C2
Brook Pk YO21 ....32 A7
Brook St
Castleford WF10 ....201 B6
18 Earby BB18 ....172 A1
Hebden BD23 ....135 A2
Hellifield BD23 ....154 B3
Ilkley LS29 ....218 B4
12 Scarborough YO12 ....212 F6
Selby YO8 ....232 C4
Skipton BD23 ....216 F4
York YO31 ....233 B4
Brook View BD23 ....173 B4
Brookacre LA6 ....103 D3
Brooke Cl
Harrogate HG1 ....219 E7
12 Kirkbymoorside YO62 ....70 B1
Brookfield HG3 ....161 A5
Brookfield Cl HG3 ....161 A5
Brookfield Cres HG3 ....161 A5
Brookfield Ct 5 WF6 ....200 B1
Brookfield Garth HG3 ....161 A5
Brookfield Way
7 Earby BB18 ....172 A1
Hampsthwaite HG3 ....160 F5
Brookland 1 LA6 ....102 F2
Brooklands
43 Filey YO14 ....101 B3
York YO10 ....229 D4
Brooklands Cl 44 YO14 ....101 B3
Brooklands Cres DL6 ....210 E5
Brooklands Sch BD23 ....216 F2
Brooklands Terr BD23 ....216 F3
Brooksbank Rd TS7 ....7 D7
Brookside
Collingham LS22 ....188 A8
Hovingham YO62 ....119 E6
Skelton & Brotton TS12 ....9 D8
Sleights YO22 ....32 B6
Brookside Ave 1 DL8 ....63 B2
Brookside Cl 2 DL8 ....63 B2
Brookwood Way TS16 ....5 E4
Broom House La
Egton YO21 ....30 F4
Ugthorpe YO21 ....12 B2
Broom Rd LS24 ....189 D5
Broom Wlk YO12 ....212 E7
Broome Cl
14 Pontefract WF6 ....200 A2
York YO32 ....225 F5
Broome Way YO32 ....226 A5
Broomfield HG3 ....160 E6
Broomfield Ave DL7 ....210 D2
Broomfield CP Sch DL7 ....210 D2
Broomhill WF10 ....201 A3
Broomhill Cl 23 WF11 ....202 A2
Broomhill Cres 25 WF11 ....202 A2
Broomhill Dr 26 WF11 ....202 A2
Broomhill Gr 19 WF11 ....202 A2
Broomhill Pl 22 WF11 ....202 A2
Broomhill Sq 24 WF11 ....202 A2
Broomhill Wlk 21 WF11 ....202 A2
Brootes La BD23 ....107 C2
Brotes La YO26 ....164 B5
Brotherton Cty Prim Sch WF11 ....201 E4
Brough Ave 5 DL9 ....41 A5
Brough Hall* DL10 ....41 B4
Brough Mdws 4 DL10 ....41 D5
Brough Rd 23 DL9 ....40 E4
Brougham Cl YO30 ....227 F8
Brougham St
Darlington DL3 ....3 C7
Skipton BD23 ....217 A3
Broughton Ave BD23 ....216 D3
Broughton Cres BD23 ....216 C3
Broughton Gr BD23 ....216 D3
Broughton Rd
Broughton YO17 ....121 C3
11 East Ayton/West Ayton YO13 ....99 A7
Malton YO17 ....215 A5
Skipton BD23 ....216 C3
Broughton Way
4 Harrogate HG2 ....220 C3
York YO10 ....229 B4
Brow La LA2 ....129 D6
Browcliff BD20 ....174 C2
Brown Bank La BD20 ....174 D2
Brown Bank Rd
Kirkby Malzeard HG4 ....111 F5
Norwood HG3 ....177 B8
Brown Cow Rd YO8 ....204 C8
Brown Howe Rd YO18 ....51 A1
Brown La YO26 ....141 F1
Brown Moor 22 YO41 ....168 D2
Brown Rigg Rd YO13 ....53 F5
Browney Croft YO10 ....233 C1
Browning Cl 3 DL9 ....40 E4
Brownlow St YO31 ....233 C4
Brownmoor La
Huby YO61 ....144 A2
Sutton-on-the-Forest YO61 ....166 B8
Brownroyd 14 BB18 ....172 B1
Browns Ct 4 BD20 ....173 E3
Browns Fold 3 BD23 ....134 E3
Brown's Terr 4 TS13 ....11 F7
Browsfield Rd 24 LS29 ....174 F4
Broxa Hill YO13 ....74 C6
Broxa La YO13 ....74 D5
Broxa Moor La YO13 ....74 C7
Bruce Way 5 YO18 ....95 F6
Brunel Ct 12 YO26 ....227 F5
Brunel Way DL1 ....3 D5
Brunsell La YO26 ....163 F7
Brunswick Cl 2 YO32 ....167 C8
Brunswick Dr HG1 ....219 B2
Brunswick Pl 1 HG1 ....219 D1
Brunswick Sh Ctr YO11 ....213 A5
Brunswick St
Whitby YO21 ....208 D6
York YO23 ....228 B1
Brunt Acres Rd DL8 ....56 D4
Brunthwaite La BD20 ....174 E1
Brunton Bank DL8 ....59 A5
Brunton La HG5 ....163 B6
Brunton Rd LA2 ....131 A6
Bry Hills YO12 ....99 D6
Bryan Cl 13 DL2 ....3 E1
Bryden Cl DL6 ....210 E2
Bryony Ct YO8 ....232 B2
Bryony Rd 4 HG3 ....161 B3
Bryony Wlk 5 HG3 ....161 B3
Bubwith Cty Prim Sch YO8 ....199 D7
Buck Haw Brow BD24 ....131 B4
Buck La YO60 ....147 B6
Buck Stone La BD22 ....187 C5
Buckden Cl 1 YO61 ....143 D8
Buckden Wood La BD23 ....107 D8
Buckingham Sq
8 Helmsley YO62 ....92 F6
7 Helmsley YO62 ....92 F6
Buckingham St YO1 ....233 B1
Buckingham Way WF11 ....201 F4
Buckle Ct YO8 ....232 B7
Buckle La WF6 ....200 A1
Bucks La 1 BD24 ....131 D2
Buess La DL1 ....4 A7
Buffet Hill La LA2 ....129 D7
Bugthorpe La YO41 ....169 D5
Bugthorpe La Town E YO41 ....169 E5
Bull Alley La DN14 ....204 B3
Bull Balk YO41 ....185 E4
Bull Hill DL8 ....61 E8
Bull Ing La BD23 ....134 D3
Bull La Huby YO61 ....166 B7
York YO10 ....228 F3
Bull Moor La YO60 ....168 A8
Bull Piece La YO17 ....122 D3
Bullamoor Cl DL6 ....210 F5
Bullamoor Cty Jun Sch DL6 ....210 F5
Bullamoor Rd DL6 ....210 E5
Buller St YO8 ....232 B6
Bullock La YO7 ....89 A5
Bullytree La LS25 ....195 E2
Bulmer Hill YO60 ....146 B6
Bungalow Rd BD20 ....187 D7
Bunkers Hill
Aberford LS25 ....194 F7
1 Skipton BD23 ....217 A4
BUPA Belvedere Hospl YO11 ....213 A3
Burdale Cl YO17 ....215 F2
Burdike Ave YO30 ....228 A8
Burdock Cl 10 HG3 ....161 B3
Burdyke Inf Sch YO30 ....228 B8
Burgate YO18 ....95 F7
Burgoyne Cl HG4 ....113 D3
Burke Rd YO17 ....215 C5
Burke St HG1 ....219 E5
Burlands La YO26 ....182 F7
Burley Ave HG3 ....161 A2
Burley Bank Cl HG3 ....161 A3
Burley Bank Rd HG3 ....161 A3
Burley Cl LS25 ....195 F2
Burley in Wharfedale Sch LS29 ....176 C1
Burley La HG3 ....161 A3
Burley Mid Sch LS29 ....176 C1
Burlington Ave YO10 ....228 F4
Burlyn Rd 3 YO14 ....127 A8
Burma Rd DL2 ....3 F2
Burn Bridge La HG3 ....222 C2
Burn Bridge Oval HG3 ....222 C3
Burn Bridge Rd HG3 ....222 C3
Burn Hall Cl YO8 ....203 D7
Burn La YO8 ....203 D6
Burn Wood Ct TS21 ....5 A7
Burnby Cl HG3 ....219 B5
Burneston C of E Prim Sch DL8 ....87 E8
Burneston Hargill DL8 ....87 F8
Burnett Cl HG3 ....140 A2
Burnham Rd LS25 ....194 C3
Burnholme Ave YO31 ....229 B6
Burnholme Com Coll YO31 ....229 A5
Burnholme Dr YO31 ....229 A6
Burnholme Gr YO31 ....229 A5
Burniston Gdns YO13 ....75 D7
Burniston Gr YO10 ....229 A4
Burniston Rd YO12 ....212 E8
Burnley Rd BB8 ....186 A1
Burnleys Ct LS26 ....200 B4
Burnleys Dr LS26 ....200 B4
Burnleys Mews LS26 ....200 B4
Burnleys View LS26 ....200 B5
Burnmoor Cres LA6 ....103 D3
Burnmoor Dr TS16 ....5 D5
Burnroyd Ave 17 BD20 ....187 E7
Burns Ct YO24 ....230 B7
Burns Hill 4 LS29 ....174 F4
Burns Way
Boston Spa LS23 ....188 E7
Harrogate HG1 ....219 E7
Burnsall Cl 6 YO14 ....101 A3
Burnsall Dr YO26 ....227 E4
Burnsall La BD23 ....135 A1
Burnsall Mews BD20 ....174 B2
Burnsall Prim Sch BD23 ....157 B8
Burnside 4 YO11 ....100 A6
Burnside Ave BD23 ....216 F2
Burnside Cl HG1 ....219 B5
Burnside Cres BD23 ....216 F2
Burnside Dr HG1 ....219 B5
Burnside Rd
Darlington DL1 ....3 E4
Harrogate HG1 ....219 B5
Burnside Wlk HG1 ....219 B5
Burnt La HG4 ....87 A1
Burnt Yates C of E Endowed Prim Sch HG3 ....160 F8
Burnthouse Bank DL6 ....45 B3
Burr Bank 15 YO11 ....213 B6
Burrard Ave DL10 ....209 B7
Burrill Ave YO30 ....228 B8
Burrill Dr 13 YO32 ....166 D5
Burrill Rd DL8 ....62 F2
Burrow Rd LA6 ....102 B7
Burstall Dr 2 DL9 ....209 C1
Burtersett Rd DL8 ....56 D4
Burton Ave YO30 ....228 B7
Burton Comm La LS25 ....202 A6
Burton Fields Cl 12 YO41 ....168 D2
Burton Fields Rd 4 YO41 ....168 D2
Burton Fleming Rd YO25 ....126 B3
Burton Gn YO30 ....228 B8
Burton Hill 3 LA6 ....102 F3
Burton La YO61 ....141 D8
Burton Leonard C of E Prim Sch HG3 ....140 A2
Burton Rd LA2 ....128 E8
Burton Salmon CP Sch LS25 ....201 F6
Burton Stone La YO30 ....233 A4
Burtondale Rd 1 YO12 ....99 F7
Burtree Ave YO30 ....224 B4
Burtree La YO21 ....29 B5
Burwains La BD23 ....155 F5
Burwen Castle (Roman Fort)* BD23 ....172 C4
Burwen Castle Rd BD23 ....172 C4
Busby La TS9 ....26 C4
Busk La LS24 ....196 C8
Busky Dike La LS21 ....159 E2
Butcher La Potto DL6 ....25 C2
Whitley DN14 ....207 A6
Butcher Terr YO23 ....228 C1
Butcher's La YO25 ....126 E3
Butler Rd HG1 ....219 E5
Butt Fields La DN14 ....203 F1
Butt Hedge YO26 ....182 A5
Butt Hill 22 Haxby YO32 ....166 D5
Kippax LS25 ....194 D1
Butt La
Carlton Husthwaite YO7 ....116 F7
Guisborough TS14 ....9 A6
Wold Newton YO25 ....126 A3
Buttacre La YO23 ....182 D2
Butter Mkt 8 DN14 ....204 C1
Butterbur Way 34 HG3 ....161 B3
Buttercrambe Rd YO41 ....168 C3
Buttercup Cl 6 HG3 ....161 B3
Butterfield Cl HG3 ....140 B5
Butterfield Dr TS16 ....5 D5
Butterfly World* TS18 ....5 E6
Buttermere Ave
Middlesbrough TS5 ....6 E8
4 Wetherby LS22 ....180 B3
Buttermere Ct 9 YO8 ....232 B6
Buttermere Dr YO30 ....224 E1
Butters Cl 20 YO32 ....166 D5
Butterwick La YO17 ....120 F8
Butterwick Rd
Barton-le-Street YO17 ....120 E5
Foxholes YO17 ....125 B1
Langtoft YO25 ....151 C7
Butthouse Rigg DL11 ....35 F8
Buttle La 3 DN14 ....204 C1
Butts BB18 ....171 D1
Butts Cl 19 YO41 ....168 D2
Butts Hill YO14 ....127 C6
Butts La Bainbridge DL8 ....81 B8
Barton-le-Willows YO60 ....146 D2
Bentham LA2 ....129 A8
Egglescliffe TS16 ....5 D4
Monk Fryston LS25 ....201 E8
South Milford LS25 ....195 E1
Butts The 12 WF8 ....201 B1
Buxton Ave TS7 ....7 B5
Byards Pk 6 HG5 ....221 A7
Byefield Gr YO13 ....99 B8
Byemoor Ave TS9 ....8 A1
Byemoor Cl TS9 ....8 A1
Byland Abbey (rems of)* YO61 ....91 E1
Byland Ave
Northallerton DL6 ....210 E5
Thirsk YO7 ....211 C3
York YO31 ....228 E8
Byland Ct 5 YO21 ....208 B6
Byland Gr HG1 ....219 F6
Byland Mews HG5 ....221 D4
Byland Pl
Harrogate HG1 ....219 F6
Northallerton DL6 ....210 E5
Byland Rd
Harrogate HG1 ....219 F6
Whitby YO21 ....208 B6
Bylands Way DL3 ....3 A6
Byng Rd DL9 ....209 F1
Byram Cl 3 DL6 ....210 E3
Byram Ct 4 DL6 ....210 E3
Byram Park Ave WF11 ....201 F4
Byram Park Rd WF11 ....202 A4
Byron Ave 3 DN6 ....206 E1
Byron Ct DL2 ....22 D7
Byron Dr YO30 ....227 F8
Byron Rd 21 BB8 ....186 A3
Byron St 2 BD23 ....217 A3
Byron Wlk Mews HG2 ....219 D2
Byward Dr YO12 ....99 F7
Byway The DL1 ....3 E5
By-Ways HG2 ....222 D6

C

Cabin La 2 HG3 ....137 F1
Caburn Cl 2 YO12 ....212 B5
Caedmon Ave YO21 ....208 B8
Caedmon Cl YO31 ....229 A7
Caedmon Sch YO21 ....208 D5
Cairnborrow 4 YO24 ....230 B7
Caithness Cl 10 YO30 ....224 E3
Calcaria Cres LS24 ....189 D5
Calcaria Rd LS24 ....189 E5
Calcutt HG5 ....221 A4
Caldbeck Cl 1 YO30 ....225 A1
Calder Ave YO26 ....227 B8

Calder Cres DN14 207 F6
Caledonia St YO12 212 E5
Caledonian Way DL1 3 F8
Calf Cl YO32 225 D8
Calf Hall La BB18 171 D1
Calf Wood La BD20 172 E1
California Dr WF10 200 B3
California Gr 7 TS9 8 A2
California Rd YO22 208 E5
Calton La BD23 155 A6
Calvert Cl YO32 225 C7
Calvert Hos DL11 36 C4
Calverts Garth YO60 145 D5
Cam Gill Rd BD23 108 B4
Cam High Rd BD23 79 D5
Cam La BD23 172 A3
Camblesforth CP Sch YO8 204 C4
Cambrian Cl 2 YO32 225 F3
Cambridge Ave TS7 7 B5
Cambridge Cres 5 HG1 219 D2
Cambridge Pl
7 Harrogate HG1 219 D2
1 Scarborough YO12 212 E4
Cambridge Rd
Harrogate HG1 219 D2
Middlesbrough TS5 6 E8
Cambridge St
Harrogate HG1 219 D2
Normanton South WF6 200 A1
Scarborough YO12 212 F6
4 York YO24 228 A3
Cambridge Terr
4 Harrogate HG1 219 D2
1 Scarborough YO11 213 A4
Camden Rd WF10 201 B4
Camela La YO8 204 B6
Cameron Gr YO23 228 C1
Camm La DN14 204 C3
Cammock La BD24 131 D2
Camp Hill Cl HG4 214 D3
Campbell Ave
Ripon HG4 113 D3
York YO24 227 E2
Campbell St 11 BD20 187 E8
Campion Cl YO13 75 D5
Campion Dr TS14 8 D6
Campion Gr
Coulby Newham TS7 7 B6
6 Harrogate HG3 161 B3
Campion La TS15 25 B4
Campion Rd DL1 3 D7
Campleshon Rd YO23 228 B1
Campsall Balk DN6 206 E1
Campsall Hall Rd 12 DN6 206 E1
Campsall Park Rd 11 DN6 206 E1
Campsmount Sch DN6 206 D1
Camwal Rd HG1 220 C4
Camwal Terr 5 HG1 220 C4
Cana La HG4 114 E2
Canaan La DL8 60 E2
Canal Garth DN14 207 F6
Canal Rd
Cottingwith YO42 193 C5
Ripon HG4 214 D4
Selby YO8 232 D4
Canal St BD23 216 F4
Canal View YO8 232 D3
Canal Yd 8 BD23 216 F4
Canberra Rd TS7 7 B6
Canby La 4 HG3 179 E6
Candler Ave 12 YO13 99 A7
Candler St YO12 212 E5
Canham Gr YO10 229 D3
Cannon Hall La DN14 202 F1
Cannon St WF10 200 F3
Canon Gr TS15 5 E2
Canon Lee Sch YO30 228 A8
Canons Garth La 2 YO62 92 F6
Canterbury Cl
9 Haxby YO32 166 D5
Whitby YO21 208 C5
Canterbury Ct 5 WF8 201 C2
Canton Gdns TS5 6 E6
Caper Hill YO21 29 F1
Captain Cook & Staithes Heritage Ctr★ TS13 13 K2
Captain Cook Birthplace Mus★ TS7 7 B7
Captain Cook Cres YO22 208 E6
Captain Cook Meml Mus★ YO22 208 E7
Captain Cook Prim Sch TS7 7 B6
Captain Cook's Cl
Hinderwell TS13 11 D8
Staithes TS13 13 K1
Captain Cook's Cres TS7 7 C6
Captain Cook's Mon★ TS9 8 D1
Captain Cook's Schoolroom Mus★ TS9 8 A1
Captain Cook's Way TS9 8 A1
Cardale Pk HG3 222 A6
Cardan Dr LS29 218 E4
Cardinal Cl 18 LS25 195 F4
Cardinals Cl 3 YO8 197 B8
Careless House La HG3 138 E4
Carentan Cl 6 YO8 232 B6
Carey St YO10 228 D1
Cargate Hill 32 YO14 101 B3
Cargo Fleet La TS3 7 C8
Carl St YO23 228 C2
Carla Beck La BD23 173 B4
Carlbury Ave TS5 6 D6
Carlbury Cres DL3 3 A5
Carless La YO14 100 F4
Carleton Ave BD23 216 E3
Carleton Dr DL3 3 A5
Carleton Endowed Prim Sch BD23 173 B4
Carleton La BD23 173 A4
Carleton New Rd BD23 216 E3
Carleton Rd BD23 216 E1
Carleton St
3 Skipton BD23 216 F3
17 York YO26 227 F5
Carlile Hill TS8 6 E5
Carline Mead 23 HG3 161 B3
Carlisle St 16 YO26 227 F5
Carlton & Faceby C of E Prim Sch TS9 26 A3
Carlton App 1 LS22 180 B3
Carlton Ave Thirsk YO7 211 B1
York YO10 229 B3
Carlton Cl
4 Carlton Miniott YO7 89 C4
Eggborough DN14 202 F1
19 Normanton South WF6 200 A1
Carlton Dr TS17 6 A6
Carlton Gdns 1 WF6 200 B1
Carlton La YO62 92 F7
Carlton Miniott CP Sch YO7 89 B4
Carlton Moor Cres DL1 3 E4
Carlton Rd
Carlton Miniott YO7 89 A3
Catterick Garrison DL9 40 F4
9 Filey YO14 101 B3
Harrogate HG2 222 D7
Helmsley YO62 92 F7
Sutton upon Derwent YO41 185 C1
Carlton St WF6 200 A2
Carlton Terr 6 YO11 213 A4
Carlton Twrs★ DN14 204 D2
Carlton View WF10 200 C7
Carlton-in-Snaith CP Sch DN14 204 C3
Carlyle Cres WF10 201 A4
Carlyle Rd WF10 201 A4
Carmel Gr DL3 3 B4
Carmel RC Aided Comp Sch DL3 3 A5
Carmel Rd N DL3 3 B5
Carmel Rd S DL3 3 B4
Carmelite St YO1 233 C2
Carmires Ave
Haxby YO32 166 F5
Knaresborough HG5 221 C8
Carnagil Rd DL9 209 B1
Carnagill CP Sch DL9 40 D4
Carney St TS12 9 D7
Carnot St YO26 227 F5
Carnoustie Cl 1 YO26 227 B4
Carnoustie Dr TS16 5 E5
Carnoustie Gdns 20 WF6 200 B1
Carnoustie Way TS8 7 C5
Caroline Cl 5 YO24 227 F3
Carousel Wlk LS25 195 F4
Carpenters Yd YO17 215 C4
Carpley Green Rd DL8 57 D3
Carr Ave LS25 195 F4
Carr Bridge La DL6 24 D3
Carr Cl
18 Hemingbrough YO8 198 F1
Rainton with Newby YO7 114 F6
Ripon HG4 214 B3
Carr Field La YO26 141 F1
Carr Fields La YO12 99 B5
Carr Head La BD20 187 B7
Carr Hill YO60 145 D5
Carr Hill La YO21 32 B7
Carr Hill Ridge YO21 32 B7
Carr House La
Cayton YO11 100 A5
Heslerton YO17 98 A1
Carr Inf Sch YO26 227 C5
Carr Jun Sch YO26 227 C5
Carr La Ampleforth YO62 92 B1
Azerley HG4 113 A7
Barlby with Osgodby YO8 232 F5
Barlow YO8 204 C7
Castleford WF10 200 F3
Cawton YO62 119 C8
Cayton YO11 100 B4
East Ayton YO13 99 B7
Escrick YO19 192 B5
Glaisdale YO21 30 D4
Gristhorpe YO11 100 E4
Heslerton YO17 124 A8
Kilburn High & Low YO61 91 B3
Little Ouseburn YO26 164 A7
Long Drax YO8 204 F6
Muston YO14 100 F3
Newby & Scalby YO13 75 C5
Newton on Derwent YO41 185 F4
Rainton with Newby YO7 114 F6
Roecliffe YO51 140 E3
Sheriff Hutton YO60 145 E6
Stillington YO61 144 C6
Sutton-on-the-Forest YO61 144 D2
Thirlby YO7 90 F6
Thormanby YO61 116 E4
Wetherby LS22 180 D4
Carr La *continued*
Wistow YO8 197 A3
York YO26 227 D5
Carr Leys La YO7 66 A5
Carr Mill Mews BD22 187 B5
Carr Rd 7 BB18 171 D2
Carr Side Rd YO26 163 F8
Carr St YO8 232 F4
Carr The HG3 222 E2
Carr Wood Rd WF10 200 F3
Carrbank La YO32 167 E3
Carrfield YO24 230 C8
Carrfield Dr LS15 194 B8
Carrfield La LS15 194 B8
Carrfield Rd LS15 194 B8
Carrick Gdns YO24 227 E3
Carrier's Row BB8 186 B2
Carrington Ave 1 YO26 227 E5
Carrnock Ct 3 YO32 225 F1
Carrol Cl DL6 210 F2
Carroll Pl 2 DL2 22 C8
Carron Cres YO24 230 B7
Carrs Mdw YO19 192 B5
Carrs The YO21 208 A2
Carrside 2 YO11 99 F6
Carseylands Hill BD23 155 A4
Cart Riggin YO7 66 A8
Carter Ave YO31 228 F5
Carter La 22 YO62 70 B1
Carter's La Ilkley LS29 218 E6
Longnewton TS16 5 A4
Cartmell Terr DL3 3 C6
Cass House Rd TS8 6 E4
Cass La
Knaresborough HG5 221 A4
South Milford LS25 195 E1
Castelo Gr 1 YO18 96 A6
Castle Bank DL6 25 E1
Castle C of E Jun Sch HG5 221 B6
Castle Cl Cawood YO8 197 A8
1 Haxby YO32 166 D5
Killinghall HG3 161 C5
Middleton St George DL2 4 C3
Northallerton DL7 210 D5
2 Spofforth HG3 179 E6
1 Thornton Dale YO18 96 D5
Castle Dyke Wynd TS16 5 E3
Castle End DL8 59 B6
Castle Garth
Pontefract WF8 201 C1
4 Thornton Dale YO18 96 D5
Castle Gate 4 LS29 218 B4
Castle Gdns YO11 213 B6
Castle Hill
8 Hunmanby YO14 126 F8
2 Ilkley LS29 218 B4
Richmond DL10 209 C6
4 Settle BD24 131 E2
Castle Hill Cl HG2 222 B6
Castle Hill Dr HG2 222 B6
Castle Hill Glade HG2 222 B6
Castle Hill Gr HG2 222 B6
Castle Hill La YO8 204 F5
Castle Howard★ YO60 120 D1
Castle Howard Dr YO17 215 A4
Castle Howard Rd YO17 215 A4
Castle Ings 1 HG3 179 E5
Castle Ings Cl 1 HG5 221 A5
Castle Ings Rd 3 HG5 221 A5
Castle La Danby YO21 29 D6
10 East Ayton/West Ayton YO13 99 B8
Castle Mdws DL8 87 A7
Castle Rd Colne BB8 186 A4
1 Ilkley LS29 218 B4
Killinghall HG3 161 C5
18 Pickering YO18 95 F7
Scarborough YO11 213 A6
Thornton Dale YO18 96 D5
Whitby YO21 208 A6
Castle Rise 1 YO13 99 A7
Castle Sch WF10 201 B4
Castle Side YO60 145 C5
Castle St Skipton BD23 217 A3
Spofforth HG3 179 E6
Castle Steads (Fort)★ DL8 84 C8
Castle Steads★ DL11 19 D6
Castle Terr
Richmond DL10 209 C6
16 Scarborough YO11 213 B6
Castle View
7 Newby & Scalby YO13 75 D5
Sheriff Hutton YO60 145 C5
Castle View Terr BD23 216 F4
Castle Yd 3 LS29 218 B4
Castlebergh Hospl BD24 131 C2
Castlebergh La 5 BD24 131 E2
Castleford High Sch WF10 200 F4
Castleford La
Featherstone WF7 200 D2
Knottingley WF11 201 D3
Castleford Mus Room★ WF10 200 E4
Castleford Normanton & District Hospl WF10 200 D3
Castleford Park Sch WF10 200 F4
Castleford Rd WF6 200 B2
Castleford Redhill Mid Sch WF10 201 B4
Castleford RUFC WF10 200 C3
Castleford Sta WF10 200 E4
Castleford Three Land Ends Jun & Inf Sch WF10 200 D4
Castleford Tigers RLFC WF10 200 F5
Castlegate
East Ayton/West Ayton YO13 99 A7
6 Helmsley YO62 92 F6
Kirkbymoorside YO62 70 B1
3 Knaresborough HG5 221 B5
Malton YO17 215 C4
19 Pickering YO18 95 F7
Scarborough YO11 213 B7
Thirsk YO7 211 B2
York YO1 233 B2
Castlekeep Cl DL10 209 C8
Castlemount Ave YO13 75 D6
Castlereagh Cl TS21 5 A7
Castleton Ave
Middlesbrough TS5 6 D8
Northallerton DL7 210 C1
Castleton Moor Sta YO21 29 A7
Castleton Prim Sch YO21 29 A7
Castleton Rd DL9 40 F4
Castley La LS21 178 A1
Cat Bank DL11 39 C6
Cat La Balne DN14 207 E5
Bilbrough YO23 182 D1
Upper Poppleton YO26 182 D8
Cathcart Cl DN14 206 F7
Cathedral C of E Prim Sch HG4 214 D5
Cathedral Cl HG4 214 D5
Catherine Love Dr 15 YO61 143 C8
Catherine St 2 TS12 9 F7
Cattal Moor La YO26 181 B8
Cattal St YO26 164 A2
Cattal Sta YO26 164 A2
Catterick Bridge★ DL10 41 C6
Catterick La DL10 41 D3
Catterick Race Course DL10 41 C5
Catterick Rd DL9 40 E4
Catterton La LS24 190 A8
Cattle La LS25 194 F8
Cattlelaith La WF11 201 E2
Catton La YO7 115 A7
Catton Moor La YO7 114 F8
Caudle Hill WF11 201 C6
Causeway BD23 81 E3
Causeway The DL1 3 E5
Cautley Dr HG3 161 C5
Cautley Gr HG3 161 C5
Cavalry Ct 9 YO12 75 F5
Cavendish Ave
Harrogate HG2 219 E1
8 Pontefract WF8 201 C2
Cavendish Ct HG2 222 F8
Cavendish Gr YO10 229 D3
Cavendish Rd TS4 7 A8
Cavendish St
Barnoldswick BB18 171 D1
Harrogate HG1 219 E5
Skipton BD23 216 F3
Cavendish Terr 8 HG4 214 C4
Caversham Rd TS4 7 A8
Cawcliff La YO18 97 A5
Cawdel Cl 4 LS25 195 F2
Cawdel Way LS25 195 F2
Cawder Ghyll BD23 217 A1
Cawder La BD23 217 A1
Cawder Rd BD23 217 A1
Cawood C of E Prim Sch YO8 197 B8
Cawood Cres LS24 190 C1
Cawood Dr TS5 6 F7
Cawood Rd
Stillingfleet YO19 191 D3
Wistow YO8 197 C7
Cawthorn Ave HG2 220 B2
Cawthorn Pl HG2 220 B3
Cawthorne Cres YO14 101 A3
Cawthorne La YO18 71 D3
Cawton Rd YO62 118 F8
Caxton Ave YO26 227 D6
Caxton Cl 1 DL10 41 C7
Caxton Gdns 4 WF8 201 B2
Caxton Way YO11 99 F6
Cayley Cl YO30 224 F1
Cayley La YO13 98 C5
Caymer Rd YO11 100 A7
Cayton Cty Prim Sch YO11 100 B6
Cayton Low Rd YO11 99 F6
Cayton Low Road Ind Est YO11 100 A6
Cecil Rd 7 YO14 127 A8
Cecil St HG1 219 E5
Cecilia Pl 3 YO24 228 A3
Cedar Cl
Hambleton YO8 197 B1
Ripon HG4 214 B3
Cedar Cres YO8 197 D2
Cedar Dr
Coulby Newham TS8 6 D4
Tadcaster LS24 189 D6
Cedar Glade YO19 184 E7
Cedar Gr Barton DL10 21 C7
3 Filey YO14 101 B4
Sutton BD20 187 E7
York YO31 229 B7
Cedar Grange HG2 222 D7
Cedar Mews 4 DL2 22 D8
Cedar Rd DL3 3 B6
Cedar Ridge LS25 194 E5
Cedar Vale 8 YO62 70 B1
Cedarhurst Dr TS12 9 F7
Cedarwood 3 DL2 4 C4
Cedarwood Ave 1 TS9 26 C8
Cedarwood Cl 8 YO24 227 B1
Cedarwood Glade TS8 6 E4
Celtic Cl YO26 227 B5
Cemetery La DL3 3 A5
Cemetery Rd
40 Earby BB18 172 A1
Normanton South WF6 200 B1
Thirsk YO7 211 A3
York YO10 233 C1
Centenary Rd DN14 205 F3
Central Av 6 YO61 143 D8
Central Dr
Castleford WF10 200 C4
Northallerton DL6 210 E4
Central St TS16 5 E3
Central Way 6 TS9 8 A2
Centre La LS24 189 E6
Centre Rd BD20 186 D7
Centurian Cl 7 DL10 41 E4
Centurion Way YO30 225 B3
Century Wlk 1 HG2 220 B3
Ceres Rd LS22 180 C3
Chacksfield Rd 17 DL10 41 E4
Chadderton Cl TS12 9 E8
Chadderton Dr TS17 6 C7
Chain Bar La HG3 161 A4
Chain La HG5 221 C6
Chair Wlk HG4 139 B8
Chaldon Cl 4 YO32 167 A6
Chaldron Way TS16 5 D6
Chalfield Cl TS17 6 B4
Chalfonts YO24 227 F1
Chalford Oaks TS5 6 D8
Challacombe Cres TS17 6 A3
Challoner Rd TS15 5 D2
Chaloner St TS14 8 F6
Chaloner's Cres YO24 230 D7
Chaloner's Rd YO24 230 D8
Chamber End Fold 5 BD23 134 E3
Chancery Ct YO24 227 C3
Chancery Rise TS18 6 A6
Chandler Cl DL10 209 F8
Chandlers Ct YO11 213 B2
Chandlers Ridge Prim Sch TS7 7 D5
Chandlers Wharf YO17 215 C3
Chanting Hill Cl YO60 146 E6
Chantry Ave 14 YO26 165 F1
Chantry Bank DL8 59 D3
Chantry Cl YO24 230 C8
Chantry Ct HG3 161 C7
Chantry Dr
East Ayton/West Ayton YO13 99 B8
2 Ilkley LS29 218 B3
Chantry Gap 11 YO26 165 F1
Chantry Garth DL8 59 D3
Chantry Gr 13 YO26 165 F1
Chantry La
Bishopthorpe YO23 231 B4
Scotton HG5 162 A6
Stutton with Hazlewood LS24 189 B3
Chantry Rd
9 East Ayton/West Ayton YO13 99 B8
Northallerton DL7 210 B3
Chapel Balk Rd YO8 198 F1
Chapel Bridge★ DL11 1 C7
Chapel Cl
Bilton-in-Ainsty with Bickerton LS22 181 B5
21 Helmsley YO62 92 F6
Rawcliffe DN14 205 A1
Chapel Croft 7 BD23 134 E3
Chapel Ct
Gargrave BD23 155 D1
Huby YO61 144 A4
Chapel Fields Rd YO26 227 A3
Chapel Fold 6 BD23 134 E3
Chapel Garth
Dalton YO7 115 E7
Markington with Wallerthwaite HG3 139 C3
Thrintoft DL7 63 F7
Chapel Gate
Kirkby Malham BD23 154 F8
Malham BD23 132 F1
Sherburn YO17 124 D6
Chapel Haddlesey C of E Prim Sch YO8 203 B5
Chapel Hill
Boroughbridge YO51 141 C5
Kearby with Netherby LS22 179 B1
Skipton BD23 217 A5
Chapel Hill La LS21 178 A1
Chapel La
Askham Bryan YO23 182 F3
Barwick in Elmet LS15 194 C8
Boston Spa LS23 188 E7
Brayton YO8 232 B1
Brompton YO13 98 B7
5 Burton in Lonsdale LA6 102 F3

Chapel La *continued*
13 Easingwold YO61 . . . . .143 C8
18 Eastfield YO11 . . . . . . .100 B6
Finghall DL8 . . . . .61 E4
Halton East BD23 . . . . . . .174 C8
Harome YO62 . . . . .93 C4
Hebden BD23 . . . . .135 A2
Horton in Ribblesdale
BD24 . . . . .105 C3
Ilkley LS29 . . . . .218 A4
Langtoft YO25 . . . . .151 D5
Little Smeaton WF8 . . . . . .206 B3
Marton-le-Moor HG4 . . . . .114 F1
Rawcliffe DN14 . . . . .205 A2
Reighton YO14 . . . . .127 E5
3 Riccall YO19 . . . . .192 A1
2 Spofforth HG3 . . . . . . .179 E5
3 Thornton Dale YO18 . . . .96 D5
Tollerton YO61 . . . . .143 A3
Weston YO60 . . . . .147 B4
Chapel of Our Lady*
YO11 . . . . .213 C7
Chapel Rd
23 Scarborough YO11 . . . .213 A6
Settrington YO17 . . . . . . .122 D1
Chapel Riggs 4 DL10 . . .41 E4
Chapel Row YO10 . . . . .233 C1
Chapel Sq 7 BD24 . . . . .131 E2
Chapel St
8 Addingham LS29 . . . . .174 F4
6 Beadlam YO62 . . . . .93 D7
Carleton BD23 . . . . .173 B4
Cattal YO26 . . . . .164 A1
22 Earby BB18 . . . . .172 A1
27 Filey YO14 . . . . .101 B3
Grassington BD23 . . . . . .134 E3
Hambleton YO8 . . . . .196 F1
Hillam LS25 . . . . .202 B7
Kirk Hammerton YO26 . . .164 C2
Knaresborough HG5 . . . . .221 B5
Middleton St George DL2 . . . .4 C4
Nunnington YO62 . . . . .93 E2
12 Settle BD24 . . . . .131 D2
Tadcaster LS24 . . . . .189 E6
Thirsk YO7 . . . . .211 B2
Chapel Wlk
Long Preston BD23 . . . . . .153 F5
4 Riccall YO19 . . . . .192 A1
Chapman Cl 1 YO32 . . .167 C8
Chapman La 8 HG4 . . . . .86 C3
Chapman Sq HG1 . . . . .219 B2
Chapmans Ct YO24 . . . .230 D6
Chapman's La YO30 . . .165 E7
Chapter House St YO1 .233 B3
Charles Ave HG1 . . . . .219 E5
Charles Ct DL10 . . . . . .209 F7
Charles Moor YO31 . . . .228 F7
Charles St YO8 . . . . . . .232 B6
Charles Wesley Dr
YO8 . . . . .232 B2
Charlock TS8 . . . . .7 B4
Charlton Ave
Knaresborough HG5 . . . . .221 B6
2 Whitby YO21 . . . . .208 B7
Charlton Ct 10 HG5 . . . .221 B6
Charlton Dr HG5 . . . . . .221 B6
Charlton Gr 12 HG5 . . . .221 B6
Charlton Manor Dr 13
HG5 . . . . .221 B6
Charlton St YO23 . . . . .228 C2
Charnwood Dr TS7 . . . . . .7 D6
Charrington Ave TS17 . . . .6 A6
Charter Ave DN14 . . . . .205 A1
Charters The YO8 . . . . .198 B5
Chartwell Cl TS17 . . . . . . .6 B4
Chase Garth Rd 16
YO61 . . . . .143 C8
Chase Side Ct YO24 . . .230 E8
Chase The
11 Boroughbridge YO51 . .141 B4
Garforth LS25 . . . . .194 D4
Hurworth-on-Tees DL2 . . . . .3 E1
Knaresborough HG5 . . . . .221 D5
Norton YO17 . . . . .215 E2
Chastworth Ct HG1 . . . .219 D4
Chatham Rd HG4 . . . . . .113 D2
Chatsworth Ave 7 WF8 201 C2
Chatsworth Dr
16 Haxby YO32 . . . . .166 F5
2 Wetherby LS22 . . . . . .180 B3
Chatsworth Gdns
YO12 . . . . .212 E7
Chatsworth Gr
4 Boroughbridge YO51 . .141 B5
Harrogate HG1 . . . . .219 C4
Chatsworth Pl HG1 . . . .219 D4
Chatsworth Rd HG1 . . .219 D4
Chatsworth Terr
2 Harrogate HG1 . . . . . .219 E4
4 York YO26 . . . . .227 E4
Chaucer Gn HG1 . . . . . .219 F7
Chaucer St 7 YO10 . . . .228 E3
Chaumont Way 1 YO32 167 D2
Chauvel Cl DL9 . . . . . . .209 C2
Cheapside
2 Knaresborough HG5 . .221 B5
12 Normanton South WF6 .200 A1
11 Settle BD24 . . . . .131 D2
Cheapsides Rd YO17 . . .215 B8
Checker La YO19 . . . . . .198 A7
Chelkar Way YO30 . . . .224 F1
Chelmsford Rd HG1 . . .219 E2
Cheltenham Ave
Ilkley LS29 . . . . .218 E4
Middlesbrough TS7 . . . . . . .7 B5
Cheltenham Cres
6 Harrogate HG1 . . . . . .219 D2
7 Harrogate HG1 . . . . . .219 D3
Cheltenham Mount
HG1 . . . . .219 D3
Cheltenham Par HG1 . .219 D3
Cheltenham Rd 8 HG1 .219 D3
Chelwood Wlk 12 YO26 .227 E4
Chepstow Ct 14 DL1 . . . . .3 F6
Cherry Ave
Malton YO17 . . . . .215 D6
Swinton YO17 . . . . .121 B4
Cherry Cl YO21 . . . . . .208 B6
Cherry Garth YO31 . . . .229 B5
Cherry Garth Rd DL7 . .210 C3
Cherry Gr 7 Bedale DL8 . .63 B3
2 Ilkley LS29 . . . . .175 C2
16 Poppleton YO26 . . . . . .165 F1
Cherry Hill La YO23 . . .233 B1
Cherry La YO24 . . . . . .230 F8
Cherry Orch 2 YO32 . . .225 D8
Cherry Paddock
4 Haxby YO32 . . . . .225 D8
Kexby YO41 . . . . .168 C2
Cherry Rd 4 YO14 . . . . .127 A8
Cherry St YO23 . . . . . .233 B1
Cherry Tree Ave
Newton-on-Ouse YO30 . . .165 B6
1 Scarborough YO12 . . . .212 B5
York YO32 . . . . .225 D4
Cherry Tree Cl 13 YO8 . .197 D1
Cherry Tree Dr YO14 . . .101 A4
Cherry Tree Gdns 7
DL9 . . . . .209 B1
Cherry Tree Way 14 DL9 .41 A5
Cherry Tree Wlk
Amotherby YO17 . . . . . . .121 A4
7 Barlby YO8 . . . . .198 B4
Cherry Wood Cres
YO19 . . . . .231 E5
Cherrytree Cl HG4 . . . . .140 E7
Cherrywood Ave 4 TS9 . .26 C8
Cherwell Croft YO8 . . . .196 F1
Cherwell Ct YO8 . . . . . .196 F1
Cheshire Ave YO32 . . . .167 A6
Cheshire Sq 5 YO7 . . . . .89 B1
Chesler-Pit La YO61 . . .117 F2
Chesney Fields 4 YO24 227 D1
Chessingham Gdns
YO24 . . . . .230 E6
Chessingham Pk YO19 .184 F6
Chester Court Rd YO8 .204 A6
Chester La DL6 . . . . .65 D8
Chesterton Ave TS17 . . . . .6 A6
Chestnut Ave
2 Airmyn DN14 . . . . .205 E4
Harrogate HG1 . . . . .219 F3
10 Hemingbrough YO8 . . .198 F1
Malton YO17 . . . . .215 D5
Thornton Dale YO18 . . . . .96 D6
2 Topcliffe YO7 . . . . .89 A1
1 Topcliffe YO7 . . . . .89 B1
Welburn YO60 . . . . .146 E6
York YO31 . . . . .228 F6
Chestnut Bank YO12 . . .212 D6
Chestnut Cl
3 Catterick DL10 . . . . . . .41 D5
4 Ilkley LS29 . . . . .218 E3
Richmond DL10 . . . . .209 C8
Scarborough YO12 . . . . . .212 D6
Chestnut Cres
6 Catterick Garrison DL9 . .40 F5
1 Catton YO7 . . . . .89 A1
Chestnut Croft 7 YO8 . .198 F1
Chestnut Ct 9 YO8 . . . .198 F1
Chestnut Dr
17 Barnoldswick BB18 . . .171 D1
8 Hemingbrough YO8 . . . .198 F1
Middlesbrough TS7 . . . . . . .7 C6
Chestnut Garth 4 YO8 .198 F1
Chestnut Gr
Harrogate HG1 . . . . .219 E6
Norton YO17 . . . . .215 F2
York YO26 . . . . .227 C4
Chestnut Mews YO8 . . .197 A8
Chestnut Rd
Cawood YO8 . . . . .197 A8
Eaglescliffe TS16 . . . . .5 E6
Chestnut Rise 6 YO8 . . .198 F1
Chestnuts The
6 Haxby YO32 . . . . .225 C8
Hensall DN14 . . . . .203 D2
Pontefract WF8 . . . . .201 C2
Chevin Dr YO14 . . . . . .101 A3
Cheviot Cl 1 YO32 . . . . .225 F3
Chew La
Gargrave BD23 . . . . .155 D1
Seamer YO12 . . . . .99 D6
Chichester Cl 18 YO13 . . .75 D5
Chieftain Rd DL9 . . . . . .40 C4
Chiltern Ave WF10 . . . .200 C3
Chiltern Way YO32 . . . .225 F5
Chilvers Ct 4 YO8 . . . . .232 A1
Chimes Rd YO8 . . . . . . .232 C6
China St DL3 . . . . .3 D7
Chippendale Jun Sch
LS21 . . . . .176 F1
Chippendale Rise 8
LS21 . . . . .177 A1
Chippenham Rd TS4 . . . . .7 A7
Cholmley Way YO22 . . .208 F3
Christ Church C of E Sch
BB8 . . . . .186 A3
Christ Church Oval
HG1 . . . . .219 E2
Christchurch C of E Prim Sch
BD23 . . . . .216 F3
Christina St 5 HG1 . . . .219 C5
Christ's Hospl DL8 . . . . .63 A1
Christy Gate Rd YO21 . . .28 E4
Chubb Hill Rd YO21 . . .208 C6
Chudleigh Rd
Harrogate HG1 . . . . .219 E3
1 York YO26 . . . . .227 F5
Church Ave
Clapham LA2 . . . . .130 C8
4 Dacre HG3 . . . . .137 F1
Harrogate HG1 . . . . .219 D5
Swillington LS26 . . . . . . .194 A1
Church Balk YO19 . . . . .184 E7
Church Bank
Aysgarth DL8 . . . . .58 F3
Hunton DL8 . . . . .61 F7
Kirkby Malzeard HG4 . . . .112 D5
Church Cl
Askham Bryan YO23 . . . . .182 F3
Bagby YO7 . . . . .90 C3
4 Bubwith YO8 . . . . .199 D7
Carleton BD23 . . . . .173 B4
18 Filey YO14 . . . . .101 B4
1 Hambleton YO8 . . . . . .196 F1
Killinghall HG3 . . . . .219 A8
Kirby Hill YO51 . . . . .141 B7
Middleton St George DL2 . . . .4 C3
Newby & Scalby YO13 . . . . .75 C5
Sawley HG4 . . . . .138 E6
Sharow HG4 . . . . .214 F7
4 Swillington LS26 . . . . .194 A1
5 Tollerton YO61 . . . . . .143 B3
Wheldrake YO19 . . . . . . .193 A7
Church Cliff Dr 9 YO14 101 B4
Church Cres
Stutton with Hazlewood
LS24 . . . . .189 D4
Swillington LS26 . . . . . . .194 A1
Church Croft
Barkston Ash LS24 . . . . . .195 F7
Gargrave BD23 . . . . .172 C8
Church Cswy LS23 . . . . .188 F8
Church Ct 18 WF6 . . . . .200 A1
Church Dike La YO8 . . .204 F5
Church Dr
Great Ayton TS9 . . . . .7 F1
Lockwood TS12 . . . . .9 E7
Church End
Cawood YO8 . . . . .197 B8
Sheriff Hutton YO60 . . . . .145 D5
Church Farm YO7 . . . . .211 A6
Church Farm Cl YO23 . .182 C6
Church Farm View
LS15 . . . . .194 C8
Church Fenton La
LS24 . . . . .190 B3
Church Fenton Sta
LS24 . . . . .196 A8
Church Field La 2
YO26 . . . . .164 A8
Church Field Rd DN6 . .206 E1
Church Fields 17 WF6 . .200 A1
Church Garth DL6 . . . . . .23 C3
Church Gdns LS25 . . . .194 C3
Church Gn 3 YO41 . . . .185 C2
Church Hill
4 Bramham LS23 . . . . . .188 E5
Crayke YO61 . . . . .118 A1
Easingwold YO61 . . . . . .117 C1
10 Hunmanby YO14 . . . . .126 F8
Hunsingore LS22 . . . . . . .180 E8
Malton YO17 . . . . .215 C4
Newby & Scalby YO13 . . . . .75 C5
North Rigton LS17 . . . . . .178 B3
Reighton YO14 . . . . .127 C6
3 Selby YO8 . . . . .232 D5
Sherburn in Elmet LS25 . . .195 E4
5 Spofforth HG3 . . . . . . .179 E6
Stillingfleet YO19 . . . . . .191 D3
Thorner LS14 . . . . .188 A3
Thornton Dale YO18 . . . . . .96 D6
8 Wistow YO8 . . . . .197 D6
Church La
Allerston YO18 . . . . .97 B5
Appleton Roebuck YO23 . .190 F4
Aysgarth DL8 . . . . .58 F3
Bagby YO7 . . . . .90 C3
Barton DL10 . . . . .21 C8
Bishopthorpe YO23 . . . . .231 A4
Bolton Percy YO23 . . . . . .190 D4
Boroughbridge YO51 . . . . .141 B5
Brompton YO13 . . . . .98 C5
Burnsall BD23 . . . . .157 A8
Carlton DN14 . . . . .204 C3
Catton YO41 . . . . .185 D8
Cayton YO11 . . . . .100 B6
Collingham LS22 . . . . . . .180 A1
Cropton YO18 . . . . .71 B4
Cundall with Leckby
YO61 . . . . .115 E3
Dunnington YO19 . . . . . . .184 F7
Elslack BD23 . . . . .172 D4
4 Elvington YO41 . . . . . .185 C2
Faceby TS9 . . . . .25 F1
Fylingdales YO22 . . . . .33 C4
Garforth LS25 . . . . .194 C4
Gargrave BD23 . . . . .172 D8
Gateforth YO8 . . . . .202 F8
Gilling East YO62 . . . . . . .118 F7
Guisborough TS7 . . . . .7 E5
Guisborough TS9 . . . . .8 A4
Guisborough TS14 . . . . .8 F7
Hampsthwaite HG3 . . . . . .161 A6
17 Haxby YO32 . . . . .166 E5
Hebden BD23 . . . . .135 A1
Hensall DN14 . . . . .203 C1
Hutton Buscel YO13 . . . . . .98 F7
Ingleby Greenhow TS9 . . . . .27 B5
Kelbrook & Sough BB18 . . .186 A8
Church La *continued*
Kellington DN14 . . . . .202 E3
Kirby Hall YO26 . . . . .164 B7
Kirby Hill YO51 . . . . .141 B7
Knaresborough HG5 . . . . .221 A6
Langtoft YO25 . . . . .151 C5
Low Worsall TS15 . . . . .24 A8
Marton cum Grafton
YO51 . . . . .141 D1
Martons Both BD23 . . . . .172 A5
Micklefield LS25 . . . . . . .194 F4
Mickletown LS26 . . . . . . .200 B5
Middlesbrough TS5 . . . . .6 E7
Middlesbrough TS7 . . . . .7 D7
Middleton YO18 . . . . .95 E8
Middleton St George DL2 . . . .4 C3
Milby YO51 . . . . .141 B7
4 Monk Fryston LS25 . . . .202 A8
Moor Monkton YO26 . . . . .165 B2
Nether Poppleton YO26 . . .224 B3
New Earswick YO32 . . . . .225 F5
11 Normanton South WF6 .200 A1
North Featherstone
WF7 . . . . .200 E1
Pannal HG3 . . . . .222 D4
Poppleton YO26 . . . . .224 A3
Redmire DL8 . . . . .59 C5
Ripon HG4 . . . . .214 B5
Sadberge DL2 . . . . .4 C7
Scarborough YO11 . . . . . .213 B7
4 Selby YO8 . . . . .232 D5
Sessay YO7 . . . . .116 C6
Settrington YO17 . . . . . . .122 D1
Sinnington YO62 . . . . .71 A1
Skelton YO30 . . . . .224 B5
Slingsby YO62 . . . . .120 B6
2 Snaith DN14 . . . . .204 C1
South Stainley with Cayton
HG3 . . . . .139 E2
9 Spofforth HG3 . . . . . . .179 E6
Stainburn LS21 . . . . .177 E3
Stainforth BD24 . . . . .131 E6
10 Stamford Bridge YO41 .168 D2
Strensall YO32 . . . . .167 A7
Stutton with Hazlewood
LS24 . . . . .189 E4
Swillington LS26 . . . . . . .194 A1
Terrington YO60 . . . . . . .119 F1
Thormanby YO61 . . . . . . .116 F5
Thornton Dale YO18 . . . . . .96 D6
Thwing YO25 . . . . .126 A1
Tunstall LA6 . . . . .102 B4
Welburn YO60 . . . . .146 E6
Weston LS21 . . . . .176 D1
Westow YO60 . . . . .147 B4
Wheldrake YO19 . . . . . . .193 A7
Whitby YO22 . . . . .208 E7
Whorlton DL6 . . . . .25 D1
Wigglesworth BD23 . . . . .153 D3
Wighill LS24 . . . . .181 D1
Wintringham YO17 . . . . . .123 C4
York YO1 . . . . .233 B2
Church Mdw DL10 . . . . . .21 D8
Church Mdws 9 LS23 . . .188 E6
Church Mews
13 Boroughbridge YO51 . .141 B5
Sherburn in Elmet LS25 . . .195 F4
2 York YO26 . . . . .227 C3
Church Rd
26 Glusburn BD20 . . . . . .187 E7
Great Preston LS26 . . . . .200 C8
Linton BD23 . . . . .134 E2
Pontefract WF6 . . . . .200 A3
Scotton DL9 . . . . .40 E4
Stainton Dale YO13 . . . . . .54 A7
Stamford Bridge YO41 . . .168 D2
Thornton in Craven
BD23 . . . . .171 F3
York YO10 . . . . .229 D4
Church Rise YO19 . . . . .167 F1
Church Row
Hurworth-on-Tees DL2 . . . . .3 E1
Melsonby DL10 . . . . .20 F7
Church Side LS26 . . . . .200 B5
Church Sq YO21 . . . . . .208 C7
Church St
Addingham LS29 . . . . . . .175 A4
Amotherby YO17 . . . . . . .121 B4
Asenby YO7 . . . . .115 B7
Barkston Ash LS24 . . . . . .195 F7
Bellerby DL8 . . . . .60 D7
Bilton-in-Ainsty with Bickerton
YO26 . . . . .181 D5
Boston Spa LS23 . . . . . . .188 E8
Broughton BD23 . . . . . . .172 D7
Bubwith YO8 . . . . .199 D7
Carleton BD23 . . . . .173 B4
Church Fenton LS24 . . . . .196 B7
Copmanthorpe YO23 . . . .230 B2
Danby YO21 . . . . .29 B7
Dunnington YO19 . . . . . . .184 E7
5 Easingwold YO61 . . . . .143 C8
5 Filey YO14 . . . . .101 B3
Gargrave BD23 . . . . .155 D1
13 Glusburn BD20 . . . . . .187 E8
Goldsborough HG5 . . . . .163 A3
Guisborough TS14 . . . . .8 F7
5 Helmsley YO62 . . . . . . .92 F6
Heslerton YO17 . . . . .123 E7
Hovingham YO62 . . . . . . .119 E6
Ilkley LS29 . . . . .218 A4
Ingleton LA6 . . . . .103 D4
Kirk Hammerton YO26 . . .164 C2
Kirkby Malzeard HG4 . . . .112 D5
24 Kirkbymoorside YO62 . . .70 B1
Knottingley WF11 . . . . . .201 E4
Long Preston BD23 . . . . . .153 F4
6 Masham HG4 . . . . .86 C3
Church St *continued*
6 Middleham DL8 . . . . . . .60 E2
Norton YO17 . . . . .215 D3
Nunnington YO62 . . . . .93 E2
2 Scarborough YO11 . . . .213 B6
Settle BD24 . . . . .131 D3
4 Skipton BD23 . . . . . . .216 F3
5 Staithes TS13 . . . . .13 K2
Trawden BB8 . . . . .186 B1
Ulleskelf LS24 . . . . .190 C3
Well DL8 . . . . .87 A4
West Tanfield HG4 . . . . . . .87 A1
Whitby YO22 . . . . .208 E6
Whixley YO26 . . . . .164 A5
York YO1 . . . . .233 B2
Church Stairs St 3
YO11 . . . . .213 B6
Church View
12 Airmyn DN14 . . . . . . .205 E4
3 Brompton DL6 . . . . .43 F3
16 Hurworth DL2 . . . . .3 E1
Kirby Hill YO51 . . . . .141 B7
Ledston LS25 . . . . .194 E1
Norton DN6 . . . . .206 E1
Sherburn YO17 . . . . .124 D8
Sherburn in Elmet LS25 . . .195 F4
South Milford LS25 . . . . .195 F2
Thirsk YO7 . . . . .211 A3
Church View Mews 7
LS23 . . . . .188 E7
Church Wind
Alne YO61 . . . . .142 F4
Burneston DL8 . . . . .87 E7
Church Wlk
Lindrick with Studley
Royal & Fountains HG4 . .139 B7
1 Willerby YO12 . . . . .99 D2
5 Wistow YO8 . . . . .197 D6
Church Wynd DL10 . . . .209 C7
Churchfield Dr 28 YO32 .166 E5
Churchfield La
Castleford WF10 . . . . . . .200 F3
Little Smeaton DN6 . . . . .206 C4
Churchill Cl 13 TS9 . . . . . .8 A2
Churchill Way 4 BD20 . .187 F8
Churchside Villas
LS26 . . . . .200 B5
Churchville LS25 . . . . .195 A4
Churchville Ave LS25 . .194 F4
Churchville Dr LS25 . . .195 A4
Churchville Terr LS25 . .195 A4
Churwell Cl WF10 . . . . .200 E3
Cinder La
Castleford WF10 . . . . . . .200 E4
Clifford LS23 . . . . .188 F7
Lindley LS21 . . . . .177 C3
Upper Poppleton YO26 . . .165 F1
Upper Poppleton YO26 . . .227 A7
York YO26 . . . . .228 A4
York YO31 . . . . .228 E6
Citadilla Cl 5 DL10 . . . . .41 C7
Clack La DL6 . . . . .45 A4
Clapdale Dr LA2 . . . . . .130 C8
Clapdale Way 2 LA2 . . . .130 C8
Clapgate Bank DL11 . . . .39 D8
Clapham C E Prim Sch
LA2 . . . . .130 C7
Clapham Sta LA2 . . . . . .130 A6
Clare Ave DL3 . . . . .3 A5
Claremont 23 YO14 . . . .101 B3
Claremont Dr TS7 . . . . . . .7 C5
Claremont La HG3 . . . . .140 B5
Claremont St BB8 . . . . .186 A3
Claremont Terr YO31 . . .233 B4
Clarence Ave 47 YO14 . . .101 B3
Clarence Dr Filey YO14 . .101 B3
Harrogate HG1 . . . . .219 B3
Clarence Pl
7 Scarborough YO11 . . . .213 A6
2 Whitby YO21 . . . . .208 D7
Clarence Rd
Middlesbrough TS7 . . . . . . .7 D5
2 Scarborough YO12 . . . .213 A7
Scorton DL10 . . . . .41 F7
Clarence St
2 Barnoldswick BB18 . . .171 E1
6 Colne BB8 . . . . .186 A3
1 Trawden Forest BB8 . . .186 B1
York YO31 . . . . .233 B4
Clarendon Rd
Boston Spa LS23 . . . . . . .188 E8
Great Burdon DL1 . . . . .3 F7
Thornaby TS17 . . . . .6 B7
Clarendon St 15 BB8 . . .186 A3
Clareton La HG5 . . . . . .163 B6
Clark Ct WF7 . . . . .200 E1
Clark St 7 YO12 . . . . . .213 A7
Clarkson Ct 12 WF6 . . . .200 B1
Clarkson Dr LS25 . . . . .201 F6
Clarkson St 2 YO21 . . .208 D7
Claro Ave HG1 . . . . . . .219 F4
Claro Mews 4 HG5 . . . .221 A5
Claro Pk HG1 . . . . .219 F4
Claro Rd
Harrogate HG1 . . . . .219 F3
Ripon HG4 . . . . .214 C4
Claro Way HG1 . . . . . . .219 F4
Claude Ave TS5 . . . . .6 E8
Claver Cl DL6 . . . . .45 D8
Clavery Ley La YO62 . . . .67 E1
Claxton Ave DL3 . . . . .3 A6
Clay Bank TS9 . . . . .27 A3
Clay Hill YO41 . . . . . . .169 C3
Clay La Bubwith YO8 . . .199 C5
Camblesforth YO8 . . . . . .204 C6
Cliffe YO8 . . . . .198 D4
Clay Pit La YO51 . . . . .141 A4
Clay Pl 3 YO24 . . . . . . .227 D1

Claygate YO31 229 B6
Claypenny Hospl YO61 117 D1
Claypit La
Carlton DN14 204 C3
Ledston WF10 201 A8
Clayton Hall Rd BD20 187 F7
Clayton Mews 8 WF6 200 A2
Clayton Pl 9 WF6 200 A2
Clayton St 7 BB18 171 E1
Cleasby La DL2 2 F1
Cleasby Way TS16 5 D6
Clement St 4 YO23 233 B1
Clementhorpe YO23 233 B1
Clevedon House Sch LS29 176 A1
Clevegate TS7 7 C5
Cleveland Ave
Darlington DL3 3 C5
Knottingley WF11 201 F2
Scalby YO12 212 D8
Stokesley TS9 26 C8
Cleveland Coll of Art & Design TS5 6 E8
Cleveland Dr DL7 210 D2
Cleveland Rd Boltby YO7 91 B8
Catterick Garrison DL9 40 F4
Scarborough YO12 212 E6
Scorton DL10 41 F7
Cleveland Rein YO7 66 A3
Cleveland St
Darlington DL1 3 D6
Great Ayton TS9 8 A2
Guisborough TS14 8 E6
York YO24 228 A4
Cleveland Terr DL3 3 B5
Cleveland Trad Est DL1 3 D6
Cleveland View 1 TS9 25 F1
Cleveland Way
1 Carlton Miniott YO7 89 C4
York YO32 225 F3
Cliff Bridge Pl 6 YO11 213 A5
Cliff Bridge Terr 7 YO11 213 A5
Cliff Brow TS13 11 C7
Cliff Cres LS25 194 E1
Cliff Dr 24 DL8 60 D5
Cliff Gate Rd DL11 35 E4
Cliff Hill Rd DN6 206 D2
Cliff La
Newholm-cum-Dunsley YO21 13 B2
Snainton YO13 97 F5
Whitwell-on-the-Hill YO60 146 E4
Wilton YO18 97 A5
Wrelton YO18 95 B8
Cliff Rd
Stainton Dale YO13 54 A8
Staithes TS13 13 K2
Cliff St YO21 208 D7
Cliff The YO22 32 B6
Cliffe Prim Sch YO8 198 E2
Cliffe Rd HG2 219 B1
Clifford Ave LS29 218 A5
Clifford Moor Rd LS23 188 D8
Clifford Rd
Boston Spa LS23 188 F8
Ilkley LS29 218 A6
Clifford St
3 Barnoldswick BB18 171 E1
1 Skipton BD23 216 F3
York YO1 233 B2
Clifford's Terr 25 YO14 101 B3
Cliffords Twr★ YO1 233 B1
Clifton Ave TS18 5 E6
Clifton Dale YO30 228 A6
Clifton La LS21 176 F3
Clifton Moor Gate YO30 225 A2
Clifton Moor Ret Pk YO30 224 E3
Clifton Moorgate YO30 225 B3
Clifton Pl 3 YO30 228 A7
Clifton Prep Sch YO30 233 A4
Clifton Rd Darlington DL1 3 D4
Ilkley LS29 218 D3
York YO30 233 A4
Clifton St Earby BB18 186 A8
5 Scarborough YO12 212 F6
Trawden Forest BB8 186 A1
Clifton Without Jun Sch YO30 227 F8
Clint Bank HG3 160 E6
Clint Bank La HG3 160 F6
Clint Garth HG3 160 F8
Clipt La YO7 65 D2
Clitheroe St 2 BD23 216 D3
Clive Gr YO24 227 F2
Clive Rd 1 HG3 179 E6
Clock Twr★ HG4 214 C6
Clockhill Field La YO26 163 F3
Clockwood Gdns TS16 5 E3
Clogger La BD23 172 D3
Cloggerby Rigg DL11 35 E5
Cloisters The
15 Hemingbrough YO8 198 F1
Wilberfoss YO41 185 F6
York YO31 233 C3
Cloisters Wlk YO31 233 C3
Close La BD22 187 B5
Close Rd WF10 200 F4
Close The
Barwick in Elmet LS15 194 B7
Close The *continued*
Boroughbridge YO51 141 A3
Boston Spa LS23 188 E8
Cawood YO8 197 A7
6 Collingham LS22 188 A8
11 East Ayton/West Ayton YO13 99 B8
4 Fylingdales YO22 33 D4
Hunmanby Sands YO14 101 C1
Longnewton TS21 4 F7
Neasham DL2 4 A1
Northallerton DL7 210 B2
Norton DN6 206 E2
Riccall YO19 198 A8
Scalby YO12 212 B8
Skipton BD23 216 F3
Studley Roger HG4 113 D1
Thirsk YO7 211 C1
Thorner LS14 188 A3
Thornton Dale YO18 96 D5
Towton LS24 189 E2
York YO30 227 F8
Clotherholme Rd HG4 214 A5
Clough La DN6 207 B2
Clover Hill BD23 217 B5
Clover Way 9 HG3 161 B3
Cloverley Cl YO41 168 C2
Clowbeck Ct DL3 3 B8
Coach La
10 Hurworth-on-Tees DL2 3 E1
Lindley LS21 177 D3
Coach Rd
Harrogate HG1 219 F2
Sheriff Hutton YO60 145 D4
Sleights YO22 32 A6
Coach St BD23 216 F4
Coach Street Yd 13 BD23 216 F4
Coachman's Ct 6 HG2 220 B1
Coal Pit La
Kirk Smeaton WF8 206 A2
Rimington BB7 171 A1
Coalmire La DL6 45 D7
Coarse La HG3 159 A4
Coastal Rd YO13 75 D7
Coastguard Hill YO14 127 E5
Coates Ave BB18 171 E2
Coates Fields BB18 171 E2
Coates La
Barnoldswick BB18 171 E2
Kettlewell with Starbotton BD23 107 F5
Coate's La BD20 173 F2
Coates Lane Inf Sch BB18 171 E2
Coates Marsh La DN14 204 B2
Coatham Ave DL2 4 D3
Coatham La TS21 5 B7
Cob Castle★ DL8 63 B1
Cob La BB18 186 A6
Cobble Carr TS14 8 E6
Cobblers La WF8 201 C1
Cobbler's La WF8 201 C1
Cobblers Lane Inf Sch WF8 201 D1
Cobby Syke Rd HG3 159 F1
Cobcroft La WF11 206 B8
Cobden St
Barnoldswick BB18 171 D1
Darlington DL1 3 E5
Thornaby TS17 6 B8
Coble La YO60 145 D5
Cobshaw La DL8 62 F6
Cochrane St YO8 232 D3
Cock Garth YO17 122 D1
Cock La Gainford DL2 1 E8
Piercebridge DL2 2 A7
Cock Lodge (site of)★ YO7 115 C6
Cockburn St 5 TS12 9 F7
Cocked Hat HG4 139 C8
Cockerhill La YO62 93 E7
Cockerton C of E Prim Sch DL3 3 A6
Cockerton Gn DL3 3 B6
Cockhill La BB8 186 A4
Cocking La LS29 174 E3
Cocklakes La YO7 114 F1
Cockmoor Rd YO13 74 A1
Cockpit Cl HG4 113 C7
Cockrah Rd YO13 74 F2
Cockret Cl 8 YO8 232 B6
Cockret Ct YO8 232 B7
Cockret Rd YO8 232 B7
Cockshaw Bank La HG4 113 B4
Cockshott Pl 5 LS29 174 F4
Coda Ave YO23 231 B3
Codlin Rd 1 TS15 25 C5
Coeside YO24 230 B7
Coggan Way YO23 230 F4
Colber La HG3 138 F2
Colbert Ave LS29 218 E5
Colburn CP Sch DL9 41 A5
Colburn Dr DL9 40 F5
Colburn La DL9 40 F6
Colburn Sidings DL9 40 F4
Cold Bath Pl HG2 219 C1
Cold Bath Rd HG2 222 C8
Cold Cotes Rd HG3 160 B4
Cold Kirby Rd YO7 91 C8
Coldhill La LS25 195 C6
Coldie Hill 11 TS15 25 C5
Coldstone La YO7 88 B2
Coldyhill La YO12 212 B8
Cole St YO31 233 B4
Coledale Cl 2 YO30 224 F1
Colenso St YO23 233 B1
Coleridge Dr HG1 219 E7
Coleridge Gdns DL1 3 D3
Coleridge Way 1 WF8 201 B1
Colescliffe Cres YO12 212 C8
Colescliffe Rd YO12 212 C8
Colin St 14 BB18 171 D2
Coll of St John The YO31 233 B3
College Ave YO11 213 A2
College Ct
1 Low Bradley BD20 173 E3
4 Scarborough YO11 212 F4
College Farm Cl DN14 207 A8
College Farm La LS22 180 A2
College Gr WF10 200 D3
College La
Bradleys Both BD20 173 E3
5 Masham HG4 86 C3
Scarborough YO11 213 A1
College of Law YO23 231 B7
College of Ripon & York St Johns
York YO10 229 B3
York YO31 233 B3
College Rd
Bradleys Both BD20 173 E3
Copmanthorpe YO23 230 A3
Harrogate HG2 222 B8
Ripon HG4 214 B6
College St
Harrogate HG2 222 B8
York YO1 233 B3
Colley Broach Rd YO61 117 F7
Collier Hag La YO23 182 B3
Collier La
Lotherton cum Aberford LS25 195 A6
West Layton DL11 20 A8
Colliergate YO1 233 B2
Collin Ave TS4 6 F8
Collin Bank HG3 160 E6
Collinge Rd 9 BD22 187 B6
Collingham Way 12 YO14 101 A3
Collingwood Ave YO24 227 F2
Collingwood Gdns YO17 215 A3
Collingwood Rd WF6 200 A2
Collin's Hill HG3 223 D7
Collinsons La YO17 122 F5
Colliwath La DL8 60 F4
Colne & Broughton Rd BD23 172 C4
Colne Rd
Barnoldswick BB18 171 D1
Cowling BD22 187 A5
Earby BB18 172 A1
Kelbrook & Sough BB18 186 A8
Sutton BD20 187 C7
Trawden Forest BB8 186 A1
Colonel's Wlk 9 WF8 201 B1
Colorado Way WF10 200 F2
Colstan Rd DL6 210 E3
Colton Junc LS24 190 E7
Colton La YO23 190 E6
Coltsgate Hill HG4 214 B6
Columbine Gr 33 HG3 161 B3
Columbus Ravine YO12 212 F7
Colville Cres 8 DL9 41 A5
Colville Rd 12 DL9 41 A5
Comfort La DL10 20 C5
Comfrey Cl 32 HG3 161 B3
Comfrey Manor TS8 7 B4
Commercial St
9 Barnoldswick BB18 171 D1
Harrogate HG1 219 D3
Norton YO17 215 D3
Scarborough YO12 212 E5
10 Settle BD24 131 E2
Tadcaster LS24 189 E6
Commercial Yd 1 HG5 221 B6
Common Balk La HG3 140 A3
Common Croft La YO26 165 E1
Common Holme La LS29 175 C3
Common La Beal DN14 202 D3
Burn YO8 203 E7
Carlton Husthwaite YO7 116 F8
Catton YO41 185 E8
Coverham with Agglethorpe DL8 60 A2
Dunnington YO19 184 F5
Fangfoss YO41 169 B1
Glaisdale YO21 29 F1
Hambleton YO8 196 D2
Harome YO62 93 E5
Hartley CA17 14 A8
Knottingley WF11 202 B1
Norton DN6 206 E2
Scruton DL7 63 E7
South Milford LS25 195 F2
Sutton upon Derwent YO41 193 C8
Temple Hirst YO8 203 F4
Thorganby YO19 192 F5
Ulleskelf LS24 190 C2
Walden Stubbs DN6 206 F4
Warthill YO19 167 F2
West Witton DL8 59 F2
York YO10 229 B1
Common Rd
Barkston Ash LS24 195 F7
Church Fenton LS24 196 A7
Common Rd *continued*
Dunnington YO19 184 F7
Skipwith YO8 192 E1
Strensall YO60 145 D1
Commondale Sta YO21 9 E1
Compton La LS23 188 A7
Compton St YO30 228 A6
Conan Dr DL10 209 D8
Conan Gdns DL10 209 D8
Concorde Pk YO30 225 A3
Concorde Way TS18 5 F7
Coney Moor Gr LS26 200 C6
Coney St YO1 233 B2
Coneycroft 10 YO19 184 F7
Coneygarth La
Dunnington YO19 184 E5
Tunstall LA6 102 A4
Conference Ct YO17 215 B4
Conifer Cl 6 YO32 225 D3
Conifers Cl 2 YO8 197 D1
Coniscliffe Mews DL3 3 A4
Coniscliffe Rd DL3 3 A4
Coniston Ave BB18 171 D2
Coniston Cl 1 YO30 224 E1
Coniston Dr
Castleford WF10 201 C4
York YO10 229 B4
Coniston Gdns 6 YO12 99 F7
Coniston Gr
1 Colne BB8 186 A3
Middlesbrough TS5 6 E7
Coniston Rd HG1 220 B4
Coniston Way
3 Eastfield YO12 99 F7
Thirsk YO7 89 C4
Conistone La BD23 108 B3
Connaught Rd
Ilkley LS29 218 D3
Middlesbrough TS7 7 D6
Connaught Way YO32 225 F6
Cononley La BD20 173 D1
Cononley Prim Sch BD20 173 D2
Cononley Rd BD20 187 D8
Cononley Sta BD20 173 D1
Conowl Cl 23 YO62 92 F6
Conroy Cl 11 YO61 143 D8
Consort St BD23 217 B4
Constable Burton Hall★ DL8 61 C6
Constable Rd
Hunmanby YO14 127 A8
Ilkley LS29 218 D3
Constable Ridge Rd HG3 160 B2
Constantine Ave
10 Colburn DL9 41 A5
York YO10 229 A4
Constantine Gr 11 DL9 41 A5
Constitution Hill 3 BD24 131 E2
Conway Cl 2 YO30 224 E3
Conway Cres BB18 171 E1
Conyers Ave DL3 3 A6
Conyers Cl DL10 209 D8
Conyers Ings YO13 99 A7
Conyers La DL8 61 D6
Conyers Rd DL7 22 E2
Conyers Sch TS15 5 E2
Cookgate TS7 7 C5
Cooks Cl 2 DL6 45 A7
Cooks Gdns 3 YO13 75 D5
Cook's Row 5 YO11 213 B6
Coolham La BB18 186 B8
Coombe Dr DL1 3 F6
Coombes Cl YO61 144 C3
Coomboots Brow YO13 75 A6
Cooper Cl DL6 25 D2
Cooper La
Blubberhouses LS21 159 C1
Potto DL6 25 D2
Cooper Lane Shepherd LS21 159 C2
Cooper Rd 49 YO14 101 B3
Coopers Dr YO23 230 B3
Copgrove La HG5 162 D8
Copgrove Rd HG3 140 A2
Cophill La YO7 66 A4
Copley La LS25 195 B7
Copmanroyd LS21 177 A2
Copmanthorpe Jun Sch YO23 230 B3
Copmanthorpe La YO23 230 E3
Copmanthorpe Prim Sch YO23 230 B3
Copmanthorpe Recn Ctr & Sports Club YO23 230 B2
Copper Beeches The 2 YO19 184 E7
Copperclay Wlk YO61 117 D1
Copperfield Cl YO17 215 C5
Coppergate
1 Riccall YO19 191 F1
York YO1 233 B2
Coppergate Wlk YO1 233 B2
Coppertop Mews 4 WF8 201 C2
Coppice Ave HG1 219 C4
Coppice Beck Ct HG1 219 D3
Coppice Cl
Harrogate HG1 219 C4
10 Haxby YO32 166 E5
Coppice Dr HG1 219 C3
Coppice Gate HG1 219 C4
Coppice La YO18 71 B1
Coppice Rise HG1 219 C5
Coppice The
Barwick in Elmet LS15 194 B7
Bishopthorpe YO23 230 F4
Brayton YO8 197 C1
Ilkley LS29 218 A6
Leeming DL7 63 F3
14 Sherburn in Elmet LS25 195 F4
19 Sutton BD20 187 E7
Coppice Valley CP Sch HG1 219 C5
Coppice Valley Pool HG1 219 D4
Coppice View HG1 219 C4
Coppice Way HG1 219 C5
Coppy La
Cononley BD20 173 C2
Sutton BD22 187 E4
Coppy Rd LS29 174 F4
Coppy Wood Dr LS29 218 B7
Copse Hill 1 YO14 101 A4
Copse The
3 North Featherstone WF7 200 E1
5 Scarborough YO12 212 B5
Copsewood Wlk 5 TS9 26 C8
Copwood Gr 7 YO32 225 C8
Corban La YO32 166 B6
Corban Way 21 YO32 166 D5
Corber Hill 7 DL6 43 F3
Corbie Way YO18 96 A7
Corby Ave TS5 6 D8
Cordike La
Birdsall YO17 148 D6
Langton YO17 147 F6
Cordilleras La DL11 39 C8
Corn Mill Gdns YO12 212 D7
Corn Mill La 39 LS29 176 D1
Cornbell Gate 4 HG4 113 D2
Cornborough Av YO31 228 F6
Cornborough Rd YO60 145 C5
Cornel Rise 26 HG3 161 B3
Cornelian Ave YO11 100 B8
Cornelian Cl
1 Scarborough YO11 100 B8
Scarborough YO11 213 C1
Cornelian Dr
2 Scarborough YO11 100 B8
Scarborough YO11 213 C1
Cornelius Cswy YO8 198 E8
Corner Cl 17 YO32 166 D5
Cornfield Rd TS17 6 A8
Cornflower Way 1 HG3 161 B3
Cornforth Hill DL10 209 B6
Cornlands YO17 215 D2
Cornlands Rd YO24 227 B1
Cornmill Cl YO8 197 B8
Cornwall Ave
Darlington DL1 3 E6
Silsden BD20 174 B1
Cornwall Dr YO10 231 E8
Cornwall Rd HG1 219 B2
Cornwood Way 11 YO32 225 C8
Coronation Ave
6 Colburn DL9 41 A5
Harrogate HG2 222 E7
1 Hinderwell TS13 11 F7
Coronation Gr HG2 222 E7
Coronation Hospl LS29 218 C3
Coronation Pl DL10 209 A7
Coronation Rd
Crakehall DL8 62 E5
Harrogate HG2 222 E7
Coronation St 8 BB18 171 E1
Corporation Rd DL3 3 C6
Corpse Rd
North Otterington DL7 64 E5
Thornton-le-Moor DL6 65 A4
Cosmo Ave YO31 229 A5
Costa La YO18 95 D6
Costa Way YO18 95 E7
Cotchers La LS24 195 D8
Cotcliffe Bank DL6 65 E5
Cote Hill Rd HG3 160 B4
Cote La Healey HG4 85 D5
Sproxton YO62 92 C4
Cotescue Bank DL8 60 C1
Cotswold Dr LS25 194 C3
Cotswold Way YO32 226 A5
Cottage Cl DL6 210 E5
Cottage La YO60 145 C4
Cottagers La DL2 2 C3
Cottam La YO25 151 C5
Cotterdale Cl HG5 221 C6
Cotterdale Holt 9 LS22 180 A1
Cottom La YO42 193 C2
Cotton Tree La BB8 186 A3
Coulby Farm Way TS8 7 A5
Coulby La YO18 97 A6
Coulby Manor Way TS8 6 F6
Coulby Newham Sec Sch TS8 7 A5
Coulson Cl 5 YO32 167 C8
Coulter Beck La LA6 102 D7
Coulthurst Craven Sports Ctr The BD23 216 F3
Coulton La YO62 119 A6
Count De Burgh Terr 4 YO23 228 B1
County Cricket Gd YO12 212 F7
County Par HG1 219 F3
County Sq HG1 219 F3

Coupland Rd
Garforth LS25 ....194 C4
1 Selby YO8 ....232 C6
Courby Hill HG4 ....86 F2
Courcey Gr YO23 ....227 C4
Court Dr YO8 ....232 A4
Court Green Cl YO13 .....54 D1
Court La BD23 ....217 A4
Court Moor La YO62 ......70 A4
Court The 6 DL8 ....63 A2
Courtneys Selby YO8 .....232 B4
Wheldrake YO19 ....193 A8
Courts Cl 7 DN14 ....205 E4
Courtyard The
Bishopthorpe YO23 ....231 B4
11 Pontefract WF8 ....201 C2
Coutances Way LS29 .....218 F5
Cove Rd BD23 ....132 F2
Cover La
Carlton Town DL8 ....83 E7
Marton-le-Moor HG4 ....114 E1
Coverdale Dr
1 Knaresborough HG5 ....221 A7
Scarborough YO12 ....212 B4
Coverdale Garth 2
LS22 ....188 A8
Coverdale La TS13 ......12 A4
Coverham Abbey (rems of)★
DL8 ....60 C1
Coverham Cl DL7 ....210 C1
Coverham La DL8 ....60 C1
Covert The
9 Topcliffe YO7 ....89 B1
York YO24 ....230 F7
Cow & Calf Rocks★
LS29 ....218 D2
Cow Close La
Kirkby Malham BD23 ....154 E8
Lockwood TS12 ....10 A4
Cow Gate La BD23 ....171 B7
Cow La Cowling BD22 ....187 B6
Knottingley WF11 ....202 A2
Lothersdale BD20 ....172 F1
Middleton Tyas DL10 ......21 C4
Womersley DN6 ....206 D6
Cow Pasture La YO42 ....193 C3
Cow Wath Bank YO22 .....51 E8
Cow Wath Cl 30 YO12 ...75 D5
Cowbar Bank 1 TS13 ....13 K2
Cowbar La TS13 ....13 J2
Cowcliff Hill YO17 .....148 F6
Cowgarth La 15 BD8 ....172 B1
Cowgill St 17 BB18 .....172 A1
Cowhouse Bank YO62 .....68 F3
Cowie Dr YO8 ....232 D5
Cowland La YO7 ....88 D3
Cowley Cl TS16 ....5 E7
Cowley Rd TS5 ....6 E7
Cowling Hill La BD22 ...186 F7
Cowling La DL8 ....62 D3
Cowling Prim Sch
BD22 ....187 A6
Cowling Rd DL8 ....62 D2
Cowlings Cl 16 YO14 ...127 A8
Cowpasture Rd LS29 .....218 C3
Cowper La YO23 ....191 C8
Cowper St 3 BD23 ....217 A3
Cowton Castle★ DL7 ....22 D1
Cowton La YO14 ....127 C6
Cowton Way TS16 ....5 D6
Coxlea Gr YO31 ....229 B6
Coxwold Dr DL1 ....3 D4
Coxwold Hill 5 LS22 ....180 C4
Coxwold Pottery★
YO61 ....117 D7
Coxwold View 3 LS22 ...180 C3
Crab La Harrogate HG1 ..219 D6
Seamer YO12 ....99 E6
Crab Tree La WF8 ....206 A1
Crabmill La YO61 ....143 D8
Crabtree Gn LS22 ....188 A8
Crabtree Gr 1 YO32 ....225 D4
Crabtree Hill LS22 .....188 A8
Cracoe Prim Sch
BD23 ....156 B6
Cradley Dr TS5 ....6 E6
Crag Bank YO21 ....28 B8
Crag Cl 33 BD20 ....187 E7
Crag Gdns LS23 ....188 E5
Crag Hill La HG3 ....161 B6
Crag Hill Rd YO13 ......53 F8
Crag La
Bradleys Both BD20 ....173 E2
Felliscliffe HG3 ....160 D4
Huby LS17 ....178 B2
Killinghall HG3 ....161 B1
Killinghall HG3 ....161 C5
Knaresborough HG5 ....221 B5
North Rigton LS17 ....178 B3
Pannal HG3 ....178 C8
Sutton BD20 ....187 D6
Crag Side Rd DL8 ....57 B2
Crag The 3 LS23 ....188 E5
Crag View
Cononley BD20 ....173 D1
Threshfield BD23 ....134 B3
Weeton LS17 ....178 B2
Crag View Rd BD23 ......217 B3
Cragdale 13 BD24 ......131 D2
Cragdale Rise 1 HG5 ...221 D6
Cragg Bottom Rd
BD22 ....187 C1
Cragg Dr LS22 ....218 F3
Cragg Hill Rd BD24 ....105 C3
Cragg La LA2 ....130 C4

Craggs La
Arrathorne DL10 ....41 A4
Tatham LA2 ....129 A3
Craig St DL3 ....3 C6
Craiglands Pk LS29 .....218 C3
Craiglands Rd LS29 .....218 C3
Craigmore Dr LS29 ......218 E4
Craigs Way YO7 ....211 C4
Crake La HG3 ....159 F6
Crakehall C of E Prim Sch
DL8 ....62 E4
Cranberry TS8 ....7 B5
Cranbrook Ave YO26 .....227 C5
Cranbrook Rd YO26 ......227 C5
Cranbrooks The YO19 ....192 F8
Cranfield Pl 4 YO24 ...230 C8
Cranford Gdns TS5 ......6 D8
Crank La DL7 ....63 B7
Crankley La YO61 ....143 B7
Cranwell Gr TS17 ......6 B6
Craven Bank La BD24 ....131 B3
Craven Coll BD24 ....131 D2
Craven Cres 3 LS29 ....174 F4
Craven Ct
Cowling BD22 ....187 C6
Northallerton DL7 ....210 B3
Richmond DL10 ....209 B6
Silsden BD20 ....174 C1
Craven Dr BD20 ....174 C1
Craven Garth 5 DN14 ...202 D4
Craven Mus★ BD23 .....131 D2
Craven Ridge La BD24 ...131 A2
Craven Ridge La Ends
BD24 ....131 B3
Craven St 8 Colne BB8 ..186 A3
Harrogate HG1 ....219 D4
Scarborough YO11 ....213 A4
Skipton BD23 ....216 F3
Craven Way
6 Boroughbridge YO51 ...141 B4
Dent LA10 ....78 B8
Cravendale Rd 4 DL9 ...40 F5
Cravengate DL10 ....209 B6
Craven's Hill YO13 .....54 C3
Crawford Cl YO26 ....181 C7
Crawley Way YO31 ......229 B6
Cray Thorns Cres YO7 ...115 A4
Crayke C of E Prim Sch
YO61 ....117 F1
Crayke Castle★ YO61 ...117 F1
Crayke La YO61 ....118 A2
Crayke Manor★ YO61 ...117 F2
Crescent Ave YO21 .....208 C7
Crescent Back Rd 8
YO11 ....213 A5
Crescent Ct LS29 ....218 A4
Crescent Gdns HG1 ......219 C2
Crescent Hill 58 YO14 ..101 B3
Crescent Par LS29 ......214 C6
Crescent Rd
Harrogate HG1 ....219 C2
Ripon HG4 ....214 B6
Crescent Terr 6 LS29 ...218 B4
Crescent The
13 Bedale DL8 ....63 B3
Burton Fleming YO25 .....126 E3
Carlton TS9 ....26 A2
Eaglescliffe TS16 ....5 D4
Filey YO14 ....101 B3
Garforth LS25 ....194 D4
2 Hartwith cum Winsley
HG3 ....138 A1
17 Helmsley YO62 ....92 F4
Ilkley LS29 ....218 E5
Kelfield YO19 ....191 D1
Kexby YO41 ....185 C5
Kippax LS25 ....194 D1
Micklefield LS25 ....195 A3
Middlesbrough TS7 ....7 D6
Middleton St George DL2 .4 E4
North Rigton LS17 ....178 B3
Northallerton DL6 ....210 E4
Otley LS21 ....177 A1
6 Riccall YO19 ....197 F8
Richmond DL10 ....209 D7
Ripon HG4 ....214 B6
Scalby YO12 ....212 B4
Scarborough YO11 ....213 A5
Sicklinghall LS22 ....179 E3
Stainton Dale YO13 ......54 A8
Stamford Bridge YO41 ....168 D2
Thornaby TS17 ....6 B8
Thornton Dale YO18 ......96 D5
York YO24 ....233 A1
Crest Hill LS26 ....194 A1
Crest The LS26 ....194 A1
Crestbrooke DL7 ....210 D2
Crestholme Cl 6 HG5 ...221 D5
Crewe Rd WF10 ....201 B4
Creyke View DN14 ......205 A1
Crichton Ave YO30 ......228 B8
Cricket La TS6 ....7 E8
Cricketers Way 8 LS25 ..195 F4
Cridling Gdns DN6 ......206 F2
Crimple Ave LS22 ......180 A8
Crimple La HG3 ....223 D7
Crimple Mdws HG3 ....222 D3
Crinan Ct
Pontefract WF6 ....200 A2
3 York YO32 ....225 F6
Crindle Carr La DL7 ....65 B3
Cringle Moor Chase
TS9 ....26 F4
Cringles La BD20 ....174 C4
Cringley La DL8 ....57 E5
Crocus Ct 20 DL9 ......41 A5
Croft Ave
8 Knottingley WF11 .....202 A3

Croft Ave continued
Middlesbrough TS5 ....6 D8
4 Normanton South WF6 ..200 B2
Otley LS21 ....176 F1
Croft C of E Prim Sch
DL2 ....22 C8
Croft Cl
Carlton Husthwaite YO7 ..116 F7
14 Easingwold YO61 .....143 C8
Ingleton LA6 ....103 D3
Croft Ct YO23 ....231 A4
Croft Dr LS23 ....188 E6
Croft Farm Cl YO23 .....230 B3
Croft Gdns YO7 ....211 B1
Croft Head Terr 2
BD20 ....187 E7
Croft Heads YO7 ....211 B1
Croft Hill Carthorpe DL8 .87 E7
32 Glusburn BD20 ....187 E7
Croft Hills TS9 ....26 A7
Croft House Dr 8 LS21 ..176 F1
Croft House Fold 10
LS29 ....175 A4
Croft House La BD23 ....135 A1
Croft La
Carlton Husthwaite YO7 ..116 F8
Newton Kyme cum Toulston
LS24 ....189 B7
Snainton YO13 ....97 F5
Walton LS23 ....181 A2
Croft Motor Racing Circuit★
DL2 ....22 C5
Croft Rd
Bramham cum Oglethorpe
LS23 ....188 E6
Camblesforth YO8 ....204 D4
Catterick Garrison DL9 ...209 E1
Eaglescliffe TS16 ....5 D4
Hurworth DL2 ....3 B2
Ingleton LA6 ....103 D2
Croft St 12 Earby BB18 ..172 A1
1 Glusburn BD20 ....187 E7
Croft The Beadlam YO62 .93 D7
Burton in Lonsdale LA6 ...102 F3
Castleford WF10 ....200 F3
5 Collingham LS22 ......188 A8
Draughton BD23 ....174 F4
16 Filey YO14 ....101 B3
1 Filey YO14 ....101 B3
Knottingley WF11 ....202 A3
Langthorpe YO51 ....141 A7
Scalby YO12 ....212 B4
Sheriff Hutton YO60 .....145 D5
Stirton with Thorlby
BD23 ....216 C6
Thirsk YO7 ....211 B1
West Tanfield DL8 ....87 B3
Crofters Gn HG3 ....219 A8
Croftlands 7 WF11 .....202 A3
Crofts Ave
4 Pickering YO18 ....96 A6
Richmond DL10 ....209 D7
Crofts The
1 Glusburn BD20 ....173 F1
1 Sutton BD20 ....187 E6
Croftside 1 YO26 ....227 B3
Croftway
Barwick in Elmet LS15 ...194 C8
Camblesforth YO8 ....204 C5
Selby YO8 ....232 C4
Sherburn in Elmet LS25 ..195 F4
2 York YO26 ....227 B3
Crombie Ave YO30 ......228 B7
Cromer St YO30 ....228 B7
Cromwell Ave 22 YO14 ..101 B3
Cromwell Cl 5 WF11 ....201 E4
Cromwell Cres 6 WF8 ...201 C1
Cromwell Dr DL7 ....64 A6
Cromwell Gdns 6 YO11 ..212 F4
Cromwell Par 5 YO11 ...212 F4
Cromwell Rd
Harrogate HG2 ....222 E7
Scarborough YO11 ....212 F4
York YO1 ....233 B1
Cromwell Rise LS25 ....200 D8
Cromwell St 9 BD23 ....217 A3
Cromwell Terr 7 YO11 ..212 F4
Crook Bank La DL11 ....38 F6
Crook La HG4 ....85 E5
Crooked La YO26 ....164 C2
Crookland La YO32 .....166 F5
Croom Medieval Village★
YO25 ....150 B4
Croome Dale La YO17 ...150 C6
Croome Rd YO25 ....150 B4
Cropstones LS23 ....188 F5
Cropton La YO18 ....71 B2
Cropton Rise YO12 .....212 B4
Cropton Way TS8 ....7 B5
Crosby Rd DL6 ....210 E4
Crosby St DL3 ....3 C7
Crosland Cl 22 YO62 ...92 F6
Cross Bank BD23 ....217 B6
Cross End Fold 3 LS29 .175 A4
Cross Gate YO13 ....97 D5
Cross Haw La 3 LA2 ....130 C8
Cross Head Bank DL8 ...60 D7
Cross Hill
Fairburn WF11 ....201 D6
Sutton-under-Whitestonecliffe
YO7 ....90 D5
Cross Hills La YO8 .....232 A5
Cross La Bentham LA2 ...129 D3
Brompton DL6 ....43 D5
Burneston DL8 ....87 E8
Burniston YO13 ....75 D7
Farndale East YO62 ......48 E4
Flaxton YO60 ....167 E8

Cross La continued
Fulford YO19 ....231 F5
Giggleswick BD24 ....130 F2
Great Ouseburn YO26 .....164 B8
Little Ayton TS9 ....27 A8
Pickhill with Roxby YO7 ..88 C6
Scalby YO12 ....212 C8
Sinnington YO62 ....95 A8
Snainton YO13 ....97 F3
Stonebeck Up HG3 ....110 B5
Cross Lane Hospl
YO12 ....212 D8
Cross Lanes DL10 ......209 E7
Cross Queen St 9 WF6 ..200 A1
Cross Rd LA2 ....128 E7
Cross Rein Bank DL7 ....23 A1
Cross Row Boosbeck TS12 .9 E7
Swillington LS15 ....194 A3
Cross St 6 Cowling BD22 .187 B6
14 Earby BB18 ....172 A1
Scarborough YO11 ....213 A6
Skipton BD23 ....216 F3
5 York YO24 ....227 C3
Cross The LS15 ....194 B8
Cross Top DL8 ....57 E7
Crossbeck Cl LS29 ......218 B3
Crossbeck Rd
Ilkley LS29 ....218 B3
Northallerton DL6 ....210 F5
Crossbeck Way TS7 .....7 D8
Crosscliff TS8 ....6 F5
Crossdale Rd YO18 .....72 E3
Crossfield Cl 2 DL2 ....3 E1
Crossfield Cres YO19 ...231 E6
Crossfields TS8 ....7 A4
Crossgate La
22 Pickering YO18 ......95 F6
10 Pickering YO18 ......96 A6
Crossgates HG3 ....138 B5
Crosshill La DN14 ......207 E6
Crosshills Rd BD20 .....173 D1
Crossings The 13 DN14 ..205 E4
Crosslands Rd 2 YO10 ..231 E8
Crossley Pl BD23 ....216 F4
Crossley St 8 LS22 .....180 C3
Crossman Dr 2 WF6 .....200 B2
Crossmoor La YO32 .....166 E6
Crossway The
Darlington DL1 ....3 E5
2 York YO31 ....228 E8
Crossways YO10 ....229 C2
Crossways Cres HG2 ....220 D3
Crossways Dr HG2 ......220 D2
Crossways The LS21 ....177 A1
Crow Hill La HG3 ....160 C4
Crow Nest Rd LA2 ......130 F6
Crowberry Dr HG3 ......161 B3
Crowdy Cl YO22 ....208 E4
Crowfoot La DL6 ....43 D5
Crowgarth HG4 ....140 D7
Crown Cres YO11 ....213 A4
Crown Gr YO17 ....215 E3
Crown Sq 26 YO62 .....70 B1
Crown St
34 Burley in Warfedale
LS29 ....176 C1
Darlington DL3 ....3 C5
Crown Terr YO11 ....213 A4
Crowood Ave TS9 ....26 C8
Crowtrees LA2 ....128 E8
Crummack La LA2 ......130 E8
Crummock 3 YO24 ......230 C7
Cuddy Brown Cl 7 YO18 .96 A6
Cuddy La DL6 ....45 B4
Culvert La BD23 ....216 A4
Cumberland Cl 8 YO32 ..167 B6
Cumberland Gdns
DL10 ....21 C4
Cumberland Rd WF10 ....201 C5
Cumberland St
6 Skipton BD23 ....216 F3
York YO1 ....233 B2
Cumbernauld Rd TS17 ...6 C7
Cumbrian Ave 4 YO32 ...167 B6
Cundall Ave YO7 ....115 B6
Cundall Cl 6 YO7 ......167 C8
Cundall Manor Sch
YO61 ....115 E3
Cundall Way HG2 ....222 C8
Cunliffe Rd LS29 ......218 B4
Cunningham Ave TS17 ...6 B6
Cunningham Rd DL9 ....40 F4
Cupid's Alley YO17 ....149 B6
Curfew Rd HG4 ....214 C3
Curlew Cl 11 Ilkley LS29 .175 C2
Leyburn DL8 ....60 E4
Curlew Cres 2 YO12 ....99 F6
3 Filey YO14 ....101 A3
Curlew Dr Eastfield YO12 .99 E6
Curlew Glebe 8 YO19 ...184 F7
Curly Hill LS29 ....218 A5
Currer La LS29 ....175 B6
Currie Cl DL9 ....209 C2
Curson Terr YO8 ....198 E3
Curtain La DL11 ....1 D5
Curtain The DL11 ......1 D4
Curteis Dr DL10 ....41 D8
Curzon Terr YO23 ......228 B1
Custance Wlk YO23 .....233 A1
Cut Rd WF11 ....201 D6
Cut Throat La HG3 .....138 F1
Cutler La LS26 ....200 C6
Cutpurse La DL10 ......209 C8
Cutsyke Ave WF10 .....200 D3
Cutsyke Crest WF10 ....200 D3
Cutsyke Rd WF10 ......200 D2
Cycle St 4 YO10 ......229 A3
Cygnet Cl 7 YO14 .....101 A4

Cygnet St YO23 ....233 A1
Cypress Cl DL3 ....3 B4
Cypress Gdns HG4 ......214 B3
Cypress Rd TS7 ....7 C6

D

Dacre Ct LS24 ....195 D7
Dacre Hall Pk HG3 .....159 F7
Dacre La HG3 ....159 D7
Dacre Pasture La
HG3 ....159 D6
Daffy La YO61 ....117 C1
Dairy La HG3 ....159 E6
Daisy Cl 13 DL9 ....41 A5
Daisy Hill BD20 ....174 C1
Dakyn Cl DL7 ....22 F2
Dalacres Cres BD23 ....217 D8
Dalacres Dr BD23 ......217 D8
Dalby Ave HG2 ....220 D1
Dalby Bank YO60 ......119 C2
Dalby Cl YO12 ....212 B5
Dalby Ct HG2 ....220 D1
Dalby Forest Dr YO18 ..96 E8
Dalby Mead YO32 ......225 F1
Dalby Way TS8 ....7 A5
Dale Ave YO13 ....75 C8
Dale Bank HG1 ....219 B3
Dale Cl Burniston YO13 ..75 C8
Hampsthwaite HG3 ....161 A5
7 Hurworth-on-Tees DL2 ..3 E1
Selby YO8 ....232 C3
Thornton Watlass HG4 ....86 D8
Dale Cres BD23 ....173 A4
Dale Croft 20 LS29 ....175 C2
Dale Dike Gr YO30 .....224 F2
Dale Edge 11 YO11 ....99 F7
Dale End Danby YO21 ...29 C7
Kirkbymoorside YO62 .....70 B1
Dale End Rd YO62 ......70 A7
Dale Garth YO12 ....212 D4
Dale Gr DL8 ....60 D6
Dale Rd Carleton BD23 ..173 A4
Darlington DL3 ....3 B5
Sadberge DL2 ....4 C7
Dale Rise YO13 ....75 C8
Dale St Earby BB18 ....172 B1
York YO23 ....233 A1
Dale Stone Cl WF11 ....201 D5
Dale The LS25 ....188 F1
Dale View 6 Earby BB18 .172 A1
Ilkley LS29 ....175 C2
Dale Way 2 DL8 ....60 D5
Dalefield Ave WF6 .....200 A1
Dalefield Rd WF6 ......200 A1
Dalehouse Bank TS13 ...13 J1
Dales Ave BD23 ....217 C7
Dales Countryside Mus★
DL8 ....56 D5
Dale's La YO31 ....228 F4
Dales Park Rd TS8 .....6 E5
Dales Sch DL7 ....64 C7
Dalesbridge Outdoor Ctr★
LA2 ....130 C2
Daleside Ave HG2 ......222 E5
Daleside Dr HG2 ....222 E5
Daleside Gdns HG2 .....222 E5
Daleside Pk HG3 ....160 A6
Daleside Rd
Farndale East YO62 ......48 C7
Farndale West YO62 .....48 B6
Harrogate HG2 ....222 E5
Rosedale East Side YO18 .49 C5
Rosedale West Side YO18 .49 C3
Dalewood Wlk 3 TS9 ....26 C8
Dalguise Gr YO31 ......233 C4
Dallamires Cl HG4 .....214 D3
Dallamires La HG4 .....214 E3
Dallamires Way N
HG4 ....214 D4
Dallamires Way S
HG4 ....214 D3
Dalmally Cl YO24 ......230 B2
Dalton Hill YO19 ......193 A8
Dalton La Dalton YO7 ...115 C7
Wothersome LS23 ....188 C5
Dalton Terr YO24 ......228 A3
Dam Bank YO8 ....232 C6
Dam Head Rd 14 BB18 ..171 D1
Dam Hill YO23 ....182 B4
Dam La
Appleton Roebuck YO23 ..190 F4
Leavening YO17 ....147 E1
Markington with Wallerthwaite
HG3 ....139 C3
Saxton with Scarthingwell
LS24 ....195 C7
Selby YO8 ....197 B3
Dame La DL8 ....58 F1
Danby C of E Prim Sch
YO21 ....29 A6
Danby Castle★ YO21 ...29 D6
Danby La DL7 ....43 C5
Danby St DL9 ....40 F4
Danby Sta YO21 ....29 C7
Dandy Mill Ave WF8 ....201 C1
Dandy Mill Croft 8
WF8 ....201 C1
Dandy Mill View WF8 ...201 C1
Dane Ave
Thorpe Willoughby YO8 ...197 B1
York YO26 ....227 C2
Dane Rd DL9 ....209 E1
Danebury Cres YO26 ....227 C4
Danebury Dr YO26 ......227 C4
Danelaw Fields 1 DL6 ..43 F3
Danelaw Rd 2 DL6 .....43 F3

Danes Croft **2** YO10 . . .231 D8
Danes Ct **5** YO19 . . .198 A8
Danes Dyke **34** YO12 . . .75 D5
Danescroft YO8 . . . . .232 C2
Danesfort Ave YO24 . . . .227 D2
Danesgate YO26 . . . . . . .227 C4
Danesmead YO10 . . . . . . .231 D8
Danesmoor Cres DL3 . . . .3 B5
Daneswell Cl **3** YO41 . . .168 D2
Dangerous Cnr 160 A2
Dansk Way LS29 . . . . . . .218 D5
Danum Ave YO7 . . . . .211 A1
Danum Dr YO10 . . . . .231 E8
Danum Rd YO10 . . . . .231 E8
Darbie Cl YO32 . . . . .225 D4
D'arcy Ct DL9 . . . . .40 F4
D'arcy Rd YO8 . . . . .232 E4
Dark La
  Barwick in Elmet & Scholes
  LS15 . . . . .194 B8
  Brompton YO13 . . . . .98 C5
  Earby BB18 . . . . .172 B1
  Newsham DL11 . . . . .19 C8
  Sinnington YO62 . . . . .71 A1
  Spofforth with Stockeld
  HG5 . . . . .179 F7
  Stainburn LS21 . . . . .177 E2
  Sutton BD22 . . . . .187 B1
Darkfield La WF8 . . . . . .201 C2
Darley Carr HG3 . . . . . . .159 F6
Darley Cl **7** YO41 . . . . .168 D2
Darley CP Sch HG3 . . . . .160 A6
Darley Mill Ctr ★ HG3 . .159 F6
Darley Rd HG3 . . . . .160 D6
Darling La YO23 . . . . . . .191 C8
Darlington (Bank Top) Sta
  DL1 . . . . .3 D4
Darlington Arts Ctr ★ 3 C5
Darlington Back La DL2 . .4 E8
Darlington Coll of Tech
  DL3 . . . . .3 B5
Darlington Meml Hospl
  DL3 . . . . .3 C6
Darlington Rd
  Easby DL10 . . . . .20 F1
  Longnewton TS21 . . . . . . .5 A7
  Northallerton DL6 . . . . . .210 C4
  Richmond DL10 . . . . .209 E8
  Stockton-on-Tees TS18 . . . .5 E8
Darlington Rly Ctr & Mus ★
  DL3 . . . . .3 C6
Darlington Rugby Football
  Club DL1 . . . . .3 C3
Darnborough St YO23 . . .233 B1
Darnbrook Rd **2** BB18 . .171 D1
Darnbrook Wlk YO23 . . . .229 B5
Darnholme La YO22 . . . . .51 D5
Darnton Dr TS4 . . . . .7 A7
Darrowby Cl YO7 . . . . . . .211 C4
Darrowby Dr DL3 . . . . .3 C6
Daskett Hill YO60 . . . . . .145 D5
Dauby La YO41 . . . . .185 B3
Davenport Rd TS15 . . . . . .5 D2
David La YO18 . . . . .72 F5
Davis Ave WF10 . . . . .201 B3
Davison Rd DL1 . . . . .3 D7
Davison St TS12 . . . . .9 F7
Davygate YO1 . . . . .233 B2
Daw La YO23 . . . . .191 A5
Dawcross Rise HG3 . . . . .222 B3
Dawes Ave WF10 . . . . . . .201 A3
Dawnay Cl **5** YO12 . . . . .99 F7
Dawnay Garth
  Shipton YO30 . . . . .165 E5
  2 Snaith DN14 . . . . . . .204 B1
Dawney La YO61 . . . . . . .143 B6
Dawson St **16** BD23 . . . .217 A3
Dawson Terr HG1 . . . . . . .219 D4
Dawson's La HG4 . . . . . . .85 F4
Dawtrie St WF10 . . . . . . .201 B4
Day La HG3 . . . . .159 E4
Daysfoot Ct **8** YO10 . . .228 E3
De Brus Rd DL6 . . . . .210 D8
De Brus Pk TS8 . . . . .7 C4
De Brus Way TS14 . . . . . . .8 F7
De Ferrers Rd DL6 . . . . . .210 D8
De Ferrieres Ave HG1 . . . .219 D4
De Gaunte Rd DL6 . . . . . .210 E8
De Grey Ct YO30 . . . . . . .233 A4
De Grey Pl **2** YO23 . . . .231 B3
De Grey St YO31 . . . . . . .233 B4
De Grey Terr YO31 . . . . . .233 B4
De Lacy Ave **1** WF7 . . . .200 E1
De Lisle Cres DL9 . . . . . .209 C2
De Mowbray Ct YO23 . . . .182 D3
Deacon Ct **3** YO8 . . . . .232 B4
Deacons Ct YO23 . . . . . . .230 B2
Dealtry Ave **1** YO32 . . . .225 C4
Dean Edge Rd BD22 . . . .187 C1
Dean Hall Brow YO22 . . . .32 C5
Dean La BD22 . . . . .187 F3
Dean Rd Norton YO17 . . . .215 E3
  Scarborough YO12 . . . . . .212 E4
Dean St **1** Ilkley LS29 . . .218 C5
  Trawden Forest BB8 . . . . .186 A1
Deane Pl HG2 . . . . .220 B3
Deangate YO1 . . . . .233 B3
Deanhead Gr YO30 . . . . .224 E2
Deans Cl YO23 . . . . .230 F4
Deans Sq YO7 . . . . .115 C7
Debruse Ave TS15 . . . . . .5 D2
Dee Cl YO24 . . . . .230 B7
Deep Dale LS23 . . . . .180 E1
Deep Ghyll Croft HG4 . . .214 C3
Deep Ghyll Wlk HG4 . . . .214 C3
Deepdale
  Guisborough TS14 . . . . . .8 D6

Deepdale continued
  7 Hutton Rudby TS15 . . .25 C5
  5 York YO24 . . . . .230 D8
Deepdale Ave
  Eastfield YO11 . . . . .100 A8
  Middlesbrough TS4 . . . . . .7 A8
  Scarborough YO11 . . . . . .213 A5
Deepdale La
  Boston Spa LS23 . . . . . . .180 D1
  Dent LA10 . . . . .77 F8
Deepdale Way **7** DL1 . . . .3 F6
Deepfurrows La YO41 . . . .185 D3
Deeping Way YO8 . . . . . .232 A6
Deer Hill Gr YO30 . . . . . .224 F3
Deer Park Ct **1** LS25 . . .202 A8
Deerstone Way **22** YO19 .184 F7
Deighton La
  Brompton DL6 . . . . .43 E5
  Little Smeaton DL6 . . . . . .23 E1
Deighton Rd
  Coulby Newham TS4 . . . . .7 A7
  Spofforth with Stockeld
  HG3 . . . . .179 F6
  Wetherby LS22 . . . . .180 C4
Deigton Gate Jun & Inf Sch
  LS22 . . . . .180 C4
Del Pyke YO31 . . . . .233 C4
Delamere Cl **6** YO12 . . .166 D5
Delamere Cres HG2 . . . . .220 D1
Delamere Rd TS3 . . . . .7 B8
Delaney Cl **19** BD24 . . . .131 D2
Delf La YO7 . . . . .66 A4
Dell The **5** YO30 . . . . . .224 B5
Delves La YO22 . . . . .30 C4
Delwood YO10 . . . . .231 D7
Dene Cl DN14 . . . . .203 C2
Dene Gr DL3 . . . . .3 C6
Dene Mdw **1** YO13 . . . . .99 B8
Dene Park Cl HG1 . . . . . .219 F6
Dene Pk HG1 . . . . .219 F5
Dene The DL6 . . . . .210 C5
Dene The YO12 . . . . .212 E7
Deneside Rd DL3 . . . . .3 B6
Denesway LS25 . . . . .194 D3
Denevale TS15 . . . . .5 E3
Denison Ave **8** YO12 . . . .99 D6
Denison Rd YO8 . . . . .232 E4
Dennis La BD20 . . . . .174 A2
Dennis St YO1 . . . . .233 C2
Dennison St
  1 York YO31 . . . . .228 C4
  York YO31 . . . . .233 C4
Dentdale Dr HG5 . . . . . . .221 C6
Denton Rd LS29 . . . . .218 A5
Denton Terr WF10 . . . . . .200 F4
Denver Dr DL2 . . . . .4 D4
Denver Rd **6** DN6 . . . . . .206 F2
Denwell Terr WF8 . . . . . .201 B1
Depot La **11** YO12 . . . . .212 E4
Deramore Dr YO10 . . . . . .229 C3
Deramore Dr W YO10 . . . .229 C3
Derby Rd TS14 . . . . .8 E6
Derby The TS7 . . . . .7 B6
Dere Street Roman Rd ★
  DL11 . . . . .2 B2
Derrings La YO61 . . . . . . .142 D6
Derventio Roman Fort ★
  YO17 . . . . .215 D4
Derwent Ave
  Garforth LS25 . . . . .194 C3
  5 Scarborough YO12 . . .212 E4
  York YO31 . . . . .228 F4
Derwent Cl **2** Colne BB8 .186 A3
  Elvington YO41 . . . . .185 B3
  2 Stamford Bridge YO41 .168 D2
Derwent Ct YO41 . . . . . . .185 C2
Derwent Dr
  4 Barlby YO8 . . . . .198 B5
  Castleford WF10 . . . . . . .201 C5
  Wheldrake YO19 . . . . . . .192 F7
Derwent Est YO19 . . . . . .184 E7
Derwent Inf Sch YO10 . . .229 B4
Derwent Jun Sch
  YO10 . . . . .229 B4
Derwent Pk YO19 . . . . . . .193 A8
Derwent Rd
  Harrogate HG1 . . . . .220 B3
  Huttons Ambo YO17 . . . . .215 A2
  Whitby YO21 . . . . .208 A7
  York YO10 . . . . .231 D8
Derwent St **12** YO12 . . .212 E4
Derwent Swimming Pool &
  Fitness Ctr YO17 . . . . . .215 D4
Desmond Rd DL2 . . . . .4 C3
Deveron Way YO24 . . . . . .230 B7
Devil's Arrows Standing
  Stones ★ YO51 . . . . . . .141 B5
Devon Pl YO10 . . . . .228 F3
Devonshire Dr YO12 . . . . .212 E7
Devonshire Gn HG4 . . . . .114 F1
Devonshire Pl
  Harrogate HG1 . . . . .219 E3
  12 Skipton BD23 . . . . . .216 F4
Devonshire Rd DL1 . . . . . . .3 E6
Devonshire St **13** BD23 . .217 A3
Devonshire Way HG1 . . . .219 F4
Dew La TS7 . . . . .7 D7
Dewbury Cl TS8 . . . . .7 B4
Dewsbury Terr YO1 . . . . . .233 A1
Dexta Way DL7 . . . . .210 C3
Diamond Gr HG1 . . . . . . .220 C4
Diamond Pl HG1 . . . . . . .220 C4
Diamond Rd TS17 . . . . . . .6 B8
Diamond St YO31 . . . . . . .233 C4
Dibble Bridge Bank
  YO21 . . . . .28 F6
Dibdale Rd DL2 . . . . .4 A1

Dick La BD22 . . . . .187 B6
Dick Scot La DL11 . . . . . .19 D7
Dickens Cl **1** YO32 . . . . .225 F1
Dickens Rd YO17 . . . . . . .215 C6
Dickey La YO8 . . . . .197 D3
Dickson Rd **4** YO24 . . . .227 B1
Dicky Grounds La
  YO17 . . . . .121 D8
Dijon Ave YO24 . . . . .227 C2
Dike La HG3 . . . . .159 C8
Dikehollin La DL8 . . . . . . .58 E2
Dikelands Cl **19** YO26 . . .165 F1
Dikelands La YO26 . . . . . .165 F1
Dikes La TS9 . . . . .8 C2
Dilys Gr **5** YO26 . . . . . . .227 E4
Dimmingdale Rd TS12 . . . .10 A3
Dinsdale Ave TS5 . . . . .6 E7
Dinsdale Cl **7** DL2 . . . . .4 C4
Dinsdale Ct **6** DL2 . . . . .4 C4
Dinsdale Dr TS16 . . . . .5 E5
Dinsdale La DL2 . . . . .4 C4
Diomed Ct TS7 . . . . .7 B7
Dishforth Airfield
  YO7 . . . . .115 A2
Dishforth Airfield CP Sch
  YO7 . . . . .115 B2
Dishforth C of E Prim Sch
  YO7 . . . . .114 F4
Dishforth Rd
  Copt Hewick HG4 . . . . . . .114 B2
  Sharow HG4 . . . . .214 F6
Disraeli Cl YO32 . . . . .225 E1
Dixon La YO1 . . . . .233 C1
Dixon Rd DL1 . . . . .219 D4
Dixon St BD20 . . . . .187 E1
Dixon Terr HG1 . . . . .219 D4
Dixons Bank TS8 . . . . .7 C5
Dixsons Yd YO1 . . . . .233 C2
Dob Park Rd LS21 . . . . . .176 F3
Dobella Ave DN14 . . . . . .205 A1
Dobella La DN14 . . . . . . .205 B1
Doctor Laithe **3** BD23 . .134 D2
Doctor's Hill LA2 . . . . . . .128 E8
Doctors La WF10 . . . . . . .200 D7
Doctor's La TS15 . . . . . . .25 C5
Dodder Carr Rd TS13 . . . .10 F3
Dodford Rd TS8 . . . . .6 F5
Dodgson La
  Lothersdale BD20 . . . . . .186 D8
  Thornton in Craven
  BB18 . . . . .172 C1
Dodgson Terr YO26 . . . . . .227 D4
Dodmire Jun & Inf Sch
  DL1 . . . . .3 E4
Dodsworth Ave YO31 . . . .228 E7
Doe Park La YO41 . . . . . .169 B3
Doe Pk YO30 . . . . .224 F2
Dog Hill DL8 . . . . .60 E3
Dog Hill Brow BD24 . . . . .131 A2
Dog Kennel La YO18 . . . . .96 C5
Dolegate YO41 . . . . .168 F4
Dolly La YO7 . . . . .64 C8
Dolphin Ctr The DL1 . . . . . .3 C5
Dolphin Way YO14 . . . . . .100 F5
Don Ave YO24 . . . . .230 E8
Don Pedro Ave WF6 . . . . .200 B1
Don Pedro Cl WF6 . . . . . .200 B1
Donald Smith Ct DL8 . . . .61 C5
Doncaster Rd
  Brayton YO8 . . . . .232 B3
  Knottingley WF11 . . . . . .201 E2
  North Elmsall WF9 . . . . . .206 A1
Doran Cl **45** YO14 . . . . .101 B3
Dorchester Rd LS24 . . . . .189 D5
Doriam Ave YO31 . . . . . . .225 F2
Doriam Dr YO31 . . . . .225 F2
Dorkings The TS9 . . . . . . .26 E5
Dorset Cl HG1 . . . . .219 A3
Dorset Cres HG1 . . . . . . .219 A3
Dorset Rd TS14 . . . . .8 E5
Dorset St BD23 . . . . .217 A3
Dorts Cres LS24 . . . . .190 C1
Dotcliffe Rd BB18 . . . . . .186 A7
Doublegates Ave **6**
  HG4 . . . . .113 D2
Doublegates Cl **8** HG4 . .113 D2
Doublegates Gn **9** HG4 .113 D2
Doublegates Wlk **7**
  HG4 . . . . .113 D2
Doubting Castle ★
  YO21 . . . . .10 D1
Douglas Cl TS18 . . . . .5 F7
Douglas St **3** YO8 . . . . .232 C5
Douky Bottom Cave ★
  BD23 . . . . .133 F7
Dove Cl LS22 . . . . .180 B4
Dove Cote Gdns DN14 . . .203 D2
Dove St YO23 . . . . .233 A1
Dove Way YO62 . . . . .94 C8
Dovecot Cl YO14 . . . . . . .100 E4
Dovecote Dr WF10 . . . . . .200 F4
Dovecote Garth **5**
  YO41 . . . . .185 B2
Dovecote Mews YO7 . . . . .115 C7
Dovedale Ave YO12 . . . . .212 D8
Dovelands Rd YO13 . . . . . .54 B4
Dovelands **14** BD20 . . . .187 E6
Dowber Way YO7 . . . . . . .211 D4
Dower Chase YO19 . . . . . .192 A6
Dower Pk YO19 . . . . .192 B6
Dowkell La LS23 . . . . .180 F1
Downdale Rd YO13 . . . . . .54 B4
Downdinner Hill YO8 . . . .208 C6
Downholme Rd DL9 . . . . .209 B1
Downland Cres WF11 . . . .202 A2
Downside Rd TS5 . . . . .6 D8
Dragon Ave HG1 . . . . .219 E3
Dragon Par HG1 . . . . .219 E3

Dragon Rd HG1 . . . . .219 E3
Dragon Terr HG1 . . . . .219 E3
Drake Cl YO21 . . . . .208 B5
Drake St **2** YO23 . . . . . .233 B1
Drakes Cl YO32 . . . . .225 F5
Drapers Croft YO23 . . . . .230 B4
Drax CP Sch YO8 . . . . . . .204 F5
Dreaken Fold **4** YO13 . . .99 A7
Drebley La BD23 . . . . .157 D6
Dresser Cl DL10 . . . . .209 C8
Driffield Rd YO25 . . . . . . .151 C4
Driffield Terr YO24 . . . . . .228 A2
Drift La HG4 . . . . .138 B8
Dringfield Cl **2** YO24 . . .230 D8
Dringhouses Prim Sch
  YO24 . . . . .230 F8
Dringthorpe Rd YO24 . . . .230 F7
Drive The
  Harrogate HG1 . . . . .220 C5
  Harrogate HG2 . . . . .222 B5
  7 High & Low Bishopside
  HG3 . . . . .137 C4
  Kippax LS25 . . . . .194 D1
  12 Swillington LS26 . . . .194 A1
  Threshfield BD23 . . . . . . .134 B3
Drome Rd YO23 . . . . .230 C2
Drovers Ct **8** YO61 . . . .143 C8
Drovers Way YO7 . . . . . . .211 D4
Drovers Wlk **3** BD23 . . .154 B3
Druggist La **16** LS29 . . . .174 F4
Druggon Rd DL9 . . . . .40 E3
Druids Mdw **3** YO51 . . .141 B5
Drummond View
  YO23 . . . . .231 B4
Drury Cl HG3 . . . . .222 F2
Drury La HG3 . . . . .222 F2
Drury St DL3 . . . . .3 C6
Dryden Cl HG1 . . . . .219 E7
Dryhurst Cl **9** DN6 . . . . .206 F2
Dubbing Garth La DL11 . . .37 B4
Dubb's La BD24 . . . . .81 C1
Duchess of Kents Military
  Hospl DL9 . . . . .40 F4
Duchy Ave
  3 Harrogate HG2 . . . . .219 C1
  11 Scalby YO13 . . . . . . .75 D5
Duchy Gr **4** HG2 . . . . . .219 C1
Duchy Nuffield Hospl
  HG2 . . . . .219 C1
Duchy Rd HG1 . . . . .219 B2
Duck Hill HG4 . . . . .214 C5
Duck La YO12 . . . . .125 C8
Duck St LA2 . . . . .128 A6
Duck St La HG3 . . . . .136 D2
Duckett Cl DL10 . . . . .209 F8
Duckett St BD23 . . . . .217 A3
Dudley Mews YO31 . . . . . .233 C4
Dudley Rd DL1 . . . . .4 A5
Dudley St YO31 . . . . .233 C4
Dudley Wlk HG4 . . . . .214 B3
Duffield Cres **1** LS25 . . .195 F4
Dugdale La BB7 . . . . .152 C1
Duke St
  6 Burton in Lonsdale LA6 .102 F3
  High Bentham LA2 . . . . . .129 A8
  Settle BD24 . . . . .131 D2
  Skipton BD23 . . . . .217 A4
  20 Trawden Forest BB8 . . .186 A3
Duke's La YO25 . . . . .126 A1
Dukes Wharf YO23 . . . . . .233 B1
Dukesway TS17 . . . . .6 B5
Dulverton Cl **13** WF8 . . .201 C2
Dulverton Rise WF8 . . . . .201 C2
Dulverton Way **12** WF8 . .201 C2
Dumb Tom's La LA6 . . . . .103 B1
Dumfries Sq **3** DL9 . . . . .40 E4
Duna Way YO62 . . . . .70 C3
Duncan Cl **6** HG1 . . . . . .219 C5
Duncan St HG1 . . . . .219 C5
Dunce Mire Rd LS25 . . . . .202 A8
Duncombe Cl
  2 Eastfield YO12 . . . . . .99 F7
  Malton YO17 . . . . .215 A4
Duncombe La YO32 . . . . . .167 B8
Duncombe Pk ★ YO62 . . . .92 E6
Duncombe Pl YO1 . . . . . . .233 B3
Dundas Gdns YO21 . . . . .208 B6
Dundas St
  Richmond DL10 . . . . .209 C7
  York YO1 . . . . .233 C2
Dunderdale Cres
  WF10 . . . . .201 B5
Dunelm Wlk DL1 . . . . .3 E7
Dunhill Rd DN14 . . . . . . .205 F2
Dunkeswick La LS17 . . . . .178 D4
Dunn Gr **3** YO11 . . . . . .100 A7
Dunnington C of E Prim Sch
  YO19 . . . . .184 E7
Dunnington Dr YO8 . . . . . .196 E1
Dunroyal Cl YO61 . . . . . . .141 F8
Dunroyal YO61 . . . . .141 F8
Dunsley Cres YO21 . . . . . .208 A6
Dunsley La YO21 . . . . .32 A1
Dunslow Ct **1** YO11 . . . . .99 F6
Dunslow Rd YO11 . . . . . . .99 F6
Dunsmore Ct TS8 . . . . .6 C4
Dunwell Ave **2** YO12 . . .212 B7
Durham La TS16 . . . . .5 D5
Durham Lane Ind Pk
  TS16 . . . . .5 D6
Durham Lane Prim Sch
  TS16 . . . . .5 D5
Durham Pl **5** YO12 . . . . .213 A7
Durham St
  6 Scarborough YO12 . . .212 E7
  6 Scarborough YO12 . . .213 A7
Durham Way HG3 . . . . . . .219 A5
Durlston Dr YO32 . . . . . . .167 A7

Duxbury St **11** BB18 . . . .172 B1
Dyke Hall La LA10 . . . . . . .78 A8
Dykelands Cl YO19 . . . . . .192 F7
Dykes La YO23 . . . . .230 A1
Dyon La YO8 . . . . .199 B3
Dyon Rd YO8 . . . . .199 D7
Dyson la DL11 . . . . .18 G7

E

Eagle Pk TS8 . . . . .7 C5
Eaglescliffe Sta TS16 . . . . .5 E6
Earby Springfield Prim Sch
  BB18 . . . . .172 B1
Earfit La YO23 . . . . .191 A8
Earl Edwin Dr DL10 . . . . .209 D8
Earle St YO31 . . . . .233 C4
Earlham St **10** BB18 . . . .172 B1
Earls Court Rd TS8 . . . . . . .6 F5
Earls View **3** BD20 . . . . .187 E6
Earlsdon Ave TS5 . . . . .6 D7
Earlsway TS17 . . . . .6 C5
Earswick Chase YO32 . . . .225 F7
Earswick Village YO32 . . .225 F7
Easby Abbey (rems of) ★
  DL10 . . . . .209 E5
Easby Ave TS5 . . . . .6 F8
Easby Cl **4** Bedale DL8 . . .63 B2
  7 Ilkley LS29 . . . . .175 C2
Easby Dr LS29 . . . . .175 C2
Easby La Easby TS9 . . . . . .27 A8
  Great Ayton TS9 . . . . .7 F1
Easby Low Rd DL10 . . . . .209 D7
Easingwold CP Sch
  YO61 . . . . .117 C1
Easingwold Sch YO61 . . . .143 C8
Eason Rd YO24 . . . . .230 E8
Eason View YO24 . . . . . . .230 E8
Easson Rd DL3 . . . . .3 C5
East Acres WF11 . . . . .201 F4
East Ave
  8 Easingwold YO61 . . . .143 D8
  18 Glusburn BD20 . . . . .187 E6
  21 Scalby YO13 . . . . . . .75 D5
East Ayton CP Sch
  YO13 . . . . .99 A8
East Bank **2** LS25 . . . . . .195 F4
East Barnby La YO21 . . . . .12 C3
East Beck Ct LS21 . . . . . .176 C3
East Brow Rd YO18 . . . . . .72 C4
East Carr **18** YO11 . . . . .100 B6
East Castle St **6** BD23 . .217 A3
East Cl DL2 . . . . .4 C7
East Comm La YO8 . . . . . .232 F4
East Cowton C of E Prim Sch
  DL7 . . . . .22 E1
East Cres YO21 . . . . .208 D7
East Down WF10 . . . . .201 A4
East End YO60 . . . . .145 D4
East Garforth Cty Prim Sch
  LS25 . . . . .194 D3
East Garforth Sta
  LS25 . . . . .194 D3
East Gate YO13 . . . . .98 D6
East Heslerton La
  YO17 . . . . .124 A8
East Ings La YO18 . . . . . . .95 F4
East La Ampleforth YO62 . . .92 D1
  Castle Bolton with East &
  West Bolton DL8 . . . . . . .59 B6
  Embsay BD23 . . . . .217 D7
  Yafforth DL7 . . . . .43 C1
East Lea View **21** YO11 . .100 B4
East Moor Gdns YO19 . . . .231 F5
East Mount YO17 . . . . . . .215 C4
East Mount Rd
  Darlington DL1 . . . . .3 D6
  York YO24 . . . . .233 A1
East Neville St **14** BD23 .217 A3
East Par Harrogate HG1 . . .219 E2
  Ilkley LS29 . . . . .218 C4
  York YO31 . . . . .228 E5
East Park Rd
  Harrogate HG1 . . . . .219 E2
  15 Scalby YO13 . . . . . . .75 D5
  5 Spofforth HG3 . . . . . .179 E5
East Rd Melsonby DL10 . . .20 F7
  Northallerton DL6 . . . . . .210 E4
  Norton YO17 . . . . .215 E3
East Sandgate **4** YO11 . .213 B6
East Side **5** TS15 . . . . . .25 D5
East St Gargrave BD23 . . .155 D1
  Gayles DL11 . . . . .19 E6
  Swinton YO17 . . . . .121 B4
East Terr YO17 . . . . .215 E3
East View Barton DL10 . . .21 D8
  7 Campsall DN6 . . . . . .206 E1
  Kippax LS25 . . . . .194 D1
  10 Knottingley WF11 . . . .202 A2
  Middleton St George DL2 . .4 D3
  Sherburn in Elmet LS25 . . .195 F3
  3 Trawden BB8 . . . . . . .186 B1
East View Ct HG5 . . . . . . .162 F3
East Way Whitby YO21 . . .208 B7
  York YO31 . . . . .225 E2
East Whitby CP Sch
  YO22 . . . . .208 F4
East Witton Rd DL8 . . . . . .60 E2
Eastborough YO11 . . . . . . .213 B6
Eastbourne Comp Sch
  DL1 . . . . .3 E5
Eastbourne Gdns TS3 . . . . .7 C8
Eastbourne Gr YO31 . . . . .228 F5
Eastbourne Rd DL1 . . . . . . .3 D5

Eastburn Jun & Inf Sch BD20 187 F7
Eastbury Cl TS17 6 B4
Eastby Rd HG1 219 F6
Eastern Terr YO31 228 E6
Easterside La YO62 67 F4
Easterside Prim Sch TS4 7 A7
Easterside Rd TS4 7 A7
Eastfield
Amotherby YO17 121 B4
Knaresborough HG5 221 D6
Eastfield Ave
Haxby YO32 225 C7
Norton YO17 215 E3
Richmond DL10 209 D8
Eastfield Cl LS24 189 F7
Eastfield Cres YO10 229 C2
Eastfield Ct YO10 229 C2
Eastfield Dr 14 WF8 201 C1
Eastfield Gr WF6 200 B2
Eastfield La
Dunnington YO19 184 F8
Kellington DN14 202 F4
Spennithorne DL8 61 A3
Thoralby DL8 58 E2
Eastfield Rd
Norton YO17 215 E3
Pickering YO18 96 A6
Eastfields TS9 26 C7
Eastgate 16 Helmsley YO62 92 F6
Pickering YO18 96 A6
3 Seamer YO12 99 D6
Eastholme Dr YO30 224 E1
Easthorpe Dr YO26 224 A1
Easton La YO21 29 D6
Eastward Ave YO10 231 E7
Eastway YO11 100 A7
Eastway Cl 2 YO62 70 C1
Eaton Ct 7 YO24 230 B8
Eaton Rd LS29 218 A3
Eavestone Gr HG3 219 A4
Ebenezer Terr 9 HG1 219 D2
Ebor Cl DL10 21 A1
Ebor Ct
Northallerton DL7 210 D3
7 Selby YO8 232 C6
Ebor Mount LS25 194 D1
Ebor Prep Sch YO30 228 A7
Ebor Rise HG1 219 B2
Ebor St Selby YO8 232 C5
York YO23 233 B1
Ebor Way
7 Poppleton YO26 165 F1
Poppleton YO26 224 A2
Ebsay Dr YO30 225 A1
Eden Ave YO8 232 D3
Eden Camp Modern History Mus* YO17 215 E8
Eden Cl
2 Hurworth-on-Tees DL2 3 D1
1 Hutton Rudby TS15 25 C4
York YO24 230 C7
Eden Cres DL1 3 C4
Eden Crest DL2 1 D7
Eden La DL2 1 D8
Eden Park Rd 2 TS15 25 C4
Eden Pk DL2 1 D7
Eden Rd DL7 210 B2
Edendale WF10 200 F4
Edenhouse Rd YO17 215 E8
Edens Way HG4 214 C2
Edge Dell YO12 99 E8
Edge La
Grassington BD23 134 F3
Long Preston BD23 153 E6
Edgecombe Dr DL3 3 A6
Edgehill Rd YO12 212 E2
Edgemoor Rd DL1 3 E3
Edgerton Cl LS24 189 D6
Edgerton Ct LS24 189 D6
Edgerton Dr LS24 189 D6
Edgerton Garth LS24 189 D6
Edgware Rd YO10 228 E2
Edinburgh Dr DL3 3 A4
Edmondson St 17 BB18 171 D2
Edmondson's La BD23 172 C5
Edmund Wilson Swimming Baths YO24 227 D1
Edward St
27 Earby BB18 172 A1
Pontefract WF6 200 A3
Egglescliffe C of E Sch TS16 5 E4
Egglescliffe Sch TS16 5 D4
Eggleston View DL3 3 A6
Eggshell La LA2 130 C8
Eglington Ave TS14 8 F6
Egremont Cl 11 YO41 168 D2
Egton Ave TS7 7 C5
Egton C of E Prim Sch YO21 31 B5
Egton Cliff YO21 31 A4
Egton La YO21 31 B3
Egton Sta YO21 31 A4
Eight Acre La HG4 113 A5
Eighth Ave YO31 228 F5
El Alamein Rd 5 DL9 209 C1
Elbolton Cave* BD23 156 E8
Elder Rd DL6 210 D4
Elder's St YO11 213 A6
Eldmire La YO7 115 D6
Eldon St YO31 233 C4
Eldon Terr YO31 233 C4
Eldroth Rd LA2 130 C5
Eldwick Cl YO30 224 F2
Eleanor Dr HG2 220 C1
Eleanor Rd HG2 220 C1
Electric Ave HG1 219 B5
Elgin Rd TS17 6 B6
Elgin St 16 YO21 208 D6
Elizabeth Ct
7 Selby YO8 232 B6
Sherburn in Elmet LS25 195 E4
Elizabeth Dr WF10 201 B4
Elizabethan Ct 4 WF8 201 C1
Elland Ct 12 DL1 3 F6
Ellarfield La LS25 195 F5
Ellen Gr HG1 220 C4
Ellenthorpe La YO51 141 D6
Eller Gates YO21 30 C6
Eller Gill La BD23 172 D4
Eller Mews 3 BD23 216 E3
Ellerbeck Ct TS9 26 D6
Ellerbeck Way
Great & Little Broughton TS9 26 D6
Middlesbrough TS7 7 D8
Whitby YO22 208 E4
Ellerburn Rd YO18 96 F7
Ellerby Bank TS13 11 F4
Ellerby La TS13 11 F5
Ellerclose Rd 23 DL8 60 D5
Ellerholme La DL11 38 F5
Ellerington Cl LA6 103 D3
Ellerker La LS14 188 A3
Ellerker Rd LS14 188 A3
Ellers La DL8 59 A2
Ellers Rd BD20 187 E6
Ellerton Priory (rems of)* DL11 39 A4
Ellerton Rd TS18 5 D8
Elliot Ct YO10 231 D7
Elliot St BD23 216 F4
Elliott St BD20 174 B1
Ellis Ct HG1 219 B2
Ellis La LS25 194 C5
Ellison Ave 32 YO12 75 D5
Ellwood Cotts BD24 131 D1
Elm Ave Kippax LS25 194 C2
Northallerton DL6 210 F5
Elm Cl
Barnoldswick BB18 171 D1
10 Filey YO14 101 B4
Hipswell DL9 209 F1
Northallerton DL6 210 F5
Elm Ct DL6 210 E5
Elm Dr TS7 7 B6
Elm End 9 YO32 166 E5
Elm Gn 7 YO62 92 F7
Elm Gr Sherburn YO17 124 D8
Thornaby TS17 6 B8
4 Whitby YO21 208 B6
York YO31 225 F2
Elm Pl WF11 201 F2
Elm Rd 34 Glusburn BD20 187 E7
Guisborough TS14 8 F7
Harrogate HG1 219 E5
Ripon HG4 214 B2
9 Scarborough YO12 212 E4
3 Topcliffe YO7 89 B1
Elm St YO8 232 D6
Elm Tree Ave 9 YO26 165 F1
Elm Tree Rise HG3 140 B5
Elm Tree Sq BD23 217 D8
Elm View YO18 96 A6
Elm Wlk 6 DL10 41 D5
Elma Gr YO30 224 E2
Elmet Dr LS15 194 C8
Elmet Rd LS15 194 C7
Elmete Ave LS25 195 F4
Elmete Rd WF10 201 B5
Elmfield Ave YO31 228 F8
Elmfield Rd
3 Glusburn BD20 187 F8
Hurworth DL2 3 D1
Hurworth-on-Tees DL2 22 D8
Elmfield Terr YO31 228 F7
Elmlands Gr YO31 228 F8
Elmpark Vale YO31 229 A8
Elmpark View YO31 229 A8
Elmpark Way YO31 229 A8
Elms Cl 2 YO19 191 F1
Elmslac Cl
9 Helmsley YO62 92 F6
1 Helmsley YO62 92 F6
Elmslac Rd 3 YO62 92 F7
Elmtree Gdns 3 YO26 227 C3
Elmville Ave YO12 212 E6
Elmwood Ave LS15 194 B8
Elmwood Chase LS15 194 B8
Elmwood Cl 6 TS9 26 C8
Elmwood La LS15 194 B8
Elmwood Rd TS16 5 E6
Elmwood St 4 HG1 219 E4
Elphin Bridge La YO61 117 B6
Elslack La BD23 172 C4
Elston Cl YO30 228 A8
Elston Pl YO8 232 C6
Eltham Cres TS17 6 C6
Elton La HG3 160 E6
Elton Par DL3 3 B5
Elton Rd DL3 3 B5
Elvington C of E Prim Sch YO41 185 B3
Elvington Ind Est YO41 185 A3
Elvington La YO19 184 E5
Elvington Pk YO41 185 A3
Elvington Terr YO10 228 E4
Elwick Ave TS5 6 E7
Elwick Gr YO10 229 C4
Elwick La YO26 164 B7
Ely Cl HG3 219 A5
Embleton Dr 1 YO30 224 F1
Embleton Rd LS26 200 B4
Embsay C of E Prim Sch BD23 217 D8
Embsay Junc BD23 217 C6
Embsay Sta BD23 217 D7
Embsay Steam Rly* BD23 217 E7
Emerald St YO31 233 C4
Emerson Ave TS5 6 F8
Emerson Cl 2 DL6 25 D1
Emerson Rd DL2 3 E1
Emery Cl DL2 3 E1
Emgate 2 DL8 63 A3
Emley Moor Rd DL1 3 E4
Emmerson St 2 YO31 228 E5
Emmet La HG3 160 C5
Emmott Ct BB8 186 C3
Emmott La BB8 186 B4
Emsworth Dr TS16 5 D5
Enclosure Gdns 1 YO10 229 B1
Endcliff Cres YO12 212 D8
Endeavour Wharf 6 YO21 208 D6
Endfields Rd 1 YO10 231 E8
Endsleigh Dr TS5 6 D8
Enfield Chase TS14 8 F5
Enfield Cl 4 DL9 40 E4
Enfield Cres
2 York YO24 227 F3
1 York YO24 228 A3
Engine Shed La BD23 216 D3
England La WF11 201 F2
English Martyrs RC Prim Sch YO24 227 F3
Ennerdale Ave YO31 229 B5
Enter La LA6 103 D3
Enterpen TS15 25 C4
Enterprise Way
Bradleys Both BD20 173 D4
Sherburn in Elmet LS25 196 B4
Whitby YO22 32 F8
Eppleby Forcett C of E Prim Sch DL11 1 D4
Epsom Ct 11 DL1 3 F6
Eridge Rd TS14 8 F6
Ermysted St 4 BD23 217 A4
Ermysteds Gram Sch BD23 216 F4
Eryholme La DL2 22 F7
Escrick C of E Prim Sch YO19 192 A5
Escrick Ct YO19 192 B5
Escrick Park Gdns YO19 192 B5
Escrick St YO10 233 C1
Esher Ave TS6 7 E8
Eshington La DL8 58 F2
Eshton Rd BD23 155 D2
Esk Dr YO26 227 B8
Esk Leisure Ctr YO21 208 C7
Esk Rd DL1 3 D3
Eskdale Ave
Normanton WF6 200 A2
York YO10 229 C3
Eskdale Cl
5 Pontefract WF6 200 A2
Sleights YO22 32 A5
Eskdale Croft WF6 200 A2
Eskdale Ct 12 WF6 200 A2
Eskdale Cty Modern Sch YO22 208 E3
Eskdale Rd YO22 208 F3
Eskdaleside YO22 31 F5
Eskew La LA2 128 E7
Eskitt Hill YO12 212 D4
Esp La BB18 171 C1
Esplanade
Harrogate HG2 219 C2
Scarborough YO11 213 A4
Whitby YO21 208 D7
York YO26 233 A2
Esplanade Cres YO11 213 B2
Esplanade Gdns YO11 213 A4
Esplanade Rd YO11 213 A3
Estell La YO13 74 C5
Estill Cl 2 YO11 100 B6
Estoril Rd S DL1 3 F4
Ethel Cres HG5 221 C6
Ethel St 12 BB18 171 E1
Etive Pl YO24 230 B7
Eton Dr 7 YO32 166 D5
Eton Rd Goole DN14 205 F3
Middlesbrough TS5 6 E8
Ettersgill Dr DL3 3 A5
Ettington Ave TS3 7 B8
Etty Ave YO10 229 A4
Euclid Ave HG1 219 B5
Eva Ave YO30 224 D2
Evelyn Cres YO30 228 B7
Evelyn Ct 5 HG3 161 B2
Evelyn Dr YO12 212 D4
Evergreen Way 1 YO8 197 D1
Everingham Rd TS15 5 D2
Eversley Ave LS25 195 F3
Eversley Ct LS25 195 F4
Eversley Garth Cres LS25 195 F4
Eversley Mount LS25 195 F3
Evesham Rd TS3 7 B8
Ewart St YO12 212 E3
Ewden Cl 16 YO14 101 A3
Ewe Leys La YO7 66 A5
Ewelands Hill YO7 90 C7
Exchange St 8 WF6 200 A1
Exelby Cl DL8 63 D1
Exelby La DL7 63 D3
Exeter Cres 10 HG3 161 B3
Exeter Dr DL1 3 F7
Express Way WF6 200 A3

F

Faber Cl YO23 230 B3
Faber St YO31 228 E5
Faceby Rd TS9 26 A2
Fadmoor Bank YO62 69 E6
Fadmoor La YO62 69 F4
Fair Head La YO22 31 D4
Fairburn Cty Prim Sch WF11 201 D6
Fairburn Dr LS25 194 D3
Fairburn Sports & Recn Ctr WF11 201 D6
Fairfax 15 YO41 168 D2
Fairfax Ave
Harrogate HG2 220 B2
North Featherstone WF7 200 E1
Selby YO8 232 B4
Fairfax Cl
2 Ampleforth YO62 92 C1
Bolton Percy YO23 190 D4
Fairfax Cres YO26 181 C7
Fairfax Croft YO23 230 B2
Fairfax House* YO1 233 C2
Fairfax Rd DL2 4 D4
Fairfax St
1 Scarborough YO12 212 E5
10 Skipton BD23 217 A3
York YO1 233 B1
Fairfax Wlk 3 HG2 220 B3
Fairfield
Fairburn WF11 201 D7
Thirsk YO7 211 C4
Fairfield Ave TS7 7 D7
Fairfield Cl 16 LS25 195 F4
Fairfield Cres YO12 212 B8
Fairfield La LS25 202 A6
Fairfield Link LS25 195 F4
Fairfield Rd
Staithes TS13 13 K2
Stokesley TS9 26 B7
Tadcaster LS24 189 E6
Fairfield St DL3 3 C6
Fairfield Way
9 Tadcaster LS24 189 E6
Whitby YO22 208 F3
Fairfields Dr YO30 224 B5
Fairheath Rd LA2 128 E5
Fairholme La DL7 64 A4
Fairmead Ct YO22 208 E4
Fairmead Way YO22 208 E4
Fairview TS21 5 A7
Fairview Gdns DL10 209 C8
Fairway
Normanton South WF6 200 B1
4 Scalby YO12 75 E5
York YO30 228 A8
Fairway App WF6 200 B1
Fairway Ave WF6 200 B1
Fairway Cl
8 Normanton South WF6 200 B1
15 Sherburn in Elmet LS25 195 F4
Fairway Dr
Normanton South WF6 200 B1
18 Poppleton YO26 165 F1
Fairway Gdns 4 WF6 200 B1
Fairway Mdws 9 WF6 200 B1
Fairway The
Darlington DL1 3 E5
Middlesbrough TS8 7 C5
8 North Featherstone WF7 200 E1
Northallerton DL7 210 C3
Sherburn in Elmet LS25 195 F4
Tadcaster LS24 189 E5
Fairways Ave HG2 220 E3
Fairways Cl HG2 220 E3
Fairways Dr HG2 220 D3
Fairwood Pk TS8 7 C5
Fairy Hill La WF8 201 B3
Fairy La YO18 71 C3
Falcon Ave 7 YO12 99 E6
Falcon Cl 10 Haxby YO32 166 F5
1 Scotton DL9 40 F2
17 Settle BD24 131 D2
Falcon Dr WF10 200 E3
Falcon Gdns 20 BD24 131 D2
Falcon Terr 11 YO21 208 D6
Falcon Way TS14 8 D6
Falcon Wlk TS15 6 C2
Falconberg Way TS15 5 D2
Falconer St 11 YO24 227 F3
Falconers Rd YO11 213 A5
Falkland Rd 2 DL9 40 F5
Falkland St YO1 233 B1
Fall La Pannal HG3 222 B2
Thornthwaite with Padside HG3 159 A6
Falling Foss (Waterfall)* YO22 32 C2
Fallow Field 1 BD23 217 B5
Falmer Rd DL1 3 D4
Falmouth Ave WF6 200 A2
Falmouth Cres 20 WF6 200 A2
Falmouth Dr DL3 3 C8
Falmouth Rd WF6 200 A2
Falsgrave Cres YO30 228 B7
Falsgrave Mews 6 YO12 212 E5
Falsgrave Rd YO12 212 F5
Fanacurt Rd TS14 8 D6
Fancy Bank TS14 9 B6
Fanny La Knayton YO7 65 F2
Stutton with Hazlewood LS24 189 D4
Far La
Hutton Buscel YO13 98 F8
Kettlewell with Starbotton BD23 108 A3
Far Mead Croft 3 LS29 176 C1
Farfield YO26 227 C6
Farfield Ave HG5 221 C4
Farfield La YO19 184 E8
Farfield Mount 2 HG5 221 C4
Farfields Cl TS21 4 F6
Farm Cl YO21 208 A7
Farm Croft BD23 216 F1
Farm Garth TS9 8 A2
Farm La TS17 6 A5
Farm Way YO8 232 B7
Farmanby Cl 12 YO18 96 D5
Farmbank Rd TS7 7 E7
Farmers Way YO23 230 B3
Farmlands Rd 1 YO24 230 D8
Farmstead Rise YO32 225 D7
Farnborough Ct 10 DL2 4 C4
Farndale Ave
Northallerton DL7 210 C2
York YO10 229 D4
Farndale Cl 1 YO32 166 F5
Farndale Cres DL3 3 B6
Farndale Dr TS14 8 D6
Farndale Rd HG5 221 D6
Farndale St YO10 228 D2
Farnham La HG5 162 D7
Farnley C of E Prim Sch LS21 177 B3
Farnley Hall* LS21 177 B2
Farnley La LS21 177 B2
Farnley Pk LS21 177 C2
Farrar St YO10 228 E3
Farriers Croft 2 YO23 230 B3
Farside Garth YO13 75 D6
Farside Rd YO13 99 A7
Farthingale Way TS8 6 E4
Favell Ave WF6 200 A1
Faven Field Rd YO7 211 D4
Faverdale DL3 3 B7
Faverdale N DL3 3 B7
Faverdale Rd DL3 3 B7
Faverdale W DL3 3 B7
Favordale Rd BB8 186 A3
Fawcett Ave TS8 6 E4
Fawcett St YO10 233 C1
Fawdington Rd YO61 115 F2
Fawkes Dr YO26 227 C4
Fearby Rd Fearby HG4 85 F4
Masham HG4 86 A4
7 Stockton-on-Tees TS18 5 D8
Fearnhead TS8 7 C5
Feasegate YO1 233 B2
Featherbeck Cl LA6 103 D3
Featherbed La
Bilton-in-Ainsty with Bickerton LS24 181 C3
Ellerbeck DL6 44 E4
Federation St 12 BB18 171 D1
Feeding Pasture La YO60 147 B7
Feetham Ave DL1 3 F7
Feethams Sports Gd DL1 3 C5
Felbrigg La TS17 6 A4
Feldom La DL11 19 E1
Felixstowe Dr 10 DL9 40 E4
Fell La Cracoe BD23 156 B7
Winton CA17 14 C8
Fell Rd LA6 77 A4
Fell View BD23 217 E8
Fell View Sq 4 BD23 134 E2
Fellbrook Ave YO26 227 B4
Felliscliffe Cty Prim Sch HG3 160 C4
Fenby Ave DL1 3 E4
Fence Dike La DL7 63 C7
Fenton Ave BB18 171 E2
Fenton Cl 10 YO11 100 B7
Fenton La Malton YO17 215 C8
Sherburn in Elmet LS25 196 A5
Fenton St Boosbeck TS12 9 D7
38 Burley in Warfedale LS29 176 C1
Fenwick Cl 1 YO11 100 B6
Fenwick Comm La DN6 207 D2
Fenwick La DN6 207 B1
Fenwick St YO23 228 C2
Fenwick's La YO10 231 D7
Ferguson Cl DL7 210 C3
Ferguson Way YO32 225 F1
Fern Bank Ave BB18 171 D2
Fern Cl YO32 226 A4
Fern Gdns 1 LS29 218 A3
Fern St YO31 233 C4
Ferndale Rd YO8 232 C4
Fernie Rd TS14 8 F5
Fernlea Cl YO8 232 D4
Fernley Green Cl 6 WF11 202 A2
Fernway YO10 229 C3
Fernwood TS8 7 A4
Fernwood Cl 9 DL6 43 F3
Ferry Cl 11 YO8 198 F1
Ferry Farm Cl 2 YO19 191 D8
Ferry La Airmyn DN14 205 F4
Bishopthorpe YO23 231 B4
Bubwith YO8 199 C5
Snaith & Cowick DN14 204 C1

Ferry La *continued*
Thorganby YO19 193 B5
Ferrybridge By-Pass
WF11 201 E3
Ferrybridge Inf Sch
WF11 201 E3
Ferrybridge Rd
Castleford WF10 200 F4
Pontefract WF8 201 C1
Ferrybridge Service Area
WF11 201 E1
Fetter La YO1 233 B2
Feversham Cres 4
YO31 228 C7
Feversham Dr 16 YO62 70 B1
Feversham Rd YO62 92 F7
Fewster Way YO10 233 C1
Fewston Cl 11 YO14 101 A3
Fewston Cres HG1 219 B4
Fewston Dr 9 YO30 224 F1
Field Ave YO8 197 B1
Field Cl YO21 208 A7
Field Cl Rd 16 YO13 75 D5
Field Dr 1 Pickering YO18 95 F6
Tadcaster LS24 189 F7
Field Gr 7 DL9 40 E3
Field Head YO41 185 F6
Field House Rd 2 YO21 208 C7
Field La Aberford LS25 194 F8
Burniston YO13 75 D8
Gowdall DN14 207 F8
Hambleton YO8 196 F1
Hensall DN14 203 D2
Heslington YO10 229 C2
Newby & Scalby YO13 75 E5
Rawcliffe DN14 205 A1
Wistow YO8 197 C7
Field Lane Sports Ctr
YO8 197 B1
Field Rd YO8 203 A5
Field View
Norton YO17 215 E2
York YO31 228 C7
Fieldhead Cl 12 WF8 201 C1
Fieldhead Dr
Barwick in Elmet LS15 194 C8
15 Glusburn BD20 187 E7
Fieldhead Paddock
LS23 188 E8
Fielding's Yd DL10 209 A7
Fieldside YO12 212 D7
Fieldstead Cres YO12 212 B8
Fieldway
Harrogate HG1 219 F7
Ilkley LS29 218 E4
Fieldway Cl HG1 219 F7
Fifth Ave 24 Colburn DL9 41 A5
York YO31 228 F4
Filey Ave HG4 214 A6
Filey Brigg Nature Reserve★
YO14 101 D4
Filey C of E Inf Sch
YO14 101 B3
Filey Cl 12 DL9 40 E4
Filey CP Sch YO14 101 B3
Filey Folk Mus★ YO14 101 B3
Filey Rd Folkton YO11 100 A2
Hunmanby YO14 127 A8
Scarborough YO11 213 A2
Filey Sch YO14 101 A3
Filey Sta YO14 101 B3
Filey Terr YO30 228 C7
Finden Gdns HG3 160 F5
Fine Garth Cl LS23 188 E6
Finkills Way DL7 210 C6
Finkle Cl 4 HG4 214 C5
Finkle Hill LS25 195 F5
Finkle St Hensall DN14 203 D2
12 Knaresborough HG5 221 A6
Malham BD23 133 A1
3 Malton YO17 215 C4
Richmond DL10 209 C6
5 Ripon HG4 214 C5
Selby YO8 232 C5
Sheriff Hutton YO60 145 C5
Thirsk YO7 211 C3
Finsbury Ave YO23 228 C1
Finsbury St YO23 228 C1
Fir Gr TS17 6 B8
Fir Heath Cl 5 YO24 227 C1
Fir Tree Cl Hilton TS15 6 C2
Thorpe Willoughby YO8 197 B2
Fir Tree Dr Filey YO14 101 B4
11 Norton DN6 206 E2
Fir Tree La YO8 197 B2
Fir Tree View LS26 200 C6
Fir Tree Way YO8 197 B2
Fir Trees The YO8 197 B2
Firbank Cl 9 YO32 167 A7
Firbeck Rd LS23 188 E6
Firby La HG4 214 B5
Firby Rd Bedale DL8 63 A2
Richmond DL10 209 B8
Firs Ave Harrogate HG2 222 E6
Ripon HG4 214 D4
Firs Cl HG2 222 E6
Firs Cres HG2 222 E5
Firs Dr HG2 222 E6
Firs Gate HG2 222 E5
Firs Gr HG2 222 E5
Firs Rd HG2 222 E6
Firs View HG2 222 E5
First Ave 23 Colburn DL9 41 A5
Harrogate HG2 220 C3
Menwith with Darley
HG3 160 A4
10 Pickering YO18 95 F7
9 Wetherby LS22 180 C3

First Ave *continued*
York YO31 228 F6
First Comm La YO8 197 D4
Firth Moor Jun Sch DL1 3 F4
Firth St BD23 217 A2
Firthfields LS25 194 D4
Firthland Rd YO18 95 F7
Firthmoor Cres DL1 3 E4
Firtree Ave TS6 7 E8
Firtree Cl
4 Earswick YO32 225 F7
York YO24 227 E3
Firtree Cres LS24 189 D5
Firville Ave WF6 200 A1
Firwood Whin 5 YO32 225 F3
Fishbeck La BD20 174 D2
Fishburn Rd 4 YO21 208 D5
Fisher Green La HG4 214 F4
Fisher Row 14 HG4 86 C3
Fisher St 6 HG5 221 B5
Fishergate
3 Boroughbridge YO51 141 B5
Knottingley WF11 201 E3
17 Ripon HG4 214 C5
York YO10 233 C1
Fishergate Prim Sch
YO10 233 C1
Fishergreen HG4 214 D4
Fishers Garth 10 YO18 95 F6
Fitzalan Rd 18 DL8 63 A2
Fitzjohn Cl YO17 215 C6
Fitzwilliam Dr
Darlington DL1 3 D7
Malton YO17 215 A4
Five Hills La DL10 21 D5
Five Lane Ends HG4 86 D5
Flake La TS13 12 A3
Flamingo Land Zoo & Family Funpark★ YO17 95 D2
Flashley Carr La DN6 207 F1
Flask La DL8 87 C3
Flass La WF10 200 E3
Flat Cliffs YO14 101 C1
Flat La
Bolton-on-Swale DL10 41 E6
Hellifield BD23 153 F3
Flats Bank DL11 19 F6
Flats La
Barwick in Elmet LS15 194 B7
Thirkleby High & Low
with Osgodby YO7 90 D1
West Witton DL8 59 D4
Flatts La
Eston & South Bank TS6 7 F7
Welburn YO62 94 A7
Wombleton YO62 93 F6
Flavian Gr YO30 227 F8
Flaxdale Cl 4 HG5 221 D6
Flaxley Ct YO8 232 B5
Flaxley Rd YO8 232 A7
Flaxman Ave YO10 229 A4
Flaxman Croft YO23 230 B3
Flaxmill Cl DL11 18 G7
Flaxton Rd YO32 167 B7
Fleck Way TS17 6 B5
Fleet Bank La YO61 143 C1
Fleet La
Barmby on the Marsh
DN14 205 A7
Mickletown LS26 200 A6
Tockwith YO26 181 C7
Fleetham La
Cundall with Leckby YO7 115 C4
Kirkby Fleetham with Fencote
DL7 63 C8
Fleets La BD23 156 A6
Fleming Ave 3 YO31 228 E7
Fletcher Ct 14 YO32 166 E5
Fletcher's Croft YO23 230 C3
Flintmill La LS23 180 E2
Flints Terr DL10 209 C7
Flixton Carr La YO11 99 F4
Flock Leys 24 YO13 75 D5
Flora Ave DL3 3 B5
Florence Ct 12 YO51 141 B5
Florence Gr YO30 224 D2
Florence Rd HG2 219 B1
Flotmanby La YO14 100 D2
Flow Edge DL8 57 F7
Flower Ct 19 YO11 100 B6
Flower Garth
40 Filey YO14 101 B3
Scarborough YO12 212 C6
Flowergate 12 YO21 208 D7
Fog La YO42 193 E4
Fold La BD22 187 B6
Fold The Filey YO14 101 B1
Thornton in Craven
BD23 172 A3
Foldshaw La HG3 159 C8
Folk Mus★ DL11 38 C6
Folks Cl 13 YO32 166 F5
Follifoot C of E Prim Sch
HG3 223 F4
Follifoot La HG3 223 B2
Follifoot Rd HG3 222 F3
Folliott Ward Cl YO17 215 B5
Folly La
Barnoldswick BB18 171 D1
Bramham cum Oglethorpe
LS23 188 E5
Folly View 2 LS23 188 E5
Fontenay Rd DL10 209 D8
Fonteyn Ct TS8 6 F5
Forcett Cl
East Layton DL11 20 C8
Middlesbrough TS5 6 E7
Forcett Gdns DL11 1 D3

Forcett La DL10 20 D5
Fordlands YO8 197 B2
Fordlands Cres YO19 231 E5
Fordlands Rd YO19 231 E6
Fordon La
Willerby YO12 125 E7
Wold Newton YO25 126 A6
Fordon Pl TS4 7 A8
Fordyce Rd TS8 6 E4
Fore La Cowesby YO7 66 B4
West Tanfield DL8 87 D3
Whorlton DL6 25 F1
Foreshore Rd YO11 213 A5
Forest Ave HG2 220 D3
Forest Cl
3 Harrogate HG2 220 D3
27 Haxby YO32 166 E5
Forest Cres HG2 220 D4
Forest Dr Colburn DL9 41 A5
Dishforth YO7 115 A4
Middlesbrough TS7 7 D7
Forest Gdns HG2 220 D3
Forest Gr
Harrogate HG2 220 D3
York YO31 228 F6
Forest Grange Cl 2
HG2 220 D4
Forest La Alne YO61 143 B5
Fulford YO19 184 A2
Harrogate HG2 220 D3
Kirklevington TS15 24 D8
Strensall YO32 167 A8
Forest Lane Head
HG2 220 D5
Forest Moor Dr HG5 220 F3
Forest Moor Rd HG5 220 E3
Forest Mount 3 HG2 220 D4
Forest of Galtres Prim Sch
YO30 165 F5
Forest Rd
Appletreewick HG3 157 F8
Northallerton DL6 210 E5
Pickering YO18 96 A6
Forest Rise HG2 220 D3
Forest Sch The HG5 221 C6
Forest Way
Harrogate HG2 220 D3
York YO31 228 F6
Foresters Ct 5 YO12 75 F5
Foresters Wlk YO41 168 C1
Forester's Wlk YO24 227 B1
Forestgate YO32 225 C7
Forge Cl YO32 226 A2
Forge Gn HG3 223 F4
Forge Hill La WF11 201 F3
Forge La
Deighton YO19 192 A7
Kirkby Fleetham with Fencote
DL7 42 C1
Tollerton YO61 143 A3
Forge Valley Wood Reserve★
YO13 75 A1
Forge Way DL1 3 D6
Forkers La YO17 122 D2
Forrester's Cl 3 DN6 206 E2
Forth St YO26 227 F6
Fortune Cl HG5 220 E7
Fortune Hill HG5 220 E8
Foss Ave LS22 180 B4
Foss Bank YO31 233 C3
Foss Ct YO31 225 E1
Foss Field La YO23 191 B8
Foss Garth YO41 185 F5
Foss Islands Rd YO31 233 C3
Foss La YO22 32 C2
Foss Wlk YO26 227 B8
Fossdale Cl 5 HG5 221 D6
Fosse Way LS25 194 D3
Fossgate YO1 233 C2
Fossland View 4 YO32 167 A7
Fossway
Stamford Bridge YO41 168 D1
York YO31 228 D7
Foster Ave
Normanton South WF6 200 A1
Silsden BD20 174 B1
Foster Cl 31 LS29 176 C1
Foster Gate YO8 232 D4
Foster Rd 4 BB18 171 D2
Foster Wlk LS25 195 F4
Fostergate YO8 197 A8
Foston C of E Prim Sch
YO60 146 A3
Foston Gr 4 YO31 228 F8
Foston La YO60 146 B2
Fother Ingay Dr DL1 3 F8
Fothergill Way 3 YO51 141 B4
Fothill La YO13 98 E6
Foulbridge La YO13 97 F3
Foulds Rd BB8 186 A1
Foulgate Nook La
HG4 112 B6
Foundry La 5 WF11 202 A2
Fountain St TS14 8 F6
Fountains Abbey★
HG4 139 B7
Fountains Ave
Boston Spa LS23 188 E8
Harrogate HG1 219 F6
Ingleby TS17 6 B5
Fountains C of E Prim Sch
HG4 138 D8
Fountains Cl
Guisborough TS14 8 F6
1 Whitby YO21 208 C6
Fountains Dr TS5 6 E8
Fountains Gate HG4 112 F1
Fountains La HG4 139 B7

Fountains Mill★ HG4 139 B7
Fountains Pl DL6 210 E6
Fountains Rd DL6 210 E6
Fountains View DL3 3 A6
Fountains Way
Knaresborough HG5 221 C4
Morton-on-Swale DL7 64 A7
Fountayne Rd
13 Hunmanby YO14 126 F8
13 Hunmanby YO14 126 F8
Fountayne St YO31 228 C7
Four La Ends
Burythorpe YO17 147 D4
Lawkland BD24 130 F3
Four Lanes Ends BB7 152 C1
Four Riggs DL3 3 C5
Fouracre Dr 11 YO22 32 A6
Fourth Ave
26 Colburn DL9 41 A5
York YO31 228 E5
Fox Cl 6 DL2 22 D8
Fox Covert YO31 225 F2
Fox Covert Cl 15 DL8 63 B3
Fox Covert Rd WF8 206 C1
Fox Ct HG1 219 E4
Fox Garth
5 Brafferton YO61 115 F1
Poppleton YO26 224 A3
Fox Glade YO41 168 C2
Fox Heads La LS22 179 D4
Fox Hill La YO8 232 A3
Fox La
Chapel Haddlesey YO8 203 C5
Hambleton LS25 196 D1
Thornton-le-Dale YO18 96 C3
Thorpe Willoughby YO8 197 B1
Fox Terr WF8 201 C1
Foxberry Ave TS5 6 D6
Foxbridge Way WF6 200 C2
Foxcliff WF11 201 E5
Foxcroft 3 YO32 225 C7
Foxdale Ave YO8 197 B1
Foxglove Cl
2 Killinghall HG3 161 B3
Northallerton DL7 210 C1
Foxglove Ct 19 DL9 41 A5
Foxhill La YO8 232 A3
Foxholme La HG4 86 B3
Foxthorn Paddock
YO10 229 D3
Foxton Cl YO24 230 C8
Foxton La DL6 44 E2
Foxwood La
3 York YO24 227 C1
York YO24 230 C8
Foxwood Sch BD24 105 C4
Frances Rd DL10 209 C7
Frances St YO10 228 D1
Francis Ct 7 YO8 197 B2
Frank La YO26 164 F4
Frank St
24 Barnoldswick BB18 171 D1
4 Barnoldswick BB18 171 E1
9 Barnoldswick BB18 171 E1
Franklin Mount HG1 219 D4
Franklin Rd HG1 219 D3
Franklin Sq HG1 219 D4
Franklin St 7 YO12 212 F6
Frank's La YO26 164 A5
Fraser Rd 8 TS18 5 E8
Frazer Ct YO30 227 E8
Frederic St YO30 233 A3
Freebrough Rd TS12 10 A4
Freehold La YO17 215 D8
Freely La LS23 188 E5
Freeman's Way HG3 223 D8
Freemans Way
Leeming DL7 63 C4
Wetherby LS22 180 D3
Freeston Ct 16 WF6 200 A2
Freeston Dr 18 WF6 200 A2
French Rd DL9 209 C2
French St HG1 219 F4
Frenchgate DL10 209 C6
Friarage CP Sch YO11 213 B6
Friarage Gdns DL6 210 D5
Friarage Hospl DL6 210 E5
Friarage Mount DL6 210 E5
Friarage St DL6 210 D5
Friargate
Scarborough YO11 213 A6
York YO1 233 B2
Friars Cl YO19 184 D7
Friar's Gdns 10 YO11 213 A6
Friars Hill YO62 95 A8
Friars Mdw YO8 232 C8
Friars Pardon DL2 3 E1
Friar's Way 11 YO11 213 A6
Friar's Wlk YO31 228 E8
Friary Com Hospl
DL10 209 B7
Friendship Ct 2 YO8 232 C6
Frith Mews 4 YO8 232 C6
Frobisher Dr 5 YO21 208 C5
Frogmire Cl 4 HG5 221 B7
Frogmire Dr HG5 221 B7
Frogmire Rd HG5 221 B7
Front Nook 2 DL8 58 F1
Front St
Appleton Wiske DL6 24 B3
6 Bramham LS23 188 E5
Burton Fleming YO25 126 E3
Burton Leonard HG3 140 A2
Castleford WF10 200 F3
Grosmont YO22 31 C4
Langtoft YO25 151 C5
Lastingham YO62 70 E5
Naburn YO19 191 D8

Front St *continued*
Thirsk YO7 211 C1
Topcliffe YO7 115 C7
Wold Newton YO25 126 A4
York YO24 227 C3
Front The DL2 4 D3
Fryer Cres DL1 3 F7
Fryston Comm La
LS25 202 A8
Fryston La WF11 201 C3
Fryston Rd WF10 201 B5
Fryton La YO62 120 A7
Fryup Cres TS14 8 E5
Fulbeck Rd TS3 7 D8
Fulford Cross YO10 228 D1
Fulford Cross Specl Sch
YO10 228 D1
Fulford Pk YO10 231 D7
Fulford Rd
Scarborough YO11 212 F3
York YO10 231 D8
Fulford Sch YO10 231 E7
Fulfordgate YO10 231 E7
Fulham La DN14 206 E7
Fuller-Good Rd 14 DL10 41 E4
Fullicar La DL6 43 F3
Fulmar Head TS14 8 D6
Fulthorpe Ave DL3 3 A5
Fulthorpe Gr DL3 3 A5
Fulwith Ave HG2 222 E5
Fulwith Cl HG2 222 F5
Fulwith Dr HG2 222 F5
Fulwith Gate HG2 222 F5
Fulwith Gr HG2 222 F5
Fulwith Mill La HG2 222 F5
Fulwith Rd HG2 222 F5
Fummerber La LA2 130 C5
Furlong Rd 23 YO41 168 D2
Furlongs Ave YO17 215 F3
Furnace La HG4 87 A1
Furness Dr
Bentham LA2 129 A8
York YO30 224 E1
Furnessford Rd LA2 128 D6
Furnwood 2 YO32 225 D7
Furrows The 16 YO11 100 B7
Fushetts La LA2 129 A8
Fyling Rd YO21 208 A6
Fylingdales Ave 6
YO30 224 E1
Fylingdales C of E Prim Sch
YO22 33 C4

G

Gable Ct YO7 115 A4
Gable Pk YO23 182 C6
Gables Cl 8 DN14 202 D4
Gables The
15 Hurworth-on-Tees DL2 3 E1
Knaresborough HG5 221 A8
Middlesbrough TS7 7 B6
Scriven HG5 162 C5
Gainford C of E Prim Sch
DL2 1 C7
Gainforth Wath Rd
YO13 53 F5
Gainsborough Ct
BD23 216 E4
Gaits DL8 56 C4
Gale Bank DL8 60 B3
Gale Farm Ct 6 YO24 227 C3
Gale Garth YO61 142 F4
Gale Gate YO26 142 A1
Gale La Beadlam YO62 93 D6
Stainburn LS21 177 E3
Thorganby YO19 192 F4
York YO24 227 C2
Gale Rd YO61 142 F4
Gale The YO19 191 D4
Gallabar La YO51 141 E1
Galley Hill Prim Sch
TS14 8 D6
Galligap La YO10 229 C4
Gallogate La LS17 178 C1
Gallops The
Norton YO17 215 E2
York YO24 230 B8
Gallowfields Rd DL10 209 B7
Gallowfields Trad Est The
DL10 209 B8
Gallowgate DL10 209 C7
Gallowheads La YO62 95 A6
Gallows Hill
Castleford WF10 201 B4
Ripon HG4 214 C2
Gallows Hill Dr HG4 214 C2
Gallows Hill La YO13 98 D5
Gallows Hill Pk HG4 214 D2
Galmanhoe La YO30 233 A3
Galphay La HG4 113 A3
Galtres Ave YO31 229 B7
Galtres Dr 7 YO61 143 D8
Galtres Gr YO30 227 F7
Galtres Rd
Northallerton DL6 210 E6
York YO31 229 B7
Galtres Sch YO31 229 B5
Ganton Cl 1 YO21 208 C5
Ganton Hill YO12 125 B7
Ganton Pl YO24 230 E7
Ganton Rd YO25 125 C4
Gaol The YO61 144 E7
Gap Rd YO14 127 D8

Garbett Way 1 YO23 ...231 B3
Garburn Gr 3 YO30 ....224 E1
Garbutt Gr YO26 ......227 D5
Garbutt La
4 Whorlton DL6 ....25 D1
1 Whorlton DL6 ....25 D1
Garbutts La TS15 ....25 B5
Garden Cl
3 Glusburn BD20 ......187 D7
Sherburn in Elmet LS25 ...195 E4
Garden Flats La YO19 ..184 E7
Garden House Cl LS26 .200 B6
Garden La
11 Knottingley WF11 ....202 A3
Sherburn in Elmet LS25 ...195 E4
Garden Pl YO1 ....233 C2
Garden St
Castleford WF10 ....200 E3
13 Normanton South WF6 .200 A1
York YO31 ....233 B4
Garden Village LS25 ...195 A3
Garden Way 3 YO18 ....95 F6
Gardeners Cl 8 YO23 ..230 B3
Gardeners Row YO25 ..150 B3
Gardens Rd BD23 .....155 D2
Gardens The 15 YO14 ...101 B4
Garfield Rd YO12 ......212 E6
Garfield Terr YO26 .....227 F5
Garforth Barleyhill Infants Sch LS25 ....194 C3
Garforth Com Coll LS25 ....194 C3
Garforth Green Lane Prim Sch LS25 ....194 D3
Garforth Leisure Ctr LS25 ......194 D3
Garforth St Benedicts RC Prim Sch LS25 ....194 C4
Garforth Sta LS25 ....194 C4
Gargrave C of E Prim Sch BD23 ......155 C1
Gargrave House Gdn BD23 ......155 C1
Gargrave Rd
Broughton BD23 ....172 D6
Skipton BD23 ....216 D4
Gargrave Sta BD23 ....172 C8
Garibaldi St 1 YO11 ...213 B6
Garland St 2 YO26 ....227 E4
Garlands Hill 3 YO11 ...212 F3
Garlands The
Scarborough YO11 ......212 F3
York YO30 ....228 A8
Garman Carr La YO8 ..197 D6
Garnet Brow La LA2 ....130 D2
Garnet La 1 LS24 .....189 D5
Garnet Rd TS17 ....6 B8
Garnet Terr YO26 ....227 E5
Garrick Cl YO8 ....232 B1
Garrow Hill YO10 ......228 F2
Garrow Hill Ave YO10 ..229 A3
Garroway Way YO10 ....184 A4
Garrowby Hill YO41 ....169 F3
Garrowby Rd YO42 ....169 F2
Garrowby St YO41 .....169 E3
Garrowby View 5 YO41 168 D2
Garrs End La BD23 .....134 E3
Garrs La 10 BD23 ......134 E3
Gars The LA2 ....128 A6
Garsbeck Way TS7 ......7 D8
Garsdale Fold 8 LS22 ..180 A1
Garsdale Rd HG5 ......221 D6
Garsdale Sta LA10 ......55 A6
Garth Ave
Collingham LS22 ....188 A8
4 North Duffield YO8 ....199 A7
Garth Cl 11 Catterick DL10 41 D5
Hambleton YO8 ....196 E1
6 Wistow YO8 ....197 D6
Garth Dr YO8 ....196 E1
Garth End
Collingham LS22 ....188 A8
Kirk Deighton LS22 ......180 B5
Garth End Rd YO13 ......99 A7
Garth Glebe 8 YO8 ....198 B5
Garth Grange 3 YO30 ..164 F7
Garth La
Hambleton YO8 ....196 E1
Snainton YO13 ....98 A5
Garth Mdws 13 DL10 ....41 D5
Garth Mill 1 DN14 .....202 D4
Garth Morrell YO8 ....232 C2
Garth Rd
4 Hambleton YO8 ......196 E1
York YO32 ....225 F4
Garth Terr YO30 ....228 B7
Garth The
8 Collingham LS22 .....188 A8
Sinnington YO62 ....95 A8
4 Stokesley TS9 ....26 C7
Tunstall DL10 ....41 B2
Whitby YO21 ....208 B7
Garth View YO8 ....196 E1
Garthends La 3 YO8 ...198 F1
Garthorne Ave DL3 ......3 A5
Garths End 20 YO32 ....166 F5
Garth's End YO10 .....231 E8
Garthway 4 YO32 .....225 D3
Gas House La LA2 ....129 A8
Gas St BD23 ....216 F3
Gas Works La LS23 ....188 F8
Gascoigne Ave LS15 ...194 B7
Gascoigne Cres HG1 ...219 F4
Gascoigne Ct LS15 ....194 B7
Gascoigne Rd LS15 ....194 B7
Gascoigne View LS15 ..194 B7
Gascoigne Wood Mine LS25 ......196 C2
Gate Bridge Rd HG4 ...112 D2
Gate La Borrowby YO7 ...65 E4
Low Coniscliffe & Merrybent DL2 ....2 E4
Gate Way YO21 ....29 B4
Gatecliff Brow BD23 ...155 F4
Gateforth Ct YO8 ......196 F1
Gateforth La YO8 ......196 F1
Gateforth New Rd YO8 .....203 A8
Gatehead La YO42 ....193 D7
Gatehowe Rd YO17 ....170 A7
Gatela Rd YO13 ....53 D2
Gateland Cl YO32 .....225 C7
Gateland Field La DN14 .....205 B6
Gatenby Garth YO61 ...143 B8
Gatesgarth Cl YO12 ...212 B8
Gatherley Rd DL10 .....41 C7
Gauber Rd LA6 ....78 F1
Gaudy La DL8 ....56 C3
Gauk St WF11 ....201 D6
Gaul Rd DL9 ....209 E1
Gaw La BD23 ....174 C8
Gawtersike La YO62 ....94 B8
Gay La LS24 ....196 C7
Gay Mdws YO32 ....167 D2
Gaylands La BB18 ......172 B1
Gayle La DL8 ....56 C4
Gayton Sands TS5 ....6 D6
Gazelle Way YO7 ....115 B1
Geecroft La LS22 ......179 D3
Geldof Rd YO32 ....225 F1
General La YO42 ......193 E6
Geneva Cres DL1 ....3 D4
Geneva La DL1 ....3 D4
Geneva Rd DL1 ....3 E5
Gennell La YO60 ......145 E1
Gentian Glade HG3 ....219 A4
George Cayley Dr YO30 ......225 A3
George Ct YO31 ....233 C3
George Hudson St YO1 ....233 B2
George St
15 Addingham LS29 .....174 F4
Carleton BD23 ....173 B4
19 Earby BB18 ....172 A1
3 Scarborough YO12 ....213 A6
4 Selby YO8 ....232 D6
17 Skipton BD23 ....217 A3
Snaith DN14 ....204 C1
12 Whitby YO21 ....208 D6
7 Wistow YO8 ....197 D6
York YO1 ....233 C1
George Terr 1 YO8 ....198 B4
Gerard Ave YO31 ......229 A5
Germain Rd YO8 ......232 E4
Germany La YO19 .....231 E6
Gerrick La TS12 ....10 C3
Gerrie St TS12 ....9 D7
Ghyll Brow YO21 ....30 D4
Ghyll La BB18 ....171 E2
Ghyll Mdws BB18 ......171 E2
Ghyll Mews LS29 ......218 A3
Ghyll The DL10 ....209 D8
Ghyll Way BD23 ....173 D4
Ghyll Wood 28 LS29 ....175 C2
Gibb St BD22 ....187 B6
Gibbet Hill YO61 ......117 C5
Gibside La BD20 ......173 C1
Gibson Cl 2 YO8 .....196 F1
Gibson La LS25 ....194 D1
Gibson Lane Jun Sch LS25 .....194 D1
Giggleswick CP Sch BD24 ....131 D3
Giggleswick Sch BD24 ....131 C2
Giggleswick Sta BD24 .131 C1
Gilcar St WF6 ....200 B2
Gilcar Way WF6 ....200 B3
Gildercliffe YO12 .....212 C7
Giles Ave YO31 ....229 A5
Gill Bank Rd LS29 .....218 A6
Gill Cl 6 LS29 ....174 E4
Gill Croft YO61 ....117 C1
Gill La Cowling BD22 ...187 A6
Kearby with Netherby LS22 ....179 C1
Nesfield with Langbar LS29 ....175 B4
Rosedale West Side YO18 ..49 E2
Gillamoor Ave YO31 ...229 B5
Gillamoor Bank YO62 ...70 A5
Gillamoor C of E Prim Sch YO62 ....70 A4
Gillamoor Rd YO62 .....70 A2
Gillann St 15 WF11 ....202 A2
Gillgate Rd HG4 ......112 B4
Gilling Castle* YO62 ...118 E7
Gilling Cres DL1 ....3 E4
Gilling Rd Aske DL10 ....20 E1
Richmond DL10 ....209 D7
Gilling Way YO17 ......215 C5
Gillings Ct YO7 ....211 B3
Gillingwood Cl DL10 ...209 C8
Gillingwood Rd YO30 ...224 F3
Gills Fold 8 BD23 .....134 E2
Gills The LS21 ....177 A1
Gillygate YO31 ....233 B3
Gillylees YO12 ....212 C5
Gilmonby Rd TS3 ....7 B8
Gilsforth Hill YO26 ....164 A3
Gilsforth La YO26 .....164 A3
Gilstead Way LS29 .....218 B5
Gilsthwaite La YO26 ...164 A3
Gindhill La LS21 ......178 A4
Ginnel The 1 HG1 .....219 D2
Gipsey Cnr YO19 ......184 E3
Girls High Sch BD23 ...216 E4
Girton Wlk DL1 ....3 D7
Girvan Cl YO24 ....230 B7
Gisburn Rd
Barnoldswick BB18 .....171 D2
Hellifield BD23 ....154 B3
Gisburn Road CP Sch BB18 ....171 D1
Gisburn St
Barnoldswick BB18 ......171 D2
Skipton BD23 ....216 D3
Givendale Gr 3 YO10 ..229 C4
Givendale Rd YO12 ....212 D8
Glade Rd YO19 ....192 B2
Glade The
Escrick YO19 ....192 A6
Scarborough YO11 ......212 F3
York YO31 ....229 B7
Gladstone La YO12 ....212 E5
Gladstone Rd YO12 ....212 E5
Gladstone Road Jun & Inf Sch YO12 ....212 E5
Gladstone St
Darlington DL3 ....3 C5
Harrogate HG2 ....222 E7
Normanton South WF6 ..200 B2
Scarborough YO12 .....212 E6
14 Skipton BD23 ....216 F4
York YO31 ....233 C4
Glaisby Ct YO31 ....229 A6
Glaisdale Ave TS5 ....6 F8
Glaisdale CP Sch YO21 .30 D4
Glaisdale Hall La YO21 ..30 C4
Glaisdale Rd TS15 ....5 F3
Glaisdale Sta YO21 .....30 E4
Glasgow Dr 3 DL9 .....209 C1
Glasshoughton Fst Sch WF10 ......200 F4
Glasshouses CP Sch HG3 ....137 D3
Glaves Cl YO13 ....99 B7
Glebe Ave
Full Sutton YO41 ....169 A2
Harrogate HG2 ....219 C2
York YO26 ....227 D5
Glebe Cl Barton DL10 ...21 C7
15 Bedale DL8 ....63 A2
Bolton Percy YO23 .....190 D4
Kirby Hill YO51 ....141 B7
Manfield DL2 ....2 C4
3 Strensall YO32 ......167 B7
Glebe Ct DL10 ....21 A7
Glebe Field Dr 11 LS22 .180 B3
Glebe Gdns TS13 ....11 A8
Glebe La DL2 ....2 C4
Glebe Mdw HG4 ....214 F6
Glebe Rd Campsall DN6 .206 E1
Darlington DL1 ....3 D8
Harrogate HG2 ....219 C1
Stokesley TS9 ....26 C7
Glebe Sq DL7 ....63 C5
Glebe St WF10 ....200 E4
Glebe Way 26 YO32 ....166 E5
Gledstone Rd BD23 ....171 E5
Gledstone View 8 BB18 ....171 D2
Glen Ave YO31 ....228 E5
Glen Cl
Newby & Scalby YO13 .....75 C5
York YO10 ....231 E6
Glen Esk Rd YO22 ....208 C3
Glen Rd YO31 ....228 E5
Glencoe Cl LS25 ......200 C8
Glencoe Croft LS25 ...200 C8
Glencoe Gdns LS25 ...200 C8
Glencoe St 1 YO30 ....228 B7
Glencoe Terr LS25 ....200 C8
Glendale
Guisborough TS14 ....8 D5
9 Hutton Rudby TS15 ....25 C5
Glendale Rd TS5 ....6 F8
Gleneagles Rd
Darlington DL1 ....3 F8
Middlesbrough TS4 ....7 A8
North Featherstone WF7 .....200 E1
Glenfield Ave LS22 ....180 C2
Glenmore Dr YO17 ....215 E2
Glenn Cres TS7 ....7 B5
Glenridding YO24 .....230 D7
Glenside YO12 ....212 E7
Globe St
10 Harrogate HG2 ......220 C3
9 Scarborough YO11 ....213 B6
Gloucester Ave BD20 ..174 B1
Glusburn CP Sch BD20 ....187 E7
Glynndale Dr YO12 ....212 A8
Glynwed Ct 2 BD23 ....216 E3
Goat La BD24 ....131 F7
Goathland CP Sch YO22 ....51 C8
Goathland Gr TS14 ......8 E5
Goats Rd DL11 ....18 D2
Godfrey Rd 12 DL10 ....41 E4
Godley Cl DL9 ....209 C2
Godwinsway 18 YO41 ..168 D2
Goker La YO51 ....141 E1
Gold Thread La 5 YO8 .197 B8
Golden Acres DL7 ......22 E2
Golden Butts Rd LS29 .218 C4
Goldhill La YO7 ....90 D6
Goldsborough C of E Prim Sch HG5 ....162 F3
Goldsborough Ct HG5 .163 A3
Goldsborough La YO21 ..12 C4
Golf Links Ave 5 LS24 .189 D5
Golf Links Cres 4 LS24 189 D5
Golf Links Ct LS24 ....189 E5
Good Hope Cl WF6 ....200 B2
Goodall Cl 31 BB18 ....172 A1
Goodenber Rd LA2 ....129 A8
Goodramgate YO1 .....233 B2
Goodrick Cl HG2 ......222 B5
Goodsyard The YO8 ...232 D5
Goodwood Ave LS25 ..194 C1
Goodwood Cl YO12 ...212 B6
Goodwood Gr YO24 ....227 F1
Goodwood Rd 3 DL9 ....40 E3
Goody Cross LS26 .....194 B1
Goody Cross La LS26 ..194 A1
Goole Coll DN14 ......205 F2
Goole Gram Sch DN14 .205 F3
Goose Green Cl 2 DL9 ...40 E3
Goose La YO61 ....144 C1
Goose Mire La YO12 ....99 C6
Goose Track La YO60 ..145 C3
Goosecroft Gdns DL6 ..210 D5
Goosecroft La
East Harlsey DL6 ....44 D6
Northallerton DL6 ......210 D5
Gooselands BD24 .....153 C6
Gooselands Hill BD23 .107 D2
Goosepastures TS16 .....5 E3
Gordale Cl 3 BB18 ....171 D1
Gordale La BD23 ......133 A2
Gordale Mount HG5 ...221 C6
Gordon Ave HG1 ......219 E6
Gordon Cres DL10 ....209 D8
Gordon St
28 Glusburn BD20 ......187 E7
Ilkley LS29 ....218 C4
Scarborough YO12 .....212 E5
York YO10 ....228 E3
Gordon Terr BD20 .....173 C1
Gore La DN14 ....207 B5
Gore Sands TS5 ....6 D6
Gormire Ave 2 YO31 ...225 E2
Gormire Cl YO7 ....211 D3
Gorse Cl YO8 ....232 C2
Gorse Hill 1 YO19 .....184 F7
Gorse La LS25 ....195 D3
Gorse Paddock YO32 ..225 F2
Goschen St 8 BD23 ....217 A3
Goslipgate 9 YO18 .....95 F6
Gough Rd DL9 ....40 D4
Gouldings Cl YO11 ....100 A7
Goulton La TS9 ....25 E3
Gouthwaith Cl YO30 ...224 F2
Government House Rd YO30 ....228 A6
Gowans The YO61 .....144 C3
Gowdall Broach DN14 .207 E8
Gowdall La
Pollington DN14 ....207 F7
Snaith & Cowick DN14 ...204 B1
Gowdall Rd DN14 .....203 E2
Gower Rd Aske DL10 ....20 D1
Richmond DL10 ....209 C8
York YO24 ....230 E8
Gowland La YO13 ......54 B2
Gowthorpe YO8 ....232 C5
Gracious St Huby YO61 .144 A4
7 Knaresborough HG5 ..221 B5
Grafton Cl TS14 ....8 F6
Grafton La YO51 ......141 C3
Grafton St WF10 .....200 F3
Graham Cl YO11 ......213 B7
Graham Cres YO12 ....212 C5
Graham Dr WF10 .....201 A4
Graham Rd HG4 ....113 D3
Graham Sch YO12 .....212 B5
Grainbeck La HG3 ....219 A7
Grainger Row HG4 ....214 D5
Grainger St DL1 ....3 D4
Grains La BD23 ....154 E8
Grammar Sch La DL6 ..210 D3
Grampian Cl 4 YO32 ..225 F5
Granary Ct YO1 ....233 B3
Granby Pk HG1 ....219 F3
Granby Rd HG1 ....219 F3
Grandage La BD22 ....187 A7
Grange Ave Aiskew DL7 ..63 C4
Filey YO14 ....101 B3
Garforth LS25 ....194 C3
Harrogate HG1 ....219 D5
3 Hurworth-on-Tees DL2 ...3 D1
5 Hurworth-on-Tees DL2 ..22 D8
Ilkley LS29 ....218 D4
Scarborough YO12 .....212 E4
Spofforth HG3 ....179 E6
Tadcaster LS24 ....189 F6
Thorp Arch LS23 ....181 A2
3 Willerby YO12 ....99 D2
Grange Cl 10 Bedale DL8 .63 A2
Bishop Thornton HG3 ....138 F1
Dishforth YO7 ....114 F4
Full Sutton YO41 ....169 A2
Ilkley LS29 ....218 D4
Lebberston YO11 ....100 D5
Northallerton DL7 ......210 C3
Skelton YO30 ....224 B5
Grange Cl E DL7 ....63 E7
Grange Cres
Middlesbrough TS7 ....7 B5
10 Tadcaster LS24 ......189 E6
Grange Ct YO12 ....99 D7
Grange Dr TS9 ....26 C7
Grange Est LS29 ......218 D4
Grange Garth YO10 ...228 D2
Grange La 1 Dacre HG3 .137 F1
Rufforth YO26 ....227 A2
Scackleton YO62 ....119 C3
Stonebeck Down HG3 ....137 A6
Sutton BD22 ....187 F2
Grange Park Cl WF10 .200 D7
Grange Park Rd HG4 ..214 B2
Grange Rd 19 Bedale DL8 .63 A2
Brompton-on-Swale DL10 ..41 B6
Burley in Warfedale LS29 ....176 C1
8 Campsall DN6 ....206 E1
Castleford WF10 ....201 B5
Colburn DL9 ....40 F5
5 Dacre HG3 ....137 F1
Darlington DL1 ....3 C4
Farnhill BD20 ....173 E1
Goole DN14 ....205 F2
Tadcaster LS24 ....189 E6
Thornaby TS17 ....6 B8
Grange St YO10 ....228 D2
Grange Terr HG4 ......114 B8
Grange The
Kirby Hill YO51 ....141 A7
Thirsk YO7 ....211 B2
Grange View
11 Otley LS21 ....176 F1
Towton LS24 ....189 E2
Grangefield Ave 32 LS29 ....176 C1
Granger Ave YO26 .....227 C4
Grangeside DL3 ....3 B4
Grant Cl DL6 ....45 B4
Grantham Dr YO26 ....227 E4
Grantley Cl HG3 ......219 A4
Grantley Dr HG3 ......219 A4
Grantley Hall Coll HG4 ....138 E8
Grantley Pl HG3 ......219 A4
Grants Ave YO10 .....231 E8
Granville Rd
21 Filey YO14 ....101 B3
4 Harrogate HG1 ....219 D3
Scarborough YO11 ......213 A3
Granville Sq 3 YO11 ...213 A2
Granville St
20 Normanton South WF6 .200 A1
Skipton BD23 ....216 E4
Granville Terr 4 YO10 ..228 E3
Grape La Whitby YO22 ..208 E7
York YO1 ....233 B3
Grasmere Ave LS22 ....180 A3
Grasmere Cl 4 BB8 ....186 A3
Grasmere Cres HG2 ...222 C7
Grasmere Dr YO10 ....229 B4
Grasmere Gr 5 YO30 ...224 F1
Grass Croft TS21 ....5 A7
Grass Wood La BD23 ..134 C3
Grassfield Cl HG3 ....137 B4
Grassgill La DL8 ....59 E3
Grassholme YO24 .....230 C7
Grassington Ave DL7 ..210 C2
Grassington C of E Prim Sch BD23 ....134 E2
Grassington Rd
Middlesbrough TS4 ....7 A8
Skipton BD23 ....216 F5
Gravel Hole La
Sowerby YO7 ....89 E3
Thirsk YO7 ....211 C1
Gravelhill La DN14 ...206 F7
Gravelly Hill La LS17 ..178 A2
Gray La YO62 ....70 D1
Gray St 13 Whitby YO21 ..208 D6
York YO23 ....233 A1
Grays Rd YO62 ....69 F6
Grayshon Dr YO26 ....227 B5
Grayston Plain La HG3 ....160 F4
Graystonber La LA2 ...130 E7
Great & Little Preston C of E Inf Sch LS26 ....200 C8
Great & Little Preston Prim Sch LS26 ....200 C8
Great Auk TS14 ....8 D6
Great Ave DL10 ....209 A7
Great Ayton Sta TS9 ....8 B1
Great Cl YO8 ....197 B8
Great Close La BD24 ..153 A6
Great Croft Cl 9 BB18 .171 D2
Great Moor Rd YO13 ...74 D2
Great North Rd
Ledsham LS25 ....195 C1
Micklefield LS25 ....194 F5
Great North Way YO26 ....227 B8
Great Ouseburn Cty Prim Sch YO26 ....164 B8
Great Pasture LS29 ...176 C1
Great Sike Rd YO17 ...215 D8
Great Smeaton Cty Prim Sch DL6 ....23 C3
Greatwood Ave BD23 ..217 A3
Greatwood Prim Sch BD23 ....217 A2
Greavefield La WF8 ...201 D1
Greaves Smithy LS29 .175 B4
Grebe Ave DL9 ....40 E2
Green Ave LS25 ....194 C2
Green Balk
Great & Little Broughton TS9 ....26 F5
Millington YO42 ....170 D1
Green Bank BB18 .....171 E2
Green Bank La HG4 ...139 A6
Green Cl
Bradleys Both BD20 .....173 D3
2 Linton-on-Ouse YO30 ..164 F8

Green Cl *continued*
Middlesbrough TS7 ....7 D5
Steeton with Eastburn BD20 ....187 F7
York YO30 ....228 A8
Green Cres The YO62 ..120 B5
Green Croft Gdns 24 YO11 ....100 B6
Green Dike YO32 ....225 C8
Green Dikes La YO25 ...151 F1
Green Dyke La YO62 ...120 C5
Green Dykes YO17 ....215 A3
Green Dykes La YO10 ..228 F3
Green End Ave 35 BB18 .172 A1
Green End Rd 34 BB18 .172 A1
Green Gate
Exelby, Leeming & Newton DL8 ....63 D2
Hawsker-cum-Stainsacre YO22 ....33 A6
Kirkby Malham BD23 .....154 F8
West Witton DL8 ....59 C3
Green Gate La
Crakehall DL8 ....62 E5
Kildale YO21 ....27 F8
Long Preston BD23 ....153 F5
Green Haggs La HG3 ..223 F1
Green Hammerton C of E Prim Sch YO26 ....164 B3
Green Head La BD24 ..131 E2
Green Hill YO62 ....118 E6
Green Hill La BD22 ....187 A5
Green Hills YO60 ....168 B7
Green Hills La DL7 .....64 B6
Green Howards & Regimental Mus★ DL10 ....209 C6
Green Howard's Dr 8 YO12 ....75 F5
Green Howards Rd
Pickering YO18 ....96 A6
Richmond DL10 ....209 B8
Green Island YO12 .....99 D7
Green La
Addingham LS29 ....174 F4
Appleton Roebuck YO23 ..191 B6
Barmby on the Marsh DN14 ....205 A6
Barton-le-Street YO17 ....120 E8
Bedale DL8 ....62 F3
Bishopthorpe YO24 ....231 A6
Boston Spa LS23 ....188 F7
Bradleys Both BD20 ....174 A3
Burton Leonard HG3 ....140 B2
Burton-on-Yore HG4 ....86 D6
Castleford WF10 ....200 E3
Castleford WF10 ....200 F5
Cawton YO62 ....119 B6
Collingham LS22 ....188 A8
Coneythorpe & Clareton HG5 ....163 B5
Constable Burton DL8 .....61 A6
Cottingwith YO42 ....193 C5
Cundall with Leckby YO61 ....115 D4
Darlington DL1 ....3 D8
Dishforth YO7 ....115 A2
East Rounton TS15 ....24 F4
Fadmoor YO62 ....69 E3
Farndale West YO62 ....48 E1
Folkton YO12 ....99 F1
Garforth LS25 ....194 D4
Glusburn BD20 ....187 D7
Great Ouseburn YO26 ....142 A1
Halton East BD23 ....157 C1
Harome YO62 ....93 C5
Harrogate HG2 ....222 C6
Heck DN14 ....207 D8
Horton BD23 ....171 B5
Hudswell DL11 ....39 F5
Hutton Rudby TS15 ....25 B4
Ilkley LS29 ....176 C2
Ingleton LA6 ....103 E2
Kippax LS25 ....194 C2
Kirby Wiske YO7 ....88 F7
Kirkby Overblow LS17 ....178 D2
Kirklevington TS15 ....5 E2
Langtoft YO25 ....151 D5
Lebberston YO11 ....100 D5
Ledston WF10 ....200 E7
Little Ayton TS9 ....27 A8
Littlethorpe HG4 ....140 A7
Marrick DL11 ....38 E7
Maunby YO7 ....64 D1
Menwith with Darley HG3 ....160 A6
Mickletown LS26 ....200 C5
Middlesbrough TS5 ....6 E8
Moor Monkton YO26 .....164 F1
Newby TS7 ....7 C3
North Cowton DL7 ....22 B2
North Duffield YO8 ....198 F8
Otley LS21 ....176 F1
Ripon HG4 ....113 C3
Sawley HG4 ....138 E7
Scalby YO12 ....212 C8
Selby YO8 ....232 A3
South Stainley with Cayton HG3 ....161 E8
Stutton with Hazlewood LS24 ....189 D4
Sutton BD22 ....187 F2
Sutton-on-the-Forest YO61 ....144 E4
Thirsk YO7 ....211 F3
Weaverthorpe YO17 ....124 F1
Welbury DL6 ....44 C8
Wensley DL8 ....60 A4
Whitby YO22 ....208 E5
Green La *continued*
Whorlton DL6 ....45 F7
Wigginton YO32 ....166 D5
Winksley HG4 ....112 F2
Wressle DN14 ....205 D8
York YO30 ....225 A1
York YO24 ....227 D2
Green La E YO7 ....211 B1
Green La W YO7 ....211 A1
Green Lane Prim Sch TS5 ....6 E8
Green Mdw BB8 ....186 A1
Green Mdws YO31 ....229 A7
Green Park Ave 15 YO11 ....100 B6
Green Park Rd 14 YO11 .100 B6
Green Pastures DL8 ....62 C5
Green Row LS26 ....200 B5
Green St
7 Cowling BD22 ....187 B6
Darlington DL1 ....3 D5
Green Sward YO31 ....229 A8
Green Sykes Rd BD20 ..187 F4
Green The Brompton DL6 .43 F3
Castleford WF10 ....201 B4
1 Clapham LA2 ....130 C8
Cleasby DL2 ....2 F4
Coniston with Kilnsey BD23 ....134 B6
20 Dunnington YO19 .....184 F7
Garforth LS25 ....194 D3
Hellifield BD23 ....154 B3
High Coniscliffe DL2 ....2 C6
Kettlewell with Starbotton BD23 ....108 B3
Kirkby Malzeard HG4 ....112 D5
8 Kirklevington TS15 .....24 E8
Linton-on-Ouse YO30 .....164 F8
Longnewton TS21 ....5 A7
9 Otley LS21 ....176 F1
Rawcliffe DN14 ....205 A1
Scalby YO12 ....212 B7
Seamer TS9 ....6 F1
6 Seamer YO12 ....99 D6
1 Skelton YO30 ....224 B5
Slingsby YO62 ....120 B5
10 Thirsk YO7 ....211 C3
Tockwith YO26 ....181 C7
2 Tollerton YO61 ....143 B3
7 Topcliffe YO7 ....89 B1
Wistow YO8 ....197 D6
York YO26 ....227 C3
Green Village YO7 .....88 C5
Green Way
Glusburn BD20 ....187 E8
Harrogate HG2 ....222 C6
Middlesbrough TS7 ....7 D5
York YO32 ....225 F4
Green Ways 2 YO8 ....197 D6
Green Wlk 5 BB18 ....172 A1
Greenacre Cl TS9 ....7 F1
Greenacres Hunton DL8 ..61 E7
Morton-on-Swale DL7 .....64 A6
Skipton BD23 ....217 B5
Stainton & Thornton TS8 .....6 D5
York YO32 ....225 F4
Greenacres Cl 8 YO8 ..197 D1
Greenacres Cres 7 YO8 ....197 D1
Greenacres Dr 4 YO8 ..197 D1
Greenacres Gr 3 YO8 ..197 D1
Greenbank 5 DL6 .....210 E2
Greenbank Cl WF10 ...200 D3
Greenbank Rd DL3 ....3 C6
Greenberfield La BB18 ....171 E2
Greencliffe Dr YO30 ...228 A6
Greencroft Ct 14 YO19 ..184 F7
Greencroft La 17 YO19 ..184 F7
Greendown Cl LS29 ....218 D4
Greenfield Ave LS25 ...194 D1
Greenfield Cl DL2 ....3 E1
Greenfield Dr
6 Brayton YO8 ....197 D1
Eaglescliffe TS16 ....5 D5
Greenfield Gdns BD20 .187 F7
Greenfield Park Dr YO31 ....229 A7
Greenfield Rd 8 YO11 .213 A4
Greenfield St 5 BD23 ..216 D3
Greenfields DN14 .....207 F6
Greenfields Ave HG2 ..220 C2
Greenfields Dr HG2 ...220 C2
Greenfields Rd HG2 ...220 C2
Greenfinch Cl 1 YO12 ...99 E6
Greenfoot La LA2 .....128 E8
Greengales Ct YO19 ...193 A8
Greengales La YO19 ...193 A8
Greengate
Malton YO17 ....215 C4
Scarborough YO12 ....212 D4
Greengate Dr HG5 .....221 B8
Greengate La
Cliffe YO8 ....198 F6
Kirkby Fleetham with Fencote DL7 ....42 B1
Knaresborough HG5 .....221 B8
Thornton-le-Dale YO18 ....96 C6
Greengate Rd WF8 .....206 C1
Greengate View HG5 ..221 B8
Greengates La YO61 ...142 E3
Greenhill Cres DL6 ....210 E3
Greenhill La YO7 ....66 B4
Greenholme Cl
1 Boroughbridge YO51 ..141 B6
7 Burley in Warfedale LS29 ....176 C1
Greenhow Hill HG3 ....136 C2
Greenhow Hill Rd HG3 ....159 B6
Greenhow Pk LS29 ....176 B1
Greenhowsyke La DL6 .210 E4
Greenland La YO17 .....95 B3
Greenlands TS15 ....25 C6
Greenlands La YO8 ...197 C3
Greenlands Rd YO18 ....95 F6
Greenless La DL11 ....1 A2
Greenmires La LS21 ...177 E4
Greenroyd Gr 13 BD20 ..187 E6
Greens Yd YO22 ....208 E7
Greensborough Ave 3 YO26 ....227 B5
Greenshaw Dr YO32 ...225 C8
Greenside 18 YO19 .....184 F7
Greenside Cl 24 YO19 ...184 F7
Greenside Ct 9 DL2 ....3 E1
Greenside Wlk 23 YO19 .184 F7
Greenstead Rd YO12 ...212 B8
Greenway The
2 Haxby YO32 ....225 C7
2 Middleton St George DL2 .4 C4
Greenways Dr 1 YO8 ..197 D6
Greenways The DL7 ....63 C8
Greenwodd Rd HG3 ...137 B4
Greenwood Ave HG3 ..137 B4
Greenwood Gr YO24 ...230 C8
Greet's Hill YO17 .....169 E7
Gregory Cl YO30 ....224 C5
Grenadier Dr DL6 .....210 F3
Grendon Gdns 1 DL2 .....4 C4
Grenley St 8 WF11 ....202 A2
Grenville Rd TS17 ....6 B6
Grenwich Cl 5 YO30 ...224 E3
Gresham Cl DL1 ....3 D7
Gresley Ct 3 YO26 ....227 B4
Greta Heath 2 LA6 ...102 F2
Grewelthorpe C of E Prim Sch HG4 ....112 C7
Grey Cl YO61 ....144 C3
Grey St HG2 ....222 E7
Grey Thorn La HG5 ....163 D3
Grey Towers Dr TS7 .....7 D5
Greyfriars Cl DL3 ....2 F5
Greylands Park Ave YO12 ....212 C8
Greylands Park Dr YO12 ....212 C8
Greylands Park Gr 3 YO12 ....212 C8
Greylands Park Rd YO12 ....212 C8
Greystoke Rd YO30 ....224 E1
Greystone Cl 2 LS29 ..176 C1
Greystone Ct YO32 ....225 C7
Greystone Head HG4 ..112 A4
Greystone La
Aldbrough DL2 ....2 A4
Stanwick St John DL11 .....1 E4
Greystone Pk LS25 ....188 F1
Greystonegill La LA2 ..129 D7
Greystones Ave HG3 ...161 B4
Greystones Cl LS25 ...188 F1
Greystones La BD22 ...187 E4
Grimbald Crag Cl HG5 ....221 D4
Grimbald Crag Rd HG5 ....221 E4
Grimbald Crag Way HG5 ....221 D4
Grimbald Rd HG5 .....221 C5
Grimbald Way 3 HG5 ..221 C4
Grimston La YO17 .....148 D7
Grimston Rd 12 YO14 ...127 A8
Grimwith Garth YO30 ..224 F2
Grimwith Rd BD23 .....135 E2
Grindale Rd YO16 .....127 F2
Grinkle La TS13 ....10 F5
Grinton Rd TS18 ....5 D8
Grisedale Cres TS16 .....5 E4
Gristhwaite La YO7 .....89 D1
Grosmont Sta YO22 .....31 C4
Grosvenor Cres 2 YO11 ....213 A4
Grosvenor Gdns LS17 ..178 B2
Grosvenor Gr HG1 .....219 F6
Grosvenor House Sch HG3 ....160 D6
Grosvenor Pl TS14 ....8 E6
Grosvenor Rd
Harrogate HG1 ....219 E6
Scarborough YO11 ....212 F4
York YO30 ....233 A4
Grosvenor Sq 3 YO30 ..164 F8
Grosvenor Terr YO30 ...233 A4
Grove Ave 25 LS29 .....175 C2
Grove Bank 4 TS15 .....24 E8
Grove Cl HG4 ....214 C3
Grove Cres
Boston Spa LS23 ....188 F8
South Milford LS25 ....195 F2
Grove Gdns 12 YO26 ...165 F1
Grove Hill Rd 4 YO14 ..101 B4
Grove La
Knottingley WF11 ....201 F2
Ripon HG4 ....214 C3
Grove Park Ave HG1 ...219 E4
Grove Park Ct HG1 ....219 E4
Grove Park La HG1 ....219 E4
Grove Park Terr HG1 ..219 E4
Grove Park View HG1 ..219 E4
Grove Park Wlk HG1 ..219 E4
Grove Pk 7 YO8 ....198 B5
Grove Rd
Boston Spa LS23 ....188 F8
14 Filey YO14 ....101 B4
Harrogate HG1 ....219 D4
Grove Rd *continued*
Ilkley LS29 ....218 A3
Grove Road CP Sch HG1 ....219 E4
Grove St 38 Earby BB18 .172 A1
9 Harrogate HG2 ....220 C3
Norton YO17 ....215 E3
15 Whitby YO21 ....208 D6
Grove Terr 11 DL8 ....60 E2
Grove Terrace La YO31 ....233 C4
Grove The
Eaglescliffe TS15 ....5 E2
Guisborough TS14 ....8 D5
Harrogate HG1 ....219 E3
1 Hutton Rudby TS15 .....25 D5
Ilkley LS29 ....218 A4
Kellington DN14 ....203 A3
Kippax LS25 ....194 D1
Middlesbrough TS5 ....6 E6
Middlesbrough TS7 ....7 B7
Normanton South WF6 ...200 A1
Norton YO17 ....215 E2
1 Seamer YO12 ....99 D6
Skipton BD23 ....217 C3
Swillington LS26 ....194 A1
York YO24 ....230 E6
Grove View YO30 .....228 A6
Groves La YO31 ....233 C4
Grundy Way 11 DL10 .....41 E4
Grunton La DL2 ....2 C4
Grysedale La BD23 ....134 B2
Guadaloupe Rd DL9 ....40 C4
Guards Ct 10 YO12 .....75 F5
Guildford Rd TS6 ....7 E8
Guisborough Mus★ TS14 ....8 F7
Guisborough Rd
Aislaby YO21 ....31 F8
Great Ayton TS9 ....7 F1
Lockwood TS12 ....10 A5
Middlesbrough TS7 ....7 D5
Thornaby TS17 ....6 B8
Whitby YO21 ....208 A5
Guisborough RUFC TS14 .8 F6
Guisborough Swimming Pool TS14 ....8 E7
Gunby Rd YO8 ....199 D5
Gunbywood Rd YO8 ...199 D6
Guncroft La YO62 .....69 D1
Guning La DL11 ....36 B4
Gunnergate La TS8 .....7 B5
Gurney Pease Prim Sch DL1 ....3 D6
Gurney St DL1 ....3 D6
Guy La YO7 ....114 F2
Gyll Hall La DL10 ....41 E1
Gypsy La
Castleford WF10 ....201 B3
Middlesbrough TS7 ....7 C6
Gypsy Lane Sta TS7 .....7 D6

H

Habton La YO17 ....121 B7
Habton Rd YO17 ....95 D1
Hackforth & Hornby C of E Prim Sch DL8 ....62 E8
Hackforth Rd 2 TS18 ....5 D8
Hackness C of E Prim Sch YO13 ....74 E5
Hackness Dr YO12 ....212 A8
Hackness Rd YO12 ....212 A8
Haddlesey Rd WF11 ...202 D5
Haddocks La YO61 ....142 B4
Hadrian Ave YO10 .....229 B3
Hag La
Cottingwith YO42 ....193 C4
Raskelf YO61 ....142 E8
South Kilvington YO7 ....211 D6
Sproxton YO62 ....92 D4
Youlton YO61 ....142 F2
Hagg La Colton LS24 ....190 E8
Cottingwith YO42 ....193 E8
Cowesby YO7 ....66 C4
Dunnington YO19 ....184 F6
Hemingbrough YO8 ....198 F3
South Milford LS25 ....196 C2
Hagg Rd YO62 ....69 F2
Hagg Side La YO13 .....97 D6
Haggersgate 10 YO21 ...208 D7
Haggitt Hill La DL6 .....24 E3
Haggs La DN6 ....207 D2
Haggs Rd HG3 ....223 C4
Hague Ave 31 YO12 .....75 D5
Hagworm Hill★ YO12 .....75 C2
Haig Rd DL9 ....209 C2
Haig St YO8 ....232 B6
Haigh La DN14 ....207 A6
Hailsham Ave TS17 ....6 B5
Hailstone Dr DL6 .....210 F5
Hales La YO8 ....204 E5
Haley's Terr YO31 .....228 D8
Half Acres Jun & Inf Sch WF10 ....200 E4
Half Moon St 1 YO30 ...164 F7
Halfpenny Cl HG5 .....221 C7
Halfpenny La HG5 .....221 B7
Halifax Ct 7 YO30 .....225 A1
Halifax Way YO41 .....185 A3
Hall Arm La YO51 .....141 D5
Hall Ave 10 BD20 .....187 E6
Hall Brow BD23 ....155 A5
Hall Cl 5 Airmyn DN14 ..205 E4
Austwick LA2 ....130 E7
Burley in Warfedale LS29 ....176 B1
Hall Cl *continued*
Cawood YO8 ....191 D1
11 Glusburn BD20 ....187 E6
Hall Croft BD23 ....216 E4
Hall Ct WF11 ....201 E4
Hall Dr
Burley in Warfedale LS29 ....176 B1
Glusburn BD20 ....187 E6
Middlesbrough TS5 ....6 F7
Hall Farm Cl 4 YO19 ...197 F8
Hall Farm Pk LS25 ....194 F4
Hall Garth 25 YO18 .....95 F7
Hall Garth Cl LS24 ....190 C3
Hall Garth★ LS25 .....195 E4
Hall Gdns BD20 ....173 F1
Hall Green La LS17 ...178 C4
Hall Ings La YO62 .....70 E4
Hall La Askwith LS21 ...176 C4
Blubberhouses LS21 .....159 C2
Caldwell DL11 ....1 C4
Church Fenton LS24 .....196 C7
Harome YO62 ....93 C4
Harrogate HG1 ....219 E6
Hawnby DL6 ....46 B1
Huddleston with Newthorpe LS25 ....195 C3
Leathley LS21 ....177 D1
Ledston WF10 ....200 F7
Myton-on-Swale YO61 ....142 A6
Norton DN6 ....206 E2
Hall Mdws BB8 ....186 A2
Hall Moor Cl 7 TS15 .....24 E8
Hall Orchards Ave LS22 ....180 D3
Hall Park Cl 23 YO13 ....75 D5
Hall Park Croft LS25 ..200 D8
Hall Park Gr 25 YO13 ....75 D5
Hall Park Mdws LS25 ..200 D8
Hall Park Orch LS25 ...200 D8
Hall Park Rd
Hunmanby YO14 ....126 F8
Walton LS23 ....181 A2
Hall Pasture 9 YO22 ....32 A6
Hall Pk Wistow YO8 ....198 A5
York YO10 ....229 B1
Hall Rd
Swillington LS26 ....194 A1
Trawden Forest BB8 .....186 A2
Hall Rise
Burley in Warfedale LS29 ....176 B1
12 Haxby YO32 ....166 F5
Hall Sq 5 YO51 ....141 B5
Hall Tower Hill★ LS15 .194 B8
Hall View Gr DL3 ....3 A6
Hall Way 9 BD20 ....187 E6
Halladale Cl 1 YO24 ....230 B7
Hallam Cl 41 YO14 .....101 B3
Hallam La LS21 ....176 D3
Hallam's Yd 4 BD23 ...216 F4
Hallard Way 7 YO32 ....167 B7
Hallcroft Dr 13 LS29 ...175 A4
Hallcroft La YO23 .....230 A3
Hallfield Ave LS25 .....194 F4
Hallfield La
Nawton YO62 ....69 C3
Wetherby LS22 ....180 C3
Hallfield Rd YO31 .....228 E5
Hallfield Terr LS25 ....194 F4
Hallgarth Alne YO61 ...142 F4
Great & Little Broughton TS9 ....26 E5
Hallgarth Comp Sch TS5 .6 E7
Hallwith Rd DL8 ....61 A3
Halnaby Ave DL3 ....2 F5
Halstead Rd HG2 ....222 E7
Hambleton Ave
Northallerton DL7 ....210 C2
Thirsk YO7 ....211 D3
York YO10 ....229 C4
Hambleton C of E Prim Sch YO8 ....196 F1
Hambleton Cl
12 Easingwold YO61 .....143 D8
11 Thirsk YO7 ....211 C3
Hambleton Ct
Great Smeaton DL6 ....23 C3
Knaresborough HG5 .....221 C6
Hambleton Dr YO7 ....211 C3
Hambleton Garth 21 YO61 ....143 C8
Hambleton Gate TS9 ...26 C7
Hambleton Gr HG5 ....221 B6
Hambleton La YO61 .....91 F2
Hambleton Leisure Ctr DL6 ....210 D6
Hambleton Pl YO7 .....211 C3
Hambleton Rd
6 Catterick Garrison DL9 ..40 E3
Harrogate HG1 ....219 F4
Norton YO17 ....215 E2
Hambleton Terr YO31 ..228 C7
Hambleton View
10 Haxby YO32 ....166 D5
Thirsk YO7 ....211 D3
4 Tollerton YO61 ....143 B3
Hambleton Way
Easingwold YO61 ....143 D8
York YO32 ....225 F3
Hamer Bank YO18 .....49 F4
Hamerton Cl 11 YO14 ...127 A8
Hamerton Rd 10 YO14 ..127 A8
Hamhall La DL7 ....63 D6
Hamilton Ave HG2 .....222 E8

Hamilton Cl YO13 . . . . . . .75 C5
Hamilton Ct WF6 . . . . .200 A2
Hamilton Dr
  Darlington DL1 . . . . .3 D8
  York YO24 . . . . .227 E2
Hamilton Dr E YO24 . . .227 F2
Hamilton Dr W YO24 . . .227 E2
Hamilton Gn YO17 . . . . .215 B3
Hamilton Way YO24 . . . .227 E2
Hamlet The 🟨 DN14 . . .202 F2
Hamley La YO62 . . . . .70 F3
Hammer Rd HG4 . . . . . . .85 B7
Hammersike Rd
  Cawood YO8 . . . . .196 F5
  Wistow YO8 . . . . .197 A4
Hammerton Cl
  Green Hammerton YO26 .164 D3
  🟨 York YO26 . . . . .227 B3
Hammerton Dr
  Garforth LS25 . . . . .194 D3
  Hellifield BD23 . . . . .154 B3
Hammerton Sta YO26 . . .164 D2
Hammond Dr DL1 . . . . .3 C4
Hammond Rd YO13 . . . . .54 A8
Hampden St YO1 . . . . . . .233 B1
Hampden Way TS17 . . . . .6 B6
Hampshire Cl
  Ilkley LS29 . . . . .218 D4
  🟨 Pontefract WF8 . . . . .201 C2
Hampsthwaite C of E Prim
  Sch HG3 . . . . .161 A5
Hampsthwaite Rd
  HG1 . . . . .219 C4
Hampton Rd YO12 . . . . .212 E5
Hancow Rd
  Hartoft YO18 . . . . .50 A1
  Rosedale East Side YO18 . .49 F3
Handale Cl TS14 . . . . .9 A6
Handley Cl
  Stockton-on-Tees TS18 . . . .5 F7
  York YO30 . . . . .225 A2
Hang Bank DL10 . . . . . . .21 B8
Hanger La DN14 . . . . . . .204 B3
Hanghow La DL8 . . . . . . .84 C8
Hanging Stone La YO18 . .49 E4
Hangingstone Rd
  LS29 . . . . .218 D2
Hankins La YO42 . . . . . . .193 D1
Hanover Pl WF11 . . . . . .201 D4
Hanover Rd 🟨 YO11 . . . .212 F5
Hanover St 🟨 BD20 . . . .173 E1
Hanover St E 🟨 YO26 . . .227 F5
Hanover St W 🟨 YO26 . . .227 F5
Hansom Pl YO31 . . . . . . .228 C7
Hanson Ave WF6 . . . . . .200 A1
Harborough Cl 🟨 YO14 .126 F8
Harbour Rise 🟨 DL8 . . . .63 A2
Harbour View 🟨 DL8 . . . .63 A3
Harcourt Ave YO12 . . . . .212 E3
Harcourt Cl
  Bishopthorpe YO23 . . . . .231 A4
  Wheldrake YO19 . . . . . . .192 F7
Harcourt Dr
  Addingham LS29 . . . . . . .174 F5
  Harrogate HG1 . . . . .219 E2
Harcourt Pl 🟨 YO11 . . . .213 A5
Harcourt Rd 🟨 HG1 . . . .219 E3
Harcourt St YO31 . . . . . .228 E5
Hard Gate BD23 . . . . . . .134 A3
Hard Stiles DL11 . . . . . . .39 E4
Hardcastle Ave 🟨 WF8 . .201 B1
Harden Cl YO30 . . . . . . .224 F2
Harden Rd BB18 . . . . . . .186 A7
Hardenshaw La YO18 . . . .204 B4
Hardigate Rd YO18 . . . . . .72 B7
Hardings La
  Glusburn BD20 . . . . .187 F8
  Middleton LS29 . . . . .218 A8
Hardisty Hill HG3 . . . . . .159 C3
Hardrada Way 🟨 YO41 . .168 D1
Hardy Mdws 🟨 BD23 . . . .134 E2
Hardy St YO8 . . . . .232 E4
Harebell Cl
  🟨 Harrogate HG3 . . . . .161 B3
  Northallerton DL7 . . . . . .210 C1
Harecroft Rd 🟨 LS21 . . . .177 A1
Haregill Bank HG4 . . . . . .85 E6
Harehills La BD22 . . . . . .187 E1
Haresfield Way TS17 . . . . .6 A5
Harewell Cl HG3 . . . . . . .137 D3
Harewell La 🟨 HG3 . . . .137 F1
Harewood Ave
  🟨 Normanton South WF6 .200 B2
  🟨 Scalby YO12 . . . . . . .75 E5
  🟨 Scalby YO12 . . . . . .212 D8
Harewood Chase DL7 . . .210 B2
Harewood Dr 🟨 YO14 . . .101 A3
Harewood La DL7 . . . . . .210 C3
Harewood Rd
  Collingham LS22 . . . . . . .188 A8
  Harrogate HG3 . . . . .219 A5
  Ripon HG4 . . . . .214 B3
  Skipton BD23 . . . . .216 E4
Harford Rd YO11 . . . . . .100 B6
Hargill
  Gilling with Hartforth & Sedbury
    DL10 . . . . .20 E4
  Harmby DL8 . . . . .60 E4
  West Witton DL8 . . . . . . .59 C3
Hargill Cl DL8 . . . . .60 E4
Hargill Dr DL8 . . . . .59 C6

Hargill Rd DL8 . . . . .61 E4
  🟨 Finghall DL8 . . . . . . .61 E4
  🟨 Leeming DL7 . . . . . . .63 D4
  Redmire DL8 . . . . .59 C7
Hargrove Rd HG2 . . . . . .220 B2
Harington Ave YO10 . . . .228 F4
Harker Hill DL8 . . . . .56 C4
Harker St 🟨 WF11 . . . . .202 A2
Harkness Cl DL7 . . . . . . .63 C4
Harkness Dr DL7 . . . . . . .63 C4
Harland Ct YO61 . . . . . . .144 C3
Harley Cl YO12 . . . . .212 E5
Harley Cres DL9 . . . . .40 F4
Harley La DL9 . . . . .40 F4
Harley St 🟨 YO12 . . . . .212 E5
Harlow Ave HG2 . . . . . . .222 B7
Harlow Cl 🟨 YO24 . . . . .227 F2
Harlow Cres HG2 . . . . . .222 B7
Harlow Grange Pk
  HG3 . . . . .178 C8
Harlow Manor Pk
  HG2 . . . . .222 B8
Harlow Moor Dr HG2 . . .219 B1
Harlow Moor Rd HG2 . . .219 A1
Harlow Oval HG2 . . . . . .222 B8
Harlow Park Cres
  HG2 . . . . .222 B7
Harlow Park Dr HG2 . . . .222 B7
Harlow Park Rd HG2 . . . .222 B7
Harlow Pines HG2 . . . . . .222 A7
Harlow Rd YO24 . . . . . . .227 F2
Harlow Terr HG2 . . . . . . .219 B1
Harlsey Castle ★ DL6 . . . .44 D5
Harlsey Cres TS18 . . . . . . .5 E8
Harlsey Rd TS18 . . . . .5 E8
Harmby Rd 🟨 DL8 . . . . . .60 D5
Harness La 🟨 YO51 . . . .141 B4
Harold Ct YO24 . . . . .227 D3
Harold St YO8 . . . . .232 F4
Harolds Way 🟨 YO41 . . .168 D1
Harome Heads La YO62 . .93 B6
Harome Heads Rd
  YO62 . . . . .93 C6
Harper Gr BD20 . . . . . . .187 E6
Harper La HG3 . . . . .159 C6
Harper St
  Barnoldswick BB18 . . . . .171 D1
  🟨 Selby YO8 . . . . .232 C5
Harper Terr 🟨 TS18 . . . . .5 E8
Harpers Sq 🟨 BD20 . . . .187 E6
Harpers Terr DL2 . . . . .4 B5
Harr Gill DL8 . . . . .58 A6
Harris Dr 🟨 DL10 . . . . . . .41 E4
Harris St DL1 . . . . .3 E4
Harrison Gr HG1 . . . . . . .220 C4
Harrison St
  Barnoldswick BB18 . . . . .171 E1
  York YO31 . . . . .228 F6
Harrogate Coll HG1 . . . . .219 D2
Harrogate Ctr The ★
  HG1 . . . . .219 D3
Harrogate District Hospl
  HG2 . . . . .220 A2
Harrogate Gram Sch
  HG2 . . . . .222 C8
Harrogate Granby High Sch
  HG1 . . . . .220 A4
Harrogate Hill Jun Sch
  DL3 . . . . .3 D7
Harrogate Ladies Coll
  HG1 . . . . .219 C3
Harrogate Leisure Ctr
  HG2 . . . . .222 E7
Harrogate Rd
  Bishop Monkton HG3 . . . .139 E5
  Boroughbridge HG5 . . . . .141 A2
  Ferrensby HG5 . . . . .162 E7
  Green Hammerton YO26 . .164 B3
  Kirkby Overblow HG3 . . . .222 D1
  Knaresborough HG5 . . . . .220 F5
  Littlethorpe HG4 . . . . . . .214 C1
  Spofforth with Stockeld
    LS22 . . . . .180 A4
  Weeton LS17 . . . . .178 B2
Harrogate Rossett Acre CP
  Sch HG2 . . . . .222 C7
Harrogate RUFC HG1 . . .219 F3
Harrogate Sta HG1 . . . . .219 D2
Harrogate Town AFC
  HG2 . . . . .220 A2
Harrow Cliff La YO8 . . . . .96 E4
Harrow Glade 🟨 YO30 . .225 F3
Harrow Rd TS5 . . . . .6 E8
Harrowing Dr 🟨 YO21 . .208 C6
Harry Moor La YO8 . . . . .197 B2
Harryfield La YO61 . . . . .144 C7
Hart Hill Cres YO41 . . . . .169 A2
Hartburn Village TS18 . . . .5 E8
Hartforth La DL10 . . . . . . .20 E4
Hartington St 🟨 BB8 . . .186 A3
Hartley La CA17 . . . . .14 A7
Hartley Pl BD22 . . . . .187 B6
Hartley Rd HG2 . . . . .222 B7
Hartley St 🟨 BB18 . . . . .172 A1
Hartlington Raikes
  BD23 . . . . .157 B8
Hartoft St YO10 . . . . . . .228 D2
Hartwith Ave 🟨 HG3 . . .138 A1
Hartwith Bank HG3 . . . . .138 A1
Hartwith Cl HG3 . . . . . . .219 A4
Hartwith Dr HG3 . . . . . . .219 B4
Hartwith Gn 🟨 HG3 . . . .138 A1
Hartwith Way HG3 . . . . .219 B4
Harvard Ct YO12 . . . . . . .212 A8
Harvest Cl 🟨 WF8 . . . . .201 C2
Harvest Croft LS29 . . . . .176 B1
Harvest Way YO11 . . . . .100 B7

Harwood Dale Rd YO13 . .54 A1
Hassacarr La YO19 . . . . .184 F6
Hastings Cl 🟨 YO30 . . . .225 A1
Hastings Cres WF10 . . . .201 A4
Hatcase La 🟨 YO18 . . . . .95 F7
Hatfield Ave TS5 . . . . .6 E8
Hatfield Cl 🟨 YO30 . . . .224 E3
Hatfield Rd DL7 . . . . . . .210 D3
Hatkill La YO41 . . . . .169 B1
Hatterboard Dr YO12 . . .212 C6
Hatters Cl YO23 . . . . . . .230 B3
Haugh La YO8 . . . . .202 F8
Haughton Comp Sch
  DL1 . . . . .3 E7
Haughton Rd
  Darlington DL1 . . . . .3 D6
  York YO30 . . . . .228 C7
Hauling La YO19 . . . . . . .191 C6
Hauxley Ct LS29 . . . . . . .218 D5
Havelock St TS17 . . . . .6 B8
Haven The 🟨 LS25 . . . . .195 F2
Havercroft Rd 🟨 YO14 . .127 A8
Havernook La HG4 . . . . . .86 A3
Havers Hill YO11 . . . . . . .100 A6
Haverthwaites Dr
  LS25 . . . . .188 F1
Havertop La WF6 . . . . . .200 C1
Havikil La HG5 . . . . .162 A5
Havikil Pk HG5 . . . . .162 A6
Haviland Rd TS17 . . . . . . .6 B6
Havre Pk 🟨 BB18 . . . . . .171 E1
Haw Gr BD23 . . . . .154 B3
Haw Hill View WF6 . . . . .200 A2
Haw La BD23 . . . . .154 B3
Haw Pk 🟨 BD23 . . . . . .217 E8
Hawber Cote Dr BD20 . . .174 C1
Hawber La BD20 . . . . . . .174 C1
Hawdon Ave YO8 . . . . . .232 D5
Hawes CP Sch DL8 . . . . . .56 D4
Hawes Rd HG1 . . . . .220 B4
Hawes Visitor Ctr ★
  DL8 . . . . .56 D4
Hawke Garth 🟨 YO14 . . .127 A8
Hawkridge Cl TS17 . . . . . .6 A3
Hawkshead Cl 🟨 YO24 . .230 B8
Hawkstone TS8 . . . . .7 C4
Hawkstone Cl TS14 . . . . . .8 E6
Hawkswell La DL8 . . . . . .40 E1
Hawkswood 🟨 DL2 . . . . . .3 D1
Hawley St BB8 . . . . .186 B3
Hawse Rd YO8 . . . . .204 E8
Hawshaw Rd BD22 . . . . .186 F2
Hawsker C of E Prim Sch
  YO22 . . . . .33 A7
Hawsker Intake Rd
  YO22 . . . . .32 F5
Hawsker La
  Hawsker-cum-Stainsacre
    YO22 . . . . .13 F1
  Whitby YO22 . . . . .208 F6
Hawson Cl 🟨 YO11 . . . . .100 B7
Hawthorn Ave
  🟨 Knaresborough HG5 . .221 B7
  Knottingley WF11 . . . . . .201 E2
  Malton YO17 . . . . .215 D5
  Tadcaster LS24 . . . . .189 C5
Hawthorn Cl
  🟨 Addingham LS29 . . . .174 E4
  🟨 Pickering YO18 . . . . .96 A6
  Stutton with Hazlewood
    LS24 . . . . .189 E5
Hawthorn Cres TS7 . . . . . .7 C6
Hawthorn Croft 🟨 LS24 .189 D5
Hawthorn Dr
  🟨 Topcliffe YO7 . . . . . .89 B1
  Wilberfoss YO41 . . . . . . .185 E5
  Wistow YO8 . . . . .198 A5
Hawthorn Garth DN14 . . .202 F4
Hawthorn Gr YO31 . . . . .228 E5
Hawthorn La YO18 . . . . . .96 A6
Hawthorn Spinney
  YO32 . . . . .225 E3
Hawthorn St 🟨 YO31 . . .228 E5
Hawthorn Terr Ctr 🟨
  YO32 . . . . .225 D3
Hawthorn Terr N
  YO32 . . . . .225 D4
Hawthorn Terr S
  YO32 . . . . .225 D3
Hawthorn Way YO11 . . . .101 C1
Hawthorn Wlk 🟨 YO11 . .100 A7
Hawthorne Ave
  🟨 Haxby YO32 . . . . . . .166 E5
  🟨 Scotton DL9 . . . . . . .40 F2
Hawthorne Cl YO13 . . . . .75 D7
Hawthorne Dr
  Barnoldswick BB18 . . . . .171 E2
  Guisborough TS14 . . . . . . .8 E6
Hawthorns
  🟨 Riccall YO19 . . . . . . .197 F8
  🟨 Riccall YO19 . . . . . . .197 F8
Hawthorns La BD23 . . . . .133 B2
Hawthorns The
  🟨 Glusburn BD20 . . . . .187 E7
  🟨 Great Ayton TS9 . . . . .8 A2
Haxby Moor Rd YO32 . . .166 F7
Haxby Rd Clifton YO31 . .225 D1
  Middleton St George DL2 . .4 C5
  New Earswick YO32 . . . . .225 D6
  York YO31 . . . . .233 B4
Haxby Road Prim Sch
  YO31 . . . . .228 D7
Hay Brow Cl YO13 . . . . . .75 C5
Hay Brow Cres YO13 . . . .75 C5
Hay La YO13 . . . . .75 C5
Hay-a-Park La HG5 . . . . .221 D7
Hayfield Ave LS23 . . . . . .188 E8
Hayforth Cl YO30 . . . . . .225 A2

Haygate La YO18 . . . . . . .95 F5
Haygill Nook BD23 . . . . .174 B5
Hayhills La BD23 . . . . . . .174 B2
Hayton Wood View
  LS25 . . . . .194 F8
Haywain The LS29 . . . . . .218 D3
Haywra Cres 🟨 HG1 . . . .219 E3
Haywra St HG1 . . . . .219 D3
Hazel Bank HG5 . . . . . . .162 C6
Hazel Cl Pannal HG3 . . . .222 C3
  York YO32 . . . . .225 D2
Hazel Ct 🟨 DL8 . . . . .63 B3
Hazel Dr HG3 . . . . .222 C3
Hazel Garth YO31 . . . . . .229 B7
Hazel Gr
  Middlesbrough TS7 . . . . . . .7 C6
  Pontefract WF8 . . . . .201 C1
  Sutton BD20 . . . . .187 E7
Hazel Grove Rd BD20 . . .187 E7
Hazel Hill YO12 . . . . .75 A2
Hazel Old La DN14 . . . . .203 C2
Hazel Rd
  🟨 Boroughbridge YO51 .141 B4
  🟨 Filey YO14 . . . . .101 A4
  Knottingley WF11 . . . . . .201 E1
Hazel Rise LS26 . . . . .200 B5
Hazelheads La HG5 . . . . .221 C8
Hazelmere Ct YO32 . . . . .225 E3
Hazelnut Gr YO32 . . . . . .225 B2
Hazelwood Ave
  Garforth LS25 . . . . .194 D3
  York YO10 . . . . .229 D4
Hazing La DN14 . . . . . . .207 B6
Hazler La BD23 . . . . .157 D7
Headingley Cres 🟨 DL1 . . .3 F6
Headingley Rd 🟨 DN6 . .206 E2
Headland Cl 🟨 YO32 . . .166 E5
Headland La YO18 . . . . . . .72 A6
Headlands La
  Howgrave HG4 . . . . .87 F2
  Knottingley WF11 . . . . . .201 F2
  Pontefract WF8 . . . . .201 B1
Headlands Prim Sch
  YO32 . . . . .225 D8
Headlands Rd YO62 . . . . .70 E2
Headlands The DL3 . . . . . .3 A5
Headley Cl 🟨 YO30 . . . . .225 B1
Headley La LS23 . . . . . . .188 F5
Heads Bank DL8 . . . . .58 F3
Heads La BB18 . . . . .186 A7
Heads Rd Newton YO18 . .51 B1
  Pickering YO18 . . . . .71 F8
Headwell La LS24 . . . . . .195 E7
Healaugh La YO26 . . . . . .181 F4
Healaugh Priory ★
  LS24 . . . . .181 E1
Heald Brow BB18 . . . . . .171 D2
Heald St WF10 . . . . .200 F4
Healdfield Rd WF10 . . . . .201 A4
Healdwood Rd WF10 . . . .201 A4
Healey Gr YO31 . . . . .228 F8
Healthfield Prim Sch
  DL1 . . . . .3 E5
Heath Cl 🟨 YO24 . . . . . .227 F2
Heath Cres BD20 . . . . . . .173 E3
Heath Croft YO10 . . . . . .231 F7
Heath Dr
  Boston Spa LS23 . . . . . . .188 D8
  🟨 Low Bradley BD20 . . .173 E3
Heath Gr HG2 . . . . .219 B1
Heath Moor Dr YO10 . . . .231 F8
Heath Pk 🟨 LS29 . . . . . .175 C2
Heath Ride YO32 . . . . . . .167 B8
Heathcliff Gdns 🟨
  YO12 . . . . .212 C8
Heather Bank
  🟨 Stamford Bridge YO41 .168 D2
  York YO10 . . . . .229 C4
Heather Brow 🟨 BB18 . .172 B1
Heather Cl 🟨 Selby YO8 .232 C3
  🟨 Whorlton DL6 . . . . . .25 D1
  York YO32 . . . . .226 A4
Heather Croft 🟨 YO31 . .225 E2
Heather Dr YO22 . . . . . . .208 E3
Heather View BD23 . . . . .217 B3
Heather Way 🟨 HG3 . . . .161 B3
Heatherdene LS24 . . . . . .189 E6
Heatherdene Rd 🟨 DL9 . .40 F4
Heathfield Dr HG5 . . . . . .221 C6
Heathfield Pk DL2 . . . . . . .4 C5
Heathfield Rd 🟨 YO10 . .229 A3
Heathness Rd LS29 . . . . .174 E5
Heathrow TS17 . . . . .6 C7
Heathrow Cl 🟨 DL2 . . . . .4 C4
Hebden Bank HG3 . . . . . .138 F4
Hebden Rd BD23 . . . . . . .134 E2
Hebdon Rise 🟨 YO26 . . .227 D4
Heber Dr YO22 . . . . .172 A5
Heber's Ghyll Dr 🟨
  LS29 . . . . .175 C2
Heber's Gr 🟨 LS29 . . . . .175 C2
Hebron Rd TS9 . . . . .26 C7
Heck & Pollington Lake
  DN14 . . . . .207 E7
Heck Gill La HG3 . . . . . . .160 A5
Heck La DN14 . . . . .207 C6
Heckler Cl 🟨 HG4 . . . . . .214 C4
Heckler La HG4 . . . . .214 C4
Heddon Gr TS17 . . . . .6 A3
Hedley St TS14 . . . . .8 F7
Height La BD23 . . . . .174 C6
Height Lands La YO23 . . .182 D6
Heights La BD20 . . . . . . .174 A2
Helena St LS25 . . . . .200 C6
Helks Brow LA2 . . . . .128 E2
Hell Wath Gr HG4 . . . . . .214 A2
Hell Wath La
  Littlethorpe HG4 . . . . . . .214 A2

Hell Wath La continued
  Markingfield Hall HG4 . . . .139 E6
Hellifield CP Sch
  BD23 . . . . .154 B3
Hellifield Rd BD23 . . . . . .155 A6
Hellifield Sta BD23 . . . . .154 B4
Helmsdale YO24 . . . . . . .230 C6
Helmsley Castle ★
  YO62 . . . . .92 E6
Helmsley Cty Prim Sch
  YO62 . . . . .92 F7
Helmsley Dr TS14 . . . . . . .8 F7
Helmsley Gr 🟨 YO32 . . .166 D5
Helmsley Rd TS9 . . . . . . .26 C7
Helmsley Way DL7 . . . . .210 C2
Helperby & Myton La
  YO61 . . . . .142 A7
Helperby La YO51 . . . . . .141 C7
Helredale Gdns YO22 . . .208 E4
Helredale Rd YO22 . . . . .208 E4
Helston Rd WF6 . . . . . . .200 A2
Helwath Rd YO13 . . . . . . .53 D5
Helwith Rd DL11 . . . . .38 E7
Hemingbrough CP Sch
  YO8 . . . . .198 F1
Hemingford Gdns TS15 . . .5 E2
Hemishor Dr LS26 . . . . . .200 C8
Hemlington Hall Rd TS8 . .6 E5
Hemlington Hall Sch
  TS8 . . . . .6 E5
Hemlington Lake & Recn Ctr
  TS8 . . . . .6 E5
Hemlington Rd TS8 . . . . . .6 E5
Hemlock Ave YO31 . . . . .225 E1
Hempbridge Cl YO8 . . . . .232 A5
Hempbridge Rd YO8 . . . .232 A5
Hempland Ave YO31 . . . .228 F6
Hempland Dr YO31 . . . . .229 A7
Hempland Inf Sch
  YO31 . . . . .229 A6
Hempland Jun Sch
  YO31 . . . . .229 B6
Hempland La YO31 . . . . .229 A7
Hemsby Rd WF10 . . . . . .200 E3
Henbusk La LA2 . . . . .130 A8
Hendon Garth YO30 . . . .225 A1
Henlow La YO60 . . . . . . .147 B4
Henrietta Cl DL10 . . . . . .209 F8
Henrietta St YO22 . . . . . .208 E7
Henry Moore Jun Sch
  WF10 . . . . .200 E3
Henry St BD23 . . . . .216 F1
Hensall CP Sch DN14 . . .203 C1
Hensall Sta DN14 . . . . . .203 C1
Henshaws Coll HG1 . . . . .220 B5
Henside La BD24 . . . . . . .132 A5
Henside Rd BD24 . . . . . . .132 B6
Henson Gr WF10 . . . . . . .201 A4
Henwick Hall La YO8 . . . .232 C1
Hepton Hill YO17 . . . . . . .120 F2
Hepworth's La DN14 . . . .204 C2
Herbert St 🟨 YO10 . . . . .228 E3
Herberts Way YO31 . . . . .228 F7
Hercules St DL1 . . . . .3 E7
Herdborough Rd
  YO11 . . . . .100 A1
Herdsman Dr YO23 . . . . .230 C3
Herdsman Rd 🟨 YO24 . .230 D8
Herdwick Cl 🟨 YO30 . . .225 B1
Hereford Rd HG1 . . . . . . .219 A2
Hergill La Baldersby HG4 .88 C1
  Kirby Hill DL11 . . . . .19 F5
  Kirkby Fleetham with Fencote
    DL7 . . . . .63 C8
Herisson Cl 🟨 YO10 . . . . .95 F7
Heritage Ctr The ★ TS12 . .9 D6
Herman Wlk YO24 . . . . . .230 C8
Hermitage The ★ HG4 . . .86 C8
Hermitage Way YO22 . . . .32 A5
Heron Ave YO24 . . . . . . .230 C8
Heron Cl 🟨 Bedale DL8 . .63 B3
  🟨 Thornton Dale YO18 . .96 D5
Heron Dr DL1 . . . . .3 E5
Heron Gate TS14 . . . . .8 D6
Heron La YO12 . . . . .99 E6
Heron Rise YO32 . . . . . . .225 F5
Heron Tree Cl DL8 . . . . . .60 D7
Heron Way YO7 . . . . .215 C4
Herriot Way YO7 . . . . . . .211 C4
Hertford Cl 🟨 YO11 . . . .100 A7
Hertford Vale C of E Prim
  Sch YO12 . . . . .99 D2
Hesketh Ave TS4 . . . . .7 A4
Hesketh Bank YO10 . . . . .229 D3
Heslaker La BD23 . . . . . .216 C1
Hesleden Ave TS5 . . . . . . .6 D6
Hesley La BD24 . . . . .153 A6
Heslin Cl 🟨 YO32 . . . . . .225 C4
Heslington Croft YO10 . . .231 F7
Heslington Ct 🟨 YO10 . .229 B1
Heslington La
  Heslington YO10 . . . . . . .229 A1
  York YO10 . . . . .231 E8
Heslington Prim Sch
  YO10 . . . . .229 C1
Heslington Rd YO10 . . . . .228 D2
Hessay Pl 🟨 YO26 . . . . . .227 A3
Hetherton St YO30 . . . . .233 A3
Hetton Garth 🟨 DL8 . . . .60 D5
Hewison Rd DL1 . . . . .3 F8
Hewitts La BD20 . . . . . . .172 F2
Hewley Ave YO10 . . . . . .229 A6
Hewley Dr 🟨 YO13 . . . . .99 A7
Heworth YO31 . . . . .229 A6
Heworth ARLFC YO31 . . .229 A8

Heworth C of E Prim Sch YO31 228 F6
Heworth Dr YO21 208 B6
Heworth Gn YO31 233 C4
Heworth Hall Dr YO31 228 F6
Heworth Pl YO31 228 F6
Heworth Rd YO31 228 F6
Heyford Rd YO7 115 B1
Heygate Bank YO18 49 F3
Heygate La LS23 188 F6
Heyshaw Rd HG3 159 C8
Heythrop Dr
Guisborough TS14 8 F6
Middlesbrough TS5 6 D7
Heywood Rd HG2 219 C1
Hibernia St YO12 212 E5
Hicks La LS26 200 B6
Hickstead Ct 16 DL1 3 F6
Hidcote Gdns TS17 6 A4
High Back Side YO18 95 E8
High Bank
Ampleforth YO62 92 B2
Bradleys Both BD20 173 E3
5 Threshfield BD23 134 D2
High Bank Cl 7 LS29 174 F4
High Barmer YO13 75 B7
High Bentham CP Sch LA2 129 B8
High Bond End HG5 221 A7
High Bradley La BD20 173 E4
High Catton Rd YO41 185 D8
High Church Wynd TS16 5 D3
High Cleugh HG4 214 A4
High Coniscliffe C of E Sch DL2 2 C6
High Cragwell YO21 31 F7
High Crest 6 HG3 137 C4
High Croft 7 YO14 126 F8
High Croft Way 5 BD20 173 E1
High Eggborough La DN14 203 A1
High Fell Cl BD24 131 D1
High Field YO10 229 D4
High Fold BB18 186 A7
High Garth
Eastfield YO11 100 A7
Richmond DL10 209 B8
High Gill Rd TS7 7 D6
High Gn Catterick DL10 41 D4
Hebden BD23 135 A2
High Green Dr BD20 174 B1
High Hill Gr St 14 BD24 131 D2
High Hill La BD24 131 E2
High La Beadlam YO62 93 C8
Birstwith HG3 160 C5
Cowling BD22 187 A4
Cropton YO18 71 C4
Dalby-cum-Skewsby YO60 119 A2
Dalton DL11 19 D7
Fylingdales YO22 33 C5
Gillamoor YO62 70 A6
Grassington BD23 134 E3
Grinton DL11 37 D4
Hawes DL8 56 F4
Howsham YO60 147 B1
Kirby Sigston DL6 44 E1
Leake DL6 65 E6
Maltby TS15 6 C4
Muston YO14 100 F1
Myton-on-Swale YO61 142 B6
Newsham DL11 18 G7
Reeth, Fremington & Healaugh DL11 37 F5
Spofforth with Stockeld HG3 179 C4
Sutton upon Derwent YO41 185 D3
Thirlby YO7 90 D6
Thornton Watlass DL8 62 C2
West Scrafton DL8 83 F6
West Witton DL8 59 D2
High Leir La YO7 67 D1
High Market Pl 27 YO62 70 B1
High Mdw
Gowdall DN14 204 A1
Selby YO8 232 B6
High Mill Dr 1 YO12 75 E5
High Mill La LS29 175 A5
High Moor Edge YO12 212 A7
High Moor La
Boroughbridge HG5 141 A2
Brearton HG3 161 F8
Newton-on-Ouse YO30 165 C8
Scotton HG5 162 A5
High Moor Rd
North Rigton HG3 178 A5
Skelton YO51 140 F7
High Moor Way 11 YO11 100 A6
High Newbiggin St YO31 233 B3
High Oaks YO31 229 B7
High Ousegate YO1 233 B2
High Peak TS14 8 F5
High Peter La HG3 140 A3
High Petergate YO1 233 B3
High Rd LA2 128 F5
High Riding Aske DL10 20 D1
Richmond DL10 209 C8
High Rifts TS8 6 E5
High Riggs La YO18 96 C3
High Row
Bugthorpe YO41 169 D4
Caldwell DL11 1 C4
Darlington DL1 3 C5
Melsonby DL10 20 F7
High Skellgate 7 HG4 214 C5
High St Airmyn DN14 205 E3
Ampleforth YO62 92 C3
Aske DL10 20 E2
Austwick LA2 130 E7
Barmby on the Marsh DN14 205 A7
Barnby YO21 12 C4
Barton-le-Street YO17 120 E5
Beadlam YO62 93 D7
Boosbeck TS12 9 D8
6 Boroughbridge YO51 141 B5
Boston Spa LS23 188 E8
Boston Spa LS23 188 F7
Bramham LS23 188 E5
Buckton/Bempton YO13 97 D6
Burniston YO13 75 C8
Burton in Lonsdale LA6 102 F3
Carlton DN14 204 C2
Castleford WF10 200 E4
Catterick DL10 41 D5
Cawood YO8 197 B8
Cottam YO25 150 E5
Cropton YO18 71 B4
Danby YO21 29 A6
Eaglescliffe TS15 5 D4
13 Eastfield YO11 100 A6
Gargrave BD23 155 D1
Glaisdale YO21 30 D4
Glusburn BD20 187 E6
Great Ayton TS9 7 F1
Great Broughton TS9 26 E4
Hampsthwaite HG3 160 F5
Harrogate HG2 220 C4
4 Helmsley YO62 92 F6
Heslerton YO17 123 F6
Hinderwell TS13 11 F7
Hovingham YO62 119 E6
Husthwaite YO61 117 B6
Ingleton LA6 103 D4
Kippax LS25 194 D1
Kirby Grindalythe YO17 149 D8
5 Knaresborough HG5 221 B5
Knottingley WF11 201 E5
Langtoft YO25 151 C8
Lastingham YO62 70 E5
9 Leyburn DL8 60 D5
Lingdale TS12 9 F7
Lockwood TS12 10 A5
Markington with Wallerthwaite HG3 139 C4
Mickleby TS13 12 A4
Middlesbrough TS7 7 C8
Newton Mulgrave TS13 11 E4
Normanton South WF6 200 A1
Northallerton DL7 210 D6
Norton DN6 206 E2
Old Byland & Scawton YO62 92 A4
Oldstead YO7 91 E5
Pateley Bridge HG3 137 B4
Rawcliffe DN14 205 A1
Rillington YO17 122 F5
Scalby YO13 75 D5
6 Settle BD24 131 E2
Settrington YO17 122 F1
Sherburn YO17 124 D7
Skipton BD23 217 A4
Slingsby YO62 120 B5
Snainton YO13 98 A5
Snaith DN14 204 B1
South Milford LS25 195 E2
Spofforth HG3 179 E5
3 Staithes TS13 13 K2
Stillington YO61 144 B6
Stokesley TS9 26 C7
Swinton YO17 121 B4
Tadcaster LS24 189 E6
Thornton Dale YO18 96 E6
Thornton-le-Clay YO60 146 A4
Wharram YO17 149 A6
Whitby YO21 208 B3
Whixley YO26 164 A4
Whorlton DL6 45 D8
Wombleton YO62 93 E7
Wrelton YO18 71 C1
High St Agnesgate HG4 214 C5
High Stakesby Rd YO21 208 A6
High Stell DL2 4 C4
High Town Bank Rd YO7 91 C5
High Trace DL6 210 E2
High Trees Ct LS25 195 F4
High Trees Sch LS23 188 F7
High View HG3 160 F8
High Wheatley LS29 218 E3
High Wlk YO12 212 E7
High Wood LS29 218 F3
Highbank Gr 1 HG2 220 D4
Highbury Ave TS5 6 F8
Highcliff Rd TS14 8 E4
Highcliffe Ct YO30 228 A6
Highcroft
Collingham LS22 188 A8
9 Grassington BD23 134 E3
Highdale Ave 5 YO12 212 D8
Highdale Rd YO12 212 E7
Higher Hartley St 2 BD20 187 D7
Higher Lodge St 1 BD20 187 D7
Higher Rd BD23 152 F4
Higherlands Cl BD23 155 D1
Highfield
Pollington DN14 207 F7
Scarborough YO12 212 E4
Highfield Ave WF8 201 D2
Highfield Cl YO25 126 A4
Highfield Cres YO8 198 B5
Highfield Ct YO8 232 B1
Highfield Dr
Allerton Bywater WF10 200 C7
Garforth LS25 194 C3
Highfield Gn
Allerton Bywater WF10 200 C7
Sherburn in Elmet LS25 195 F3
Highfield Gr WF10 200 C7
Highfield La
Barwick in Elmet & Scholes LS15 194 B7
Fangfoss YO41 169 B1
Gillamoor YO62 69 F5
Huddleston with Newthorpe LS25 195 B2
Nawton YO62 69 C2
Scagglethorpe YO17 122 E2
Womersley DN6 206 D5
Highfield Pl 1 WF10 200 D7
Highfield Rd
Aberford LS25 194 F8
29 Earby BB18 172 A1
Malton YO17 215 C5
Ripon HG4 214 B3
Whitby YO21 208 A7
Highfield View 3 YO8 198 B4
Highfield Villas LS25 195 F3
Highfields La YO7 115 A1
Highgate Balne DN14 207 D6
Glusburn BD20 187 D8
Highgate Pk HG1 219 F3
Highgrove Cl 7 YO30 224 E3
Highland Cl 9 WF8 201 C1
Highlands Ave 5 YO32 167 B7
Highlands Cl YO14 101 B1
Highmoor Cl YO24 230 D8
Highmoor Rd
Darlington DL1 3 F4
York YO24 230 D8
Highthorn Rd YO31 225 E2
Highthorne La YO61 117 B5
Highway BD24 131 E3
Hilbeck Gr YO31 229 B6
Hilbra Ave YO32 225 D6
Hilda St 6 Selby YO8 232 C5
3 York YO10 228 E3
Hildenley Cl 6 YO12 212 B5
Hilderthorpe TS7 7 C6
Hildewell 3 TS13 11 F7
Hildyard Cl TS9 26 C8
Hill Bank HG5 163 B7
Hill Cl DL11 38 B6
Hill Crest YO19 167 F1
Hill Crest Gdns YO24 227 F1
Hill End La BD22 186 F5
Hill Field YO8 232 B8
Hill Foot La HG3 222 B2
Hill House La DL2 4 C8
Hill La BB8 186 B4
Hill Rd WF10 200 F3
Hill Rise
Middleton St George DL2 4 D3
Skipton BD23 216 E5
Hill Rise Ave HG2 222 B8
Hill Rise Cl HG2 222 B8
Hill Side DL2 3 A3
Hill St
6 Barnoldswick BB18 171 E1
York YO24 227 E3
Hill The DL8 56 D4
Hill Top
24 Burley in Warfedale LS29 176 C1
Castleford WF10 200 C4
Ilkley LS29 218 A2
Knottingley WF11 201 F2
Hill Top Ave HG1 219 D6
Hill Top Cl
Embsay BD23 217 C8
Harrogate HG1 219 D6
Stutton with Hazlewood LS24 189 D4
Hill Top Cres HG1 219 D6
Hill Top Ct DL7 22 C3
Hill Top Dr HG1 219 D6
Hill Top Gr HG1 219 E6
Hill Top La Earby BB18 172 A1
Pannal HG3 222 A4
Hill Top Mount HG1 219 D6
Hill Top Rd
Harrogate HG1 219 D6
4 Wistow YO8 197 D6
Hill Top Rise HG1 219 E6
Hill Top View HG3 159 F8
Hill Top Wlk HG1 219 D6
Hill View
Langthorpe YO51 141 A6
Stillington YO61 144 C6
York YO31 229 C7
Hillam Comm La LS25 202 B7
Hillam Hall La 4 LS25 202 A7
Hillam Hall View 3 LS25 202 A7
Hillam La
Burton Salmon LS25 201 F7
Hillam LS25 202 A7
Hillam Rd YO8 202 F8
Hillary Garth 9 YO26 227 E4
Hillbank Gr HG1 220 D4
Hillbank Rd HG1 220 D4
Hillbank View HG1 220 C4
Hillcrest
8 Monk Fryston LS25 202 A8
Tadcaster LS24 189 D5
Hillcrest Ave
Newby & Scalby YO12 75 E5
Hillcrest Ave *continued*
Poppleton YO26 224 A2
Silsden BD20 174 C1
Hillcrest Cl WF10 201 B3
Hillcrest Ct 2 LS24 189 D5
Hillcrest Dr
Castleford WF10 201 B3
Loftus TS13 10 D8
Hillcrest Gdns YO51 141 A7
Hillcrest Gr 2 YO12 75 E5
Hillcrest Mount WF10 201 B3
Hillgarth WF11 201 F2
Hillgarth Ct 4 YO41 185 B2
Hillhouse DL2 4 C7
Hilliam Hall Cl 5 LS25 202 A7
Hillingdon Rd TS4 7 B8
Hillocks La TS12 10 A5
Hills La BD23 155 E5
Hillsborough Terr 5 YO30 228 C7
Hillshaw Parkway HG4 214 D5
Hillside Byram WF11 201 E4
Follifoot HG3 223 F4
3 Ingleby Arncliffe DL6 45 A7
Hillside Cl
18 Addingham LS29 174 F4
9 Monk Fryston LS25 202 A8
Threshfield BD23 134 B3
Hillside Cres BD23 217 C3
Hillside Dr BD23 134 B3
Hillside Gdns
Langtoft YO25 151 D5
Scarborough YO12 212 E1
Hillside Rd HG3 222 E3
Hillside Way YO17 150 B8
Hilltop Cres DL9 40 E4
Hilton Cl DL6 210 E8
Hilton Gn DL6 210 D8
Hilton Grange DL6 210 E8
Hilton La 7 HG5 221 A6
Hilton Rd TS9 6 F1
Hilton Sq DL6 210 E8
Hincks Hall La HG3 139 C3
Hinderwell CP Sch YO12 212 D2
Hinderwell La
Hinderwell TS13 11 E8
Staithes TS13 13 K1
Hinderwell Pl YO12 212 E2
Hinderwell Rd YO12 212 E1
Hindle Dr 39 YO14 101 B3
Hinsley La DN14 204 C2
Hinton Ave 1 YO24 230 C8
Hinton Cl 9 WF8 201 C2
Hinton La WF11 201 D3
Hipswell C of E Prim Sch DL9 209 F1
Hipswell Rd DL9 209 E1
Hipswell Rd W DL9 209 C1
Hird Ave 22 DL8 63 A2
Hird Rd TS15 5 D2
Hirds Yd 2 BD23 216 F3
Hirst Courtney & Temple Hirst CP Sch YO8 203 E3
Hirst La HG3 160 E5
Hirst Rd YO8 204 A3
Hirst St WF10 200 C8
Hirstead Gdns YO12 212 B8
Hirstead Rd YO12 212 B8
Hob Cote La BD22 187 F1
Hob Moor Dr YO24 227 E2
Hob Moor Inf Sch YO24 227 D2
Hob Moor Jun Sch YO24 227 E2
Hobart Rd WF10 201 B5
Hobb Nook La LS21 176 D4
Hobbs Cl DL9 209 C2
Hobgate YO24 227 D3
Hobmoor Terr YO24 227 F1
Hobson Cl YO23 230 B1
Hodge La WF8 206 B3
Hodgson Fold LS29 174 E5
Hodgson Hill YO13 54 B4
Hodgson La YO26 182 F8
Hodgson's La LS25 196 A5
Hogg La YO17 148 E6
Holbeck Ave
Middlesbrough TS5 6 E6
Scarborough YO11 213 B2
Holbeck Cl YO11 213 B2
Holbeck Hill YO11 213 B1
Holbeck Rd YO11 213 A2
Holbecks La YO51 141 F3
Holburns Croft 3 YO10 229 B1
Holden Gdns YO8 197 D2
Hole House La BB7 152 B2
Hole La BD20 174 A2
Holes La WF11 201 E2
Holgate DL6 45 E8
Holgate Bank HG5 163 A8
Holgate Bridge Gdn 7 YO24 228 A3
Holgate Cl YO17 215 C5
Holgate Lodge Dr YO26 227 E4
Holgate Rd YO24 233 A1
Holl Gate DL8 59 E3
Hollicarrs Cl YO19 192 A2
Hollies The YO8 198 C4
Hollin Gate LS21 176 E1
Hollin Hall Dr LS29 175 C2
Hollin La LA2 129 F6
Hollin Top La YO21 29 C7
Hollings The LS26 200 A6
Hollington St 14 BB8 186 A3
Hollingwood Gate 31 LS29 175 C2
Hollingwood Rise 32 LS29 175 C2
Hollinhurst Brow LA2 128 F2
Hollins DL8 60 B3
Hollins Beck Cl LS25 200 D8
Hollins Cl HG3 161 A5
Hollins Cres HG1 219 C4
Hollins Gr WF10 200 C7
Hollins Hall HG3 161 A4
Hollins La Firby DL8 63 B1
Hampsthwaite HG3 161 A4
Melmerby HG4 114 B8
Middleton Quernhow HG4 88 C1
Rosedale East Side YO18 49 D4
Hollins Mews HG1 219 C4
Hollins Rd
10 Barnoldswick BB18 171 D1
Harrogate HG1 219 C4
Hollis Cres YO32 167 B6
Hollow Gill Brow BD24 153 C5
Hollow Moor La DL8 62 E7
Holly Bank Gr 3 YO24 227 F2
Holly Bank Rd YO24 227 F2
Holly Cl
Acaster Malbis YO23 191 C8
Full Sutton YO41 169 A2
Thirsk YO7 211 B2
Wrelton YO18 71 C1
Holly Ct 11 HG5 221 B6
Holly Garth 1 YO61 115 F1
Holly Garth Cl TS9 7 F1
Holly Gr Selby YO8 232 B3
8 Thorpe Willoughby YO8 197 B2
Holly Pk LS17 178 B3
Holly Rd 10 Bedale DL8 63 B3
Boston Spa LS23 188 D8
Holly Tree Croft 2 YO19 184 F7
Holly Tree Ct 2 YO21 208 B6
Holly Tree Garth YO32 167 E3
Holly Tree La
Dunnington YO19 184 F7
Haxby YO32 225 D8
Holly Wlk YO12 212 D7
Hollybush Ave TS17 6 B5
Hollybush Gn LS22 188 B8
Hollygarth La DN14 202 D4
Hollyhurst Rd DL3 3 C6
Hollyrood Rd YO30 224 E3
Hollywalk Ave TS6 7 E8
Hollywood YO8 232 B7
Holm Hill YO13 54 C2
Holm La LA2 130 E6
Holme Cl Earby BB18 186 A8
23 Sutton BD20 187 E7
Holme Cres BB8 186 A2
Holme Croft 1 BD23 134 D2
Holme Farm La LS23 188 A5
Holme Green Rd YO23 190 F4
Holme Hill 2 YO11 100 A6
Holme Hill La YO10 184 C4
Holme Ings LS29 175 B4
Holme La
Glusburn BD20 187 E7
Halton East BD23 174 B8
Newbiggin DL8 58 E1
Rudby TS9 25 E7
Selby YO8 232 D6
Holme St 17 BB8 186 A3
Holme The TS9 26 E4
Holmebeck La HG4 88 B1
Holmefield Cl 3 YO8 232 A1
Holmefield Ct 2 YO8 232 A1
Holmefield La YO10 229 A1
Holmefield Rd
Glusburn BD20 187 E7
Ripon HG4 214 C3
Holmefields Rd TS6 7 E8
Holmes Dr 2 YO19 192 A1
Holmes House* YO8 199 B3
Holmfield HG4 112 D7
Holmfield Cl WF8 201 C2
Holmfield Cres HG4 214 C3
Holmfield La WF8 201 C2
Holmstead Ave YO21 208 A5
Holmtree La HG4 113 B8
Holmwood Ave TS5 6 F8
Holray Pk DN14 204 C2
Holroyd Ave YO31 229 A5
Holtby Gr YO12 212 D5
Holtby La Holtby YO19 167 D1
Stockton on the Forest YO32 226 F2
Holy Family RC High Sch DN14 204 C3
Holy Family RC Prim Sch DL3 3 B6
Holy Family RC Sch WF8 201 D1
Holy Rood La LS25 201 C8
Holy Trinity C of E Inf Sch HG4 214 B6
Holy Trinity Prim Sch HG4 214 B5
Holyrood Ave DL3 3 A5
Holystone Dr TS17 6 A4
Holywell Gn TS16 5 E5
Holywell La
Castleford WF10 201 A3
North Cowton DL7 22 C2
Home Farm Cl LA2 128 A6

Home Office Emergency Planning Coll YO61 ..143 D6
Homefield Cl YO23 ....230 A2
Homestead Cl
Eggborough DN14 ....203 A2
2 York YO32 ....225 F1
Homestead Rd HG1 ...219 E2
Honey Pot 5 YO8 .....199 D7
Honey Pot Rd 2 DL10 ...41 C6
Honeypot La DL3 ....3 C7
Honeysuckle Cl
Romanby DL7 ....210 C1
Selby YO8 ....232 C2
Honister Gr TS5 ....6 D7
Hood La YO13 ....54 D2
Hoodstorth La HG3 ....158 F6
Hook La DN14 ....205 F4
Hook Pasture La
DN14 ....205 F1
Hookstone Ave HG2 ...222 E7
Hookstone Chase
HG2 ....220 D2
Hookstone Chase CP Sch
HG2 ....220 D2
Hookstone Cl HG2 ....220 C2
Hookstone Dr HG2 ....223 A8
Hookstone Garth HG3 .159 E5
Hookstone Grange Ct 3
HG2 ....220 C2
Hookstone Grange Way 2
HG2 ....220 C2
Hookstone Oval 7 HG2 220 B1
Hookstone Pk HG2 ....220 D2
Hookstone Rd HG2 ....222 E7
Hookstone Way HG2 ...220 D2
Hookstone Wood Rd
9 Harrogate HG2 ......220 B1
Harrogate HG2 ....223 B8
Hope St 30 Filey YO14 ...101 B3
Knaresborough HG5 .....221 B5
Scarborough YO12 ......213 A6
York YO10 ....233 C1
Hopetown La DL3 ....3 C6
Hopgrove La N YO32 ...226 C3
Hopgrove La S YO32 ...226 E3
Hopper Hill Rd YO11 ....99 F6
Hopper La LS21 ....159 C2
Hopperton St HG5 ....163 E4
Hopps's Rd 6 BD20 ....187 E8
Horn La BD20 ....174 B3
Hornbeam Cres HG2 ...222 F8
Hornbeam Park Ave
HG2 ....222 F7
Hornbeam Park Sta
HG2 ....222 F7
Hornbeam Sq N HG2 ..223 A7
Hornbeam Sq S HG2 ..223 A7
Hornbeam Sq W HG2 ..222 F7
Hornblower Cl 5 HG4 .113 D2
Hornby Castle* DL8 ....62 C8
Hornby Cl 1 DL2 ....3 E1
Hornby Rd
Appleton Wiske DL6 ......24 A3
Roeburndale LA2 ....128 A2
Wray-with-Botton LA2 ...128 A6
Horndale Rd 5 YO14 ....101 B4
Horne Rd DL9 ....40 F4
Horner Ave YO61 ......144 A5
Horner Cl YO61 ....144 A5
Horner St YO30 ....228 B7
Hornsea Rd TS8 ....6 E5
Hornsey Garth 25 YO32 .166 E5
Horse Bell Gate LA6 ...103 D4
Horse Course La YO17 .122 E1
Horse Mill La HG3 ....139 D5
Horsefair 2 YO51 ......141 B5
Horseman Ave YO23 ...230 A3
Horseman Cl 2 YO23 ...230 A3
Horseman Dr YO23 ....230 A3
Horseman La YO23 ....230 A3
Horsemarket Rd YO17 .215 B4
Horseshoe Cave*
BD24 ....132 A3
Horseshoe The YO24 ..230 E7
Horseway Gn YO18 .....49 D4
Horsfield Way YO19 ...184 F7
Horsman Ave YO10 ....233 C1
Horton in Ribblesdale C of E Prim Sch BD24 ......105 D3
Horton in Ribbleside Sta
BD24 ....105 C3
Hospital Fields Rd
YO10 ....228 D1
Hospital La YO8 ....197 B4
Hospital Rd YO17 .....215 B4
Hospitum The* YO30 ..233 A3
Hostess La YO18 ....72 E4
Hotham Ave YO26 .....227 B2
Hothfield Street Jun Sch
BD20 ....174 C1
Houghton Ave WF11 ...201 D2
Houndgate DL1 ....3 C5
Houndsway 6 YO24 ....230 B8
House of Correction Mus*
HG4 ....214 D5
Hovingham C of E Prim Sch
YO62 ....119 E6
Hovingham Dr YO12 ...212 B4
Hovingham Hall*
YO62 ....119 E6
How Hill Rd HG4 .....139 B6
How Stean Gorge*
HG3 ....110 B4
Howard Dr YO30 ......224 E2
Howard Link YO30 ....224 D2
Howard Rd
Catterick Garrison DL9 ...209 E1
Towthorpe YO32 ....167 B6
Howard St
3 Scarborough YO12 ....213 A7
York YO10 ....228 D2
Howden Dike TS15 ......5 E2
Howden La YO19 ......231 E1
Howden Rd
4 Barlby YO8 ....198 B4
Romanby DL7 ....210 B2
Silsden BD20 ....174 C1
Howdenshire Way
DN14 ....205 F6
Howdlands La HG4 ....140 E7
Howe Ave DL10 ....41 E3
Howe Bank YO21 ....29 B7
Howe End YO62 ....70 B1
Howe Field Rd YO26 ..142 A2
Howe Hill Bank TS8 .....7 B2
Howe Hill Cl YO26 ....227 E4
Howe Hill La DL10 .....41 C6
Howe Hill Rd YO26 ....227 E4
Howe La YO41 ....170 A5
Howe Rd Malton YO17 ..122 A6
Norton YO17 ....215 E3
Howe St YO24 ....227 D3
Howes Rd 8 YO14 .....127 A8
Howgate DL8 ....57 F6
Howgill La
Barden BD23 ....157 E6
Rimington BB7 ....171 A1
Howhill Quarry Rd
HG3 ....178 B7
Howhill Rd HG3 ......178 B8
Howker La YO61 ......116 F2
Howl Gate YO41 ......185 E8
Howlbeck Rd TS14 ......8 E7
Howldale La
Appleton-le-Moors YO62 ...70 F4
3 Beadlam YO62 ....93 D7
Howlgate La YO21 .....13 A1
Howsham Gates*
YO60 ....146 F2
Howsham Hall Prep Sch
YO60 ....146 F2
Howson La BD24 ......131 E4
Hoxton Rd YO12 ......212 F6
Hoylake Rd TS4 ....6 F8
Hoylake Way TS16 ......5 E4
Hubert St 2 YO23 .....228 B1
Huby Prim Sch YO61 ..144 A4
Huby Rd YO61 ....144 B3
Hudgin La Lockton YO18 ..72 E4
Wykeham YO13 ....98 D4
Hudson Cl
Malton YO17 ....215 C6
Stamford Bridge YO41 ...168 D2
2 Tadcaster LS24 ....189 E6
Hudson Cres 2 YO30 ..228 A7
Hudson St
Whitby YO21 ....208 D7
6 York YO30 ....228 C7
Hudson View 1 LS24 ..189 E6
Hudson Way LS24 .....189 E6
Hugden Cl YO18 ....96 A6
Hugden Way YO17 ....215 F4
Huggate Hill YO17 ....170 E7
Hugh Field La YO8 ....199 A8
Hugh Field North La
YO8 ....193 A1
Hugh St WF10 ....200 E4
Hull Rd Cliffe YO8 .....198 E2
Hemingbrough YO8 ......199 B1
Heslington YO19 ....229 E3
Humber Dr 5 YO32 ....167 B6
Humber Rd TS17 ....6 B7
Hummersknott Ave DL3 ..3 A5
Hummersknott Comp Sch
DL3 ....3 A4
Humphrey Balk La
YO7 ....114 D8
Humphrey Hill DL8 .....58 D1
Hundale Rd 5 TS15 .....25 C5
Hunday Field Rd YO51 .141 E2
Hundens Day Hospl DL1 ..3 E5
Hundens La DL1 ....3 D6
Hungate
Bishop Monkton HG3 .....140 A5
Brompton YO13 ....98 C5
Pickering YO18 ....95 F6
York YO1 ....233 C2
Hungate Cl LS24 ......195 D8
Hungate Ct 11 YO14 ...126 F8
Hungate Cty Prim Sch
LS25 ....195 F4
Hungate La YO14 .....126 F8
Hungate Rd LS25 .....195 F4
Hunger Hill LS29 .....218 C7
Hungerhill La YO62 ....93 F6
Hunmanby CP Sch
YO14 ....126 F8
Hunmanby Rd
Burton Fleming YO25 ....126 E3
Reighton YO14 ....127 C6
Hunmanby St YO14 ...100 F2
Hunmanby Sta YO14 ..127 A7
Hunt Ct YO31 ....233 C3
Hunt House Rd YO22 ...51 B6
Hunt St WF10 ....200 D4
Hunter St 8 YO21 .....208 D7
Hunters Cl
Dunnington YO19 ....184 E7
19 Easingwold YO61 ....143 C8
10 Haxby YO32 ....225 C8
4 Hurworth-on-Tees DL2 ...3 D1
Hunters Croft BD23 ...156 F1
Hunters Gn DL2 ....4 C3
Hunters Ride DL6 ......24 B3
Hunters Row 6 YO51 ..141 B4
Hunters Way
Norton YO17 ....215 D2
Selby YO8 ....232 B4
York YO24 ....230 F7
Hunters Wlk
Barlow YO8 ....204 D7
Kirk Deighton LS22 .....180 C4
Hunters Wood Way 21
YO19 ....184 F7
Huntington Prim Sch
YO32 ....225 F4
Huntington Rd YO31 ..233 C4
Huntington Sch YO32 .225 E3
Hunton CP Sch DL8 ....61 F7
Hunton Rd DL8 ....40 E1
Huntriss Row YO11 ...213 A6
Huntsmans La YO41 ..168 C2
Huntsman's Wlk YO24 .227 B1
Hurdle Cl YO17 ......215 E2
Hurgill Rd DL10 ......209 A7
Hurn Rd YO61 ....144 A4
Hurns La YO30 ....224 A7
Hurrell La YO18 ....96 E5
Hurricane Way YO30 ..224 E3
Hurrs Rd 3 BD23 ......217 B4
Hurst Hill HG3 ....159 F7
Hurstleigh Terr HG1 ..220 A3
Hurst's Yd YO1 ....233 C2
Hurworth Comp Sch
DL2 ....22 D8
Hurworth Cty Inf Sch
DL2 ....3 E1
Hurworth House Sch
DL2 ....3 E1
Hurworth Rd
Hurworth DL2 ....3 F1
Hurworth-on-Tees DL2 ....22 D8
Neasham DL2 ....4 A1
Hussars Ct 6 YO12 .....75 F5
Husthwaite C of E Prim Sch
YO61 ....117 B5
Husthwaite Rd
Coxwold YO61 ....117 D7
Easingwold YO61 ....117 B2
Hutchinson Dr DL6 ...210 E3
Hutchinson St 1 YO8 ..232 B6
Hutton Ave DL1 ....3 E7
Hutton Bank
3 Hutton Rudby TS15 ....25 D5
Ripon HG4 ....214 D7
Hutton Cl YO26 ......224 A2
Hutton Cross Rd YO13 ..98 E8
Hutton La
Guisborough TS14 ....8 E5
Hutton Conyers HG4 .....114 A4
Sharow HG4 ....214 E8
Hutton Rae La YO7 ...116 D7
Hutton Rudby CP Sch
TS15 ....25 C5
Hutton St YO26 ......182 A5
Hutton View Rd HG4 ..214 C7
Hutton Village Rd TS14 ..8 D5
Hutton's Mon* DL11 ...39 C6
Hutts La HG4 ....112 C7
Hyde Park Rd
Harrogate HG1 ....219 E3
Knaresborough HG5 .....221 B8
Hydro Cl LS29 ....218 F3
Hyrst Gr YO31 ....228 E6

I

Ian St TS17 ....6 B8
I'anson Cl DL8 ....60 D6
I'anson Rd DL10 ......209 D7
Ibbetson Cl 16 HG4 ....86 C3
Iburndale La YO22 .....32 A6
Iddison Dr DL8 ....63 A2
Ikin Way YO32 ....225 F6
Iles La HG5 ....221 B5
Ilkeston Ave DN14 ....205 F3
Ilkley Gr TS14 ....8 E5
Ilkley Gram Sch LS29 .218 C3
Ilkley Hall Mews 5
LS29 ....218 B3
Ilkley Hall Pk 4 LS29 ..218 B3
Ilkley Rd
Addingham LS29 ....175 A4
Ilkley LS29 ....176 C1
Ilkley Sch LS29 ....218 E5
Ilkley Sta LS29 ....218 B4
Ilkley Swimming Baths
LS29 ....218 C5
Ilton Bank HG4 ....85 E1
Ilton Garth YO30 .....225 A2
Imperial Athletic Club
HG2 ....222 F8
Imperial Ave TS17 ....6 B8
In Moor La HG3 ......109 F6
Ingdale Howl YO62 ....92 C7
Ingdale La YO7 ....66 C3
Ingfield La BD24 .....131 D2
Ingham Cl YO22 ....32 A6
Ingleborough Ave
YO10 ....229 B4
Ingleborough Dr 4
BB18 ....171 D1
Ingleborough Park Cl
LA6 ....103 D3
Ingleborough Park Dr
LA6 ....103 D3
Inglebrook Sch WF8 ..201 B1
Ingleby Arncliffe C of E Prim Sch DL6 ....45 A8
Ingleby Dr LS24 ......189 E6
Ingleby Greenhow C of E Prim Sch TS9 ....27 C5
Ingleby Manor* TS9 ....27 C4
Ingleby Mill Prim Sch
TS17 ....6 A4
Ingleby Rd
Great & Little Broughton
TS9 ....27 A5
Great Broughton TS9 .....26 E5
Ingleby Way TS17 ....6 B5
Ingleton CP Sch LA6 ..103 D3
Ingleton Dr 16 YO61 ..143 D8
Ingleton Ind Est LA6 ..103 D3
Ingleton Mid Sch LA6 .103 D3
Ingleton Wlk 3 YO31 ..229 A5
Ingman Lodge Rd BD24 .78 F1
Ingram Ave YO30 .....228 C8
Ingramgate YO7 ......211 C3
Ingrish La YO23 .....182 C1
Ings Cl 6 Pickering YO18 ..95 F6
5 Willerby YO12 ....99 D2
Ings CP Sch BD23 ....216 D3
Ings Ct DN14 ....202 F4
Ings Dr
Low Bradley BD20 ....173 E3
Mickletown LS26 ....200 C6
Ings Field Rd YO26 ...142 A3
Ings La
Ainderby Quernhow YO7 ...88 D4
Beal DN14 ....202 D4
Bishop Monkton HG3 .....140 B5
Bishop Wilton YO42 .....169 D2
Bradleys Both BD20 .....173 E3
Brompton YO13 ....98 C4
Carlton DN14 ....204 E2
Cawood YO8 ....197 D8
Cononley BD20 ....173 D2
Cottingwith YO42 ....193 C5
Crakehall DL8 ....62 F5
Ebberston & Yedingham
YO13 ....97 E4
Great Preston WF10 .....200 E6
Harome YO62 ....93 D4
Hensall DN14 ....203 D2
Husthwaite YO61 ....117 A6
Hutton Buscel YO13 ......99 A3
Kellington DN14 ....202 F4
21 Kirkbymoorside YO62 ...70 B1
Kirkbymoorside YO62 .....94 B7
Lastingham YO62 ....70 F5
Lillings Ambo YO60 .....145 C2
Nether Poppleton YO26 ..224 B1
Pickering YO18 ....95 E4
Riccall YO19 ....197 E8
Skipton BD23 ....216 D2
Snape with Thorp DL8 ....87 B7
Stillington YO61 ....144 A6
Thorganby YO19 ....193 B5
Thorp Arch LS23 ....189 A8
Tollerton YO61 ....143 B2
Welburn YO62 ....94 A5
Wheldrake YO19 ....193 B7
Wighill LS24 ....189 D8
4 Willerby YO12 ....99 D2
Wistow YO8 ....198 A6
Ings Mere Ct WF11 ...201 C6
Ings Rd Cliffe YO8 ....198 D2
Dunsforths YO26 ....142 A3
Snaith DN14 ....204 C1
Thorganby YO19 ....193 B4
Ulleskelf LS24 ....190 C3
West Ayton YO13 ....99 B6
Wilberfoss YO41 ....185 E6
Ings Terr YO22 ....31 C4
Ings View 2 Bedale DL8 ..63 B3
Castleford WF10 ....201 A4
Mickletown LS26 ....200 C6
York YO30 ....224 D2
Ingsgarth YO18 ....95 F6
Ingthorns La LS25 ....195 F1
Ingthorpe La
Martons Both BD23 .....171 E7
Monk Fryston LS25 .....196 A1
Inhams La YO26 ......141 F2
Inholmes La
Tadcaster LS24 ....189 D6
Walton LS23 ....181 B2
Inman Gr HG5 ....221 B8
Inman Terr YO26 .....227 D4
Inman Wlk HG5 ....221 B8
Inn La 10 YO61 ....143 C8
Innisfree Cl HG2 .....220 B1
Institute St 4 BD20 ...187 E7
Intake Ave YO30 .....228 C8
Intake La
Acaster Malbis YO23 ....191 C7
Beal WF11 ....202 D5
Carlton Miniott YO7 .....89 C4
Dunnington YO19 ....184 F7
Grassington BD23 ....134 E3
Habton YO17 ....121 E7
Heck DN14 ....207 C8
Tollerton YO61 ....143 B4
West Haddlesey YO8 .....202 F6
Intakefield Rd YO8 ....199 D7
Invicta Ct YO24 ......230 B8
Ireby Rd LA6 ....102 F3
Ireton St 3 YO12 .....212 E5
Iron Row LS29 ....176 C1
Irton Moor La YO12 ...212 A1
Irwin Ave YO31 ....228 E6
Islebeck La YO7 ......115 F8
Iver Cl YO26 ....227 C5
Ivy Bank Ct 4 YO13 ....75 D5
Ivy Cl HG3 ....223 F4
Ivy Cres DL8 ....62 B4
Ivy House Cl 6 YO11 ..100 B6
Ivy House Gdns BD23 ..155 D1
Ivy La LS23 ....188 E8

J

Jack Field La BD20 ...187 D6
Jack Hill La LS21 .....176 F6
Jack Hole YO61 ....142 F4
Jack La Crayke YO61 ...118 A1
Stillington YO61 ....144 C7
Wigglesworth BD23 .....153 C4
Jackson Cl YO11 ......100 B6
Jackson Dr TS9 ....26 C8
Jackson La YO41 ......185 E4
Jackson St
24 Glusburn BD20 ....187 E7
York YO31 ....233 C4
Jackson's La
Bradleys Both BD20 .....173 F3
Eastfield YO11 ....100 A8
Scarborough YO11 ....213 A1
Jackson's Wlk YO23 ..182 D3
Jacobi Cl YO30 ....228 A7
Jacques Gr BD20 ......174 C1
Jacques' La YO8 ......198 E4
Jaffa Rd DL9 ....209 E2
Jagger La DL10 ....20 E6
Jagoe Rd 8 BB18 ......172 A1
James Backhouse Pl
YO24 ....227 E3
James Cl LS25 ....194 D4
James Ct DL10 ....209 F7
James La DL10 ....41 A2
James Nicholson Way
YO30 ....225 A2
James Pl 2 YO12 .....213 A6
James St 20 Earby BB18 .172 A1
10 Glusburn BD20 ....187 E8
Harrogate HG1 ....219 D2
Scarborough YO12 ....213 A6
Selby YO8 ....232 C5
York YO10 ....228 E4
Jameson Cres YO12 ...212 D5
Jamesville Way YO7 ...115 B6
Jamieson Terr YO23 ..228 B1
Janesway LS25 ....194 C1
Janet's Foss* BD23 ..133 B2
Jasmine Cl
10 Snaith DN14 ....204 C1
York YO32 ....225 D2
Jasper La HG3 ....179 A3
Jay Ave TS17 ....6 B4
Jaywick Cl 3 YO32 ...167 B8
Jedburgh Dr DL3 ....2 F7
Jedwell Cl YO32 ......225 D5
Jennifer Gr 4 YO24 ...227 F2
Jenny Field Dr HG3 ...219 B4
Jenny Frisk Rd TS12 .....9 E6
Jenny Gill Cres BD23 .217 B3
Jenny La DN14 ....207 B5
Jerry Carr Bank YO62 ..92 B1
Jerry Croft 2 BD23 ...217 A4
Jerry La BD20 ....174 F1
Jersey Ct YO12 ....99 C7
Jervaulx Abbey* HG4 ..85 D8
Jervaulx Dr HG5 ......221 D4
Jervaulx Rd DL7 ....64 A6
Jervis Rd YO24 ....230 E8
Jesmond Ct YO17 .....215 E3
Jesmond Gr 5 TS18 ......5 E8
Jesmond Rd
Darlington DL1 ....3 F7
Harrogate HG1 ....220 A3
Jew Leys La YO23 ....190 F3
Jewbury YO31 ....233 C3
Jewitt La LS22 ....188 B8
Jin-Whin Hill WF10 ...200 C4
Jobbing Cross YO61 ..116 C3
Jockey La
Huntington YO32 ....225 F2
5 Knaresborough HG5 ....221 A6
Joffre Ave WF10 ......200 F3
John Breckon Rd YO21 ..28 D5
John Dixon La DL1 ......3 D5
John of Gaunt's Castle*
HG3 ....160 B1
John St Darlington DL1 ...3 D6
11 Earby BB18 ....172 A1
35 Filey YO14 ....101 B3
Great Ayton TS9 ....8 A2
11 Harrogate HG1 ....219 D2
Selby YO8 ....232 D6
Whitby YO21 ....208 D7
York YO31 ....228 E6
Johnson Cl 1 YO7 .....211 C3
Johnson St YO8 ......232 B6
Johnson Way YO7 .....211 D2
Jolby La Cleasby DL10 ...2 E1
Croft-on-Tees DL2 ....22 B8
Newton Morrell DL10 .....21 F8
Jonah's La HG3 ....160 B1
Jonathan Garth 17 LS29 174 F4
Jorvik Viking Ctr*
YO1 ....233 C2
Joseph Rowntree Sch
YO32 ....225 E5
Jowett's La BD20 .....174 B4
Jowland Winn La YO8 .204 A4
Jubbergate YO1 ....233 B2
Jubilee Bank TS7 ....7 C8
Jubilee Cave* BD24 ...131 F4
Jubilee Rd
Norton YO17 ....215 E3
Wistow YO8 ....197 D6
Jubilee Terr YO26 ....227 F5
Julia Ave YO32 ....226 B2
Junction Farm Prim Sch
TS16 ....5 D5

Juniper Cl YO32 ......225 D3
Juniper Gr TS21 ....5 C8
Juniper Way 28 HG3 ...161 B3
Jura Dr DL1 ....3 E8
Jute Rd YO26 ....227 B5
Jutland Rd DL9 ....209 C2

K

Kader Ave TS5 ....6 D7
Kader Prim Sch TS5 .....6 E7
Kail La BD23 ....156 F8
Kangel Cl HG4 ....214 E3
Kareen Ave 3 YO12 .....99 E6
Kathryn Ave YO32 ......226 A2
Kay House La TS15 .....24 D5
Kaye Dr YO8 ....198 B4
Kays Bank YO61 ....117 C5
Kearby Cliff LS22 .....179 B1
Kearsley Cl TS16 ....5 E7
Kearsley Rd HG4 ....214 B7
Kearton DL11 ....37 D6
Keasden Rd LA2 ....130 A3
Keats Cl
4 Pontefract WF8 ......201 B1
York YO30 ....227 F8
Keats Wlk HG1 ....219 E7
Keble Cl YO23 ....231 B3
Keble Dr YO23 ....231 A2
Keble Garth LS25 ......194 E1
Keble Gdns YO23 ......231 B2
Keble Park Cres YO23 .231 A2
Keble Pk N YO23 ......231 A3
Keble Pk S YO23 ......231 A2
Keeper's Cl YO61 .....118 A1
Keepers Gate 18 YO18 ...95 F6
Keeper's Hill YO25 ....150 A1
Keepers Way 11 YO19 ..184 F7
Keighley Rd
Bradleys Both BD20 .....173 D3
5 Colne BB8 ....186 A3
Cowling BD22 ....187 B6
2 Glusburn BD20 ....187 F7
Ilkley LS29 ....218 A2
Laneshaw Bridge BB8 ....186 D3
Skipton BD23 ....216 F2
Trawden Forest BB8 .....186 B3
Keilder Rise TS8 ....6 F5
Keith Ave YO32 ....226 A4
Keith Rd TS4 ....6 F8
Kelbrook Prim Sch
BB18 ....186 A7
Kelbrook Rd BB18 .....171 D1
Kelcbar Cl LS24 ......189 D6
Kelcbar Hill LS24 .....189 D6
Kelcbar Way LS24 .....189 D6
Kelcow Caves* BD24 ..131 D3
Keld Bank HG4 ....85 E3
Keld Cl Pickering YO18 ...95 E7
Scalby YO12 ....212 B8
Keld Head Orch 1 YO62 .70 B1
Keld Head Rd YO62 .....70 A1
Keld La
Hutton-le-Hole YO62 ......70 C5
Newton YO18 ....72 A5
Thorpe Bassett YO17 ....123 A3
Keld Runnels Rd YO13 ..75 A4
Keldale 4 YO32 ....166 F5
Keldale Gdns HG4 .....214 F6
Keldgate Rd YO18 ......72 A3
Keldhead YO18 ....95 E8
Keldheads La DL8 ....59 F5
Kelfield Rd 9 YO19 ....197 F8
Kell Bank C of E Prim Sch
HG4 ....85 E3
Kell Beck 1 LS21 ......176 F1
Kell Syke La BD23 .....155 A6
Kellington La DN14 ....202 F2
Kellington Prim Sch
DN14 ....202 F3
Kemmel Cl DL9 ....40 E2
Kempton Cl 2 YO24 ...227 D1
Kempton Ct 15 DL1 ....3 F6
Kendal Cl
6 Dunnington YO19 .....184 F7
Hellifield BD23 ....154 B3
Kendal Dr WF10 ....201 B4
Kendal Gdns YO26 ....181 D7
Kendal La YO26 ....181 D7
Kendal Rd
Harrogate HG1 ....220 B3
Long Preston BD23 ......154 A3
Kendalmans 4 BD24 ...131 D2
Kendrew Cl 11 Bedale DL8 63 A2
3 York YO32 ....225 F3
Kenilworth Ave HG2 ...222 D7
Kenilworth Dr
3 Earby BB18 ....172 A1
Earby BB18 ....186 A8
Kenlay Cl YO32 ....225 D4
Kennedy Dr 32 YO32 ...166 E5
Kennels La LS14 ......188 A4
Kennet La LS25 ....194 D3
Kennion Ct 2 HG2 .....220 B3
Kennion Rd HG2 ....220 B3
Kenrick Pl 5 YO26 .....227 B5
Kensal Rise YO10 .....228 D2
Kensington Ave
Eston & South Bank TS6 .....7 E8
Thorner LS14 ....188 A3
Kensington Ct 1 YO24 .230 F8
Kensington Gdns DL1 ....3 E5
Kensington Rd YO30 ...224 D2
Kensington Sq 10 HG2 ..219 C2
Kensington St YO23 ...228 B1
Kent Ave HG1 ....219 B3
Kent Cl HG4 ....214 A2
Kent Dr HG1 ....219 B3
Kent Rd Goole DN14 ....205 F2
Guisborough TS14 ....8 E5
Harrogate HG1 ....219 B3
Selby YO8 ....232 A6
Kent Rd N HG1 ....219 B3
Kent Rise HG1 ....219 A2
Kent St YO10 ....233 C1
Kentmere Dr YO30 ....224 F1
Kenton Cl 4 TS18 ....5 E8
Kershaw Ave WF10 ....201 A4
Kerver La YO19 ....184 F7
Kesteven Rd TS4 ....7 A7
Kestrel Dr 7 DL9 ....40 F2
Kestrel View 2 YO12 ....99 E6
Kestrel Wood Way
YO31 ....225 F2
Keswick Dr WF10 .....201 C5
Keswick Gr TS5 ....6 D7
Keswick Way 5 YO32 ..225 F5
Kettle Spring La HG3 ..139 B1
Kettlesbeck Brow LA2 .130 C5
Kettlestring La YO30 ..225 A3
Kettlewell CP Sch
BD23 ....108 A3
Kettlewell La DL8 ......57 A5
Kex Gill Rd HG3 ....158 F2
Kexby Ave YO10 ......228 F3
Kexby Bridge* YO41 ..185 C6
Kexby House* YO41 ...185 C6
Kexby Stray YO41 .....185 A5
Key La YO61 ....118 A1
Key Way YO19 ....231 F5
Keys Beck Rd YO18 ....71 F8
Khyber Pass YO21 .....208 D7
Kiddal La LS15 ....188 C2
Kidstones Bank DL8 ....81 E3
Kielder Dr DL1 ....3 F7
Kielder Oval HG2 ......220 D2
Kilburn Rd YO10 ......228 D2
Kildale Sta YO21 ....27 E8
Kildare Garth 5 YO62 ...70 C1
Kildwick C of E Prim Sch
BD20 ....187 F8
Kilgram La HG4 ....85 E8
Kilham Rd YO25 ....151 D5
Killerby Dr 2 DL10 ......41 E4
Killerby La YO11 ......100 C5
Killin Rd DL1 ....3 E7
Killinghall C of E Prim Sch
HG3 ....161 C5
Kilmarnock Rd DL1 ....3 E8
Kiln Hill La
Lawkland LA2 ....131 A6
Silsden BD20 ....174 A3
Kiln La LA2 ....128 A6
Kilners Croft 11 LS29 ..174 F4
Kilnsey Fold BD20 .....174 B2
Kilnwick Ct DL7 ....210 D3
Kilton La TS12 ....9 F7
Kilton Thorpe La TS13 ..10 B8
Kimberlows Wood Hill 3
YO10 ....229 C3
Kinbrace Dr YO24 .....230 B7
King Edward Ave
WF10 ....200 C7
King Edward Rd HG4 ..214 C3
King Edward St
27 Glusburn BD20 ......187 E7
Normanton South WF6 ...200 A1
King Edward's Dr
HG1 ....219 D5
King George Rd 1 HG4 214 C3
King Hill YO14 ....101 A2
King James Rd HG5 ...221 B5
King James's Gram Sch
HG5 ....221 B5
King Rudding Cl 6
YO19 ....198 A8
King Rudding La YO19 .198 B8
King St
Castleford WF10 ....200 F3
6 Cawood YO8 ....197 B8
Muston YO14 ....100 F2
Normanton South WF6 ...200 A1
Pateley Bridge HG3 ......137 B4
Richmond DL10 ....209 C6
Ripon HG4 ....214 C4
Scarborough YO11 ....213 A6
York YO1 ....233 B2
Kingfisher Cl 7 YO12 ....99 F6
Kingfisher Ct 3 DL9 .....40 F2
Kingfisher Dr
3 Bedale DL8 ....63 B3
Guisborough TS14 ....8 D6
14 Pickering YO18 ....95 F6
Whitby YO22 ....208 E3
Kingfisher Reach
17 Boroughbridge YO51 ..141 B5
5 Collingham LS22 .....180 A1
Kings Acre YO31 ......229 B6
Kings Ave 2 LS29 .....218 A4
Kings Cl 5 YO8 ....198 B5
King's Cl 9 DL10 ....41 D5
Kings Cl 19 LS29 ......175 C2
King's Gate LA2 ....130 D3
King's Gdns YO7 ......211 B1
Kings Keld Bank DL8 ...86 F8
Kings La YO13 ....97 D5
Kings Lea YO8 ....199 A8
Kings Manor Comp Sch
TS5 ....6 E7
Kings Mdws YO7 ....89 E3
Kings Mead HG4 ......214 B7
Kings Mill La 8 BD24 ..131 D2
Kings Moor Rd YO32 ..167 D2
King's Rd 6 HG1 ......219 D3
Kings Rd Ilkley LS29 ...218 A4
Kings Rd continued
Knaresborough HG5 .....221 C6
King's Sq YO1 ....233 C2
King's St 7 BD23 .....217 B4
Kingsclere YO32 ......225 F6
Kingsland Terr 11 YO26 .227 F5
Kingsley Ave WF11 ....201 D3
Kingsley Cl HG1 ......220 C3
Kingsley Dr
Harrogate HG1 ....220 A4
2 Middleham DL8 ....60 E2
Kingsley Park Mews 1
HG1 ....220 C3
Kingsley Park Rd HG1 .220 C3
Kingsley Rd
Harrogate HG1 ....220 B5
Trawden Forest BB8 .....186 B3
Kingsthorpe YO24 .....227 D2
Kingston Ave HG4 .....214 C3
Kingston Cres YO8 ....196 E2
Kingston Dr
Hambleton YO8 ....196 E1
16 Normanton WF6 .....200 B1
Norton YO17 ....215 E2
Kingston Garth 2 YO22 .33 C3
Kingston Gr 5 YO12 ...212 B7
Kingstonia Gdns 3
HG4 ....214 C3
Kingsway
Garforth LS25 ....194 B3
Harrogate HG1 ....219 E3
Pontefract WF8 ....201 B2
Scalby YO12 ....212 C8
Skipton BD23 ....217 B4
6 Stamford Bridge YO41 .168 D2
Weeton LS17 ....178 B2
Kingsway Dr
Harrogate HG1 ....219 E2
4 Ilkley LS29 ....218 A4
Kingsway Jun Sch
YO30 ....228 B7
Kingsway N YO30 .....228 B7
Kingsway W YO24 .....227 D1
Kingswood Gr YO24 ...227 D3
Kinloss Cl TS17 ....6 C7
Kinsey Cave* BD24 ...131 C4
Kintyre Dr TS17 ....6 B6
Kiplin Hall* DL10 ....42 B4
Kipling Gr WF8 ....201 B2
Kippax Greenfield Prim Sch
LS25 ....194 D1
Kippax Inf Sch LS25 ..194 D1
Kippax Leisure Ctr
LS25 ....200 D8
Kippax North Jun & Inf Sch
LS25 ....194 C2
Kir Cres YO24 ....227 C3
Kirby Hill C of E Prim Sch
YO51 ....141 B7
Kirby La
Ebberston & Yedingham
YO17 ....97 E1
Sledmere YO25 ....150 A4
Kirby Misperton La
YO17 ....121 C7
Kirby Misperton Rd
YO17 ....95 F2
Kirk Balk YO17 ....169 E8
Kirk Balk La YO60 ....168 B7
Kirk Bank
Conistone with Kilnsey
BD23 ....134 B4
Kirkby Malzeard HG4 ....112 A5
Kirk Fenton C of E Prim Sch
LS24 ....196 B8
Kirk Gate
Brompton YO13 ....98 C7
Silpho YO13 ....74 E6
Kirk Hammerton C of E Prim
Sch YO26 ....164 C2
Kirk Hammerton La
YO26 ....164 C3
Kirk Hills LS14 ....188 A3
Kirk Ings La YO7 ....66 B7
Kirk La
Embsay with Eastby
BD23 ....217 E8
Tockwith YO26 ....181 C7
Kirk Rd Eaglescliffe TS15 ...5 F2
Northallerton DL7 ....210 B3
Kirk Smeaton C of E Prim
Sch WF8 ....206 B3
Kirk Syke La BD23 ....155 A5
Kirk View 1 YO26 .....227 C3
Kirkby & Great Broughton C
of E Prim Sch TS9 .....26 E5
Kirkby Ave HG4 ....214 A6
Kirkby Cl HG4 ....214 A6
Kirkby Dr HG4 ....214 A6
Kirkby Fleetham C of E Prim
Sch DL7 ....42 C1
Kirkby in Malhamdale Prim
Sch BD23 ....154 F8
Kirkby La
Gillamoor YO62 ....70 A3
Kearby with Netherby
HG3 ....179 B2
Kirkby TS9 ....26 D6
Kirkby Fleetham with Fencote
DL7 ....42 C2
Sicklinghall LS22 ....179 D3
Kirkby Malzeard C of E Prim
Sch HG4 ....112 D5
Kirkby Overblow C of E Prim
Sch HG3 ....179 A4
Kirkby Rd
North Stainley with Sleningford
HG4 ....113 C4
Kirkby Rd continued
Ripon HG4 ....214 A6
Selby YO8 ....232 B7
Kirkbymoorside Com Prim
Sch YO62 ....70 B1
Kirkbymoorside CP Sch
YO62 ....70 A1
Kirkcroft YO32 ....225 C8
Kirkdale La YO62 ....93 F8
Kirkdale Manor YO62 ...93 D8
Kirkdale Rd YO10 .....229 D4
Kirkfield Ave LS14 .....188 A3
Kirkfield Cres LS14 ....188 A3
Kirkfield La LS14 ......188 A3
Kirkfield Rd DL3 ....3 D8
Kirkgate
Knaresborough HG5 .....221 A6
7 Middleham DL8 ....60 E2
12 Ripon HG4 ....214 C5
Settle BD24 ....131 D2
Sherburn in Elmet LS25 ..195 E4
Silsden BD20 ....174 C1
Thirsk YO7 ....211 B3
Kirkgate La YO62 ....70 F4
Kirkham Augustinian Priory
(rems of)* YO60 .....146 F4
Kirkham Ave 1 YO31 ..228 E8
Kirkham Bridge*
YO60 ....146 F4
Kirkham Cl 6 YO21 ....208 C6
Kirkham Ct 5 HG5 .....221 C4
Kirkham Gr HG1 ......219 F6
Kirkham Pl HG1 ....219 F6
Kirkham Rd
Harrogate HG1 ....219 F6
Middlesbrough TS7 ....7 D6
Whitby YO21 ....208 C6
Kirkham View YO60 ...147 B4
Kirkhaw La WF11 .....201 D4
Kirkland Cl YO8 ....232 D4
Kirklands YO32 ....167 B6
Kirklands La YO41 ....169 C2
Kirklevington Cty Prim Sch
TS15 ....24 F8
Kirkstall Dr BB18 .....171 E2
Kirkstone Dr YO31 ....229 A6
Kirkstone Rd HG1 ....220 B4
Kirkwell YO23 ....231 A4
Kit La BD20 ....174 B3
Kitchen Dr YO8 ....232 D4
Kitchener Rd
Ripon HG4 ....113 D3
Scotton DL9 ....40 E4
Kitchener St Selby YO8 .232 B6
York YO31 ....228 D7
Kitemere Pl 2 YO24 ...230 B8
Kitter La YO21 ....31 C8
Kitty Garth YO19 ......193 A7
Knapping Hill HG1 ....219 C5
Knapton Cl 1 YO32 ...167 B6
Knapton La YO26 .....227 B4
Knapton Wold Rd
YO17 ....123 C5
Knaresborough Ave TS7 ..7 B5
Knaresborough Castle*
HG5 ....221 A5
Knaresborough Rd
Bishop Monkton HG3 ....140 B4
Harrogate HG2 ....219 F2
Little Ribston LS22 ......180 A8
Ripon HG4 ....214 C3
Knaresborough Sta
HG5 ....221 A6
Knaresborough Swimming
Pool HG5 ....221 B5
Knavesmire Cl YO62 ....93 C5
Knavesmire Cres
YO23 ....228 B1
Knavesmire Prim Sch
YO23 ....228 B1
Knavesmire Rd YO23 ..228 A1
Knayton C of E Prim Sch
YO7 ....65 E3
Kneeton La DL10 ....21 C5
Knightsway LS25 ......194 B3
Knipe Point Dr 8 YO11 .100 B8
Knoll The
3 Bramham LS23 ....188 E6
York YO24 ....227 B2
Knolls Cl 11 YO11 .....100 B7
Knolls La YO62 ....67 F5
Knot La BB7 ....171 A5
Knott La
Easingwold YO61 ....143 C8
Steeton with Eastburn
BD20 ....187 F7
Knott Rd YO18 ....49 D5
Knottingley England Lane
Jun & Inf Sch WF11 ..202 A2
Knottingley High Sch
WF11 ....202 A2
Knottingley Rd WF8 ...201 D1
Knottingley Rugby Union
Club WF11 ....202 A3
Knottingley Sta WF11 ..201 F2
Knotto Bottom Cl DL6 .210 F3
Knotto Bottom Way
DL6 ....210 F3
Knotts La BD23 ....152 E1
Knowle La
Ilton-cum-Pott HG4 ....85 D1
Kirby Knowle YO7 ....66 C2
Knowles Cl 5 TS15 .....24 E8
Knox Ave HG1 ....219 C5
Knox Chase HG1 ......219 C6
Knox Cl HG1 ....219 D6
Knox Dr HG1 ....219 C6
Knox Gdns HG1 ....219 C6
Knox Gr HG1 ....219 C6
Knox La Harrogate HG1 .219 D6
Scarborough YO11 ....213 B1
Knox Mill Bank HG3 ..219 B7
Knox Mill Cl HG3 .....219 B7
Knox Mill La HG3 .....219 B7
Knox Pk HG3 ....219 B7
Knox Rd HG1 ....219 D6
Knox Rise HG1 ....219 C6
Knox Way HG1 ....219 C5
Kyle Cl 3 YO61 ....143 B3
Kyle Way YO26 ....227 B8
Kyme Castle* LS24 ...189 C7
Kyme St YO1 ....233 B1

L

La Bassee Rd DL9 .....209 D1
Laburnum Ave
Fylingdales YO22 ....33 C4
Thornaby TS17 ....6 B7
Laburnum Cl
5 Catterick Garrison DL9 209 B1
Rufforth YO23 ....182 C6
7 Snaith DN14 ....204 C1
3 Thorpe Willoughby YO8 197 B1
Laburnum Dr HG3 ....140 A5
Laburnum Garth 6
YO31 ....228 F8
Laburnum Gr
Harrogate HG1 ....219 E6
Richmond DL10 ....209 D8
Stillingfleet YO19 ....191 D4
Whitby YO21 ....208 B6
Laburnum Rd TS7 ....7 D8
Lacey Ave YO12 ....99 D7
Lachman Rd BB8 ......186 A2
Lack La YO62 ....93 C2
Lackon Bank HG3 .....160 D6
Lacy Gr LS22 ....180 C2
Ladgate La TS5 ....6 F6
Lady Balk La WF8 ....201 B1
Lady Edith's Ave YO12 .212 B6
Lady Edith's Cres
YO12 ....212 B6
Lady Edith's Dr YO12 ..212 A6
Lady Edith's Pk YO12 ..212 B7
Lady Elizabeth Hastings C of
E Sch
Collingham LS22 ....180 A1
Thorp Arch LS23 ....180 F1
Lady Grace's Ride
YO12 ....212 A3
Lady Hamilton Gdns
YO24 ....227 E2
Lady Hullocks Ct 12 TS9 .26 C7
Lady La HG3 ....222 A5
Lady Lumleys Sch YO18 .95 F7
Lady Rd YO30 ....228 B7
Ladycarr La YO61 .....143 E8
Ladysmith Ave YO21 ..208 C7
Ladysmith Mews 13
YO32 ....167 A7
Ladysmith Rd DL9 ......40 C4
Ladywell La YO51 .....141 C5
Ladywell Rd YO51 .....141 B5
Lairs Cres YO13 ....98 A5
Lairs La YO13 ....98 A5
Lairum Rise LS23 ......188 E7
Laith Staid La LS25 ...195 D4
Laithbutts La LA2 .....130 B8
Lake View WF8 ....201 B2
Lakeber Ave LA2 ......129 A8
Lakeber Dr LA2 ....129 A8
Lakeside
Acaster Malbis YO23 .....191 C7
Darlington DL1 ....3 C4
Hunmanby Sands YO14 ...101 B1
Lakeside Cl LS29 .....218 A5
Lakeside Gr 1 YO32 ...167 B8
Lakeside Mdws 1 WF8 .201 B2
Lakeside Prim Sch
YO30 ....224 F2
Lakeside Way YO17 ...215 D2
Laking La YO25 ....126 A3
Lamb Inn Rd 9 WF11 ..202 A2
Lamb La TS17 ....6 A4
Lambert Ct YO1 ......233 B1
Lambert Meml Hospl
YO7 ....211 B2
Lambert St
11 Skipton BD23 ....217 A3
2 Trawden BB8 ....186 B1
Lambeth St 18 BB8 ....186 A3
Lambourne Dr TS7 ......7 C6
Lamb's La TS9 ....27 B4
Lambs La 12 YO18 ......95 F7
Lamel St YO10 ....229 A3
Lamplugh Cres YO23 ..231 B3
Lanacar La DL8 ....56 A4
Lancar Cl 18 YO32 ....166 D5
Lancaster Cl 9 YO13 ...75 D5
Lancaster Park Rd
HG2 ....220 A3
Lancaster Rd
Harrogate HG2 ....219 C1
North Cowton DL7 ....22 C2
Lancaster St 6 YO11 ..213 A6
Lancaster Way
17 Scalby YO13 ....75 D5
York YO30 ....225 A1
Lancers Ct 4 YO12 .....75 F5
Landalewood Rd YO30 .224 F2
Landau Cl YO30 ......227 F8

Landing La
Asselby DN14 .205 D6
Barlby with Osgodby YO8 .232 F8
22 Haxby YO32 .166 F5
Haxby YO32 .225 E7
Hemingbrough YO8 .204 F8
Riccall YO19 .197 F8
York YO26 .227 E6
Landing Rd YO8 .203 A7
Landings The 21 YO32 .166 F5
Lands La HG5 .220 E7
Lane Ends La BD22 .187 B7
Lane Foot Rd HG3 .159 E8
Lane House La BB8 .186 B1
Lane House Rd BD22 .187 A6
Lane The
Gate Helmsley YO41 .168 B2
Mickleby TS13 .12 A4
Lanehead La DL11 .18 H8
Lanehouse Rd TS17 .6 B8
Laneshawbridge CP Sch BB8 .186 B3
Lang Ave YO10 .229 A4
Lang Gate YO13 .74 E4
Lang Kirk Cl 2 BD20 .173 F1
Lang Rd
Bishopthorpe YO23 .230 F4
York YO32 .225 F6
Langbar Rd LS29 .218 A6
Langbaurgh Cl TS9 .8 A2
Langbaurgh Rd TS15 .25 C4
Langber End La LA6 .103 D1
Langber La BD23 .154 A6
Langbourne Rd YO21 .208 D6
Langburn La YO21 .29 A7
Langburn's Bank YO21 .29 A7
Langcliffe Ave HG2 .222 E8
Langcliffe Ave E HG2 .222 E8
Langcliffe CP Sch BD24 .131 E4
Langcliffe Garth BD23 .108 B3
Langcliffe Rd BD24 .131 D3
Langdale TS14 .8 D6
Langdale Ave
3 Pontefract WF6 .200 A2
York YO31 .229 B6
Langdale Dr 2 WF6 .200 A2
Langdale Gr YO8 .232 B3
Langdale Mews 4 WF6 200 A2
Langdale Rd 3 YO12 .212 F7
Langer Hill La HG3 .160 B5
Langford Cl 21 LS29 .176 C1
Langford Ct 17 LS29 .176 C1
Langford La LS29 .176 C1
Langford Mews 19 LS29 176 C1
Langford Rd LS29 .176 C1
Langford Ride 30 LS29 .176 C1
Langholm Cres DL3 .3 C5
Langholme Dr YO26 .227 C6
Langhorne Dr 2 DL11 .38 B6
Langley Ct 1 YO32 .225 F6
Langley Dr YO17 .215 E1
Langleys Rd 6 DN6 .206 E1
Langrickgate La YO42 .193 C5
Langsett Ave 7 YO14 .101 A3
Langsett Gr YO30 .224 F3
Langstrothdale Rd BD24 .105 D7
Langthwaite La DL8 .59 C3
Langtoft CP Sch YO25 .151 C5
Langton CP Sch YO17 .147 F5
Langton Crossroads YO17 .148 B6
Langton Ct 1 YO32 .167 A6
Langton La YO17 .148 C8
Langton Rd
Langton YO17 .148 A7
Norton YO17 .215 E2
Langwith Ave LS22 .188 A8
Langwith Stray YO10 .184 C2
Lansdown Rd DN14 .205 F2
Lansdown Way 7 YO32 .166 F5
Lansdowne Rd TS15 .5 E3
Lansdowne Terr 5 YO10 .228 E3
Lanshaw Bank BD23 .175 A7
Lanshaw Croft YO30 .224 F1
Lantsbury Dr TS13 .10 D8
Larch Gr 1 Filey YO14 .101 B4
Pannal HG3 .222 E2
Larch Rd 6 YO7 .89 A1
Larch Rise 4 YO61 .117 D1
Larchfield YO31 .229 C7
Larchfield Com TS8 .6 F4
Larchfield Sports Ctr DL3 .3 C5
Larchfield St DL3 .3 C5
Lark Hill HG4 .214 A7
Lark Hill Cres 13 HG4 .113 D2
Lark Hill Dr HG4 .214 A6
Lark La HG4 .214 A6
Larkfield Cl
1 Copmanthorpe YO23 .230 A3
Harrogate HG2 .222 A7
Larkfield Dr HG2 .222 A7
Larkfield Rd
Harrogate HG2 .222 A7
Selby YO8 .232 A4
Larkfield Way HG2 .222 A7
Larkhill Cl HG4 .214 A6
Larkspur Gr 14 HG3 .161 B3
Larkspur Rd TS7 .7 A6
Larpool Cres YO22 .208 E4
Larpool Dr YO22 .208 D3
Larpool La YO22 .208 D4
Larsen Rd DN14 .205 F2
Larun Beat The TS15 .5 E2
Lascelles Ct DL6 .210 E4
Lascelles Gr HG2 .219 B1
Lascelles La
Malton YO17 .215 E6
Northallerton DL6 .210 E4
Lascelles Rd HG2 .222 B8
Latimer La TS14 .8 E6
Latimer Rd DL1 .3 E7
Lauderdale Dr TS14 .8 F6
Laughton Ave YO12 .212 C5
Laundry La LA6 .103 D3
Laundry Rd
4 Filey YO14 .101 B3
3 Harrogate HG1 .220 C4
Lauradale La BD23 .134 D1
Laurel Ave TS4 .7 A8
Laurel Cl Burniston YO13 .75 D8
Gateforth YO8 .197 B1
Laurel Croft BD23 .217 D8
Laurels Garth YO60 .145 C5
Laurels The 6 DL6 .210 E2
Laurence Jackson Sch TS14 .8 F7
Lavender Ct 21 DL9 .41 A5
Lavender Gr YO26 .227 E5
Laveracks Ind Est YO41 .185 B3
Laverton Gdns HG3 .219 A4
Law La HG3 .138 F1
Lawn Ave LS29 .176 C1
Lawn La DN6 .207 E3
Lawn Rd 35 LS29 .176 C1
Lawnfield Dr HG3 .140 B5
Lawnfield Rd HG3 .140 B5
Lawns Rd YO21 .29 E6
Lawns The HG2 .222 C8
Lawnswood Dr YO30 .227 F8
Lawnway YO31 .229 A7
Lawrence Cl YO12 .212 A8
Lawrence Cres DL10 .209 E8
Lawrence Gr YO12 .212 A8
Lawrence St YO10 .228 E3
Lawsings Brow LA2 .130 B5
Lawson Ave 1 YO51 .141 B4
Lawson Rd YO24 .230 F7
Lawsons Cl YO14 .126 F7
Layerthorpe YO31 .233 C3
Layfield Prim Sch TS15 .5 D2
Lazenby Dr 10 LS22 .180 B3
Lazenby Moor La HG5 .141 A2
Le Cateau CP Sch DL9 .40 F4
Le Cateau Rd DL9 .40 E4
Lea Croft LS23 .188 E7
Lea La YO61 .143 F4
Lea Way YO32 .226 A4
Lead La Brompton DL6 .43 F3
Nether Silton YO7 .66 B7
Ripon HG4 .214 B3
Westerdale YO21 .28 E4
Lead Mill La YO1 .233 C1
Leadhall Ave HG2 .222 D6
Leadhall Cl HG2 .222 D6
Leadhall Cres HG2 .222 E6
Leadhall Dr HG2 .222 D7
Leadhall Gdns HG2 .222 D6
Leadhall Gr HG2 .222 D6
Leadhall La HG2 .222 D6
Leadhall Rd HG2 .222 C6
Leadhall View HG2 .222 C5
Leadhall Way HG2 .222 C6
Leading Post St 8 YO11 .213 B6
Leadley Croft YO23 .230 A1
Leafield Rd DL1 .3 D4
Leahope Ct TS17 .6 C6
Leahurst Cl YO17 .215 E2
Leake La YO7 .65 F6
Leake St
Castleford WF10 .200 F4
York YO10 .228 E3
Lealholm C of E Sch YO21 .30 C6
Lealholm Cres TS3 .7 C8
Lealholm La YO21 .30 B5
Lealholm Sta YO21 .30 B6
Leamington Rd LS29 .218 C5
Leamington Terr LS29 .218 C5
Leas Head Rd YO22 .32 B2
Leas La YO18 .95 F5
Leas The
11 Brafferton YO61 .115 F1
Darlington DL1 .3 D8
8 Eastfield YO11 .99 F7
Lease Rigg La YO22 .31 A3
Leases La DL10 .41 E2
Leases Rd DL7 .63 C5
Leasmires Ave 10 YO61 .143 D8
Leat Cl YO17 .215 D2
Leather Bank LS29 .176 C1
Leathley La LS21 .177 D1
Leavening CP Sch YO17 .147 E2
Leck C of E Sch LA6 .102 E7
Leconfield Garth HG3 .223 F5
Ledbury Way TS14 .8 E6
Ledesway 1 BD23 .134 E3
Ledgate La LS25 .201 E6
Ledston Ave LS25 .194 D3
Ledston Hall* WF10 .200 F8
Ledston Mill La WF10 .200 F8
Leech La DL10 .41 E4
Leeds Barnsdale Rd WF10 .200 D3
Leeds La LS26 .194 A3
Leeds Rd
Allerton Bywater WF10 .200 D7
Barwick in Elmet & Scholes LS15 .194 A7
Castleford WF10 .200 E3
Collingham LS22 .188 A8
Great Preston WF10 .200 C7
Harrogate HG2 .219 D1
Ilkley LS29 .218 D5
Kippax LS25 .194 C2
Mickletown LS26 .200 A6
Pannal HG3 .222 F3
Selby YO8 .232 A4
Tadcaster LS24 .189 D5
Leeman Rd YO26 .233 A2
Leeming & Londonderry CP Sch DL7 .63 D4
Leeming La
Brough with St Giles DL10 .41 D5
Burneston DL8 .87 F8
4 Burton in Lonsdale LA6 102 F3
Catterick DL10 .41 E4
Kirklington-cum-Upsland YO7 .88 A6
Langthorpe YO51 .141 B6
Leeming DL7 .63 C4
Melmerby HG4 .114 D8
Theakston DL7 .63 E1
Thornthwaite with Padside HG3 .159 D5
Lees La DL7 .210 B1
Leeside YO24 .230 E8
Legion St LS25 .195 F2
Legram La YO26 .163 D8
Legram Rd YO26 .163 D8
Leicester Way
Aislaby TS16 .5 D4
York YO1 .233 C1
Leighton Cl YO12 .99 E6
Leighton Croft 3 YO30 .224 F1
Leighton Rd 6 TS18 .5 D8
Leith Rd DL3 .3 A5
Lendal YO1 .233 B2
Lendales La YO18 .95 E3
Lennerton La LS25 .196 C3
Lennox Ave DL10 .209 D7
Lennox Cl 2 YO14 .127 A8
Lennox Pl HG4 .113 D3
Leonard St 15 BB18 .171 D1
Leppington Dr YO12 .212 C4
Leppington La YO17 .147 D1
Lerecroft Rd YO24 .230 D8
Lesley Ave YO10 .231 E8
L'espec St DL7 .210 D3
Leven Bank Rd TS15 .5 F2
Leven Cl TS16 .5 D4
Leven Ct TS9 .8 A1
Leven Rd Eaglescliffe TS15 .5 E3
Stokesley TS9 .26 B7
York YO24 .230 D7
Leven Wynd 9 TS9 .26 C7
Levendale 6 TS15 .25 C5
Levendale Prim Sch TS15 .5 F3
Levens Cl HG3 .161 B4
Levenside Great Ayton TS9 .7 F1
4 Hutton Rudby TS15 .25 D5
Stokesley TS9 .26 C7
Levick Cres TS5 .6 D8
Levisham St YO10 .228 D2
Levisham Sta YO18 .72 B5
Lewes Rd DL1 .3 D4
Lewis Cl
1 Croft-on-Tees DL2 .22 C8
Northallerton DL6 .210 F5
Lewis Rd DL6 .210 F5
Lexden Ave TS5 .6 D8
Leyburn Com Prim Sch DL8 .60 D5
Leyburn Gr 1 TS18 .5 D8
Leyburn Pl 8 YO14 .101 A3
Leyburn RC Prim Sch DL8 .60 D5
Leyburn Rd Askrigg DL8 .57 F6
Darlington DL1 .3 D7
Masham HG4 .86 B4
Middleham DL8 .60 E3
Scotton DL9 .40 C4
Leyes The YO10 .229 C4
Leyfield Cl 1 YO32 .167 A7
Leyland Cl BB8 .186 A2
Leyland Cres 3 HG1 .220 A3
Leyland Rd
Harrogate HG1 .220 A3
York YO31 .229 A5
Leys La
Boston Spa LS23 .188 D8
Darrington WF11 .206 A8
Glusburn BD20 .187 B8
Knottingley WF11 .201 F1
Little Smeaton WF8 .206 B4
Leys Rd WF11 .206 A7
Leysthorpe La YO62 .93 B2
Liardet Rd DL10 .41 E4
Lichfield Ct 6 YO23 .228 B1
Lichfield Gr HG3 .219 A4
Lickley St HG4 .214 D5
Lidget La HG5 .163 B5
Lidget Rd BD20 .173 E3
Lidgett Gr YO26 .227 B6
Lidgett Grove Sch YO26 .227 B6
Lidgett La LS25 .194 C3
Lidice Rd DN14 .205 E2
Lidsty Hill YO62 .70 E5
Lifeboat Mus* YO21 .208 D7
Light Bank La BD20 .174 E2
Light La DL8 .59 E5
Lightfoots Ave YO12 .212 D3
Lightfoots Cl YO12 .212 C3
Lightfoot's La YO12 .212 D3
Lightfoots Rd YO12 .212 D3
Lightmire La YO26 .142 A1
Lightwater Valley Miniature Rly* HG4 .113 C6
Lightwater Valley Theme Pk* HG4 .113 C6
Lilac Ave
Appleton Roebuck YO23 .190 F5
Thornaby TS17 .6 B7
York YO10 .229 B3
Lilac Cl 7 LS29 .175 A4
Lilac Gr Harrogate HG1 .219 E6
New Earswick YO32 .225 D4
Lilac Rd TS7 .7 D7
Lilac Wlk YO12 .212 D7
Lilbourne Dr YO30 .228 A8
Lile Cl DL10 .209 C7
Lilla Cl YO21 .208 A6
Lilling Ave 3 YO31 .228 E8
Lilling La YO60 .145 E3
Lilling Low La YO60 .145 C2
Lilly Gate La HG3 .162 A8
Limber Hill YO21 .30 E4
Lime Ave YO31 .228 F7
Lime Chase 10 YO62 .70 B1
Lime Cl 10 LS29 .174 E4
Lime Gr Harrogate HG1 .219 F3
4 Whitby YO21 .208 C6
Lime Kiln La LS22 .180 B5
Lime La DL8 .87 F2
Lime Rd Eaglescliffe TS16 .5 E6
Guisborough TS14 .8 E7
Sinnington YO62 .94 D8
Lime St HG1 .219 F3
Lime Tree Ave
8 Easingwold YO61 .117 D1
Malton YO17 .215 D6
York YO32 .225 D3
Lime Tree Gr YO8 .232 A6
Lime Tree Mews 15 YO19 .184 F7
Limebar Bank Rd YO51 .141 D1
Limebar La YO51 .141 C2
Limegarth 10 YO26 .165 F1
Limehouse La BD23 .216 E1
Limekiln Bank HG4 .113 C1
Limekiln Hill YO25 .150 B3
Limekiln La
Burton Leonard HG3 .140 A1
East Layton DL11 .1 B1
8 Eastfield YO11 .100 B6
Folkton YO11 .100 A2
Halton West BD23 .154 A1
North Stainley with Sleningford HG4 .113 C5
Snape with Thorp HG4 .86 D5
Limekiln Rd YO7 .65 F5
Limes The
Burniston YO13 .75 C8
Helmsley YO62 .92 F6
Stockton on the Forest YO32 .167 D2
Limestone Gr YO13 .75 C8
Limestone La YO13 .75 A5
Limestone Rd YO13 .75 B7
Limestone Way YO13 .75 C8
Limetree Cl 2 YO8 .197 B1
Lime-Tree Cres LS25 .194 E1
Limetrees WF8 .201 D2
Limpsey Gate La YO18 .72 D6
Limpton Gate TS15 .5 E2
Linacre Way DL1 .3 D7
Lincoln Gr HG3 .219 A5
Lincoln Rd 30 BB18 .172 A1
Lincoln St YO26 .227 F5
Lindale 2 YO24 .230 C7
Linden Ave Darlington DL3 .3 B5
Great Ayton TS9 .7 F1
Linden Cl Great Ayton TS9 .7 F2
4 Hutton Rudby TS15 .25 C4
Sleights YO21 .32 B7
York YO32 .225 F5
Linden Cres
Great Ayton TS9 .7 F1
5 Hutton Rudby TS15 .25 C4
Middlesbrough TS7 .7 B6
Linden Dr Hurworth DL2 .3 D1
1 Hurworth-on-Tees DL2 .22 D8
Linden Gdns DL10 .209 D7
Linden Gr Great Ayton TS9 .7 F1
Thornaby TS17 .6 B8
1 York YO30 .228 A8
Linden Rd 9 Earby BB18 172 A1
Great Ayton TS9 .7 F1
Northallerton DL6 .210 E4
Scalby YO12 .212 A8
Linden Way
9 Thorpe Willoughby YO8 197 B2
Wetherby LS22 .180 B4
Lindhead CP Sch YO13 .75 C8
Lindhead Rd YO13 .75 B8
Lindisfarne Rd TS3 .7 C8
Lindley Rd YO30 .224 F1
Lindley St Skipton BD23 .216 F2
York YO24 .227 F3
Lindley Wood Gr YO30 .224 E3
Lindon Rd DL10 .20 F1
Lindrick Cl 3 HG4 .214 B2
Lindrick Way HG3 .219 A4
Lindsay Rd LS25 .194 C3
Lindsey Ave YO26 .227 D4
Ling Croft LS23 .188 D8
Ling Hill YO12 .212 B7
Ling La YO41 .185 F6
Ling Trod YO17 .123 D4
Lingcrag Gdns BD22 .187 B6
Lingcroft Cl YO8 .204 D4
Lingcroft La
Naburn YO19 .231 E3
Tockwith LS22 .181 A6
Lingdale Prim Sch TS12 .9 F7
Lingdale Rd
Lockwood TS12 .9 E7
Thornaby TS17 .6 C7
Lingerfield Prim Sch HG5 .162 B7
Lingfield Ash TS8 .7 A5
Lingfield Cl DL1 .4 A5
Lingfield Prim Sch TS7 .7 B5
Lingfield Rd TS15 .5 F3
Lingfield Way DL1 .4 A5
Lingham La YO7 .115 A3
Linghaw La LA2 .129 C7
Lingholm Cres 9 YO11 .99 F7
Lingholm La YO11 .100 D4
Lingmoor La YO62 .70 E3
Lingrow Cl 3 TS13 .12 A7
Link Ave YO30 .228 C8
Link Rd YO31 .225 E2
Link The
Copmanthorpe YO23 .230 A3
Middlesbrough TS3 .7 C8
Northallerton DL7 .210 B2
Northallerton DL6 .210 E4
Selby YO8 .232 A4
York YO10 .231 E8
Link Wlk 5 YO11 .100 A6
Linkfoot La YO62 .93 A6
Links Cl HG2 .220 E3
Links Dr LA2 .129 A8
Links Prim Sch The TS16 .5 E5
Links The
7 North Featherstone WF7 .200 E1
Tadcaster LS24 .189 E5
Links Way HG2 .220 E3
Linkway DN6 .206 E2
Linnburn Mews 1 LS29 218 B3
Linnet Way YO24 .230 C8
Linton Ave 9 LS22 .180 B3
Linton Cl
Cloughton YO13 .54 D1
19 Filey YO14 .101 B3
Linton Comm LS22 .179 F1
Linton Ct 8 BD23 .216 F3
Linton Falls 1 BD23 .134 E2
Linton La LS22 .180 B2
Linton Mdw 5 YO30 .164 F7
Linton Mdws 7 LS22 .180 B3
Linton Pl 4 YO30 .164 F7
Linton Rd
Collingham LS22 .180 A1
Poppleton YO26 .224 A1
Wetherby LS22 .180 B3
Linton Rise 17 DL9 .40 E4
Linton St 5 YO26 .227 E5
Linton Woods YO30 .165 A7
Linton Woods La YO30 .165 A8
Linton-on-Ouse Cty Prim Sch YO30 .165 A7
Linwith La DN14 .204 C3
Linwood Ave TS9 .26 C8
Lisheen Ave WF10 .200 F4
Lismore Pl YO12 .212 E1
Lismore Rd YO12 .212 E1
Lister Hill 5 BD20 .187 E6
Lister St LS29 .218 A4
Lister Way YO30 .228 A7
Lisvane Ave YO12 .212 D4
Litley Bank YO7 .66 B5
Little Ave YO30 .228 B8
Little Ayton La TS9 .8 A1
Little Beck Bank YO22 .32 C4
Little Beck La YO22 .32 B3
Little Catterton La LS24 .190 A7
Little Church La LS26 .200 B5
Little Comm La DN14 .207 C5
Little Croft HG3 .139 C4
Little Crossing HG4 .214 E2
Little Field La YO18 .72 C5
Little Garth YO26 .224 A2
Little Hallfield Rd YO31 .228 E5
Little Harries La HG4 .214 A7
Little Heck Comm La DN14 .203 D1
Little Hutton La DL11 .1 A4
Little Ings Cl LS24 .196 C8
Little Ings La YO51 .141 C5
Little King St HG3 .137 B4
Little La Brompton DL6 .44 A3
12 Easingwold YO61 .143 C8
Ellerton YO42 .193 C1
11 Haxby YO32 .166 E5
Ilkley LS29 .218 C4
Little Smeaton DN6 .206 D4
North Stainley with Sleningford HG4 .113 C4
Little Mdws YO32 .225 D8
Little Moor Cl YO13 .54 C1
Little Moor La YO8 .232 A8
Little Stonegate YO1 .233 B3
Little Studley Cl HG4 .214 C7
Little Studley Rd HG4 .214 C7
Little Westfield YO25 .151 C3
Little Wood St YO17 .215 E3
Littlebeck Dr DL1 .3 E7

Littleboy Dr TS17 ... 6 C8
Littledale YO18 ... 95 F7
Littlefield Cl 5 YO26 ... 165 F1
Littleside DL8 ... 83 E7
Littlethorpe Cl HG3 ... 219 A4
Littlethorpe La HG4 ... 214 D2
Littlethorpe Pk HG4 ... 214 E3
Littlethorpe Rd HG4 ... 214 E3
Littondale Ave HG5 ... 221 D6
Liverton La TS13 ... 10 D6
Liverton Mill Bank TS12 ... 10 B6
Liverton Rd TS13 ... 10 D7
Livingstone Rd YO12 ... 212 E6
Livingstone St YO26 ... 227 F5
Lloyd Cl YO10 ... 229 B1
Lob La YO41 ... 168 D2
Lochrin Pl 2 YO26 ... 227 B4
Lock Cl DN14 ... 207 F6
Lock La
Castleford WF10 ... 200 E5
Normanton WF6 ... 200 A3
Lock Lane Sports Ctr WF10 ... 200 F5
Lock Wlk DL10 ... 41 E4
Locker La HG4 ... 214 C4
Lockey Croft YO32 ... 225 C8
Lockfield Dr BB18 ... 171 E2
Lockgate Rd DN14 ... 207 C4
Lockheed Cl TS18 ... 5 F7
Lockton Cres TS17 ... 6 A6
Lockton Ct LS24 ... 196 B7
Lockton La YO18 ... 72 E4
Lockton Rd YO21 ... 208 A6
Lockwood Chase YO13 ... 54 D1
Lockwood Prim Sch TS12 ... 9 D7
Lockwood St YO31 ... 233 C3
Loders Gn
5 Eastfield YO11 ... 99 F6
10 Eastfield YO11 ... 100 A6
Lodge Cl 7 YO11 ... 100 B6
Lodge Gdns
Gristlthorp YO14 ... 100 E4
5 Snaith DN14 ... 204 C1
Lodge La 5 Brompton DL6 43 F3
Danby YO21 ... 29 D7
Gowdall DN14 ... 203 F1
Newby with Mulwith HG4 ... 140 E6
Wennington LA2 ... 102 B1
Lodge Rd
Hutton-le-Hole YO62 ... 70 C5
Lythe YO21 ... 12 E3
Settle BD24 ... 153 E8
Lodore Gr TS5 ... 6 D7
Lofthouse Endowed Prim Sch HG3 ... 110 B4
Lofthouse La YO41 ... 185 D7
Loftus Cl YO12 ... 212 B4
Lombards Wynd DL10 ... 209 C7
Londesborough Gr 5 YO8 ... 197 B2
Londesborough Pk 10 YO12 ... 99 D6
Londesborough Rd YO12 ... 212 E4
Londesborough St 5 YO8 ... 232 C5
London La DN6 ... 207 D1
Long Acre Wlk HG3 ... 222 E2
Long Ashes Leisure Ctr BD23 ... 134 B3
Long Band DL8 ... 58 A8
Long Bank DL11 ... 19 C6
Long Bank La BD23 ... 153 E1
Long Causeway Rd
Danby YO21 ... 29 E3
Hutton Buscel YO13 ... 99 A4
Long Close La YO10 ... 233 C1
Long Crag View 1 HG3 ... 161 B2
Long Cswy
Halton East BD23 ... 174 B8
Thirkleby High & Low with Osgodby YO7 ... 90 D1
Long Furrow YO32 ... 225 C8
Long Gate BD22 ... 187 D4
Long Gn 7 BB18 ... 172 B1
Long Heads La LS25 ... 195 F1
Long Hill End BD22 ... 187 B5
Long Ing La BB18 ... 171 E1
Long La
Barwick in Elmet LS15 ... 194 C7
Borrowby YO7 ... 65 E5
Brompton DL6 ... 44 A6
Catton YO41 ... 185 D6
Cawood YO8 ... 197 A6
Cowling BD22 ... 187 B7
East Ayton YO13 ... 99 B7
Ellerton YO42 ... 193 F1
Farndale East YO62 ... 48 F4
Felliscliffe HG3 ... 160 E3
Gayles DL11 ... 19 E6
Heck DN14 ... 207 D8
Heslington YO10 ... 184 C3
Kirk Smeaton WF8 ... 206 B1
Laneshaw Bridge BB8 ... 186 B4
Lockwood TS12 ... 10 B5
Normanby YO62 ... 95 A4
Picton TS15 ... 24 E6
Seamer YO12 ... 99 E6
Slingsby YO62 ... 120 D6
Tatham LA2 ... 128 E7
Well DL8 ... 87 C4
Long Level LA6 ... 102 C8
Long Mann Hills Rd YO8 ... 232 B4
Long Marston C of E Prim Sch YO26 ... 182 A6
Long Mdw 12 Colne BB8 ... 186 A3
Skipton BD23 ... 217 B5
Long Mdw Gate LS25 ... 194 C2
Long Mdws
Garforth LS25 ... 194 C3
6 Ilkley LS29 ... 176 C1
Rillington YO17 ... 122 F5
Long Newton La TS21 ... 5 A6
Long Preston Endowed Prim Sch BD23 ... 153 F5
Long Preston Sta BD23 ... 153 F4
Long Rampart YO42 ... 193 D3
Long Riddings LS29 ... 174 F5
Long Ridge Dr YO26 ... 224 A1
Long Ridge La YO26 ... 224 A1
Long Royd Rd BB18 ... 172 A1
Long St Asenby YO7 ... 115 B6
Easingwold YO61 ... 143 C8
Thirsk YO7 ... 211 C3
Topcliffe YO7 ... 115 C6
Long Stoop Standing Stone★ HG3 ... 160 A2
Long Swales La HG4 ... 112 D5
Long Trods 5 YO8 ... 232 C6
Long Wlk
Knaresborough HG5 ... 221 A6
Scarborough YO12 ... 212 D7
Longacre WF10 ... 200 E3
Longbank Rd TS7 ... 7 D7
Longber La LA6 ... 102 D4
Longcroft 2 YO32 ... 166 E5
Longcroft Rd 1 LS29 ... 218 E3
Longdale Ave 18 BD24 ... 131 D2
Longdike La
Kippax LS25 ... 200 E8
Thornton Steward HG4 ... 61 E1
Longfield Comp Sch DL3 ... 3 C8
Longfield Ct 21 BB18 ... 171 D1
Longfield Rd DL3 ... 3 C7
Longfield Terr YO30 ... 233 A3
Longland La YO26 ... 164 A3
Longlands Field Rd YO26 ... 163 D8
Longlands La
Boroughbridge YO51 ... 141 A3
Danby YO21 ... 29 B6
Hetton BD23 ... 155 F5
Sicklinghall LS22 ... 179 E3
Thornton-le-Dale YO18 ... 96 E5
Longlands Rd YO17 ... 123 B3
Longmans Hill CP Sch YO8 ... 232 C3
Longtons La BD23 ... 152 F4
Longwestgate YO11 ... 213 B6
Longwood Bank DL10 ... 209 D5
Longwood Link 8 YO30 224 E3
Longwood Rd YO30 ... 224 F3
Lonsdale Mdws LS23 ... 188 E8
Lonsdale Pl 12 YO13 ... 99 B8
Lonsdale Rd YO11 ... 213 A3
Loos Rd DL9 ... 40 F3
Loraine Cres DL1 ... 3 C4
Lord Ave TS17 ... 6 B5
Lord Mayor's Wlk YO31 ... 233 B3
Lord's Close Rd LA2 ... 129 B3
Lords La DL8 ... 41 F1
Lord's La DL8 ... 63 C2
Lords La DL8 ... 62 E8
Lords Moor La YO32 ... 167 C7
Lordship La YO8 ... 232 D8
Loriners Dr 7 YO23 ... 230 B3
Loring Rd YO13 ... 54 A7
Lorne St YO23 ... 228 B1
Lorraine Ave 3 YO41 ... 185 B2
Loscoe Cl WF6 ... 200 C2
Loscoe La WF7 ... 200 C1
Loshpot La LS22 ... 180 C5
Lothersdale CP Sch BD20 ... 186 F8
Lothersdale Rd BD20 ... 187 B8
Lotherton La LS25 ... 195 A7
Lotherton Way LS25 ... 194 C4
Louisa St DL1 ... 3 D5
Lousy Hill La YO22 ... 32 C3
Louvain St 5 BB18 ... 171 D2
Love La Brawby YO17 ... 94 F1
Castleford WF10 ... 200 E3
Easby DL10 ... 209 E4
8 Leyburn DL8 ... 60 D5
Whitby YO21 ... 208 A7
York YO24 ... 228 A2
Lovers' La DL7 ... 64 F2
Low Bank
4 Embsay BD23 ... 217 E8
Over Silton DL6 ... 66 A8
Low Bentham CP Sch LA2 ... 128 F8
Low Bentham Rd LA2 ... 128 F8
Low Catton Rd YO41 ... 185 C8
Low Cl LS29 ... 218 A5
Low Croft 6 YO32 ... 167 A7
Low Demesne LA6 ... 103 D3
Low Demesne Cl LA6 ... 103 D3
Low Farm LS26 ... 200 C8
Low Farm Cl YO23 ... 190 D4
Low Field La
Cold Kirby YO7 ... 91 D7
Goldsborough HG5 ... 163 A1
Marton cum Grafton YO51 ... 141 E2
Staveley HG5 ... 140 E1
Low Fields Dr YO24 ... 227 C3
Low Fold BB18 ... 186 A7
Low Garth YO22 ... 32 A6
Low Garth Link 17 LS25 ... 195 F4
Low Garth Rd LS25 ... 195 F4
Low Gate DL8 ... 57 F5
Low Gate La HG4 ... 138 F7
Low Gn Catterick DL10 ... 41 D4
Copmanthorpe YO23 ... 230 B2
13 Knottingley WF11 ... 202 A2
Menwith with Darley HG3 ... 160 A6
Low House La
Carlton Miniott YO7 ... 89 C2
Dishforth YO7 ... 115 B2
Low Hutton Pk YO60 ... 147 C6
Low La Askrigg DL8 ... 58 B4
Carperby-cum-Thoresby DL8 ... 58 F4
Cononley BD20 ... 173 C2
Cowling BD22 ... 187 A8
Cropton YO18 ... 71 B4
Dalby-cum-Skewsby YO60 ... 119 B2
Dalton DL11 ... 19 D7
Embsay with Eastby BD23 ... 217 E8
Grassington BD23 ... 134 E3
Grinton DL11 ... 37 E5
Grinton DL11 ... 38 C5
Heslington YO10 ... 229 D1
Howsham YO60 ... 147 A1
Hutton-Sessay YO7 ... 116 B7
Leck LA6 ... 102 D7
Leyburn DL8 ... 60 C4
Maltby TS17 ... 6 B3
Menwith with Darley HG3 ... 159 F6
Mickleby TS13 ... 12 A3
Middlesbrough TS5 ... 6 E6
Muker DL11 ... 36 C4
Newsham DL11 ... 18 H7
Reeth, Fremington & Healaugh DL11 ... 37 F5
Silsden BD20 ... 174 B3
Spofforth with Stockeld HG3 ... 179 C4
Stainburn LS21 ... 177 F3
Sutton-under-Whitestonecliffe YO7 ... 90 E6
Swinton YO17 ... 121 C4
Thirkleby High & Low with Osgodby YO7 ... 90 C1
West Rounton DL6 ... 24 D3
Westow YO60 ... 147 C4
Wigglesworth BD23 ... 153 D3
Low Mdw YO8 ... 232 C6
Low Mill Cl YO10 ... 229 D3
Low Mill La LS29 ... 175 A4
Low Mill Rd HG4 ... 214 D4
Low Moor Ave 3 YO10 ... 231 F8
Low Moor La
Askham Richard YO23 ... 182 D3
Brearton HG5 ... 162 B7
East Harlsey DL6 ... 44 C7
Fearby HG4 ... 85 F3
Hessay YO26 ... 182 C8
Rillington YO17 ... 122 E6
Low Moor Rd YO18 ... 71 F5
Low Moor S La YO17 ... 122 D6
Low Moorgate YO17 ... 122 F5
Low Ousegate YO1 ... 233 B2
Low Park Rd LS29 ... 176 A3
Low Peter La HG3 ... 140 A3
Low Petergate YO1 ... 233 B3
Low Poppleton La YO26 ... 227 B7
Low Rd Gainford DL2 ... 1 C7
Gowdall DN14 ... 204 A1
Irton YO12 ... 75 B3
Kellington DN14 ... 202 F4
Kirby Grindalythe YO17 ... 149 F7
Newby & Scalby YO12 ... 212 A6
Thirkleby High & Low with Osgodby YO7 ... 116 E8
Low Skellgate HG4 ... 214 C5
Low Sleights Rd LA6 ... 104 B7
Low St Aiskew DL7 ... 63 C6
Austwick LA2 ... 130 E7
Burton in Lonsdale LA6 ... 102 F3
Carlton DN14 ... 204 C2
Husthwaite YO61 ... 117 B6
Kirkby Fleetham with Fencote DL10 ... 41 F2
Knottingley WF11 ... 201 E4
Lastingham YO62 ... 70 E5
Nunnington YO62 ... 93 E2
Oswaldkirk YO62 ... 92 F3
Ripon HG4 ... 214 D5
22 Scalby YO13 ... 75 D5
Sherburn in Elmet LS25 ... 195 F4
Thornton-le-Clay YO60 ... 146 A4
Low Stanghow Rd TS12 ... 9 F6
Low Town Bank Rd YO61 ... 91 B4
Low Tun Way YO62 ... 69 A2
Low Wath Rd HG3 ... 137 B4
Low Way 5 LS23 ... 188 E5
Low Well Pk YO19 ... 192 F7
Low Westfield Rd YO23 ... 230 A1
Low Wood La
Glaisdale YO21 ... 30 C6
Leyburn DL8 ... 60 C4
Low Wood Rise LS29 ... 218 F3
Lowcroft 9 LS22 ... 188 A8
Lowcross Ave TS14 ... 8 E5
Lowcross Dr TS9 ... 26 E5
Lowdale Ave YO12 ... 212 E8
Lowdale Ct 4 YO22 ... 32 A6
Lower Clark St
2 Scarborough YO12 ... 212 F6
13 Scarborough YO12 ... 213 A7
Lower Constable Rd LS29 ... 218 D3
Lower Croft St 39 BB18 ... 172 A1
Lower Darnborough St YO23 ... 233 B1
Lower Derwent Valley Nature Reserve★ YO42 ... 199 C8
Lower Flat Cliffs YO14 ... 101 C1
Lower Friargate YO1 ... 233 B2
Lower Greenfoot 15 BD24 ... 131 D2
Lower Mickletown LS26 ... 200 C6
Lower Oxford St WF10 ... 200 E4
Lower Park Marina★ BB18 ... 171 E1
Lower Priory St YO1 ... 233 A1
Lower Station Rd 3 WF6 ... 200 A1
Lower Union St BD23 ... 216 F3
Lower Wellington Rd LS29 ... 218 B4
Lower William St 3 YO12 ... 212 F6
Loweswater Rd 5 YO30 224 E1
Lowfield
3 Eastfield YO11 ... 100 A6
Hawes DL8 ... 56 C4
Lowfield Dr YO32 ... 166 E5
Lowfield La
Beamsley BD23 ... 174 F7
Kirkby Fleetham with Fencote DL7 ... 42 D2
Langthorpe YO51 ... 141 A6
Rufforth YO26 ... 227 A4
Scrayingham YO41 ... 169 A7
Sharow HG4 ... 214 F6
Snape with Thorp DL8 ... 87 A7
Lowfield Rd
Barlby with Osgodby YO8 ... 198 B5
Hillam LS25 ... 202 C8
Malton YO17 ... 215 C6
Lowfield Sch YO24 ... 227 D3
Lowfields 2 YO12 ... 99 D2
Lowfields Ave TS17 ... 6 A5
Lowfields La YO7 ... 88 C6
Lowgate DN14 ... 207 D5
Lowgill La LA2 ... 128 F4
Lowick YO24 ... 230 C7
Lowkber La LA6 ... 103 E2
Lowlands Dr DL7 ... 63 C5
Lowmoor Rd YO8 ... 198 E6
Lown Hill YO24 ... 227 C2
Lowna Rd YO62 ... 70 B5
Lownorth Rd YO13 ... 53 C2
Lowskellgate 15 HG4 ... 214 C5
Lowther Cres 3 LS26 ... 194 A1
Lowther Ct YO31 ... 233 C4
Lowther Dr
Garforth LS25 ... 194 C3
Selby YO8 ... 232 E3
2 Swillington LS26 ... 194 A1
Lowther St YO31 ... 233 C4
Lowther Terr YO24 ... 228 A3
Loxley Cl YO30 ... 224 F2
Loyne Pk LA6 ... 102 A7
Lucas Ave YO30 ... 228 C8
Lucas Gr N YO26 ... 181 C7
Lucas Gr S YO26 ... 181 C7
Lucas Rd YO26 ... 181 C7
Lucerne Dr TS14 ... 8 E6
Lucia La TS14 ... 8 E6
Lucky La YO7 ... 89 E8
Lucombe Way YO32 ... 225 D4
Luddith Rd YO17 ... 148 D5
Ludlow Ave LS25 ... 194 D4
Lulsgate TS17 ... 6 C7
Lumb Gill La LS29 ... 175 A3
Lumb La BD22 ... 187 A5
Lumb Mill Way BD23 ... 157 E7
Lumby Hill LS25 ... 202 A8
Lumby La
Monk Fryston LS25 ... 202 A8
South Milford LS25 ... 196 A1
Lumley Cl YO7 ... 211 D2
Lumley La Azerley HG4 ... 112 D8
Kirkby Fleetham with Fencote DL7 ... 42 B1
Lumley Rd YO30 ... 228 B7
Lumley St WF10 ... 200 D3
Lunar Pk★ YO11 ... 213 C6
Luncarr La HG4 ... 114 B2
Lund Cl YO32 ... 225 C8
Lund Head La HG3 ... 179 B2
Lund La Bubwith YO8 ... 199 C4
Cliffe YO8 ... 198 D4
Hampsthwaite HG3 ... 161 A5
Lund Rd YO62 ... 70 B7
Lund Sand La
Easingwold YO61 ... 143 A8
Raskelf YO61 ... 117 A1
Lund Sike La LS25 ... 195 F2
Lundgreen La YO61 ... 144 A3
Lund's Twr★ BD20 ... 187 C6
Lundy Cl 10 YO30 ... 225 A1
Lunebeck Wlk TS17 ... 6 C6
Lunedale Ave
Knaresborough HG5 ... 221 C5
Middlesbrough TS5 ... 6 E8
Lunedale Rd DL3 ... 3 A6
Lunn La DN14 ... 202 D3
Lunnfields La WF11 ... 201 E6
Lupton Bank HG3 ... 137 D3
Lupton Cl HG3 ... 137 D3
Lutton La YO17 ... 123 F4
Luttons CP Sch YO17 ... 150 B8
Lutyens The 22 LS29 ... 175 C2
Lycett Rd YO24 ... 230 F6
Lych Gate 14 DL2 ... 3 E1
Lydford Rd 18 DL10 ... 41 E4
Lydham Ct 2 YO24 ... 230 C8
Lyell St YO12 ... 212 E6
Lynbrook Cl YO7 ... 211 B4
Lyndale LS25 ... 200 D8
Lyndale Ave YO10 ... 229 C3
Lyndale Gr 14 WF6 ... 200 B1
Lynden Way YO24 ... 227 D3
Lyndhurst Cl
2 Norton DN6 ... 206 F2
9 Whitby YO21 ... 208 D6
Lyndhurst Dr 1 DN6 ... 206 F2
Lyndhurst Rise 3 DN6 ... 206 F2
Lyndon Ave
Bramham LS23 ... 188 E6
Garforth LS25 ... 194 C4
Lyndon Cl 1 LS23 ... 188 E6
Lyndon Cres 4 LS23 ... 188 E6
Lyndon Rd LS23 ... 188 E6
Lyndon Sq 2 LS23 ... 188 E6
Lyndon Way LS23 ... 188 E6
Lynmouth Cl TS8 ... 6 E5
Lynndale Ave 6 BD20 ... 187 F8
Lynton Ave LS23 ... 188 E8
Lynton Cl YO8 ... 232 B1
Lynton Gdns
Brayton YO8 ... 232 B1
Darlington DL1 ... 3 E5
Harrogate HG1 ... 220 A3
Lynton Way DL6 ... 210 D3
Lynwith Cl DN14 ... 204 C3
Lynwith Ct DN14 ... 204 C3
Lynwith Dr DN14 ... 204 C3
Lynwood Ave 3 YO23 ... 230 A3
Lynwood View 4 YO23 ... 230 A3
Lynx La YO7 ... 115 B1
Lyon Rd BD20 ... 187 F7
Lyonette Rd DL1 ... 3 E7
Lyons Rd DL10 ... 209 C8
Lys Cres DL9 ... 209 D1
Lysander Cl YO30 ... 225 A3
Lytham Cl BD23 ... 217 C3
Lytham Gdns BD23 ... 217 C3
Lytham Rd DL1 ... 3 D8
Lythe Bank Lythe YO21 ... 12 F4
Sutton with Howgrave DL8 ... 87 F2
Lythe C of E Prim Sch YO21 ... 12 E3
Lythe Fell Rd LA2 ... 129 B2
Lythe La LA2 ... 129 A2

M

M62 Trad Est DN14 ... 205 F2
Mac Arthur Cl YO7 ... 211 B2
Macdonell Cl 1 DL9 ... 209 C1
Mackeridge La YO62 ... 48 F4
Mackie Dr TS14 ... 8 F7
Mackinnon Ave 1 WF6 ... 200 B2
Maclagan Rd YO23 ... 230 F4
Mafeking St HG1 ... 219 F4
Magazine La YO8 ... 198 B3
Magazine Rd YO8 ... 198 B4
Magdalen's Cl HG4 ... 214 D6
Magdalen's Rd HG4 ... 214 D6
Magister Rd TS17 ... 6 B7
Magnolia Gr YO32 ... 225 D2
Maida Gr YO10 ... 228 D2
Maiden Bower (Motte & Bailey)★ YO7 ... 115 D5
Maiden Castle★ DL11 ... 38 A5
Maiden Greve YO17 ... 215 A4
Maidensgrave Henge★ YO25 ... 126 F1
Maidstone Dr TS7 ... 7 C6
Main Ave YO31 ... 228 F5
Main Rd Drax YO8 ... 204 F5
Gainford DL2 ... 1 D7
Hambleton YO8 ... 196 E1
Hellifield BD23 ... 154 B3
Stainforth BD24 ... 131 E6
Steeton with Eastburn BD20 ... 187 F7
Weaverthorpe YO17 ... 124 E1
Main St Aberford LS25 ... 194 F8
Addingham LS29 ... 174 F4
Allerston YO18 ... 97 B5
Alne YO61 ... 142 F4
Amotherby YO17 ... 121 A4
Appleton Roebuck YO23 ... 190 F5
Askham Bryan YO23 ... 182 F3
Askrigg DL8 ... 57 E6
Asselby DN14 ... 205 D7
Austwick LA2 ... 130 E7
Aysgarth DL8 ... 58 E3
Barkston Ash LS24 ... 195 E7
Barwick in Elmet LS15 ... 194 B8
3 Beal DN14 ... 202 D4
Bentham LA2 ... 128 E8
Bilbrough YO23 ... 182 C1
Bilton-in-Ainsty with Bickerton LS22 ... 181 A5
Bishop Monkton HG3 ... 140 B5
Bishopthorpe YO23 ... 231 A4
Boroughbridge YO51 ... 141 A3
4 Brafferton YO61 ... 115 F1

Main St *continued*
Brafferton YO61 141 F8
Bubwith YO8 199 C7
Bugthorpe YO41 169 D4
Burley in Warfedale LS29 176 C1
Burton Salmon LS25 201 F6
Church Fenton LS24 196 B7
Cliffe YO8 198 E2
Cononley BD20 173 D1
Copmanthorpe YO23 230 A2
Cottingwith YO42 193 C5
Darley HG3 160 A6
Deighton YO19 192 A7
Earby BB18 186 A7
East Ayton/West Ayton YO13 99 A7
Eastfield YO11 100 B6
Ebberston & Yedingham YO13 97 D5
Ellerton YO42 193 C1
Elvington YO41 185 C2
Embsay BD23 217 E8
Escrick YO19 192 B5
Farnhill BD20 173 E1
Folkton YO11 100 A2
Follifoot HG3 223 F5
Ganton YO12 125 A8
Garforth LS25 194 C3
Gillamoor YO62 70 A4
Gilling East YO62 118 F7
Glusburn BD20 187 E7
Gowdall DN14 204 A1
13 Grassington BD23 134 E3
Great Ouseburn YO26 164 B8
Great Preston WF10 200 D6
Gristlthorp YO14 100 E4
Harome YO62 93 C5
Healaugh LS24 181 F2
Hebden BD23 135 A1
Heck DN14 207 C8
Helperby YO61 142 A8
Hemingbrough YO8 198 F1
Hensall DN14 203 D2
Hessay YO26 182 B8
High Bentham LA2 129 A8
Hovingham YO62 119 E6
Huby YO61 144 A4
Ingleton LA6 103 D3
Irton YO12 99 C6
Kelfield YO19 191 D1
Kellington DN14 202 F3
Kirk Deighton LS22 180 B5
Kirk Smeaton WF8 206 B3
Kirkby Malham BD23 154 F8
Kirkby Malzeard HG4 112 C5
Langcliffe BD24 131 E4
Ledston WF10 200 F7
Linton LS22 180 A1
Little Ouseburn YO26 164 A7
Long Preston BD23 153 F5
Low Bradley BD20 173 E3
Menwith with Darley HG3 160 A4
Mickletown LS26 200 B6
Middleton YO18 95 E8
Monk Fryston LS25 201 F8
1 Naburn YO19 191 D8
Newton Kyme cum Toulston LS24 189 C7
North Duffield YO8 199 A8
Pannal HG3 222 D3
Pollington DN14 207 F6
Poppleton YO26 165 F1
Rathmell BD24 153 C6
Reighton YO14 127 E5
Riccall YO19 198 A8
Ryther cum Ossendyke LS24 190 E2
Saxton with Scarthingwell LS24 195 D7
Scholes LS15 194 A7
Scotton HG5 162 A6
Seamer YO12 99 D6
Sheriff Hutton YO60 145 D5
Shipton YO30 165 F5
Sicklinghall LS22 179 D3
Sinnington YO62 95 A8
Stainforth BD24 131 E6
Stamford Bridge YO41 168 D2
Staveley HG5 140 E1
Stillington YO61 144 C6
Threshfield BD23 134 C2
Thwing YO25 126 B1
Tollerton YO61 143 A3
Ulleskelf LS24 190 C3
Walton LS23 181 A2
Wath HG4 114 A8
Weeton LS17 178 C1
West Tanfield HG4 87 A1
Westow YO60 147 B4
Wheldrake YO19 192 F7
Whittington LA6 102 A7
Wilberfoss YO41 185 E5
Wombleton YO62 93 E6
Womersley DN6 206 C6
Wray-with-Botton LA2 128 A6
York YO26 227 A5
York YO10 229 B1
York YO10 231 D8
Mains La YO60 146 D5
Mains The BD24 131 D3
Mainsfield Cl 1 BD24 131 D3
Mainsfield Rise 2 BD24 131 D3
Maison Dieu DL10 209 D7
Major St DL3 3 C6
Malais La BD20 187 D7
Malbys Gr YO23 230 B2
Malden Rd HG1 220 B3
Malham Gr YO31 229 B5
Malham Moor La BD23 133 F4
Malham Rakes BD23 133 A2
Malham Tarn Field Ctr* BD24 132 F6
Malham Visitor Ctr* BD23 133 A1
Malham Way HG5 221 D6
Malim Rd DL1 3 F5
Mallard Cl 8 Filey YO14 101 A4
12 Pickering YO18 95 F6
Mallard Rd 4 DL9 40 F2
Mallard View YO17 215 D2
Mallard Way
4 Eastfield YO12 99 F6
11 Haxby YO32 166 F5
Mallard Wlk 14 YO51 141 B5
Mallinson Cl HG2 222 D6
Mallinson Cres HG2 222 E6
Mallinson Gate HG2 222 E6
Mallinson Gr HG2 222 D6
Mallinson Oval HG2 222 D6
Mallinson Way HG2 222 D6
Mallison Hill Dr 5 YO61 117 D1
Mallorie Cl HG4 214 A5
Mallorie Ct HG4 214 B5
Mallorie Park Dr HG4 214 A4
Mallory Cl YO32 225 D4
Mallory Ct 17 DL1 3 F6
Mallowdale TS7 7 C5
Malltraeth Sands TS17 6 D6
Malpas Dr DL7 210 D4
Malpas Rd
Brompton YO13 98 C4
Northallerton DL7 210 D3
Malsis Prep Sch BD20 187 C7
Malt Dubs Cl LA6 103 D3
Malt Kiln La YO23 190 F5
Malt Kiln Terr LS24 189 D4
Maltby Rd TS8 6 D4
Malthouse La HG3 222 D2
Maltings Ct Alne YO61 143 A5
6 Selby YO8 232 C6
Maltings The
8 Brafferton YO61 115 F1
13 Pontefract WF8 201 B1
Thirsk YO7 211 B2
Maltkiln La
Castleford WF10 200 F4
Killinghall HG3 161 C6
Malton Ave YO31 228 E6
Malton CP Sch YO17 215 D5
Malton Gate YO18 96 D5
Malton La
Allerston YO18 97 B4
Flaxton YO60 146 A1
Kirby Grindalythe YO17 150 A8
Malton Mus* YO17 215 C4
Malton Norton & District Hospl YO17 215 B4
Malton Rd
Hunmanby YO14 126 F8
Huntington YO32 226 A1
Leavening YO17 147 E2
Pickering YO18 95 F6
Rillington YO17 122 E4
Scampston YO17 123 B7
Slingsby YO62 120 B5
Swinton YO17 121 C4
York YO31 228 F7
Malton Rugby Club YO17 215 E5
Malton St Marys RC Prim Sch YO17 215 D5
Malton Sch YO17 215 A5
Malton St YO61 117 D6
Malton Sta YO17 215 C3
Malton Way YO30 227 F8
Malvern Ave YO26 227 D5
Malvern Cl
Huntington YO32 226 A5
8 Hurworth-on-Tees DL2 3 E1
Stokesley TS9 26 C7
Malvern Cres
Darlington DL3 2 F7
Scarborough YO12 212 D5
Malvern Dr
Middlesbrough TS5 6 E6
Stokesley TS9 26 C7
Malvern Rd WF11 201 F2
Manchester Rd BB18 171 D1
Mancroft YO32 225 C8
Mandale Mill Prim Sch TS17 6 B8
Mandale Rd TS5 6 D8
Manfield C of E Prim Sch DL2 2 B4
Mangrill La LS14 188 C3
Manham Hill YO11 99 F7
Mankin La HG4 214 D1
Manley Cl YO32 225 D4
Manley Dr LS22 180 A3
Manley Gr LS29 218 D4
Manley Rd LS29 218 E4
Manley Rise LS29 218 D3
Manor Ave YO12 212 D6
Manor Beeches The 3 YO19 184 E7
Manor C of E Sch YO26 227 C7
Manor Chase YO26 181 F6
Manor Cl
Burton in Lonsdale LA6 102 F3
5 Hemingbrough YO8 198 F1
Ingleton LA6 103 D3
Kirk Smeaton WF8 206 B3
13 Kirkbymoorside YO62 70 B1
Low Worsall TS15 24 B8
6 North Duffield YO8 199 A7
12 Norton DN6 206 E2
5 Stokesley TS9 26 C7
Topcliffe YO7 115 C6
Wath HG4 114 B7
Whitby YO21 208 B6
Manor Cres HG5 221 C6
Manor Ct
6 Bubwith YO8 199 D7
Fairburn WF11 201 D7
Follifoot HG3 223 F5
Kirkby Malzeard HG4 112 D5
Knaresborough HG5 221 B5
2 York YO32 225 F6
Manor Dr
2 Brafferton YO61 115 F1
Camblesforth YO8 204 C4
4 Dunnington YO19 184 E7
Harrogate HG2 222 C8
Hilton TS15 6 C2
Kirby Hill YO51 141 A7
Knaresborough HG5 221 C6
5 North Duffield YO8 199 A7
North Featherstone WF7 200 E1
Pickering YO18 95 E7
Scotton HG5 162 A6
Manor Dr N YO26 227 D4
Manor Dr S YO26 227 D4
Manor Farm Cl
1 Brayton YO8 232 A1
Carlton DN14 204 C2
Copmanthorpe YO23 230 A2
Kellington DN14 202 F3
Manor Farm Ct YO8 203 C4
Manor Farm Way TS8 6 F5
Manor Fold HG3 223 F5
Manor Garth
Haxby YO32 225 B8
Kellington DN14 202 F3
12 Kirklevington TS15 24 E8
Ledsham LS25 201 B8
7 Norton DN6 206 F2
1 Riccall YO19 198 A8
7 Spofforth HG3 179 E6
Manor Garth Rd LS25 194 E1
Manor Gdns
6 Hunmanby YO14 127 A8
Killinghall HG3 161 C5
Scarborough YO12 212 E6
Thorner LS14 188 A3
Manor Gn DL8 62 C6
Manor Gr Colburn DL9 40 F5
Great Broughton TS9 26 E5
Manor Heath YO23 230 A3
Manor House Art Gall & Mus* LS29 218 B4
Manor Inf Sch The HG5 221 B6
Manor La
Healaugh LS24 181 E1
Rawcliffe YO30 224 D2
Manor Orchards HG5 221 B6
Manor Park Ave
Great Preston WF10 200 D7
Pontefract WF8 201 C2
Manor Park Cl YO30 224 E2
Manor Park Gr YO30 224 E2
Manor Park Rd YO30 224 E2
Manor Pk
Arkendale HG5 163 A7
Cowling BD22 187 B6
Ledston WF10 200 F7
Swinton YO17 121 C4
Manor Rd Beal DN14 202 C4
Darlington DL3 3 C4
Easingwold YO61 117 C1
Fylingdales YO22 33 C4
Harrogate HG2 222 B8
Hurworth-on-Tees DL2 3 D1
Killinghall HG3 161 C5
Knaresborough HG5 221 B6
Scarborough YO12 212 E5
Stutton with Hazlewood LS24 189 D4
Manor Rise LS29 218 D4
Manor Vale La 28 YO62 70 B1
Manor View
Oswaldkirk YO62 93 A1
Rillington YO17 122 F5
Manor View Rd YO11 100 D5
Manor Way
Glusburn BD20 187 E6
York YO30 224 E2
Manor Wood TS8 6 F6
Manorcroft WF6 200 A1
Manorfields 11 DL2 3 E1
Manse Cres 23 LS29 176 C1
Manse La HG5 221 D4
Manse Rd LS29 176 C1
Manse Way BD20 187 E7
Mansfield Ave TS17 6 B8
Mansfield Rd LS29 176 B1
Mansfield St YO31 233 C3
Manston Ct 14 DL2 4 C4
Manston La LS15 194 A5
Manton Ave TS5 6 D8
Maple Ave
Bishopthorpe YO23 231 A3
Malton YO17 215 D6
Maple Cl 5 Colburn DL9 40 F5
Maple Cl *continued*
Hambleton YO8 197 B1
Knaresborough HG1 220 D5
2 South Milford LS25 195 F2
Maple Croft YO61 144 A5
Maple Ct YO10 231 E6
Maple Dr YO12 212 D7
Maple Gr 12 Brayton YO8 197 D1
7 Linton-on-Ouse YO30 164 F7
York YO10 228 D1
Maple La YO61 144 A5
Maple Rd DL10 209 A8
Maple Tree Ave YO8 198 B4
Maplewood Paddock 2 YO24 227 C1
Mar Head Balk HG5 163 A7
Marage Rd YO7 211 B3
Marazion Dr DL3 3 C8
Marbeck La HG5 140 F2
March St
Normanton South WF6 200 A1
York YO31 233 C4
Marchlyn Cres TS17 5 F4
Marcus St DN14 205 F2
Marderby La YO7 90 C7
Maresfield Rd DL9 40 E3
Margaret Rd HG2 219 B1
Margaret St YO10 233 C1
Margerison Cres LS29 218 E3
Margerison Rd LS29 218 E3
Maria St 15 LS29 176 C1
Marias Ct 9 YO11 213 A6
Marigold Cl YO8 232 C2
Marina Ave 3 DN14 204 B1
Marina Cres BD23 216 D3
Marina Rd DL3 3 D8
Marina Way HG4 214 A2
Marine Dr YO11 213 C7
Marine Espl YO13 54 A8
Marine Villa Rd WF11 201 F2
Mariner's Terr 16 YO14 101 B3
Marion Ave TS16 5 D4
Marishes La
Allerston YO17 97 A2
Thornton-le-Dale YO17 96 E1
Marishes Low Rd YO17 122 B8
Mark House La BD23 155 C1
Mark La
Fylingdales YO22 33 C3
Kirk Deighton LS22 180 B5
Markenfield Hall* HG4 139 D6
Markenfield Rd HG3 219 B5
Market Flat La HG5 162 C6
Market Hill 5 YO51 141 B6
Market La YO8 232 C5
Market Pl 4 Bedale DL8 63 A3
2 Cawood YO8 197 B8
7 Easingwold YO61 143 C8
11 Helmsley YO62 92 F6
10 Helmsley YO62 92 F6
25 Kirkbymoorside YO62 70 B1
3 Knaresborough HG5 221 B6
Malton YO17 215 C4
9 Masham HG4 86 C3
9 Middleham DL8 60 E2
6 Normanton South WF6 200 A1
Pickering YO18 95 F7
Richmond DL10 209 C6
11 Selby YO8 232 C5
10 Settle BD24 131 D2
9 Snaith DN14 204 C1
Thirsk YO7 211 B3
12 Wetherby LS22 180 C3
11 Whitby YO22 208 D7
Market Pl E 20 HG4 214 C5
Market Pl N 19 HG4 214 C5
Market Pl S 21 HG4 214 C5
Market Pl W 22 HG4 214 C5
Market St Malton YO17 215 C4
Normanton South WF6 200 A1
24 Scarborough YO11 213 A6
York YO1 233 B2
Market Way 25 YO11 213 A6
Market Weighton Rd YO8 198 B6
Markham Cres YO31 233 B4
Markham St YO31 233 B4
Markington C of E Prim Sch HG3 139 C3
Marl Hill La BD20 186 D8
Marlborough Ave
3 Byram WF11 201 F4
Tadcaster LS24 189 D5
3 Whitby YO21 208 B7
Marlborough Cl YO30 224 D3
Marlborough Dr
Darlington DL1 3 C4
Tadcaster LS24 189 D5
Marlborough Gr
Ilkley LS29 218 D3
Ripon HG4 214 B6
York YO10 228 D2
Marlborough Rd HG1 219 E2
Marlborough Sq LS29 218 C3
Marlborough St 11 YO12 213 A7
Marmiam Dr 2 YO32 167 D2
Marmion Ct HG4 87 A1
Marmion Twr* HG4 87 A1
Marne Cl 1 DL9 209 B1
Marne Rd DL9 209 D1
Marr The YO14 100 F5
Marrick Priory (rems of)* DL11 38 E4
Marrick Rd TS18 5 D8
Marridales DL8 56 D4
Marriforth La HG4 61 F2
Mars La TS13 11 A4
Marsett La DL8 57 B2
Marsh Croft WF11 201 E4
Marsh End WF11 202 A3
Marsh La Asselby DN14 205 D7
Barlow YO8 204 B8
2 Beal DN14 202 D4
Bolton Percy YO23 190 D3
Byram cum Sutton WF11 201 F4
Cawood YO8 197 D8
Ingleby Greenhow TS9 27 B5
Knottingley WF11 202 A2
West Haddlesey YO8 202 F5
Marsh Lane Gdns DN14 202 F4
Marsh Rd WF10 200 D3
Marshall Dr YO18 96 A7
Marshfield Rd 7 BD24 131 D2
Marston Ave YO26 227 B3
Marston Bsns Pk YO26 181 B7
Marston Cres YO26 227 B3
Marston La YO26 182 A8
Marston Moor Rd DL1 3 F4
Marston Rd YO26 181 D7
Marston Way 3 LS22 180 B3
Marten Cl 2 YO30 228 A8
Martin Cheeseman Ct 3 YO24 230 C8
Martindale Rd DL1 3 D7
Martinet Rd TS17 6 B7
Marton Abbey (Priory)* YO61 144 C8
Marton Ave TS4 7 B8
Marton Cum Grafton C of E Prim Sch YO51 141 D1
Marton La
Arkendale HG5 163 B8
Wrelton YO18 95 C7
Marton Manor Prim Sch TS7 7 B6
Marton Moor Rd TS7 7 D5
Marton Rd
Coulby Newham TS4 7 A7
Gargrave BD23 172 C8
Marton YO62 94 F6
Sinnington YO62 95 A7
Marton St BD23 216 D3
Marton Sta TS7 7 C7
Martonside Way TS4 7 A8
Marvell Rise HG1 219 E7
Marwood Dr TS9 7 F1
Marwoods C of E Inf Sch TS9 7 F1
Mary La YO26 141 F3
Mary St 3 BD20 173 F1
Marygate Barton DL10 21 D7
York YO30 233 A3
Marygate La YO30 233 A3
Marykirk Rd TS17 6 B6
Masefield Cl HG1 219 E7
Masham Bank HG4 85 D8
Masham C of E Prim Sch HG4 86 C3
Masham Cl HG2 220 C1
Masham La DL8 87 A4
Masham Rd Firby DL8 62 F1
Harrogate HG2 220 C1
Snape with Thorp DL8 86 E8
Mask La YO41 185 D4
Masongill Fell La LA6 103 A6
Masonic La YO7 211 B3
Maspin Moor Rd LS25 202 C7
Massa Flatts Wood BD23 216 E5
Massey St YO8 232 C5
Master Rd TS17 6 B7
Master's Gate YO18 49 D4
Mastil Cl DL8 62 D5
Mastiles La BD23 134 A6
Matfen Ave TS7 7 D6
Matthew La
Bradleys Both BD20 173 E3
Green Hammerton YO26 164 C4
Mattison Way YO24 227 E2
Maud La LS21 177 A6
Maude Rd DL9 209 A1
Maudon Ave YO18 96 A6
Maudon Gr YO17 215 F4
Maufe Way 3 LS29 218 B3
Maunby La YO7 64 D1
Mawson Gr DL6 65 B5
Mawson La HG4 214 C4
Maxim Cl 5 DL9 40 E4
Maxwell Rd LS29 218 D3
May Beck Farm Trail YO22 32 D1
Mayfair Ave TS6 7 E8
Mayfair Rd DL1 3 D8
Mayfield DL7 64 F2
Mayfield Ave
Ilkley LS29 218 D4
7 Scalby YO12 75 E5
Mayfield Cl
3 Glusburn BD20 187 E7
Ilkley LS29 218 D4
Mayfield Cres TS16 5 D5
Mayfield Dr
5 Brayton YO8 232 A1
4 Seamer YO12 99 D6
Mayfield Gdns LS29 218 D5
Mayfield Gr
Harrogate HG1 219 D3
York YO24 230 E8
Mayfield Pl
Harrogate HG1 219 D3
3 Whitby YO21 208 C5

Mayfield Rd
Brayton YO8 232 A1
Ilkley LS29 218 C4
Middlesbrough TS7 7 D6
Whitby YO21 208 B5
Mayfield Terr HG1 219 D3
Maypole Gdns YO8 197 B8
Maypole Gr 3 YO19 191 D8
Maypole Mews LS15 194 B8
Maythorn Rd YO31 225 E2
Maythorpe YO23 182 C6
Mayville Ave YO12 212 E6
Mcdonald Rd HG4 113 D3
Mcmullen Rd DL1 3 E6
Mead Cres TS17 6 C8
Meadlands YO31 229 B6
Meadow Ave 5 HG4 214 B2
Meadow Brook Chase 19 WF6 200 B1
Meadow Cl
Cononley BD20 173 D2
7 Eastfield YO11 100 A6
Hampsthwaite HG3 160 F5
Northallerton DL7 210 D2
Thorpe Willoughby YO8 197 C2
Meadow Croft
Brayton YO8 232 A2
Cononley BD20 173 C2
Meadow Ct
Rillington YO17 122 F5
Scruton DL7 63 E7
6 Willerby YO12 99 D2
3 York YO24 230 E8
Meadow Dale Ct TS12 9 F7
Meadow Dr
7 East Ayton/West Ayton YO13 99 B8
Harrogate HG1 219 E7
Scruton DL7 63 E7
Thorpe Willoughby YO8 197 B2
Meadow Garth
2 Tadcaster LS24 189 F6
Thorpe Willoughby YO8 197 C2
Meadow Gate HG1 219 E6
Meadow Gr 20 DL8 63 A2
Meadow La
Cononley BD20 173 C2
2 Darley HG3 160 A6
8 Eastfield YO11 100 A6
1 Haxby YO32 225 D8
Northallerton DL6 210 E6
Snape DL8 87 A7
Meadow Lea 21 BD20 187 E7
Meadow Pl 5 YO8 232 B6
Meadow Rd
Garforth LS25 194 D4
Knaresborough HG5 221 B7
2 Pickering YO18 95 F7
Meadow Rise
Harrogate HG1 219 E7
2 Skipton BD23 217 B5
Meadow Spring Bank HG4 214 C7
Meadow Springs Way 3 YO61 143 D8
Meadow Vale
Green Hammerton YO26 164 C3
2 Ripon HG4 214 B2
Meadow View
Barwick in Elmet & Scholes LS15 194 B8
Harrogate HG1 219 E6
Sherburn in Elmet LS25 195 F4
Meadow Way
Barnoldswick BB18 171 E2
Harrogate HG1 219 E7
3 Tadcaster LS24 189 F6
York YO32 225 F4
York YO31 228 F7
Meadowbank Rd TS7 7 D7
Meadowbeck Cl YO10 229 B4
Meadowcroft
Draughton BD23 174 B7
Harrogate HG1 219 E6
Meadowcroft Dr HG3 140 A5
Meadowfield
Amotherby YO17 121 A4
9 Bedale DL8 63 B3
1 Bubwith YO8 199 D7
Lythe YO21 13 A3
8 Stokesley TS9 26 C8
Meadowfield Dr TS16 5 D5
Meadowfield Rd
9 Colburn DL9 41 A5
Darlington DL3 3 A7
Meadowfields YO21 208 C6
Meadowfields Cl 9 YO61 143 D8
Meadowfields Ct 17 YO21 208 D6
Meadowfields Dr YO31 225 D2
Meadowings The TS15 5 D2
Meadowlands Cl 2 TS13 11 A8
Meadows The
Carlton DN14 204 C3
Coulby Newham TS8 7 B5
Hambleton YO8 196 F1
8 Middleton St George DL2 4 C4
7 Monk Fryston LS25 202 A8
Riccall YO19 197 F8
Richmond DL10 209 E7
Scalby YO12 212 B7
2 Skelton YO30 224 B5
South Milford LS25 195 F2
Meadowside CP Sch HG5 221 C7
Meads La YO12 99 E5
Meads The
3 Eastfield YO11 99 F6
9 Eastfield YO11 100 A6
Meadway YO8 197 D2
Meadway Dr YO8 197 D2
Meagill La LS21 159 E2
Meagill Rise LS21 176 E1
Meanee Rd 11 DL9 40 F2
Medbourne Gdns TS5 6 E6
Megson Pl YO7 211 C4
Melander Cl YO26 227 B4
Melander Gdns 5 YO32 225 D7
Melbourne Dr YO7 90 E5
Melbourne Pl YO7 211 B2
Melbourne St YO10 228 D2
Melcombe Ave 11 YO32 167 A7
Meldyke La TS8 6 D5
Mellersh Rd 16 DL10 41 E4
Melling with Wrayton C of E Sch LA6 102 A2
Melltown's Gn YO7 88 C6
Melmerby Green La HG4 114 C6
Melmerby Green Rd HG4 114 B6
Melmerby Ind Est HG4 114 B6
Melrose Cl 1 YO31 229 A5
Melrose Cres
Bishop Monkton HG3 140 A5
Guisborough TS14 9 A6
Melrose Dr 16 LS29 176 C1
Melrose Rd HG3 140 A5
Melrose St 4 YO12 212 F6
Melrosegate YO31 228 F5
Melsonby Methodist Prim Sch DL10 20 F7
Melton Ave YO30 227 F8
Melton Dr
Bishopthorpe YO23 231 A3
York YO30 227 F8
Melville Gr 1 LS29 218 E4
Melville Terr 52 YO14 101 B3
Melwood Gr YO26 227 B5
Mendip Cl 2 YO32 225 F5
Menethorpe La YO17 147 D7
Menin Rd DL9 209 B1
Menwith Hill Rd HG3 159 D4
Mercer Art Gall* HG2 219 C3
Mercer Dr DL9 209 C1
Merchant Adventurers Hall* YO1 233 C2
Merchant Taylors Hall* YO31 233 C3
Merchant Way YO23 230 B3
Merchantgate YO1 233 C2
Merchant's Row 10 YO11 213 B6
Mercury Rd DL10 209 A8
Mere La YO11 212 F1
Mere View Gdns YO12 99 F8
Merewood Rd WF10 200 C4
Merlin Covert 4 YO31 225 F3
Merlinwood BD23 172 B4
Merrington Ave TS17 6 D6
Merry Dale YO11 100 A7
Merrybank La LS17 178 A3
Merrybent Dr DL2 2 F5
Merryfield HG2 222 B7
Mesnes La DL8 59 D3
Messines Rd DL9 40 E3
Metcalfe La YO19 229 C5
Metes La YO12 99 E5
Methley Cty Jun Sch LS26 200 B6
Methley La LS26 200 A6
Methley Park Hospl LS26 200 A6
Methley Rd WF10 200 D4
Methodist Prim Sch DL11 36 E5
Meuse Cl 4 DL9 209 C1
Mewburn Rd DL3 3 C8
Mewith La LA2 129 B6
Mews The WF6 200 A2
Meynell Rd DL3 3 C7
Michael Mount Rd YO11 213 C1
Michael Syddall C of E Prim Sch DL10 41 E5
Micklebury La HG4 86 A3
Mickleby Dr YO21 208 B6
Mickleby La TS13 11 F4
Mickledale La YO26 163 D8
Micklefield C of E Sch LS25 195 A4
Micklefield Sta LS25 195 A3
Micklegate
17 Pontefract WF8 201 B1
1 Selby YO8 232 D5
York YO1 233 A2
Micklegate Bar Mus* YO24 233 A1
Micklethwaite View LS22 180 C2
Mickletown Rd LS26 200 B6
Middle Bank Rd TS7 7 D7
Middle Banks 24 YO32 166 E5
Middle Head Rd YO18 71 E8
Middle La Brayton YO8 232 C1
Brompton YO13 98 C7
Collingham LS22 180 B1
Hutton Buscel YO13 74 E1
Kettlewell with Starbotton BD23 108 A3
14 Knottingley WF11 202 A2
Snainton YO13 97 F4
Middle Moor La DL11 39 F5
Middle Oxford St WF10 200 E4
Middle Rd TS17 6 A5
Middle St Gayles DL11 19 E6
Swinton YO17 121 B4
Wilberfoss YO41 185 F5
Middle Wlk YO12 212 E7
Middlebrook Gdns YO8 232 A2
Middlecave Cl YO17 215 A4
Middlecave Dr YO17 215 A4
Middlecave Rd YO17 215 B4
Middlecroft Dr YO32 167 A7
Middlecroft Gr 2 YO32 167 B7
Middlefield Cl YO17 124 E1
Middlefield La
Kirk Smeaton WF8 206 A2
Melmerby DL8 84 A8
Middleham Ave YO31 228 E8
Middleham C of E Prim Sch DL8 60 E2
Middleham Castle* DL8 60 E2
Middlesbrough Coll TS5 6 E8
Middlesbrough Rd TS7 7 E6
Middlesbrough Rugby & Cricket Clubs TS5 6 E8
Middlethorpe Dr YO24 230 E7
Middlethorpe Gr YO24 230 F7
Middleton Ave
Ilkley LS29 218 B6
Thornaby TS17 6 B6
Middleton Carr La YO18 95 D7
Middleton Cl YO17 122 D1
Middleton La
Middleton YO18 95 E8
Middleton St George DL2 4 C3
Middleton Rd
Hutton Rudby TS15 25 D6
Ilkley LS29 218 A4
Pickering YO18 95 E7
Sadberge DL2 4 C7
York YO24 227 C2
Middleton St George Cty Prim Sch DL2 4 C4
Middleton Tyas C of E Prim Sch DL10 21 C5
Middleton Tyas La DL10 21 B4
Middleway BD20 174 C1
Middlewood Cl
3 Fylingdales YO22 33 C3
Rufforth YO23 182 C6
Middlewood Cres 5 YO22 33 C3
Middlewood Garth 4 YO22 33 C3
Middlewood La YO22 33 C3
Middycar Bank HG4 138 F6
Midge Hall Cl 18 LS29 176 C1
Midgeley Gate HG5 162 F2
Midgley Cl
4 Embsay BD23 217 C7
21 Stamford Bridge YO41 168 D2
Midgley Rd LS29 176 C1
Midgley Rise 2 WF8 201 B2
Midhope Way 15 YO14 101 A3
Midland St BD23 216 E3
Midway Ave YO26 224 A1
Mightens' Bank DL8 60 D4
Milbank Rd DL3 3 B5
Milburn La YO7 89 D3
Mildred Gr 5 YO24 227 F2
Mildred Sylvester Way WF6 200 B1
Mile Hill Coldhill La LS25 195 E5
Mile Planting DL10 209 F8
Milestone Ave YO23 182 C6
Milford Mews 7 YO32 225 D7
Milford Rd LS25 195 F3
Milford Way 8 YO32 225 D7
Milking Hill YO61 118 B4
Mill Balk DN14 207 C8
Mill Bank
Bishop Thornton HG3 138 F1
Fylingdales YO22 33 D2
Lindrick with Studley Royal & Fountains HG4 113 A3
Norton YO17 215 E3
Mill Bank Rd YO18 72 D5
Mill Bridge BD23 216 F4
Mill Brow LA2 128 E2
Mill Brow Rd BB18 172 B1
Mill Cl
Monk Fryston LS25 202 A8
Ravensworth DL11 19 F6
Settle BD24 131 D2
3 Spofforth HG3 179 E6
Mill Croft
Cowling BD22 187 B6
Richmond DL10 209 A7
Mill Dam LS23 188 F7
Mill Dam La WF8 201 C1
Mill Dike La YO7 116 F8
Mill Field La YO61 91 B1
Mill Field Rd YO8 203 B5
Mill Flats La DL8 60 F3
Mill Garth 14 YO8 198 F1
Mill Gate
Gilling with Hartforth & Sedbury DL10 20 E3
Harrogate HG1 219 C7
Knayton with Brawith YO7 65 E2
Mill Green Way The YO22 51 D8
Mill Hill Escrick YO19 192 B5
16 Normanton South WF6 200 A1
Mill Hill Cl 8 DL6 43 F3
Mill Hill CP Sch DL6 210 E4
Mill Hill Cres DL6 210 E3
Mill Hill Dr YO32 225 F4
Mill Hill La
Giggleswick BD24 131 C3
Northallerton DL6 210 E3
Mill Hills La DL11 38 E4
Mill House YO7 65 D1
Mill La
Acaster Malbis YO23 191 C8
Ampleforth YO62 118 C8
Askham Richard YO23 182 D2
Askrigg DL8 57 E6
Aysgarth DL8 58 E3
Barlow YO8 204 B7
Bellerby DL8 60 E8
Bentham LA2 128 F7
Bewerley HG3 137 B4
Boroughbridge YO51 141 B5
Brayton YO8 203 C8
Buckton/Bempton YO13 97 D5
Burniston YO13 75 C8
Burton Leonard HG3 140 B2
Carlton DN14 204 D3
Castleford WF10 200 E5
Cayton YO11 100 C6
Constable Burton DL8 61 C5
Darlington DL1 3 F6
Earby BB18 172 B1
Easingwold YO61 117 D1
3 East Ayton/West Ayton YO13 99 A7
Eskdaleside cum Ugglebarnby YO22 32 B6
Exelby, Leeming & Newton DL7 63 D3
Faceby TS9 25 F2
Farndale East YO62 48 E4
Farndale West YO62 48 F1
Gargrave BD23 155 D1
Great Ouseburn YO26 164 C8
Hambleton YO8 196 F1
Haxby YO32 166 D5
Hebden BD23 135 A1
2 Hemingbrough YO8 198 F1
Hessay YO23 182 B7
High Coniscliffe DL2 2 C6
Kearby with Netherby LS22 179 C2
Kirk Hammerton YO26 164 C2
Knaresborough HG5 221 F8
Langtoft YO25 151 C7
Leyburn DL8 60 E4
6 Linton-on-Ouse YO30 164 F7
Long Preston BD23 153 F4
Longnewton DL2 4 F6
Low Bradley BD20 173 E3
Mickletown LS26 200 B6
Middleton St George DL2 4 D5
Muston YO14 101 A2
Nether Silton YO7 66 B6
Newland YO8 205 A3
Pannal HG3 222 E2
Pickering YO18 95 F6
Pontefract WF8 201 C2
Rawcliffe DN14 204 F1
Redmire DL8 59 C5
1 Riccall YO19 192 A1
Ryther cum Ossendyke LS24 190 E1
1 Scarborough YO12 212 E3
Scruton DL7 63 E5
Sherburn in Elmet LS25 195 F2
Skipton BD23 216 F3
Sledmere YO25 149 F3
Snape with Thorp DL8 87 B7
South Milford LS25 195 F2
Spofforth with Stockeld HG3 179 E6
Stillington YO61 144 C6
Stutton with Hazlewood LS24 189 E4
Swinden BD23 154 B1
Thirkleby High & Low with Osgodby YO7 90 D2
Thormanby YO61 116 E5
Thrintoft DL7 63 F8
Whitwood WF10 200 B2
Wilberfoss YO41 185 E6
York YO31 228 E6
Youlton YO61 142 F2
Mill Lane Ave YO60 145 C5
Mill Mount YO24 228 A3
Mill Mount Ct YO24 228 A3
Mill Race The 4 DL2 22 C8
Mill Rd
Burton Fleming YO25 126 D4
Gillamoor YO62 70 A5
Goldsborough HG5 221 F3
Mill Riggs TS9 26 D7
Mill Rise DL6 210 E2
Mill Row BD20 187 F7
Mill St
6 Barnoldswick BB18 171 D1
Glusburn BD20 187 F7
Guisborough TS14 8 F6
Harome YO62 93 C4
Norton YO17 215 E3
Scarborough YO12 212 F5
York YO1 233 C1
Mill View
5 Burley in Warfedale LS29 176 C1
Mill View *continued*
Knottingley WF11 201 D2
Mill Wynd TS16 5 E3
Millbank Ct YO7 89 D4
Millbank La TS17 6 B7
Millbeck Gn LS22 188 A8
Millenium Rd BD20 173 D4
Millers Cl YO17 215 D2
Millers Croft 6 YO23 230 B3
Millers La TS12 9 F6
Millers Rd 2 YO7 211 C3
Millfield YO51 141 D2
Millfield Ave
Northallerton DL6 210 E3
York YO10 228 F3
Millfield Cl
Eaglescliffe TS16 5 D4
1 Leeming DL7 63 D4
Pickering YO18 95 F6
Wilberfoss YO41 185 E5
Millfield Cres DL6 210 E3
Millfield Dr YO8 204 D4
Millfield Gdns YO26 224 A2
Millfield Glade HG2 220 D4
Millfield La
Easingwold YO61 117 C1
Nether Poppleton YO26 227 B8
Poppleton YO26 224 A2
York YO10 229 A3
Millfield Rd
17 Hemingbrough YO8 198 F1
Hemingbrough YO8 204 F8
York YO23 228 B2
Millfield Rise YO61 117 C1
Millfield St HG3 137 B4
Millfields BD20 174 B1
Millgarth Ct 7 LS22 188 A8
Millgate 10 Masham HG4 86 C3
Richmond DL10 209 C6
Selby YO8 232 C6
Thirsk YO7 211 B3
Millgates YO26 227 C6
Millholme Rise BD23 217 C8
Millings La YO51 141 B7
Millrace Cl YO17 215 D2
Millside YO17 215 D2
Millthorpe Sch YO23 228 B2
Millway YO62 92 C1
Milner La LS24 195 D8
Milner Rd DL1 3 D4
Milner St YO24 227 D3
Milners La HG1 219 F7
Milnthorpe Cl 6 LS23 188 E6
Milnthorpe Garth 7 LS23 188 E6
Milnthorpe Gdns 5 LS23 188 E6
Milnthorpe La LS23 188 E6
Milnthorpe Way LS23 188 D5
Milson Gr YO10 229 A3
Milton Ave
Malton YO17 215 D5
Scarborough YO12 212 E3
Milton Carr 8 YO30 224 F1
Milton Cl HG1 219 E7
Milton Gr 11 BB18 171 D2
Milton Rd Malton YO17 215 C5
Pannal HG3 222 E3
Milton St Darlington DL1 3 E5
4 Skipton BD23 217 A3
York YO10 228 F3
Minchin Cl 3 YO30 225 B1
Mine Mus* BB18 172 A2
Minors Cres DL3 3 A7
Minskip Rd HG5 140 F2
Minster Ave YO31 225 F2
Minster Cl
3 Haxby YO32 225 C8
23 Ripon HG4 214 C5
Minster Rd HG4 214 C5
Minster Sch The YO1 233 B3
Minster View YO32 225 C8
Minster Wlk 12 DL2 3 E1
Minster Yd YO1 233 B3
Minsterley Dr TS5 6 D7
Minter Cl 2 YO24 227 B1
Mire Bank La DL8 56 F4
Mire Close La BD22 187 A8
Mire Ridge BB8 186 A2
Mire Syke La HG5 162 A5
Mires La Carthorpe DL8 87 D6
Ulleskelf LS24 190 B1
Mirkhill Rd YO8 232 B6
Miry La LS15 188 C1
Missies La HG4 112 C3
Mistral Ct YO31 228 E8
Mitchell Ave TS17 6 B7
Mitchell La Alne YO61 142 F4
Catton YO41 185 D8
Settle BD24 131 E1
Mitchel's La YO10 231 F8
Miterdale 4 YO24 230 C7
Mitford Cl 3 YO14 126 F8
Mitford Rd 2 YO14 126 F8
Mitford St 24 YO14 101 B3
Mitton La BD20 172 D1
Moat Field YO10 229 C4
Moat Way YO8 197 D1
Moatside Ct YO31 233 B3
Mock Beggar Hall* BD23 157 D7
Moiser Cl YO32 225 D4
Mole End 15 YO18 95 F6
Monash Ave DL9 209 C1
Monckton Dr WF10 201 B3

Monk Ave YO31 ......228 F7
Monk Bar Ct YO31 ......233 B3
Monk Bar Mus★ YO31 .233 C3
Monk Fryston C of E Prim
Sch LS25 ....202 A8
Monk Fryston Prim Sch
LS25 ....202 A8
Monk Gardens La YO62 .93 A7
Monk Gn YO61 ....142 F4
Monk Ing Rd HG3 .....159 E8
Monk La YO8 ....232 C7
Monkbridge Ct YO31 ..233 C4
Monket House Bank
YO62 ....48 C4
Monkgate YO31 ......233 C3
Monkgate Cloisters
YO31 ....233 C3
Monkhill Ave WF8 ...201 B1
Monkhill Dr WF8 ....201 B1
Monkhill La WF8 ....201 B2
Monkhill Mount WF8 ..201 B1
Monkholme La BD23 ..134 C2
Monkroyd Ave BB18 ...171 D1
Monks Cross Dr YO32 .226 A3
Monks Cross Link
YO32 ....226 B4
Monk's Rd BD23 ......107 D2
Monkswell Pk HG5 ...221 D5
Monkton Rd
5 York YO31 ......225 F1
York YO31 ....228 E8
Monmouth Dr TS16 ....5 E5
Monmouth St 10 BB8 ..186 A3
Mons Cl DL9 ....209 B1
Mons Rd
Catterick Garrison DL9 .209 D1
Colburn DL9 ....40 F4
Montague Cres LS25 ..194 D4
Montague Rd YO23 ...231 A3
Montague St YO23 ....228 C1
Montague Wlk 6 YO6 .165 F1
Montagu's Harrier TS14 .8 D6
Montgomery Rd DL9 ..209 C2
Montgomery St YO23 .217 A3
Montpellier Gdns 2
HG1 ....219 C2
Montpellier Hill HG2 .219 C2
Montpellier Mews 3
HG1 ....219 C2
Montpellier Rd 1 HG1 .219 C2
Montpellier Sq 3 HG1 .219 C2
Montpellier St 4 HG1 .219 C2
Montrose Ave YO31 ...228 D8
Moody Sty La 4 BD23 .134 E3
Mook St YO60 ....169 B8
Moor Ave 1 LS23 ....188 E7
Moor Carr La YO8 ....198 A5
Moor Cl Killinghall HG3 .219 A8
10 Kirklevington TS15 ..24 E8
Lockwood TS12 ....10 A5
Wheldrake YO19 .....192 F8
Moor Cres BD23 .....217 B4
Moor Croft 8 BD23 ...134 E3
Moor End La
Crakehall DL8 ....62 C3
Sowerby YO7 ....90 A2
Moor End Rd YO13 ....53 F2
Moor Gn TS7 ....7 D5
Moor Gr YO17 ....230 E8
Moor Hill YO17 .....147 E7
Moor House La YO61 .116 B1
Moor La
Addingham LS29 .....174 D5
Aislaby YO21 ....31 F7
Aldfield HG4 ....138 F8
Arkendale HG5 .....162 F7
Arrathorne DL10 .....41 A2
Askwith LS21 ....176 D4
Bagby YO7 ....90 C4
6 Barlby YO8 ......198 B5
Bilton-in-Ainsty with Bickerton
YO26 ....181 D5
Bishopthorpe YO23 ...230 E2
Borrowby TS13 ....11 C4
Brawby YO17 ....94 F2
Brompton YO13 ....74 B1
Broughton YO17 ....121 C4
Burton Leonard HG3 .140 B4
Carthorpe DL8 ....87 D4
Catterton LS24 .....190 A8
Cleasby DL2 ....2 F1
Cliffe YO8 ....198 F4
Cloughton YO13 ......54 C1
Collingham LS23 ....188 C8
Coneythorpe & Clareton
HG5 ....163 B6
Copmanthorpe YO23 ..230 A1
Cropton YO18 ....71 B6
Crosby DL8 ....65 C5
Dalton DL11 ....19 C6
Dalton YO7 ....116 B8
Dishforth YO7 .....114 F3
Earswick YO32 .....226 D8
East Ayton/West Ayton
YO13 ....99 B8
East Layton DL11 .....20 B8
Eastfield YO11 .....100 A6
Elslack BD23 ......172 D3
Embsay with Eastby
BD23 ....156 F1
Full Sutton YO41 ...168 F1
Grassington BD23 ...134 E3
Great Ouseburn YO26 .163 D7
Great Ribston with Walshford
LS22 ....180 E8

Moor La continued
Halton East BD23 ...157 B1
Haxby YO32 ....166 D7
Hunton DL8 ....61 E8
Hutton-le-Hole YO62 ..70 C5
Kearby with Netherby
HG3 ....179 B2
Kelfield YO19 .....191 E2
Kirby Hill HG4 ....140 F8
Long Preston BD23 ..153 F5
Milby YO51 ....141 C7
Murton YO19 ......229 F8
Myton-on-Swale YO61 .142 B5
Naburn YO19 ......191 D8
Nether Silton DL6 ....66 C8
Newsham DL11 ......19 A7
Newsham with Breckenbrough
YO7 ....65 A1
Newton-on-Ouse YO30 .165 C7
Rufforth YO23 .....182 E6
Ryther cum Ossendyke
LS24 ....196 E8
Scalby YO12 ......212 A8
Settrington YO17 ..122 C1
Skelton YO30 .....224 D6
Snape with Thorp DL8 ..86 E6
Steeton with Eastburn
BD20 ....187 F7
Stillington YO61 ...143 F6
Strensall YO32 ....167 B7
Stutton with Hazlewood
LS24 ....189 D4
Thirkleby High & Low with
Osgodby YO7 ......90 C1
Thirsk YO7 ....89 D5
Tholthorpe YO61 ...142 D6
Thormanby YO61 ...116 E5
Thornton Steward HG4 .61 E2
Thornton-le-Clay YO60 .145 F2
Thorp Arch LS23 ...180 E3
Threshfield BD23 ..134 B2
Welburn YO62 ......94 A5
West Tanfield HG4 ...87 B2
Weston LS21 ......176 E2
Wilstrop YO26 ....181 D8
Yafforth DL7 ....43 B2
York YO24 ....230 C6
Moor Lane Trad Est
LS25 ....196 A3
Moor Lee La
Eggborough DN14 ..207 B8
Heck DN14 ....203 B1
Moor Park Cl
2 Addingham LS29 ..174 E4
Pannal HG3 ......219 A1
Moor Park Cres 3 LS29 174 E4
Moor Park Dr LS29 ..174 E4
Moor Park Gr 2 LS29 .174 F4
Moor Park Way 1 LS29 174 E4
Moor Pk TS7 ....7 D5
Moor Rd Askrigg DL8 ..57 E6
Bishop Monkton HG3 .139 F5
Filey YO14 ....101 B1
Hunmanby YO14 ...127 B7
Ilkley LS29 ....218 F1
Knayton with Brawith YO7 .65 F3
Leyburn DL8 ....60 C5
Marton cum Grafton
YO51 ....141 C2
Melsonby DL10 .....20 F6
Muston YO14 .....101 A2
9 Sherburn in Elmet LS25 195 F4
Stamford Bridge YO41 .168 D2
Wykeham YO13 ....74 B4
Moor Side LS23 ....188 D8
Moor View 2 TS13 ...11 F7
Moor Way YO32 ....226 A4
Moorber La BD23 ..171 E8
Moorberries TS15 ....6 C2
Moorbridge Croft 6
LS25 ....196 A4
Moorcock La HG3 ...159 F5
Moorcroft Rd YO24 .230 D7
Moore Ave YO10 ...229 B4
Moorfield Dr YO41 .185 E6
Moorfield Rd LS29 ..218 F4
Moorfield Sch LS29 .218 C3
Moorfield Way YO41 .185 E6
Moorfields
Raskelf YO61 ......116 F2
3 Wistow YO8 ....197 D6
Moorfields La YO62 ..93 E5
Moorfoot La BD20 ..173 D2
Moorgarth Ave
10 York YO24 .....227 F2
3 York YO24 .....228 A2
Moorgate YO24 ....227 D3
Moorgate Dr LS25 ..194 D1
Moorgate Rd LS25 ..194 D2
Moorhill La YO17 ..147 E6
Moorhouse Cl 3 WF6 .200 B2
Moorhouse La YO7 ...89 D8
Moorland Ave 6 BB18 .172 B1
Moorland Cl
5 Embsay BD23 ...217 E8
Harrogate HG2 ....220 D4
Moorland Garth 2
YO32 ....167 A7
Moorland Rd
Harrogate HG2 ....220 D4
Scarborough YO12 .212 F7
York YO10 ....231 D8
Moorland Rise YO12 .217 E8
Moorland View HG2 .220 D4
Moorlands Ilkley LS29 .218 F4
Skelton YO32 .....166 B5

Moorlands La
Skelton YO30 .....224 C6
1 Tollerton YO61 ...143 B3
Moorlands Pk YO21 ..29 A6
Moors Ctr The★ YO21 .29 D7
Moorsholm La TS13 ..10 C6
Moorside
Melling-with-Wrayton
LA6 ....102 A2
Scalby YO12 ......212 A8
Moorside Ave HG4 ..214 B2
Moorside Cl HG4 ...102 A4
Moorside Cty Jun & Inf Sch
HG4 ....214 B3
Moorside Dale 6 HG4 .214 B2
Moorside La
Addingham LS29 ...175 A3
Askwith LS21 .....176 C4
Moorside Rd DL10 ..209 E8
Moorside View HG4 .214 C2
Moorview Rd
Northallerton DL6 ..210 F5
Skinton BD23 .....217 B3
Moorview Way BD23 .217 B4
Morehall Cl YO30 ..224 F2
Morgan Dr TS14 .....8 E6
Morgan St 4 YO12 .212 F5
Morley Dr 10 YO13 ..99 A7
Morley Gate DL11 ...37 C5
Mornington Cres HG1 .219 E4
Mornington Rd LS29 .218 C4
Mornington Terr HG1 .219 E3
Morpeth Ave
Coulby Newham TS4 ...7 A7
Darlington DL1 ......3 E7
Morpeth Gate DL8 ...58 F1
Morrets La YO8 ....197 A1
Morrison Rd TS14 ....8 F7
Morritt Cl 3 YO31 ..228 F8
Morton Carr La TS7 ...7 E6
Morton La YO8 ....203 A8
Morton Rd DL1 ......4 A5
Mosber La BD23 ...172 C8
Moss Arc HG4 .....214 C5
Moss End La BD22 .186 F5
Moss Green La
Brayton YO8 ......232 A2
Hirst Courtney YO8 .203 F3
Moss Haven DN6 ...207 D1
Moss Hill La YO8 ..164 D5
Moss Rd DN6 .....207 B1
Moss Side BB18 ...171 E1
Moss St YO24 .....233 A1
Moss Way YO8 ....195 F7
Mossburn Dr YO62 .119 E6
Mossdale Gr TS14 ....8 D6
Mossra HG4 ....85 F4
Mosswood Cres TS5 ...6 D7
Mosswood La YO61 .118 A1
Mossy La 8 DL8 ...56 C4
Moulton Hall★ DL10 .21 D2
Moulton La DL7 ....22 C3
Mounstrall La DL7 ..43 C1
Mount Ave YO8 ...232 B6
Mount Bank DL6 ...45 A5
Mount Cres YO17 ..215 B5
Mount Dr DL8 .....60 D5
Mount Ephraim 6
YO24 ....228 A3
Mount Farm Cl YO22 .208 E3
Mount Gdns HG2 ..222 A4
Mount Gr YO8 ....232 B3
Mount Grace Priory★
DL6 ....45 B5
Mount Leven Rd TS15 ..5 F3
Mount Par
5 Harrogate HG1 ..219 D3
York YO24 ....228 A3
Mount Park Ave YO12 .212 E5
Mount Park Rd 2 YO12 212 E4
Mount Pk YO19 ...198 A8
Mount Pleasant
26 Addingham LS29 ..174 F4
High Bentham LA2 .129 A8
Kippax LS25 ......200 D5
Newby & Scalby YO13 ..75 C5
Mount Pleasant Cl 9 DL2 .3 A7
Mount Pleasant E 2
YO22 ....33 D4
Mount Pleasant Grange
TS18 ....6 A8
Mount Pleasant N 1
YO22 ....33 D4
Mount Pleasant Prim Sch
DL3 ....3 A7
Mount Pleasant S 3
YO22 ....33 D4
Mount Rd Malton YO17 .215 B4
Northallerton DL6 ..210 F6
Mount Sch The YO24 .228 A3
Mount St HG2 .....222 A4
Mount The
Barwick in Elmet & Scholes
LS15 ....194 B7
Castleford WF10 ..201 B4
Malton YO17 .....215 B4
Selby YO8 ....232 B3
8 Thornton Dale YO18 ..96 D5
York YO24 ....233 A1
Mount Vale YO24 ..228 A3
Mount Vale Dr YO24 .228 A3
Mount View YO14 ..101 A4
Mount View Ave YO12 212 E6
Mount View Cl 4 YO12 .212 E6
Mount View Rd 3 YO11 100 B6
Mountside YO11 ...212 F3
Mouseman Visitor Ctr★
YO61 ....91 B2

Mowbray Castle (site of)★
HG4 ....112 D5
Mowbray Cres
17 Bedale DL8 .....63 A2
Hovingham HG4 ...119 E6
Kirkby Malzeard HG4 .112 D5
Mowbray Dr
4 Hurworth-on-Tees DL2 .3 E1
York YO26 ....227 C4
Mowbray Pl YO7 ...211 B2
Mowbray Rd
5 Catterick DL10 ...41 D5
Northallerton DL6 ..210 E6
Mowbray Sch DL8 ...63 A2
Mowbray Sq HG1 ..219 E3
Mowbray Terr HG4 ...87 A2
Mowden Inf Sch DL3 ..3 A6
Mowthorp Rd YO12 ..75 A3
Mowthorpe La YO60 .145 F8
Mowthorpe Medieval
Village★ YO17 ...149 C6
Moxby YO61 ......144 A3
Moxby Priory★ YO61 .144 D5
Muddy La TS8 .....7 A3
Muff La TS8 ....7 A3
Muirfield Ave WF7 .200 E1
Muirfield Rd TS16 ...5 E5
Muirfield Way 6 YO26 227 B5
Mulberry Ct YO32 ..225 F6
Mulberry Dr 7 YO32 .166 E5
Mulberry Garth LS23 .188 F8
Mulgrave Castle★
YO21 ....12 E2
Mulgrave Cres YO21 .208 B8
Mulgrave Dr 6 DL7 .210 D2
Mulgrave Pl YO11 ..213 B7
Mulgrave Rd YO21 .208 A8
Mulgrave View YO22 ..32 F7
Mullberry Gdns LS26 .200 A5
Mulwith Cl YO31 ...229 A6
Mulwith La HG4 ...140 E6
Muncaster Way YO22 .208 E3
Muncastergate YO31 .228 E7
Murchison Pl 8 YO12 .212 F6
Murchison St YO12 .212 E6
Murray St 31 Filey YO14 .101 B3
Scarborough YO12 .212 F5
York YO24 ....227 F3
Murray Wlk DL3 .....3 A5
Murrayfield Way 5 DL1 .3 F6
Murrough Wilson Pl 8
YO31 ....228 C7
Murton Bank YO62 ..67 E3
Murton Garth YO19 .229 F6
Murton La YO19 ..184 D7
Murton Way YO19 ..229 E5
Muscoates La YO62 ..93 F3
Museum of Craven Life★
BD24 ....131 E2
Museum St YO1 ...233 B2
Music in Miniature Ex★
YO22 ....33 D3
Musterfield La HG4 .113 A8
Muston Rd Filey YO14 .101 A3
Hunmanby YO14 ..126 F8
Mutton Scalp Rd TS12 ..9 E7
My Love La HG3 ...159 C5
Myer's Green La YO26 .161 B5
Myers La DL7 ......64 A8
Myra Bank La YO61 .117 F3
Myrtle Ave
Bishopthorpe YO23 .231 B3
Selby YO8 ....232 B3
Myrtle Gdns DL1 ....3 D8
Myrtle Rd
Eaglescliffe TS16 ...5 E6
3 Harrogate HG2 ..219 E3
Myrtle Sq 2 HG1 ..219 E3
Myson Ave WF8 ...201 C2
Myton La YO61 ...142 C5
Myton Rd TS17 .....6 A4

N

Nab View BD20 ....174 C2
Nabs View YO12 ..212 A7
Naburn La
Deighton YO19 ....192 A7
Fulford YO19 .....231 D4
Naburn Park Mews
YO19 ....191 E8
Nairn Cl YO24 ....230 C6
Nairnhead Cl TS8 ...6 E5
Nalton Cl YO23 ...230 A1
Nalton St YO8 ....232 C5
Nanny Goat La
Barwick in Elmet & Scholes
LS25 ....194 B4
Hunton DL8 ....61 E8
Nanny La LS24 ....196 C7
Nansen St YO12 ..212 E6
Nap Cote La HG4 ..112 E4
Napier Cres YO12 ...99 D7
Napier Rd HG4 ....113 D3
Nares St YO12 ....212 E6
Narrow La YO42 ..193 D7
Narrowfield 8 YO22 .32 A6
Nasterfield Nature Reserve★
HG4 ....87 B2
Nat La LS17 ......178 A3
National Rly Mus★
YO26 ....228 A4
Nattrass Wlk 7 DL8 ..63 B2
Navigation Rd YO1 .233 C2
Nawton Cty Sch YO62 .93 D7

Nawton Rd YO62 ....93 E7
Neasham Ct TS9 ....26 C8
Neasham Hill DL2 ....4 B1
Neasham Rd
Darlington DL1 ......3 D4
Low Dinsdale DL2 ....4 B3
Neile Cl DL3 ....210 D4
Nell Bank Ctr★ LS29 .218 D6
Nelson Rd LS29 ...218 A4
Nelson St
7 Normanton South WF6 .200 B2
Scarborough YO12 .212 F6
Skipton BD23 .....217 A3
York YO31 ....233 C4
Nelson's La YO24 .227 F1
Nesfield Cl
17 Eastfield YO11 .100 B6
Harrogate HG1 ....219 B5
Nesfield Rd LS29 ..218 A5
Nesfield View 12 LS29 .175 C2
Ness La
Pickhill with Roxby YO7 .88 B6
Tockwith YO26 ....181 C8
Ness Rd 5 YO8 ...232 D6
Nessgate YO1 ....233 B2
Nestfield St 4 DL1 .232 B2
Nether Way 20 YO26 .165 F1
Netherby Cl 6 YO22 ..32 A6
Netherby La
Huttons Ambo YO60 .147 B6
Sinnington YO62 ...71 A1
Netheredge Cl HG5 .220 A5
Netheredge Dr HG5 .220 E8
Netherfield Cl WF10 .200 C3
Nethergill La BD20 .173 B1
Netherside Hall Sch
BD23 ....134 C2
Netherwindings 18
YO32 ....166 F5
Netherwoods 6 YO32 .167 B8
Nettledale Cl 1 TS13 .12 A7
Nettledale La YO13 ..97 F6
Nevern Cres TS17 ...5 F4
Neville Cres BD23 ..155 D1
Neville Dr YO23 ...231 A3
Neville Gr LS26 ...194 A1
Neville Pits La DN14 .207 B4
Gargrave BD23 ...155 D1
Neville St
Normanton South WF6 .200 A1
Skipton BD23 .....217 A3
York YO31 ....233 C4
Neville Terr YO31 .233 C4
Neville Wlk DL10 ..209 D7
Nevinson Gr YO10 .231 E8
Nevis Way YO24 ..230 B7
Nevison Ave WF8 ..201 C2
New Brook St LS29 .218 B5
New Close La LA2 ..130 C2
New Dales La BD20 .173 D4
New Earswick Prim Sch
YO32 ....225 D4
New Fen La YO8 ..197 A6
New Forge Ct 15 YO32 .166 F5
New Hall Rd WF8 ..201 C2
New House La BD23 .153 F5
New Ings La YO18 ...96 E4
New Inn La DL8 .....87 F4
New La Aislaby YO18 ..95 D8
Beal DN14 ....202 D3
Bishopthorpe YO23 .231 A4
Burton Salmon WF11 .201 E6
Green Hammerton YO26 .164 C3
Hawes DL8 ....56 E4
Huntington YO32 ..226 A4
Kildwick BD20 ....173 F1
Lillings Ambo YO60 .145 C3
Little Ouseburn YO26 .164 A8
Long Marston YO23 .182 B3
Neasham DL2 ....4 B3
Newland YO8 .....205 A3
Ravensworth DL11 ..20 A4
Selby YO8 ....232 C5
Sherburn in Elmet LS25 .195 F3
Sheriff Hutton YO60 .145 D5
Stainburn LS21 ...177 E4
Strensall YO32 ...167 B8
West Tanfield DL8 ...87 C2
York YO32 ....225 F1
York YO24 ....227 E3
New Laithe Cl 5 BD23 .217 B5
New Lennerton La
LS25 ....196 C4
New Mill La LS23 ..188 F7
New Millgate YO8 .232 C6
New Park CP Sch
HG1 ....219 C5
New Park Rd 4 YO12 .212 E4
New Park Row YO1 .219 C5
New Parks Cres 8
YO12 ....212 E6
New Potter Grange Rd
DN14 ....205 E2
New Quay Rd YO21 .208 D6
New Queen St 10 YO12 .213 D7
New Rd Allerston YO13 ..73 D6
Allerton Mauleverer
with Hopperton HG5 .163 E4
Appleton Roebuck YO23 .190 E5
Appletreewick BD23 .157 E8
Beningbrough YO30 .165 C6
Birstwith HG3 ....160 B6
Bramham LS23 ...188 E6
Earby BB18 ......172 A1
Fylingdales YO22 ...33 D4
Glaisdale YO21 ....29 C3
Guisborough TS14 ...8 F6

New Rd *continued*
Heck DN14 .....203 D1
Hessay YO26 .....182 C8
Hunmanby YO14 .....126 F7
Kirby Grindalythe YO17 ...149 B6
Kirby Hall YO26 .....164 B8
Kirkbymoorside YO62 .....70 B1
Knottingley WF11 .....201 D3
Ledsham LS25 .....201 B8
Lillings Ambo YO60 .....145 D3
Long Drax YO8 .....204 E6
Newsham DL11 .....18 J8
North Stainley with Sleningford HG4 .....113 B8
Norton DN6 .....206 F2
Rainton with Newby YO7 ..114 E6
Raskelf YO61 .....116 E3
Reighton YO14 .....127 E5
Richmond DL10 .....209 C6
Rosedale East Side YO18 ...49 E3
Scotton HG5 .....162 A5
Settrington YO17 .....122 D1
Spaunton YO62 .....70 E5
Stapleton WF8 .....206 B5
Terrington YO60 .....119 E2
Thornton in Lonsdale LA6 .....103 B4
Ulleskelf LS24 .....190 B3
Westerdale YO21 .....28 F6
Wheldrake YO19 .....192 C7
Whixley YO26 .....164 A4
New Row
15 Boroughbridge YO51 ...141 B5
Eppleby DL11 .....1 D4
Trawden Forest BB8 .....186 B2
New St Carleton BD23 ..173 B4
Kippax LS25 .....194 D1
Langcliffe BD24 .....131 E4
Tadcaster LS24 .....189 E6
York YO1 .....233 B2
New Sturton La LS25 ..194 D4
New Walk Terr YO10 ...228 D2
New Way YO21 .....29 C4
Newall Ave LS21 .....176 F1
Newall Carr Rd LS21 ...176 F3
Newall Hall Pk 10 LS21 .177 A1
Newbiggin
Malton YO17 .....215 B5
Richmond DL10 .....209 B6
Newborough YO11 ....213 A6
Newborough St YO30 ..233 A4
Newbridge La BD23 ...174 B8
Newburgh Priory* YO61 .....117 E7
Newbury Ave YO24 ...227 D1
Newby Cl HG4 .....214 D4
Newby CP Sch YO12 ..212 B8
Newby Cres HG3 .....219 A4
Newby Farm Cl 35 YO12 .75 D5
Newby Farm Cres 36 YO12 .....75 D5
Newby Farm Rd YO12 ..75 D5
Newby Hall* HG4 .....140 C6
Newby Hall C of E Prim Sch HG4 .....140 E7
Newby La DN14 .....207 F8
Newby Pk* HG4 .....140 D6
Newby St HG4 .....214 D4
Newby Terr YO31 .....228 C7
Newcastle Farm Ct 4 WF11 .....201 D6
Newchase Ct YO11 .....99 F6
Newcoln Rd YO12 .....212 E1
Newcroft YO8 .....232 B4
Newdale 3 YO32 .....166 F5
Newfield Ave 6 WF6 ....200 B1
Newfield Cl 7 WF6 ....200 B1
Newfield Cres
Middlesbrough TS17 .....6 D7
Normanton South WF6 ...200 B1
Newfield Ct 3 WF6 ....200 B1
Newfield La LS25 .....201 B8
Newgate 2 Malton YO17 215 C4
York YO1 .....233 B2
Newgate Bank YO62 ....68 A4
Newgate Ct YO1 .....233 B2
Newham Bridge Prim Sch TS5 .....6 F8
Newham Way TS8 .....7 B5
Newhay La YO8 .....198 E1
Newhold LS25 .....194 D4
Newington Rd TS4 .....7 A8
Newkin DL8 .....57 D5
Newlaithes Cres WF6 ..200 B1
Newland Ave 1 HG2 ...220 A1
Newland Park Cl YO10 .....229 A3
Newland Park Dr YO10 .....228 F3
Newlands DL6 .....210 F4
Newlands Ave
Scarborough YO12 .....212 E8
3 Whitby YO21 .....208 C7
Newlands Ct YO7 .....211 D3
Newlands Dr
2 Glusburn BD20 .....187 F8
Ripon HG4 .....214 B3
York YO26 .....227 B6
Newlands La
Burniston YO13 .....54 D1
Upper Poppleton YO26 ...182 E8
Wintringham YO17 .....123 F3
Newlands Park Ave YO12 .....212 D8
Newlands Park Cres YO12 .....212 D8
Newlands Park Dr YO12 .....212 D8
Newlands Park Gr 2 YO12 .....212 D8
Newlands Park Rd YO12 .....212 D8
Newlands Rd
Bishopthorpe YO23 .....230 F4
Darlington DL3 .....3 B6
Newlands Sch TS4 .....6 F7
Newlyn Dr DL3 .....3 C8
Newmarket St BD23 ...217 A4
Newnham St HG2 .....220 A3
Newnham Terr HG2 ...220 A3
Newport Ave YO8 .....232 B4
Newport St
Goole DN14 .....205 F2
5 Pontefract WF8 .....201 B1
Newsham Hill DL11 .....18 J8
Newsham La
Barugh (Great & Little) YO17 .....95 A1
Habton YO17 .....121 A8
Newsham Rd YO7 .....211 A3
Newsham Way DL7 ....210 B1
Newstead La HG4 .....85 C7
Newstead Prim Sch TS14 .....8 E5
Newsteads 12 DL8 .....63 B3
Newthorpe Rd 2 DN6 ..206 E2
Newton Cres 4 DL7 .....63 D4
Newton Dr TS17 .....6 B6
Newton House Ct YO61 .....144 C3
Newton La
Archdeacon Newton DL2 ....2 F8
Ledsham WF10 .....201 A6
Newton Mulgrave TS13 ....11 F6
Newton Pk YO30 .....165 B7
Newton Rd
Great Ayton TS9 .....8 A2
Tollerton YO61 .....143 B3
Newton St YO21 .....208 D6
Newton Terr YO1 .....233 B1
Newtondale Cl HG5 ...221 D6
Newtondale Forest Dr YO18 .....72 B6
Newtondale Halt YO18 ..51 D1
Nicholas Gdns YO10 ...228 F3
Nicholas St YO10 .....228 F3
Nichols Way LS22 .....180 A3
Nicholson Ave HG4 ...113 D3
Nickey Nackey La YO8 .197 B8
Nicklaus Dr TS16 .....5 E5
Nickstream La DL3 .....3 A7
Nidd Bank HG5 .....220 F7
Nidd Cl YO26 .....227 B8
Nidd Dr HG3 .....160 E6
Nidd Gr YO24 .....230 E8
Nidd La Birstwith HG3 ..160 E7
Ripley HG3 .....161 D7
Nidd Orch 4 HG3 .....160 A6
Nidd Rise HG3 .....160 E6
Nidd Viaduct* HG3 ....219 E8
Nidd Wlk HG3 .....137 B4
Nidderdale Dr HG5 ....221 D5
Nidderdale Lodge HG5 .....221 E5
Nidderdale Mus* HG3 .....137 B4
Nidderdale Recn Ctr HG3 .....137 A5
Niddside HG3 .....160 A6
Niffany Gdns 7 BD23 ..216 D3
Nigel Gr 7 YO24 .....227 F2
Nightingale Cl YO32 ...225 E1
Nightingale Dr HG2 ...220 B3
Nightingale La 9 YO12 ..99 F6
Nile Rd LS29 .....218 B4
Ninelands La LS25 ...194 D3
Ninelands Lane CP Sch LS25 .....194 D4
Ninevah La WF10 .....200 C7
Ninth Ave YO31 .....228 F5
No Man's Moor La DL8 .61 E3
Noel's Ct DL10 .....41 E5
Nook The LS25 .....195 F2
Nooking The YO61 .....117 B6
Nora Ave HG5 .....221 C6
Norby YO7 .....211 B3
Norby Front St YO7 ...211 B4
Norfolk Cl WF11 .....201 E4
Norfolk Cres TS3 .....7 C8
Norfolk Gdns YO26 ...181 C7
Norfolk Rd HG2 .....222 D7
Norfolk St YO23 .....228 C2
Norman Cl
22 Pickering YO18 .....95 F7
7 Thorpe Willoughby YO8 197 B1
Norman Cres 11 YO14 ..101 B3
Norman Dr YO26 .....227 B6
Norman Rd Aske DL10 ...20 D1
Catterick Garrison DL9 ...209 E1
Richmond DL10 .....209 C8
Norman Sq DL10 .....209 D8
Norman St 5 YO10 ....229 A3
Normanby Prim Sch TS6 .7 F8
Normanby Rd
Middlesbrough TS7 .....7 D8
Northallerton DL7 .....210 D2
Normandy Cl 4 YO8 ...232 B6
Normanton Comm Sch WF6 .....200 B2
Normanton Freeston High Sch WF6 .....200 A1
Normanton Ind Est WF6 .....200 B1
Normanton Public Baths WF6 .....200 A1
Normanton Sta WF6 ...200 A2
Normanton Town Mid Sch WF6 .....200 A1
Norseman Cl 7 YO19 ..197 F8
Norseway 2 YO41 .....168 D1
North & South Cowton CP Sch DL7 .....22 C3
North App LS24 .....189 A2
North Ave
Castleford WF10 .....200 C4
12 Glusburn BD20 .....187 E6
North Back La YO60 ...119 E1
North Baileygate WF8 .201 B1
North Bay Rly* YO12 ..212 E8
North Burton La YO14 .127 B4
North Cl 5 WF7 .....200 E1
North Cliff Ave YO12 ....75 F5
North Cliff Ctry Pk* YO14 .....101 C4
North Cotes Rd
Hunmanby YO25 .....126 C5
Wold Newton YO25 .....125 E5
North Cres LS25 .....195 F5
North Croft Grove Rd 1 LS29 .....218 A4
North Dr Kippax LS25 ..194 D2
Sherburn in Elmet LS25 ...195 F5
North Duffield CP Sch YO8 .....199 A8
North End Bedale DL8 ...63 A3
2 Hutton Rudby TS15 .....25 C5
Osmotherley DL6 .....45 B4
North Field Ave YO23 ..190 F5
North Field Cl YO23 ...190 F5
North Field La
Askham Bryan YO23 .....182 F3
Upper Poppleton YO26 ...182 F7
North Field Way YO23 .190 F5
North Garth La YO60 ..145 D5
North Gr 2 LS22 .....180 C3
North Grove Ave 6 LS22 .....180 C4
North Hill Rd YO7 .....115 B2
North La Eastfield YO11 .100 B6
Gainford DL2 .....1 D8
Great Timble LS21 .....176 E8
Huntington YO32 .....226 D5
Hutton Hang DL8 .....61 C4
Wheldrake YO19 .....192 F7
York YO32 .....225 F5
York YO24 .....230 E8
North Leas Ave YO12 ..212 D8
North Lodge Ave 2 HG1 .....219 C5
North Marine Rd YO12 .....212 F7
North Moor 7 YO32 ....225 F5
North Moor Gdns YO32 .....225 F5
North Moor La YO61 ..118 C5
North Moor Rd
Easingwold YO61 .....117 B2
York YO32 .....225 F5
North Par
10 Burley in Warfedale LS29 .....176 C1
Ilkley LS29 .....218 C4
Skipton BD23 .....217 A2
York YO30 .....233 A3
North Park Rd HG1 ...219 E2
North Prom YO21 .....208 C7
North Rd Darlington DL1 ...3 D7
5 Fairburn WF11 .....201 D6
Glusburn BD20 .....187 E7
Grosmont YO22 .....31 C4
Hackforth DL8 .....62 E8
3 Middleham DL8 .....60 E2
Norton YO17 .....215 E3
Ripon HG4 .....214 D6
Stokesley TS9 .....26 C7
Whitby YO21 .....208 D6
North Road Prim Sch DL1 .....3 D7
North Road Sta DL1 .....3 D6
North Ribblesdale RUFC BD24 .....131 D2
North Riding Rise DL7 ..65 B3
North Rigton C of E Prim Sch LS17 .....178 C4
North Side TS15 .....25 C5
North St
Addingham LS29 .....175 A4
Barmby on the Marsh DN14 .....205 A7
Barnoldswick BB18 .....171 D1
Castleford WF10 .....201 B6
Folkton YO11 .....100 A2
Gargrave BD23 .....155 D1
31 Glusburn BD20 .....187 E7
14 Glusburn BD20 .....187 E8
Newby & Scalby YO13 .....75 C6
Ripon HG4 .....214 C6
Scarborough YO11 .....213 A6
Silsden BD20 .....174 C1
Wetherby LS22 .....180 C3
York YO1 .....233 B2
North Stainley C of E Prim Sch HG4 .....113 C8
North Street La 22 YO11 .....213 A6
North Terr Gainford DL2 ...1 D7
4 Scarborough YO11 ...213 A6
Whitby YO21 .....208 C7
North View
Knottingley WF11 .....201 F2
Little Ribston LS22 .....180 A8
North York Craven Inst of Further Ed BD23 .....217 A4
North Yorkshire Moors Rly* YO18 .....95 F7
Northallerton Coll DL6 .....210 E4
Northallerton Rd
Brompton DL6 .....210 E7
Dalton-on-Tees DL2 .....22 E6
Leeming DL7 .....63 C4
Thirsk YO7 .....211 A6
Thornaby TS17 .....6 B7
Northallerton Rigg DL6 .43 D4
Northallerton Rugby Club DL6 .....210 D8
Northallerton Sta DL7 .210 C3
Northcarrs La YO61 ...144 A4
Northcliffe Gr 3 TS15 ...25 C5
Northcote Ave YO24 ...227 E3
Northcote Fold 3 LS22 .180 A1
Northcroft 5 YO32 .....166 F5
Northfield 3 YO8 .....198 B5
Northfield Cl
Stokesley TS9 .....26 C7
Womersley DN6 .....206 C6
Northfield Ct LS24 ....196 B8
Northfield Dr
Pontefract WF8 .....201 C1
Stokesley TS9 .....26 C8
Northfield La
Church Fenton LS24 .....196 B8
Pockley YO62 .....69 B2
3 Riccall YO19 .....191 F1
South Milford LS25 .....195 E2
Womersley DN6 .....206 C7
Northfield Pl LS22 ....180 C3
Northfield Rd YO8 .....199 E8
Northfield Sch YO26 ...227 B5
Northfield Way YO13 ...75 D6
Northfields
4 Hutton Rudby TS15 .....25 C5
5 Strensall YO32 .....167 B8
Northfields Ave 4 BD24 .....131 D3
Northfields Cres 5 BD24 .....131 D3
Northfields La YO61 ...142 C6
Northgate Darlington DL1 ..3 D5
Guisborough TS14 .....8 F7
Hunmanby YO14 .....126 F8
Muston YO14 .....100 F1
Pontefract WF8 .....201 B1
Northgate Cl 15 WF8 ...201 B1
Northgate Jun Sch TS14 .8 F7
Northgate La
1 Linton LS22 .....180 A1
Warthill YO41 .....168 A3
Northgate Lodge 11 WF8 .....201 B1
Northgate Rise 2 LS22 .180 A1
Northlands Ave 1 YO32 225 F7
Northleach Dr TS8 .....6 F5
Northminster Bsns Pk YO26 .....182 F7
Northolme Dr YO30 ...224 E1
Northstead Cty Prim Sch YO12 .....212 D8
Northstead Manor Dr YO12 .....212 E7
Northumberland Ct 8 HG1 .....219 D2
Northumberland Rd TS17 .....6 B8
Northway Pickering YO18 .95 E7
11 Scarborough YO12 ....212 F6
6 Whitby YO21 .....208 B7
Northwell Gate LS21 ...176 F1
Northwold Rd YO11 ...100 A7
Norton & Kirk Smeat WF8 .....206 C3
Norton Back La DL2 .....4 D8
Norton Cl HG4 .....114 A8
Norton Comm La DN6 .206 F2
Norton Comm Rd DN6 .....207 A1
Norton Comp Sch YO17 .....215 E2
Norton Conyers* HG4 .....113 F7
Norton CP Sch YO17 ..215 E3
Norton Cres DL2 .....4 C8
Norton Cty Jun & Inf Sch DN6 .....206 E2
Norton Grove Ind Est YO17 .....215 F3
Norton Mill La DN6 ...206 E2
Norton Priory DN6 ....206 E2
Norton Rd
Norton YO17 .....215 C3
Sadberge DL2 .....4 C7
Norton Twr* BD23 ....156 B4
Norway Dr YO10 .....231 D8
Norwich Cl YO13 .....75 D6
Norwich Dr HG3 .....219 A5
Norwood Ave LS29 ....176 C1
Norwood Bottom Rd LS21 .....177 A5
Norwood Cl
38 Burley in Warfedale LS29 .....176 C1
2 Knaresborough HG5 ..221 B8
Norwood Ct 1 HG5 ....221 B7
Norwood Gr HG3 .....219 B4
Norwood La
Glusburn BD20 .....187 B8
Pannal HG3 .....177 E7
Norwood Pl 8 YO12 ...212 F5
Norwood St
Normanton WF6 .....200 B2
Scarborough YO12 .....212 F5
Nossill La DL8 .....59 C3
Nosterfield Rd HG4 .....87 B2
Notagreen Rd DL11 .....39 F6
Nought Bank Rd HG3 ..137 B3
Nought Moor Rd HG3 .137 B2
Nova Scotia Way 4 YO19 .....198 A8
Nun Monkton Prim Sch YO26 .....165 A5
Nuneaton Dr TS8 .....6 E5
Nunmill St YO23 .....228 C2
Nunnery La
Darlington DL3 .....3 A5
York YO23 .....233 B1
Nunnington Cres HG3 .219 A5
Nunnington Hall* YO62 .....93 F2
Nuns Green La YO21 ....29 E3
Nunthorpe Ave YO23 ..228 B2
Nunthorpe Cres YO23 ..228 B1
Nunthorpe Gr YO23 ...228 B2
Nunthorpe Prim Sch TS7 .....7 E6
Nunthorpe Rd YO23 ...233 A1
Nunthorpe Sta TS7 .....7 E6
Nurseries The
3 Easingwold YO61 .....143 C8
East Ayton YO13 .....99 C8
10 Leyburn DL8 .....60 D5
3 Whitby YO21 .....208 B6
Nursery Ct YO26 .....224 A2
Nursery Dr YO24 .....227 E3
Nursery Gdns YO10 ...229 C3
Nursery La 4 LS29 ....175 A4
Nursery Rd YO26 .....224 A2
Nursery Way 8 LS23 ...188 E7
Nutgill La Bentham LA2 .129 D8
Ingleton LA2 .....103 D1
Nutwith La HG4 .....112 B8
Nydd Vale Rd HG1 ....219 D3

O

Oak Ave
Appleton Roebuck YO23 ..190 E3
Garforth LS25 .....194 C4
Killinghall HG3 .....161 B2
Oak Beck Rd HG1 .....219 B5
Oak Beck Way HG1 ....219 B6
Oak Busk La YO60 ....145 F1
Oak Cl Filey YO14 .....101 B4
9 Kirkbymoorside YO62 .....70 B1
Oak Cres LS25 .....194 C4
Oak Dr Garforth LS25 ...194 C4
5 Thorpe Willoughby YO8 197 B1
3 Topcliffe YO7 .....89 A1
Oak Field YO8 .....232 A1
Oak Field Ave YO22 .....51 D8
Oak Glade 6 YO31 .....225 F3
Oak Gr DL6 .....210 E6
Oak Hill TS8 .....7 B5
Oak La HG3 .....159 F8
Oak Rd Eaglescliffe TS16 ...5 E6
Garforth LS25 .....194 C4
Guisborough TS14 .....8 F7
2 North Duffield YO8 ....199 A7
Ripon HG4 .....214 B2
Scarborough YO12 .....212 D4
Tockwith LS22 .....180 E7
Whitby YO21 .....208 B6
Oak Ridge 6 LS22 .....180 B3
Oak Rise 4 YO26 .....227 C3
Oak St 3 YO26 .....227 E5
Oak Terr HG2 .....219 C2
Oak Tree Cl
2 Bedale DL8 .....63 A2
Strensall YO32 .....167 B7
Tees-side Airport DL2 .....4 E4
Oak Tree Ct 7 YO8 ....199 D7
Oak Tree Dr DL8 .....62 F2
Oak Tree Gr YO32 .....225 D3
Oak Tree La YO32 .....225 C7
Oak Tree Rd 7 DL8 .....63 A2
Oak Tree Way 10 YO32 ..167 B7
Oak Wood Rd LS22 ....180 B4
Oakbank HG1 .....219 C4
Oakburn Rd LS29 .....218 A3
Oakbusks La YO61 ....142 F4
Oakdale HG1 .....219 A3
Oakdale Ave HG1 .....219 B4
Oakdale Glen HG1 ....219 B3
Oakdale Manor HG1 ...161 B2
Oakdale Pl HG1 .....219 B4
Oakdale Rd YO30 .....224 F2
Oakdale Rise HG1 ....219 C4
Oaken Grove Sch YO32 .....166 F5
Oakenshaw Dr TS5 .....6 E7
Oaker Bank HG3 .....161 B2
Oakfields DL10 .....21 D4
Oakhill Cres 3 YO32 ...167 A6
Oakland Ave YO31 ....229 A7
Oakland Comp Sch TS5 ..6 D8
Oakland Dr YO31 .....229 A7
Oaklands
Camblesforth YO8 .....204 C5
9 Great Ayton TS9 .....8 A2
5 Ilkley LS29 .....218 A3
5 Pickering YO18 .....96 A6
6 Strensall YO32 .....167 B7
Oaklands Cres YO8 ....204 C5
Oaklands Rd TS6 .....7 F8
Oaklands Sch YO24 ...227 C2

Oaklands Small Sch
DN14 . . . . .205 E4
Oaklands Sports Ctr
YO24 . . . . .227 C2
Oaklands The DL2 . . . . . .4 D3
Oakley Bank YO22 . . . . .208 B2
Oakley Cl TS14 . . . . .8 F5
Oakley Rd TS12 . . . . .9 E7
Oakney Wood Dr YO8 . .232 D1
Oakridge Cty Prim Sch
TS13 . . . . .11 F7
Oakridge View 3 HG3 .161 B3
Oaks La LS23 . . . . .188 E8
Oaks The
Coulby Newham TS8 . . . . . .6 E5
Dalton YO7 . . . . .115 F7
7 Masham HG4 . . . . .86 C3
Oaksfield LS26 . . . . .200 B5
Oaktree Ave DL9 . . . . . . .40 E2
Oaktree Bank YO7 . . . . . .65 F3
Oaktree Dr DL7 . . . . . . .210 C1
Oaktree Gr 5 TS18 . . . . . .5 D8
Oaktree Junc DL2 . . . . . . .4 D4
Oakville Ave YO12 . . . . .212 E6
Oakwood Cl LS24 . . . . . .196 B7
Oakwood Pk DN14 . . . . .207 F6
Oatlands Cty Inf Sch
HG2 . . . . .222 E7
Oatlands Cty Jun Sch
HG2 . . . . .222 F7
Oatlands Dr
Harrogate HG2 . . . . .222 F8
11 Otley LS21 . . . . .177 A1
Oatlands St 3 TS13 . . . . .11 A8
Occaney La HG3 . . . . . . .162 D8
Occupation La LS24 . . . .188 E2
Occupation Rd TS6 . . . . . .7 F8
Ocean Rd YO21 . . . . . . .208 C7
Ocean Terr YO14 . . . . . .100 F6
Ochrepit Hill YO42 . . . . .170 A2
Oddie's La LA6 . . . . .103 D5
Offerton Dr TS8 . . . . .6 F5
Ogleforth YO31 . . . . . . .233 B3
Okehampton Dr TS7 . . . . .7 B6
Olav Rd DL10 . . . . .209 C7
Old Barber HG1 . . . . . . .219 D6
Old Boys Sch La 4 YO8 197 B8
Old Brewery Gdns 5
LS24 . . . . .189 F6
Old Bridge Rise 7 LS29 218 A4
Old Chapel Cl 7 HG3 . .161 B2
Old Church La YO26 . . . .164 C2
Old Church La 9 HG3 . .137 C4
Old Church Sch DL8 . . . . .60 E2
Old Coach Rd HG3 . . . . .137 F2
Old Coppice 14 YO32 . .166 F5
Old Courthouse Museum★
HG5 . . . . .221 A5
Old Dike Lands YO32 . . .225 C8
Old Farm Cl 5 YO18 . . . .95 F7
Old Farm Way YO8 . . . .232 B2
Old Garth Croft 3
WF11 . . . . .201 D6
Old Gayle La DL8 . . . . . . .56 D4
Old Great North Rd
WF11 . . . . .201 E4
Old Hall Cl BD20 . . . . . .187 D7
Old Hall Croft BD23 . . . .155 D1
Old Hall La
Gilling with Hartforth & Sedbury
DL10 . . . . .20 D3
Kexby YO41 . . . . .185 C5
Old Hall Rd BD20 . . . . . .187 D7
Old Hall Way BD20 . . . . .187 D7
Old La Addingham LS29 . .175 B3
Broughton BD23 . . . . . . .172 D5
Cowling BD22 . . . . .187 B5
Earby BB18 . . . . .172 A4
Hambleton YO8 . . . . .196 E1
Hirst Courtney YO8 . . . . .203 F3
Horton in Ribblesdale
BD24 . . . . .105 A7
Ilkley LS29 . . . . .218 D3
Kelbrook & Sough BB18 . .186 A6
Long Marston YO26 . . . . .182 A6
Old Lane Ct LS24 . . . . . .190 E7
Old London Rd LS24 . . .189 D3
Old Malton Rd
Malton YO17 . . . . .215 D5
7 Willerby YO12 . . . . . . .99 D2
Old Maltongate YO17 . .215 C4
Old Market Pl 6 HG4 . . .214 C5
Old Mill Cl 8 LS29 . . . . .176 C1
Old Mill Row 3 YO7 . . .211 C3
Old Mill View YO60 . . . .145 C5
Old Mill Wynd TS9 . . . . . .8 A1
Old Moor La YO24 . . . . .230 E7
Old Moor Rd LA2 . . . . . .128 B8
Old Oliver La BD24 . . . .152 F6
Old Orch YO32 . . . . . . .225 D8
Old Orch The
1 Easingwold YO61 . . . . .143 C8
Fulford YO10 . . . . .231 E7
Shipton YO30 . . . . .165 F5
Old Park La YO21 . . . . . . .31 D6
Old Park Mews HG4 . . . .214 B5
Old Quarry La LS25 . . . .195 E1
Old Raike BD23 . . . . . . .152 F4
Old Rd
Appleton Roebuck YO23 . .190 E5
Clapham LA2 . . . . .130 C8
Garsdale LA10 . . . . .55 A6
Ingleton LA6 . . . . .103 E3
Kirkby Overblow LS17 . . .178 E1

Old Rd continued
Kirkbymoorside YO62 . . . . .70 B1
Thornton in Craven
BD23 . . . . .172 A3
Old Sawmill The BD24 . .153 B7
Old Sch The LS23 . . . . . .188 E7
Old School Hall LS29 . . .174 F4
Old School La YO8 . . . . .198 B5
Old St The LS24 . . . . . . .190 E8
Old Station Rd 4 YO2 . .92 C1
Old Station Way 20
LS29 . . . . .174 F4
Old Station Yd★ YO62 . .92 F6
Old Stone Trough La
BB18 . . . . .186 A6
Old Stubble The 6 TS13 .13 K2
Old Sutton Rd YO7 . . . . .211 E3
Old Trough Way HG1 . . .219 C6
Old Vicarage La 5
LS25 . . . . .202 A8
Old Village The YO32 . . .225 F5
Old Wife's Way YO18 . . . .73 A8
Olde Mkt The TS16 . . . . . .5 D3
Oldfield La
Collingham LS22 . . . . . . .180 C1
Spaunton YO62 . . . . .70 E4
Sutton BD22 . . . . .187 F1
Oldgate La LS25 . . . . . . .195 D6
Oldham Cl TS12 . . . . .9 E8
Oldham St TS12 . . . . .9 D7
Oldstead Rd YO61 . . . . . .91 B3
Olicana Pk LS29 . . . . . . .218 B5
Olive Gr HG1 . . . . .220 B4
Olive Way HG1 . . . . .220 B4
Olive Wlk HG1 . . . . .220 B4
Oliver La YO17 . . . . .121 C8
Oliver St 4 YO11 . . . . . .213 A4
Oliver's Cl 18 YO14 . . . .126 F8
Oliver's Mount Rd
YO11 . . . . .212 F2
Olliver La DL10 . . . . .20 F1
Olliver Rd DL10 . . . . . . .209 E8
Olympia Cres YO8 . . . . . .232 E6
Omega St 7 HG1 . . . . . .219 C5
Onams La YO60 . . . . .69 F4
One Acre Garth 2 YO8 .196 E1
Onhams La YO60 . . . . . .146 E4
Oran La DL10 . . . . .41 E4
Orcaber La LA2 . . . . .130 E6
Orchard Cl
Appleton Roebuck YO23 . .190 F5
Barkston Ash LS24 . . . . .195 E7
Dalton-on-Tees DL2 . . . . .22 D7
1 Great Ayton TS9 . . . . . .8 A2
6 Hartwith cum Winsley
HG3 . . . . .137 F1
1 Knaresborough HG5 . . .221 B8
Monk Fryston LS25 . . . . .202 A8
9 Norton DN6 . . . . .206 E2
Selby YO8 . . . . .232 A4
Sharow HG4 . . . . .214 F6
6 South Milford LS25 . . .195 F2
York YO31 . . . . .227 C1
Orchard Cotts 4 YO19 . .184 F7
Orchard Ct
Bramham cum Oglethorpe
LS23 . . . . .188 F5
8 Knaresborough HG5 . . .221 B5
Orchard Dr
Fairburn WF11 . . . . .201 D7
Hambleton YO8 . . . . .196 F2
Linton LS22 . . . . .180 A2
Orchard Gdns YO31 . . . .225 E2
Orchard Gr 4 DL6 . . . . . .43 F3
Orchard Head Cres
WF8 . . . . .201 C2
Orchard Head Dr WF8 .201 C2
Orchard Head Jun & Inf Sch
WF8 . . . . .201 C2
Orchard Head La WF8 .201 B2
Orchard La
8 Addingham LS29 . . . . .175 A4
Barkston Ash LS24 . . . . .195 F6
Hebden BD23 . . . . .135 A2
Ripley HG3 . . . . .161 C7
Thirsk YO7 . . . . .211 B1
Orchard Paddock
34 Haxby YO32 . . . . .166 E5
3 Haxby YO32 . . . . .225 D8
Orchard Rd
Malton YO17 . . . . .215 B4
Selby YO8 . . . . .232 A4
3 Sleights YO22 . . . . .32 A6
Upper Poppleton YO26 . . .224 A1
Orchard The
5 Ampleforth YO62 . . . . .92 C1
Burniston YO13 . . . . .75 D8
6 North Featherstone
WF7 . . . . .200 E1
Sadberge DL2 . . . . .4 C7
Scalby YO12 . . . . .212 C7
Snainton YO13 . . . . .98 A4
Thirsk YO7 . . . . .211 C4
Tholthorpe YO61 . . . . . . .142 D5
Orchard View
Markington with Wallerthwaite
HG3 . . . . .139 E3
3 Skelton YO30 . . . . . . .224 B5
Orchard Way
Hensall DN14 . . . . .203 C2
Middlesbrough TS7 . . . . . . .7 D8
Selby YO8 . . . . .232 A4
1 Strensall YO32 . . . . . . .167 B7
Thorpe Willoughby YO8 . .197 B2
York YO24 . . . . .227 B1
Orchards The
2 Beadlam YO62 . . . . . . .93 D7
6 Brafferton YO61 . . . . .115 F1

Orchards The continued
Leavening YO17 . . . . . . .147 E1
Mickletown LS26 . . . . . . .200 B5
Ripon HG4 . . . . .214 C6
Westow YO60 . . . . .147 B6
Orchid Cl 17 DL9 . . . . . . .41 A5
Orchid Way 8 HG3 . . . . .161 B3
Ordmerstones La YO18 . .96 C4
Ordnance La YO10 . . . . .228 D1
Oriel Bank YO11 . . . . . . .212 F3
Oriel Cl YO11 . . . . .212 F3
Oriel Cres YO11 . . . . . . .212 F3
Oriel Gr YO30 . . . . .224 F2
Ormesby Bank TS7 . . . . . .7 D7
Ormesby Cres DL7 . . . . .210 D2
Ormesby Cty Modern Sch
TS3 . . . . .7 D8
Ormesby Prim Sch TS7 . .7 D8
Ormesby Rd TS3 . . . . .7 C8
Orms Gill Green La
BD23 . . . . .154 D6
Orpington Rd TS3 . . . . . . .7 C8
Orrin Cl YO24 . . . . .230 C7
Osbaldwick La YO10 . . .229 B4
Osbaldwick Link Rd
YO19 . . . . .229 D4
Osbaldwick Prim Sch
YO10 . . . . .229 C4
Osbaldwick Village
YO10 . . . . .229 C4
Osborne Cl HG1 . . . . . . .219 D4
Osborne Gdns HG1 . . . .219 D4
Osborne Pk YO12 . . . . . .212 D5
Osborne Rd HG1 . . . . . .219 D4
Osborne Wlk HG1 . . . . .219 D4
Osbourne Dr 4 YO30 . . .224 E3
Osgodby Cres YO11 . . . .100 B8
Osgodby Gr 9 YO11 . . . .100 B8
Osgodby Hall Rd YO11 . .100 B7
Osgodby Hill YO11 . . . . .100 B8
Osgodby La 12 YO11 . . .100 B8
Osgodby Way 11 YO11 . .100 B8
Osgoodby Bank YO7 . . . .90 F3
Osmington Gdns 10
YO32 . . . . .167 A7
Osmotherley CP Sch
DL6 . . . . .45 B4
Osprey Cl
4 Collingham LS22 . . . . .180 A1
Guisborough TS14 . . . . . . .8 D6
5 Scotton DL9 . . . . .40 F2
4 York YO24 . . . . .230 B8
Osprey Garth 4 YO12 . . .99 E6
Ostler's Cl YO23 . . . . . . .230 C3
Ostman Rd YO26 . . . . . .227 C5
Oswaldene DL6 . . . . .45 B4
Oswaldkirk Bank YO62 . .93 A1
Oswestry Gn TS4 . . . . .7 A7
Oswin Gr DL10 . . . . .20 E4
Oswy St 5 YO21 . . . . . . .208 D5
Otley Rd
Harrogate HG2 . . . . .222 B8
Killinghall HG3 . . . . .161 B4
Pannal HG3 . . . . .178 A7
Skipton BD23 . . . . .217 B4
Stainburn HG3 . . . . .177 F6
Otley St BD23 . . . . .217 A4
Otter Dr 13 YO18 . . . . . . .95 F6
Otter Way TS17 . . . . .6 A5
Otterbeck Way 16 DL8 . .63 B3
Otterwood Bank 6
YO24 . . . . .227 B1
Otterwood La YO24 . . . .227 B1
Otterwood Paddock
YO41 . . . . .168 C2
Oucher La HG3 . . . . .140 B2
Oughtershaw Rd BD23 . .80 B6
Oulston Rd YO61 . . . . . .117 C1
Our Ladys RC Prim Sch
YO24 . . . . .227 A1
Ouse Acres YO26 . . . . . .227 D6
Ouse Bank YO8 . . . . .232 E5
Ouseburn Ave YO26 . . . .227 C6
Ousecliffe Gdns YO30 . .228 A6
Ousegate YO8 . . . . .232 D5
Ouston Cl LS24 . . . . .189 F6
Ouston La LS24 . . . . . . .189 F6
Out Gang La BD23 . . . . .107 F1
Outgaits Cl 4 YO14 . . . .126 F8
Outgaits La
Hunmanby YO14 . . . . . . .127 A8
21 Pickering YO18 . . . . . .95 F6
Thornton-le-Dale YO18 . . .96 E6
Outgang Rd
Malton YO17 . . . . .215 B5
Pickering YO18 . . . . .96 A6
Scampston YO17 . . . . . . .122 F7
Outgang The YO17 . . . . .122 F4
Outgate Cnr DL6 . . . . .23 F4
Outwood La LS24 . . . . . .190 C2
Oval The
Harrogate HG2 . . . . .222 D8
Hurworth DL2 . . . . .3 F1
Kellingley DN14 . . . . . . .202 C3
Middlesbrough TS5 . . . . . . .6 E6
Otley LS21 . . . . .176 F1
3 Scarborough YO11 . . . .100 B8
Skipton BD23 . . . . .217 B3
Over Nidd HG1 . . . . .219 C6
Overburn Rd 8 BD20 . . .187 E6
Overdale YO11 . . . . .100 A7
Overdale Cl YO24 . . . . . .230 D8
Overdale CP Sch
YO11 . . . . .100 A7

Overdale Ct BD23 . . . . . .217 A5
Overdale Grange 3
BD23 . . . . .217 B5
Overdale Rd TS3 . . . . .7 C8
Overgreen Cl YO13 . . . . . .75 D8
Overgreen La YO13 . . . . .75 C8
Overgreen View YO13 . . .75 D8
Overscar La YO18 . . . . . . .72 E3
Overton Rd YO30 . . . . . .165 F3
Ovington La DL11 . . . . . . .1 A6
Ovington Terr YO23 . . . .228 B2
Owler Park Rd LS29 . . . .175 C3
Owlwood Cl 7 YO19 . . . .184 E7
Owlwood La 6 YO19 . . . .184 E7
Owmen Field La YO62 . . .93 C5
Owston Ave 2 YO10 . . . .229 A3
Owston Rd 1 YO14 . . . . .126 F8
Ox Calder Cl 16 YO19 . . .184 E7
Ox Carr La YO32 . . . . . . .167 B6
Ox Cl YO41 . . . . .168 D2
Ox Close La
Eldmire with Crakehill
YO7 . . . . .115 E5
Myton-on-Swale YO61 . . .141 F5
North Deighton LS22 . . . .180 B7
Whixley YO26 . . . . .163 F5
Ox Moor La
Cattal YO26 . . . . .164 A1
Hunsingore LS22 . . . . . . .180 E8
Oxcliff YO12 . . . . .212 C8
Oxclose La Huby YO61 . .144 B4
Hutton-le-Hole YO62 . . . . .70 C4
Oxcroft 23 YO62 . . . . . . .70 B1
Oxen La YO8 . . . . .198 E3
Oxenby Pl 12 YO61 . . . .117 C1
Oxford Dr LS25 . . . . .194 D1
Oxford Pl HG1 . . . . .219 D2
Oxford St
Harrogate HG1 . . . . .219 D2
6 Normanton South WF6 .200 B2
Scarborough YO12 . . . . . .212 F6
Skelton & Brotton TS12 . . .9 D7
5 York YO24 . . . . .228 A3
Oxford Terr 2 HG1 . . . . .219 D1
Oxmoor La LS24 . . . . . . .196 D2
Oxpasture Cl YO12 . . . . .212 C4
Oxton Dr LS24 . . . . .189 F6
Oxton La LS24 . . . . .189 F6
Oyster Park Inf Sch
WF10 . . . . .201 B4
Oyster Park Mid Sch
WF10 . . . . .201 B4

P

Packhorse Bridge★
Dacre HG3 . . . . .159 D6
Romanby DL7 . . . . .210 B4
Pad Cote La BD22 . . . . . .187 B5
Padbury Ave 50 YO14 . .101 B3
Padbury Cl 46 YO14 . . . .101 B3
Paddock Cl
Copmanthorpe YO23 . . . .230 A2
Norton YO17 . . . . .215 D9
2 Pickering YO18 . . . . . . .95 F6
Paddock Hill YO17 . . . . .215 A4
Paddock House La
LS22 . . . . .179 E1
Paddock Rise 13 YO61 . .117 D1
Paddock The
14 Airmyn DN14 . . . . . . .205 E4
Appleton Wiske DL6 . . . . .24 B3
Burton Salmon LS25 . . . .201 F6
1 Linton-on-Ouse YO30 . .164 F8
Melmerby HG4 . . . . .114 B7
Middleton St George DL2 . .4 C3
Newby Wiske DL7 . . . . . . .64 E2
8 Selby YO8 . . . . .232 C6
Stokesley TS9 . . . . .26 C8
9 Whitby YO21 . . . . .208 D7
Wilberfoss YO41 . . . . . . .185 E5
York YO26 . . . . .227 C6
Paddock Way YO26 . . . .227 C6
Paddocks The HG3 . . . . .223 F4
Page La YO62 . . . . .93 E6
Pagnell Ave YO8 . . . . . . .232 E4
Painsthorpe La YO41 . . .170 B5
Painter La YO8 . . . . .196 E2
Palace Rd HG4 . . . . .214 B7
Pale La Carleton BD23 . . .216 E1
Gateforth YO8 . . . . .202 F7
Paley Green La BD24 . . .131 B2
Pallet Hill 10 DL10 . . . . . .41 D5
Palmer Gr YO8 . . . . .232 A3
Palmer La YO1 . . . . .233 C2
Palmes Cl YO19 . . . . .191 E8
Panman La YO19 . . . . . . .184 E8
Pannal Ash Cl HG2 . . . . .222 C8
Pannal Ash Cres HG2 . . .222 B7
Pannal Ash Dr HG2 . . . . .222 B7
Pannal Ash Gr HG2 . . . . .222 B7
Pannal Ash Rd HG2 . . . . .222 B7
Pannal Ave HG3 . . . . . . .222 E2
Pannal Bank HG3 . . . . . .222 E2
Pannal Cl 3 HG3 . . . . . . .208 B5
Pannal CP Sch HG3 . . . . .222 E1
Pannal Gn HG3 . . . . .222 E2
Pannal Rd HG3 . . . . .223 D4
Pannal Sta HG3 . . . . . . .222 E2
Pannett Way 3 YO1 . . . .208 D6
Pannierman La TS9 . . . . . .7 D1
Panorama Cl 10 HG3 . . .137 C4
Panorama Dr LS29 . . . . .175 C1
Panorama Wlk HG3 . . . . .137 C4
Pant La LA2 . . . . .130 E7

Parade Ct YO31 . . . . . . .228 F6
Parade The HG1 . . . . . . .219 E2
Paradise YO11 . . . . .213 C6
Paradise Cotts YO17 . . . .170 F8
Paradise Field Est 2
YO61 . . . . .143 D8
Paradise La Dalton YO7 .115 F7
Stutton with Hazlewood
LS24 . . . . .189 C5
Paradise Rd YO7 . . . . .67 A2
Paragon St YO1 . . . . . . .233 C1
Parish Ghyll Dr LS29 . . .218 A3
Parish Ghyll La LS29 . . .218 A3
Parish Ghyll Rd LS29 . . .218 A3
Parish Ghyll Wlk LS29 . .218 A3
Park Ave Barlow YO8 . . .204 D4
Castleford WF10 . . . . . . .200 F4
Glusburn BD20 . . . . .187 E2
Great Preston WF10 . . . . .200 B4
Harrogate HG2 . . . . .219 C1
Hellifield BD23 . . . . .154 B3
Kippax LS25 . . . . .194 E1
Knaresborough HG5 . . . .221 B8
New Earswick YO32 . . . . .225 D5
Normanton South WF6 . . .200 A1
Scarborough YO12 . . . . . .212 D4
Sherburn in Elmet LS25 . .195 E4
Skipton BD23 . . . . .216 F4
Swillington LS26 . . . . . . .194 A1
Thornaby TS17 . . . . .6 B8
Park Ave S HG2 . . . . .222 D8
Park Bank YO21 . . . . .29 E7
Park Chase
Harrogate HG1 . . . . .219 E3
Hornby DL8 . . . . .62 C5
Park Cl 5 Airmyn DN14 . .205 E4
1 Easingwold YO61 . . . . .143 D8
8 Knaresborough HG5 . . .221 B6
Skelton YO30 . . . . .224 B4
Park Cres
6 Addingham LS29 . . . . .175 A4
Castleford WF10 . . . . . . .201 B4
Darlington DL1 . . . . .3 D4
Embsay BD23 . . . . .217 C2
Hellifield BD23 . . . . .154 B3
York YO31 . . . . .233 C4
Park Crest HG5 . . . . .221 B6
Park Dale WF10 . . . . . . .201 B5
Park Dr Campsall DN6 . . .206 E1
Glusburn BD20 . . . . .187 E2
7 Harrogate HG2 . . . . . . .219 D1
Harrogate HG2 . . . . .222 D8
Knaresborough HG5 . . . .221 B6
13 Masham HG4 . . . . . . .86 C3
Park Edge HG2 . . . . .222 F8
Park End Prim Sch TS3 . .7 C8
Park Gate
Knaresborough HG5 . . . .221 B8
Strensall YO32 . . . . .167 B8
Park Gr
Knaresborough HG5 . . . .221 B8
Norton YO17 . . . . .215 C3
Selby YO8 . . . . .232 B4
Swillington LS26 . . . . . . .200 A8
York YO31 . . . . .233 C4
Park Grove Sch YO31 . . .233 C4
Park Hill BB18 . . . . .171 E4
Park House Gn
Harrogate HG1 . . . . .219 C5
7 Spofforth HG3 . . . . . . .179 E5
Park House La LA2 . . . . .128 D5
Park La Balne DN14 . . . .207 C5
Barlow YO8 . . . . .204 C7
Bishop Wilton YO42 . . . . .169 F1
Borrowby YO7 . . . . .65 E4
Buckden BD23 . . . . .81 E2
Burn YO8 . . . . .203 D7
Carleton BD23 . . . . .173 A3
Cowling BD22 . . . . .186 F5
Darlington DL1 . . . . .3 D4
6 Easington TS13 . . . . . . .11 A8
Glusburn BD20 . . . . .187 E2
Great Preston WF10 . . . . .200 F1
Guisborough TS14 . . . . . . .8 E6
Kippax LS25 . . . . .200 E8
Kirkbymoorside YO62 . . . .70 B1
Knaresborough HG5 . . . .221 C6
Ledsham LS25 . . . . .201 B8
Luttons YO17 . . . . .150 C8
Mickletown LS26 . . . . . . .200 A5
5 Middleham DL8 . . . . . . .60 E2
North Featherstone WF8 . .200 F1
North Stainley with Sleningford
HG4 . . . . .113 C5
Spofforth with Stockeld
HG3 . . . . .179 D5
Tatham LA2 . . . . .128 B8
West Tanfield HG4 . . . . . .113 A8
Wilberfoss YO41 . . . . . . .185 E5
Womersley DN6 . . . . .206 B4
York YO24 . . . . .227 F3
Park Lands 4 HG3 . . . . .179 E5
Park Lane Cl YO42 . . . . .169 F1
Park Lane Inf Sch TS14 . .8 E7
Park Mount 6 HG3 . . . . .179 E5
Park Nook Rd YO8 . . . . .196 F4
Park Par
Harrogate HG1 . . . . .219 F2
Knaresborough HG5 . . . .221 B6
Park Pl Darlington DL1 . . . .3 D5
Hellifield BD23 . . . . .154 B3
4 Knaresborough HG5 . . .221 B6
Park Rd Airmyn DN14 . . .205 E4
Asenby YO7 . . . . .115 B6
Barlow YO8 . . . . .204 C7
Castleford WF10 . . . . . . .201 A3
Cowling BD22 . . . . .187 B6
Glusburn BD20 . . . . .187 E4

Park Rd *continued*
8 Harrogate HG2 219 D1
Harrogate HG2 222 D8
Norton-on-Derwent YO17 215 C3
Pontefract WF8 201 A1
6 Scarborough YO12 212 E4
Spofforth HG3 179 E5
Park Rise 17 YO14 126 F8
Park Row
Knaresborough HG5 221 B5
Selby YO8 232 D5
Park Side BB18 186 A8
Park Sq
2 Knaresborough HG5 221 B6
9 Ripon HG4 214 C4
Park St 16 Glusburn BD20 187 E8
1 Harrogate HG1 219 C5
Hovingham YO62 119 E6
Masham HG4 86 C3
Pickering YO18 95 F7
Ripon HG4 214 B5
Scarborough YO12 212 D4
Selby YO8 232 D5
1 Skipton BD23 216 F4
York YO24 233 A1
Park Terr YO21 208 D6
Park The 14 YO13 75 D5
Park View
Castleford WF10 201 B3
Glaisdale YO21 30 D4
Harrogate HG1 219 E2
22 Leyburn DL8 60 D5
Middleton Tyas DL10 21 C4
Skipton BD23 216 D4
Swillington LS26 194 A1
Park View Dr BD23 134 B3
Park Way
Kirk Hammerton YO26 164 C2
Knaresborough HG5 221 B8
Park Wood BD23 216 D5
Park Wood Cl BD23 216 E5
Park Wood Cres BD23 216 D5
Park Wood Way BD23 216 D5
Park Wynd DL10 209 C6
Parker Ave YO26 227 B2
Parker Dr 21 DL8 63 A2
Parker La YO26 164 C3
Parker St 15 BD20 187 E8
Parkers Mount 20 YO62 70 B1
Parkfield Ave TS5 6 E8
Parkfield Cl YO12 212 D4
Parkfield Gdns YO12 212 D4
Parkfield La WF7 200 E1
Parkgate DL1 3 D5
Parkgate La DL10 41 B7
Parkin Ave YO8 232 E4
Parkinson App LS25 194 C4
Parkinson's La LS21 159 E2
Parkinson's Yd 5 DL10 209 C6
Parkland Dr
Darlington DL3 3 A6
Tadcaster LS24 189 F6
Parkland Way YO32 225 D8
Parklands
Castleford WF10 200 F4
Ilkley LS29 218 D4
Parklands The
1 Ingleby Arncliffe DL6 45 A7
Scruton DL7 63 D7
Parkshill Ct DL10 20 F7
Parkside DL1 3 C4
Parkside Cl YO24 227 E3
Parkside Prim Sch DN14 205 F3
Parkway The YO12 212 B7
Parkways YO8 232 B3
Parkwood Dr 6 TS18 5 E8
Parliament Ave YO17 215 E4
Parliament St
Harrogate HG1 219 C3
Norton YO17 215 E3
York YO1 233 B2
Parliament Terr 2 HG1 219 D2
Parlington Ct LS15 194 C8
Parlington Dr LS25 194 E8
Parlington La LS25 194 E7
Parlington Mdw LS15 194 C7
Parlington Villas LS25 194 E8
Parrock St 7 BB18 171 D1
Parson Back La DL6 25 B2
Parsonage Rd LS26 200 C6
Parsonage The 10 HG5 221 A6
Parsons Cl 10 DN14 205 E4
Parson's Cl YO21 208 A7
Parsons Close La BD24 131 A2
Parson's La
1 Addingham LS29 174 E4
Hutton Rudby DL6 25 A2
Parsons La YO26 165 E1
Parson's Wlk 11 DN14 205 E4
Pasley Rd HG4 113 D3
Pasture Ave LS25 196 A4
Pasture Cl
Barnoldswick BB18 171 E2
4 Sherburn in Elmet LS25 196 A4
Skelton YO30 224 B5
Skipton BD23 217 B5
2 Strensall YO32 167 B6
Wistow YO8 197 D6
Pasture Cres
Filey YO14 101 A4
3 Knaresborough HG5 221 B7
Pasture Ct LS25 195 F4
Pasture Dr Bedale DL8 63 A2
Castleford WF10 200 D3
Pasture Farm Cl YO10 231 D6
Pasture Field La YO22 32 C5
Pasture Fold 4 LS29 176 C1
Pasture Hill YO17 169 E8
Pasture La
Ellerton YO42 193 C1
Helperby YO61 142 B8
Heworth YO31 229 B8
Hovingham YO62 119 E6
Kearby with Netherby LS22 179 C1
Malton YO17 215 C5
Marton-le-Moor HG4 140 D8
2 Seamer YO12 99 D6
Pasture Rd
Embsay with Eastby BD23 217 C8
Lockton YO18 73 A5
Pasture View LS25 195 F4
Pasture Way
Castleford WF10 200 D3
Sherburn in Elmet LS25 195 F4
Wistow YO8 197 D6
Pastures The
Carlton DN14 204 C3
Coulby Newham TS8 7 B5
16 Eastfield YO11 100 B6
Sherburn YO17 124 D7
4 York YO24 230 E8
Pateley Moor Cres DL2 3 E3
Pately Pl 1 YO26 227 D4
Paterson Cres DL6 210 E4
Patience La HG4 114 D3
Patrick Pool YO1 233 B2
Patterdale Dr YO30 224 E1
Patterham La DL8 59 D4
Paul's Row 5 YO17 215 C4
Pavement YO1 233 B2
Paver La YO1 233 C2
Pavilion Sq 7 HG2 219 C1
Peacock's Cl DL7 63 E7
Peacocks Cl TS9 26 C8
Peak Scar Rd YO62 67 C3
Pear Tree Acre LS23 180 F1
Pear Tree Ave
Long Drax YO8 204 F7
8 Poppleton YO26 165 F1
Pear Tree Cl
Skeeby DL10 20 F1
York YO32 225 F4
Pear Tree Wlk YO17 215 B4
Pearl Rd TS17 6 B8
Pearl St HG1 220 C4
Pearson Garth YO13 99 A7
Pearson St WF6 200 A3
Peart La BD23 154 C8
Peartree Ct YO1 233 C3
Pease Ct
Guisborough TS14 8 D5
4 Lingdale TS12 9 F7
Pease St Darlington DL1 3 E5
6 Lingdale TS12 9 F7
Peasey Hills Rd YO17 215 C5
Peasholm Ave YO12 212 F7
Peasholm Cres YO12 212 F7
Peasholm Dr YO12 212 E7
Peasholm Gap YO12 212 F8
Peasholm Gdns YO12 212 F7
Peasholm Rd YO12 212 F8
Peasholme Bridge YO12 212 E7
Peasholme Gn YO1 233 C2
Peasland La YO7 66 B5
Peaslands La YO18 96 D5
Peat La HG3 137 B3
Peatmoor La DL8 58 E5
Peckett's Holt HG1 219 D7
Peckett's Way HG1 219 D7
Peckfield HG4 214 C2
Peckfield Cl HG3 160 F5
Peckitt St YO1 233 B1
Peel Cl YO10 229 A1
Peel Gn BD23 154 B2
Peel Pl 11 LS29 176 C1
Peel St Thornaby TS17 6 B8
York YO1 233 C1
Pefham La YO17 170 F4
Pegman Cl TS14 8 F7
Peirse Cl DL8 63 A2
Pelham Pl 15 YO32 167 A7
Pellentine Rd HG3 223 F4
Pemberton Cres TS4 7 A8
Pemberton Rd WF10 201 A4
Pembroke St
10 Skipton BD23 216 F3
York YO30 228 B7
Pembroke Way YO21 208 C5
Pembury Mews DL10 41 B6
Penders La TS15 5 E1
Penderyn Cres TS17 5 F4
Pendle St 4 BD23 216 D3
Pendleton Rd DL1 3 D7
Pendragon Castle* CA17 14 A1
Penhill Ct DL7 210 C1
Penhowe La YO17 147 D4
Penistone Rd TS3 7 C8
Penley's Grove St YO31 233 C4
Penn La DL8 56 D4
Penn Rd DL10 209 B7
Pennine Way BD20 172 E2
Pennine Cl YO32 225 F4
Pennine View
Burneston DL8 87 E8
Northallerton DL7 210 B2
Pennine Way
11 Barnoldswick BB18 171 D1
Pennine Way *continued*
Ingleby TS17 6 A4
Penniston La YO13 97 C4
Penny Gn BD24 131 D1
Penny La
1 Easingwold YO61 117 D1
Ripon HG4 214 C7
Penny Pot Gdns 4 HG3 161 B2
Penny Pot La
Felliscliffe HG3 160 D2
Killinghall HG3 161 A2
Penny Royal Cl 7 HG3 161 B3
Pennycarr La YO61 143 D7
Pennyman Prim Sch TS3 7 D8
Pennypot La TS18 5 E7
Pennywort Gr 15 HG3 161 B3
Penrith Cres WF10 201 B5
Penrith Rd TS3 7 B8
Pentland Dr YO32 225 E3
Penton Rd 20 YO11 100 B6
Penyghent Ave YO31 229 A5
Pen-y-Ghent Way 5 BB18 171 D1
Penyghent Way TS17 6 A3
Peppercorn Cl 6 YO26 227 E4
Peppergarth The DL7 210 B3
Peppermint Dr 15 DL9 41 A5
Peppermint Way YO8 232 A5
Per Ardua Way 6 DL10 41 E4
Percy Cross Rigg YO21 9 A1
Percy Dr 4 DN14 205 E4
Percy Rd Darlington DL3 3 C7
14 Hunmanby YO14 127 A8
Percy St YO31 233 B3
Percy's La YO1 233 C2
Perie Ave HG4 113 D3
Perry Ave TS17 6 B5
Peter Hill Dr YO30 228 A8
Peter La
Burton Leonard HG3 140 A2
York YO1 233 B2
Petercroft Cl 5 YO19 184 F7
Petercroft La YO19 184 F7
Peterhouse Cl DL1 3 D7
Petersbottom La LA2 129 B4
Petersway YO30 233 A4
Petre Ave YO8 232 E3
Petty Whin Cl 25 HG3 161 B3
Petyt Gr BD23 217 A4
Pheasant Dr 5 YO24 230 B8
Philadelphia Terr 2 YO23 228 B2
Philip La YO8 196 E2
Philippa's Dr HG2 222 D8
Philpin La LA6 104 C8
Phlashetts La DL8 87 A4
Phoenix Pk TS8 6 F6
Piave Rd DL9 40 D4
Piccadilly YO1 233 C2
Pick Haven Garth DN14 202 F3
Pickard Cl BB18 171 E2
Pickard La BD20 174 C1
Pickering Castle* YO18 95 F7
Pickering Cty Inf Sch YO18 96 A7
Pickering Cty Jun Sch YO18 95 F7
Pickering Rd
East Ayton/West Ayton YO13 99 A7
Thornaby TS17 6 B8
Thornton-le-Dale YO18 96 C6
Pickeringmoor La YO7 64 C2
Pickhill C of E Prim Sch YO7 88 C6
Picking Croft La HG3 161 B5
Pickrowfield La LS25 196 C6
Pickwick Cl YO17 215 C5
Piece Croft 2 BD23 134 D2
Piece Fields 4 BD23 134 D2
Pier Rd YO21 208 D7
Piercy End YO62 70 B1
Pierremont Rd DL3 3 B6
Piggy La DL2 1 C7
Pighill Nook Rd LS25 202 C7
Pike Hills Mount YO23 230 A3
Pike La BD24 131 E4
Pike Rd 8 YO18 95 F6
Pikepurse La DL10 209 D8
Pilgrim St YO31 233 B4
Pill White La LS21 177 C3
Pilmoor Cl DL10 209 E8
Pilmoor Dr DL10 209 E8
Pindar Leisure Ctr YO11 100 A6
Pindar Rd YO11 100 A6
Pindar Sch YO11 100 A6
Pinders Cres WF11 201 E3
Pinders Gn LS26 200 B4
Pinders Green Ct LS26 200 B5
Pinders Green Dr LS26 200 B5
Pinders Green Fold LS26 200 B5
Pine Cl
Castleford WF10 200 F3
Skipton BD23 216 E4
Pine Croft HG4 112 F2
Pine Gr 1 DL6 210 E3
Pine Hill TS8 7 B5
Pine Rd Guisborough TS14 8 E7
Middlesbrough TS7 7 D8
Pine St HG1 219 E5
Pine Tree Ave YO17 122 F5
Pine Tree Cl YO8 197 B2
Pine Tree La 1 LS25 202 A7
Pinelands 4 YO32 225 D7
Pinelands Way YO10 229 C3
Pines Gdns 29 LS29 175 C2
Pines The LS17 178 B2
Pinetree Gr DL2 4 C4
Pinewood Ave YO14 101 B4
Pinewood Cl
5 Easington TS13 11 A8
2 Ilkley LS29 218 A3
5 Whitby YO21 208 C6
Pinewood Dr
Camblesforth YO8 204 D4
Scarborough YO12 212 D5
Pinewood Gate HG2 222 A7
Pinewood Gr
13 Bedale DL8 63 A2
6 York YO31 225 E2
Pinewood Hill 4 YO10 229 C3
Pinewood Rd TS7 7 C6
Pinewood Wlk 7 TS9 26 C8
Pinfold Ave LS25 195 F4
Pinfold Cl
Bilton-in-Ainsty with Bickerton LS22 181 B5
5 Riccall YO19 192 A1
3 Sherburn in Elmet LS25 195 F4
Pinfold Ct
Kirkby Malzeard HG4 112 D5
4 Sherburn in Elmet LS25 195 F4
4 York YO30 228 A7
Pinfold Dr DL6 210 E5
Pinfold Garth
Malton YO17 215 A4
6 Sherburn in Elmet LS25 195 F4
1 Sherburn in Elmet LS25 196 A4
Pinfold Gn HG5 140 E1
Pinfold Hill YO8 197 D6
Pinfold La
Asselby DN14 205 F6
Kirk Smeaton WF8 206 B3
Mickletown LS26 200 C5
Moss DN6 207 D1
Norton DN6 206 E2
Norwood HG3 177 A8
Pollington DN14 207 F6
Pinfold Rise LS25 194 F8
Pinfold The 5 BD23 216 F4
Pinfold View DN14 207 F6
Pinfold Way
5 Sherburn in Elmet LS25 195 F4
2 Sherburn in Elmet LS25 196 A4
Pinhaw Rd BD23 217 A2
Pinnacle View BD22 187 A5
Pioneer Way WF10 200 C2
Piper Hill 1 WF11 201 D6
Piper La Cowling BD22 187 B5
Thirsk YO7 211 C3
Piper Rd DL6 45 F6
Pipers Acre 4 YO18 95 F7
Pipers La YO26 141 F1
Pippin Rd YO17 215 B4
Pippin's App 17 WF6 200 A2
Pit Ings La YO7 115 F6
Pit La Micklefield LS25 195 A4
Mickletown LS26 200 B6
Pitman Rd YO17 215 C5
Place Hill DL11 38 B6
Plane Tree Way YO14 101 A4
Planetree La
Kirkby Fleetham with Fencote DL7 42 A1
Thornville YO26 164 A1
Plantation Ave HG3 222 A8
Plantation Cl HG2 222 A8
Plantation Dr
Barlby with Osgodby YO8 198 B5
York YO26 227 C6
Plantation Gr YO26 227 C6
Plantation Rd HG2 222 A8
Plantation Terr HG2 222 A8
Plantation The BD23 152 E3
Plantation Way 28 YO32 166 E5
Pleasance The 6 LS26 194 A1
Pleasant Mount YO22 208 F3
Pleasant View 5 BB18 172 B1
Plews Way DL7 63 C5
Plompton Cl HG2 220 D1
Plompton Dr HG2 220 D2
Plompton Gr 3 HG2 220 D2
Plompton Rd HG3 223 F5
Plompton Way 1 HG2 220 D2
Plompton Wlk 2 HG2 220 D2
Plough Garth The DN14 202 F3
Ploughlands 1 YO32 225 C7
Ploughman's Cl YO23 230 C3
Ploughmans Ct 14 YO11 100 B7
Ploughmans' La YO32 225 C7
Plover Gdns 1 YO12 99 F6
Plum St YO17 215 D3
Plumer Ave YO31 229 A5
Plumer Rd DL9 209 B1
Plumpton La HG4 139 D8
Plumpton Pk HG2 220 D3
Plumpton Rocks* HG5 179 D8
Pluntrain Dale La YO18 96 B7
Pocklington La YO42 169 F2
Pockthorpe La YO25 151 F2
Pocock Pl DL10 41 E4
Polam Hall Sch DL1 3 C4
Polam La DL1 3 C4
Pole Rd BD22 187 F4
Pollard Cl YO32 225 E3
Pollard Gdns YO12 212 C4
Pollington Balne C of E Sch DN14 207 F6
Polperro Cl 21 WF6 200 A2
Pond Farm Cl TS13 11 F7
Pond Field Cl DL3 3 A4
Pond St 3 YO8 232 D6
Pondfields Dr LS25 194 D1
Pontefract C of E Sch WF8 201 B1
Pontefract Castle* WF8 201 C1
Pontefract Monkhill Sta WF8 201 B1
Pontefract Mus* WF8 201 B1
Pontefract New Coll WF8 201 A1
Pontefract Park Race Course* WF8 200 F2
Pontefract Rd
Castleford WF10 200 F4
Knottingley WF11 201 D2
Normanton South WF6 200 B2
Pool Ct 20 YO18 95 F6
Pool La YO26 164 E4
Poole La LS25 201 F6
Pope St WF6 200 B3
Poplar Ave
Castleford WF10 201 B4
6 Hutton Rudby TS15 25 D5
4 Kirkbymoorside YO62 70 B1
3 Wetherby LS22 180 C4
Poplar Cres
Harrogate HG1 219 F6
Northallerton DL7 210 C2
Poplar Dr WF6 200 A3
Poplar Gdns YO8 204 F5
Poplar Gn HG5 162 A6
Poplar Gr
Harrogate HG1 219 F6
York YO32 225 E3
Poplar Pl TS14 8 E7
Poplar Row 6 YO21 208 D7
Poplar St YO26 227 E5
Poplar Way HG1 219 F6
Poplars La YO17 123 A7
Poplars The
11 Brayton YO8 197 D1
2 Glusburn BD20 187 E6
Knottingley WF11 202 A1
Poppleton Hall Gdn YO26 224 A3
Poppleton Rd YO26 227 E4
Poppleton Road Prim Sch YO26 227 E5
Poppleton Sta YO26 182 F8
Poppy Cl YO8 232 C2
Poppy Ct 16 DL9 41 A5
Porch Farm Cl YO62 120 B5
Porch The DL10 21 D7
Pornic Ave YO13 75 D5
Porritt La YO12 99 D7
Portal Rd YO26 227 B6
Portholme Cres 7 YO8 232 C5
Portholme Dr YO8 232 C4
Portholme Rd YO8 232 C5
Portisham Pl 12 YO32 167 A7
Portland St YO31 233 B4
Portland Way DL7 63 C5
Portman Rise TS14 8 F5
Post Office Row DN14 205 A1
Postern Cl YO23 233 B1
Postern La YO42 193 D6
Pot Bank HG3 178 A8
Potlands DL7 63 C4
Pott Bank HG4 85 A1
Pott Moor High Rd HG4 110 F8
Potter Hill 11 YO18 95 F7
Potter La DL7 64 A5
Pottergate
Gilling East YO62 118 F7
14 Helmsley YO62 92 F6
Richmond DL10 209 C7
Potters Dr 4 YO23 230 B3
Potter's Side La YO21 9 D1
Potterton Cl LS15 194 C8
Potterton La
Barwick in Elmet LS15 194 C8
Barwick in Elmet & Scholes LS15 188 C1
Pottery La
Bishop Monkton HG4 140 A6
Knottingley WF11 201 E3
Littlethorpe HG4 214 E1
York YO31 228 E7
Pottery St WF10 200 D4
Potticar Bank YO62 119 D4
Pounteys Cl 4 DL2 4 C4
Powell St
Harrogate HG1 219 F4
Selby YO8 232 B6
Prail Cl 13 WF8 201 C1
Precentor's Ct YO31 233 B3
Preen Dr TS5 6 D8
Premier Rd TS7 7 D7
Premiere Pk 30 LS29 175 C2
Preston Field Cross Rd YO13 74 E1
Preston Hall Mus* TS18 5 F6
Preston La
Great Preston WF10 200 C7

Preston La *continued*
Preston-on-Tees TS18 ......5 E7
Preston Prim Sch TS16 ...5 E6
Preston View LS26 ....194 A1
Preston Way TS9 ....26 C8
Prestwick Ct
15 Middleton St George DL2 .4 C4
Rufforth YO26 ....227 B5
Pretoria St WF10 ......200 F4
Price's La YO23 ....233 B1
Priest Bank DL8 ....57 B4
Priest Bank Rd 4 BD20 .173 F1
Priest Cl YO14 ....126 F8
Priest Gill Bank DL11 ...19 F5
Priest La
Dunnington YO19 ....184 F5
Ripon HG4 ....214 D4
Priestcarr La YO26 ....163 D8
Primrose Ave
Hunmanby Sands YO14 ..101 B1
Swillington LS26 ....194 A1
Primrose Cl
Guisborough TS14 ....8 E6
13 Killinghall HG3 ....161 B3
Ripon HG4 ....214 C6
Primrose Ct 18 DL9 .....41 A5
Primrose Dene WF11 ..201 E4
Primrose Dr
Filey YO14 ....101 B1
Ripon HG4 ....214 C6
Primrose Gr YO8 ......232 A6
Primrose Hill
9 Knottingley WF11 ....202 A3
2 Skipton BD23 ....216 F4
Primrose Hill Cl LS26 ..194 A1
Primrose Hill Dr
Great & Little Preston
LS26 ....200 A8
15 Swillington LS26 .....194 A1
Primrose Hill Garth
LS26 ....200 A8
Primrose Hill Gdns
LS26 ....194 A1
Primrose Hill Gn LS26 .200 A8
Primrose Hill Gr 16
LS26 ....194 A1
Primrose La LS23 ......188 E8
Primrose Vale 1 WF11 .202 A2
Primrose Valley Rd
YO14 ....101 B1
Prince Henry Rd LS21 .177 A1
Prince Henrys Gram Sch
LS21 ....177 A1
Prince of Wales Terr
YO11 ....213 A4
Prince Rupert Dr
YO26 ....181 C7
Prince St WF10 ....200 C8
Princes Cres BD23 ....217 B4
Princes Dr BD23 ......217 A4
Princes Sq
12 Harrogate HG1 ......219 D2
Thornaby TS17 ....6 B6
Princes Villa Rd HG1 ..219 E2
Princess Ave HG5 .....221 C5
Princess Cl HG4 ......214 C6
Princess Ct 11 WF6 ....200 B1
Princess Dr HG5 ....221 C5
Princess Gr 4 HG5 .....221 C5
Princess La 12 YO11 ....213 B6
Princess Mead HG5 ...163 A3
Princess Mount 3 HG5 221 C5
Princess Pl 5 YO21 ....208 D6
Princess Rd
Darlington DL3 ....3 D8
Ilkley LS29 ....218 A3
Malton YO17 ....215 C4
Ripon HG4 ....214 C6
Strensall YO32 ....167 B7
Princess Royal La 4
YO11 ....212 F3
Princess Royal Pk 1
YO11 ....213 A3
Princess Royal Rd
HG4 ....214 C3
Princess Royal Terr
YO11 ....213 A3
Princess Royal Way
HG3 ....222 E1
Princess Sq 11 YO11 ...213 B6
Princess St
Castleford WF10 ....200 F5
Normanton South WF6 ..200 A1
Scarborough YO11 ......213 B6
Prior Ave DL10 ....209 B7
Prior Pursgrove Coll
TS6 ....7 E8
Prior Wath Rd YO13 ....54 A5
Priorpot Way YO17 ....215 F4
Prior's La BD23 ....174 C8
Prior's Wlk YO26 ......227 D6
Priorwood Gdns TS17 ....6 A4
Priory Cl
Guisborough TS14 ....8 F7
Northallerton DL6 ....210 E5
Wilberfoss YO41 ....185 F6
Priory La 1 DN14 ....204 C1
Priory Park Cl 3 LS25 ..202 A8
Priory Park Gr 2 LS25 ..202 B8
Priory Pk YO21 ....31 C4
Priory Pl YO11 ....100 B7
Priory Rd DN6 ....206 E2
Priory St YO1 ....233 A1
Priory View 2 BD23 ....217 E8
Priory Way
4 Ingleby Arncliffe DL6 ...45 A7
1 Snaith DN14 ....204 B1
Priory Wood Way
YO31 ....225 F2
Prissick Sports Ctr TS4 ..7 B8
Pritchett Rd TS3 ....7 C8
Promenade La HG1 ...219 C3
Prospect Ave
Normanton South WF6 ..200 A2
Sherburn in Elmet LS25 ..195 F4
Prospect Bank LS23 ...188 F6
Prospect Cl
Camblesforth YO8 ....204 D5
Harrogate HG2 ....220 C3
Pollington DN14 ....207 F6
Prospect Cres
13 Harrogate HG1 ......219 D2
Scarborough YO12 ......212 D6
Prospect Ct 3 LS24 ....189 E6
Prospect Dr LS24 ......189 E6
Prospect Field
5 Fylingdales YO22 ......33 D4
Hawsker-cum-Stainsacre
YO22 ....33 A6
Prospect Hill YO21 ....208 C5
Prospect Mount Rd
YO12 ....212 C6
Prospect Pk YO12 .....212 D6
Prospect Pl
Harrogate HG1 ....219 D2
Northallerton DL6 ....210 F4
28 Scarborough YO11 ....213 A6
Skipton BD23 ....216 F4
Thornton-le-Dale YO18 ....96 D6
Wistow YO8 ....197 D6
Prospect Rd
Harrogate HG2 ....220 C3
9 Scarborough YO12 ....212 F6
Prospect St 14 BD20 ...187 E7
Prospect Terr
Fulford YO10 ....231 D6
1 Lingdale TS12 ....9 F7
Micklefield LS25 ....195 A3
York YO1 ....233 B1
Prospect View DL6 ....210 E4
Prospect Way
5 Leeming DL7 ....63 D4
Selby YO8 ....232 D4
Providence Gn 16 WF8 .201 C2
Providence Pl
13 Filey YO14 ....101 B3
Mickletown LS26 ....200 D6
15 Scarborough YO11 ....213 A6
Skipton BD23 ....217 A4
Providence Terr HG1 ..219 D4
Pry Hills La
Hartoft YO18 ....71 A8
Rosedale East Side YO18 ...49 F2
Pudding Hill Rd DL11 ....1 B6
Pudding La YO13 ....97 F5
Pudding Pie Hill*
YO7 ....211 D1
Pulleyn Cl 3 YO32 .....167 C8
Pulleyn Dr YO24 ....227 F1
Pump Hill 4 HG5 ....221 A6
Pump La
Kirklevington TS15 ....24 F8
4 Malton YO17 ....215 C4
Purey Cust Nuffield Hospl
The YO31 ....233 B3
Pursglove Prior Coll
TS14 ....8 F7
Pye Busk Cl LA2 ....129 B8
Pye La HG3 ....160 F8

Q

Quaker Cl
1 Reeth, Fremington &
Healaugh DL11 ....38 B6
Scarborough YO12 ......212 C5
Quaker Gn 1 YO24 .....230 C7
Quaker La DL6 ....210 D5
Quaker's La DL6 ....44 D7
Quakers La DL10 ....209 B7
Quant Mews YO10 .....229 B3
Quarry Ave 20 WF11 ....202 A2
Quarry Banks YO7 .....116 E7
Quarry Dr TS8 ....6 E5
Quarry Gate YO13 ....74 C1
Quarry Hill YO17 ....120 F4
Quarry Hill La LS22 ....180 B3
Quarry La
Harrogate HG1 ....219 C6
Osmotherley DL6 ....45 C5
Pateley Bridge HG3 .....137 C4
Quarry Moor La HG4 ..214 C3
Quarry Mount YO12 ...212 E3
Quarry Rd Norton DN6 ..206 F2
Richmond DL10 ....209 B7
Ripon HG4 ....214 B2
Quay St YO11 ....213 B6
Quay The YO8 ....232 D6
Queen Anne's Ct 3 DL8 .63 A2
Queen Anne's Dr 4 DL8 .63 A2
Queen Anne's Rd
YO30 ....233 A3
Queen Elizabeth Dr 10
YO13 ....75 D5
Queen Elizabeth Sixth Form
Coll DL3 ....3 C5
Queen Ethelburgas Coll
YO26 ....164 C6
Queen Ethelburga's Dr 6
HG3 ....161 B2
Queen Ethelburga's Pa 8
HG3 ....161 B2
Queen Margarets Ave 4
WF11 ....201 E4
Queen Margarets Cl 3
WF11 ....201 E4
Queen Margaret's Dr
WF11 ....201 E4
Queen Margaret's Rd 6
YO11 ....212 F3
Queen Margarets Sch
YO19 ....192 A5
Queen Marys Sch YO7 .115 A7
Queen Par HG1 ....219 E2
Queen St
10 Cowling BD22 ....187 B6
Great Preston LS26 .....200 C7
Normanton South WF6 ..200 A1
18 Ripon HG4 ....214 C5
Scarborough YO11 ......213 A6
Skelton & Brotton TS12 .....9 D7
York YO24 ....233 A2
Queen Street Jun & Inf Sch
WF6 ....200 A1
Queen Victoria St
YO23 ....228 B1
Queens Ave DL9 ....40 E3
Queen's Cl 8 HG2 ......219 C1
Queen's Dr LS29 ....218 A3
Queens Dr
9 Stokesley TS9 ....26 C8
Whitby YO22 ....208 E3
Queen's Drive La LS29 .218 A3
Queens Garth BD23 ...172 A3
Queen's Gdns
4 Ilkley LS29 ....218 A3
Tadcaster LS24 ....189 E6
Queen's Par YO12 .....213 A7
Queen's Park Dr
WF10 ....201 A4
Queen's Rd
Harrogate HG2 ....219 C1
Ilkley LS29 ....218 A3
Queens Rd
Knaresborough HG5 .....221 C6
Richmond DL10 ....209 C7
Queen's St 6 BD23 ....217 B4
Queen's Staith Rd
YO1 ....233 B2
Queen's Terr
3 Filey YO14 ....101 B3
Scarborough YO12 ......213 A7
Queen's Way YO62 .....70 B1
Queensbury Ct 15 WF6 .200 B1
Queensway WF8 ......201 C2
Queenswood Gr YO24 .227 D2
Quentin Rd 19 DL9 ......40 E4
Quernmore Dr BB18 ...186 A7

R

Rabbit La YO17 ....215 F8
Raby La DL7 ....22 E3
Raby Pk LS22 ....180 B3
Raby Terr DL3 ....3 C5
Racca Ave 11 WF11 ....202 A2
Racca Gn WF11 ....202 A2
Race La Carlton YO8 ...204 B4
Sessay YO61 ....116 C4
Racecourse Ct DL10 ...209 A8
Racecourse La DL7 ...210 D3
Racecourse Mews
YO7 ....211 A2
Racecourse Rd
East Ayton/West Ayton
YO13 ....99 B8
Irton YO12 ....212 A1
Richmond DL10 ....209 B8
York YO23 ....231 B8
Rachel La DL11 ....20 B5
RAF Leeming CP Sch
DL7 ....63 F3
Rag Robin Turn YO7 ....66 D6
Raghill La YO61 ....142 A8
Raglan St HG1 ....219 D2
Raglan Terr 3 YO21 ....208 D5
Raikes Ave BD23 ......216 F5
Raikes La BD23 ....156 A6
Raikes' La YO22 ....32 E3
Raikes Rd BD23 ....216 F5
Raikes The HG3 ....137 E3
Raikeswood Cres
BD23 ....216 E5
Raikeswood Dr BD23 ..216 E5
Raikeswood Rd BD23 ..216 E5
Railer Bank HG4 ......112 E6
Railway Ave WF8 ......201 B1
Railway Rd
Follifoot HG3 ....223 C7
Ilkley LS29 ....218 B4
Railway St 16 Leyburn DL8 60 D5
Norton YO17 ....215 C3
Slingsby YO62 ....120 B5
Railway Terr
Hurworth-on-Tees DL2 ...22 D8
5 Normanton South WF6 .200 A1
Thirsk YO7 ....211 B2
York YO24 ....228 A4
Railway View DL7 .....210 D3
Raincliffe Ave
29 Filey YO14 ....101 B3
Scarborough YO12 ......212 C5
Raincliffe Cres YO12 ..212 C5
Raincliffe Gr YO12 ....212 C4
Raincliffe Sch YO12 ...212 B6
Raincliffe St 4 YO8 ....232 C5
Raindale Rd YO18 ....71 F6
Raines Dr 5 BD20 ......173 E3
Raines La BD23 ....134 D3
Raines Lea BD23 ....134 D3
Raines Mdws 6 BD23 ..134 D2
Raines Rd BD24 ....131 C1
Rainford Cl 7 YO12 .....99 D6
Rainhall Cres BB18 ....171 E1
Rainhall Rd BB18 ......171 D1
Rainham Cl TS17 ....6 B4
Rainhill Road Cty Prim Sch
BB18 ....171 D1
Rainsborough Way 3
YO30 ....228 A8
Rainsburgh La YO25 ...126 A3
Raisdale Rd TS9 ....26 D1
Rake La YO21 ....30 D6
Rake The LA6 ....103 D4
Rakehill Rd LS15 ......194 B8
Raker Cl YO19 ....192 F7
Rakes BD23 ....134 C1
Rakes La BD23 ....171 B5
Raleigh St YO12 ....212 E6
Ralph Butterfield Sch
YO32 ....166 F5
Ralph Garth YO26 ....181 D7
Rampart The YO23 ....190 D4
Ramsay Cl YO31 ......233 C4
Ramsden Cl WF11 .....201 D4
Ramsden St LS25 .....200 C8
Ramsey Ave YO23 .....231 B3
Ramsey St YO12 ....212 E6
Ramshaw Dr BD23 ....217 A1
Ramshill Rd YO11 .....213 A4
Randal La HG3 ....160 D4
Range Rd DL8 ....40 A2
Rankin's Well Rd 4
BD23 ....217 B4
Rantreefold Rd LA2 ...128 F4
Rape Close La YO62 ..118 E4
Rape La YO62 ....93 B7
Raper La YO61 ....117 B3
Raper View LS25 ....194 F8
Rarber Top La LA6 ....103 D2
Rarey Dr YO17 ....124 E1
Raskelf Rd
7 Brafferton YO61 ......115 F1
Easingwold YO61 ....117 B1
Ratcliffe Ct YO30 ......224 C5
Ratcliffe St YO30 ......228 B7
Rathmall La YO26 .....164 C2
Rathmell C of E Prim Sch
BD24 ....153 B7
Rattan Row YO25 .....151 C6
Ratten Row Hunton DL8 ..61 E7
Seamer YO12 ....99 C5
Raven Cl 10 Eastfield YO12 99 F6
Featherstone WF7 ....200 D1
Raven Gr YO26 ....227 C4
Raven Hall Rd YO13 ....53 F7
Ravens Close Brow
LA2 ....102 C1
Ravenscroft Way
BB18 ....171 E2
Ravensdale Rd DL3 ......3 B4
Ravensthorpe Prep Sch
DL3 ....3 B5
Ravensville 1 BD20 ....187 F7
Ravensworth C of E Prim Sch
DL11 ....20 A6
Ravensworth Castle*
DL11 ....20 A6
Ravine Hill 17 YO14 ....101 B4
Ravine Rd YO14 ....101 B4
Ravine Top 7 YO14 ....101 B3
Raw Bank DL11 ....37 E8
Raw La Fylingdales YO22 ..33 B4
Kirkby Wharfe with
North Milford LS24 .....190 A3
Towton LS24 ....189 F3
Raw Pasture Bank
YO22 ....33 B5
Raw Pasture La YO22 ...33 C5
Rawcliff Rd YO18 ....72 A5
Rawcliffe Ave YO30 ...227 F8
Rawcliffe Cl YO30 .....224 E2
Rawcliffe Croft YO30 ..224 D2
Rawcliffe Dr YO30 ....227 F8
Rawcliffe in Snaith Prim Sch
DN14 ....205 A2
Rawcliffe Inf Sch
YO30 ....224 E1
Rawcliffe La YO30 .....224 F1
Rawcliffe Rd DN14 ....205 D2
Rawcliffe Way YO30 ..224 E2
Rawdon Ave YO10 .....228 F4
Rawfield La WF11 .....201 D7
Rawlinson Rd DL9 .....209 D2
Rawson St HG1 ....219 E5
Ray Bridge La BD23 ...155 D1
Ray Dike Cl YO32 .....225 C7
Ray La HG4 ....114 B1
Raydale Cl 2 HG5 .....221 D5
Raygill La BD20 ....186 E8
Rayleigh Rd HG2 ......222 E8
Raylton Ave TS7 ....7 B5
Rayner St HG4 ....214 C5
Read Cl YO8 ....204 F5
Read Sch YO8 ....204 F5
Real Aeroplane Mus The*
YO8 ....199 D5
Reas La YO51 ....141 D1
Reasty Hill YO13 ....53 E1
Reasty Rd YO13 ....53 D2
Recreation Rd
17 Pickering YO18 ....95 F6
2 Selby YO8 ....232 D6
Rectory Cl
Bolton Percy YO23 ......190 D4
Rectory Cl *continued*
Heslerton YO17 ....123 F6
Rectory Gdns YO23 ....228 B1
Rectory La
Guisborough TS14 ....8 E6
3 Hurworth-on-Tees DL2 ..22 C8
Longnewton TS21 ....5 A7
Skipton BD23 ....217 A4
Thornton-le-Dale YO18 ....96 E5
Red Bank Cl HG4 .....214 A3
Red Bank Dr HG4 .....214 A3
Red Bank Rd HG4 .....214 A3
Red Barnes Way DL1 .....3 E6
Red Brae Bank HG3 ...137 A3
Red Brow YO13 ....74 C5
Red Gate DL8 ....57 C6
Red Hall La TS15 ....6 A1
Red Hall Prim Sch DL1 ...3 F6
Red Hill La LS25 ....195 E1
Red Hills La HG3 ......140 B3
Red Hills Rd HG4 ......214 B7
Red House Prep Sch
YO26 ....165 D3
Red La
Green Hammerton YO26 ..164 C3
4 Masham HG4 ....86 C3
Red Lion St BB18 ......172 B1
Red Scar Dr YO12 .....212 A7
Red Scar La
Newby & Scalby YO12 .....75 C4
Scalby YO12 ....212 A8
Red Twr* YO1 ....228 E4
Red Way Brompton DL6 ..43 F6
Danby YO21 ....29 E6
Farndale East YO62 ....48 E4
Nether Silton DL6 ....45 D1
Redcap La YO42 ....193 C5
Redcar Rd
Guisborough TS14 ....8 F7
Thornaby TS17 ....6 B7
Redcliff Cl 12 YO11 ....100 B7
Redcliffe Ct YO12 .....212 D7
Redcliffe Gdns YO12 ..212 C6
Redcliffe La YO11 .....100 D6
Redcliffe Rd YO12 .....212 D6
Redcoat W 1 YO24 ....230 B8
Redeness St YO31 .....228 E5
Redhill Ave WF10 .....201 A3
Redhill Cl HG1 ....219 D6
Redhill Dr WF10 ....201 A3
Redhill Field La YO23 .182 D1
Redhill Inf Sch WF10 ..201 B4
Redhill Rd
Castleford WF10 ....201 A4
Harrogate HG1 ....219 C6
Redhouse La YO8 ......204 F6
Redlish Rd HG3 ....136 E1
Redman Cl YO10 ......231 C8
Redmayne Sq YO32 ...167 B8
Redmires Cl YO30 .....225 A2
Redruth Dr 22 WF6 ....200 A2
Redshaw Cl 1 HG4 ....214 C4
Redshaw Gr 2 HG4 ....214 C4
Redthorn Dr YO31 .....225 F1
Redwood Dr 6 YO32 ...166 E5
Reebys La LA2 ....129 F5
Reedshaw La BD22 ....186 F5
Reeth Rd
Middlesbrough TS5 ....6 E8
Richmond DL10 ....209 A7
2 Stockton-on-Tees TS18 ...5 E8
Reeval Cl 13 BB18 .....172 B1
Reeves The YO24 ......227 C1
Regency Ave TS6 ....7 E8
Regency Ct
3 Ilkley LS29 ....218 A3
Northallerton DL6 ....210 F3
Regency Mews 2 YO24 .230 F8
Regency Pk TS17 ....6 B4
Regent Ave
Harrogate HG1 ....219 E3
Skipton BD23 ....217 B5
Regent Cres BD23 .....217 B5
Regent Dr BD23 ....217 B5
Regent Gr HG1 ....219 E4
Regent Mount 2 HG1 ..220 C4
Regent Par HG1 ....219 E3
Regent Pl HG1 ....220 C4
Regent Rd Ilkley LS29 ..218 A4
Skipton BD23 ....217 B5
Regent St
Castleford WF10 ....200 E4
Harrogate HG1 ....219 F3
Normanton WF6 ....200 B2
1 Scarborough YO12 ....213 A6
York YO10 ....228 E3
Regent Terr HG1 ....219 E3
Regents Ct 14 YO26 ....227 F5
Reginald Gr YO23 .....228 C1
Reid Street Prim Sch
DL3 ....3 C6
Reid Terr TS14 ....8 F6
Reighton Ave YO30 ....227 F8
Reighton Dr 10 YO30 ...224 F1
Rein Ct LS25 ....194 F8
Reins HG5 ....163 A7
Reivaulx Dr TS5 ....6 F8
Renfield Gr WF6 ......200 B2
Renshaw Gdns 8 YO26 .227 E4
Renton Cl HG3 ....140 B5
Reservoir La 7 YO11 ...100 B8
Residence La HG4 .....214 D5
Resolution Way YO21 ..208 B5
Retreat Hospl The
YO10 ....228 F2
Reygate Gr YO23 .....230 B2
Reynard Crag La HG3 .160 C6
Reynolds St 15 YO14 ...101 B3

Rhode's Hill La LS23 ... 188 F6
Rhodes La LS23 ... 188 D7
Rhodes St WF10 ... 200 D4
Rhyddings Gdns LS29 ... 218 D4
Rianbow La YO17 ... 215 C6
Ribble Dr DL1 ... 3 C3
Ribblehead Sta LA6 ... 78 E1
Ribblehead Viaduct* LA6 ... 78 D2
Ribston Rd
Little Ribston LS22 ... 180 A7
Spofforth with Stockeld HG3 ... 179 F6
Ribstone Gr YO31 ... 229 B6
Riccal Dr
25 Helmsley YO62 ... 92 F6
Huttons Ambo YO17 ... 121 C1
Riccal Moor La YO62 ... 93 E4
Riccall CP Sch YO19 ... 191 F1
Riccall La YO19 ... 191 D1
Rice Gate YO13 ... 74 D8
Rice La Aldwark YO61 ... 142 C2
Flaxton YO60 ... 145 F2
Richard St YO8 ... 232 B5
Richard Taylor C of E Prim Sch HG1 ... 219 E6
Richard Thorntons C of E Prim Sch LA6 ... 102 E3
Richardson Ct YO8 ... 196 F1
Richardson Rd TS17 ... 6 A7
Richardson St YO23 ... 228 C2
Richmond Ave
Harrogate HG2 ... 222 C7
Knottingley WF11 ... 201 D3
Richmond C of E Prim Sch DL10 ... 209 D7
Richmond Castle* DL10 ... 209 C6
Richmond Cl HG2 ... 222 C7
Richmond Garth HG4 ... 112 C5
Richmond Holt HG2 ... 222 C7
Richmond Methodist Prim Sch DL10 ... 209 E7
Richmond Pl LS29 ... 218 C3
Richmond Rd
12 Barnoldswick BB18 ... 171 D2
Barton DL10 ... 21 E6
Brompton-on-Swale DL10 ... 41 A6
Croft-on-Tees DL10 ... 21 F6
Harrogate HG2 ... 222 C7
Hipswell DL9 ... 209 D1
Leyburn DL8 ... 60 D5
Skeeby DL10 ... 20 F1
Richmond Sch
Richmond DL10 ... 209 C6
Richmond DL10 ... 209 D7
Richmond St YO31 ... 228 E5
Richmond Swimming Pool & Gemini Fitness Ctr DL10 ... 209 D6
Richmondfield Ave LS15 ... 194 C7
Richmondfield Cl LS15 ... 194 C7
Richmondfield Cres LS15 ... 194 C7
Richmondfield Cross LS15 ... 194 C7
Richmondfield Dr LS15 ... 194 B7
Richmondfield Garth LS15 ... 194 C8
Richmondfield Gr LS15 ... 194 C7
Richmondfield La LS15 ... 194 C7
Richmondfield Mount LS15 ... 194 C7
Richmondfield Way LS15 ... 194 C8
Richmondshire Mus* DL10 ... 209 C7
Richmondshire Sports Ctr DL10 ... 209 C8
Ridding Cres DN14 ... 205 A1
Ridding Gate 5 LS21 ... 176 F1
Ridding La DN14 ... 205 A1
Riddings Rd LS29 ... 218 B3
Riders La YO60 ... 146 F2
Ridge Gn YO13 ... 75 D5
Ridge La Roxby TS13 ... 11 A6
Silsden BD20 ... 174 B4
Sleights YO21 ... 32 B7
Staithes TS13 ... 13 H1
Ridge Rd LS25 ... 200 E8
Ridge The
Coulby Newham TS8 ... 7 A4
Linton LS22 ... 180 B2
Ridgedale Mount WF8 ... 201 B2
Ridgeway Darlington DL3 ... 3 C8
10 Eastfield YO11 ... 99 F7
Skipton BD23 ... 216 E6
York YO26 ... 227 B3
Ridgeway The WF11 ... 201 F2
Riding Cl 4 BB18 ... 171 E1
Ridings The
7 Boroughbridge YO51 ... 141 B4
Norton YO17 ... 215 D2
Ridley Ave TS5 ... 6 E8
Ridleys Fold 14 LS29 ... 174 F4
Ridsdale St DL1 ... 3 D5
Rievaulx Abbey* YO62 ... 92 B8
Rievaulx Ave HG5 ... 221 C4
Rievaulx Bank YO62 ... 92 B8
Rievaulx Cl HG5 ... 221 C4
Rievaulx Ct 6 HG5 ... 221 C4
Rievaulx Dr DL7 ... 64 A6
Rievaulx Rd YO21 ... 208 C6
Rievaulx Terr* YO62 ... 92 B7
Rievaulx Way TS14 ... 8 F6
Riffa La LS21 ... 177 E2
Rigg Bank HG4 ... 85 E3
Rigg The TS15 ... 5 E2
Rigg View YO22 ... 32 F7
Riggs Rd YO17 ... 121 F5
Riggs Spring 8 HG3 ... 137 F1
Rigton Hill LS17 ... 178 B4
Riley St 41 BB18 ... 172 A1
Rillington CP Sch YO17 ... 122 F5
Rimington Ave DL10 ... 209 D6
Rimington Way YO11 ... 100 B7
Ringing Keld Hill YO13 ... 54 A3
Ringstone Rd YO30 ... 224 F3
Ringstones La LA2 ... 129 A4
Ringway LS25 ... 194 B3
Ringway Gr 11 DL2 ... 4 C4
Ringwood Rd DL9 ... 40 F3
Ripley Bank HG3 ... 137 C4
Ripley Castle* HG3 ... 161 C7
Ripley Cl
11 Kirkbymoorside YO62 ... 70 B1
Normanton South WF6 ... 200 B1
Ripley Dr
Harrogate HG1 ... 219 C6
Normanton South WF6 ... 200 B2
Ripley Endowed Prim Sch HG3 ... 161 C7
Ripley Gr 3 YO32 ... 166 E5
Ripley Rd
Knaresborough HG5 ... 220 E8
Nidd HG3 ... 161 E6
Scotton HG5 ... 162 A5
Ripley Way HG1 ... 219 C6
Ripley's Rd YO13 ... 54 B1
Ripon & District Hospl HG4 ... 214 B5
Ripon By-Pass HG4 ... 214 C2
Ripon Cath HG4 ... 214 C5
Ripon Cathedral Choir Sch HG4 ... 214 A3
Ripon Coll HG4 ... 214 A5
Ripon Dr DL1 ... 3 D3
Ripon FC HG4 ... 214 B5
Ripon Gram Sch HG4 ... 214 A6
Ripon Greystone CP Sch HG4 ... 214 C2
Ripon Horn The* HG4 ... 214 C5
Ripon Leisure Ctr HG4 ... 214 D3
Ripon Race Course* HG4 ... 214 F2
Ripon Rd
Harrogate HG3 ... 219 A7
Middlesbrough TS7 ... 7 E6
Ripley HG3 ... 161 D8
South Stainley with Cayton HG3 ... 139 E2
Ripon Rugby Club HG4 ... 214 B5
Ripon Swimming Baths HG4 ... 214 B5
Ripon Way
Carlton Miniott YO7 ... 89 C4
Harrogate HG1 ... 219 C5
Rise Carr Prim Sch DL3 ... 3 C7
Rise Richmond DL7 ... 210 C3
Rise The
Huttons Ambo YO60 ... 147 C6
Knottingley WF11 ... 201 E4
Leavening YO17 ... 147 E1
Thornton Dale YO18 ... 96 D5
Riseber DL8 ... 60 C5
Risedale Rd DL9 ... 209 B1
Risedale Sch DL9 ... 209 F1
Risewood YO41 ... 168 B2
Rishworth Gr YO30 ... 224 F2
Rivadale View LS29 ... 218 B5
Rivelin Way
10 Filey YO14 ... 101 A3
York YO30 ... 224 F2
Rivendell BD23 ... 134 B3
River Cl 2 YO8 ... 198 B5
River La
Brompton-on-Swale DL10 ... 41 B6
Kilburn High & Low YO61 ... 91 B2
West Haddlesey YO8 ... 203 A5
River Pl BD23 ... 155 D1
River Rd YO61 ... 91 C2
River St 1 Selby YO8 ... 232 D6
Trawden BB8 ... 186 B2
York YO23 ... 233 B1
River View
1 Barlby YO8 ... 198 B5
Boston Spa LS23 ... 188 F8
River View Rd HG4 ... 214 C7
Riverdale 4 DN14 ... 202 D4
Rivergarth DL1 ... 3 F7
Riversdale
17 Haxby YO32 ... 166 F5
5 Settle BD24 ... 131 D2
Riversdene TS9 ... 26 B7
Riverside Clapham LA2 ... 130 C8
Gargrave BD23 ... 155 D1
Rawcliffe DN14 ... 205 A2
28 Scalby YO12 ... 75 D5
Riverside Ave LS21 ... 177 A1
Riverside Cl
1 Elvington YO41 ... 185 C2
Farnley LS21 ... 177 A1
Riverside CP Sch LS24 ... 189 E6
Riverside Cres
5 Otley LS21 ... 177 A1
York YO32 ... 225 F6
Riverside Ct DN14 ... 205 A2
Riverside Dr 3 LS21 ... 177 A1
Riverside Gdns
2 Boroughbridge YO51 ... 141 B6
2 Elvington YO41 ... 185 C2
2 Poppleton YO26 ... 165 F1
Riverside Mews 6 YO7 ... 211 C3
Riverside Pk 4 LS21 ... 177 A1
Riverside Rd DL10 ... 209 C6
Riverside View YO17 ... 215 B3
Riverside Way DL1 ... 3 E7
Riverside Wlk
Airton BD23 ... 155 A6
Ilkley LS29 ... 218 A5
1 Poppleton YO26 ... 165 F1
5 Strensall YO32 ... 167 A7
Riverslea TS9 ... 26 B7
Riversvale Dr 21 YO26 ... 165 F1
Riversway BD23 ... 155 C1
RNLI Mus* YO21 ... 208 D7
Roach Grange Ave LS25 ... 194 D2
Roall La DN14 ... 202 F4
Robert St HG1 ... 219 D1
Robert Wilkinson Prim Sch YO32 ... 167 A7
Roberts Cres HG1 ... 219 D5
Robertson Rd
Colburn DL9 ... 40 F4
Ripon HG4 ... 113 D3
Robin Cl 6 WF8 ... 201 B2
Robin Gr 6 YO24 ... 227 F3
Robin Hood Cl YO21 ... 29 A6
Robin Hood Rd YO13 ... 53 F8
Robin Hood's Bay Rd YO22 ... 33 A3
Robin La Bentham LA2 ... 103 A1
High Bentham LA2 ... 129 A8
Huby YO61 ... 144 A4
Robinson Dr
Harrogate HG2 ... 222 B6
York YO24 ... 227 B2
Robinson Rd 13 DL10 ... 41 E4
Robinson St WF10 ... 200 D6
Robson Ave TS17 ... 6 B5
Roche Ave
Harrogate HG1 ... 219 F6
York YO31 ... 228 E8
Rock Hill WF10 ... 201 A3
Rockingham Ave YO31 ... 229 A5
Rockingham Cl YO17 ... 215 A3
Rockingham Ct LS24 ... 189 E2
Rockingham Dr YO12 ... 212 B7
Rockland Gdns YO12 ... 212 D5
Rockley Grange Gdn LS25 ... 194 B3
Rocks La YO13 ... 75 D7
Rocks La Cl YO13 ... 75 D7
Rockville Dr BD23 ... 217 C8
Rockwell Ave DL1 ... 3 E7
Rockwood Cl 1 BD23 ... 216 E4
Rockwood Dr BD23 ... 216 E5
Rodney Terr 15 HG4 ... 86 C3
Roe La LS25 ... 202 C7
Roebuck La LS21 ... 176 F2
Roecliffe C of E Prim Sch YO51 ... 140 F4
Roecliffe La YO51 ... 141 B5
Roedean Dr TS16 ... 5 E4
Roger La TS8 ... 6 C4
Roker Rd HG1 ... 219 E4
Rolston Ave 3 YO31 ... 225 E2
Roman Ave N 17 YO41 ... 168 D2
Roman Ave S YO41 ... 168 D1
Roman Cl
Newby & Scalby YO12 ... 212 A7
4 Tadcaster LS24 ... 189 E6
Roman Cres DL9 ... 209 C1
Roman Fort of Olicana* LS29 ... 218 B4
Roman Rd TS5 ... 6 E8
Roman Signal Sta* YO21 ... 12 D6
Roman Town Mus* YO51 ... 141 C5
Roman Way YO12 ... 212 A7
Romanby CP Sch DL7 ... 210 B2
Romanby Rd DL7 ... 210 C3
Romans Cl YO19 ... 197 F8
Romany Rd 11 TS9 ... 8 A2
Rombalds Dr BD23 ... 217 A2
Rombalds La LS29 ... 218 E3
Rombald's View LS29 ... 218 D5
Rombalds View LS21 ... 176 E1
Romille St 15 BD23 ... 217 A3
Ronaldshay Cl DL10 ... 209 E8
Ronaldshay Dr DL10 ... 209 E8
Ronway Ave HG4 ... 214 B2
Rook St
25 Barnoldswick BB18 ... 171 D1
Lothersdale BD20 ... 186 F8
Rookery Rd BB18 ... 171 E1
Rookwood Ave LS25 ... 200 C8
Rookwood Rd TS7 ... 7 D6
Roomer La HG4 ... 86 B1
Rope Wlk BD23 ... 217 A4
Roper Ct DL10 ... 209 C7
Ropers Ct YO23 ... 230 C3
Ropery La YO17 ... 124 E1
Ropery The
15 Pickering YO18 ... 95 F7
Whitby YO22 ... 208 E6
Ropery Wlk YO17 ... 215 C4
Ropewalk The YO31 ... 228 E5
Rosamund Ave 21 YO18 ... 95 F7
Roscoe St YO12 ... 212 F5
Rose Ave
Sherburn in Elmet LS25 ... 195 F3
Whitby YO21 ... 208 B7
Rose Cres
Richmond DL10 ... 209 B7
Sherburn in Elmet LS25 ... 195 F3
Rose Ct LS25 ... 194 D4
Rose Hill Dr 13 TS9 ... 26 C7
Rose Hill Way TS9 ... 26 C7
Rose La LS24 ... 196 A7
Rose Lea Cl 2 LS25 ... 202 A7
Rose St YO31 ... 228 C7
Rose Tree Gr YO32 ... 225 D4
Rose Wood Prim Sch TS8 ... 7 A4
Roseberry Ave
Great Ayton TS9 ... 8 A2
Stokesley TS9 ... 26 D8
Roseberry CP Sch TS9 ... 8 A2
Roseberry Cres TS9 ... 8 A2
Roseberry Dr 8 TS9 ... 8 A2
Roseberry Gn HG4 ... 113 C7
Roseberry Gr YO30 ... 224 F3
Roseberry La
Guisborough TS9 ... 8 B3
Stillington YO61 ... 144 B6
Roseberry Mount TS14 ... 8 E6
Roseberry Rd TS9 ... 8 A2
Roseberry Topping* TS9 ... 8 C3
Rosebery Ave YO12 ... 212 E3
Rosebery St YO26 ... 227 F6
Rosecomb Way 6 YO32 ... 225 D7
Rosecroft Ave TS13 ... 10 D8
Rosecroft La TS13 ... 10 D7
Rosecroft Sch TS13 ... 10 D8
Rosecroft Way YO30 ... 227 E8
Rosedale HG3 ... 222 D3
Rosedale Abbey CP Sch YO18 ... 49 E2
Rosedale Ave YO26 ... 227 C4
Rosedale Chy Bank YO18 ... 49 E1
Rosedale Cl
Pannal HG3 ... 222 D3
3 Whitby YO21 ... 208 C6
Rosedale Cres
Darlington DL3 ... 3 A6
Guisborough TS14 ... 8 D6
Rosedale La
Hinderwell TS13 ... 11 F8
Staithes TS13 ... 13 L1
Rosedale St YO10 ... 228 D2
Rosehill TS9 ... 8 A1
Rosehill Sq 11 HG5 ... 221 B5
Rosehurst Gr HG3 ... 222 E2
Roseland Dr TS7 ... 7 C7
Rosemary Ct
20 Easingwold YO61 ... 143 C8
6 Tadcaster LS24 ... 189 E6
York YO1 ... 233 C2
Rosemary La 1 DL10 ... 209 C6
Rosemary Pl YO1 ... 233 C2
Rosemary Row 5 LS24 ... 189 E6
Rosemoor Cl
Coulby Newham TS8 ... 7 B5
19 Hunmanby YO14 ... 126 F8
Rosemount Rd 2 YO21 ... 208 C5
Rosendale Ave YO17 ... 215 F2
Roseville Ave
Harrogate HG1 ... 220 A3
Scarborough YO12 ... 212 E6
Roseville Dr HG1 ... 220 A3
Roseville Rd HG1 ... 220 A3
Roseway HG1 ... 219 E5
Roseworth TS9 ... 26 E5
Rosley St BB8 ... 186 B3
Roslyn Rd HG2 ... 220 A2
Rossett Ave HG2 ... 222 C6
Rossett Beck HG2 ... 222 C6
Rossett Cres HG2 ... 222 D6
Rossett Dr HG2 ... 222 C6
Rossett Garth HG2 ... 222 C6
Rossett Gdns HG2 ... 222 C6
Rossett Green La HG2 ... 222 C5
Rossett Holt Ave HG2 ... 222 C7
Rossett Holt Cl HG2 ... 222 C8
Rossett Holt Dr HG2 ... 222 C7
Rossett Holt Gr HG2 ... 222 C7
Rossett Holt View HG2 ... 222 C7
Rossett Park Rd HG2 ... 222 D6
Rossett Sch HG2 ... 222 B6
Rossett Way HG2 ... 222 C7
Rossiter Dr WF11 ... 201 E2
Rosslyn St 1 YO30 ... 228 A6
Rossway DL1 ... 3 F8
Rostle Top Rd 10 BB18 ... 172 A1
Rotary Way HG4 ... 214 D6
Roth Hill La YO19 ... 192 E3
Rothbury Cl HG2 ... 220 D2
Rothbury St YO12 ... 212 E5
Rothesay Gr TS7 ... 7 D6
Rothwell Methley CP Inf Sch LS26 ... 200 B5
Rotunda Mus* YO11 ... 213 A5
Rough Rd HG3 ... 161 A2
Roughaw Cl BD23 ... 216 F2
Roughaw Rd BD23 ... 217 A2
Roughley Bank DL7 ... 63 C5
Rougier St YO1 ... 233 A2
Round Hill Link YO30 ... 224 F2
Roundell Rd BB18 ... 171 E2
Roundhill Ave TS17 ... 5 F4
Roundhill Cl 5 DL2 ... 3 E1
Roundhill Jun Sch WF11 ... 201 D3
Roundhill Rd DL2 ... 3 E1
Routh Wlk 5 YO21 ... 208 D7
Rowan Ave
3 Filey YO14 ... 101 A4
Malton YO17 ... 215 D6
York YO32 ... 225 D4
Rowan Cl
Gateforth YO8 ... 197 B1
Scarborough YO12 ... 212 C6
Rowan Ct 8 DL10 ... 41 D5
Rowan Dr 5 TS9 ... 8 A2
Rowan Fields YO12 ... 99 E7
Rowan Garth 22 BD20 ... 187 E7
Rowan Lea HG2 ... 222 B7
Rowan Pl YO32 ... 225 D4
Rowan Sq 6 DL9 ... 209 B1
Rowans The YO7 ... 115 F7
Rowans Way DL7 ... 210 B4
Rowden La HG3 ... 160 F5
Rowedale Cl 15 YO14 ... 126 F8
Rowen Ave 6 YO61 ... 117 D1
Rowland Keld TS14 ... 8 E5
Rowland St 18 BD23 ... 217 A3
Rowlandhall La DN14 ... 199 E1
Rowley Ct 2 YO32 ... 225 F7
Rowley Dr LS29 ... 218 F3
Rowmans The YO30 ... 224 C4
Rowntree Ave YO30 ... 228 C8
Roxburghe Dale WF7 ... 200 C1
Roxby Ave TS14 ... 8 E5
Roxby Gdns
4 Eastfield YO12 ... 99 F7
5 Thornton Dale YO18 ... 96 D5
Roxby La Roxby TS13 ... 11 C7
Staithes TS13 ... 13 J1
Roxby Rd YO18 ... 96 D5
Roxby Terr 6 YO18 ... 96 D5
Royal Albert Dr YO12 ... 212 F8
Royal Ave YO11 ... 212 F4
Royal Chase YO24 ... 230 F8
Royal Cres YO21 ... 208 C7
Royal Crescent La 8 YO11 ... 212 F4
Royal Dragoon Guard Association Regimental Mus* YO1 ... 233 B2
Royal George Dr TS16 ... 5 D5
Royal Hall* HG1 ... 219 D3
Royal Par 8 HG1 ... 219 C2
Royal Pump House Mus* HG2 ... 219 C2
Royd Cl 18 BD20 ... 187 E7
Royd The TS15 ... 5 D2
Royds Ave WF10 ... 201 B4
Royd's Rd YO8 ... 202 F6
Ruby St 3 YO23 ... 228 B1
Rudbeck Cl HG2 ... 220 C1
Rudbeck Cres HG2 ... 220 C1
Rudbeck Dr HG2 ... 220 C1
Rudby Bank TS15 ... 25 D5
Rudby Lea TS15 ... 25 D6
Rudcarr La YO19 ... 167 E1
Rudda Rd YO13 ... 53 F6
Rudding Dower HG3 ... 223 E7
Rudding La
Follifoot HG3 ... 223 C5
North Rigton HG3 ... 222 A1
Ruddings YO19 ... 193 A8
Ruddings Cl 9 YO32 ... 225 C8
Ruddings La
Cowesby YO7 ... 66 C4
Crakehall DL8 ... 62 D4
Ellerton YO42 ... 193 E2
Ruddings Rd YO18 ... 72 B3
Ruddings The YO8 ... 232 A4
Rudgate
Bilton-in-Ainsty with Bickerton YO26 ... 181 B6
Newton Kyme cum Toulston LS24 ... 189 B6
Walton LS23 ... 181 B1
Rudgate Gr YO26 ... 164 A4
Rudgate Pk LS23 ... 181 A2
Rudstone Gr LS25 ... 195 F4
Ruebury La DL6 ... 45 B4
Rues La LS21 ... 176 C8
Ruff La YO61 ... 142 B5
Ruffa La YO18 ... 96 A6
Ruffhams Cl YO19 ... 192 F8
Ruffin La YO17 ... 147 D5
Rufford Cl TS14 ... 8 F5
Rufforth Prim Sch YO23 ... 182 C6
Rumford Way DL8 ... 60 D6
Rumple Croft 4 LS21 ... 176 F1
Runnymede TS7 ... 7 D5
Runs Bank DL8 ... 60 D8
Runswick Ave
Middlesbrough TS5 ... 6 E6
Whitby YO21 ... 208 B6
York YO26 ... 227 B4
Runswick La TS13 ... 11 F7
Rupert Rd LS29 ... 218 A5
Rushmere TS8 ... 7 B5
Rusholme La YO8 ... 205 A5
Rushton Ave 21 BB18 ... 172 A1
Rushwood Cl 6 YO32 ... 166 F5
Ruskin Ave
Middlesbrough TS5 ... 6 D7
6 Skipton BD23 ... 216 D3
Ruskin Cl DL2 ... 22 D7
Ruskin Dr WF10 ... 201 A4
Russell St
Harrogate HG2 ... 222 E7
Skipton BD23 ... 217 A3

Russell St *continued*
York YO23 228 B2
Russet Dr YO31 229 B5
Russet Gr YO12 212 C8
Russett Rd YO17 215 B4
Ruston La YO13 98 D7
Ruswarp Bank YO21 208 B3
Ruswarp C of E Prim Sch YO21 208 B3
Ruswarp La YO21 208 B4
Ruswarp Sta YO22 208 C3
Rutland Cl
Copmanthorpe YO23 230 A3
Harrogate HG1 219 A2
Rutland Dr HG1 219 A2
Rutland Pl 4 YO62 92 F7
Rutland Rd HG1 219 B2
Rutland St 38 YO14 101 B3
Rutmoor Rd YO18 71 E8
Rutson Hospl DL7 210 D5
Ryburn Cl YO30 224 F2
Rycroft Rd 3 YO12 75 E5
Rydal Ave
Middlesbrough TS5 6 E8
York YO31 229 A6
Rydal Cl 2 YO7 89 C4
Rydal Cres 7 YO12 99 F7
Rydal Pl 3 BB8 186 A3
Rydal Rd Darlington DL1 3 E4
Harrogate HG1 220 B3
Ryder Cres 3 YO62 70 B1
Ryder's Wynd 3 DL10 209 C6
Rye Cl Haxby YO32 225 C8
Huttons Ambo YO17 121 C1
Rye Hill Way TS8 7 B4
Ryecroft 7 YO32 167 A6
Ryecroft Ave
10 Norton DN6 206 E2
York YO24 230 C7
Ryecroft Cl YO31 229 C8
Ryecroft Gdns DN14 203 A2
Ryecroft Rd
Glusburn BD20 187 D8
Norton DN6 206 E1
Ryecroft Way 2 BD20 187 E8
Ryedale Cl
Helmsley YO62 92 F7
Norton YO17 215 F1
Pontefract WF6 200 A3
Ulleskelf LS24 190 B2
Ryedale Folk Mus* YO62 70 C5
Ryedale Indoor Bowls Ctr YO17 215 E4
Ryedale Leisure Ctr YO18 95 F7
Ryedale Pk LS29 218 D3
Ryedale Pl WF6 200 A3
Ryedale Sch YO62 93 D7
Ryedale Swimming Pool YO62 93 D4
Ryedale View 2 YO62 70 B1
Ryedale Way YO8 232 C3
Ryefield Cl 12 YO11 99 F7
Ryefield Rd 1 YO11 100 A6
Ryegate 18 YO62 92 F6
Ryehill Cl YO32 225 D5
Ryeland St 9 BD20 187 E8
Ryelands Pk 1 TS13 11 A8
Ryemoor Rd YO32 225 C8
Rylatt Pl YO26 227 B3
Rylstone Dr 1 BB18 171 D1
Rymer Way 4 YO7 211 C3
Ryndle Cres YO12 212 E8
Ryndle Wlk YO12 212 E8
Ryndleside YO12 212 E7
Ryngwoode Dr YO17 215 C6
Ryton Old La YO17 121 F5
Ryton Old Rd YO17 122 A5
Ryton Stile Rd YO17 215 C7

S

Sackville Rd BD20 174 C1
Sackville St
20 Barnoldswick BB18 171 D1
Skipton BD23 217 A3
Sacred Heart Cath Prim Sch LS29 218 D4
Sacred Heart RC Prim Sch DL7 210 D2
Sadberge C of E Sch DL2 4 C8
Sadberge Ct YO10 229 C3
Sadberge Rd DL2 4 C5
Saddle Cl YO17 215 D2
Saddlers Cl
1 Copmanthorpe YO23 230 B3
Huntington YO32 225 F2
Saddlers Croft 8 LS29 218 A4
Saddlers La WF11 201 E5
Saddlers Way YO26 182 A6
Sadler Dr TS7 7 B6
Sadler Forster Way TS17 6 B5
Sadlers Ct YO61 143 A5
Saffron Dr 6 DN14 204 C1
Saffron Mdw 19 HG3 161 B3
Sails Dr YO10 229 B3
St Aelreds Cl YO31 228 F4
St Aelreds RC Prim Sch YO31 229 B5
St Aidans C of E High Sch HG2 219 F1
St Aidan's Rd DL9 209 D1
St Aidans Rd LS26 200 C8
St Alkelda's Rd 1 DL8 60 E2
St Andrew Pl YO1 233 C2
St Andrewgate YO1 233 B2
St Andrew's Ave HG2 220 A3
St Andrew's Cres HG2 220 A3
St Andrews Dr WF7 200 E1
St Andrews Gate HG4 112 D5
St Andrew's Gr 1 HG2 220 B2
St Andrews Gr 2 DL7 210 D2
St Andrew's Par 3 HG2 220 A2
St Andrew's Pl 2 HG2 220 A2
St Andrew's Rd
Castleford WF10 201 B5
4 Harrogate HG2 220 B3
St Andrews Rd YO21 208 B5
St Andrew's St 1 HG2 220 A2
St Andrew's Wlk HG2 220 A2
St Anne's Cres 3 DL10 41 E4
St Annes Gdns DL2 4 C3
St Ann's Ct YO10 228 D2
St Ann's Staith 13 YO21 208 D7
St Anthonys Ave 2 DL7 210 E2
St Athan's Wlk HG2 222 D7
St Aubyn's Pl YO24 228 A2
St Augustines RC Jun & Infants Sch DL3 3 C5
St Augustines RC Prim Sch TS8 7 B5
St Augustines RC Sch YO12 212 C4
St Barnabas Ct 13 YO26 227 F5
St Bedes Ave 4 DL7 210 D2
St Bedes RC Prim Sch DL1 3 D8
St Benedict Rd YO23 233 A1
St Bernadettes RC Prim Sch TS7 7 D6
St Boltophs Cl 4 WF11 202 A2
St Catherines YO30 224 D6
St Catherines Cl YO30 224 C5
St Catherine's Rd HG2 219 F1
St Chads Wharf YO23 231 C8
St Christopher Cl 3 DL7 210 D2
St Christophers Dr 27 LS29 174 F4
St Clares Abbey DL3 3 B5
St Clares RC Prim Sch TS5 6 D6
St Clement's Gr YO23 228 C2
St Clement's Rd HG2 220 A2
St Cuthbert Dr DL7 210 B3
St Cuthbert's Ave 4 DL9 41 A5
St Cuthberts C of E Prim Sch HG3 137 B4
St Cuthbert's Gn DL10 21 D8
St Davids Gr TS17 5 F4
St Davids Rd LS21 176 F1
St Davids Sec Sch TS5 6 E7
St David's View 9 DN14 205 E4
St Denys' Rd YO1 233 C2
St Edmunds Cl 1 DL10 41 C6
St Edwards Cl 2 WF11 201 F4
St Edward's Cl YO24 230 F8
St Edward's RC Prim Sch LS23 188 E8
St Edwin's Cl DL2 2 C6
St Francis Xavier Sch DL10 209 E8
St Gabriels RC Prim Sch TS7 7 D8
St George's Ave HG2 222 D7
St Georges Gr 3 DL7 210 E2
St George's Pl YO24 227 F2
St Georges RC Prim Sch
Eastfield YO11 100 A7
York YO10 228 D2
St George's Rd HG2 222 D7
St George's Wlk HG2 222 D6
St Giles' Cl 1 DL9 41 A5
St Giles Cl YO7 211 C3
St Giles Ct YO31 233 B3
St Giles Rd YO30 224 B5
St Giles Way YO23 230 A2
St Gregory's Cl DL8 62 E4
St Heddas RC Prim Sch YO21 31 A4
St Helena 11 YO51 141 B5
St Helens Cl DL7 64 A7
St Helen's Dr LS25 194 F4
St Helens Dr DL7 64 A7
St Helen's La
Borrowby YO7 65 E4
Reighton YO14 127 C6
St Helen's Rd
Harrogate HG2 223 A8
5 York YO24 230 E8
St Helen's Rise YO19 193 A7
St Helen's Sq
26 Scarborough YO11 213 A6
York YO1 233 B2
St Helen's Way LS29 218 D4
St Hilary Cl DL10 209 B7
St Hilda's Bsns Ctr YO22 208 E6
St Hildas C of E Sch YO62 92 C1
St Hilda's Cres YO17 124 E8
St Hilda's Gdns 4 YO21 208 C7
St Hildas RC Prim Sch YO21 208 D5
St Hilda's Rd HG2 219 F1
St Hildas Rd 5 DL7 210 D2
St Hilda's St YO17 124 D7
St Hilda's Terr YO21 208 D6
St Hilda's Wlk 6 YO62 92 C1
St Ians Croft 32 LS29 174 F4
St Ives Cl 3 WF8 201 B2
St Ives Cres WF10 201 B3
St James C of E Sch LS22 180 C3
St James Cl
Melsonby DL10 20 F7
York YO30 224 E3
St James Ct DN14 205 A1
St James' Dr HG2 222 E8
St James Dr DL7 210 D2
St James Gn 9 YO7 211 C3
St James' Mdw 16 YO51 141 B5
St James Mount YO24 228 A2
St James Pl 5 YO24 227 D1
St James' Rd LS29 218 A3
St James Rd
Northallerton DL7 210 B2
Scarborough YO12 212 E4
St James Terr YO8 232 C5
St James's St 7 LS22 180 C3
St John Fisher RC High Sch HG2 223 A8
St John Mews YO8 232 B7
St John of God Hospl DL10 41 F7
St John St
Harrogate HG1 219 D2
York YO31 233 B3
St John the Baptist RC Aided Prim Sch WF6 200 B1
St Johns Ave 25 LS29 174 F4
St John's Ave
42 Filey YO14 101 B3
Milby YO51 141 B7
Scarborough YO12 212 E5
St Johns C of E Prim Sch DL1 3 E4
St John's Cl
Aberford LS25 188 F1
Bishop Monkton HG3 140 B5
St Johns Cl
Northallerton DL6 210 E2
Sharow HG4 214 F7
St John's Cres
Bishop Monkton HG3 140 A5
Harrogate HG1 219 D5
3 Leeming DL7 63 D4
York YO31 233 C4
St Johns Ct LS24 190 C3
St John's Dr
Harrogate HG1 219 D6
North Rigton LS17 178 B4
St John's Garth LS25 194 F8
St John's Gr HG1 219 C5
St Johns Pk DL11 2 A1
St John's Rd
Bishop Monkton HG3 140 A5
Clifford LS23 188 E7
Harrogate HG1 219 D5
Ilkley LS29 218 E4
2 Leeming DL7 63 D4
Scarborough YO12 212 E5
Scotton HG5 162 A6
9 Stamford Bridge YO41 168 D2
St Johns Rd DL9 209 F1
St Johns Residential Sch for the Deaf LS23 188 E8
St John's St BD20 173 C1
St John's View LS23 188 E8
St John's Way
Bishop Monkton HG3 140 A5
Harrogate HG1 219 D6
St John's Wlk
Harrogate HG1 219 D6
Milby YO51 141 B7
St Joseph's Cl 2 YO12 212 C8
St Josephs RC Prim Sch
Harrogate HG1 219 C5
Loftus TS13 10 D8
Pickering YO18 95 F7
Tadcaster LS24 189 E6
Wetherby LS22 180 C3
St Josephs RC Sch
Barnoldswick BB18 171 D2
Castleford WF10 200 F4
St Joseph's St LS24 189 E6
St Lawrences C of E Prim Sch YO10 228 E3
St Leonards Ave YO8 198 B4
St Leonards Cl 30 LS29 174 F4
St Leonard's Cl
1 Harrogate HG2 220 B1
8 Malton YO17 215 C4
St Leonard's Cres YO12 212 D8
St Leonard's Oval HG2 220 A1
St Leonard's Pl YO30 233 B3
St Leonards Rd TS14 8 E6
St Leonard's Rd HG2 220 A1
St Luke's Cl
6 Boston Spa LS23 188 E7
Harrogate HG1 219 D4
St Lukes Cl DL7 22 C2
St Luke's Cres YO12 212 C6
St Luke's Gr YO30 228 B7
St Lukes Hospl TS4 7 A8
St Luke's Mount HG1 219 D4
St Margaret's Ave LS26 200 B6
St Margaret's Cl 3 HG5 221 A6
St Margarets Cl DL2 4 C3
St Margaret's Garth 2 HG5 221 A6
St Margaret's Gdns 1 HG5 221 A6
St Margaret's Rd
Knaresborough HG5 221 A6
St Margaret's Rd *continued*
Mickletown LS26 200 B6
St Margaret's Terr
6 Ilkley LS29 218 B3
York YO1 228 E4
St Mark's Ave HG2 222 D7
St Mark's Cl 1 YO12 212 C8
St Marks Gr YO30 224 E2
St Martins Ave 2 LS21 176 F1
St Martin's Ave YO11 213 A4
St Martins C of E Prim Sch YO11 213 C1
St Martins Cl 15 DL9 40 E4
St Martin's La YO1 233 A2
St Martin's Pl 10 YO11 213 A4
St Martin's Rd 9 YO11 213 A4
St Martin's Sq 5 YO11 213 A4
St Martins Way 11 TS15 24 E8
St Marygate HG4 214 D5
St Mary's YO30 233 A3
St Mary's App YO8 196 F1
St Mary's Ave
Barnoldswick BB18 171 E2
Harrogate HG2 219 C2
12 Hemingbrough YO8 198 F1
14 Swillington LS26 194 A1
Thirsk YO7 211 C4
St Marys C of E Prim Sch
Askham Richard YO23 182 D3
Longnewton TS21 5 A7
St Marys Cath TS8 7 B5
St Mary's Cl DL10 21 D7
St Marys Cl YO42 193 C5
St Mary's Cl
15 Haxby YO32 166 E5
Ilkley LS29 218 C4
South Cowton DL7 22 E2
Thirsk YO7 211 C4
St Mary's Cres YO22 208 E6
St Mary's Ct
Allerton Bywater LS26 200 D6
York YO24 233 A1
St Mary's Dr YO7 211 C4
St Mary's Gdns BD23 173 B4
St Mary's Gr YO10 229 C4
St Marys Hospl YO12 212 F6
St Marys RC Prim Sch
Knaresborough HG5 221 A7
Richmond DL10 209 E7
Selby YO8 232 B2
St Marys Sixth Form Coll TS4 6 F7
St Mary's St 6 YO11 213 B6
St Mary's Terr YO30 233 A3
St Mary's Way YO7 211 C4
St Mary's Wlk
Harrogate HG2 219 C1
Micklefield LS25 194 F4
Middlesbrough TS5 6 E8
Scarborough YO11 213 A7
Thirsk YO7 211 C4
St Matthew's Cl
20 Leyburn DL8 60 D5
4 Naburn YO19 191 D8
St Maurice's Rd YO31 233 C3
St Michael St 6 YO17 215 C4
St Michaels Ct 1 DL7 210 D2
St Michaels Gn 15 WF6 200 A1
St Michael's La YO11 213 C1
St Michael's Mead HG4 138 E6
St Michaels Way 29 LS29 174 F4
St Monica Hospl YO61 143 C8
St Monicas Ct 4 YO61 143 D8
St Nicholas Cl
Copmanthorpe YO23 230 A3
Richmond DL10 209 F8
St Nicholas Cliff 5 YO11 213 A5
St Nicholas Cres YO23 230 A3
St Nicholas Croft YO23 182 E3
St Nicholas Dr DL10 209 F7
St Nicholas Gdns TS15 5 F2
St Nicholas Pl 1 YO10 228 F3
St Nicholas Rd
Copmanthorpe YO23 230 A3
Harrogate HG2 220 B2
Ilkley LS29 218 A5
St Nicholas St
Norton YO17 215 D3
Scarborough YO11 213 A6
St Nicholas Way 22 YO32 166 E5
St Olave's Cl HG4 214 A3
St Olave's Rd YO30 233 A4
St Olave's Sch YO30 233 A3
St Oswalds C of E Prim Sch YO10 231 E7
St Oswalds Cl 14 DL9 40 E4
St Oswald's Cl
Catton YO41 185 F6
Oswaldkirk YO62 93 A1
St Oswalds Cl YO7 89 F3
St Oswalds Ct 6 YO14 101 B3
St Oswalds Rd 18 DL9 40 E4
St Oswald's Rd YO10 231 D8
St Patricks RC Comp Sch TS17 6 C7
St Patricks RC Prim Sch TS17 6 B8
St Patrick's Way HG2 220 B2
St Paulinas RC Prim Sch TS14 8 D6
St Paulinus Dr DL7 210 B3
St Pauls C of E Prim Sch YO24 228 A3
St Paul's Cl DL10 41 B6
St Pauls Cl 4 DL7 210 E2
St Pauls Ct 3 WF8 201 C2
St Paul's Dr DL10 41 B6
St Paul's Gr LS29 218 D4
St Pauls Mews YO24 228 A3
St Paul's Rd TS17 6 B8
St Pauls Rise LS29 174 F4
St Paul's Sq YO24 228 A3
St Paul's Terr
Darlington DL3 3 C7
York YO24 228 A4
St Peter St YO17 215 D3
St Peters C of E Prim Sch HG2 219 D1
St Peter's Cl 2 DL9 41 A5
St Peters Cl YO26 227 A5
St Peter's Cres YO17 215 D3
St Peters Ct 31 LS29 174 F4
St Peter's Ct YO22 208 F4
St Peter's Garth LS14 188 A3
St Peter's Gr YO30 233 A4
St Peters RC Prim Sch YO12 212 D8
St Peter's Rd Drax YO8 204 F5
Whitby YO22 208 F4
St Peters Sch YO30 233 A4
St Peter's Sq 7 HG2 219 C2
St Philip's Gr YO30 228 A8
St Philip's Way 33 LS29 176 C1
St Princes Sq 14 HG1 219 D2
St Richards Rd 3 LS21 176 F1
St Robert's Gdns HG5 221 B4
St Roberts Mews 4 HG1 219 D1
St Roberts RC Prim Sch HG1 219 F4
St Robert's Rd HG5 221 B4
St Ronan's Cl 3 HG2 220 A1
St Ronan's Rd 2 HG2 220 A1
St Sampsons Sq YO1 233 B2
St Saviourgate YO1 233 C2
St Saviour's Pl YO1 233 C2
St Sepulchre St 7 YO11 213 B6
St Simon's Chapel (rems of)* DL8 84 A7
St Stephen's Cl BD23 216 F4
St Stephens Gdns 1 DL7 210 E2
St Stephens RC Prim Sch BD23 216 F4
St Stephen's Rd YO24 227 C2
St Stephen's Sq YO24 227 C1
St Swithin's Wlk YO26 227 E4
St Teresa's RC Prim Sch DL1 3 E4
St Thomas' Pl YO31 233 B4
St Thomas St YO11 213 A6
St Thomas's Cl 2 YO10 229 C4
St Thomas's Way YO26 164 C3
St Trinians Cl DL10 209 F8
St Trinians Dr DL10 209 F8
St Wilfred Dr DL7 210 B3
St Wilfrids Cath High Sch WF7 200 E1
St Wilfrid's Cl 1 YO32 167 B6
St Wilfrid's Cres 9 YO8 197 D1
St Wilfrid's Gdns HG4 214 C6
St Wilfrid's Pl 2 HG4 214 C5
St Wilfrids RC Prim Sch
Ripon HG4 214 B5
York YO31 233 C3
St Wilfrid's Rd
1 Ripon HG4 214 C5
8 Strensall YO32 167 B6
St Williams Coll YO31 233 B3
St Winifred's Ave HG2 219 F1
St Winifred's Cl HG2 219 F1
St Winifred's Rd HG2 219 F1
St Wulstan Cl YO31 228 E7
Salents La YO17 148 C4
Salerno Cl 6 DL9 209 C1
Salisbury Cl 15 WF6 200 A2
Salisbury Dr 9 HG3 161 B3
Salisbury Rd YO26 227 F5
Salisbury St
Scarborough YO12 212 E3
Skipton BD23 216 E5
Sallow Heath 16 HG3 161 B3
Salmon La DL8 87 B6
Salmond Rd 5 YO24 227 B1
Salt Pans Rd YO13 54 D2
Saltburn Rd TS17 6 B8
Salter Rd YO11 99 F6
Salterforth La BB18 171 E1
Salterforth Rd BB18 172 A1
Saltergate Bank YO18 72 F8
Saltergate Cty Jun & Inf Sch HG3 219 A5
Saltergate Dr HG3 161 B3
Saltergill La TS15 24 C8
Saltergill Sch TS15 5 D1
Salters Ave DL1 3 E6
Salters La DL1 3 F4
Salters La N DL1 3 D8
Salters La S DL1 3 E7
Saltersgill Ave TS4 6 F8
Salton La
Nunnington YO62 94 B1
Salton YO62 94 E3
Salutation Rd DL3 3 A4
Sam La YO61 142 D8
San Carlos Cl 1 DL9 40 E3

Sand Hutton C of E Prim Sch
YO41 . . . .**168** B5
Sand Hutton Ct YO41 . .**168** B5
Sand La
Barlby with Osgodby
YO8 . . . .**198** B4
Bubwith YO8 . . . .**199** D5
Hesterton YO17 . . . . . .**123** F7
Huby YO61 . . . .**144** A5
Oldstead YO61 . . . .**91** D3
Sherburn YO17 . . . . . .**124** D7
South Milford LS25 . . . .**195** F2
Stillington YO61 . . . . . .**144** A6
Wistow YO8 . . . .**197** E6
Sandacre Ct YO26 . . . .**227** D5
Sandbeck DL10 . . . . . .**209** C5
Sandbeck Ind Est
LS22 . . . .**180** C4
Sandbeck La LS22 . . . .**180** C4
Sandbeck Way LS22 . . .**180** C4
Sandcroft Cl 4 YO24 . .**230** D8
Sandcroft Rd YO24 . . . .**230** D8
Sanders Way WF6 . . . . .**41** E4
Sanderson Ave WF6 . . .**200** A1
Sanderson Rd DL2 . . . . . .**3** F1
Sandfield La YO7 . . . . . .**88** D4
Sandfield Terr 4 LS24 . .**189** F6
Sandgate 14 YO22 . . . .**208** D7
Sandgate Dr LS25 . . . .**194** D1
Sandgate La LS25 . . . .**194** E2
Sandgate Rise LS25 . . .**194** E1
Sandgate Terr LS25 . . .**194** E1
Sandhill Cl
Harrogate HG1 . . . .**219** F6
Pontefract WF8 . . . .**201** B2
Sandhill Dr HG1 . . . . . .**219** F6
Sandhill La
Bedale DL8 . . .**63** B3
Brayton YO8 . . . .**197** D2
Sutton upon Derwent
YO41 . . . .**185** E2
Sandhill Rise WF8 . . . .**201** B2
Sandhill Way HG1 . . . .**219** F6
Sandholme 2 YO32 . . .**166** F5
Sandholme Cl
14 Easingwold YO61 . .**143** D8
2 Settle BD24 . . . .**131** D2
Sandholmes La YO7 . . . .**89** E3
Sandhurst Gdns 4
YO12 . . . .**212** B7
Sandhutton La YO7 . . . . .**89** B4
Sandiacres 5 YO8 . . . .**197** D1
Sandmartin Ct YO24 . .**230** D8
Sandmoor Cl 5 YO21 . .**208** B5
Sandown Cl Bagby YO7 . .**90** B3
York YO24 . . . .**227** C2
Sandpiper Cl
6 Eastfield YO12 . . . . .**99** E6
1 Filey YO14 . . . .**101** A3
Sandpit La YO62 . . . . . .**69** B1
Sandriggs DL3 . . . .**3** B7
Sandringham Cl YO32 . .**225** C7
Sandringham Rd
Byram cum Sutton WF11 .**201** E4
Lockwood TS12 . . . .**9** F6
2 Ripon HG4 . . . .**214** C3
6 Wetherby LS22 . . . .**180** C3
Sandringham St
4 Scarborough YO12 . .**212** F7
York YO10 . . . .**228** D2
Sandrock Rd 3 WF8 . . .**201** C1
Sands Cl YO14 . . . .**127** D7
Sands La
Hunmanby YO14 . . . . . .**127** A8
Rillington YO17 . . . .**122** F5
Sands Rd YO14 . . . . . .**127** D7
Sandsend Rd
Newholm-cum-Dunsley
YO21 . . . .**13** A3
Whitby YO21 . . . .**208** A8
Sandside YO11 . . . .**213** B6
Sandsprunt La YO13 . . . .**97** C6
Sandstock Rd YO31 . . . .**229** B7
Sandwath La LS24 . . . .**196** A8
Sandway Ave 12 YO8 . .**197** B1
Sandway Cl 11 YO8 . . .**197** B1
Sandway Dr
Camblesforth YO8 . . . . .**204** D4
1 Thorpe Willoughby YO8 **197** B1
Sandwith La YO8 . . . . .**204** B4
Sandwood Pk TS14 . . . . .**8** D5
Sandy Bank
Northallerton DL6 . . . . .**210** F3
Romanby DL6 . . . .**65** A7
Sandy Flatts La TS5 . . . . .**6** F6
Sandy Gap YO32 . . . . .**225** C2
Sandy Gate HG3 . . . . .**159** A6
Sandy La Alne YO61 . . .**143** A4
Dalton YO7 . . . .**116** A8
5 Embsay BD23 . . . . .**217** C2
Harton YO60 . . . .**168** B8
16 Haxby YO32 . . . . . .**166** E5
High & Low Bishopside
HG3 . . . .**137** D3
Humberton YO61 . . . . .**141** D8
North Duffield YO8 . . . . .**198** F8
Ripon HG4 . . . .**214** B2
Scampston YO17 . . . . .**123** B5
Stockton on the Forest
YO32 . . . .**167** E4
Sandy Leas La TS21 . . . . .**5** A8
Sandy Rise YO8 . . . . . .**232** C2
Sandybed Cres YO12 . .**212** C4
Sandybed La
Scarborough YO12 . . . . .**212** C4
Wykeham YO13 . . . .**98** F6
Sandyforth La BD22 . . .**186** E5

Sandyland 29 YO32 . . .**166** E5
Sandyridge YO26 . . . . .**224** A1
Sarah's Croft BD23 . . . .**155** A1
Sargent Ave YO23 . . . .**230** F4
Saunters Way WF6 . . . .**200** A2
Savile Rd
Castleford WF10 . . . . . .**200** E4
Mickletown LS26 . . . . . .**200** B6
Saville Gr YO30 . . . . . .**228** A8
Saville St YO17 . . . . . .**215** C4
Saw Wells La LS24 . . . .**195** F6
Sawley Cl BD23 . . . . . .**217** C7
Sawley Moor La HG4 . . .**138** D6
Sawley St 1 BD23 . . . .**216** D3
Sawmill La YO62 . . . . .**92** F6
Sawyer's Cres BD23 . . .**230** C2
Sawyers Garth 9 LS29 . .**175** A4
Sawyers Wlk 9 YO19 . . .**184** F7
Saxford Way 8 YO32 . .**166** D5
Saxon Cl Shipton YO30 . .**165** F5
6 Thorpe Willoughby YO8 **197** B1
Saxon Dr YO17 . . . . . .**122** F5
Saxon Pl YO31 . . . . . .**228** E7
Saxon Rd
Catterick Garrison DL9 . .**209** E1
Ripon HG4 . . . .**214** D5
Stamford Bridge YO41 . .**168** D2
Whitby YO21 . . . .**208** B7
Saxon Vale YO30 . . . . .**165** F5
Saxonfield 5 . . . .**7** A6
Saxton C of E Prim Sch
LS24 . . . .**195** D7
Saxton Ct LS24 . . . . . .**195** D8
Saxton La LS24 . . . . . .**195** E8
Saxty Way YO7 . . . . . .**211** A1
Scabbate Gate BD23 . .**108** B3
Scackleton Bank
YO62 . . . .**119** C4
Scackleton La 1 YO62 . .**119** C3
Scafell Cl 4 YO30 . . . .**224** E1
Scagglethorpe La
YO17 . . . .**122** C4
Scaife Gdns YO31 . . . .**228** C7
Scaife Shay La YO7 . . .**116** A7
Scaife St YO31 . . . . . .**228** C7
Scalby Ave YO12 . . . . .**212** B8
Scalby Beck Rd 27 YO13 . .**75** D5
Scalby Cty Modern Sch
YO12 . . . .**212** B8
Scalby Mills Rd YO12 . . .**75** F5
Scalby Rd YO12 . . . . . .**212** D5
Scaldhill La YO51 . . . .**141** C7
Scale Hill LS21 . . . . . .**177** D2
Scale The BD23 . . . . . .**157** D3
Scallow Bank La DL8 . . .**59** B6
Scalm La
Hambleton YO8 . . . . . .**196** F2
Selby YO8 . . . .**197** A4
Scampton Cl TS17 . . . . . .**6** A6
Scar Close Nature Reserve*★*
LA6 . . . .**104** D8
Scar Fold 9 BD23 . . . .**134** E2
Scar Hos DL11 . . . .**35** F5
Scar Rd BD23 . . . .**171** E6
Scar St BD23 . . . .**134** E2
Scarah Bank HG3 . . . .**161** B8
Scarah La HG3 . . . . . .**140** A2
Scarbeck Bank DL11 . . . .**19** D7
Scarborough Art Gall*★*
YO11 . . . .**213** A5
Scarborough Castle*★*
YO11 . . . .**213** C7
Scarborough Coll
YO11 . . . .**213** A2
Scarborough Football Club
YO12 . . . .**212** B7
Scarborough General Hospl
YO12 . . . .**212** B6
Scarborough Indoor Pool*★*
YO12 . . . .**212** E8
Scarborough Rd
Gristhorpe YO14 . . . . . .**101** A4
Heslerton YO17 . . . . . .**123** F6
Langtoft YO25 . . . .**151** C7
Norton YO17 . . . .**215** E4
Norton-on-Derwent
YO17 . . . .**122** A3
Seamer YO12 . . . .**99** D6
Stainton Dale YO13 . . . . .**53** F8
Scarborough RUFC
YO12 . . . .**212** A8
Scarborough Sixth Form Coll
YO12 . . . .**212** A8
Scarborough Sports Ctr
YO11 . . . .**213** A2
Scarborough Sta
YO11 . . . .**212** F5
Scarborough Terr
YO30 . . . .**233** B4
Scarcroft Hill YO24 . . . .**228** B2
Scarcroft La YO23 . . . .**233** A1
Scarcroft Prim Sch
YO23 . . . .**233** A1
Scarcroft Rd YO24 . . . .**233** A1
Scardale Cres YO12 . . .**212** E8
Scardale Ct YO8 . . . . .**232** A2
Scarer's La YO26 . . . . .**142** B2
Scargill Rd HG1 . . . . . .**219** B4
Scarhouse La DL11 . . . .**17** E2
Scarlet Balk La YO17 . .**122** C1
Scarth Cl 3 TS12 . . . .**9** F7
Scarth Nick
Preston-under-Scar DL8 . .**59** A6
Whorlton DL6 . . . .**45** D6
Scarthingwell Cres
LS24 . . . .**195** D8
Scarthingwell La LS24 . .**195** E8
Scate Moor La YO26 . . .**163** F3

Scaudercroft 13 YO19 . .**184** F7
Scawling End Rd YO61 . .**91** C3
Scawthorpe Cl WF8 . . .**201** C1
Scawton Ave 1 YO31 . . .**225** E2
Scholes La BD22 . . . . .**187** F1
Scholes Park Ave 3
YO12 . . . .**75** F5
Scholes Park Cliff 1
YO12 . . . .**75** F5
Scholes Park Dr 2 YO12 . .**75** F5
Scholes Park Rd YO12 . . .**75** F5
Scholla La DL6 . . . .**210** F5
Scholla View DL6 . . . . .**210** F5
School Cl Huby YO61 . .**144** A4
Selby YO8 . . . .**232** B3
16 Stamford Bridge YO41 **168** D2
School Croft WF11 . . . .**201** E4
School Fields BB18 . . . .**172** A2
School Garth YO7 . . . . . .**89** C3
School Hill
Bainbridge DL8 . . . .**57** D5
8 Settle BD24 . . . .**131** E2
School House Dr YO12 . .**99** D6
School La
Addingham LS29 . . . . . .**174** F5
Askham Richard YO23 . .**182** D3
Bellerby DL8 . . . .**60** D7
Bishopthorpe YO23 . . . .**231** A4
Burton Fleming YO25 . . .**126** E3
Collingham LS22 . . . . . .**188** A8
Copmanthorpe YO23 . . .**230** A2
Dacre HG3 . . . .**159** F8
Earby BB18 . . . .**172** A1
Easington BB7 . . . .**152** B3
Eppleby DL11 . . . .**1** D4
Great Ayton TS9 . . . .**8** A1
Laneshaw Bridge BB8 . .**186** C3
Lawkland LA2 . . . .**130** D3
Lotherton cum Aberford
LS25 . . . .**194** F8
Malton YO17 . . . .**215** C4
4 Nawton YO62 . . . . . .**93** D7
Newton-le-Willows DL8 . . .**62** B4
Osmotherley DL6 . . . . . .**45** B4
23 Poppleton YO26 . . .**165** F1
South Milford LS25 . . . .**195** F2
8 Spofforth HG3 . . . . .**179** E6
Thornton-le-Beans DL6 . .**65** B5
Walton LS23 . . . .**180** F2
Wray-with-Botton LA2 . .**128** A6
York YO10 . . . .**229** B1
York YO10 . . . .**231** E7
School Rd
Hemingbrough YO8 . . . .**198** F1
Wetherby LS22 . . . .**180** C3
School St
Castleford WF10 . . . . . .**200** F5
2 Earby BB18 . . . .**186** A7
York YO24 . . . .**227** D3
Schoolgate LS15, ...**194** C8
Score Ray La YO26 . . . .**164** A5
Scoreby La YO41 . . . . .**168** B3
Scoresby Terr 2 YO21 . .**208** D5
Scosthrop La BD23 . . . .**154** E6
Scotch Cnr
Middleton Tyas DL10 . . . .**21** B4
Oldstead YO61 . . . .**91** C4
Scotch George La
HG5 . . . .**221** A7
Scotchman La YO60 . . .**168** A8
Scotpit La DL6 . . . .**43** E4
Scots Dike Terr DL10 . .**209** D6
Scots Dyke Cl DL10 . . . .**20** F7
Scott Cl
35 Glusburn BD20 . . . .**187** E7
13 Swillington LS26 . . .**194** A1
Scott Moncrieff Rd
YO32 . . . .**167** B6
Scott Rd YO8 . . . .**232** C6
Scott St YO23 . . . .**228** C2
Scotton Bank DL8 . . . . .**40** D2
Scotton Ct HG5 . . . . . .**162** A6
Scotton Dr HG5 . . . . . .**220** C8
Scotton Gdns 8 DL9 . . . .**40** E3
Scotton Gr
Knaresborough HG5 . . . .**220** C8
Scotton HG5 . . . .**162** A5
Scotton Pk DL9 . . . .**40** E3
Scotton Rd DL9 . . . .**40** E3
Scriftain La LS22 . . . . .**180** C5
Scriven Gr 9 YO32 . . . .**166** F5
Scriven Rd HG5 . . . . . .**221** A7
Scroggs La DL8 . . . .**86** C7
Scrogs La DL8 . . . .**59** B6
Scrope Ave 4 YO31 . . .**228** E5
Scugdale Rd DL6 . . . . . .**45** E8
Scurragh House La
DL10 . . . .**21** C2
Scurragh La DL10 . . . . .**21** B2
Sea App YO14 . . . .**100** F4
Sea Cliff Cres YO11 . . . .**213** B2
Sea Cliff Rd YO11 . . . . .**213** B2
Sea Life Ctr*★* YO12 . . .**75** F5
Sea View YO11 . . . . . .**101** C1
Sea View Cl 5 YO11 . . .**100** B8
Sea View Cres YO11 . . .**100** B8
Sea View Dr 13 YO11 . . .**100** B8
Sea View Gdns 6 YO11 . .**100** B8
Sea View Gr 4 YO11 . . .**100** B8
Seafield Ave 1 YO11 . . .**100** B7
Seafire Cl YO30 . . . . . .**225** A4
Seagram Cres DL10 . . .**209** C8
Seakel La YO23 . . . . . .**182** C2
Seal Bank BD23 . . . .**81** D1
Seamer & Irton CP Sch
YO12 . . . .**99** D6

Seamer Moor Hill
YO12 . . . .**212** B1
Seamer Moor La YO12 . .**212** B1
Seamer Rd
East Ayton YO13 . . . .**99** B1
Eastfield YO12 . . . .**99** F8
Hilton TS8 . . . .**6** C2
Maltby TS8 . . . .**6** B1
Scarborough YO12 . . . . .**212** B3
Seamer St 2 YO12 . . . .**212** E3
Seamer Sta YO11 . . . . . .**99** F6
Seaton Cl YO10 . . . . . .**229** C4
Seaton Cres TS13 . . . . .**13** K2
Seaton Cty Prim Sch
TS13 . . . .**13** K2
Seaton Garth TS13 . . . . .**13** K2
Seave Cl YO26 . . . .**164** D2
Seavegate 4 YO13 . . . . .**99** B8
Seavegate Cl 3 YO13 . . .**99** B8
Seaview Ave 5 YO11 . . . .**75** E5
Seavy Rd DN14 . . . . . .**205** F2
Second Ave
Menwith with Darley
HG3 . . . .**160** A4
9 Pickering YO18 . . . . .**95** F7
Wetherby LS22 . . . .**180** C3
York YO31 . . . .**228** F6
Second Common La
YO8 . . . .**197** C4
Sedber La 5 BD23 . . . .**134** E2
Sedbergh Dr LS29 . . . .**218** B3
Sedbergh Pk LS29 . . . .**218** B3
Sedbusk La DL8 . . . .**56** D6
Sedge Rise LS24 . . . . .**189** D5
Sedgefield Rd TS6 . . . . . .**6** E5
Sedley Cl HG1 . . . .**219** E7
Seed Hill LA6 . . . .**103** D4
Sefton Ave YO31 . . . . .**228** F8
Sefton Dr LS29 . . . . . .**218** B3
Sefton Way TS15 . . . .**5** D2
Seg La YO8 . . . .**204** F3
Seggans Rd YO26 . . . .**142** A1
Segrave Rd 9 YO7 . . . . .**40** E4
Segrave Wlk 10 YO26 . .**227** E4
Selbourne 9 BB18 . . . .**172** B1
Selby Abbey YO8 . . . . .**232** D5
Selby Abbey Prim Sch
YO8 . . . .**232** C5
Selby Coll YO8 . . . .**232** D4
Selby Cres DL3 . . . .**3** A7
Selby High Sch YO8 . . .**232** B4
Selby Rd
Eggborough DN14 . . . . .**202** F1
Fulford YO19 . . . .**231** E6
Garforth LS25 . . . .**194** B3
Ledston LS25 . . . .**195** A2
Riccall YO19 . . . .**198** A8
Swillington LS15 . . . . . .**194** A3
Wistow YO8 . . . .**197** D6
Womersley DN14 . . . . . .**207** A4
Selby Town Football Club
YO8 . . . .**232** B5
Seldon Rd YO26 . . . . . .**227** E5
Self Gdns YO62 . . . .**70** B3
Selside Shaw DL8 . . . .**105** A7
Selstone Cres 7 YO22 . . .**32** A6
Seph Way YO17 . . . . . .**215** A2
Sergeant Bank HG4 . . . .**86** B8
Sessay C of E Prim Sch
YO7 . . . .**116** C5
Sessions House Yd 10
WF8 . . . .**201** B1
Settle C of E Prim Sch
BD24 . . . .**131** E2
Settle High Sch BD24 . .**131** E2
Settle Junc BD24 . . . . .**153** D8
Settle Mid Sch BD24 . . .**131** D3
Settle Rd BD23 . . . . . .**155** A6
Settle Sta BD24 . . . . . .**131** D3
Settle Swimming Pool
BD24 . . . .**131** D3
Settrington C of E Prim Sch
YO17 . . . .**122** D1
Settrington Rd YO12 . . .**212** B5
Seven St YO17 . . . . . .**121** C1
Seven Wells YO17 . . . .**121** A4
Seventh Ave YO31 . . . .**228** F5
Severfield Rd YO7 . . . .**211** D2
Severn Dr
Garforth LS25 . . . .**194** C3
Guisborough TS14 . . . . . .**8** E6
Severn Gn YO26 . . . . . .**227** C8
Severn Way DL1 . . . .**3** D3
Severus Ave YO26 . . . .**227** D4
Severus St YO24 . . . . . .**227** D4
Sewell's Cave*★ LA2 . . .**131** A5
Sewerbridge La WF7 . . .**200** C1
Sexhow La TS9 . . . .**25** F4
Seymour Gr
Eaglescliffe TS16 . . . .**5** D4
York YO31 . . . .**228** F6
Shackleton Cl YO21 . . .**208** C5
Shady La BD20 . . . . . .**173** C2
Shaftesbury Ave
Goole DN14 . . . .**205** F3
Kellingley DN14 . . . . . .**202** C3
Shaker Stile Rd YO18 . . .**96** B7
Shakespeare Ave 2
DN6 . . . .**206** E1
Shakespeare Cl 3 DL10 . .**41** C7
Shakespeare Cres
WF10 . . . .**201** B3
Shallowdale Gr 1 YO10 .**229** C3
Shambles YO1 . . . .**233** B2
Shambles La YO7 . . . . .**114** D5

San - Sho 267

Shambles The 2 YO17 . .**215** B4
Shandon Pk TS8 . . . .**7** B5
Shandy Hall*★ YO61 . . .**117** D8
Shannon Cl 26 LS29 . . .**175** C2
Shannon Lea DL2 . . . .**4** D4
Sharow C of E Prim Sch
HG4 . . . .**214** F7
Sharow La HG4 . . . . . .**214** E6
Sharp Hill La YO8 . . . . .**204** F6
Sharphaw Ave BD23 . . .**217** A2
Sharphaw View BD23 . .**155** D1
Shaw Ave WF6 . . . . . .**200** B1
Shaw Barn La LS22 . . .**180** B3
Shaw Cl WF6 . . . .**200** B1
Shaw Cres YO61 . . . . .**144** A5
Shaw Dr YO62 . . . .**70** B4
Shaw La Farnham HG5 . .**162** C7
Fenwick DN6 . . . .**207** D2
North Rigton HG3 . . . . .**178** B6
Spofforth with Stockeld
HG3 . . . .**179** D7
Shaw Rise WF6 . . . . . .**200** B1
Shawclose La YO62 . . . .**67** E4
Shawcroft Ct DL10 . . . .**209** E8
Shawl Terr 11 DL8 . . . . .**60** D5
Shaws La
Barwick in Elmet & Scholes
LS15 . . . .**194** B7
Hawes DL8 . . . .**56** E4
Shaw's Terr YO24 . . . . .**233** A1
Sheep Rake La YO25 . . .**151** F4
Sheep St 11 BD23 . . . .**216** F4
Sheepcote La HG3 . . . .**159** F5
Sheepdyke La YO14 . . .**127** A8
Sheepfoot Hill YO17 . . .**215** D4
Sheepwalk La
Castleford WF10 . . . . . .**201** B3
Kirby Grindalythe YO17 . .**150** B7
Sheepwash Bank YO7 . . .**66** D5
Sheepwash La DN14 . . .**207** A7
Sheldrake Cl 9 YO11 . . .**101** A4
Sheldrake Rd WF10 . . .**200** E3
Shelley Cl YO11 . . . . . .**100** B6
Shelley Ct HG1 . . . . . .**219** E7
Shelley Dr WF11 . . . . .**201** D2
Shelley Gr YO30 . . . . .**224** F1
Shelley Rd TS4 . . . .**6** F8
Shelton Ave 2 YO13 . . . .**99** B8
Shepherd Ct TS12 . . . . . .**9** E7
Shepherd Gate LS22 . . .**130** F5
Shepherd Hill DL6 . . . . .**45** D8
Shepherdfields La
YO60 . . . .**146** E5
Shepherdies The HG4 . .**113** C8
Shepherds Dr 13 YO11 . .**100** B7
Shepherd's Rd YO62 . . . .**70** B4
Sherbrooke Cl 18 YO62 . .**70** B1
Sherburn C of E Prim Sch
YO17 . . . .**124** D7
Sherburn High Sch
LS25 . . . .**195** F3
Sherburn Rd YO8 . . . . .**232** A8
Sherburn St 1 YO8 . . . .**197** B8
Sherburn in Elmet Sta
LS25 . . . .**196** A4
Sheridan Rd BB8 . . . . .**186** B3
**Sheriff Hutton Castle (rems
of)*★** YO60 . . . .**145** D5
Sheriff Hutton CP Sch
YO60 . . . .**145** C5
Sherriff Hutton House*★
. . . .**145** D4
Sherringham Dr BD24 . .**230** D8
Sherwood Brow BD24 . .**131** D7
Sherwood Cl
Hunton DL8 . . . .**61** E7
18 Norton DN6 . . . . . .**206** E1
Sherwood Dr HG2 . . . .**220** D2
Sherwood Gr
Huntington YO32 . . . . .**225** C1
York YO26 . . . .**227** B6
Sherwood St 5 YO12 . . .**212** F5
Shetland Cl TS5 . . . .**6** E6
Shilton Garth Cl 3
YO32 . . . .**225** F7
Shipton Low Rd YO30 . .**165** E5
Shipton Rd
Clifton YO30 . . . .**227** F8
Rawcliffe YO30 . . . .**224** C2
York YO30 . . . .**228** A7
Shipton St 3 YO30 . . . .**228** B7
Shipton Street Inf Sch
YO30 . . . .**228** B7
Shipyard Rd YO8 . . . . .**232** E5
Shirbutt La YO26 . . . . .**182** C8
Shire Cl 18 YO11 . . . . .**100** B7
Shire Croft 17 YO11 . . .**100** B7
Shire Fold YO11 . . . . . .**100** B7
Shire Garth DL6 . . . .**24** B1
Shire Gr YO17 . . . .**95** D2
Shire Rd YO7 . . . .**211** B4
Shirehorse Ctr*★ YO13 . .**54** C5
Shires Croft BD23 . . . .**217** E8
Shires La BD23 . . . . . .**217** D8
Shirley Ave Ripon HG4 . .**214** B4
York YO26 . . . .**227** C6
Shoebridge Ave BD20 . .**187** F7
Shop Hill YO17 . . . .**33** B4
Shop La Cowling BD22 . .**187** A6
Danby YO21 . . . .**29** B3
Middleton YO18 . . . .**95** D7
Short La
Farndale East YO62 . . . .**48** F4
West Haddlesey YO8 . . .**202** F6
Short Lee La BD23 . . . .**216** F6

Short Rd YO7 .....115 B2
Shortacre La YO42 ....193 C2
Shortbank Cl BD23 ...217 B3
Shortbank Rd BD23 ...217 B3
Shortsill La HG5 .....163 B5
Shotel Cl YO30 .....227 F8
Showfield Cl LS25 ...195 E4
Showfield Ct **17** YO61 ...143 C8
Showfield La YO17 ...215 C6
Shrubberies The YO8 ...198 E2
Shute Rd DL9 ...209 E1
Shutt La DL8 ...56 E6
Shuttleworth St **36**
BB18 ...172 A1
Shuttocks Fold LS25 ...194 D2
Sicklinghall CP Sch
LS22 ...179 D3
Sicklinghall Rd LS22 ...179 F3
Side Gate YO12 ...99 D1
Sidegate La YO30 ...186 F8
Sidgwick Ct **7** BD23 ...217 A3
Siding La YO8 ...198 B5
Sidings La YO61 ...143 B4
Sidings The
Settle BD24 ...131 D2
Skipton BD23 ...216 E3
Sidmouth Sq **9** DL9 ...40 E4
Signals Ct **7** YO12 ...75 F5
Sigston Castle* DL6 ...44 D2
Sike La YO7 ...115 B4
Sikelands La DL11 ...38 F4
Silicar La HG4 ...88 B1
Sills La YO30 ...165 B5
Silly La LA2 ...129 A2
Silsden Rd
Addingham LS29 ...174 D4
Low Bradley BD20 ...173 C4
Silver Garth DL10 ...21 C7
Silver Hill DL7 ...22 C2
Silver Mdws DL10 ...21 D7
Silver St Askrigg DL8 ...57 E5
Barton DL10 ...21 C7
Fairburn WF11 ...201 D6
Hackforth DL8 ...62 B5
4 Knaresborough HG5 ...221 B5
Masham HG4 ...86 C3
Reeth, Fremington & Healaugh
DL11 ...38 B6
3 Riccall YO19 ...198 A8
8 Scarborough YO11 ...213 A6
Thirsk YO7 ...211 C1
Whitby YO21 ...208 D7
Whitley DN14 ...207 A4
York YO1 ...233 B2
Silverdale Cl **5** HG3 ...160 A6
Silverdale Ct YO24 ...230 D7
Silverdale Rd BD24 ...131 E8
Silverfields Rd HG1 ...220 A3
Silverton Rd TS14 ...8 F5
Silverwood Ave **5**
YO14 ...101 A3
Sim Balk La YO24 ...230 E5
Simbach Cl BD23 ...217 B3
Simon Howe YO12 ...124 F6
Simpson Ave **6** YO14 ...126 F8
Simpson Cl BB18 ...171 E5
Simpson Lane Jun & Inf Sch
WF11 ...201 E2
Simpsons La WF11 ...201 E2
Simpson's Yd **3** YO8 ...232 D4
Sinderby La YO7 ...88 B4
Sinks La DL8 ...62 C4
Sinnington Cl TS14 ...8 F6
Sinnington Cliff Rd
YO62 ...95 A8
Sinnington CP Sch
YO62 ...94 F8
Sinnington Rd TS17 ...6 B6
Sir John's La LS25 ...195 E4
Sirocco Ct YO31 ...228 D8
Sissy Bank DL8 ...59 D6
Sitwell Gr YO26 ...227 C5
Sitwell St YO12 ...212 E5
Siward St YO10 ...229 A3
Sixth Ave YO31 ...228 E5
Sked Dale YO17 ...124 E6
Skates La YO61 ...144 B3
Skegmer La YO60 ...145 F4
Skelda Rise LS29 ...218 B3
Skelder Rd YO21 ...31 C5
Skeldergate YO1 ...233 B2
Skelf St LS24 ...190 C1
Skelgate La DL11 ...38 B6
Skellbank HG4 ...214 B4
Skellbank Cl HG4 ...214 B4
Skelldale Cl HG4 ...214 C4
Skelldale View HG4 ...214 C4
Skellfield Terr HG4 ...214 D4
Skellgill La DL8 ...57 C6
Skelton Ct **3** YO30 ...228 A6
Skelton Ellers TS14 ...9 A3
Skelton La
Givendale HG4 ...140 C8
Marske DL11 ...39 B7
Skelton Prim Sch
YO30 ...224 C5
Skelton Rd
Skelton YO51 ...140 E6
Thornaby TS17 ...6 B8
Skelton Windmill*
YO51 ...140 F8
Skerne Park Cty Inf Sch
DL1 ...3 D4

Skerne Park Cty Jun Sch
DL1 ...3 C4
Skeugh Head La DL11 ...35 E6
Skeugh La YO61 ...144 D6
Skewsby Gr YO31 ...225 F1
Skibeden BD23 ...217 E6
Skibeden Ct **4** BD23 ...217 B5
Skiddaw YO24 ...230 C7
Skiddaw Ct TS7 ...7 C6
Skinner La YO1 ...233 B2
Skinner St YO21 ...208 D7
Skiplam Cl **4** YO12 ...212 B5
Skiplam Rd YO62 ...69 D2
Skipper La YO25 ...125 E3
Skipton Castle*
BD23 ...217 A5
Skipton Cres HG1 ...219 D5
Skipton General Hospl
BD23 ...216 F3
Skipton High Sch
BD23 ...216 E5
Skipton Hospl BD23 ...216 E3
Skipton Old Rd BB8 ...186 A3
Skipton Parish Church Sch
BD23 ...217 A3
Skipton Rd
Addingham LS29 ...174 E5
Barnoldswick BB18 ...171 E2
Bradleys Both BD20 ...173 D4
Colne BB8 ...186 A2
Cononley BD20 ...173 C2
Earby BB18 ...172 A3
Embsay with Eastby
BD23 ...217 C2
Farnhill BD20 ...187 E8
Felliscliffe HG3 ...160 E3
Fewston LS21 ...159 D2
Gargrave BD23 ...155 D1
Glusburn BD20 ...187 F8
Harrogate HG3 ...219 A5
Hellifield BD23 ...154 B3
Ilkley LS29 ...218 A4
Silsden BD20 ...174 B1
Skipton BD23 ...217 B6
Skipton RUFC BD23 ...216 D3
Skipton St HG1 ...219 D4
Skipton Sta BD23 ...216 E3
Skipwith Comm Nature
Reserve* YO8 ...198 E8
Skipwith Rd YO19 ...192 B6
Skirt Bank YO7 ...66 C7
Skottowe Cres TS9 ...7 F2
Skottowe Dr TS9 ...7 F2
Skuff Rd BD23 ...157 B8
Skurkhill La YO62 ...92 E7
Skyreholme Bank
BD23 ...157 F7
Skyreholme La BD23 ...157 E7
Slack La HG3 ...160 B4
Slackgap La CA17 ...14 A8
Sladeburn Dr **2** DL6 ...210 E3
Slaidburn La LA2 ...129 B4
Slate Hill YO21 ...29 D4
Slates La LS29 ...218 B7
Slayde The TS15 ...5 E2
Sled Gates YO22 ...33 B3
Sled La DL10 ...41 F4
Sledgate YO17 ...122 F5
Sledgate Garth YO17 ...122 F5
Sledmere Rd YO25 ...151 B6
Sledmere Sch YO25 ...150 B3
Sleigh La YO60 ...120 A1
Sleightholme Dale Rd
YO62 ...69 D5
Sleightholme Moor Rd
DL11 ...16 D7
Sleights C of E Prim Sch
YO22 ...32 A6
Sleights La
Acklam YO17 ...169 E7
Amotherby YO17 ...121 A6
Birstwith HG3 ...160 C4
Rainton with Newby YO7 ...114 E3
Sleights Rd YO62 ...69 D6
Sleights Sta YO22 ...32 A7
Sleights The LS17 ...178 A7
Slessor Rd
8 Catterick DL10 ...41 E4
York YO24 ...227 B1
Slice La LS24 ...190 A6
Slim Rd DL9 ...209 C2
Slingsby Ave HG5 ...221 A4
Slingsby Bank YO62 ...120 C4
Slingsby Castle (rems of)*
YO62 ...120 B5
Slingsby Cres HG1 ...219 F4
Slingsby Cty Prim Sch
YO62 ...120 B5
Slingsby Garth **19** YO62 ...70 B1
Slingsby Gdns DL7 ...210 E3
Slingsby Gr YO24 ...230 E8
Slip Inn Bank DL11 ...19 E6
Slippery Ford La
BD22 ...187 E3
Smales' St YO1 ...233 B1
Smary La YO19 ...184 D1
Smawthorne Ave
WF10 ...200 E4
Smawthorne Gr WF10 ...200 E4
Smawthorne La WF10 ...200 E4
Smay La YO22 ...33 D3
Smearbottoms La
BD23 ...157 F7
Smeathorns Rd TS12 ...9 F4
Smeatley's La DN6 ...206 C4
Smeaton Gr
5 Swillington LS26 ...194 A1
York YO26 ...227 C5

Smeaton Rd YO41 ...185 D7
Smiddy Hill
19 Pickering YO18 ...95 F6
Walton LS23 ...181 A2
Smiddyfields **5** YO22 ...32 A6
Smirthwaite View **14**
WF6 ...200 A1
Smith Cl YO10 ...231 F8
Smith La HG4 ...114 A4
Smith St **19** BB18 ...171 D1
Smithfield **17** HG4 ...214 B2
Smithfield Rd DL1 ...3 D4
Smithgutter La DL10 ...21 C4
Smithie Cl YO32 ...225 D5
Smith's La Egton YO22 ...30 E3
Flaxton YO60 ...145 D1
Smithson Ave WF10 ...201 B3
Smithson Cl DL10 ...21 D2
Smithson Ct YO17 ...215 D5
Smithson Gr **4** YO51 ...141 B4
Smithson's La HG3 ...177 A8
Smithy La Denton LS29 ...176 A4
Scotton HG5 ...162 A6
Thornton in Lonsdale
LA6 ...103 A4
Ulleskelf LS24 ...190 C2
Smuts Rd DL9 ...209 D1
Smythy La YO25 ...125 D4
Snainton C of E Prim Sch
YO13 ...98 A5
Snainton La YO13 ...97 F7
Snaith Rd
Pollington DN14 ...207 F7
Rawcliffe DN14 ...205 B2
Snaith Sta DN14 ...204 C1
Snaizeholme Rd DL8 ...55 E1
Snape CP Sch DL8 ...87 A7
Snape Castle* DL8 ...87 A7
Snape Hill YO62 ...93 E7
Snargate Hill YO61 ...118 E3
Sneaton La YO22 ...208 B1
Sneaton Thorpe La
YO22 ...32 E5
Sneck Gate La TS8 ...7 B2
Sneck Yate Bank YO7 ...67 A2
Snipe Cl **5** YO14 ...101 A4
Snipe La Hurworth DL2 ...3 C3
Loftus TS13 ...11 A6
Snowden Carr Rd
LS21 ...176 E5
Snowden Cl **4** HG4 ...214 B2
Snowdon Cl YO23 ...182 D3
Snowfield La YO61 ...142 F5
Snydale Ave WF6 ...200 B1
Snydale Cl WF6 ...200 B1
Snydale Ct **10** WF6 ...200 B1
Snydale Gr WF6 ...200 B1
Snydale Rd WF6 ...200 A1
Sober Hall Ave TS17 ...6 A4
Socarrs La YO62 ...119 F7
Sockburn La DL2 ...23 B8
Somerset Cl **6** YO30 ...224 E3
Somerset Rd
2 Harrogate HG2 ...219 C1
York YO31 ...228 D8
Somerset Terr YO11 ...213 A5
Somme Barracks DL9 ...40 F3
Sommerset Pastures
YO61 ...116 F2
Sorrel Gr **29** HG3 ...161 B3
Sorrell Gr TS14 ...8 D6
Sough La BD23 ...186 B8
Sour La BD23 ...216 B6
Sourby La LS21 ...176 D7
Soursikes Field Rd
YO51 ...141 D5
South App
Aberford LS25 ...188 F1
Bramham cum Oglethorpe
LS23 ...188 C5
Stutton with Hazlewood
LS24 ...189 A2
South Ave
Castleford WF10 ...200 C4
20 Scalby YO13 ...75 D5
South Back La
Stillington YO61 ...144 C6
Terrington YO60 ...119 E1
Tollerton YO61 ...143 B2
South Baileygate WF8 ...201 C1
South Bank Ave YO23 ...228 B1
South Beech Ave HG2 ...220 C3
South Cleveland Hospl
TS4 ...7 B8
South Cliff Dr YO14 ...101 B1
South Craven Sch
BD20 ...187 E7
South Cres HG4 ...214 C4
South Crescent Ave **54**
YO14 ...101 B3
South Crescent Cl **51**
YO14 ...101 B3
South Crescent Rd
YO14 ...101 B3
South Dowber La YO7 ...211 D4
South Down Rd **3** YO32 ...225 F5
South Dr HG2 ...222 E8
South Duffield Rd
YO8 ...198 C4
South End Bedale DL8 ...63 A3
Burniston YO13 ...75 D7
Osmotherley DL6 ...45 B3
South End Ave **6** DL8 ...63 A3
South End Cl YO13 ...75 D7
South End La DN14 ...207 B4
South Field La YO26 ...181 B6
South Gate **18** YO62 ...92 F6

South Grange Rd HG4 ...214 B2
South Hawksworth St **7**
LS29 ...218 B4
South Ings La LS29 ...218 B4
South Kilvington C of E Prim
Sch YO7 ...211 B4
South La
Bishop Wilton YO42 ...169 F1
Cawood YO8 ...197 B2
Thornton Dale YO18 ...96 D6
South Milford CP Sch
LS25 ...195 F2
South Milford Sta
LS25 ...195 F2
South Moor La
Garriston DL7 ...61 A7
Sowerby DL7 ...89 D3
South Otterington C of E
Prim Sch DL7 ...64 C2
South Par
Hurworth-on-Tees DL2 ...22 C8
Ilkley LS29 ...218 A4
Northallerton DL7 ...210 D3
Norton YO17 ...215 E3
8 Selby YO8 ...232 C5
York YO24 ...233 A1
South Park Ave TS6 ...7 E8
South Park La LS22 ...180 A8
South Park Rd HG1 ...219 E1
South Ridge LS25 ...194 D1
South Ruddings La
YO19 ...192 F7
South Side TS15 ...25 C5
South St
Barmby on the Marsh
DN14 ...205 A7
Burton Fleming YO25 ...126 E2
Scalby YO13 ...75 D5
7 Scarborough YO11 ...213 A4
South Town La TS13 ...10 E8
South Vale DL6 ...210 E2
South View
Burniston YO13 ...75 D7
Castleford WF10 ...201 B5
3 Glusburn BD20 ...173 E1
Healaugh LS24 ...182 A2
Hunton DL8 ...61 E7
19 Leyburn DL8 ...60 D5
Northallerton DL6 ...210 F6
2 Rudby TS15 ...25 D5
South View Terr BD20 ...174 B1
South Wood La **11** BD23 ...134 E3
Southdean **48** YO14 ...101 B3
Southdene DL8 ...6 F6
Southend Ave **1** ...3 C4
Southend Gdns **8** YO21 ...208 C6
Southey St **1** BD23 ...217 A3
Southfield **1** YO17 ...122 D3
Southfield Ave HG4 ...214 B2
Southfield La
6 Hurworth-on-Tees DL2 ...3 E1
Rufforth YO23 ...182 D6
Southfield Cres **2**
YO24 ...230 E8
Southfield La
28 Addingham LS29 ...174 F4
Kellington DN14 ...202 E2
Southfield Rd
28 Addingham LS29 ...174 F4
Burley in Warfedale
LS29 ...176 C1
Littlethorpe HG4 ...214 B2
Southfield Terr
22 Addingham LS29 ...174 F4
7 Skipton BD23 ...216 F3
Southfields Rd YO32 ...167 B7
Southgate
Eastfield YO12 ...99 E6
Pickering YO18 ...95 F7
Ripon HG4 ...214 C4
Southgate Ave HG4 ...214 C4
Southgate Cl **7** HG4 ...214 C4
Southlands
4 Haxby YO32 ...166 E5
1 Helmsley YO62 ...92 F6
16 Hemingbrough YO8 ...198 F1
High & Low Bishopside
HG3 ...137 B4
Southlands Cl
Escrick YO19 ...192 B6
8 South Milford LS25 ...195 F2
Southlands Gr YO12 ...212 B7
Southlands Rd YO23 ...228 B2
Southlea YO17 ...122 F5
Southmoor La WF11 ...202 B1
Southmoor Rd YO19 ...192 F5
Southolme Cl **22** YO51 ...141 B5
Southolme Dr **7** YO30 ...224 F1
Southolme Wlk **23** YO51 ...141 B5
Southway
Harrogate HG2 ...222 C8
Ilkley LS29 ...218 D3
Southwold **7** YO11 ...100 B7
Southwold Cl **5** YO11 ...100 B7
Southwold Rise **6**
YO11 ...100 B7
Southwood TS8 ...7 A5
Sovereign Gdns **2** WF6 ...200 A1
Sovereign Pk HG1 ...219 D2
Sowarth Field **21** BD24 ...131 C2
Sowerby Cres TS9 ...26 C7
Sowerby Cty Prim Sch
YO7 ...211 B1
Sowerby Rd Thirsk YO7 ...211 B2
York YO26 ...227 B4
Sowerby Terr YO7 ...211 B2
Sowerby Way TS16 ...5 D5

Sowgate La WF8 ...201 D2
Spa Complex The*
YO11 ...213 B4
Spa La Harrogate HG2 ...220 C3
Middleton YO18 ...95 B6
Spa St Gainford DL2 ...1 C7
Harrogate HG2 ...220 C3
Spa St HG2 ...220 C3
Spa Terr **3** HG2 ...220 C3
Spalding Ave YO30 ...228 B7
Sparrington La HG5 ...144 B5
Sparrow Hall Dr DL1 ...3 E8
Sparrow La TS14 ...8 F5
Spartal La LS25 ...200 E4
Spaunton Bank YO62 ...70 E5
Spaunton La YO62 ...70 E4
Spawd Bone La WF11 ...201 E2
Speculation St York ...228 E4
Speedwell Rd WF10 ...200 E4
Speeton Ave TS5 ...6 F7
Spellow Cres HG5 ...140 E4
Spellow Gr HG5 ...140 E4
Spen Brow LA2 ...128 E6
Spen Common La
LS24 ...188 F3
Spence Ct **4** TS9 ...8 A2
Spenceley Pl DL11 ...2 A2
Spencer Cl **5** BD20 ...187 E8
Spencer St
29 Glusburn BD20 ...187 E8
3 York YO23 ...233 B1
Spencer Wlk BD23 ...217 C3
Spencer's Holt HG1 ...219 D7
Spencer's Way HG1 ...219 D7
Speng La YO26 ...182 B5
Spennithorne C of E Prim
Sch DL8 ...60 E4
Spey Bank YO24 ...230 C6
Spiker's Hill La YO13 ...74 F2
Spindle Cl YO24 ...230 C8
Spink La WF8 ...201 B1
Spinksburn La HG3 ...159 F1
Spinner La HG3 ...161 A8
Spinney The
Darlington DL3 ...3 B8
Draughton BD23 ...174 B7
6 Easingwold YO61 ...143 C8
Knaresborough HG5 ...221 C6
3 Scarborough YO12 ...212 B5
Tees-side Airport DL2 ...4 D4
York YO24 ...230 D7
Spinniker Dr **4** YO21 ...208 C5
Spital Bridge YO22 ...208 E5
Spital Field Ct **1** YO17 ...215 C4
Spital Rd YO12 ...99 E3
Spital St YO17 ...215 B4
Spital The TS15 ...5 D3
Spitalcroft HG5 ...221 B4
Spitalfields TS15 ...5 D2
Spitfire Ct DL10 ...41 F6
Spitfire Way LS15 ...196 B4
Spitlands La HG5 ...163 B4
Spittal Hardwick La
WF10 ...201 B3
Spittlerush La DN6 ...206 D2
Spofforth Castle*
HG3 ...179 D6
Spofforth Hill LS22 ...180 B3
Spofforth Rd
Follifoot HG3 ...223 F4
North Deighton LS22 ...180 A3
Spofforth Prim Sch
HG3 ...179 E5
Spofoth La LS22 ...180 A2
Spout La LA2 ...102 B2
Spring Bank YO12 ...212 B3
Spring Bank Cl HG4 ...214 C2
Spring Bank Rd HG4 ...214 C2
Spring Cl Garforth LS25 ...194 C3
12 Sleights YO22 ...32 A6
Spring Ct HG3 ...160 E6
Spring Field Garth
YO17 ...215 D3
Spring Gdns **10** YO11 ...100 B6
Spring Gr
Harrogate HG1 ...219 C3
Laneshaw Bridge BB8 ...186 B3
Spring Hall Garth
YO17 ...215 A3
Spring Hill
Stonegrave YO62 ...93 C2
Welbury DL6 ...24 B1
Whitby YO21 ...208 D6
Spring Hill Sch HG4 ...113 E4
Spring Hill Terr **10**
YO21 ...208 D6
Spring La Birdforth YO7 ...116 F8
Kirkby Overblow HG3 ...179 A2
Long Marston YO26 ...182 A5
Pannal HG3 ...222 C3
Wetherby LS22 ...180 C3
York YO1 ...229 A1
Spring Mount HG1 ...219 C3
Spring Rise BD23 ...174 B3
Spring St
11 Easingwold YO61 ...117 D1
2 Easingwold YO61 ...143 C8
Spring Vale YO21 ...208 C6
Spring Way TS18 ...5 F8
Spring Wlk YO8 ...232 A1
Springbank
Marton cum Grafton
YO51 ...141 E2
Swillington LS25 ...194 B3
Springbank Ave YO19 ...184 E1

Springfield
Bentham LA2 .....129 B8
Clifford LS23 .....188 E7
4 Scarborough YO11 .....213 B6
Skeeby DL10 .....21 A1
Stokesley TS9 .....26 C7
Springfield Ave
4 Earby BB18 .....172 B1
Harrogate HG1 .....219 C3
Ilkley LS29 .....218 C4
11 Pontefract WF8 .....201 C1
Springfield Cl
Barlby with Osgodby YO8 .....198 B5
20 Boroughbridge YO51 .....141 B5
Heworth YO31 .....229 C7
1 Leyburn DL8 .....60 D5
5 Pateley Bridge HG3 .....137 C4
Ripon HG4 .....214 B7
Thirsk YO7 .....211 B4
Springfield Cres
Bentham LA2 .....129 B8
3 Kirk Smeaton WF8 .....206 C3
Springfield Ct
7 Grassington BD23 .....134 E2
Sherburn in Elmet LS25 .....195 F5
Springfield Cty Prim Sch DL1 .....3 E7
Springfield Dr
9 Barlby YO8 .....198 B5
19 Boroughbridge YO51 .....141 B5
Springfield Gdns 1 TS9 .....26 C7
Springfield Gr
21 Boroughbridge YO51 .....141 B5
Kirklevington TS15 .....5 F1
Springfield La
3 Kirkbymoorside YO62 .....70 C1
Tockwith YO26 .....181 C7
Springfield Mews HG1 .....219 C3
Springfield Mount LS29 .....174 F5
Springfield Rd
18 Boroughbridge YO51 .....141 B5
Darlington DL1 .....3 E7
6 Grassington BD23 .....134 E2
4 Poppleton YO26 .....165 F1
Sherburn in Elmet LS25 .....195 F5
Springfield Rise 1 YO26 .....164 A8
Springfield Terr YO17 .....124 D7
Springfield Way
4 Pateley Bridge HG3 .....137 C4
York YO31 .....229 B7
Springfields
18 Knottingley WF11 .....202 A2
5 Skipton BD23 .....217 B4
Springfields Ave 17 WF11 .....202 A2
Springhead Specl Sch YO12 .....212 E2
Springhill Cl YO12 .....212 E4
Springhill Ct 7 LS24 .....189 E6
Springhill La YO12 .....212 D3
Springhill Rd YO12 .....212 E4
Springmead Dr LS25 .....194 C3
Springmount 3 BB18 .....172 B1
Springs La
Ellerton-on-Swale DL10 .....41 F4
Ilkley LS29 .....218 C4
Walton LS23 .....180 F3
Whashton DL11 .....20 B4
Springs Leisure Ctr TS17 .....6 B8
Springs The 4 DL8 .....60 E2
Springwater Sch HG2 .....220 D4
Springwell Ave 11 LS26 .....194 A1
Springwell Cl 8 BD22 .....187 B6
Springwell Gdns 3 DL7 .....210 D4
Springwell La DL7 .....210 B4
Springwell Rd 10 LS26 .....194 A1
Springwell Terr E 1 DL7 .....210 D4
Springwell Terr W 2 DL7 .....210 D4
Springwood YO32 .....225 D7
Spruce Cl YO32 .....225 D2
Spruce Gill Ave 4 DL8 .....63 B3
Spruce Gill Dr 5 DL8 .....63 B3
Spruisty Rd HG1 .....219 C4
Spurn Lightship★ YO23 .....233 B1
Spurriergate YO1 .....233 B2
Square The
Boston Spa LS23 .....188 F8
Castleford WF10 .....201 B4
Ingleton LA6 .....103 D4
Kippax LS25 .....194 D1
Knottingley WF11 .....201 E3
Leeming DL7 .....63 F3
1 Tadcaster LS24 .....189 F6
Stable Rd YO8 .....204 D7
Stabler Cl 15 YO32 .....166 D5
Stablers Wlk
Earswick YO32 .....225 F7
13 Pontefract WF6 .....200 A2
Stables La LS23 .....188 F8
Stackhouse La
Giggleswick BD24 .....131 D4
Lawkland BD24 .....130 F2
Stainburn Ave WF10 .....201 A3
Stainburn La LS21 .....177 E2
Staindale TS14 .....8 D6
Staindale Cl YO30 .....224 E2
Staindrop Dr TS5 .....6 E7
Staindrop Rd DL3 .....3 A6
Stained Glass Ctr★ YO11 .....100 C5
Stainforth Gdns TS17 .....6 B5
Stainforth La BD24 .....131 D5
Stainforth Rd BD24 .....131 E4
Stainsacre La
Hawsker-cum-Stainsacre YO22 .....32 F6
Whitby YO22 .....208 F3
Stainsby Rd TS5 .....6 D8
Stainton Rd TS9 .....6 F1
Stainton Way
Coulby Newham TS8 .....7 A5
Stainton & Thornton TS8 .....6 E5
Staithe St 3 YO8 .....199 D7
Staithes Cl 4 YO26 .....227 B4
Staithes La TS13 .....13 K2
Stake Rd DL8 .....57 C1
Stakesby Com Prim Sch YO21 .....208 B6
Stakesby Rd YO21 .....208 B6
Stakesby Vale YO21 .....208 C6
Stamford Bridge Prim & Inf Sch YO41 .....168 D2
Stamford Bridge Rd YO19 .....184 E7
Stamford Bridge W YO41 .....168 C2
Stamford St E 10 YO26 .....227 F5
Stamford St W 8 YO26 .....227 F5
Stammergate YO7 .....211 C3
Stammergate La LS22 .....180 A1
Stamp Hill Cl 7 LS29 .....174 E4
Stan Valley 2 WF8 .....206 C3
Standard Way DL6 .....210 B6
Standard Way Ind Est DL6 .....210 C6
Standridge Clough Lan BB18 .....172 B1
Standroyd Dr BB8 .....186 A3
Standroyd Rd BB8 .....186 A3
Stang La
Arkengarthdale DL11 .....17 E3
Farnham HG5 .....162 C7
Hope DL11 .....18 A8
Stang Top
Arkengarthdale DL11 .....17 F5
Hope DL11 .....18 A6
Stanghow Rd TS12 .....9 F8
Stangs La BD23 .....157 D6
Stanhope Dr HG2 .....220 B2
Stanhope Gr TS5 .....6 E8
Stanhope Rd N DL3 .....3 C5
Staniland Dr YO8 .....232 A5
Stanley Ave YO32 .....225 D7
Stanley Cl
4 Catterick Garrison DL9 .....40 E3
22 Eastfield YO11 .....100 B6
Stanley Gr Aske DL10 .....20 D1
Richmond DL10 .....209 D8
Stanley St
Castleford WF10 .....200 F4
4 Scarborough YO12 .....213 A7
York YO31 .....233 C4
Stansfield Brow BD20 .....187 A8
Stansfield Dr WF10 .....201 B4
Stansfield Rd WF10 .....201 A4
Stanstead Way TS17 .....6 C7
Stansted Gr DL2 .....4 D4
Stanyforth Cres YO26 .....164 C2
Stape Rd YO18 .....71 F7
Stape Sch YO18 .....71 F7
Stapleton Bank DL2 .....3 A2
Stapleton Cl
3 Bedale DL8 .....63 B2
11 Seamer YO12 .....99 D6
Stapley La DL8 .....87 F4
Star Carr La YO12 .....99 E4
Starbeck Cl 4 YO21 .....208 B5
Starbeck CP Sch HG2 .....220 D4
Starbeck Sta HG2 .....220 C4
Starbeck Swimming Baths HG2 .....220 D3
Starfits La
Fadmoor YO62 .....69 F3
Welburn YO62 .....94 A8
Stark Bank Rd HG4 .....85 C7
Starkey Cres YO31 .....229 A5
Starkey La 5 BD20 .....173 F1
Starmire BD22 .....187 A6
Starra Field La YO26 .....163 F5
Station Ave
20 Filey YO14 .....101 B3
23 Filey YO14 .....101 B3
Harrogate HG1 .....219 E2
Whitby YO21 .....208 B7
York YO32 .....225 D3
York YO1 .....233 A2
Station Bridge HG1 .....219 D2
Station Cl Dacre HG3 .....159 F8
6 East Ayton/West Ayton YO13 .....99 A7
Hambleton YO8 .....196 F2
Sharow HG4 .....214 D7
Station Dr HG4 .....214 D7
Station Fields LS25 .....194 C4
Station La
Barmby on the Marsh DN14 .....205 B7
Burton Leonard HG3 .....139 F3
Cliffe YO8 .....198 E3
Cloughton YO13 .....54 D1
Gristhorpe YO14 .....100 E4
Morton-on-Swale DL7 .....64 A7
Shipton YO30 .....165 E5
Station Par HG1 .....219 D2
Station Rd
Ampleforth YO62 .....92 C1
Beadlam YO62 .....93 D7
Brompton DL6 .....43 F4
Station Rd *continued*
Brompton-on-Swale DL10 .....41 B6
Burley in Warfedale LS29 .....176 C1
Carlton DN14 .....204 C3
Castleford WF10 .....200 E4
Cayton YO11 .....100 B5
Church Fenton LS24 .....196 B7
Clapham LA2 .....130 C7
Copmanthorpe YO23 .....230 B2
Danby YO21 .....29 A7
Fylingdales YO22 .....33 C4
Gainford DL2 .....1 C8
Gilling East YO62 .....118 F8
Glusburn BD20 .....187 E8
Goldsborough HG5 .....163 A3
Great Ayton TS9 .....8 A1
Great Preston WF10 .....200 E6
Hambleton YO8 .....196 F1
Haxby YO32 .....166 F5
Hellifield BD23 .....154 B4
Helmsley YO62 .....92 F6
Hensall DN14 .....203 C1
Heslerton YO17 .....97 D1
High Bentham LA2 .....129 A8
Hinderwell TS13 .....11 F7
Horton in Ribblesdale BD24 .....105 C3
Ilkley LS29 .....218 B4
Kildale YO21 .....27 E8
Kippax LS25 .....200 C8
Kirk Hammerton YO26 .....164 D2
9 Knaresborough HG5 .....221 A6
Long Preston BD23 .....153 F4
Menwith with Darley HG3 .....160 A6
Mickletown LS26 .....200 A6
Middleton St George DL2 .....4 C5
Normanton WF6 .....200 A2
Norton DN6 .....206 F2
Nunnington YO62 .....93 E2
Pannal HG3 .....222 E2
24 Poppleton YO26 .....165 F1
Poppleton YO26 .....182 F8
Rawcliffe DN14 .....205 A1
Riccall YO19 .....198 A8
Richmond DL10 .....209 C7
Scalby YO13 .....75 D5
Scruton DL7 .....63 E6
Selby YO8 .....232 D5
Settle BD24 .....131 C2
Sleights YO22 .....32 A6
Snainton YO13 .....97 F4
South Otterington DL7 .....64 F2
Sowerby YO7 .....211 A2
Stainton Dale YO13 .....54 A8
Stokesley TS9 .....26 C7
Tadcaster LS24 .....189 D6
Thirsk YO7 .....89 D4
Threshfield BD23 .....134 D2
Tollerton YO61 .....143 B3
Wharram YO17 .....148 F4
Whixley YO26 .....164 A3
Wistow YO8 .....197 C6
Womersley DN6 .....206 D5
York YO1 .....233 A2
Station Rise YO1 .....233 A2
Station Sq
4 Strensall YO32 .....167 B7
4 Whitby YO21 .....208 D6
Station Terr
4 Boroughbridge YO51 .....141 B6
Great Preston WF10 .....200 E6
Station View
Cliffe YO8 .....198 D3
2 Harrogate HG1 .....220 C3
Seamer YO12 .....99 E7
8 Skipton BD23 .....216 D3
Station Way YO17 .....215 C3
Staupes Rd HG3 .....160 B4
Staveley CP Sch HG5 .....140 E1
Staxton Carr La YO12 .....99 D3
Staxton Hill YO12 .....125 C8
Staynor Ave YO8 .....232 E3
Stead La LS14 .....188 A3
Stean La HG3 .....110 A4
Steelmoor La YO60 .....146 C2
Steeple Cl 4 YO32 .....166 D5
Steeton La LS24 .....190 D7
Steeton Way LS25 .....195 E2
Steincroft Rd 7 LS25 .....195 F2
Stella Gdns 10 WF8 .....201 C1
Stelling Rd DL11 .....38 E7
Stephen Bank DL11 .....18 H8
Stephen's Wlk YO8 .....232 B1
Stephenson Cl
Knaresborough HG5 .....221 B4
York YO31 .....225 E1
Stephenson Rd 2 DL10 .....41 C7
Stephenson Way YO26 .....227 F5
Stephenson's La YO26 .....164 A2
Stephensons Way LS29 .....218 C4
Stephenwath La YO41 .....169 C5
Stepin Turn YO62 .....49 B1
Stepney Ave YO12 .....212 D4
Stepney Cl YO12 .....212 C5
Stepney Dr YO12 .....212 C5
Stepney Gr YO12 .....212 C5
Stepney Hill YO12 .....212 B3
Stepney Rd YO12 .....212 D4
Stepney Rise YO12 .....212 D5
Sterne Ave YO31 .....229 A5
Sterne Way YO61 .....144 C3
Stewart La YO19 .....191 C4
Stillington Cty Prim Sch YO61 .....144 C7
Stillington Rd
Easingwold YO61 .....143 D8
Huby YO61 .....144 A4
Stinton La
Boroughbridge YO51 .....141 C4
Helperby YO61 .....142 A8
Stirling Gr YO10 .....231 F8
Stirling Rd
Burley in Warfedale LS29 .....176 B1
York YO30 .....224 F3
Stirling Way TS17 .....6 B6
Stirrup Cl Norton YO17 .....215 E2
York YO24 .....230 B8
Stirton La BD23 .....216 C5
Stirtonber BD23 .....216 E5
Stittenham Hill YO60 .....146 A6
Stobarts La TS15 .....5 B1
Stock Stile La HG3 .....160 D5
Stockdale Cl 9 HG5 .....221 B5
Stockdale Ct DL6 .....210 F3
Stockdale La BD24 .....131 F2
Stockdale Wlk HG5 .....221 B5
Stockeld La LS22 .....179 E3
Stockeld Rd LS29 .....218 A4
Stockeld Way LS29 .....218 A5
Stockfield La YO51 .....141 D2
Stockfield Park House★ LS22 .....179 F4
Stockhill Cl 1 YO19 .....184 E7
Stockholm Cl 1 YO10 .....231 D8
Stocking Hill TS9 .....25 E2
Stocking La
Hambleton YO8 .....196 E1
Hillam LS25 .....202 B7
Knottingley WF11 .....202 B2
Lotherton cum Aberford LS25 .....195 A7
Stockinger La LS29 .....174 F4
Stockings La YO62 .....92 F2
Stocks La 1 HG3 .....160 A6
Stockshill YO12 .....99 D6
Stockshott La BD20 .....173 C2
Stockton Football Club TS17 .....6 C8
Stockton La
Heworth YO32 .....226 D1
York YO31 .....229 A7
Stockton on the Forest Cty Prim Sch YO32 .....167 D3
Stockton Rd
Darlington DL1 .....3 F7
Sadberge DL2 .....4 C7
South Kilvington YO7 .....211 B6
Stockwell Ave
Ingleby TS17 .....6 B5
Knaresborough HG5 .....221 B7
Stockwell Cres 5 HG5 .....221 B7
Stockwell Ct 9 HG5 .....221 B6
Stockwell Dr HG5 .....221 B7
Stockwell Gr HG5 .....221 B7
Stockwell La HG5 .....221 B6
Stockwell Pl HG5 .....221 B7
Stockwell Rd HG5 .....221 B6
Stockwell View HG5 .....221 B7
Stockwith La YO8 .....204 A4
Stokelake Rd 5 HG1 .....219 E3
Stokesley CP Sch TS9 .....26 C7
Stokesley Leisure Ctr TS9 .....26 D7
Stokesley Rd
Brompton DL6 .....44 A3
Coulby Newham TS7 .....7 B7
Guisborough TS14 .....8 C6
Middlesbrough TS7 .....7 B6
Northallerton DL6 .....210 E7
Stokesley Sch TS9 .....26 D7
Stone Bramble 22 HG3 .....161 B3
Stone Bridge Dr YO41 .....185 F5
Stone Ct 6 YO13 .....75 D5
Stone Dale YO42 .....170 D3
Stone Garth 3 YO62 .....92 F6
Stone Gate YO26 .....164 A4
Stone Head La BD22 .....186 E6
Stone Man La DL11 .....19 C5
Stone Quarry Rd YO13 .....75 C8
Stone Riggs YO32 .....167 D2
Stone Rings Cl HG2 .....222 E5
Stone Rings La HG2 .....222 E5
Stone Stoup Hill TS9 .....27 C5
Stonebeck Ave HG1 .....219 B4
Stonebeck Gate La YO21 .....29 D4
Stonebow The
Thornton-le-Beans DL6 .....65 B5
York YO1 .....233 C2
Stonebridgegate HG4 .....214 D5
Stonecrop Ave 5 HG3 .....161 B3
Stonecrop Dr 1 HG3 .....161 B3
Stonecross Rd YO21 .....208 A6
Stoned Horse La YO26 .....164 C4
Stonefall Ave HG2 .....220 C3
Stonefall Dr HG2 .....220 B2
Stonefall Mews HG2 .....220 C3
Stonefall Pl 2 HG2 .....220 B2
Stonefield Ave YO61 .....143 C8
Stonefield Garth 9 YO61 .....143 C8
Stonefield La 4 YO61 .....143 C8
Stonegate
Hunmanby YO14 .....126 F8
York YO1 .....233 B2
Stonehaven Way DL1 .....3 F8
Stonelands Ct 2 YO30 .....225 A1
Stoneleigh Gate YO26 .....164 B3
Stonepit Balk YO17 .....149 C5
Stonepit Hill YO17 .....149 C4
Stonepit La
Birdsall YO17 .....148 D6
Gristhorpe YO14 .....100 E5
Stonesdale Cl 3 HG5 .....221 D5
Stonesdale La DL11 .....35 E8
Stonethwaite 5 YO24 .....230 C7
Stoney Bank Rd BB18 .....172 B1
Stoney Haggs Rd YO12 .....99 E7
Stoneyborough Cl YO7 .....211 C4
Stoneybrough La YO7 .....211 C4
Stony Cross YO62 .....93 E7
Stony La
East Harlsey DL6 .....44 F5
8 Scalby YO13 .....75 D5
Stonygate Bank DL11 .....20 A5
Stoop Cl YO32 .....225 C8
Stooperdale Ave DL3 .....3 B7
Stoopes Hill 8 BB18 .....172 B1
Storey Cl 26 YO62 .....92 F6
Storiths La BD23 .....175 A8
Storking La YO41 .....185 F6
Storr La YO13 .....74 E5
Storth Gill La BD24 .....131 A1
Stourton Rd LS29 .....175 C3
Stow Ct YO32 .....225 E3
Strafford Rd 15 DL10 .....41 E4
Straight La
Addingham LS29 .....174 E3
Aldwark YO61 .....142 C3
Burton Leonard HG3 .....140 A3
Holtby YO19 .....184 F8
Middleham DL8 .....60 F2
Straights The DL8 .....58 C4
Strait La
Copt Hewick HG4 .....114 B2
Danby YO21 .....29 C6
Hurworth DL2 .....3 F1
Stainton & Thornton TS8 .....6 D5
Weeton LS17 .....178 B2
Well DL8 .....87 A3
Straits La YO13 .....99 A3
Stranglands La WF11 .....201 C3
Stratford Way YO32 .....225 E3
Strathmore Dr 9 TS15 .....24 E8
Strathmore Rd LS29 .....218 E4
Straw Gate DL2 .....3 A2
Strawberry Ct YO12 .....212 D4
Strawberry Dale HG1 .....219 D3
Strawberry Dale Ave 3 HG1 .....219 D3
Strawberry Dale Sq 1 HG1 .....219 D3
Strawberry Dale Terr 2 HG1 .....219 D3
Strawgate Gr DL2 .....3 A3
Stray Garth YO31 .....228 F7
Stray Rd
Harrogate HG2 .....222 D8
York YO31 .....229 B6
Stray Rein HG2 .....219 E1
Stray The Darlington DL1 .....3 E5
Henderskelfe YO60 .....146 D8
Longnewton TS21 .....5 A7
Stray Wlk HG2 .....222 E8
Straylands Gr YO31 .....228 F8
Street 1 LS23 .....189 A8
Street 2
Thorp Arch LS23 .....181 A1
Walton LS23 .....189 A8
Street 3 LS23 .....181 A1
Street 5 LS23 .....181 A1
Street 6 LS23 .....181 A2
Street 7 LS23 .....181 B1
Street 8 LS23 .....181 B1
Street Head La BD22 .....187 F1
Street La Bewerley HG3 .....137 B4
Bubwith YO8 .....199 F5
Colton LS24 .....190 D7
Glaisdale YO21 .....29 E3
Middleton YO18 .....95 E7
Pickhill with Roxby YO7 .....88 B6
Street The 8 LS29 .....174 E4
Strensall Dr 11 YO12 .....75 F5
Strensall Pk YO32 .....167 A5
Strensall Rd
Earswick YO32 .....226 A7
York YO32 .....225 F6
Stretton Cl WF7 .....200 D1
Strickland Rd 13 YO14 .....127 A8
Strikes La BD20 .....187 F6
Stripe La
Hartwith cum Winsley HG3 .....160 B8
Skelton YO30 .....224 B5
Stripe The 6 TS9 .....26 C7
Stuart Ave DL10 .....209 C8
Stuart Cl
4 Scarborough YO11 .....100 B7
4 Strensall YO32 .....167 C8
Stuart Gr
Eggborough DN14 .....203 A2
1 Pontefract WF6 .....200 A2
9 Thorpe Willoughby YO8 .....197 B1
Stuart Rd
Pontefract WF8 .....201 B1
York YO24 .....227 D1
Stuart St
10 Barnoldswick BB18 .....171 E1
Pontefract WF8 .....201 B1
Stubbing La BD23 .....81 B1
Stubbing Nook La DL8 .....62 B2
Stubbs La
Cridling Stubbs WF11 .....206 A8
Norton DN6 .....206 E2

Stubbs La *continued*
Stainton Dale YO13 ... 53 F5
Stubbs Rd DN6 ... 206 D3
Stubden Gr YO30 ... 224 F2
Stubham Rise LS29 ... 218 A5
Stud Fold Bank HG3 ... 110 B3
Studford Ring★ YO62 ... 92 C2
Studley Cl DL7 ... 210 B2
Studley La HG4 ... 113 C1
Studley Rd
Harrogate HG1 ... 219 D3
Ripon HG4 ... 214 A4
Studley Roger HG4 ... 113 D1
Stumpcross Ct 14 WF8 ... 201 C2
Stumpcross La WF8 ... 201 C2
Stumpcross Way 15
WF8 ... 201 C2
Stumps La HG3 ... 160 A5
Stunstead Rd BB8 ... 186 B2
Sturdee Gr YO31 ... 228 D7
Sturdy House La
Marske DL11 ... 19 E2
Whashton DL11 ... 20 A4
Sturton Grange La
LS25 ... 194 D4
Sturton La LS25 ... 194 D4
Stuteville Cl 4 YO62 ... 70 C1
Stutton Rd LS24 ... 189 D4
Stygate La DN6 ... 206 E1
Sudforth La DN14 ... 202 C3
Suffield Hill YO13 ... 75 A5
Sugar Hill 9 LS29 ... 174 F4
Summer Hill Rd LS26 ... 200 B6
Summerbridge CP Sch
HG3 ... 138 A1
Summerfield Cl 1
WF11 ... 201 F4
Summerfield Dr WF11 ... 201 F4
Summerfield La YO22 ... 33 A7
Summerfield Rd YO24 ... 230 C7
Sun La LS29 ... 176 C1
Sun Lounge Theatre
YO14 ... 101 B3
Sun St Cononley BD20 ... 173 C1
4 Cowling BD22 ... 187 B6
Thornaby TS17 ... 6 A8
Sunderland Rd BD20 ... 173 E3
Sundew Heath 24 HG3 ... 161 B3
Sunmoor Dr BD23 ... 217 A4
Sunningdale LS25 ... 194 F4
Sunningdale Cl 1 YO26 227 B5
Sunningdale Dr TS16 ... 5 E5
Sunningdale Gr 1
YO21 ... 208 B5
Sunningdales WF6 ... 200 B1
Sunny Bank 3 WF11 ... 202 A2
Sunny Bank Rd 6 BD20 187 E7
Sunnybank Rd LS25 ... 195 A3
Sunnycrest Ave DL10 ... 209 D8
Sunnydale 3 YO32 ... 225 D7
Sunnyside Prim Sch TS8 . 7 A6
Sunset Dr LS29 ... 218 D5
Sunstar Gr TS7 ... 7 B6
Sur Gate
Harwood Dale YO13 ... 53 F1
Suffield-cum-Everley
YO13 ... 74 F8
Surrey Way YO30 ... 227 F8
Surtees St Darlington DL3 . 3 C6
York YO30 ... 228 B7
Sussex Cl Bedale DL8 ... 63 A2
York YO10 ... 229 C2
Sussex Rd YO10 ... 229 C2
Sussex St Bedale DL8 ... 63 A2
14 Scarborough YO11 ... 213 A6
Sussex Way 14 YO32 ... 167 A7
Sutcliffe Ct 6 YO21 ... 208 B6
Sutherland Rd YO18 ... 71 C6
Sutherland St YO23 ... 228 B1
Sutor Cl YO23 ... 230 B3
Sutton Ave 7 DL9 ... 41 A5
Sutton Bank YO7 ... 91 A5
Sutton Bridge★ YO41 ... 185 C2
Sutton C of E Prim Sch
YO7 ... 90 E5
Sutton CP Sch BD20 ... 187 E7
Sutton Ct 5 YO7 ... 211 C3
Sutton Dr DL7 ... 210 C2
Sutton Grange Cl HG3 . 219 B4
Sutton in Craven C of E Prim
Sch BD20 ... 187 E7
Sutton La Byram WF11 ... 201 E4
Byram cum Sutton
WF11 ... 202 A4
Ellington High & Low HG4 ... 86 A5
Fearby HG4 ... 85 F4
Steeton with Eastburn
BD20 ... 187 F7
Sutton on Derwent C of E
Prim Sch YO41 ... 185 C2
Sutton Rd YO7 ... 211 E3
Sutton St YO17 ... 215 D3
Sutton Way
Middlesbrough TS4 ... 6 F8
York YO30 ... 228 B8
Sutton-on-the-Forest C of E
Prim Sch YO61 ... 144 C3
Swadford St BD23 ... 216 F4
Swain Ct DL6 ... 210 D5
Swainby Abbey★ DL8 ... 88 B8
Swainby Ellers DL6 ... 25 D1
Swainby La DL8 ... 87 F7
Swainsea Dr 3 YO18 ... 95 F7
Swainsea La YO18 ... 95 F8
Swainstead Raike
BD24 ... 153 B8
Swainston Cl TS5 ... 6 E7
Swale Ave YO24 ... 230 E8
Swale Hall La DL11 ... 38 B5
Swale La Catterick DL10 ... 41 E5
Pickhill with Roxby YO7 ... 88 C7
Swale Pasture La DL10 ... 41 E5
Swale View YO7 ... 115 B6
Swaledale Ave DL3 ... 3 B6
Swaledale Rd 22 DL9 ... 40 E4
Swalegate DL10 ... 209 C8
Swallow Cl TS14 ... 8 D6
Swan Cl YO19 ... 192 A7
Swan Farm Ct YO19 ... 192 A7
Swan Hill Rd YO11 ... 213 A6
Swan La YO7 ... 65 F2
Swan Rd HG1 ... 219 C2
Swan St BD23 ... 173 B4
Swan Syke Dr 8 DN6 ... 206 F2
Swang Rd YO13 ... 75 A6
Swanhills La YO13 ... 98 F3
Swanland Rd YO62 ... 92 F7
Swann St YO23 ... 233 A1
Swarcliffe Rd HG1 ... 220 B4
Swartha La BD20 ... 174 D2
Swarthlands La YO13 ... 75 D7
Sweeming La LS25 ... 196 C5
Sweet Bits La HG5 ... 221 C8
Sweet Briar
18 Harrogate HG3 ... 161 B3
Harrogate HG3 ... 219 A4
Sweetbecks Cl 12 YO11 . 100 A6
Swillington La LS26 ... 194 A2
Swillington Prim Sch
LS26 ... 194 A1
Swinburn Ct 12 HG4 ... 86 C3
Swinburn Rd 11 HG4 ... 86 C3
Swinburne Cl HG1 ... 219 E7
Swinburne Rd TS16 ... 5 E6
Swindale La TS12 ... 9 F5
Swindon La HG3 ... 178 E4
Swinegate YO1 ... 233 B2
Swineherd La YO62 ... 70 C1
Swinneybeck Bank
HG4 ... 85 E5
Swinsty Ct YO30 ... 224 F1
Swinton Ct HG2 ... 222 B8
Swinton La YO17 ... 121 B3
Swire Way DL10 ... 20 F7
Swires La BD20 ... 173 C3
Swordfish Way LS25 ... 196 B4
Sycamore Ave
4 Catton YO7 ... 89 A1
Filey YO14 ... 101 A4
Kippax LS25 ... 194 C1
Knottingley WF11 ... 201 E1
Malton YO17 ... 215 D5
Richmond DL10 ... 209 A8
York YO32 ... 225 D4
Sycamore Cl
Bishop Monkton HG3 ... 140 A5
Clint HG3 ... 160 F8
1 Haxby YO32 ... 225 D7
3 Hurworth-on-Tees DL2 ... 3 E1
Selby YO8 ... 232 A4
Skelton YO30 ... 224 C5
Slingsby YO62 ... 120 B5
Spennithorne DL8 ... 60 F4
Sycamore Ct
2 Catterick DL10 ... 41 D5
2 Pontefract WF8 ... 201 C1
Sycamore Dr
11 Addingham LS29 ... 175 A4
9 Bedale DL8 ... 63 A2
Harrogate HG2 ... 220 C3
Norton-le-Clay YO7 ... 115 B1
Sycamore Gr BD20 ... 187 F7
Sycamore La DL7 ... 63 D4
Sycamore Pl YO30 ... 233 A3
Sycamore Rd
Barlby with Osgodby
YO8 ... 198 B5
Ripon HG4 ... 214 B2
Sycamore Terr YO30 ... 233 A3
Sycamore View 17 YO26 165 F1
Sycamore Way 16 BB18 . 171 D1
Sydall's Way 1 DL10 ... 41 E4
Sydney St 5 YO12 ... 212 F7
Sykehead La YO62 ... 93 D6
Sykes Barrel 3 BD24 ... 131 D3
Sykes Gr HG1 ... 219 C5
Sykes La YO61 ... 143 B3

T

Tabard Hamlet 5 DN14 . 202 F2
Tabard Rd 6 DN14 ... 202 F2
Tabards The 7 DN14 ... 202 F2
Tadcaster Albion FC
LS24 ... 189 E6
Tadcaster East CP Sch
LS24 ... 189 F6
Tadcaster Gram Sch
LS24 ... 189 B5
Tadcaster Leisure Ctr
LS24 ... 189 E6
Tadcaster Rd YO24 ... 230 F8
Tadcaster Road Dringhouses
YO23 ... 230 E5
Tadcaster Sports & Leisure
Ctr LS24 ... 189 E6
Talbot St WF6 ... 200 A1
Tameside TS9 ... 26 C8
Tamworth Rd 9 YO30 ... 225 A1
Tanfield Dr 1 LS29 ... 176 C1
Tanfield La HG4 ... 114 A8
Tang Hall La YO31 ... 229 A5
Tang Hall Prim Sch
YO31 ... 228 F5
Tang Rd HG3 ... 160 D4
Tanner Row YO1 ... 233 A2
Tanner's Moat YO1 ... 233 A2
Tannery Ct 10 HG5 ... 221 B5
Tannery La DL7 ... 210 D5
Tanpit La
Easingwold YO61 ... 143 C8
Walden Stubbs DN6 ... 206 E3
Tanshelf Sta WF8 ... 201 A1
Tansy Cl 2 HG3 ... 161 B3
Tansy Rd 3 HG3 ... 161 B3
Tanton Rd TS9 ... 7 B1
Tarbard Ave 14 HG4 ... 113 D2
Tarbert Cres 2 YO24 ... 230 B7
Tarn Moor Cres BD23 ... 216 E6
Tarr Steps TS17 ... 6 A3
Tasmania Sq TS7 ... 7 C6
Tate Cl YO8 ... 197 D6
Tate Rd DL10 ... 209 C8
Tatham Fells Sch LA2 ... 128 F3
Tatton Cl YO30 ... 225 A1
Taylor Gr LS26 ... 200 C6
Taylor Hill YO18 ... 71 F7
Taylor La LS15 ... 194 A7
Taylor St 8 BB18 ... 171 D1
Teal Cl Castleford WF10 . 200 E3
2 Filey YO14 ... 101 A3
Teal Dr YO24 ... 230 C8
Teal La 6 YO18 ... 95 F7
Teal Rd DL1 ... 3 E5
Teasel Gr 31 HG3 ... 161 B3
Tebay Cl TS7 ... 7 D8
Tedder Ave TS17 ... 6 B6
Tedder Prim Sch TS17 ... 6 C6
Tedder Rd YO24 ... 227 B1
Tedworth Cl TS14 ... 8 F5
Tees Bank Ave TS18 ... 5 E6
Tees Grange Ave DL3 ... 3 A5
Tees View Hurworth DL2 ... 3 C1
Hurworth-on-Tees DL2 ... 22 C8
Teesdale Ave DL3 ... 3 A4
Teesdale Rd DL9 ... 40 E4
Teesgate TS17 ... 6 C8
Teeside Tertiary Coll
TS4 ... 7 B8
Teesside High Sch TS16 ... 5 E5
Teesside Ind Est TS17 ... 6 C5
Teesside International
Airport DL2 ... 4 F4
Teesway DL2 ... 4 A1
Telford Cl WF10 ... 200 D4
Telford Terr 1 YO24 ... 228 B2
Templar Cl DN14 ... 202 F1
Templar Gdns LS22 ... 180 C4
Templar Way YO8 ... 232 C2
Temple Ave YO10 ... 229 B4
Temple Bank DL8 ... 59 A3
Temple Garth YO23 ... 230 C1
Temple La
Burton cum Walden DL8 ... 82 D3
Copmanthorpe YO23 ... 230 C1
Temple Manor★ YO8 ... 203 D4
Temple Rd YO23 ... 230 F4
Temple St WF10 ... 200 E4
Templemead YO31 ... 228 E8
Tems Side 3 BD24 ... 131 D2
Tems St 2 BD24 ... 131 D2
Ten Thorn La YO26 ... 227 A4
Tennant Cl DL7 ... 210 B6
Tennant St YO8 ... 232 B6
Tennent Rd YO24 ... 227 B2
Tennis Court La YO61 . 143 A3
Tennyson Ave
1 Campsall DN6 ... 206 E1
Harrogate HG1 ... 219 E7
Scarborough YO12 ... 212 F7
York YO30 ... 228 C7
Tennyson Way 3 WF8 ... 201 B1
Tenter Hill LS23 ... 188 D5
Tentergate Ave 4 HG5 . 221 A7
Tentergate Cl 3 HG5 ... 221 A7
Tentergate Gdns 2
HG5 ... 221 A7
Tentergate La HG5 ... 221 A7
Tentergate Rd 5 HG5 ... 221 A7
Tenters Cl WF11 ... 201 E3
Tern Pk 6 LS22 ... 180 A1
Terrington Bank YO60 . 119 C2
Terrington C of E Prim Sch
YO60 ... 119 E1
Terrington Hall Sch
YO60 ... 119 F1
Terrington South Bank
YO60 ... 119 D1
Terrington View YO60 . 145 C5
Terry Ave YO1 ... 233 B1
Terry St YO23 ... 228 C1
Tetherings La YO13 ... 98 F5
Tewit Well Ave HG2 ... 222 D8
Tewit Well Rd HG2 ... 222 E7
Thackadale La YO17 ... 121 A1
Thackeray Gr TS5 ... 6 E8
Thacking La LA6 ... 103 D4
Thames Ave
Guisborough TS14 ... 8 E6
Thornaby TS17 ... 6 B7
Thanet Rd YO24 ... 227 D1
Thanets Ct 9 BD23 ... 216 F3
Thatch Cl YO8 ... 232 C4
Thatchers Croft YO23 ... 230 C3
Theakston Brewery Visitor
Ctr★ HG4 ... 86 C4
Theakston Hargill DL8 ... 87 E8
Theakston La DL10 ... 209 C5
Theresa Cl 6 YO31 ... 225 F1
Thickrash Brow LA2 ... 129 A7
Thief La Barlow YO8 ... 232 F1
York YO10 ... 228 F3
Thiefgate La HG4 ... 86 E3
Thiefhole La DL7 ... 65 B3
Third Ave
10 Wetherby LS22 ... 180 C3
York YO31 ... 228 F5
Thirkleby Way YO10 ... 229 C4
Thirlmere Cl 3 YO7 ... 89 C4
Thirlmere Dr YO31 ... 229 A6
Thirsk Athletic Club
YO7 ... 211 A3
Thirsk Bank
Angram Grange YO61 ... 117 B8
Thornton-le-Moor DL7 ... 65 B3
Thirsk Bsns Pk YO7 ... 211 B2
Thirsk CP Sch YO7 ... 211 C4
Thirsk Ind Pk YO7 ... 211 D2
Thirsk Mus★ YO7 ... 211 B3
Thirsk Race Course★
YO7 ... 211 A3
Thirsk Rd
Eaglescliffe TS15 ... 5 E2
Easingwold YO61 ... 117 B1
Kirkby TS9 ... 26 C6
Romanby DL6 ... 210 F1
Thirsk Sch YO7 ... 211 B1
Thirsk Sta YO7 ... 89 D4
Thirsk Swimming Pool
YO7 ... 211 C2
Thirty Acre La HG5 ... 163 A6
Thirwall Dr TS17 ... 6 A4
Thistle Cl
Northallerton DL7 ... 210 D1
Selby YO8 ... 232 C2
Thistle Hill HG5 ... 221 B3
Thistle Rise TS8 ... 6 F6
Thistlebar Rd YO51 ... 141 D2
Thomas Gill Rd 7 HG3 . 137 F1
Thomas St 6 Selby YO8 . 232 D6
2 York YO10 ... 228 E3
Thomason Foss (Waterfall)★
YO22 ... 31 C1
Thompson Cl
9 Barlby YO8 ... 198 B4
29 Scalby YO12 ... 75 D5
Thompson Dr 2 YO32 ... 167 B8
Thompson Pl 6 YO26 ... 227 E5
Thompson St E DL1 ... 3 D7
Thompson St W DL3 ... 3 C7
Thoresby La DL8 ... 59 B5
Thoresby Rd YO24 ... 227 B1
Thorington Gdns TS17 ... 6 B4
Thorn Nook YO31 ... 228 F8
Thorn Tree Ave 6 YO14 101 B4
Thorn Wath La YO62 ... 48 E4
Thornaby Com Sch TS17 . 6 B7
Thornaby Rd TS17 ... 6 B7
Thornaby Swimming Baths
TS17 ... 6 A8
Thornaby Village Prim Sch
TS17 ... 6 B7
Thornborough Cres 4
DL8 ... 60 D5
Thornbrough Rd DL6 ... 210 E3
Thornburgh Rd 6 YO11 ... 99 F6
Thorncroft 8 YO19 ... 184 F7
Thorndale St BD23 ... 154 B3
Thornden Bldgs YO8 ... 232 D5
Thorndikes La HG5 ... 141 A2
Thorne Cl 13 WF6 ... 200 B1
Thorner C of E Prim Sch
LS14 ... 188 A3
Thorner Gr BD20 ... 174 C2
Thorner La LS23 ... 188 B5
Thorner Rd LS23 ... 188 B4
Thornfield Ave
Dishforth YO7 ... 115 A4
5 York YO31 ... 228 F8
Thornfield Bsns Pk
DL7 ... 210 B6
Thornfield Dr 7 YO31 ... 225 E2
Thornfield Gr TS5 ... 6 E8
Thornfield Rd DL8 ... 87 C3
Thornhill
6 Eastfield YO11 ... 100 A6
Northallerton DL6 ... 210 E3
Thornhill Rd WF10 ... 200 F3
Thornhills 19 YO32 ... 166 F5
Thornlands 9 YO61 ... 117 D1
Thornley Ave DL7 ... 210 D3
Thorns La YO51 ... 140 F4
Thornthwaite Brow
HG3 ... 159 E5
Thornton Cl
15 Easingwold YO61 ... 143 D8
Stainton & Thornton TS8 ... 6 D4
Thornton in Craven CP Sch
BD23 ... 172 A3
Thornton La Dent LA10 ... 78 A4
Marishes YO17 ... 96 B1
Thornton in Lonsdale
LA6 ... 103 C4
Thornton-on-the-Hill
YO61 ... 117 D4
Thornton le Dale C of E Prim
Sch YO18 ... 96 C5
Thornton Moor Cl
YO30 ... 224 F2
Thornton Rd
Coulby Newham TS8 ... 6 D4
Pickering YO18 ... 96 A6
Thornton St
14 Burley in Warfedale
LS29 ... 176 C1
Darlington DL3 ... 3 C5
3 Skipton BD23 ... 216 D3
Thornton Vale TS8 ... 6 E4
Thornton Watlass C of E Prim
Sch HG4 ... 86 D8
Thorntree Gdns DL2 ... 4 C4
Thorntree La DN14 ... 207 C6
Thorntree Rd
Northallerton DL6 ... 210 F6
Thornaby TS17 ... 6 B7
Thornview Rd BD23 ... 154 B3
Thornwood Ave TS17 ... 6 A5
Thornwood Covert 1
YO24 ... 227 C1
Thorny Hill La YO51 ... 141 E2
Thorny La YO42 ... 169 F2
Thorp Arch Pk LS23 ... 180 F1
Thorp Arch Trad Est
LS23 ... 189 A8
Thorpe Bassett La
YO17 ... 122 E1
Thorpe Chase HG4 ... 214 E3
Thorpe Green Bank 1
YO22 ... 33 C3
Thorpe Green La
YO26 ... 164 B7
Thorpe La
Ampleforth YO62 ... 118 B8
Cawood YO8 ... 197 B8
Cracoe BD23 ... 156 C7
Fylingdales YO22 ... 33 C4
Thorpe BD23 ... 156 D8
Thorpe Rd HG4 ... 86 C2
Thorpe St YO23 ... 228 B2
Thorpe Willoughby Cty Prim
Sch YO8 ... 197 B1
Threapland BD23 ... 156 C7
Three Tuns Wynd 7 TS9 . 26 C7
Threshfield Prim Sch
BD23 ... 134 D2
Thrintoft La DL7 ... 64 A7
Thrintoft Moor La DL7 ... 64 A8
Thrope La HG3 ... 110 C4
Throstle Farm Sch
WF11 ... 201 F1
Throstle Nest Cl LS21 ... 176 E1
Throstle Nest Dr HG2 . 222 D6
Throxenby Gr 3 YO12 ... 212 B7
Throxenby La YO12 ... 212 B7
Thruscross La HG3 ... 159 B5
Thrussendale Rd
YO17 ... 169 E8
Thurland Castle★ LA6 . 102 B3
Thwaite Holme La DL8 ... 57 F5
Thwaite La LA2 ... 128 E5
Thwaites Ave LS29 ... 218 C4
Thwaites La
Markington with Wallerthwaite
HG3 ... 139 D5
Nether Silton YO7 ... 66 C7
Thirkleby High & Low with
Osgodby YO7 ... 90 E1
Thweng Way TS14 ... 8 E5
Thwing Rd YO25 ... 126 E2
Tib Garth LS22 ... 180 A2
Tibby Butts 26 YO13 ... 75 D5
Tickergate La DL7 ... 63 A8
Tidkin La TS14 ... 8 E6
Tile Cl BD23 ... 217 B3
Tillman Cl 6 BD24 ... 131 D2
Tilmire Cl 2 YO10 ... 231 F8
Timble Gr HG1 ... 219 B5
Timmys La DL2 ... 3 F1
Tindall St YO12 ... 212 F5
Tinker La YO23 ... 182 D6
Tinkers' La HG3 ... 139 A1
Tinkingfield La LS22 ... 181 A5
Tinkler La YO51 ... 141 C6
Tinkler's La WF11 ... 202 D6
Tinley Garth YO62 ... 70 B1
Tinley Gdns 14 YO62 ... 70 B1
Tintagel Ct WF6 ... 200 A2
Tiplady Cl 18 YO61 ... 143 C8
Tippaty La WF11 ... 202 A4
Tirril Way TS7 ... 7 C5
Tisbury Rd YO26 ... 227 E4
Tithe Barn Fold LS15 ... 194 B8
Tithe Barn Rd 2 WF11 . 202 A2
Tithe Barn Way DN14 ... 202 F3
Tithe Cl YO24 ... 227 B1
Tithe Way HG4 ... 114 F1
Tivoli Pl LS29 ... 218 C3
Toadham La DN14 ... 207 C5
Toby Ct YO32 ... 167 A7
Toc La YO18 ... 97 C5
Tockwith C of E Prim Sch
YO26 ... 181 C7
Tockwith La YO26 ... 181 D6
Tockwith Rd
Long Marston YO26 ... 181 F6
Tockwith LS22 ... 180 F7
Tod Holes La BD23 ... 153 B4
Todd La DL7 ... 63 B8
Todds Ct 8 YO7 ... 211 C3
Todley Hall Rd BD22 ... 187 F3
Todmanhaw La BD23 ... 153 E3
Toft Gn YO1 ... 233 A2
Toft Ings La YO61 ... 143 B8
Tofta Rd YO13 ... 54 A5
Tofting La YO17 ... 148 B5
Tofts Cl TS15 ... 24 B8
Tofts Fort The★ DL11 ... 1 E2
Tofts La Danby YO21 ... 29 B5
Follifoot HG3 ... 223 F4
Humberton YO61 ... 141 F8
Pickering YO18 ... 95 F3
Tholthorpe YO61 ... 142 D6
Welbury DL6 ... 24 B1
Tofts Rd YO18 ... 95 F3
Toll Bar Cl 3 YO8 ... 196 E1

Toll Bar Rd WF10 ...200 C4
Toll Bar Way LS24 ...189 F7
Tollergate YO11 ...213 A7
Tollerton Rd YO30 ...165 B7
Tollesby La TS7 ...7 B6
Tollesby Rd TS5 ...6 F8
Tom Cat La
Bilton-in-Ainsty with Bickerton LS22 ...181 A5
Birdsall YO17 ...148 B4
Tom Dando Cl WF6 ...200 C1
Tom Hall Ct 12 DL8 ...63 A2
Tom La Cowling BD22 ...186 E7
Dunsforths YO26 ...141 F3
Tom Smith's Cross YO62 ...92 B4
Tomahawk Trail WF10 ...200 F3
Tomgill Bank DL8 ...58 E2
Tomlinson Way LS25 ...195 E4
Top Fold WF11 ...201 D6
Top House Farm Mews 2 WF11 ...201 D6
Top La Colne BB8 ...186 B2
Copmanthorpe YO23 ...230 B3
Norwood LS21 ...177 A6
Top Stone Cl LS25 ...201 F6
Topcliff Ct YO8 ...232 B7
Topcliffe C of E Prim Sch YO7 ...115 C7
Topcliffe Rd
Sowerby YO7 ...89 E3
Thirsk YO7 ...211 B1
Thornaby TS17 ...6 C7
Toremill Cl YO32 ...225 D4
Torrance Dr DL1 ...3 F8
Torridon Pl YO24 ...230 B7
Torrs Rd HG1 ...220 A3
Tostig Ave YO26 ...227 C5
Tostig Cl 14 YO41 ...168 D2
Toulston La LS23 ...188 F5
Tout Hill YO60 ...146 E5
Tow Scar Rd LA6 ...103 C5
Tow Top La BD20 ...173 A1
Tower Cres LS24 ...189 D6
Tower Croft 7 YO61 ...117 D1
Tower Rd Darlington DL3 ...3 B6
Ripon HG4 ...214 C6
Tower St
Harrogate HG1 ...219 D1
York YO1 ...233 B1
Tower Street Castle W 4 DL10 ...209 C6
Tower The* HG4 ...139 B6
Tower View DN14 ...204 C2
Towers Paddock WF10 ...201 A4
Town End Ave DN14 ...204 C3
Town End Cl
16 Glusburn BD20 ...187 E7
9 Pickering YO18 ...96 A6
Town End Gdns 3 YO32 ...166 D5
Town Farm Cl 15 YO62 ...70 B1
Town Green Dr TS9 ...26 E5
Town Head Ave 1 BD24 ...131 E2
Town Head Way 14 BD24 ...131 D2
Town Hill LS23 ...188 E5
Town St
Bishop Thornton HG3 ...138 F1
Brandsby-cum-Stearsby YO61 ...118 D3
Malton YO17 ...215 E6
Nidd HG3 ...161 E7
Scampston YO17 ...123 A6
Settrington YO17 ...122 C1
Townend Ct 3 YO26 ...164 A8
Townend Pl 5 BD20 ...187 E7
Townend Rd YO42 ...193 D1
Townend St YO31 ...233 B4
Townhead 2 BD24 ...131 E2
Townhead Fold 12 LS29 ...174 F4
Townhead La LA2 ...130 E8
Towthorpe Moor La YO32 ...167 C5
Towthorpe Rd YO32 ...166 F5
Towton Ave
9 York YO24 ...227 F2
1 York YO24 ...228 A2
Toy Mus* YO12 ...212 F5
Trafalgar Ct 10 HG1 ...219 D1
Trafalgar Rd
11 Harrogate HG1 ...219 D1
Ilkley LS29 ...218 B4
Trafalgar Sq YO12 ...212 F7
Trafalgar St YO23 ...228 B1
Trafalgar St W YO12 ...212 F6
Trafalgar Terr YO12 ...212 F7
Trafford Ct 9 DL1 ...3 F6
Trafford Rd 4 DN6 ...206 E2
Train La 14 YO18 ...95 F7
Tranby Ave YO10 ...229 D4
Tranmire Cl YO7 ...211 D4
Tranmore La DN14 ...203 B3
Trans Wlk LS24 ...190 B1
Tranter Rd TS4 ...6 F8
Trapping Hill HG3 ...110 C4
Trattles Hill YO13 ...54 D2
Travellers Garth YO17 ...121 C1
Trawden CP Sch BB8 ...186 A1
Trawden Rd BB8 ...186 A3
Treesdale Rd 1 HG2 ...219 C1
Trefoil Cl TS14 ...8 D6
Trefoil Dr 4 HG3 ...161 B3
Trefoil Wood TS7 ...7 B7
Trencar La YO61 ...91 A2
Trenchard Ave TS17 ...6 B6
Trenchard Rd YO26 ...227 B6
Trenchard St 8 YO7 ...89 B1
Trenholme La TS15 ...25 B3
Trent Ave
Garforth LS25 ...194 D3
Pontefract WF6 ...200 A2
4 York YO32 ...225 F6
Trent Way YO24 ...230 D7
Trentholme Dr 2 YO24 ...228 A2
Trevine Gdns TS17 ...5 F4
Trevor Gr 8 YO24 ...227 F2
Trimdon Ave TS5 ...6 D6
Trinity Cl 1 YO11 ...212 F3
Trinity Gdns 2 YO11 ...212 F3
Trinity La Ripon HG4 ...214 B5
York YO1 ...233 A2
Trinity Pk HG4 ...214 B6
Trinity Rd Darlington DL3 ...3 C5
Harrogate HG2 ...219 D1
Scarborough YO11 ...212 F3
Trinket La LA2 ...128 B6
Trip Garth LS22 ...180 A1
Trip La Collingham LS22 ...180 A1
Sicklinghall LS22 ...179 F1
Triplins La HG4 ...113 B6
Troon Cl 2 YO26 ...227 B5
Trousdale Hill YO60 ...147 A7
Troutbeck 7 YO24 ...230 C7
Troutbeck Cl 11 YO18 ...95 F6
Troutsdale Ave YO30 ...224 E2
Trumfleet La DN6 ...207 D1
Trundles La 7 WF11 ...202 A2
Truro Cres 8 HG3 ...161 B3
Truro Dr 19 WF6 ...200 A2
Truro Rd 7 HG3 ...161 B3
Truro Wlk 23 WF6 ...200 A2
Trust Fold LS25 ...201 E6
Tudor Cl 10 YO8 ...197 B1
Tudor Rd
Richmond DL10 ...209 D7
York YO24 ...227 C2
Tudor Way YO32 ...167 C8
Tuke Ave YO10 ...229 B4
Tumbledown Cl 5 DL9 ...40 E3
Tune St YO8 ...198 B4
Tunstall Rd
Catterick DL10 ...41 D4
Harrogate HG2 ...220 B3
Turbary Rd LA6 ...103 B7
Turfy Hill DL8 ...56 C4
Turker Cl DL6 ...210 E5
Turker La DL6 ...210 F6
Turkey La YO7 ...114 F8
Turnberry Ave TS16 ...5 E4
Turnberry Dr YO26 ...227 B4
Turnberry Way TS8 ...7 C5
Turner Cl DL9 ...209 C2
Turner Cres 6 LS21 ...177 A1
Turner La 4 LS29 ...174 E4
Turner's Croft YO10 ...229 A1
Turners Sq 9 YO8 ...232 C5
Turnham La YO8 ...198 C2
Turnhead Cres YO8 ...198 B5
Turnhead Ct YO8 ...198 B6
Turnmire Rd 1 YO24 ...230 E8
Turnpike La LS22 ...181 B5
Turnpike Rd LS24 ...189 F7
Turnshaw Rd BD22 ...187 F1
Turpin La LS25 ...196 A2
Turton Rd TS15 ...5 D2
Turver's La WF11 ...202 C2
Tuscany Way WF6 ...200 A3
Tuthill 18 YO11 ...213 B6
Tutin Rd DL7 ...63 C5
Tweed Ave TS17 ...6 B7
Twelve Acre Bank DL8 ...40 E1
Twin Pike Way 14 YO32 ...166 D5
Twine Wlk 7 LA6 ...102 F3
Twizzie Gill View 7 TS13 ...11 A8
Two Laws Rd BB8 ...187 B1
Tyler Cl WF6 ...200 C1
Tyn Garth YO19 ...191 D8
Tyne Cres DL1 ...3 D3
Typhoon Cl DL10 ...41 F6
Tyseley Gr 4 BB18 ...172 A1
Tyson Pl HG2 ...220 B2

U

Uldale Cl 5 HG5 ...221 D5
Uldale Dr TS16 ...5 E4
Ulla Gn LS24 ...190 B1
Ulleskelf Sta LS24 ...190 B2
Ullswater YO24 ...230 D7
Ullswater Ave TS5 ...6 E8
Ullswater Dr LS22 ...180 B3
Ullswater Rise 5 LS22 ...180 B3
Ulnaby La DL2 ...2 C7
Under Cliffe 17 YO18 ...95 F7
Undercliffe Rise LS29 ...218 E2
Undercroft 7 YO19 ...184 F7
Underlands La HG4 ...114 C7
Underwit Rd YO8 ...204 C4
Union La YO8 ...232 C4
Union St 28 Filey YO14 ...101 B3
Harrogate HG1 ...219 D3
2 Knaresborough HG5 ...221 A5
12 Scarborough YO11 ...213 A6
Union Terr
5 Skipton BD23 ...216 F3
York YO31 ...233 B4
Unity Cl HG1 ...219 D5
Unity Gr HG1 ...219 D5
Unity St 1 BB18 ...186 A7
University Coll of Ripon & York St John HG4 ...214 B6
University College of Scarborough YO12 ...213 B1
University of York
Heslington YO10 ...228 F1
York YO10 ...228 E3
York YO10 ...229 B2
York YO30 ...233 A3
University Rd YO10 ...228 F2
Upgang La YO21 ...208 B7
Upgarth Cl 2 TS13 ...12 A7
Uplands BD23 ...217 B5
Uplands Ave 8 YO13 ...99 B8
Uplands Rd DL3 ...3 B5
Uplands The YO12 ...212 A7
Upper Carr La YO18 ...96 A4
Upper Green La TS18 ...6 A7
Upper Hanover St 6 YO26 ...227 F5
Upper Newborough St 1 YO30 ...228 C7
Upper Nidderdale High Sch HG3 ...137 B4
Upper Poppleton Jun Sch YO26 ...165 F1
Upper Price St YO23 ...233 A1
Upper Sackville St 5 BD23 ...217 A3
Upper St Paul's Terr YO24 ...228 A4
Upper Union St BD23 ...216 F3
Upper Wharfdale Mus* BD23 ...134 E2
Upper Wharfedale Sch BD23 ...134 D2
Uppercommon La DN14 ...202 F3
Uppercroft 4 YO32 ...225 C8
Uppergate LA6 ...103 D4
Upsall Dr DL3 ...3 C4
Upsall La
South Kilvington YO7 ...211 C7
Thornbrough YO7 ...90 A8
Upsall YO7 ...66 B1
Upwell Rd DL7 ...210 D4
Ure Bank HG4 ...214 D7
Ure Bank Terr HG4 ...214 C7
Ure Bank Top HG4 ...214 D7
Urlay Nook Rd TS16 ...5 C5
Usher La YO32 ...166 F6

V

Vale Ave WF11 ...201 E2
Vale Cres
Bishop Wilton YO42 ...169 F2
Knottingley WF11 ...201 E2
Vale Crest WF11 ...201 E2
Vale Sch WF11 ...201 E2
Vale The
10 Collingham LS22 ...188 A8
Middlesbrough TS5 ...6 F8
Skelton YO30 ...224 B5
Vale View HG4 ...114 B2
Valley Bridge Par YO11 ...213 A5
Valley Dr
Barnoldswick BB18 ...171 E2
Eaglescliffe TS15 ...5 E3
Great Preston LS26 ...200 C8
Harrogate HG2 ...219 C1
Ilkley LS29 ...218 D4
Valley Gdns TS16 ...5 D4
Valley Gdns* HG2 ...219 C2
Valley Mount HG2 ...219 C2
Valley Rd
Barnoldswick BB18 ...171 E1
3 Darley HG3 ...160 A6
32 Earby BB18 ...172 A1
Harrogate HG2 ...219 C2
Ilkley LS29 ...218 D5
Kippax LS25 ...194 C2
Northallerton DL6 ...210 F3
Scarborough YO12 ...212 E4
Whitby YO21 ...208 A8
Valley Ridge LS25 ...194 C2
Valley St N DL1 ...3 D5
Valley View
3 Ampleforth YO62 ...92 C1
Clint HG3 ...160 F8
Danby YO21 ...29 C6
3 Glusburn BD20 ...187 E8
Wheldrake YO19 ...192 F7
Valuation La 1 YO51 ...141 B5
Vanbrugh Dr YO10 ...229 C3
Vane Ct TS21 ...4 F7
Vane Terr DL3 ...3 C5
Vasey Cl 5 DL8 ...63 B2
Vaughan Rd 10 DN6 ...206 E1
Vavasour Ct YO23 ...230 B2
Venables Rd TS14 ...8 E7
Vernon Cl YO23 ...231 A3
Vernon Gr 4 YO12 ...212 D8
Vernon Pl 3 YO11 ...213 A5
Vernon Rd
Harrogate HG2 ...222 E7
2 Scarborough YO11 ...213 A5
Trawden Forest BB8 ...186 B3
York YO30 ...224 E2
Vesper Dr YO24 ...227 B3
Vesper Wlk YO32 ...225 F6
Vicar Hill La YO7 ...116 D8
Vicarage Cl
2 Bubwith YO8 ...199 D7
12 Hunmanby YO14 ...126 F8
Seamer YO12 ...99 D6
Vicarage Gdns 1 YO10 ...229 C4
Vicarage La
Bishop Wilton YO42 ...169 F2
Bramham LS23 ...188 E5
10 Knaresborough HG5 ...221 A6
Naburn YO19 ...191 E8
Sherburn YO17 ...124 D8
Vicarage Rd
Barnoldswick BB18 ...171 E2
16 Catterick Garrison DL9 ...40 E4
3 Kelbrook & Sough BB18 ...186 A7
Vicars Cl YO23 ...230 B2
Vicars Croft DL6 ...210 E5
Vicar's La YO61 ...144 C6
Vicars Terr WF10 ...200 D6
Vickers Rd 2 DL9 ...40 E4
Victor St YO1 ...233 B1
Victoria Ave
10 Filey YO14 ...101 B3
Harrogate HG1 ...219 D2
Ilkley LS29 ...175 C2
Knaresborough HG5 ...221 B8
Ripon HG4 ...214 D5
Thirsk YO7 ...211 B2
Victoria Cave* BD24 ...131 F4
Victoria Cl
Great Preston WF10 ...200 E6
Ilkley LS29 ...218 A4
Victoria Ct 15 YO26 ...227 F5
Victoria Dr 9 LS29 ...175 C2
Victoria Emb DL1 ...3 C4
Victoria Farm Cl YO23 ...182 C6
Victoria Gdns 17 LS29 ...175 C2
Victoria Gr
5 Ilkley LS29 ...175 C2
Ripon HG4 ...214 C5
Victoria Par 13 YO11 ...212 F5
Victoria Park Ave 2 YO12 ...212 F7
Victoria Park Mount YO12 ...212 E7
Victoria Pk 1 YO12 ...212 F7
Victoria Pl 3 YO21 ...208 D6
Victoria Rd
1 Barnoldswick BB18 ...171 E1
28 Burley in Warfedale LS29 ...176 C1
Cowling BD22 ...187 B6
Darlington DL1 ...3 C5
Earby BB18 ...172 A1
Glusburn BD20 ...187 E7
Harrogate HG2 ...219 C1
11 Ilkley LS29 ...175 C2
1 Malton YO17 ...215 B4
Richmond DL10 ...209 B7
Scarborough YO11 ...212 F5
Thornaby TS17 ...6 B8
Victoria St
24 Earby BB18 ...172 A1
Glusburn BD20 ...187 E7
Great Preston WF10 ...200 D6
Pontefract WF8 ...201 B2
Scarborough YO12 ...212 F6
Settle BD24 ...131 E2
10 Skipton BD23 ...216 F4
1 York YO23 ...233 B1
Victoria Terr
1 Harrogate HG1 ...220 C4
3 Skipton BD23 ...216 F4
Victoria Way 2 YO32 ...228 F8
Victoria Works Ind Est BD20 ...187 F8
Victory Rd LS29 ...218 B4
Viewley Hill Ave TS8 ...6 F5
Viewley Hill Sch TS8 ...6 F5
Viking Cl 20 YO41 ...168 D2
Viking Dr 5 YO19 ...197 F8
Viking Rd
Stamford Bridge YO41 ...168 D2
York YO26 ...227 C5
Vikings Ct 6 DL6 ...43 F3
Villa Cl YO8 ...198 F1
Villa Fields 4 DN14 ...204 C1
Villa Gr 2 YO31 ...228 E6
Village Farm Ct 7 DN14 ...202 D4
Village Fold DL7 ...42 B1
Village Garth 1 YO32 ...166 E5
Village Paddock TS18 ...5 E8
Village Rd TS15 ...24 B8
Village St YO30 ...224 E3
Village The
Boston Spa LS23 ...180 F1
Haxby YO32 ...166 E5
Skelton YO30 ...224 B5
Stockton on the Forest YO32 ...167 D3
Strensall YO32 ...167 B7
Village Wy DL7 ...42 B1
Villiers Ct 6 YO62 ...92 F6
Vimy Rd DL9 ...40 E3
Vincent St 9 YO12 ...213 A7
Vincent Way YO24 ...230 C8
Vine Cl TS14 ...8 F6
Vine Farm Cl YO26 ...164 A4
Vine St Darlington DL3 ...3 B6
Norton YO17 ...215 E4
6 Scarborough YO12 ...212 F6
York YO23 ...228 C2
Vinstra Cl DL10 ...209 D8
Virginia Gdns TS5 ...6 E6
Vivars Way YO8 ...232 D5
Vivers Pl 1 YO62 ...70 C1
Vivis La YO18 ...95 F6
Volta St YO8 ...232 E4
Vulcan Way TS17 ...6 B6
Vyner St Ripon HG4 ...214 D4
York YO31 ...228 C7

W

Waddington St 37 BB18 ...172 A1
Wade House La YO8 ...204 F4
Waggoners Dr 3 YO23 ...230 B3
Wain Cl
15 Eastfield YO11 ...100 B7
South Milford LS25 ...195 E2
Wain Gap LS25 ...195 F2
Waincroft 8 YO32 ...167 A6
Waindyke Way WF6 ...200 B1
Wainers Cl 5 YO23 ...230 B3
Wainfleet Rd HG1 ...219 D6
Waingates La YO51 ...140 F4
Wainman's Cl BD22 ...187 B6
Wain's Gr YO24 ...230 D7
Wain's La YO12 ...99 D2
Wain's Rd YO24 ...230 D8
Wainstones Cl TS9 ...7 F1
Wainstones Dr TS9 ...7 F1
Waite La YO13 ...53 F2
Waithwith Rd DL9 ...209 B1
Waitlands La DL11 ...20 A7
Wakefield Coll WF10 ...200 D3
Wakefield Rd
Garforth LS25 ...194 B3
10 Normanton South WF6 ...200 A1
Swillington LS26 ...194 A2
Wakeman Rd HG4 ...214 C3
Walburn Head DL11 ...39 D3
Walden Stubbs Rd DN6 ...206 E2
Wales St DL3 ...3 C7
Walker Cl BD20 ...187 D7
Walker Dr YO24 ...230 C8
Walker La
Menwith with Darley HG3 ...160 A6
Wheldrake YO19 ...192 F7
Walker St YO21 ...208 D6
Walker's La BD20 ...174 B4
Walkers Row TS14 ...8 F7
Walkerville Ave 22 DL9 ...41 A5
Walkington La YO30 ...165 B8
Wallgates La YO17 ...215 D4
Walmgate YO1 ...233 C2
Walmsley Gdns YO12 ...212 C5
Walney Rd YO31 ...229 A5
Walnut Cl
Saxton with Scarthingwell LS24 ...195 D8
York YO10 ...229 A1
Walnut Gr HG1 ...219 E6
Walpole St YO31 ...228 D7
Walton Ave
Gargrave BD23 ...155 C1
Middlesbrough TS5 ...6 E8
Pannal HG3 ...222 F2
Walton Chase LS23 ...180 F2
Walton Cl
Gargrave BD23 ...172 C8
Huby YO61 ...144 A4
Walton Head La HG3 ...178 F4
Walton Pk HG3 ...222 E2
Walton Pl Pannal HG3 ...222 E2
York YO26 ...227 B3
Walton Rd
Walton LS23 ...181 A2
Wetherby LS22 ...180 E2
Walton St
5 Cowling BD22 ...187 B6
Skipton BD23 ...216 F1
Walworth Ave HG2 ...220 B3
Walworth St N 4 YO26 ...227 F5
Walworth St S 9 YO26 ...227 F5
Wand Hill TS12 ...9 E8
Wand La DN14 ...203 C3
Wandale La YO17 ...95 A2
Wandales Cl YO17 ...215 F3
Wandales Cl YO13 ...75 D8
Wandales Dr YO13 ...75 D8
Wandales La YO60 ...146 B6
Wandales Rd YO13 ...75 D8
Wandell Balk YO61 ...144 B6
Wandels La YO21 ...29 B6
Wandesford Gr DL9 ...209 F1
Wandhill 31 YO32 ...166 E5
Wandhill Gdns TS12 ...9 E8
Wandhill La YO7 ...66 D1
Wandle The YO26 ...227 A2
Wansbeck 3 YO24 ...230 B7
Wapping La YO62 ...94 C7
War Dike La YO13 ...54 B6
War Field La LS22 ...180 F6
Warbler Cl TS17 ...6 A5
Ward Ct YO23 ...233 B1
Ward St BD23 ...217 A4
Wardale Ave TS5 ...6 E6
Wardrop Rd DL9 ...209 C1
Wareham Rd YO11 ...99 F6
Warehill La YO61 ...143 C2
Warlbeck 23 LS29 ...175 C2
Warley Wise La BB8 ...186 D6
Warren Ave WF11 ...201 E2
Warren La
Bramham cum Oglethorpe LS24 ...189 A5
Brearton HG3 ...162 A8
Kirkby Malzeard HG4 ...112 D4
Warren Pl HG1 ...219 D5
Warrenner La DL10 ...20 C6
Warth La LA6 ...103 C3

Warthill C of E Prim Sch
YO19 . . . . .167 F2
Warwick Cl YO60 . . . . . . .145 D5
Warwick Cres HG2 . . . . . .222 E8
Warwick Dr **2** BD18 . . .172 A1
Warwick Pl **2** YO62 . . . . .92 F7
Warwick St YO31 . . . . . . .228 D7
Wasdale Cl **2** YO30 . . . .224 E1
Wash Beck La YO62 . . . . . .93 F6
Washbeck Cl YO12 . . . . . .212 E4
Washbrook Dr DL3 . . . . .3 C8
Washburn Cl **13** YO14 . . .101 A3
Washburn Dr **4** BD20 . .187 E8
Washfold La DL8 . . . . .60 B6
Washford Cl TS17 . . . . .6 A3
Washington Ave DL2 . . . . . . .4 D4
Washington Cl HG4 . . . . . .214 E2
Washington Cl TS16 . . . . . . .5 D5
Wass Bank Rd YO61 . . . . . .91 F2
Wass Way TS16 . . . . .5 D5
Waste La YO62 . . . . .48 F2
Watchet Rd **11** DL9 . . . . .40 E4
Water Bag Bank **8** HG5 .221 A6
Water End YO26 . . . . .227 E5
Water Gap YO17 . . . . .97 B5
Water Garth DN14 . . . . . . .202 F4
Water Hill La YO8 . . . . . . .232 D6
Water Houses BD24 . . . . . .132 E6
Water La
Camblesforth YO8 . . . . . . .204 D5
8 Clifton YO30 . . . . .225 A1
Dalton YO7 . . . . .115 E7
Dunnington YO19 . . . . . . .184 F7
Eggborough DN14 . . . . . . .203 A2
Exelby, Leeming & Newton
DL7 . . . . .63 D4
Hemingbrough YO8 . . . . . .198 F1
Huttons Ambo YO60 . . . . . .147 C6
Kirby Grindalythe YO17 . . .149 B6
Kirby Underdale YO41 . . . .170 A1
Kirk Smeaton WF8 . . . . . . .206 C3
Knaresborough HG5 . . . . . .221 C8
Loftus TS13 . . . . .10 E8
North Stainley with Sleningford
HG4 . . . . .113 C6
7 Pontefract WF8 . . . . . .201 C1
South Stainley with Cayton
HG3 . . . . .139 D2
Thorpe Bassett YO17 . . . . .123 A3
Welburn YO60 . . . . .146 E7
Whitby YO21 . . . . .208 B3
York YO30 . . . . .228 A7
Water Skellgate HG4 . . . . .214 C5
Water Slack La YO26 . . . . .164 C5
Water St Earby BB18 . . . . .172 A1
Gargrave BD23 . . . . .155 D1
Malton YO17 . . . . .215 C4
Skipton BD23 . . . . .216 F4
Water Street CP Sch
BD23 . . . . .216 F4
Water Way Garth
DN14 . . . . .207 F6
Water World York★
YO32 . . . . .226 A2
Waterdale Pk YO31 . . . . . .225 E1
Waterfall Fold **1** WF8 . .201 C2
Waterfalls Wlk LA6 . . . . . .103 D6
Watergate
Mickletown LS26 . . . . .200 A5
7 Pontefract WF8 . . . . . .201 B1
Watergate Rd HG3 . . . . . .139 A4
Waterhouse La **29** YO11 213 A6
Waterings **19** YO32 . . . . .166 D5
Waterloo YO22 . . . . .31 C4
Waterloo Cl WF10 . . . . . . .200 C3
Waterloo Rd BB18 . . . . . . .186 A7
Waterloo St
Harrogate HG1 . . . . .219 E4
2 Richmond DL10 . . . . . .209 C6
Waterman Ct **3** YO24 . . .227 B1
Watermill Croft HG4 . . . . .113 C7
Watermill La HG4 . . . . . . .113 C7
Waters End DL2 . . . . .1 D7
Waters La DL10 . . . . .20 E3
Watershed Mill Bsns Ctr
BD24 . . . . .131 D3
Waterside
3 Boroughbridge YO51 . .141 B6
Knaresborough HG5 . . . . . .221 A5
4 Ripon HG4 . . . . .214 C4
7 Thirsk YO7 . . . . .211 C3
Watersole La LS22 . . . . . . .180 C3
Waterstead Cres 1
YO21 . . . . .208 D5
Waterways Mus & Adventure
Ctr The★ LS14 . . . . . .205 F1
Watery La Airton BD23 . . . .155 A5
Giggleswick BD24 . . . . . . .131 C1
Snape with Thorp DL8 . . . . .86 F7
Wath La Catton YO41 . . .185 C8
Copgrove HG3 . . . . .140 D1
High & Low Bishopside
HG3 . . . . .137 B6
Humberton YO61 . . . . .141 E8
Ulleskelf LS24 . . . . .190 B2
Wath Rd HG3 . . . . .137 B5
Wathcote Cl DL10 . . . . . . .209 F8
Wathcote Pl DL10 . . . . . . .209 F8
Wathgill Camp DL11 . . . . . .39 C3
Watlass La DL8 . . . . .86 E8
Watlass Moor La HG4 . . . . .86 D7
Watling Cl DL11 . . . . .19 E6
Watling Rd WF10 . . . . .201 C1
Watson Cl **9** YO14 . . . . .127 A8

Watson St
4 Normanton South WF6 .200 A1
York YO24 . . . . .228 A3
Watson Terr **2** YO24 . . . .228 A3
Watson's Houses 7
BD23 . . . . .216 F4
Watson's La
Newton Kyme cum Toulston
LS24 . . . . .189 B7
Norwood HG3 . . . . .177 B8
Reighton YO14 . . . . .127 D6
Wattle Syke LS22 . . . . . . .180 B1
Wattlers Cl YO23 . . . . . . .230 C3
Wattlesyke LS22 . . . . .188 C3
Wavell Cty Jun Sch
DL9 . . . . .209 D1
Wavell Rd DL9 . . . . .209 D1
Wavell St YO8 . . . . .232 A6
Waveney Gr YO30 . . . . . . .228 B8
Waver La DL8 . . . . .43 F8
Wavertree Cl DN14 . . . . . .204 C2
Waverley Cres HG2 . . . . . .222 E8
Waverley St YO31 . . . . . . .233 C3
Waydale Cl YO62 . . . . .70 A2
Wayne Tarbard Cl **12**
HG4 . . . . .113 D2
Waynefleet Gr **3** YO10 .229 A3
Wayside Ave HG2 . . . . . . .220 B1
Wayside Cl **4** HG2 . . . . .220 B1
Wayside Cres HG2 . . . . . . .220 B1
Wayside Gr HG2 . . . . .220 A1
Wayside Terr LS17 . . . . . . .178 B2
Wayside The DL2 . . . . .3 E1
Wayside Wlk **5** HG2 . . .220 B1
Weaponness Dr YO11 . . . .213 A5
Weaponness La
Eastfield YO11 . . . . .99 F8
Scarborough YO11 . . . . . . .212 F1
Weaponness Pk YO11 . . . .213 A2
Weaponness Valley Cl 5
YO11 . . . . .212 F3
Weaponness Valley Rd
YO11 . . . . .212 E3
Weardale TS14 . . . . .8 D5
Weardale Rd **20** DL9 . . . .40 E4
Weary Bank TS15 . . . . .25 B8
Weavers Cl YO23 . . . . .230 B3
Weavers Ct **3** TS9 . . . . . .26 C7
Weavers Gn DL7 . . . . .210 C3
Weaverthorpe C of E Prim
Sch YO17 . . . . .124 E2
Webster Pl **1** WF6 . . . . .200 A1
Weddall Cl YO24 . . . . .227 F1
Wedderburn Ave HG2 . . . .220 C2
Wedderburn Cl HG2 . . . . .220 C3
Wedderburn Cty Inf Sch
HG2 . . . . .220 B2
Wedderburn Dr HG2 . . . . .220 B2
Wedderburn Lodge 2
HG2 . . . . .220 B1
Wedderburn Rd HG2 . . . . .220 B2
Weedling Gate LS24 . . . . . .189 D4
Weeland Ct **16** WF11 . . .202 A2
Weeland Rd Beal DN14 . . .202 E3
Hensall DN14 . . . . .203 E2
Weeton La LS17 . . . . .178 D1
Weeton Sta LS17 . . . . .178 B2
Weets View BB18 . . . . .171 E2
Welbeck Ave DL1 . . . . .3 E7
Welborn Cl YO10 . . . . .229 A4
Welborn Ct YO11 . . . . .99 F2
Welbourn Dr **12** YO12 . . .99 D6
Welburn Cty Prim Sch
YO60 . . . . .146 D6
Welburn Gr TS7 . . . . .7 D7
Welburn Hall Sch YO62 . . .94 A7
Welburn La YO60 . . . . .147 A8
Welbury Cl **2** BB18 . . . . .172 B1
Welfare Ave LS15 . . . . . . .194 C8
Welford Rd **36** YO14 . . . .101 B3
Welham Hill YO17 . . . . . . .147 E7
Welham Rd YO17 . . . . .215 D3
Well Bank DL8 . . . . .87 A4
Well Cl
Great & Little Preston
LS25 . . . . .200 C8
3 Whitby YO21 . . . . .208 D7
Well Close Terr 4
YO21 . . . . .208 D7
Well La Kippax LS25 . . . . . .194 D1
Redmire DL8 . . . . .59 C5
Seamer TS9 . . . . .6 F2
Snape with Thorp DL8 . . . . .87 A6
South Milford LS25 . . . . . .195 F2
Yearsley YO61 . . . . .118 C5
Welland Dr LS25 . . . . .194 D3
Welland Rise YO26 . . . . . . .227 D5
Wellbrook Cl TS17 . . . . .6 B7
Wellesley Cl YO30 . . . . . . .225 A2
Wellfield La **13** LS29 . . . .176 C1
Wellhouse St **5** BB18 . . .171 E1
Wellington Ct **3** HG2 . . .219 C2
Wellington Mews 9
HG4 . . . . .214 C5
Wellington Rd
Ilkley LS29 . . . . .218 B4
Richmond DL10 . . . . .209 B7
2 Whitby YO21 . . . . .208 D6
Wellington Row YO1 . . . . .233 A2
Wellington Sq **6** HG2 . . .219 C2
Wellington Terr YO21 . . .208 D7
Wellington Way **4** DL10 . .41 C7
Wellingtonia Dr **5** DN6 . .206 E1

Wells Cl YO8 . . . . .232 A5
Wells La Barton DL10 . . . . .21 D7
Kellington DN14 . . . . .202 E3
Malton YO17 . . . . .215 C4
Wells Prom LS29 . . . . .218 B4
Wells Rd LS29 . . . . .218 B3
Wells Wlk Ilkley LS29 . . . .218 B4
13 Pickering YO18 . . . . . .95 F7
Wellspring Cl TS17 . . . . .6 D7
Welton Ave YO26 . . . . .227 D5
Welwyn Dr YO10 . . . . .231 E8
Wemyss Rd **11** HG4 . . . . .113 D2
Wendel Ave LS15 . . . . .194 B8
Wendy Ave HG4 . . . . .214 B3
Wenham Rd YO24 . . . . . . .230 C8
Wenlock Dr YO19 . . . . .192 B6
Wenlock Terr YO10 . . . . . . .228 D1
Wenning Ave LA2 . . . . .129 A7
Wenning Bank LA2 . . . . . . .130 A6
Wennington Hall Sch
LA2 . . . . .102 B1
Wennington Rd LA2 . . . . . .128 A6
Wennington Sta LA2 . . . . . .128 B8
Wensley Gr HG2 . . . . .222 D7
Wensley Rd
Harrogate HG2 . . . . .222 D7
15 Leyburn DL8 . . . . .60 D5
Northallerton DL7 . . . . .210 B2
Wensleydale Ave **2**
BD23 . . . . .217 B4
Wensleydale Dr YO10 . . . .229 D4
Wensleydale Rd **21** DL9 . .40 E4
Wensleydale Rugby Club
DL8 . . . . .60 C5
Wensleydale Sch DL8 . . . . .60 D5
Wentcliffe Dr BB18 . . . . . . .172 A1
Wentdale **11** WF8 . . . . . .206 C3
Wentworth Ave YO61 . . . . .116 F5
Wentworth Cl
Camblesforth YO8 . . . . . . .204 D4
Harrogate HG2 . . . . .220 D4
Kellington DN14 . . . . .203 A2
Wentworth Cres
Harrogate HG2 . . . . .220 D3
2 Whitby YO21 . . . . .208 B5
Wentworth Gate LS22 . . . .180 A3
Wentworth Rd YO24 . . . . .228 B2
Wentworth St YO17 . . . . . .215 B5
Wentworth Way
Eaglescliffe TS16 . . . . .5 A4
5 Hunmanby YO14 . . . . .126 F8
Wescoe Hill La LS17 . . . . . .178 B1
Wesley Pl YO1 . . . . .233 C2
Wesley Rd YO22 . . . . .33 C4
Wesley Sq **7** TS13 . . . . . .13 K2
Wesson Cl **6** DL9 . . . . . . .40 E4
West Acres **2** WF11 . . . . .201 E4
West Acres Ct **7** YO13 . . .99 A7
West Auckland Rd DL3 . . . . .3 A7
West Ave
Boston Spa LS23 . . . . .180 E1
Burton Fleming YO25 . . . . .126 E3
5 Easingwold YO61 . . . . .143 D8
Filey YO14 . . . . .101 B3
19 Scalby YO13 . . . . .75 D5
West Bank
Scarborough YO12 . . . . . . .212 E4
York YO24 . . . . .227 E3
West Bank Rd BD23 . . . . . .216 E4
West Barnby La YO21 . . . . .12 B3
West Beck Way TS8 . . . . . . .7 A6
West Burton C of E Prim Sch
DL8 . . . . .58 F1
West Cam Rd BD23 . . . . . . .79 E6
West Cl Carthorpe DL8 . . . .87 E6
Normanton WF6 . . . . .200 A1
Swinton YO17 . . . . .121 B4
West Cliff Ave **5** YO21 . . .208 B7
West Cliffe Gr HG2 . . . . . . .219 B1
West Cliffe Mews 5
HG2 . . . . .219 C1
West Cliffe Mount
HG2 . . . . .219 B1
West Cliffe Terr HG2 . . . . .219 B1
West Close Rd **13** BB18 . .171 D2
West Craven High Sch
BB18 . . . . .171 E1
West Craven Swimming Pool
BB18 . . . . .171 E1
West Croft
19 Addingham LS29 . . . .174 F4
6 Glusburn BD20 . . . . . .187 E6
West Ct **8** YO19 . . . . .197 F8
West Dale LS23 . . . . .180 E1
West Dike Rd YO18 . . . . . . .71 F5
West Edge Rd WF8 . . . . . . .206 A3
West End
Boston Spa LS23 . . . . .180 E1
Guisborough TS14 . . . . .8 E6
Hurworth-on-Tees DL2 . . . . .3 E1
Hutton Rudby TS15 . . . . . . .25 C5
Kirkbymoorside YO62 . . . . .70 B1
Muston YO14 . . . . .100 F2
Osmotherley DL6 . . . . .45 B4
Pollington DN14 . . . . .207 F6
Rawcliffe DN14 . . . . .205 A2
Sheriff Hutton YO60 . . . . . .145 C5
Stokesley TS9 . . . . .26 C7
Strensall YO32 . . . . .167 A7
West End App LS24 . . . . . .190 B3
West End Ave
Appleton Roebuck YO23 . . .190 F5
Harrogate HG2 . . . . .222 B7
Richmond DL10 . . . . .209 A7
West End Cl
North Duffield YO8 . . . . . . .199 A8
9 Strensall YO32 . . . . . .167 B7
West End Ct **5** YO11 . . . .100 B6

West End Gdns
Egglescliffe TS16 . . . . .5 D4
Pollington DN14 . . . . .207 F6
West End Rd DN6 . . . . .206 E2
West End View **4** YO11 . .100 B6
West End Way TS18 . . . . . . .5 F8
West Field La
Arkendale HG5 . . . . .163 A8
East Witton Town DL8 . . . . .60 F1
Upper Poppleton YO26 . . . .165 E1
West Field Rd **2** BB18 . . .171 D2
West Fields YO62 . . . . .70 B1
West Garforth Jun Sch
LS25 . . . . .194 C3
West Garth
Cayton YO11 . . . . .100 B6
Sherburn YO17 . . . . .124 D8
Ulleskelf LS24 . . . . .190 B3
West Garth Gdns 28
YO11 . . . . .100 B6
West Gate
Thornton-le-Dale YO18 . . . . .96 C5
Wetherby LS22 . . . . .180 B3
Wykeham YO13 . . . . .98 D6
West Gr
Bishop Thornton HG3 . . . . .139 A2
Swinton YO17 . . . . .121 B4
West Grove Rd HG1 . . . . . .219 D4
West Hall La LS29 . . . . . . .175 A5
West Heslerton C of E Prim
Sch YO17 . . . . .123 F6
West Ing La BD23 . . . . .171 A5
West Ings Cl **4** WF11 . . . .202 A3
West Ings Cres 5
WF11 . . . . .202 A3
West Ings Ct **1** WF11 . . . .202 A3
West Ings La **2** WF11 . . . .202 A3
West Ings Mews 6
WF11 . . . . .202 A3
West Ings Way **3** WF11 . .202 A3
West La
Appleton Wiske DL6 . . . . . .24 A3
Askwith LS21 . . . . .176 C3
Azerley HG4 . . . . .112 F3
Bewerley HG3 . . . . .136 E4
Boston Spa LS23 . . . . .180 E1
Burn YO8 . . . . .203 C6
Burniston YO13 . . . . .54 C1
Burton Fleming YO25 . . . . .126 E3
Caldwell DL11 . . . . .1 B4
Caldwell DL11 . . . . .1 D5
Cononley BD20 . . . . .173 C2
Dalton-on-Tees DL2 . . . . . .22 D6
Danby YO21 . . . . .29 C8
East Layton DL11 . . . . .20 A8
Embsay BD23 . . . . .217 D8
Hampsthwaite HG3 . . . . . .161 A4
Hornby DL6 . . . . .23 F4
Littlethorpe HG4 . . . . .214 A2
2 Low Bradley BD20 . . . .173 E3
Melsonby DL10 . . . . .20 E7
Mickleby TS13 . . . . .12 A4
Nether Silton YO7 . . . . .66 B7
North Deighton LS22 . . . . .179 F6
Snainton YO13 . . . . .97 F5
Stillington YO61 . . . . .143 F7
Sutton BD20 . . . . .187 E6
Sykehouse DN14 . . . . .207 F2
Whixley YO26 . . . . .163 F5
West Lea Ave HG2 . . . . . . .222 B7
West Lodge Gdns
YO17 . . . . .215 A4
West Lund **17** YO62 . . . . .70 B1
West Lund La YO62 . . . . . . .94 B8
West Mead WF10 . . . . .201 A4
West Moor La DL8 . . . . .61 C4
West Moor Rd
Darlington DL2 . . . . .3 E3
Raskelf YO61 . . . . .116 E2
West Mount LS29 . . . . .189 E5
West Oaks Sch LS23 . . . . . .188 E3
West Par LS29 . . . . .218 C4
West Parade Rd 11
YO12 . . . . .212 F5
West Park Ave YO12 . . . . . .212 C8
West Park Cres YO12 . . . . .212 C7
West Park Rd **13** YO13 . . .75 D5
West Park St **2** HG2 . . . .219 D1
West Pasture
Kirkbymoorside YO62 . . . . .70 B1
7 Pickering YO18 . . . . . .95 F6
West Pk YO8 . . . . .232 A4
West Rd Carleton BD23 . . .173 A4
12 Filey YO14 . . . . .101 B3
Melsonby DL10 . . . . .20 F7
West Row DL2 . . . . .4 C7
West Side Rd YO13 . . . . . . .53 A1
West Sq **7** YO11 . . . . .212 F5
West St
Castleford WF10 . . . . .200 D4
Eaglescliffe TS15 . . . . .5 D4
Gargrave BD23 . . . . .155 D1
Gayles DL11 . . . . .19 E6
Harrogate HG1 . . . . .219 C5
Ilkley LS29 . . . . .218 B4
Muston YO14 . . . . .100 F2
Normanton South WF6 . . . .200 A1
Scarborough YO11 . . . . . . .213 A4
Swinton YO17 . . . . .121 B4
West Tanfield C of E Prim
Sch YO7 . . . . .87 A1
West Thorpe YO24 . . . . . . .230 D8
West Vale **37** YO14 . . . . .101 B3
West View
Carleton BD23 . . . . .173 B4
Darlington DL3 . . . . .3 A5
Draughton BD23 . . . . .174 B7
Kippax LS25 . . . . .194 D1

West View continued
Mickletown LS25 . . . . .195 A3
North Deighton LS22 . . . . .180 A6
Sherburn in Elmet LS25 . . .195 E3
West View Ave **25** LS29 . .176 C1
West View Rd **26** LS29 . . .176 C1
West View Terr TS16 . . . . . .5 C1
West Villa YO61 . . . . .144 A4
West Way YO61 . . . . .118 A1
West Wood La YO23 . . . . . .182 A6
Westacres **5** DL2 . . . . .4 C4
Westbeck Gdns TS5 . . . . . .6 F8
Westborough **1** YO11 . . .213 A5
Westbourne Ave
Harrogate HG2 . . . . .222 B8
Whitby YO21 . . . . .208 A6
Westbourne Cl YO21 . . . . .208 A6
Westbourne Cres
LS25 . . . . .194 B3
Westbourne Gdns
YO8 . . . . .232 C4
Westbourne Gr
8 Pickering YO18 . . . . . .95 F6
3 Ripon HG4 . . . . .214 C5
11 Scarborough YO11 . . .213 A4
Selby YO8 . . . . .232 C4
Whitby YO21 . . . . .208 A6
Westbourne Pk YO12 . . . . .212 E4
Westbourne Rd
Scarborough YO11 . . . . . . .212 F3
Selby YO8 . . . . .232 C4
Whitby YO21 . . . . .208 A6
Westbourne Terr YO7 . . . . .211 C2
Westbury Cty Jun Sch
TS17 . . . . .6 B8
Westbury St TS17 . . . . .6 B8
Westcliff Prim Sch
YO21 . . . . .208 C7
Westcroft La YO8 . . . . .196 E1
Westdene HG2 . . . . .222 B7
Westend La DN14 . . . . .207 B6
Westerdale **4** YO18 . . . . .95 F6
Westerdale Ct **2** YO30 . . .228 A6
Western Ave WF8 . . . . .201 C1
Western CP Sch HG2 . . . . .219 C1
Western Ct **18** WF11 . . . .201 C1
Western Gales Way
WF6 . . . . .200 B1
Western Rd Goole DN14 . . .205 F3
Skipton BD23 . . . . .217 B3
Western Way **1** YO18 . . . .95 C1
Westerns La HG3 . . . . .139 C4
Westfield YO8 . . . . .232 B4
Westfield Ave
Castleford WF10 . . . . .200 E2
3 Eggborough DN14 . . . .202 F2
Rawcliffe DN14 . . . . .205 A1
6 Scalby YO12 . . . . .75 E5
Selby YO8 . . . . .232 B4
Westfield Cl
2 Eggborough DN14 . . . .202 F2
21 Haxby YO32 . . . . . . .166 E5
South Milford LS25 . . . . . .195 E2
Westfield Cres LS24 . . . . . .189 E6
Westfield Ct **1** LS25 . . . . .195 F2
Westfield Cty Inf Sch
YO24 . . . . .227 B2
Westfield Cty Jun Sch
YO26 . . . . .227 A2
Westfield Dr
Hurworth-on-Tees DL2 . . . . .3 E1
York YO10 . . . . .231 D8
Westfield Gn YO26 . . . . . . .181 C7
Westfield Gr
Allerton Bywater WF10 . . . .200 D7
4 Eggborough DN14 . . . .202 F2
12 Haxby YO32 . . . . . . .166 E5
Westfield La
Exelby, Leeming & Newton
DL8 . . . . .63 C2
Kippax LS25 . . . . .194 C1
Ledsham LS25 . . . . .195 C1
Lockton YO18 . . . . .72 E4
Normanby YO62 . . . . .94 F4
Norton WF8 . . . . .206 C2
South Milford LS25 . . . . . .195 F2
Thirsk YO7 . . . . .211 A3
Thoralby DL8 . . . . .58 D1
Thorganby YO19 . . . . .193 A5
Thornton-le-Dale YO18 . . . .96 C5
Westfield Pl
19 Haxby YO32 . . . . . . .166 E5
York YO24 . . . . .227 A1
Westfield Rd
1 Eggborough DN14 . . . .202 F2
20 Haxby YO32 . . . . . . .166 E5
3 North Duffield YO8 . . . .199 A7
Rawcliffe DN14 . . . . .205 A1
Selby YO8 . . . . .232 B4
2 Stokesley TS9 . . . . .26 C7
Tockwith YO26 . . . . .181 C7
Westfield Sq **8** LS24 . . . .189 E6
Westfield Terr
2 Great Preston WF10 . . .200 D7
Tadcaster LS24 . . . . .189 E6
9 Thornton Dale YO18 . . .96 D5
Westfield Way YO17 . . . .215 F4
Westfields
Castleford WF10 . . . . .200 E3
Richmond DL10 . . . . .209 B7
Scorton DL10 . . . . .41 F7
Westfields Ct DL10 . . . . . . .209 B7
Westfold YO17 . . . . .215 F4
Westgarth LS22 . . . . .180 A2
Westgate
22 Barnoldswick BB18 . . .171 D1
Guisborough TS14 . . . . .8 F6

Westgate *continued*
Malton YO17 215 E6
Pickering YO18 95 E7
Rillington YO17 122 F5
Ripon HG4 214 C5
Tadcaster LS24 189 E6
Thirsk YO7 211 B2
Westgate Carr Rd YO18 95 D5
Westgate La
Malton YO17 215 D6
Thornton in Lonsdale LA6 103 C5
Westgate Rd DL3 3 B7
Westholme 10 TS15 25 C5
Westholme Bank DL8 58 F2
Westholme Cres 2 HG4 86 C3
Westholme Ct 3 HG4 86 C3
Westholme Dr YO30 224 E1
Westholme Rd 1 HG4 86 C3
Westland Cl 3 BD20 187 F7
Westlands
Bilton-in-Ainsty with Bickerton YO26 181 D5
6 Kirklevington TS15 24 E8
Pickering YO18 96 A7
Stokesley TS9 26 B7
Westlands Ave 1 YO21 208 C7
Westlands Gr YO31 228 F7
Westlands La YO7 211 A4
Westlands Rd DL3 3 B6
Westminster Cl HG3 222 C3
Westminster Cres HG3 222 D2
Westminster Dr HG3 222 D3
Westminster Gate HG3 222 C3
Westminster Gr HG3 222 D3
Westminster Rd
Pannal HG3 222 C3
York YO30 228 A6
Westminster Rise HG3 222 D2
Westmoreland St
Darlington DL3 3 C7
1 Harrogate HG1 219 E3
19 Skipton BD23 217 A3
Westmount Cl HG4 214 B6
Weston Cres 7 LS21 176 F1
Weston Dr LS21 176 E1
Weston La LS21 176 F1
Weston Moor Rd LS21 176 E4
Weston Park View LS21 176 E1
Weston Rd LS29 218 B4
Weston Ridge LS21 176 F1
Westover Rd YO12 212 F4
Westpit La YO32 167 A7
Westridge Cres 1 DL9 40 F5
Westside Cl YO17 215 B4
Westside Rd
Bransdale YO62 48 B5
Fadmoor YO62 69 E7
Westview Cl
3 Low Bradley BD20 173 E3
York YO26 227 B7
Westville Ave LS29 218 A4
Westville Cl 6 LS29 218 A4
Westville House Prep Sch LS29 218 D7
Westville Oval HG1 219 C6
Westville Rd LS29 218 A4
Westway Eastfield YO11 99 F7
Harrogate HG2 222 B8
Westwood
Carleton BD23 173 B4
Scarborough YO11 212 F5
Westwood Cl 2 YO11 212 F4
Westwood Dr LS29 218 A2
Westwood Gdns 3 YO11 212 F4
Westwood La
Ampleforth YO62 92 A2
West Tanfield HG4 86 E1
Westwood Mews
Carleton BD23 173 B4
12 Dunnington YO19 184 F7
Westwood Rd
Ripon HG4 214 A2
Scarborough YO11 212 F4
Westwood Terr YO23 228 B1
Westwood Way LS23 188 E8
Wetherby Bsns Pk LS22 180 C3
Wetherby High Sch LS22 180 C3
Wetherby Jun Sch LS22 180 C3
Wetherby La LS22 180 D7
Wetherby Leisure Ctr LS22 180 C2
Wetherby Race Course★ LS22 180 E3
Wetherby Rd
8 Boroughbridge YO51 141 B4
Bramham cum Oglethorpe LS23 188 E6
Harrogate HG2 220 B1
Kirk Deighton LS22 180 B5
Knaresborough HG5 221 D4
Sicklinghall LS22 179 E3
Tadcaster LS24 189 D6
Walton LS23 180 F2
Wetherby LS22 180 B2
York YO26 227 B3
Wethercote La YO7 67 C1
Wetlands La DL11 18 G7
Weydale Ave YO12 212 E8
Weymouth Ave TS8 7 A7
Weymouth Rd 1 HG1 219 E4
Whaddon Chase TS14 8 F6
Whaites La YO7 115 C5
Whales La DN14 202 E3
Wham La BD24 130 F1
Wharfe Dr YO24 230 D8
Wharfe Gr 8 LS22 180 B3
Wharfe La
Grassington BD23 134 D3
Kearby with Netherby LS22 179 B1
Wharfe Pk 2 LS29 175 A4
Wharfe View
Grassington BD23 134 D3
Kirkby Overblow HG3 179 A4
Wharfe View Rd LS29 218 B4
Wharfedale YO14 101 A3
Wharfedale Ave HG2 222 A7
Wharfedale Cl 1 BD23 217 B4
Wharfedale Cres
Harrogate HG2 222 B7
Tadcaster LS24 189 E6
Wharfedale Dr
Ilkley LS29 218 C4
Normanton WF6 200 A3
Wharfedale General Hospl LS21 176 F1
Wharfedale Pl HG2 222 A7
Wharfedale RUFC BD23 134 D3
Wharfedale View 6 LS29 174 F4
Wharfeside Ave BD23 134 D3
Wharfeside La LS29 218 C5
Wharncliffe Pl 14 YO14 101 A3
Wharnscliffe Dr YO30 224 F2
Wharton Ave YO30 228 B7
Wharton Rd 8 YO41 168 D2
Whartons Prim Sch The LS21 177 A2
Whartons The LS21 177 A1
Whashton Rd Aske DL10 20 C1
Richmond DL10 209 C8
Wheatcroft 6 YO32 167 A6
Wheatcroft Ave YO11 213 B1
Wheatcroft Cty Prim Sch YO11 213 B1
Wheatdale Rd LS24 190 B2
Wheatear La TS17 6 A5
Wheatfield La YO32 225 C8
Wheatlands
Great Ayton TS9 8 A2
Ilkley LS29 218 C4
Wheatlands Ave 8 BD20 187 E8
Wheatlands Dr 4 TS13 11 A8
Wheatlands Gr
Harrogate HG2 222 E8
York YO26 227 C6
Wheatlands La
7 Glusburn BD20 187 E8
Roecliffe YO51 140 E4
Wheatlands Rd HG2 222 E7
Wheatlands Rd E HG2 222 E8
Wheatlands Way HG2 222 F8
Wheatley Ave
Ilkley LS29 218 E3
Normanton South WF6 200 A1
Wheatley Dr YO32 225 C8
Wheatley Gdns 2 LS29 218 E3
Wheatley Gr LS29 218 E3
Wheatley La 3 LS29 218 E3
Wheatley Rd LS29 218 C3
Wheatley Rise LS29 218 E3
Wheeldale Cres TS17 6 B7
Wheeldale Rd YO18 51 A4
Wheelgate YO17 215 C4
Wheelgate Sq 7 YO17 215 C4
Wheelhouse The 4 YO30 224 B5
Wheels La YO8 204 F3
Wheelwright Cl
Copmanthorpe YO23 230 B2
Sutton upon Derwent YO41 185 C1
Wheldale La WF10 201 B5
Wheldon Rd WF10 201 A5
Wheldrake C of E Prim Sch YO19 193 A8
Wheldrake Ings Nature Reserve★ YO19 193 C7
Wheldrake La
Deighton YO19 184 B1
Escrick YO19 192 B5
Whenby Gr YO31 225 F1
Whenby La YO60 145 C6
Whernside TS7 7 C5
Whernside Ave YO31 229 A5
Whessoe Rd DL3 3 C8
Whin Bank YO12 212 D5
Whin Cl
3 Strensall YO32 167 B6
York YO24 230 F7
Whin Garth YO24 230 F6
Whin Gn YO22 32 A6
Whin Hill YO17 147 E1
Whin La
South Milford LS25 195 D2
Warlaby DL7 64 C5
Whin Rd YO24 230 F6
Whinbeck Ave WF6 200 B1
Whinbush Way DL1 3 F8
Whinchat Tail TS14 8 D6
Whincup Ave HG5 221 B6
Whincup Cl 6 HG5 221 B6
Whincup Gr 7 HG5 221 B6
Whinfield Rd DL1 3 E7
Whinfield Road Jun & Inf Sch DL1 3 F7
Whinfields The 1 HG3 138 A1
Whingroves TS17 6 C8
Whinmoor Hill YO7 66 C2
Whinney La HG3 222 A5
Whinney Mire La LA2 103 E1
Whinny Bank YO61 117 C8
Whinny Gill Rd BD23 217 B3
Whinny Hagg La YO8 197 A2
Whinny Hill DL9 40 E3
Whinny La YO60 168 A7
Whinnythwaite La YO26 181 C8
Whins La
Spofforth with Stockeld HG3 179 E4
Thorp Arch LS23 180 F1
Whins The YO12 212 A7
Whinstone Prim Sch TS17 6 A5
Whinstone View 13 TS9 8 A2
Whinwath La DL8 87 F4
Whipley Bank HG3 161 A8
Whipley La HG3 161 A7
Whip-ma-whop-ma-gate YO1 233 C2
Whipperdale Bank DL8 60 A8
Whiston Dr 18 YO14 101 B3
Whit Moor Rd HG3 158 F5
Whitby Archives & Heritage Ctr★ YO22 208 E7
Whitby Ave
Guisborough TS14 8 F6
York YO31 229 A7
Whitby Benedictine Abbey (rems of)★ YO22 208 E7
Whitby Com Coll YO21 208 C5
Whitby Dr YO31 229 A7
Whitby Gate YO18 96 D6
Whitby Hospl YO21 208 D6
Whitby Mus & Art Gall★ YO21 208 C6
Whitby Pavilion & Theatre YO21 208 C8
Whitby Rd
Guisborough TS14 9 A7
Pickering YO18 96 B8
Staithes TS13 13 K2
Whitby Sta YO21 208 D6
Whitby Town Football Club YO21 208 B7
Whitby Way DL3 3 A7
Whitcliffe Ave HG4 214 B4
Whitcliffe Cres HG4 214 B3
Whitcliffe Dr HG4 214 B3
Whitcliffe Gr HG4 214 B3
Whitcliffe La
Littlethorpe HG4 139 D8
Ripon HG4 214 A2
Whitcliffe Pl DL10 209 A7
White Bridge Rd YO21 208 B8
White Canons Ct 4 DL10 209 E8
White Canons Wlk 3 DL10 209 E8
White Cross Rd YO31 228 D7
White Cross Way YO41 169 A2
White Friars Cl DL10 209 F8
White Friars Gdns 6 DL10 209 E8
White Friars Wlk 5 DL10 209 E8
White Gate
Heslerton YO17 123 E6
Sherburn YO17 124 C6
White Gate Hill YO11 100 B2
White Hart Cres 4 DL1 3 F6
White Hill La BD20 172 E1
White Hills Croft BD23 216 E6
White Hills La BD23 216 E6
White Horse Cl 6 YO32 225 F5
White Horse Fold WF10 200 F7
White Horse La 9 YO12 99 D6
White Horse Mews 3 HG3 179 E5
White Horse of Kilburn★ YO61 91 B4
White House Croft TS21 5 A7
White House Dale YO24 227 F1
White House Dr YO24 227 F1
White House Gdns 4 YO24 228 A2
White House Gr 1 YO41 185 B2
White House Rise YO24 227 F1
White La BD22 187 F1
White Lands DL10 209 E7
White Lee Ave BB8 186 B1
White Ley Rd DN6 206 C1
White Leys Rd YO21 208 A7
White Lilac Cl DL10 209 E7
White Lodge YO8 232 B4
White Pastures DL10 209 E7
White Point Ave 1 YO21 208 B7
White Point Rd YO21 208 B8
White Rose Ave 3 YO32 225 D3
White Rose Cl
Huby YO61 144 A5
8 Linton-on-Ouse YO30 164 F7
White Rose Cl *continued*
Nether Poppleton YO26 224 C1
White Rose Cres DL10 209 E7
White Rose Gr 5 YO32 225 D3
White Rose Way
Nether Poppleton YO26 227 C8
Thirsk YO7 211 D4
White Sprunt Hill YO17 125 A1
White St YO8 232 B6
White Wall La HG3 160 D4
White Way YO13 54 C1
White Way Heads YO18 51 F4
Whitebridge Dr DL1 3 D8
Whitecarr La YO62 95 A5
Whitecliffe Cres LS26 194 A1
Whitecliffe Dr 1 LS26 194 A1
Whitecliffe Rise LS26 194 A1
Whitecote La LS25 195 D2
Whitecross Hill DL8 87 F3
Whitefield Bglws DN14 206 F8
Whitefield La DN14 202 E1
Whitefields Dr DL10 209 E7
Whitefields Gate 1 DL10 209 E8
Whitefields Wlk 2 DL10 209 E8
Whitefriars Ct 9 BD24 131 D2
Whitegate Cl 7 TS13 13 K2
Whitegate La HG4 114 F1
Whitehill Rd BD22 187 E3
Whitehouse Ave LS26 200 B8
Whitehouse Cres LS26 200 B8
Whitehouse Dr LS26 200 B8
Whitehouse La
Great & Little Preston LS26 200 B8
Swillington LS26 194 B2
Whitelass Cl YO7 211 B4
Whitemoor La YO8 198 C6
Whiteoak Ave YO61 143 C8
Whitepits La LA2 129 A5
Whiterose Dr YO41 168 D2
Whiterow Rd DL8 82 F7
Whitestone Dr YO31 225 E2
Whitethorn Cl YO31 225 E2
Whitewall YO17 215 D1
Whitewall Corner Hill YO17 147 E8
Whiteway Head HG5 221 A4
Whitfield Ave YO18 96 A6
Whitkirk Pl 17 YO14 101 B3
Whitley & Eggborough Cty Prim Sch DN14 202 F1
Whitley Bridge Sta DN14 202 F1
Whitley Cl YO30 225 A1
Whitley Pl WF10 200 E6
Whitley Rd
Elvington YO41 185 A3
Norton-le-Clay YO7 115 B1
Thornaby TS17 6 B6
Whitley Thorpe La DN14 206 F7
Whitsundale Cl 4 HG5 221 D5
Whittle St 6 YO7 89 B1
Whitton Croft Rd 9 LS29 218 B4
Whitton Pl YO10 229 C4
Whitwell Rd YO60 146 E5
Whitwood Common La WF10 200 C3
Whitwood La WF10 200 C3
Whitworth Way BB18 171 E2
Whixley Field La YO26 164 B4
Whixley La YO26 163 E2
Whorlton Castle (rems of)★ DL6 25 D1
Whorlton La DL6 45 E8
Whorlton Parochial Sch DL6 45 D8
Whyett Bank YO21 28 F6
Wickets The 8 TS15 25 C5
Widdale Rd HG5 221 D5
Widdale Sch DL8 55 E2
Widdowfield St DL3 3 C6
Wide Howe La YO7 114 E8
Wide La YO14 127 E5
Widgeon Cl 4 YO14 101 A4
Wigby Cl HG3 140 A2
Wigginton Prim Sch YO32 166 D5
Wigginton Rd YO31 233 B4
Wigginton Terr YO31 228 C8
Wigglesworth Sch BD23 153 C3
Wighill Garth LS24 189 E6
Wighill La
Healaugh LS24 181 F3
Healaugh LS24 189 E7
Wighill St 25 BD20 187 E7
Wilberforce Ave YO30 228 B7
Wilberfoss Sch YO41 185 E6
Wilcock La BD20 173 F2
Wild Rd DL1 4 A4
Wilfreds Gr 8 YO8 198 B4
Wilfreds Rd 5 YO8 198 B4
Wilken Cres TS14 8 F7
Wilkinson St TS12 9 E7
Wilkinson Way
6 Otley LS21 176 F1
3 Strensall YO32 167 A7
Willance Gr DL10 209 A7
Willaston Cres HG2 220 A2
Willaston Rd 1 HG1 220 A3
Willerby Carr La YO12 99 C3
Willgutter La BD22 187 F1
William Crossthwaite TS17 6 B4
William Jacques Dr YO8 198 E2
William Plows Ave YO10 228 E2
William Rd YO8 198 B4
William St 16 BB18 172 A1
William's Hill Ring & Bailey★ DL8 60 E2
Williamson Cl 14 HG4 214 C5
Williamson Dr 8 HG4 214 C5
Willins Cl 13 TS15 25 C5
Willis St YO10 228 E3
Willitoft Rd YO8 199 F6
Willoughby Way YO24 230 B8
Willow Ave
Catterick Garrison DL9 209 B1
Clifford LS23 188 E7
Willow Bank YO32 225 E4
Willow Bank Dr 1 WF8 201 C1
Willow Beck Rd DL6 210 D6
Willow Bridge La YO7 115 F8
Willow Chase The TS21 4 F7
Willow Cl
20 Burley in Warfedale LS29 176 C1
2 Filey YO14 101 B4
Willow Cres
Clifford LS23 188 E7
Richmond DL10 209 D8
Willow Ct Kexby YO41 168 C2
2 North Featherstone WF7 200 E1
16 Pickering YO18 95 F6
Willow Dr 6 Bedale DL8 63 B3
Eston & South Bank TS6 7 E8
1 North Duffield YO8 199 A7
Willow Garth
Ferrensby HG5 162 F7
Scalby YO12 212 A7
10 Thornton Dale YO18 96 D5
Willow Garth Ave BD20 187 E8
Willow Garth La DN6 207 A1
Willow Glade
5 Boston Spa LS23 188 E7
York YO32 225 F3
Willow Gr
3 Boston Spa LS23 188 E7
Earswick YO32 226 A7
Harrogate HG1 219 E5
York YO31 228 F7
Willow La
Boston Spa LS23 188 E7
North Featherstone WF7 200 E1
Willow La E 4 WF7 200 E1
Willow Park Rd YO41 185 F5
Willow Rd
9 Campsall DN6 206 E1
Darlington DL3 3 B6
10 Knottingley WF11 202 A3
Northallerton DL7 210 D2
Willow Rise
5 Kirkbymoorside YO62 70 B1
Tadcaster LS24 189 D5
Thorpe Willoughby YO8 197 B1
Willow Tree Gdns 9 LS29 176 C1
Willow View 1 DL10 41 D5
Willow Way 4 BD20 187 E6
Willow Wlk 1 HG4 214 B2
Willowbank TS8 7 A5
Willowbridge Rd WF8 206 C2
Willowbridge Way WF10 200 C3
Willowdene La WF8 201 B2
Willowgate 24 YO18 95 F7
Willows Ave TS8 6 C4
Willows The
1 Hambleton YO8 196 E1
Middlesbrough TS7 7 C6
8 Strensall YO32 167 B7
Willymath Cl YO13 75 D7
Wilmot Rd LS29 218 C4
Wilson St
Castleford WF10 200 E4
Guisborough TS14 8 F6
Lockwood TS12 9 F7
16 Pontefract WF8 201 B1
Sutton BD20 187 F7
Wilson's La 5 YO13 99 A7
Wilsthorpe Gr 1 YO10 231 F8
Wilstrop Farm Rd YO23 230 A2
Wilton Carr La YO18 97 A3
Wilton Ings La YO18 97 A4
Wilton La TS14 8 F7
Wilton Rd LS29 218 A3
Wilton Rise YO24 227 F3
Wimbledon Cl 2 DL1 3 F6
Wimpole Cl 6 YO30 225 A1
Winchester Ave 3 YO26 227 E4
Winchester Gr 1 YO26 227 E4
Winchester Way DL1 3 F6
Windermere YO24 230 D7
Windermere Ave BB8 186 A3
Windermere Dr WF11 201 F1
Windgate Hill La YO8 197 B6
Windle La BD20 173 D1
Windleston Dr TS3 7 B8
Windmill Gdns YO8 232 B7

Windmill Gr LS24 ....189 D5
Windmill La
Norton DN6 ....206 D1
York YO10 ....229 B2
Windmill Mdws YO41 ..185 E6
Windmill Rd LS23 ....188 F6
Windmill Rise
Aberford LS25 ....194 F7
Tadcaster LS24 ....189 D5
York YO26 ....227 E3
Windrose Cl WF6 ....200 A2
Windross Sq 11 YO61 ...143 C8
Windsor Ave
Richmond DL10 ....209 D8
Skipton BD23 ....217 A4
Windsor Cl 17 WF6 ....200 B1
Windsor Cres
Middlesbrough TS7 ....7 D6
7 Whitby YO21 ....208 D6
Windsor Dr
2 Haxby YO32 ....166 D5
Lockwood TS12 ....9 F7
Windsor Garth YO24 ..227 D1
Windsor La HG5 ....221 B5
Windsor Pl BB18 ....171 E2
Windsor Rd
24 Catterick Garrison DL9 ..40 E4
4 Harrogate HG2 ....220 A1
Ripon HG4 ....214 C3
Thornaby TS17 ....6 B7
Windsor St 1 YO23 ....228 B1
Windsor Terr YO21 ....208 D6
Windy Hill LA2 ....129 B8
Winewall La BB8 ....186 B2
Winewall Rd 16 BB8 ....186 A3
Winksley Banks Rd
HG4 ....112 E2
Winksley Gr HG3 ....219 A4
Winn La YO7 ....115 C6
Winnow La LS23 ....188 D8
Winscar Gr 9 YO30 ....224 E3
Winston Ave BD20 ....187 F8
Winston Ct
Northallerton DL6 ....210 E6
Norton YO17 ....215 E3
Winter Gap La BD20 ...186 D8
Winter Gn 21 HG3 ....161 B3
Winterburn La BD23 ...155 D5
Winterscale St YO10 ...228 D2
Winthropp Cl YO17 ...215 C5
Winton Rd DL6 ....210 E6
Wise House La YO17 ...215 F7
Wisker La YO32 ....226 C7
Wisp Hill 12 BD23 ....134 E3
Wistow Parochial C of E Prim
Sch YO8 ....197 D6
Wistow Rd YO8 ....232 A8
Wistowgate YO8 ....197 B8
Witch La YO25 ....127 B2
Witham Dr YO32 ....226 A6
Withington Rd 6 YO62 ...92 F7
Witton Cres DL3 ....3 A7
Witton Steeps DL8 ....59 E2
Wobeck La HG4 ....114 B7
Wold La Willerby YO12 ...99 D1
Willerby YO12 ....125 E8
Wold Newton GM Sch
YO25 ....126 A4
Wold Newton Rd
YO25 ....126 E3
Wold Rd YO17 ....149 E8
Wold St YO17 ....215 D3
Wold View YO14 ....100 F2
Wold View Gr 5 YO12 ...99 E6
Woldcroft YO41 ....185 C2
Wolfe Ave YO31 ....228 F5
Wolsey Ave YO8 ....197 B8
Wolsey Cl 11 LS25 ....195 F4
Wolsey Croft LS25 ....195 F4
Wolsey Dr YO23 ....231 A3
Wolsey Gdns 12 LS25 ...195 F4
Wolsingham Dr TS5 ....6 E7
Wolsley St YO10 ....228 E3
Wolviston Ave YO10 ...229 C3
Womersley C of E Prim Sch
DN6 ....206 C6
Womersley Rd WF11 ...202 A2
Wood Acre Cl BD23 ....134 C3
Wood Aven Cl 35 HG3 ..161 B3
Wood Cl
Bradleys Both BD20 ....173 D3
Skipton BD23 ....216 E5
7 Strensall YO32 ....167 A7
14 Thorpe Willoughby
YO8 ....197 B1
Wood End La DL8 ....59 D5
Wood End Mus★
YO11 ....213 A5
Wood Gate YO13 ....74 A1
Wood Gn WF10 ....200 C3
Wood Hill Cl YO51 ....141 D1
Wood La
Acaster Selby YO23 ....191 B2
Austwick LA2 ....131 A8
Birkin WF11 ....202 D6
Gainford DL2 ....1 D8
10 Grassington BD23 ....134 E2
Great Preston LS26 ....200 C7
Low Coniscliffe & Merrybent
DL2 ....2 E4
Spennithorne DL8 ....61 A3
Thorp Arch LS23 ....180 F2
13 Thorpe Willoughby
Y... ....197 B1
...hfield BD23 ....134 B3
Wood La continued
Whitwood WF10 ....200 C3
Wood Lea 1 WF11 ....201 E4
Wood Park Cl HG2 ....220 B1
Wood Row LS26 ....200 A6
Wood St
Castleford WF10 ....200 E4
Norton YO17 ....215 D3
York YO31 ....228 E6
Wood View
Airmyn DN14 ....205 E3
Embsay BD23 ....217 C7
Harrogate HG1 ....219 C3
Wood View Ave WF10 ..200 D4
Wood Way YO32 ....226 A4
Woodall Ave YO12 ....212 F7
Woodall Ct 9 YO8 ....197 D6
Woodbine Cl 12 TS9 ....8 A2
Woodbine Terr 9 HG1 .219 D3
Woodburn Dr 3 DL8 ....60 D5
Woodcock Cl
Eston & South Bank TS6 ....7 F8
9 Haxby YO32 ....166 F5
Woodcock Dr 8 DL9 ....40 F2
Woodcrest Rd DL3 ....3 B4
Wooden Hill La DL7 ....210 B2
Woodend WF10 ....200 C7
Woodend Cres WF10 ..200 C7
Woodfield Ave HG1 ..219 E4
Woodfield Cl HG1 ....219 E4
Woodfield CP Sch
HG1 ....219 F5
Woodfield Dr
Harrogate HG1 ....219 E4
6 Low Bradley BD20 ....173 E3
Woodfield Gdns 5 HG1 219 E4
Woodfield Gr HG1 ....219 E4
Woodfield Inf Sch
HG1 ....219 F5
Woodfield Pl 6 HG1 ..219 E4
Woodfield Rd
Goole DN14 ....205 F3
Harrogate HG1 ....219 F7
Woodfield Sq HG1 ....219 E4
Woodford Pl 1 YO24 ..227 D1
Woodgate YO12 ....212 D5
Woodgate La LS17 ....178 B2
Woodhall Dr HG1 ....219 F6
Woodhall Gr
Harrogate HG1 ....219 F6
Mickletown LS26 ....200 B6
4 Stockton-on-Tees TS18 ....5 D8
Woodhall La
Hemingbrough YO8 ....199 B3
Womersley DN6 ....206 D6
Woodhead Field La
YO62 ....70 A4
Woodhill View 3 LS22 .180 C3
Woodhouse Gr 4 YO31 .229 A5
Woodhouse La BD23 ..157 B7
Woodhouse Rd
Guisborough TS14 ....8 E6
Thorganby YO19 ....193 A3
Woodland Ave
Scarborough YO12 ....212 D6
9 Swillington LS26 ....194 A1
Woodland Chase
YO30 ....225 B1
Woodland Cl YO12 ....212 D6
Woodland Cres 8 LS26 194 A1
Woodland Dr DL7 ....63 F3
Woodland Gr
Scarborough YO12 ....212 C6
7 Swillington LS26 ....194 A1
Woodland Pl
New Earswick YO32 ....225 E4
Scarborough YO12 ....212 C6
Woodland Ravine
YO12 ....212 D6
Woodland Rd DL3 ....3 B6
Woodland Rise YO12 ..212 D6
Woodland St 3 BD22 ....187 B6
Woodland Terr DL3 ....3 B5
Woodland View 5 YO7 ...89 A1
Woodland Way
8 Airmyn DN14 ....205 E4
Longnewton TS21 ....4 F7
York YO32 ....225 F4
Woodlands
Escrick YO19 ....192 B5
Ilkley LS29 ....218 D4
Woodlands Ave
Harrogate HG2 ....220 B1
Haxby YO32 ....225 C8
Norton YO17 ....215 E2
Rillington YO17 ....122 F5
Tadcaster LS24 ....189 D5
Woodlands Cl
Goldsborough HG5 ....163 A3
Harrogate HG2 ....220 C2
15 Ilkley LS29 ....175 C2
Sherburn in Elmet LS25 ...195 F2
Woodlands Cres HG2 ..220 C2
Woodlands Croft
LS25 ....200 D8
Woodlands Ct 3 HG2 ..220 B1
Woodlands Cty Jun Sch
HG2 ....220 B2
Woodlands Dr
Egglescliffe TS15 ....5 E3
Garforth LS25 ....194 D3
Harrogate HG2 ....220 C1
Scarborough YO12 ....212 B5
Skipton BD23 ....216 E5
Woodlands Gn 3 HG2 ..220 B1
Woodlands Gr
Harrogate HG2 ....220 C2
8 Ilkley LS29 ....175 C2
Woodlands Gr continued
Kippax LS25 ....200 E8
Rillington YO17 ....122 F5
York YO31 ....229 A7
Woodlands La LS25 ....202 B7
Woodlands Rd
Harrogate HG2 ....220 C2
Rillington YO17 ....122 F5
Woodlands Rise
1 Harrogate HG2 ....220 C2
14 Ilkley LS29 ....175 C2
Norton DN6 ....206 E1
Woodlands Sch The
YO12 ....212 B5
Woodlands The TS7 ....7 D5
Woodlands View
Barlby with Osgodby
YO8 ....198 B4
Kippax LS25 ....200 E8
3 Tadcaster LS24 ....189 D5
2 Thornton Dale YO18 ....96 D5
Woodlands Way
Hurworth DL2 ....3 D1
7 Hurworth-on-Tees DL2 ..22 D8
Woodlands Wlk
Harrogate HG2 ....220 C2
Skipton BD23 ....216 E5
Stokesley TS9 ....26 C8
Woodlea Ave YO26 ....227 C4
Woodlea Bank YO26 ....227 D4
Woodlea Cres YO26 ....227 D4
Woodlea Gr YO26 ....227 D5
Woodleigh Cl 2 YO32 ..167 A6
Woodleigh Sch YO17 ..148 A6
Woodley Gr TS7 ....7 D7
Woodman La LA6 ....102 B6
Woodman Terr BD23 ....216 F4
Woodmanwray La
HG3 ....159 C8
Woodpark Ave HG5 ....221 A7
Woodpark Dr HG5 ....221 A7
Woodpecker Rd 12
LS29 ....176 C1
Woodrow Ave TS7 ....7 B6
Woodrow Cres LS26 ....200 A6
Woodroyd Gdns LS29 ..218 F3
Woodruff Cl 27 HG3 ....161 B3
Woodrush TS8 ....7 B4
Wood's Cl YO13 ....75 C8
Wood's Gr YO13 ....75 C8
Woods La YO26 ....142 B2
Woods Pl LS29 ....218 C4
Woodside
Castleford WF10 ....201 B4
Harrogate HG1 ....219 E2
Hutton Rudby TS15 ....25 C6
5 Leyburn DL8 ....60 D5
Woodside Ave YO31 ....229 A6
Woodside Cl 3 YO61 ....117 D1
Woodside Gr
Allerton Bywater WF10 ..200 C7
3 Stockton-on-Tees TS18 ...5 E8
Woodside La BD20 ....173 C2
Woodside Rd
Ganton YO12 ....125 A8
Silsden BD20 ....174 B1
Woodside St WF10 ....200 C7
Woodthorpe Prim Sch
YO24 ....230 C7
Woodvale TS8 ....7 B5
Woodvale Rd DL3 ....3 B4
Woodville Ave
Middlesbrough TS4 ....6 F8
3 Scalby YO12 ....212 D8
Woodville Terr YO8 ....232 E3
Wooldale Dr YO14 ....101 B4
Wooler St YO12 ....212 E5
Woolmoor Cl YO7 ....211 D4
Woolnough Ave YO10 ..229 B3
Woolpots La YO61 ....117 B4
Woolsington Dr DL2 ....4 C4
Worcester Dr YO31 ....229 B5
Wordsworth App 2
WF8 ....201 B1
Wordsworth Ave 4
DN6 ....206 E1
Wordsworth Cl YO13 ....75 C5
Wordsworth Cres
Harrogate HG2 ....222 C8
York YO24 ....230 D7
Wordsworth Dr WF11 ..201 D3
Workhouse Museum★
HG4 ....214 C6
Worsall Rd TS15 ....5 D2
Worsall Toll Bar TS15 ...24 B7
Worsendale Rd YO42 ..169 F2
Worsley Cl TS16 ....5 E7
Worsley Cres TS7 ....7 B5
Worsley Ct YO17 ....215 A3
Woundales La
Knayton with Brawith YO7 ..65 F4
Upsall YO7 ....66 A2
Wrangham Dr 1 YO14 .127 A8
Wray with Botton Endowed
Sch LA2 ....128 A6
Wray's Ave YO31 ....225 E1
Wrea Head Cl 2 YO13 ...75 D5
Wrea La 1 YO12 ....212 F6
Wreaks La HG4 ....111 E6
Wreaks Rd
Birstwith HG3 ....160 E6
Harrogate HG1 ....220 B3
Wrelton Cliff Rd YO18 ..95 B8
Wrelton Hall Gdns
YO18 ....71 C1
Wren Croft 5 WF8 ....201 B2
Wren Hall La YO8 ....204 E6
Wren La 2 YO8 ....232 D5
Wrenbeck Ave 1 LS21 .177 A1
Wrenbeck Cl 2 LS21 ..177 A1
Wrenbeck Dr LS21 ....177 A1
Wressle Sta YO8 ....199 D2
Wrexham Rd LS29 ....176 B1
Wreyfield Dr YO12 ....212 C7
Wright St 30 BD20 ....187 E7
Wrights La WF11 ....206 B8
Wycar 1 DL8 ....63 A2
Wycliffe Ave
Northallerton DL7 ....210 C2
York YO10 ....229 B3
Wycliffe Rd DL7 ....22 E1
Wycoller Ctry Pk★
BB8 ....186 D2
Wydale La YO13 ....98 B6
Wydale Rd YO10 ....229 D4
Wydale Rise YO13 ....98 A5
Wydra La HG3 ....159 F1
Wykeham Abbey★
YO13 ....98 E5
Wykeham Ave TS14 ....8 E5
Wykeham C of E Prim Sch
YO13 ....98 E6
Wykeham Carr Rd
YO13 ....98 E3
Wykeham Dale YO62 ....93 B8
Wykeham La YO13 ....98 E7
Wykeham Rd YO17 ....122 A5
Wykeham St YO12 ....212 E5
Wykeham Way TS8 ....7 A6
Wylam Ave DL1 ....3 D7
Wynbrook Ct YO13 ....75 C5
Wynd Cl 12 TS15 ....25 C5
Wynd The 3 Bedale DL8 ..63 A3
Hawes DL8 ....56 D4
Hutton Rudby TS15 ....25 D5
Skeeby DL10 ....20 F1
Wyvil Cres LS29 ....218 E4
Wyvil Rd LS29 ....218 E5
Wyville Gr DL8 ....61 E7

Y

Yafforth Rd DL7 ....210 B6
Yall Flat La YO21 ....29 B6
Yan Brow YO62 ....70 C3
Yarborough Cl DL10 ....41 B2
Yarburgh Cl 4 DN14 ..204 B1
Yarburgh Gr 2 YO26 ..227 E5
Yarburgh Way YO10 ..229 C3
Yarde Ave DL10 ....41 E4
Yarker Bank La DL8 ....60 C6
Yarlside La BD23 ....171 B4
Yarm Back La TS18 ....5 D8
Yarm Cty Jun Sch TS15 ...5 E2
Yarm La TS9 ....7 D1
Yarm Rd Darlington DL1 ...3 E5
Egglescliffe TS16 ....5 E5
Hilton TS15 ....6 C2
Middleton St George DL2 ...4 C4
Yarm Road Ind Est DL1 ...3 F5
Yarm Sch TS15 ....5 E3
Yarm Sta TS15 ....5 E2
Yarrow Dr HG3 ....161 B3
Yatts Rd YO18 ....96 A8
Yaud Sike La YO18 ....95 E5
Yeadon Wlk 12 DL2 ....4 C4
Yealand Ave BD24 ....131 D3
Yearby Cl TS5 ....6 D7
Yearsley Cres YO31 ....228 D7
Yearsley Gr YO31 ....225 E1
Yearsley Grove Jun Sch
YO32 ....225 F1
Yearsley Moor Bank
YO62 ....118 B7
Yearsley Swimming Baths
YO31 ....228 D8
Yederick Rd YO13 ....98 B8
Yedingham Priory (site of)★
YO17 ....97 D2
Yedmandale Rd
2 East Ayton/West Ayton
YO13 ....99 A7
Hutton Buscel YO13 ....98 F7
Yeomans Mount HG3 ..137 B4
Yew Tree Cl
Acaster Malbis YO23 ....191 C8
Harrogate HG2 ....222 C4
8 Low Bradley BD20 ....173 E3
Rufforth YO23 ....182 C6
Selby YO8 ....232 C6
13 Sleights YO22 ....32 A6
Yew Tree Gdns HG2 ....222 B5
Yew Tree La HG2 ....222 C5
Yew Tree Mews YO19 ..229 C5
Yew Tree Pk DN14 ....207 A7
Yew Tree Wlk HG2 ....222 B6
Yew Wlk The TS21 ....4 F7
Yewbank Cl 3 LS29 ....218 A4
Yewbank Terr LS29 ....218 A4
Yewdale Rd HG2 ....220 A1
Yiewsley Dr DL3 ....3 A5
YMCA Leisure Ctr
YO11 ....213 A6
Yoadwath Bank YO62 ...70 C3
Yoredale Ave
Darlington DL3 ....3 B6
17 Leyburn DL8 ....60 D5
York Abbey★ YO30 ....233 A3
York Barbican Leisure Ctr
YO10 ....233 C1
York Bridge Rd YO61 ..143 B2
York Castle Mus★
YO1 ....233 C1
York City Art Gall★
YO30 ....233 B3
York City Football Club
YO30 ....233 A4
York Cl 2 HG5 ....221 C5
York Coll of Further & Higher
Ed YO24 ....230 E6
York Cricket & RUFC
YO30 ....227 F7
York District Hospl
YO30 ....233 B4
York Dungeon★ YO1 ..233 B2
York Garth 1 HG5 ....221 C5
York Ind Pk YO17 ....121 C1
York La Flaxton YO60 ....167 E8
Knaresborough HG5 ....221 B5
York Minster★ YO1 ....233 B3
York Pl Harrogate HG2 ..219 E1
Knaresborough HG5 ....221 B5
Scarborough YO11 ....213 A5
York Race Course (The
Knavesmire)★ YO24 ..228 A1
York Rd Bagby YO7 ....211 D2
Barlby YO8 ....198 B5
Bilbrough YO23 ....182 B2
Bilton-in-Ainsty with Bickerton
LS22 ....181 A4
Boroughbridge YO51 ....141 B5
37 Burley in Warfedale
LS29 ....176 C1
Cliffe YO8 ....198 E3
Cottam YO25 ....151 B2
Dunnington YO19 ....184 D6
Easingwold YO61 ....143 C7
Flaxby HG5 ....163 B5
Green Hammerton YO26 ..164 B3
Harrogate HG1 ....219 C2
Haxby YO32 ....225 D7
Kilham YO25 ....151 F3
Kirk Hammerton YO26 ....164 C3
Knaresborough HG5 ....221 D5
Leavening YO17 ....147 E2
Long Marston YO26 ....182 A6
Malton YO17 ....215 A3
Middlesbrough TS7 ....7 D6
Naburn YO19 ....191 D8
North Duffield YO8 ....199 A8
Riccall YO19 ....192 A1
Sledmere YO25 ....150 E1
Sowerby YO7 ....211 E1
Stillingfleet YO19 ....191 D4
Strensall YO32 ....167 A6
Sutton-on-the-Forest
YO61 ....144 C2
Sutton-on-the-Forest
YO61 ....166 C8
Tadcaster LS24 ....189 F6
Wetherby LS22 ....180 C3
York YO26 ....227 C3
York Rugby League Club
YO32 ....226 A2
York Sixth Form Coll
YO24 ....230 E6
York St
Barnoldswick BB18 ....171 D1
Castleford WF10 ....200 E4
Crathorne TS15 ....24 E6
5 Dunnington YO19 ....184 E7
12 Glusburn BD20 ....187 E8
1 Selby YO8 ....232 C5
York Sta YO24 ....233 A2
York Steiner Sch
YO10 ....228 D1
York View DL10 ....209 E8
York Villas WF6 ....200 A1
Yorkdale Ct 4 YO8 ....196 F1
Yorkdale Dr 3 YO8 ....196 F1
Yorkersgate YO17 ....215 B4
Yorkshire Air Mus★
YO41 ....184 F3
Yorkshire Carriage Mus★
DL8 ....58 F3
Yorkshire Coast Coll
YO12 ....212 B6
Yorkshire Dales National
Park Ctr★ BD24 ....131 D3
Yorkshire Mus★ YO30 ..233 A3
Yorkshire Mus of Farming★
YO19 ....229 F5
Young Bank La YO62 ...70 C2
Young's Ct LS25 ....194 F7
Young's Dr 3 HG3 ....161 B2
Youngs Way 10 DL10 ....41 E4
Ypres Rd DL9 ....209 D1
Yule La YO26 ....164 C3

Z

Zetland Dr DL10 ....209 F8
Zetland St DL6 ....210 D4

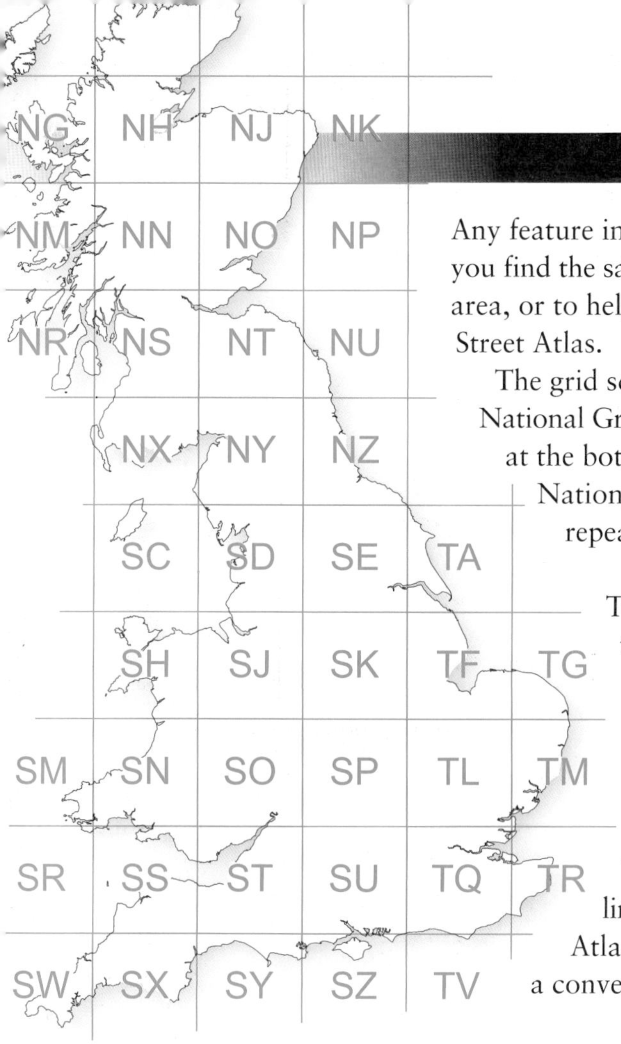

NG NH NJ NK

NM NN NO NP

NR NS NT NU

NX NY NZ

SC SD SE TA

SH SJ SK TF TG

SM SN SO SP TL TM

SR SS ST SU TQ TR

SW SX SY SZ TV

Any feature in this atlas can be given a unique reference to help you find the same feature on other Ordnance Survey maps of the area, or to help someone else locate you if they do not have a Street Atlas.

The grid squares in this atlas match the Ordnance Survey National Grid and are at 500 metre intervals. The small figures at the bottom and sides of every other grid line are the National Grid kilometre values (**00** to **99** km) and are repeated across the country every 100 km (see left).

To give a unique National Grid reference you need to locate where in the country you are. The country is divided into 100 km squares with each square given a unique two-letter reference. Use the administrative map to determine in which 100 km square a particular page of this atlas falls.

The bold letters and numbers between each grid line (**A** to **F**, **1** to **8**) are for use within a specific Street Atlas only, and when used with the page number, are a convenient way of referencing these grid squares.

Example   *The railway bridge over DARLEY GREEN RD in grid square B1*

Step 1: Identify the two-letter reference, in this example the page is in **SP**

Step 2: Identify the 1 km square in which the railway bridge falls. Use the figures in the southwest corner of this square: Eastings **17**, Northings **74**. This gives a unique reference: **SP 17 74**, accurate to 1 km.

Step 3: To give a more precise reference accurate to 100 m you need to estimate how many tenths along and how many tenths up this 1 km square the feature is (to help with this the 1 km square is divided into four 500 m squares). This makes the bridge about **8** tenths along and about **1** tenth up from the southwest corner.

This gives a unique reference: **SP 178 741**, accurate to 100 m.

Eastings (read from left to right along the bottom) come before Northings (read from bottom to top). If you have trouble remembering say to yourself "Along the hall, THEN up the stairs"!

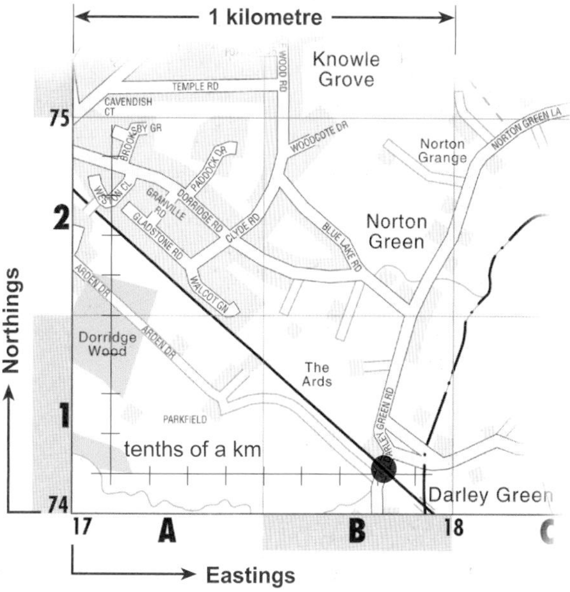

Name and Address	Telephone	Page	Grid reference

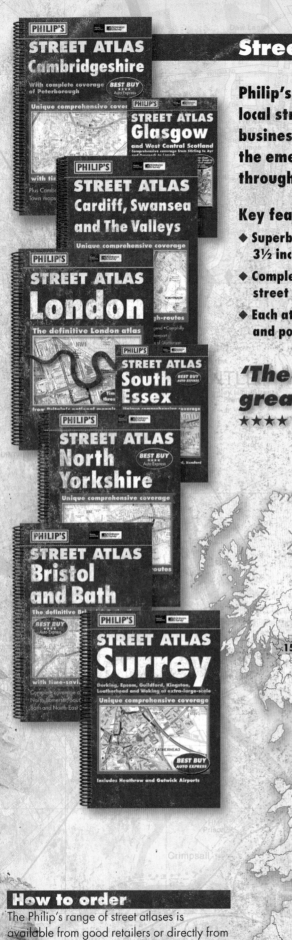